Digital Image Processing

S Esakkirajan • T Veerakumar
Badri Narayan Subudhi

Digital Image Processing

Illustration using Python

 Springer

S Esakkirajan
Department of Instrumentation and Control
Engineering
PSG College of Technology
Coimbatore, Tamil Nadu, India

T Veerakumar
Department of Electronics and
Communication Engineering
National Institute of Technology Goa
Cuncolim, Goa, India

Badri Narayan Subudhi (iD)
Department of Electrical Engineering
Indian Institute of Technology
Jammu, Jammu and Kashmir, India

ISBN 978-981-96-6381-1   ISBN 978-981-96-6382-8   (eBook)
https://doi.org/10.1007/978-981-96-6382-8

This Springer imprint is published by the registered company Springer Nature Singapore Pte Ltd.
The registered company address is: 152 Beach Road, #21-01/04 Gateway East, Singapore 189721,
Singapore

If disposing of this product, please recycle the paper.

Preface

This book represents the culmination of over a decade of teaching experience in the field of digital image processing. It results from the combined expertise of three authors. Image processing is a rapidly growing field with widespread applications in science and engineering. Digital images play a crucial role in various areas, including medical imaging, multimedia communications, and autonomous vehicle navigation. The primary aim of this book is to implement a wide range of image processing algorithms using Python, bringing a practical approach to the theory of digital image processing. Each chapter begins with clearly defined learning objectives and includes a rich collection of Python programs to illustrate key concepts. Additionally, exercises and objective questions enhance the learning experience, followed by a bibliography for further reading. A distinctive feature of this book is the collection of Python programs that effectively demonstrate digital image processing concepts. Throughout the text, physical interpretations of mathematical concepts are provided to aid understanding. While there are numerous software options for mathematical analysis, this book chooses to utilize Python for implementing digital image processing algorithms. Python is an open-source programming language with robust scientific computing libraries, making it an essential tool in both teaching and research. The libraries employed in this text include OpenCV, NumPy, SciPy, scikit-learn, Pillow, Matplotlib, and TensorFlow. The objective is not to teach Python programming per se, but rather to use it as a tool to illustrate image processing concepts. Each chapter features carefully selected examples and sample problems that reinforce the fundamental concepts presented.

Target Audience

This book is suited for undergraduate students, postgraduate students, research scholars, practicing engineers, and faculty members working in image processing and computer vision. The reader is assumed to be familiar with basic Python programming.

Highlights of the Book

The salient features of the book are summarized below:

- Wide range of topics covered starting from the concept of pixels to image analysis using deep learning.
- Step-by-step implementation of digital image processing algorithms in Python with detailed inference of results.
- Exercise at the end of each chapter to enhance the understanding of concepts. This will help the reader to implement digital image processing algorithms using Python.
- Objective-type questions at the end of each chapter. This will help the reader to prepare for a competitive examination.

Chapter Organization

The book comprises of 11 chapters. Chapter 1 introduces the basics of digital images, including image sampling, quantization, dithering, image resolution, and image file formats. Generation of different types of test image patterns is discussed in depth in this chapter. Chapter 2 focuses on two-dimensional convolution and correlation. Convolution is a powerful mathematical operation that is used to extract information from images. The spatial and frequency domain method of performing convolution and correlation is discussed in this chapter. This chapter also discusses template matching as one of the important applications of correlation. Chapter 3 is devoted to image transforms. Different transforms discussed in this chapter include Fourier transform, discrete cosine transform, Hadamard transform, Wavelet transform, Hough transform, and Radon transform. The properties and applications of the above-mentioned transforms are discussed in detail in this chapter.

A detailed discussion on spatial domain and transform domain image enhancement is done in Chapter 4. The concepts discussed in this chapter include gray-level transformation, contrast enhancement using histogram processing, and spatial and frequency domain filtering of the image. Chapter 5 deals with image denoising and image restoration. This chapter examines different types of noises that can get into a digital image and methods to mitigate the noise. This chapter also discusses different types of degradations and methods to restore the degraded image. Binary and grayscale morphological operations are discussed in Chapter 6. Morphological operations like dilation, erosion, opening, and closing are illustrated with Python examples. In addition to morphological operations, morphological algorithms like hit or miss transform, top-hat transform, black-hat transform, and thinning are discussed with suitable Python examples.

Chapter 7 is dedicated to image segmentation. Edge-based segmentation, threshold-based segmentation, region-based segmentation, and graph-based segmentation are discussed in depth in this chapter. Chapter 8 focuses on feature extraction. Both conventional and modern feature extraction techniques are covered in this chapter. Conventional techniques include Gray level co-occurrence matrix (GLCM), local binary pattern (LBP), scale invariant feature transform (SIFT), and histogram of oriented gradient (HOG). Modern techniques of feature extraction discussed in this chapter are convolutional neural network based deep feature extraction, and auto encoder based feature extraction. Detailed discussion on lossless and lossy compression algorithms are given in Chapter 9. Lossless compression algorithms discussed in this chapter are run length coding, Huffman coding, arithmetic coding, and dictionary based coding. Lossy compression algorithms discussed in this chapter are transform based coding. Chapter 10 is devoted to colour image processing. The concepts discussed in this chapter are colour models, pseudo-colouring, colour image enhancement, segmentation, and compression. Chapter 11 performs image analysis using machine learning and deep learning approaches. Both supervised and unsupervised machine and deep learning algorithms are covered in this chapter.

Coimbatore, Tamil Nadu, India   S Esakkirajan
Cuncolim, Goa, India   T Veerakumar
Jammu, Jammu and Kashmir, India   Badri Narayan Subudhi

Acknowledgements

The authors would like to thank the almighty who has granted countless blessings, knowledge, protection, courage, and opportunity to accomplish the book. The authors wish to thank Shri L. Gopalakrishnan, Managing Trustee, PSG Institutions; Dr. K. Prakasan, Principal, PSG College of Technology, Coimbatore; Prof. O. R. Jaiswal, Director, National Institute of Technology, Goa; and Prof. Manoj Singh Gaur, Director, Indian Institute of Technology, Jammu for their constant encouragement in this successful endeavour.

Dr. S Esakkirajan would like to thank his parents, Mr. G. Sankaralingam and Mrs. S. Saraswathi, his wife, Mrs. K. Sornalatha, and his sons, Azhakuvignesh and Krishnan. He would like to thank his students, Mr. Senthil Murugan, Mr. Vijay Bhaskar, Ms. B. Keerthiveena and Mr. Upendra Vishwanath, for their continual support and encouragement.

Dr. T Veerakumar would like to thank his parents, Mr. N. Thangaraj and Mrs. T. Muniammal, brothers, Mr. Tamilselvan and Mr. Karlmarks, and sister, Mrs. Muniponnu, for their wholehearted support. He would like to thank his wife, Banupriya, and daughters, Harini and Ishani, for tolerating his late coming home and their support in completing this work on time. He would also like to thank his life guru, Prof. S Esakkirajan, for his encouragement and support during his life.

Dr. Badri Narayan Subudhi would like to express his gratitude to his parents, Mr. Ananda Chandra Subudhi and Ms. Subasini Subudhi, wife Ms. Bandanarani Subudhi, and children Aaradhya and Anwit, for their unflagging love and support throughout life. He would also like to thank his brother, Rashimi Ranjan Subudhi, and Prof. Sarat Kumar Patra for their encouragement and support during his life.

Contents

About the Authors

S Esakkirajan is a Professor in the Department of Instrumentation and Control Systems Engineering, PSG College of Technology, Coimbatore. He did a B.Sc. in Physics from Sadakathullah Appa College, Palayamkottai, B.Tech. in Instrumentation Engineering from Cochin University of Science and Technology, Cochin, M.E. in Applied Electronics from PSG College of Technology, and Ph.D. in Image Processing from Anna University. He co-authored the textbooks *Digital Image Processing* and *Digital Signal Processing*, published by McGraw Hill, and another textbook *Digital Signal Processing: Illustration Using Python*, published by Springer. He has published around 65 research articles in reputed journals and conferences. His research interests include digital signal processing and digital image processing.

T Veerakumar is an Associate Professor in the Department of Electronics and Communication Engineering, National Institute of Technology, Goa. He graduated with a B.E. in Electronics and Communication Engineering degree from RVS College of Engineering and Technology, Dindigul, in 2004. He did an M.E. degree in Applied Electronics from PSG College of Technology, Coimbatore, in 2006, and Ph.D. in Image Denoising from Anna University, Chennai, in 2013. He co-authored the textbooks *Digital Image Processing* and *Digital Signal Processing*, published by McGraw Hill, and another textbook *Digital Signal Processing: Illustration Using Python*, published by Springer. He has published around 70 research articles in reputed journals and conferences. His areas of interest include signal and image processing, biomedical image processing, object detection, and tracking.

Badri Narayan Subudhi received an M.Tech. degree in Electronics and System Communication from National Institute of Technology, Rourkela, India, in 2009. He worked on his Ph.D. from Machine Intelligence Unit, Indian Statistical Institute, Kolkata, India, in 2014. He is currently an Associate Professor at Indian Institute of Technology, Jammu. Prior to this, he was working as an Assistant Professor at NIT Goa from July 2014 to November 2017. He received a CSIR senior research fellowship for the year 2011–2015. He was nominated as the Young Scientist Awardee by

Indian Science Association for the year 2011–2012. He was awarded the Young Scientist Travel grant from DST, Government of India, and Council of Scientific and Industrial Research, India, 2011. He received the Bose-Ramagnosi Award for the year 2010 from DST, Government of India, under India-Trento Programme for Advanced Research (ITPAR). He was a visiting scientist at the University of Trento, Italy, from August 2010 to February 2011. His research interests include video processing, image processing, pattern recognition, machine learning, deep learning, and medical image processing. He co-authored the textbooks *Digital Signal Processing*, published by McGraw Hill, and *Digital Signal Processing: Illustration Using Python*, published by Springer. He has published around 80 research papers in reputed journals and conferences. He is a Senior Member of IEEE.

Abbreviations

ANN	Artificial Neural Network
ASM	Attribute Selection Measure
BMP	Bit map file format
BRIEF	Binary Robust Independent Elementary Feature
CCV	Colour Coherence Vector
CLAHE	Contrast Limited Adaptive Histogram Equalization
CMY	Cyan, Magenta, Yellow
CNN	Convolutional Neural Network
CR	Compression Ratio
CV	Computer Vision
DBN	Deep Belief Network
DCT	Discrete Cosine Transform
DL	Deep Learning
DPCM	Differential Pulse Code Modulation
FAST	Features from Accelerated Segment Test
FNN	Feed Forward Neural Network
GAN	Generative Adversarial Network
GLCM	Gray Level Co-occurrence Matrix
GMM	Gaussian Mixture Model
GRU	Gated Recurrent Unit
HOG	Histogram Oriented Gradient
HSV	Hue Saturation Value
ICA	Independent Component Analysis
ISOMAP	Isometric Mapping
JPEG	Joint Photographic Expert Group
KNN	K-Nearest Neighbour
LBP	Local Binary Pattern
LDA	Linear Discriminative Analysis
LoG	Laplacian of Gaussian
LSTM	Long Short Term Memory
LZW	Lembel-Ziv-Welch

ML	Machine Learning
MSE	Mean Square Error
MSR	Multi-Scale Retinex
NLM	Non-Local Mean Filter
NN	Neural Network
PCA	Principal Component Analysis
PIXEL	Picture Element
PNG	Portable Network Graphics
PSF	Point Spread Function
PSNR	Peak Signal to Noise Ratio
RAG	Region Adjacency Graph
RBFN	Radial Basis Function Network
RBM	Restricted Boltzmann Machine
ReLU	Rectified Linear Unit
ResNet	Residual Network
RGB	Red, Green, Blue
RLE	Run Length Encoding
RMSE	Root Mean Square Error
RNN	Recurrent Neural Network
SIFT	Scale Invariant Feature Transform
SLIC	Simple Linear Iterative Clustering
SOM	Self-Organizing Map
SSR	Single Scale Retinex
SVD	Singular Value Decomposition
SVM	Support Vector Machine
TIFF	Tagged Image File Format
t-SNE	t-distributed Stochastic Neighbour Embedding
TVF	Total Variation Filter
UMAP	Uniform Manifold Approximation and Projection
VAE	Variational Auto Encoder
VGG	Visual Geometry Group
VQ	Vector Quantization
XOR	Exclusive OR
YOLO	You Only Look Once

Chapter 1
Elements of Digital Image Processing

Learning Objectives

After completing this chapter, the reader should be able to

- Read and display images of different file formats
- Perform basic mathematical operations on the input image
- Perform sampling and quantization of the image
- Implement different dithering algorithms on the input image
- Generation of different types of test patterns as images

Roadmap of the Chapter

The concepts discussed in this chapter are illustrated in the form of a roadmap, which is given in Fig. 1.1.

The concepts to be discussed in this chapter include the resolution of digital images, sampling and quantization of images, different mathematical operations that can be performed on the image, and the generation of various types of test image patterns.

PreLab Questions

1. What is a pixel?
2. What is gray level with respect to digital image?
3. Mention the factor that decides the spatial resolution of a digital image.
4. Define gray level resolution of the digital image.
5. Mention the steps involved in the image digitization.
6. What is aliasing in digital image processing?
7. Why quantization is considered as an irreversible phenomenon?
8. Explain the terms "brightness" and "contrast" of a digital image.

Supplementary Information The online version contains supplementary material available at https://doi.org/10.1007/978-981-96-6382-8_1.

S Esakkirajan et al., *Digital Image Processing*, https://doi.org/10.1007/978-981-96-6382-8_1

1

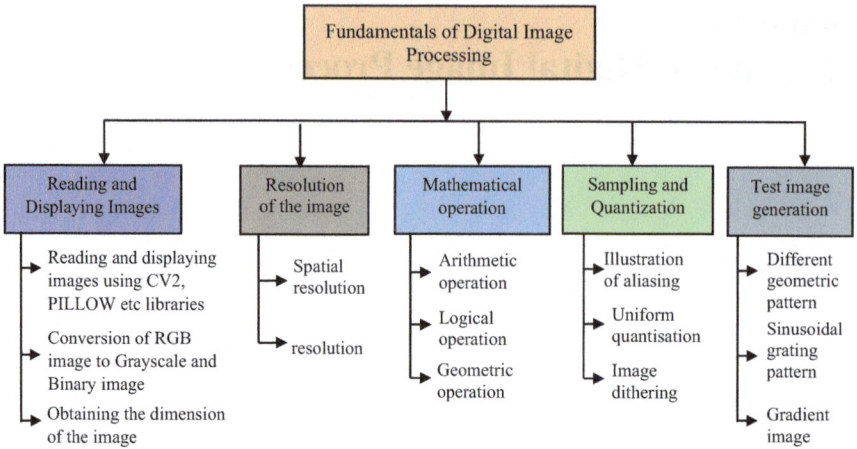

Fig. 1.1 Roadmap of this Chapter

 9. What is image dithering? Mention different types of image dithering techniques.
10. Mention the popular types of image file formats used to store the digital image.

1.1 Definition of Image and Pixel

This section begins with the definition of the digital image. An image is composed of small elements called pixels. The definition of the pixel is also discussed in this section.

1.1.1 Image

Image is a multidimensional function. It is represented as $f(x, y, z, \lambda)$. $f(x, y, z, \lambda)$ represents three-dimensional colour image, whereas $f(x, y, \lambda)$ represents two-dimensional "colour image" and $f(x, y)$ represents the "grayscale image". If the image $f(x, y)$ takes only two values, either "0" or "1", it is called a "binary image". An image is a numerical representation of visual information.

1.1.2 Pixel

Pixel is the smallest unit in a digital image. Pixel stands for "Picture element". Each pixel is specified by a location and the value. The pixel's value is termed the "gray level".

1.2 Reading and Displaying Images Using Different Libraries

This section deals with reading and displaying images using different libraries such as CV2, Matplotlib, and Scikitlearn.

1.2.1 Reading and Displaying an Image Using OpenCV

This section discusses the approach to reading and displaying images using the library "*cv2*". Here, "*cv*" stands for "*computer vision*".

Experiment 1.1: Read and Display RGB Image
The Python code that reads and displays RGB images is given in Fig. 1.2a, and the corresponding output is shown in Fig. 1.2b.

Inference

- The built-in function "*cv2.imread*" is used to read the image, "*cv2.imshow*" is used to display the image. *cv2.waitKey*() method waits until one exits or clicks the close button.

Experiment 1.2: Display the RGB Image as a Grayscale Image
This experiment discusses the read and display the colour image as grayscale image using Python. The Python code given in Fig. 1.3 reads a colour image and displays it as a grayscale image.

Inference

- From Fig. 1.3b, it is possible to observe that the colour image is displayed as a grayscale image.

Fig. 1.2 Computer vision library to read and display images: (**a**) Python code, (**b**) output image

```
import cv2
img=cv2.imread('krish.jpg')
cv2.imshow('testimage',img)
cv2.waitKey(0)
```

(a) Python Code   **(b) Output image**

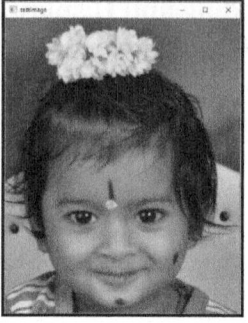

```
import cv2
img=cv2.imread('krish.jpg',0)
cv2.imshow('testimage',img)
cv2.waitKey(0)
```

(a) Python Code   (b) Output image

Fig. 1.3 Display the colour image as a grayscale image: (**a**) Python code, (**b**) output image

1.2.2   Reading the Image Using OpenCV and Displaying Using Matplotlib

This section aims to illustrate ways to read the image using "*opencv*" library and display the image using "*matplotlib*" library.

Experiment 1.3: Read the Image Using cv2 Library and Display the Image Using Matplotlib Library

In this experiment, the colour image is read using the built-in function "*cv2.imread*". It is then converted from BGR to RGB format. After converting it into RGB format, the built-in function available in "*matplotlib*" (*plt.imshow*) library is used to display the image. The Python code that does this task is shown in Fig. 1.4a, and the corresponding output is shown in Fig. 1.4b.

Inference

- In this experiment, the cv2 library is used to read the image and convert it into RGB format, and the built-in function "*plt.imshow*" is used to display the image.

Experiment 1.4: Read the Colour Image Using cv2 Library and Display It as a Grayscale Image Using Matplotlib Library

This experiment deals with the read the colour image using "cv2" library and display it as a grayscale image using "matplotlib" library. The Python code that uses the "cv2" library to read the colour image and using the "matplotlib" library to display it as the grayscale image is given in Fig. 1.5a, and the corresponding result is shown in Fig. 1.5b.

Inference

- The colour image is read using the "*cv2*" library, and it is converted to a grayscale image. The grayscale image is displayed using "*matplotlib*" library. Here, "cmap" stands for "colourmap".

```
import cv2
import matplotlib.pyplot as plt
#Step 1: Reading the image
img=cv2.imread('testimg.jpg')
#Step 2: Converting the image to RGB format
image = cv2.cvtColor(img, cv2.COLOR_BGR2RGB)
#Step 3: Displaying the image using matplotlib
plt.subplot(1,2,1),plt.imshow(img),
plt.title('Input image'),plt.axis('off')
plt.subplot(1,2,2),plt.imshow(image),
plt.title('RGB format'),plt.axis('off')
plt.tight_layout()
```

(a) Python Code   **(b) Output image**

Fig. 1.4 CV library to read the image and "matplotlib" library to display the image: (**a**) Python code, (**b**) output image

```
import cv2
import matplotlib.pyplot as plt
#Step 1: Reading the image
img=cv2.imread('testimg.jpg',0)
#Step 2: Displaying the image using
matplotlib
plt.subplot(1,2,1),plt.imshow(img),
plt.title('without cmap'),plt.axis('off')
plt.subplot(1,2,2),
plt.imshow(img,cmap='gray')
plt.title('with cmap'),plt.axis('off')
plt.tight_layout()
```

(a) Python Code   **(b) Output image**

Fig. 1.5 Reading a colour image and displaying it as a grayscale image: (**a**) Python code, (**b**) output image

1.2.3   Reading and Displaying Image Using Matplotlib

This section discusses the read and display image using "matplotlib" library.

Experiment 1.5: Image Read and Display Using "Matplotlib"
This experiment aims to read and display the colour image using "matplotlib" library in Python. The Python code that uses the "matplotlib" library to read and display images is given in Fig. 1.6a, and the corresponding output is shown in Fig. 1.6b.

Inference

- From Fig. 1.6a, it is possible to observe that "image" command is imported from "matplotlib" library to read an image and "imshow" command is used to display the image.

```
import matplotlib.pyplot as plt
from matplotlib import image as mpimg
img=mpimg.imread('testimg2.jpg')
plt.imshow(img),plt.axis('off')
```

(a) Python Code   (b) Output image

Fig. 1.6 Display of colour image using matplotlib: (a) Python code, (b) output image

```
from PIL import Image
img=Image.open('A-Z.png')
img.show()
```

ABCDEFGHIJKLMNO
PQRSTUVWXYZ

(a) Python Code   (b) Output image

Fig. 1.7 Python code to read the image using PILLOW library: (a) Python code, (b) output image

1.2.4   PILLOW Library to Read and Display the Image

This section discusses the read and display of the image using "PILLOW" library.

Experiment 1.6: Read and Display the Digital Image Using "PILLOW" Library

The Python code that performs the read and display of the digital image using the PILLOW library is given in Fig. 1.7a, and the corresponding output is shown in Fig. 1.7b.

Inferences

- In this experiment, the module "Image" is imported from PIL package.
- The image is read using the variable "img". The built-in function "*show*()" is called to display the image, which is stored in the variable "img".

1.2.5   Image Read and Display Through "Scikit" Learn

Scikit-image is a sub-module of scikit-learn that can be used to read and display the image.

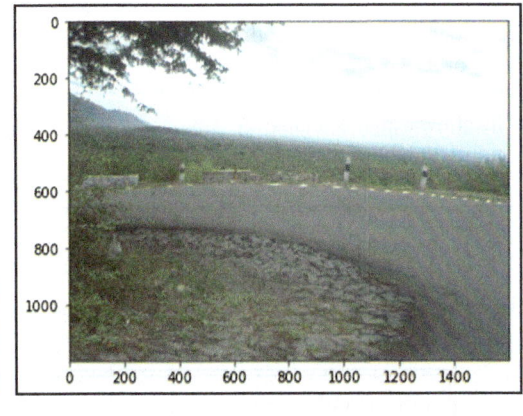

```
from skimage import io
img=io.imread('testimg.jpg')
io.imshow(img)
```

(a) Python Code   **(b) Output image**

Fig. 1.8 Scikit library function to read and display image: (**a**) Python code, (**b**) output image

Experiment 1.7: Read and Display the Digital Image Using "Scikit" Learn Library

This experiment discusses the digital image read and display using "scikit" learn library. The Python code that performs the digital image's read and display using the scikit learn library is shown in Fig. 1.8a, and the corresponding output is shown in Fig. 1.8b.

Inferences

- From Fig. 1.8a, it is possible to infer that the "io" command is imported from the "skimage" library, the "imread" command is used to read, and "imshow" command is used to display the image.
- Figure 1.8b shows the test image, which is a "curve road".

1.3 Height and Width of the Image

The height and width of the image have to be known for image processing and application. Here, "height" represents the number of rows in an image, and "width" denotes the number of columns in an image.

Experiment 1.8: Obtain the Height and Width of the Image

The objective of this experiment is to obtain the height and width of the image using "cv2" library. The Python code that performs this task is shown in Fig. 1.9a, and the corresponding output is shown in Fig. 1.9b.

Inference

- From Fig. 1.9b, it is possible to interpret that the input image has 256 rows and 256 columns.

```
#Obtaining the height and width of the image
import cv2
img=cv2.imread('cameraman.tif',0)
height,width=img.shape[:2]
print("Height of the image is:",height)
print("Width of the image is:",width)
```

```
Height of the image is: 256
Width of the image is: 256
```

(a) Python Code   **(b) Output image**

Fig. 1.9 Display the height and width of the digital image: (**a**) Python code, (**b**) output image

```
import cv2
import numpy as np
cv2.namedWindow("output", cv2.WINDOW_NORMAL)
img_color=cv2.imread('tstimage3.jpg')
img_gray = cv2.cvtColor(img_color, cv2.COLOR_BGR2GRAY)
cv2.imshow('output',img_color)
cv2.waitKey(0)
cv2.imshow('output',img_gray)
cv2.waitKey(0)
```

Fig. 1.10 Python code to convert colour image to a grayscale image

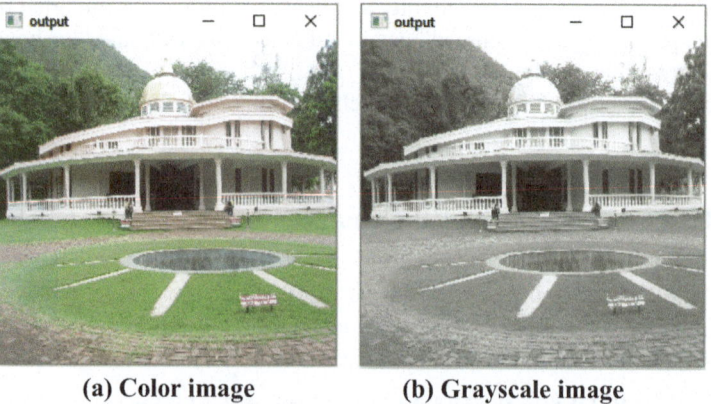

(a) Color image   **(b) Grayscale image**

Fig. 1.11 Result of the Python code shown in Fig. 1.10: (**a**) colour image, (**b**) grayscale image

Experiment 1.9: Converting Colour image to a Grayscale Image

The built-in function "*cvtColor*" in the cv2 library can be used to convert the colour image into a grayscale image. The Python code that performs this task is given in Fig. 1.10, and the corresponding output is shown in Fig. 1.11.

Inference

- The colour image is read in BGR format, and then it is converted to grayscale image using the built-in function "*cvtColor*", which is available in "cv2" library.

1.4   Resolution of Digital Image

Resolution refers to small details in the digital image that can be seen with distinction. Two types of resolutions associated with digital image are (1) spatial resolution and (2) gray level resolution.

1.4.1   Spatial Resolution

Spatial resolution is governed by the density of pixels used to construct a digital image. The greater the spatial resolution, the more pixels are used to display the image.

Experiment 1.10: Illustration of Change in the Spatial Resolution of the Image

In this experiment, a Cameraman image of size 256×256 is taken. The image is subsampled from 256×256 to 16×16. The Python code that performs this operation of downsampling the dimension is given in Fig. 1.12, and the corresponding output is shown in Fig. 1.13.

Inferences

- As the spatial resolution of the image is reduced from 128×128 to 16×16, it is possible to observe that the "checkerboard" pattern-like distortion appears in the image.

```
import cv2
import matplotlib.pyplot as plt
im=cv2.imread('cameraman.tif',0)
im1=cv2.resize(im,(128,128))
im2=cv2.resize(im,(64,64))
im3=cv2.resize(im,(32,32))
im4=cv2.resize(im,(16,16))
plt.figure(figsize=(8,6))
plt.subplot(1,4,1),plt.imshow(im1,cmap='gray'),plt.title('128 x 128'),plt.axis('off')
plt.subplot(1,4,2),plt.imshow(im2,cmap='gray'),plt.title('64 x 64'),plt.axis('off')
plt.subplot(1,4,3),plt.imshow(im3,cmap='gray'),plt.title('32 x 32'),plt.axis('off')
plt.subplot(1,4,4),plt.imshow(im4,cmap='gray'),plt.title('16 x 16'),plt.axis('off')
```

Fig. 1.12 Python illustration of spatial resolution

Fig. 1.13 Result of Python code shown in Fig. 1.12

```
#Gray level resolution of digital image
import cv2
import matplotlib.pyplot as plt
import numpy as np
im=cv2.imread('cameraman.tif',0)
b=[1,2,3,4,5,6,7,8]
for i in range(len(b)):
    L=2**b[i]
    im1=np.uint8(np.floor(np.double(im/L)))
    im2=cv2.normalize(im1,None,0,255,norm_type=cv2.NORM_MINMAX)
    plt.subplot(2,4,i+1)
    plt.imshow(im2,cmap='gray'),plt.xticks([]),plt.yticks([])
    plt.title('b={}'.format(8-b[i]))
plt.tight_layout()
```

Fig. 1.14 Illustration of intensity level resolution of the image

- This means that the smallest detail in the image cannot be seen with distinction if the spatial resolution of the image is decreased.

1.4.2   Gray Level Resolution

Gray level resolution is the smallest discernible change in the intensity level of the digital image. Digital images with the higher gray level resolution are composed of a larger number of gray shades and are displayed at a more significant bit of depth.

Experiment 1.11: Illustration of Gray Level Resolution

This experiment deals with the illustration of gray level resolution using Python. The Python code used to illustrate the gray level resolution of a digital image is given in Fig. 1.14, and the corresponding output is shown in Fig. 1.15.

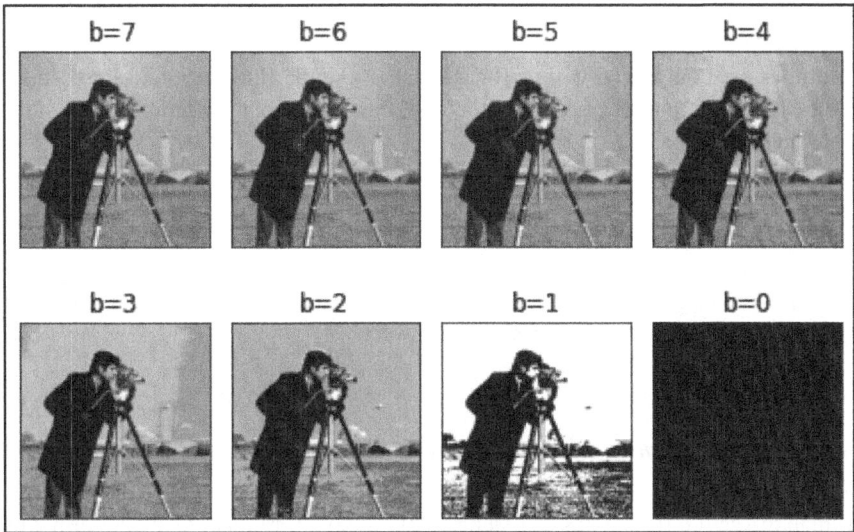

Fig. 1.15 Result of the Python code shown in Fig. 1.14

Inferences

- As the number of bits (b) used to represent the digital image decreases, the quality of the image decreases.
- With $b = 1$, it is possible to observe that the grayscale image appears as a black and white image.

1.5 Image File Format

Image file formats provide a standardized method of organizing and storing image data. Standardization helps to share the images in different systems. Different types of file formats include (1) tagged image file format (TIFF), (2) portable network graphics (PNG), (3) joint photographic expert group (JPEG), and (4) bitmap file format (BMP). Each file format offers different levels of quality, performance, and scalability. The choice of image file format will depend on the intended use of the image, balance between file size and image quality, and the type of image being stored.

1.5.1 Tagged Image File Format

Tagged image file format has either ".tif" or ".tiff" extension. Tiff file format was originally created for storing scanned photos. TIFF is used as a lossless image storage format that uses no compression at all.

Advantage of Tagged Image File Format

TIFF files are compatible with software such as Adobe Illustrator and Photoshop. Professional photographers and editors use this file format to produce and store high-quality photos.

Drawback of TIFF File Format

TIFF files are large due to incredible details and resolution. Because of this reason, it is not a suitable file format for use on the web.

1.5.2   Bitmap Image File Format

Bitmap image file format has an extension of ".bmp". It is a native image format in Microsoft Windows operating system. There is no compression or information loss with bitmap image file format, which allows images to have high quality at the expense of large file size.

Advantages of Bitmap File Format

BMP files are device independent and can be stored across multiple devices without loss in quality. They can handle multiple colour depths.

Drawbacks of Bitmap File Format

BMP files are larger in size as they store the pixel data without any compression. BMP file formats are not preferable when sharing images online or storing large number of images on a device with limited storage capacity.

1.5.3   Joint Photographic Experts Group

Joint photographic expert group (JPEG) file format has an extension of ".jpg" or ".jpeg". It employs lossy compression algorithm to make the file size smaller. The compression creates a loss in quality but is not visually perceivable. JPEG file format is widely employed in digital cameras. JPEG2000 offers a lossless and lossy compression scheme.

Advantages of JPEG File Format

JPEG file format is supported by all browsers and image viewers. Because of lossy compression, the file size of JPEG files is less; hence, the image files can be effectively stored and efficiently transmitted.

Drawback of JPEG File Format

Lossy compression of JPEG files may cause the appearance of artefacts such as blocking artefacts and ringing artefacts, thus affecting the image quality.

1.5.4   Portable Network Graphics

Portable network graphics (PNG) employs a lossless compression algorithm. PNG files are able to handle up to 16 million colours. The PNG format is widely used on websites to display high-quality digital images.

Advantages of PNG File Format

PNG employs a lossless compression algorithm; hence, the image quality is well preserved in PNG file format. PNG file format supports for transparent backgrounds. This feature is useful for creating images that need to be placed over different backgrounds.

Drawback of PNG File Format

PNG file format tends to create large files due to their lossless compression method. PNG file format does not support animation.

Experiment 1.12: Comparison of File Size Versus File Format
This experiment tries to compare the file size versus file formats. For this, a 256 × 256 grayscale "cameraman image" in PNG format is read. This image is stored in different file formats, such as .tif, .png, .jpg, and .bmp. The Python code to extract the file size of the image in different image file format is given in Fig. 1.16, and its corresponding result of a bar chart of image file format versus file size is shown in Fig. 1.17.

```
#Image file format
import cv2
import os
import matplotlib.pyplot as plt
#Step 1: Reading the input image
img = cv2.imread('cameraman.tif', 0)
#Step 2: Writing the image in different file formats
cv2.imwrite('cameraman.jpg', img)
cv2.imwrite('cameraman.png', img)
cv2.imwrite('cameraman.bmp', img)
#Step 3: Extracting the file size
image_format = ['tif', 'jpg', 'png', 'bmp']
sizes = []
for imgFormat in image_format:
    sizes.append(os.path.getsize('cameraman.'+imgFormat))
plt.bar(image_format, sizes),plt.xlabel('Image File Format')
plt.ylabel('File Size'),plt.title('Image File Format Vs Size')
```

Fig. 1.16 Python code to extract the file size in different image file formats

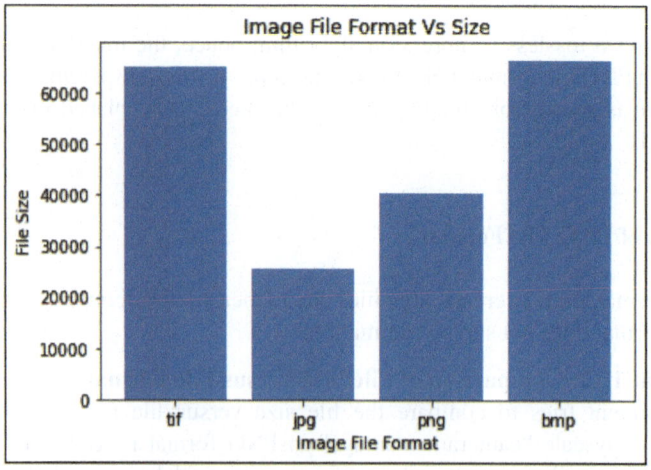

Fig. 1.17 Result of Python code shown in Fig. 1.16

Inferences

• From Fig. 1.17, it is possible to infer that in both ".bmp" and ".tif" file formats, the file size is large because both file formats employ lossless compression or no compression.

- Among the file formats considered in this example, ".jpg" file format occupies minimum space.

Experiment 1.13: Comparison of File Size Quality Factor

This experiment tries to obtain a comparison between the file size versus quality factor. For this, a 256×256 grayscale "cameraman" image is read in ".png" format. The image is stored in ".jpg" format with different quality factors, namely 10, 20, 70, and 100. The objectives are (1) to plot a graph of file size versus quality factor and (2) to display the images that are stored with different quality factors. The Python code that performs the above-mentioned task is given in Fig. 1.18, and the corresponding output is shown in Fig. 1.19.

```
# Image file size Vs Quality factor
import cv2
import os
import matplotlib.pyplot as plt
#Step 1: Reading the input image
img = cv2.imread('cameraman.tif', 0)
#Step 2: Writing the image in jpg format with different quality factors
cv2.imwrite('img_trial10.jpg', img, [int(cv2.IMWRITE_JPEG_QUALITY), 10])
cv2.imwrite('img_trial20.jpg', img, [int(cv2.IMWRITE_JPEG_QUALITY), 20])
cv2.imwrite('img_trial50.jpg', img, [int(cv2.IMWRITE_JPEG_QUALITY), 50])
cv2.imwrite('img_trial75.jpg', img, [int(cv2.IMWRITE_JPEG_QUALITY), 75])
cv2.imwrite('img_trial100.jpg', img, [int(cv2.IMWRITE_JPEG_QUALITY),100])
#Step 3: Extract the file size in different quality factor
s1=os.path.getsize('img_trial10.jpg')
s2=os.path.getsize('img_trial20.jpg')
s3=os.path.getsize('img_trial50.jpg')
s4=os.path.getsize('img_trial75.jpg')
s5=os.path.getsize('img_trial100.jpg')
QF = ['10', '20', '50', '75', '100']
sizes=[s1,s2,s3,s4,s5]
fig = plt.figure(figsize=(8,6)),plt.subplot(2,3,1),plt.bar(QF,sizes),plt.xlabel('Quality Factor'),
plt.ylabel('File Size'),plt.title('Quality Factor Vs File Size')
#Step 4: Read the images which is stored in different quality factor
img1=cv2.imread('img_trial10.jpg',0)
img2=cv2.imread('img_trial20.jpg',0)
img3=cv2.imread('img_trial50.jpg',0)
img4=cv2.imread('img_trial75.jpg',0)
img5=cv2.imread('img_trial100.jpg',0)
#Step 5: Displaying the results
plt.subplot(2,3,2),plt.imshow(img1,cmap='gray'),plt.title('Quality factor=10'),plt.axis('off'),
plt.subplot(2,3,3),plt.imshow(img2,cmap='gray'),plt.title('Quality factor=20'),plt.axis('off'),
plt.subplot(2,3,4),plt.imshow(img3,cmap='gray'),plt.title('Quality factor=70'),plt.axis('off'),
plt.subplot(2,3,5),plt.imshow(img4,cmap='gray'),plt.title('Quality factor=100'),plt.axis('off'),
plt.subplot(2,3,6),plt.imshow(img5,cmap='gray'),plt.title('Quality factor=100'),plt.axis('off')
plt.tight_layout()
```

Fig. 1.18 Python code to store the image in .jpg format with different quality factors

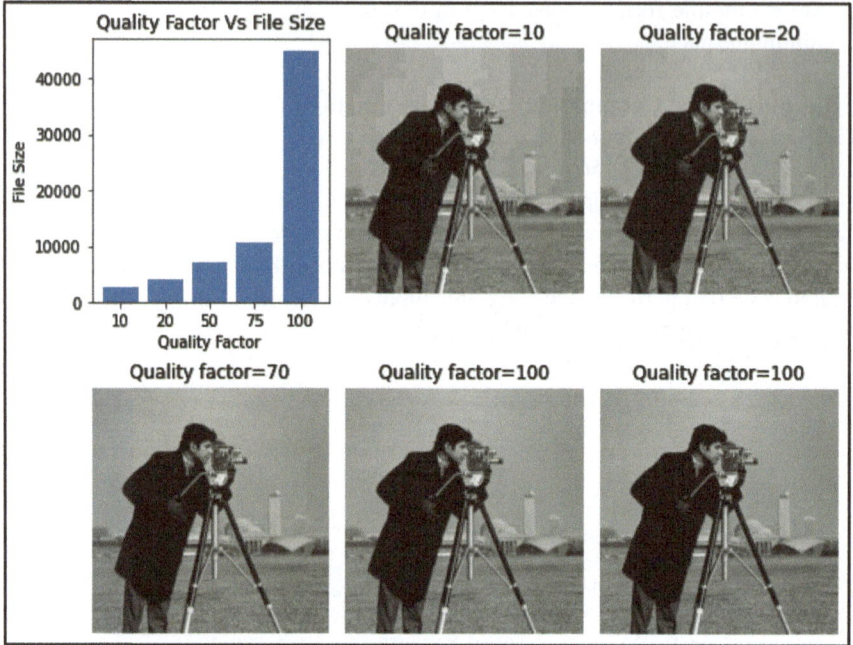

Fig. 1.19 Simulation results

Inferences

- From Fig. 1.19, it is possible to observe that the file size depends on the quality factor. With the increase in quality factor, the file size increases.
- Also, it is possible to observe with a low-quality factor, the visual quality of the image is poor. With the increase in quality factor, the visual quality of the image is good.
- From Fig. 1.19, it can be concluded that to get a better-quality image, the quality factor should be high. With an increase in quality factor, the file size increases.

1.6   Operations in Digital Image

The mathematical operations performed in the digital image can be classified as (1) arithmetic operation, (2) logical operation, and (3) geometric transformation. The arithmetic operation includes addition, subtraction, multiplication, and division. The logical operations include AND, OR, XOR, and NOT operations. The geometric transformation includes rotation, scaling, and translation.

1.6.1 Arithmetic Operation on Images

The arithmetic operations considered in this section include (1) addition, (2) subtraction, (3) multiplication, and (4) division.

Addition of Two Images

Let $f_1[m,n]$ and $f_2[m,n]$ represent the two images, then the addition of these two images is represented as

$$g[m,n] = f_1[m,n] + f_2[m,n] \qquad (1.1)$$

Experiment 1.14: Write a Python Code to Perform the Addition of Two Images

The built-in function "*add*" in "cv2" library can perform the arithmetic addition operation of two images. While performing the arithmetic addition operation between two images, it is necessary to ensure that the dimensions of the two images should be the same. The Python code that performs the task of image addition is shown in Fig. 1.20, and the corresponding output is shown in Fig. 1.21.

Inference

- In Fig. 1.21, the first image has a horizontal line; the second image has a vertical line; the addition of these two images shows both horizontal and vertical lines.

```
#Addition of images
import cv2
import matplotlib.pyplot as plt
import numpy as np
#Step 1: Generation of first image
img1=np.zeros([256,256])
img1[128,:]=255
#Step 2: Generation of second image
img2=np.zeros([256,256])
img2[:,128]=255
#Step 3: Performing image addition
img3=cv2.add(img1,img2)
#Step 4: Displaying the images
plt.subplot(1,3,1),plt.imshow(img1,cmap='gray'),plt.axis('off')
plt.title('Image1'),plt.subplot(1,3,2),plt.imshow(img2,cmap='gray'),
plt.axis('off'),plt.title('Image2'),plt.subplot(1,3,3),
plt.imshow(img3,cmap='gray'),plt.axis('off'),plt.title('Image1+Image2')
plt.tight_layout()
```

Fig. 1.20 Python code to perform the addition of two images

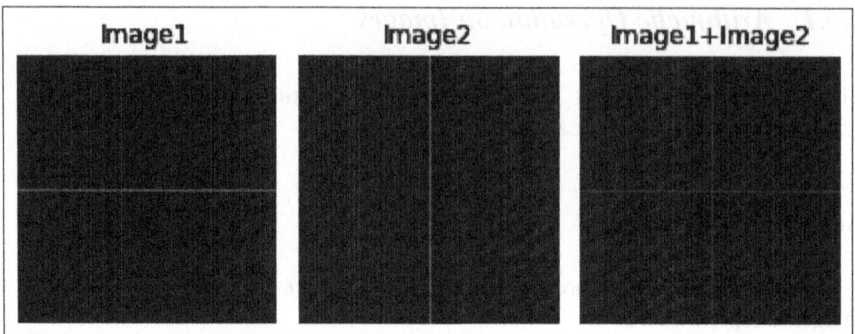

Fig. 1.21 Result of image addition

Weighted Addition of Two Images

The expression for weighted addition of two images $f_1[m,n]$ and $f_2[m,n]$ is given by

$$g[m,n] = \alpha f_1[m,n] + \beta f_2[m,n] \qquad (1.2)$$

In the above expression, "α" and "β" are the weights associated with the images $f_1[m,n]$ and $f_2[m,n]$, respectively.

Experiment 1.15: Weighted Addition of Two Images
The Python code that performs the weighted addition of two images is shown in Fig. 1.22, and the corresponding output is shown in Fig. 1.23.

Inferences
The following inferences can be drawn from Fig. 1.23:

- The input Image-1 is an image with a horizontal line, whereas the input Image-2 is an image with a vertical line.
- When 0.15 and 0.85 weights are given to Image-1 and Image-2, respectively, then the weighted addition results in an image that resembles Image-2, which is an image with the vertical line because more weightage is given to Image-2. Hence, the output image resembles Image-2.
- When 0.85 and 0.15 weights are given to Image-1 and Image-2, respectively, then the weighted addition results in an image that resembles Image-1, which is an image with a horizontal line because more weight is given to Image-1. Hence, the output image resembles Image-1.

Image Subtraction

The expression for the subtraction of two images $f_1[m,n]$ and $f_2[m,n]$ is given by

$$g[m,n] = f_1[m,n] - f_2[m,n] \qquad (1.3)$$

```
#Weighted addition of images
import cv2
import matplotlib.pyplot as plt
import numpy as np
#Step 1: Generation of first image
img1=np.zeros([256,256])
img1[128,:]=255
#Step 2: Generation of second image
img2=np.zeros([256,256])
img2[:,128]=255
#Step 3: Performing weighted image addition
img3=cv2.addWeighted(img1,0.15,img2,0.85,0)
img4=cv2.addWeighted(img1,0.85,img2,0.15,0)
#Step 4: Displaying the images
plt.subplot(2,2,1),plt.imshow(img1,cmap='gray'),plt.axis('off')
plt.title('Im1'),plt.subplot(2,2,2),plt.imshow(img2,cmap='gray'),
plt.axis('off'),plt.title('Im2'),plt.subplot(2,2,3),
plt.imshow(img3,cmap='gray'),plt.axis('off'),plt.title('0.15*Im1+0.85*Im2')
plt.subplot(2,2,4),plt.imshow(img4,cmap='gray'),plt.axis('off')
plt.title('0.85*Im1+0.15*Im2')
plt.tight_layout()
```

Fig. 1.22 Python code to perform weighted addition of two images

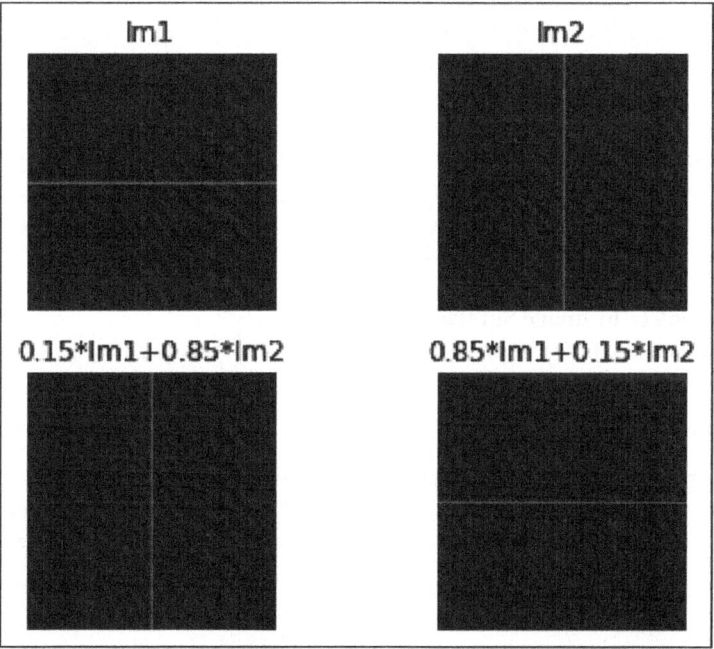

Fig. 1.23 Result of weighted addition of two images

```
#Image subtraction
import numpy as np
import matplotlib.pyplot as plt
import cv2
#Step 1: Generation of first image
img1=np.zeros([256,256])
r=40  #Radius of the circle
for i in range(0,256):
   for j in range(0,256):
      if (i-128)**2 + (j-128)**2 < r**2:
         img1[i,j]=255
#Step 2: Generation of second image
img2=np.zeros([256,256])
img2[118:138,118:138]=255
#Step 3: Subtraction of two images
img3=cv2.subtract(img1,img2)
#Step 4: Displaying the results
plt.subplot(1,3,1),plt.imshow(img1,cmap='gray'),plt.axis('off')
plt.title('Image1'),plt.subplot(1,3,2),plt.imshow(img2,cmap='gray'),
plt.axis('off'),plt.title('Image2'),plt.subplot(1,3,3),
plt.imshow(img3,cmap='gray'),plt.axis('off'),plt.title('Image1-Image2')
plt.tight_layout()
```

Fig. 1.24   Python code to perform image subtraction

The steps involved in the image subtraction are as follows:

- Step 1: Generation of first image. The first image is an image of a circle.
- Step 2: Generation of second image. The second image is an image of a square.
- Step 3: Subtraction of the images generated in Step 1 and Step 2, respectively.
- Step 4: Displaying the input images and the subtracted image.

Experiment 1.16: Image Subtraction
The Python code that performs the image subtraction mentioned in the above steps is given in Fig. 1.24, and the corresponding output is shown in Fig. 1.25.

Inferences

- The first image is an image of a circle. The second image is a square.
- Upon subtracting the second image (square) from the first image (circle), it is possible to observe that the square portion appears dark inside the circle.

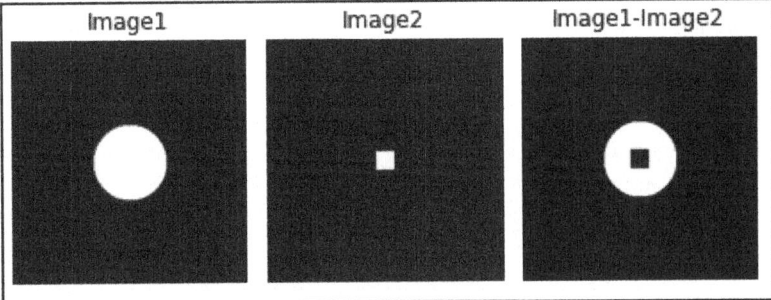

Fig. 1.25 Result of image subtraction

Image Multiplication

Image multiplication is used to obtain the product of two images. The product of two images $f_1[m,n]$ and $f_2[m,n]$ is given by

$$g[m,n] = f_1[m,n] \times f_2[m,n] \qquad (1.4)$$

Experiment 1.17: Image Multiplication
The Python code that performs the product of two images is given in Fig. 1.26, and the corresponding output is displayed in Fig. 1.27.

Inferences

- Image-1 is a white circle on a black background, whereas Image-2 is a black circle on a white background.
- Black corresponds to a gray level of "0", whereas white corresponds to a gray level of "1" or "255". Upon multiplying any number with zero, the result is zero. This is because the products of Image-1 and Image-2 result in a black circle inside a white circle.

Division of Image

The division of two images $f_1[m,n]$ and $f_2[m,n]$ is represented as

$$g[m,n] = \frac{f_1[m,n]}{f_2[m,n]} \qquad (1.5)$$

Experiment 1.18: Image Division
The Python code that performs the image's division is shown in Fig. 1.28, and the corresponding output is shown in Fig. 1.29.

```
#Image multiplication
import numpy as np
import matplotlib.pyplot as plt
import cv2
#Step 1: Generation of first image
img1=np.zeros([256,256])
r=40  #Radius of the circle
for i in range(0,256):
    for j in range(0,256):
        if (i-128)**2 + (j-128)**2 < r**2:
            img1[i,j]=255
#Step 2: Generation of second image
img2=np.ones([256,256])
r=20  #Radius of the circle
for i in range(0,256):
    for j in range(0,256):
        if (i-128)**2 + (j-128)**2 < r**2:
            img2[i,j]=0
#Step 3: Multiplication of two images
img3=cv2.multiply(img1,img2)
#Step 4: Displaying the results
plt.subplot(1,3,1),plt.imshow(img1,cmap='gray'),plt.axis('off')
plt.title('Image-1'),plt.subplot(1,3,2),plt.imshow(img2,cmap='gray'),
plt.xticks([]),plt.yticks([])
plt.title('Image-2'),plt.subplot(1,3,3),plt.imshow(img3,cmap='gray'),plt.axis('off')
plt.title('Image-1 x Image-2')
plt.tight_layout()
```

Fig. 1.26 Python code to obtain the product of two images

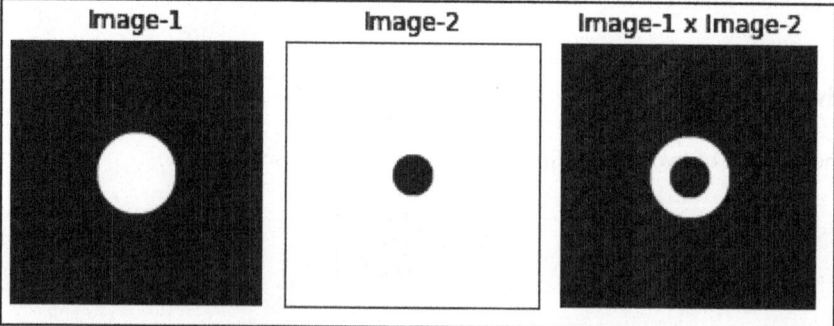

Fig. 1.27 Result of the product of two images

```
#Division of image
import cv2
import matplotlib.pyplot as plt
#Step 1: Reading the image
img=cv2.imread('C.png')
#Step 2: Obtaining the inverse of the image
img1=255-img
#Step 3: Perform the division operation
img2=cv2.divide(img,img1)
#Step 4: Displaying the result
plt.subplot(1,3,1),plt.imshow(img,cmap='gray'),plt.title('$f_1[m,n]$'),plt.xticks([]),plt.yticks([])
plt.subplot(1,3,2),plt.imshow(img1,cmap='gray'),plt.axis('off'),plt.title('$f_2[m,n]$'),
plt.subplot(1,3,3),plt.imshow(img2,cmap='gray'),plt.axis('off'),plt.title('g[m,n]')
plt.tight_layout()
```

Fig. 1.28 Python code to perform division operation

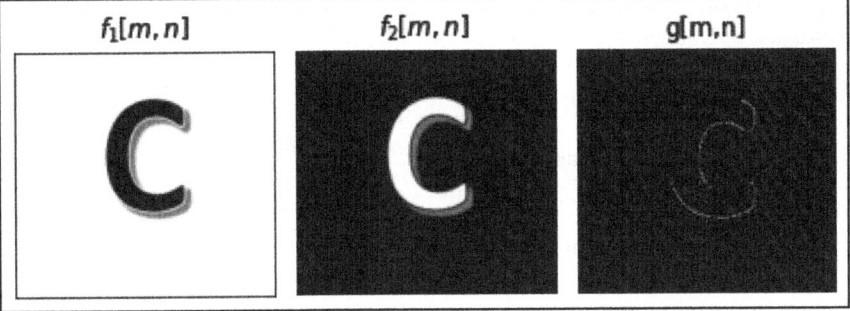

Fig. 1.29 Result of image division operation

Inferences

- The input image $f_1[m,n]$ is an alphabet "C" that appears black and white.
- The image $f_2[m,n]$ is obtained by taking the negative of the image $f_1[m,n]$.
- The image $g[m,n]$ is the result of the division of image $f_1[m,n]$ by image $f_2[m,n]$.

1.6.2 Logical Operation

Boolean logic compares two images on a pixel-by-pixel basis and generates an output image. The logical operation results in a binary image. The result of logical operation is either "yes" or "no". The logical operations can be either (1) binary operation or (2) unary operation. Examples of binary operations include AND, OR, XOR, and so on. Example of unary operation is NOT operation. This section explores logical operations such as AND, OR, XOR, and NOT.

Experiment 1.19: Perform Logical Operations

The Python code that performs the logical operation is given in Fig. 1.30, and the corresponding output is shown in Fig. 1.31. The tabular form of representation of AND, OR, and XOR operations is given in Table 1.1.

Inferences

- Two input images, "*A*" and "*B*", are generated. Image "*A*" is a circle image, and image "*B*" is a square image.
- Different logical operations performed on the input image include "AND", "OR", "XOR", and "NOT" operations.
- AND operation gives high output when both the images "*A*" and "*B*" are high. OR operation gives high output, either image "*A*" or image "*B*" is high. XOR operation gives high output when the inputs "*A*" and "*B*" are different. By performing a NOT operation on image "*B*", it is possible to observe that the white square turns out to be black.

```
#Logical operations
import cv2
import matplotlib.pyplot as plt
import numpy as np
#Step 1: Generation of image 'A'
img1=np.zeros([256,256])
img2=np.zeros([256,256])
r1=40  #Radius of the circle
for i in range(0,256):
    for j in range(0,256):
        if (i-170)**2 + (j-170)**2 < r1**2:
            img1[i,j]=255
#Step 2: Generation of image 'B'
img2[80:180,80:180]=255
#Step 3: Performing logical operations
img3=cv2.bitwise_and(img1,img2)
img4=cv2.bitwise_or(img1,img2)
img5=cv2.bitwise_xor(img1,img2)
img6=cv2.bitwise_not(img2)
#Step 4: Displaying the results
plt.subplot(2,3,1),plt.imshow(img1,cmap='gray'),plt.axis('off'),plt.title('A')
plt.subplot(2,3,2),plt.imshow(img2,cmap='gray'),plt.axis('off'),plt.title('B')
plt.subplot(2,3,3),plt.imshow(img3,cmap='gray'),plt.axis('off'),plt.title('A AND B')
plt.subplot(2,3,4),plt.imshow(img4,cmap='gray'),plt.axis('off'),plt.title('A OR B')
plt.subplot(2,3,5),plt.imshow(img5,cmap='gray'),plt.axis('off'),plt.title('A XOR B')
plt.subplot(2,3,6),plt.imshow(img6,cmap='gray'),plt.title('NOT (B)')
plt.xticks([]),plt.yticks([])
plt.tight_layout()
```

Fig. 1.30 Program to perform logical operations

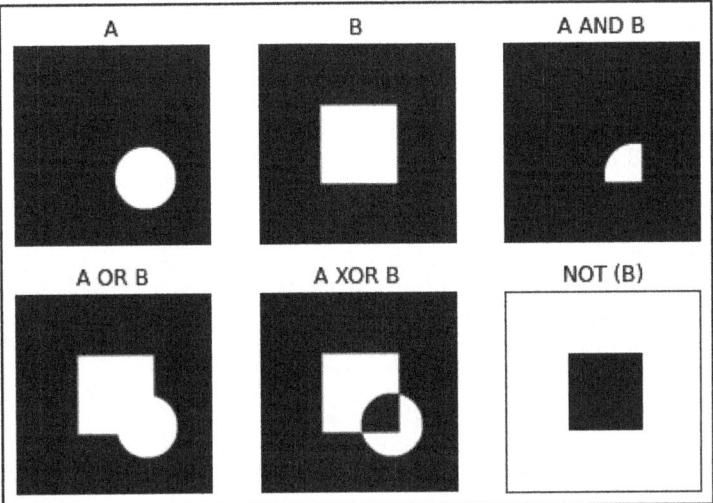

Fig. 1.31 Results of logical operations

Table 1.1 Summary of Boolean logic

Image A	Image B	AND logic	OR logic	XOR logic
0	0	0	0	0
0	1	0	1	1
1	0	0	1	1
1	1	1	1	0

1.6.3   Geometric Transformation of the Image

Different geometric operations discussed in this section include (1) scaling of the image, here scaling could be either downscaling or upscaling; (2) rotation of the image in different orientations; (3) flipping the image, which includes flipping along the x-axis, flipping along the y-axis, and flipping along both axes; and (4) translation of the image refers to the spatial shift of the image.

Experiment 1.20: Resizing the Image
The built-in function "*resize*" available in "cv2" library can be used to either upscale (increase) or downscale (decrease) the dimension of the input image. The Python code that performs this task is shown in Fig. 1.32 and the corresponding outputs are shown in Fig. 1.33 and Fig. 1.34.

Inferences

- The input image dimension is 144×256; this image is downscaled by a factor of 2 to obtain the resized Image-1, which has a dimension of 72×128.
- The input image is upscaled by a factor of 2 to obtain the resized Image-2.

```
import cv2
img=cv2.imread('tstimage2.jpg',1)
h,w,c=img.shape
print(f"Height and width of original image: {h}, {w}" )
newsize=(128,128)
resize_img1 = cv2.resize(img,(0,0),fx=0.5,fy=0.5)
resize_img2 = cv2.resize(img,(0,0),fx=2,fy=2)
h_new1,w_new1,c_new1=resize_img1.shape
h_new2,w_new2,c_new2=resize_img2.shape
print(f"Height and width of Resized image1: {h_new1}, {w_new1}" )
print(f"Height and width of Resized image2: {h_new2}, {w_new2}" )
cv2.imwrite('original_image.tif',img)
cv2.imwrite('resized_image1.tif',resize_img1)
cv2.imwrite('resized_image2.tif',resize_img2)
```

Fig. 1.32   Image resizing program

(a) Original image   **(b) Downscaled image**

(c) Upscaled image

Fig. 1.33 Original and resized images: (**a**) original image, (**b**) downscaled image, (**c**) upscaled image

Fig. 1.34 Dimension of the input and resized images

> Height and width of original image: 144, 256
> Height and width of Resized image1: 72, 128
> Height and width of Resized image2: 288, 512

Fig. 1.35 Python code to perform cropping operation

```
#Cropping the image
import cv2
img=cv2.imread('test1.jpg', cv2.IMREAD_GRAYSCALE)
img1=img[40:245,200:390]
cv2.imwrite('original.jpg',img)
cv2.imwrite(cropped.jpg',img1)
```

(a) Original image   **(b) Cropped image**

Fig. 1.36 Original and the cropped image: (**a**) original image, (**b**) cropped image

- Upon downscaling the image, the information is lost; upon interpolation, the pixelation effect can be observed. Different types of interpolation techniques, such as bilinear, bicubic, and spline interpolation techniques, can be used to minimize the impact of pixelation.

Experiment 1.21: Cropping the Image

Cropping the image refers to selecting a portion of the image that is significant when compared to the entire image. It is used to reduce the dimension of the input image. The Python code that performs the cropping operation on the image is shown in Fig. 1.35, and the corresponding output is shown in Fig. 1.36.

Inferences

- The original image contains an apple with a background, whereas in the cropped image, the apple is segregated from the background.
- The cropping operation extracts the region of interest from the entire image.

```
#Image rotation
import numpy as np
import matplotlib.pyplot as plt
import imutils
img=np.zeros([256,256])
img[128,:]=255
angle=[45,90,135,180,270]
plt.figure(1),plt.subplot(2,3,1),plt.imshow(img,cmap='gray'),plt.axis('off')
plt.title('Input image')
for i in range(len(angle)):
    img1=imutils.rotate(img,angle[i])
    plt.figure(1),plt.subplot(2,3,i+2),plt.imshow(img1,cmap='gray')
    plt.title(r'$\theta={}^\circ$'.format(angle[i])),plt.axis('off')
plt.tight_layout()
```

Fig. 1.37 Python code to perform rotation of the input image

Experiment 1.22: Rotating the Image

Two different methods to rotate the given image is discussed in this section. One way to rotate the input image is to use the library "*imutils*" and the other is to use the "*opencv*" library.

Method 1: Using the Library "Imutils"

The library "*imutils*" can be used to rotate the image in different angles. The Python code that rotates the input image using the built-in function "*rotate*" available in the library "*imutils*" is shown in Fig. 1.37, and the corresponding output is displayed in Fig. 1.38.

Inferences

The following are the inferences from Fig. 1.38:

- The input image is an entirely black image with a horizontal white line.
- The input image is rotated through different angles, namely 45°, 90°, 135°, 180°, and 270°. From the resultant image, it is possible to observe that the input image is rotated as per the specification.

Method 2: Image Rotation Using "cv2" Library

The cv2 library can be used to rotate the input image by constructing the rotation matrix. The rotation matrix is given by $R = \begin{bmatrix} \cos\theta & -\sin\theta \\ \sin\theta & \cos\theta \end{bmatrix}$. The height and width of the image are obtained using "*img.shape*" command, and it is then divided by 2 to obtain the centre of the image. The built-in function in "cv2" library "*getRotation Matrix2D()*" takes the argument of the point with which the image has to be rotated, and the angle of rotation and the factor with the image has to be resized. If the factor

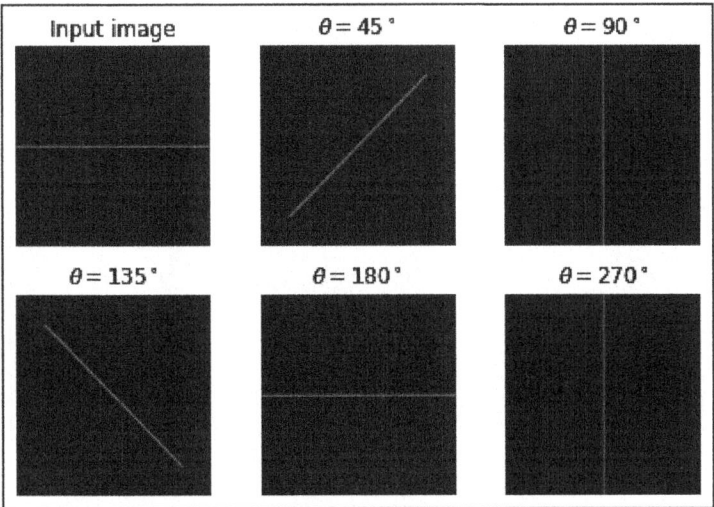

Fig. 1.38 Input image and rotated image at different angles

```
#Image rotation using cv2 library
import numpy as np
import matplotlib.pyplot as plt
import cv2
img=np.zeros([256,256])
img[100:180,100:200]=255
plt.figure(1),plt.subplot(2,3,1),plt.imshow(img,cmap='gray'),plt.axis('off')
plt.title('Input image')
(h, w) = img.shape[:2]
(cX, cY) = (w // 2, h // 2)
angle=[45,90,135,180,225]
for i in range(len(angle)):
    rot_mat = cv2.getRotationMatrix2D((cX, cY), angle[i], 1.0)
    im_rot = cv2.warpAffine(img, rot_mat, (w, h))
    plt.figure(1),plt.subplot(2,3,i+2),plt.imshow(im_rot,cmap='gray')
    plt.title(r'$\theta={}^\circ$'.format(angle[i])),plt.axis('off')
plt.tight_layout()
```

Fig. 1.39 Python code to rotate the input image

is "1", then the output image dimension is the same as the input image dimension.
The rotation matrix is applied to the input image using the built-in function "*warpAffine*" available in cv2 library. The Python code that performs the task is shown in
Fig. 1.39, and the corresponding output is shown in Fig. 1.40.

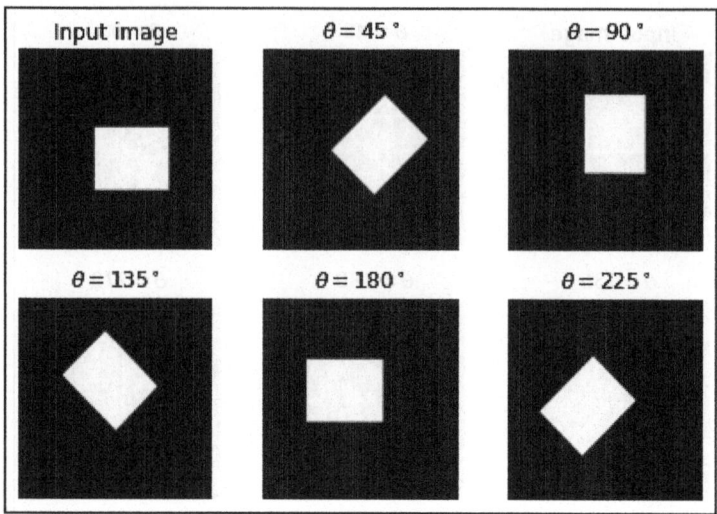

Fig. 1.40 Input and rotated image

Inferences

The following are the inferences from Fig. 1.40:

- The input image is a rectangle in a black background.
- The input image is rotated through different angles, namely 45°, 90°, 135°, 180°, and 225°. From the resultant image, it is possible to observe that the input image is rotated as per the specifications.

Experiment 1.23: Flipping the Image

Flipping in the image refers to the reversal of the input image along the x-axis, along the y-axis, and along both axes. The syntax of the built-in function "*cv2.flip*" is cv2.flip(inputimage, code), if the code is "0" then the input image will be flipped along x-axis, if it is "1" then the input image will be flipped along y-axis, and if the code is "−1" then the image will be flipped along x and y axes. The Python code that performs this task is shown in Fig. 1.41, and the corresponding output is shown in Fig. 1.42.

Inference

- From Fig. 1.42, it is possible to observe that the image of the alphabet "C" is flipped along x-axis, y-axis, and both the axes.

```
#Flipping of the image
import cv2
import matplotlib.pyplot as plt
#Step 1: Reading the image
img=cv2.imread('C.png',0)
#Step 2: Flipping the image
img1=cv2.flip(img,0)
img2=cv2.flip(img,1)
img3=cv2.flip(img,-1)
#Step 3: Displaying the results
plt.figure(figsize=(10,8))
plt.subplot(1,4,1),plt.imshow(img,cmap='gray'),plt.title('Input image')
plt.xticks([]),plt.yticks([]),plt.subplot(1,4,2),plt.imshow(img1,cmap='gray'),
plt.title('Flipped image(x-axis)'),plt.xticks([]),plt.yticks([]),plt.subplot(1,4,3),
plt.imshow(img2,cmap='gray'),plt.title('Flipped image(y-axis)'),plt.xticks([]),plt.yticks([])
plt.subplot(1,4,4),plt.imshow(img3,cmap='gray'),plt.title('Flipped image(both axis)')
plt.xticks([]),plt.yticks([]),plt.tight_layout()
```

Fig. 1.41 Python code to flip the image

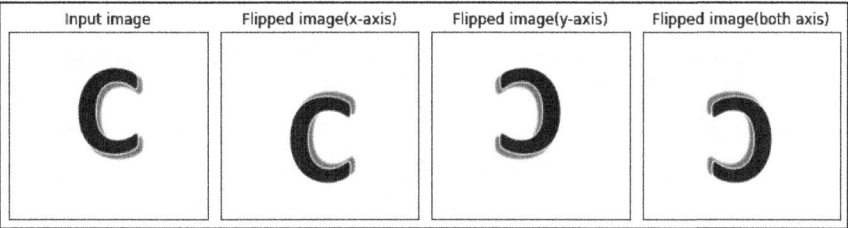

Fig. 1.42 Flipping of the image along x-axis, y-axis, and both x and y axes

Experiment 1.24: Translation of the Image

Translation refers to shifting of the image. The image can be shifted/translated along x-axis as well as along y-axis. Translation is achieved by using the transformation matrix, which is given by

$$M = \begin{bmatrix} 1 & 0 & t_x \\ 0 & 1 & t_y \end{bmatrix}$$

In the above expression, t_x refers to translation along x-axis, and t_y refers to translation along y-axis. The Python code that performs the image's translation is shown in Fig. 1.43, and the corresponding output is shown in Fig. 1.44.

```
#Translation of the image
import cv2
import matplotlib.pyplot as plt
import numpy as np
#Step 1: Generation of image 'A'
img=np.zeros([256,256])
r=50  #Radius of the circle
for i in range(0,256):
    for j in range(0,256):
        if (i-128)**2 + (j-120)**2 < r**2:
            img[i,j]=255
plt.figure(figsize=(8,6)),plt.subplot(2,3,1),plt.imshow(img,cmap='gray'),plt.axis('off'),
plt.title('Input image')
rows,cols = img.shape
M1= np.float32([[1,0,50],[0,1,0]])
M2= np.float32([[1,0,-50],[0,1,0]])
M3=np.float32([[1,0,0],[0,1,50]])
M4= np.float32([[1,0,0],[0,1,-50]])
im1 = cv2.warpAffine(img,M1,(cols,rows))
im2 = cv2.warpAffine(img,M2,(cols,rows))
im3 = cv2.warpAffine(img,M3,(cols,rows))
im4 = cv2.warpAffine(img,M4,(cols,rows))
plt.subplot(2,3,2),plt.imshow(im1,cmap='gray'),plt.axis('off')
plt.title('Translation along x-axis'),plt.subplot(2,3,3),plt.imshow(im2,cmap='gray'),
plt.axis('off'),plt.title('Translation along x-axis'),plt.subplot(2,3,5),plt.imshow(im3,cmap='gray'),
plt.axis('off'),plt.title('Translation along y-axis'),plt.subplot(2,3,6),plt.imshow(im4,cmap='gray'),
plt.axis('off'),plt.title('Translation along y-axis')
plt.tight_layout()
```

Fig. 1.43   Python code to perform translation of the image

Inferences

From Fig. 1.44, the following inferences can be drawn:

- The input image is of dimension 256×256 with a circle centred at (128, 128).
- The output Image-1 is obtained by applying the transformation matrix "M_1" to the input image, which shifts the image along the x-axis towards the right.
- The output Image-2 is obtained by applying the transformation matrix "M_2" to the input image, which shifts the image along the x-axis towards left.
- The output Image-3 is obtained by applying the transformation matrix "M_3" to the input image, which shifts the image along the y-axis towards bottom.
- The output Image-4 is obtained by applying the transformation matrix "M_4" to the input image, which shifts the image along the y-axis towards the top.

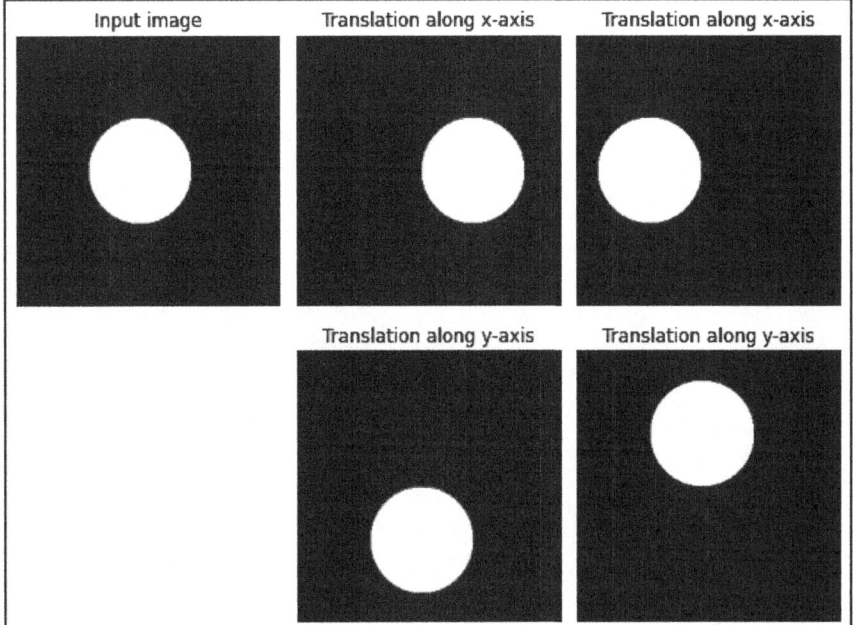

Fig. 1.44 Result of translation of the image

1.7 Image Sampling

Analog images must be sampled and quantized to store and process using a computer. Before sampling, it is necessary to ensure that the signal is band-limited. The analog image is sampled on a discrete grid, and each sample is quantized to an integer value representing a gray level. The digitized image can be processed by means of a computer. This process is illustrated in Fig. 1.45.

In Fig. 1.45, $f(x, y)$ represents the input analog image, $fs[m, n]$ represents the sampled image, and after quantization, the digital image is represented as $f[m, n]$.

1.7.1 Band Limited Image

An image is band-limited if its Fourier transform is zero outside the bounded region in the frequency plane. Let $f(x, y)$ represents the input image in the spatial domain; upon taking Fourier transform, let its spectrum be represented by $F(\omega_1, \omega_2)$. If one assumes that the spectrum is circularly symmetric, then the spectrum of the input image is depicted in Fig. 1.46. From Fig. 1.46, it is possible to observe that

$$F\left(\omega_1, \omega_2\right) = 0, \left|\omega_1\right| > \omega_{10}, \left|\omega_2\right| > \omega_{20} \tag{1.6}$$

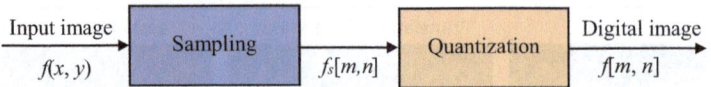

Fig. 1.45 Analog image to a digital image

Fig. 1.46 Spectrum of the
input signal

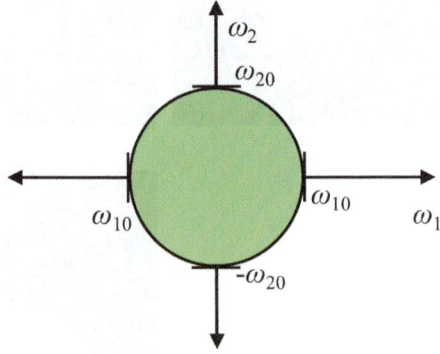

If an image satisfies the above-mentioned criterion, it is claimed to be a band-limited image.

1.7.2   Spectrum of the Sampled Image

The Fourier transform of the sampled image is a scaled, periodic replication of the spectrum of the input image. This is illustrated in Fig. 1.47. From the figure, it is possible to observe the spectrum replication in ω_1 and ω_2 axes. The expression for the sampled spectrum is given by

$$F_s\left(\omega_1,\omega_2\right)=\frac{1}{\Delta x \Delta y}\sum_{k=-\infty}^{\infty}\sum_{l=-\infty}^{\infty}F\left(\omega_1-\frac{2\pi k}{\Delta x},\omega_2-\frac{2\pi l}{\Delta y}\right) \tag{1.7}$$

where $\Delta x = \dfrac{1}{\omega_{xs}}$ and $\Delta y = \dfrac{1}{\omega_{ys}}$. Equation (1.7) can be expressed as

$$F_s\left(\omega_1,\omega_2\right)=\frac{1}{4\pi^2}\omega_{xs}\omega_{ys}\sum_{k=-\infty}^{\infty}\sum_{l=-\infty}^{\infty}F\left(\omega_1-k\omega_{xs},\omega_2-l\omega_{ys}\right) \tag{1.8}$$

Equation (1.8) justifies that the sampled signal spectrum gets replicated along ω_1 and ω_2 axes. The frequencies $2\omega_{10}$ and $2\omega_{20}$ are termed as Nyquist frequencies. In order to reconstruct the image exactly from the samples, the sampling frequency should be greater than or equal to twice the frequency associated with the finest detail in the image. Violation of the sampling theorem results in overlapping the spectrum in the frequency domain, termed "aliasing".

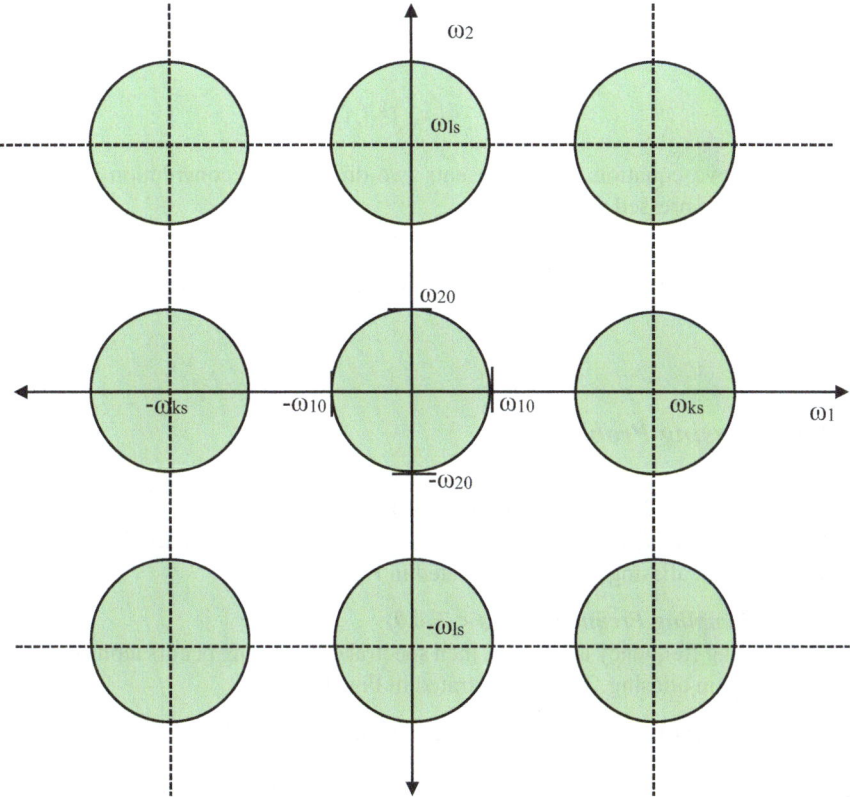

Fig. 1.47 Spectrum of sampled image

1.7.3   Reconstruction of the Image

If the sampling frequencies along the "*x*" and "*y*" directions are chosen in such a way that $\omega_{xs} > 2\omega_{10}$ and $\omega_{ys} > 2\omega_{20}$, then it is possible to recover $F(\omega_1, \omega_2)$ from $Fs(\omega_1, \omega_2)$ using 2D ideal low-pass filter whose frequency response is given by

$$H\left(\omega_1, \omega_2\right) = \begin{cases} \Delta x \Delta y, & \omega_1, \omega_2 \in R, \\ 0, & \text{otherwise.} \end{cases} \tag{1.9}$$

The spectrum of the reconstructed image is given by

$$\hat{F}\left(\omega_1, \omega_2\right) = H\left(\omega_1, \omega_2\right) F_s\left(\omega_1, \omega_2\right) \tag{1.10}$$

A typical choice of "*R*" is a rectangular region for which the impulse response is a "sinc" function, which is given by

$$h\left(x, y\right) = sinc\left(x\omega_{xs}\right) sinc\left(y\omega_{ys}\right) \tag{1.11}$$

We know that convolution in the spatial domain is equivalent to multiplication in the frequency domain and vice versa. Using this idea, Eq. (1.10) can be expressed as

$$\hat{f}(x,y) = h(x,y) * f_s(x,y) \tag{1.12}$$

In the above equation, "*" represents two-dimensional convolution. Equation (1.12) can be expressed as

$$\hat{f}(x,y) = \sum_{m=-\infty}^{\infty} \sum_{n=-\infty}^{\infty} f(m\Delta x, n\Delta y) \operatorname{sinc}\left(\omega_{xs}(x - m\Delta x)\right) \operatorname{sinc}\left(\omega_{ys}(y - n\Delta y)\right) \tag{1.13}$$

1.7.4   Aliasing Problem

Case (i): Sampling Frequency ($\omega xs < 2\omega 10$)
If the sampling frequency $\omega_{xs} < 2\omega_{10}$, then spectral overlapping occurs along ω_1 axis, which results in aliasing. This is illustrated in Fig. 1.48.

Case (ii): Sampling Frequency ($\omega ys < 2\omega 20$)
If the sampling frequency $\omega_{ys} < 2\omega_{20}$, then spectral overlapping occurs along ω_2 axis, which results in aliasing. This is illustrated in Fig. 1.49.

Case (iii): Sampling Frequency ($\omega xs < 2\omega 10$ and $\omega ys < 2\omega 20$)
If the sampling frequency $\omega_{xs} < 2\omega_{10}$ and $\omega_{ys} < 2\omega_{20}$, then spectral overlapping occurs along ω_1 and ω_2 axes, which results in aliasing. This is illustrated in Fig. 1.50.

Experiment 1.25: Image Sampling
In this experiment, a sinusoidal grating pattern with horizontal frequency $fx = 4$ Hz and $fy = 5$ Hz is generated. This image is sampled at four different sampling frequencies, namely, 10 Hz, 20 Hz, 50 Hz, and 100 Hz. The Python code that performs this task is shown in Fig. 1.51. The original and the reconstructed image are shown in Fig. 1.52.

Inferences
From Fig. 1.52, it is possible to observe the following:

- The input signal is a sinusoidal grating pattern. The frequencies along x and y directions are different.
- The input image is sampled at four different sampling frequencies.
- When the sampling frequency is less, the reconstructed image differs from the original image. This is termed as "aliasing".
- With increasing sampling frequency, the reconstructed image resembles the original image. This means there is no aliasing.

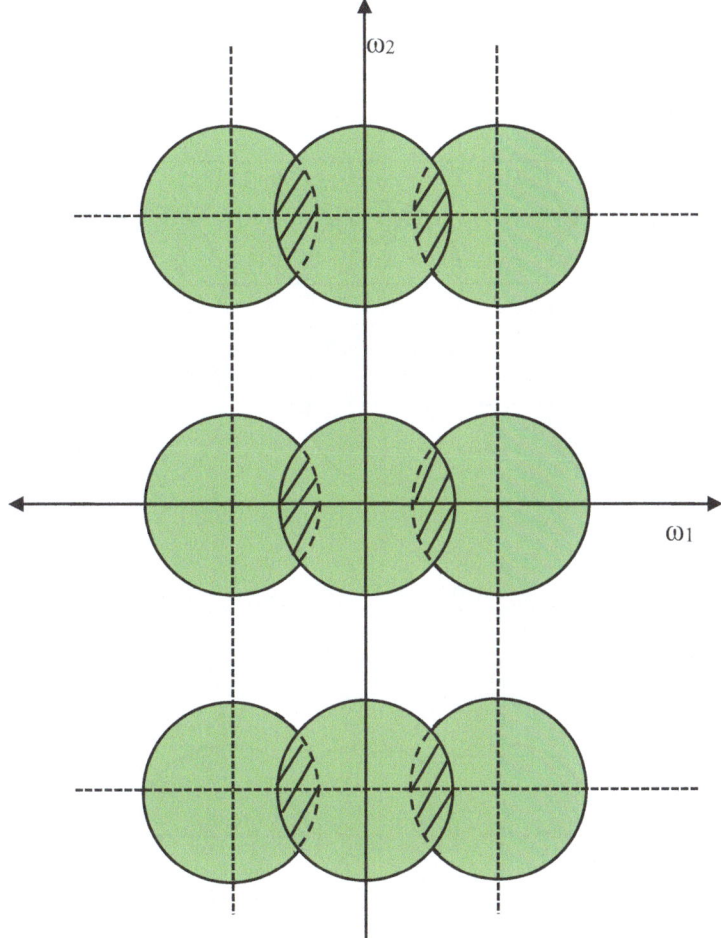

Fig. 1.48 Aliasing due to spectral overlapping along ω_1 axis

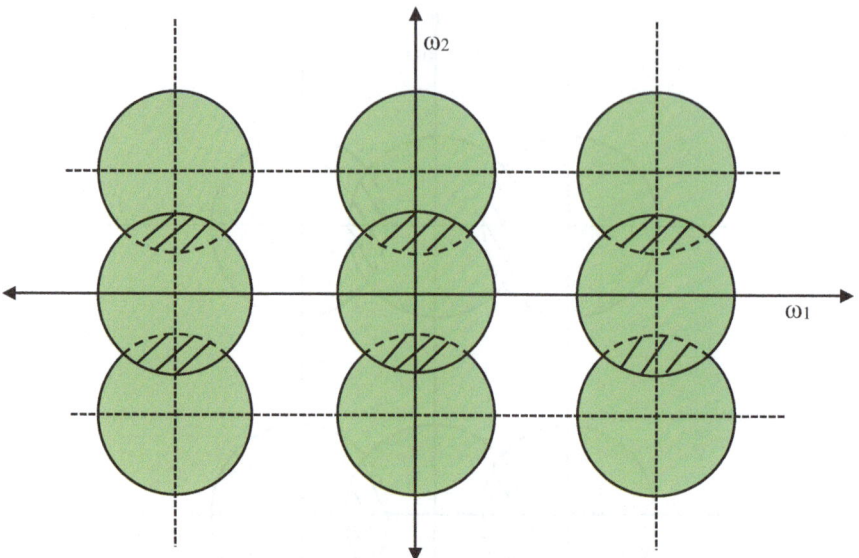

Fig. 1.49 Aliasing due to spectral overlapping along ω_2 axis

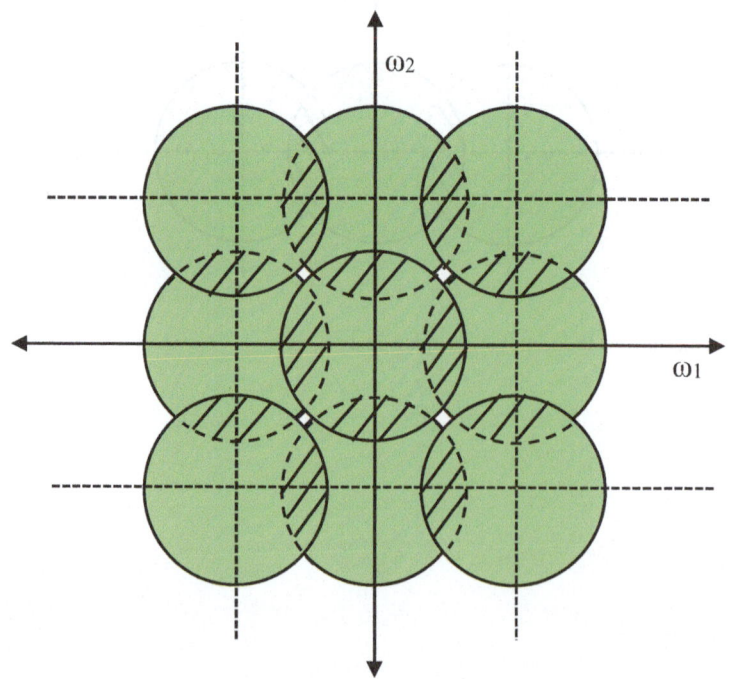

Fig. 1.50 Aliasing due to spectral overlapping along ω_1 and ω_2 axes

```
#Sampling of the image
import numpy as np
import matplotlib.pyplot as plt
#Step 1: Generation of input image
x=np.arange(-.5,.5,1/100)
y=np.arange(-.5,.5,1/100)
X,Y=np.meshgrid(x,y)
fx,fy=4,5
img=np.sin(2*np.pi*(fx*X+fy*Y))
plt.figure(figsize=(8,6)),plt.subplot(2,3,1),plt.imshow(img,cmap='gray'),
plt.axis('off'),plt.title('Input image')
#To generate sampled image
fxs = [10,20,50,75,100]; #Sampling frequency along x-direction
fys = [10,20,50,75,100]; #Sampling frequency along y-direction
for i in range(len(fxs)):
    deltax = 1/fxs[i];
    deltay = 1/fys[i];
    xs=np.arange(-.5,.5,deltax)
    ys=np.arange(-.5,.5,deltay)
    Xs,Ys= np.meshgrid(xs,ys)
    imgs=np.sin(2*np.pi*(fx*Xs+fy*Ys))
    Ir=np.zeros(np.shape(img))
    Nx=np.shape(imgs)[1]
    Ny=np.shape(imgs)[0]
#To obtain the reconstructed image
    for n in range(1,Nx):
        for m in range(1,Ny):
            sincx=np.sinc(np.pi*(x - (n-0.5*Nx)*deltax)/deltax)
            sincx = np.tile(sincx, ([np.shape(img)[0], 1]))
            sincy=np.sinc(np.pi*(y - (m-0.5*Ny)*deltay)/deltay)
            sincy = np.tile(sincy.reshape(np.shape(sincy)[0],1), ([1,np.shape(img)[1]]))
            Ir = Ir + imgs[m][n]*sincx*sincy
            plt.subplot(2,3,i+2),plt.imshow(Ir,cmap='gray'),plt.axis('off')
            plt.title('$f_{{xs}}={}$, $f_{{ys}}={}$'.format(fxs[i],fys[i]))
plt.tight_layout()
```

Fig. 1.51 Python code to illustrate sampling and aliasing

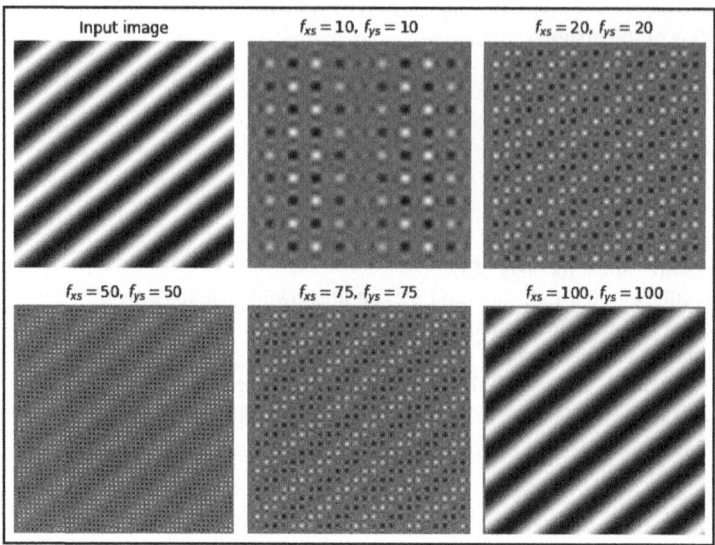

Fig. 1.52 Original and reconstructed images

1.8   Quantization of the Image

The process of representing a continuous function with discrete values is termed as "quantization". It is the process of mapping a large set of values into a smaller set of values. It is a many-to-one mapping, hence it is an irreversible operation. Quantization leads to loss of information. Quantization is performed to represent an image with a minimum number of bits so that the image can be effectively stored and easily transmitted. Quantization converts the continuously varying brightness of an image into a discrete set of levels. This is represented in Fig. 1.53. In the figure x-axis represents the input values and the y-axis represents the output values. Here T_1 to T_4 represents the threshold values. If the spacing between the threshold and the quantization levels is constant, then the quantization is termed as uniform quantization.

1.8.1   Terminologies Related to the Quantization of the Image

Some terminologies that are common in image quantization are (1) dynamic range, (2) reconstruction level, and (3) step size of the quantizer. Dynamic range is the difference between the maximum and minimum gray levels of the image. If "b" is the number of bits used to represent the gray level of the image, then the reconstruction level is given by $L = 2^b$. The bit depth that implies the number of bits used to represent the image determines the accuracy and the quality of the quantized value.

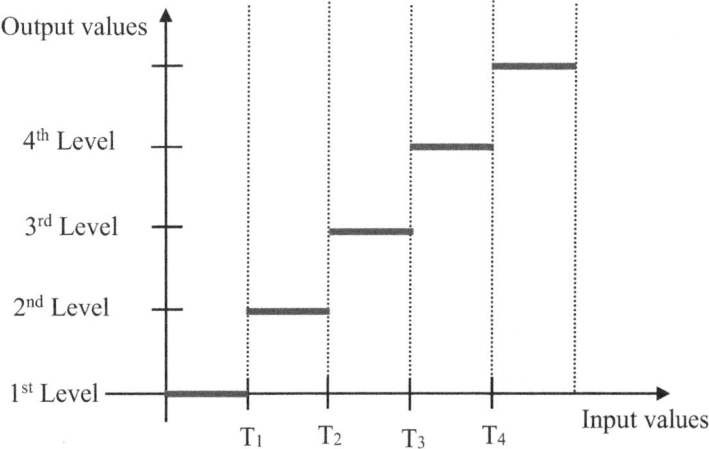

Fig. 1.53 Transfer characteristics of a uniform quantizer

Quantizing an image with lesser number of bits introduces "false contours". The step size of the quantizer is given by $\Delta = \dfrac{DR}{L}$, where "DR" represents the dynamic range and "L" represents the reconstruction level. The reconstruction level is provided by $L = 2^b$, where "b" is the number of bits used to represent the pixel value. Equal distances between adjacent decision levels and adjacent reconstruction levels lead to uniform quantization.

Experiment 1.26: Transfer Characteristics of Uniform Quantization
The Python code that plots the transfer characteristics of uniform quantization for different reconstruction levels is shown in Fig. 1.54, and the corresponding output is shown in Fig. 1.55.

Inferences
From the transfer characteristics shown in Fig. 1.55, it is possible to infer the following:

- The transfer characteristics of uniform quantizer follow stair step waveform.
- With the increase in the number of reconstruction levels, it is possible to observe that the transfer characteristics are a straight line. This implies that the output signal follows the input signal when the number of reconstruction levels is high.

Experiment 1.27: Python Illustration of Uniform Quantization
This experiment illustrates the uniform quantization using Python. The Python code that performs uniform quantization of the input image with different reconstruction levels is shown in Fig. 1.56, and the corresponding output is shown in Fig. 1.57.

```
#Transfer characteristics of uniform quantizer
import numpy as np
import matplotlib.pyplot as plt
#Step 1: Generation of input image
x = np.linspace(-20,20)
# Uniform Quantization
b=[1,2,4,8]  #Number of bits used to represent pixel
plt.figure(figsize=(8,6))
for i in range(len(b)):
    dr = np.max(x) - np.min(x) #Dynamic range
    l = 2 ** b[i]   #Reconstruction level
    q = dr / l     #Quantization step size
    y= np.floor(x/ q) * q + (q / 2)
    plt.subplot(2,2,i+1),plt.plot(x,y),plt.xlabel('Input Values'),
    plt.ylabel('Output Values'),plt.title('L={}'.format(2**b[i]))
plt.tight_layout()
```

Fig. 1.54 Python code to obtain the transfer characteristics of uniform quantizer

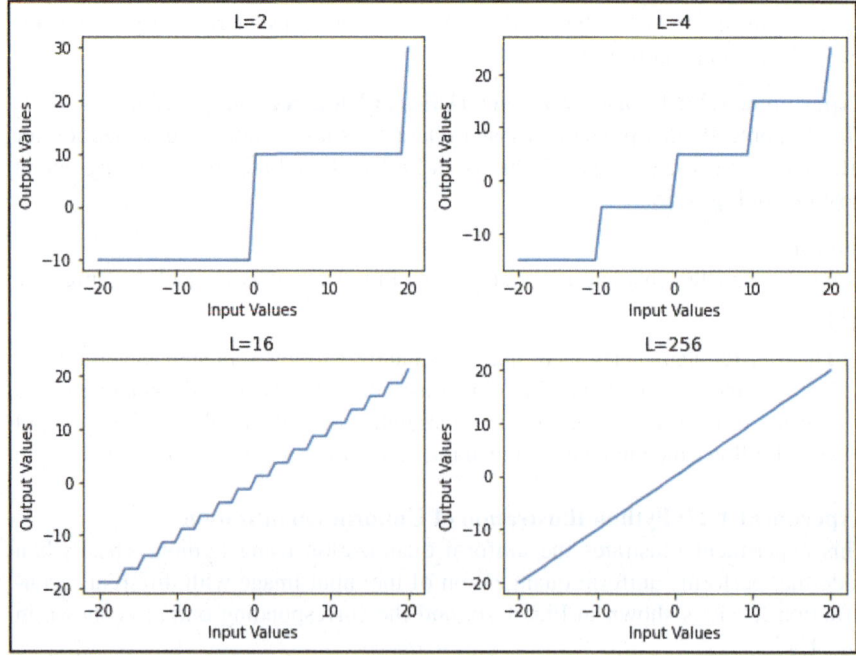

Fig. 1.55 Transfer characteristics of uniform quantizer

```
#Uniform quantization of the image
import numpy as np
import matplotlib.pyplot as plt
#Step 1: Generation of input image
im = np.arange(256).reshape(16, 16)
# Uniform Quantization
b=[1,2,4,6,8]  #Number of bits used to represent pixel
plt.figure(figsize=(8,6))
plt.subplot(2,3,1),plt.imshow(im,cmap='gray'),plt.title('Input image')
ax=plt.gca()
ax.get_xaxis().set_visible(False),ax.get_yaxis().set_visible(False)
for i in range(len(b)):
    dr = np.max(im) - np.min(im) #Dynamic range
    l = 2 ** b[i]   #Reconstruction level
    q = dr / l     #Quantization step size
    q_im = np.floor(im/q)*q + (q/2)
    q_im[q_im.shape[0]-1,q_im.shape[1]-1]=q_im[q_im.shape[0]-1,q_im.shape[1]-2]
    q_im.astype(np.uint8)
    plt.subplot(2,3,i+2),plt.imshow(q_im,cmap='gray'),
    plt.xticks([]),plt.yticks([])
    plt.title('L={}'.format(2**b[i]))
plt.tight_layout()
```

Fig. 1.56 Python code to perform uniform quantization of the image

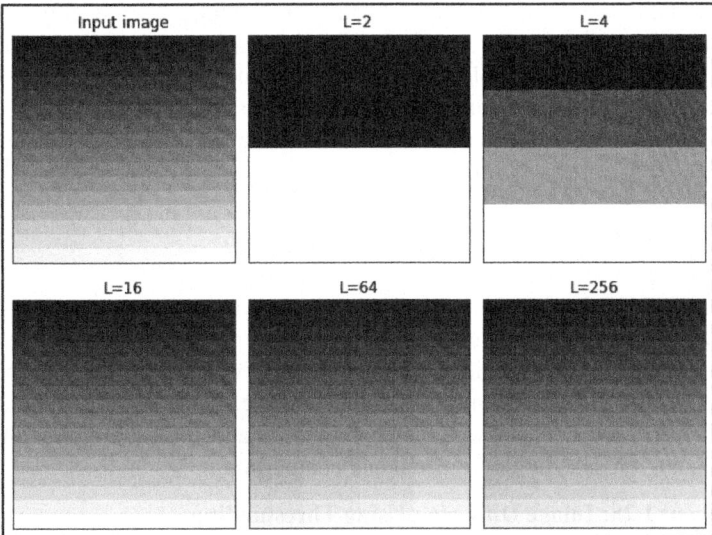

Fig. 1.57 Original and reconstructed image with different levels of reconstruction

Inferences

From Fig. 1.57, it is possible to observe the following facts:

- The input image gray level varies gradually (vertically) from black to white.
- With a number of reconstruction levels, $L = 2$, the reconstructed image has two distinct gray levels.
- With the number of reconstruction level $L = 4$, it is possible to observe that the reconstructed image has four distinct gray levels.
- With the increase in the number of reconstruction levels, the reconstructed image resembles the input image.

1.9 Image Dithering

Dithering is a process by which images with a finite number of gray levels appear as continuous-tone images. That is, an attempt is made to create an illusion. Broadly, image dithering can be classified as (1) average dithering or thresholding, (2) random dithering, (3) ordered dithering, and (4) error diffusion dithering.

1.9.1 Average Dithering or Thresholding

In average dithering or thresholding, each input image pixel is compared with a fixed threshold value. Thresholding results in a binary image. Three different types of thresholding include (1) global threshold, (2) local threshold, and (3) adaptive threshold. In the global threshold, a single threshold value is used for the entire image.

If $f(x, y)$ represents the input image, "T" represents the threshold value, then the expression for the thresholded image ($g(x, y)$) is given by

$$g(x,y) = \begin{cases} 1, & \text{if } f(x,y) > T, \\ 0, & \text{if } f(x,y) \le T. \end{cases} \tag{1.14}$$

If the value of "T" is fixed for the entire image, it is termed as "global threshold". Thus, thresholding can be considered as two-level or one-bit quantization.

In local thresholding technique, unique threshold value is chosen for subimage, which is obtained by partitioning the whole image. In adaptive thresholding, a threshold has to be calculated for each pixel in the image. It is the simplest dithering algorithm but it results in loss of detail and contouring.

Experiment 1.28: Image Dithering Using Thresholding

The aim of this experiment is to perform image dithering using thresholding technique. The Python code that performs thresholding of the input grayscale image using (1) OTSU threshold algorithm and (2) arbitrary threshold, is shown in Fig. 1.58, and the corresponding output is shown in Fig. 1.59.

```
import cv2
import matplotlib.pyplot as plt
#Step 1:Reading the image
img=cv2.imread('cameraman.tif',0)
#Step 2: Threshold using OTSU algorithm
(thresh, im_bw) = cv2.threshold(img, 128, 255, cv2.THRESH_BINARY | cv2.THRESH_OTSU)
#Step 3: Arbitrary threshold
arb_thresh=128
im1=img>arb_thresh
#Step 3: Displaying the result
plt.figure(figsize=(8,6)),plt.subplot(1,3,1),plt.imshow(img,cmap='gray')
plt.title('Original image'),plt.xticks([]),plt.yticks([]),plt.subplot(1,3,2),
plt.imshow(im_bw,cmap='gray'),plt.title('Thresholded image(OTSU)'),
plt.xticks([]),plt.yticks([]),plt.subplot(1,3,3),plt.imshow(im1,cmap='gray')
plt.title('Arbitrary threshold'),plt.xticks([]),plt.yticks([])
plt.tight_layout()
```

Fig. 1.58 Python code to perform dithering using thresholding

Fig. 1.59 Result of thresholded image

Inferences

From Fig. 1.58, it is possible to observe the following facts:

- The input image is a grayscale image. The grayscale image is thresholded using (1) OTSU algorithm using the built-in function "threshold" function available in cv2 library.
- Arbitrary threshold is done using the threshold value of "128". An 8-bit image takes gray level from 0 to 255, the mid value "128" is chosen as the arbitrary threshold value.

From Fig. 1.59, the following inferences can be drawn:

- The input image is termed as an original image, which is a grayscale image.
- Two different types of thresholding are applied to the input image. The OTSU threshold value for the input image is 88, whereas the arbitrary threshold value is chosen as 128.

- Both the threshold images are binary image, which takes either "0" or "1" value. Thresholding can be considered as one-bit quantizer.

1.9.2   Random Dithering

In random dithering, each pixel value is compared against a random threshold, resulting in a noisy image. Random dithering does not generate patterned artefacts. Random dithering can be considered as random noise binarization. The drawback of random dithering is that the noise tends to swamp the details of the image. Random dithering is based on the fact that the human eye is more tolerant to high-frequency noise than contours or aliasing.

Experiment 1.29: Random Dithering
The objective of this experiment is to perform random dithering using Python. The Python code that performs random dithering of the input "cameraman" image is shown in Fig. 1.60a, and the corresponding output is shown in Fig. 1.60b.

```
#Random dithering
import cv2
import numpy as np
import matplotlib.pyplot as plt
import random
#Step 1: Reading the input image
img=cv2.imread('cameraman.tif',0)
[m,n]=img.shape
#Step 2: Performing random dithering
bw=np.zeros((m,n))
for x in range(m):
    for y in range(n):
        if random.randrange(255)<img[x,y]:
            bw[x,y]=255
        else:
            bw[x,y]=0
#Step 3: Displaying the result
plt.subplot(1,2,1),
plt.imshow(img,cmap='gray'),
plt.title('Original image'),
plt.xticks([]),plt.yticks([])
plt.subplot(1,2,2),
plt.imshow(bw,cmap='gray'),
plt.title('Random dithered image'),
plt.xticks([]),plt.yticks([])
plt.tight_layout()
```

| **(a) Python Code** | **(b) Dithering Output** |

Fig. 1.60 Random dithering: (**a**) Python code, (**b**) dithering output

```
#Comparison of thresholding and Random dithering
import cv2
import numpy as np
import matplotlib.pyplot as plt
import random
#Step 1: Reading the input image
img=cv2.imread('cameraman.tif',0)
[m,n]=img.shape
#Step 2: Thresholding of the image
(thresh, im_bw) = cv2.threshold(img, 128, 255, cv2.THRESH_BINARY | cv2.THRESH_OTSU)
#Step 3: Performing random dithering
bw=np.zeros((m,n))
for x in range(m):
  for y in range(n):
      if random.randrange(255)<img[x,y]:
        bw[x,y]=255
      else:
        bw[x,y]=0
#Step 3: Displaying the result
plt.figure(figsize=(8,6)),plt.subplot(1,3,1),plt.imshow(img,cmap='gray'),plt.title('Input image')
plt.xticks([]),plt.yticks([]),plt.subplot(1,3,2),plt.imshow(im_bw,cmap='gray'),
plt.title('Thresholded image'),plt.xticks([]),plt.yticks([]),plt.subplot(1,3,3),
plt.imshow(bw,cmap='gray'), plt.title('Random dithered image'),plt.xticks([]),plt.yticks([])
plt.tight_layout()
```

Fig. 1.61 Comparison of thresholding and random dithering

Inferences

The following inferences can be made from this experiment:

- From Fig. 1.60a, it is possible to observe that the built-in function "*randrange()*" available in "random" library is used to generate the random number.
- From Fig. 1.60b, it is possible to observe that a random dithered image is free from false contouring.

Experiment 1.30: Comparison of Thresholding and Random Dithering

The objective of this experiment is to compare the thresholding with random dithering. The Python code that illustrates this task is shown in Fig. 1.61, and the corresponding output is shown in Fig. 1.62.

Inferences

The following inferences can be made from this experiment:

- Figure 1.62 shows the result of thresholding and random dithering applied to the grayscale image.
- A thresholded image is a binary image with a gray level of either "0" or "1".
- Random dithered images attempt to create an illusion of a continuous tone image.

Fig. 1.62 Result of the Python code shown in Fig. 1.61

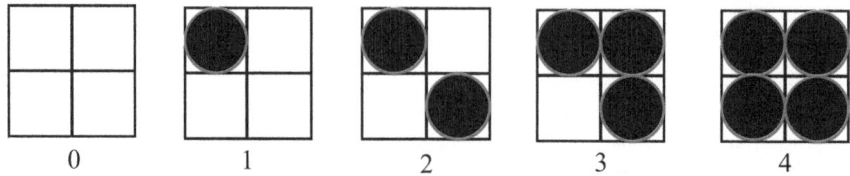

$$0 \qquad 1 \qquad 2 \qquad 3 \qquad 4$$

Fig. 1.63 2×2 dither pattern

1.9.3   Ordered Dithering

In ordered dithering, a comparison of blocks of the original to a two-dimensional grid of threshold called a dither pattern is done. Each element of the original block is quantized according to the corresponding threshold value in the dither pattern. Ordered dithering uses a fixed pattern. This means that the values in the dither matrix are fixed. For every pixel in the image, the value of the pattern at the corresponding location is used as a threshold. Different patterns can generate different dithering effects. 2×2 dither matrix generates 5 gray levels, which is illustrated in Fig. 1.63. 3×3 dither matrix exhibits 10 gray levels, which is shown in Fig. 1.64. A "$n \times n$" dither matrix exhibits $n^2 + 1$ gray levels.

The dither pattern through "Bayer" matrix is obtained according to the recurrence $B_k = \begin{pmatrix} B_{k-1} & B_{k-1} + 2.2^{-2k} \\ B_{k-1} + 3.2^{-2k} & B_{k-1} + 1.2^{-2k} \end{pmatrix}$ with $B_0 = (0)$. With this relation, the Bayer matrix of size 2×2 is given by

$$B_1 = \frac{1}{4}\begin{pmatrix} 0 & 2 \\ 3 & 1 \end{pmatrix}$$

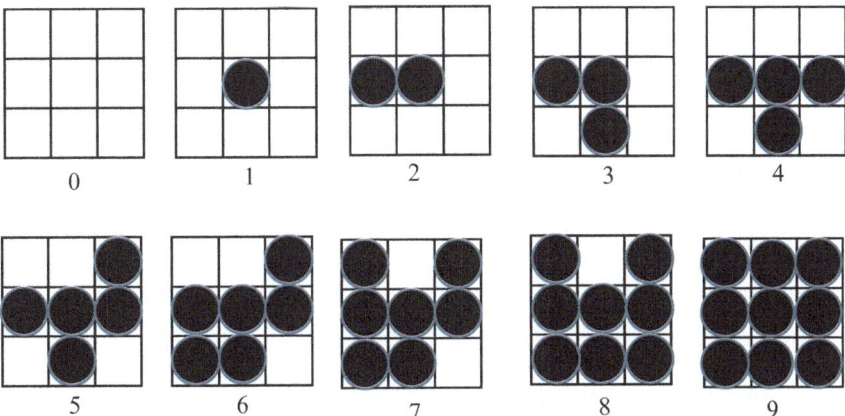

Fig. 1.64 3 × 3 dither pattern

Similarly, Bayer matrix of size 4 × 4 is given by

$$\frac{1}{16}\begin{pmatrix} 0 & 8 & 2 & 10 \\ 12 & 4 & 14 & 6 \\ 3 & 11 & 1 & 9 \\ 15 & 7 & 13 & 5 \end{pmatrix}$$

Experiment 1.31: Plotting Bayer Matrix of Size 2 × 2, 4 × 4, 8 × 8, and 16 × 16
The aim of this experiment is to plot the various size of the Bayer matrix using Python. The Python code that plots the Bayer matrix of different dimensions is shown in Fig. 1.65, and the corresponding output is shown in Fig. 1.66.

Inference

• Bayer pattern attempts to get different shades of gray, from black to white.

Pseudo-Code for Ordered Dithering of Grayscale Image
The pseudo-code of ordered dithering is given in Fig. 1.67. Let $f(x,y)$ represents the input image, $g(x,y)$ represents the output image, and $D(x,y)$ represents the dither matrix.

Experiment 1.32: Ordered Dithering of Grayscale Image
This experiment discusses the implementation of ordered dithering of grayscale image in the Python environment. The Python code that performs ordered dithering of input grayscale image for Bayer pattern of size 2 × 2 and 4 × 4 is given in Fig. 1.68, and the corresponding output is shown in Fig. 1.69.

Inferences
The following inferences can be drawn from this experiment:

```
#Plotting Bayer pattern
import numpy as np
import matplotlib.pyplot as plt
#Step 1: Generation of Bayer matrix
def Bayer_matrix(n):
  if n == 1:
    return np.array([[0]])
  else:
    first = (n ** 2) * Bayer_matrix(int(n/2))
    second = (n ** 2) * Bayer_matrix(int(n/2)) + 2
    third = (n ** 2) * Bayer_matrix(int(n/2)) + 3
    fourth = (n ** 2) * Bayer_matrix(int(n/2)) + 1
    first_col = np.concatenate((first, third), axis=0)
    second_col = np.concatenate((second, fourth), axis=0)
    return (1/n**2) * np.concatenate((first_col, second_col), axis=1)
n=[2,4,8,16]
#Step 2: Plotting the Bayer pattern
plt.figure(figsize=(8,6))
for i in range(len(n)):
  dithermat=Bayer_matrix(n[i])
  plt.subplot(1,4,i+1),plt.imshow(dithermat,cmap='gray'),
  plt.xticks([]),plt.yticks([])
  plt.title('Bayer matrix ({} x {})'.format(n[i],n[i]))
plt.tight_layout()
```

Fig. 1.65 Python code to plot the Bayer pattern

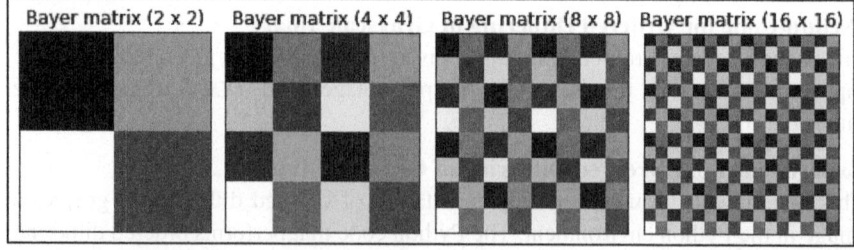

Fig. 1.66 Plot of Bayer matrix of different dimensions

Fig. 1.67 Pseudo-code for
ordered dithering of image

```
for x=0 to x_max
    for y=0 to y_max
        i = x mod n
        j= y mod n
        if f(x,y)>D(i,j)
                    g(x,y)=1
        else
                    g(x,y)=0
        end
    end
end
```

- The input image to the ordered dithering is a grayscale image. Two Bayer patterns of size 2×2 and 4×4 are defined to perform ordered dithering of the input grayscale image.
- The result of ordered dithering is shown in Fig. 1.69. With the increase in the size of the Bayer pattern, the output image appears to be a continuous tone image.

1.9.4   Error Diffusion Dithering

In error diffusion dithering, the quantization error is spread over neighbouring pixels. The error is dispersed to pixels on the right and below. This is illustrated in Fig. 1.70.

In Fig. 1.70, C_j represents the "j^{th}" column and R_j and R_{j+1} represent the "j^{th}" and "$(j + 1)^{th}$" rows. In Fig. 1.70, α, β, γ, and δ are weights with which the error is spread to the neighbouring pixels. It can be observed from Fig. 1.70 that $\alpha + \beta + \gamma + \delta = 1$. One of the popular algorithms for error diffusion is "Floyd–Steinberg" algorithm. The steps of Floyd–Steinberg algorithm are given below:

1. Initialize an output image matrix with zeros.
2. Quantize the current pixel using the threshold "T", and place the result in the output matrix.
3. Compute the quantization error by subtracting the binary pixel from the grayscale pixel.

```
#Ordered dithering of grayscale image
import numpy as np
import cv2
import matplotlib.pyplot as plt
#Step 1: Reading the input image
img=cv2.imread('cameraman.tif',0)
#Step 2: Defining the dither matrix
BP_2=(1/4)*np.array([[0,2],[3,1]])
BP_4 = (1 / 16) * np.array([[0, 8, 2, 10],[12, 4, 14, 6],[3, 11, 1, 9],[15, 7, 13, 5]])
#Step 3: Obtaining the dither matrix
outputimg1 = np.array(img, dtype=float) /np.max(img)
outputimg2 = np.array(img, dtype=float) /np.max(img)
h1, w1 = outputimg1.shape
output1 = np.zeros([h1, w1], dtype=bool)
for j in range(h1):
     for i in range(w1):
        if outputimg1[j][i] < BP_2[j % 2][i % 2]:
            output1[j][i] = 0
        else:
            output1[j][i] = 1
h2, w2 = outputimg2.shape
output2 = np.zeros([h2, w2], dtype=bool)
for j in range(h2):
     for i in range(w2):
        if outputimg2[j][i] < BP_4[j % 4][i % 4]:
            output2[j][i] = 0
        else:
            output2[j][i] = 1
#Step 4: Plotting the result
plt.figure(figsize=(8,6)),plt.subplot(1,3,1),plt.imshow(img,cmap='gray')
plt.title('Input image'),plt.xticks([]),plt.yticks([]),plt.subplot(1,3,2),
plt.imshow(output1,cmap='gray'),plt.title('2 x 2 ordered dither'),plt.xticks([]),
plt.yticks([]),plt.subplot(1,3,3),plt.imshow(output2,cmap='gray'),
plt.title('4 x 4 ordered dither'),plt.xticks([]),plt.yticks([])
plt.tight_layout()
```

Fig. 1.68   Ordered dithering of grayscale image

4. Add scaled versions of this error to the "future" pixels of the original image. This
    is represented as:

$$f(x+1,y)+=\frac{7}{16}\times\alpha$$

$$f(x-1,y-1)+=\frac{3}{16}\times\beta$$

Fig. 1.69 Result of ordered dithering

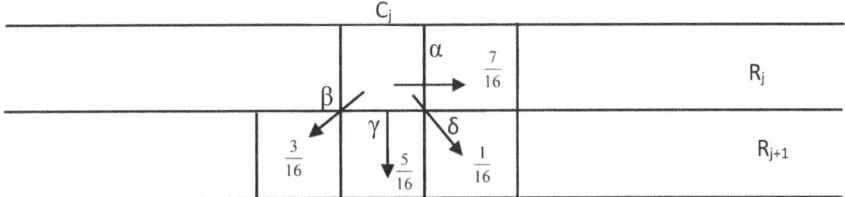

Fig. 1.70 Illustration of error diffusion phenomenon

$$f\left(x,y-1\right)+=\frac{5}{16}\times\gamma$$

$$f\left(x+1,y-1\right)+=\frac{1}{16}\times\delta$$

Let $f(x, y)$ represents the current pixel, then $f(x + 1, y)$ represents pixel to the right of $f(x,y)$, whereas $f(x - 1, y - 1)$ represents below left pixel of $f(x,y)$, $f(x,y - 1)$ represents pixel below $f(x,y)$, and $f(x + 1, y + 1)$ represent below right pixel of $f(x,y)$.

5. Proceed to the next pixel.

Experiment 1.33: Error Diffusion Dithering of Grayscale Image

This experiment deals with the implementation of error diffusion dithering of grayscale image. The Python code that performs error diffusion dithering using the Floyd–Steinberg algorithm is shown in Fig. 1.71, and the corresponding output is shown in Fig. 1.72.

Inference

• The error diffusion dithering attempts to generate a continuous tone image by diffusing the error.

```
#Error diffusion dithering
import numpy as np
import cv2
import matplotlib.pyplot as plt
#Step 1: Reading the input image
img=cv2.imread('cameraman.tif',0)
img1= np.array(img, dtype=float) /np.max(img)
h, w = img1.shape
output = np.copy(img1) + np.random.random_sample([h, w])
#Step 2: Defining the weights
alpha,beta,theta,delta=7/16,3/16,5/16,1/16
#Step 3: Floyd-Steinberg algorithm
for j in range(h):
    for i in range(w):
        x = i if j % 2 == 0 else w - 1 - i
        original_pixel = output[j][x]
        new_pixel = round(original_pixel)
        output[j][x] = new_pixel
        error = original_pixel - new_pixel
        if j < h - 1 and 0 < x < w - 1 and j % 2 == 0:
            output[j][x + 1] += error * alpha
            output[j + 1][x - 1] += error * beta
            output[j + 1][x] += error * theta
            output[j + 1][x + 1] += error * delta
        if j < h - 1 and 0 < x < w - 1 and j % 2 == 1:
            output[j][x - 1] += error * alpha
            output[j + 1][x - 1] += error * beta
            output[j + 1][x] += error *theta
            output[j + 1][x - 1] += error * delta
output=(np.clip(output, 0, 1) * 255).astype(np.uint8)
#Step 3: Displaying the result
plt.figure(figsize=(8,6)),plt.subplot(1,2,1),plt.imshow(img,cmap='gray'),
plt.title('Input image'),plt.xticks([]),plt.yticks([]),plt.subplot(1,2,2),
plt.imshow(output,cmap='gray'),plt.title('Error diffusion dither'),
plt.xticks([]),plt.yticks([])
plt.tight_layout()
```

Fig. 1.71 Python code to perform error diffusion dithering

Fig. 1.72 Result of Python code shown in Fig. 1.71

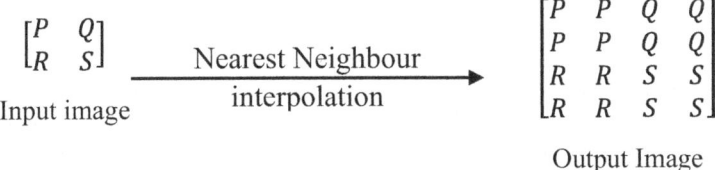

Output Image

Fig. 1.73 Nearest neighbour interpolation

1.9.5   Image Interpolation

Interpolation is based on the principle of using known data to estimate values at unknown points. Widely used interpolation techniques are (1) nearest neighbour, (2) bilinear, (3) bicubic, and (4) cubic spline. Each method of interpolation has its own advantages and drawbacks.

1.9.6   Nearest Neighbour Interpolation

In nearest neighbour interpolation, each interpolated output pixel is assigned the value of the nearest sample point in the input image. The illustration of nearest neighbour interpolation technique is given in Fig. 1.73.

In Fig. 1.73, the input image is a 2×2 image, which is interpolated to 4×4 output image by assigning the value of the nearest pixel to the new pixel.

Nearest neighbour interpolation is very simple, and it uses the nearest neighbour's pixel to fill the interpolated point. The nearest neighbour method of interpolation is easy to implement. The drawback is that this method of interpolation results in blocky or pixelated results. The details and smoothness of the image is lost in nearest neighbour method of interpolation.

1.9.7 Bilinear Interpolation

In bilinear interpolation, the interpolated point is filled with four closest pixel's weighted average. This method uses two linear interpolations in horizontal and vertical directions; hence, it is termed as bilinear interpolation technique. The result obtained by the bilinear interpolation technique is smoother when compared to the result obtained using nearest neighbour interpolation.

1.9.8 Bicubic Interpolation

Bicubic interpolation uses cubic polynomials to interpolate pixel values. Bicubic interpolation is a method for image resizing that calculates new pixel values using the nearest 16 pixels. The algorithm assigns different weights to the neighbouring pixels based on their distance from the target pixel, allowing closer pixels to influence the interpolated value more. This technique produces smoother and higher quality results compared to nearest neighbour and bilinear interpolation. This is achieved at the expense of complexity to perform mathematical evaluation.

Experiment 1.34: Implementation of Different Interpolation Techniques
The objective of this experiment is to implement nearest neighbour, bilinear, and bicubic interpolation of the image. The input image is a 256 × 256 cameraman image. It is reduced to 20 × 20 to understand the impact of interpolation. The downsized image is then interpolated to a 512 × 512 image using nearest neighbour, bilinear, and bicubic interpolation. The Python code that performs this task is shown in Fig. 1.74, and the corresponding output is shown in Fig. 1.75.

Inferences
From Fig. 1.75, it is possible to observe the following:

- The input image is a 256 × 256 cameraman image with good spatial resolution. Upon resizing the 256 × 256 cameraman image to 50 × 50 resized image, the spatial resolution is lost to obtain poor quality image.
- Three different types of interpolation namely nearest neighbour, bilinear, and bicubic interpolation techniques are applied to the poor-quality image to obtain 512 × 512 image.
- It is possible to observe pixelated results in nearest neighbour interpolation.
- Compared to nearest neighbour interpolation, bilinear and bicubic interpolation techniques result in a smooth image.

```
#Image interpolation
import matplotlib.pyplot as plt
import cv2
#Step1: Reading the input image
img=cv2.imread('cameraman.tif',0)
#Step 2: Resizing the image
img1=cv2.resize(img,(50,50))
#Step 3: Inerpolation techniques
#nearest neighbor interpolation
nn_image = cv2.resize(img1, (512, 512),interpolation=cv2.INTER_NEAREST)
#Bilinear interpolation
bilinear_image = cv2.resize(img1, (512, 512),interpolation=cv2.INTER_LINEAR)
#Bicubic interpolation
bicubic_image = cv2.resize(img1, (512, 512),interpolation=cv2.INTER_CUBIC)
#Step 4: Displaying the result
fig=plt.figure(figsize=(10,8)),plt.subplot(1, 4, 1),plt.imshow(img1,cmap='gray')
plt.title('Input Image {}'.format(img1.shape),plt.axis('off'),plt.subplot(1, 4, 2),
plt.imshow(nn_image,cmap='gray'),plt.title('Nearest Neighbor {}'.format(nn_image.shape)),
plt.axis('off'),plt.subplot(1, 4, 3),plt.imshow(bilinear_image,cmap='gray')
plt.title('Bilinear {}'.format(bilinear_image.shape)),plt.axis('off')
plt.subplot(1, 4, 4),plt.imshow(bicubic_image,cmap='gray')
plt.title('Bicubic {}'.format(bicubic_image.shape)),plt.axis('off')
plt.tight_layout()
```

Fig. 1.74 Python code to perform image interpolation

Fig. 1.75 Result of image interpolation

1.10 Generation of Test Image Patterns

This section deals with the generation of different types of test image patterns. The pattern includes different two-dimensional functions such as sinusoidal grating pattern, gradient image, zone plate image generation, and geometrical shapes such as lines, circles, and concentric circles.

Experiment 1.35: Generate a 256 × 256 Black Image with a White Dot at the Centre (at the Location 128 × 128). Display the Generated Image and its 128th Row and Comment on the Observed Result

The Python code that does the task is shown in Fig. 1.76a, and the corresponding output is shown in Fig. 1.76b.

Inferences

- From Fig. 1.76a, it is possible to observe that the built-in libraries "numpy" and "matplotlib" are used in Test Image-1 generation.
- From Fig. 1.76b, it is possible to observe a white dot at the centre of black background.
- Upon visualizing the 128th row of the test image, it is possible to infer that this signal can be considered as a two-dimensional unit sample sequence $\delta[n_1, n_2]$.

Experiment 1.36: Generation of a Sequence of Dots on a Black Background

This experiment aims to generate a series of dots in a specific row of a 256×256 image. The Python code that generates a sequence of dots in a black background is shown in Fig. 1.77a, and the corresponding result is shown in Fig. 1.77b.

```
#Test image1 - White dot in black background
import numpy as np
import matplotlib.pyplot as plt
#Step 1: Generation of test image
img=np.zeros([256,256])
img[128,128]=1
#Step 2: Visualizing the result
plt.subplot(2,1,1),plt.imshow(img,cmap='gray'),plt.axis('off'),
plt.title('2D impulse function'),plt.subplot(2,1,2),plt.plot(img[128,:])
plt.title('128th row of 2D impulse function')
plt.tight_layout()
```

(a) Python code

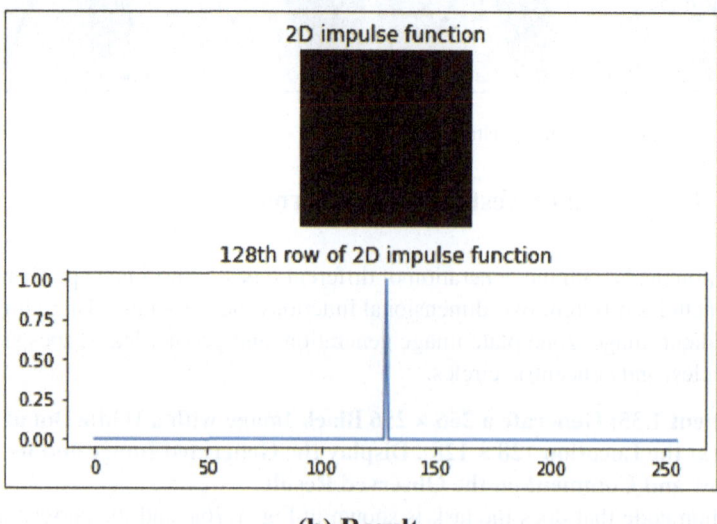

(b) Result

Fig. 1.76 Python code to generate Test Image 1: (**a**) Python code, (**b**) result

```
#Test image2 - Sequence of white dots on black background
import numpy as np
import matplotlib.pyplot as plt
#Step 1: Generation of test image
img=np.zeros([256,256])
img[128,0:256:10]=255
#Step 2: Visualizing the result
fig = plt.figure(figsize=(6,6))
plt.subplot(2,1,1),plt.imshow(img,cmap='gray',vmin=0,vmax=1)
plt.title('2D impulse function'),plt.axis('off')
plt.subplot(2,1,2),plt.plot(img[128,:])
plt.title('128th row of 2D impulse function')
plt.tight_layout()
```

(a) Python code to generate a series of dots on a black background

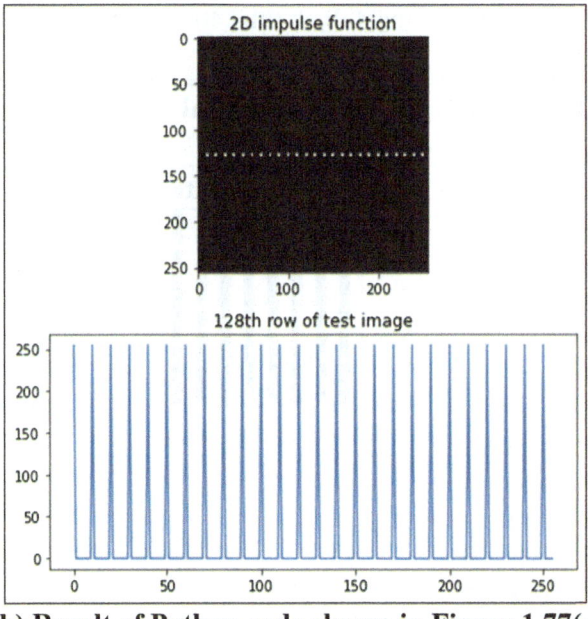

(b) Result of Python code shown in Figure 1.77(a)

Fig. 1.77 Python code and result for the generation of Test Image 2: (**a**) Python code to generate a series of dots on a black background, (**b**) result of Python code shown in Fig. 1.77(**a**)

Inference

- Upon plotting the 128th row of a series of dot images, it is possible to observe a series of impulses, which is termed a train of impulses or impulse train.

Experiment 1.37: Generation of the Stripe Pattern
The aim of this experiment is to generate the vertical stripes pattern on a black background. The Python code that performs this task is shown in Fig. 1.78a, and the corresponding output is shown in Fig. 1.78b.

```
#Generation of vertical stripe pattern
import numpy as np
import matplotlib.pyplot as plt
#Step 1: Generation of test image
img=np.zeros([64,64])
m,n=img.shape
stripe_size=4;
for i in range(0,m):
  for j in range(0,n,2*stripe_size):
    img[i,j:j+stripe_size]=1
#Step 2: Visualizing the result
plt.subplot(2,1,1),plt.imshow(img,cmap='gray')
plt.title('Vertical Stripe Pattern'),plt.xticks([]),plt.yticks([])
plt.subplot(2,1,2),plt.plot(img[4,:]),plt.title('4th row of test image')
plt.tight_layout()
```

(a) Python code to generate vertical stripes pattern

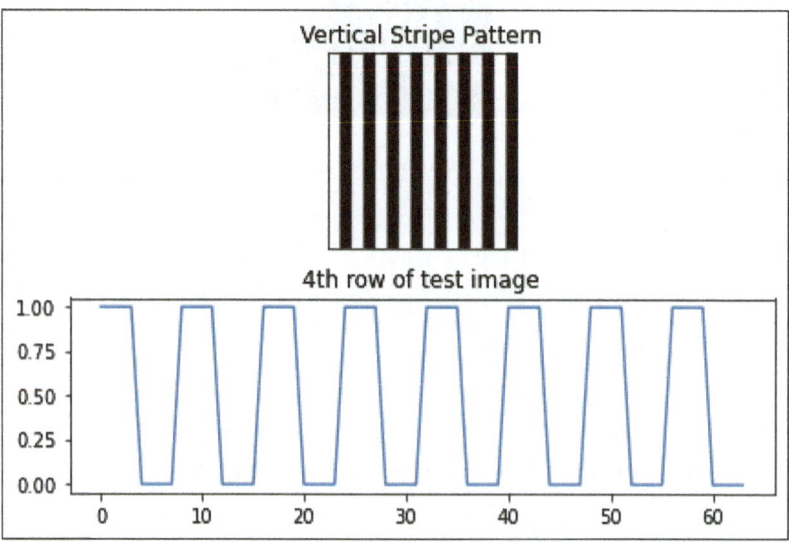

(b) Vertical stripe pattern and the profile of its fourth row

Fig. 1.78 Vertical stripe pattern and its corresponding profile: (a) Python code to generate vertical stripes pattern, (b) vertical stripe pattern and the profile of its fourth row

Inference

- The generated image is a 64 × 64 image. The plot of the fourth row of the vertical stripe pattern image exhibits a square-like pattern.

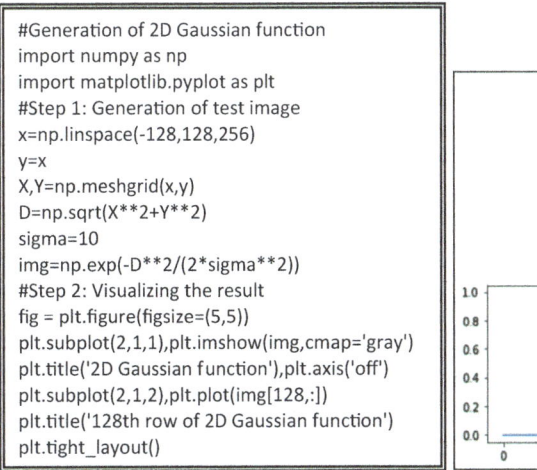

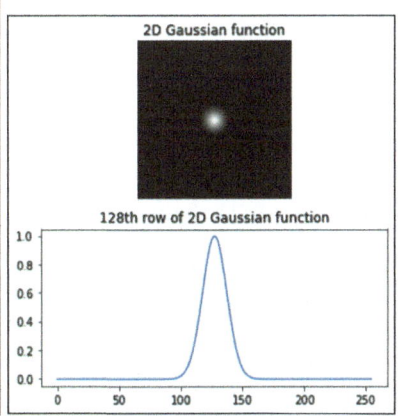

(a) Python code   (b) 2D Gaussian function and the plot of its 128

Fig. 1.79 Generation of 2D Gaussian function: (**a**) Python code, (**b**) 2D Gaussian function and the plot of its 128th row

Experiment 1.38: Generation of Two-Dimensional Gaussian Smoothing Function

The objective of this experiment is to generate the two-dimensional Gaussian function. The expression for 2D Gaussian function is given by

$$f(x,y) = \frac{1}{2\pi\sigma^2} e^{-\frac{(x^2+y^2)}{2\sigma^2}} \tag{1.15}$$

The Python code that generates the 2D Gaussian function is given in Fig. 1.79a, and the corresponding output is shown in Fig. 1.79b.

Inference

- The plot of the 128th row of the 2D Gaussian function results in a Gaussian function or normal curve. This function is used to smoothen the input image, which is termed as "Gaussian smoothing" or "weighted averaging".

Experiment 1.39: Generation of 2D Gaussian Sharpening Function

The objective of this experiment is to generate 2D Gaussian sharpening function. The Python code that generates the function is shown in Fig. 1.80a, and the corresponding output is shown in Fig. 1.80b.

Inference

- The plot of the 128th row of 2D Gaussian sharpening function is found to be inverse of the Gaussian smoothing function. Gaussian sharpening is used to enhance the fine details of the input image.

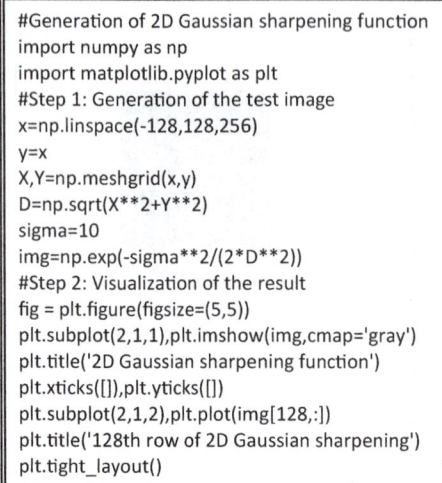

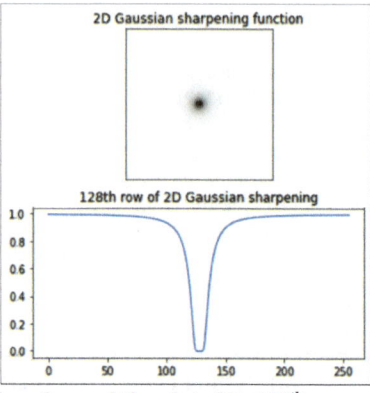

```
#Generation of 2D Gaussian sharpening function
import numpy as np
import matplotlib.pyplot as plt
#Step 1: Generation of the test image
x=np.linspace(-128,128,256)
y=x
X,Y=np.meshgrid(x,y)
D=np.sqrt(X**2+Y**2)
sigma=10
img=np.exp(-sigma**2/(2*D**2))
#Step 2: Visualization of the result
fig = plt.figure(figsize=(5,5))
plt.subplot(2,1,1),plt.imshow(img,cmap='gray')
plt.title('2D Gaussian sharpening function')
plt.xticks([]),plt.yticks([])
plt.subplot(2,1,2),plt.plot(img[128,:])
plt.title('128th row of 2D Gaussian sharpening')
plt.tight_layout()
```

(a) Python code   (b) Gaussian sharpening function and the plot of its 128th row

Fig. 1.80 Generation of 2D Gaussian sharpening function: (a) Python code, (b) Gaussian sharpening function and the plot of its 128th row

Experiment 1.40: Generation of the Sinusoidal grating Pattern

The objective of this experiment is to generate sinusoidal grating pattern. The expression for the sinusoidal grating pattern is given by

$$f(m,n) = \sin\left(2\pi\left(f_x m + f_y n\right)\right) \tag{1.16}$$

In the above equation, f_x and f_y represent the frequency along the horizontal and vertical directions, respectively. The Python code that generates the sinusoidal grating pattern is shown in Fig. 1.81a, and the corresponding output is shown in Fig. 1.81b.

Inferences

- Figure 1.81b displays the sinusoidal grating pattern with the horizontal and vertical frequency fixed as 5 units.
- The 128th row of the generated image plot clearly indicates that the generated image is a sinusoidal signal.
- The waveform starts at the origin (since $\sin(0) = 0$), and it is possible to observe five peaks in the waveform, which indicates the frequency component of the generated image.

Experiment 1.41: Generation of Cosine Grating Pattern

This experiment discusses the generation of a cosine grating pattern by replacing the trigonometric function "sin" with "cos". The Python code that modifies the sine function as a cosine function is given in Fig. 1.82a, and the corresponding output is shown in Fig. 1.82b.

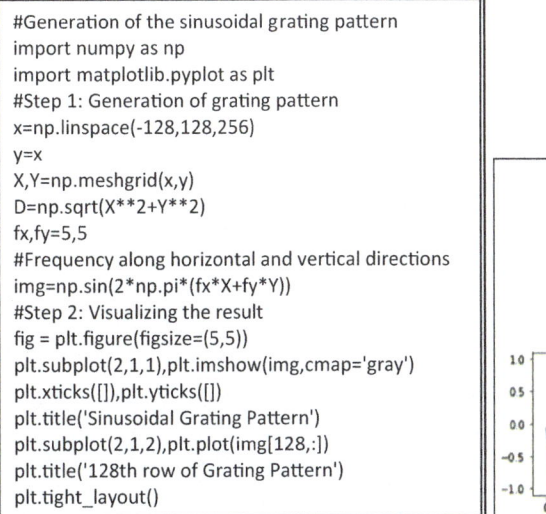
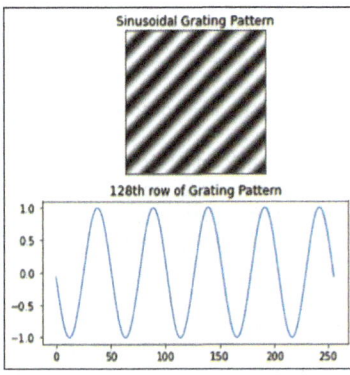

```
#Generation of the sinusoidal grating pattern
import numpy as np
import matplotlib.pyplot as plt
#Step 1: Generation of grating pattern
x=np.linspace(-128,128,256)
y=x
X,Y=np.meshgrid(x,y)
D=np.sqrt(X**2+Y**2)
fx,fy=5,5
#Frequency along horizontal and vertical directions
img=np.sin(2*np.pi*(fx*X+fy*Y))
#Step 2: Visualizing the result
fig = plt.figure(figsize=(5,5))
plt.subplot(2,1,1),plt.imshow(img,cmap='gray')
plt.xticks([]),plt.yticks([])
plt.title('Sinusoidal Grating Pattern')
plt.subplot(2,1,2),plt.plot(img[128,:])
plt.title('128th row of Grating Pattern')
plt.tight_layout()
```

(a) Python code   (b) Sinusoidal grating pattern and the plot of its 128th row

Fig. 1.81 Sinusoidal grating pattern generation: (a) Python code, (b) sinusoidal grating pattern and the plot of its 128th row

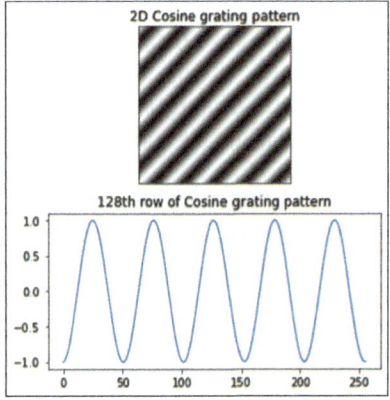

```
#Generation of Cosine grating pattern
import numpy as np
import matplotlib.pyplot as plt
#Step 1: Generation of grating pattern
x=np.linspace(-128,128,256)
y=x
X,Y=np.meshgrid(x,y)
D=np.sqrt(X**2+Y**2)
fx,fy=5,5
#Frequency along horizontal and vertical
directions
img=np.cos(2*np.pi*(fx*X+fy*Y))
#Step 2: Visualizing the result
fig = plt.figure(figsize=(5,5))
plt.subplot(2,1,1),plt.imshow(img,cmap='gray')
plt.xticks([]),plt.yticks([])
plt.title('2D Cosine grating pattern')
plt.subplot(2,1,2),plt.plot(img[128,:])
plt.title('128th row of Cosine grating pattern')
plt.tight_layout()
```

(a) Python code   (b) Result of grating pattern using cosine function

Fig. 1.82 Cosine grating pattern generation: (a) Python code, (b) result of grating pattern using cosine function

```
#Generation of grating pattern
import numpy as np
import matplotlib.pyplot as plt
#Step 1: Generation of grating pattern
x=np.linspace(-128,128,256)
y=x
X,Y=np.meshgrid(x,y)
D=np.sqrt(X**2+Y**2)
fx,fy=1,1
#Frequency along horizontal and vertical
directions
img=np.sin(2*np.pi*(fx*X+fy*Y)**2)
#Step 2: Visualizing the result
fig = plt.figure(figsize=(5,5))
plt.subplot(2,1,1),plt.imshow(img,cmap='gray')
plt.xticks([]),plt.yticks([])
plt.title('2D grating pattern')
plt.subplot(2,1,2),plt.plot(img[128,:])
plt.title('128th row of grating pattern')
plt.tight_layout()
```

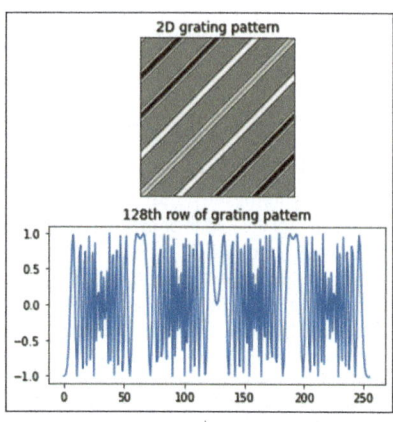

(a) Python code   (b) Result of python code shown in Figure 1.83(a)

Fig. 1.83 2D grating pattern generation: (**a**) Python code, (**b**) result of Python code shown in Fig. 1.83(**a**)

Inference

- The grating pattern generated using "cosine function" starts at -1 instead of "0". This implies that sine and cosine functions vary with respect to phase angle. The phase angle represents the starting point of the waveform.

Experiment 1.42: 2D Grating Pattern in the Form of sin(m, n)²
The objective of this experiment is to generate the signal, which is of the form $f(m,n) = \sin(2\pi(f_x m + f_y n)^2)$. The Python code that performs this task is shown in Fig. 1.83a, and the corresponding output is shown in Fig. 1.83b.

Inferences

- The signal $f(m,n) = \sin(2\pi(f_x m + f_y n)^2)$ is a non-stationary signal, which implies that the frequency of the signal varies with respect to time or space.
- Observing the 128th row of the grating pattern makes it possible to observe that the frequency varies with respect to time. Hence, the characteristics of this image are non-stationary.

Experiment 1.43: Generation of 2D "sinc" Function
The objective of this experiment is to generate the signal, which is of the form $f(m,n) = \operatorname{sinc}\left(\sqrt{m^2 + n^2}\right)$. The Python code that performs this task is shown in Fig. 1.84a, and the corresponding output is shown in Fig. 1.84b.

```
import numpy as np
import matplotlib.pyplot as plt
import matplotlib.cm as cm
x=np.linspace(-8,8,256)
y=x
X, Y = np.meshgrid(x, y)
D=np.sqrt(X**2+Y**2)
f = np.sinc(D)
fig = plt.figure(figsize=(10,8))
ax = plt.axes(projection='3d')
ax.plot_surface(X, Y, f, rstride=2, cstride=2, cmap=cm.seismic)
plt.title('2D Sinc function')
plt.figure(),plt.plot(f[128,:])
plt.title('128th row of 2D Sinc function')
plt.tight_layout()
```

(a) Python code to generate 2D Sinc function

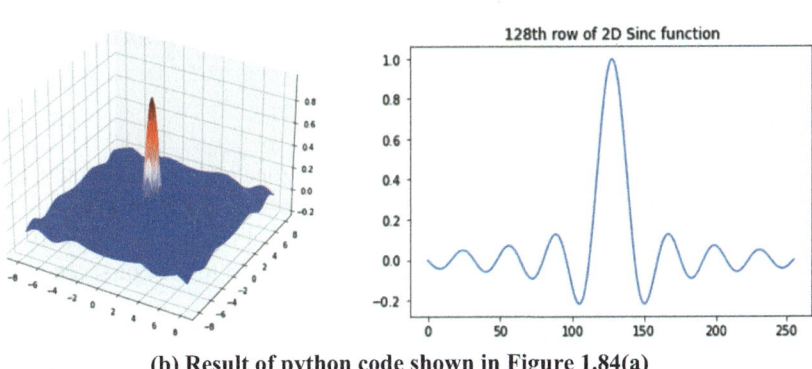

(b) Result of python code shown in Figure 1.84(a)

Fig. 1.84 2D "sinc" function generation: (**a**) Python code to generate 2D "sinc" function, (**b**) result of Python code shown in Fig. 1.84(**a**)

Inferences

- The 2D sinc function $f(x,y) = sinc\left(\sqrt{x^2 + y^2}\right)$ is generated using Python and a plotter in this experiment.
- Observing the 128th row of the 2D sinc function makes it possible to observe that it is a 1D sinc function.

Experiment 1.44: Generation of Zone Plate Image

The objective of this experiment is to generate zone plate image. A zone plate is a radially symmetric pattern with low frequencies in the middle and high frequencies near the edge. The Python code that generates the zone plate image is shown in Fig. 1.85a, and the corresponding output is shown in Fig. 1.85b.

```
#Generation of zone plate test image
import numpy as np
import matplotlib.pyplot as plt
#Step 1: Generation of image
x=np.linspace(-128,128,256)
y=x
X,Y=np.meshgrid(x,y)
D=np.sqrt(X**2+Y**2)
img=np.cos(256*np.pi*(X**2+Y**2))
#Step 2: Visualization of the result
fig = plt.figure(figsize=(5,5))
plt.subplot(2,1,1),plt.imshow(img,cmap='gray')
plt.title('Zone plate test image'),
plt.xticks([]),plt.yticks([])
plt.subplot(2,1,2),plt.plot(img[4,:])
plt.title('128th row of Zone plate')
plt.tight_layout()
```

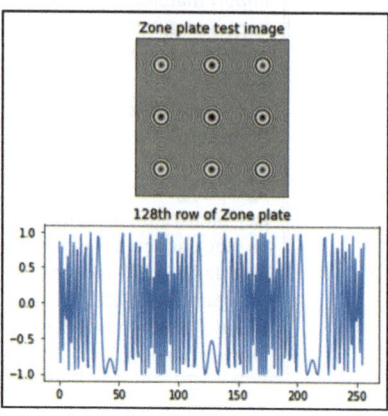

(a) Python Code   (b) Zone plate output image

Fig. 1.85 Generation of zone plate test image and its profile: (**a**) Python code, (**b**) zone plate output image

Inferences

- From Fig. 1.85b, it is possible to observe that the zone plate is a circularly symmetric diffractive structure that contains a wide range of spatial frequencies.
- The plot of the 128th row of the zone plate reveals that it is a non-stationary signal, which implies that the frequency varies with respect to time or space.

Experiment 1.45: Generation of Gradient Image

This experiment aims to generate a 256×256 gradient image whose intensity varies from black to white. The Python code that performs this task is given in Fig. 1.86a, and the corresponding output is shown in Fig. 1.86b.

Inferences

- From Fig. 1.86b, it is possible to observe that the gray level of the gradient image varies gradually from black to white.
- The plot of the 128th row of the gradient image reveals the fact that the gray level value of the image varies from 0 to 255 gradually or linearly.

Experiment 1.46: Generation of Gradient Image that Exhibits Roof Edge

The objective is to generate a gradient image whose intensity level should vary from black to white and then from white to black. The Python code that is used to generate the above-mentioned test pattern is shown in Fig. 1.87a, and the corresponding result is shown in Fig. 1.87b.

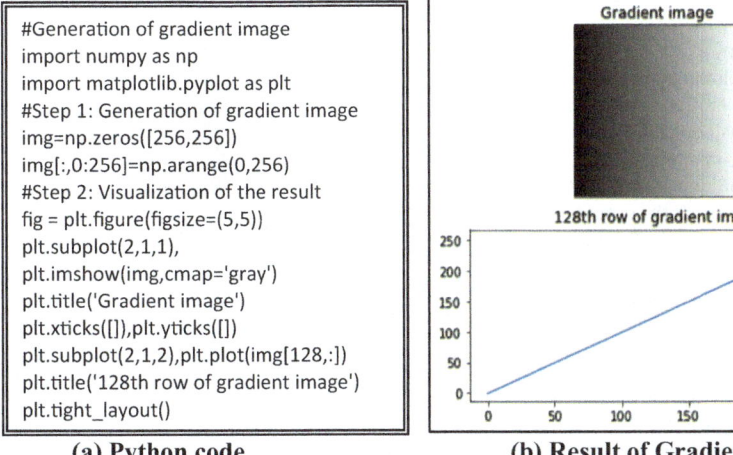

```
#Generation of gradient image
import numpy as np
import matplotlib.pyplot as plt
#Step 1: Generation of gradient image
img=np.zeros([256,256])
img[:,0:256]=np.arange(0,256)
#Step 2: Visualization of the result
fig = plt.figure(figsize=(5,5))
plt.subplot(2,1,1),
plt.imshow(img,cmap='gray')
plt.title('Gradient image')
plt.xticks([]),plt.yticks([])
plt.subplot(2,1,2),plt.plot(img[128,:])
plt.title('128th row of gradient image')
plt.tight_layout()
```

(a) Python code   **(b) Result of Gradient image**

Fig. 1.86 Gradient image and its profile: (**a**) Python code, (**b**) result of gradient image

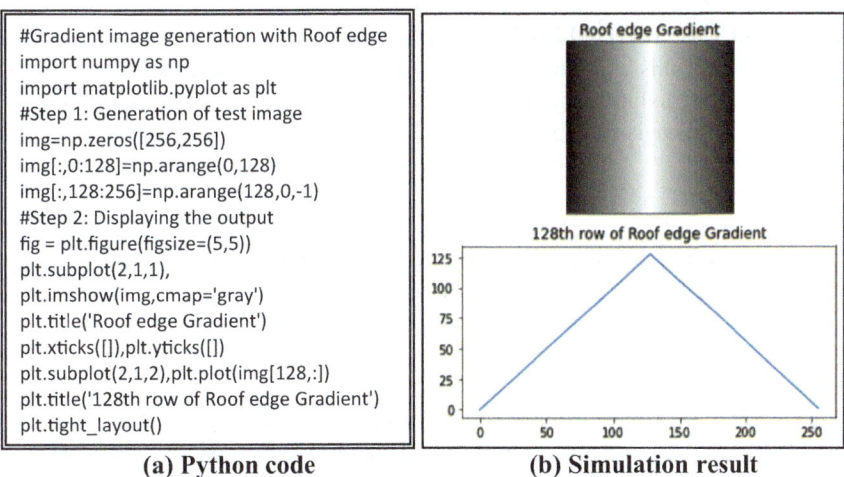

```
#Gradient image generation with Roof edge
import numpy as np
import matplotlib.pyplot as plt
#Step 1: Generation of test image
img=np.zeros([256,256])
img[:,0:128]=np.arange(0,128)
img[:,128:256]=np.arange(128,0,-1)
#Step 2: Displaying the output
fig = plt.figure(figsize=(5,5))
plt.subplot(2,1,1),
plt.imshow(img,cmap='gray')
plt.title('Roof edge Gradient')
plt.xticks([]),plt.yticks([])
plt.subplot(2,1,2),plt.plot(img[128,:])
plt.title('128th row of Roof edge Gradient')
plt.tight_layout()
```

(a) Python code   **(b) Simulation result**

Fig. 1.87 Gradient image that exhibits roof edge: (**a**) Python code, (**b**) simulation result

Inferences

- From Fig. 1.87b, it is possible to observe that the intensity of the generated test image varies from black to white and then from white to black.
- The plot of the 128th row of the generated test image shows that the generated test image exhibits a roof edge.

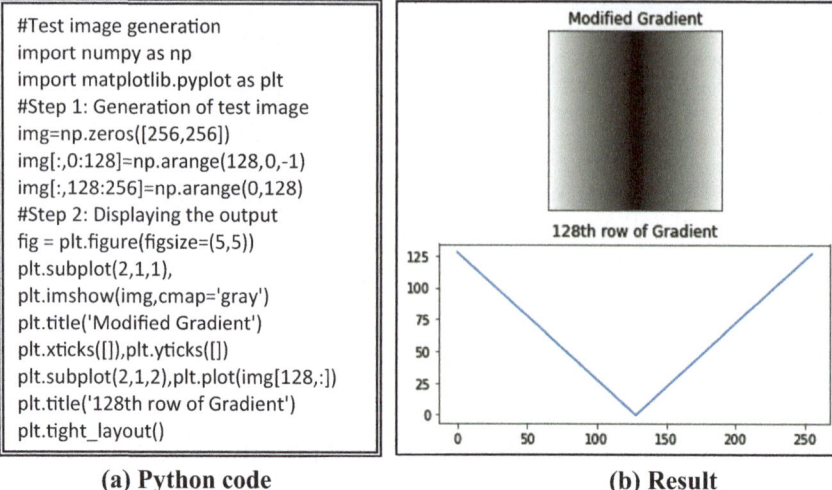

```
#Test image generation
import numpy as np
import matplotlib.pyplot as plt
#Step 1: Generation of test image
img=np.zeros([256,256])
img[:,0:128]=np.arange(128,0,-1)
img[:,128:256]=np.arange(0,128)
#Step 2: Displaying the output
fig = plt.figure(figsize=(5,5))
plt.subplot(2,1,1),
plt.imshow(img,cmap='gray')
plt.title('Modified Gradient')
plt.xticks([]),plt.yticks([])
plt.subplot(2,1,2),plt.plot(img[128,:])
plt.title('128th row of Gradient')
plt.tight_layout()
```

(a) Python code   (b) Result

Fig. 1.88   Modified gradient image generation: (**a**) Python code, (**b**) result

Experiment 1.47: Inverted Roof Gradient Image

The objective of this experiment is to generate a gradient image whose intensity varies from white to black and then from black to white. The Python code that generates the test image is shown in Fig. 1.88a, and the corresponding output is shown in Fig. 1.88b.

Inferences

- From Fig. 1.88b, it is possible to observe that the generated test image intensity varies from white to black and then from black to white.
- The plot of 128th row of the test image reveals that the edge profile is an inverted roof.

Experiment 1.48: Generation of Gradient Image whose Edge Profile Resembles "ReLU" Activation Function. Here ReLU Stands for "rectified linear unit"

This experiment aims to generate a test image whose edge profile should resemble that of "ReLU" activation function. This is achieved by generating a 256 × 256 image whose gray level is zero till 128th column. After 128th column, the gray level should vary uniformly from black to white. The Python code that performs this task is shown in Fig. 1.89a, and the corresponding result is shown in Fig. 1.89b.

Inferences

- From Fig. 1.89b, it is possible to observe that the gray level of the test image is zero from 0 to 128th column.
- After 128th column, the gray level varies linearly to a value of 255. The plot of 128th row of the test image resembles that of "ReLU" activation function.

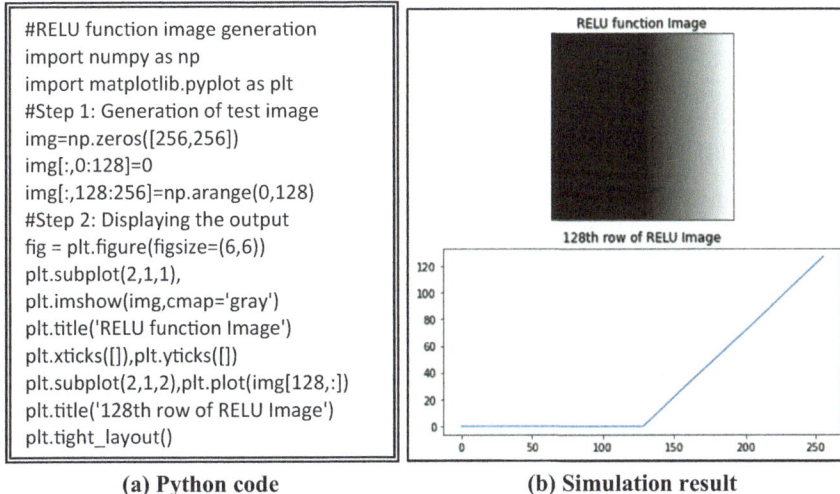

```
#RELU function image generation
import numpy as np
import matplotlib.pyplot as plt
#Step 1: Generation of test image
img=np.zeros([256,256])
img[:,0:128]=0
img[:,128:256]=np.arange(0,128)
#Step 2: Displaying the output
fig = plt.figure(figsize=(6,6))
plt.subplot(2,1,1),
plt.imshow(img,cmap='gray')
plt.title('RELU function Image')
plt.xticks([]),plt.yticks([])
plt.subplot(2,1,2),plt.plot(img[128,:])
plt.title('128th row of RELU Image')
plt.tight_layout()
```

(a) Python code   (b) Simulation result

Fig. 1.89   Generation of ReLU function image: (a) Python code, (b) simulation result

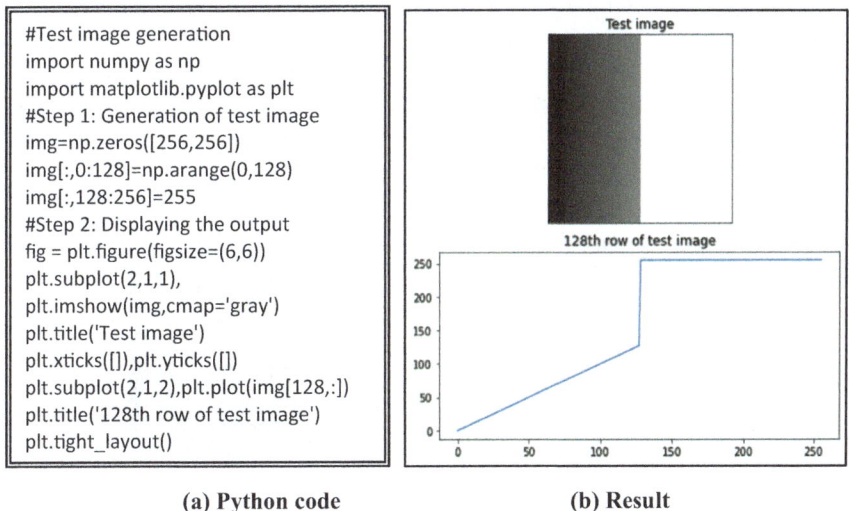

```
#Test image generation
import numpy as np
import matplotlib.pyplot as plt
#Step 1: Generation of test image
img=np.zeros([256,256])
img[:,0:128]=np.arange(0,128)
img[:,128:256]=255
#Step 2: Displaying the output
fig = plt.figure(figsize=(6,6))
plt.subplot(2,1,1),
plt.imshow(img,cmap='gray')
plt.title('Test image')
plt.xticks([]),plt.yticks([])
plt.subplot(2,1,2),plt.plot(img[128,:])
plt.title('128th row of test image')
plt.tight_layout()
```

(a) Python code   (b) Result

Fig. 1.90   Generation of ramp with step image: (a) Python code, (b) result

Experiment 1.49: Generation of Test image whose Profile Resembles the Ramp and Step Function

The objective of this experiment is to generate a 256×256 test image whose gray level should vary linearly from 0 to 128 along the column. After 128th column, the gray level should take the maximum value of 255. The Python code that performs this task is shown in Fig. 1.90a, and the corresponding output is shown in Fig. 1.90b.

Inferences

- From Fig. 1.90b, it is possible to observe that the intensity of the test image varies linearly from 0 to 128 along the column.
- After the 128th column, the gray level takes the value of 255, which can be considered saturation in the case of an 8-bit image.

Task: Modify the Python code shown in Fig. 1.90a such that the output is a flipped version of the output shown in Fig. 1.90b.

Experiment 1.50: White Square on a Black Background
In this experiment, a white square is generated on a black background. The test image is of size 256 × 256. The Python code that performs this task is shown in Fig. 1.91a, and the corresponding output is shown in Fig. 1.91b.

Inferences

- From Fig. 1.91b, it is possible to observe that the test image is a square image on a black background.
- The plot of 128th row of the generated test image resembles that of a pulse function. The square image is obtained because the length and width are equal.
- A rectangle image will be generated if the height and width are different.

Experiment 1.51: Generation of Checkerboard Pattern
The objective of this experiment is to generate 16 × 16 checkerboard pattern image. The Python code that accomplishes this task is given in Fig. 1.92a, and the corresponding output is shown in Fig. 1.92b.

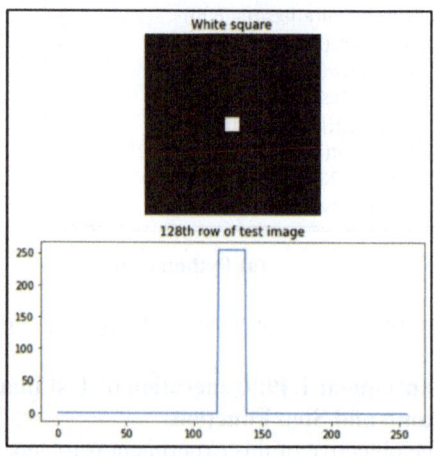

```
#White square on a black background
import numpy as np
import matplotlib.pyplot as plt
#Step 1: Generation of test image
img=np.zeros([256,256])
img[118:138,118:138]=255
#Step 2: Displaying the output
fig = plt.figure(figsize=(6,6))
plt.subplot(2,1,1),
plt.imshow(img,cmap='gray')
plt.title('White square')
plt.xticks([]),plt.yticks([])
plt.subplot(2,1,2),plt.plot(img[128,:])
plt.title('128th row of test image')
plt.tight_layout()
```

(a) Python code   (b) Simulation output

Fig. 1.91 Generation of white square with black background: (**a**) Python code, (**b**) simulation output

```
#Generation of checkerboard pattern
import numpy as np
import matplotlib.pyplot as plt
#Step 1: Generation of checkerboard pattern
img=np.zeros([16,16])
m,n=img.shape
img1=np.zeros([m**2,n**2])
p,q=0,0
for i in range(0,m):
  for j in range(0,n):
    img1[p:p+m,q:q+n]=((-1)**(i+j))*np.ones([m,n])
    q=q+n;
    if q>=n**2:
      q=0
  p=p+m
#Step 2: Displaying the output
fig = plt.figure(figsize=(6,6))
plt.subplot(2,1,1),plt.imshow(img1,cmap='gray')
plt.title('Checkerboard Pattern')
plt.xticks([]),plt.yticks([])
plt.subplot(2,1,2),plt.plot(img1[4,:])
plt.title('4th row of test image')
plt.tight_layout()
```

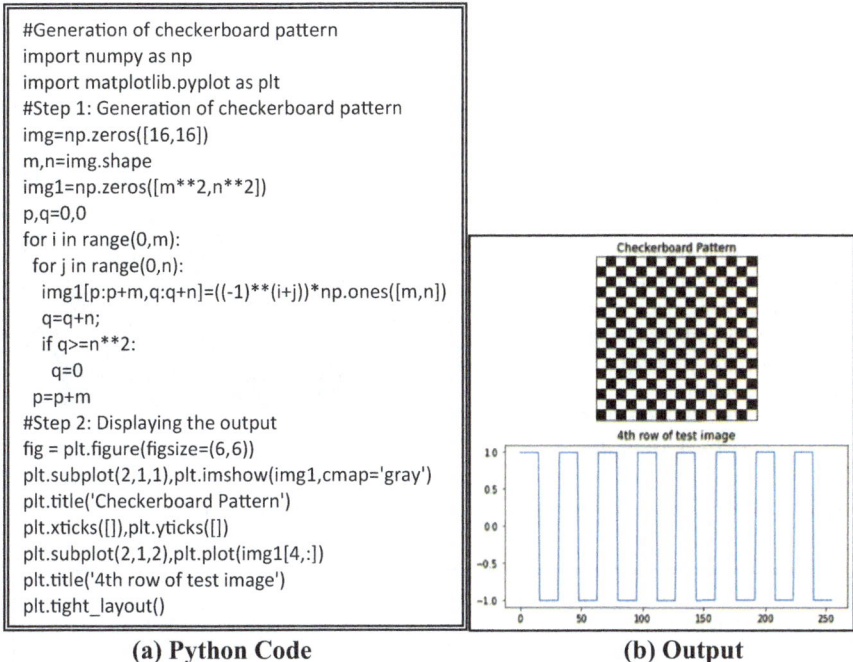

| (a) Python Code | (b) Output |

Fig. 1.92 Generation of checkerboard pattern: (**a**) Python code, (**b**) output

Inferences

- The checkerboard pattern test image gray level patch varies alternately between black and white.
- The plot of the fourth row of the checkerboard pattern reveals the fact that the profile of the generated image resembles that of a square function.

Aliter: Generation of Checkerboard Image Using the Idea of Outer product of Two Vectors

The alternate approach to generate checkerboard pattern is explained here using the concept of outer product. The outer product of two vectors results in a matrix, which can be visualized as an image. As an example, consider a vector "v" that is given by $v = [1, -1]$. The outer product of this vector is given by

$$v \otimes v = \begin{bmatrix} 1 \\ -1 \end{bmatrix} \begin{bmatrix} 1 & -1 \end{bmatrix} \tag{1.17}$$

$$v \otimes v = \begin{bmatrix} 1 & -1 \\ -1 & 1 \end{bmatrix} \tag{1.18}$$

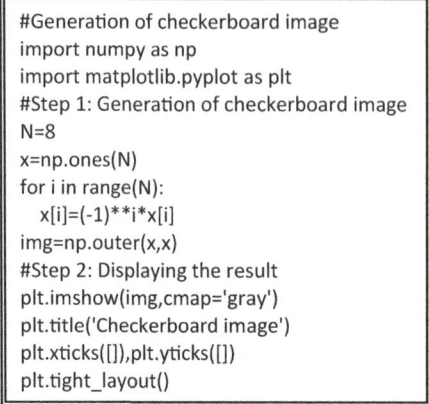

```
#Generation of checkerboard image
import numpy as np
import matplotlib.pyplot as plt
#Step 1: Generation of checkerboard image
N=8
x=np.ones(N)
for i in range(N):
    x[i]=(-1)**i*x[i]
img=np.outer(x,x)
#Step 2: Displaying the result
plt.imshow(img,cmap='gray')
plt.title('Checkerboard image')
plt.xticks([]),plt.yticks([])
plt.tight_layout()
```

(a) Python code   (b) Simulation result

Fig. 1.93 Generation of checkerboard image: (**a**) Python code, (**b**) simulation result

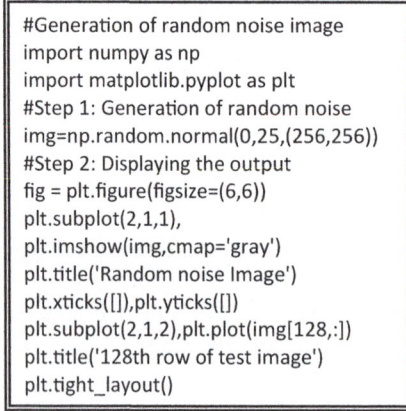

```
#Generation of random noise image
import numpy as np
import matplotlib.pyplot as plt
#Step 1: Generation of random noise
img=np.random.normal(0,25,(256,256))
#Step 2: Displaying the output
fig = plt.figure(figsize=(6,6))
plt.subplot(2,1,1),
plt.imshow(img,cmap='gray')
plt.title('Random noise Image')
plt.xticks([]),plt.yticks([])
plt.subplot(2,1,2),plt.plot(img[128,:])
plt.title('128th row of test image')
plt.tight_layout()
```

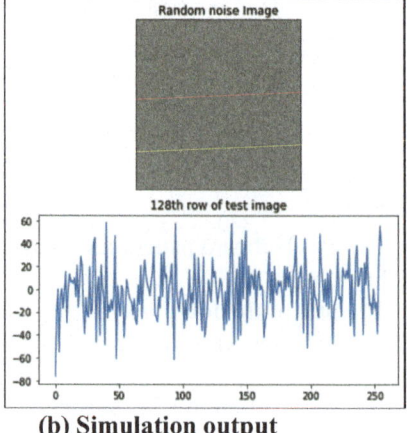

(a) Python code   (b) Simulation output

Fig. 1.94 Generation of random noise image: (**a**) Python code, (**b**) simulation output

Thus, outer product of two vectors results in a matrix. This idea is used to generate the checkerboard pattern. The Python code that performs this task is shown in Fig. 1.93a, and the corresponding output is shown in Fig. 1.93b.

Experiment 1.52: Generation of Random Noise that Follows a Normal Distribution

This experiment discusses the generation of random noise, which follows a normal distribution using Python. To generate a random noise that follows normal distribution, the mean and standard deviation are chosen as 0 and 25, respectively. The Python code that performs this task is shown in Fig. 1.94a, and the corresponding output is shown in Fig. 1.94b.

Inferences

- From Fig. 1.94b, it is possible to observe that the random noise exhibits random fluctuation of pixel value.
- The plot of the 128th row of the test image reveals that the profile of the image is similar to that of a one-dimensional noisy signal.

Experiment 1.53: Generation of Test image that Exhibits Step-like Change in the Gray Level

The objective of this experiment is to generate 256 × 256 image that exhibits step-like change in the gray level along the column of the image. From 0 to 128th column, the pixel value is 255, and from the column 128th to 256th the gray level value is 0. The Python code that performs this task is shown in Fig. 1.95a, and the corresponding result is shown in Fig. 1.95b.

Inferences

- From Fig. 1.95b, it is possible to observe that the test image exhibits a step-like change in the gray level along the column of the image.
- The 128th row plot of the test image resembles that of a step function.

Experiment 1.54: Write a Python Code to Generate a 256 × 256 Test Image in Such a Way that Pixels Lying above the Leading Diagonal Should Take a Value of "0" and pixels Lying below the Leading Diagonal Should Take a Value of "255"

The Python code that performs the above-mentioned task is shown in Fig. 1.96a, and the corresponding output is shown in Fig. 1.96b.

```
#Generation of test image
import numpy as np
import matplotlib.pyplot as plt
#Step 1: Generation of test image
img=np.zeros([256,256])
img[0:256,0:128]=255
#Step 2: Displaying the output
fig = plt.figure(figsize=(6,6))
plt.subplot(2,1,1),
plt.imshow(img,cmap='gray')
plt.title('Step like image')
plt.xticks([]),plt.yticks([])
plt.subplot(2,1,2),plt.plot(img[128,:])
plt.title('128th row of test image')
plt.tight_layout()
```

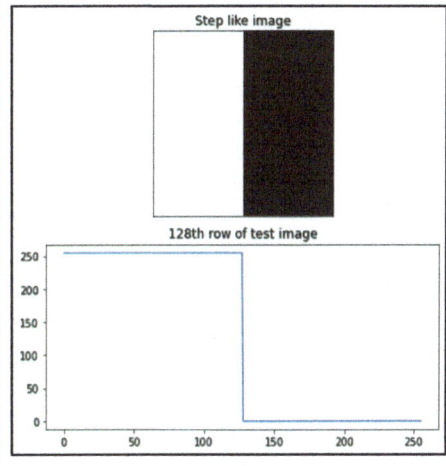

(a) Python code	**(b) Output**

Fig. 1.95 Generation of step-like image: (**a**) Python code, (**b**) output

```
#Generation of test image
import numpy as np
import matplotlib.pyplot as plt
# step 1 - Generate the test image
img = np.zeros([256,256])
m,n=img.shape
for i in range(0,m):
  for j in range(0,n):
    if i > j:
      img[i,j] = 255
#Step 2: Displaying the result
fig = plt.figure(figsize=(6,6))
plt.subplot(2,1,1),
plt.imshow(img,cmap='gray')
plt.title('Test image')
plt.xticks([]),plt.yticks([])
plt.subplot(2,1,2), plt.plot(img[125,:])
plt.title('128th row of test image')
plt.tight_layout()
```

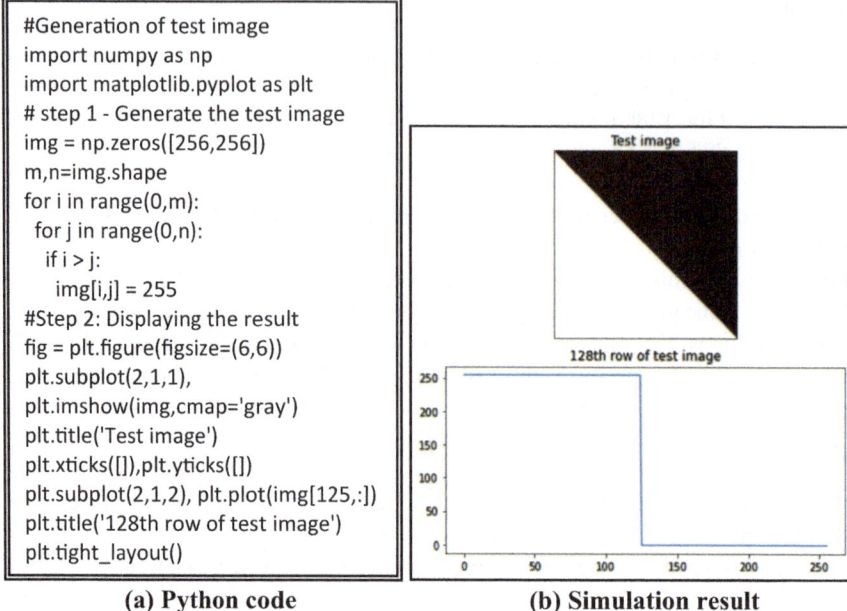

(a) Python code   **(b) Simulation result**

Fig. 1.96 Python code and simulation result of Experiment 1.54: (**a**) Python code, (**b**) simulation result

Inferences

- From Fig. 1.96b, it is possible to observe that the test image takes a value of "255" below the leading diagonal and takes a value of "0" above the leading diagonal, hence the image appears as white below the leading diagonal and black above the leading diagonal.
- The plot of the 128th row of the test image shows that the image exhibits a step-like transition at a gray level along the 128th row of the image.

1.10.1   Generation of Geometric Shapes

This section deals with generation of test images that exhibit different geometric shapes such as line, square, rectangle, circle, ellipse, and so on.

Experiment 1.55: Generation of Test image with Different Lines
The objective of this experiment is to generate test image with horizontal, vertical, diagonal, and combined lines in a black background. The Python code that performs this task is shown in Fig. 1.97, and the corresponding output is shown in Fig. 1.98.

```
#Generation of test image with lines
import numpy as np
import matplotlib.pyplot as plt
#Step 1: Generation of the different lines
img1=np.zeros([256,256])
img2=np.zeros([256,256])
img3=np.zeros([256,256])
img4=np.zeros([256,256])
img1[128,:]=1;#Horizontal line
img2[:,128]=1;#Vertical line
m,n=img3.shape;# Diagonal lines
for i in range(0,m):
    for j in range(0,n):
        if (i==j) | (i==256-j):
            img3[i,j]=1
img4=img1+img2+img3;# Combined
#Step 2: Displaying the result
plt.figure(figsize=(8,6)),plt.subplot(1,4,1),plt.imshow(img1,cmap='gray',vmin=0,vmax=1)
plt.title('Horizontal line'),plt.axis('off'),plt.subplot(1,4,2)
plt.imshow(img2,cmap='gray',vmin=0,vmax=1),plt.title('Vertical line'),plt.axis('off')
plt.subplot(1,4,3),plt.imshow(img3,cmap='gray',vmin=0,vmax=1)
plt.title('Diagonal lines'),plt.axis('off'),plt.subplot(1,4,4)
plt.imshow(img4,cmap='gray',vmin=0,vmax=1)
plt.title('Combined lines'),plt.axis('off')
plt.tight_layout()
```

Fig. 1.97 Python code for generation of test image with lines

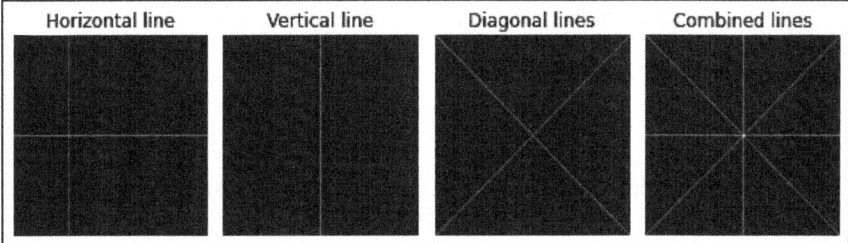

Fig. 1.98 Test image with lines

Inference

- From Fig. 1.98, it is possible to observe that an image has horizontal, vertical, diagonal, and combined lines on a black background.

Experiment 1.56: Generate a Set of Vertical Lines Such that the Spacing between the Lines Is 25 Units

The Python code that generates a set of vertical lines with the spacing between the lines as 25 units is shown in Fig. 1.99a, and the corresponding output is shown in Fig. 1.99b.

```
#Generation of a set of vertical lines
import numpy as np
import matplotlib.pyplot as plt
img=np.zeros([255,255])
img[:,0:255:25]=255
plt.imshow(img,cmap='gray'),
plt.axis('off')
plt.title('Test image4'),
plt.tight_layout()
```

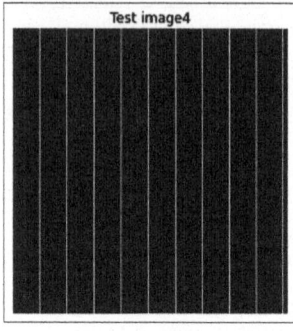

(a) Python Code   (b) Result

Fig. 1.99 Python code to generate a set of vertical lines: (a) Python code, (b) result

```
#Generation of the box-like pattern
import numpy as np
import matplotlib.pyplot as plt
img=np.zeros([256,256])
img[:,0:255:25]=255  #Set of vertical lines
img[0:255:25,:,]=255 #Set of horizontal lines
plt.imshow(img,cmap='gray'),
plt.axis('off')
plt.title('Test image5'),
plt.tight_layout()
```

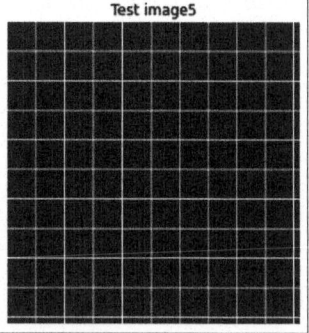

(a) Python Code   (b) Result

Fig. 1.100 Python code to generate box pattern: (a) Python code, (b) result

Inferences

- From Fig. 1.99b, it is possible to observe that an image of size 255×255 with a black background is generated in which the vertical lines with the spacing between the lines as 25 units are generated.
- The total number of lines is 10, which can be verified by observing the result.

Experiment 1.57: Generate a Set of Vertical and Horizontal Lines Such that the Spacing between the Lines Is 25 Units

This experiment uses Python to discuss the generation of a set of vertical and horizontal lines with a gap of 25. The intersection of the horizontal and the vertical line will generate a box-like pattern. The Python code that generates the box-like pattern is shown in Fig. 1.100a, and the corresponding output is shown in Fig. 1.100b.

```
#Test image - Circle image
import numpy as np
import matplotlib.pyplot as plt
img=np.zeros([256,256])
r=40  #Radius of the circle
for i in range(0,256):
    for j in range(0,256):
        if (i-128)**2 + (j-128)**2 < r**2:
            img[i,j]=255
plt.imshow(img,cmap='gray'),plt.axis('off')
plt.title('Test image 7')
plt.tight_layout()
```

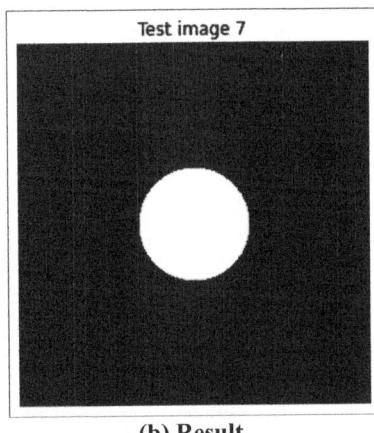

| (a) Python Code | (b) Result |

Fig. 1.101 Python code to generate the image of the circle: **(a)** Python code, **(b)** result

Inference

- From Fig. 1.100b, it is possible to observe that there are 100 square boxes.

Experiment 1.58: Generate a Circle Image on a Black Background. The Centre of the Circle Is at (128, 128) and the Radius of the Circle Is 40 Units

The Python code that generates the circle image is shown in Fig. 1.101a, and the corresponding output is shown in Fig. 1.101b.

Inferences

- From Fig. 1.101a, it is possible to observe that the equation $(x - a)^2 + (y - b)^2 = r^2$ is used to generate the circle, where "a" and "b" represent the centre.
- In this experiment, the centre is chosen as (128, 128), and the radius is chosen as 40.

Experiment 1.59: Generation of Concentric Circle Image

The Python code to generate a concentric circle image is shown in Fig. 1.102a, and the corresponding output is shown in Fig. 1.102b.

Inference

- From Fig. 1.102b, it is possible to observe that the concentric circle has the same centre with a different radius.

Experiment 1.60: Generate the Image of an Ellipse in the Black Background. The Centre of the Ellipse Is at (128, 128), the Length of the Major Axis Is 200, and the Length of the Minor Axis Is 100

The equation of the ellipse with the centre at (h, k) is given by

$$\frac{(x-h)^2}{a^2} + \frac{(y-k)^2}{b^2} = 1 \tag{1.19}$$

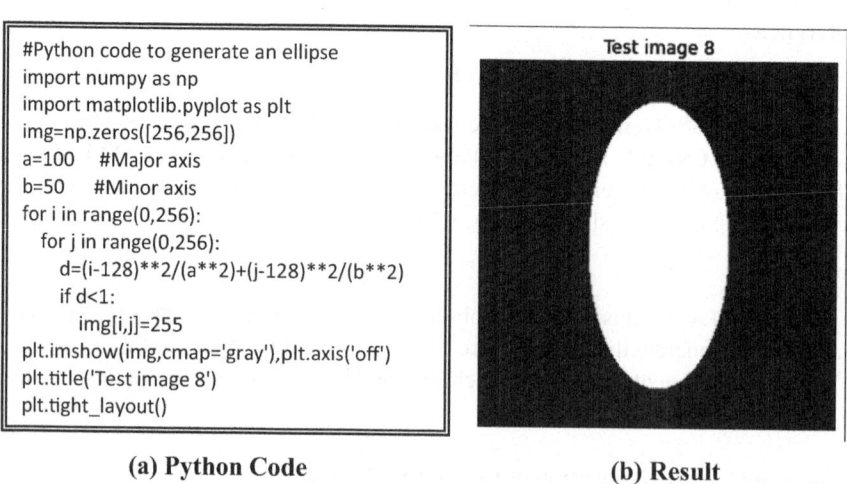

```
import numpy as np
import matplotlib.pyplot as plt
a = np.zeros([256,256]);
a[128,128]=255;
radii = [20,50,80,110]
for current_radius in radii:
    for i in range(256):
        for j in range(256):
            temp = np.sqrt(((i-128)**2 + (j-128)**2))
            if temp <current_radius and temp >
(current_radius -1 ):
                a[i,j] = 255
plt.title("Concentric Circle"),plt.axis('off')
plt.imshow(a,cmap='gray'),plt.show()
```

(a) Python code   **(b) Result**

Fig. 1.102   Python code to generate concentric circle image: **(a)** Python code, **(b)** result

```
#Python code to generate an ellipse
import numpy as np
import matplotlib.pyplot as plt
img=np.zeros([256,256])
a=100    #Major axis
b=50     #Minor axis
for i in range(0,256):
    for j in range(0,256):
        d=(i-128)**2/(a**2)+(j-128)**2/(b**2)
        if d<1:
            img[i,j]=255
plt.imshow(img,cmap='gray'),plt.axis('off')
plt.title('Test image 8')
plt.tight_layout()
```

(a) Python Code   **(b) Result**

Fig. 1.103   Python code to generate the image of an ellipse: **(a)** Python code, **(b)** result

In this experiment, the values "h" and "k" are mentioned as (128, 128). The length of the major axis is $2a$, which is specified as 200, hence $a = 100$. Similarly, the length of the minor axis is $2b$, which is specified as 100, hence $b = 50$. The Python code that generates the ellipse is shown in Fig. 1.103a, and the corresponding output is shown in Fig. 1.103b.

Inference

- From Fig. 1.103b, it is possible to infer that the generated image contains elliptic shape in white foreground.

```
#Generation of an equilateral triangle
import numpy as np
import matplotlib.pyplot as plt
#Step 1: Generation of the image
center_x = 128
center_y = 128
side = 100
size = 256
img = np.zeros([size,size])
for i in range(side+2):
    img[center_x + i - side//2,center_y - int(i/1.7)
:center_y + int(i/1.7) ] = 255
#Step 2: Displaying the result
plt.imshow(img,cmap='gray',vmin = 0,vmax = 255)
plt.title('Equilateral triangle'),plt.axis('off')
plt.tight_layout()
```

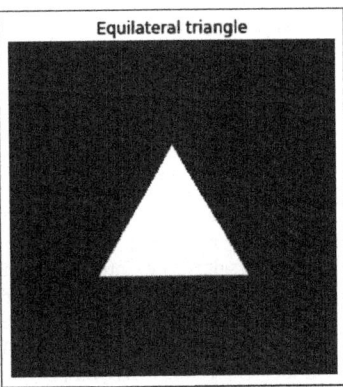

(a) Python code   **(b) Equilateral triangle output**

Fig. 1.104 Generation of equilateral triangle: (**a**) Python code, (**b**) equilateral triangle output

Task: In the Python program, which is shown in Fig. 1.103a, interchange the values of "a" and "b", that is, change the major axis to minor and vice versa and obtain the result. Comment on the observed result.

Experiment 1.61: Generation of Equilateral Triangle Image
The objective of this experiment is to generate the image of an equilateral triangle. The Python code that performs this task is shown in Fig. 1.104a, and the corresponding output is shown in Fig. 1.104b.

Inference

- From Fig. 1.104b, it is possible to observe that the generated image is an equilateral triangle image since all the sides are equal in length.

Experiment 1.62: Generation of Hexagon Image
This experiment discusses the generation of hexagonal shape image using Python. The Python code that is used to generate a hexagon image is given in Fig. 1.105a, and the corresponding output is shown in Fig. 1.105b.

Inferences

- With respect to Fig. 1.105a, the term "apothem" refers to a line from the centre of a regular polygon at right angles to any of its sides. First, the apothem of the hexagon is found using the formula: $\text{Apothem} = \dfrac{\sqrt{3}}{2} \times \text{side}$.
- From Fig. 1.105b, it is possible to observe that the generated shape is a hexagon with six sides.

```
#Generation of hexagon image
import numpy as np
import matplotlib.pyplot as plt
center_x = 128
center_y = 128
side = 50
apothem = int(np.sqrt(3)/2*side)
c = int((side**2 - apothem**2)**(1/2))
size = 256
img = np.zeros([size,size])
for i in range(apothem+1):
  img[center_x - i,center_y - side//2 - c + int(i/1.7):
center_y + side//2 + c - int(i/1.7)] = 255
  img[center_x + i,center_y - side//2 - c + int(i/1.7):
center_y + side//2 + c - int(i/1.7)] = 255
plt.imshow(img,cmap = 'gray',vmin = 0,vmax = 255)
plt.title('Hexagon'),plt.axis('off')
plt.tight_layout()
```

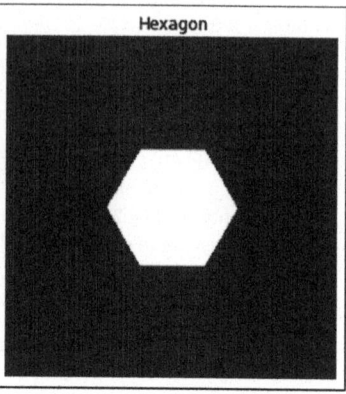

(a) Python code   **(b) Hexagon shape output**

Fig. 1.105 Generation of hexagon shape image: (**a**) Python code, (**b**) hexagon shape output

```
import numpy as np
import matplotlib.pyplot as plt
center_x = 128
center_y = 128
size = 256
img = np.zeros([size,size])
#Coordinates of pentagon
x = [center_x, center_x + 50, center_x + 31,
center_x - 31, center_x - 50, center_x]
y = [center_y - 60, center_y - 20, center_y + 50,
center_y + 50, center_y - 20, center_y - 60]
#Filling the pentagon
plt.fill(x,y, 'w')
plt.imshow(img,cmap = 'gray',vmin = 0,vmax =
255)
plt.title('Pentagon'),plt.axis('off')
plt.tight_layout()
```

(a) Python code   **(b) Pentagon shape output**

Fig. 1.106 Generation of pentagon shape image: (**a**) Python code, (**b**) pentagon shape output

Experiment 1.63: Generation of Pentagon Image

This experiment discusses the generation of pentagon shape image using Python. The Python code that generates a pentagon-shape image is given in Fig. 1.106a, and the corresponding output is shown in Fig. 1.106b.

Inference

- From Fig. 1.106b, it is possible to infer that the image generated is a pentagon shape, which is confirmed by the number of sides being five and the length being uniform. Thus, the output image is a regular pentagon.

Exercises

1. Generate a checkerboard pattern image of size 32×32 and write a Python code to compute the number of black and white pixels in that image.
2. Write a Python code to read an input image and plot a specific row of the image.
3. Read the input image in the variable im, reduce the dimension of the image by half along the y-direction and store it in variable im1, reduce the dimension of the image by half along the x-direction and store it in the variable im2. Plot the image and print the dimensions of the input and output images.
4. Read an input image and try to add a border to the input image.
5. Write a Python program to shuffle all the pixels in the input image.
6. Perform uniform quantization of the input image. Now add uniform random noise to the input image to get the noisy image. Perform the uniform quantization of the noisy image. Compare the quantization result of noise free and noisy image and comment on the observed output.
7. Read a 256×256, 8-bit "cameraman" image. Divide the image into four quadrants. Now, obtain the resultant image by interchanging the quadrants as shown in the following figure:

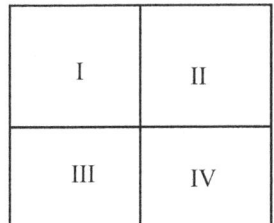

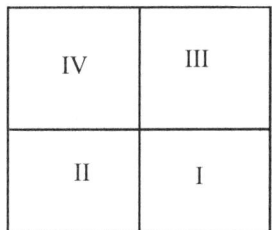

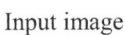

Input image   Quadrant interchanged
                                        image

8. Generate a 32×32 image with all the elements taking a value of 255 (i.e. a white image). Let us name this image as $f(m,n)$. Now multiply each pixel of $f(m,n)$ with $(-1)^{m+n}$ to obtain the image $g[m,n]$. This is given by $g[m,n] = (-1)^{m+n}f[m,n]$. What would be the nature of $g[m,n]$? Comment on the observed result.
9. Images are stored in the form of a matrix. If "A" represents a matrix, then $(A^T)^T = A$. Upon taking two times, the transpose of a matrix results in the same matrix. Write a Python code to illustrate this property.
10. Prove that matrix subtraction is not commutative. If "A" and "B" are two matrices then $A - B \neq B - A$.

Objective Questions

1. Assume that the grayscale image is read in the variable "img". Then, the built-in function shown in the following figure will give

```
Import cv2
Img=cv2.imread('cameraman.tif',0)
print(img.shape[0])
```

    A. Width of the image
    B. Height of the image
    C. Number of channels in the image
    D. Gray level resolution of the image

2. A grayscale image of dimension 256×256 is read in the variable "img". After executing the following Python code, what will the dimension of "img1" be?

```
Import cv2
Img=cv2.imread('cameraman.tif',0)
img1=img[::2,::2]
```

    A. 256×256
    B. 128×128
    C. 64×64
    D. 32×32

3. If the variable "img" holds 256×256 grayscale image, then the command that is used to extract the 128th row of the image is.

    A. img[128,:]
    B. img[:,128]
    C. img[128,128]
    D. img[127,:]

4. If the variable "img" holds 256×256 grayscale image, after executing the following Python code segment, what is the dimension of the image "img1"?

```
import cv2
import numpy as np
img=cv2.imread('cameraman.tif',0)
h,w=img.shape[:2]
img1=np.zeros([2*h,2*w])
```

    A. 256×256
    B. 128×128
    C. 512×512
    D. 1024×1024

5. If the variable "img" holds a grayscale image, then the Python command to access the last element in the image "img" is.

   A. img[0,0]
   B. img[1]
   C. img[-1,-1]
   D. img[end,end]

6. If the variable "img" holds a grayscale image, then the Python command to access the first element in the image "img" is

   A. img[0,0]
   B. img[1]
   C. img[-1,-1]
   D. img[end,end]

7. If the variable "img" holds an 8-bit grayscale image, upon executing the following Python code shown below, the variable "img1" holds

   ```
   Img1=img>128
   ```

   A. 8-bit grayscale image
   B. 16-bit grayscale image
   C. 4-bit grayscale image
   D. 2-bit binary image.

8. If the data type variable "img" holds an 8-bit grayscale image is "uint8", upon executing the following Python code shown below, the datatype of the variable "img1" is

   ```
   Img1=img>128
   ```

   A. uint8
   B. uint16
   C. float32
   D. Boolean

9. The reason for aliasing while performing the downsampling operation is

   A. Sampling introduces new frequency components in the image
   B. Sampling leads to the addition of low-frequency noise
   C. Sampled high-frequency components result in apparent low-frequency components.
   D. Sampling leads to furious high-frequency noise.

10. The input image to the built-in function "*transpose*" available in "numpy"
    library is a cameraman image as shown below. After the transpose operation,
    the modified image is

A.

B.

C.

D.

11. What output image will be if the following Python code is executed?

```
import numpy as np
import matplotlib.pyplot as plt
img=np.zeros([256,256])
img[118:138,118:138]=255
plt.imshow(img,cmap='gray')
```

   A. Horizontal white line in a black background
   B. White square in a black background
   C. White triangle in a black background
   D. Vertical line in a black background

12. A 2 × 2 dither matrix exhibit

   A. 4 gray levels
   B. 5 gray levels
   C. 6 gray levels
   D. 7 gray levels

13. A $n \times n$ dither matrix exhibit

   A. n^2 gray levels
   B. $n^2 + 1$ gray levels
   C. $n^2 - 1$ gray levels
   D. $\log(n^2)$ gray levels

14. The operation that converts a grayscale image to a binary image is

   A. Image sharpening
   B. Image smoothing
   C. Thresholding
   D. Image stitching

15. Floyd–Steinberg algorithm is an example of

   A. Average dithering
   B. Random dithering
   C. Ordered dithering
   D. Error diffusion dithering

16. An 8-bit image will exhibit

   A. 2 gray
   B. 8 gray levels
   C. 64 gray levels
   D. 256 gray levels

17. The use of an insufficient number of gray levels in smooth areas of digital images will result in

   A. Sharpening of the image
   B. Smoothening of the image
   C. False contours in the image
   D. Negative of the image

18. Identify the unary logic operation

   A. AND operation
   B. OR operation
   C. XOR operation
   D. NOT operation

19. Let the variable "img" hold a 32×32 checkerboard pattern. Upon taking bitwise XOR operation of the image "img" with itself will result in

   A. 32×32 checkerboard pattern
   B. 32×32 image with all the pixels values as "0"
   C. 32×32 image with all the pixels values as "255"
   D. 32×32 with all pixel values as '128".

20. Let the variable "img" holds a colour image, and then the Python command img[:,:,2] extracts

   A. Blue component of the image
   B. Green component of the image
   C. Red component of the image
   D. All three components of the image

21. Which operation is often employed to mitigate the problem of aliasing?

   A. Low-pass filtering
   B. High-pass filtering
   C. Better focusing
   D. Subtracting out the image mean

22. Discretization of pixel intensities of an image is termed as

   A. Sampling
   B. Quantization
   C. Encoding
   D. Interpolation

Answers to Objective Questions

Q. No.	01	02	03	04	05	06	07	08	09	10
Key	B	B	D	C	C	A	D	D	C	D

Q. No.	11	12	13	14	15	16	17	18	19	20	21	22
Key	B	B	B	C	D	D	C	D	B	C	A	B

Answers to PreLab Questions

1. Pixel stands for "picture element". It is the smallest unit of a digital image. Each pixel is characterized by a location and a value.
2. The value taken by the pixel is termed as gray level. Binary image takes the value of either "0" or "1". An 8-bit grayscale image can take value from 0 to 255, where "0" corresponds to black and "255" corresponds to white.
3. The spatial resolution depends on the density of the pixels that constitutes the digital image. The spatial resolution refers to the number of pixels utilized in construction of the image.
4. Gray level resolution refers to the smallest discernible change in gray level. Digital images having higher gray level resolution are composed with a larger number of shades of gray are displayed at a greater bit depth than with lower gray level resolution.
5. The steps involved in converting the analog image to a digital image are (1) sampling, (2) quantization, and (3) encoding.
6. Aliasing is an undesirable effect that occurs one under sample an image. Here under sampling refers to the choice of the sampling rate, which is less than twice the highest frequency present in the signal.
7. Quantization is mapping large set of values to a smaller set of values. Because of this uniqueness is lost, hence quantization is considered as irreversible phenomenon.
8. Brightness refers to the overall lightness or darkness of the image. Contrast is defined as a separation in intensity level between the dark and bright areas of an image.
9. Dithering is a process by which image with a finite number of gray levels is made to appear as continuous-tone image. Broadly, image dithering can be classified as (1) average dithering or thresholding, (2) random dithering, (3) ordered dithering, and (4) error diffusion dithering.
10. The popular image file formats employed to store the image include (1) tagged image file format (TIFF), (2) joint photographic expert group (JPEG), (3) bitmap file format, (BMP), (4) portable network graphics (PNG), and (5) encapsulated post script (EPS).

Bibliography

1. Rafael C. Gonzalez and Richard E. Woods, "Digital Image Processing", Pearson Education, 2018.
2. Alasdair McAndrew, "A Computational Introduction to Digital Image Processing", Chapman and Hall, 2021.
3. S. Jayaraman, S. Esakkirajan and T. Veerakumar, "Digital Image Processing", McGraw Hill, 2020.
4. Anil K. Jain, "Fundamentals of Digital Image Processing", Pearson Education, 2015.
5. Manas Kamal Bhuyan, "Computer Vision and Image Processing", CRC Press, 2019.

Chapter 2
Two-Dimensional Convolution and Correlation

Learning Objectives

After completing this chapter, the reader should be able to

- Perform linear convolution between two matrices in spatial domain
- Perform linear convolution in transform domain
- Understand the properties and applications of convolution
- Perform correlation in spatial and transform domain
- Understand the relationship between convolution and correlation

Roadmap of the Chapter

The concepts discussed in this chapter are illustrated in the form of the roadmap given in Fig. 2.1.

PreLab Questions

1. What are the mathematical operations involved in computing the convolution between two matrices?
2. Mention the properties satisfied by convolution operation.
3. What is the equivalent operation to convolution in frequency domain or transform domain?
4. What is the autocorrelation function of white noise?
5. Mention one application of convolution operation.
6. Mention one application of correlation operation.
7. Mention two characteristics of autocorrelation function?
8. What is the relation between convolution and correlation operation?
9. What is the objective of template matching?
10. Is it possible to perform convolution operation in transform domain?

Supplementary Information The online version contains supplementary material available at https://doi.org/10.1007/978-981-96-6382-8_2.

S Esakkirajan et al., *Digital Image Processing*, https://doi.org/10.1007/978-981-96-6382-8_2

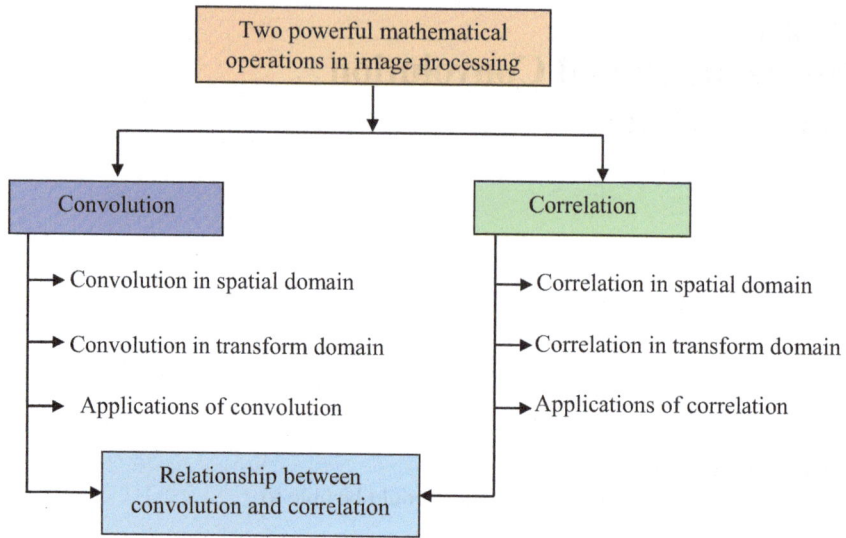

Fig. 2.1 Roadmap of the Chapter

Fig. 2.2 Linear shift invariant system

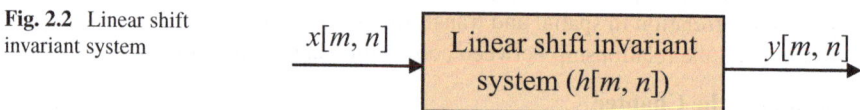

2.1 Two-Dimensional Convolution

If a system satisfies the linearity and shift-invariant properties, then the system is called a linear shift-invariant (LSI) system. Let us consider a 2D linear shift-invariant system ($h[m,n]$) as shown in Fig. 2.2. The input to the linear shift-invariant system is represented by $x[m,n]$, and the output of the system is represented as $y[m,n]$. The system is characterized by the impulse response $h[m,n]$.

The relationship between the input and output of linear shift invariant system is represented as

$$y[m,n] = x[m,n] * h[m,n] \qquad (2.1)$$

where "*" denotes convolution operation. The linear shift invariant system is completely characterized by its impulse response. The mathematical expression of 2D convolution operation is given by

$$y[m,n] = \sum_{k=0}^{M-1}\sum_{l=0}^{N-1} x[k,l] h[m-k,n-l] \qquad (2.2)$$

where M and N represent the row and column of an input image $x[m,n]$.

Case (i): Identity System
If $h[m, n] = \delta[m, n]$, the system acts as an identity system. For an identity system, the output of the system is the same as its input.

Case (ii): Low-Pass Filter
If the impulse response of the system is $h[m,n] = \dfrac{1}{M \times M} \times ones\left(M, M\right)$, the system behaves like a low-pass filter. For example, $h[m,n] = \dfrac{1}{9}\begin{bmatrix} 1 & 1 & 1 \\ 1 & 1 & 1 \\ 1 & 1 & 1 \end{bmatrix}$, then the

system behaves like a low-pass filter. Low-pass filter has the tendency to blur the edges. Low-pass filtering is considered as a smoothing operation.

Case (iii): High-Pass Filter
If the impulse response of the system is $h[m,n] = \begin{bmatrix} 0 & -1 & 0 \\ -1 & 4 & -1 \\ 0 & -1 & 0 \end{bmatrix}$, then the system

acts as high-pass filter. High-pass filter has the tendency to sharpen the edges. A high-pass filter is also termed as a sharpening operation.

2.2 2D Convolution in Spatial Domain

This section discusses the computation of 2D convolution in spatial domain. For this, let us consider an input signal as $x[m,n] = \begin{bmatrix} 1 & 2 \\ 3 & 4 \end{bmatrix}$ and an LSI system as $h[m,n] = \begin{bmatrix} 5 & 6 \\ 7 & 8 \end{bmatrix}$. The expression for two-dimensional convolution between two inputs $x[m, n]$ and $h[m, n]$ is given by

$$y[m,n] = x[m,n] * h[m,n]$$

The above equation can be expressed as

$$y[m,n] = \sum_{k=0}^{M-1}\sum_{l=0}^{N-1} x[k,l]h[m-k,n-l] \tag{2.3}$$

To compute the output y[0, 0], substitute $m = n = 0$ in Eq. (2.3), we get

$$y[0,0] = \sum_{k=0}^{1}\sum_{l=0}^{1} x[k,l]h[-k,-l] \tag{2.4}$$

To compute the output y[0, 1], substitute $m = 0$ and $n = 1$ in Eq. (2.3), we get

$$y[0,1] = \sum_{k=0}^{1}\sum_{l=0}^{1} x[k,l]h[-k,1-l] \tag{2.5}$$

To compute the output y[0, 2], substitute $m = 0$ and $n = 2$ in Eq. (2.3), we get

$$y[0,2] = \sum_{k=0}^{1}\sum_{l=0}^{1} x[k,l]h[-k,2-l] \tag{2.6}$$

Upon observing Eqs. (2.4), (2.5), and (2.6), it is possible to interpret that while performing 2D convolution between two inputs $x[m,n]$ and $h[m,n]$, one matrix is unaltered while the other matrix is folded and shifted. This idea is used to perform 2D convolution operation.

Step 1: Folding of the second input $h[m,n]$ to obtain $h[-m,-n]$.

The input $h[m,n]$ is given by $h[m,n] = \begin{bmatrix} 5 & 6 \\ 7 & 8 \end{bmatrix}$. Upon folding along "$m$" axis, the

folded matrix is given by $h[-m,n] = \begin{bmatrix} 6 & 5 \\ 8 & 7 \end{bmatrix}$. Now folding the resultant matrix

along "n" axis results in $h[-m,-n] = \begin{bmatrix} 8 & 7 \\ 6 & 5 \end{bmatrix}$.

Step 2: Zero padding of the input $x[m,n]$

Upon zero padding of the input $x[m,n]$, we get

$$x[m,n] = \begin{bmatrix} 0 & 0 & 0 & 0 \\ 0 & 1 & 2 & 0 \\ 0 & 3 & 4 & 0 \\ 0 & 0 & 0 & 0 \end{bmatrix}$$

It is possible to observe that a 2×2 matrix upon zero padding along rows and columns results in a 4×4 matrix.

Step 3: Computing the value of the output y[0, 0]

The graphical way of computing the output y[0, 0] is illustrated as follows:

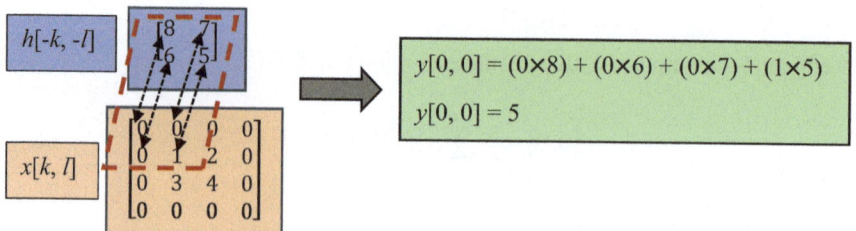

The output $y[0, 0]$ is obtained by performing element-by-element multiplication of $x[k, l]$ with $h[-k, -l]$ to get the value as $y[0, 0] = 5$.

Step 4: To compute the output $y[0, 1]$

The graphical way of computing the output $y[0, 1]$ is illustrated as follows:

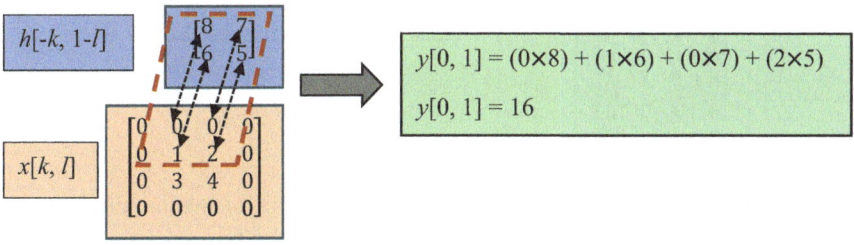

The output $y[0, 1]$ is obtained by performing element-by-element multiplication of $x[k, l]$ with $h[-k, 1 - l]$ to get the value as $y[0, 1] = 16$.

Step 5: To compute $y[0, 2]$

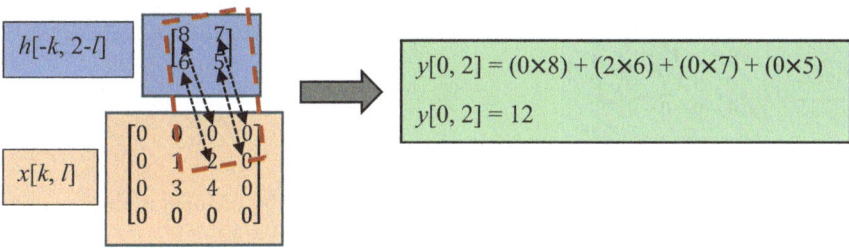

The output $y[0, 2]$ is obtained by performing element-by-element multiplication of $x[k, l]$ with $h[-k, 2 - l]$ to obtain the value as $y[0, 2] = 12$.

Step 6: To compute $y[1, 0]$

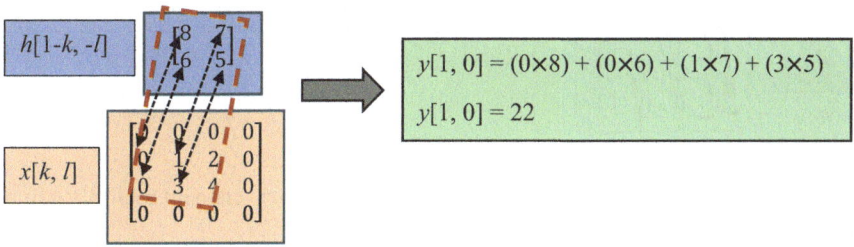

The output $y[1, 0]$ is obtained by performing element-by-element multiplication of $x[k, l]$ with $h[1 - k, -l]$ to obtain the value as $y[1, 0] = 22$.

Step 7: To compute y[1, 1]

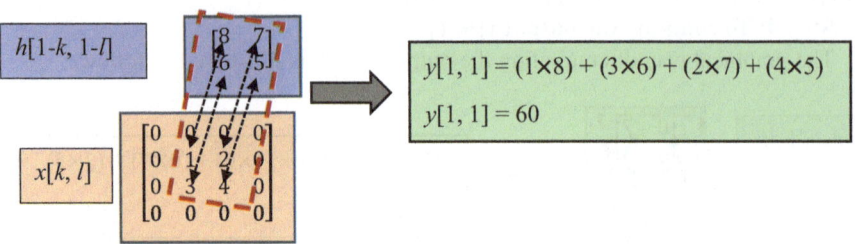

The output $y[1, 1]$ is obtained by performing element-by-element multiplication of $x[k, l]$ with $h[1 - k, 1 - l]$ to obtain the value as $y[1, 1] = 60$.

Step 8: To compute y[1, 2]

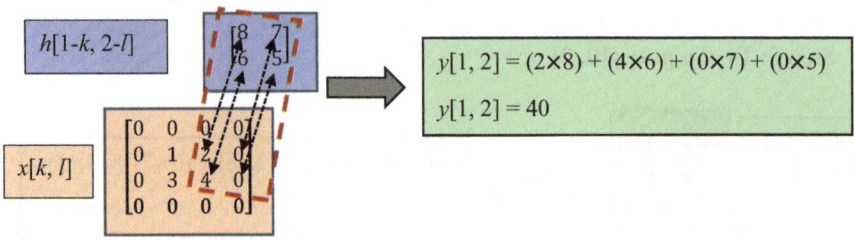

The output $y[1, 2]$ is obtained by performing element-by-element multiplication of $x[k, l]$ with $h[1 - k, 2 - l]$ to obtain the value as $y[1, 2] = 40$.

Step 9: To compute y[2, 0]

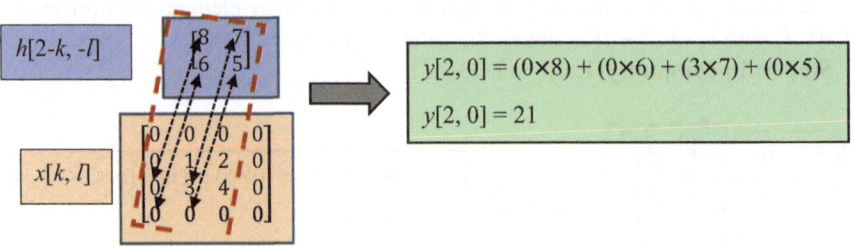

The output $y[2, 0]$ is obtained by performing element-by-element multiplication of $x[k, l]$ with $h[2 - k, -l]$ to obtain the value as $y[2, 0] = 21$.

Step 10: To compute y[2, 1]

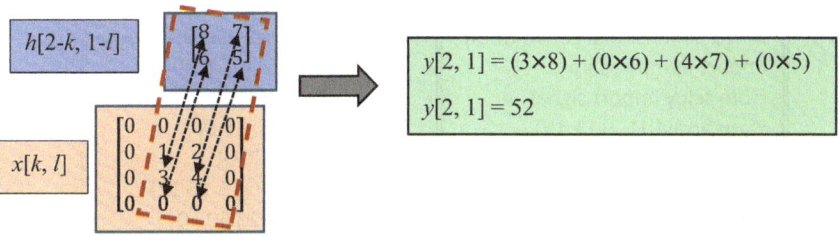

The output $y[2, 1]$ is obtained by performing element-by-element multiplication of $x[k, l]$ with $h[2 - k, 1 - l]$ to obtain the value as $y[2, 1] = 52$.

Step 11: To compute $y[2, 2]$

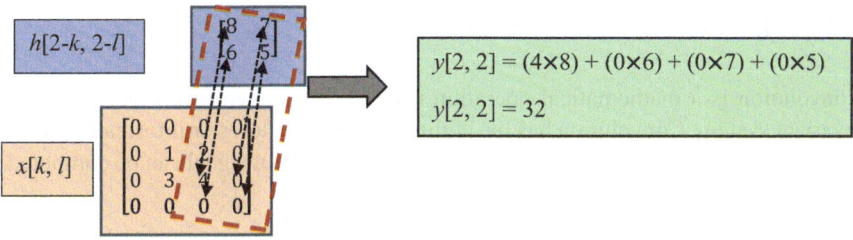

The output $y[2, 2]$ is obtained by performing element-by-element multiplication of $x[k, l]$ with $h[2 - k, 2 - l]$ to obtain the value as $y[2, 2] = 32$.

Consolidating the above results, it can be written as

$$\begin{bmatrix} 1 & 2 \\ 3 & 4 \end{bmatrix} * \begin{bmatrix} 5 & 6 \\ 7 & 8 \end{bmatrix} = \begin{bmatrix} 5 & 16 & 12 \\ 22 & 60 & 40 \\ 21 & 52 & 32 \end{bmatrix}$$

Experiment 2.1: Computation of 2D Convolution

This experiment discusses the implementation of 2D convolution using Python. The Python code that performs the 2D convolution between the matrices $\begin{bmatrix} 1 & 2 \\ 3 & 4 \end{bmatrix}$ and $\begin{bmatrix} 5 & 6 \\ 7 & 8 \end{bmatrix}$ is given in Figure 2.3a and the corresponding result is shown in Figure 2.3b.

Inference

The experimental result obtained using the built-in function "convolve2d" available in "*scipy*" library is in agreement with the theoretical result.

```
#Two dimensional convolution
import numpy as np
from scipy import signal
x=np.array([[1,2],[3,4]])
h=np.array([[5,6],[7,8]])
y=signal.convolve2d(x,h)
print('x:',x),print('h:',h)
print('y:',y)
```

```
x: [[1 2]
 [3 4]]
h: [[5 6]
 [7 8]]
y: [[ 5 16 12]
 [22 60 40]
 [21 52 32]]
```

(a) Python code   **(b) Result of linear convolution**

Fig. 2.3 Computation of 2D convolution: (**a**) Python code, (**b**) result of linear convolution

2.3   Significance of Convolution

Convolution is a mathematical operation that can be applied to linear time/shift-invariant system. Convolution has the ability to extract features or information from the input signal. Many of the 2D system operations on input signal can be computed by using the 2D convolution operation.

2.3.1   Identity System

The input to the linear shift-invariant (LSI) system ($h[m, n]$) is denoted as ($x[m, n]$). The impulse response of the system is $h[m, n] = \delta[m, n]$. The output of the system is given by

$$y[m,n] = x[m,n] * h[m,n]$$

The impulse response of a 2D LSI system is a 2D impulse function, which is represented as

$$h[m,n] = \delta[m,n]$$

Substituting the 2D impulse function in the system output equation, we get

$$y[m,n] = x[m,n] * \delta[m,n]$$

The convolution of any signal with an impulse signal results in the same signal, hence the output is given by

$$y[m,n] = x[m,n]$$

The output image is the same as the input image.

Experiment 2.2: Implementation of Identity System

This experiment deals with the implementation of an identity system using Python. If the impulse response of linear shift-invariant system is $h[m, n] = \delta[m, n]$, then the system acts as an identity system. The Python code for an implementation of identity system is given in Fig. 2.4 and the corresponding output is shown in Fig. 2.5.

Inferences

In this experiment, the input signal $x[m, n]$ is a Cameraman image, and the impulse response is a 2D impulse function. The output signal $y[m, n]$ is a Cameraman image, which is the same as the input signal, as shown in Fig. 2.5. Therefore, this operation is termed as identity operation because the output signal is same as the input signal.

Fig. 2.4 Python code for identity operation

```
#Identity operation
import cv2
import numpy as np
from scipy import signal
import matplotlib.pyplot as plt
x=cv2.imread('cameraman.tif',0)
kernel=np.zeros([3,3])
kernel[1,1]=1
y=signal.convolve2d(x,kernel,'same')
fig = plt.figure(figsize=(8,8))
plt.subplot(1,3,1),plt.imshow(x,cmap='gray')
plt.title('x[m,n]'),plt.axis('off')
plt.subplot(1,3,2),plt.imshow(kernel,cmap='gray')
plt.title('h[m,n]=$\delta[m,n]$'),plt.axis('off')
plt.subplot(1,3,3),plt.imshow(y,cmap='gray')
plt.title('y[m,n]'),plt.axis('off')
plt.tight_layout()
```

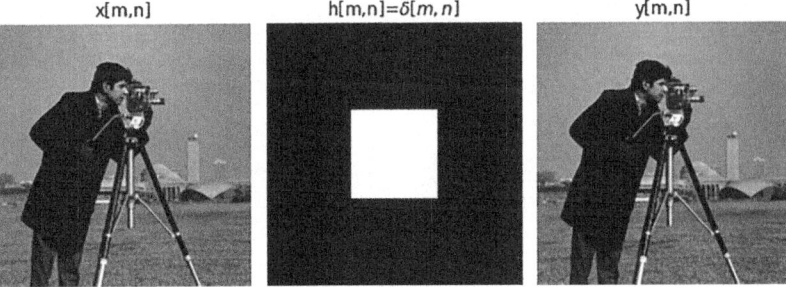

Fig. 2.5 Result of identity operation

2.3.2 Spatial Shift Operation

The spatial shift of an input image can be done by convolving an input image with a shifted 2D impulse function. The mathematical expression of a spatial shift operation is given by

$$y[m,n] = x[m,n] * \delta[m - m_0, n] \tag{2.7}$$

The above expression is simplified as

$$y[m,n] = x[m - m_0, n] \tag{2.8}$$

Similarly,

$$y[m,n] = x[m,n] * \delta[m,n - n_0] = x[m,n - n_0] \tag{2.9}$$

The shift along both "m" and "n" direction is accomplished using the relation

$$y[m,n] = x[m,n] * \delta[m - m_0, n - n_0] = x[m - m_0, n - n_0] \tag{2.10}$$

Experiment 2.3: Implementation of Spatial Shift Operation

This experiment discusses the implementation of spatial shift operation on given input image using Python. The spatial shift operation on input image is performed by convolving shifted 2D impulse function. The Python code that illustrates the spatial shift operation is shown in Fig. 2.6, and the corresponding output is shown in Fig. 2.7.

Inferences

The following inferences can be drawn from Fig. 2.7:

- $x[m, n]$ represents the input signal, which is a "Cameraman image".
- $y_1[m, n]$ represents the spatial shift along the column, which is obtained by convolving the input image with $\delta[m, n - n_0]$.
- $y_2[m, n]$ represents spatial shift along the row, which is obtained by convolving the input image with $\delta[m - m_0, n]$.
- $y_3[m, n]$ represents the spatial shift along both row and column, which is obtained by convolving the input image with $\delta[m - m_0, n - n_0]$.

2.3.3 Gaussian Smoothing

Gaussian smoothing is an important operation in image enhancement, which acts like a low-pass filter. The expression for 2D Gaussian function is given by

```
#Spaital shift operation
import cv2
import numpy as np
from scipy import signal
import matplotlib.pyplot as plt
#Step 1: Defining the input signal x[m,n]
x=cv2.imread('cameraman.tif',0)
#Step 2: Defining the spatial shift kernels
kernel_1=np.zeros([20,20])
kernel_1[10,19]=1
kernel_2=np.zeros([20,20])
kernel_2[19,10]=1
kernel_3=np.zeros([20,20])
kernel_3[19,19]=1
#Step 3: Obtaining the output
y1=signal.convolve2d(x,kernel_1,'same')
y2=signal.convolve2d(x,kernel_2,'same')
y3=signal.convolve2d(x,kernel_3,'same')
# Step 4: Displaying the result
fig = plt.figure(figsize=(12,12))
plt.subplot(3,3,1),plt.imshow(x,cmap='gray')
plt.title('x[m,n]'),plt.axis('off')
plt.subplot(3,3,2),plt.imshow(kernel_1,cmap='gray')
plt.title('h[m,n]=$\delta[m,n-9]$'),plt.axis('off')
plt.subplot(3,3,3),plt.imshow(y1,cmap='gray')
plt.title('$y_1[m,n]$'),plt.axis('off')
plt.subplot(3,3,4),plt.imshow(x,cmap='gray')
plt.title('x[m,n]'),plt.axis('off')
plt.subplot(3,3,5),plt.imshow(kernel_2,cmap='gray')
plt.title('h[m,n]=$\delta[m-9,n]$'),plt.axis('off')
plt.subplot(3,3,6),plt.imshow(y2,cmap='gray')
plt.title('$y_2[m,n]$'),plt.axis('off')
plt.subplot(3,3,7),plt.imshow(x,cmap='gray')
plt.title('x[m,n]'),plt.axis('off')
plt.subplot(3,3,8),plt.imshow(kernel_3,cmap='gray')
plt.title('h[m,n]=$\delta[m-9,n-9]$'),plt.axis('off')
plt.subplot(3,3,9),plt.imshow(y3,cmap='gray')
plt.title('$y_3[m,n]$'),plt.axis('off')
plt.tight_layout()
```

Fig. 2.6 Python code to perform spatial shift of the input image through convolution

$$f[m,n] = \frac{1}{2\pi\sigma^2} e^{\frac{-(m^2+n^2)}{2\sigma^2}} \tag{2.11}$$

In the above expression, "σ" represents the standard deviation. The Gaussian kernel is used to smoothen the input signal.

Fig. 2.7 Result of spatial shift operation

Experiment 2.4: Gaussian Smoothing Using 2D Convolution
This experiment aims to perform the Gaussian smoothing operation on the input image using 2D convolution. The Python code that performs the input signal's Gaussian smoothing is given in Fig. 2.8, and the corresponding output is shown in Fig. 2.9.

Inferences
The following inferences can be made from Fig. 2.9:

- The Gaussian kernel is generated as per Eq. (2.11), and the variance is chosen as 5.
- The 2D Gaussian function is convolved with the input image to obtain the output image. By observing the input and output image, it is possible to interpret that the output image is a blurred or smoothened version of the input image.
- This blurring effect is used to minimize the impact of additive noise in digital image.

```
#Gaussian smoothing
import numpy as np
import matplotlib.pyplot as plt
import cv2
from scipy import signal
#Step 1: Defining the input signal x[m,n]
img_in=cv2.imread('cameraman.tif',0)
#Step 2: Generation of 2D Gaussian kernel
x=np.linspace(-10,10,20)
y=np.linspace(-10,10,20)
X,Y=np.meshgrid(x,y)
D0=3
kernel=(1/(2*np.pi*D0))*np.exp(-(X**2+Y**2)/(2*D0**2))
#Step 3: Obtaining the output image
img_out=signal.convolve2d(img_in,kernel,'same')
#Step 4: Displaying the result
plt.subplot(1,3,1),plt.imshow(img_in,cmap='gray')
plt.title('Input image'),plt.axis('off')
plt.subplot(1,3,2),plt.imshow(kernel,cmap='gray'),plt.axis('off')
plt.title('Gaussian kernel')
plt.subplot(1,3,3),plt.imshow(img_out,cmap='gray')
plt.title('Output image'),plt.axis('off')
plt.tight_layout()
```

Fig. 2.8 Python code to perform Gaussian smoothing

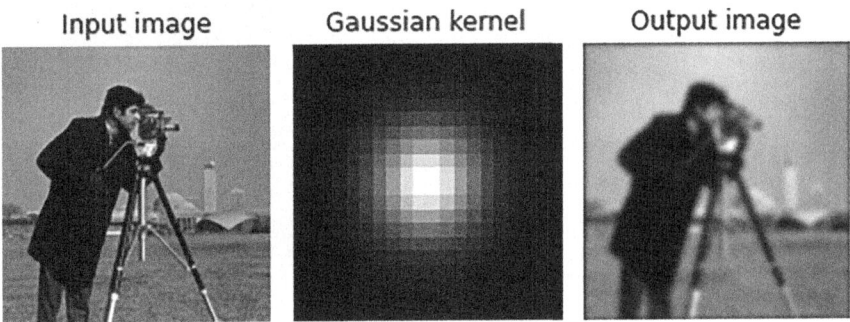

Fig. 2.9 Result of Gaussian smoothing

2.3.4   Image Sharpening

Image sharpening can be performed by applying a high-pass filter kernel to the input image. The image sharpening kernels are used to extract the edge details in the input image. The kernel, which is used to extract the edge information from the input image, is given by $\begin{bmatrix} 0 & 1 & 0 \\ 1 & -4 & 1 \\ 0 & 1 & 0 \end{bmatrix}$.

```
#Image sharpening
import numpy as np
import matplotlib.pyplot as plt
import cv2
from scipy import signal
#Step 1: Defining the input signal x[m,n]
img_in=cv2.imread('testimage_edge.jpg',0)
#Step 2: Defining the kernel
kernel=np.array([[0,1,0],[1,-4,1],[0,1,0]])
#Step 3: Obtaining the output image
img_out=signal.convolve2d(img_in,kernel,'same')
img_out = np.clip(img_out, 0, 255).astype(np.uint8)
#Step 4: Displaying the result
fig = plt.figure(figsize=(8,8)),plt.subplot(1,3,1),plt.imshow(img_in,cmap='gray')
plt.title('Input image'),plt.axis('off'),plt.subplot(1,3,2),
plt.imshow(kernel,cmap='gray'),plt.title('Kernel'),plt.xticks([]),plt.yticks([])
plt.subplot(1,3,3),plt.imshow(img_out,cmap='gray'),
plt.title('Output image'),plt.axis('off')
plt.tight_layout()
```

Fig. 2.10 Python code to enhance the edge detail in the input image

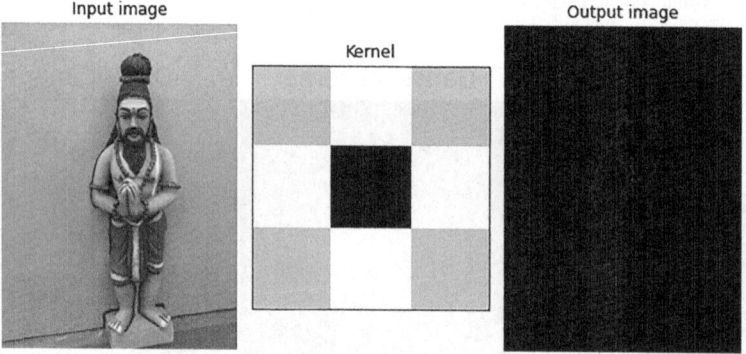

Fig. 2.11 Result of image sharpening

Experiment 2.5: Implementation of Image sharpening Operation

This experiment deals with the image sharpening operation on the input image. The Python code that is used to extract the edge information from the input image is given in Fig. 2.10, and the corresponding output is shown in Fig. 2.11.

Inference

From Fig. 2.11, it is possible to observe that the edge details are clearly visible in the output image. The filter kernel extracts the edge details in the input image.

```
#Directional filtering
import numpy as np
import matplotlib.pyplot as plt
from scipy import signal
import cv2
#Step 1: Reading the input image
img=cv2.imread('X.png',0)
#Step 2: Generating directional kernel
k1=np.array([[0,0,0],[-0.5,1,-0.5],[0,0,0]]) #Horizontal direction
k2=np.array([[0,-0.5,0],[0,1,0],[0,-0.5,0]]) #Vertical direction
k3=np.array([[-0.5,0,0],[0,1,0],[0,0,-0.5]]) #Diagonal direction
k4=np.array([[0,0,-0.5],[0,1,0],[-0.5,0,0]]) #Diagonal direction
#Step 3: Performing convolution
img1=signal.convolve2d(img,k1,'same')
img1 = np.clip(img1, 0, 255).astype(np.uint8)
img2=signal.convolve2d(img,k2,'same')
img2 = np.clip(img2, 0, 255).astype(np.uint8)
img3=signal.convolve2d(img,k3,'same')
img3 = np.clip(img3, 0, 255).astype(np.uint8)
img4=signal.convolve2d(img,k4,'same')
img4 = np.clip(img4, 0, 255).astype(np.uint8)
#Step 4: Displaying the results
fig = plt.figure(figsize=(10,6)),plt.subplot(3,4,2),plt.imshow(img,cmap='gray'),
plt.title('Input image'),plt.xticks([]),plt.yticks([])
plt.subplot(3,4,5),plt.imshow(k1,cmap='gray'),plt.title('Horizontal Kernel'),
plt.xticks([]),plt.yticks([]),plt.subplot(3,4,9),plt.imshow(img1,cmap='gray')
plt.title('Horizontal edge detection'),plt.xticks([]),plt.yticks([])
plt.subplot(3,4,6),plt.imshow(k2,cmap='gray'),plt.title('Vertical Kernel')
plt.xticks([]),plt.yticks([]),plt.subplot(3,4,10),plt.imshow(img2,cmap='gray')
plt.title('Vertical edge detection'),plt.xticks([]),plt.yticks([])
plt.subplot(3,4,7),plt.imshow(k3,cmap='gray'),plt.title('Diagonal Kernel')
plt.xticks([]),plt.yticks([]),plt.subplot(3,4,11),plt.imshow(img3,cmap='gray')
plt.xticks([]),plt.yticks([]),plt.title('Diagonal edge detection')
plt.subplot(3,4,8),plt.imshow(k4,cmap='gray'),plt.title('Diagonal Kernel')
plt.xticks([]),plt.yticks([]),plt.subplot(3,4,12),plt.imshow(img4,cmap='gray')
plt.xticks([]),plt.yticks([]),plt.title('Diagonal edge detection')
plt.tight_layout()
```

Fig. 2.12 Python code to perform directional filtering of the input image

Experiment 2.6: Directional Edge Detection

This experiment deals the directional edge detection from an input image using Python. The kernel used to detect the horizontal edge is $\begin{bmatrix} 0 & 0 & 0 \\ -0.5 & 1 & -0.5 \\ 0 & 0 & 0 \end{bmatrix}$, the

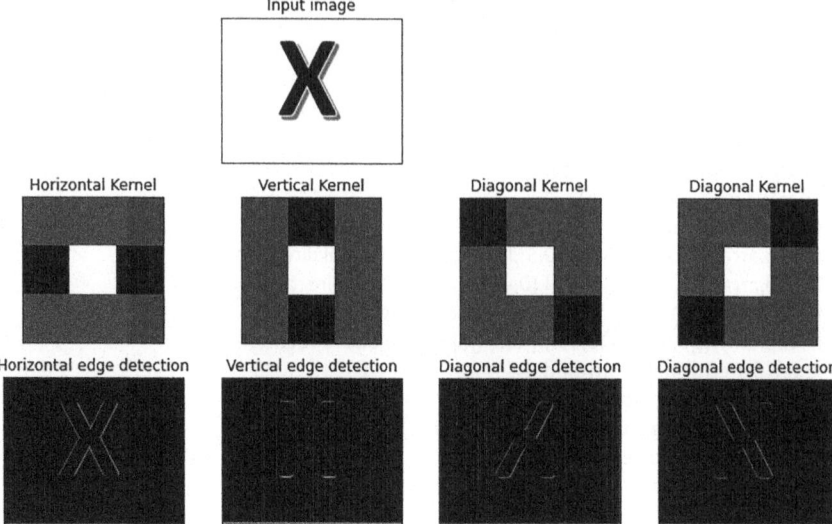

Fig. 2.13 Result of directional filtering

kernel used to detect the vertical edge is $\begin{bmatrix} 0 & -0.5 & 0 \\ 0 & 1 & 0 \\ 0 & -0.5 & 0 \end{bmatrix}$, and the kernel used to

detect the diagonal edges is $\begin{bmatrix} -0.5 & 0 & 0 \\ 0 & 1 & 0 \\ 0 & 0 & -0.5 \end{bmatrix}$ and $\begin{bmatrix} 0 & 0 & -0.5 \\ 0 & 1 & 0 \\ -0.5 & 0 & 0 \end{bmatrix}$, respectively.

The Python code that illustrates the impact of the directional kernel on the input image is shown in Fig. 2.12, and the corresponding output is shown in Fig. 2.13.

Inference
Directional filtering has the ability to extract the horizontal, vertical, and diagonal edge informations from the input image.

Experiment 2.7: Linear convolution between Two-Step Signals
Step signal exhibits sudden change from one value to the other. In terms of the image, a step image is a half black and half white. The black corresponds to gray level "0", whereas white corresponds to gray level "1", and sudden change in gray level 0 to 1 is considered as step image. The objective of this experiment is to perform linear convolution between two images that exhibits step change in gray level from "0 to 1". The Python code that performs this task is given in Fig. 2.14, and the corresponding output is shown in Fig. 2.15.

Inferences
From Fig. 2.15, the following inferences can be drawn:

- Image-1 and Image-2 exhibit step-like changes in the gray level from black to white.

```
#Linear convolution of two step signals
import numpy as np
import matplotlib.pyplot as plt
from scipy import signal
#Step 1: Generation of input images
img1=np.ones([16,16])
img1[0:16,0:8]=0
img2=img1
#Step 2: Perform linear convolution
img_out=signal.convolve2d(img1,img2,'same')
#Step 3: Displaying the result
plt.subplot(1,3,1),plt.imshow(img1,cmap='gray')
plt.title('Image-1'),plt.xticks([]),plt.yticks([])
plt.subplot(1,3,2),plt.imshow(img2,cmap='gray')
plt.title('Image-2'),plt.xticks([]),plt.yticks([])
plt.subplot(1,3,3),plt.imshow(img_out,cmap='gray')
plt.title('Linear convolution result'),plt.xticks([]),
plt.yticks([])
plt.tight_layout()
```

Fig. 2.14 Python code to perform convolution between two-step images

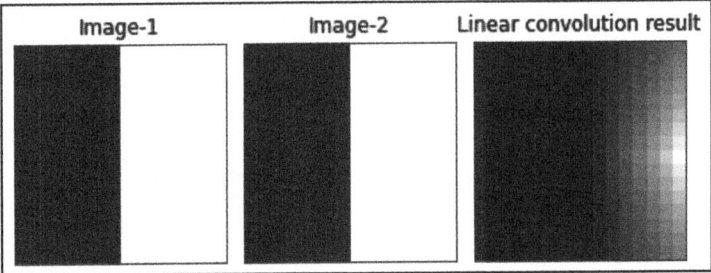

Fig. 2.15 Result of linear convolution

- The result of linear convolution exhibits slow variation in gray level from black to white.
- The output image exhibits ramp-like change in the gray level.
- It is a well-known fact that the convolution of two-step signals results in a ramp signal. In this case, Image-1 and Image-2 are similar to that of two-step signals; their linear convolution results in an image that shows a ramp-like change in the gray level from black to white.

Experiment 2.8: Convolution of Two Gaussian Functions

This Python experiment aims to prove that the convolution of two Gaussian functions will result in another Gaussian function. To illustrate this, two images, which follow Gaussian distribution with zero mean and variance 10 and 20, are generated as Image-1 and Image-2, respectively. The linear convolution between these two images is performed to verify whether the output image is a Gaussian or not. The Python code to perform this task is shown in Fig. 2.16, and the corresponding output is shown in Fig. 2.17.

Inferences

The following inferences can be drawn from this experiment:

- Image-1 is a Gaussian function with zero mean and variance = 10.
- Image-2 is a Gaussian function with zero mean and variance = 20.
- The linear convolution of Image-1 with Image-2 results in another Gaussian function, which is evident from the profile of the resultant image.
- This result implies that convolution of two Gaussian functions will result in an another Gaussian function.

```
#Linear convolution of two Gaussian functions
import numpy as np
import matplotlib.pyplot as plt
from scipy import signal
#Step 1: Generation of input images
x=np.linspace(-128,128,256)
y=x
X,Y=np.meshgrid(x,y)
D=np.sqrt(X**2+Y**2)
sigma1,sigma2=10,20
img1=(1/(2*np.pi*sigma1))*np.exp((-D**2)/(2*sigma1**2))
img2=(1/(2*np.pi*sigma2))*np.exp((-D**2)/(2*sigma2**2))
#Step 2: Perform linear convolution
img_out=signal.convolve2d(img1,img2)
#Step 3: Displaying the result
plt.subplot(2,3,1),plt.imshow(img1,cmap='gray'),plt.title('Image-1'),plt.axis('off')
plt.subplot(2,3,2),plt.imshow(img2,cmap='gray'),plt.title('Image-2'),plt.axis('off')
plt.subplot(2,3,3),plt.imshow(img_out,cmap='gray')
plt.title('Linear convolution result'),plt.axis('off'),plt.subplot(2,3,4),
plt.plot(img1[128,:]),plt.title('Profile of Image-1'),plt.subplot(2,3,5),
plt.plot(img2[128,:]),plt.title('Profile of Image-2'),plt.subplot(2,3,6),
plt.plot(img_out[256,:]),plt.title('Profile of output image')
plt.tight_layout()
```

Fig. 2.16 Python code to perform linear convolution between two Gaussian function

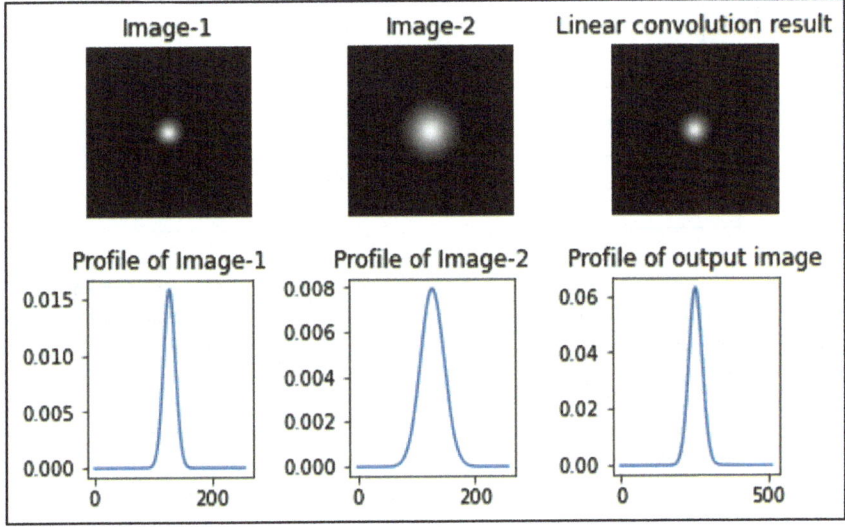

Fig. 2.17 Result of linear convolution between two Gaussian functions

2.4 Convolution in Frequency Domain

Convolution in spatial domain is equivalent to multiplication in the frequency domain. The flow chart to compute linear convolution using the transform domain (Fourier domain) is given in Fig. 2.18. In the figure, $x[m, n]$ and $h[m, n]$ represent the two input matrices. The objective is to compute linear convolution between these two matrices. To perform the linear convolution between the given two matrices, zero padding is done first to obtain the matrices $x_1[m, n]$ and $h_1[m, n]$. After zero padding, Fourier transform of these two matrices is taken to obtain $X_1[k, l]$ and $H_1[k, l]$. Then, the two matrices are multiplied to obtain $Y_1[k, l]$. Upon taking the inverse Fourier transform of $Y_1[k, l]$, the result of linear convolution $y_1[m, n]$ is obtained.

Experiment 2.9: Computation of Linear convolution Using Transform
The objective of this experiment is to obtain the result of linear convolution in the spatial domain and in the frequency domain and to prove the fact that "convolution in the spatial domain is equivalent to multiplication in the transform domain". To illustrate this fact, two input matrices, namely $x[m, n]$ and $h[m, n]$, are defined, and the linear convolution between these two matrices is obtained using the "convolve2d" built-in function available in the "*scipy*" library. The linear convolution is then performed in transform domain by first zero padding the two matrices $x[m, n]$ and $h[m, n]$ to obtain $x_1[m, n]$ and $h_1[m, n]$, respectively. Then, the Fourier transform

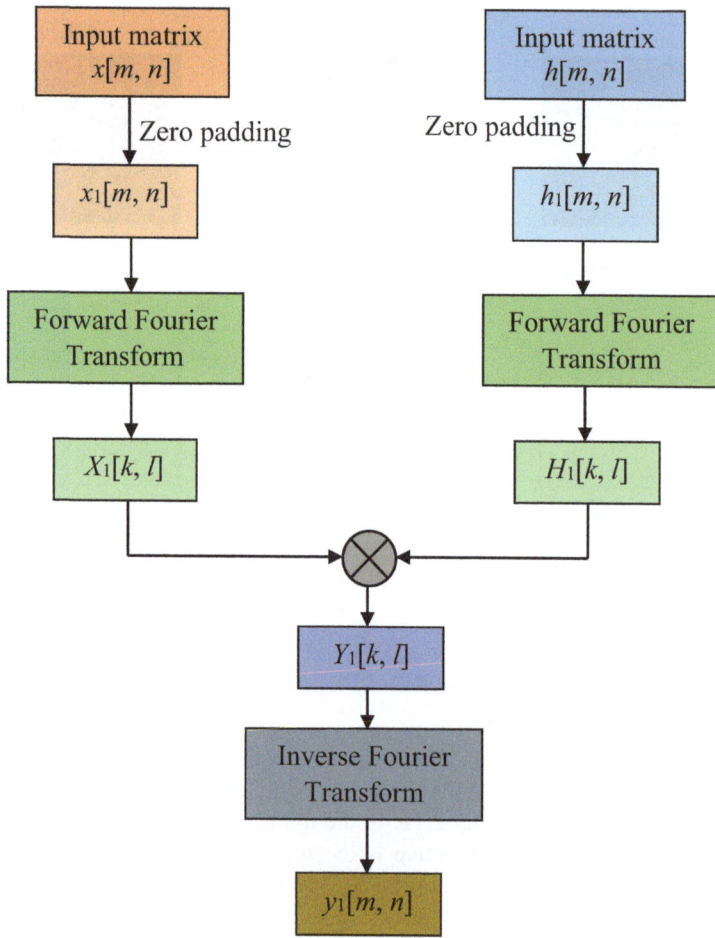

Fig. 2.18 Flow chart to compute linear convolution between two matrices in transform domain

of the zero-padded matrices is obtained as $X_1[k, l]$ and $H_1[k, l]$. The matrices $X_1[k, l]$ and $H_1[k, l]$ are multiplied to obtain $Y_1[k, l]$. Upon taking the inverse Fourier transform of $Y_1[k, l]$, the matrix $y_1[m, n]$ is obtained. The Python code for this procedure is given in Fig. 2.19, and its corresponding result is shown in Fig. 2.20.

Inference

From Fig. 2.20, it is possible to observe that the result of linear convolution in spatial and transform domain are same. This implies that "convolution in spatial domain is equivalent to multiplication in the transform domain and vice versa".

```
# Computation of linear convolution in transform
import numpy as np
from scipy import signal
#Step 1: Defining the input matrices
x=np.array([[1,2],[3,4]])
h=np.array([[5,6],[7,8]])
print('x:',x),print('h:',h)
#Step 2: Linear convolution in spatial domain
y=signal.convolve2d(x,h)
#Step 3: Zero padding of the input matrices
x1=np.pad(x, [(0, 1), (0, 1)], mode='constant')
h1=np.pad(h, [(0, 1), (0, 1)], mode='constant')
print('x after padding:',x1),print('h after padding:',h1)
#Step 4: Taking Forward transform
X1=np.fft.fft2(x1)
H1=np.fft.fft2(h1)
#Step 5: Multiplication of the spectrum
Y1=np.multiply(X1,H1)
#Step 6: Taking Inverse Fourier transform
y1=np.fft.ifft2(Y1)
#Step 7: Comparing the result
print('Result of linear convolution in spatial domain:',y)
print("Result of linear convolution in transform domain:",np.abs(y1))
```

Fig. 2.19 Python code to perform linear convolution in transform domain

2.5 Correlation

Correlation is a mathematical operation that is used to obtain the relative similarity between two signals. Two types of correlation include (1) autocorrelation and (2) cross-correlation. If one finds the relative similarity between two signals that originated from the same source, it is termed autocorrelation. On the other hand, if one is interested in finding the relative similarity between two signals from different sources, then it is termed cross-correlation. The mathematical expression for the correlation between two signals is represented as $f[m, n]$ and $g[m, n]$ is expressed as

$$f[m,n] \text{''} g[m,n] = \sum_a \sum_b f[a,b] g[m+a,n+b] \tag{2.12}$$

where "•" denotes correlation operation. Mathematically, convolution and correlation are similar operations. Convolution is used to extract features from the input image, whereas correlation is used to obtain the relative similarity between the two images. Correlation is used for template matching.

```
x: [[1 2]
 [3 4]]
h: [[5 6]
 [7 8]]
x after padding: [[1 2 0]
 [3 4 0]
 [0 0 0]]
h after padding: [[5 6 0]
 [7 8 0]
 [0 0 0]]
Result of linear convolution in spatial domain: [[ 5 16 12]
 [22 60 40]
 [21 52 32]]
Result of linear convolution in transform domain: [[ 5. 16. 12.]
 [22. 60. 40.]
 [21. 52. 32.]]
```

Fig. 2.20 Comparing the result of linear convolution in spatial and transform domain

2.5.1   *Correlation in Spatial Domain*

This section explains the computation of autocorrelation of the input signal $f[m,n] = \begin{bmatrix} 1 & 2 \\ 3 & 4 \end{bmatrix}$ in spatial domain. The steps involved in the computation of auto-correlation are as follows:

Step 1: Zero padding of the input signal

Zero padding of the input image along a row and column of the image is given as follows:

$$\begin{bmatrix} 0 & 0 & 0 & 0 \\ 0 & 1 & 2 & 0 \\ 0 & 3 & 4 & 0 \\ 0 & 0 & 0 & 0 \end{bmatrix}$$

Step 2: To determine the output $r_{xx}[0, 0]$

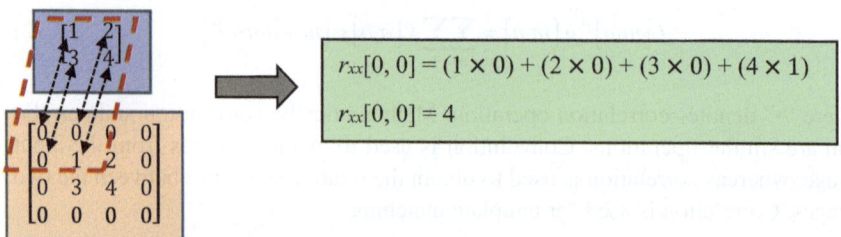

$r_{xx}[0, 0] = (1 \times 0) + (2 \times 0) + (3 \times 0) + (4 \times 1)$

$r_{xx}[0, 0] = 4$

The first value of the autocorrelation function is 4.
Step 3: To compute $r_{xx}[0, 1]$

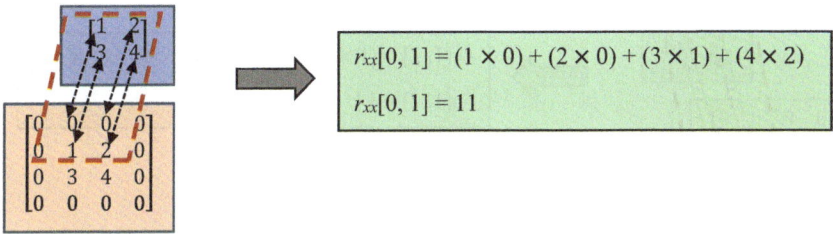

$r_{xx}[0, 1] = (1 \times 0) + (2 \times 0) + (3 \times 1) + (4 \times 2)$

$r_{xx}[0, 1] = 11$

The second value of the autocorrelation is 11.
Step 4: To compute $r_{xx}[0, 2]$

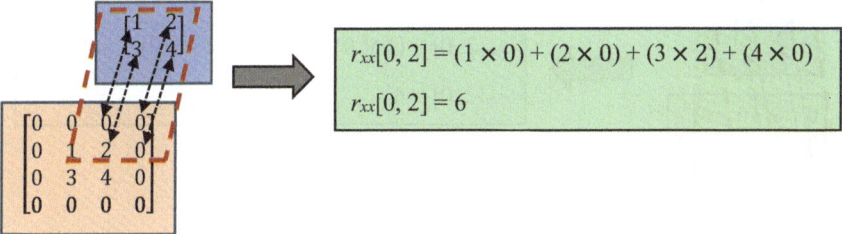

$r_{xx}[0, 2] = (1 \times 0) + (2 \times 0) + (3 \times 2) + (4 \times 0)$

$r_{xx}[0, 2] = 6$

The second value of the autocorrelation is 6.
Step 5: To compute $r_{xx}[1, 0]$

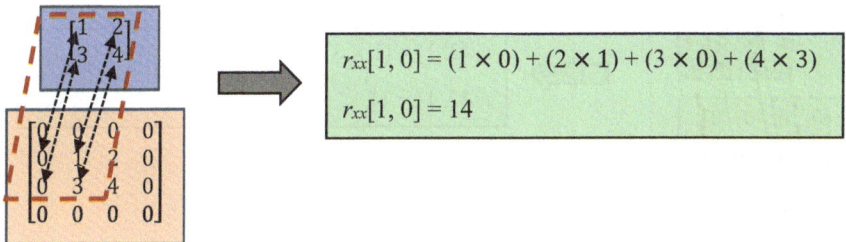

$r_{xx}[1, 0] = (1 \times 0) + (2 \times 1) + (3 \times 0) + (4 \times 3)$

$r_{xx}[1, 0] = 14$

The value of the autocorrelation function $r_{xx}[1, 0] = 14$.
Step 6: To compute $r_{xx}[1, 1]$

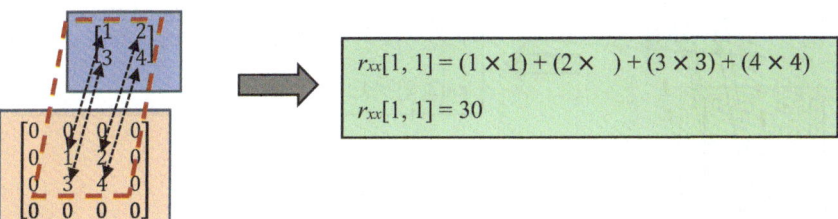

$r_{xx}[1, 1] = (1 \times 1) + (2 \times \quad) + (3 \times 3) + (4 \times 4)$

$r_{xx}[1, 1] = 30$

The value of the autocorrelation function $r_{xx}[1, 1] = 30$.
Step 7: To compute $r_{xx}[1, 2]$

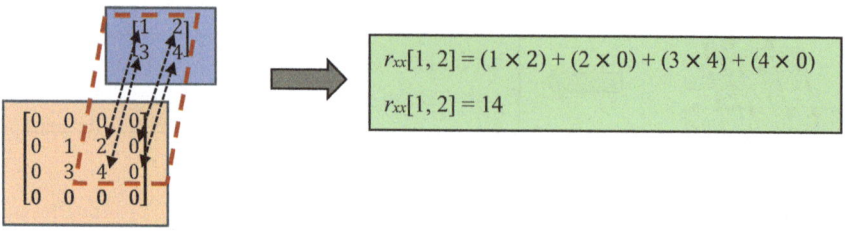

$$r_{xx}[1, 2] = (1 \times 2) + (2 \times 0) + (3 \times 4) + (4 \times 0)$$
$$r_{xx}[1, 2] = 14$$

The value of the autocorrelation function $r_{xx}[1, 2] = 14$.
Step 8: To compute $r_{xx}[2, 0]$

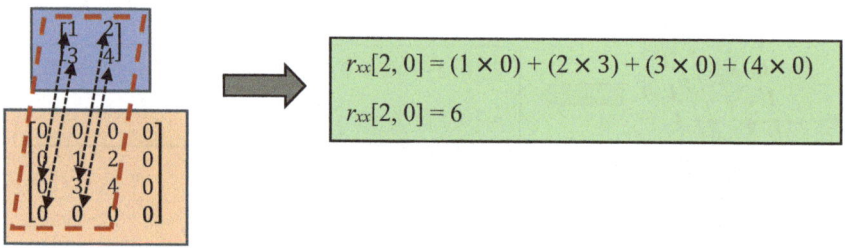

$$r_{xx}[2, 0] = (1 \times 0) + (2 \times 3) + (3 \times 0) + (4 \times 0)$$
$$r_{xx}[2, 0] = 6$$

The value of the autocorrelation function $r_{xx}[2, 0] = 6$.
Step 9: To compute $r_{xx}[2, 1]$

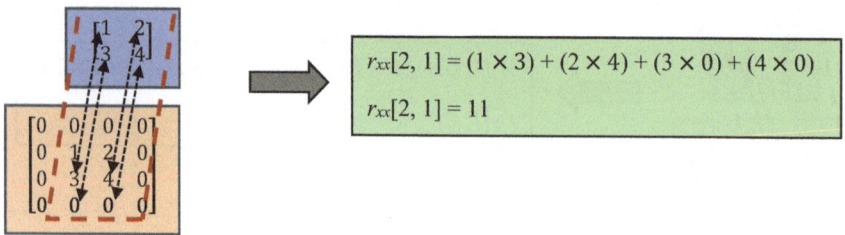

$$r_{xx}[2, 1] = (1 \times 3) + (2 \times 4) + (3 \times 0) + (4 \times 0)$$
$$r_{xx}[2, 1] = 11$$

The value of the autocorrelation function $r_{xx}[2, 1] = 11$.
Step 10: To compute $r_{xx}[2, 2]$

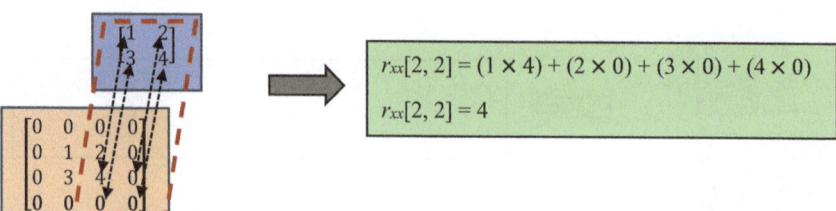

$$r_{xx}[2, 2] = (1 \times 4) + (2 \times 0) + (3 \times 0) + (4 \times 0)$$
$$r_{xx}[2, 2] = 4$$

The value of the autocorrelation function $r_{xx}[2, 2] = 4$.

Combining the results of Step 2 to Step 10, the result of autocorrelation between two matrices is given by

$$\begin{bmatrix} 1 & 2 \\ 3 & 4 \end{bmatrix} \bullet \begin{bmatrix} 1 & 2 \\ 3 & 4 \end{bmatrix} = \begin{bmatrix} 4 & 11 & 6 \\ 14 & 30 & 14 \\ 6 & 11 & 4 \end{bmatrix}$$

In the above expression, "•" denotes the correlation between the two signals. In the autocorrelation output, the origin is located at the center of the matrix, corresponding to the value 30.

Experiment 2.10: Computation of 2D Autocorrelation

This experiment discusses the computation of 2D autocorrelation of 2D signal using Python. The built-in function "*correlated2d*" available in "*scipy*" library can be used to perform the correlation between the two matrices. The Python code that performs the autocorrelation between the two matrices is given in Figure 2.21a, and the corresponding result is shown in Figure 2.21b.

Inferences

From the result of autocorrelation, it is possible to observe the following facts:

• The autocorrelation function exhibits even symmetry.
• Autocorrelation achieves maximum value at zero lag, which is "30" in this case.
• The maximum value of autocorrelation is obtained when the two signals exactly match. Hence, correlation can be used to perform "template matching".

2.5.2   *Correlation in Frequency Domain*

The flow chart to compute correlation in transform domain (Fourier domain) is given in Fig. 2.22. In the figure, $x[m, n]$ and $h[m, n]$ represent the two input matrices. The objective is to compute correlation between these two matrices. To perform the

```
# Computation of 2D Correlation
import numpy as np
from scipy import signal
x=np.array([[1,2],[3,4]])
y=signal.correlate2d(x,x)
print('Autocorrelation result:',y)
```

```
[[ 4 11  6]
 [14 30 14]
 [ 6 11  4]]
```

(a) Python code   **(b) Result of autocorrelation**

Fig. 2.21 Python code and its result of autocorrelation: (**a**) Python code, (**b**) result of autocorrelation

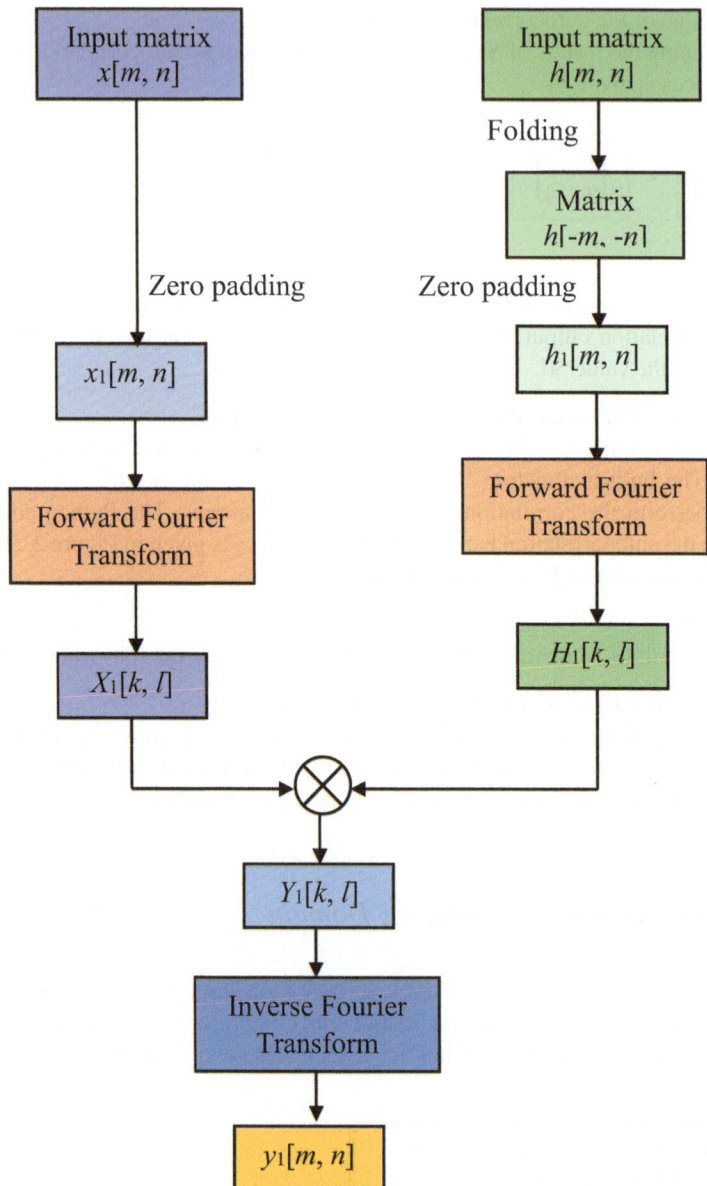

Fig. 2.22 Correlation through transform domain

correlation between the given two matrices, the matrix $h[m, n]$ is folded to obtain $h[-m, -n]$. Then zero padding is done first to obtain the matrices $x_1[m, n]$ and $h_1[m, n]$. After zero padding, Fourier transform of these matrices are taken to obtain $X_1[k, l]$ and $H_1[k, l]$. Then, the two matrices are multiplied to obtain $Y_1[k, l]$. Upon taking the inverse Fourier transform of $Y_1[k, l]$, the result of correlation $y_1[m, n]$ is obtained.

```
#Correlation through transform domain
import numpy as np
from scipy import signal
#Step 1: Defining the input matrices
x=np.array([[1,2],[3,4]])
h=x
#Step 2: Flipping the matrix 'h'
h1=h[:,::-1] #Equivalent to fliplr
h2=h1[::-1,]#Equivalent to flip ud
#Step 2: Linear correlation in spatial domain
y=signal.correlate2d(x,h)
#Step 3: Zero padding of the input matrices
x1=np.pad(x, [(0, 1), (0, 1)], mode='constant')
h1=np.pad(h2, [(0, 1), (0, 1)], mode='constant')
#Step 4: Taking Forward transform
X1=np.fft.fft2(x1)
H1=np.fft.fft2(h1)
#Step 5: Multiplication of the spectrum
Y1=np.multiply(X1,H1)
#Step 6: Taking Inverse Fourier transform
y1=np.fft.ifft2(Y1)
#Step 7: Comparing the result
print('Result of correlation in Spatial domain:',y)
print('Result of correlation in Transform
domain:',np.abs(y1))
```

```
Result of correlation in spatial
domain: [[ 4 11  6]
 [14 30 14]
 [ 6 11  4]]
Result of correlation in transform
domain: [[ 4. 11.  6.]
 [14. 30. 14.]
 [ 6. 11.  4.]]
```

(a) Python code   **(b) Result**

Fig. 2.23 Python code and its result of 2D correlation: (**a**) Python code, (**b**) result

Experiment 2.11: Computation of 2D autocorrelation in Transform Domain
This experiment aims to compute the 2D autocorrelation using Fourier transform.
For this, 2D input matrix is chosen as $x[m,n] = \begin{bmatrix} 1 & 2 \\ 3 & 4 \end{bmatrix}$. The Python code to compute the 2D autocorrelation using Fourier transform is given in Figure 2.23a, and its corresponding output is shown in Figure 2.23b.

Inferences
The following inferences can be made from this experiment:

• From Figure 2.23a, it is possible to observe that both the inputs are the same ($h = x$). fft.fft2 Python command is used here to compute the Fourier transform of the input matrices (X1, H1) and outputs are multiplied by using (Y1 = np. multiply(X1,H1)). The multiplied output is applied as an input to the inverse Fourier transform "np.fft.ifft2(Y1)".

• Figure 2.23b shows that the output of the transform domain resembles the output of the spatial domain approach. From this, 2D correlation operation can be performed through the transform domain also.

2.6 Relationship between Convolution and Correlation

Correlation can be performed in terms of convolution provided one of the signals is folded. The correlation between two one-dimensional signals $x[n]$ and $y[n]$ is given by

$$r_{xy}(l) = x[n] * y[-n] \tag{2.13}$$

The same idea can be extended to two-dimensional autocorrelation of two 2D signals $x[m, n]$ and $y[m, n]$ and is represented as

$$r_{xy}(l,k) = x[m,n] * y[-m, -n] \tag{2.14}$$

From the above relation, it is possible to infer that correlation can be performed in terms of convolution provided the second sequence or the signal is folded.

Experiment 2.12: Relationship Between convolution and Correlation
The objective of this experiment is to perform two-dimensional correlation between the matrices using "*convolve2d*" built-in function, which is available in "*scipy*" library. To perform correlation in terms of convolution, it is necessary that the second sequence should be folded. The Python code that performs correlation in terms of the "*convolve2d*" built-in function is given in Figure 2.24a, and the corresponding output is shown in Figure 2.24b.

```
# Relation between correlation and
Convolution
import numpy as np
from scipy import signal
#Step 1: Defining the input matrices
x=np.array([[1,2],[3,4]])
h=x
#Step 2: Fold the second signal
h1=h[:,::-1] #Equivalent to fliplr
h2=h1[::-1,:]#Equivalent to flip ud
#Step 2: Linear convolution
y=signal.convolve2d(x,h2)
#Step 3: Printing the result
print('Input x:',x),print('Input h:', h),
print('Flipped h:', h2)
print('Correlation using Convolution:', y)
```

```
Input x: [[1 2]
 [3 4]]
Input h: [[1 2]
 [3 4]]
Flipped h: [[4 3]
 [2 1]]
Correlation using Convolution: [[ 4 11  6]
 [14 30 14]
 [ 6 11  4]]
```

(a) Python code   (b) Correlation result

Fig. 2.24 Python code to perform correlation in terms of convolution: (a) Python code, (b) correlation result

Inference

The result of this code exactly matches the theoretical result. This experiment illustrates the fact that correlation can be performed in terms of convolution.

2.7 Autocorrelation and Cross-Correlation

Autocorrelation is finding the relative similarity of the signal with itself, whereas cross-correlation is finding the relative similarity between two different signals. Autocorrelation is an even function, whereas cross-correlation is not an even function.

Experiment 2.13: Comparison between autocorrelation and Cross-Correlation

This experiment reveals the difference between autocorrelation and cross-correlation. The Python code that depicts the output of autocorrelation and cross-correlation is given in Fig. 2.25, and the corresponding output is shown in Fig. 2.26. In this experiment, two test images are generated. The "Test Image-1" is white above the main diagonal and black below the main diagonal. The "Test Image-2" is black above the main diagonal and white below the main diagonal. First, the auto-correlation of "Test Image-1" with itself is performed, and then the cross-correlation between "Test Image-1" and "Test Image-2" is performed.

Fig. 2.26 Result of autocorrelation and cross-correlation

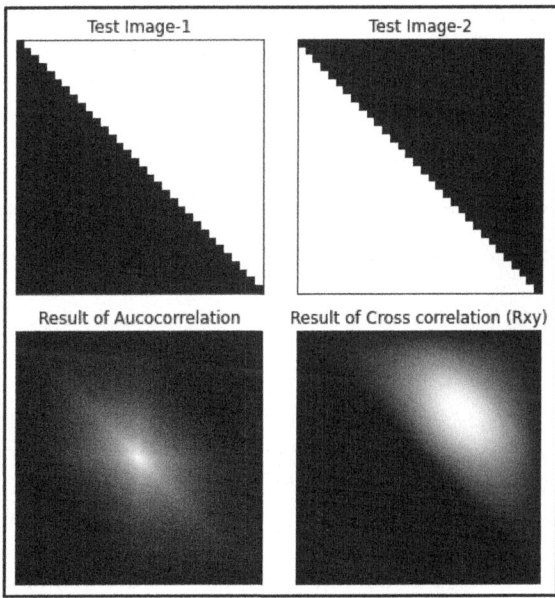

```
#Autocorrelation and Cross-correlation
import numpy as np
import matplotlib.pyplot as plt
from scipy import signal
#Step 1: Generation of test image
#Test image 1
x=np.zeros([32,32])
for i in range(0,32):
   for j in range(0,32):
      if(i<j):
         x[i,j]=255
#Test image 2
y=np.zeros([32,32])
for i in range(0,32):
   for j in range(0,32):
      if(i>j):
         y[i,j]=255
rxx=signal.correlate2d(x,x);#Step 2: Performing the autocorrelation
rxy=signal.correlate2d(x,y);#Step 3: Performing the cross correlation
fig = plt.figure(figsize=(6,6));#Sep 4: Displaying the result
plt.subplot(2,2,1),plt.imshow(x,cmap='gray')
plt.title('Test Image-1'),plt.xticks([]),plt.yticks([])
plt.subplot(2,2,2),plt.imshow(y,cmap='gray')
plt.title('Test Image-2'),plt.xticks([]),plt.yticks([])
plt.subplot(2,2,3),plt.imshow(rxx,cmap='gray')
plt.title('Result of Aucocorrelation'),plt.axis('off')
plt.subplot(2,2,4),plt.imshow(rxy,cmap='gray')
plt.title('Result of Cross correlation (Rxy)'),plt.axis('off')
plt.tight_layout()
```

Fig. 2.25 Python code to perform autocorrelation and cross-correlation

Inferences

From Fig. 2.26, the following inferences can be drawn:

- Two test images "Test Image-1" and "Test Image-2" are generated.
- The autocorrelation of "Test Image-1" with itself is performed.
- The cross-correlation between "Test Image-1" and "Test Image-2" is performed.
- The result of autocorrelation indicates that the autocorrelation function is an even function.
- The result of the cross-correlation function indicates that the cross-correlation function is not even symmetrical.

2.8   Application of Correlation

Template matching is one of the applications of autocorrelation function. The template is basically a subimage that contains the shape or the object one wishes to find in an image. The process of searching the template within an input image is called as "template matching".

Figure 2.27 has a source image with different shapes such as triangle, pentagon, square, and hexagon. The template is basically a subimage; in this illustration, it is a square shape. The objective is to find where exactly in the source image the template matches, which is termed as template matching. The process involves moving the template over the source image and noting the positions at which a match occurs.

Let the source image be denoted by $s[m, n]$ and the template be represented by $t[m, n]$. The objective is to minimize the energy that will lead to the matching of the template over the source image. The energy to be minimized is expressed as

$$E[i,j] = \sum_m \sum_n \left(s[m,n] - t[m-i, n-j] \right)^2 \tag{2.15}$$

The above equation can be expanded as

$$E[i,j] = \sum_m \sum_n \left(s^2[m,n] + t^2[m-i, n-j] - 2s[m,n]t[m-i, n-j] \right) \tag{2.16}$$

Minimizing the energy is now equivalent to maximizing the term $2s[m, n]t[m-i, n-j]$ in the above expression. The expression

$$R_{st}[i,j] = \sum_m \sum_n s[m,n]t[m-i, n-j] \tag{2.17}$$

The above expression is the cross-correlation between the source image and the template. The template will be matched with the source image in the location where cross-correlation is the maximum value. Normalized cross-correlation is considered if the template matching has to be insensitive to changes in brightness. The expression for normalized cross-correlation is given by

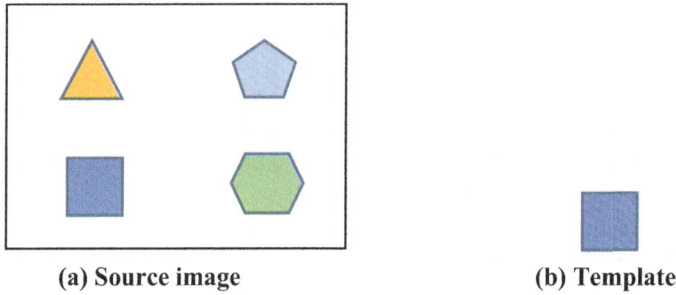

(a) **Source image**   (b) **Template**

Fig. 2.27   Illustration of template matching: (**a**) source image, (**b**) template

$$N_{st}[i,j] = \frac{\sum_m \sum_n s[m,n]t[m-i,n-j]}{\sqrt{\sum_m \sum_n s^2[m,n]}\sqrt{\sum_m \sum_n t^2[m-i,n-j]}}$$ (2.18)

Normalized cross-correlation takes values between -1 and $+1$. The cross-correlation value of $+1$ indicates that the template and the source image match perfectly.

Experiment 2.14: Template Matching

This experiment discusses the template-matching process using Python. For this, the input image consists of alphabets from "*A*" to "*Z*". The template is chosen as one of the alphabets. In our case, the template is the character "*W*". The template matching is performed using the built-in function "*matchTemplate*" available in the "cv2" library. The Python code that performs this task is shown in Fig. 2.28, and the corresponding output is shown in Fig. 2.29.

```
#Template matching
import numpy as np
import matplotlib.pyplot as plt
import cv2
#Step 1: Reading the input image and template
img = cv2.imread('A-Z.png',0)
template = cv2.imread('template.png',0)
#Displaying the input and template
plt.figure(1),plt.subplot(2,1,1),plt.imshow(img,cmap='gray')
plt.title('Test image'),plt.xticks([]),plt.yticks([])
plt.subplot(2,1,2),plt.imshow(template,cmap='gray')
plt.title('Template image'),plt.xticks([]),plt.yticks([])
#Step 2: Perform template matching
img_copy = img.copy()
res = cv2.matchTemplate(img, template,cv2.TM_CCORR_NORMED)
#Step 3: Bounding box for matched character
min_val, max_val, min_loc, max_loc = cv2.minMaxLoc(res)
top_left = max_loc
h,w=template.shape
bottom_right = (top_left[0] + w, top_left[1] + h)
cv2.rectangle(img, top_left, bottom_right, 0, 2)
plt.figure(2),plt.imshow(img, cmap="gray"),plt.xticks([]),plt.yticks([])
plt.title('Image after template matching'),
plt.tight_layout()
```

Fig. 2.28 Python code to perform template matching

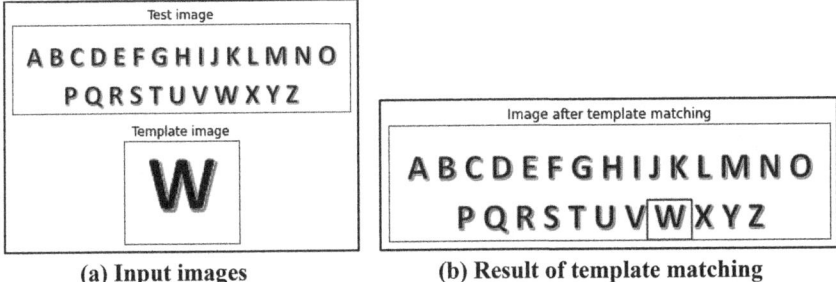

(a) Input images   (b) Result of template matching

Fig. 2.29 Template matching result: (**a**) input images, (**b**) result of template matching

Inferences

- The input image has alphabets "*A* to *Z*". The template image is the letter "*W*".
- The objective is to find where the template matches with respect to the input test image.
- The bounding box clearly indicates that the template matching is correctly performed.

Exercises

1. Write a Python code to plot the 3D plot of a Gaussian kernel and comment on the observed result.
2. Write a Python code to illustrate the fact that convolution operation obeys commutative property.
3. Write a Python code to illustrate the fact that convolution operation obeys associative property.
4. Write a Python code to perform autocorrelation of the matrix $x = \begin{bmatrix} 1 & 2 & 3 \\ 4 & 5 & 6 \\ 7 & 8 & 9 \end{bmatrix}$

   with itself. Display the result of autocorrelation and comment on the observed result.
5. Write a Python code to obtain the autocorrelation of the white noise image.

Objective Questions

1. Statement 1: Convolution is applicable to linear time-variant system
   Statement 2: Convolution is applicable to linear time-invariant system

   A. Statements 1 and 2 are true
   B. Statement 1 is true, Statement 2 is false
   C. Statement 1 is false, Statement 2 is true
   D. Statements 1 and 2 are false

2. The result of the convolution operation $y[m,n] = x[m,n] * \delta[m,n]$ is

   A. $y[m,n] = 0$

   B. $y[m,n] = x[m,n]$

   C. $y[m,n] = x[-m,n]$

   D. $y[m,n] = x[m,-n]$

3. Convolution in spatial domain is equivalent to

   A. Addition in frequency domain
   B. Subtraction in frequency domain
   C. Multiplication in frequency domain
   D. Division in frequency domain

4. Autocorrelation function is

   A. Even function
   B. Odd function
   C. Either even function or odd function
   D. Neither even nor odd function

5. The operation that can be used for template matching is

   A. Convolution
   B. Correlation
   C. Spectral estimation
   D. Deconvolution

6. Statement 1: Autocorrelation is an even function
  Statement 2: Cross-correlation is an even function

   A. Statements 1 and 2 are true
   B. Statement 1 is true, Statement 2 is false
   C. Statement 1 is false, Statement 2 is true
   D. Statements 1 and 2 are false

7. Autocorrelation of white noise results in

   A. Impulse function
   B. Step function
   C. Sinc function
   D. Sinusoidal function

8. Assertion: Autocorrelation of a white noise is an impulse function
  Reason: Successive samples of white noise are uncorrelated

   A. Assertion and reason are true
   B. Assertion is true; reason is false
   C. Assertion is false; reason may be true
   D. Assertion and reason are false

9. Linear convolution of two-step signals results in

   A. Step signal
   B. Ramp signal
   C. Impulse signal
   D. Sinc signal

10. Linear convolution of two Gaussian functions will result in

    A. Step function
    B. Sinc function
    C. Gaussian function
    D. Impulse function

Answers to Objective Questions

Q. No.	01	02	03	04	05	06	07	08	09	10
Key	C	B	C	A	B	B	A	A	B	C

Answers to PreLab Questions

1. The mathematical operations such as addition, multiplication, and shift operations are involved in computing the convolution between the two matrices.
2. Convolution obeys (1) commutative property (2) associative property, and (3) distributive property.
3. Convolution in spatial domain is equivalent to multiplication in the transform domain.
4. Autocorrelation of white noise results in impulse function, which implies that successive samples of white noise are uncorrelated.
5. Convolution is used to extract information from the signal or image.
6. Correlation is used to find the relative similarity between two signals. Correlation is employed in template matching.
7. Autocorrelation is finding the relative similarity of the signal to itself. Autocorrelation is an even function. Autocorrelation function attains maximum value at zero lag.
8. Correlation is basically convolution between two signals, with one of the signals being folded.
9. Template matching is a method for searching and finding the location of a template image in a larger image. Cross-correlation measure is used in the template matching process.
10. Yes, convolution in time or spatial domain is equivalent to multiplication in transform domain.

Bibliography

1. Jae S. Lim, "Two dimensional signal and image processing", Prentice Hall, 1989.
2. Don Dudgeon, and Russel M. Mersereau, "Multidimensional Digital Signal Processing", Prentice Hall, 1984.
3. S. Jayaraman, S. Esakkirajan, and T. Veerakumar, "Digital Image Processing", McGraw Hill, 2020.
4. John W. Woods, "Multidimensional Signal, Image and Video Processing and Coding", Academic Press, 2006.
5. Tamal Bose, "Digital Signal and Image Processing", Wiley, 2010.

Chapter 3
Image Transforms

Learning Objectives

After reading this chapter, the reader should be familiar with the following concepts:

- Importance of magnitude and phase of Fourier transform
- Energy compaction property of transform
- Properties of two-dimensional discrete Fourier transform
- Multidirectional image analysis using wavelet and wavelet packet transform
- Understanding the principle and application of Radon and Hough transform

Roadmap of the Chapter

The transforms discussed in this chapter are given in the form of the roadmap in Fig. 3.1.

Based on nature of basis function, transform can be broadly classified into transform with sinusoidal basis function and transform with non-sinusoidal basis function. Examples of transforms with sinusoidal basis functions are (1) Fourier transform, whose basis function is a complex exponential function and (2) Discrete Cosine Transform, whose basis function is a cosine function. Haar and Hadamard transform belongs to the category of transform with non-sinusoidal basis function. Transform that has the ability to perform multi-resolution analysis of the signal are "wavelet and wavelet packet transform". The transforms that express a signal in terms of its projections are the Radon transform and Hough transform. Radon transform is widely used in computed tomography; Hough transform is widely used to detect lines and shapes in an image.

PreLab Questions

1. Mention two needs of image transform.
2. What is the basis function of Fourier transform?

Supplementary Information The online version contains supplementary material available at https://doi.org/10.1007/978-981-96-6382-8_3.

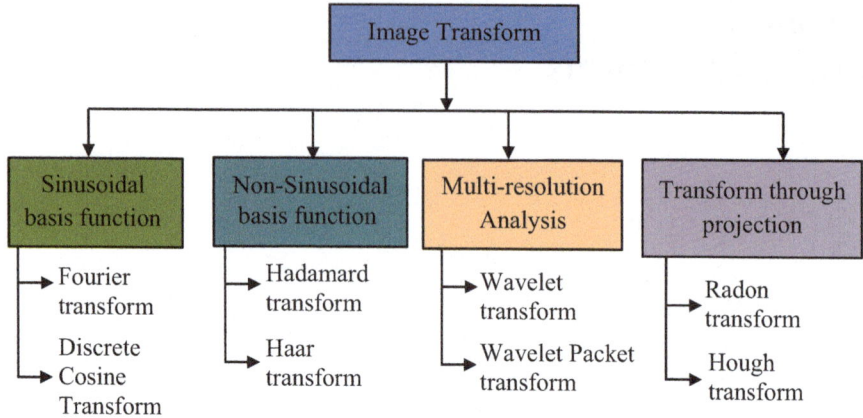

Fig. 3.1 Roadmap of Chapter

3. What do you understand by energy compaction property of image transform?
4. Mention two applications of Fourier transform in image processing.
5. Mention two essential qualities of image transform.
6. Which transform has the ability to perform multi-resolution analysis of the image?
7. What is sinogram of an image?
8. Mention one application of Hough transform in image processing.
9. Mention the transform employed in JPEG and JPEG 2000 standards.
10. Mention the condition for the function to be called as a wavelet.

3.1   Fourier Transform

The three flavours of two-dimensional Fourier transform are (1) continuous space and continuous frequency Fourier transform, (2) discrete space and continuous frequency Fourier transform, and (3) discrete space and discrete frequency Fourier transform.

3.1.1   Continuous Space and Continuous Frequency Fourier Transform

Let $f(x, y)$ represent continuous space 2D signal (image), then the Fourier transform of continuous space signal is continuous frequency signal, which is represented as

$$F(k,l) = \int_{-\infty}^{\infty}\int_{-\infty}^{\infty} f(x,y) e^{-j2\pi(xk+yl)} dx dy \qquad (3.1)$$

The expression for inverse Fourier transform is given by

$$f(x,y) = \frac{1}{(2\pi)^2} \int_{-\infty}^{\infty} \int_{-\infty}^{\infty} f(k,l) e^{j2\pi(xk+yl)} dk dl \qquad (3.2)$$

Fourier transform is a complex-valued function, hence it can be represented as

$$F(k,l) = R(k,l) + jI(k,l) \qquad (3.3)$$

The magnitude of the transform is given by

$$|F(k,l)| = \sqrt{R^2(k,l) + I^2(k,l)} \qquad (3.4)$$

The phase of the transform is given by

$$\varphi(k,l) = \tan^{-1}\left[\frac{I(k,l)}{R(k,l)}\right] \qquad (3.5)$$

3.1.2   Discrete Space and Continuous Frequency Fourier Transform

Discrete space and continuous frequency two-dimensional Fourier transform is equivalent to discrete-time Fourier transform (DTFT) of one-dimensional signal. The expression for the forward transform is given by

$$F(k,l) = \sum_{m=0}^{N-1} \sum_{n=0}^{N-1} f(m,n) e^{-j\frac{2x}{N}(mk+nl)} \qquad (3.6)$$

The expression for the inverse Fourier transform is given by

$$f(m,n) = \frac{1}{(2\pi)^2} \int_{k=-\pi}^{\pi} \int_{l=-\pi}^{\pi} F(k,l) e^{j(mk+nl)} dk dl \qquad (3.7)$$

3.1.3   Discrete Space and Discrete Frequency Fourier Transform

The expression for the forward discrete space and discrete frequency Fourier transform is given by

$$F(k,l) = \sum_{m=0}^{N-1} \sum_{n=0}^{N-1} f(m,n) e^{-j\frac{2\pi}{N}(mk+nl)} \qquad (3.8)$$

In the above expression, $f(m, n)$ is a $N \times N$ image, whereas $F(k, l)$ represents the Fourier transform of $f(m, n)$. The expression for inverse Fourier transform is given by

$$f(m,n) = \frac{1}{N \times N} \sum_{k=0}^{N-1} \sum_{l=0}^{N-1} F(k,l) e^{j\frac{2\pi}{N}(mk+nl)} \tag{3.9}$$

From Eqs. (3.8) and (3.9), it is possible to observe that the basis function of Fourier transform is a complex exponential signal. According to Fourier transform, signals can be represented as a weighted sum of sinusoids.

Experiment 3.1: DFT Basis for $N = 4$

The basis function of Fourier transform is complex exponential function. The Python code that plots the discrete Fourier transform (DFT) basis for $N = 4$ is shown in Fig. 3.2, and the corresponding output is shown in Fig. 3.3.

Inferences

- Figure 3.2 shows the Python code used to plot the DFT basis for $N = 4$.
- From Fig. 3.3, it is possible to observe that for $N = 4$, 16 blocks are displayed as 16 images.

Task: Change the value of N and comment on the observed DFT basis.

```
#DFT basis function
import numpy as np
from scipy.fft import fft
import matplotlib.pyplot as plt
N = int(input(Enter the N point DFT:))
dft_basis = np.zeros((N*N,N*N))
k = 0
for i in range(N):
    for j in range(N):
        g = np.zeros((N,N))
        g[i,j]=1
        dft_basis[k,:] = fft(fft(g.T,norm='ortho').T,norm='ortho').flatten()
        k+=1
dft_basis = dft_basis/np.max(np.absolute(dft_basis))
fig, axes = plt.subplots(N, N, figsize=(8, 8))
for idx, ax in enumerate(axes.flat):
    img = np.real(dft_basis[idx].reshape(N, N))
    ax.imshow(img, cmap='gray', interpolation='nearest', vmin=-1, vmax=1)
    ax.set_xticks([]),ax.set_yticks([])
    # Thin black border
    for spine in ax.spines.values():
        spine.set_edgecolor('black')
        spine.set_linewidth(0.5)
plt.subplots_adjust(wspace=0.05, hspace=0.05) # control spacing between images
plt.suptitle(f2D {N}-point DFT Basis (Real Part))
plt.show()
```

Fig. 3.2 DFT basis image for $N = 4$

2D 4-point DFT Basis (Real Part)

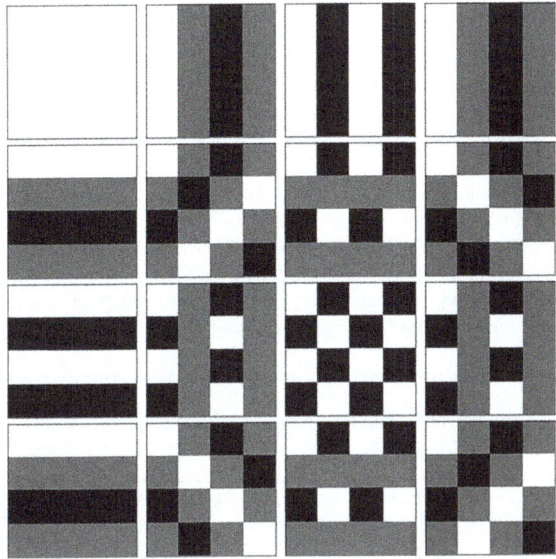

Fig. 3.3 DFT basis for $N = 4$

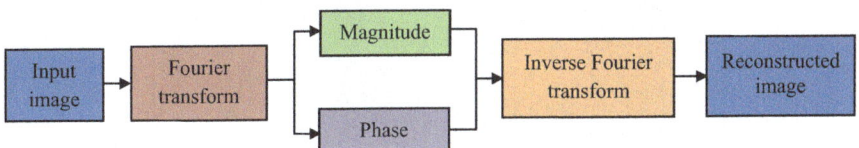

Fig. 3.4 Illustration of the problem statement

Experiment 3.2: Image Reconstruction from Magnitude and phase of Fourier Transform

Fourier transform is complex in nature. Upon taking the Fourier transform of an image, two information, namely magnitude and phase, are obtained. The objective of this experiment is to read an input image and obtain the magnitude and phase information by taking the Fourier transform. Use the magnitude and phase information to reconstruct the image. This is illustrated in Fig. 3.4.

The Python code that performs the above-mentioned task is shown in Fig. 3.5, and the corresponding output is shown in Fig. 3.6.

Inferences

- Figure 3.5 shows that the "numpy" library is used to compute the Fourier and inverse Fourier transform.
- From Fig. 3.6, it is possible to observe that the reconstructed image is similar to that of the input image.
- Thus, Fourier transform is a reversible transform.

```
#Reading and displaying image
import cv2
import numpy as np
import matplotlib.pyplot as plt
img=cv2.imread('cameraman.tif',0);#Step 1:Read the input image
IMG=np.fft.fft2(img);#Step 2: Obtain the FT of the image
#Step 3: Extract the magnitude and phase information
magnitude=np.abs(IMG)
phase=np.angle(IMG)
#Step 4: Combine the magnitude and phase information
imgcom=np.multiply(magnitude,np.exp(1j*phase))
rimg=np.real(np.fft.ifft2(imgcom));#Step 5: Inverse FT
#Step 6: Display the result
plt.subplot(1,2,1),plt.imshow(img,cmap='gray'),plt.title('Input image'),plt.axis('off')
plt.subplot(1,2,2),plt.imshow(rimg,cmap='gray'),plt.title('Reconstructed image'),plt.axis('off')
plt.tight_layout()
```

Fig. 3.5 Python code that performs Fourier decomposition and reconstruction

Fig. 3.6 Result of the Python code shown in Fig. 3.5

Experiment 3.3: Image Reconstruction from Magnitude-Alone, Phase-Alone, Both Magnitude and Phase

Read the input image. Take the Fourier transform of the input image. Reconstruct the image using (1) magnitude-alone information, (b) phase-alone information, and (3) using both magnitude and phase information. The Python code that does the above-mentioned task is shown in Fig. 3.7, and the corresponding output is shown in Fig. 3.8.

Inferences

- From Fig. 3.8, it is possible to understand the impact of magnitude and phase information.
- For perfect reconstruction, both magnitude and phase informations are necessary.

Experiment 3.4: Phase Interchange

Read two images namely "Cameraman" image (Image-1) and "Clock" image (Image-2). Extract the magnitude and phase information of the two images. Combine

```
#Displaying original, Magnitude alone, Phase alone and combined image
import numpy as np
import cv2
import matplotlib.pyplot as plt
img=cv2.imread('cameraman.tif',0);#Step 1: Read the input image
#Step 2: Take the Fourier transform of the input image
IMG=np.fft.fft2(img)
#Step 3: Extract the magnitude and phase information
Mag=np.abs(IMG)
Ph=np.angle(IMG)
magimg=np.real(np.fft.ifft2(Mag));#Step 4: Magnitude alone reconstruction
#Step 5: Phase alone reconstruction
phimg = np.real(np.fft.ifft2(np.exp(1j*Ph)))
#Step 6: Combined magnitude and phase reconstruction
comimg=np.multiply(Mag,np.exp(1j*Ph))
comimg=np.real(np.fft.ifft2(comimg))
#Step 7: Displayin the results
fig=plt.figure(figsize=(8,6)),plt.subplot(1,4,1),plt.imshow(img,cmap='gray'),
plt.title('Input image'),plt.axis('off'),plt.subplot(1,4,2),
plt.imshow(np.uint8(magimg),cmap='gray'),plt.title('Magnitude alone'),
plt.axis('off'),plt.subplot(1,4,3),plt.imshow(phimg,cmap='gray'),
plt.title('Phase alone'),plt.axis('off'),plt.subplot(1,4,4),
plt.imshow(comimg,cmap='gray'),plt.title('Mag. and Phase'),plt.axis('off')
plt.tight_layout()
```

Fig. 3.7 Python code to perform magnitude-alone, phase-alone, and combined image reconstruction

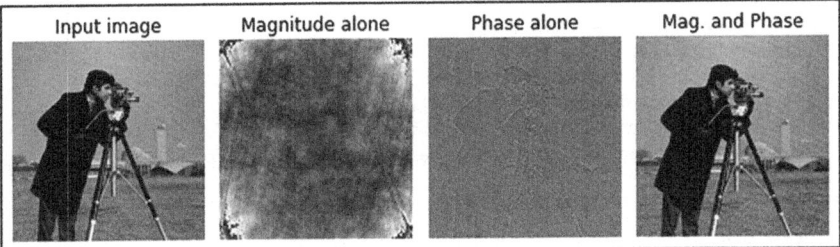

Fig. 3.8 Result of the Python code shown in Fig. 3.7

the phase information of "Cameraman" image with the magnitude of "Clock" image. Similarly, combine the phase information of the "Clock" image with the magnitude of the "Cameraman" image. This is generally termed as a phase interchange. After phase interchange, perform inverse Fourier transform of the phase interchanged images and comment on the observed output.

The block diagram that depicts the idea of phase interchange is shown in Fig. 3.9.

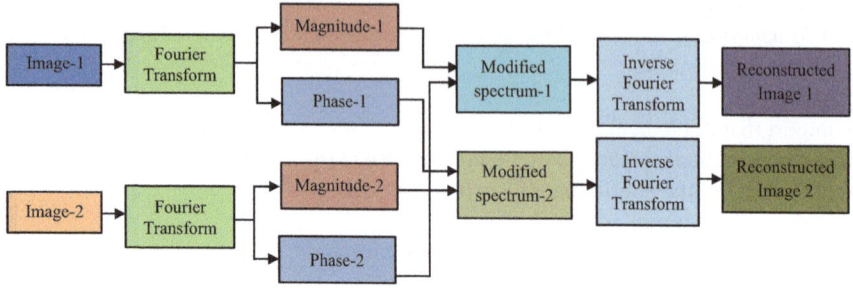

Fig. 3.9 Block diagram representation of phase interchange

```
#Phase interchange
import numpy as np
import cv2
import matplotlib.pyplot as plt
#Step1: Reading the two images
im1=cv2.imread('cameraman.tif')
im2=cv2.imread('rice.tif')
#Step 2: Extracting the magnitude and phase of image 1
IM1=np.fft.fft2(im1)
Mag_1=np.abs(IM1)
Ph_1=np.angle(IM1)
#Step 3: Extracting the magnitude and phase of image 2
IM2=np.fft.fft2(im2)
Mag_2=np.abs(IM2)
Ph_2=np.angle(IM2)
#Step 4: Phase interchange
rimg1=np.multiply(Mag_1,np.exp(1j*Ph_2))
rimg2=np.multiply(Mag_2,np.exp(1j*Ph_1))
#Step 5: Obtaining the Inverse Fourier transform
imgCombined1= np.real(np.fft.ifft2(rimg1))
imgCombined2= np.real(np.fft.ifft2(rimg2))
#Step 6: Plotting the result
fig=plt.figure(figsize=(9,6)),plt.subplot(1,4,1),plt.imshow(im1),plt.title('IM-1'),plt.axis('off')
plt.subplot(1,4,2),plt.imshow(im2),plt.title('IM-2'),plt.axis('off'),plt.subplot(1,4,3),
plt.imshow(imgCombined1/255),plt.title('IM1-phase interchange'),plt.axis('off'),plt.subplot(1,4,4),
plt.imshow(imgCombined2/255),plt.title('IM2-phase interchange'),plt.axis('off')
plt.tight_layout()
```

Fig. 3.10 Python code that performs the phase interchange

The Python code that performs the phase interchange operation is shown in Fig. 3.10, and the corresponding output is shown in Fig. 3.11.

Inferences

- After phase interchange, "Cameraman" image resembles more or less like "Clock" image and "Clock" image resembles "Cameraman" image.
- This experiment illustrates the importance of phase of Fourier transform.

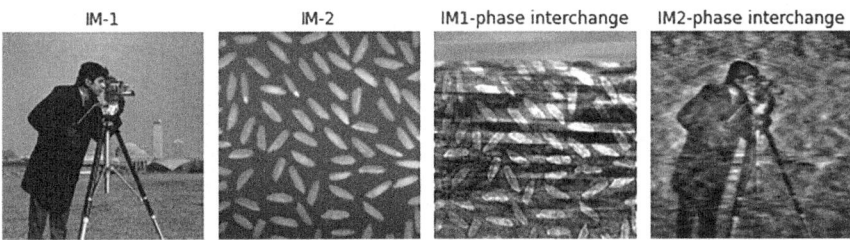

IM-1   IM-2   IM1-phase interchange   IM2-phase interchange

Fig. 3.11 Result of phase interchange operation

```
#Plotting the power spectra of the images
import numpy as np
import cv2
import matplotlib.pyplot as plt
#Step1: Reading the two images
im1=cv2.imread('cameraman.tif',0)
im2=cv2.imread('Clock.tiff',0)
#Step 2: Obtain the Fourier transform of the two images
IM1=np.fft.fft2(im1)
IM2=np.fft.fft2(im2)
#Step 3: Shift the DC frequency to the centre
IM1=np.fft.fftshift(IM1)
IM2=np.fft.fftshift(IM2)
#Step 4:Obtain the Power spectrum of the two images
PS1=20*np.log(np.abs(IM1))
PS2=20*np.log(np.abs(IM2))
#Step 5: Plotting the images and their power spectra
fig=plt.figure(figsize=(8,4)),plt.subplot(1,4,1),plt.imshow(im1,cmap='gray'),
plt.title('Cameraman image'),plt.axis('off'),plt.subplot(1,4,2),plt.imshow(PS1,cmap='gray'),
plt.title('Power spectrum'),plt.axis('off'),plt.subplot(1,4,3),plt.imshow(im2,cmap='gray'),
plt.title('Clock image'),plt.axis('off'),plt.subplot(1,4,4),plt.imshow(PS2,cmap='gray'),
plt.title('Power spectrum'),plt.axis('off'),plt.tight_layout()
```

Fig. 3.12 Python code to obtain the power spectra of images

Experiment 3.5: Power Spectrum of the Input Image

Let $f[m, n]$ represents the Cameraman image. Let $F[k, l]$ represents the Fourier transform of the Cameraman image. Then the expression for power spectrum is given by $20 \log_{10}|F[k, l]|$. The Python code that obtains the power spectrum of the Cameraman and Clock images is shown in Fig. 3.12, and the corresponding output is shown in Fig. 3.13.

Inference

There is a significant difference between the power spectra of Cameraman and Clock image. Thus, power spectra can be used as one of the features to distinguish the images.

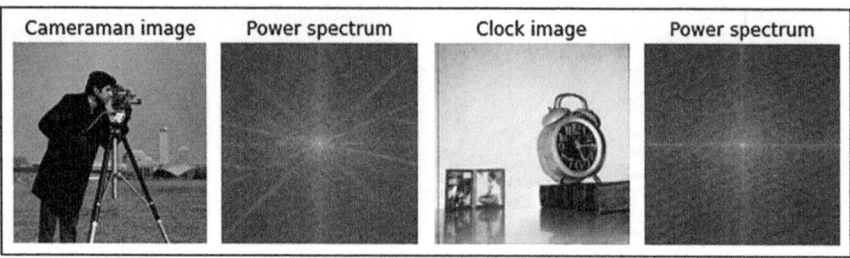

Fig. 3.13 Power spectra of Cameraman and Clock images

```
#Impact of zeroing specific rows in the centre-shifted spectrum
import numpy as np
import cv2
import matplotlib.pyplot as plt
#Step1: Reading the two images
im1=cv2.imread('cameraman.tif',0)
#Step 2: Obtain the spectrum of the image
IM1=np.fft.fft2(im1)
IM1=np.fft.fftshift(IM1)
#Step 3: Remove specific rows in the spectrum
rows_remove=[1,50,100,128]
fig = plt.figure(figsize=(12,8))
for i in range(len(rows_remove)):
  IM1[rows_remove[i]]=0
 #Step 4: Reconstruct the image
  RIMG1=np.fft.ifftshift(IM1)
  RIMG2=np.fft.ifft2(RIMG1)
  fig.add_subplot(1, 4,i+1),plt.imshow(np.real(RIMG2),cmap='gray'),
  plt.axis('off'),plt.title(f'Removed row in spectrum: {rows_remove[i]}')
plt.tight_layout()
```

Fig. 3.14 Python code to modify the magnitude of Fourier transform

Experiment 3.6: Modifying the Magnitude of Fourier Transform

Read the Cameraman image. Take the two-dimensional Fourier transform. Use "fft-shift" to shift the DC frequency towards the centre. In the shifted spectrum, make the rows "1, 50, 100, and 128" to take a value of zero. Then take the inverse Fourier transform to obtain the reconstructed image. Comment on the obtained recon-structed image.

The Python code that does the above-mentioned task is shown in Fig. 3.14, and the corresponding output is shown in Fig. 3.15.

Fig. 3.15 Result of Python code shown in Fig. 3.14

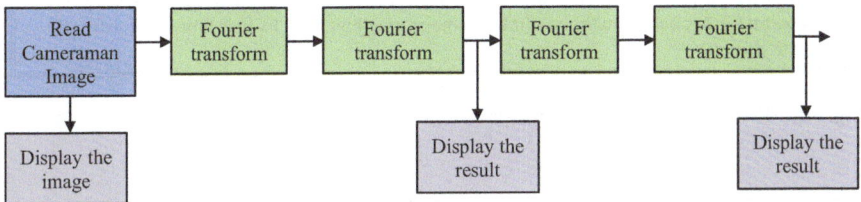

Fig. 3.16 Block diagram depicting problem statement

Inferences

- Zeroing the first, 50th, and 100th rows has little impact in the reconstructed image.
- On the other hand, removing row 128th shows significant degradation in the image quality.
- The DC values will be around the pixel location (128, 128). Removing the DC values will have a significant impact on the reconstructed image quality.

Experiment 3.7: Taking Fourier Transform more than Once

Read Clock image. Take Fourier transform four times. Display the result of taking Fourier transform two times and four times and comment on the observed result. The problem statement is depicted in Fig. 3.16.

The Python code that performs the above-mentioned task is shown in Fig. 3.17, and the corresponding output is shown in Fig. 3.18.

Inferences

- Fourier transform is merely a rotation operation.
- Taking Fourier transform once is a rotation by 90°.
- Taking Fourier transform twice is equivalent to rotation by 180°.
- Taking Fourier transform four times is equivalent to rotation by 360°.

Hence, the result of taking Fourier transform four times resembles the input image. This is shown in Fig. 3.19.

```
#Taking FFT 4 times is equal to bringing the image back
import cv2
import matplotlib.pyplot as plt
import numpy as np
#Read the input image
img=cv2.imread('cameraman.tif',0)
IMG1=np.fft.fft2(img);#FT once
IMG2=np.fft.fft2(IMG1);#FT twice
IMG3=np.fft.fft2(IMG2);#FT thrice
IMG4=np.fft.fft2(IMG3);#FT four times
#Displaying the results
plt.subplot(1,3,1),plt.imshow(img,cmap='gray'),plt.title('Input image'),plt.axis('off')
plt.subplot(1,3,2),plt.imshow(np.real(IMG2),cmap='gray'),plt.title('FT twice'),plt.axis('off')
plt.subplot(1,3,3),plt.imshow(np.real(IMG4),cmap='gray'),plt.title('FT four times'),plt.axis('off')
plt.tight_layout()
```

Fig. 3.17 Python code to obtain Fourier transformed results

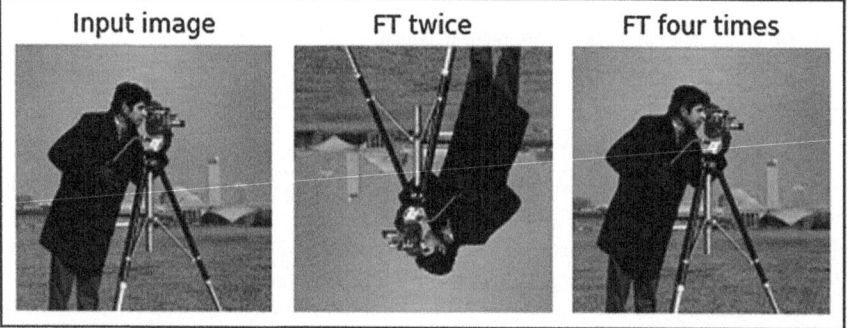

Fig. 3.18 Result of the Python code shown in Fig. 3.17

Fig. 3.19 Figure to illustrate that Fourier transform is a rotation operation

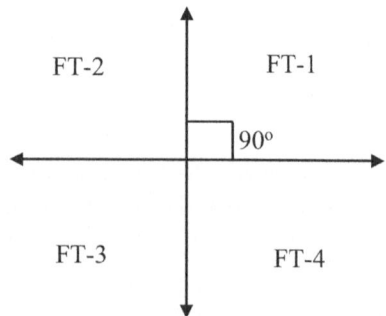

3.2 Properties of Fourier Transform

The properties of Fourier transform discussed in this section include (1) linearity property, (2) spatial shift property, (3) scaling property, (4) rotation property, (5) frequency shift property, and (6) convolution property.

3.2.1 Linearity Property

Transform is linear if it obeys the superposition principle. The superposition principle involves satisfying homogeneity and additivity properties. Let $f_1[m, n]$ and $f_2[m, n]$ represent two matrices or images and their corresponding Fourier transform are represented as $F_1[k, l]$ and $F_2[k, l]$, respectively. Fourier transform is linear if the following criterion is satisfied:

$$FT\left\{af_1[m,n]+bf_2[m,n]\right\} = aF_1[k,l]+bF_2[k,l] \qquad (3.10)$$

Experiment 3.8: Linearity Property of Fourier Transform

To verify the linearity property, the scaling factors are chosen as $a = 1$ and $b = 2$, respectively. The matrices $f_1[m, n]$ and $f_2[m, n]$ are chosen as $f_1[m,n] = \begin{bmatrix} 1 & 0 \\ 0 & 1 \end{bmatrix}$ and $f_2[m,n] = \begin{bmatrix} 1 & 1 \\ 1 & 1 \end{bmatrix}$. The objective is to verify that Eq. (3.10) is true. The Python code that performs this operation is shown in Figure 3.20a, and the corresponding output is shown in Figure 3.20b.

Inference

- From Figure 3.20b, it is possible to interpret that the Fourier transform satisfied both homogeneity and additive properties; hence, the Fourier transform is a linear transform.

3.2.2 Spatial Shift Property

The spatial shift of an image results in a phase shift in the Fourier domain. This is represented as

$$2D\_DFT\left\{f[m-m_0,n]\right\} = e^{-j\frac{2\pi}{N}m_0 k} F[k,l] \qquad (3.11)$$

If the shift is along "n", then the spatial shift property is expressed as

```
#Linearity property of Fourier Transform
import numpy as np
a,b=1,2
#Step 1: Defining the two matrices f1 and f2
f1=np.array([[1, 0],[0,1]])
f2=np.array([[1, 1],[1,1]])
#Step 2: Taking the Fourier transform
F1=np.fft.fft2(f1)
F2=np.fft.fft2(f2)
f3=a*f1+b*f2
F3=np.fft.fft2(f3)
F4=a*F1+b*F2
#Step 3: Verifying property
if np.array_equal(F3,F4):
    print('FT is linear')
else:
    print('FT is non-linear')
```

Fourier Transform is linear

(a) Python code   **(b) Result**

Fig. 3.20 Verification of superposition principle: (**a**) Python code, (**b**) result

$$2D\_DFT\{f[m,n-n_0]\} = e^{-j\frac{2\pi}{N}n_0l}F[k,l] \tag{3.12}$$

If the shift is along both "m" and "n" axis in the spatial domain, it is expressed as

$$2D\_DFT\{f[m-m_0,n-n_0]\} = e^{-j\frac{2\pi}{N}(m_0k+n_0l)}F[k,l] \tag{3.13}$$

From Eqs. (3.11), (3.12), and (3.13), it is possible to observe the fact that the impact of spatial shift is observed in the phase shift of the spectrum.

Experiment 3.9: Spatial Shift Results in Phase Shift
The objective of this experiment is to prove that spatial shift results in phase shift. Two images "Image-1" and "Image-2" are generated. Both images are square images on a black background. The location of the square in Image-1 is different from Image-2. In other words, Image-2 can be considered as a spatial shift version of Image-1. Then the magnitude and phase spectrum of the two images are obtained. The Python code that performs this task is shown in Fig. 3.21, and the corresponding output is shown in Fig. 3.22.

Inferences
The following inferences can be made from Experiment 3.9:

- Image-2 can be considered as a spatially shifted version of Image-1.
- The magnitude spectrum of two images, which are labelled as "M1" and "M2" in Fig. 3.22, are alike.

```
#Spatial shift results in phase shift
import numpy as np
import matplotlib.pyplot as plt
#Step 1: Generating the images
img1=np.zeros([256,256])
img1[60:76,60:78]=255
img2=np.zeros([256,256])
img2[188:204,188:204]=255
IMG1=np.fft.fft2(img1)
M1=np.fft.fftshift(IMG1)
IMG2=np.fft.fft2(img2)
M2=np.fft.fftshift(IMG2)
A1=(np.angle(IMG1))
A2=(np.angle(IMG2))
fig=plt.figure(figsize=(8,6)),plt.subplot(2,3,1),plt.imshow(img1,cmap='gray')
plt.title('Image-1'),plt.xticks([]),plt.yticks([]),plt.subplot(2,3,2),
plt.imshow(np.abs(M1),cmap='gray'),plt.title('M1'),plt.xticks([]),plt.yticks([])
plt.subplot(2,3,3),plt.imshow(np.unwrap(A1),cmap='gray'),plt.title('A1'),plt.xticks([]),
plt.yticks([]),plt.subplot(2,3,4),plt.imshow(img2,cmap='gray'),plt.title('Image-2'),
plt.xticks([]),plt.yticks([]),plt.subplot(2,3,5),plt.imshow(np.abs(M2),cmap='gray')
plt.title('M2'),plt.xticks([]),plt.yticks([]),plt.subplot(2,3,6),
plt.imshow(np.unwrap(A2),cmap='gray'),plt.title('A2'),plt.xticks([]),plt.yticks([])
plt.tight_layout()
```

Fig. 3.21 Python code to illustrate that spatial shift results in phase shift

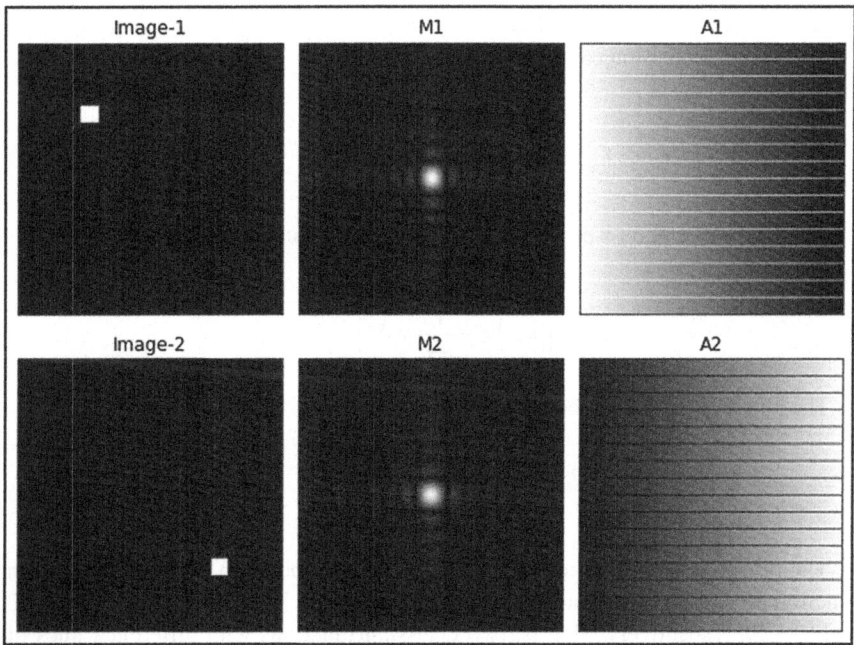

Fig. 3.22 Magnitude and phase spectrum of two images

- The phase spectrum of the two images is different.
- This experiment illustrates the fact that spatial shift results in phase shift.

3.2.3   Scaling Property of Fourier Transform

If $F[k, l]$ represents the spectrum of the image $f[m, n]$, then the scaled version of the signal $f[am, bn]$ has the following Fourier transform:

$$2D\_DFT\{f[am,bn]\} = \frac{1}{|ab|}F\left[\frac{k}{a},\frac{l}{b}\right]$$ (3.14)

Equation (3.14) can be interpreted as "Compression in spatial domain is equivalent to expansion in frequency domain and vice versa".

Experiment 3.10: Fourier Transform of Gaussian Function
Scaling property can be illustrated by taking Fourier transform of a two-dimensional Gaussian function. The Python code that obtains the spectrum of 2D-Gaussian function is discussed as follows.
The general expression for Gaussian function is

$$f[m,n] = \frac{1}{2\pi\sigma_m\sigma_n}e^{-\frac{(m-\mu_m)^2}{2\sigma_m^2}}e^{-\frac{(n-\mu_n)^2}{2\sigma_n^2}}$$ (3.15)

The above expression can be written as

$$f[m,n] = \frac{1}{2\pi\sigma_m\sigma_n}e^{-\left(\frac{(m-\mu_m)^2}{2\sigma_m^2}+\frac{(n-\mu_n)^2}{2\sigma_n^2}\right)}$$ (3.16)

If $\mu_m = \mu_n = 0$ and $\sigma_m = \sigma_n = \sigma$, the above expression can be written as

$$f[m,n] = \frac{1}{2\pi\sigma^2}e^{-\left(\frac{(m)^2}{2\sigma^2}+\frac{(n)^2}{2\sigma^2}\right)}$$ (3.17)

The above equation can be simplified as

$$f[m,n] = \frac{1}{2\pi\sigma^2}e^{-\left(\frac{m^2+n^2}{2\sigma^2}\right)}$$ (3.18)

The objective of this experiment is to obtain the spectrum of the 2D Gaussian function for two different values of standard deviations. The values chosen are $\sigma = 2$ and $\sigma = 20$, respectively. That is, two Gaussian functions with different values of

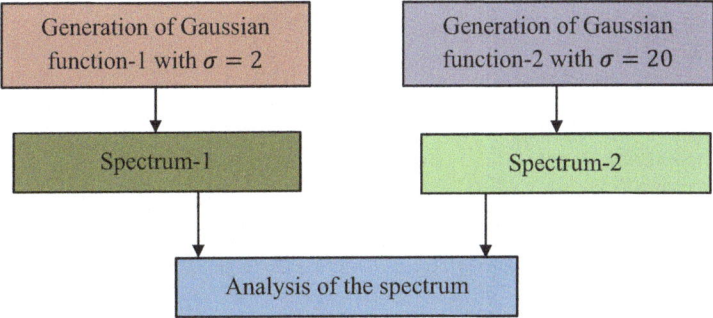

Fig. 3.23 Block diagram of problem statement

standard deviations are generated. Then the Fourier transform of the generated Gaussian function is obtained. The problem statement is depicted in Fig. 3.23. The Python code that implements this task is shown in Fig. 3.24, and the corresponding output is shown in Fig. 3.25.

Inferences

From Fig. 3.25, the following inferences can be drawn:

- Fourier transform of a Gaussian function results in another Gaussian function.
- Compression in spatial domain leads to expansion in frequency domain and vice versa.

Experiment 3.11: Scaling Property of Fourier Transform

Generate the following test image. The test image is a black image with two white dots at the location (110, 110) and (120, 120). Obtain the Fourier transform of the image.

The Python code that generates the spectrum of the dark image with two white dots at the spatial location (110, 110) and (120, 120) is shown in Figure 3.26a, and the corresponding output is shown in Figure 3.26b.

Now increase the spacing between the two dots. That is, the dot should be at the spatial location (110, 110) and (140, 140). The Python code that does this task is shown in Figure 3.27a. This implies that expansion happens in spatial domain. The impact of expansion in the frequency domain can be visualized by observing the output, which is shown in Figure 3.27b.

Inferences

The following inferences can be drawn from Experiment 3.11:

- The spectral line is widely spaced if the points are closely spaced in spatial domain.
- If the points are well separated in the spatial domain (the distance between points in the spatial domain is increased), the spectral lines are closely spaced.
- This experiment illustrates the fact that "Compression in one domain is equivalent to expansion in another domain and vice versa".

```
#Fourier transform of Gaussian function
import numpy as np
import matplotlib.pyplot as plt
M=256
x=np.linspace(-M/2,M/2,M+1)
y=np.linspace(-M/2,M/2,M+1)
X,Y=np.meshgrid(x,y)
#Step 1: Generation of Gaussian functions
sigma1,sigma2=2,20
img1=1./(2.* np.pi *sigma1*sigma1)*np.exp(-((X)**2. / (2. * sigma1**2.) + (Y)**2. / (2.*
sigma1**2.)))
img2=1./(2.* np.pi *sigma2*sigma2)*np.exp(-((X)**2. / (2. * sigma2**2.) + (Y)**2. / (2.*
sigma2**2.)))
#Step 2: Obtaining the spectrum of the Gaussian function
IMG1=np.fft.fft2(img1)
IMG1=np.fft.fftshift(IMG1)
IMG2=np.fft.fft2(img2)
IMG2=np.fft.fftshift(IMG2)
#Step 3: Plotting the results
fig=plt.figure(figsize=(8,6)),plt.subplot(1,4,1),plt.imshow(img1,cmap='gray'),
plt.title('Image-1'),plt.axis('off'),plt.subplot(1,4,2),plt.imshow(np.abs(IMG1),cmap='gray'),
plt.title('Spectrum-1'),plt.axis('off'),plt.subplot(1,4,3),plt.imshow(img2,cmap='gray'),
plt.title('Image-2'),plt.axis('off'),plt.subplot(1,4,4),plt.imshow(np.abs(IMG2),cmap='gray'),
plt.title('Spectrum-2'),plt.axis('off'),plt.tight_layout()
```

Fig. 3.24   Fourier transform of Gaussian function

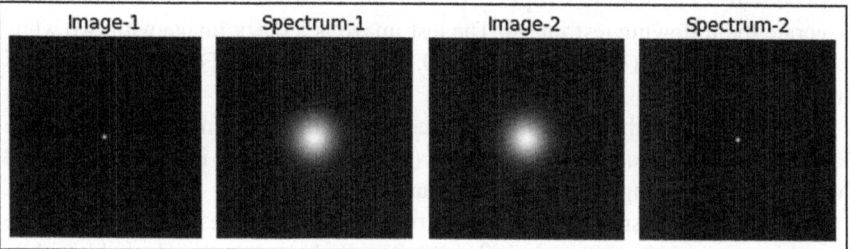

Fig. 3.25   Gaussian functions and their spectra

3.2.4   Rotation Property of Fourier Transform

According to rotation property of 2D DFT, if an image is rotated by an angle "θ", then its spectrum will be rotated by an angle "θ".

Experiment 3.12: Fourier Transform of Horizontal and Vertical Lines

Generate two images which contains horizontal and vertical lines on a black background. Obtain their magnitude spectrum and comment on the observed result.

Let horizontal line and vertical line images be termed Image-1 and Image-2, and their corresponding magnitude spectra be Spectrum-1 and Spectrum-2. The Python

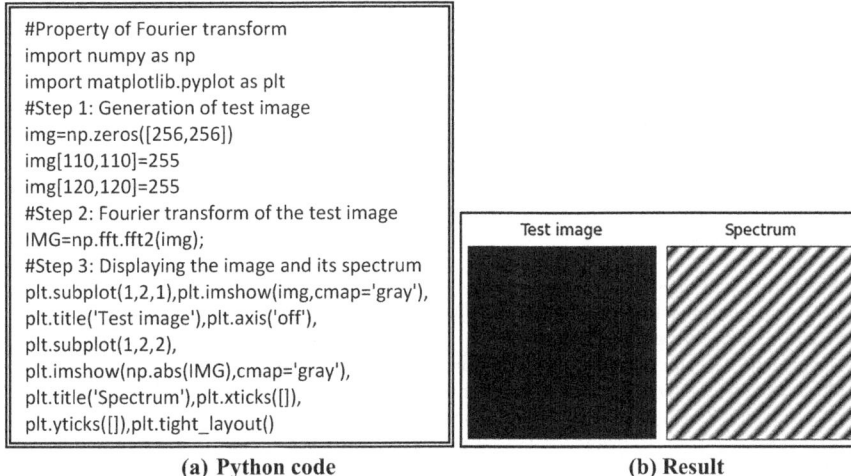

(a) Python code   (b) Result

Fig. 3.26 Fourier transform of two dots and the corresponding spectrum: (**a**) Python code, (**b**) result

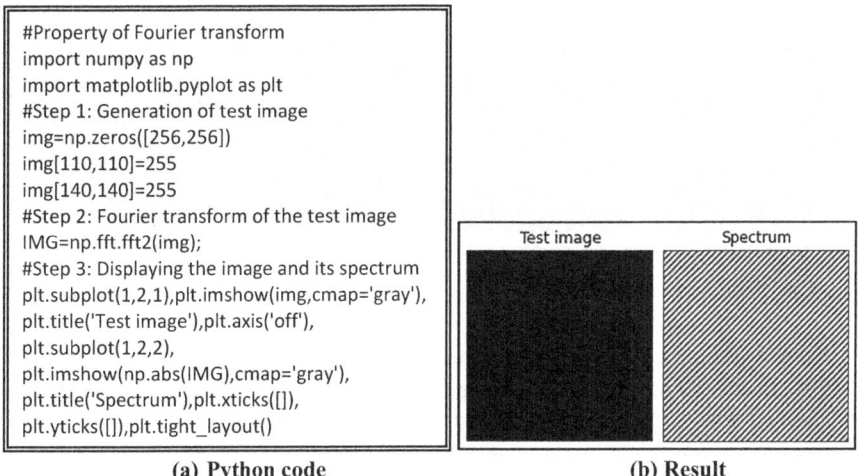

(a) Python code   (b) Result

Fig. 3.27 Increases the spacing between the dots in the image: (**a**) Python code, (**b**) result

code that generates the test images and their corresponding magnitude spectra is shown in Fig. 3.28, and the corresponding output is shown in Fig. 3.29.

Inferences

From Fig. 3.29, it is possible to observe the following:

- Magnitude spectra of horizontal line is a vertical line.
- Magnitude spectra of vertical line is a horizontal line.

```
#Magnitude spectrum of horizontal and vertical line
import numpy as np
import matplotlib.pyplot as plt
#Step 1: Generation of image
img=np.zeros([256,256])
img_hline=np.copy(img)
img_hline[128,:]=255
img_vline=np.copy(img)
img_vline[:,128]=255
#Step 2: Obtaining the Fourier transform
IMG_hline=np.fft.fftshift(np.fft.fft2(img_hline))
IMG_vline=np.fft.fftshift(np.fft.fft2(img_vline))
#Step 3: Displaying the result
plt.subplot(1,4,1),plt.imshow(img_hline,cmap='gray'),plt.title('Image-1'),plt.axis('off')
plt.subplot(1,4,2),plt.imshow(np.abs(IMG_hline),cmap='gray'),plt.title('Spectrum-1'),plt.axis('off')
plt.subplot(1,4,3),plt.imshow(img_vline,cmap='gray'),plt.title('Image-2'),plt.axis('off')
plt.subplot(1,4,4),plt.imshow(np.abs(IMG_vline),cmap='gray'),plt.title('Spectrum-2'),plt.axis('off')
plt.tight_layout()
```

Fig. 3.28 Python code to obtain the magnitude spectra of horizontal and vertical line

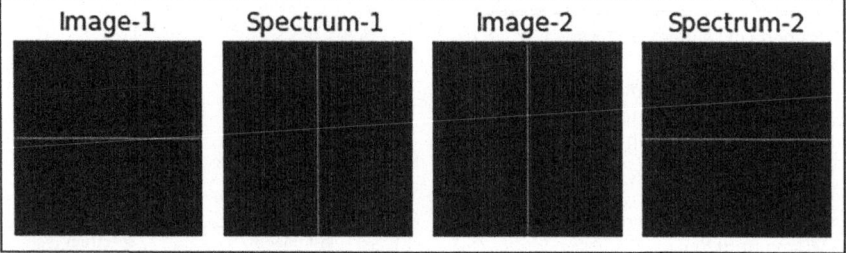

Fig. 3.29 Result of Python code shown in Fig. 3.28

- Here, a vertical line can be considered as a horizontal line rotated by an angle of 90°. In this Experiment 3.12, Image-2 is obtained by rotating Image-1 by an angle of 90°. Spectrum-2 is a rotated version of Spectrum-1 by an angle of 90°.
- Rotation of an image by an angle "θ" results in rotation of the spectrum by an angle "θ".

Experiment 3.13: Rotation Property of Fourier Transform
In this experiment, the Gaussian function is chosen to illustrate the rotation property of the Fourier transform instead of horizontal and vertical lines.

The general expression for Gaussian function is

$$f[m,n] = \frac{1}{2\pi\sigma_m\sigma_n} e^{-\frac{(m-\mu_m)^2}{2\sigma_m^2}} e^{-\frac{(n-\mu_n)^2}{2\sigma_n^2}} \tag{3.19}$$

The above expression can be written as

$$f[m,n] = \frac{1}{2\pi\sigma_m\sigma_n} e^{-\left(\frac{(m-\mu_m)^2}{2\sigma_m^2} + \frac{(n-\mu_n)^2}{2\sigma_n^2}\right)} \tag{3.20}$$

In this experiment, the value of the standard deviation along x and y directions are made different by choosing $\sigma_m = 10$, $\sigma_n = 30$ for Image-1 and $\sigma_m = 30$, $\sigma_n = 10$ for Image-2. The Fourier transform of the two test images are obtained as IMG1 and IMG2. The problem statement is represented in the form of a block diagram, which is shown in Fig. 3.30.

The Python code that implements the above-mentioned task is shown in Fig. 3.31, and the corresponding output is shown in Fig. 3.32.

Inferences

- This experiment illustrates the fact that for every action in spatial domain, there is a reaction in spectral domain. Image-1 is elongated along y-direction, whereas its spectrum (Spectrum-1) is elongated in x-direction. On the other hand, Image-2 is elongated in x-direction, whereas its spectrum is elongated in y-direction.
- This experiment also illustrates the fact that rotation of an image by an angle "θ" results in rotation of the spectrum by an angle "θ".

3.2.5 *Frequency Shift Property of Fourier Transform*

According to frequency shift or modulation property, multiplying an image $f[m, n]$ by a cosine signal will result in the shift in the spectrum of the image.

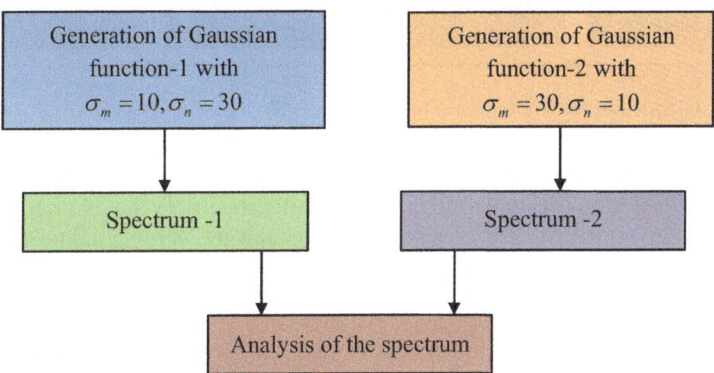

Fig. 3.30 Block diagram depicting the problem statement

```
#Fourier transform of Gaussian functions
import numpy as np
import matplotlib.pyplot as plt
M=256
x=np.linspace(-M/2,M/2,M+1)
y=np.linspace(-M/2,M/2,M+1)
X,Y=np.meshgrid(x,y)
#Step 1: Generation of the images
sigma_m1,sigma_n1,sigma_m2,sigma_n2=10,30,30,10
mean_m,mean_n=0,0
img1=1./(2.* np.pi *sigma_m1 * sigma_n1) * np.exp(-((X - mean_m)**2. / (2. * sigma_m1**2.) +
(Y - mean_n)**2. / (2.* sigma_n1**2.)))
img2=1./(2.* np.pi *sigma_m2 * sigma_n2) * np.exp(-((X - mean_m)**2. / (2. * sigma_m2**2.) +
(Y - mean_n)**2. / (2.* sigma_n2**2.)))
#Step 2: Obtaining the spectrum of the images
IMG1=np.fft.fft2(img1)
IMG1=np.fft.fftshift(IMG1)
IMG2=np.fft.fft2(img2)
IMG2=np.fft.fftshift(IMG2)
#Step 3: Plotting the results
plt.subplot(1,4,1),plt.imshow(img1,cmap='gray'),plt.title('Image-1'),plt.axis('off')
plt.subplot(1,4,2),plt.imshow(np.abs(IMG1),cmap='gray'),plt.title('Spectrum-1'),plt.axis('off')
plt.subplot(1,4,3),plt.imshow(img2,cmap='gray'),plt.title('Image-2'),plt.axis('off')
plt.subplot(1,4,4),plt.imshow(np.abs(IMG2),cmap='gray'),plt.title('Spectrum-2'),plt.axis('off')
plt.tight_layout()
```

Fig. 3.31 Python code that obtains the Fourier transform of two Gaussian functions

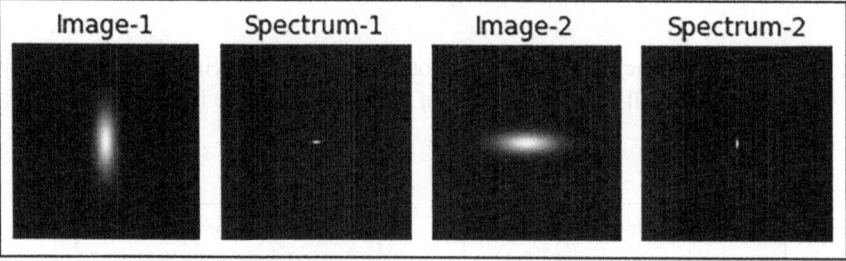

Fig. 3.32 Fourier transform of Gaussian functions

Experiment 3.14: Frequency Shift Property of DFT

The Python code that illustrates the frequency shift property or modulation property of the Fourier transform is shown in Fig. 3.33, and the corresponding output is shown in Fig. 3.34.

The steps involved in Python implementation are as follows:

Step 1: Generation of the test image. In this case, the test image is a white circle on a black background. The radius of the circle is fixed at 50.

Step 2: Generation of sinusoidal signal. Here, the frequency of the signal along the x and y directions is kept at 15.

```
#Frequency shift property of FT
import numpy as np
import matplotlib.pyplot as plt
#Step 1: Generation of image 1
img1=np.zeros([256,256])
R=50  #Radius
for i in range(0,256):
    for j in range(0,256):
        D=((i-128)**2 + (j-128)**2)**0.5
        if(D<=R):
            img1[i,j]=1/(np.pi*R**2)
#Step 2: Generation of sinusoidal grating pattern
x=np.arange(-.5,.5,1/256)
y=np.arange(-.5,.5,1/256)
X,Y=np.meshgrid(x,y)
fx,fy=15,15
img2=np.cos(2*np.pi*(fx*X+fy*Y))
#Step 3: Multiplying the image with sinusoidal signal
img3=np.multiply(img1,img2)
#Step 4: Obtaining the spectrum of the images
IM1=np.fft.fft2(img1)
IM2=np.fft.fft2(img2)
IM3=np.fft.fft2(img3)
#Step 5: Displaying the results
fig=plt.figure(figsize=(8,6)),plt.subplot(2,3,1),plt.imshow(img1,cmap='gray'),
plt.title('Input image'),plt.axis('off'),plt.subplot(2,3,4),
plt.imshow(np.fft.fftshift(np.abs(IM1)),cmap='gray'),plt.title('Input image spectrum'),
plt.axis('off'),plt.subplot(2,3,2),plt.imshow(img2,cmap='gray')
plt.title('Sinusoidal image'),plt.xticks([]),plt.yticks([]),plt.subplot(2,3,5),
plt.imshow(np.fft.fftshift(np.abs(IM2)),cmap='gray'),plt.title('Spectrum of sinusoidal signal'),
plt.xticks([]),plt.yticks([]),plt.subplot(2,3,3),plt.imshow(img3,cmap='gray')
plt.title('Modulated image'),plt.xticks([]),plt.yticks([]),plt.subplot(2,3,6),
plt.imshow(np.fft.fftshift(np.abs(IM3)),cmap='gray'),plt.title('Spectrum of modulated image'),
plt.axis('off'),plt.tight_layout()
```

Fig. 3.33 Python code to illustrate frequency shift property of Fourier transform

Step 3: Modulation of the input test image with the sinusoidal signal to obtain the modulated image.

Step 4: Obtaining the spectrum of the input image, sinusoidal image, and the modulated image.

Step 5: Dealing with displaying the result using subplot.

Inferences

- From Fig. 3.34, it is possible to observe that shift in the magnitude spectrum of the Fourier transform of the modulated image.
- Thus, multiplying a signal with a sinusoidal signal will result in a frequency shift in the spectrum of the modulated signal.

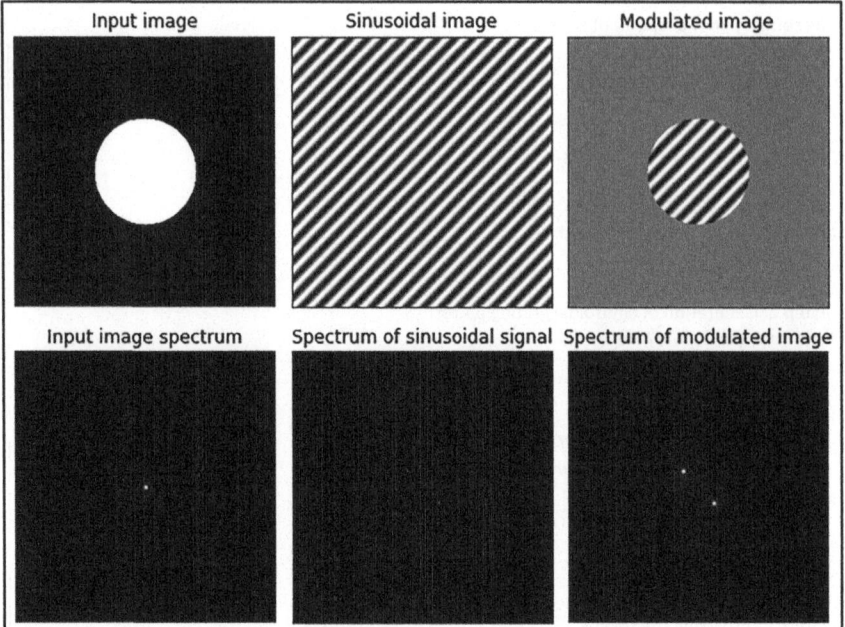

Fig. 3.34 Result of Python code shown in Fig. 3.33

3.2.6   Convolution Property

According to convolution property, convolution in spatial domain is equivalent to multiplication in the frequency domain. This is expressed as

$$f_1[m,n] * f_2[m,n] = F^{-1}\left\{F_1[k,l] \times F_2[k,l]\right\} \qquad (3.21)$$

Equation (3.21) is illustrated in the form of a block diagram, which is shown in Fig. 3.35. In Fig. 3.35, $f_1[m, n]$ and $f_2[m, n]$ represent two images in spatial domain.

Experiment 3.15: Convolution Property of DFT

In this experiment, $f_1[m, n]$ is a white square on a black background, whereas $f_2[m, n]$ represents two-dimensional delta function. It is well known that convolution of any function with a delta function will result in the same function. Hence, convolution of $f_1[m, n]$ with $f_2[m, n]$ results in $f_3[m, n]$. As per convolution property, $f_3[m, n] = f_4[m, n]$. The Python code that illustrates the convolution property is shown in Fig. 3.36, and the corresponding output is shown in Fig. 3.37.

Inferences

- From Fig. 3.37, Image-1 is a white square in a black background, whereas Image-2 is a 2D delta function.

Fig. 3.35 Illustration of
convolution property of
Fourier transform

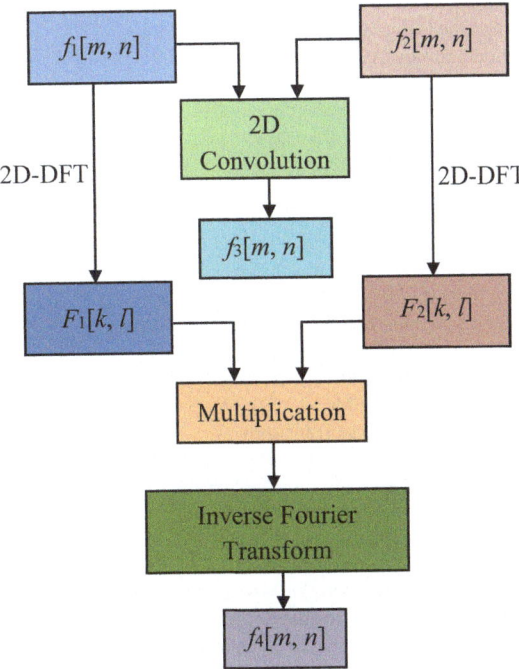

- Convolution of any function with 2D delta function results in the same function. This is reflected in the result of convolution.
- Fourier transform of 2D delta function results in 2D dc function, which is reflected in the result.
- The result obtained using convolution is the same as the result obtained by the inverse Fourier transform (IFT) of multiplication of the spectrum of the two images. Hence, convolution in spatial domain is equal to multiplication in the frequency domain.

3.3   Discrete Cosine Transform

Discrete Cosine Transform (DCT) expresses a finite sequence of data points in terms of a sum of cosine functions at different frequencies. DCT is a real transform. Upon taking DCT of an image, the coefficients of DCT are always real. Fast algorithms exist to compute DCT, and DCT has a good energy compaction property. Because of this property, DCT is used in JPEG image compression standard. The expression for forward two-dimensional DCT of the image $f[m, n]$ is expressed as

```
# Convolution property of Fourier transform
import numpy as np
import matplotlib.pyplot as plt
from scipy.signal import convolve2d
#Step 1: Generation of images
img1=np.zeros([32,32])
img1[12:20,12:20]=255
img2=np.zeros([32,32])
img2[16,16]=255
#Step 2: Perform the Convolution
img3=convolve2d(img1,img2,mode='same')
#Step 3: Obtain the spectrum of the two images
IMG1=np.fft.fftshift(np.fft.fft2(img1))
IMG2=np.fft.fftshift(np.fft.fft2(img2))
IMG3=np.multiply(IMG1,IMG2); #Step 4: Multiply the spectrum
#Step 5: Take Inverse Transform
rimg=np.fft.fftshift(np.fft.ifft2(IMG3))
fig=plt.figure(figsize=(8,6)),plt.subplot(2,3,1),plt.imshow(img1,cmap='gray')
plt.title('Image-1'),plt.axis('off'),plt.subplot(2,3,2),plt.imshow(img2,cmap='gray')
plt.title('Image-2'),plt.axis('off'),plt.subplot(2,3,3),plt.imshow(img3,cmap='gray')
plt.title('Result of Convolution'),plt.axis('off'),plt.subplot(2,3,4),
plt.imshow(np.abs(IMG1),cmap='gray'),plt.title('Spectrum on Image-1'),plt.axis('off')
plt.subplot(2,3,5),plt.imshow(np.abs(IMG2),cmap='binary'),plt.title('Spectrum on Image-2'),
plt.xticks([]),plt.yticks([]),plt.subplot(2,3,6),plt.imshow(np.abs(rimg),cmap='gray')
plt.title('IFT of Spectrum Multiplication'),plt.axis('off')
plt.tight_layout()
```

Fig. 3.36 Python code to illustrate convolution property

$$F[k,l] = \alpha[k]\alpha[l]\sum_{m=0}^{N-1}\sum_{n=0}^{N-1}f[m,n]\cos\left(\frac{[2m+1]\pi k}{2N}\right)\cos\left(\frac{[2n+1]\pi l}{2N}\right) \quad (3.22)$$

where

$$\alpha[p] = \begin{cases} \sqrt{\dfrac{1}{N}}, & p=0, \\ \sqrt{\dfrac{2}{N}}, & 1 \le p \le N-1. \end{cases} \quad (3.23)$$

The expression for inverse 2D DCT is given by

$$f[m,n] = \sum_{k=0}^{N-1}\sum_{l=0}^{N-1}\alpha[k]\alpha[l]F[k,l]\cos\left(\frac{[2m+1]\pi k}{2N}\right)\cos\left(\frac{[2n+1]\pi l}{2N}\right) \quad (3.24)$$

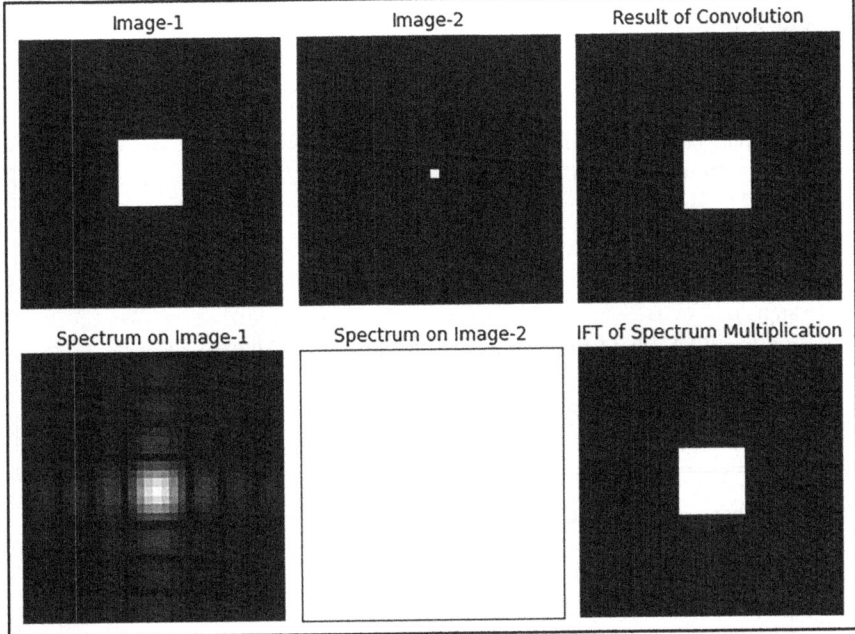

Fig. 3.37 Result of Python code shown in Fig. 3.36

Experiment 3.16: Plotting the DCT Basis function for N = 4

The Python code that plots the DCT basis function for N is shown in Fig. 3.38, and the corresponding output is shown in Fig. 3.39. Execute the Python code given in Fig. 3.38 and enter the value of N as 4.

Inferences

The following inferences can be observed from this experiment:

- DCT basis image for $N = 4$ is shown in Fig. 3.39.
- The top left basis function assumes a constant value, which is referred to as a DC coefficient.
- Change in gray level in every row of the DCT matrix is termed as sequency.
- The basis function exhibits a progressive increase in frequency both in vertical and horizontal directions.

Experiment 3.17: Energy Compaction of DCT

Generate 4×4 checkerboard pattern. This checkerboard pattern is the input image. Take the forward Discrete Cosine Transform of this input image so as to obtain 16 DCT coefficients. Make the maximum valued DCT coefficient is to zero. After this, take inverse Discrete Cosine Transform and comment on the observed result.

The steps involved in the task are shown in Fig. 3.40.

```
#Plotting the DCT basis function for N=4
import numpy as np
from scipy.fft import dct
import graphlearning as gl
N = int(input("Enter the N point DFT:"))
dct_basis = np.zeros((N*N,N*N))
k = 0
for i in range(N):
  for j in range(N):
    g = np.zeros((N,N))
    g[i,j]=1
    dct_basis[k,:] = dct(dct(g.T,norm='ortho').T,norm='ortho').flatten()
    k+=1
dct_basis = dct_basis/np.max(np.absolute(dct_basis))
gl.utils.image_grid(dct_basis,n_rows=N,n_cols=N,title='2D {} point DCT'.format(N))
```

Fig. 3.38   Python code to plot the basis function of DCT basis for $N = 4$

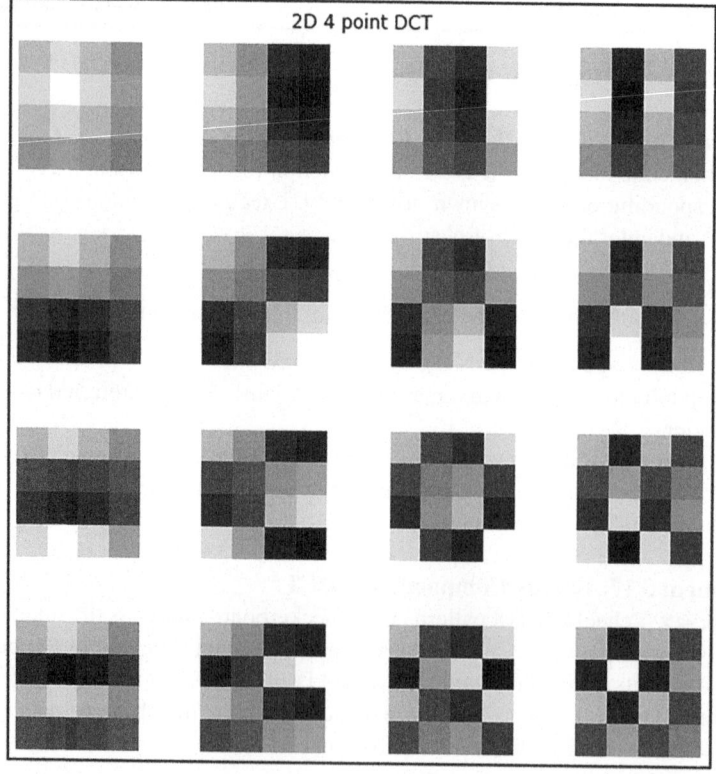

Fig. 3.39   DCT basis for $N = 4$

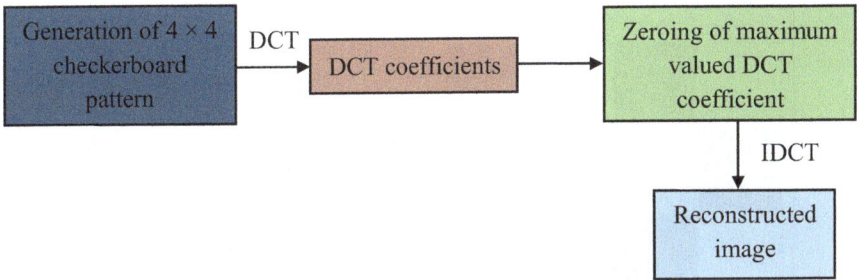

Fig. 3.40 Illustration of problem statement

```
# Importance of DC coefficient in DCT
from scipy.fftpack import dct, idct
import numpy as np
import matplotlib.pyplot as plt
#Step 1: Generation of 4 x 4 checkerboard pattern
im=np.ones([4,4])
m,n=im.shape[:2]
for i in range(0,m):
   for j in range(0,n):
      im[i,j]=(-1)**(i+j)*im[i,j]
#Step 2: Taking the DCT of the image
IM=dct(dct(im.T,norm='ortho').T,norm='ortho')
#Step 3: Find the index corresponding to the maximum value
max_xy = np.where(IM == IM.max() )
#Step 4: Make the largest value coefficient to zero
IM[max_xy[0],max_xy[1]]=0
#Step 5: Taking IDCT of the image
im_r=idct(idct(IM.T,norm='ortho').T,norm='ortho')
#Step 6: Displaying the result
plt.subplot(1,2,1),plt.imshow(im,cmap='gray'),plt.title('Input image'),
plt.xticks([]),plt.yticks([]),plt.subplot(1,2,2),plt.imshow(im_r,cmap='gray')
plt.title('Reconstructed image'),plt.xticks([]),plt.yticks([])
plt.tight_layout()
```

Fig. 3.41 Python code to perform zeroing of maximum DCT coefficient

The Python code that performs this task is shown in Fig. 3.41, and the corresponding output is shown in Fig. 3.42.

Inferences

- The input image is a checkerboard pattern. Upon making the maximum value of DCT coefficient is to zero, the reconstructed image is different from the input image.

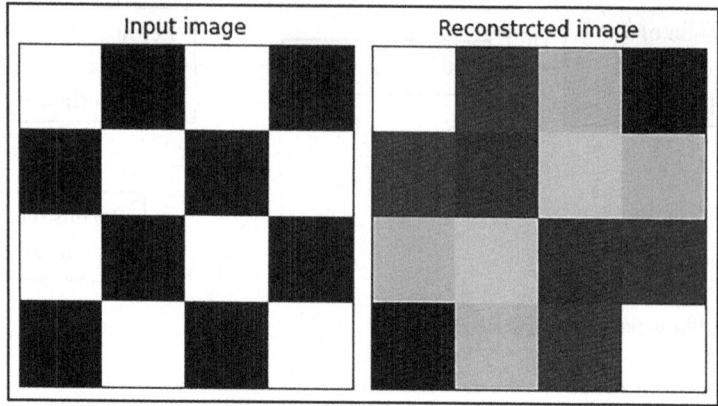

Fig. 3.42 Result of Python code shown in Fig. 3.41

- This experiment illustrates that the value of DCT coefficient is related to the energy in the signal. If the maximum valued DCT coefficient is set to zero, then much of the information is lost. Hence, the reconstructed image is different from the input image.

Experiment 3.18: Reconstruct the Original Image from a Minimum Number of DCT Coefficients

Generate 4×4 checkerboard pattern. This checkerboard pattern is the input image. Take the forward Discrete Cosine Transform of this input image so as to obtain 16 DCT coefficients. Make the minimum valued DCT coefficient to zero. After this, take inverse DCT and comment on the observed result.

The Python code that takes the DCT of the input image and sets the minimum valued DCT coefficient of the input image to zero, then obtains the reconstructed image by taking inverse DCT, is shown in Fig. 3.43, and the corresponding output is shown in Fig. 3.44.

Inferences

- The Python code generates the checkerboard pattern. Then DCT is taken on the checkerboard pattern to obtain the DCT coefficients.
- The minimum valued DCT coefficient is set to zero. Then inverse DCT is taken to obtain the reconstructed image.
- From Fig. 3.44, it is possible to interpret that the reconstructed image resembles the input image. The minimum valued DCT coefficient contains less information about the input image; hence, zeroing it does not affect the quality of the image.

Experiment 3.19: DCT Block Processing

Generate 16×16 checkerboard pattern image. Divide the image into 8×8 sub-blocks. Apply DCT to each subblock to get the transform coefficients. Use the same

```
# Energy compaction of DCT transform
from scipy.fftpack import dct, idct
import numpy as np
import matplotlib.pyplot as plt
#Step 1: Generation of 4 x 4 checkerboard pattern
im=np.ones([4,4])
m,n=im.shape[:2]
for i in range(0,m):
    for j in range(0,n):
        im[i,j]=(-1)**(i+j)*im[i,j]
#Step 2: Taking the DCT of the image
IM=dct(dct(im.T,norm='ortho').T,norm='ortho')
#Step 3: Find the index corresponding to the maximum value
max_xy = np.where(IM == IM.min() )
#Step 4: Make the largest value coefficient to zero
IM[max_xy[0],max_xy[1]]=0
#Step 5: Taking IDCT of the image
im_r=idct(idct(IM.T,norm='ortho').T,norm='ortho')
#Step 6: Displaying the result
plt.subplot(1,2,1),plt.imshow(im,cmap='gray'),plt.title('Input image'),
plt.xticks([]),plt.yticks([]),plt.subplot(1,2,2),plt.imshow(im_r,cmap='gray'),
plt.title('Reconstructed image'),plt.xticks([]),plt.yticks([])
plt.tight_layout()
```

Fig. 3.43 Python code that sets the minimum valued DCT coefficient to zero

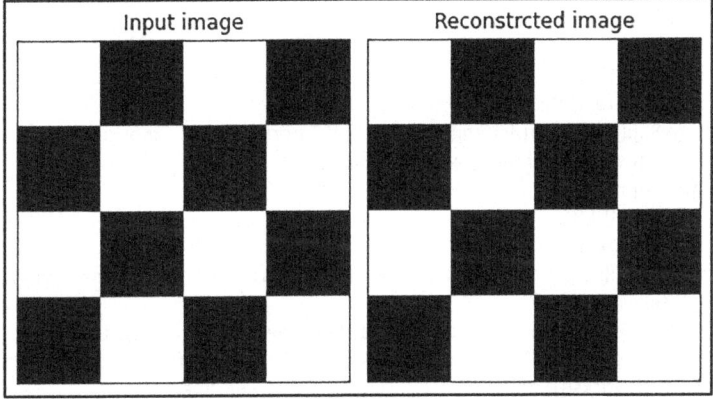

Fig. 3.44 Result of Python code shown in Fig. 3.43

block processing approach to obtain the inverse DCT of each block to get the reconstructed image. Comment on the observed result.

The following steps are involved in this experiment:

Step 1: Generation of test image.
Step 2: Divide the image into 8 × 8 blocks and apply DCT to each block.
Step 3: Apply inverse DCT to each block to obtain the reconstructed image.
The Python code that performs this task is shown in Fig. 3.45, and the corresponding output is shown in Fig. 3.46.

Inferences
The following inferences can be drawn from Fig. 3.46:

- The input image is 16 × 16 checkerboard pattern image.
- The image is divided into 8 × 8 subblocks. By dividing 16 × 16 image into 8 × 8 subblocks, one obtains 4 subblocks.
- The Inverse Discrete Cosine Transform (IDCT) is applied to each subblock to obtain the reconstructed image.

```
# DCT block processing
import numpy as np
import matplotlib.pyplot as plt
from scipy.fftpack import dct,idct
from numpy import r_
#Step 1: Generation of test image
img=np.zeros([16,16])
img[1::2, ::2] = 1
img[::2, 1::2] = 1
imsize = img.shape
#Step 2: DCT for 8 x 8 subblock
IM = np.zeros(imsize)
for i in r_[:imsize[0]:8]:
    for j in r_[:imsize[1]:8]:
        IM[i:(i+8),j:(j+8)] = dct(dct(img[i:(i+8),j:(j+8)].T,norm='ortho').T,norm='ortho')
#Step 3: Reconstruction of the image from subblock
rimg=np.zeros(imsize)
for i in r_[:imsize[0]:8]:
    for j in r_[:imsize[1]:8]:
        rimg[i:(i+8),j:(j+8)] =idct(idct(IM[i:(i+8),j:(j+8)].T,norm='ortho').T,norm='ortho')
#Step 4: Displaying the result
plt.subplot(1,3,1),plt.imshow(img,cmap='gray'),plt.title('Input Image'),plt.xticks([]),
plt.yticks([]),plt.subplot(1,3,2),plt.imshow(IM,cmap='gray'),plt.title('DCT coefficients'),
plt.xticks([]),plt.yticks([]),plt.subplot(1,3,3),plt.imshow(rimg,cmap='gray')
plt.title('Reconstructed image'),plt.xticks([]),plt.yticks([])
plt.tight_layout()
```

Fig. 3.45 Python code to perform block processing of the input image

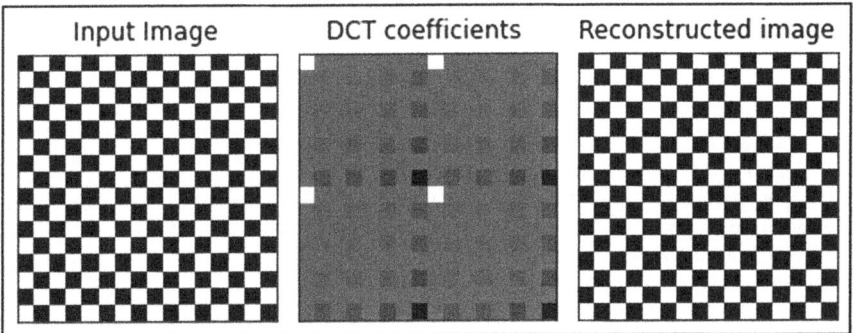

Fig. 3.46 Input and reconstructed image

- The reconstructed image resembles the input image, which implies that DCT is a reversible transform.

Experiment 3.20: Block Processing of DCT

Generate 16×16 checkerboard pattern image. Divide the image into 8×8 subblocks. Then 4 subblocks will be obtained. This makes the largest coefficient value in the first and last subblock to zero. After zeroing out the maximum DCT coefficients in the first and last block, perform inverse DCT of each block to obtain the reconstructed image. Plot the input image, modify DCT coefficients, and reconstruct image and comment on the observed results.

The following steps are involved in this experiment:

Step 1: Generation of test image.
Step 2: Divide the image into 8×8 blocks and apply DCT to each block.
Step 3: Making the largest coefficient (DC coefficient) in the first and the last block to zero.
Step 4: Apply inverse DCT to each block to obtain the reconstructed image.

The Python code that performs this task is shown in Fig. 3.47, and the corresponding output is shown in Fig. 3.48.

Inferences

The following inferences can be drawn from Fig. 3.48:

- The input image is 16×16 checkerboard pattern image.
- The image is divided into 8×8 subblocks. By dividing 16×16 image into 8×8 subblocks, one obtains 4 subblocks.
- The DC coefficients in the first and last block are forced to make a zero value.
- The Inverse Discrete Cosine Transform (IDCT) is applied to each subblock to obtain the reconstructed image.
- The reconstructed image in the first and last blocks differs from the input images.

```
import numpy as np
import matplotlib.pyplot as plt
from scipy.fftpack import dct,idct
from numpy import r_
#Step 1: Generation of test image
img=np.zeros([16,16])
img[1::2, ::2],img[::2, 1::2] = 1, 1
imsize = img.shape
#Step 2: DCT for 8 x 8 subblock
IM = np.zeros(imsize)
for i in r_[:imsize[0]:8]:
    for j in r_[:imsize[1]:8]:
        IM[i:(i+8),j:(j+8)] = dct(dct(img[i:(i+8),j:(j+8)].T,norm='ortho').T,norm='ortho')
IM[0,0], IM[8,8]=0, 0; #Step 3: Setting the DC coefficients to zero
#Step 4: Reconstruction of the image from subblock
rimg=np.zeros(imsize)
for i in r_[:imsize[0]:8]:
    for j in r_[:imsize[1]:8]:
        rimg[i:(i+8),j:(j+8)] =idct(idct(IM[i:(i+8),j:(j+8)].T,norm='ortho').T,norm='ortho')
#Step 5: Displaying the result
plt.subplot(1,3,1),plt.imshow(img,cmap='gray'),plt.title('Input Image'),plt.xticks([]),
plt.yticks([]),plt.subplot(1,3,2),plt.imshow(IM,cmap='gray'),plt.title('DCT coefficients'),
plt.xticks([]),plt.yticks([]),plt.subplot(1,3,3),plt.imshow(rimg,cmap='gray')
plt.title('Reconstructed image'),plt.xticks([]),plt.yticks([])
plt.tight_layout()
```

Fig. 3.47 Python code to perform block processing of the image

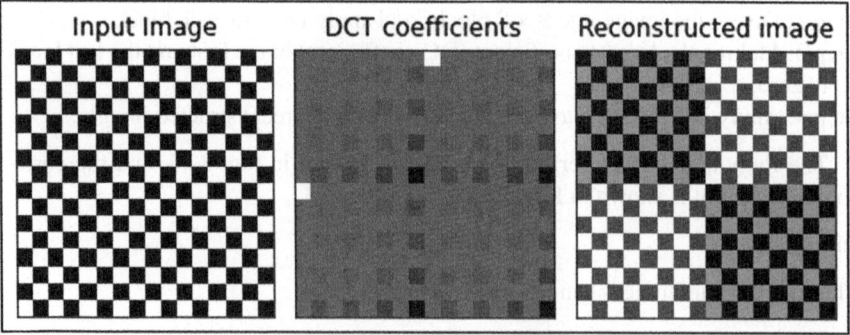

Fig. 3.48 Result of Python code shown in Fig. 3.47

- This experiment illustrates the fact that much of the information is contained in the low frequency coefficients (DC coefficients). Forcing the DC coefficients to zero value makes the reconstructed image different from the input image.

3.4 Hadamard Transform

Hadamard transform projects image into a set of square functions to obtain the Hadamard coefficients. The expression for 2D Hadamard transform of the input signal $f[m, n]$ is given by

$$F[k,l] = \sum_{m=0}^{N-1}\sum_{n=0}^{N-1} f[m,n](-1)^{\sum_{i=0}^{n-1}(b_i(m)b_i(k)+b_i(n)b_i(l))} \tag{3.25}$$

In the above expression, $b_i(m)$ refers to "i^{th}" bit position in the binary value of "m". The expression for the inverse Hadamard transform is given by

$$f[m,n] = \frac{1}{N^2}\sum_{k=0}^{N-1}\sum_{l=0}^{N-1} F[k,l](-1)^{\sum_{i=0}^{n-1}(b_i(m)b_i(k)+b_i(n)b_i(l))} \tag{3.26}$$

Hadamard transform matrix can be constructed using the relation

$$H_{2N} = \begin{bmatrix} H_N & H_N \\ H_N & -H_N \end{bmatrix} \tag{3.27}$$

If $H_2 = \begin{bmatrix} 1 & 1 \\ 1 & -1 \end{bmatrix}$, then the matrix H_4 can be constructed using the above relation as

$$H_4 = \begin{bmatrix} H_2 & H_2 \\ H_2 & -H_2 \end{bmatrix} \tag{3.28}$$

The above equation can be expressed as

$$H_4 = \begin{bmatrix} 1 & 1 & 1 & 1 \\ 1 & -1 & 1 & -1 \\ 1 & 1 & -1 & -1 \\ 1 & -1 & -1 & 1 \end{bmatrix} \tag{3.29}$$

The Hadamard matrix satisfies the following relation:

$$H \times H^T = N \times I \tag{3.30}$$

In the above expression, "I" represents the identity matrix.

Experiment 3.21: Plotting Hadamard Basis Functions
The objective of this experiment is to plot the Hadamard matrix for $N = 2, 4, 8$, and 16. The Python code that performs this action is given in Fig. 3.49, and the corresponding output is shown in Fig. 3.50.

Inferences

- The Hadamard basis images takes a value of either "+1" or "−1", which is reflected in Fig. 3.50.

```
#Plot the Hadamard basis images
from scipy.linalg import hadamard
import matplotlib.pyplot as plt
N=[2,4,8,16]
fig = plt.figure(1)
for i in range(len(N)):
    H=hadamard(N[i])
    plt.subplot(1,4,i+1), plt.imshow(H,cmap='gray'),plt.title('N = {}'.format(N[i]))
    plt.xticks([]),plt.yticks([])
plt.tight_layout()
```

Fig. 3.49 Python code to plot the Hadamard basis images

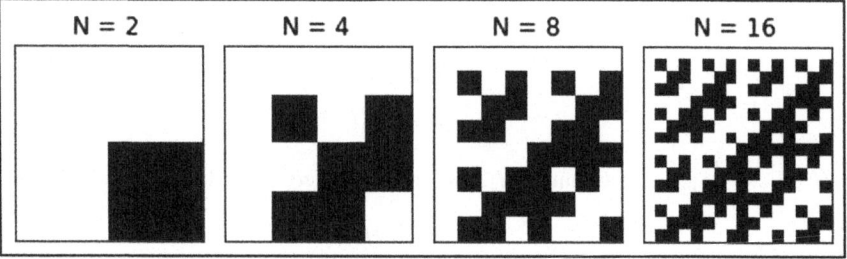

Fig. 3.50 Hadamard basis images

- For the value of "+1", the image is white; for the value of "−1", the image is black.

Experiment 3.22: Examine whether Hadamard Matrix Is Symmetric or Not
A matrix "A" is symmetric if it satisfies the following condition:

$$A = A^T \tag{3.31}$$

Interchanging of rows and columns results in the same matrix. The Python code that examines whether the Hadamard matrix is symmetric or not is given in Fig. 3.51a, and the corresponding output is shown in Fig. 3.51b.

Inference

- From Fig. 3.51b, it is possible to conclude that Hadamard matrix is symmetric.

Experiment 3.23: Examine Whether the Hadamard Basis Matrix Is Orthogonal or Not?
A square matrix "A" is orthogonal if it satisfies the following condition:

$$H \times H^T = N \times I \tag{3.32}$$

The Python code that examines whether the Hadamard basis matrix is orthogonal or not is given in Fig. 3.52, and the corresponding outputs are shown in Fig. 3.53(a, b).

```
import numpy as np
from scipy.linalg import hadamard
N=4 #Dimension of the matrix
#Step 1: Obtaining the Hadamard matrix
D = hadamard(N)
#Step 2: Performing the transpose operation
D1=np.transpose(D)
#Step 3: Checking the condition
if np.array_equal(D,D1):
    print('Hadamard matrix is symmetric')
else:
    print('Hadamard matrix is not symmetric')
```

Hadamard matrix is symmetric

(a) Python Code   **(b) Result**

Fig. 3.51 Verification of symmetry property of Hadamard matrix: (**a**) Python code, (**b**) result

```
#Orthogonal nature of Hadamard matrix
from scipy.linalg import hadamard
import numpy as np
import matplotlib.pyplot as plt
N=32
H=hadamard(N)
y=np.matmul(H,H)
y1=N*np.eye(N)
if np.array_equal(y,y1):
    print('Orthogonal basis')
else:
    print('Non-orthogonal basis')
plt.imshow(y,cmap='gray'),plt.xticks([]),plt.yticks([])
```

Fig. 3.52 Orthogonal property of Hadamard matrix

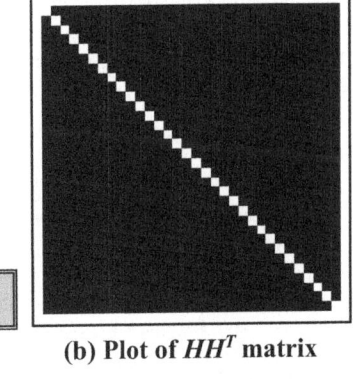

Hadamard matrix is symmetric

(a) Result   **(b) Plot of HH^T matrix**

Fig. 3.53 Result of Python code shown in Fig. 3.52: (**a**) result, (**b**) plot of HH^T matrix

Inferences

- From Fig. 3.53b, it is possible to observe that the HH^T matrix has an element of "1" only in the diagonal; all the other elements are zero.
- This illustrates the fact that $HH^T = N \times I$, where "I" is the identity matrix.
- An identity matrix is a square matrix with all the elements equal to zero except the diagonal elements.

Experiment 3.24: Obtaining the Rank of Hadamard Matrix

The rank of a matrix refers to the maximum number of linearly independent columns or rows present in the matrix. The Python code that checks whether the Hadamard matrix is a full rank matrix or not is shown in Figure 3.54a, and the corresponding output is shown in Figure 3.54b.

Inference

- From Figure 3.54b, it is possible to observe that the Hadamard matrix is a full rank matrix. This implies that the rows and columns of Hadamard matrix are linearly independent.

Experiment 3.25: Hadamard Transform of an Image

This Python experiment illustrates the impact of zeroing specific rows of the Hadamard transformation matrix. The problem statement is illustrated in the form of a block diagram, which is depicted in Fig. 3.55.

The input image is a 256 × 256 Cameraman image. Upon taking forward Hadamard transform, 256 × 256 Hadamard coefficients are obtained. The first 50 rows of the Hadamard coefficients are forced to make zero values. Inverse Hadamard transform is taken to obtain the reconstructed image after zeroing out the first 50 rows of the transformed image.

The Python code that performs the task mentioned in the problem statement is shown in Fig. 3.56, and the corresponding output is shown in Fig. 3.57.

```
#Rank of Hadamard matrix
from scipy.linalg import hadamard
from numpy.linalg import matrix_rank
N=8 #Dimension of the matrix
H=hadamard(N)
R=matrix_rank(H)
if N==R:
    print('Full rank matrix: R = {}'.format(R))
else:
    print('Not a full rank matrix R = {}'.format(R))
```

Full rank matrix: R = 8

(a) Python Code   (b) Result

Fig. 3.54 Rank of Hadamard matrix: (a) Python code, (b) result

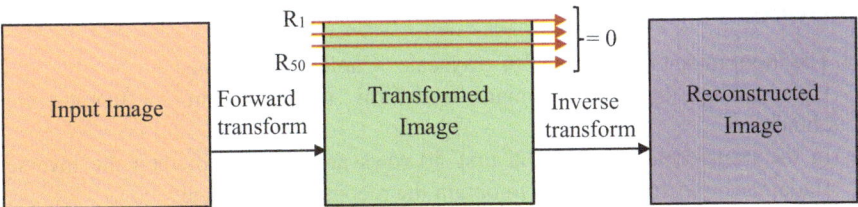

Fig. 3.55 Illustration of problem statement

```
from scipy.linalg import hadamard
import numpy as np
import cv2
import matplotlib.pyplot as plt
#Reading the input image
img=cv2.imread('cameraman.tif',0)
height,width=img.shape[:2]
#Computing the Forward Hadamard transform
H=hadamard(height)
IMG1=np.matmul(H,img);#H*img
IMG=np.matmul(IMG1,H);#IMG1*H^T
#Manipulating the transform coefficients
for i in range(0,50):
    IMG[i,:]=0
#Performing Inverse transform
rimg1=np.matmul(H,IMG)
rimg=1/(height*width)*np.matmul(rimg1,H)
#Displaying the result
plt.subplot(1,3,1),plt.imshow(img,cmap='gray'),plt.title('Input image'),plt.xticks([]),
plt.yticks([]),plt.subplot(1,3,2),plt.imshow(IMG,cmap='gray'),plt.title('Transformed image'),
plt.xticks([]),plt.yticks([]),plt.subplot(1,3,3),plt.imshow(rimg,cmap='gray'),
plt.title('Reconstructed image'),plt.xticks([]),plt.yticks([]),plt.tight_layout()
```

Fig. 3.56 Python code to perform the task mentioned in the problem statement

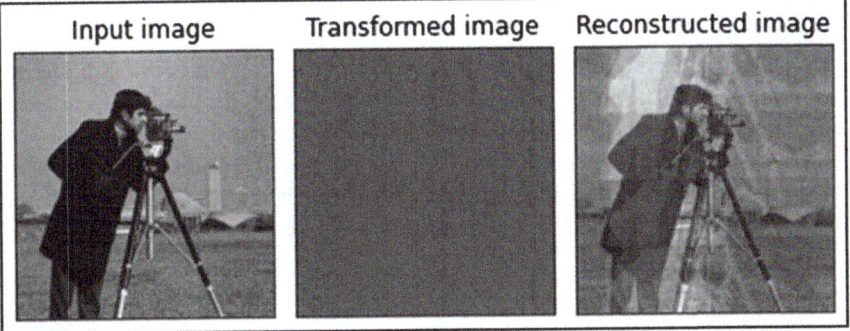

Fig. 3.57 Result of Python code shown in Fig. 3.56

Inferences

- The input image is a 256 × 256, grayscale "Cameraman" image.
- Upon taking forward Hadamard transform, the transform coefficients are obtained.
- In the transformed image, the first 50 rows are made zero; then the inverse Hadamard transform is taken to obtain the reconstructed image.
- The reconstructed image is distorted as expected. This is because the information contained in the first 50 rows is not preserved in the reconstructed image.

3.5   Radon Transform

Radon transform is a mapping from the Cartesian coordinate (x, y) to a distance and angle coordinate (ρ, θ) known as a polar coordinate. The Radon transform of the image $f(x, y)$ is represented as

$$R(\rho,\theta) = \int_{-\infty}^{\infty}\int_{-\infty}^{\infty} f(x,y)\delta(\rho - x\cos\theta - y\sin\theta)\,dxdy \qquad (3.33)$$

In the above expression,

$$\rho = x\cos\theta + y\sin\theta \qquad (3.34)$$

The discrete Radon transform of the image $f[m, n]$ is given by

$$R(\rho,\theta) = \sum_{m=0}^{N-1}\sum_{n=0}^{N-1} f[m,n]\delta(\rho - x\cos\theta - y\sin\theta) \qquad (3.35)$$

The Radon transform maps a 2D function $f(x, y)$ into a "Sinogram". Sinogram is a 2D function representing the original function $f(x, y)$ into the projection data space.

3.5.1   Inverse Radon Transform

One of the approach to obtain the image $f(x, y)$ from sinogram is through filtered back propagation. The back projection operation propagates the measured sinogram back into the image space along the projection paths. The reconstruction is based on Fourier Slice Theorem. According to the Fourier Slice Theorem, the 1D Fourier transform of the projection function is equal to the 2D Fourier transform of the image evaluated on the line that the projection was taken on.

3.5.2 Central Slice Theorem

The Central Slice Theorem, also termed as Projection-Slice Theorem or Fourier Slice Theorem, relates the Fourier transform of a projection to the Fourier transform of the original object.

The Fourier transform of the projection $(R(\rho, \theta))$ is represented as $G(\omega, \theta)$, which is represented as

$$G(\omega,\theta) = \int_{-\infty}^{\infty} R(\rho,\theta) e^{-j2\pi\rho\omega} d\rho \tag{3.36}$$

Substituting the expression for $R(\rho, \theta)$ from Eq. (3.33), we get

$$G(\omega,\theta) = \int_{-\infty}^{\infty} \int_{-\infty}^{\infty} \int_{-\infty}^{\infty} f(x,y) \delta(\rho - x\cos\theta - y\sin\theta) dx\, dy \left(e^{-j2\pi\rho\omega}\right) d\rho \tag{3.37}$$

Rearranging the above equation, we get

$$G(\omega,\theta) = \int_{-\infty}^{\infty} \left\{ \int_{-\infty}^{\infty} \int_{-\infty}^{\infty} f(x,y) \delta(\rho - x\cos\theta - y\sin\theta) dxdy \right\} e^{-j2\pi\rho\omega} d\rho \tag{3.38}$$

The above equation can be written as

$$G(\omega,\theta) = \int_{-\infty}^{\infty} \int_{-\infty}^{\infty} f(x,y) \left\{ \int_{-\infty}^{\infty} \delta(\rho - x\cos\theta - y\sin\theta) e^{-j2\pi\rho\omega} \right\} dxdy \tag{3.39}$$

The impulse function is represented as

$$\delta(\rho - x\cos\theta - y\sin\theta) = \begin{cases} 1, & \rho = x\cos\theta + y\sin\theta \\ 0, & \text{otherwise} \end{cases} \tag{3.40}$$

Evaluating the delta function in Eq. (3.39), we get

$$G(\omega,\theta) = \int_{-\infty}^{\infty} \int_{-\infty}^{\infty} f(x,y) e^{-j2\pi\omega(x\cos\theta + y\sin\theta)} dxdy \tag{3.41}$$

Substituting $u = \omega\cos\theta$ and $v = \omega\sin\theta$ in the above expression, we get

$$G(\omega,\theta) = \int_{-\infty}^{\infty} \int_{-\infty}^{\infty} f(x,y) e^{-j2\pi(ux+vy)} dxdy \tag{3.42}$$

The above expression is 2D-Fourier transform of $f(x, y)$ along the line $u = \omega\cos\theta$ and $v = \omega\sin\theta$.

Computing Inverse Radon transform involves the following steps:

1. Obtain Radon transform $R(\rho, \theta)$ of the input image $f(x, y)$.
2. Back project the Radon transform data.

3. Take the Fourier transform of back projected data.
4. Multiply the back projected data with the filter. Different filters include Ram-Lak filter, Shepp-Logan filter, Hamming filter, cosine filter, and so on.
5. Perform inverse Fourier transform to obtain the reconstructed image $\hat{f}(x,y)$.

Experiment 3.26: Computation of Sinogram
Obtain the sinogram of an image with a value of 255 at the centre, and all the other values are zero. It is a 2D impulse function that has a value of 255 at the centre, and at all other instances, it takes a value of zero.

The Python code that obtains the sinogram of the input signal specified in the problem statement is shown in Fig. 3.58, and the corresponding output is shown in Fig. 3.59.

```
# Radon Transform
import numpy as np
import matplotlib.pyplot as plt
from skimage.transform import radon
#Step 1: Generation of image
img=np.zeros([256,256])
img[128,128]=255
#Step 2: Obtaining the sinogram
theta = np.linspace(0., 180., max(img.shape), endpoint=False)
sinogram=radon(img,theta=theta)
#Step 3: Displaying the result
plt.subplot(1,2,1),plt.imshow(img,cmap='gray',interpolation='nearest', vmin=0, vmax=255)
plt.title('Image'),plt.axis('off'),plt.subplot(1,2,2),plt.imshow(sinogram,cmap='gray')
plt.title('Sinogram'),plt.axis('off'),plt.tight_layout()
```

Fig. 3.58 Python code for sinogram computation

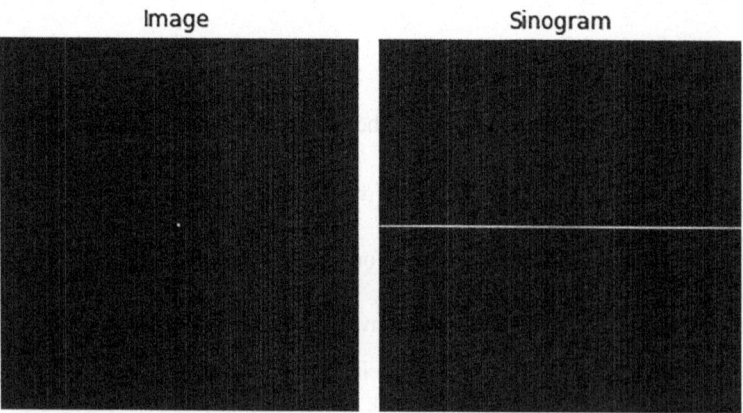

Fig. 3.59 Result of Python code shown in Fig. 3.58

```
import numpy as np
import matplotlib.pyplot as plt
from skimage.transform import radon
#Step 1: Generation of images
img1=np.zeros([256,256])
img1[128,:]=255
img2=np.zeros([256,256])
img2[:,128]=255
#Step 2: Obtaining the sinogram
theta = np.linspace(0., 180., max(img1.shape), endpoint=False)
sinogram1=radon(img1,theta=theta)
sinogram2=radon(img2,theta=theta)
#Step 3: Displaying the result
plt.subplot(1,4,1),plt.imshow(img1,cmap='gray'),plt.title('Image-1'),plt.axis('off')
plt.subplot(1,4,2),plt.imshow(sinogram1,cmap='gray',interpolation='nearest', vmin=0, vmax=255)
plt.title('Sinogram-1'),plt.xticks([]),plt.yticks([]),plt.subplot(1,4,3),plt.imshow(img2,cmap='gray')
plt.title('Image-2'),plt.axis('off'),plt.subplot(1,4,4),
plt.imshow(sinogram2,cmap='gray',interpolation='nearest', vmin=0, vmax=255)
plt.title('Sinogram-2'),plt.xticks([]),plt.yticks([])
plt.tight_layout()
```

Fig. 3.60   Python code to obtain the sinogram of horizontal line

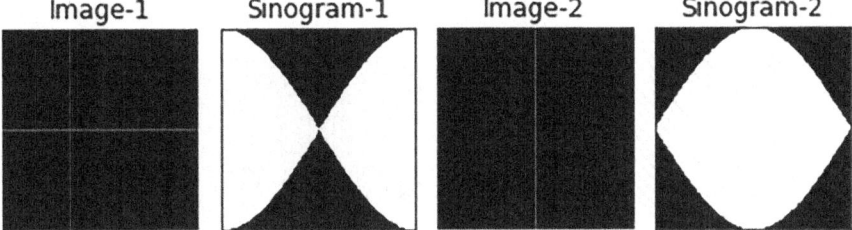

Fig. 3.61   Result of Python code shown in Fig. 3.60

Experiment 3.27: Computation of Sinogram of Two Different Line Images
Generate two images, the first image is a horizontal line image on a black background and the second is a vertical line image on a black background. For the generated images, obtain the sinogram and comment on the observed result.

The Python code that generates a horizontal white line on a black background and obtains the sinogram of the generated image is given in Fig. 3.60, and the corresponding output is shown in Fig. 3.61.

Inference

- From Fig. 3.61, it is possible to observe sinusoidal oscillation pattern in the sinogram for the horizontal and the vertical lines.

```
import numpy as np
import matplotlib.pyplot as plt
from skimage.transform import radon
#Step 1: Generation of sinusoidal grating
sz=[256,256]    #Size of the image
phi=np.pi/4    #Phase angle
radius = (int(sz[0]/2.0), int(sz[1]/2.0))
theta = np.pi/4
omega = [np.cos(theta), np.sin(theta)]
[x, y] = np.meshgrid(range(-radius[0], radius[0]+1), range(-radius[1], radius[1]+1))
sine_grating = np.cos(omega[0] * x  + omega[1] * y + phi)
#Step 2: Sinogram of sinusoidal grating
theta = np.linspace(0., 180., max(sine_grating.shape), endpoint=False)
sinogram=radon(sine_grating,theta)
#Step 3: Displaying the results
plt.subplot(1,2,1),plt.imshow(sine_grating,cmap='gray'),plt.title('Image-1'),plt.xticks([]),
plt.yticks([]),plt.subplot(1,2,2),
plt.imshow(sinogram,cmap='gray',interpolation='nearest', vmin=0, vmax=255)
plt.title('Sinogram-1'),plt.axis('off'),plt.tight_layout()
```

Fig. 3.62 Python code for sinogram of sinusoidal grating pattern

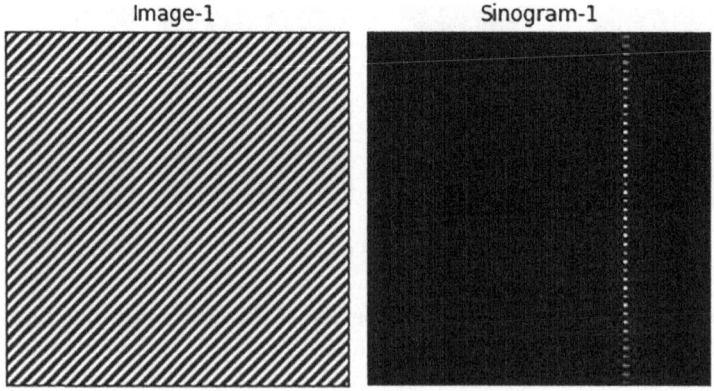

Fig. 3.63 Sinogram of sinusoidal grating

Experiment 3.28: Sinogram of Sinusoidal grating Pattern

The objective of this experiment is to obtain the sinogram of sinusoidal grating pattern. The Python code that performs this task is shown in Fig. 3.62, and the corresponding output is shown in Fig. 3.63.

Inference

- The sinogram of sinusoidal grating pattern results in a straight line.

Experiment 3.29: Inverse Radon Transform Through Filtered Back Projection Algorithm

Generate a circle image on a black background. This is the input image. For this image, obtain the sinogram of the image using forward Radon transform. After obtaining the sinogram, obtain the inverse Radon transform using a filtered back projection algorithm for different projection angles.

The built-in function "radon" and "iradon" available in the "skimage" library is used to obtain the sinogram and the reconstructed image. The following steps are involved in performing the desired task:

Step 1: Generation of the test image.

Step 2: Obtaining the sinogram of the test image using the built-in function "radon" available in the "skimage" library. Here, the projection angle varies from 45°, 90°, and 180°.

Step 3: Obtain the inverse Radon transform for different projection angle using the built-in function "iradon".

Step 4: Use subplot to display the input image and the reconstructed images.

The Python code that performs the above-mentioned tasks is shown in Fig. 3.64, and the corresponding output is shown in Fig. 3.65.

Inferences

From Fig. 3.65, the following inferences can be drawn:

- The input image is a white circle on a black background.
- In the figure, "RI" stands for "Reconstructed Image" for different projections. Different projection angles chosen in this experiment are 45°, 90°, and 180°.
- As the number of projections (the length of theta) increases, the reconstructed image more accurately approximates the original image.
- The vector theta must contain monotonically increasing angular values with a constant incremental angle. The filter chosen for reconstruction is ramp filter. Other filter options include "cosine", "Hamming", and "Hanning" filters.

3.6 Hough Transform

Hough transform is widely used to detect shapes such as lines, circles, and ellipses in images. The Hough transform was introduced by Paul Hough in 1962. Hough transform is a mapping from Cartesian coordinate to Polar coordinate. The polar coordinate is termed as "parameter plane" or "parameter space". A line in the Cartesian plane is a point in the parameter plane. Similarly, a point in the Cartesian plane is a line in the parameter plane.

```
#Image reconstruction from projection
import numpy as np
import matplotlib.pyplot as plt
from skimage.transform import radon,iradon
#Step 1: Generation of test image
img=np.zeros([256,256])
m,n=np.shape(img)
r=40
for i in range(0,m):
    for j in range(0,n):
        if (i-128)**2+(j-128)**2<=r**2:
            img[i,j]=255
#Step 2: Obtaining the Radon transform
theta1 = np.linspace(0.,45., max(img.shape), endpoint=False)
theta2 = np.linspace(0.,90., max(img.shape), endpoint=False)
theta3 = np.linspace(0.,180., max(img.shape), endpoint=False)
sinogram1=radon(img,theta1)
sinogram2=radon(img,theta2)
sinogram3=radon(img,theta3)
#Step 3: Image reconstruction
r_img1 = iradon(sinogram1, theta=theta1, filter_name='ramp')
r_img2 = iradon(sinogram2, theta=theta2, filter_name='ramp')
r_img3 = iradon(sinogram3, theta=theta3, filter_name='ramp')
#Step 4: Displaying the results
plt.subplot(1,4,1),plt.imshow(img,cmap='gray'),plt.title('Input image'),
plt.axis('off'),plt.subplot(1,4,2),plt.imshow(r_img1,cmap='gray')
plt.title('RI:'r'$\theta=45^0$'),plt.xticks([]),plt.yticks([])
plt.subplot(1,4,3),plt.imshow(r_img2,cmap='gray'),plt.title('RI:' r'$\theta=90^0$'),
plt.xticks([]),plt.yticks([]),plt.subplot(1,4,4),plt.imshow(r_img3,cmap='gray')
plt.title('RI:'r'$\theta=180^0$'),plt.xticks([]),plt.yticks([])
plt.tight_layout()
```

Fig. 3.64 Python code to obtain reconstructed image from different projections

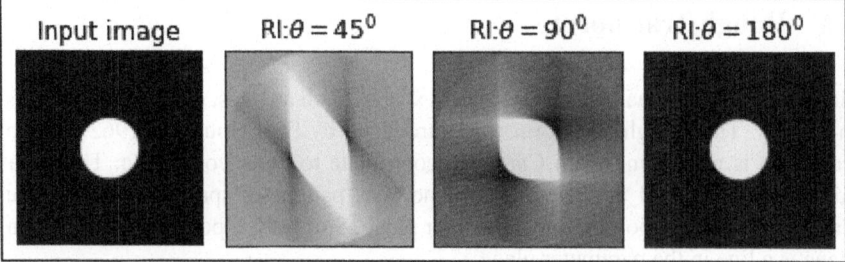

Fig. 3.65 Reconstructed image from different projection angle

3.6.1 Line Detection

The equation of a straight line in the image space with slope "m" and y-intercept "b" is given by

$$y = mx + b \qquad (3.43)$$

The expression of the line in polar coordinate is given by

$$\rho = x\cos(\theta) + y\sin(\theta) \qquad (3.44)$$

In the above equation, "ρ" is the norm distance of the line from origin and "θ" is the angle between the norm and the horizontal x-axis. This is illustrated in Fig. 3.66. The angle "θ" in polar coordinate takes a value in the range of $-90°$ to $+90°$. The maximum norm distance is expressed as

$$\rho_{max} = \sqrt{x^2 + y^2} \qquad (3.45)$$

Steps followed in Hough transform in line detection are summarized as follows: Extract the edges of the image using a suitable edge detection algorithm.

Step 1: Initialize the parameter space "r"s and "θ"s.
Step 2: Create the accumulator array and initialize it to zero.
Step 3: For each edge pixel.
Step 4: For each theta (θ).
Step 5: Compute $r = x*\cos(\theta) + y*\sin(\theta)$.
Step 6: Increment the accumulator at "r" and "θ".
Step 7: Find maximum values in the accumulator that correspond to the line.

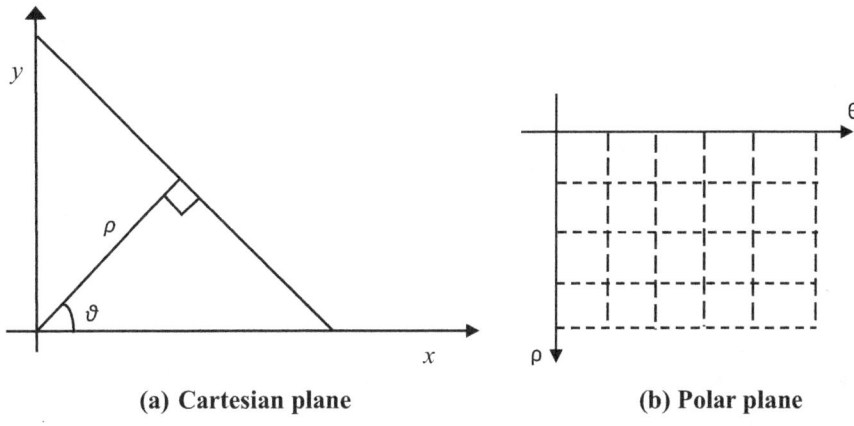

(a) Cartesian plane   **(b) Polar plane**

Fig. 3.66 Straight line in Cartesian and polar coordinate: (**a**) Cartesian plane, (**b**) polar plane

Experiment 3.30: Hough Transform Without Built-in Function

This experiment deals with the implementation of Hough transform without built-in function. For this, a test image with the size of 50 × 50 with all the pixels are black except the centre pixel (25, 25), which is white. The image can be considered as a 2D impulse signal. The generated 2D impulse signal is applied to Hough transform to obtain the Hough transform result.

The steps involved in implementing the task expressed in experiment are as follows:

Step 1: Generation of test image.
Step 2: Obtaining the Hough transform of the test image.
Step 3: Displaying the results.

The Python code that performs these steps is given in Fig. 3.67, and the corresponding output is shown in Fig. 3.68.

Inference

- A point in the image plane (Cartesian coordinate) is mapped to a curve in the parameter space (Hough space).

```
import numpy as np
import matplotlib.pyplot as plt
#Step 1: Generation of test image
img = np.zeros((50,50))
img[25,25] = 255
#Step 2: Obtaining the Hough transform
Ny = img.shape[0]
Nx = img.shape[1]
Maxdist = int(np.round(np.sqrt(Nx**2 + Ny ** 2)))
thetas = np.deg2rad(np.arange(-180, 180))
rs = np.linspace(-Maxdist, Maxdist, 2*Maxdist)
acc = np.zeros((2 * Maxdist, len(thetas)))
for y in range(Ny):
    for x in range(Nx):
        if img[y,x] > 0:
            for k in range(len(thetas)):
                r = x*np.cos(thetas[k]) + y * np.sin(thetas[k])
                acc[int(r) + Maxdist,k] += 1
#Step 3: Displaying the results
plt.subplot(1,2,1),plt.imshow(img,cmap='gray'),plt.title('Test image'),plt.axis('off')
plt.subplot(1,2,2),plt.imshow(acc,cmap='gray'),plt.title('Hough transform'),
plt.axis('off'),plt.tight_layout()
```

Fig. 3.67 Python code to obtain the Hough transform of test image

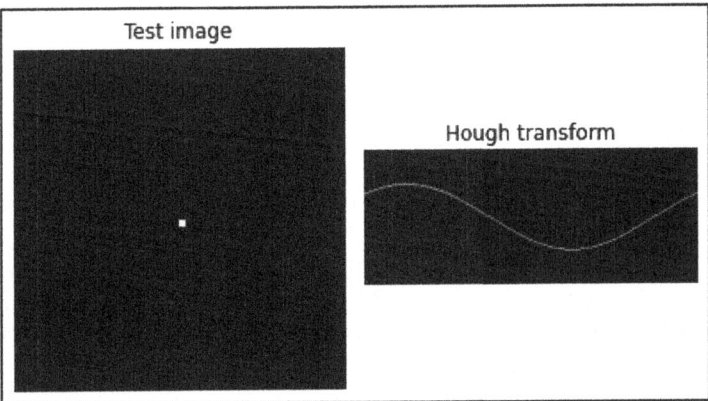

Fig. 3.68 Result of Python code shown in Fig. 3.67

Experiment 3.31: Hough Transform Without Built-in Function

Generate a 50 × 50 black image with a white vertical line. Obtain the Hough transform of the generated image and comment on the observed result. The Python code that performs the mentioned task is given in Fig. 3.69, and the corresponding output is shown in Fig. 3.70.

Inferences

- From Fig. 3.69, it is possible to observe that logarithm operation is performed in the accumulator value to compress the dynamic range.
- From Fig. 3.70, it can be inferred that the generated image corresponds to a vertical line, which produces a bright spot in the Hough space.

Experiment 3.32: Hough Transform Using Built-in Function from Skimage Library

Generate two test images. Test Images 1 and 2 are diagonal lines on a black background. Obtain the Hough transform of the generated images. Plot the images and the corresponding Hough transform and comment on the observed result. The Python code that generates the test images and the corresponding Hough transform is shown in Fig. 3.71, and the corresponding output is shown in Fig. 3.72.

Inference

- From Fig. 3.72, it is possible to observe that the test image has two diagonal lines on a black background, and the corresponding Hough transform shows peaks in two different locations corresponding to the lines.

Experiment 3.33: Counting the Number of Lines in the Image Using Hough Transform

Write a Python code to generate 10 vertical lines on a black background. Use Hough transform to compute the number of lines in the image. Comment on the observed result.

```
import numpy as np
import matplotlib.pyplot as plt
#Step 1: Generation of test image
img = np.zeros((50,50))
img[:,25] = 255
#Step 2: Obtaining the Hough transform
Ny = img.shape[0]
Nx = img.shape[1]
Maxdist = int(np.round(np.sqrt(Nx**2 + Ny ** 2)))
thetas = np.deg2rad(np.arange(-90, 90))
rs = np.linspace(-Maxdist, Maxdist, 2*Maxdist)
acc = np.zeros((2 * Maxdist, len(thetas)))
for y in range(Ny):
    for x in range(Nx):
        if img[y,x] > 0:
            for k in range(len(thetas)):
                r = x*np.cos(thetas[k]) + y * np.sin(thetas[k])
                acc[int(r) + Maxdist,k] += 1
#Step 3: Displaying the results
plt.subplot(1,2,1),plt.imshow(img,cmap='gray'),plt.title('Test image'),plt.xticks([]),
plt.yticks([]),plt.subplot(1,2,2),plt.imshow(np.log10(1+acc),cmap='gray')
plt.title('Hough transform'),plt.xticks([]),plt.yticks([])
plt.tight_layout()
```

Fig. 3.69 Hough transform of a vertical line

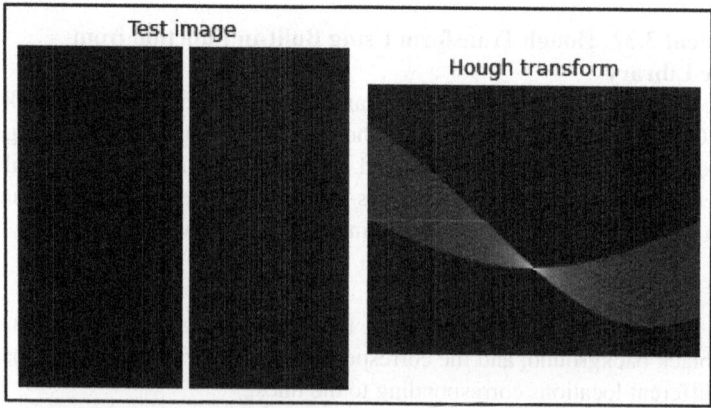

Fig. 3.70 Result of Python code shown in Fig. 3.69

```
from skimage.transform import hough_line
import numpy as np
import matplotlib.pyplot as plt
#Step 1: Generation of test images
img1=np.zeros([256,256])
img2=np.zeros([256,256])
m,n=img1.shape
for i in range(0,m):
   for j in range(0,n):
      if (i==j):
         img1[i,j]=1
for i in range(0,m):
   for j in range(0,n):
      if (i==256-j):
         img2[i,j]=1
#Step 2: Obtaining the Hough transform
angle=np.linspace(-np.pi/2,np.pi/2,360,endpoint=False)
h1, theta1, d1 = hough_line(img1, angle)
h2, theta2, d2 = hough_line(img2, angle)
#Step 3: Displaying the results
fig=plt.figure(figsize=(8,6)),plt.subplot(1,4,1),plt.imshow(img1,cmap='gray'),
plt.title('Test Image -1'),plt.xticks([]),plt.yticks([]),plt.subplot(1,4,2),
plt.imshow(np.log(1+h1),cmap='gray'),plt.title('Hough transform of Image-1'),plt.xticks([]),
plt.yticks([]),plt.subplot(1,4,3),plt.imshow(img2,cmap='gray'),plt.title('Test Image -2'),
plt.xticks([]),plt.yticks([]),plt.subplot(1,4,4),plt.imshow(np.log(1+h2),cmap='gray'),
plt.title('Hough transform of Image-2'),plt.xticks([]),plt.yticks([]),plt.tight_layout()
```

Fig. 3.71 Generation of test images and obtaining their Hough transform

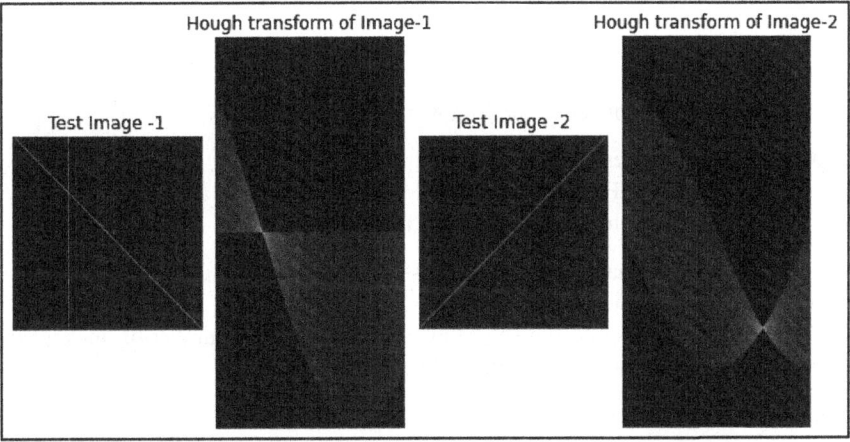

Fig. 3.72 Test images and their Hough transform

```
from skimage.transform import hough_line
import numpy as np
import matplotlib.pyplot as plt
#Step 1: Generation of test image
img=np.zeros([256,256])
img[:,10:255:26]=1
plt.imshow(img,cmap='gray'),plt.title('Input Image'),
plt.xticks([]),plt.yticks([])
#Step 2:Hough transform
angle=np.linspace(-np.pi/2,np.pi/2,360,endpoint=False)
h, theta, d = hough_line(img, angle)
#Step 3: To compute the number of lines
count = (h == 256).sum();
```

Fig. 3.73 Python code to compute the number of lines in the image

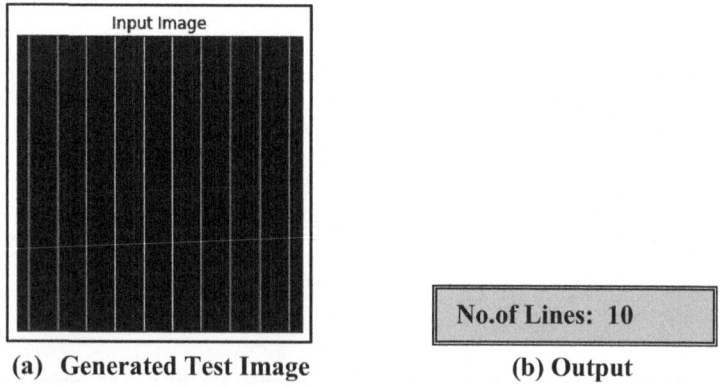

(a) **Generated Test Image**   **(b) Output**

Fig. 3.74 Simulation result: (a) generated test image, (b) output

The given task comprises of the following three steps:

Step 1: Generation of test image.
Step 2: Computing the Hough transform of the test image.
Step 3: To count the number of lines in the image.

The Python code that performs this task is shown in Fig. 3.73 and the corresponding output is shown in Fig. 3.74.

Upon executing the code shown in Fig. 3.73, the count of number of lines given in Figure 3.74a is 10, which is resulted in Figure 3.74b.

Inferences

- The built-in functions used in Fig. 3.73 is given in Table 3.1.
- From Figure 3.74a, it is possible to observe that the generated test image has 10 vertical lines.

Table 3.1 Built-in functions used in the program

S. no.	Built-in function	Library	Purpose
1	Hough_line	Skimage.Transform	To detect the straight lines in the given image
2	Zeros	Numpy	To create matrix of zeros
3	Sum	Numpy	To obtain the count of given number

```
from skimage.transform import hough_line
import numpy as np
import matplotlib.pyplot as plt
#Step 1: Generation of test image
img=np.zeros([256,256])
img[:,10:255:26]=1
img[10:255:26,:]=1
plt.imshow(img,cmap='gray'),plt.title('Input Image')
plt.xticks([]),plt.yticks([])
#Step 2:Hough transform
angle=np.linspace(-np.pi/2,np.pi/2,360,endpoint=False)
h, theta, d = hough_line(img, angle)
#Step 3: To compute the number of lines
count = (h == 256).sum()
print('No.of Lines: ',count);
```

Fig. 3.75 Python code to perform the desired task

- Upon executing the code, the number of lines generated by the code is 10, which is in agreement with the visual result shown in Figure 3.74b.

Experiment 3.34: Modify the code given in Experiment 3.33 to generate both horizontal and vertical lines in the black background. Now, the total number of lines generated is 20. Comment on the observed output.
The Python code that performs the above-mentioned task is shown in Fig. 3.75, and the corresponding output is shown in Fig. 3.76.

Inferences

- From Fig. 3.75, the code is intended to generate both horizontal and vertical lines.
- From Figure 3.76a, it is verified that the code generates both horizontal and vertical lines.
- Now, the test image has 10 horizontal lines and 10 vertical lines. Hence, the total number of lines should be 20, which is verified from Figure 3.76b.

3.6.2 *Hough Transform to Detect Circle in the Image*

Circles are a common geometric structure of interest in computer vision applications. The equation of a circle in the Cartesian plane is expressed as

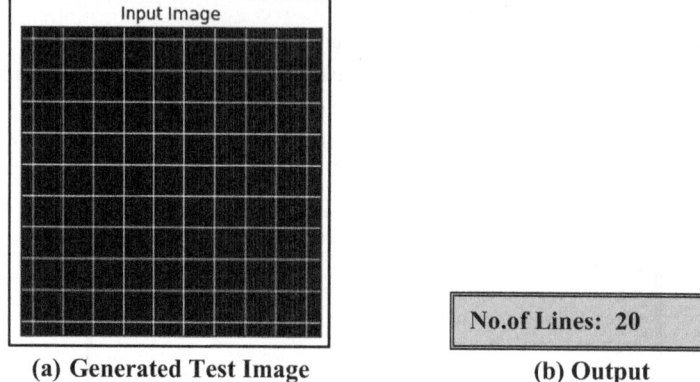

(a) Generated Test Image   (b) Output

Fig. 3.76 Simulation result: (**a**) generated test image, (**b**) output

$$(x-a)^2 + (y-b)^2 = r^2 \qquad (3.46)$$

In Eq. (3.46), "a" and "b" represent the centre of the circle and "r" represents the radius of the circle. The equation of the circle in the parameter plane is given by

$$x = a + r\cos(\theta) \qquad (3.47)$$

$$y = b + r\sin(\theta) \qquad (3.48)$$

The circle detection problem is reduced to a triplet (a, b, and r) search problem. The angle (θ) sweeps through the full 360° range of the points (x, y).

The pseudo-code for circle detection using Hough transform is given as follows:

- Initialize the accumulator ($H[a, b, r]$) to all zeros.
- Find the edge image using any edge detector.
- For $r = 0$ to diagonal image length.
- For each edge pixel (x, y) in the image.
- For $\theta = 0$ to 360°.
- $a = x - r*\cos\theta$,
- $b = y - r*\sin\theta$,
- $H[a, b, r] = H[a, b, r] + 1$.
- Find the [a, b, r] value(s), where $H[a, b, r]$ is above a suitable threshold value.

Experiment 3.35: Circles Detection Using Hough Transform

The objective of this experiment is to detect the circle present in the test image. The built-in function "HoughCircles" in "cv2" library is utilized to detect the circle in the image. The Python code that performs this task is shown in Fig. 3.77, and the corresponding output is shown in Fig. 3.78.

The built-in function used in the program are summarized in Table 3.2.

```
import numpy as np
import cv2
import matplotlib.pyplot as plt
img = cv2.imread('Coin.png');# Read image
img = cv2.medianBlur(img,3);# Smooth it
img_copy = img.copy()
img_gray = cv2.cvtColor(img_copy,cv2.COLOR_BGR2GRAY);# Convert to grayscale
# Apply Hough transform to greyscale image
circles = cv2.HoughCircles(img_gray,cv2.HOUGH_GRADIENT,1,40,
            param1=160,param2=55,minRadius=0,maxRadius=0)
circles = np.uint16(np.around(circles))
# Draw the circles
for i in circles[0,:]:
    cv2.circle(img_copy,(i[0],i[1]),i[2],(255,0,0),5); # draw the outer circle
    cv2.circle(img_copy,(i[0],i[1]),2,(0,0,255),10);# draw the center of the circle
plt.subplot(1,2,1),plt.imshow(img),plt.title('Input image'),plt.xticks([]),plt.yticks([])
plt.subplot(1,2,2),plt.imshow(img_copy),plt.title('Detected circles'), plt.xticks([]),
plt.yticks([]),plt.tight_layout()
```

Fig. 3.77 Python code to detect circle in the test image

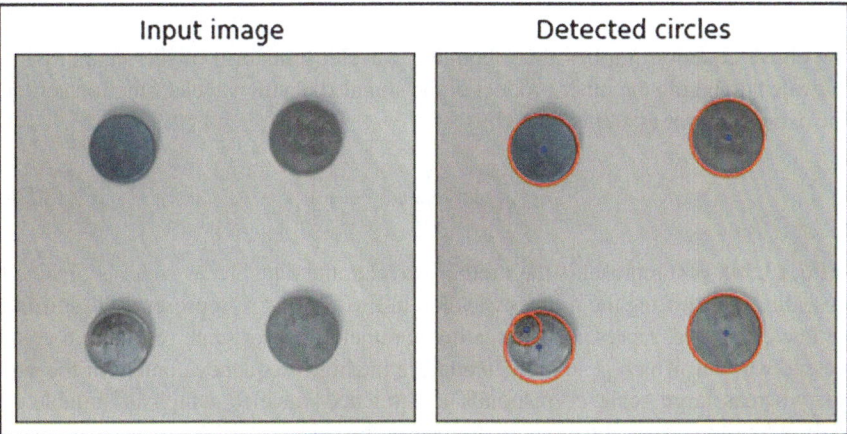

Fig. 3.78 Result of circle detection program

The variable "param1" is the first parameter, which is the higher threshold passed to the Canny edge detector. In Experiment 3.35, "param1" is chosen as 160, whereas "param2" is the accumulator threshold for the circle centres. In this experiment, it is chosen as 55.

From Fig. 3.78, it is possible to observe that the input test image has four coins and all four coins are detected by the Hough transform. The detected circle is shown in red, and the centre of the circle is marked in blue.

Table 3.2 Built-in functions used in the program

S. no.	Built-in function	Library	Purpose
1	Imread	cv2	To read the input test image
2	Median blur	cv2	To minimize the impact of salt and pepper noise in the digital image
3	HoughCircles	cv2	Hough transform to detect the circle in the image
4	HoughGradient	cv2	The edge image is calculated using canny edge detector. The gradient information is computed using the Sobel operator.
5	Circle	cv2	To draw a circle on any image

3.7   Wavelet Transform

Wavelets are oscillatory functions of finite duration. Wavelet transform provides localization in both the spatial domain as well as in the frequency domain. It can perform multi-resolution analysis of the signal. The main advantage of wavelet transforms is the ability to obtain information on the time, location, and frequency of a signal simultaneously. The wavelet transform of the signal $x(t)$ is given by

$$W_x(a,b) = \langle x(t), \psi_{a,b}(t) \rangle \tag{3.49}$$

The above equation implies that obtaining wavelet transform of the signal $x(t)$ is equivalent to taking the inner product of the signal $x(t)$ with wavelet function $\psi_{a,b}(t)$. The expression for $\psi_{a,b}(t)$ is given by

$$\psi_{a,b}(t) = \frac{1}{\sqrt{a}} \psi\left(\frac{t-b}{a}\right) \tag{3.50}$$

In Eq. (3.50), $\psi(t)$ represents the mother wavelet, the daughter wavelet is obtained by scaling and shifting the mother wavelet. In Eq. (3.50), "b" represents the shifting parameter and "a" represents the scaling parameter. Lower scale results in a compressed wavelet, which is suitable to analyse the high-frequency content of the signal, whereas large scale corresponds to stretched wavelet, which is suitable to analyse low-frequency information content in the signal.

Two broad categories of wavelet transform are (1) continuous wavelet transform and (2) discrete wavelet transform. Continuous wavelet transform (CWT) takes every possible set of scale and translation parameter value. Hence, it is a redundant transform. In discrete wavelet transform (DWT), the scaling and shifting are chosen to the power of 2, which is termed as "dyadic scaling and shifting". DWT can be realized through filterbank or lifting scheme. Multi-level wavelet analysis of the signal is shown in Fig. 3.79.

In Fig. 3.79, A_1 and D_1 represent the approximation and detail in the first level of decomposition. A_2 and D_2 represent the approximation and detail in the second level of decomposition and so on. Here, the approximation and details are the subbands

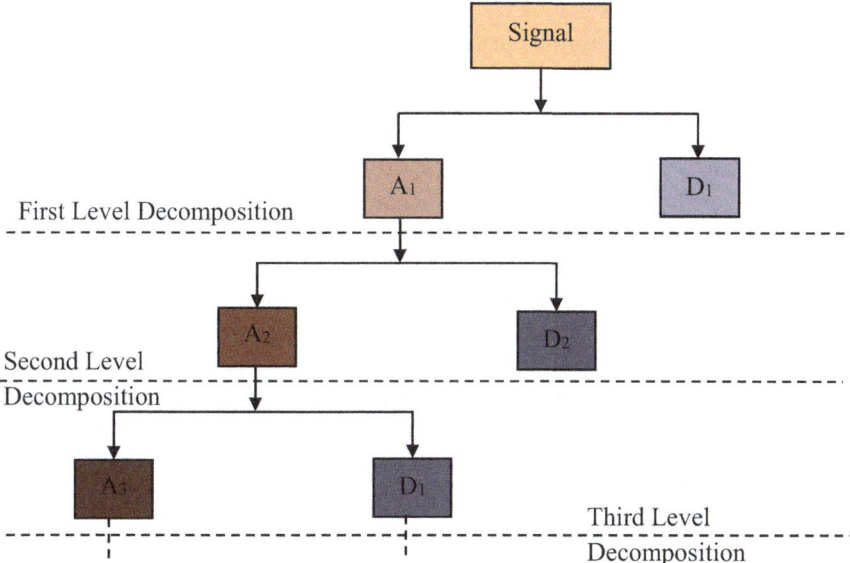

Fig. 3.79 Multi-level decomposition of the signal

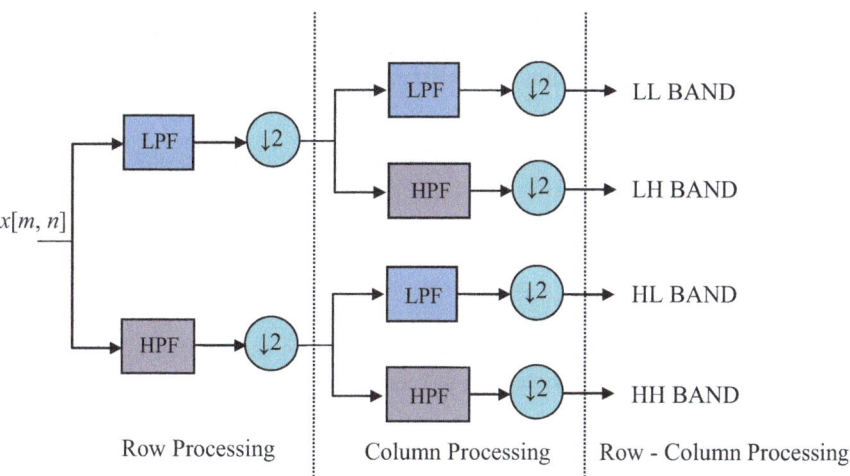

Fig. 3.80 First-level wavelet decomposition of 2D signal

of the signal. In wavelet transform, successive decomposition is performed in the approximation with the assumption that much of the signal energy is in approximation. For a 2D signal, the subbands obtained using filterbank is shown in Fig. 3.80.

In Fig. 3.80, $x[m, n]$ represents the input 2D signal, h_0 and h_1 represent the low- and high-pass filters. After first level decomposition, the input signal $x[m, n]$ is decomposed into four subbands: *LL, LH, HL,* and *HH*. Here, *LL* band represents the approximation, *LH* represents the vertical detail, *HL* represents the horizontal detail, and *HH* represents the diagonal detail. The signal is decomposed into subbands through wavelet filters.

Important wavelet families include Haar, Daubechies, Symlet, Coiflet, and biorthogonal wavelets. Wavelet selection for a particular application depends on properties of wavelets such as orthogonal, symmetry, vanishing moments, regularity, and so on. Orthogonal basis allows one to reconstruct the signal from its transform coefficients by summing the basis functions weighted by the transform coefficients. The regularity of wavelet is associated with the rate of decay of scaling functions and ultimately with the number of vanishing moments of scaling and wavelet functions.

In Table 3.3, the terms "*d*" and "*r*" represent decomposition and reconstruction, respectively. *Nr*, *N*, *Nd* refer to the order.

Wavelet transform has good energy compaction, which implies that the signal energy is concentrated in a small fraction of wavelet coefficients. This sparse representation property of wavelet transform makes it a good tool for data compression and denoising. Wavelet transform is used in JPEG 2000 compression standard.

3.7.1   PyWavelets

PyWavelets is a free Open Source library for wavelet transforms in Python. PyWavelet is a Python package to implement continuous and discrete wavelet transform. A wide variety of predefined wavelets are provided and it is possible for users to specify custom wavelet filter banks.

Experiment 3.36: First-Level Wavelet Decomposition of the Image
Read an input image and perform first-level wavelet decomposition of the image using the "Haar" wavelet. Perform inverse wavelet transform to obtain the reconstructed image. Display the input image, first-level wavelet coefficients (approximation, horizontal detail, vertical detail, and diagonal detail), and the reconstructed image. Comment on the observed result.

The Python library "pywavelet" is used to perform the image decomposition using the "Haar" wavelet. The steps in the code are as follows:

Table 3.3 Wavelet families and its properties

S. no.	Wavelet family	Member of wavelet	Orthogonal	Compact support	Filter length	Vanishing moment
1	Daubechies	"db1" to "db45"	Yes	Yes	2N	N
2	Coiflet	Coif1, Coif5	Yes	Yes	6N	2N-1
3	Symlet	"sym1", "sym45"	Yes	Yes	2N	N
4	Biorthogonal	"bior3.5", "bior3.3", "bior3.7"	No	Yes	$Max(2N_r, 2N_d) + 2$	N_r

Table 3.4 Built-in functions to perform wavelet decomposition and reconstruction

S. no.	Built-in function	Library	Purpose
1	dwt2	Pywt	To perform wavelet decomposition of the input image
2	idwt2	Pywt	To perform inverse wavelet transform of the wavelet coefficients

```
#Wavelet decomposition of the image
import matplotlib.pyplot as plt
import pywt
import cv2
#Step 1: Reading the input image
img = cv2.imread('apple.jpg',0)
fig=plt.figure(figsize=(8,4)),plt.figure,plt.subplot(2,3,1),plt.imshow(img,cmap='gray'),
plt.title('Input image'),plt.xticks([]),plt.yticks([])
#Step 2: Performing Wavelet Decomposition
coeffs = pywt.dwt2(img, 'haar')
cA, (cH, cV, cD) = coeffs
plt.subplot(2,3,2),plt.imshow(cA,cmap='gray'),plt.title('Approximation (LL)'),
plt.xticks([]),plt.yticks([]),plt.subplot(2,3,3),plt.imshow(cH,cmap='gray'),
plt.title('Horizontal detail (LH)'),plt.xticks([]),plt.yticks([])
plt.subplot(2,3,4),plt.imshow(cV,cmap='gray'),plt.title('Vertical detail (HL)'),
plt.xticks([]),plt.yticks([]),plt.subplot(2,3,5),plt.imshow(cD,cmap='gray'),
plt.title('Diagonal detail (HH)'),plt.xticks([]),plt.yticks([])
#Step 3: Inverse Wavelet transform
img_r=pywt.idwt2(coeffs,'haar')
plt.subplot(2,3,6),plt.imshow(img_r,cmap='gray'),plt.title('Reconstructed image'),
plt.xticks([]),plt.yticks([]),plt.tight_layout()
```

Fig. 3.81 Python code to perform wavelet decomposition and reconstruction

Step 1: Reading the input image.
Step 2: Perform first-level wavelet decomposition.
Step 3: Perform inverse wavelet transform to obtain the reconstructed image.

The built-in functions used in the program are given in Table 3.4.

The Python code that performs the desired task is shown in Fig. 3.81, and the corresponding output is shown in Fig. 3.82.

Inferences

- The input image is an "apple" image. The size of the input image is 277×432. It is a rectangular array of pixels.
- Upon performing first-level wavelet decomposition, one gets approximation, as well as horizontal, vertical, and diagonal details.
- The approximation is a low-pass filtered image; hence, it resembles the input image. The details are high-pass/band-pass filtered image.
- Since all the coefficients are used to obtain the reconstructed image, the reconstructed image resembles the input image.

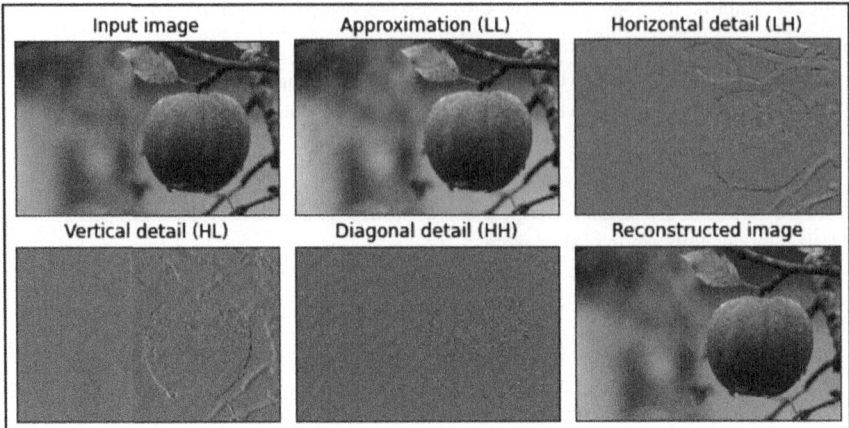

Fig. 3.82 Simulation result

Experiment 3.37: Analysing the Impact of Zeroing the Wavelet Coefficients
Read an input image and perform first-level wavelet decomposition using
"Daubechies" wavelet. After performing first-level wavelet decomposition, four
subbands are obtained, which are an approximation, horizontal detail, vertical
detail, and diagonal detail. This experiment studies the impact of zeroing the
approximation, horizontal, vertical, and diagonal details.

The Python code that performs the first-level wavelet decomposition and analyses the impact of zeroing the approximation, horizontal, vertical, and diagonal detail
is shown in Fig. 3.83, and the corresponding output is shown in Fig. 3.84.

Inferences

- The first-level wavelet decomposition of the input "crow" image is done using
  Daubechies wavelet (db4).
- Figure 3.84 shows the reconstructed image by nullifying the approximation,
  horizontal, and vertical details. In this figure, "RI" represents the reconstructed image.
- From Fig. 3.84, it is possible to infer that zeroing the approximation coefficients
  leads to the loss of all the image information because much of the information in
  the image is in low-frequency coefficients. Nullifying the horizontal, vertical,
  and diagonal details has less impact on the reconstructed image.
- From Fig. 3.84, it is possible to observe that by retaining all the wavelet coefficients, the output image resembles the input image, which implies that the wavelet transform is reversible. Wavelet coefficients can exactly reconstruct the image.

Experiment 3.38: Multi-Level Wavelet Decomposition
The multi-level wavelet decomposition can be performed using the built-in function
"wavedec2" available in the "pywt" library. Perform second-level wavelet

```
import matplotlib.pyplot as plt
import pywt
import cv2
#Step 1: Reading the input image
img = cv2.imread('crow.jpg',0)
fig=plt.figure(figsize=(6,4)),plt.subplot(2,3,1),plt.imshow(img,cmap='gray'),
plt.title('Input image'),plt.xticks([]),plt.yticks([])
#Step 2: Performing Wavelet Decomposition
cA,(cH,cV,cD)= pywt.dwt2(img, 'db4')
#Step 3: Nullifying the wavelet coefficients
rimg1=pywt.idwt2((None,(cH,cV,cD)),'db4')
rimg2=pywt.idwt2((cA,(None,cV,cD)),'db4')
rimg3=pywt.idwt2((cA,(cH,None,cD)),'db4')
rimg4=pywt.idwt2((cA,(cH,cV,None)),'db4')
rimg=pywt.idwt2((cA,(cH,cV,cD)),'db4')
plt.subplot(2,3,2),plt.imshow(rimg1,cmap='gray'),plt.title('RI:Zeroing LL'),plt.xticks([]),
plt.yticks([]),plt.subplot(2,3,3),plt.imshow(rimg2,cmap='gray'),plt.title('RI:Zeroing LH'),
plt.xticks([]),plt.yticks([]),plt.subplot(2,3,4),plt.imshow(rimg3,cmap='gray'),
plt.title('RI:Zeroing HL'),plt.xticks([]),plt.yticks([]),plt.subplot(2,3,5),
plt.imshow(rimg4,cmap='gray'),plt.title('RI:Zeroing HH'),plt.xticks([]),plt.yticks([])
plt.subplot(2,3,6),plt.imshow(rimg,cmap='gray'),plt.title('RI:using all coefficients'),
plt.xticks([]),plt.yticks([]),plt.tight_layout()
```

Fig. 3.83 Python code to analyse the impact of zeroing the wavelet coefficients

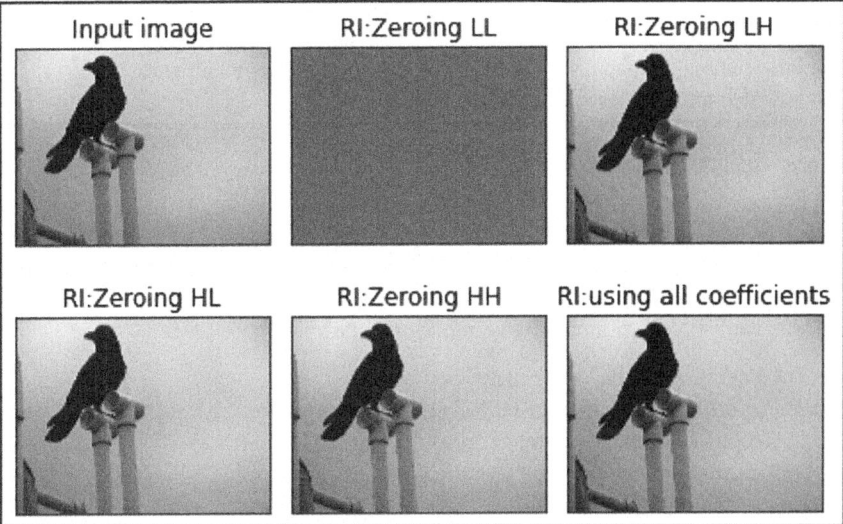

Fig. 3.84 Input and reconstructed images by nullifying the wavelet coefficients

Table 3.5 Built-in functions used in the program and its purpose

S. no.	Built-in function	Library	Purpose
1	wavedec2	Pywt	To perform 2D multi-level wavelet decomposition of the input image
2	waverec2	Pywt	To perform 2D multi-level inverse wavelet transform
3	coeffs_to_array	Pywt	Concatenation of wavelet coefficients into an array

```
#Multi-level wavelet decomposition
import numpy as np
import matplotlib.pyplot as plt
import pywt
#Step 1: Test image generation
x = np.arange(0,2,(1/128))
y = np.arange(0,2,(1/128))
xv,yv = np.meshgrid(x,y)
img = 0.5 + 0.5*np.cos(64*np.pi*((xv)**2 + (yv-1)**2))
#Step 2: Performing second level wavelet decomposition
coeffs=pywt.wavedec2(img, wavelet='haar', mode='periodization',level=2)
#Step 3: Displaying the wavelet decomposed image
arr,coeff_slices=pywt.coeffs_to_array(coeffs)
#Step 4: Reconstruction of the image
img_r=pywt.waverec2(coeffs,'haar',mode='periodization')
plt.subplot(1,3,1),plt.imshow(img,cmap='gray'),plt.title('Input image'),
plt.xticks([]),plt.yticks([]),plt.subplot(1,3,2),plt.imshow(arr,cmap='gray')
plt.title('Subbands'),plt.xticks([]),plt.yticks([]),plt.subplot(1,3,3),
plt.imshow(img_r,cmap='gray'),plt.title('Reconstructed image'),plt.xticks([]),
plt.yticks([]),plt.tight_layout()
```

Fig. 3.85 Multi-level wavelet decomposition and reconstruction of the test image

decomposition of the "zone plate" image to obtain the subbands. Pass subbands to "waverec2" function to obtain the reconstructed image. Comment on the observed result.

Three steps involved in the above-mentioned task are as follows:

Step 1: Generation of the "zone plate" test image.
Step 2: Performing second-level wavelet decomposition on the test image.
Step 3: Reconstruction of the image from the subbands.
The built-in function used in this task are summarized in Table 3.5.

The Python code that uses the built-in functions listed in Table 3.5 to perform the desired task is shown in Fig. 3.85, and the corresponding output is shown in Fig. 3.86.

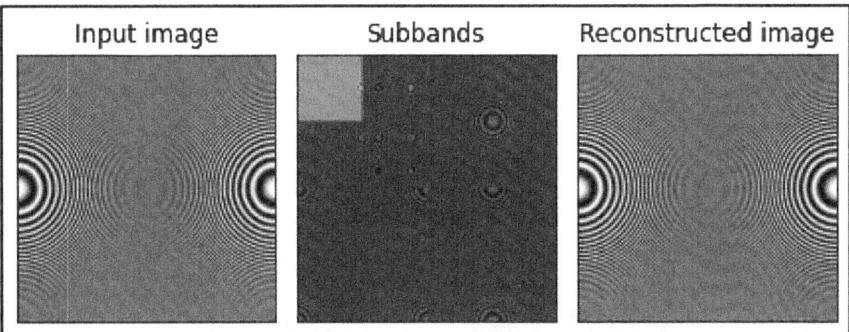

Fig. 3.86 Multi-level wavelet decomposition and reconstruction result

Inferences

The following inferences can be drawn from Figs. 3.85 and 3.86:

- The input test image is a "zone plate" image.
- Two-level wavelet decomposition is performed on the test image using "Haar" wavelet.
- Upon performing two-level wavelet decomposition, seven subbands are obtained, which are shown in Fig. 3.86.
- The subbands are used to obtain the reconstructed image. The reconstructed image resembles the input image.

3.8   Wavelet Packet Transform

In wavelet packet transform (WPT), decomposition is done in both approximation and detail, whereas in wavelet transform, decomposition is performed only in approximation subband. The third-level wavelet decomposition and the wavelet packet decomposition are illustrated in Figs. 3.87 and 3.88, respectively.

From Figs. 3.87 and 3.88, it is possible to infer that there are more subbands in the wavelet packet. The computational complexity increases with an increase in the number of subbands. To overcome this problem, best subband selection is incorporated in wavelet packet decomposition.

Experiment 3.39: Second-Level Wavelet Packet Decomposition of the Image

Read the input image. Perform second-level wavelet packet decomposition of the input image using "Haar" wavelet. Display the subbands obtained in second-level wavelet packet decomposition and comment on the observed result.

The Python code that performs the second-level wavelet packet decomposition of the input image is shown in Fig. 3.89, and the corresponding result is shown in Fig. 3.90.

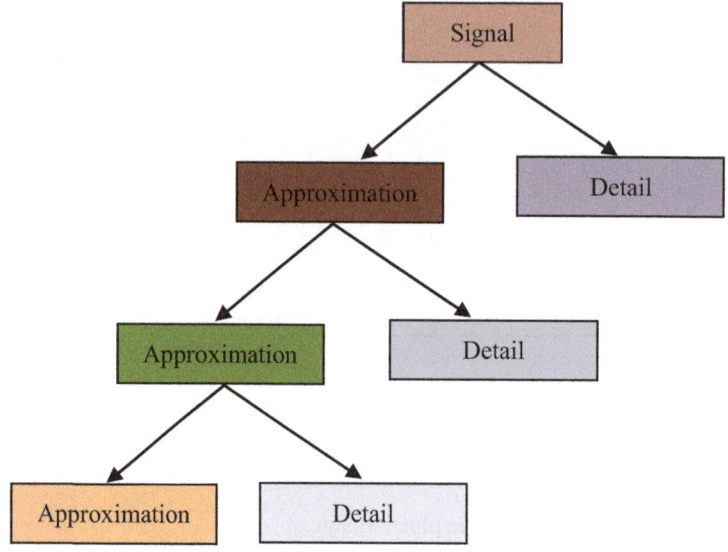

Fig. 3.87 Third-level wavelet decomposition

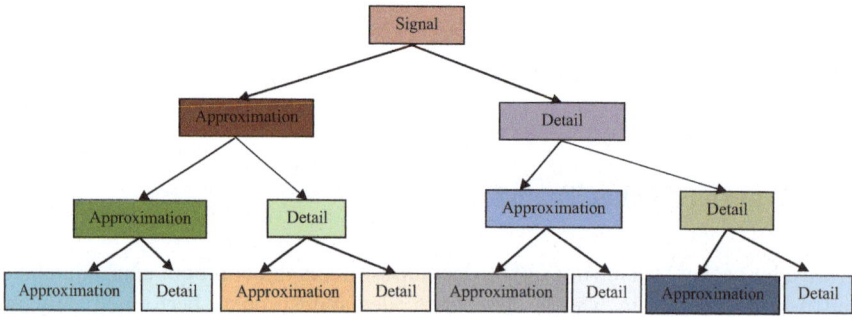

Fig. 3.88 Third-level wavelet packet decomposition

Inferences

- The input image is 256 × 256 "Cameraman" image.
- Second-level wavelet packet decomposition is performed using the built-in function "WaveletPacket2D", which is available in the "pywt" library. The wavelet used to decompose the input image is "Haar" wavelet.
- The second-level wavelet packet decomposition results in 16 subbands each of size 64 × 64. The approximation resembles the input image, and the details correspond to the fine details and the edges in the input image.

```
import matplotlib.pyplot as plt
import pywt
import cv2
#Step 1: Reading the input image
img=cv2.imread('cameraman.tif',0)
#Step 2: Performing Wavelet Packet Decomposition
coeffs=pywt.WaveletPacket2D(img,'haar')
#Step 3: Displying the second level subbands
paths = [node.path for node in coeffs.get_level(2)]
fig=plt.figure(figsize=(8,8))
for i in range(len(paths)):
    plt.subplot(4,4,i+1),plt.imshow(coeffs[paths[i]].data,cmap='gray'),
    plt.title((paths[i].upper())),plt.xticks([]),plt.yticks([])
plt.tight_layout()
```

Fig. 3.89 Python code corresponding to second-level wavelet packet decomposition

3.8.1 *Wavelet and Wavelet Packet Decomposition*

In wavelet transform, successive decomposition is performed in the approximation, assuming that much of the signal information is contained in the approximation. In wavelet packet decomposition, successive decomposition is performed in both approximation and detail. In this section, a comparison of wavelet and wavelet packet decomposition is done by considering the second-level decomposition of the image. This is illustrated in Fig. 3.91.

From Fig. 3.91, second-level wavelet decomposition results in seven subbands, whereas wavelet packet decomposition results in 16 subbands. The number of subbands in wavelet packet decomposition is more than the wavelet decomposition. With the increase in the number of subbands, the computational complexity increases; hence, there is a need to select the best subband in wavelet packet decomposition. Entropy-based best subband selection was proposed by Coifman and Wickerhauser.

Experiment 3.40: Comparison of Wavelet and Wavelet Packet Transforms
The Python code that performs second-level wavelet and wavelet packet decomposition of the input image using "Haar" wavelet is shown in Fig. 3.92, and the corresponding output is shown in Fig. 3.93.

Inferences

- The input image is alphabet image of letter "*A*".
- Second-level wavelet decomposition is performed using the function "wavedec2" available in the "pywt" library.
- Second-level wavelet packet decomposition is performed using the built-in function "WaveletPacket2D" using "Haar" wavelet, which is available in the "pywt" library.

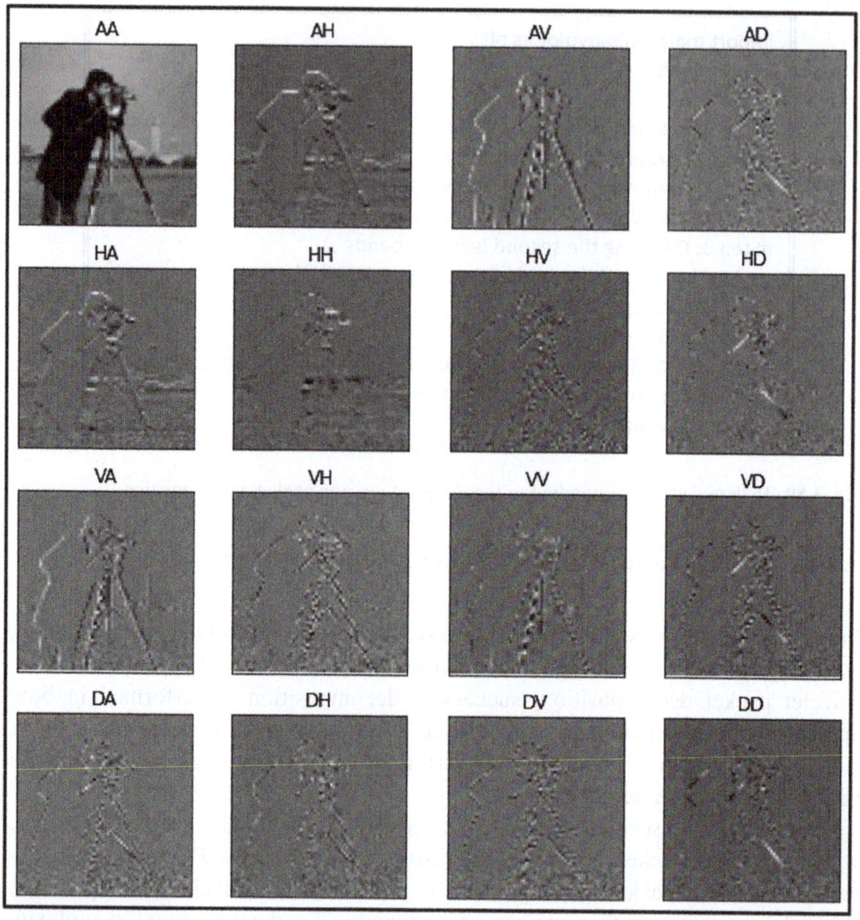

Fig. 3.90 Subbands corresponding to second-level wavelet packet decomposition

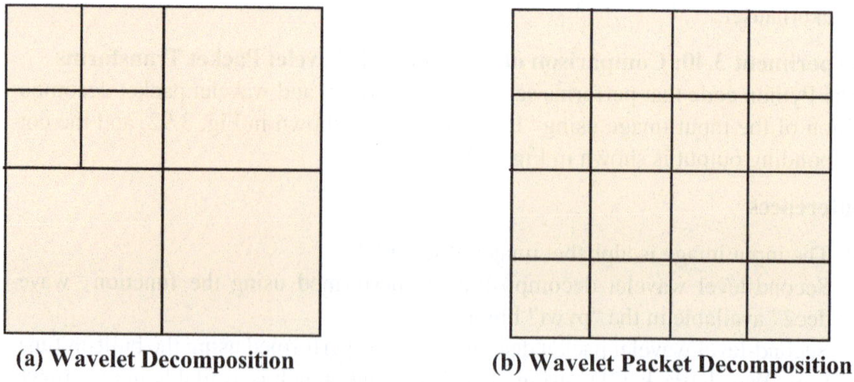

Fig. 3.91 Wavelet and wavelet packet decomposition: (a) wavelet decomposition, (b) wavelet packet decomposition

```
import matplotlib.pyplot as plt
import pywt
import cv2
#Step 1: Reading the input image
img=cv2.imread('A.png',0)
fig=plt.figure(figsize=(8,4))
plt.subplot(1,2,1),plt.imshow(img,cmap='gray'),plt.title('Input image')
plt.xticks([]),plt.yticks([])
#Step 2: Performing Wavelet Decomposition
coeffs1=pywt.wavedec2(img, wavelet='haar', mode='periodization',level=2)
arr,coeff_slices=pywt.coeffs_to_array(coeffs1)
plt.subplot(1,2,2),plt.imshow(arr,cmap='gray'),plt.xticks([]),plt.yticks([])
plt.title('2nd level Wavelet Decomposition')
#Step 3: Performing Wavelet Packet Decomposition
coeffs=pywt.WaveletPacket2D(img,'haar',maxlevel=2)
#Step 3: Displying the second level subbands
paths = [node.path for node in coeffs.get_level(2)]
fig=plt.figure(figsize=(8,8))
for i in range(len(paths)):
    plt.subplot(4,4,i+1),plt.imshow(coeffs[paths[i]].data,cmap='gray'),plt.title((paths[i].upper()))
    plt.suptitle('2nd level Wavelet Packet Decomposition'),plt.xticks([]),plt.yticks([])
plt.tight_layout()
```

Fig. 3.92 Python code to perform wavelet and wavelet packet decomposition

- Seven subbands are obtained using second-level wavelet decomposition, whereas
  in second-level wavelet packet decomposition, 16 subbands are obtained.

3.9   Singular Value Decomposition (SVD)

A singular value decomposition is used to represent a matrix "A" in the form of
product of three matrices, which is given by

$$A = USV^T \tag{3.51}$$

where U and V are orthonormal matrices and S is the diagonal matrix with positive
real values. Here, the input image matrix is decomposed into three matrices, which
are based on the eigen values and eigen vectors of the input matrix. The eigen values
are arranged in the descending order in the form of diagonal entries giving rise to
singular matrix or diagonal matrix.

Experiment 3.41: Computation of SVD
Write a Python code to compute the SVD and reconstruct the original image with
low rank singular components.

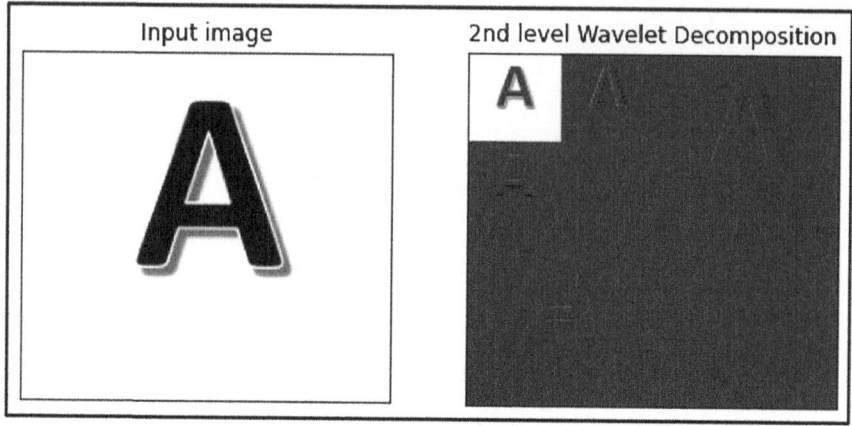

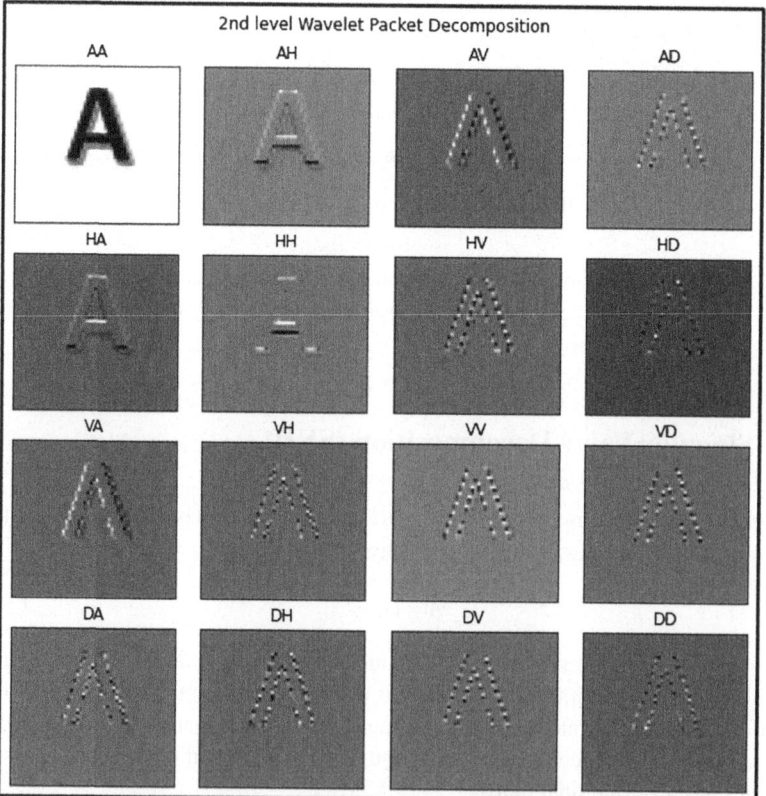

Fig. 3.93 Result of wavelet and wavelet packet decomposition

```
import cv2
import numpy as np
import matplotlib.pyplot as plt
import seaborn as sns
A = cv2.imread('crow.jpg',0);
fig=plt.figure(figsize=(8,4)),plt.subplot(1,2,1),plt.imshow(A,cmap='gray'),
plt.title('Input Image'),plt.xticks([]),plt.yticks([])
U, S, V = np.linalg.svd(A, full_matrices=False)# Singular Value Decomposition
#Average Energy distribution of singular value
S_En_d = np.round(S**2/np.sum(S**2),decimals=5)
plt.subplot(1,2,2),sns.barplot(x=list(range(1, 16)),y=S_En_d[0:15], color="gray")
plt.title('Energy Distribution'),plt.xlabel('Singular Vector')
plt.ylabel('Average Energy'),plt.tight_layout()
# Reconstruction of Original Image with number of singular values
no_sing=[5, 10, 15, 20, 25, S.shape[0]]
plt.figure(figsize=(10, 7))
for i in range(len(no_sing)):
    Rec_I = U[:, :no_sing[i]] @ np.diag(S[:no_sing[i]]) @ V[:no_sing[i], :]
    plt.subplot(2, 3, i+1),plt.imshow(Rec_I, cmap='gray'),plt.xticks([]),plt.yticks([])
    plt.title(f'Rec_I-no.of singular values = {no_sing[i]}')
plt.tight_layout()
```

Fig. 3.94 Python code to perform SVD

This experiment deals with the implementation of SVD using Python. The Python code to perform this task is shown in Fig. 3.94, and its simulation result is shown in Fig. 3.95.

Inferences

From Figs. 3.94 and 3.95, the following inferences can be made:

- From Fig. 3.94, it is possible to infer that "np.linalg.svd" command is used for the SVD computation, which is imported from the "numpy" linear algebra library.
- Figure 3.95 shows the distribution of average energy of the singular values up to 15, and it is also possible to know that the singular values are arranged in descending order.
- Figure 3.95 displays the reconstruction of the original image from the limited number of singular values, which are varied from 5, 10, 15, 20, 25, and whole singular values are used for the reconstruction. From this figure, it is possible to conclude that SVD can be used for image or data compression.

Exercise

1. Write a Python code to prove that DFT matrices are symmetric.
2. Write a Python code to illustrate the fact that the DCT matrix is not symmetric.

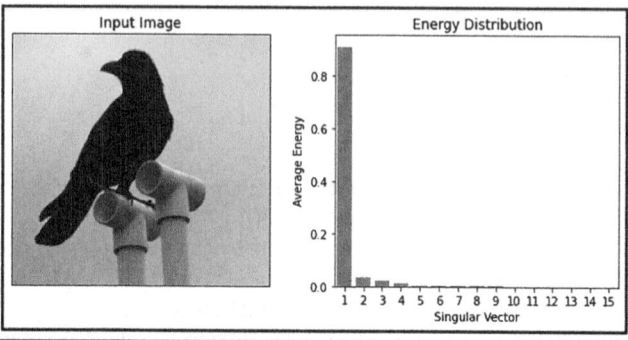

Fig. 3.95 Simulation result of SVD

3. Generate 16×16 checkerboard pattern image. The first task is to divide the image into 8×8 subblocks and apply a Discrete Cosine Transform (DCT) to each block. The second task is to obtain DCT for the entire image. Display the two results and comment on the observed result. (block processing vs entire image processing).

4. Prove Parseval's relation for Fourier transform of an image.

5. The objective of this exercise is to verify the fact that "Sine function" and "Cosine function" exhibit same magnitude spectrum but different phase spectrum.

6. Radon transform of a test image of size 256×256, which is black in colour. In the black background, generate 10 horizontal lines. Obtain the sinogram of the generated image and comment on the observed result.

7. Generate a white circle of radius "20" in a black background (256 × 256). Perform first-level wavelet decomposition using "Haar" wavelet to obtain approximation, horizontal detail, vertical detail, and diagonal detail. Obtain the energy of each subband and comment on the observed result.

8. Interchanging the approximation coefficients of wavelet between two images. Read the two images, where Image-1 is a Cameraman image and Image-2 is a Clock image. Perform first-level wavelet decomposition using "Haar" wavelet to obtain LL1, LH1, HL1, and HH1 for Cameraman image and LL2, LH2, HL2, and HH2 for Clock image. Interchange LL1 with LL2 and perform inverse wavelet transform and comment on the observed result.

9. Interchanging horizontal, vertical, and diagonal details of wavelet coefficients between two images.

10. Write a Python code to apply a SVD on a grayscale image and make it zeros for the first five singular values in the diagonal matrix and reconstruct the original image and comment on the observed result.

Objective Questions

1. What will be the output after executing the following Python code?

```
import numpy as np
x=np.array([[1,1],[1,1]])
X=np.fft.fft2(x)
print(np.abs(X))
```

A. $\begin{bmatrix} 4 & 4 \\ -4 & -4 \end{bmatrix}$

B. $\begin{bmatrix} 4 & 4 \\ 4 & 4 \end{bmatrix}$

C. $\begin{bmatrix} 4 & 0 \\ 0 & 0 \end{bmatrix}$

D. $\begin{bmatrix} 4 & -4 \\ 4 & -4 \end{bmatrix}$

2. What will be the output if the following Python code is executed?

```
import numpy as np
A=np.fft.fft(np.eye(4))
print(A)
```

A. $\begin{bmatrix} 1 & 1 & 1 & 1 \\ 1 & -j & -1 & j \\ 1 & -1 & 1 & -1 \\ 1 & j & -1 & -j \end{bmatrix}$

B.
$$\begin{bmatrix} 1 & 1 & 1 & 1 \\ 1 & 0 & -1 & 0 \\ 1 & -1 & 1 & -1 \\ 1 & 0 & -1 & 0 \end{bmatrix}$$

C.
$$\begin{bmatrix} 1 & 1 & 1 & 1 \\ j & -j & j & -j \\ 1 & -1 & 1 & -1 \\ -j & j & -j & j \end{bmatrix}$$

D.
$$\begin{bmatrix} 1 & 0 & 0 & 0 \\ 0 & 1 & 0 & 0 \\ 0 & 0 & 1 & 0 \\ 0 & 0 & 0 & 1 \end{bmatrix}$$

3. After executing the following Python code, what will the rank of matrix "A" be?

```
import numpy as np
from numpy.linalg import
matrix_rank
N=8
A=np.fft.fft(np.eye(N))
print(matrix_rank(A))
```

A. 2
B. 4
C. 6
D. 8

4. What value would be stored in the variable "X" if the following Python code is executed?

```
from scipy.fftpack import dct
import numpy as np
x=np.ones([2,2])
X=dct(dct(x.T,norm='ortho').T, norm='ortho')
```

A. $X = \begin{bmatrix} 1 & 0 \\ 0 & 0 \end{bmatrix}$

B. $X = \begin{bmatrix} 2 & 0 \\ 0 & 0 \end{bmatrix}$

C. $X = \begin{bmatrix} 3 & 0 \\ 0 & 0 \end{bmatrix}$

D.
$$X = \begin{bmatrix} 4 & 0 \\ 0 & 0 \end{bmatrix}$$

5. Assertion: The DCT coefficients of an image is real
Reason: The basis function of Discrete Cosine Transform is a cosine function

   A. Assertion and Reason are true
   B. Assertion is true, Reason is false
   C. Assertion is false, Reason may be true
   D. Assertion and Reason are false

6. Statement 1: Discrete Fourier Transform (DFT) matrix is symmetric
Statement 2: Discrete Cosine Transform (DCT) matrix is symmetric

   A. Statements 1 and 2 are true
   B. Statement 1 is true, statement 2 is false
   C. Statement 1 is false, statement 1 is true
   D. Statements 1 and 2 are false

7. The transform employed in JPEG compression standard is

   A. Fourier transform
   B. Discrete Cosine Transform
   C. Hadamard transform
   D. Slant transform

8. The term "sinogram" is associated with

   A. Fourier transform
   B. Hadamard transform
   C. Radon transform
   D. Discrete Cosine Transform

9. The number of subbands after first-level of wavelet decomposition of the image is

   A. 1
   B. 2
   C. 3
   D. 4

10. The number of subbands after second-level wavelet and wavelet packet decomposition are respectively

   A. 8, 16
   B. 7, 16
   C. 7, 7
   D. 16, 16

11. Match Group I with Group II

    Group I   Group II

    P. Fourier Transform   I. Multi-resolution Analysis
    Q. Discrete Cosine Transform   II. To detect shapes in the image
    R. Wavelet Transform   III. JPEG standard
    S. Hough Transform   IV. Transform whose coefficients are complex

    A. P-I, Q-II, R-III, S-IV
    B. P-IV, Q-III, R-II, S-I
    C. P-IV, Q-III, R-I, S-II
    D. P-II, Q-I, R-III, S-IV

12. The transform that has the ability to perform multi-resolution analysis of the image is

    A. Discrete Fourier Transform
    B. Discrete Cosine Transform
    C. Hadamard Transform
    D. Wavelet Transform

Answers to Objective Questions

Q. No.	01	02	03	04	05	06	07	08	09	10	11	12
Key	C	A	D	B	A	B	B	C	D	B	C	D

Answers to PreLab Questions

1. Two needs of transform are (1) transform is a tool to analyse the image and (2) transform allows one to extract information from the image.
2. The basis function of Fourier transform is "complex exponential" function.
3. Energy compaction refers to the fact that much of the image energy must be packed to few transform coefficients. Energy compaction is an important property with respect to image compression.
4. Fourier transform can be used to (1) perform filtering of the image and (2) denoise the image. Fourier transform can also be employed to detect periodic noise in digital image.
5. The two essential features of image transform are (1) transform should represent wide classes of image, (2) transform should have good energy compaction property, and (3) fast algorithms should exist so that the transform is computationally efficient.
6. Wavelet transform has the ability to perform multi-resolution analysis of the image. The image can be analysed in different scales.
7. A sonogram is a collection of projections at different angles. Radon transform data is often termed as sonogram.

8. Hough transform is used to detect shapes such as lines and circles in an image.
9. Discrete Cosine Transform (DCT) is employed in JPEG standard and wavelet transform is employed in JPEG2000 standard.
10. The function should be oscillatory. This means that the average value of the signal should be equal to zero. The energy of the function should be finite.

Bibliography

1. Alexander D. Poularikas, "Transforms and Applications Handbook", CRC Press, 2010.
2. K.R. Rao and P.C. Yip, "The Transform and Data Compression Handbook", CRC Press, 2018.
3. Anil K. Jain, "Fundamentals of Digital Image Processing", Pearson Education, 2015.
4. Jae S. Lim, "Two Dimensional Signal and Image Processing", Prentice Hall, 1989.
5. Richard Szeliski, "Computer Vision: Algorithms and Applications", Springer, 2011.

Chapter 4
Image Enhancement

Learning Objectives

After completing this chapter, the reader should be able to

- Perform spatial domain image enhancement
- Perform frequency domain image enhancement
- Implement histogram equalization, adaptive histogram equalization
- Implement Homomorphic filter
- Implement single-scale and multiscale retinex algorithms

Roadmap of the Chapter

The roadmap of this chapter is given in the form of a flow chart, which is shown in Fig. 4.1.

PreLab Questions

1. What is the objective of image enhancement?
2. Distinguish between the brightness and contrast of a digital image.
3. What is simultaneous contrast?
4. If an 8-bit image ($x[m, n]$) undergoes image negative to obtain the output image ($y[m, n]$), what is the mathematical relation between the output image ($y[m, n]$) and the input image ($x[m, n]$)?
5. What is histogram of an image? What information does it convey?
6. Whether multiple images can have the same histogram? Justify your answer.
7. From the histogram, will it be possible to obtain the image in a unique way? Justify your answer.
8. Distinguish between high-pass and high-boost filters in digital image processing.

Supplementary Information The online version contains supplementary material available at https://doi.org/10.1007/978-981-96-6382-8_4.

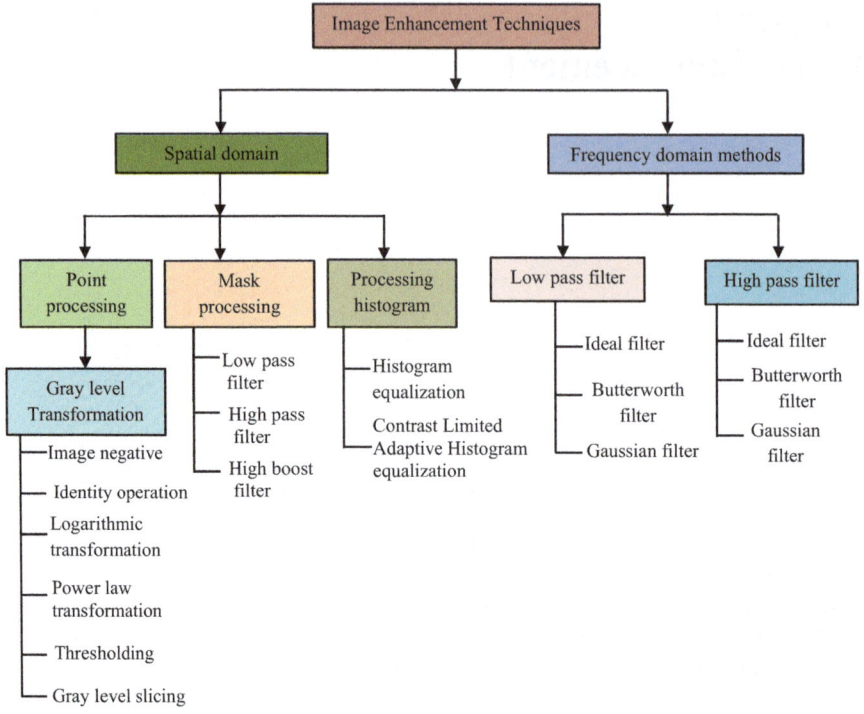

Fig. 4.1 Road map of this Chapter

9. What is an idempotent operation? Why histogram equalization is considered as an idempotent operation?
10. A grayscale image is fed to the thresholding operation. What will be the nature of output image?
11. Averaging filter results in blurring of the input image. What is the purpose of applying an averaging filter even after knowing that it is going to blur the image?
12. What is the purpose of taking logarithm operation in homomorphic filtering?
13. Mention the steps involved in frequency domain-based image filtering.
14. An image is filtered in the frequency domain with the filter whose transfer function is given by $H[k, l] = -4\pi^2(k^2 + l^2)$. Explain the effect of filtering in the output image.
15. What is the principle of the retinex algorithm? What are the types of retinex algorithms?

4.1   Objectives of Image Enhancement

The objective of image enhancement is to improve the visual quality of the image with respect to human visual perception so that the enhanced image is ready for high-level processing and analysis by an automated system. Visual quality of the image can be improved by removing undesirable noise, edge sharpening, pseudo-colouring, interpolation, geometric operations, and so on. Image enhancement results are evaluated subjectively by human observers.

Image enhancement can be achieved in two broad ways: (1) spatial domain methods and (2) frequency domain methods. Spatial domain techniques are based on direct manipulation of pixels in an image. Frequency domain techniques are based on modifying the coefficients of an image. This is depicted in Fig. 4.1. The spatial domain methods can be classified as point operation, mask operation, and histogram-based operation. In frequency domain method, the spectrum of the input image is modified to realize low-pass, high-pass, and band-pass filters. Three different approaches to realize low-pass and high-pass filters are ideal filters, Butterworth filter, and Gaussian filter.

4.2 Image Brightness

Brightness is the intensity of a pixel in an image relative to another pixel. The brightness of the image can be increased by adding a constant value to each pixel of the image. The darkness of an image can be decreased by subtracting a constant value from each pixel of the image.

Experiment 4.1: Changing the Brightness of an Image
In this experiment, the input image is read, and then a bright image is obtained by increasing the intensity of each pixel of the image. The dark image is obtained by decreasing the pixel value of each pixel of the image. The Python code that performs this task is shown in Fig. 4.2, and the corresponding output is shown in Fig. 4.3.

```
#Changing the brightness of the image
import cv2
import matplotlib.pyplot as plt
#Step 1: Reading the input image
img=cv2.imread('tstimage_brightness.jpg',0)
#Step 2: Increasing the brightness of the image
img1=img+115
#Step 3: Decreasing the brightness of the image
img2=img-15
#Step 4: Displaying the results
plt.subplot(1,3,1),plt.imshow(img,cmap='gray'),plt.title('Input image'),plt.xticks([]),plt.yticks([])
plt.subplot(1,3,2),plt.imshow(img1,cmap='gray'),plt.title('Output image-1'),plt.xticks([]),
plt.yticks([]),plt.subplot(1,3,3),plt.imshow(img2,cmap='gray'),plt.title('Output image-2'),
plt.xticks([]),plt.yticks([])
plt.tight_layout()
```

Fig. 4.2 Python code to change the brightness of the image

Fig. 4.3 Result of brightness change in the input image

Inferences

From Figs. 4.2 and 4.3, the following conclusions can be drawn:

- From Fig. 4.2, it is possible to observe that a constant value of "115" is added to each pixel of the input image to increase the brightness of the image. The result is shown as "Output Image-1" in Fig. 4.3. From the result, it is possible to observe that the brightness of the image is increased.
- From Fig. 4.2, it is possible to observe that a constant value of "15" is subtracted from each pixel of the input image to decrease the brightness of the image. The result is shown as "Output Image-2" in Fig. 4.3. From the result it is possible to observe that the brightness of the image is decreased. The image has become darker.

4.3   Image Contrast

Contrast is a measure of the difference in brightness between the light and dark areas of an image. In a low-contrast image, the image values are concentrated in a narrow range. Contrast enhancement techniques attempt to change the pixel values such that the pixel values are distributed over a wide range. Low-contrast images are due to insufficient lighting, the small dynamic range of the optical sensors, and natural phenomena such as fog, mist, and so on. It is difficult to extract information from low-contrast image, hence it is necessary to perform contrast enhancement. Contrast enhancement provides meaningful information for real-time image processing applications.

4.3.1   Simultaneous Contrast

The human visual system does not possess an absolute sense of gray levels in an image. The brightness or darkness of a region in an image depends on the gray level in the adjoining regions. This is termed as simultaneous contrast.

Experiment 4.2: Simultaneous Contrast

The objective of this experiment is to illustrate simultaneous contrast in digital image. The Python code to illustrate the phenomenon is given in Fig. 4.4, and the corresponding output is shown in Fig. 4.5.

Inferences

- The brightness of the inner square in all three images, namely Image-1, Image-2 and Image-3, are the same.
- The inner square takes the gray level value of 100 in all the three images.
- The inner square appears darker as one progresses from Image-1 to Image-3 because the background is lighter as one progresses from Image-1 to Image-3.

```
#Simultaneous contrast
import numpy as np
import matplotlib.pyplot as plt
#Step 1: Generation of image 1
img1=np.zeros([256,256])
img1[108:148,108:148]=100
#Step 2: Generation of image 2
img2=np.zeros([256,256])
img2=img2+80
img2[108:148,108:148]=100
#Step 3: Generation of image 3
img3=np.zeros([256,256])
img3=img3+200
img3[108:148,108:148]=100
#Step 4: Displaying the results
plt.subplot(1,3,1),plt.imshow(img1,cmap='gray',vmin=0,vmax=256),plt.title('Image-1'),
plt.xticks([]),plt.yticks([]),plt.subplot(1,3,2),plt.imshow(img2,cmap='gray',vmin=0,vmax=256)
plt.title('Image-2'),plt.xticks([]),plt.yticks([]),plt.subplot(1,3,3),
plt.imshow(img3,cmap='gray',vmin=0,vmax=256),plt.title('Image-3'),plt.xticks([]),plt.yticks([])
plt.tight_layout()
```

Fig. 4.4 Python code to illustrate simultaneous contrast

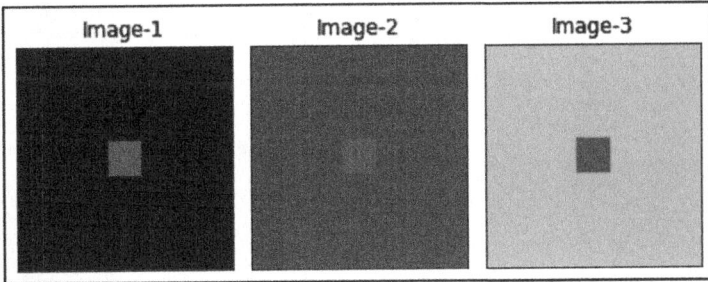

Fig. 4.5 Illustration of simultaneous contrast

- Thus, the brightness or darkness of a region in an image depends on the gray level in the adjoining regions, which is termed as simultaneous contrast.

Experiment 4.3: Illustration of Simultaneous contrast Using the Koffka–Benussi Ring

To create the Koffka–Benussi ring, a bipartite image is created, in which part of the image is black and the other part is white. A ring is generated in the bipartite image, which is termed as Koffka–Benussi ring. The Python code that generates the Koffka–Benussi ring is shown in Fig. 4.6, and the corresponding output is shown in Fig. 4.7.

```
#Generation of the Koffka-Benussi ring
import numpy as np
import matplotlib.pyplot as plt
#Step 1: Generation of bipartite image
img=np.zeros([256,256])
img[:,0:127]=255;
m,n=img.shape
#Step 2: Ring in bipartite image
a=50    #Major axis
b=100     #Minor axis
for i in range(0,m):
    for j in range(0,n):
        d=(i-128)**2/(a**2)+(j-128)**2/(b**2)
        if (d>0.5) & (d<1):
            img[i,j]=128
#Step 3: Displaying the result
plt.imshow(img,cmap='gray',vmin=0,vmax=255),plt.title('The Koffka-Benussi ring'),
plt.xticks([]),plt.yticks([]),plt.tight_layout()
```

Fig. 4.6 Python code to generate the Koffka–Benussi ring

Fig. 4.7 The Koffka–Benussi ring

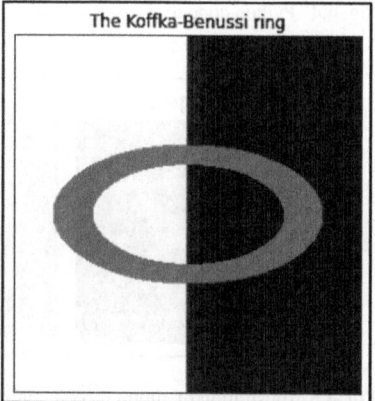

The Koffka-Benussi ring

```
# #Contrast enhancement import cv2
import matplotlib.pyplot as plt
#Step 1: Reading the input image
img_in=cv2.imread('tstimage_contrast.jpg',0)
#Step 2: Changing the contrast of the image
contrast=2
brightness=0
img_out = cv2.addWeighted(img_in, contrast, img_in, 0, brightness)
#Step 3: Displaying the results
plt.figure(figsize=(8, 6)),plt.subplot(1,2,1),plt.imshow(img_in,cmap='gray')
plt.title('Input image'),plt.axis('off'),plt.subplot(1,2,2),
plt.imshow(img_out,cmap='gray'),plt.title('Output image'),plt.axis('off')
plt.tight_layout()
```

Fig. 4.8 Python code that performs contrast enhancement

Inferences

- The same ring set on a bipartite background looks different in the two parts of the image.
- This illustrates the fact that grayscale is regarded as a subjective phenomenon.

4.3.2 Contrast Enhancement

Contrast enhancement improves the visual quality of the image by enhancing the brightness difference between objects and their backgrounds.

Experiment 4.4: Contrast Enhancement

The Python code that performs contrast enhancement is shown in Fig. 4.8, and the corresponding output is shown in Fig. 4.9. There are different approaches to image enhancement, such as contrast stretching, histogram equalization, adaptive histogram equalization, and so on. This experiment illustrates the use of the built-in function "addWeighted" function, which is available in the "cv2" library, to perform contrast enhancement.

Inferences

- The input image is a low-contrast image.
- The built-in function "addWeighted" available in "cv2" library is used to increase the contrast of the input image.
- The output image has better contrast than the input image.

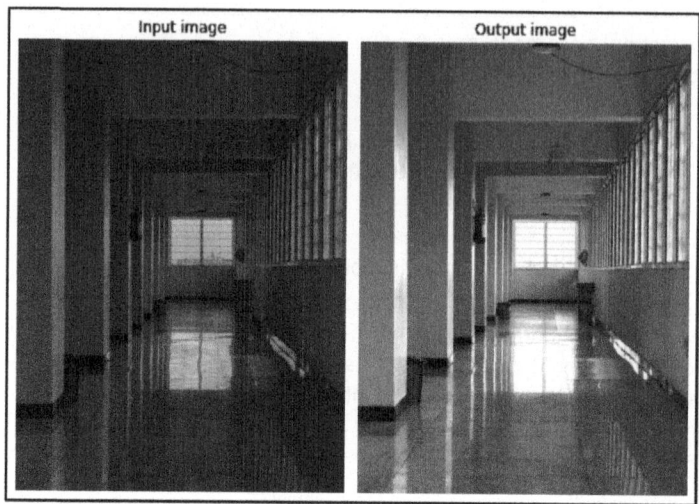

Fig. 4.9 Result of contrast enhancement

4.4 Gray Level Transformation

If $x[m, n]$ and $y[m, n]$ represent the input and output image, then the gray level transformation is expressed as

$$y[m,n] = T\{x[m,n]\} \tag{4.1}$$

In the above expression, "T" represents the mapping between the input and output image. The mapping could be either linear, non-linear, and piecewise linear mapping. Example of linear mapping include identity operation and image negative. Examples of non-linear mapping are logarithmic transformation and power-law transformation. Examples of piecewise linear mapping include contrast stretching and gray level slicing.

4.4.1 Identity Operation

If $x[m, n]$ represents the input image and $y[m, n]$ represents the output image, then the identity operation is expressed as

$$y[m,n] = x[m,n] \tag{4.2}$$

Expression (4.2) indicates that the output image is exactly equal to the input image. This operation is similar to that of a "voltage follower or buffer" in electronics, where the output signal exactly resembles the input signal.

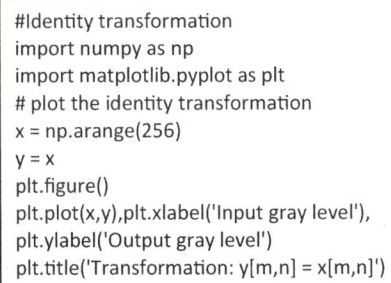

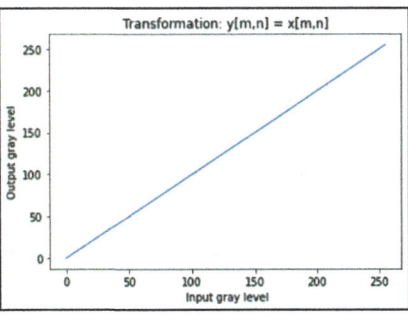

| (a) Python code | (b) Graphical representation |

Fig. 4.10 Python code that performs identity operation: (**a**) Python code, (**b**) graphical representation

Experiment 4.5: Identity Operation

The Python code that performs this identity transformation is shown in Fig. 4.10a, and the corresponding output is shown in Fig. 4.10b. This identity transformation is now applied to an input image to get an output image. The Python code for this task is shown in Fig. 4.11a, and its simulation results are displayed in Fig. 4.11b.

Inference

- By observing Fig. 4.11b, it is possible to interpret that the output image resembles the input image.

4.4.2   Negative Transformation

For an 8-bit image ($x[m, n]$), the negative transformation is expressed as

$$y[m,n] = 255 - x[m,n] \qquad (4.3)$$

Image negative enhances white or gray detail embedded in dark regions.

Experiment 4.6: Negative Transformation

The Python code that plots the negative transformation is shown in Fig. 4.12a, and the corresponding output is shown in Fig. 4.12b. This negative transformation is applied to the Cameraman image using the Python code given in Fig. 4.13a, and its simulation result is depicted in Fig. 4.13b.

Inferences

- From Fig. 4.13b, it is possible to observe that the gray level "black" changes to "white" and vice versa.
- This is equivalent to "NOT gate" operation where input "0" results in output "1" and vice versa.

```
#Identity transformation
import numpy as np
import matplotlib.pyplot as plt
import cv2
#Step 1: Read the input image
input_img=cv2.imread('cameraman.tif',0)
M,N = input_img.shape
#Step 2: Template for the output image
out_img=np.zeros((M,N))
#Step 3: Applying the gray level transformation
for m in range(M):
  for n in range(N):
    out_img[m,n] = input_img[m,n]
plt.subplot(1,2,1),plt.imshow(input_img,cmap='gray'),plt.title('Input image'),plt.axis('off'),
plt.subplot(1,2,2),plt.imshow(out_img,cmap='gray'),plt.title('Output image'),plt.axis('off')
plt.tight_layout()
```

(a) Python Code

(b) Simulation result

Fig. 4.11 Applying the identity transformation to the input image: (**a**) Python code, (**b**) simulation result

4.4.3   Logarithmic Transformation

The logarithmic transformation maps a narrow range of low input gray level values into a wider range of output values. The expression for logarithmic transformation is given by

$$y[m,n] = C \log(1 + x[m,n])$$ (4.4)

where

$$C = \frac{255}{\log(1 + 255)}$$ (4.5)

```
#Negative transformation
import numpy as np
import matplotlib.pyplot as plt
# plot the negative transformation
x = np.arange(256)
y = 255-x
plt.figure(),plt.plot(x,y),
plt.xlabel('Input gray level'),
plt.ylabel('Output gray level')
plt.title('Negative transformation: y[m,n] = 255 - x[m,n]')
```

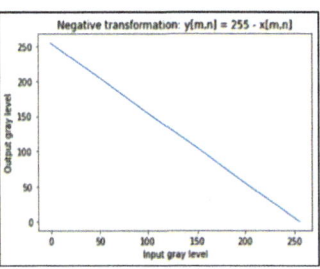

(a) Python code   **(b) Graphical representation**

Fig. 4.12 Python code for the negative transformation: (**a**) Python code, (**b**) graphical representation

```
#Negative transformation
import numpy as np
import matplotlib.pyplot as plt
import cv2
#Step 1: Read the input image
input_img=cv2.imread('cameraman.tif',0)
M,N = input_img.shape
#Step 2: Template for the output image
out_img=np.zeros((M,N))
#Step 3: Applying the gray level transformation
for m in range(M):
  for n in range(N):
    out_img[m,n] = 255-input_img[m,n]
plt.subplot(1,2,1),
plt.imshow(input_img,cmap='gray'),
plt.title('Input image')
plt.axis('off'),plt.subplot(1,2,2),
plt.imshow(out_img,cmap='gray'),
plt.title('Output image'),plt.axis('off')
plt.tight_layout()
```

(a) Python code   **(b) Simulation Result**

Fig. 4.13 Applying negative transformation to the input image: (**a**) Python code, (**b**) simulation Result

Logarithmic transformation compresses the dynamic range of images with large variations in pixel values.

Experiment 4.7: Logarithmic Transformation

The Python code that performs logarithmic transformation is shown in Fig. 4.14, and the corresponding output is shown in Fig. 4.15.

```
#Logarithmic transformation
import numpy as np
import matplotlib.pyplot as plt
# plot the negative transformation
x = np.arange(256)
c=255/np.log(1+255)
y = c*np.log(1+x)
plt.figure()
plt.plot(x,y),plt.xlabel('Input gray level'),
plt.ylabel('Output gray level')
plt.title('Logarithmic transformation: y[m,n]=clog(1+x[m,n])')
```

Fig. 4.14 Python code that performs logarithmic transformation

Fig. 4.15 Result of the Python code shown in Fig. 4.14

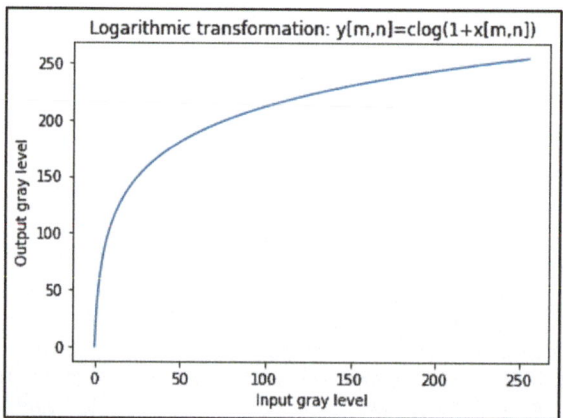

The Python code that applies this logarithmic transformation to the input Cameraman image is shown in Fig. 4.16, and the corresponding output is shown in Fig. 4.17.

Inference

- From Fig. 4.17, it is possible to infer that dark pixels in the image are expanded as compared to higher pixel values.

4.4.4 Power Law Transformation

The power-law transformation is also called as "gamma transformation". It uses a power-law function to enhance the pixel intensity of an image. This technique is versatile, and it allows the enhancement of specific details in an image.

```
import numpy as np
import cv2
import matplotlib.pyplot as plt
#Step 1: Read the input image
input_img=cv2.imread('cameraman.tif',0)
M,N = input_img.shape
#Step 2: Template for the output image
out_img=np.zeros((M,N))
c=255/np.log(1+255)
#Step 3: Applying the gray level transformation
for m in range(M):
  for n in range(N):
    out_img[m,n] = c*np.log(1+input_img[m,n])
plt.subplot(1,2,1),plt.imshow(input_img,cmap='gray'),plt.title('Input image'),
plt.axis('off'),plt.subplot(1,2,2),plt.imshow(out_img,cmap='gray'),
plt.title('Output image'),plt.axis('off')
plt.tight_layout()
```

Fig. 4.16   Python code that performs logarithmic transformation

Fig. 4.17   Result of Python
code shown in Fig. 4.16

The mathematical model for power-law transformation is given by

$$y[m,n] = c \times x[m,n]^{\gamma} \tag{4.6}$$

where "c" represents the scaling factor or constant, which can be calculated by using Eq. (4.5), γ denotes the power-law factor, and x and y denote the input and output images, respectively.

If the value of γ is greater than 1, it stretches the contrast in brighter region and compresses the pixel intensity in darker regions. Similarly, if the value of γ is less than 1, it enhances the contrast and compresses the intensity in the brighter region.

Experiment 4.8: Power-Law Transformation
This experiment discusses the generation of a graphical curve of power-law transformation using Python and also shows the effect of power-law transformation on a

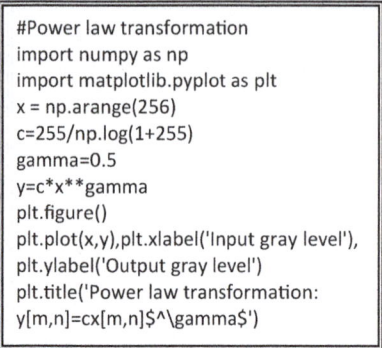

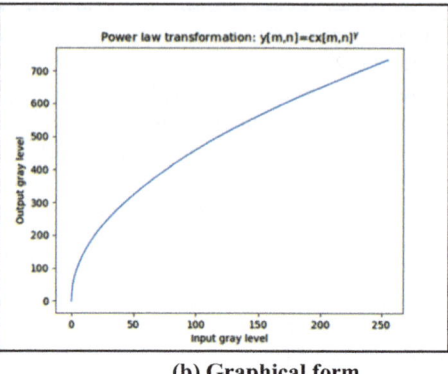

(a) Python Code	(b) Graphical form

Fig. 4.18 Power-law transformation: (**a**) Python code, (**b**) graphical form

Cameraman image. The Python code that performs the power-law transformation is shown in Fig. 4.18a, and the corresponding output is shown in Fig. 4.18b.

Applying the power-law transformation to an input Cameraman image with gamma = 0.5 and 1.5, its simulation result is commented on in this experiment. The Python code that performs the power-law transformation is shown in Fig. 4.19, and the corresponding output is shown in Fig. 4.20.

Inferences
The following inferences can be made from this experiment:

- The gamma value of 0.5 (i.e. less than "1"): brightens the input image.
- The gamma value of 2.5 (i.e. greater than "1"): darkens the input image.

4.4.5   Gray Level Slicing

Gray level slicing can be classified into (1) gray level slicing without background and (2) gray level slicing with background.

Experiment 4.9: Gray Level Slicing without Background
This method converts the grayscale image into binary. That is, the output image takes only two values (0 and 255). The Python code that performs gray level slicing without background and its simulation result is shown in Fig. 4.21.

The Python code that applies this gray level slicing without background to the input Cameraman image is shown in Fig. 4.22, and the corresponding output is shown in Fig. 4.23.

Inference

- From Fig. 4.23, it is possible to observe that the variation of the output image is only black and white. Background of the image is completely removed.

```
import numpy as np
import cv2
import matplotlib.pyplot as plt
#Step 1: Read the input image
input_img=cv2.imread('cameraman.tif',0)
M,N = input_img.shape
#Step 2: Template for the output image
out_img=np.zeros((M,N))
c=255/np.log(1+255)
gamma=[.5,2.5]
plt.figure(1)
plt.subplot(1,3,1),plt.imshow(input_img,cmap='gray'),plt.title('Input
image'),plt.axis('off')
#Step 3: Applying the gray level transformation
for i in range(len(gamma)):
   for m in range(M):
      for n in range(N):
         out_img[m,n] = c*input_img[m,n]**gamma[i]
   plt.figure(1),plt.subplot(1,3,i+2),plt.imshow(out_img,cmap='gray'),
   plt.title(f'Output: Gamma = {gamma[i]}'),plt.axis('off')
plt.tight_layout()
```

Fig. 4.19 Python code that performs power-law transformation

Fig. 4.20 Power-law transformation result

Experiment 4.10: Gray Level Slicing with Background

This method slices only the set of range of gray levels into white (i.e. 255), and the remaining gray levels are retained as it is. Therefore, it is called as gray level slicing with background. The Python code that performs gray level slicing with background is shown in Fig. 4.24a, and the corresponding output is shown in Fig. 4.24b. From Fig. 4.24b, it is possible to observe that input and output gray levels are the same except for the interval from 100 (T1) to 150 (T2).

```
#Gray level slicing without background
import numpy as np
import matplotlib.pyplot as plt
x = np.arange(256)
y=np.zeros(len(x))
T1, T2=100,150
for i in range(0,256):
   if T1 < x[i] < T2:
      y[i]=255
plt.figure(),plt.plot(x,y),
plt.xlabel('Input gray level'),
plt.ylabel('Output gray level')
plt.title('Gray level slicing without
background')
```

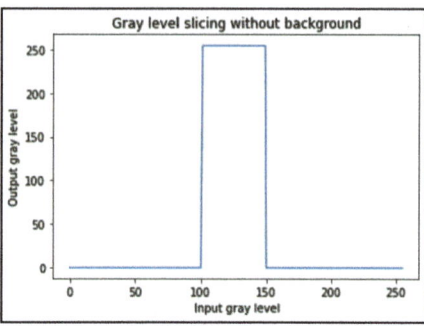

(a) Python code   **(b) Graphical representation**

Fig. 4.21 Gray level slicing without background: (**a**) Python code, (**b**) graphical representation

```
#Gray level slicing without background
import numpy as np
import matplotlib.pyplot as plt
import cv2
img_in = cv2.imread('cameraman.tif',0)
m,n=img_in.shape
img_out=np.copy(img_in)
T1=100
T2=150
for i in range(0,m):
   for j in range(0,n):
      if T1 < img_in[i,j] < T2:
         img_out[i,j]=255
      else:
         img_out[i,j]=0
plt.subplot(1,2,1),plt.imshow(img_in,cmap='gray'),plt.title('Input
Image')
plt.axis('off'),plt.subplot(1,2,2),plt.imshow(img_out,cmap='gray'),
plt.axis('off'),plt.title('Gray level slicing without background')
plt.tight_layout()
```

Fig. 4.22 Gray level slicing without background applied to an input image

Fig. 4.23 Result of Python code shown in Fig. 4.22

```
#Gray level slicing with background
import numpy as np
import matplotlib.pyplot as plt
x = np.arange(256)
y=np.copy(x)
T1, T2=100, 150
for i in range(0,256):
    if T1 < x[i] < T2:
        y[i]=255
    else:
        y[i]=x[i]
plt.plot(x,y),plt.xlabel('Input gray level'),
plt.ylabel('Output gray level')
plt.title('Gray level slicing with background')
```

(a) Python code   **(b) Graphical representation**

Fig. 4.24 Gray level slicing with background: (**a**) Python code, (**b**) graphical representation

The Python code that applies this gray level slicing with background on the Cameraman image as input is shown in Fig. 4.25, and the corresponding output is shown in Fig. 4.26.

Inferences

The following inferences can be drawn from this experiment:

- From Fig. 4.24b, it is possible to infer that the background region is in the form of linear transformation, and the region has to be highlighted in the non-linear form.
- From Fig. 4.26, it is possible to confirm that the output of the gray level slicing with the background retains the background region as it is, and the foreground region is represented in white colour.

```
#Gray level slicing with background
import numpy as np
import matplotlib.pyplot as plt
import cv2
img_in = cv2.imread('cameraman.tif',0)
m,n=img_in.shape
img_out=np.copy(img_in)
T1,T2=100,150
for i in range(0,m):
    for j in range(0,n):
        if T1 < img_in[i,j] < T2:
            img_out[i,j]=255
        else:
            img_out[i,j]=img_in[i,j]
plt.subplot(1,2,1),plt.imshow(img_in,cmap='gray'),plt.title('Input image')
plt.axis('off'),plt.subplot(1,2,2),plt.imshow(img_out,cmap='gray'),
plt.title('Output image'),plt.axis('off')
```

Fig. 4.25   Gray level slicing with background applied to input image

Fig. 4.26   Result of Python code shown in Fig. 4.25

4.4.6   Piecewise Linear Contrast Stretching

In piecewise linear contrast stretching, the contrast of the input image is improved by stretching the intensity values to fill the entire dynamic range. For an 8-bit image, $L = 256$. The x-axis represents the gray level of the input image and the y-axis represents the gray level of the output image. The piecewise linear contrast stretching graph is shown in Fig. 4.27.

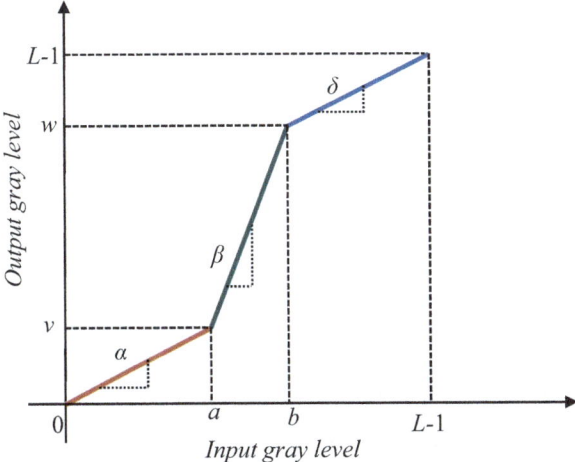

Fig. 4.27 Piecewise linear contrast stretching

There are three lines: one line from 0 to "a", the next line is from "a" to "b", and the third line is from "b" to "$L-1$". The slopes of the three lines are represented as "α", "β", and "δ", respectively. From the figure, it is possible to observe that a small change in the gray level of the input image from "a" to "b" results in a large change in the gray level of the output image from "v" to "w". The relationship between the input image (x) and the output image (y) is given by

$$y = \begin{cases} \alpha x, & for\ 0 \le x < a \\ \beta(x-a)+v, & for\ a \le x < b \\ \delta(x-b)+w, & for\ b \le x < L-1 \end{cases} \tag{4.7}$$

The expressions for the slopes of the line are given by

$$\alpha = \frac{v}{a} \tag{4.8}$$

$$\beta = \frac{w-v}{b-a} \tag{4.9}$$

and

$$\delta = \frac{L-1-w}{L-1-b} \tag{4.10}$$

Experiment 4.11: Implementation of Piecewise Linear Contrast Enhancement
This experiment aims to implement piecewise linear contrast enhancement in Python environment. The Python code that performs piecewise linear contrast

```
#Contrast stretching
import cv2
import numpy as np
import matplotlib.pyplot as plt
img=cv2.imread('testimg5.jpg',0)
enhanced_img = np.zeros_like(img)
a, b = 50, 200
v, w = 70, 120
alpha = v/a
beta= (w-v)/(b-a)
delta= (255-w)/(255-b)
for i in range(img.shape[0]):
    for j in range(img.shape[1]):
        if img[i, j] < a:
            enhanced_img[i, j] = alpha*img[i, j]
        elif img[i, j] < b:
            enhanced_img[i, j] = beta*(img[i, j] - a) + v
        else:
            enhanced_img[i, j] = delta*(img[i, j] - b) + w
plt.subplot(1, 2, 1),plt.imshow(img, cmap='gray'),plt.title('Input image'),plt.axis('off')
plt.subplot(1, 2, 2),plt.imshow(enhanced_img, cmap='gray'),plt.title('Output image'),plt.axis('off')
plt.tight_layout()
```

Fig. 4.28 Python code to perform piecewise linear contrast stretching

enhancement is given in Fig. 4.28, and the corresponding output is shown in Fig. 4.29.

Inferences

- Due to contrast stretching, the output image is brighter than the input image.
- It is due to the fact that contrast stretching increases the dynamic range of gray levels in the input image to obtain a better visual quality output image.

4.5   Bit Plane Slicing

The pixels in the digital image are represented in the form of bits. For an n-bit representation of a digital image, the spatial maps corresponding to a specific bit position are known as image's bit planes. Bit plane "$n - 1$" corresponds to the most significant bit (MSB) and the bit plane "0" to the least significant bit (LSB). Information content in natural images decreases from MSB to LSB.

Experiment 4.12: Extraction of Bit Planes of the Image
The objective of this experiment is to extract the 8-bit planes of the input grayscale image.

The Python code that performs this task is shown in Fig. 4.30, and the corresponding output is shown in Fig. 4.31.

Fig. 4.29 Result of Python code shown in Fig. 4.28

Inference

- From Fig. 4.31, it is possible to infer that much of the information about the image is in a higher-order bit plane.

Experiment 4.13: Image Reconstruction from Bit Planes
Read an input image and extract the 8-bit planes of the input image. After extracting the bit plane, the image was reconstructed using only the MSB plane and the LSB plane, and both the LSB and MSB planes were used. The Python code that performs the extraction of the bit plane and image reconstruction using the MSB, LSB, and both MSB and LSB bit plane is shown in Fig. 4.32, and the corresponding output is shown in Fig. 4.33.

Inferences
The following inferences can be drawn from Fig. 4.33:

- The reconstructed image using the MSB bit plane resembles the input image.
- The reconstructed image using the LSB bit plane is like a noisy image.
- The MSB bit plane carries vital information about the image.

Experiment 4.14: Combining Bit Planes of Two Image
The objective of this experiment is to combine the bit planes of two input images to create a new image. The bit planes of Image-1 and Image-2 are combined alternately to obtain the bit planes of the new image, which is illustrated in Fig. 4.34.

```
# #Extraction of bitplanes
import cv2
import numpy as np
import matplotlib.pyplot as plt
#Step 1: Reading the input image
img=cv2.imread('cameraman.tif',0)
#Step 2: Extracting the 8 bit planes
bp_0=np.mod(img,2)
bp_1=np.mod(np.floor(img/2),2)
bp_2=np.mod(np.floor(img/4),4)
bp_3=np.mod(np.floor(img/8),8)
bp_4=np.mod(np.floor(img/16),16)
bp_5=np.mod(np.floor(img/32),32)
bp_6=np.mod(np.floor(img/64),64)
bp_7=np.mod(np.floor(img/128),128)
#Step 3: Displaying the result
plt.figure(figsize=(8, 4)),plt.subplot(2,4,1),plt.imshow(bp_0,cmap='gray')
plt.title('Bit plane-0'),plt.xticks([]),plt.yticks([]),plt.subplot(2,4,2),
plt.imshow(bp_1,cmap='gray'),plt.xticks([]),plt.yticks([]),plt.title('Bit plane-1'),
plt.xticks([]),plt.yticks([]),plt.subplot(2,4,3),plt.imshow(bp_2,cmap='gray')
plt.title('Bit plane-2'),plt.xticks([]),plt.yticks([]),plt.subplot(2,4,4),
plt.imshow(bp_3,cmap='gray'),plt.title('Bit plane-3'),plt.xticks([]),plt.yticks([])
plt.subplot(2,4,5),plt.imshow(bp_4,cmap='gray'),plt.title('Bit plane-4')
plt.xticks([]),plt.yticks([]),plt.subplot(2,4,6),plt.imshow(bp_5,cmap='gray')
plt.title('Bit plane-5'),plt.xticks([]),plt.yticks([]),plt.subplot(2,4,7),
plt.imshow(bp_6,cmap='gray'),plt.title('Bit plane-6'),plt.xticks([]),plt.yticks([])
plt.subplot(2,4,8),plt.imshow(bp_7,cmap='gray'),plt.title('Bit plane-7')
plt.xticks([]),plt.yticks([]),plt.tight_layout()
```

Fig. 4.30 Python code to extract the bit plane of the image

Fig. 4.31 Bit planes of the image

```
# Image Reconstruction from Bitplanes
import cv2
import numpy as np
import matplotlib.pyplot as plt
#Step 1: Reading the input image
img=cv2.imread('Clock.tiff',0)
#Step 2: Extracting the 8 bit planes
bp_0=np.mod(img,2)
bp_1=np.mod(np.floor(img/2),2)
bp_2=np.mod(np.floor(img/4),4)
bp_3=np.mod(np.floor(img/8),8)
bp_4=np.mod(np.floor(img/16),16)
bp_5=np.mod(np.floor(img/32),32)
bp_6=np.mod(np.floor(img/64),64)
bp_7=np.mod(np.floor(img/128),128)
#Step 3: Reconstructed image
r1=bp_7*(2**7) #Reconstruced image using MSB plane
r2=bp_0*(2**0) #Reconstrcted image using LSB plane
r3=r1+r2 #Reconstruced image using MSB+ LSB plane
#Step 4: Displaying the result
plt.figure(figsize=(8,6)),plt.subplot(1,4,1),plt.imshow(img,cmap='gray'),
plt.title('Input image'),plt.xticks([]),plt.yticks([]),plt.subplot(1,4,2),
plt.imshow(r1,cmap='gray'),plt.title('RI: MSB plane'),plt.xticks([]),plt.yticks([])
plt.subplot(1,4,3),plt.imshow(r2,cmap='gray'),plt.title('RI: LSB plane'),
plt.xticks([]),plt.yticks([]),plt.subplot(1,4,4),plt.imshow(r3,cmap='gray'),
plt.title('RI: MSB+LSB plane'),plt.xticks([]),plt.yticks([])
plt.tight_layout()
```

Fig. 4.32 Python code to reconstruct the image from bit planes

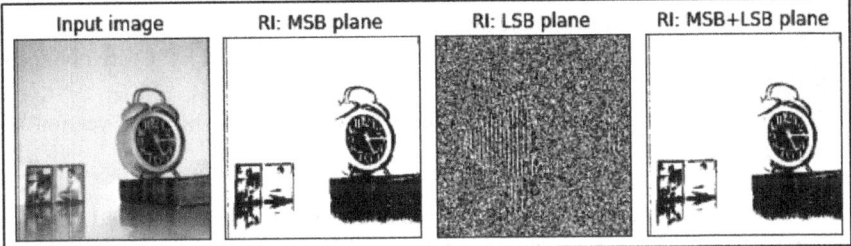

Fig. 4.33 Image reconstruction from bit plane

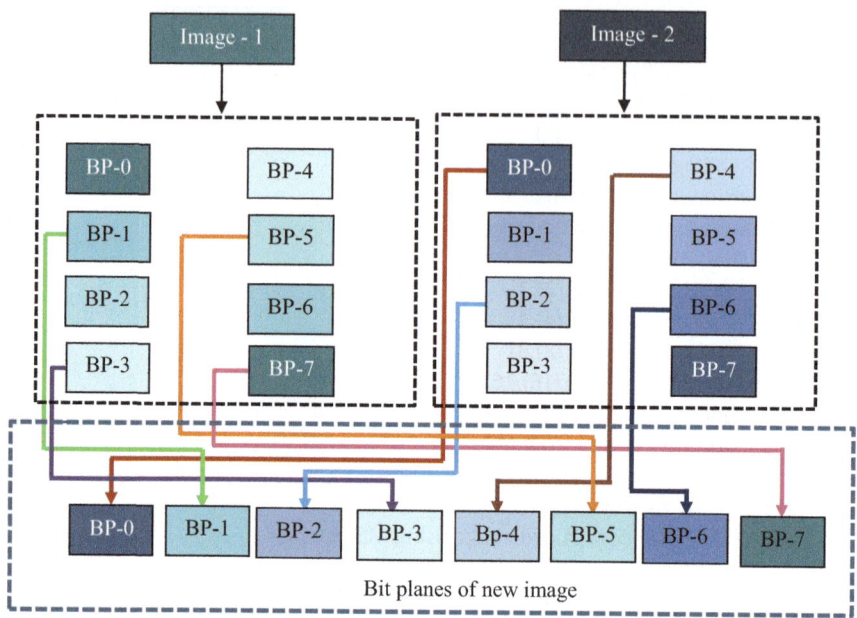

Fig. 4.34 Combining bit planes of two images alternately

From Fig. 4.34, it is possible to observe that Image-1 and Image-2 have 8-bit planes. In the figure, the term "BP" refers to "bit plane". First, the 8-bit planes (BP-0 to BP-7) of Image-1 and Image-2 are extracted. A new image is obtained by combining the odd bit plane of Image-1 with the even bit plane of Image-2. The Python code that performs the above-mentioned task is shown in Fig. 4.35, and the corresponding output is shown in Fig. 4.36.

Inference

- Image-1 is a "Cameraman image" and Image-2 is a "Rice image".
- A new image is obtained by combining the bit planes of Image-1 and Image-2. The odd bit plane of new image (BP-1, BP-3, BP-5, and BP-7) is obtained from Image-1, whereas the even bit planes (BP-0, BP-2, BP-4, and BP-6) are obtained from Image-2.
- The visual appearance of the new image is similar to the blended version of Image-1 and Image-2.

Experiment 4.15: Modify the Above Program in Such a Way that the Lower Order Bit Plane of the New Image Is Obtained from Image-1 and the Higher-Order Bit Plane of the New Image Is Obtained from Image-2 and Comment on the Observed Result

This experiment modifies the Python code given in Fig. 4.35 to combine the lower order bit planes from Image-1 and higher-order bit planes from Image-2 to form the new image and the modified Python code is given in Fig. 4.37, and its corresponding output is shown in Fig. 4.38.

```
#Combining bitplane of two images
import cv2
import numpy as np
import matplotlib.pyplot as plt
#Step 1: Read the first image
img1=cv2.imread('cameraman.tif',0)
#Step 2: Extract the eight biplanes of image-1
bpc_0=np.mod(img1,2)
bpc_1=np.mod(np.floor(img1/2),2)
bpc_2=np.mod(np.floor(img1/4),4)
bpc_3=np.mod(np.floor(img1/8),8)
bpc_4=np.mod(np.floor(img1/16),16)
bpc_5=np.mod(np.floor(img1/32),32)
bpc_6=np.mod(np.floor(img1/64),64)
bpc_7=np.mod(np.floor(img1/128),128)
#Step 3: Read the second image
img2=cv2.imread('rice.tif',0)
#Step4: Extract the eight biplanes of image-1
bpl_0=np.mod(img2,2)
bpl_1=np.mod(np.floor(img2/2),2)
bpl_2=np.mod(np.floor(img2/4),4)
bpl_3=np.mod(np.floor(img2/8),8)
bpl_4=np.mod(np.floor(img2/16),16)
bpl_5=np.mod(np.floor(img2/32),32)
bpl_6=np.mod(np.floor(img2/64),64)
bpl_7=np.mod(np.floor(img2/128),128)
#Step 5: New image using bitplanes of image-1 and image-2
img_new=bpc_7*128+bpl_6*64+bpc_5*32+bpl_4*16+bpc_3*8+bpl_2*4+bpc_1*2+bpl_0
#Step 6: Displaying the result
plt.subplot(1,3,1),plt.imshow(img1,cmap='gray'),plt.title('Image-1'),plt.axis('off')
plt.subplot(1,3,2),plt.imshow(img2,cmap='gray'),plt.title('Image-2'),plt.axis('off')
plt.subplot(1,3,3),plt.imshow(img_new,cmap='gray'),plt.title('New image'),plt.axis('off')
plt.tight_layout()
```

Fig. 4.35 Python code to combine the bit planes of two images

Inference

- The new image resembles Image-2, because the higher-order bit plane of the new image is obtained from "Rice image".

Experiment 4.16: Modify the Program in Such a Way that the Higher-Order Bit Plane of the New Image Is Obtained from Image-1, which Is a "Cameraman Image", and the Lower Order Bit Planes of the New Image Are Obtained from Image-2, which Is the "Rice Image"

This experiment modifies the Python code given in Fig. 4.35 to combine the higher-order bit planes from Image-1 and lower order bit planes from Image-2 to form the new image and the modified Python code is given in Fig. 4.39, and its corresponding output is shown in Fig. 4.40.

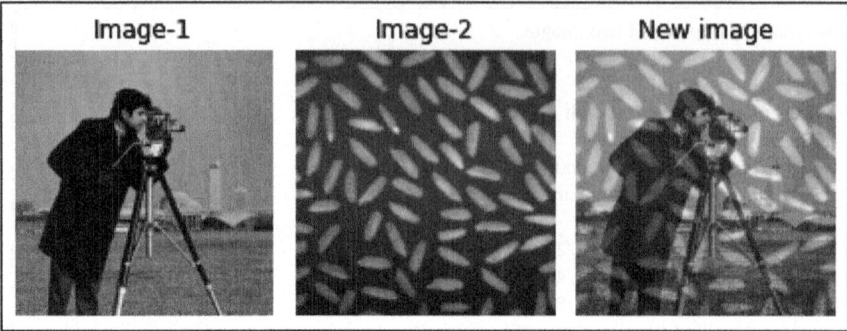

Fig. 4.36 Result of Python code shown in Fig. 4.35

```
#Combining bitplane of two images
import cv2
import numpy as np
import matplotlib.pyplot as plt
#Step 1: Read the first image
img1=cv2.imread('cameraman.tif',0)
#Step 2: Extract the eight biplanes of image-1
bpc_0=np.mod(img1,2)
bpc_1=np.mod(np.floor(img1/2),2)
bpc_2=np.mod(np.floor(img1/4),4)
bpc_3=np.mod(np.floor(img1/8),8)
bpc_4=np.mod(np.floor(img1/16),16)
bpc_5=np.mod(np.floor(img1/32),32)
bpc_6=np.mod(np.floor(img1/64),64)
bpc_7=np.mod(np.floor(img1/128),128)
#Step 3: Read the second image
img2=cv2.imread('rice.tif',0)
#Step4: Extract the eight biplanes of image-1
bpl_0=np.mod(img2,2)
bpl_1=np.mod(np.floor(img2/2),2)
bpl_2=np.mod(np.floor(img2/4),4)
bpl_3=np.mod(np.floor(img2/8),8)
bpl_4=np.mod(np.floor(img2/16),16)
bpl_5=np.mod(np.floor(img2/32),32)
bpl_6=np.mod(np.floor(img2/64),64)
bpl_7=np.mod(np.floor(img2/128),128)
#Step 5: New image using bitplanes of image-1 and image-2
img_new=bpl_7*128+bpl_6*64+bpl_5*32+bpl_4*16+bpc_3*8+bpc_2*4+bpc_1*2+bpc_0
#Step 6: Displaying the result
plt.subplot(1,3,1),plt.imshow(img1,cmap='gray'),plt.title('Image-1'),plt.axis('off')
plt.subplot(1,3,2),plt.imshow(img2,cmap='gray'),plt.title('Image-2'),plt.axis('off')
plt.subplot(1,3,3),plt.imshow(img_new,cmap='gray'),plt.title('New image'),plt.axis('off')
plt.tight_layout()
```

Fig. 4.37 Python code to obtain new image by combining the bit planes of two images

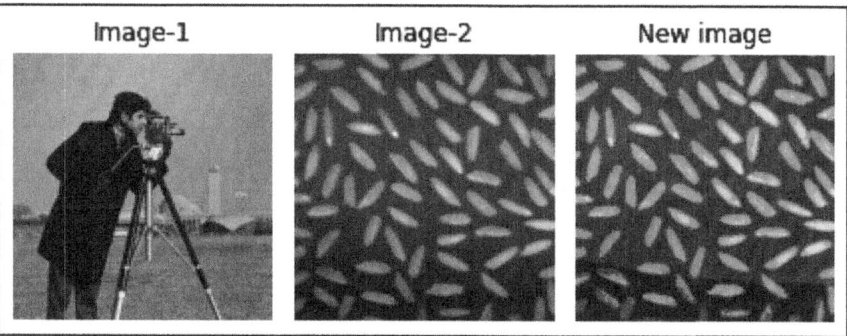

Fig. 4.38 Result of Python code shown in Fig. 4.37

```
#Combining bitplane of two images
import cv2
import numpy as np
import matplotlib.pyplot as plt
#Step 1: Read the first image
img1=cv2.imread('cameraman.tif',0)
#Step 2: Extract the eight biplanes of image-1
bpc_0=np.mod(img1,2)
bpc_1=np.mod(np.floor(img1/2),2)
bpc_2=np.mod(np.floor(img1/4),4)
bpc_3=np.mod(np.floor(img1/8),8)
bpc_4=np.mod(np.floor(img1/16),16)
bpc_5=np.mod(np.floor(img1/32),32)
bpc_6=np.mod(np.floor(img1/64),64)
bpc_7=np.mod(np.floor(img1/128),128)
#Step 3: Read the second image
img2=cv2.imread('rice.tif',0)
#Step4: Extract the eight biplanes of image-1
bpl_0=np.mod(img2,2)
bpl_1=np.mod(np.floor(img2/2),2)
bpl_2=np.mod(np.floor(img2/4),4)
bpl_3=np.mod(np.floor(img2/8),8)
bpl_4=np.mod(np.floor(img2/16),16)
bpl_5=np.mod(np.floor(img2/32),32)
bpl_6=np.mod(np.floor(img2/64),64)
bpl_7=np.mod(np.floor(img2/128),128)
#Step 5: New image using bitplanes of image-1 and image-2
img_new=bpc_7*128+bpc_6*64+bpc_5*32+bpc_4*16+bpl_3*8+bpl_2*4+bpl_1*2+bpl_0
#Step 6: Displaying the result
plt.subplot(1,3,1),plt.imshow(img1,cmap='gray'),plt.title('Image-1'),plt.axis('off')
plt.subplot(1,3,2),plt.imshow(img2,cmap='gray'),plt.title('Image-2'),plt.axis('off')
plt.subplot(1,3,3),plt.imshow(img_new,cmap='gray'),plt.title('New image'),plt.axis('off')
plt.tight_layout()
```

Fig. 4.39 Python code to combine the bit planes of two image

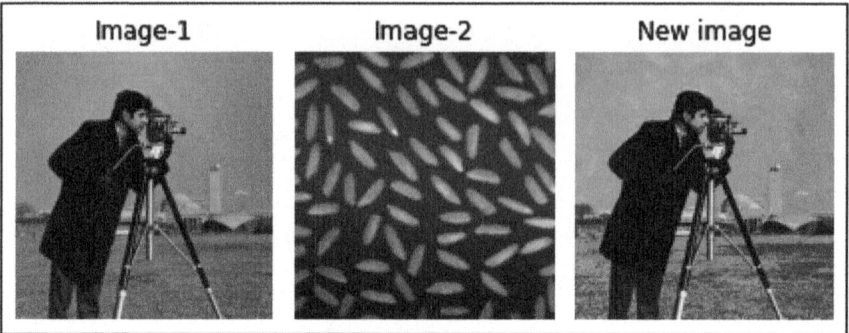

Fig. 4.40 Result of Python code shown in Fig. 4.39

Inferences

- The new image resembles Image-1 (Cameraman image) because the higher-order bit plane of the new image is obtained from the "Cameraman image".
- From this experiment, the visual quality of the new image is predominantly decided by higher-order bit plane.

4.6   Histogram of an Image

Histogram is a plot of gray level against the frequency of occurrence of grey level. A histogram does not give any information about the location of the pixels; hence, two different images can have the same histogram.

Experiment 4.17: Image Histogram "Matplotlib" Library
The following Python code is used to plot the histogram of the grayscale image using the built-in function available in the "matplotlib" library. The Python code is shown in Fig. 4.41, and the corresponding output is shown in Fig. 4.42.

Inferences

- In Fig. 4.41, the command "img.ravel()" is used to flatten the 2D array to a 1D array.
- Figure 4.42 shows the histogram plot of the Cameraman image.

Experiment 4.18: Image Histogram from "cv2" Library
The built-in function "calcHist" available in "cv2" library can be used to plot the histogram of the given image. The Python code that performs the task of plotting the histogram of "Cameraman image" using the built-in function "catechist" is shown in Fig. 4.43, and the corresponding output is shown in Fig. 4.44.

```
# Histogram of grayscale image
import matplotlib.pyplot as plt
import cv2
img=cv2.imread('cameraman.tif',0)
plt.subplot(1,2,1),plt.imshow(img,cmap='gray')
plt.title('Image'),plt.axis('off')
plt.subplot(1,2,2),plt.hist(img.ravel(),bins = 256, range = [0,256])
plt.xlabel('Gray level'),plt.ylabel('Freq of Occurrence')
plt.title('Histogram of the image')
plt.tight_layout()
```

Fig. 4.41 Python code to plot the histogram of a grayscale image

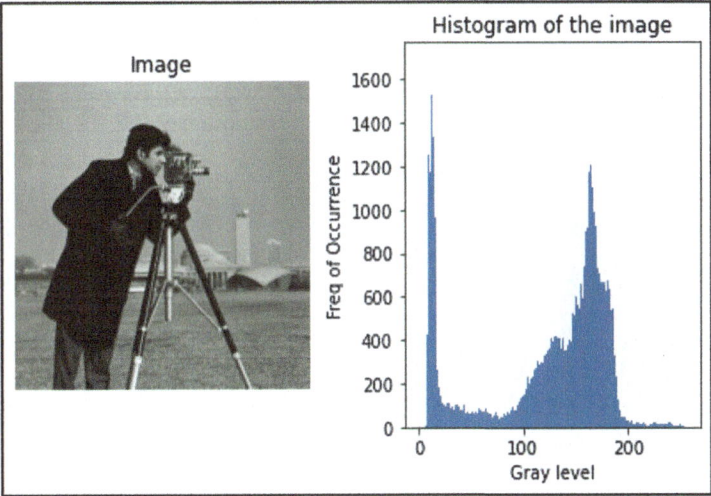

Fig. 4.42 Result of Python code shown in Fig. 4.41

Inferences

- The built-in function "calcHist" is used to plot the histogram of the grayscale image.
- This built-in function accepts the input image and returns the histogram of the input image.

Experiment 4.19: Two Different Images Can Have Same Histogram

The objective of this experiment is to prove that two different images can have the same histogram. To illustrate this fact, the input image is taken and it is flipped upside down to get the new image. Upon plotting the original image and the flipped image, it is observed that both the histograms are the same. The Python code that performs this task is shown in Fig. 4.45, and the corresponding output is shown in Fig. 4.46.

```
# Histogram plot using CV2 library
import cv2
import matplotlib.pyplot as plt
#Step 1: Reading the image
img=cv2.imread('cameraman.tif',0)
#Step 2: Obtaining the histogram
histogram = cv2.calcHist([img], [0], None, [256], [0, 256])
#Step 3: Displaying the result
plt.subplot(1,2,1),plt.imshow(img,cmap='gray'),plt.title('Image'),plt.axis('off')
plt.subplot(1,2,2),plt.plot(histogram),plt.title('Histogram of the image'),
plt.xlabel('Gray level'),plt.ylabel('Freq of Occurrence')
plt.tight_layout()
```

Fig. 4.43 Python code to obtain the histogram of grayscale image

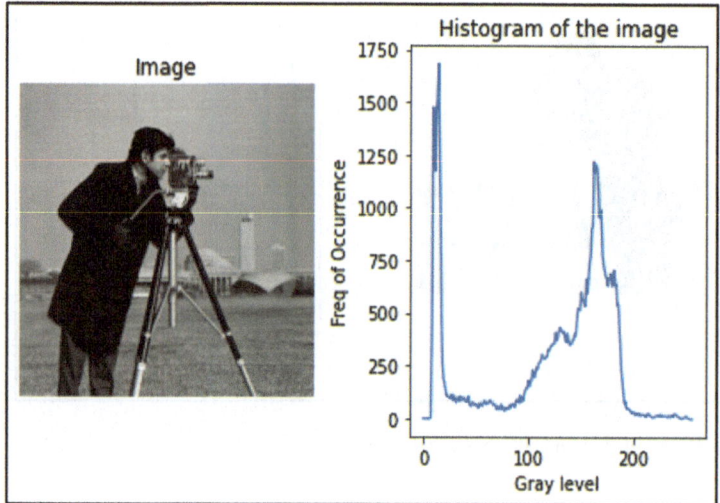

Fig. 4.44 Histogram of the grayscale image

Inferences

- From Fig. 4.46, it is possible to observe that Images 1 and 2 are different, but their histograms are identical.
- The reason is that the histogram gives only the frequency of occurrence of the gray level of the image. It does not provide any information about the pixel location.

```
# Same Histogram for two different image
import cv2
import matplotlib.pyplot as plt
#Step 1: Reading the image
img1=cv2.imread('cameraman.tif',0)
img2=img1[::-1]
#Step 2: Obtaining the histograms
histogram1 = cv2.calcHist([img1], [0], None, [256], [0, 256])
histogram2 = cv2.calcHist([img2], [0], None, [256], [0, 256])
#Step 3: Displaying the result
plt.figure(figsize=(8,6)),plt.subplot(2,2,1),plt.imshow(img1,cmap='gray')
plt.title('Image-1'),plt.axis('off'),plt.subplot(2,2,2),plt.plot(histogram1)
plt.title('Histogram of the image'),plt.xlabel('Gray level'),plt.ylabel('Freq of occurrence')
plt.subplot(2,2,3),plt.imshow(img2,cmap='gray'),plt.title('Image-2'),plt.axis('off')
plt.subplot(2,2,4),plt.plot(histogram2),plt.title('Histogram of the image')
plt.xlabel('Gray level'),plt.ylabel('Freq of occurrence')
plt.tight_layout()
```

Fig. 4.45 Python code to illustrate two different images can have the same histogram

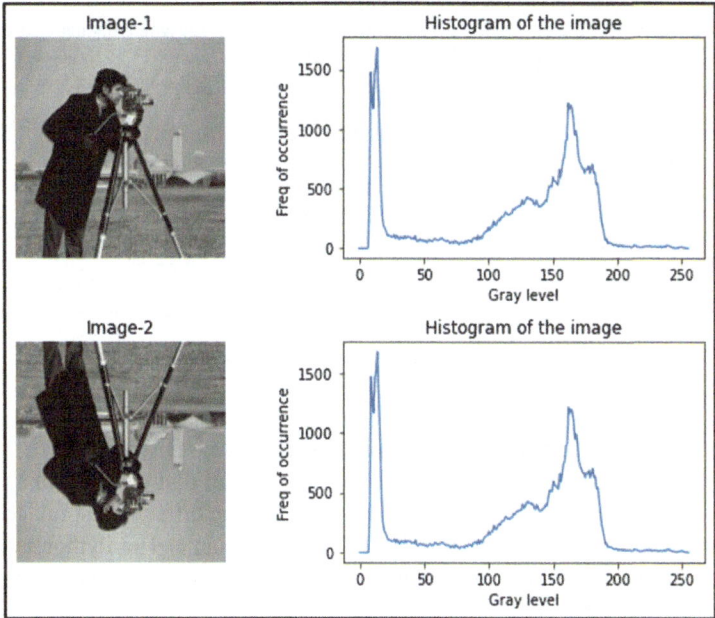

Fig. 4.46 Result of Python code shown in Fig. 4.45

```
# Same histogram plot for different images
import numpy as np
import matplotlib.pyplot as plt
import cv2
#Step 1: Generation of test image 1
img=20+np.zeros([256,256])
img[:,0:127]=150
#Step 2: Generation of test image 2
img1=20+np.zeros([32,32])
img2=150+np.zeros([32,32])
img3=cv2.hconcat([img1,img2,img1,img2,img1,img2,img1,img2])
img4=cv2.hconcat([img2,img1,img2,img1,img2,img1,img2,img1])
img5=cv2.vconcat([img3,img4])
img6=cv2.vconcat([img3,img4])
img7=cv2.vconcat([img5,img6])
img8=cv2.vconcat([img7,img7])
#Step 3: Generation of test image 3
img_1=20+np.zeros([64,64])
img_2=150+np.zeros([64,64])
img_3=cv2.hconcat([img_1,img_2,img_1,img_2])
img_4=cv2.hconcat([img_2,img_1,img_2,img_1])
img_5=cv2.vconcat([img_3,img_4])
img_6=cv2.vconcat([img_5,img_5])
#Step 3: Displaying the image and the histogram
plt.figure(figsize=(8, 8)),plt.subplot(3,2,1),plt.imshow(img,cmap='gray',vmin=0,vmax=255)
plt.title('Test image 1'),plt.xticks([]),plt.yticks([]),plt.subplot(3,2,2),
plt.hist(img.ravel(),bins=256,range=[0,256]),plt.title('Histogram 1'),plt.xlabel('Gray level'),
plt.ylabel('Freq of Occurrence'),plt.subplot(3,2,3),
plt.imshow(img8,cmap='gray',vmin=0,vmax=255),plt.title('Test image 2'),plt.xticks([]),
plt.yticks([]),plt.subplot(3,2,4), plt.hist(img8.ravel(),bins=256,range=[0,256])
plt.title('Histogram 2'),plt.xlabel('Gray level'),plt.ylabel('Freq of Occurrence'),plt.subplot(3,2,5),
plt.imshow(img_6,cmap='gray',vmin=0,vmax=255),plt.title('Test image 3'),plt.xticks([]),
plt.yticks([]),plt.subplot(3,2,6), plt.hist(img_6.ravel(),bins=256,range=[0,256])
plt.title('Histogram 3'),plt.xlabel('Gray level'),plt.ylabel('Freq of Occurrence')
plt.tight_layout()
```

Fig. 4.47 Python code to illustrate that multiple images can have the same histogram

Experiment 4.20: Multiple Images Can Have the Same Histogram

The objective of this experiment is to illustrate the fact that multiple images can have the same histogram. To demonstrate this fact, three different test images were generated, and their histograms were found to be the same. The Python code that illustrates the above problem statement is given in Fig. 4.47, and the corresponding output is shown in Fig. 4.48.

Inferences

The following inferences can be drawn from Fig. 4.48:

- Test Images 1, 2, and 3 are different. Even though Test Images 1, 2, and 3 broadly belong to the checkerboard pattern, appearance-wise they are different.
- The histograms of the three images are identical. This illustrates the fact that multiple images can have the same histogram.

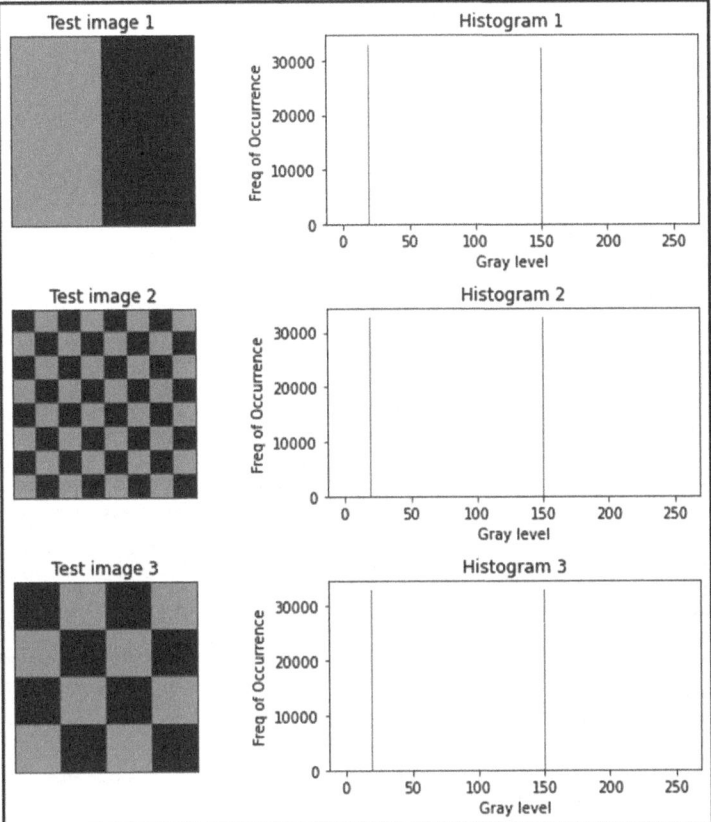

Fig. 4.48 Result of Python code shown in Fig. 4.47

Experiment 4.21: Histogram of Bright and Dark Image

The objective of this experiment is to observe the histogram of the original image and its brighter and darker versions. A constant value is added to the input image to create a brighter image. To create a darker image, a constant value is subtracted from each input image pixel. Then histogram of the original image, brighter image, and darker image has to be plotted. The Python code that performs the task mentioned in the problem statement is shown in Fig. 4.49, and the corresponding output is shown in Fig. 4.50.

Inferences

The following observations can be made from this experiment:

- The input image is read, and a brightened image is obtained by adding a "50" to each pixel in the image.
- Darken image is obtained by subtracting a value of "30" from each pixel of the input image.

```
# Histogram of bright and dark image
import cv2
import matplotlib.pyplot as plt
import numpy as np
#Step 1: Reading the input image
img1=cv2.imread('tstimg.jpg',0)
#Step2: Increasing the brightness of the image
img2=img1+50
img2 = np.clip(img2.astype(np.uint8)+50, 50, 255).astype(np.uint8)
#Step 3: Decreasing the brightness of theimage
img3=img1-30
img3 = np.clip(img3.astype(np.uint8)-30, 0, 255-30).astype(np.uint8)
#Step 3: Displaying the result
plt.figure(figsize=(10, 8)),plt.subplot(3,2,1),plt.imshow(img1,cmap='gray')
plt.title('Image-1'),plt.axis('off'),plt.subplot(3,2,2),
plt.hist(img1.ravel(),bins = 256, range = [0,256]),plt.title('Histogram 3'),
plt.xlabel('Gray level'),plt.ylabel('Freq of Occurrence'),plt.title('Histogram of the input image')
plt.subplot(3,2,3),plt.imshow(img2,cmap='gray'),plt.title('Image-2'),plt.axis('off')
plt.subplot(3,2,4),plt.hist(img2.ravel(),bins = 256, range = [0,256]),plt.title('Histogram 3'),
plt.xlabel('Gray level'),plt.ylabel('Freq of Occurrence'),plt.title('Histogram of the bright
image')
plt.subplot(3,2,5),plt.imshow(img3,cmap='gray'),plt.title('Image-3'),plt.axis('off')
plt.subplot(3,2,6),plt.hist(img3.ravel(),bins = 256, range = [0,256]),plt.title('Histogram 3'),
plt.xlabel('Gray level'),plt.ylabel('Freq of occurrence'),plt.title('Histogram of the dark image')
plt.tight_layout()
```

Fig. 4.49 Histogram of brighter and darker image

- After obtaining the brightened and darkened images, the images and their corresponding histogram are plotted, which is shown in Fig. 4.50.
- The second image is brighter; the histogram of the brighter image shifts towards the right when compared to the input image.
- The third image is darker; the histogram of the darker image shifts towards the left compared to the input image.

Experiment 4.22: Histogram of Low-Contrast and High-Contrast Image
This experiment aims to obtain the histogram of low- and high-contrast images. The Python code that performs the above-mentioned task is shown in Fig. 4.51, and the corresponding output is shown in Fig. 4.52.

Inferences
The following inferences can be drawn from Fig. 4.52:

- The histogram of the low-contrast image is a shrunk version of the input image histogram.
- The histogram of the high-contrast image is a stretched version of the input image histogram.

Experiment 4.23: Histogram of the Input Image and the Scrambled Image
In this experiment, the input image is read and then scrambled by randomly redistributing the pixel values of the input image. The histogram of the input image and

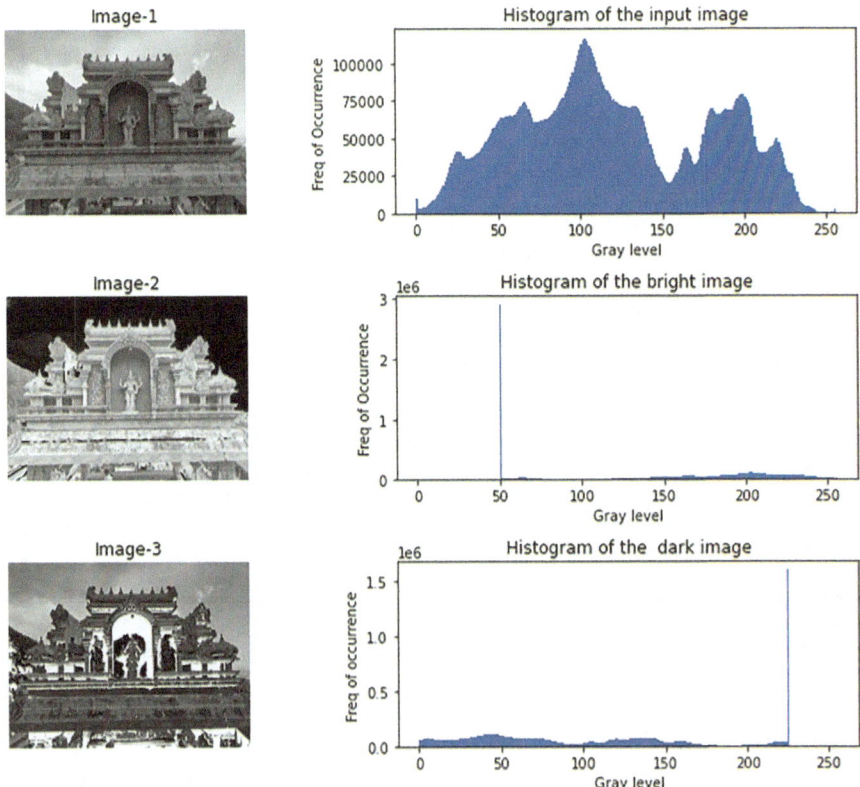

Fig. 4.50 Histogram of original, brighter, and darker image

the scrambled image is plotted. The Python code that performs this task is shown in Fig. 4.53, and the corresponding output is shown in Fig. 4.54.

Inferences

- Histogram of the input image and the scrambled image are similar. Histogram gives the frequency of occurrence of the gray level.
- It does not give any information regarding the spatial location information of the pixel.

4.7   Histogram Equalization

Histogram equalization is a statistical tool to improve the contrast of the image. Histogram equalization maps the input image histogram into an "equalized" histogram with an equal population of all gray levels.

```
# Histogram plot of low and high-contrast images
import matplotlib.pyplot as plt
import cv2
#Step 1: Read the three images
img1=cv2.imread('cameraman.tif',0)
c1,c2=0.1,1.7;#contrast
b1,b2=0,0;# brightness
img2 = cv2.addWeighted(img1,c1,img1,0,b1)
img3=cv2.addWeighted(img1,c2,img1,0,b2)
#Step 2: Displaying the images and their histogram
plt.figure(figsize=(10, 8)),plt.subplot(3,2,1),plt.imshow(img1,cmap='gray')
plt.title('Original image'),plt.axis('off'),plt.subplot(3,2,2),
plt.hist(img1.ravel(),bins = 256, range = [0,256]),plt.title('Histogram of the Original image')
plt.xlabel('Gray level'),plt.ylabel('Freq of Occurrence'),plt.subplot(3,2,3),
plt.imshow(img2,cmap='gray'),plt.title('LC image'),plt.axis('off'),plt.subplot(3,2,4),
plt.hist(img2.ravel(),bins = 256, range = [0,256]),plt.xlabel('Gray level'),
plt.ylabel('Freq of Occurrence'),plt.title('Histogram of LC image'),plt.subplot(3,2,5),
plt.imshow(img3,cmap='gray'),plt.title('HC image'),plt.axis('off'),plt.subplot(3,2,6),
plt.hist(img3.ravel(),bins = 256, range = [0,256]),plt.xlabel('Gray level'),
plt.ylabel('Freq of Occurrence'),plt.title('Histogram of HC image')
plt.tight_layout()
```

Fig. 4.51 Python code to plot the histogram of low-contrast and high-contrast image

Experiment 4.24: Histogram Equalization

This experiment focuses on achieving the histogram equalized image from the input image using the built-in function *"equalizeHist"* available in "cv2" library. The Python code that performs the histogram equalization of the input image is given in Fig. 4.55, and the corresponding output is shown in Fig. 4.56.

Inferences

The following inferences can be drawn from Figs. 4.55 and 4.56:

- The input image shows "sun rising from the cloud". After histogram equalization, the brightness of the sun is shattered.
- By observing the histogram of the input image and histogram equalized image, it is possible to infer that histogram equalization is an attempt to spread the gray level such that equalized histogram has an equal population of all gray levels.

Experiment 4.25: Histogram equalization Is an Idempotent Operation

An operation is idempotent if it produces the same results even after many times it is performed. Histogram equalization is an idempotent operation. It gives the same result if it is repeated many times. The Python code that is used to illustrate the idempotent nature of histogram equalization operation is shown in Fig. 4.57, and the corresponding output is shown in Fig. 4.58.

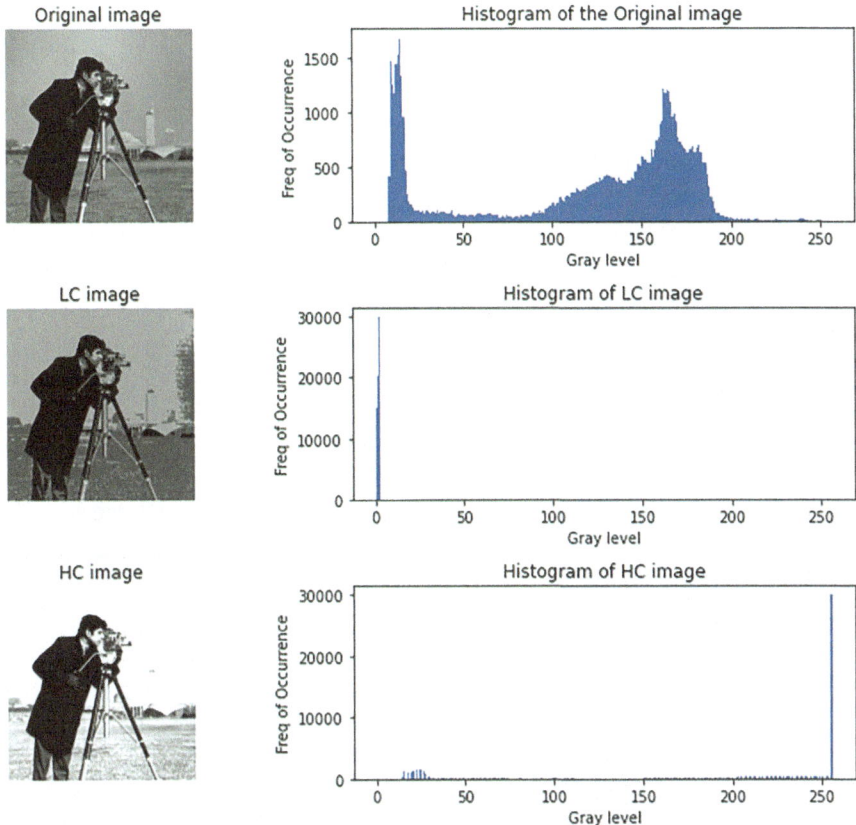

Fig. 4.52 Histogram of the input, low-contrast, and high-contrast image

Inferences
The following inferences can be drawn from Fig. 4.58:

- Histogram equalization is performed on the input image twice.
- In the figure, "HE" stands for histogram equalization. The image after perform-ing histogram equalization twice resembles the image for which histogram equalization is performed once.
- The histogram of the input image and the histogram equalized image were plotted.
- In the figure, "HE1" implies histogram equalization performed once, whereas "HE2" refers to histogram equalization performed twice. There is no change in the histogram if the histogram equalization operation is repeated. Thus, it is pos-sible to infer that histogram equalization is an idempotent operation.

```
import cv2
import matplotlib.pyplot as plt
import random
#Step 1: REading the input image
img=cv2.imread('cameraman.tif',0)
#Step 2: Scrambling the input image
scrambled_img = img.copy()
for i in range(img.shape[0]):
    for j in range(img.shape[1]):
        scrambled_img[i, j] = img[random.randint(0, img.shape[0]-1),
                            random.randint(0, img.shape[1]-1)]
#Step 3: Displaying the result
fig=plt.figure(figsize=(8,6)),plt.subplot(2,2,1),plt.imshow(img,cmap='gray')
plt.title('Input image'),plt.axis('off'),plt.subplot(2,2,2),
plt.imshow(scrambled_img,cmap='gray'),plt.title('Scrambled image'),plt.axis('off')
plt.subplot(2,2,3), plt.hist(img.ravel(),bins=256,range=[0,256])
plt.title('Histogram of input image'),plt.xlabel('Gray level'),plt.ylabel('No.of Occurrence')
plt.subplot(2,2,4), plt.hist(scrambled_img.ravel(),bins=256,range=[0,256])
plt.title('Histogram of scrambled image'),plt.xlabel('Gray level'),plt.ylabel('No.of Occurrence')
plt.tight_layout()
```

Fig. 4.53 Python code to obtain the histogram of input and scrambled image

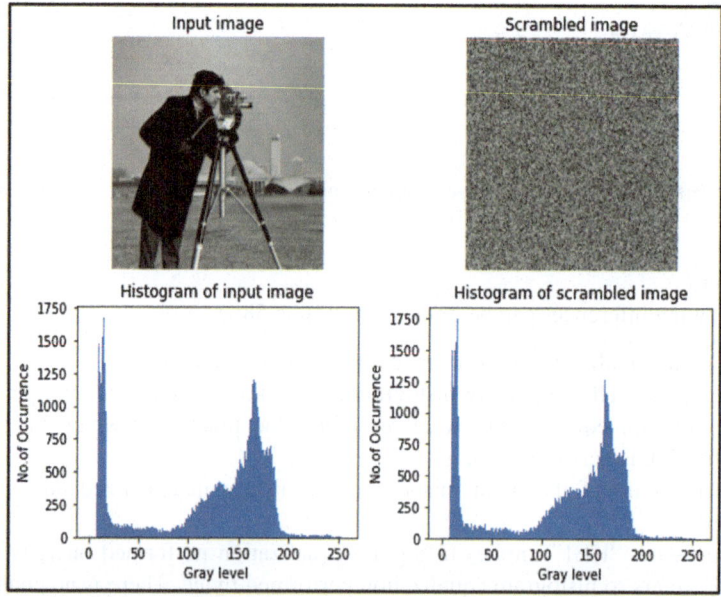

Fig. 4.54 Result of Python code shown in Fig. 4.53

```
#Histogram equalization
import cv2
import matplotlib.pyplot as plt
#Step 1: Reading the input image
img=cv2.imread('testimage.jpg',0)
#Step 2: Perform histogram equalization
img_heq=cv2.equalizeHist(img)
#Step 3: Histogram of input and equalized image
hist1 = cv2.calcHist([img], [0], None, [256], [0, 256])
hist2 = cv2.calcHist([img_heq], [0], None, [256], [0, 256])
#Step 4: Displaying the results
plt.figure(figsize=(8, 6)),plt.subplot(2,2,1),plt.imshow(img,cmap='gray')
plt.title('Input image'),plt.axis('off'),plt.subplot(2,2,2),plt.stem(hist1,markerfmt=" ")
plt.title('Histogram of the input image'),plt.xlabel('Gray level'),
plt.ylabel('Freq of Occurrence'),plt.subplot(2,2,3),plt.imshow(img_heq,cmap='gray')
plt.title('Histogram equalized image'),plt.axis('off'),plt.subplot(2,2,4),
plt.stem(hist2,markerfmt=" "),plt.title('Histogram of the equalized image')
plt.xlabel('Gray level'),plt.ylabel('Freq of Occurrence')
plt.tight_layout()
```

Fig. 4.55 Python code to perform histogram equalization

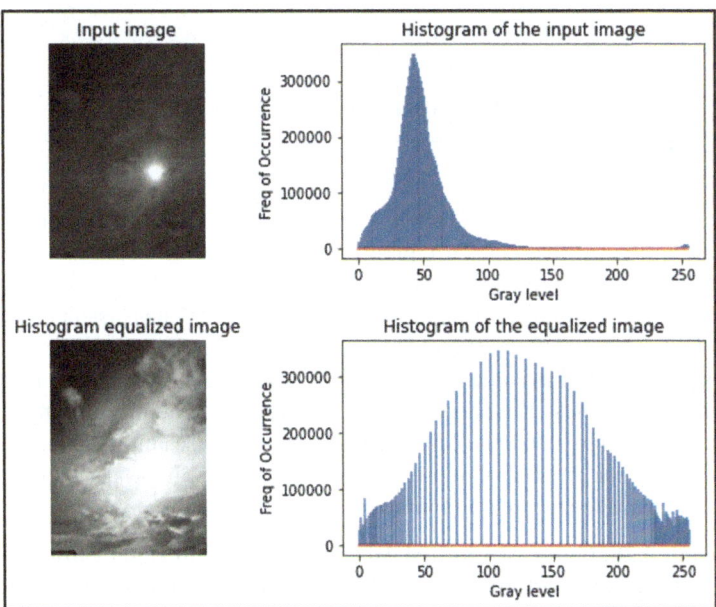

Fig. 4.56 Histogram of input image and histogram equalized image

```
#Histogram equalization is an idempotent operation
import cv2
import matplotlib.pyplot as plt
#Step 1: Reading the input image
img=cv2.imread('squares.tif',0)
#Step 2: Performing histogram equalization once
img_heq1=cv2.equalizeHist(img)
#Step 3: Repeating histogram equalization operation
img_heq2=cv2.equalizeHist(img_heq1)
#Step 4: Obtaining the histogram
histogram1 = cv2.calcHist([img], [0], None, [256], [0, 256])
histogram2 = cv2.calcHist([img_heq1], [0], None, [256], [0, 256])
histogram3 = cv2.calcHist([img_heq2], [0], None, [256], [0,256])
#Displaying the results
plt.figure(figsize=(10, 8)),plt.subplot(2,3,1),plt.imshow(img,cmap='gray')
plt.title('Input image'),plt.axis('off'),plt.subplot(2,3,2),plt.imshow(img_heq1,cmap='gray')
plt.title('HE: First time'),plt.axis('off'),plt.subplot(2,3,3),plt.imshow(img_heq2,cmap='gray')
plt.title('HE: Second time'),plt.axis('off'),plt.subplot(2,3,4),plt.plot(histogram1)
plt.title('Histogram:Input image'),plt.xlabel('Gray level'),plt.ylabel('Freq of Occurrence')
plt.subplot(2,3,5),plt.plot(histogram2),plt.title('Histogram:HE1 image')
plt.xlabel('Gray level'),plt.ylabel('Freq of Occurrence')
plt.subplot(2,3,6),plt.plot(histogram3),plt.title('Histogram:HE2 image')
plt.xlabel('Gray level'),plt.ylabel('Freq of Occurrence')
plt.tight_layout()
```

Fig. 4.57 Python code that repeats histogram equalization operation

4.8   Contrast Limited Adaptive Histogram Equalization (CLAHE)

CLAHE stands for "contrast limited adaptive histogram equalization". In CLAHE, the image is divided into several regions, and the histogram is computed for the segmented region. Multiple histograms are utilized to redistribute gray level values of the image. The interpolation technique is used to correct inconsistencies between borders. CLAHE is an effective tool for improving the local contrast in each region of an image. CLAHE has some important hyperparameters, which are (1) clip limit and (b) number of tiles. The clip limit or contrast factor is defined as a multiple of the average histogram contents. Clip limit controls the noise amplification. Number of tiles controls the amount of non-overlapping sub-areas. Improper hyperparameter selection leads to a decrease in image quality.

Experiment 4.26: Contrast Limited Adaptive Histogram Equalization
The Python code that performs contrast-limited histogram equalization of the input image for different clip levels is given in Fig. 4.59, and the corresponding output is shown in Fig. 4.60.

Inferences
From Figs. 4.59 and 4.60, the following inferences can be drawn:

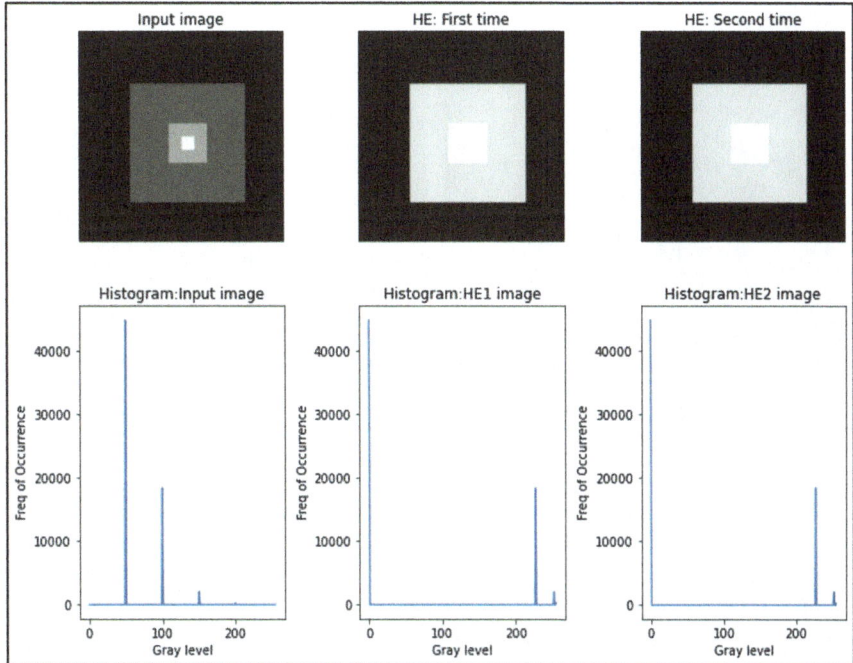

Fig. 4.58 Idempotent nature of histogram equalization operation

```
import cv2
import matplotlib.pyplot as plt
#Step 1: Reading the input image
img=cv2.imread('testimg5.jpg',0)
#Step 2: Performing histogram equalization for different CL
img_heq1=cv2.equalizeHist(img)
clahe1=cv2.createCLAHE(2.0,tileGridSize=(8,8))
clahe2=cv2.createCLAHE(3.0,tileGridSize=(8,8))
clahe3=cv2.createCLAHE(4.0,tileGridSize=(8,8))
im_clahe1=clahe1.apply(img)
im_clahe2=clahe2.apply(img)
im_clahe3=clahe3.apply(img)
#Step 3: Displaying the results
plt.figure(figsize=(8, 8))
plt.subplot(1,4,1),plt.imshow(img,cmap='gray'),plt.title('Input image'),plt.axis('off')
plt.subplot(1,4,2),plt.imshow(im_clahe1,cmap='gray'),plt.title('CLAHE:CL=2'),plt.axis('off')
plt.subplot(1,4,3),plt.imshow(im_clahe2,cmap='gray'),plt.title('CLAHE:CL=3'),plt.axis('off')
plt.subplot(1,4,4),plt.imshow(im_clahe3,cmap='gray'),plt.title('CLAHE:CL=4'),plt.axis('off')
plt.tight_layout()
```

Fig. 4.59 Python code to perform CLAHE

Fig. 4.60 Result of CLAHE for different clip limits

- The input image is a sculpture image commonly seen in temples of India.
- Upon applying CLAHE algorithm to the input image, the contrast of the input image is enhanced.
- In CLAHE, the clip limit (CL) is varied as 2, 3, and 4. The contrast of the image changes with respect to the change in clip limit. The block size is fixed as 8×8.

Experiment 4.27: Comparison of Histogram equalization and CLAHE
This experiment compares the output of histogram equalization and CLAHE-based image enhancement approaches. For this, read a gradient image. The gradient image is black at the centre and the gray level approaches white along the diagonal. The steps followed in this experiment are as follows:
Step 1: Reading the gradient image.
Step 2: Performing histogram equalization and contrast limited adaptive histogram.
equalization.
Step 3: Displaying the results.
Python code for this experiment is given in Fig. 4.61, and its corresponding output is shown in Fig. 4.62.

Inferences
The following inferences can be drawn from Fig. 4.62:

- The input image is a gradient image. The gray level at the centre of the image is black and it gradually reaches white towards the diagonal.
- Upon performing histogram equalization, the black region at the centre of the image is distributed towards the diagonal.
- Upon performing CLAHE, the black-gray level is not distributed towards the diagonal; the contrast enhancement is better in CLAHE when compared to histogram equalization.

```
import cv2
import matplotlib.pyplot as plt
#Step 1:Reading the input image
img=cv2.imread('testimg1.png',0)
#Step2: Histogram equalization
img_heq=cv2.equalizeHist(img)
#Step 3: CLAHE
clahe1=cv2.createCLAHE(3.0,tileGridSize=(8,8))
img_clahe=clahe1.apply(img)
#Step 4: Displaying the result
plt.subplot(1,3,1), plt.imshow(img,cmap='gray'),plt.title('Input image'),plt.xticks([]),
plt.yticks([]),plt.subplot(1,3,2), plt.imshow(img_heq,cmap='gray')
plt.title('HE Output'),plt.xticks([]),plt.yticks([]),plt.subplot(1,3,3),
plt.imshow(img_clahe,cmap='gray'),plt.title('CLAHE Output'),plt.xticks([]),plt.yticks([])
plt.tight_layout()
```

Fig. 4.61 Python code to perform histogram equalization and CLAHE

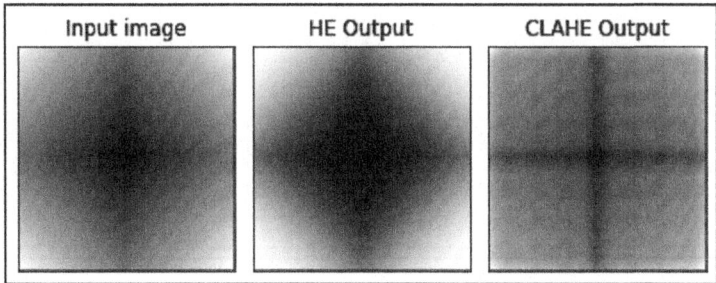

Fig. 4.62 Histogram equalization and CLAHE output

4.9 Histogram Matching

Histogram matching manipulates the pixels of the input image so that its histogram matches the histogram of the reference image. It is an attempt to modify the contrast level of the test image according to the contrast level of the reference image. The built-in function "match_histograms" available in "scikit" image library can be used to perform histogram matching.

Experiment 4.28: Histogram Matching
This experiment deals with histogram matching. Two images, "Test image" and "Reference image" are read. The histogram of the test image is modified in accordance with the histogram of the reference image using the built-in function "match_histogram" available in "scikit" image library. The Python code that performs this task is shown in Fig. 4.63, and the corresponding output is shown in Fig. 4.64.

```
#Histogram matching
import cv2
from skimage.exposure import match_histograms
import matplotlib.pyplot as plt
img=cv2.imread('testimg1.png',0)
ref=img_heq=cv2.equalizeHist(img);#cv2.imread('reference.png',0)
matched = match_histograms(img, ref)
fig=plt.figure(figsize=(8,6)),plt.subplot(1,3,1), plt.imshow(img,cmap='gray')
plt.title('Input image'),plt.xticks([]),plt.yticks([]),plt.subplot(1,3,2),
plt.imshow(ref,cmap='gray'),plt.title('Reference image'),plt.xticks([]),
plt.yticks([]),plt.subplot(1,3,3), plt.imshow(matched,cmap='gray')
plt.title('Histogram Matched Output'),plt.xticks([]),plt.yticks([])
plt.tight_layout()
```

Fig. 4.63 Python code to perform histogram matching

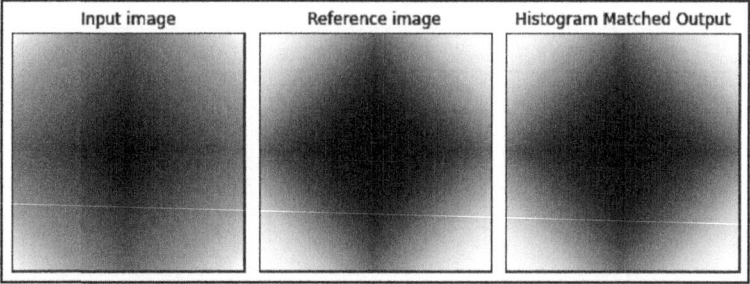

Fig. 4.64 Result of histogram matching

Inferences

The following inferences can be drawn from Fig. 4.64:

- The input image is a gradient image whose gray level gradually varies from black to white along the diagonal.
- The reference image gray level is blacker when compared to the test image.
- Upon performing histogram matching, the matched image resembles the reference image.

4.10 Spatial Domain Filtering

In linear spatial filtering, each output pixel is a weighted sum of neighbouring pixels. It is equivalent to the convolution of the image with the mask. This is represented in Fig. 4.65.

Fig. 4.65 Block diagram
of spatial domain filtering
process

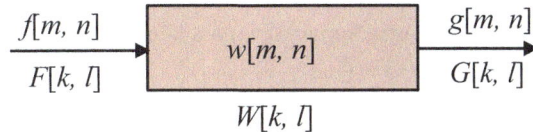

In Fig. 4.65, $f[m, n]$ represents the input image, $w[m, n]$ represents the mask of the window and $g[m, n]$ represents the output image. $F[k, l]$, $W[k, l]$, and $G[k, l]$ represent the Fourier transform of input image, window function, and output image, respectively. In spatial domain, the relationship between the input image $f[m, n]$ and the output image $g[m, n]$ is given by

$$g[m,n] = f[m,n] * w[m,n] \qquad (4.11)$$

In Eq. (4.11), "*" represents the convolution operation. In the frequency domain, the relationship between the input and output image is given by

$$G[k,l] = F[k,l] \times W[k,l] \qquad (4.12)$$

The above equation is due to the fact that convolution in the spatial domain is equivalent to multiplication in the frequency domain.

A linear spatially invariant filter can be represented with a mask that is convolved with the image pixels. The weight of 3 × 3 mask is represented as $\begin{bmatrix} w_1 & w_2 & w_3 \\ w_4 & w_5 & w_6 \\ w_7 & w_8 & w_9 \end{bmatrix}$, if the gray level of the image pixels under the mask are represented as $i_1, i_2, \ldots, i_9$. The response of the linear mask is given by $R = i_1 w_1 + i_2 w_2 + i_3 w_3 + \cdots + i_9 w_9$. Masks are usually chosen to have odd dimensions to provide a centre pixel location.

4.10.1   Low-Pass Filtering Using Box Filter

Low-pass filtering results in smoothing of the image. Smoothing is linear and spatially invariant. Low-pass filtering can be done using (1) box filter and (2) Gaussian filter. The box filter equally weights all samples within a square region of the image. The 3 × 3 mask of the box filter is given by $\dfrac{1}{9}\begin{bmatrix} 1 & 1 & 1 \\ 1 & 1 & 1 \\ 1 & 1 & 1 \end{bmatrix}$, and the 5 × 5 mask of the box filter is given by $\dfrac{1}{25}\begin{bmatrix} 1 & 1 & 1 & 1 & 1 \\ 1 & 1 & 1 & 1 & 1 \\ 1 & 1 & 1 & 1 & 1 \\ 1 & 1 & 1 & 1 & 1 \\ 1 & 1 & 1 & 1 & 1 \end{bmatrix}$. The weights of the smoothing or low-pass

```
#Spatial domain Low pass filtering
import cv2
import matplotlib.pyplot as plt
import numpy as np
#Step 1: Reading the input image
img=cv2.imread('A.png',0)
#Step 2: Defining different mask size
size=[5,11,21,25,41]
plt.figure(figsize=(8,6))
plt.figure(1),plt.subplot(2,3,1)
plt.imshow(img,cmap='gray'),plt.title('Input image')
plt.xticks([]),plt.yticks([])
#Step 3: Performing spatial filtering and displaying result
for i in range(len(size)):
    kernel=np.ones((size[i], size[i])) / (size[i] ** 2)
    im_filt=cv2.filter2D(img,-1,kernel)
    plt.figure(1),plt.subplot(2,3,i+2)
    plt.imshow(im_filt,cmap='gray'),plt.xticks([]),plt.yticks([])
    plt.title(f'kernel = {size[i]} x {size[i]}')
plt.tight_layout()
```

Fig. 4.66 Python code to perform spatial domain low-pass filtering of the image

filter are positive. The weights are typically chosen to sum to unity to maintain the average brightness value.

Experiment 4.29: Spatial domain Low-Pass Filtering

The aim of this experiment is to perform spatial domain low-pass filtering on image. For this, read an input alphabet image "A". Perform spatial domain low-pass filtering of the input image for different mask sizes, namely 5×5, 11×11, 21×21, 25×25, and 41×41. The Python code that performs spatial domain low-pass filtering of the input image is shown in Fig. 4.66, and the corresponding result is displayed in Fig. 4.67. The built-in functions used in the program and its purpose is given in Table 4.1.

Inferences

From Fig. 4.67, the following conclusions can be drawn:

- The input image is an image of an alphabet "A".
- The input image is convolved with four different smoothing filters, which is also termed as "box filters". The box filter smooth's the image by making each output pixel the average of the surrounding ones.
- It is also possible to observe that the size of the mask decides the extent of smoothing (blurring). The blurring effect is greater with the increase in the size of mask.

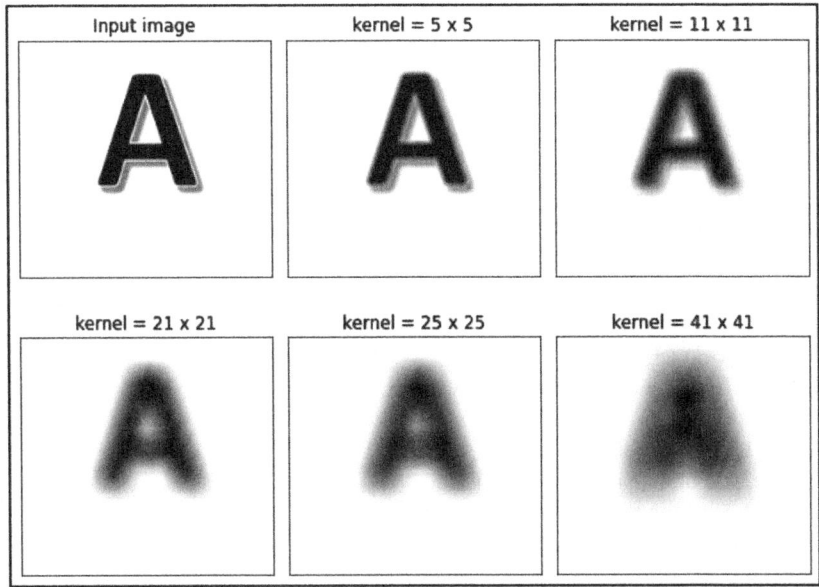

Fig. 4.67 Result of spatial domain low-pass filtering

Table 4.1 List of built-in functions used in the program

S. no.	Built-in function	Library	Purpose
1	Imread	cv2	To read the input image
2	Imshow	Matplotlib	To display the image
3	Ones	Numpy	To obtain the kernel or mask
4	filter2D	cv2	To perform 2D convolution

Experiment 4.30: Impact of Smoothing Filters

This experiment discusses the impact of various smoothing filters. Read an input image and add additive white Gaussian noise to the input image. Pass the noisy image to 5 × 5 and 11 × 11 smoothing filters. The objective of this experiment is to illustrate the fact that the low-pass filter characteristic of smoothing filters reduces high-frequency noise.

The steps involved in this experiment are as follows:

Step 1: Reading the input image.

Step 2: Adding additive white Gaussian noise to the input image. The two parameters to be considered into account in additive white Gaussian noise are mean and variance. In this example, the mean value is chosen as 0 and variance is fixed as 1000.

Step 3: Pass the noisy image to the smoothing filter. The nature of kernel used in smoothing is box kernel. The kernel size chosen in this experiment are 5 × 5 and 11 × 11.

```
# Filtering the image
import cv2
import matplotlib.pyplot as plt
import numpy as np
#Step 1: Reading the input image
img=cv2.imread('A.png',0)
#Step 2: Adding noise to the input image
mean,variance=0,1000
sigma=np.sqrt(variance)
gauss = np.random.normal(mean, sigma, img.shape)
img_noise=img+gauss
#Step 3: Defining different mask size
size1,size2=5,11
kernel1=np.ones((size1, size1)) / (size1 ** 2)
kernel2=np.ones((size2, size2)) / (size2 ** 2)
#Step 4: Filtering the noisy image
img_filt1=cv2.filter2D(img_noise,-1,kernel1)
img_filt2=cv2.filter2D(img_noise,-1,kernel2)
#Step 5: Displaying the results
plt.figure(figsize=(10,8)),plt.subplot(1,4,1),plt.imshow(img,cmap='gray')
plt.title('Input image'),plt.xticks([]),plt.yticks([]),plt.subplot(1,4,2),
plt.imshow(img_noise,cmap='gray'),plt.title('Noisy image'),plt.xticks([]),
plt.yticks([]),plt.subplot(1,4,3),plt.imshow(img_filt1,cmap='gray')
plt.title('5 x 5 Smoothing filter'),plt.xticks([]),plt.yticks([]),
plt.subplot(1,4,4),plt.imshow(img_filt2,cmap='gray')
plt.title('11 x 11 Smoothing filter'),plt.xticks([]),plt.yticks([])
plt.tight_layout()
```

Fig. 4.68 Python code to perform denoising of the image using smoothing filter

Step 4: Display the result.

The Python code that performs the above-mentioned task is shown in Fig. 4.68, and the corresponding output is shown in Fig. 4.69.

Inferences

From Fig. 4.69, the following inferences can be drawn:

- The input image is an alphabet "*A*" image. It is labelled as "Input image".
- The image is corrupted with additive white Gaussian noise which is labelled as "Noisy image".
- The noisy image is passed to a smoothing filter with kernel sizes 5 × 5 and 11 × 11.
- Upon passing the image to the smoothing filter, the impact of noise is minimized. With increase in the size of the kernel, the extent of filtering is more, and the impact of noise is minimized, but the image is more blurred.

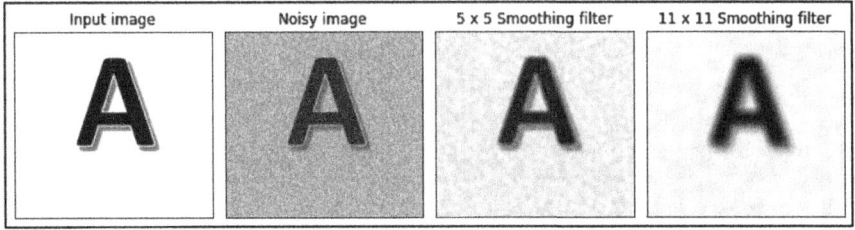

Fig. 4.69 Result of smoothing filter

- The larger smoothing filters remove more high-frequency energy. This removes more of the noise, and it also removes detail information from edges and other image features.

4.10.2 Low-Pass Filtering Using Gaussian Filter

Gaussian filter is considered as weighted average filter. The Gaussian filter smooths by replacing each image pixel with a weighted average of the neighbouring pixels such that the weight given to a neighbour decreases monotonically with distance from the central pixel. The two-dimensional zero mean discrete Gaussian function is expressed as

$$g[m,n] = e^{-\frac{\left(m^2 + n^2\right)}{2\sigma^2}}$$

(4.13)

In the above expression, σ^2 represents the variance of the Gaussian function. A larger variance implies a wider Gaussian filter and greater smoothing.

Experiment 4.31: Low-Pass Filtering Using Gaussian Filter
This experiment shows how the Gaussian filter acts as a low-pass filter. For this, read an input image and add white Gaussian noise to the input image. Pass the noisy image to 5 × 5 and 11 × 11 Gaussian filters. The Python code that performs the above-mentioned task is given in Fig. 4.70, and the corresponding output is shown in Fig. 4.71.

Inferences
From Fig. 4.71, the following inferences can be drawn:

- The input image is an alphabet "A" image. It is labelled as "Input image".
- The image is corrupted with additive white Gaussian noise, which is labelled as "Noisy image".
- The noisy image is passed to a Gaussian smoothing filter with kernel sizes 5 × 5 and 11 × 11.

```
#Gaussian smoothing of the image
import cv2
import matplotlib.pyplot as plt
import numpy as np
#Step 1: Reading the input image
img=cv2.imread('A.png',0)
#Step 2: Adding noise to the input image
mean, variance=0, 1000
sigma=np.sqrt(variance)
gauss = np.random.normal(mean, sigma, img.shape)
img_noise=img+gauss
#Step 3: Performing spatial filtering
m1, m2=5, 11
img_filt1=cv2.GaussianBlur(img_noise,(m1,m2),cv2.BORDER_DEFAULT)
img_filt2=cv2.GaussianBlur(img_noise,(m2,m2),cv2.BORDER_DEFAULT)
#Step 4: Displaying the results
plt.figure(figsize=(10,8)),plt.subplot(1,4,1),plt.imshow(img,cmap='gray'),plt.title('Input image'),
plt.xticks([]),plt.yticks([]),plt.subplot(1,4,2), plt.imshow(img_noise,cmap='gray'),
plt.title('Noisy image'),plt.xticks([]),plt.yticks([]),plt.subplot(1,4,3),
plt.imshow(img_filt1,cmap='gray'),plt.title('5 x 5 Gaussian filter'),plt.xticks([]),plt.yticks([]),
plt.subplot(1,4,4), plt.imshow(img_filt2,cmap='gray'),plt.title('11 x 11 Gaussian filter'),
plt.xticks([]),plt.yticks([]),plt.tight_layout()
```

Fig. 4.70 Python code to perform Gaussian smoothing

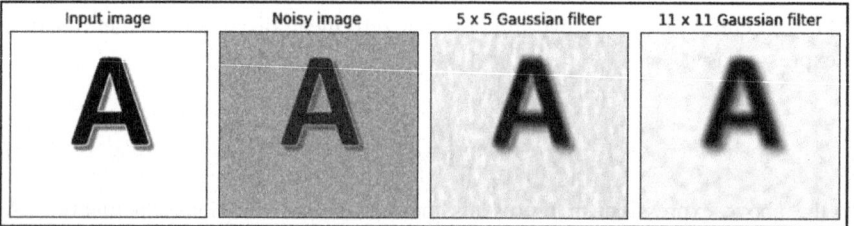

Fig. 4.71 Result of Gaussian smoothing

- Upon passing the image to the Gaussian smoothing filter, the impact of noise is minimized. With increase in the size of the kernel, the extent of filtering is more, and the impact of noise is minimized. However, it also results in increased blurring of image details.

Experiment 4.32: Comparison of Averaging Filter with a Weighted Averaging Filter

The objective of this experiment is to compare the performance of average filter with weighted average filter in the presence of noise. First the test image is generated. The test image is 256×256 image in which half of the pixel is white and the remaining half is black. The test image is corrupted with additive white Gaussian noise with zero mean and variance equals to 500. Now, the noisy image is passed through the average filter and weighted average filter, and a comparison is done with respect to the visual quality of the filtered images.

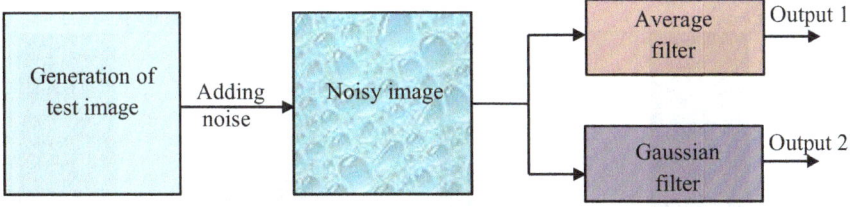

Fig. 4.72 Block diagram of the problem statement

```
#Comparison of Average with Weighted average filter
import matplotlib.pyplot as plt
import numpy as np
import cv2
#Step 1: Generation of test image
img=np.zeros([256,256])
m,n=img.shape
for i in range(0,255):
    for j in range(0,128):
        img[i,j]=255;
#Step 2: Adding noise to the input image
mean, variance=0, 500
sigma=np.sqrt(variance)
gauss = np.random.normal(mean, sigma, img.shape)
img_noise=img+gauss
mask=51
kernel_ave=np.ones((mask, mask)) / (mask ** 2)
#Step 3: Averaging filter
img_filt1=cv2.filter2D(img_noise,-1,kernel_ave)
#Step 4: Weighted averaging filter
img_filt2=cv2.GaussianBlur(img_noise,(mask,mask),cv2.BORDER_DEFAULT)
#Step5: Displaying the results
plt.figure(figsize=(10,8)),plt.subplot(1,4,1),plt.imshow(img,cma p='gray')
plt.title('Input image'),plt.xticks([]),plt.yticks([]),plt.subplot(1,4,2),
plt.imshow(img_noise,cmap='gray'),plt.title('Noisy image'),plt.xticks([]),
plt.yticks([]),plt.subplot(1,4,3),plt.imshow(img_filt1,cmap='gray')
plt.title(f'{mask} x {mask} Averaging filter'),plt.xticks([]),plt.yticks([])
plt.subplot(1,4,4),plt.imshow(img_filt2,cmap='gray')
plt.title(f'{mask} x {mask} Weighted Avg. filter'),plt.xticks([]),plt.yticks([])
plt.tight_layout()
```

Fig. 4.73 Python code to compare average filter with weighted average filter

The problem statement is depicted in the form of a block diagram, which is shown in Fig. 4.72.

The Python code that performs the task in the block diagram is shown in Fig. 4.73, and the corresponding output is shown in Fig. 4.74.

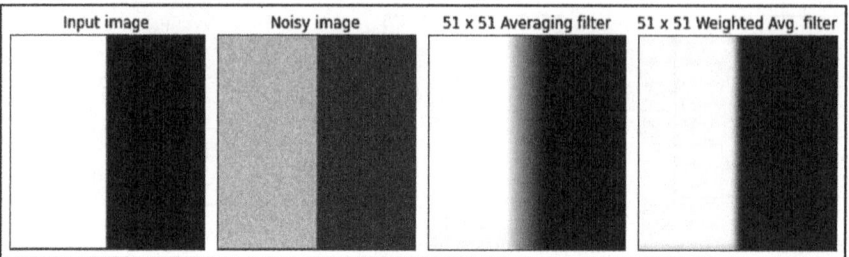

Fig. 4.74 Comparison of average filter with weighted average filter

Inferences

From Fig. 4.74, the following inferences can be drawn:

- The test image takes only two gray levels, either 0 or 255. There is an abrupt transition from white to black. It is equivalent to the unit step input signal.
- After adding white noise, the gray level white turns out to be gray. The noisy image takes a gray level between 0 and 255.
- After passing the noisy image to the averaging filter, the impact of noise is reduced, but there is a visible blurring effect. The size of the mask is 51×51; hence, the blurring effect is visible.
- After passing the noisy image to the 51×51 Gaussian filter, the impact of noise is reduced, and the blurring effect is not visible.
- If the objective is to minimize the impact of noise with less blurring effect, a weighted average filter is a better choice than an average filter.

4.10.3   High-Pass Filtering

High-pass filter enhances the edge information in the digital image. High-pass filters are also termed as sharpening filters. The second-order Laplacian operator is given by

$$\nabla^2 f = \left[f(x+1,y) + f(x-1,y) + f(x,y+1) + f(x,y-1) \right] - 4f(x,y) \quad (4.14)$$

The filter mask used to implement Laplacian operator is given as follows:

$$\nabla^2 f = \begin{bmatrix} 0 & 1 & 0 \\ 1 & -4 & 1 \\ 0 & 1 & 0 \end{bmatrix} \quad (4.15)$$

From Eq. (4.15), it is possible to interpret that the sum of the elements of the mask is equal to zero.

```
#Sharpening filter
import numpy as np
import matplotlib.pyplot as plt
import cv2
#Step 1: Read the input image
img=cv2.imread('X.png',0)
#Step 2: Define the high pass filter mask
mask=np.array([[0,1,0],[1,-4,1],[0,1,0]])
#Step 3: Perform the high-pass filtering
img1=cv2.filter2D(img,-1,mask)
#Step 4: Displaying the results
plt.subplot(1,2,1),plt.imshow(img,cmap='gray'),plt.title('Input image')
plt.xticks([]),plt.yticks([]),plt.subplot(1,2,2),plt.imshow(img1,cmap='gray'),
plt.title('High pass filtered image'),plt.xticks([]),plt.yticks([])
plt.tight_layout()
```

Fig. 4.75 Python code to perform high-pass filter

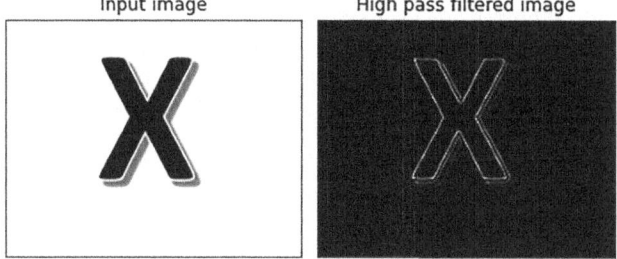

Fig. 4.76 Result of high-pass filtering

Experiment 4.33: Sharpening or High-Pass Filtering
This experiment deals with the implementation of sharpening or high-pass filtering in Python environment. For this, read the image, which is alphabet "X". Pass this image through high-pass filter whose mask is given by $h[m,n] = \begin{bmatrix} 0 & 1 & 0 \\ 1 & -4 & 1 \\ 0 & 1 & 0 \end{bmatrix}$ to obtain the output image. The Python code that performs high-pass filtering of the input image is shown in Fig. 4.75, and the corresponding output is shown in Fig. 4.76.

Inferences
The following inference can be drawn from Fig. 4.76:

- The input image is an image of alphabet "X". The image takes two gray levels, either 0 or 255.

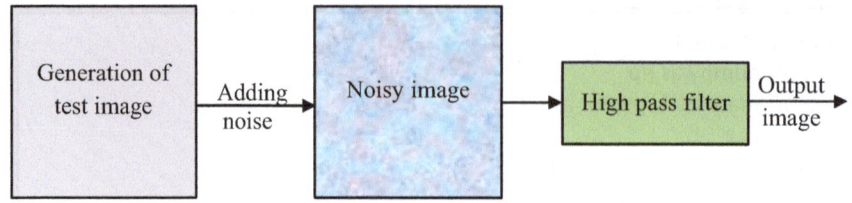

Fig. 4.77   Block diagram of high-pass filtering of noisy image

- The input image is passed through the high-pass filter. From the high-pass filtered image, it is possible to infer that the high-pass filter enhances the edge information of the input image; the background information is lost in the high-pass filtering operation. High-boost filtering is preferred to retain the background information.

Experiment 4.34: High-Pass filter in the Presence of Noise
A high-pass filter basically emphasises high-frequency components like the edges of the image. Noises are considered as high-frequency components; hence, the high-pass filter has the tendency to amplify the noise. This concept is illustrated in Fig. 4.77. To illustrate this idea, the input image is read, and then the input image is corrupted with additive white Gaussian noise with zero mean and variance equals to 100. The noisy image is then passed through a high-pass filter.

The Python code that performs the above-mentioned task is shown in Fig. 4.78, and the corresponding output is shown in Fig. 4.79.

Inferences
From Fig. 4.79, the following inferences can be drawn:

- The input image is the image of the alphabet "*X*". It takes two gray levels, either 0 or 255.
- The input image is corrupted by adding additive white Gaussian noise to obtain the noisy image.
- The noisy image is passed through high-pass filter to obtain the filtered output.
- The high-pass filter has the tendency to emphasize the high-frequency component in the image. The noise belongs to the high-frequency component; thus, the high-pass filter amplifies the noisy component in the input image.
- It is not desirable to apply a high-pass filter if the image is corrupted with noise. First, the noise impact has to be reduced, and then only a high-pass filter has to be applied.

Experiment 4.35: Low-Pass Filtering of the Input Image and Plotting the Profile of Input and Filtered Image
First, the test image is generated, which is a 256×256 image with half of the image as white and the remaining half as black. The test image is passed through a low-pass filter. Then, the profile of a single row of the input and filtered images is drawn.

```
#Sharpening filter
import numpy as np
import matplotlib.pyplot as plt
import cv2
#Step 1: Read the input image
img=cv2.imread('X.png',0)
#Step 2: Define the high pass filter mask
mask=np.array([[-1,-1,-1],[-1,8,-1],[-1,-1,-1]])
#Step 3: Adding noise to the image
mean, variance=0, 100
sigma=np.sqrt(variance)
gauss = np.random.normal(mean, sigma, img.shape)
img_noise=img+gauss
#Step 3: Perform the high-pass filtering
img1=cv2.filter2D(img_noise,-1,mask)
#Step 4: Displaying the results
plt.subplot(1,3,1),plt.imshow(img,cmap='gray'),plt.title('Input image')
plt.xticks([]),plt.yticks([]),plt.subplot(1,3,2),plt.imshow(img_noise,cmap='gray')
plt.title('Noisy image'),plt.xticks([]),plt.yticks([]),plt.subplot(1,3,3),
plt.imshow(img1,cmap='gray'),plt.title('High pass filtered image')
plt.xticks([]),plt.yticks([])
plt.tight_layout()
```

Fig. 4.78 Python code to perform high-pass filtering of noisy images

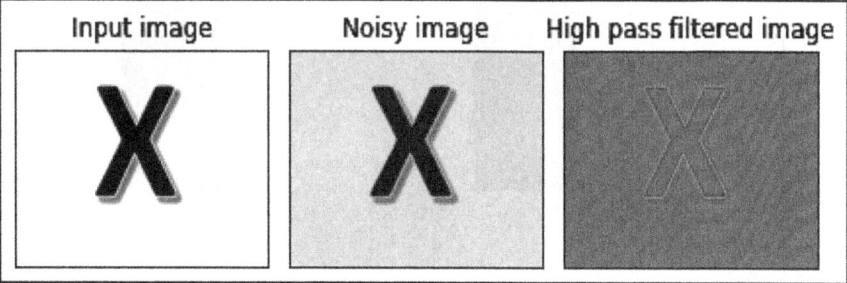

Fig. 4.79 Result of high-pass filtering of noisy image

The Python code that performs this task is shown in Fig. 4.80, and the corresponding output is shown in Fig. 4.81.

Inferences

From Fig. 4.81, the following inferences can be drawn:

- The test image exhibits an abrupt change in gray level from white to black.
- The profile, which refers to plotting the 128th row of the input test image, reveals that the gray level abruptly falls from 255 to 0. Thus, the profile is similar to a step signal.

```
#Spatial domain low pass filtering
import cv2
import numpy as np
import matplotlib.pyplot as plt
#Step 1: Generation of the test image
img=np.zeros([256,256])
img[:,0:127]=255
#Step 2: Define the mask
mask=np.ones([21,21])/(21*21)
#Step 3: To perform convolution
img_mod=cv2.filter2D(img,-1,mask)
#Step 4: Displaying the result
plt.figure(figsize=(8, 6)),plt.subplot(2,2,1),plt.imshow(img,cmap='gray'),
plt.title('Input image'),plt.xticks([]),plt.yticks([]),plt.subplot(2,2,2),
plt.imshow(img_mod,cmap='gray'),plt.title('Filtered image'),plt.xticks([]),
plt.yticks([]),plt.subplot(2,2,3),plt.plot(img[128,:]),plt.xlabel('128th Row'),
plt.ylabel('Pixel Intensity'),plt.title('Profile of input image'),
plt.subplot(2,2,4),plt.plot(img_mod[128,:]),plt.title('Profile of filtered image'),
plt.xlabel('128th Row'),plt.ylabel('Pixel Intensity')
plt.tight_layout()
```

Fig. 4.80 Spatial domain low-pass filtering of test image

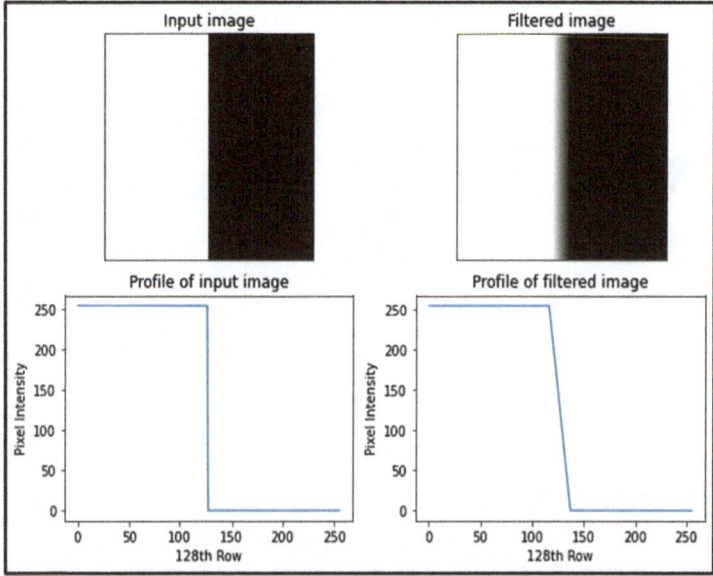

Fig. 4.81 Result of spatial domain low-pass filtering of the test image

```
#Spatial domain high pass filtering
import cv2
import numpy as np
import matplotlib.pyplot as plt
#Step 1: Generation of the test image
img=np.zeros([256,256])
img[:,0:127]=255
#Step 2: Define the mask
mask=np.array([[-1,-1,-1],[-1,8,-1],[-1,-1,-1]])
#Step 3: To perform convolution
img_mod=cv2.filter2D(img,-1,mask)
#Step 4: Displaying the result
plt.figure(figsize=(6, 6)),plt.subplot(2,2,1),plt.imshow(img,cmap='gray'),plt.title('Input image')
plt.xticks([]),plt.yticks([]),plt.subplot(2,2,2),plt.imshow(img_mod,cmap='gray'),
plt.title('Filtered image'),plt.xticks([]),plt.yticks([])
plt.subplot(2,2,3),plt.plot(img[128,:]),plt.title('Profile of input image'),
plt.xlabel('128th Row'),plt.ylabel('Pixel Intensity')
plt.subplot(2,2,4),plt.plot(img_mod[128,:]),plt.title('Profile of filtered image')
plt.xlabel('128th Row'),plt.ylabel('Pixel Intensity')
plt.tight_layout()
```

Fig. 4.82   Spatial domain high-pass filtering of test image

- Upon low-pass filtering of the input test image, the sudden variation in the input test image is changed to a gradual variation in the gray level.
- The plot of the 128th row of the filtered image shows a ramp-like signal. Thus, the step-like change in the input image gray level variation is converted to a ramp-like slow gray level variation by spatial domain low-pass filter.
- Thus, the low-pass filter converts a sharp change in the input image gray level to a gradual change in the filtered image.

Experiment 4.36: High-Pass Filtering of the Input Image and Plotting the Profile of Input and Filtered Image

First, the test image is generated, which is a 256×256 image with half of the image as white and the remaining half as black. The test image is passed through high-pass filter. Then, the profile of a single row of the input and filtered images is drawn. The Python code that performs this task is shown in Fig. 4.82, and the corresponding output is shown in Fig. 4.83.

Inferences

From Fig. 4.83, the following inferences can be drawn:

- The test image exhibits an abrupt change in gray level from white to black.
- The profile, which refers to plotting the 128th row of the input test image, reveals that the gray level abruptly falls from 255 to 0. Thus, the profile is similar to a step signal.
- The high-pass filter is basically a change detector. The high-pass filter gives an output whenever there is change in the gray level.

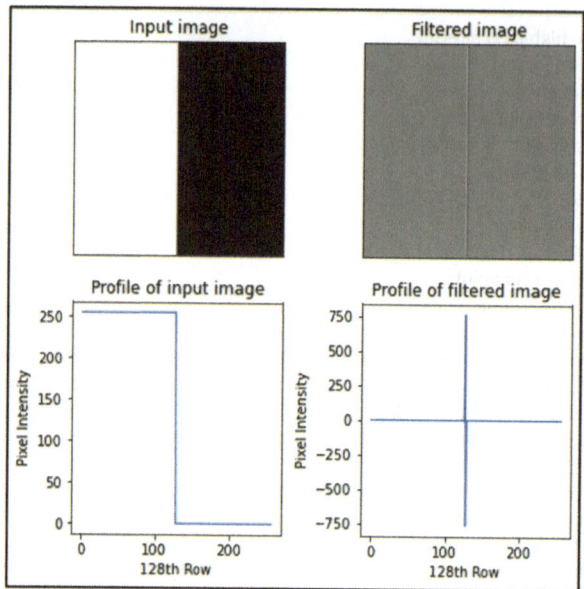

Fig. 4.83 Result of spatial domain low-pass filtering of the test image

- The plot of the 128th row of the high-pass filtered image shows a spike-like a signal. Differentiation of a constant is zero, which is why the gray level of the filtered image is zero till 128th column. At 128th column, the gray level of the filtered image abruptly changes from white to black, which is captured by a spike like signal in the filtered image.
- Thus, the high-pass filter acts like a change detector.

4.10.4   Unsharp Masking

Unsharp masking is used to crispen the edges of the digital image. Unsharp masking is done by subtracting the blurred version of the image from the input image and then adding the result to the input image. This is represented in the form of a block diagram in Fig. 4.84.

From Fig. 4.84, the expression for the image $g(x, y)$ is given by

$$g(x,y) = f(x,y) - f_{\text{smooth}}(x,y)$$ (4.16)

The expression for the output image $z(x, y)$ is given by

$$z(x,y) = f(x,y) + kg(x,y)$$ (4.17)

In the above expression, "k" represents the scaling constant.

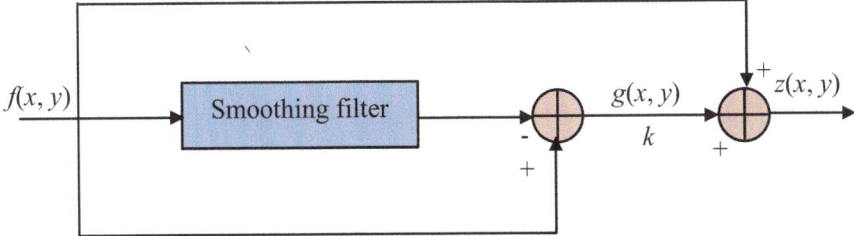

Fig. 4.84 Block diagram of unsharp masking operation

```
#Unsharp masking
import cv2
import matplotlib.pyplot as plt
#Step 1: Reading the input image
img=cv2.imread('Moth.jpg',0)
#Step 2: Obtain the blurred version of the input
im_blur=cv2.GaussianBlur(img,(11,11),10)
#Step 3: Unsharp masking
img_usm=cv2.addWeighted(img,1.0+5.0,im_blur,-4,0)
#Step 4: Displaying the result
plt.subplot(1,2,1),plt.imshow(img,cmap='gray'),plt.title('Input image')
plt.xticks([]),plt.yticks([]),plt.subplot(1,2,2),plt.imshow(img_usm,cmap='gray')
plt.title('Output of unsharp masking'),plt.xticks([]),plt.yticks([])
plt.tight_layout()
```

Fig. 4.85 Python code to perform unsharp masking

Experiment 4.37: Unsharp masking of the Input Image

In this experiment, the input image is read, and then a blurred version of it is obtained by passing it through a Gaussian low-pass filter. The smoothened version of the image is added to the original image with some weight factor. To do this "AddWeighted()" built-in function available in "cv2" library is used. The Python code that performs this action is shown in Fig. 4.85, and the corresponding output is shown in Fig. 4.86.

Inferences

The following inferences can be made from this experiment:

- The input image is an image of a "moth".
- First, the input image is passed through Gaussian low-pass filter. The mask size is 11 × 11.
- The smoothened image is added to the original image with some weight factor. In this experiment the weight factor chosen is 5. This results in unsharp masking of the input image.
- The visual quality of the unsharp masked image is better than the input image.

Fig. 4.86   Result of unsharp masking

4.10.5   High-Boost Filter

The high-pass filter emphasizes the high-frequency component of the image, but the background information is lost in the high-pass filter. A high-boost filter is used to enhance the high-frequency component of the input image. At the same time, it preserves the background information. The 3 × 3 mask used to perform high-pass

filter is $\begin{bmatrix} -1 & -1 & -1 \\ -1 & 8 & -1 \\ -1 & -1 & -1 \end{bmatrix}$, whereas the mask used to perform high-boost filtering opera-

tion is given by $\begin{bmatrix} -1 & -1 & -1 \\ -1 & 9A-1 & -1 \\ -1 & -1 & -1 \end{bmatrix}$, where $A = 1$ results in high-pass filter output and

$A > 1$ results in high-boost filtering of the input image.

Experiment 4.38: Comparison of High-Pass and High-Boost Filter
In this experiment, the input image is read first. Both a high-pass filter and a high-boost filter are applied to the input image. The Python code that performs this task is shown in Fig. 4.87, and the corresponding output is shown in Fig. 4.88.

Inferences
From Fig. 4.88, the following inferences can be drawn:

- The input image is the image of a temple. It is a grayscale image.
- Upon performing a high-pass filter, the edge information is enhanced, while the background information is lost.
- Upon performing high-boost filtering operation, the edge information is enhanced, while the background information is preserved.

```
#High pass versus High boost filter
import numpy as np
import matplotlib.pyplot as plt
import cv2
#Step 1: Read the input image
img=cv2.imread('testimage_temple.jpg',0)
#Step 2: HPF and Unsharp masking filter mask
mask_hpf=np.array([[-1,-1,-1],[-1,8,-1],[-1,-1,-1]])
mask_usm=np.array([[-1,-1,-1],[-1,10,-1],[-1,-1,-1]])
#Step 3: Performing filtering operation
img_hpf=cv2.filter2D(img,-1,mask_hpf)
img_usm=cv2.filter2D(img,-1,mask_usm)
#Step 4: Displaying the results
plt.subplot(1,3,1),plt.imshow(img,cmap='gray'),plt.title('Input image'),
plt.xticks([]),plt.yticks([]),plt.subplot(1,3,2),plt.imshow(img_hpf,cmap='gray'),
plt.title('HPF output'),plt.xticks([]),plt.yticks([]),plt.subplot(1,3,3),
plt.imshow(img_usm,cmap='gray'),plt.title('High Boost filter output')
plt.xticks([]),plt.yticks([])
plt.tight_layout()
```

Fig. 4.87 Python code to perform high-pass and high-boost filters

Fig. 4.88 Comparison of high-pass and high-boost filters

4.11 Transform Domain-Based Image Enhancement

The basic steps in transform domain-based image enhancement are depicted in Fig. 4.89.

The input image is represented as $f[m, n]$. Let $F[k, l]$ represents the spectrum of the input image. The spectrum is obtained by taking Fourier transform of the input image. The filter function is represented as $H[k, l]$. The basic model of filtering in frequency domain is expressed as

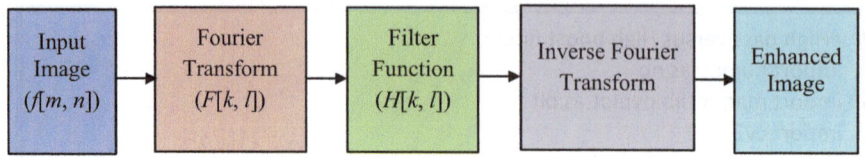

Fig. 4.89 Steps in transform domain-based image enhancement

$$G[k,l] = F[k,l] \times H[k,l] \tag{4.18}$$

Upon taking Inverse Fourier transform, the enhanced image is given by

$$g[m,n] = F^{-1}\{G[k,l]\} \tag{4.19}$$

In the above expression, F^{-1} represents the Inverse Fourier transform. The nature of filtering is decided by the filter function $H[k, l]$. Two broad classifications of filtering are low-pass filtering and high-pass filtering. Low-pass filtering is also termed a smoothing operation, and high-pass filtering operation is termed a sharpening operation.

4.11.1   Generation of Low-Pass Filter Mask

There are three types of low-pass filters considered in this section: (1) ideal filter, (2) Butterworth filter, and (3) Gaussian filter.

Ideal Low-Pass Filter

The expression for the ideal low-pass filter mask is given by

$$H[k,l] = \begin{cases} 1, & \text{if } D[k,l] \leq D_0, \\ 0, & \text{if } D[k,l] > D_0 \end{cases} \tag{4.20}$$

where $D[k,l] = \left[\left(k - \dfrac{M}{2}\right)^2 + \left(l - \dfrac{N}{2}\right)^2\right]^{\frac{1}{2}}$. In this expression, "$D_0$" represents the cut-off frequency. The ideal low-pass filters are radially symmetric about the origin.

Butterworth Filter

The expression for the Butterworth low-pass filter mask is given by

$$H[k,l] = \cfrac{1}{1 + \left[\cfrac{D[k,\ l]}{D_0} \right]^{2n}}$$

(4.21)

In the above expression, "n" refers to the order of the Butterworth filter. $D[k,l] = \left[\left(k - \dfrac{M}{2} \right)^2 + \left(l - \dfrac{N}{2} \right)^2 \right]^{\frac{1}{2}}$. In this expression, "$D_0$" represents the cut-off frequency.

Gaussian Filter

The expression for Gaussian low-pass filter mask is given by

$$H[k,l] = e^{-D^2[k,l]/2D_0^2}$$

(4.22)

where $D[k,l] = \left[\left(k - \dfrac{M}{2} \right)^2 + \left(l - \dfrac{N}{2} \right)^2 \right]^{\frac{1}{2}}$. In this expression, "$D_0$" represents the cut-off frequency.

Experiment 4.39: Generation of Low-Pass filter Mask
The Python code that generates the ideal low-pass, Butterworth low-pass, and Gaussian low-pass filter mask for $D_0 = 25$ units is given in Fig. 4.90, and the corresponding output is shown in Fig. 4.91.

Inferences
The following inferences can be made from Fig. 4.91:

- In an ideal low-pass filter mask, the boundary of the circle is well-defined. The mask takes a value of either low or high.
- In Butterworth and Gaussian low-pass filter masks, the boundary of the circle is crisp. Gradual variation in intensity can be observed.

Experiment 4.40: Transform Domain Ideal Low-Pass Filtering of the Image
This experiment aims to perform transform domain ideal low-pass filtering of the input image. The steps involved in this task are as follows:

Step 1: In this step, the input image is read. The built-in function "*imread*" available in "cv2" library is used here to perform the task of reading the input image. The input image considered in this experiment is an 8-bit grayscale Cameraman image.

Step 2: The spectrum of the input image is obtained in this step. The built-in function "*fft2*" available in "numpy" library is used to obtain the Fourier transform of the input image, which is termed as spectrum of the input image.

```
#Generation of LPF masks
import numpy as np
import matplotlib.pyplot as plt
#Step 1: Ideal LPF
N=256
x=np.arange(-N/2,N/2,1)
y=np.arange(-N/2,N/2,1)
k,l=np.meshgrid(x,y)
D=np.sqrt(k**2+l**2) #D(k,l)
D0=25
H_Ideal=D<D0        #H(k,l)
#Step 2: Butterworth LPF
n=5  #Order of Butterworth filter
H_Butter=1/(1+D/D0)**2*n
#Step 3: Gaussian LPF
H_Gaussian=np.exp(-(D**2)/(2*D0**2))
#Step 4: Plotting the LPF kernel
plt.subplot(1,3,1),plt.imshow(H_Ideal,cmap='gray'),plt.title('Ideal LPF mask'),plt.axis('off')
plt.subplot(1,3,2),plt.imshow(H_Butter,cmap='gray'),plt.title('Butterworth LPF mask'),
plt.axis('off'),plt.subplot(1,3,3),plt.imshow(H_Gaussian,cmap='gray')
plt.title('Gaussian LPF mask'),plt.axis('off')
plt.tight_layout()
```

Fig. 4.90 Python code to generate low-pass filter mask

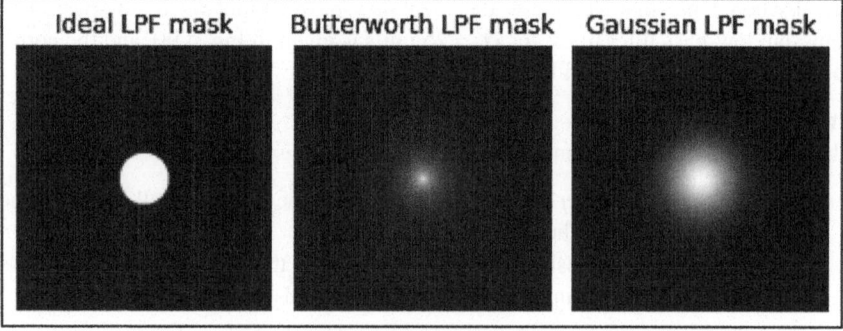

Fig. 4.91 Result of the Python code shown in Fig. 4.90

Step 3: The ideal low-pass filter mask is generated in this step. The expression for ideal low-pass filter mask is given by $H[k,l] = \begin{cases} 1, & \text{if } D[k,l] \leq D_0, \\ 0, & \text{if } D[k,l] > D_0 \end{cases}$. The value of D_0 controls the extent of smoothing.

Step 4: In this step, the spectrum of the input image is multiplied with low-pass filter mask. This is because convolution in the spatial domain is equivalent to multiplication in the frequency domain. The built-in function "*multiply*" available in the "numpy" library performs this task.

```
#Transform domain ideal LPF
import cv2
import numpy as np
import matplotlib.pyplot as plt
#Step 1: Reading the input image
img=cv2.imread('cameraman.tif',0)
#Step 2: Spectrum of the input image
IMG=np.fft.fft2(img)
IMG=np.fft.fftshift(IMG)
#Step 3: Defining Ideal LPF
N,D0 = 256, 20
x=np.arange(-N/2,N/2,1)
y=np.arange(-N/2,N/2,1)
k,l=np.meshgrid(x,y)
D=np.sqrt(k**2+l**2) #D(k,l)
H_Ideal=D<D0       #H(k,l)
#Step4: Multiplying spectrum of input image with H(k,l)
IMG_out=np.multiply(IMG, H_Ideal)
#Step 5:Inverse Fourier transform
img_out=np.fft.fftshift(IMG_out)
img_out=np.fft.ifft2(IMG_out)
#Step 6: Displaying the results
plt.figure(figsize=(9, 6)),plt.subplot(1,3,1),plt.imshow(img,cmap='gray')
plt.title('Input image'),plt.axis('off'),plt.subplot(1,3,2),plt.imshow(H_Ideal,cmap='gray')
plt.title('Ideal LPF mask'),plt.axis('off'),plt.subplot(1,3,3),
plt.imshow(np.abs(img_out),cmap='gray'),plt.title('Filtered image'),plt.axis('off')
plt.tight_layout()
```

Fig. 4.92 Python code to perform frequency domain ideal low-pass filter

Step 5: To visualize the result, the result should be in spatial domain. Inverse Fourier transform is applied to get the result in spatial domain. The built-in function "*ifft2*" available in the "numpy" library performs this task.

Step 6: This step deals with displaying the results. The input image, filter mask, and filtered image are displayed using the "subplot" available in the "matplotlib" library.

The Python code that performs the above-mentioned task is shown in Fig. 4.92, and the corresponding result is shown in Fig. 4.93.

Inferences

From Fig. 4.93, the following inferences can be drawn:

- The input image is a Cameraman image. The image has both low- and high-frequency information. The background contains low-frequency information; the edges correspond to high-frequency information.
- The radius of low-pass filter is fixed as 20. The ideal low-pass filter mask is a circle of radius 20. The white region in the circle corresponds to the passband, and the black region corresponds to the stop band.

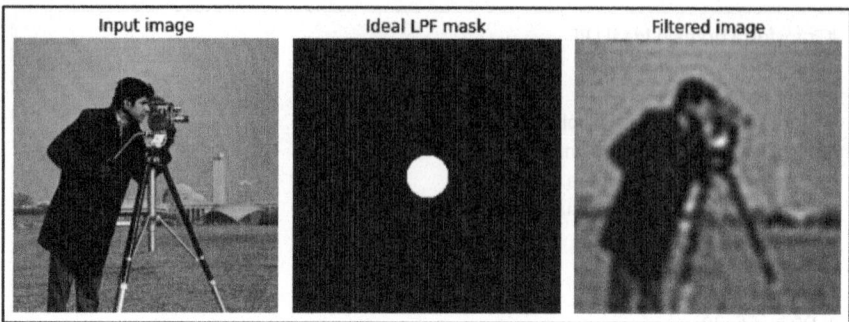

Fig. 4.93 Result of ideal low-pass filter in transform domain

- The filtered image is obtained after performing low-pass filtering of the input image. Blurring effect is visible in the filtered image. It is possible to observe the smearing of edges in the filtered image.

Experiment 4.41: Impact of Varying the Size of the Ideal Low-Pass filter Mask

The objective of this experiment is to visualize the impact of varying the radius of an ideal low-pass filter mask. Two low-pass filter masks of radius 10 and 20 are used to perform low-pass filtering of the input image. The extent of smoothing done by these two filters on the input image is analysed in this example. The Python code that performs this task is shown in Fig. 4.94, and the corresponding output is shown in Fig. 4.95.

Inferences

The following observations can be made from this experiment:

- The input image is passed through two low-pass filter masks, namely ideal LPF mask-1 and ideal LPF mask-2.
- The radius of ideal LPF mask-1 is 10, whereas the radius of ideal LPF mask-2 is 20.
- The "Filtered Image-1" is obtained by passing the input image through a low-pass filter mask-1. Since the radius is 10, a few coefficients of the input image are retained. As a result, "Filtered Image-1" is more blurred.
- With the increase in the radius of the mask, more low-frequency components are preserved in the image; hence, less blurring effect of "Filtered Image-2" is observed.
- The radius of the filter controls the extent of smoothing.

Experiment 4.42: Comparison of Ideal, Butterworth, and Gaussian LPF

The objective of this experiment is to compare the performance of ideal, Butterworth, and Gaussian lowpass filters on the input image. The problem statement is represented in the form of a block diagram, which is depicted in Fig. 4.96.

```
#Impact of LPF mask radius on extent of filtering
import cv2
import numpy as np
import matplotlib.pyplot as plt
#Step 1: Reading the input image
img=cv2.imread('cameraman.tif',0)
#Step 2: Spectrum of the input image
IMG=np.fft.fft2(img)
IMG=np.fft.fftshift(IMG)
#Step 3: Defining Ideal LPF masks
N=256
x=np.arange(-N/2,N/2,1)
y=np.arange(-N/2,N/2,1)
k,l=np.meshgrid(x,y)
D=np.sqrt(k**2+l**2) #D(k,l)
D0=[10,20] #Radius of the mask
H_Ideal1=D<D0[0]
H_Ideal2=D<D0[1]
#Step 4: Multiplication of F(k,l) with H(k,l)
IMG_out1=np.multiply(IMG, H_Ideal1)
IMG_out2=np.multiply(IMG, H_Ideal2)
#Step 5: Taking Inverse Fourier Transform
img_out1=np.fft.ifft2(IMG_out1)
img_out2=np.fft.ifft2(IMG_out2)
plt.figure(figsize=(10, 6)); #Step 6: Displaying the results
plt.subplot(2,3,1),plt.imshow(img,cmap='gray'),plt.title('Input image'),plt.axis('off')
plt.subplot(2,3,2),plt.imshow(H_Ideal1,cmap='gray'),plt.title('Ideal LPF mask-1'),plt.axis('off')
plt.subplot(2,3,3),plt.imshow(np.abs(img_out1),cmap='gray'),plt.title('Filtered image-1'),
plt.axis('off'),plt.subplot(2,3,4),plt.imshow(img,cmap='gray'),plt.title('Input image'),
plt.axis('off'),plt.subplot(2,3,5),plt.imshow(H_Ideal2,cmap='gray'),plt.title('Ideal LPF mask-2'),
plt.axis('off'),plt.subplot(2,3,6),plt.imshow(np.abs(img_out2),cmap='gray'),
plt.title('Filtered image-2'),plt.axis('off')
plt.tight_layout()
```

Fig. 4.94 Python code to analyse the impact of low-pass filter radius on the extent of smoothing

The Python code that compares different types of low-pass filter masks is given in Fig. 4.97, and the corresponding output is shown in Fig. 4.98.

Inferences

The following observations can be made from Fig. 4.98:

- The input "Cameraman" image is passed through (1) ideal low-pass filter, (2) Butterworth low-pass filter, and (3) Gaussian low-pass filter.
- The blurring effect in ideal low-pass filter is more when compared to Butterworth and Gaussian low-pass filters.
- The order of the Butterworth filter is chosen as 2 in this case. Among Butterworth and Gaussian low-pass filters, the blurring effect is more apparent in the Gaussian low-pass filter than in the Butterworth low-pass filter.

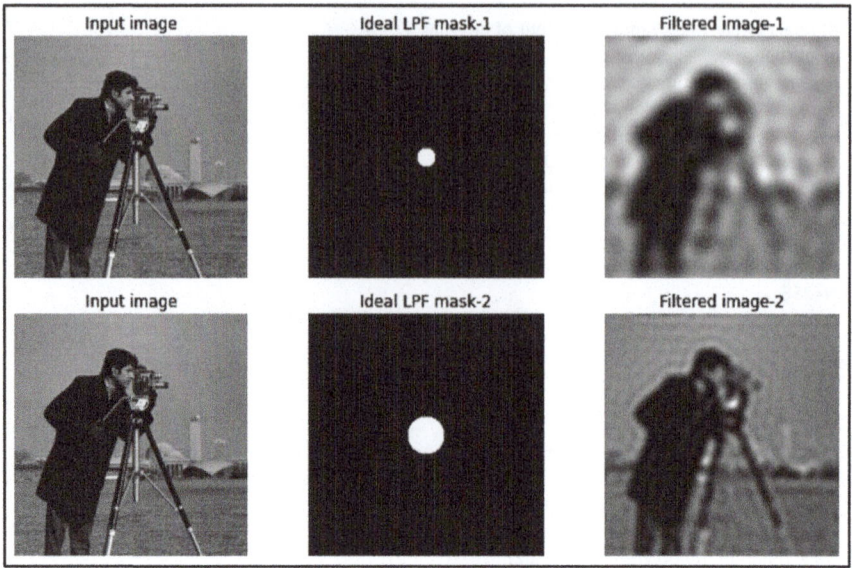

Fig. 4.95 Impact of filter mask size on the extent of smoothing

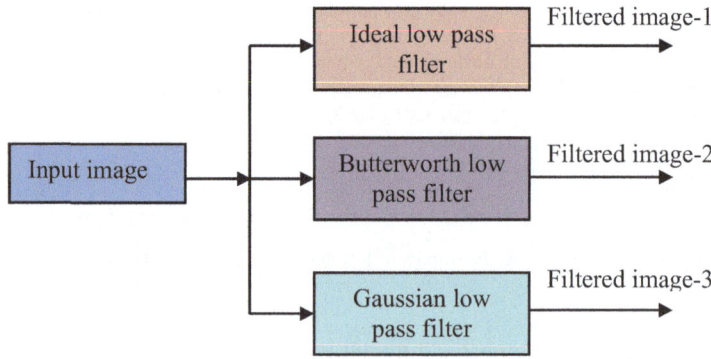

Fig. 4.96 Block diagram of the problem statement

4.11.2   Generation of High-Pass Filter Mask

The high-pass filter extracts edges and fine details in the input image. High-pass filter is used to sharpen the input image. The simplest high-pass filter is the complement of the low-pass filter. If $H[k, l]$ represents the transfer function of the low-pass filter, then the transfer function of the high-pass filter ($G[k, l]$) is expressed as

$$G[k,l] = 1 - H[k,l] \qquad (4.23)$$

```
#Comparison of Ideal, Butterworth and Gaussian LPF
import cv2
import numpy as np
import matplotlib.pyplot as plt
img=cv2.imread('cameraman.tif',0); #Step 1: Reading the input image
IMG=np.fft.fft2(img); #Step 2: Spectrum of the input image
IMG=np.fft.fftshift(IMG)
#Step 3: Defining Ideal LPF
N=256
x=np.arange(-N/2,N/2,1)
y=np.arange(-N/2,N/2,1)
k,l=np.meshgrid(x,y)
D=np.sqrt(k**2+l**2)  #D(k,l)
D0=10
H_Ideal=D<D0        #H(k,l)
#Step 4: Butterworth LPF mask
n=2   #Order of Butterworth filter
H_Butter=1/(1+D/D0)**2*n
#Step 5: Gaussian LPF mask
H_Gaussian=np.exp(-(D**2)/(2*D0**2))
#Step4: Multiplying spectrum of input image with H(k,l)
IMG_out1=np.multiply(IMG, H_Ideal)
IMG_out2=np.multiply(IMG, H_Butter)
IMG_out3=np.multiply(IMG, H_Gaussian)
#Step 5:Inverse Fourier transform
img_out1=np.fft.ifft2(IMG_out1)
img_out2=np.fft.ifft2(IMG_out2)
img_out3=np.fft.ifft2(IMG_out3)
#Step 6: Displaying the results
plt.figure(figsize=(9, 9))
plt.subplot(3,3,1),plt.axis('off')
plt.subplot(3,3,2),plt.imshow(H_Ideal,cmap='gray'),plt.title('Ideal LPF mask'),plt.axis('off')
plt.subplot(3,3,3),plt.imshow(np.abs(img_out1),cmap='gray'),plt.title('Ideal LPF image'),
plt.axis('off'),plt.subplot(3,3,4),plt.imshow(img,cmap='gray'),plt.title('Input image'), plt.axis('off')
plt.subplot(3,3,5),plt.imshow(H_Butter,cmap='gray'),plt.title('Butterworth LPF mask'),plt.axis('off')
plt.subplot(3,3,6),plt.imshow(np.abs(img_out2),cmap='gray'),plt.title('Butterworth LPF image'),
plt.axis('off'),plt.subplot(3,3,7),plt.axis('off'),plt.subplot(3,3,8),
plt.imshow(H_Gaussian,cmap='gray'),plt.title('Gaussian LPF mask'),plt.axis('off'),plt.subplot(3,3,9),
plt.imshow(np.abs(img_out3),cmap='gray'),plt.title('Gaussian LPF image'), plt.axis('off')
plt.tight_layout()
```

Fig. 4.97 Python code to compare the performance of different low-pass filters

Experiment 4.43: Generation of the High-Pass filter Mask

The objective of this experiment is to generate a high-pass filter mask. Three types of high-pass filters considered in this experiment are (1) ideal filter, (2) Butterworth filter, and (3) Gaussian filter. The expression for the filter mask is given as follows:

Ideal High-Pass Filter

The expression for ideal high-pass filter mask is given by

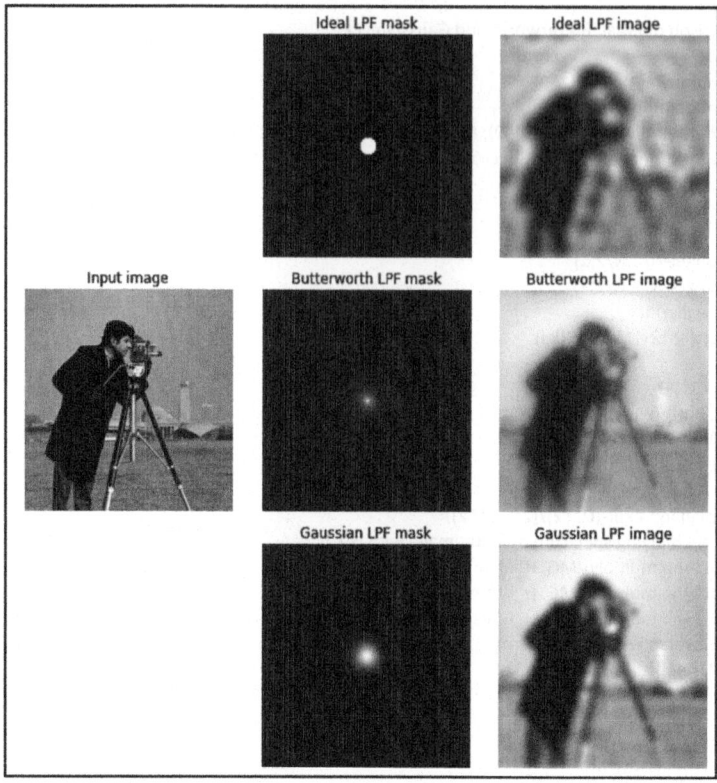

Fig. 4.98 Result of comparison of low-pass filters

$$H[k,l] = \begin{cases} 0, & \text{if } D[k,l] \leq D_0, \\ 1, & \text{if } D[k,l] > D_0 \end{cases} \tag{4.24}$$

where $D[k,l] = \left[\left(k - \dfrac{M}{2} \right)^2 + \left(l - \dfrac{N}{2} \right)^2 \right]^{\frac{1}{2}}$. The cut-off frequency of the filter is denoted as "D_0".

Butterworth Filter

The expression for Butterworth high-pass filter mask is given by

$$H[k,l] = \dfrac{1}{1 + \left[\dfrac{D_0}{D[k,l]} \right]^{2n}} \tag{4.25}$$

```
#Generation of HPF mask
import numpy as np
import matplotlib.pyplot as plt
#Step 1: Ideal HPF
N, D0 = 256, 25
x=np.arange(-N/2,N/2,1)
y=np.arange(-N/2,N/2,1)
k,l=np.meshgrid(x,y)
D=np.sqrt(k**2+l**2)  #D(k,l)
H_Ideal=D>D0        #H(k,l)
#Step 2: Butterworth HPF
n=5  #Order of Butterworth filter
H_Butter=1/((1+D0/D)**(2*n))
#Step 3: Gaussian HPF
H_Gaussian=1-np.exp(-(D**2)/(2*D0**2))
#Step 4: Plotting the LPF kernel
plt.subplot(1,3,1),plt.imshow(H_Ideal,cmap='gray'),plt.title('Ideal HPF mask')
plt.xticks([]),plt.yticks([]),plt.subplot(1,3,2),plt.imshow(H_Butter,cmap='gray'),
plt.title('Butterworth HPF mask'),plt.xticks([]),plt.yticks([])
plt.subplot(1,3,3),plt.imshow(H_Gaussian,cmap='gray'),plt.title('Gaussian HPF mask')
plt.xticks([]),plt.yticks([])
plt.tight_layout()
```

Fig. 4.99 Python code to generate low-pass filter mask

where $D(k,l) = \left[\left(k - \dfrac{M}{2} \right)^2 + \left(l - \dfrac{N}{2} \right)^2 \right]^{\frac{1}{2}}$. The cut-off frequency of the filter is denoted as "D_0" and "n" refers to the order of the Butterworth filter.

Gaussian Filter

The expression for Gaussian high-pass filter mask is given by

$$H(k,l) = 1 - e^{-D^2(k,l)/2D_0^2} \tag{4.26}$$

The Python code that generates the ideal high-pass, Butterworth high-pass, and Gaussian high-pass filter mask for $D_0 = 25$ units is given in Fig. 4.99, and the corresponding output is shown in Fig. 4.100.

Inferences

The following inferences can be made from Fig. 4.100:

- The high-pass filter mask is the complement of the low-pass filter mask.
- High-pass filtering allows one to extract the edges and fine details of the image.

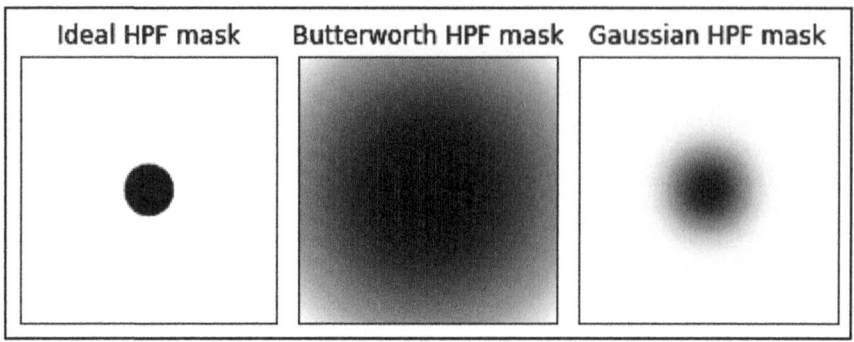

Fig. 4.100   Result of Python code shown in Fig. 4.99

Experiment 4.44: Transform Domain High-Pass Filtering of Input Image

The objective of this experiment is to visualize the impact of varying the radius of an ideal high-pass filter mask. Two high-pass filter masks of radius 10 and 80 are used to perform high-pass filtering of the input image. The Python code that performs this task is shown in Fig. 4.101, and the corresponding output is shown in Fig. 4.102.

Inferences

The following inferences can be drawn from Fig. 4.102:

- The input image is an 8-bit "Clock image" in tagged image file (tif) format. The input image is passed through two ideal high-pass filters. The radius of the high-pass filter masks is 10 and 80, respectively.
- After passing through two high-pass filters, the input image resulted in "Filtered Image-1" and "Filtered Image-2".
- With the increase in the size of the mask, the edge information is clearly obtained in the "Filtered Image-2" with the loss of background information.

Experiment 4.45: Comparing Frequency Domain High-Pass Filters

This experiment aims to compare the performance of ideal, Butterworth, and Gaussian high-pass filters on the input image. The problem statement is represented in the form of a block diagram, which is depicted in Fig. 4.103.

The Python code that performs the task of comparison of different types of high-pass filter masks is given in Fig. 4.104, and the corresponding output is shown in Fig. 4.105.

Inferences

The following inferences can be made from Fig. 4.105:

- The input "Clock image" is passed through (1) ideal, (2) Butterworth, and (3) Gaussian high-pass filters.

```
#Transform domain high-pass filtering
import cv2
import numpy as np
import matplotlib.pyplot as plt
#Step 1: Reading the input image
img=cv2.imread('Clock.tiff',0)
#Step 2: Obtaining the spectrum
IMG=np.fft.fft2(img)
IMG=np.fft.fftshift(IMG)
#Step 3: Generating high pass filter masks
N, D0 = 256, [10,80] #Radius of the mask
x=np.arange(-N/2,N/2,1)
y=np.arange(-N/2,N/2,1)
k,l=np.meshgrid(x,y)
D=np.sqrt(k**2+l**2)  #D(k,l)
H_Ideal1=D>D0[0]
H_Ideal2=D>D0[1]
#Step 4: Multiplication of F(k,l) with H(k,l)
IMG_out1=np.multiply(IMG, H_Ideal1)
IMG_out2=np.multiply(IMG, H_Ideal2)
#Step 5: Taking Inverse Fourier Transform
img_out1=np.fft.ifft2(IMG_out1)
img_out2=np.fft.ifft2(IMG_out2)
#Step 6: Displaying the results
plt.figure(figsize=(10, 6)),plt.subplot(2,3,1),plt.imshow(img,cmap='gray'),
plt.title('Input image'),plt.axis('off'),plt.subplot(2,3,2),plt.imshow(H_Ideal1,cmap='gray'),
plt.title('Ideal HPF mask-1'),plt.xticks([]),plt.yticks([])
plt.subplot(2,3,3),plt.imshow(np.abs(img_out1),cmap='gray'),plt.title('Filtered image-1')
plt.axis('off'),plt.subplot(2,3,4),plt.imshow(img,cmap='gray'),plt.title('Input image'),
plt.axis('off'),plt.subplot(2,3,5),plt.imshow(H_Ideal2,cmap='gray'),
plt.title('Ideal HPF mask-2'),plt.xticks([]),plt.yticks([]),plt.subplot(2,3,6),
plt.imshow(np.abs(img_out2),cmap='gray'),plt.title('Filtered image-2'),plt.axis('off')
plt.tight_layout()
```

Fig. 4.101 Python code to perform transform domain high-pass filtering

- The edge and background information are obtained using Gaussian high-pass filtering.
- The edge information obtained in the Butterworth high-pass filter is more precise than the ideal high-pass filter.

4.11.3 High-Frequency Emphasis Filter in Frequency Domain

The block diagram of the high-frequency emphasis filter in the spatial domain is given in Fig. 4.106. The smoothing filter in Fig. 4.106 is basically a low-pass filter. The signal $g(x, y)$ is obtained by subtracting the blurred version of the image from the input image.

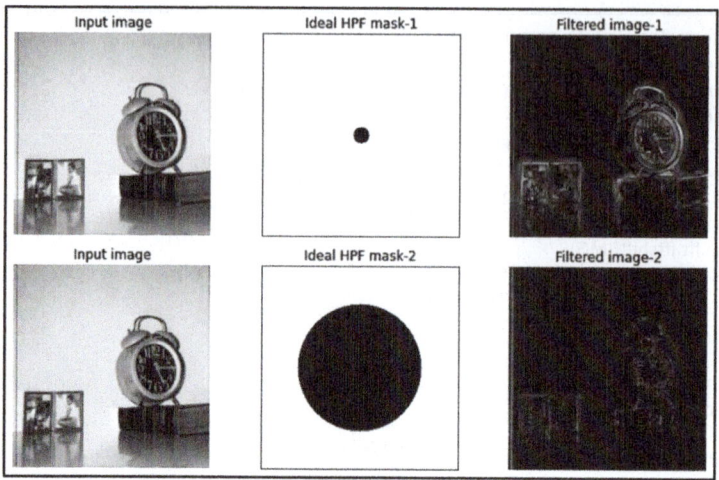

Fig. 4.102 Result of transform domain high-pass filtering operation

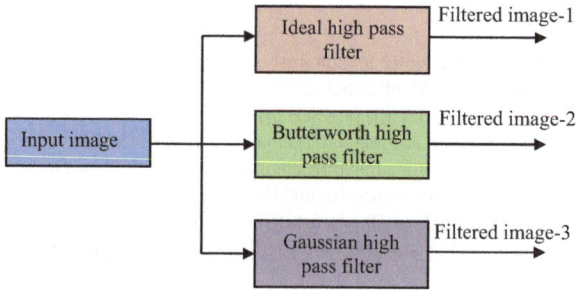

Fig. 4.103 Block diagram of the problem statement

The expression for the image $g(x, y)$ is given by

$$g(x,y) = f(x,y) - f_{lp}(x,y) \qquad (4.27)$$

In Eq. (4.27), $f_{lp}(x, y)$ represents the low-pass filtered version of the input image $f(x, y)$. The expression for the image $z(x, y)$ is given by

$$z(x,y) = f(x,y) + Kg(x,y) \qquad (4.28)$$

Substituting Eq. (4.27) in Eq. (4.28), we get

$$z(x,y) = f(x,y) + K\left[f(x,y) - f_{lp}(x,y)\right] \qquad (4.29)$$

```
#Comparing frequency domain high pass filters
import cv2
import numpy as np
import matplotlib.pyplot as plt
#Step 1: Reading the input image
img=cv2.imread('Clock.tiff',0)
#Step 2: Spectrum of the input image
IMG=np.fft.fft2(img)
IMG=np.fft.fftshift(IMG)
#Step 3: Defining the HPF masks
#Step 3a: Ideal HPF
N, D0 = 256, 30
x=np.arange(-N/2,N/2,1)
y=np.arange(-N/2,N/2,1)
k,l=np.meshgrid(x,y)
D=np.sqrt(k**2+l**2)  #D(k,l)
H_Ideal=D>D0        #H(k,l)
#Step 3b: Butterworth HPF
n=5   #Order of Butterworth filter
H_Butter=1/(1+D0/D)**2*n
#Step 3c: Gaussian HPF
H_Gaussian=1-np.exp(-(D**2)/(2*D0**2))
#Step4: Multiplying spectrum of input image with H(k,l)
IMG_out1=np.multiply(IMG, H_Ideal)
IMG_out2=np.multiply(IMG, H_Butter)
IMG_out3=np.multiply(IMG, H_Gaussian)
#Step 5:Inverse Fourier transform
img_out1=np.fft.ifft2(IMG_out1)
img_out2=np.fft.ifft2(IMG_out2)
img_out3=np.fft.ifft2(IMG_out3)
#Step 6: Displaying the results
plt.figure(figsize=(9, 9))
plt.subplot(3,3,1),plt.axis('off'),plt.subplot(3,3,2),plt.imshow(H_Ideal,cmap='gray'),
plt.title('Ideal HPF mask'),plt.xticks([]),plt.yticks([]),plt.subplot(3,3,3),
plt.imshow(np.abs(img_out1),cmap='gray'),plt.title('Ideal HPF image'),plt.axis('off')
plt.subplot(3,3,4),plt.imshow(img,cmap='gray',vmin=0,vmax=256),plt.title('Input image'),
plt.axis('off'),plt.subplot(3,3,5),plt.imshow(H_Butter,cmap='gray'),plt.title('Butterworth HPF mask')
plt.xticks([]),plt.yticks([]),plt.subplot(3,3,6),plt.imshow(np.abs(img_out2),cmap='gray'),
plt.title('Butterworth HPF image'),plt.axis('off'),plt.subplot(3,3,7),plt.axis('off'),
plt.subplot(3,3,8),plt.imshow(H_Gaussian,cmap='gray'),plt.title('Gaussian HPF mask')
plt.xticks([]),plt.yticks([]),plt.subplot(3,3,9),plt.imshow(np.abs(img_out3),cmap='gray'),
plt.title('Gaussian HPF image'),plt.axis('off')
plt.tight_layout()
```

Fig. 4.104 Python code to compare the performance of different types of high-pass filters

Taking Fourier transform on both sides of the above expression, we get

$$Z(k,l) = F(k,l) + K\left[F(k,l) - H_{lp}(k,l)F(k,l)\right] \tag{4.30}$$

In the above expression, $H_{lp}(k, l)$ represents the filter kernel corresponding to low-pass filter. Equation (4.30) can be expressed as

$$Z(k,l) = F(k,l) + KF(k,l)\left[1 - H_{lp}(k,l)\right] \tag{4.31}$$

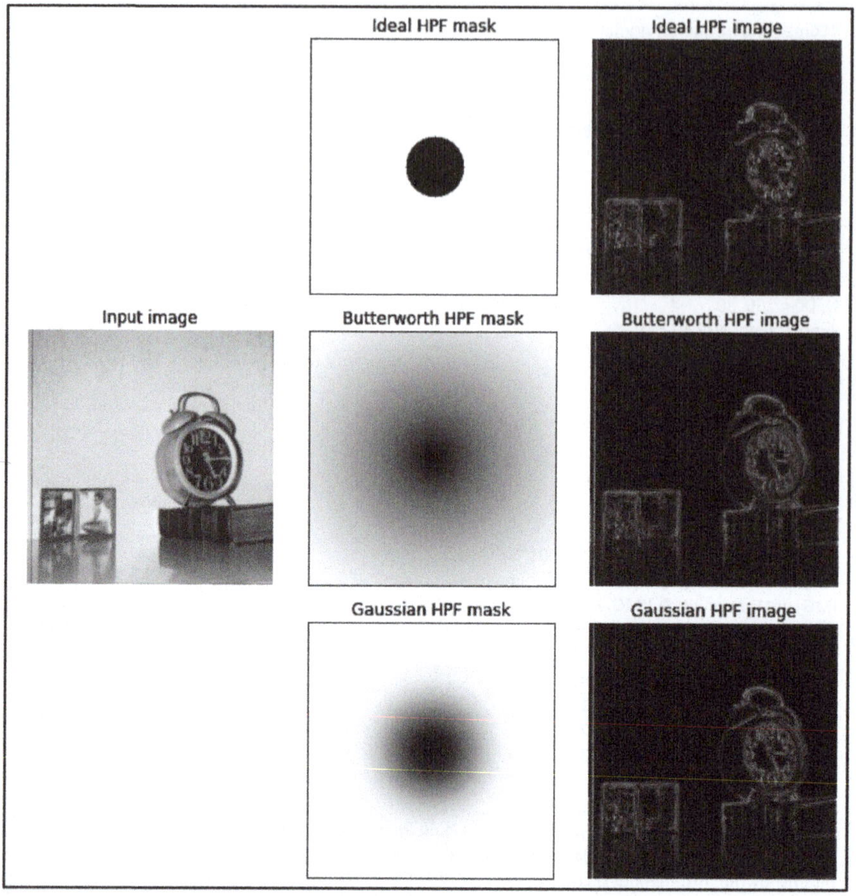

Ideal HPF mask
Ideal HPF image
Input image
Butterworth HPF mask
Butterworth HPF image
Gaussian HPF mask
Gaussian HPF image

Fig. 4.105 Result of different types of transform domain high-pass filtering

f(x, y)
Smoothing filter
g(x, y)
K
z(x, y)
+
-
+
+
+

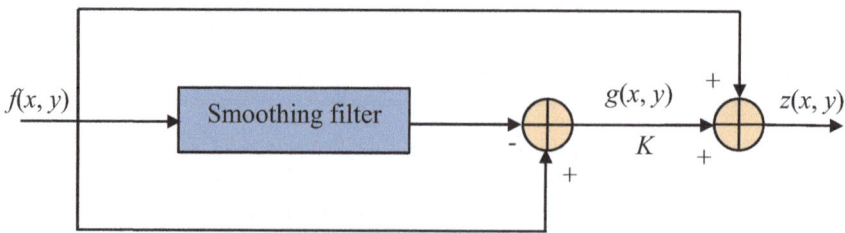

Fig. 4.106 Block diagram of high-frequency emphasis filter

The low-pass filter and high-pass filter are complementary to each other, hence

$$1 - H_{lp}(k,l) = H_{hp}(k,l) \tag{4.32}$$

Substituting Eq. (4.32) in Eq. (4.31), we get

$$Z(k,l) = F(k,l) + KF(k,l)H_{hp}(k,l) \tag{4.33}$$

The above equation can be expressed as

$$Z(k,l) = F(k,l)\left[1 + KH_{hp}(k,l)\right] \tag{4.34}$$

The constant "K" can be split as

$$Z(k,l) = F(k,l)\left[K_1 + K_2 H_{hp}(k,l)\right] \tag{4.35}$$

The above expression in spatial domain is expressed as

$$z(x,y) = F^{-1}\left\{\left[K_1 + K_2 H_{hp}(k,l)\right]F(k,l)\right\} \tag{4.36}$$

Experiment 4.46: High-Frequency Emphasis Filter (High-Boost Filter)
This experiment aims to compare high-pass filter with high-frequency emphasis filter (high-boost filter). The Python code that performs this task is shown in Fig. 4.107, and the corresponding output is shown in Fig. 4.108.

Inferences
From Fig. 4.108, the following inferences can be made:

- The high-pass filter output shows only the edge information of the input image.
- The high-boost filter output also displays the edge information and some low-frequency components.

4.11.4 Ideal Band-Pass Filter in the Frequency Domain

The transfer function of ideal band-pass filter is given by

$$H[k,l] = \begin{cases} 0, & D[k,l] < D_0 - \dfrac{W}{2}, \\ 1, & D_0 - \dfrac{W}{2} \leq D[k,l] \leq D_0 + \dfrac{W}{2}, \\ 0, & D[k,l] > D_0 + \dfrac{W}{2}. \end{cases} \tag{4.37}$$

```
#High frequency emphasis filter
import cv2
import numpy as np
import matplotlib.pyplot as plt
#Step 1: Reading the input image
img=cv2.imread('cameraman.tif',0)
M,N=img.shape
#Step 2: Obtaining the spectrum
IMG=np.fft.fft2(img)
IMG=np.fft.fftshift(IMG)
#Step 3: Generating high pass filter masks
x=np.arange(-N/2,N/2,1)
y=np.arange(-M/2,M/2,1)
k,l=np.meshgrid(x,y)
D=np.sqrt(k**2+l**2)
D0,c1,c2 = 50, 1, 10
H=1-np.exp(-(D**2)/(2*D0**2))
#Step 4: High pass filter ouptut
IMG_out1=H*IMG
img_out1=np.fft.ifft2(IMG_out1)
#Step 5: High boost filter output
IMG_out2=(c1+c2*H)*IMG
img_out2=np.fft.ifft2(IMG_out2)
#Step 6: Displaying the results
plt.subplot(1,3,1),plt.imshow(img,cmap='gray'),plt.title('Input image'),plt.axis('off')
plt.subplot(1,3,2),plt.imshow(np.abs(img_out1),cmap='gray'),plt.title('HPF output')
plt.axis('off'),plt.subplot(1,3,3),plt.imshow(np.abs(img_out2),cmap='gray')
plt.title('HBF output'),plt.axis('off')
plt.tight_layout()
```

Fig. 4.107 Python code to compare high-pass and high-boost filter

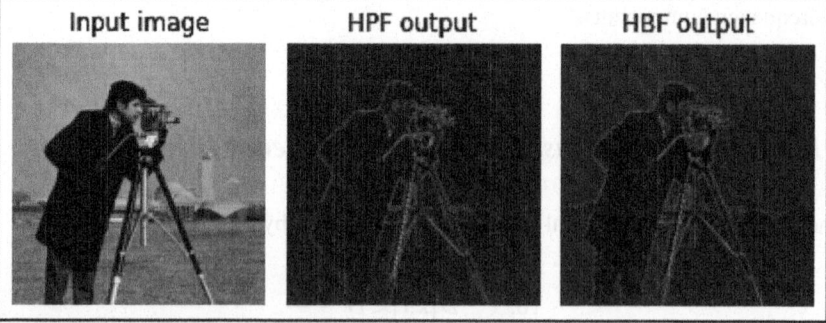

Fig. 4.108 High-pass and high-frequency emphasis filters output

```
#Generation of bandpass filter mask
import numpy as np
import matplotlib.pyplot as plt
#Step 1: Defining the dimension of the mask
N, M =256, 256
#Step 2: Defining the inner and outer radius
r_out, r_in = 80, 20
center = [int(N / 2), int(M / 2)]
#Step 3: Generation of mask
x, y = np.ogrid[:N, :M]
mask = np.logical_and(((x - center[0]) ** 2 + (y - center[1]) ** 2 >= r_in ** 2),
          ((x - center[0]) ** 2 + (y - center[1]) ** 2 <= r_out ** 2))
#Step 4: Displaying the mask
plt.imshow(mask,cmap='gray'),plt.title('Bandpass filter mask'),plt.axis('off')
```

Fig. 4.109 Python code to generate frequency domain band-pass filter

Fig. 4.110 Frequency domain band-pass filter mask

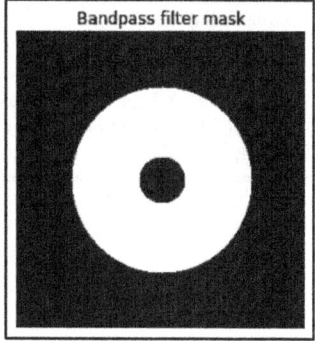

In the above expression, $D[k, l]$ is the distance from the origin, "W" is the band-width, and D_0 is the radial centre.

Experiment 4.47: Band-pass Filter Mask
The objective of this example is to generate a frequency domain band-pass filter mask. The Python code that generates the band-pass filter mask is shown in Fig. 4.109, and the corresponding output is shown in Fig. 4.110.

The built-in function that is used to generate the band-pass filter mask are summarized as follows:

(a) "*np.ogrid()*": An instance that returns an open multi-dimensional "*meshgrid*"
(b) "*np.logical_and*": Logical AND operation.

```
#Frequency domain band pass filter
import numpy as np
import matplotlib.pyplot as plt
import cv2
#Step 1: Reading the input image
img=cv2.imread('squares.tif',0)
M,N=img.shape
#Step 2: Spectrum of the input image
IMG=np.fft.fft2(img)
IMG=np.fft.fftshift(IMG)
#Step 3: Bandpass filter mask
r_out, r_in = 80, 20
center = [int(N / 2), int(M / 2)]
x, y = np.ogrid[:M, :N]
mask = np.logical_and(((x - center[0]) ** 2 + (y - center[1]) ** 2 >= r_in ** 2),
            ((x - center[0]) ** 2 + (y - center[1]) ** 2 <= r_out ** 2))
#Step 4: Multiplying F(k,l) with H(k,l)
IMG_out=np.multiply(IMG, mask)
#Step 5:Inverse Fourier transform
img_out=np.fft.ifft2(IMG_out)
#Step 6: Displaying the results
plt.figure(figsize=(9, 6))
plt.subplot(1,3,1),plt.imshow(img,cmap='gray'),plt.title('Input image'),plt.axis('off')
plt.subplot(1,3,2),plt.imshow(mask,cmap='gray'),plt.title('Ideal BPF mask'),plt.axis('off')
plt.subplot(1,3,3),plt.imshow(np.abs(img_out),cmap='gray')
plt.title('Band pass filtered image'),plt.axis('off')
plt.tight_layout()
```

Fig. 4.111 Python code to perform frequency domain band-pass filter

Inferences

- The band-pass filter mask has a white circle region in-between dark regions.
- The width of the white portion decides the portion of the input signal to be passed by the mask.

Experiment 4.48: Band-Pass Filtering of Input Image
The Python code that performs frequency domain band-pass filtering of the input image is shown in Fig. 4.111, and the result is shown in Fig. 4.112.

Inference
The following inference can be drawn from this experiment:

- The input image is graded with squares of varying grayscale values. The centre square is white in colour.
- Upon passing the graded square image through a band-pass filter, the low-frequency information, which is the background information and the high-frequency information, which is edge information, are not preserved, while the mid-frequency information is preserved.

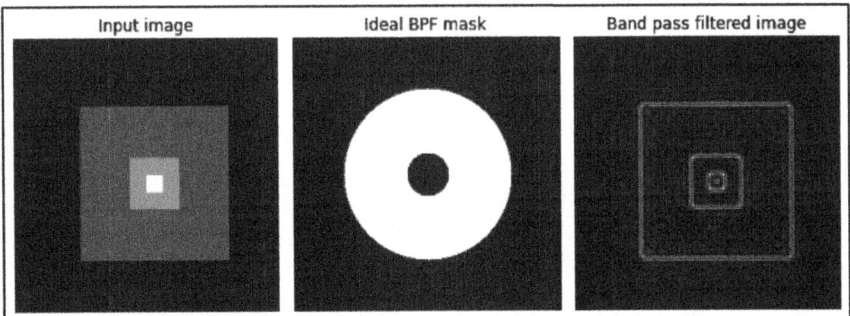

Fig. 4.112 Result of frequency domain band-pass filtering

4.11.5 Ideal Band-Reject Filter in the Frequency Domain

The transfer function of ideal band-reject filter is given by

$$H[k,l] = \begin{cases} 1, & D[k,l] < D_0 - \dfrac{W}{2}, \\ 0, & D_0 - \dfrac{W}{2} \le D[k,l] \le D_0 + \dfrac{W}{2}, \\ 1, & D[k,l] > D_0 + \dfrac{W}{2}. \end{cases} \tag{4.38}$$

In the above expression, $D[k,l]$ is the distance from the origin, "W" is the bandwidth, and D_0 is the radial centre.

Experiment 4.49: Frequency Domain Mask of Band-Reject Filter
This experiment discusses the implementation of band-reject filter mask in frequency domain. The Python code that is used to generate the frequency domain band-reject filter mask is shown in Fig. 4.113, and the corresponding result is shown in Fig. 4.114.

Inference

• The frequency domain band-reject filter mask is basically a white circle on a black background, which is surrounded by a white region.

Experiment 4.50: Frequency Domain Band-Reject Filtering of the Input Image
The aim of this experiment is to compute the band-reject filter output in the frequency domain. The Python code that performs frequency domain band-reject filtering of the input image is shown in Fig. 4.115, and the corresponding output is shown in Fig. 4.116.

```
#Generation of band reject filter mask
import numpy as np
import matplotlib.pyplot as plt
#Step 1: Defining the dimension of the mask
N, M = 256, 256
#Step 2: Defining the inner and outer radius
r_out, r_in = 80, 20
center = [int(N / 2), int(M / 2)]
#Step 3: Generation of mask
x, y = np.ogrid[:N, :M]
mask = np.logical_xor(((x - center[0]) ** 2 + (y - center[1]) ** 2 >= r_in ** 2),
            ((x - center[0]) ** 2 + (y - center[1]) ** 2 <= r_out ** 2))
#Step 4: Displaying the mask
plt.imshow(mask,cmap='gray'),plt.title('Bandreject filter mask'),
plt.xticks([]),plt.yticks([])
```

Fig. 4.113 Python code to generate frequency domain band-reject filter mask

Fig. 4.114 Frequency
domain band-reject
filter mask

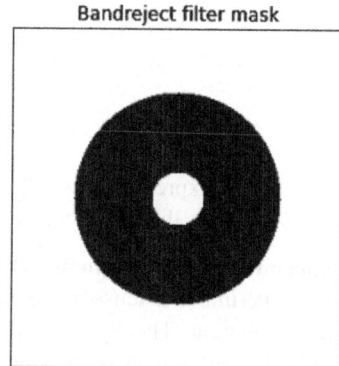

Inferences

- The band-reject filter rejects the range of frequency, and it retains the low-frequency component and the high-frequency component of the input signal.
- In the output image, the background information corresponding to the low-frequency component and the edges belonging to the high-frequency component are retained.

```
#Frequency domain band reject filter
import numpy as np
import matplotlib.pyplot as plt
import cv2
#Step 1: Reading the input image
img=cv2.imread('squares.tif',0)
M,N=img.shape
#Step 2: Spectrum of the input image
IMG=np.fft.fft2(img)
IMG=np.fft.fftshift(IMG)
#Step 3: Bandpass filter mask
r_out, r_in = 80, 20
center = [int(N / 2), int(M / 2)]
x, y = np.ogrid[:M, :N]
mask = np.logical_xor(((x - center[0]) ** 2 + (y - center[1]) ** 2 >= r_in ** 2),
                ((x - center[0]) ** 2 + (y - center[1]) ** 2 <= r_out ** 2))
#Step 4: Multiplying F(k,l) with H(k,l)
IMG_out=np.multiply(IMG, mask)
#Step 5:Inverse Fourier transform
img_out=np.fft.ifft2(IMG_out)
#Step 6: Displaying the results
plt.figure(figsize=(9, 6)),plt.subplot(1,3,1),plt.imshow(img,cmap='gray'),
plt.title('Input image'),plt.axis('off'),plt.subplot(1,3,2),plt.imshow(mask,cmap='gray')
plt.title('Ideal BRF mask'),plt.xticks([]),plt.yticks([]),plt.subplot(1,3,3),
plt.imshow(np.abs(img_out),cmap='gray'),plt.title('Band reject filtered image'),plt.axis('off')
plt.tight_layout()
```

Fig. 4.115 Python code to perform frequency domain band-reject filtering of input image

Fig. 4.116 Result of frequency domain band-reject filtering of input image

4.11.6   Laplacian Operator in the Frequency Domain

Laplacian is a differential operator that approximates the second-order derivative as

$$\nabla^2 f = \frac{\partial^2 f}{\partial x^2} + \frac{\partial^2 f}{\partial y^2} \tag{4.39}$$

In the above expression, "f" denotes the input image. The Laplacian filter highlights the regions of rapid intensity change. The Laplacian operator in the frequency domain is given by

$$H[k,l] = -4\pi^2 D^2 [k,l] \tag{4.40}$$

Experiment 4.51: Laplacian in Frequency Domain
This experiment aims to implement Laplacian operator in the frequency domain. Then, the Laplacian operator is applied to the input test image. The test image is of size 250 × 250 with alternate black and white stripe, with the stripe width being 25.

The following steps are involved in this experiment:
Step 1: Generation of test image.
Step 2: Obtaining the spectrum of the input image.
Step 3: Generation of Laplacian mask in the frequency domain.
Step 4: Multiplying the spectrum of the input image with Laplacian mask.
Step 5: Taking the Inverse Fourier transform of Step 4 result to obtain the filtered image.

The Python code that performs the above-mentioned task is shown in Fig. 4.117, and the corresponding output is shown in Fig. 4.118.

Inferences
The following observations can be made from Fig. 4.118:

• The input image has alternate stripes of black and white pixels. The width of the stripe is 25.
• Upon passing the input image to the Laplacian operator, the filtered image is obtained, which is a vertical line on a black background. Wherever there is a change from the gray level white to black and vice versa, the output will be high. Thus, the Laplacian operator acts as a change detector.

4.12   Homomorphic Filter

A grayscale image $f[m, n]$ can be expressed as

$$f[m,n] = i[m,n] \times r[m,n] \tag{4.41}$$

```
#Laplacian in the frequency domain
import numpy as np
import matplotlib.pyplot as plt
#Step 1: Generating the input image
img=np.ones([250,250])
for i in range(len(img)):
    if(int(i/25)%2==1):
        img[1:250,i]=0
#Step 2: Obtaining the spectrum
IMG=np.fft.fft2(img)
IMG=np.fft.fftshift(IMG)
#Step 3: Generating Laplacian masks
M,N=img.shape
x=np.arange(-N/2,N/2,1)
y=np.arange(-M/2,M/2,1)
k,l=np.meshgrid(x,y)
D=np.sqrt(k**2+l**2)
H=-4*np.pi*np.pi*D*D
#Step 4: Multiplying F(k,l) with H(k,l)
IMG_out=np.multiply(IMG, H)
#Step 5: Taking the Inverse Fourier transform
img_out=np.fft.ifft2(IMG_out)
#Ste6: Displaying the results
plt.figure(figsize=(8, 8)),plt.subplot(1,2,1),plt.imshow(img,cmap='gray')
plt.title('Input image'),plt.xticks([]),plt.yticks([])
plt.subplot(1,2,2),plt.imshow(np.abs(img_out),cmap='gray')
plt.title('Output image'),plt.xticks([]),plt.yticks([])
```

Fig. 4.117 Python code to implement Laplacian filter in frequency domain

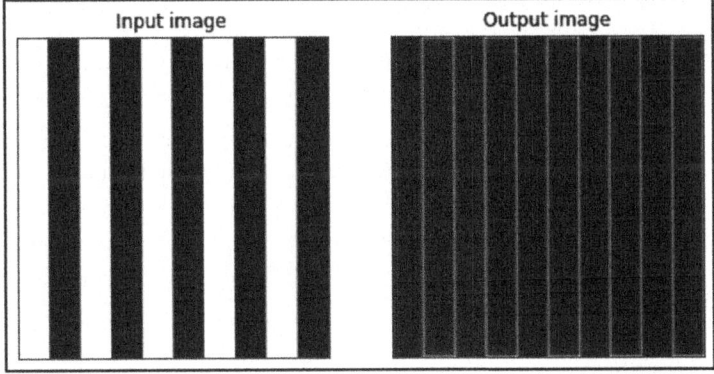

Fig. 4.118 Result of applying Laplacian operator

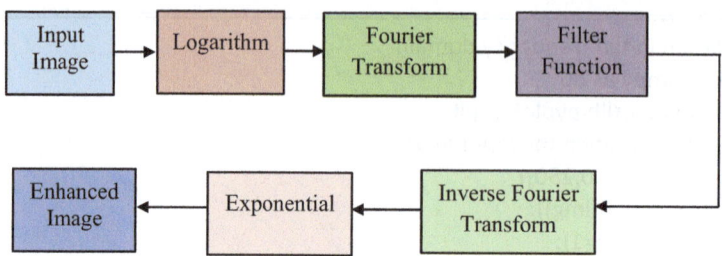

Fig. 4.119   Steps in homomorphic filter

In the above expression, $i[m, n]$ and $r[m, n]$ represent the illumination and reflectance component. In general, slow spatial variation is exhibited by the illumination component and drastic spatial variation is exhibited by the reflectance component. Logarithmic transformation is used to separate the illumination and reflectance components. After separating the illumination and reflectance components, the Fourier transform of both components is taken. This spectrum is multiplied with filter transfer function $H[k, l]$ to obtain the filtered image. However, the filtered image is in frequency domain. To bring the result back to the spatial domain, the Inverse Fourier transform is applied. The final result is obtained by applying the exponential transformation. The steps followed in the homomorphic filter is illustrated in Fig. 4.119.

Experiment 4.52: Implementation of Homomorphic Filter
The Python code that performs the homomorphic filtering operation on the input image is shown in Fig. 4.120 and the corresponding result is shown in Fig. 4.121.

Inference

- The homomorphic filter has attenuated the contribution made by illumination, and it has amplified the contribution made by reflectance, which has resulted in the enhancement of high-frequency components in the filtered image.

4.13   Retinex Algorithm

Retinex theory considers image as the product of reflectance and illumination. Retinex theory is used to enhance images under varying illumination conditions. There are two types of retinex algorithms: (1) single-scale retinex (SSR) algorithm and (2) multiscale retinex (MSR) algorithm.

```
#Homomorphic filter
import numpy as np
import matplotlib.pyplot as plt
import cv2
#Step 1: Reading the input image
img=cv2.imread('Clock.tiff',0)
#Step 2: Logarithm of input image
img_log = np.log(np.float64(img), dtype=np.float64)
#Step 3: Spectrum of log transformed image
IMG = np.fft.fft2(img_log, axes=(0,1))
IMG = np.fft.fftshift(IMG)
#Step 5: Generating the mask
gH, gL, N= 1.5, 0.5, 256
x=np.arange(-N/2,N/2,1)
y=np.arange(-N/2,N/2,1)
k,l=np.meshgrid(x,y)
D=np.sqrt(k**2+l**2)
D0=30
H=(gH-gL)*(1-np.exp(-(D**2)/(2*D0**2)))+gL
#Step 6: Multiplication
IMG_out=np.multiply(IMG, H)
#Step 7: Taking Inverse Fourier transform
img_res = np.fft.ifft2(IMG_out, axes=(0,1))
img_res = np.abs(img_res)
# Step 8: Apply exp to reverse the earlier log
img_homomorphic = np.exp(img_res, dtype=np.float64)
img_homomorphic = cv2.normalize(img_homomorphic, None, alpha=0, beta=255,
norm_type=cv2.NORM_MINMAX, dtype=cv2.CV_8U)
#Step 9: Displaying the result
plt.figure(figsize=(10, 8)),plt.subplot(1,2,1),plt.imshow(img,cmap='gray')
plt.title('Input image'),plt.axis('off')
plt.subplot(1,2,2),plt.imshow(img_homomorphic,cmap='gray')
plt.title('Filtered image'),plt.axis('off')
```

Fig. 4.120 Python code to implement homomorphic filter

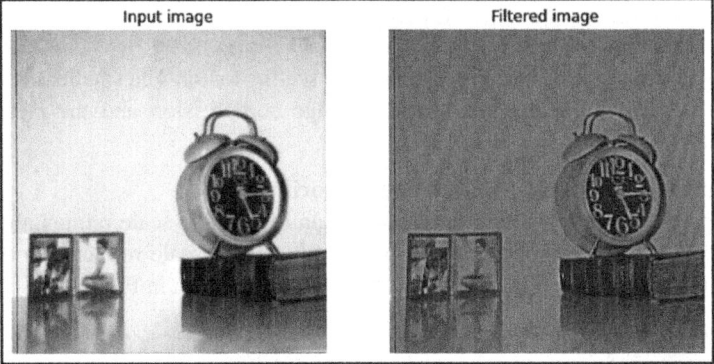

Fig. 4.121 Result of homomorphic filtering operation

```
#Single Scale Retinex (SSR)
import cv2
import matplotlib.pyplot as plt
import numpy as np
#Step 1: Reading the input image
img=cv2.imread(Clock.tiff',0)
#Step 2: Performing SSR
sigma=100
img_ssr =np.log10(img)-np.log10(cv2.GaussianBlur(img, (15,15), sigma))
res_ssr=np.asanyarray(img_ssr,dtype=np.float64)
#Step 3: Displaying the result
plt.subplot(1,2,1),plt.imshow(img,cmap='gray'),plt.title('Input image'),plt.axis('off')
plt.subplot(1,2,2),plt.imshow(res_ssr,cmap='gray')
plt.title('SSR output image'),plt.axis('off')
plt.tight_layout()
```

Fig. 4.122 Python code to perform single-scale retinex algorithm

4.13.1   Single-Scale Retinex Algorithm

Single-scale retinex considers Gaussian-filtered image as the illumination. The single-scale retinex algorithm produces a reflection image by evaluating the ambient brightness, which is represented as

$$\log\left[R_i\left(x,y\right)\right]=\log\left[I_i\left(x,y\right)\right]-\log\left[G\left(x,y\right)*I_i(x,y)\right] \tag{4.42}$$

In the above expression, $I(x, y)$ represents the input image, $R(x, y)$ represents the reflection image, and "i" represents the various colour channels. $G(x, y)$ represents the Gaussian function and "*" represents the convolution operation. The Gaussian function is given by

$$G\left(x,y\right)=ke^{-\frac{x^2+y^2}{\sigma^2}} \tag{4.43}$$

In the above expression, "σ" represents the scaling factor. The smaller the scaling factor, the greater the image's dynamic range compression and the clearer the local values.

Experiment 4.53: Single-Scale Retinex Algorithm
This experiment deals with the implementation of a single-scale retinex algorithm using Python. The Python code that performs a single-scale retinex algorithm is shown in Fig. 4.122, and the corresponding output is shown in Fig. 4.123.

Inferences
The following inferences can be made from Fig. 4.123:

Fig. 4.123 Result of single-scale retinex algorithm

- The input image is a "Clock" image in Tag Image File Format (TIFF) format.
- The image obtained using SSR algorithm has better enhancement of edges and visual quality when compared to the input image.

4.13.2 Multiscale Retinex Algorithm

Multiscale retinex is realized by averaging single-scale retinex for different value of the scale factor. The expression for multiscale retinex is given by

$$MSR = \sum_{n=1}^{N} w_n \left[\log(I_i(x,y)) - \log(F_n(x,y) * I_i(x,y)) \right] \qquad (4.44)$$

In the above expression, "N" is the number of scales and "w_n" is the weight of each scale and $F_n(x,y) = C_n e^{\left[-\frac{x^2+y^2}{2\sigma_n^2} \right]}$. The real challenge is to choose the scale values, number of scale values, and the choice of weighting factor for each scale.

Experiment 4.54: Single-Scale Retinex Versus Multiscale Retinex
This experiment compares single-scale retinex with multiscale retinex algorithm. The Python code that performs the single-scale retinex and multiscale retinex algorithms is shown in Fig. 4.124, and the corresponding result is displayed in Fig. 4.125.

Inferences

- The single-scale retinex algorithms are realized for the values of $\sigma = 1, 5, 10$, and 15. The multiscale retinex is obtained by adding the results of single-scale retinex and then dividing the result by a factor of 4.

```
#Multi Scale Retinex (MSR)
import cv2
import matplotlib.pyplot as plt
import numpy as np
#Step 1: Reading the input image
img=cv2.imread('Clock.tiff',0)
#Step 2: Performing SSR
sigma1,sigma2,sigma3,sigma4=1,5,10,15
img_ssr1 =np.log10(img)-np.log10(cv2.GaussianBlur(img, (15,15), sigma1))
img_ssr2 =np.log10(img)-np.log10(cv2.GaussianBlur(img, (15,15), sigma2))
img_ssr3 =np.log10(img)-np.log10(cv2.GaussianBlur(img, (15,15), sigma3))
img_ssr4 =np.log10(img)-np.log10(cv2.GaussianBlur(img, (15,15), sigma4))
#Obtaining MSR
img_msr=(img_ssr1 +img_ssr2 +img_ssr3 +img_ssr4)/4
res_msr=np.asanyarray(img_msr,dtype=np.float64)
res_ssr=np.asanyarray(img_ssr1,dtype=np.float64)
#Step 3: Displaying the result
plt.subplot(1,3,1),plt.imshow(img,cmap='gray'),plt.title('Input image'),plt.axis('off')
plt.subplot(1,3,2),plt.imshow(res_ssr,cmap='gray'),plt.title('SSR output image'),
plt.axis('off'),plt.subplot(1,3,3),plt.imshow(res_msr,cmap='gray')
plt.title('MSR output image'),plt.axis('off')
plt.tight_layout()
```

Fig. 4.124 Python code to compare SSR and MSR

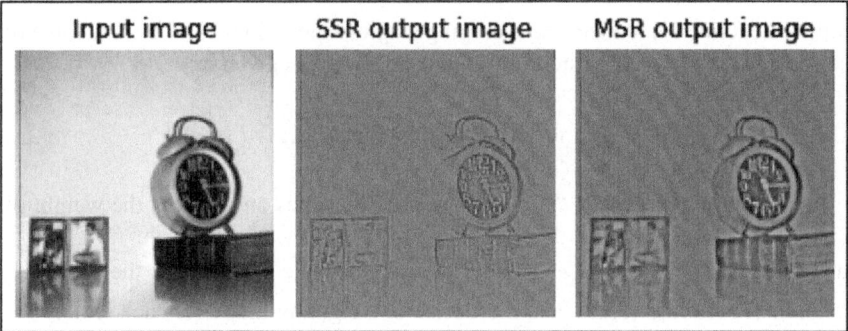

Fig. 4.125 Simulation result

- In this experiment, the multiscale retinex algorithm result is better than the single-scale retinex algorithm.
- The reason behind this result is the choice of the scaling factor.
- When the scale factor is very less, the edge enhancement happens but the background information is lost.

Exercise

1. Generate a 16×16 image that has all zero value except the centre pixel, which takes the value of 255. Pass this image through box filter of size $3 \times 3, 5 \times 5$, and 7×7. Display the input and filtered images and comment on the observed result.
2. Generate a 16×16 image that has all zero value except the centre pixel, which takes the value of 255. Pass it through $3 \times 3, 5 \times 5$, and 7×7 Gaussian kernel and comment on the observed result.
3. Generate a 256×256 test image that has a white square in a black background. Pass this test image through low-pass filter and high-pass filter. Plot the profile of 128th row of the input image, low-pass filtered image, and high-pass filtered image and comment on the observed result.
4. Generate a 7×7 image with white pixel in the centre and all the other pixels are black. The image in matrix form is represented as $\begin{bmatrix} 0 & 0 & 0 & 0 & 0 & 0 & 0 \\ 0 & 0 & 0 & 0 & 0 & 0 & 0 \\ 0 & 0 & 0 & 0 & 0 & 0 & 0 \\ 0 & 0 & 0 & 1 & 0 & 0 & 0 \\ 0 & 0 & 0 & 0 & 0 & 0 & 0 \\ 0 & 0 & 0 & 0 & 0 & 0 & 0 \\ 0 & 0 & 0 & 0 & 0 & 0 & 0 \end{bmatrix}$.

   Apply 5×5 median filter and mean filter to process the image and comment on the observed result.
5. Read an input image. Add zero mean unit variance white noise to the input image. Perform histogram equalization of the noisy image and comment on the observed result.
6. Generate a gradient image whose gray level varies gradually from black to white. After generating the gradient image, pass this image through first-order and second-order derivative filters. Plot the original image, filtered images, and their corresponding profile and comment on the observed result.

Objective Questions

1. If the variable "img_in" in the below Python code represents an 8-bit grayscale image, then "img_out" is

   ```
   Img_out=img_in +100
   ```

   A. Brighter image
   B. Darker image
   C. Contrast enhanced image
   D. Dynamic range compressed image

2. The mask generated by the following Python code is

```
import numpy as np
mask=np.array([[-1,-1,-1],[-1,8,-1],[-1,-1,-1]])
```

A. Low-pass filter
B. High-pass filter
C. Band-pass filter
D. Band-reject filter

3. The mask generated by the following Python code is

```
import numpy as np
mask=np.array([[-1,-1,-1],[-1,10,-1],[-1,-1,-1]])
```

A. Low-pass filter
B. High-pass filter
C. High-frequency emphasis filter
D. Band-pass filter

4. If the variable "img_in" in the Python code given below represents an 8-bit

```
Img_out=img_in>128
```

grayscale image, then "img_out" represents

A. Contrast enhanced grayscale image
B. Binary image
C. Dynamic range enhanced grayscale image
D. Dynamic range compressed grayscale image

5. The mask given in the following Python code belongs to

```
Import numpy as np
mask=1/16*np.array([[1,2,1], [2,4,2],[1,2,1]])
```

A. Ideal low-pass filter
B. Gaussian low-pass filter
C. Ideal high-pass filter
D. Gaussian high-pass filter

6. If "img_in" is an 8-bit input grayscale image, after executing the following Python code, what will be the nature of the output image "img_out"?

```
Img_out=255-img_in
```

A. Negative of the input image
B. Binary form of the input image
C. Output image exactly same as input image
D. Output image is contrast-enhanced version of input image

7. In the following Python code, if "h1" represents low-pass filter mask and "h2" represents the high-pass filter mask, then the mask represented by the variable "h" is

```
import numpy as np
from scipy import signal
h1=1/9*np.ones([3,3])
h2=np.array([[0,-1,0],[-1,4,-1],[0,-1,0]])
h=signal.convolve2d(h1,h2,mode='same')
```

A. Low-pass filter
B. High-pass filter
C. Band-pass filter
D. Band-reject filter

8. If "img_in" is the input image, the following Python code represents

```
Import numpy as np
Import cv2
sigma=100
img_out =np.log10(img_in)-np.log10(cv2.GaussianBlur(img_in, (15,15), sigma))
```

A. Histogram equalization
B. Unsharp masking
C. Single-scale retinex algorithm
D. Multiscale retinex algorithm

9. The measure of the difference in brightness between the light and dark areas of an image is termed as

A. Brightness of the image
B. Darkness of the image
C. Contrast of the image
D. Entropy of the image

10. The filter that is used to emphasize high-frequency components in the image, at the same time preserving the low-frequency content, is

A. Low-pass filter
B. High-pass filter
C. High-boost filter
D. Homomorphic filter

11. If the histogram of the image is concentrated on the higher side of the intensity scale, the image would probably be

A. Bright image
B. Dark image
C. Colour image
D. High-contrast image

12. Statement 1: Low-pass filter performs smoothing of the input image.
    Statement 2: High-pass filtering performs sharpening of the input image

    A. Statements 1 and 2 are true
    B. Statement 1 is true, Statement 2 is false
    C. Statement 1 is false, Statement 2 is false
    D. Statements 1 and 2 are false

13. Statement 1: Mean filter is a non-linear filter
    Statement 2: Median filter is a linear filter

    A. Statements 1 and 2 are true
    B. Statement 1 is true, Statement 2 is false
    C. Statement 1 is false, Statement 2 is false
    D. Statements 1 and 2 are false

14. What should be the value of "x" in the mask $\begin{bmatrix} -1 & -1 & -1 \\ -1 & x & -1 \\ -1 & -1 & -1 \end{bmatrix}$ such that the mask

    can be used to perform high-pass filtering of the image?

    A. −1
    B. 0
    C. 8
    D. −8

15. The operation performed as per the block diagram given below performs

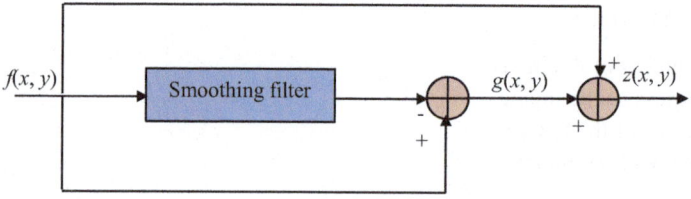

    A. Image negative
    B. Unsharp masking
    C. Bit plane slicing
    D. Contrast stretching

16. What should be the value of "x" such that the filter acts as averaging

    filter $\dfrac{1}{x}\begin{bmatrix} 1 & 1 & 1 \\ 1 & 1 & 1 \\ 1 & 1 & 1 \end{bmatrix}$?

    A. 1
    B. 3
    C. 6
    D. 9

17. A graph of gray level against the frequency of occurrence of gray level is termed as

   A. Spectrum of the image
   B. Histogram of the image
   C. Spectrogram of the image
   D. Scalogram of the image

18. Identify the idempotent operation

   A. Image negative
   B. Histogram equalization
   C. Logarithmic transformation
   D. Power-law transformation

19. A patch of 8-bit grayscale image is given by $\begin{bmatrix} 100 & 110 & 90 \\ 80 & [55] & 65 \\ 75 & 67 & 72 \end{bmatrix}$. What will be the value of the square bracketed pixel after applying "negative transformation" operation?

   A. 100
   B. 200
   C. 150
   D. 70

20. The gray level transformation, which can compress the dynamic range of images with large variations in pixel values, is

   A. Thresholding
   B. Gray level slicing
   C. Logarithmic transformation
   D. Contrast stretching

21. The mask corresponding to Laplacian operator is

   A. $\begin{bmatrix} 0 & -1 & 0 \\ -1 & -1 & -1 \\ 0 & -1 & 0 \end{bmatrix}$

   B. $\begin{bmatrix} 0 & 1 & 0 \\ 1 & 1 & 1 \\ 0 & 1 & 0 \end{bmatrix}$

   C. $\begin{bmatrix} 0 & -1 & 0 \\ -1 & 4 & -1 \\ 0 & -1 & 0 \end{bmatrix}$

   D. $\begin{bmatrix} 0 & -1 & 0 \\ -1 & -4 & -1 \\ 0 & -1 & 0 \end{bmatrix}$

22. The frequency domain mask shown below represents

    A. Low-pass filter
    B. High-pass filter
    C. Band-pass filter
    D. Band-reject filter

23. The transfer function $H[k,l] = \begin{cases} 1, & \sqrt{k^2 + l^2} \le D_0, \\ 0, & \sqrt{k^2 + l^2} > D_0 \end{cases}$, where "$D_0$" represents the cut-off frequency represents

    A. Low-pass filter
    B. High-pass filter
    C. Band-pass filter
    D. Band-reject filter

24. If $H[k, l]$ represents the transfer function of low-pass filter. Then the expression $1 - H[k, l]$ represents the transfer function of

    A. Low-pass filter
    B. High-pass filter
    C. Band-pass filter
    D. Band-reject filter

25. Assertion: Median filter is a non-linear filter.
  Reason: Median filter violates superposition principle

    A. Assertion and reason are correct
    B. Assertion is correct, reason is wrong
    C. Assertion is wrong, reason may be correct
    D. Assertion and reason are wrong

Answers to Objective Questions

Q. No.	01	02	03	04	05	06	07	08	09	10
Key	A	B	C	C	B	A	C	C	C	C
Q. No.	11	12	13	14	15	16	17	18	19	20
Key	A	A	D	C	B	D	B	B	B	C
Q. No.	21	22	23	24	25					
Key	C	C	A	B	A					

Answers to PreLab Questions

1. The objective of image enhancement is to improve the visual quality of the image so that better image can be fed to automated image processing techniques.
2. Brightness refers to the overall lightness or darkness of the image. Contrast is the difference in brightness between regions of the image.
3. Simultaneous contrast is a phenomenon in which a gray patch looks lighter when it is next to a darker patch. It is a phenomenon that manifests when two similar colours mutually influence one other, changing the way one perceives them.
4. For an 8-bit image, the expression for image negative is given by $y[m, n] = 255 - x[m, n]$. Image negative is also termed as an inversion of gray level values in a digital image whose operation is similar to that of NOT gate in digital electronics.
5. Histogram of an image is a plot of gray level values versus the number of pixels at that value. Shape of the histogram gives information about the nature of the image.

    (i) Very narrow histogram implies that the image could be low-contrast image.
    (ii) Histogram with widespread corresponds to high-contrast image.
    (iii) Histogram skewed towards higher end of gray level indicate that the image is a bright image.
    (iv) Histogram skewed towards lower end of gray level indicate that the image is a dark image.

6. Yes, multiple images can have same histogram. Histogram gives the frequency of occurrence of the gray level. It does not convey information related to the location of the pixel. Hence, multiple images can have the same histogram.
7. From the histogram, it is not possible to derive the image in a unique way, because multiple images can have the same histogram.
8. A high-pass filter is basically a change detector that will not preserve the background information, which is normally smooth or has many low-frequency components. A high-boost filter is a high-frequency emphasis filters that will preserve the background information in the digital image.
9. An idempotent operation is an operation that can be performed multiple times without changing the result beyond the initial application. Histogram equalization result will not alter beyond the initial application even if it is repeated many times, hence it is considered as an idempotent operation.
10. When a grayscale image is fed to thresholding operation, binary image will be obtained as the output. Thresholding is basically a logical operation that gives binary result.
11. Averaging filter or mean filter has the tendency to smooth the edges of the image that will result in blurring of the image. Averaging filter is a tool to minimize the impact of additive noise in digital image. Even though it has the tendency to blur the image, it has the ability to minimize the impact of additive noise, hence it is preferred.

12. Logarithm operation converts multiplication operation into an addition operation. Image is represented as

$$f(x,y) = i(x,y) \times r(x,y)$$

where $i(x, y)$ represents illuminance and $r(x, y)$ represents reflectance. To convert the multiplication into an addition, logarithmic operation is preferred. Also, logarithm operation compresses the dynamic range of the input values. Logarithmic operation is also preferable for dynamic range compression.

13. Steps involved in frequency domain-based filtering of the image are.

    (i) Compute the Fourier transform of the input image ($f[m, n]$) to obtain the coefficients $F[k, l]$.

    (ii) Multiply the Fourier coefficient of the image ($F[k, l]$) with the filter transfer function ($H[k, l]$).

    (iii) Perform Inverse Fourier transform of the result obtained in step (ii) to obtain the filtered image.

14. $H[k, l]$ represents the Laplacian mask. As a result, the output image will be the high-pass filtered version of the input image. The filter acts as an edge detector.

15. The word retinex is a combination of two words, namely retina and cortex. The fundamental idea in retinex theory is that the human visual system ensures that the perceived colour of one object remains relatively constant with different illumination conditions, which is termed as colour constancy. Two broad types of retinex algorithms are (1) single-scale retinex and (2) multiscale retinex.

Bibliography

1. Alan C. Bovik, "The Essential Guide to Image Processing", Academic Press, 2009.
2. Kenneth R. Castleman, "Digital Image Processing", Pearson Education, 2007.
3. Wilhelm Burger and Mark Burge, "Digital Image Processing: An Algorithmic Introduction using Java", Springer, 2007.
4. Scott E. Umbaugh, "Digital Image Processing and Analysis", CRC Press, 2011.
5. William K. Pratt, "Digital Image Processing", John Wiley and Sons, 2007.

Chapter 5
Image Denoising and Image Restoration

Learning Objectives

After reading this chapter, the reader should be familiar with the following concepts:

- Types of noises in digital image
- Spatial and frequency domain filters to mitigate noise
- Different types of degradation in digital image
- Inverse and Wiener filters for image restoration

Roadmap of the Chapter

The roadmap of this chapter is given in the form of a flowchart, and it is depicted in Fig. 5.1.

PreLab Questions

1. Mention some non-linear filters that are used to minimize noise in digital images.
2. Why is the median filter considered a non-linear filter?
3. List two advantages of bilateral filter.
4. Mention two disadvantages of bilateral filter.
5. An image is corrupted with periodic noise. Mention the steps to minimize the impact of the noise.
6. In which circumstances one should prefer (1) Gaussian smoothing and (2) median filtering?
7. When a degradation function in image restoration is said to be linear and shift invariant?
8. How is the degradation process modelled by assuming the degradation function to be linear and shift-invariant?

Supplementary Information The online version contains supplementary material available at https://doi.org/10.1007/978-981-96-6382-8_5.

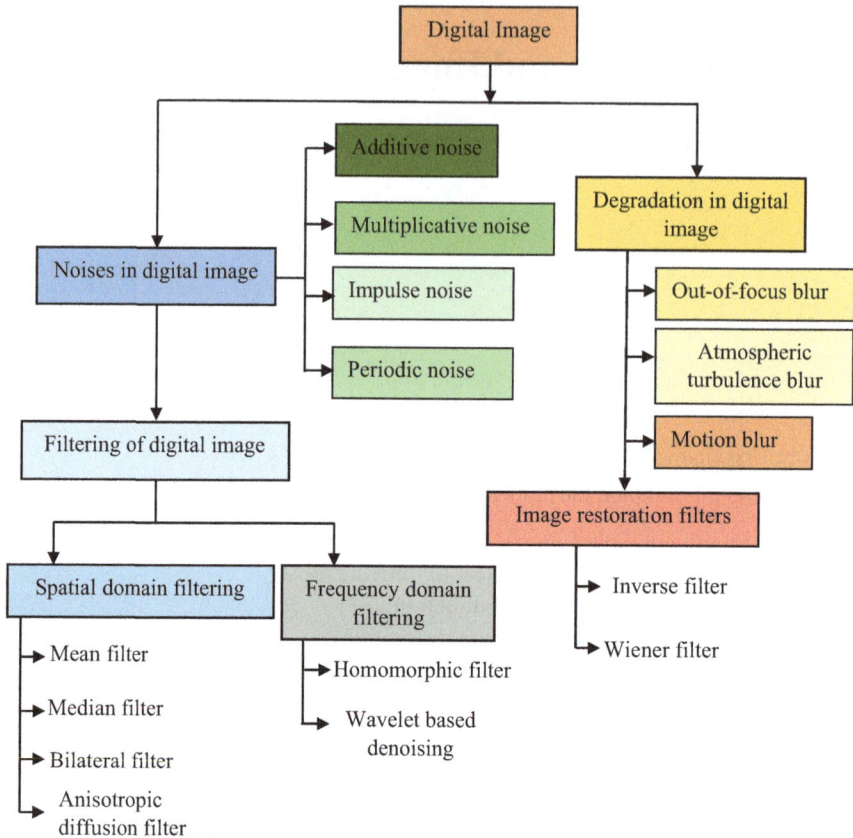

Fig. 5.1 Roadmap of this chapter

9. Mention the ways to estimate the degradation function in image restoration.
10. In which sense is the Wiener filter termed as "optimum filter"?

5.1   Introduction

The objective of this chapter is to discuss two important aspects of image processing, namely image denoising and image restoration. Different types of noise and methods to mitigate the impact of noise are discussed in this chapter. Both linear and non-linear filtering techniques for minimizing the impact of noise is given in this chapter. The second part of the chapter deals with different types of degradation and methods to restore digital image. Two prominent techniques for image restoration discussed in this chapter are (1) inverse filter and (2) Wiener filter.

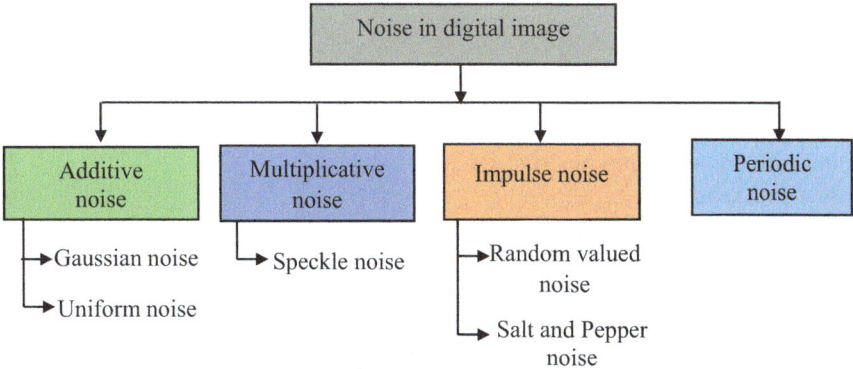

Fig. 5.2   Noise in digital image

5.2   Noises in Digital Image

Image noise is a random variation in the intensity values of the pixels. Noise occurs in digital image during acquisition, transmission, and processing. Different types of noises in digital images include (1) Gaussian noise, (2) impulse noise, (3) speckle noise, and (4) periodic noise. The classification of noise in digital images is given in Fig. 5.2.

5.2.1   Gaussian Noise

Common factors of Gaussian noise include amplifier noise, shot noise, and grain noise of film. The probability density function of Gaussian distribution is given by

$$f(x) = \frac{1}{\sqrt{2\pi}\sigma} e^{-\frac{(x-\mu)^2}{2\sigma^2}}, x \geq 0 \tag{5.1}$$

The Gaussian noise is characterized by mean "μ" and standard deviation "σ".

Experiment 5.1: Adding Gaussian Noise to the Input Image
Read an input image. Add white Gaussian noise to the input image with zero mean and standard deviation values as 50, 75, and 150. Plot the input image and the noisy image.

The Python code that adds white Gaussian noise to the input image is shown in Fig. 5.3, and the corresponding output is displayed in Fig. 5.4.

The built-in functions used in the program shown in Fig. 5.3 are summarized in Table 5.1.

```
import numpy as np
import matplotlib.pyplot as plt
import cv2
#Step 1: Reading the input image
img=cv2.imread('cameraman.tif',0)
m,n=img.shape
#Step 2: Adding white Gaussian noise to the image
gauss_noise=np.zeros((m,n),dtype=np.uint8)
mean,std1,std2,std3=0,50,75,150
gauss_noise1=(cv2.randn(gauss_noise,mean,std1)).astype(np.uint8)
gauss_noise2=(cv2.randn(gauss_noise,mean,std2)).astype(np.uint8)
gauss_noise3=(cv2.randn(gauss_noise,mean,std3)).astype(np.uint8)
noisy_img1=cv2.add(img,gauss_noise1)
noisy_img2=cv2.add(img,gauss_noise2)
noisy_img3=cv2.add(img,gauss_noise3)
#Step 3: Displaying the results
fig = plt.figure(figsize=(8,6))
plt.subplot(1,4,1),plt.imshow(img,cmap='gray'),plt.title('Input image')
plt.axis('off'),plt.subplot(1,4,2),plt.imshow(noisy_img1,cmap='gray'),
plt.title('NI:"$\sigma={}$'.format(std1)),plt.axis('off')
plt.subplot(1,4,3),plt.imshow(noisy_img2,cmap='gray'),
plt.title('NI:"$\sigma={}$'.format(std2)),plt.axis('off')
plt.subplot(1,4,4),plt.imshow(noisy_img3,cmap='gray'),
plt.title('NI:"$\sigma={}$'.format(std3)),plt.axis('off')
plt.tight_layout()
```

Fig. 5.3 Python code to add white Gaussian noise to the input image

Fig. 5.4 Result of adding white Gaussian noise to the input image

Inferences

The following inferences can be drawn for the addition of Gaussian noise:

- The input image is a "Cameraman image".
- The noise added to the input image is additive white Gaussian noise.

Table 5.1 Built-in function used to add white noise to the input image

S. No.	Built-in function	Library	Purpose
1	Randn	cv2	To generate random numbers that follow normal or Gaussian distribution
2	Add	cv2	To add two images

- The parameters of white noise are mean and standard deviation. The mean value is fixed at zero, and the standard deviation is increased to 50, 75, and 150.
- The impact of noise is more with increase in standard deviation of the noise.

5.2.2 Uniform Noise

The probability density function of uniform distribution is given by

$$f(x) = \begin{cases} \dfrac{1}{b-a}, & a \le x < b, \\ 0, & \text{otherwise.} \end{cases} \tag{5.2}$$

where "a" is the minimum value and "b" is the maximum value.

Experiment 5.2: Adding Uniform Noise to the Input Image
This experiment discusses adding uniform noise to the input image. The Python code that adds random noise which follows uniform distribution is shown in Fig. 5.5, and the corresponding output is shown in Fig. 5.6.

Inference

- The lower bound of the uniform noise is kept as "0". The upper bound varies from 50, 100, and 250. With increase in the value of the upper bound, the impact of noise is more.

5.2.3 Impulse Noise

Impulse noise is due to analog-to-digital converter saturation, transmission errors, memory errors, and faulty pixels in the camera sensors. There are two types of impulse noise: salt and pepper noise and random valued noise.

Salt and pepper noise randomly alters a certain amount of pixels into two extremes, either 0 or 255, for an 8-bit image. In salt and pepper noise, the black pixels correspond to pepper noise, which usually appears in the brighter areas of the image, whereas the white pixels correspond to salt noise, which appears in the darker areas of the image. It is expressed as

```
#Adding uniform noise to the input image
import numpy as np
import matplotlib.pyplot as plt
import cv2
#Step 1: Reading the input image
img=cv2.imread('cameraman.tif',0)
m,n=img.shape
#Step 2: Adding white Gaussian noise to the image
uni_noise=np.zeros((m,n),dtype=np.uint8)
ub1,ub2,ub3=50,100,250
uniform_noise1=(cv2.randu(uni_noise,0,ub1)).astype(np.uint8)
uniform_noise2=(cv2.randu(uni_noise,0,ub2)).astype(np.uint8)
uniform_noise3=(cv2.randu(uni_noise,0,ub3)).astype(np.uint8)
noisy_img1=cv2.add(img,uniform_noise1)
noisy_img2=cv2.add(img,uniform_noise2)
noisy_img3=cv2.add(img,uniform_noise3)
fig = plt.figure(figsize=(8,6))
plt.subplot(1,4,1),plt.imshow(img,cmap='gray'),plt.title('Input image')
plt.axis('off'),plt.subplot(1,4,2),plt.imshow(noisy_img1,cmap='gray'),
plt.title('NI:UB1={}'.format(ub1)),plt.axis('off')
plt.subplot(1,4,3),plt.imshow(noisy_img2,cmap='gray'),
plt.title('NI:UB2={}'.format(ub2)),plt.axis('off')
plt.subplot(1,4,4),plt.imshow(noisy_img3,cmap='gray'),
plt.title('NI:UB3={}'.format(ub3)),plt.axis('off')
plt.tight_layout()
```

Fig. 5.5 Python code that adds uniform white noise to the input image

Fig. 5.6 Result of adding uniform white noise to the input image

$$y[m,n] = \begin{cases} x_{\min}, & \text{with probability } P_{\min}, \\ x_{\max}, & \text{with probability } P_{\max}, \\ x[m,n], & \text{with probability } 1 - P_{\max} - P_{\min}. \end{cases} \tag{5.3}$$

where $y[m, n]$ represents the image corrupted with salt and pepper noise, $x[m, n]$ is a noise-free image, and $x_{\min}$ and $x_{\max}$ represent the minimum and maximum intensity of the pixel, respectively.

Experiment 5.3: Image Corrupted with Only Salt Noise
The objective of this experiment is to read the input image and corrupt it with only salt noise. Salt noise can be added by randomly picking the pixels and forcing its value to 255. The built-in function "randint" available in random library is used to select coordinates of the pixels randomly. The Python code that accomplishes this task is shown in Fig. 5.7, and the corresponding output is shown in Fig. 5.8.

```
#Salt noise only
import matplotlib.pyplot as plt
import cv2
import random
img=cv2.imread('cameraman.tif',0)
img_clone=img.copy()
m,n=img.shape[:2]
number_of_pixels = random.randint(100, 9000)
for i in range(number_of_pixels):
    y=random.randint(0, m - 1)
    x=random.randint(0, n - 1)
    img[x,y]=255
plt.subplot(1,2,1),plt.imshow(img_clone,cmap='gray')
plt.title('Input image'),plt.axis('off')
plt.subplot(1,2,2),plt.imshow(img,cmap='gray')
plt.title('Image with only salt noise'),plt.axis('off')
```

Fig. 5.7 Python code to corrupt the input image with only salt noise

Fig. 5.8 Input image corrupted with only salt noise

Inferences

The following inference can be made from Fig. 5.8:

- The input image is a "Cameraman" image. The image is corrupted with only salt noise. The salt noise takes a maximum gray level of 255 in the case of an 8-bit image, which appears as white.
- It is possible to observe that the noisy image has the random occurrence of white dots, which corresponds to salt noise.

Experiment 5.4: Image Corrupted with Only Pepper Noise

The objective of this experiment is to corrupt the input image with only pepper noise. Pepper noise corresponds to a "black" colour. Black takes a gray level of 0. The logic to create pepper noise is to randomly select the pixel of the input image and force it to take a value of 0. The Python code that performs this task is shown in Fig. 5.9, and the corresponding output is shown in Fig. 5.10.

Inference

- From Fig. 5.10, it is possible to observe that the input image is corrupted with a random occurrence of black dots, which corresponds to pepper noise.

Experiment 5.5: Salt and Pepper Noise Using Built-in Function from "Scikit" Library

In this example, the salt and pepper noise is added to the input image using the built-in (random_noise()) function available in "*scikit*" library. The Python code that adds the salt and pepper noise to the input image is given in Fig. 5.11, and the corresponding output is shown in Fig. 5.12.

```
#Pepper noise only
import matplotlib.pyplot as plt
import cv2
import random
img=cv2.imread('cameraman.tif',0)
img_clone=img.copy()
m,n=img.shape[:2]
number_of_pixels = random.randint(100, 9000)
for i in range(number_of_pixels):
    y=random.randint(0, m - 1)
    x=random.randint(0, n - 1)
    img[x,y]=0
plt.subplot(1,2,1),plt.imshow(img_clone,cmap='gray')
plt.title('Input image'),plt.axis('off')
plt.subplot(1,2,2),plt.imshow(img,cmap='gray')
plt.title('Image with only pepper noise'),plt.axis('off')
```

Fig. 5.9 Python code to add only pepper noise

Fig. 5.10 Input image corrupted by only pepper noise

```
import cv2
from skimage.util import random_noise
import matplotlib.pyplot as plt
#Step 1: Reading the input image
img=cv2.imread('cameraman.tif',0)
fig = plt.figure(figsize=(8,6))
plt.figure(1),plt.subplot(2,3,1),plt.axis('off')
plt.imshow(img,cmap='gray'),plt.title('Input image')
#Step 2: Adding salt and pepper noise
noise_amount=[0.01,0.1,0.2,0.5,0.8]
for i in range(len(noise_amount)):
    noise_img = random_noise(img, mode='s&p',amount=noise_amount[i])
    #Step 3: Displaying the result
    plt.subplot(2,3,i+2),plt.imshow(noise_img,cmap='gray')
    plt.title('Noise amount={}'.format(noise_amount[i])), plt.axis('off')
plt.tight_layout()
```

Fig. 5.11 Adding salt and pepper noise to the input image

Inferences

The following inferences can be made from Fig. 5.12:

- Salt and pepper noise is the random occurrence of black (gray level 0) and white (gray level 255) pixels in the input image.
- With increase in noise density, the impact of noise in the input image is visible.

Experiment 5.6: Adding Salt and Pepper Noise Using "Numpy" Library

This experiment illustrates the idea of adding salt and pepper noise to the input image using "*numpy*" library. The Python code is shown in Fig. 5.13, and the corresponding output is shown in Fig. 5.14.

Fig. 5.12 Salt and pepper noise added to the input image

Inference

- This experiment illustrates the idea of adding salt and pepper noise to the input image. By varying the probability of the noise, the impact of noise in the input image can be varied.

5.2.4   Speckle Noise

Speckle noise is a multiplicative noise. The mathematical expression for speckle noise is given by

$$g[m,n] = f[m,n] \times \eta[m,n] \tag{5.4}$$

where $f[m, n]$ represents noise-free image, $g[m, n]$ represents the noisy image, and $\eta[m, n]$ represents the speckle noise. The larger the variance of the speckle noise, the greater its influence on the gray values of the image.

```
import cv2
import numpy as np
import random
import matplotlib.pyplot as plt
#Step 1: Reading the input image
img=cv2.imread('cameraman.tif',0)
#Step 2: Adding noise to the input image
prob=0.1
output = np.zeros(img.shape,np.uint8)
thres = 1 - prob
for i in range(img.shape[0]):
    for j in range(img.shape[1]):
        rdn = random.random()
        if rdn < prob:
            output[i][j] = 0
        elif rdn > thres:
            output[i][j] = 255
        else:
            output[i][j] = img[i][j]
#Step 3: Displaying the result
plt.subplot(1,2,1),plt.imshow(img,cmap='gray'),plt.title('Input image'),
plt.axis('off'),plt.subplot(1,2,2),plt.imshow(output,cmap='gray')
plt.title('Noisy image'),plt.axis('off')
plt.tight_layout()
```

Fig. 5.13 Python code to add salt and pepper noise using "numpy" library

Fig. 5.14 Result of adding salt and pepper noise

Experiment 5.7: Adding Speckle Noise in an Image

This experiment discusses the generation of speckle noise and addition to the input image. The Python code that illustrates the generation of speckle noise is given in Fig. 5.15, and the corresponding output is shown in Fig. 5.16.

```
import numpy as np
import matplotlib.pyplot as plt
img=np.ones([256,256])
img[68:188,58:188]=255
m,n=img.shape
mean, sigma = 5, 0.05
theta=sigma**2/mean
k=mean/theta
spec_noise=np.random.randn(m,n)
noisy_img=img*spec_noise
plt.subplot(1,2,1),plt.imshow(img,cmap='gray'),plt.axis('off')
plt.title('Input image'),plt.subplot(1,2,2),plt.imshow(noisy_img,cmap='gray')
plt.title('Speckle noise'),plt.axis('off')
```

Fig. 5.15   Python code to add speckle noise to the input image

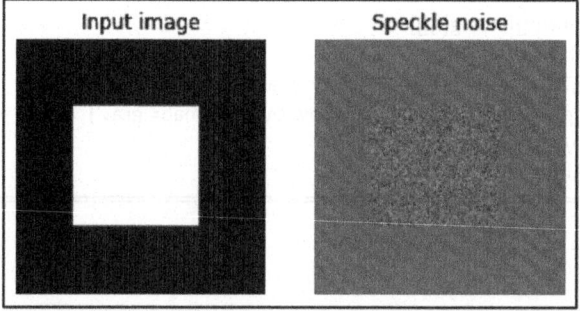

Fig. 5.16   Speckle noise to the input image

Inferences

The following inferences can be made from this experiment:

- The input image is a synthetic image, which is a white square on a black background.
- The speckle noise is a multiplicative noise. With increase in the variance of the speckle noise, the impact of noise on the input image will be more visible.
- The speckle noise creates a grain-like pattern on the input image.

5.2.5 *Poisson Noise*

Poisson noise can be modelled by a Poisson process. The Poisson distribution is expressed as

$$P\big(f\big(x=k\big)\big)=\frac{\lambda^{k}e^{-\lambda}}{k!} \tag{5.5}$$

The above model assumes that each pixel of the image $f(x)$ is drawn from Poisson distribution. In Eq. (5.5), "λ" is proportional to the number of photons that hit the receptor during the exposition time. The Poisson noise is also termed as "Shot noise".

Experiment 5.8: Generation of Poisson Noise and Addition to the Input Image
This experiment deals with the generation of Poisson noise and how to add it to the input image using Python. The Python code that adds Poisson noise to the input image is shown in Fig. 5.17, and the corresponding output is shown in Fig. 5.18.

Inferences
The following inferences can be drawn from this experiment:

- The input image is a synthetic image with a white square in a black background.
- Upon adding Poisson noise, the gray level of the input image varies, which is visible in the noisy image.
- The profile of the 128th row of the input image and the noisy image is shown in the figure, from which it is possible to infer that the input image profile is a pulse pattern with a sharp transition in the gray level value from 0 to 255 and vice versa.
- The profile of the 128th row of the noisy image indicates that there is fluctuation in the gray level in the noisy image.

```python
#Poisson noise
import numpy as np
import matplotlib.pyplot as plt
#Step 1: Generation of input image
img=np.ones([256,256])
img[68:188,58:188]=255
#Step 2: Adding Poisson noise to the input image
poisson_noise = np.sqrt(img) * np.random.normal(0, 1, img.shape)
noisy_img = img + poisson_noise
#Step 3: Displaying the result
fig = plt.figure(figsize=(8,6))
plt.subplot(2,2,1),plt.imshow(img,cmap='gray'),plt.title('Input image'),plt.axis('off')
plt.subplot(2,2,2),plt.imshow(noisy_img,cmap='gray')
plt.title('Poisson noise'),plt.axis('off'),plt.subplot(2,2,3),plt.plot(img[128,:])
plt.title('Profile of 128th row of input image'),plt.xlabel('128th Row'),
plt.ylabel('Pixel Intensity'),plt.subplot(2,2,4),plt.plot(noisy_img[128,:])
plt.title('Profile of 128th row of Noisy image'),plt.xlabel('128th Row'),plt.ylabel('Pixel Intensity')
plt.tight_layout()
```

Fig. 5.17 Python code to add Poisson noise to the input image

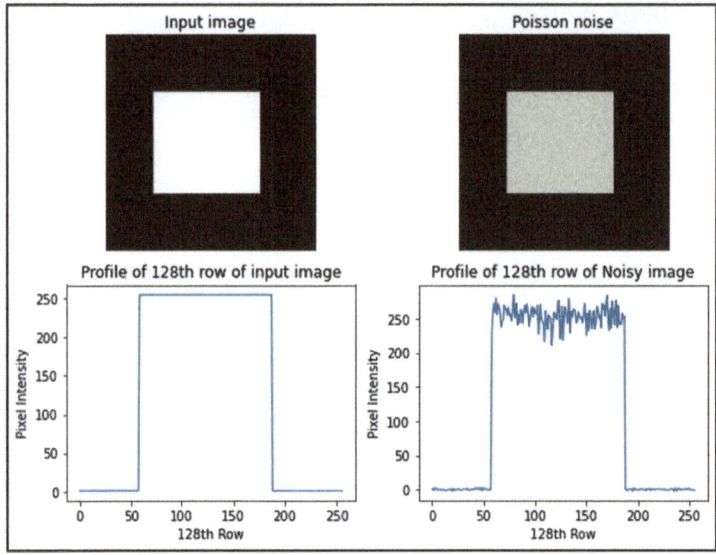

Fig. 5.18 Result of adding Poisson noise to the input image

5.2.6 Rayleigh Noise

Rayleigh noise follows Rayleigh distribution. The probability density function of Rayleigh distribution is given by

$$f(x) = \frac{x}{\sigma^2} e^{-\frac{x^2}{2\sigma^2}}, x \geq 0 \tag{5.6}$$

where "σ" represents the scale parameter. The mean and variance of Rayleigh distributions are given by

$$\text{Mean} = \sigma \sqrt{\frac{\pi}{2}} \tag{5.7}$$

$$\text{Var} = \sigma^2 \frac{4 - \pi}{2} \tag{5.8}$$

Experiment 5.9: Rayleigh Noise
This experiment discusses the generation of Rayleigh noise and adds it to the input image. The Python code that adds Rayleigh noise to the input image is shown in Fig. 5.19, and the corresponding output is shown in Fig. 5.20.

Inference

• Upon adding Rayleigh noise to the input image, it is possible to observe the fluctuation of the gray level of the input image, which is evident from Fig. 5.20.

```
#Rayleigh noise
import cv2
import matplotlib.pyplot as plt
import numpy as np
#Step 1: Generation of input image
img=np.ones([256,256])
img[68:188,58:188]=255
#Step 2: Generation of noise
noise_std = 0.05
noise = np.random.rayleigh(noise_std, img.shape)
#Step 3: Adding noise to the input image
noisy_img = cv2.addWeighted(img, 1, noise, 10, 0.0).astype(np.uint8)
#Step 4: Displaying the result
fig = plt.figure(figsize=(7,6))
plt.subplot(2,2,1),plt.imshow(img,cmap='gray'),plt.title('Input image'),plt.axis('off')
plt.subplot(2,2,2),plt.imshow(noisy_img,cmap='gray'),plt.title('Rayleigh noise'),plt.axis('off')
plt.subplot(2,2,3),plt.plot(img[150,:]),plt.xlabel('150th Row'),plt.ylabel('Pixel Intensity')
plt.title('Profile of 150th row of input image'),plt.subplot(2,2,4),plt.plot(noisy_img[150,:]),
plt.xlabel('150th Row'),plt.ylabel('Pixel Intensity'),plt.title('Profile of 150th row of Noisy image')
plt.tight_layout()
```

Fig. 5.19 Python code to add Rayleigh noise to the input image

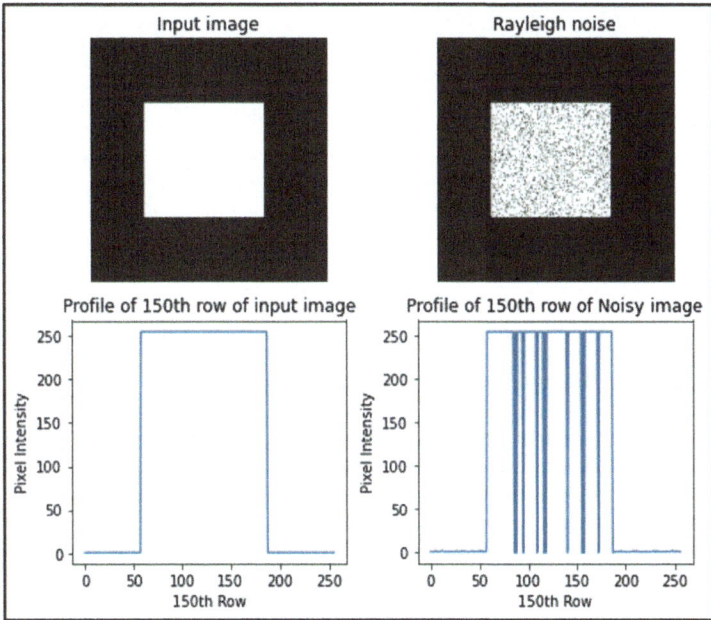

Fig. 5.20 Result of adding Rayleigh noise to the input image

5.2.7 *Periodic Noise*

Periodic noise corrupts digital images by adding repetitive patterns. Natural images get corrupted with periodic noises when sinusoidal noisy functions created by electrical interferences get added to pure image contents during image acquisition. Periodic noises mix their components with uncorrupted pixel values, which is difficult to minimize in the spatial domain.

Experiment 5.10: Periodic Noise

This example deals with the addition of a periodic pattern to the input test image, which results in periodic noise. The Python code that performs this task is shown in Fig. 5.21, and the corresponding output is shown in Fig. 5.22.

```
import matplotlib.pyplot as plt
import numpy as np
#Step 1: Generating the grating patterns
x=np.arange(-.5,.5,1/100)
y=np.arange(-.5,.5,1/100)
X,Y=np.meshgrid(x,y)
fx1,fy1,fx2,fy2,fx3,fy3=0,10,10,0,10,10
grating1=np.sin(2*np.pi*(fx1*X+fy1*Y))
grating2=np.sin(2*np.pi*(fx2*X+fy2*Y))
grating3=np.sin(2*np.pi*(fx3*X+fy3*Y))
#Step 2: Test image generation
img=np.zeros([100,100])
r=40
m,n=img.shape[:2]
for i in range(0,m):
    for j in range(0,n):
        if (i-50)**2 +(j-50)**2<r**2:
            img[i,j]=1
#Step 3: Adding noise to the input image
img1=img+grating1
img2=np.add(img,grating2)
img3=np.add(img,grating3)
#Step 4: Displaying the results
fig = plt.figure(figsize=(8,6))
plt.subplot(3,3,1),plt.imshow(img,cmap='gray'),plt.title('Test image'),plt.axis('off'),
plt.subplot(3,3,2),plt.imshow(img,cmap='gray'),plt.title('Test image'),plt.axis('off'),
plt.subplot(3,3,3),plt.imshow(img,cmap='gray'),plt.title('Test image'),plt.axis('off'),
plt.subplot(3,3,4),plt.imshow(grating1,cmap='gray'),plt.title('$f_x=0$'),plt.xticks([]),
plt.yticks([]),plt.subplot(3,3,5),plt.imshow(grating2,cmap='gray'),plt.title('$f_y=0$'),
plt.xticks([]),plt.yticks([]),plt.subplot(3,3,6),plt.imshow(grating3,cmap='gray'),
plt.title('$f_x=10,f_y=10$'),plt.xticks([]),plt.yticks([]),plt.subplot(3,3,7),
plt.imshow(img1,cmap='gray'),plt.title('Noisy image-1'),plt.xticks([]),plt.yticks([]),
plt.subplot(3,3,8),plt.imshow(img2,cmap='gray'),plt.title('Noisy image-2'),plt.xticks([]),
plt.yticks([]),plt.subplot(3,3,9),plt.imshow(img3,cmap='gray'),plt.title('Noisy image-3'),
plt.xticks([]),plt.yticks([])
plt.tight_layout()
```

Fig. 5.21 Python code to add periodic noise to the test image

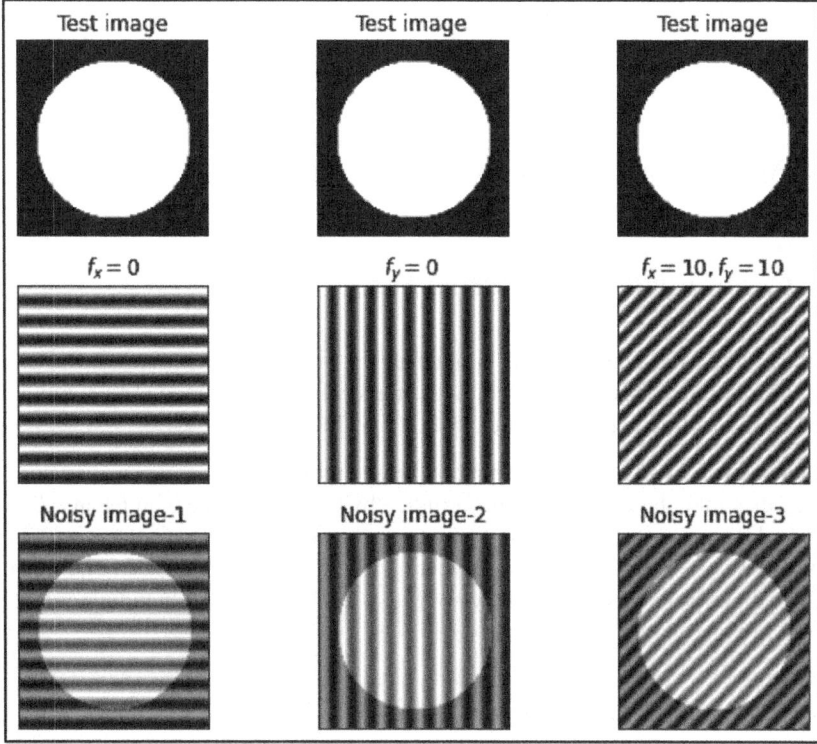

Fig. 5.22 Addition of periodic noise to the input image

Inferences

From Fig. 5.22, the following inferences can be drawn:

- The input test image is a white circle on a black background.
- Three different types of periodic noise patterns are generated. The first noise pattern is obtained by setting the frequency component along the x-axis to zero; the second noise pattern is obtained by setting the frequency component along the y-axis to zero, while the third noise pattern is obtained by retaining the frequency component along the x and y directions.
- The three different noise patterns are added to the input test image to obtain three noisy images, namely Noisy Image-1, Noisy Image-2, and Noisy Image-3, respectively.

5.3 Filters for Noise Minimization

The objective of denoising is to minimize the impact of noise so as to restore the true image. The major challenges in image denoising are as follows: (1) Edges of the image should be preserved; (2) Flat areas in the digital image should remain smooth; (3) Textures in the image should be preserved; and (4) New artifacts should not be generated. Two broad classifications of filters are (1) spatial domain filters and (2) transform domain filters. Spatial domain filters can be further classified as (1) linear filters and (2) non-linear filters. The mean filter is an example of a linear filter, whereas the median filter is an example of a non-linear filter. The mean filter is effective in minimizing the impact of Gaussian noise, and the median filter is an effective tool to minimize the impact of salt and pepper noise.

5.3.1   Mean Filter or Averaging Filter

In mean filter, the output image is obtained by replacing each pixel in the input image with the mean value of each pixel in a local neighbourhood. The commonly used neighbourhood or kernels are 3×3, 5×5, 7×7, and so on.

Experiment 5.11: Average Filtering of Noisy Image
In this example, the input image is corrupted by Gaussian noise with mean = 0 and standard deviation = 100. The noisy image is passed through two averaging filter. Filter 1 uses a 3×3 mask or kernel, whereas filter 2 uses a 9×9 mask. The Python code that performs this task is shown in Fig. 5.23, and the corresponding output is shown in Fig. 5.24.

Inferences
The following inferences can be drawn from Fig. 5.24:

- The input "Clock image" is corrupted with Gaussian noise
- The noisy image is passed through two averaging filters of kernel size 3×3 and 9×9.
- The 3×3 mean filter attempts to minimize the impact of Gaussian noise, but the noise is not completely minimized.
- The 9×9 mean filter completely minimizes the impact of noise, but the filtered image is blurred. Even though the impact of noise is minimized by 9×9 mean filter, the fine details in the image is lost, which results in blurring of the image.

5.3.2   Averaging and Weighted Averaging Filter

In the averaging filter, the pixels to be processed are given equal weightage, whereas in the weighted average filter, more weightage is given to the centre pixel and the immediate neighbours. The kernel of 3×3 average filter is given as $\dfrac{1}{9}\begin{bmatrix} 1 & 1 & 1 \\ 1 & 1 & 1 \\ 1 & 1 & 1 \end{bmatrix}$, and the kernel of 3×3 weighted average filter is given by $\dfrac{1}{16}\begin{bmatrix} 1 & 2 & 1 \\ 2 & 4 & 2 \\ 1 & 2 & 1 \end{bmatrix}$.

```
#Average filtering
import numpy as np
import cv2
import matplotlib.pyplot as plt
#Step 1: Reading the input image
img=cv2.imread('Clock.tiff',0)
m,n=img.shape
#Step 2: Adding white Gaussian noise to the image
gauss_noise=np.zeros((m,n),dtype=np.uint8)
mean,std=0,100
gauss_noise=(cv2.randn(gauss_noise,mean,std)).astype(np.uint8)
noisy_img1=cv2.add(img,gauss_noise)
#Step 3: Defining two averaging filter
kernel1=np.ones((3,3),np.float32)/9
kernel2 = np.ones((9,9),np.float32)/81
#Step 4: Passing the noisy image through averaging filter
filtered_img1 = cv2.filter2D(noisy_img1,-1,kernel1)
filtered_img2 = cv2.filter2D(noisy_img1,-1,kernel2)
#Step 5: Displaying the results
plt.figure(figsize=(8,6)),plt.subplot(1,4,1),plt.imshow(img,cmap='gray'),
plt.title('Clean image'),plt.xticks([]),plt.yticks([]),plt.subplot(1,4,2),
plt.imshow(noisy_img1,cmap='gray'),plt.title('Noisy image'),plt.xticks([]),plt.yticks([])
plt.subplot(1,4,3),plt.imshow(filtered_img1,cmap='gray'),plt.title('3 x 3 Mean filter')
plt.xticks([]),plt.yticks([]),plt.subplot(1,4,4),plt.imshow(filtered_img2,cmap='gray')
plt.title('9 x 9 Mean filter'),plt.xticks([]),plt.yticks([])
plt.tight_layout()
```

Fig. 5.23 Python code to perform average filtering of the noisy image

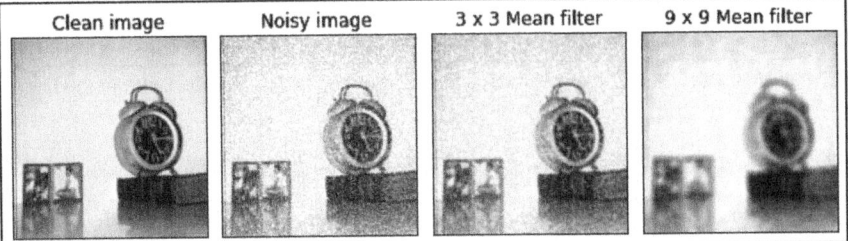

Fig. 5.24 Result of average filtering of noisy image

Experiment 5.12: Average and Weighted Average Filtering of Noisy Image
In this experiment, the input "Clock image" is corrupted with Gaussian noise with a mean value of 10 and a standard deviation of 75. The corrupted image is then passed through an averaging and weighted averaging filter to obtain the filtered image. The Python code that performs this task is given in Fig. 5.25, and the corresponding output is shown in Fig. 5.26.

```
import numpy as np
import cv2
import matplotlib.pyplot as plt
#Step 1: Reading the input image
img=cv2.imread('Clock.tiff',0)
m,n=img.shape
#Step 2: Adding white Gaussian noise to the image
gauss_noise=np.zeros((m,n),dtype=np.uint8)
mean,std=10,75
gauss_noise=(cv2.randn(gauss_noise,mean,std)).astype(np.uint8)
noisy_img=cv2.add(img,gauss_noise)
#Step 3: Defining averaging filter
ave_kernel=np.ones((3,3),np.float32)/9
wave_kernel=1/16*np.array([[1,2,1],[2,4,2],[1,2,1]])
#Step 4: Filtering of the noisy image
filtered_img1 = cv2.filter2D(noisy_img,-1,ave_kernel)
filtered_img2 = cv2.filter2D(noisy_img,-1,wave_kernel)
#Step 5: Displaying the results
plt.figure(figsize=(8,6)),plt.subplot(1,4,1),plt.imshow(img,cmap='gray')
plt.title('Clean image'),plt.xticks([]),plt.yticks([]),plt.subplot(1,4,2),
plt.imshow(noisy_img,cmap='gray'),plt.title('Noisy image'),plt.xticks([]),
plt.yticks([]),plt.subplot(1,4,3),plt.imshow(filtered_img1,cmap='gray')
plt.title('Average filter'),plt.xticks([]),plt.yticks([])
plt.subplot(1,4,4),plt.imshow(filtered_img2,cmap='gray')
plt.title('Weighted Average filter'),plt.xticks([]),plt.yticks([])
plt.tight_layout()
```

Fig. 5.25 Python code to perform averaging and weighted averaging of noisy image

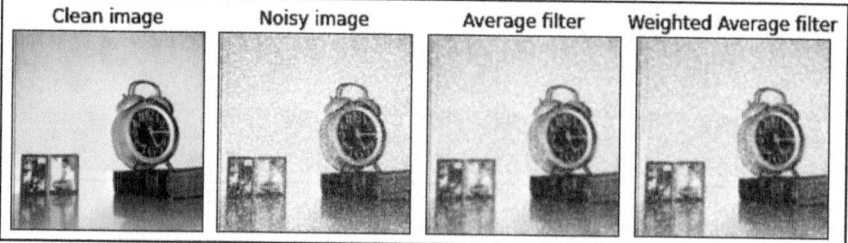

Fig. 5.26 Result of averaging and weighted averaging filter output

Inferences

From Fig. 5.26, the following inferences can be drawn:

- The input "Clock image" is a clean image. The input image is corrupted by Gaussian noise to obtain the "Noisy image".

- The noisy image is passed through 3×3 averaging and 3×3 weighted averaging filters. The visual quality of the weighted average filter appears to be better than the visual quality of the averaging filter.

5.4 Non-linear Spatial Domain Filters

A filter is non-linear if it is not obeying the superposition principle. The filter will violate either additivity property or homogeneity property. The non-linear filters discussed in this chapter are order statistics filters, which include minimum filter, maximum filter, and median filter.

5.4.1 Alpha Trimmed Mean Filter

Alpha trimmed mean filter removes the $d/2$ lowest and $d/2$ highest gray levels to process the remaining "$mn - d$ pixels" where "m" and "n" represent the number of rows and columns of the mask. The expression for alpha-trimmed mean filter is given by

$$g(x,y) = \frac{1}{mn-d} \sum_{(s,t) \in S_{xy}} f_r(s,t) \tag{5.9}$$

Alpha-trimmed mean filter is a balance between a median filter and a mean filter.

Experiment 5.13: Alpha Trimmed Mean Filter Versus Mean Filter
In this experiment, the input "Cameraman" image is corrupted with salt and pepper noise. The noisy image is then passed through mean and alpha trimmed mean filter. The mask for mean and alpha trimmed mean filter is 5×5 mask. The Python code that performs this task is shown in Fig. 5.27, and the corresponding result is shown in Fig. 5.28.

Inference

- From Fig. 5.28, the visual quality of alpha trimmed mean filter is marginally better than mean filter in minimizing the impact of salt and pepper noise in digital image.

5.4.2 Minimum Filter

The minimum filter replaces a given pixel with the minimum of all pixels within a local region of the image. The minimum filter effectively minimizes the impact of "salt noise". However, it is a poor choice if the image is corrupted with "pepper noise".

```
import cv2
import numpy as np
import matplotlib.pyplot as plt
import random
#Step 1: Reading the input image
img=cv2.imread('cameraman.tif',0)
m,n=img.shape
#Step 2: Adding salt and pepper noise to the image
prob=0.09
noisy_img = np.zeros(img.shape,np.uint8)
thres = 1 - prob
for i in range(img.shape[0]):
    for j in range(img.shape[1]):
        rdn = random.random()
        if rdn < prob:
            noisy_img[i][j] = 0
        elif rdn > thres:
            noisy_img[i][j] = 255
        else:
            noisy_img[i][j] = img[i][j]
#Step 3: Mean filter
kernel=np.ones((5,5),np.float32)/25
filtered_img1 = cv2.filter2D(noisy_img,-1,kernel)
#Step 4: Alpha trimmed mean filter
kernel_size, d=5,10
r = kernel_size // 2
padded_image = np.pad(noisy_img, r, mode='reflect')
filtered_img2 = np.zeros(noisy_img.shape)
   # loop through all pixels
for i in range(n):
  for j in range(m):
        neighbors = list(padded_image[i-r:i+r+1, j-r:j+r+1].reshape(-1))
        neighbors.sort()
        neighbors_pruned = neighbors[r:-r]
        filtered_img2[i, j] = (1/(m*n - d)) * sum(neighbors_pruned)
#Step 5: Displaying the result
plt.figure(figsize=(10,8)),plt.subplot(1,4,1),plt.imshow(img,cmap='gray'),
plt.title('Clean image'),plt.axis('off'),plt.subplot(1,4,2),plt.imshow(noisy_img,cmap='gray'),
plt.title('Noisy image'),plt.axis('off'),plt.subplot(1,4,3),plt.imshow(filtered_img1,cmap='gray')
plt.title('3 x 3 Mean filter'),plt.axis('off'),plt.subplot(1,4,4),
plt.imshow(filtered_img2,cmap='gray'),plt.title('Alpha trimmed mean filter'),plt.axis('off')
plt.tight_layout()
```

Fig. 5.27 Python code to compare mean filter with alpha trimmed mean filter

Experiment 5.14: Minimum Filter for Image Corrupted with Only Salt Noise
In this experiment, the input image is corrupted with only salt noise. The noisy image is passed through a minimum filter. The morphological operator "erode" is used to implement the minimum filter. While using the morphological operator, it is necessary to define the shape and size of the structuring element. In this case, a rectangular structuring element of size (3×3) is used. The Python code that

Fig. 5.28 Result of mean filter and alpha trimmed mean filter

```
#Minimum filter
import matplotlib.pyplot as plt
import cv2
import random
img=cv2.imread('cameraman.tif',0)
img_clone=img.copy()
m,n=img.shape[:2]
number_of_pixels = random.randint(5, 10000)
for i in range(number_of_pixels):
    y=random.randint(0, m - 1)
    x=random.randint(0, n - 1)
    img[x,y]=255
#Minimum filter
size = (3, 3)
shape = cv2.MORPH_RECT
kernel = cv2.getStructuringElement(shape, size)
min_img = cv2.erode(img, kernel)
plt.subplot(1,3,1),plt.imshow(img_clone,cmap='gray'),plt.title('Input image'),
plt.axis('off'),plt.subplot(1,3,2),plt.imshow(img,cmap='gray'),plt.title('Noisy image'),
plt.axis('off'),plt.subplot(1,3,3),plt.imshow(min_img,cmap='gray')
plt.title('Minimum filter output'),plt.axis('off')
plt.tight_layout()
```

Fig. 5.29 Python code to apply minimum filter to the image corrupted with only salt noise

implements the minimum filter is given in Fig. 5.29, and the corresponding output
is shown in Fig. 5.30.

Inferences

From Fig. 5.30, the following inferences can be drawn:

- The input image is corrupted with only salt noise. From the noisy image, it is
  possible to observe the random occurrences of white dots.
- The noisy image is passed through a minimum filter. The impact of noise is minimized. Thus, minimum filter is an effective tool to minimize salt noise only in
  digital image.

Fig. 5.30   Minimum filter for salt noise only

```
#Minimum filter: Pepper only noise
import matplotlib.pyplot as plt
import cv2
import random
img=cv2.imread('cameraman.tif',0)
img_clone=img.copy()
m,n=img.shape[:2]
number_of_pixels = random.randint(5, 10000)
for i in range(number_of_pixels):
    y=random.randint(0, m - 1)
    x=random.randint(0, n - 1)
    img[x,y]=0
#Minimum filter
size = (3, 3)
shape = cv2.MORPH_RECT
kernel = cv2.getStructuringElement(shape, size)
min_img = cv2.erode(img, kernel)
plt.subplot(1,3,1),plt.imshow(img_clone,cmap='gray'),plt.title('Input image'),
plt.xticks([]),plt.yticks([]),plt.subplot(1,3,2),plt.imshow(img,cmap='gray')
plt.title('Noisy image'),plt.xticks([]),plt.yticks([]),plt.subplot(1,3,3),
plt.imshow(min_img,cmap='gray'),plt.title('Minimum filter output'),plt.xticks([]),
plt.yticks([]),plt.tight_layout()
```

Fig. 5.31   Python code to apply minimum filter for pepper only noise

Experiment 5.15: Minimum Filter for Pepper Noise

In this experiment, the input image is corrupted with only pepper noise. The noisy image is passed through a minimum filter. The Python code that accomplishes this task is shown in Fig. 5.31, and the corresponding output is shown in Fig. 5.32.

Fig. 5.32 Minimum filter for only pepper noise

Inferences
From Fig. 5.32, the following inferences can be drawn:

- The input image is corrupted with only pepper noise.
- The pepper noise corresponds to random occurrences of black dots.
- After passing the noise through the minimum filter, it is possible to observe that the minimum filter enhances the noise.
- Thus, the minimum filter is ineffective for images corrupted with only pepper noise.

5.4.3 Maximum Filter

The maximum filter replaces a given pixel with the maximum value of all pixels within a local region of the image. The maximum filter is effective in minimizing the impact of "pepper noise". However, it is a poor choice if the image is corrupted with "salt noise".

Experiment 5.16: Maximum Filter for Image Corrupted with Only Pepper Noise
The objective of this experiment is to illustrate that maximum filter is an effective tool to minimize the impact of pepper noise only. The input image is corrupted with only pepper noise. The noisy image is passed through the maximum filter. The maximum filter is realized using morphological operation "dilation". The structuring element chosen is a rectangle, and its size is 3×3. The Python code that performs this task is shown in Fig. 5.33, and the corresponding output is shown in Fig. 5.34.

Inferences
The following inferences can be made from this experiment:

- The input image is corrupted with only pepper noise.
- This is visible by observing random occurrences of black spots in the noisy image.

```
#Maximum filter: only pepper noise
import matplotlib.pyplot as plt
import cv2
import random
img=cv2.imread('cameraman.tif',0)
img_clone=img.copy()
m,n=img.shape[:2]
number_of_pixels = random.randint(100, 10000)
for i in range(number_of_pixels):
    y=random.randint(0, m - 1)
    x=random.randint(0, n - 1)
    img[x,y]=0
#Maximum filter
size = (3, 3)
shape = cv2.MORPH_RECT
kernel = cv2.getStructuringElement(shape, size)
min_img = cv2.dilate(img, kernel)
plt.subplot(1,3,1),plt.imshow(img_clone,cmap='gray'),plt.title('Input image'),plt.axis('off')
plt.subplot(1,3,2),plt.imshow(img,cmap='gray'),plt.title('Noisy image'),plt.axis('off')
plt.subplot(1,3,3),plt.imshow(min_img,cmap='gray'),plt.title('Maximum filter output'),plt.axis('off')
plt.tight_layout()
```

Fig. 5.33 Python code to apply maximum filter to noisy image

Fig. 5.34 Maximum filter to the image corrupted by pepper noise only

- The noisy image is passed through the maximum filter.
- The maximum filter is effective in minimizing the impact of pepper noise.

Experiment 5.17: Maximum Filter for Image Corrupted with Only Salt Noise
In this experiment, an attempt is made to apply the maximum filter to the image that is corrupted by only salt noise. The Python code that performs this attempt is shown in Fig. 5.35, and the corresponding output is given in Fig. 5.36.

Inferences
The following inferences can be made from this experiment:

- The input image is corrupted by only salt noise.
- The noisy image is passed through a maximum filter.
- The maximum filter tends to magnify the impact of noise.

```
#Maximum filter: only salt noise
import matplotlib.pyplot as plt
import cv2
import random
img=cv2.imread('cameraman.tif',0)
img_clone=img.copy()
m,n=img.shape[:2]
number_of_pixels = random.randint(100, 10000)
for i in range(number_of_pixels):
    y=random.randint(0, m - 1)
    x=random.randint(0, n - 1)
    img[x,y]=255
#Maximum filter
size = (3, 3)
shape = cv2.MORPH_RECT
kernel = cv2.getStructuringElement(shape, size)
min_img = cv2.dilate(img, kernel)
plt.subplot(1,3,1),plt.imshow(img_clone,cmap='gray'),plt.title('Input image'),
plt.xticks([]),plt.yticks([]),plt.subplot(1,3,2),plt.imshow(img,cmap='gray')
plt.title('Noisy image'),plt.xticks([]),plt.yticks([]),plt.subplot(1,3,3),
plt.imshow(min_img,cmap='gray'),plt.title('Maximum filter output'),plt.xticks([]),
plt.yticks([]),plt.tight_layout()
```

Fig. 5.35 Python code to apply maximum filter to image corrupted by only salt noise

Fig. 5.36 Maximum filter output for image corrupted by only salt noise

- Thus, the maximum filter is ineffective in the minimizing salt-only noise in images.

5.4.4 Median Filter

Median filter is an effective filter in minimizing the impact of salt and pepper noise. The median filter is a non-linear filter as it violates the superposition principle.

Experiment 5.18: Median Filter

This experiment demonstrates the impact of a median filter in minimizing the impact of salt and pepper noise. The program reads the input image and corrupts the image by salt and pepper noise. The noisy image is passed through two median filters of size 3×3 and 5×5, respectively. The Python code that performs this task is shown in Fig. 5.37, and the corresponding output is shown in Fig. 5.38.

```python
#Median filter
import cv2
import numpy as np
import matplotlib.pyplot as plt
import random
#Step 1: Reading the input image
img=cv2.imread('Clock.tiff',0)
m,n=img.shape
#Step 2: Adding salt and pepper noise to the image
prob=0.2
noisy_img = np.zeros(img.shape,np.uint8)
thres = 1 - prob
for i in range(img.shape[0]):
    for j in range(img.shape[1]):
        rdn = random.random()
        if rdn < prob:
            noisy_img[i][j] = 0
        elif rdn > thres:
            noisy_img[i][j] = 255
        else:
            noisy_img[i][j] = img[i][j]
#Step 3: Median filter
kernel_1,kernel_2=3,5
filtered_img1=cv2.medianBlur(noisy_img,kernel_1)
filtered_img2=cv2.medianBlur(noisy_img,kernel_2)
#Step 4: Displaying the results
fig = plt.figure(figsize=(8,6))
plt.subplot(1,4,1),plt.imshow(img,cmap='gray'),plt.title('Clean image'),plt.axis('off')
plt.subplot(1,4,2),plt.imshow(noisy_img,cmap='gray'),plt.title('Noisy image')
plt.axis('off'),plt.subplot(1,4,3),plt.imshow(filtered_img1,cmap='gray')
plt.title('3 x 3 median filter'),plt.axis('off'),plt.subplot(1,4,4),plt.imshow(filtered_img2,cmap='gray')
plt.title('5x5 median filter'),plt.axis('off')
plt.tight_layout()
```

Fig. 5.37 Python code to perform median filtering of noisy image

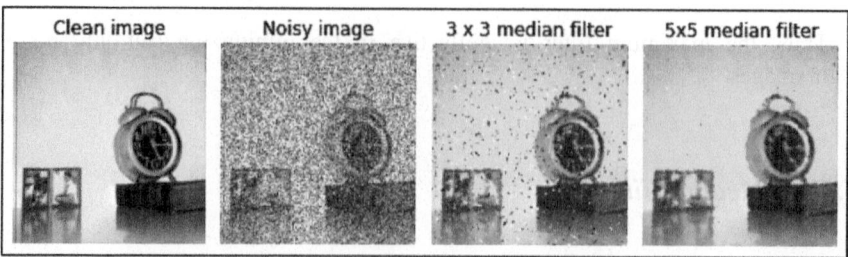

Fig. 5.38 Median filter for salt and pepper noise minimization

Inferences

The following inferences can be observed from this experiment:

- The input "Clock image" is corrupted by salt and pepper noise.
- The noisy image is passed through 3 × 3 and 5 × 5 median filter.
- With increase in the size of the window, the impact of noise is minimized at the expense of blurring the edge information.

5.5 Bilateral Filter

Tomasi and Manduchi (1998) first proposed the bilateral filter as a non-linear edge-preserving filter that combines range and domain filtering. This method is non-iterative, local, and simple. The bilateral filter takes the weighted sum of pixels in a local neighbourhood; the weights depend on both spatial and intensity distances. Mathematically, the output of the bilateral filter at a pixel location "x" is calculated as

$$\tilde{I}(x) = \frac{1}{C} \sum_{y \in N(x)} e^{-\frac{\|y-x\|^2}{2\sigma_d^2}} e^{-\frac{|I(y)-I(x)|^2}{2\sigma_r^2}} I(y) \tag{5.10}$$

where "σ_d" and "σ_r" are parameters controlling the fall-off of weights in spatial and intensity domains, respectively, $N(x)$ is a spatial neighbourhood of pixel $I(x)$, and C is the normalization constant that is given by

$$C = \sum_{y \in N(x)} e^{-\frac{\|y-x\|^2}{2\sigma_d^2}} e^{-\frac{|I(y)-I(x)|^2}{2\sigma_r^2}} \tag{5.11}$$

The first exponential term in Eq. (5.10) is a domain filtering term, and the second is an exponential term, a range filtering term. Thus, bilateral filtering is a combination of domain and range filtering. In domain filters like Gaussian filters, the filter weights are assigned using the spatial closeness, which has the tendency to blur the edges. In range filters, the filter weights are assigned according to the intensity difference. Here, the pixels with similar intensity to the central pixel are considered for blurring. Bilateral filter combines both domain and range filtering. Thus, a bilateral filter effectively smoothens the input image while preserving its edge information.

Bilateral filtering replaces the pixel value at "x" with an average of similar and nearby pixel values. In smooth regions, the bilateral filter acts as a standard domain filter, but in the case of sharp boundaries, the range filter comes into the picture. When a bilateral filter is centred on a pixel on the bright side of the boundary, for example, the range term assumes a value close to "1" for pixels on the same side and close to "0" for pixels on the dark side. Thus, the filter replaces the centre bright pixel with an average of the bright pixels in its vicinity and ignores the dark pixels. Conversely, bright pixels are ignored when the filter is centred on a dark pixel. Thus, the bilateral filter effectively preserves the edges. The two parameters "σ_d" and "σ_r" control the behaviour of the bilateral filter.

```
import numpy as np
import matplotlib.pyplot as plt
import cv2
img=cv2.imread('Clock.tiff',0)
m,n=img.shape
gauss_noise=np.zeros((m,n),dtype=np.uint8)
mean, std=0, 20
gauss_noise=(cv2.randn(gauss_noise,mean,std)).astype(np.uint8)
noisy_img=cv2.add(img,gauss_noise)
neighborhood=[5,7,9,11]
plt.figure(figsize=(8, 6)),plt.figure(1),plt.subplot(2,3,1),plt.imshow(img,cmap='gray'),
plt.title('Clean image'),plt.axis('off'),plt.subplot(2,3,2),
plt.imshow(noisy_img,cmap='gray'),plt.title('Noisy image'),plt.axis('off')
for i in range(len(neighborhood)):
    img_filtered=cv2.bilateralFilter(noisy_img,neighborhood[i],90,10)
    plt.figure(1),plt.subplot(2,3,i+3)
    plt.imshow(img_filtered,cmap='gray'),plt.axis('off')
    plt.title('Filtered image with d={}'.format(neighborhood[i]))
plt.tight_layout()
```

Fig. 5.39 Python code to perform bilateral filtering of the noisy image for different neighbourhood

Experiment 5.19: Bilateral Filtering

Read the input "Clock image". Add Gaussian noise to the input image, which has zero mean and standard deviation = 20. Now pass the noisy image through a Bilateral filter with a sigma_colour value of 90 and a sigma_space value of 10. Vary the pixel neighbourhood size as 5, 7, 9, and 11 and comment on the observed result.

The Python code that performs the above-mentioned task is shown in Fig. 5.39, and the corresponding output is shown in Fig. 5.40.

Inferences

From this experiment, the following inferences can be made:

- The input image is a 256 × 256, 8-bit Clock image.
- The Gaussian noise is added to the input image to obtain the noisy image, which is shown in Fig. 5.40.
- The filtered image for different choices of neighbourhood of pixels is shown in Fig. 5.40. From this figure, it is possible to observe that with an increase in the neighbourhood size, the impact of noise is minimized at the expense of blurring of image.
- When the neighbourhood of pixel is varied from 5, 7, 9, and 11, it is possible to observe that for the choice of "$d = 11$", the impact of noise is minimized but the blurring effect is more.

Experiment 5.20: Impact of Bilateral Filter for Different Values of Domain

Read the input "Clock image". Add Gaussian noise to the input image, with zero mean and standard deviation = 100. Now pass the noisy image through a bilateral filter with the pixel neighbourhood size as 5, sigma_colour value as 90, and sigma_space value as 50, 100, 150, and 200 and comment on the observed result.

Fig. 5.40 Display of noiseless, noisy, and filtered images

```
import numpy as np
import matplotlib.pyplot as plt
import cv2
img=cv2.imread('Clock.tiff',0)
m,n=img.shape
gauss_noise=np.zeros((m,n),dtype=np.uint8)
mean, std=0,100
gauss_noise=(cv2.randn(gauss_noise,mean,std)).astype(np.uint8)
noisy_img=cv2.add(img,gauss_noise)
sigma_domain=[50,100,150,200]
plt.figure(figsize=(8,6)),plt.figure(1),plt.subplot(2,3,1),plt.imshow(img,cmap='gray'),
plt.title('Clean image'),plt.axis('off'),plt.subplot(2,3,2),plt.imshow(noisy_img,cmap='gray'),
plt.title('Noisy image'),plt.axis('off')
for i in range(len(sigma_domain)):
    img_filtered=cv2.bilateralFilter(noisy_img,5,90,sigma_domain[i])
    plt.figure(1),plt.subplot(2,3,i+3),plt.axis('off'),   plt.imshow(img_filtered,cmap='gray')
    plt.title('Filtered image with $\sigma_d={}$'.format(sigma_domain[i]))
plt.tight_layout()
```

Fig. 5.41 Python code to perform bilateral filtering of the noisy image for different choices of domain filter

The Python code that performs the above-mentioned task is shown in Fig. 5.41, and the corresponding output is shown in Fig. 5.42.

Inferences

The following inferences can be made from Fig. 5.42:

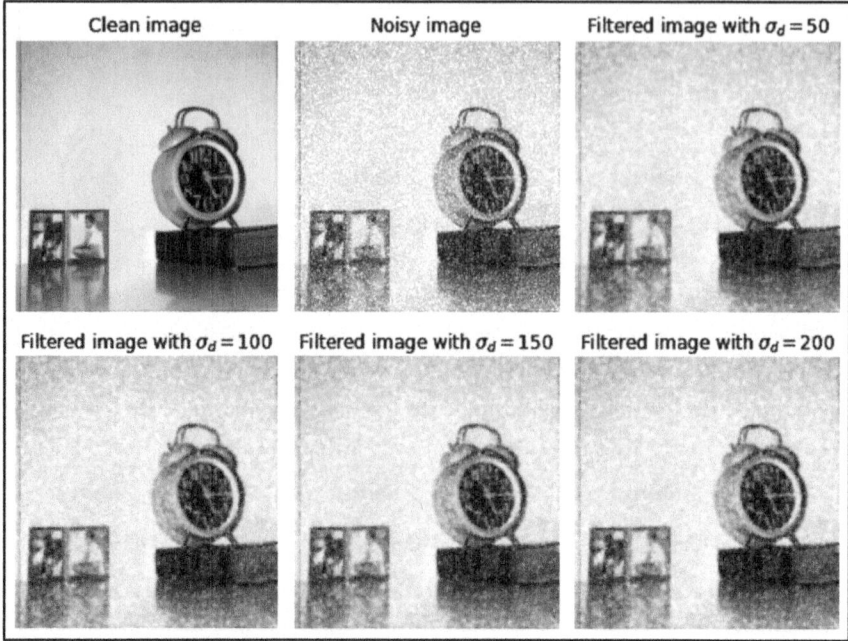

Fig. 5.42 Display of noiseless, noisy, and filtered images

- The input image is a 256 × 256, 8-bit Clock image.
- The Gaussian noise is added to the input image to obtain the noisy image.
- The filtered image for different choice of domain filter is shown in Fig. 5.42. From this figure, it is possible to observe that the impact of noise is minimized with an increase in the value of domain's filter standard deviation.

Experiment 5.21: Bilateral Filter for Different Choices of Range Filter
Read the input "Clock image". Add Gaussian noise to the input image, with zero mean and standard deviation = 100. Now pass the noisy image through a bilateral filter with the pixel neighbourhood size as 5, sigma_colour value as 50, 100, 150, and 200, and sigma_space value as 50 and comment on the observed result.

The Python code that performs the above-mentioned task is shown in Fig. 5.43, and the corresponding output is shown in Fig. 5.44.

Inferences
The following inferences can be drawn from Fig. 5.44:

- The input image is a 256 × 256, 8-bit Clock image.
- The Gaussian noise is added to the input image to obtain the noisy image, which is shown in Fig. 5.44.
- The filtered image for different choices of range filter is shown in Fig. 5.44. From this figure, it is possible to observe that with an increase in the value of the range filter's standard deviation, the impact of noise is minimized as well as the edges are preserved.

```
import numpy as np
import matplotlib.pyplot as plt
import cv2
img=cv2.imread('Clock.tiff',0)
m,n=img.shape
gauss_noise=np.zeros((m,n),dtype=np.uint8)
mean, std=0, 100
gauss_noise=(cv2.randn(gauss_noise,mean,std)).astype(np.uint8)
noisy_img=cv2.add(img,gauss_noise)
sigma_range=[50,100,150,200]
plt.figure(figsize=(8,6))
plt.figure(1),plt.subplot(2,3,1),plt.imshow(img,cmap='gray'),plt.title('Clean image')
plt.axis('off'),plt.subplot(2,3,2),plt.imshow(noisy_img,cmap='gray'),
plt.title('Noisy image'),plt.axis('off')
for i in range(len(sigma_range)):
    img_filtered=cv2.bilateralFilter(noisy_img,5,sigma_range[i],50)
    plt.figure(1),plt.subplot(2,3,i+3),plt.imshow(img_filtered,cmap='gray')
    plt.title('Filtered image with $\sigma_r={}$'.format(sigma_range[i])),    plt.axis('off')
plt.tight_layout()
```

Fig. 5.43 Python code to perform bilateral filter for different choices of sigma_colour

Fig. 5.44 Display of noiseless, noisy, and filtered images

5.6   Non-local Mean Filter

Non-local mean filter tends to minimize the impact of noise by making use of the redundancy in natural image. Redundancy exists because of repeated patterns. The non-local mean filter estimates the coefficients for averaging by comparing the similarity of patches of pixels. It is an attempt to identify the features to be preserved while eliminating the noise by averaging. To implement a non-local mean filter, weights to all other pixels must be computed at each pixel. The computational complexity of non-local mean filter is $O(DN^2)$, where "N" is the number of pixels in the image and "D" is the patch size. The computational complexity can be minimized by restricting the search to patches in a local neighbourhood.

Let the search window around the pixel be represented by Ω_s for a given image $f(m, n)$, the filtered image $\hat{f}[m, n]$ is represented as

$$\hat{f}(m,n) = \sum_{\forall k,l \in \Omega_s} w\big((m,n),(k,l)\big) \cdot f(k,l) \tag{5.12}$$

The weights $w(m,n)(k, l)$ is based on the similarity between the neighbourhoods $(N_{m, n})$ and $(N_{k, l})$ of pixels (m, n) and (k, l), where N_p is a square sub-image window centred pixel p with radius R_p. The weights are calculated using the formula

$$w(m,n)(k,l) = \frac{K\big(N_{m,n} - N_{k,l2} / h\big)}{\sum_{\forall k,l \in \Omega_s} K\big(N_{m,n} - N_{k,l2} / h\big)} \tag{5.13}$$

where $K(\chi)$ is kernel function and "h" is exponential decay control.

Experiment 5.22: Non-local Mean Filter
The built-in function "fastNlMeansDenoising()" available in computer vision library can be used to implement the non-local mean filter. The syntax of the built-in function is *cv2.fastNlMeansDenoising ('Input image', 'Output image', 'h', template window size, search window size)*

Input image: Grayscale image

Output image: Grayscale image

h: Parameter regulating filter strength.

template window size: Size in pixels of the template patch that is used to compute weights.

search window size: Size in pixels of the window that is used to calculate the weighted average for a given pixel.

In this experiment, the input image is read, and it is then corrupted with additive Gaussian noise with zero mean and standard deviation of 100. The noisy image is fed through non-local mean (NLM) filter. The template window size and the search window size of the NLM filter is fixed as 7 and 21, respectively, whereas the filter strength is varied as 10, 20, 40, and 80. The Python code that performs this task is shown in Fig. 5.45, and the corresponding output is shown in Fig. 5.46.

```
import numpy as np
import matplotlib.pyplot as plt
import cv2
img=cv2.imread('Clock.tiff',0)
m,n=img.shape
gauss_noise=np.zeros((m,n),dtype=np.uint8)
mean,std=0,100
gauss_noise=(cv2.randn(gauss_noise,mean,std)).astype(np.uint8)
noisy_img=cv2.add(img,gauss_noise)
h=[10,20,40,80]
plt.figure(figsize=(8, 6)),plt.figure(1),plt.subplot(2,3,1),plt.imshow(img,cmap='gray')
plt.title('Noise free image'),plt.axis('off'),plt.subplot(2,3,2),
plt.imshow(noisy_img,cmap='gray'),plt.title('Noisy image'),plt.axis('off')
for i in range(len(h)):
    filtered_img=cv2.fastNlMeansDenoising(noisy_img,None,h[i],7,21)
    plt.figure(1),plt.subplot(2,3,i+3),plt.imshow(filtered_img,cmap='gray')
    plt.title('Filtered image with h={}'.format(h[i])),plt.axis('off')
plt.tight_layout()
```

Fig. 5.45 Filtering of noisy image using non-local mean filter

Fig. 5.46 Output of non-local mean filter for different values of filter strength

Inferences

- The noisy image is fed as input to the non-local mean filter for different filter strength.
- With increase in filter strength, the impact of noise is minimized at the expense of blurring the edge details.
- Choosing the optimum value of filter strength parameter will suppress the impact of noise while preserving the edge information.

5.7 Anisotropic Diffusion Filter

Noise filtering is a smoothing process that tends to blur important image structures such as edges and lines. Perona and Malik proposed an anisotropic diffusion equation that tends to preserve edges in the image. Anisotropic diffusion is a non-linear partial differential equation-based diffusion process. Anisotropic diffusion filtering can successfully smooth noise while preserving the region boundaries and small structures within the image if the crucial parameters are estimated correctly. The anisotropic equation is given by

$$\frac{\partial I(x,y,t)}{\partial t} = div\left[g\left(\nabla I(x,y,t)\right)\nabla I(x,y,t)\right] \tag{5.14}$$

where "t" is the time parameter, $I(x, y, 0)$ is the original image, $\nabla I(x, y, t)$ is the gradient of the image at time "t", and $g(.)$ is the conductance function. This function is chosen in such a way that $\lim_{x \to 0} g(x) = 1$, which implies that the diffusion is maximal within the uniform region and $\lim_{x \to \infty} g(x) = 0$, which implies that the diffusion is stopped across edges. The diffusion function proposed by Perona and Malik is given by

$$g(x) = \frac{1}{1 + \left(\dfrac{x}{K}\right)^2} \tag{5.15}$$

where "K" is the gradient magnitude threshold parameter that controls the rate of diffusion. The discrete version of anisotropic diffusion equation proposed by Perona and Malik is given by

$$I_{t+1}(S) = I_t(S) + \frac{\lambda}{|\eta_S|} \sum_{p \in \eta_S} g_K\left(\left|\nabla I_{s,p}\right|\right) \nabla I_{s,p} \tag{5.16}$$

where "I" represents the digital image, "t" denotes the iteration step, "S" denotes the pixel position, "g" is the conductance function, "K" is the gradient threshold parameter, the rate of diffusion is determined by "λ", which takes a value between 0 and 1, η_S represents the spatial neighbourhood of pixels where $\eta_S = [N, S, E, W]$, where N, S, E, and W are the North, South, East, and West neighbours of pixel "S". The gradient operator in discrete form is expressed as

$$\nabla I_{s,p} = I_{t(p)} - I_{t(s)}, p \in \eta_S = \left[N, S, E, W\right] \tag{5.17}$$

From the above expression, it is possible to interpret that the gradient operator is a scalar, which is the difference between neighbouring pixels in each direction.

Experiment 5.23: Anisotropic Diffusion Filter
Generate a 256×256 test image that is half white and half black. The transition from white to black indicates the presence of an edge in the image. The test image is then corrupted with Gaussian noise with zero mean and standard deviation of 50. The noisy image is passed through (1) an averaging filter with a mask size of 21×21 and (2) an anisotropic diffusion filter with the following choice of parameters: number of iterations = 100, the conduction coefficient is represented as Kappa whose value is fixed as 10, and the gamma value is chosen as 0.9. The Python code that performs the denoising operation using an averaging filter and anisotropic diffusion filter is given in Fig. 5.47, and the corresponding result is shown in Fig. 5.48.

Inference
The following observations can be made from Fig. 5.48:

- The test image is a 256×256 grayscale image.
- The test image is corrupted with Gaussian noise.
- The noisy image is passed through an averaging filter and anisotropic diffusion filter.
- Even though the averaging filter minimizes the impact of noise, the edge in the image is smeared.
- The anisotropic diffusion filter attempts to minimize the impact of noise. It also preserves the edge information in the image.
- Anisotropic diffusion filter performs better than averaging filter to preserve the edge information.

```
import numpy as np
import cv2
import matplotlib.pyplot as plt
#Step 1: Generation of input image
img=np.zeros([256,256])
m,n=img.shape
img[:,0:127]=255
mean, sigma=0, 50
img_noise=img+np.random.normal(mean,sigma,size=img.shape)
#Averaging filter
N=21
mask=np.ones([N,N])/(N*N)
img_filt=cv2.filter2D(img_noise,-1,mask)
#Anisotropic diffusion filter
niter, kappa, gamma =100, 10, 0.9
step=(1.,1.)
imgout = img_noise.copy()
deltaS = np.zeros_like(imgout)
deltaE = deltaS.copy()
NS = deltaS.copy()
EW = deltaS.copy()
gS = np.ones_like(imgout)
gE = gS.copy()
for ii in range(niter):
    deltaS[:-1,: ] = np.diff(imgout,axis=0)
    deltaE[: ,:-1] = np.diff(imgout,axis=1)
    gS = 1./(1.+(deltaS/kappa)**2.)/step[0]
    gE = 1./(1.+(deltaE/kappa)**2.)/step[1]
    E = gE*deltaE
    S = gS*deltaS
    NS[:] = S
    EW[:] = E
    NS[1:,:] -= S[:-1,:]
    EW[:,1:] -= E[:,:-1]
    imgout += gamma*(NS+EW)
plt.figure(figsize=(8,6))
plt.subplot(1,4,1),plt.imshow(img,cmap='gray'),plt.title('Input image')
plt.xticks([]),plt.yticks([]),plt.subplot(1,4,2),plt.imshow(img_noise,cmap='gray'),
plt.title('Noisy image'),plt.xticks([]),plt.yticks([])
plt.subplot(1,4,3),plt.imshow(img_filt,cmap='gray'),plt.title('Averaging filter output')
plt.xticks([]),plt.yticks([]),plt.subplot(1,4,4), plt.imshow(imgout,cmap='gray'),
plt.title('AD filter output'),plt.xticks([]),plt.yticks([])
plt.tight_layout()
```

Fig. 5.47 Comparison of averaging filter with anisotropic filter

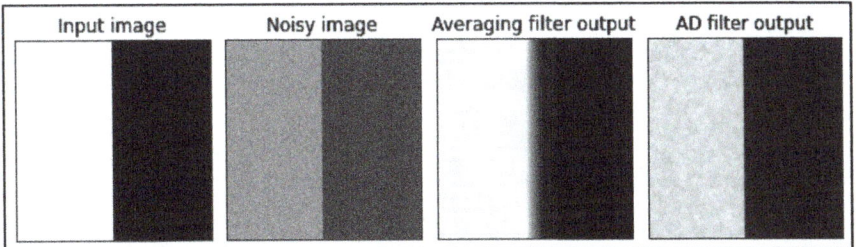

Fig. 5.48 Comparison of averaging filter with an anisotropic diffusion filter

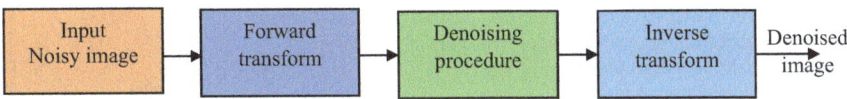

Fig. 5.49 Block diagram of transform domain-based image denoising

5.8   Transform Domain-Based Image Denoising

The basic idea in transform-based image denoising is that the characteristics of image information and noise are different in the transform domain. In transform domain filtering methods, the noisy image is transformed to another domain, then the denoising procedure is applied on the transformed image, and then the coefficients are passed through inverse transform to obtain the denoised image. The block diagram representation of transform domain-based image denoising is given in Fig. 5.49.

5.8.1   Fourier Transform-Based Image Denoising

Fourier transform is a very good tool to identify the presence of periodic noise. After identifying the location of periodic noise, notch filter can be used to minimize the impact of periodic section.

Experiment 5.24: Minimization of Periodic Noise
In this experiment, a test image is generated. The test image is a white square in a black background. Then sinusoidal grating pattern is generated. This pattern is considered as the noise. The noisy image is obtained by adding the test image with the sinusoidal grating pattern. Then, the spectrum of the noisy image is observed to find the peaks corresponding to the sinusoidal grating pattern. The inverse Fourier transform is applied to obtain the filtered image after nullifying the peak (notch filtering) corresponding to the grating pattern.

```
#Periodic noise minimisation
import matplotlib.pyplot as plt
import numpy as np
#Step 1: Image generation
img=np.zeros([256,256])
img[98:158,98:158]=1
#Step 2: Grating pattern generation
x=np.arange(-.5,.5,1/256)
y=np.arange(-.5,.5,1/256)
X,Y=np.meshgrid(x,y)
fx,fy=10,10
grating=np.sin(2*np.pi*(fx*X+fy*Y))
img_grating=img+grating;#Step 3: Grating pattern + image
img_Spec=np.fft.fftshift(np.fft.fft2(img)); # Spectrum of Original image
grating1=np.fft.fft2(img_grating);#Step 4: Spectrum of noisy image
grating2=np.fft.fftshift(grating1)
#Step 5: Manipulation of spectrum
grating2[118,118]=0
grating2[138,138]=0
#Step 6: Inverse Fourier Transform
rimg1=np.fft.ifftshift(grating2)
rimg=np.fft.ifft2(rimg1)
plt.figure(figsize=(10,6)),plt.subplot(2,3,1),plt.imshow(img,cmap='gray'),plt.title('Input image'),
plt.axis('off'),plt.subplot(2,3,2),plt.imshow(img_grating,cmap='gray'),plt.title('Noisy image'),
plt.axis('off'),plt.subplot(2,3,3),plt.imshow(np.real(rimg),cmap='gray'),plt.title('Filtered image')
plt.axis('off'),plt.subplot(2,3,4),plt.imshow(np.abs(img_Spec),cmap='gray')
plt.title('Spectrum:Input image'),plt.axis('off'),plt.subplot(2,3,5),
plt.imshow(np.abs(np.fft.fftshift(np.fft.fft2(img_grating))),cmap='gray')
plt.title('Spectrum:Noisy image'),plt.axis('off')
plt.subplot(2,3,6),plt.imshow(np.abs(np.fft.fftshift(np.fft.fft2(rimg))),cmap='gray')
plt.title('Spectrum:Filtered image'),plt.axis('off')
plt.tight_layout()
```

Fig. 5.50 Python code to illustrate periodic noise minimization

Notch filter is effective in minimizing the impact of periodic noise in the input image. Notch filter has the ability to remove specific frequency component in the input signal. The Python code that performs this task is shown in Fig. 5.50, and the corresponding output is shown in Fig. 5.51.

Inferences

The following inferences can be made from Fig. 5.51:

- The input image is a white square on a black background
- Fourier transform of square signal results in a "sinc" function. It is possible to observe 2D "sinc" function as the spectrum of input image
- The noisy image is a square image with the sinusoidal grating pattern. Fourier transform of noisy image shows prominent peaks at (118,118) and (138,138), which corresponds to the grating pattern.
- Upon nullifying the spectrum value at (118,118) and at (138,138), and taking inverse Fourier transform, the filtered image is obtained. The filtered image

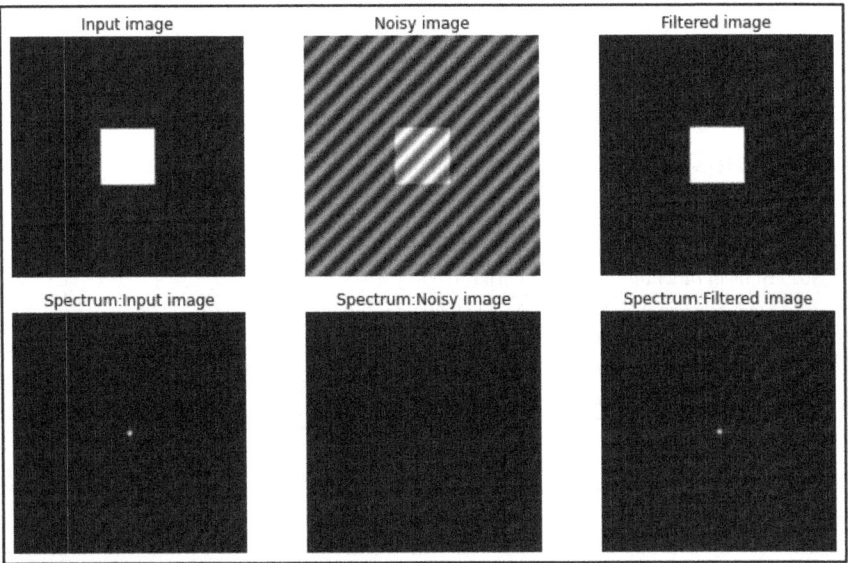

Fig. 5.51 Periodic noise minimization

resembles the input image, and its spectrum resembles the spectrum of the input image.

- In this experiment, the periodic noise components, which occur at the location (118,118) and at (138,138) in the spectrum, are nullified to minimize the impact of the grating pattern. Thus, this experiment illustrates two-dimensional notch filtering of the input image.
- The challenge is to locate the location of the peak in the spectrum, which corresponds to the periodic pattern (sinusoidal grating pattern).

Task: Write a Python code to obtain the mean square value between the input image and the filtered image.

5.8.2   Wavelet Transform-Based Image Denoising

Wavelet transform, due to its localization property, is an effective tool widely used in the area of image denoising and compression. Wavelets are used to decompose the image into different frequency regions called subbands. After decomposition, a thresholding operation is used to minimize the impact of noise. Different ways to modify the wavelet coefficients to minimize the impact of noise is termed as "shrinkage" techniques. The universal threshold commonly known as "VisuShrink" is given by

$$\lambda = \sigma \sqrt{2 \log(N)} \tag{5.18}$$

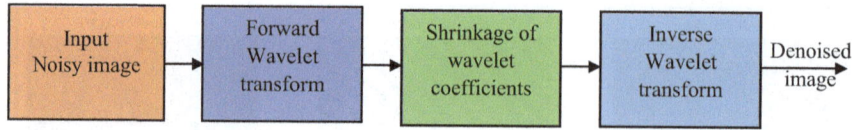

Fig. 5.52 Wavelet-based image denoising technique

Table 5.2 Built-in functions used in the program

S. No.	Built-in function	Library	Purpose
1	random.normal()	Numpy	To add white noise to the input image
2	wavedec2()	Pywt	To perform multi-level wavelet decomposition of the image
3	threshold()	Pywt	To perform thresholding of wavelet coefficients
4	waverec2()	Pywt	To perform multi-level wavelet reconstruction of the image

where "σ" represents the standard deviation of the noise and "N" represents the sample size.

After thresholding, inverse wavelet transform is taken to obtain the denoised image. The block diagram representation of wavelet-based image denoising is shown in Fig. 5.52.

Experiment 5.25: Image Denoising in Wavelet Domain Without "Scikit" Library

In this experiment, the input image is read, and then additive white Gaussian noise is added to the input image with zero mean and standard deviation of 50. Then, sub-band decomposition of the noisy image is performed using the "Haar" wavelet. The level of decomposition is fixed as 3. Then, a universal threshold of wavelet coefficient is performed to minimize the impact of noise. After that, inverse wavelet decomposition is performed to obtain the denoised image. The built-in functions used in the program are summarized in Table 5.2.

The Python code that performs wavelet-based image denoising is given in Fig. 5.53, and the corresponding output is shown in Fig. 5.54.

Inferences

- The impact of noise is minimized in the denoised image, but the edge information and background information are not preserved.
- The PSNR (peak signal-to-noise ratio) value in decibel is 20.6753. To improve the PSNR value, different choices of wavelet function and different types of shrinkage techniques have to be adopted.

Tasks

1. Perform the same experiment by changing the wavelet. Choose a wavelet other than the "Haar" wavelet and observe the output.
2. Vary the level of wavelet decomposition and observe the result.
3. Instead of "Universal threshold", use "Bayes shrink" and other shrinkage techniques and observe the result.

```
import numpy as np
import matplotlib.pyplot as plt
import cv2
import pywt
#Step 1: Reading the input image
img=cv2.imread('Clock.tiff',0)
#Step 2: Adding noise to the image
mean, sigma=0,50
img_noise=img+np.random.normal(mean,sigma,size=img.shape)
#Step 3: To perform wavelet decomposition of noisy image
wave_name = 'haar' # Define the type of wavelet base
l = 3#       Level of decomposition
coeffs = pywt.wavedec2(img_noise, wavelet=wave_name,level=l)
# Step 4: Fix the universal thershold
threshold = sigma*np.sqrt(2*np.log2(img_noise.size))
#Step 5: Perform thresholding of wavelet coefficients
list_coeffs = []
for i in range(1, len(coeffs)):
    list_coeffs_ = list(coeffs[i])
    list_coeffs.append(list_coeffs_)
for r1 in range(len(list_coeffs)):
    for r2 in range(len(list_coeffs[r1])):
        #     (soft threshold)
        list_coeffs[r1][r2] = pywt.threshold(list_coeffs[r1][r2], threshold*np.max(list_coeffs[r1][r2]))
rec_coeffs = []
rec_coeffs.append(coeffs[0])
for j in range(len(list_coeffs)):
    rec_coeffs_ = tuple(list_coeffs[j])
    rec_coeffs.append(rec_coeffs_)
#Step 6: Perform Inverse wavelet transform
denoised_img = pywt.waverec2(rec_coeffs, wavelet=wave_name)
#Step 7: To obtain the PSNR
def PSNR(original, reconstructed):
    mse = np.mean((original - reconstructed) ** 2)
    max_pixel = 255.0
    psnr1 = 20 * np.log10(max_pixel / np.sqrt(mse))
    psnr = round(psnr1,4)
    return psnr
psnr1=PSNR(img,denoised_img)
psnr2=PSNR(img,img_noise)
#Step 8: Displaying the result
plt.figure(figsize=(8,8)),plt.subplot(1,3,1),plt.imshow(img,cmap='gray'),plt.title('Input image'),
plt.axis('off'),plt.subplot(1,3,2),plt.imshow(img_noise,cmap='gray')
plt.title(r'Noisy PSNR = {} dB'.format(psnr2)),plt.axis('off'),plt.subplot(1,3,3),
plt.imshow(denoised_img,cmap='gray'),plt.title(r'Denoised PSNR = {} dB'.format(psnr1)),
plt.axis('off'),plt.tight_layout()
```

Fig. 5.53 Python code to perform wavelet-based image denoising

Experiment 5.26: Image Denoising in Wavelet Domain Using Built-in Function from "Scikit" Library

The built-in function "*denoise_wavelet*" available in "scikit" library can be used to denoise the input image, which is corrupted by additive Gaussian noise with zero mean and standard deviation = 50. The noisy image is decomposed using different

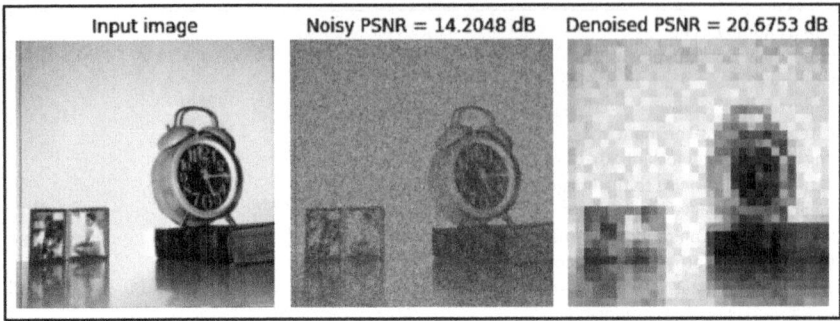

Fig. 5.54 Result of wavelet-based denoising

```
import cv2
import matplotlib.pyplot as plt
import numpy as np
from skimage.restoration import denoise_wavelet
#Step 1: Read the input image
img=cv2.imread('Clock.tiff',0)
#Step 2: Adding noise to the image
mean, sigma = 0, 50
img_noise=img+np.random.normal(mean,sigma,size=img.shape)
plt.figure(figsize=(8, 6)),plt.figure(1)
plt.subplot(2,3,1),plt.imshow(img,cmap='gray'),plt.title('Noise free image')
plt.axis('off'),plt.subplot(2,3,2),plt.imshow(img_noise,cmap='gray')
plt.title('Noisy image'),plt.axis('off')
w_name=['db1','coif1','sym3','bior1.1']
#Step 3: Denoising of the image
for i in range(len(w_name)):
    im_bayes = denoise_wavelet(img_noise,wavelet=w_name[i], method='BayesShrink',
mode='soft',rescale_sigma=False)
    plt.figure(1),plt.subplot(2,3,i+3),plt.imshow(im_bayes,cmap='gray')
    plt.title(r'Denoised using "{}"'.format(w_name[i])),plt.axis('off')
plt.tight_layout()
```

Fig. 5.55 Python code to perform image denoising using built-in function from "scikit" library

wavelets such as "Haar", "Coiflet", "Symlet", and "Biorthogonal wavelet". After decomposition, the wavelet coefficients are thresholded using "Bayes shrink" and then inverse wavelet transform is performed to obtain the denoised image. The Python code that accomplishes this task is shown in Fig. 5.55, and the corresponding output is shown in Fig. 5.56.

Inference

The denoised image using a different choice of wavelets is shown in Fig. 5.56. From the figure, it is possible to observe that the denoising ability of Haar wavelet is good but the background of the image is not well preserved. Symlet preserves the background information, but the noise minimization ability is low.

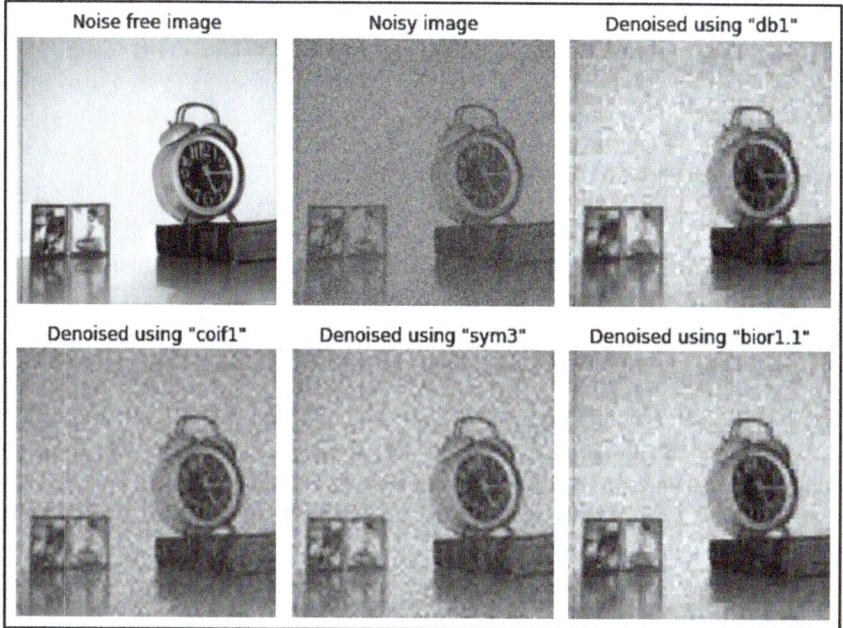

Fig. 5.56 Result of Python code given in Fig. 5.55

Fig. 5.57 Model for image degradation

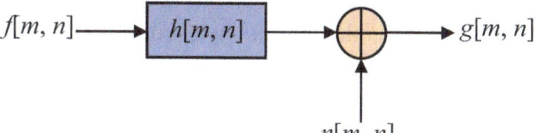

5.9   Image Restoration

Digital image restoration is a field of engineering that studies methods used to recover an original scene from degraded observations. Due to imperfections in the image capturing process, the recorded image represents the degraded version of the original scene. In this process, mathematical model of degradation is obtained first, then the inverse of the degradation is applied to recover the original image. The image degradation model is shown in Fig. 5.57. In the figure, $f[m, n]$ represents noise-free image, $h[m, n]$ represents degradation function, $\eta[m, n]$ represents the additive noise, and $g[m, n]$ represents the degraded image.

If the degradation function is assumed to be linear and shift invariant, then the expression for the degraded image is given by

$$g[m,n] = f[m,n] * h[m,n] + \eta[m,n] \tag{5.19}$$

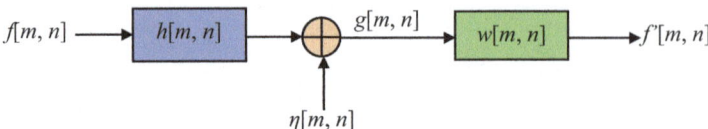

Fig. 5.58 Model of image restoration

In Eq. (5.19), "*" represents the convolution operation. Upon taking Fourier transform on both sides, the expression for the degraded image in frequency domain is expressed as

$$G[k,l] = F[k,l]H[k,l] + N[k,l] \tag{5.20}$$

The objective of image restoration is to design a system ($w[m, n]$) that operates on the observed image $g[m, n]$ to obtain the estimate of the input image $f[m, n]$, which is represented as $f'[m, n]$. This is depicted in Fig. 5.58.

In the figure, $f'[m, n]$ is the restored image, which should be as close as possible to the noise-free image $f[m, n]$.

5.10   Classification of Image Restoration Methods

Image restoration methods can be classified based on the type and amount of information related to the images involved in the problem and also the distortion. One way to classify image restoration methods is (1) deterministic or (2) stochastic methods. It can also be classified as (1) non-blind, (2) semi-blind, and (3) blind methods.

Deterministic methods work directly on image values in either spatial domain or frequency domain. Stochastic methods work on statistical properties of image of interest. In the non-blind method, it is assumed that the cause of degradation is known. In semi-blind methods, the degradation process is partly known. In blind methods, the degradation process is unknown.

5.11   Point Spread Function (PSF)

The PSF identifies the response, which is the output of the imaging system, to a point source that is the input. The pattern of the PSF is influenced by the optical device that is used to record the blurred image or by other physical or environmental events. Some of the assumptions in PSF are summarized as follows:

1. The PSF is spatially invariant in many applications but not all. The PSF is equally distributed along the spatial coordinates in the blurred image. Spatially variant PSF is computationally difficult to construct because each pixel has a different PSF.

2. The blurring is a local phenomenon. This implies that the light intensity of the PSF is confined to a small area around its centre and is zero beyond a given distance from its centre.
3. The PSF can be represented as a matrix that contains all the information about the blurring function, and its size, in general, is less than the size of the image.
4. The sum of the pixel values of the PSF array is equal to 1. This is represented as $\sum_{m=0}^{N-1}\sum_{n=0}^{N-1}h[m,n]=1$.
5. The coefficients of the matrix of the PSF have only positive values since the nature of image formation cannot be negative.

Blurring is a form of bandwidth reduction of an ideal image owing to the imperfect image formation process. It can be caused by an optical system that is out-of-focus, or it can be caused by relative motion between the camera and the scene, or it may be due to atmospheric turbulence. This section discusses the mathematical model of different types of blurs.

5.11.1 No Blur

If the image is recorded perfectly, no blur will appear in the digital image. The point spread function (PSF), in this case, can be modelled as a delta function, which is represented as

$$h[m,n] = \begin{cases} 1, & if \; m = n = 0 \\ 0, & \text{Otherwise} \end{cases} \tag{5.21}$$

Experiment 5.27: Python Code to Generate Two-Dimensional Delta Function
The Python code to generate two-dimensional delta function is shown in Fig. 5.59a, and the corresponding output is shown in Fig. 5.59b.

```
#PSF of NO blur
import numpy as np
import matplotlib.pyplot as plt
H=np.zeros([256,256])
H[128,128]=1
plt.imshow(H,cmap='gray'),
plt.title('$\delta[m,n]$')
plt.axis('off')
```

(a) Python code   **(b) 2D delta function**

Fig. 5.59 Generation of two-dimensional delta function: (a) Python code, (b) 2D delta function

Inference

- From Fig. 5.59b, it is possible to observe that the two-dimensional delta function has a value of 1 only at $m = n = 128$, and it is 0 for all the other values.

5.11.2   Out-of-Focus Blur

Image is basically a projection of a 3D scene on a 2D plane. During projection, some parts of the scene may not be focussed properly. For a circular aperture camera, the projected image of a point source is a small disc, which is known as circle of confusion. The point spread function of out-of-focus blur is given by

$$h[m,n] = \begin{cases} \dfrac{1}{\pi R^2}, & if \ \sqrt{m^2 + n^2} \le R, \\ 0, & otherwise. \end{cases} \tag{5.22}$$

where "R" represents the radius of the circle or disc.

Experiment 5.28: Generation of PSF of Out-of-Focus Blur

This experiment discusses the generation of PSF of out-of-focus blur. The Python code that generates the point spread function of out-of-focus blur for two different radius values ($R = 20$ and $R = 40$ units) is given in Fig. 5.60a, and the corresponding output is shown in Fig. 5.60b.

Inference

- Figure 5.60b shows the PSF of out-of-focus blur, which is a disc. The radius of the disc decides the extent of blur.

```
#Out-of-focus blur
import numpy as np
import matplotlib.pyplot as plt
img=np.zeros([256,256])
R=[20,40]  #Radius
fig = plt.figure(figsize=(6,6))
for k in range(len(R)):
    for i in range(0,256):
        for j in range(0,256):
            D=((i-128)**2 + (j-128)**2)**0.5
            if(D<=R[k]):
                img[i,j]=1/(np.pi*R[k]**2)
    fig.add_subplot(1,2,k+1),
    plt.imshow(img,cmap='gray')
    plt.title(f'R = {R[k]}'),plt.axis('off')
plt.tight_layout()
```

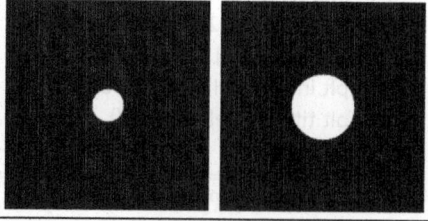

| (a) Python code | (b) Simulation result |

Fig. 5.60 Generation of PSF of out-of-focus blur: (a) Python code, (b) simulation result

```
import cv2
import numpy as np
import matplotlib.pyplot as plt

def out_of_focus(m,n,R):
    H=np.zeros([m,n]);
    for j in range(0,m):
        for k in range(0,n):
            D=((j-128)**2+(k-128)**2)**0.5
            if (D<=R):
                H[j,k]=1/(np.pi*R**2)
    return H
img=cv2.imread('Clock.tiff',0);
plt.figure(figsize=(8,6)),plt.subplot(1,4,1),plt.imshow(img,cmap='gray')
plt.xticks([]),plt.yticks([]),plt.title('Input image')
R=[1,5,10];
for i in range(0,len(R)):
    mask=out_of_focus(256, 256, R[i]);
    img_b1=cv2.filter2D(img,-1,mask);
    plt.subplot(1,4,i+2),plt.imshow(img_b1,cmap='gray'),plt.xticks([]),
    plt.yticks([]),plt.title(r'Out of focus R = {}'.format(R[i]))
plt.tight_layout()
```

Fig. 5.61 Python code for out-of-focus blurring on image

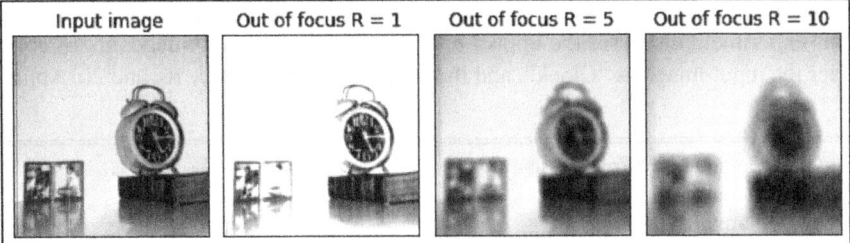

Fig. 5.62 Impact of out-of-focus blur

Experiment 5.29: Apply the Out-of-Focus Blur to the "Clock" Image, Plot the Output, and Comment on the Observed Result

This experiment deals with the impact of out-of-focus blur in image processing. Here, input image is considered as "Clock.tiff" and the radius of the out-of-focus blur is chosen as 1, 5, and 10. The Python code to perform this task is shown in Fig. 5.61, and its simulation result is displayed in Fig. 5.62.

Inference

- From Fig. 5.62, it is possible to observe that the radius (R) of the out-of-focus blur decides the impact of the blurring. The higher value of "R" blurs more on the input image.

5.11.3   Atmospheric Turbulence Blur

Atmospheric turbulence blur is due to the turbulent atmosphere of the earth. Atmosphere is an unstable random medium. Its temperature, pressure, density, and water vapour content are constantly changing. When a light is propagated in the atmosphere, it is affected by molecular absorption, scattering of aerosol, and turbulence disturbances. This leads to change in the refractive index of a layer that distorts the image to be observed. This affects the quality of the captured image. The mathematical model of atmospheric turbulence blur is given as Gaussian function. The expression for the point spread function of Gaussian blur with zero mean and variance σ^2 is given by

$$h[m,n] = \frac{1}{2\pi\sigma^2} e^{\frac{-(m^2+n^2)}{2\sigma^2}} \tag{5.23}$$

Experiment 5.30: PSF of Gaussian Blur
The Python code to generate Gaussian blur for different values of standard deviation is given in Fig. 5.63, and the corresponding output is shown in Fig. 5.64.

Inference

- From Fig. 5.64, it is possible to observe that the extent of blur increases with increase in the value of standard deviation.

Experiment 5.31: Visualize the Impact of Gaussian Blur on Image
This experiment discusses the impact of Gaussian blur on input image. Let us consider the input image as "Clock", and the standard deviation is 5, 10, and 20. Apply

```
#Point spread function of Gaussian blur
import numpy as np
import matplotlib.pyplot as plt
M=256
x=np.linspace(-M/2,M/2,M+1)
y=np.linspace(-M/2,M/2,M+1)
X,Y=np.meshgrid(x,y)
c,r = 4,1
# Generation of Gaussian functions
sigma1=[5,10,20,50]
fig = plt.figure(figsize=(6,6))
for k in range(len(sigma1)):
    H=1./(2.* np.pi *sigma1[k]*sigma1[k])*np.exp(-((X)**2. / (2. * sigma1[k]**2.) +
        (Y)**2. / (2.* sigma1[k]**2.)))
    fig.add_subplot(r, c,k+1),plt.imshow(H,cmap='gray'),plt.axis('off')
    plt.title(f'$\sigma$ = {sigma1[k]}')
plt.tight_layout()
```

Fig. 5.63 Python code to generate PSF of Gaussian blur

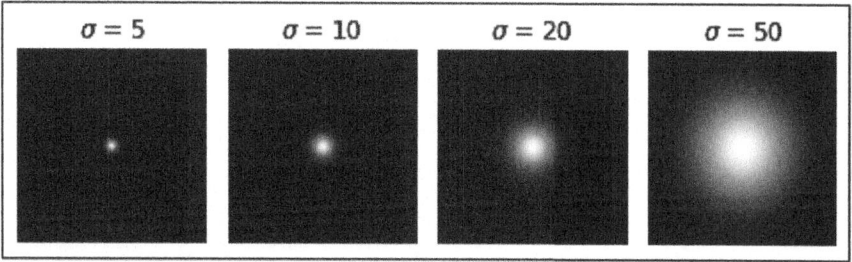

Fig. 5.64 PSF of Gaussian blur for different values of standard deviation

```
# Gauss blur on input image
import cv2
import numpy as np
import matplotlib.pyplot as plt
def gauss_blur(M,sigma):
  x=np.linspace(-M/2,M/2,M+1)
  y=np.linspace(-M/2,M/2,M+1)
  X,Y=np.meshgrid(x,y)
  H=1./(2.* np.pi *sigma**2)*np.exp(-((X)**2./(2. * sigma**2.)+
     (Y)**2./(2.* sigma**2.)))
  return H
img=cv2.imread('Clock.tiff',0);
plt.figure(figsize=(8,6)),plt.subplot(1,4,1),plt.imshow(img,cmap='gray')
plt.xticks([]),plt.yticks([]),plt.title('Input image')
sigma=[1,5,10];
for i in range(0,len(sigma)):
  mask=gauss_blur(256,sigma[i]);
  img_b1=cv2.filter2D(img,-1,mask);
  plt.subplot(1,4,i+2),plt.imshow(img_b1,cmap='gray'),plt.xticks([]),
  plt.yticks([]),plt.title(r'Gauss blur Sigma = {}'.format(sigma[i]))
plt.tight_layout()
```

Fig. 5.65 Python code for Gaussian blur

this Gaussian blur to the input image. The Python code to perform the above-mentioned task is given in Fig. 5.65, and its corresponding simulation result is depicted in Fig. 5.66.

Inference

- From Fig. 5.66, it is possible to infer that standard deviation plays a major role in the blur. If the value is high, it blurs more.

Fig. 5.66 Visual impact of Gaussian blur

5.11.4   Motion Blur

The expression for the PSF of motion blur is given by

$$h[m,n] = \begin{cases} \dfrac{1}{L}, & 0 \leq |m| \leq L\cos(\theta), \quad |n| = L\sin(\theta), \\ 0, & \text{otherwise.} \end{cases} \tag{5.24}$$

where "L" represents the length of the blur and θ represents the angle of the blur.

Experiment 5.32: Generation of PSF of Motion Blur
The Python code that generates the PSF of motion blur for angle $\theta = 45°$ and motion length = 180 units is shown in Fig. 5.67, and the corresponding output is shown in Fig. 5.68.

Inference

- From Fig. 5.68, it is possible to confirm that the PSF of a motion blur is a line inclined at an angle of 45° and −45°.

Experiment 5.33: Impact of Motion Blur on Image
This experiment deals with the impact of motion blur on input image. Let us consider the motion distance is 20 and motion angles are 45°, −45°, and 90°. The Python code to perform this task is given in Fig. 5.69, and its simulation result is displayed in Fig. 5.70.

Inferences
The following inferences can be made from Fig. 5.70:

- The motion blur exists in the output image based on the motion distance and angle.
- For the motion angle 45°, the output shows clearly the motion occurs in the direction of 45°.
- For the motion angle −45°, the output image contains the motion blur towards −45° angle.

```
#PSF of motion blur
import numpy as np
import matplotlib.pyplot as plt
import math
H1=np.zeros([256,256])
H2=np.zeros([256,256])
m1,n1=H1.shape
x_center = (m1-1)/2
y_center = (n1-1)/2
motion_dis=180
motion_angle1=45
motion_angle2=-45
sin_val1 = math.sin(motion_angle1 * math.pi / 180)
cos_val1 = math.cos(motion_angle1 * math.pi / 180)
sin_val2 = math.sin(motion_angle2 * math.pi / 180)
cos_val2 = math.cos(motion_angle2 * math.pi / 180)
for i in range(motion_dis):
    x_offset1 = round(sin_val1 * i)
    y_offset1 = round(cos_val1 * i)
    x_offset2 = round(sin_val2 * i)
    y_offset2 = round(cos_val2 * i)
    H1[int(x_center - x_offset1),int(y_center + y_offset1)]= 1
    H2[int(x_center - x_offset2),int(y_center + y_offset2)]= 1
plt.subplot(1,2,1),plt.imshow(H1,cmap='gray'),plt.axis('off'),plt.title('45$^{o}$')
plt.subplot(1,2,2),plt.imshow(H2,cmap='gray'),plt.axis('off'),plt.title('-45$^{o}$')
```

Fig. 5.67 Python code to generate PSF of motion blur

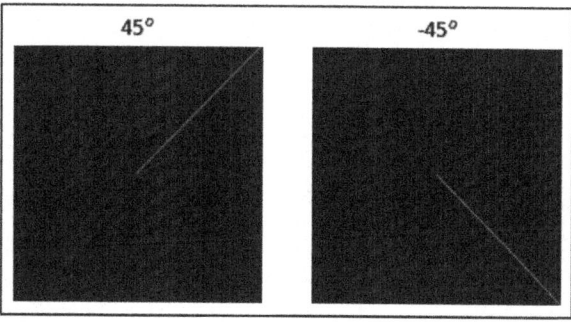

Fig. 5.68 PSF of motion blur for angle 45° and −45°

- Similarly, for the motion angle 90°, the output images clearly indicates that the motion occurs along y direction.

Task: Increase the motion distance value in the Python code given in Fig. 5.69 and comment on the observed result.

```python
# Motion blur on input image
import cv2
import numpy as np
import matplotlib.pyplot as plt
import math
def motion_blur(motion_dis,motion_angle):
  H=np.zeros([256,256])
  m,n=H.shape;
  x_center = (m-1)/2
  y_center = (n-1)/2
  sin_val = math.sin(motion_angle * math.pi / motion_dis)
  cos_val = math.cos(motion_angle * math.pi / motion_dis)
  for i in range(motion_dis):
    x_offset = round(sin_val * i)
    y_offset = round(cos_val * i)
    H[int(x_center - x_offset),int(y_center + y_offset)]= 1/motion_dis
  return H
img=cv2.imread('Clock.tiff',0);
plt.figure(figsize=(10,8)),plt.subplot(1,4,1),plt.imshow(img,cmap='gray')
plt.xticks([]),plt.yticks([]),plt.title('Input image')
angle=[0,-45,90];
for i in range(0,len(angle)):
  mask=motion_blur(20,angle[i]);
  img_b1=cv2.filter2D(img,-1,mask);
  plt.subplot(1,4,i+2),plt.imshow(img_b1,cmap='gray'),plt.xticks([]),
  plt.yticks([]),plt.title(r'Motion blur angle = {}$^o$'.format(angle[i]))
plt.tight_layout()
```

Fig. 5.69 Python code for motion blur on input image

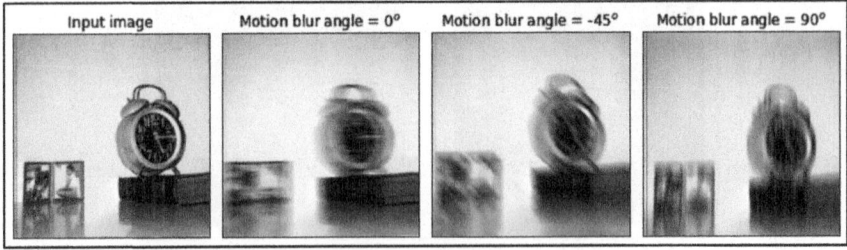

Fig. 5.70 Simulation result of Python code in Fig. 5.69

5.12   Image Restoration Filters

Image restoration filter attempts to find the reason (point spread function) for the degradation and then applies the inverse of the degradation function to obtain the restored image. Three types of image restoration filters discussed in this section are (1) inverse filter, (2) pseudo-inverse filter, and (3) Wiener filter.

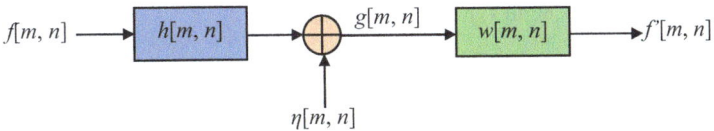

$f[m, n] \longrightarrow$ $h[m, n]$ $\longrightarrow \oplus \xrightarrow{g[m, n]}$ $w[m, n]$ $\longrightarrow f'[m, n]$

$\eta[m, n]$

Fig. 5.71 Image restoration model

5.12.1   Inverse Filter

The general framework of image restoration is given in Fig. 5.71. In the figure, $f[m, n]$ represents the input image, $h[m, n]$ represents the mathematical model of degradation, $\eta[m, n]$ represents the additive noise, $g[m, n]$ represents the observed image, $w[m, n]$ represents the restoration filter, and $f'[m, n]$ represents the restored image.

If the point spread function (PSF) of the degradation is assumed to be linear and space invariant, the expression for the observed image in spatial domain is expressed as

$$g[m,n] = f[m,n] * h[m,n] + \eta[m,n] \tag{5.25}$$

Upon taking Fourier transform on both sides, we get

$$G[k,l] = F[k,l] \times H[k,l] + N[k,l] \tag{5.26}$$

If the degradation model is known, the expression for the inverse filter is given by

$$w[m,n] = \frac{1}{h[m,n]} \tag{5.27}$$

In the frequency domain, the above expression is given by

$$W[k,l] = \frac{1}{H[k,l]} \tag{5.28}$$

From Fig. 5.71, the expression for the restored image is given by

$$f'[m,n] = g[m,n] * w[m,n] \tag{5.29}$$

Upon taking the Fourier transform on both sides, we get

$$F'[k,l] = G[k,l] \times W[k,l] \tag{5.30}$$

Substituting Eq. (5.26) in Eq. (5.30), we get

$$F'[k,l] = \left(F[k,l] H[k,l] + N[k,l] \right) W[k,l] \tag{5.31}$$

Substituting Eq. (5.28) in Eq. (5.31), we get

$$F'[k,l] = \frac{F[k,l]H[k,l] + N[k,l]}{H[k,l]} \tag{5.32}$$

The above equation can be simplified as

$$F'[k,l] = F[k,l] + \frac{N[k,l]}{H[k,l]} \tag{5.33}$$

In the absence of noise, the second term in Eq. (5.33) vanishes, and the restored image is identical to the noise-free image.

Drawbacks of Inverse Filter

1. The noise component is a random function whose Fourier transform ($N[k, l]$) is unknown.
2. If the degradation filter $H[k, l]$ is zero at some selected frequencies (k, l), then inverse filter may not exist. This is possible in the case of linear motion blur and out-of-focus blur.
3. Inverse filter performs well in the absence of noise. In the presence of noise, noise values can have influence in $H[k, l]$ that has small magnitude. This in general corresponds to high frequencies, which result in blurring of fine details of the image.

Experiment 5.34: Inverse Filtering

Apply a Gaussian blur to the input image to obtain the degraded image. To this degraded image, apply inverse filter and comment on the observed output. The block diagram that depicts the problem statement is shown in Fig. 5.72.

The Python code that performs the above-mentioned task is shown in Fig. 5.73, and the corresponding output is shown in Fig. 5.74.

Inferences

- From Fig. 5.73, it is possible to observe that the Fourier transform of the input image is computed, and it is multiplied by the PSF of Gaussian blur. Then, inverse Fourier transform of multiplied output is performed to get a blur image.
- For the restoration process, the multiplied output is divided by the PSF of the Gaussian function, and then the inverse Fourier transform is taken to get a restored image.

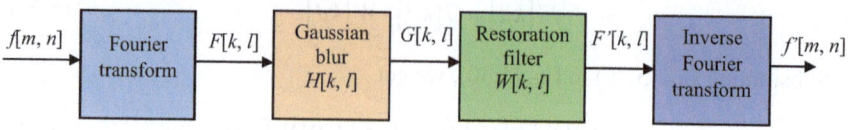

Fig. 5.72 Inverse filter frame work

```
#Inverse filtering - Image restoration
import numpy as np
import matplotlib.pyplot as plt
import cv2
img=cv2.imread('cameraman.tif',0);#Step 1: Reading th input image
IMG=np.fft.fft2(img);#Step 2: Obtaining the spectrum of input image
IMG=np.fft.fftshift(IMG)
M,D0=255,10
x=np.linspace(-M/2,M/2,M+1)
y=np.linspace(-M/2,M/2,M+1)
X,Y=np.meshgrid(x,y)
D=np.sqrt(X**2+Y**2)
H=np.exp(-D**2/(2*D0**2));#Step 3:Gaussian blur
G=np.multiply(IMG,H)#Step 4: Obtaining the degraded image
g=np.fft.ifft2(np.fft.ifftshift(G))#Blurred image in spatial domain
F_hat = G / H;#Step 5: Applying Inverse Filter
a = np.nan_to_num(F_hat)
f_hat = np.fft.ifft2( np.fft.ifftshift(a) )
#Step 5: Displaying the results
plt.subplot(1,4,1),plt.imshow(img,cmap='gray'),plt.title('Input image'),plt.xticks([]),
plt.yticks([]),plt.subplot(1,4,2),plt.imshow(H,cmap='gray'),plt.title('PSF'),plt.xticks([]),
plt.yticks([]),plt.subplot(1,4,3),plt.imshow(np.abs(g),cmap='gray'),plt.title('Blurred image'),
plt.xticks([]),plt.yticks([]),plt.subplot(1,4,4),plt.imshow(np.abs(f_hat),cmap='gray'),
plt.title('Restored image'),plt.xticks([]),plt.yticks([])
plt.tight_layout()
```

Fig. 5.73 Python code that performs inverse filtering

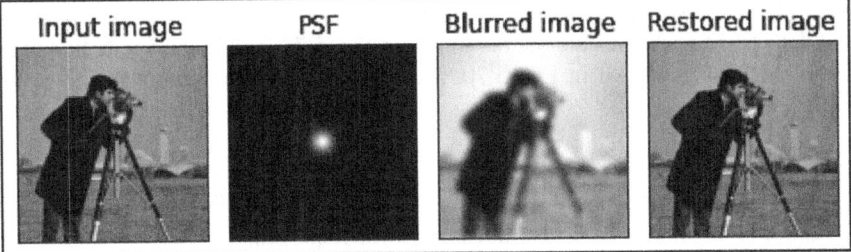

Fig. 5.74 Result of inverse filtering operation

- From Fig. 5.74, it is possible to infer that the PSF of the Gaussian function blurs the input image, and inverse filtering gets back the restored image from the blurred image. The blurring effect is purely based on the value of the radius of the PSF.
- This experiment concludes that if the exact PSF is known and the blurred image is without noise, the inverse filter can restore the original image from the blurred image.

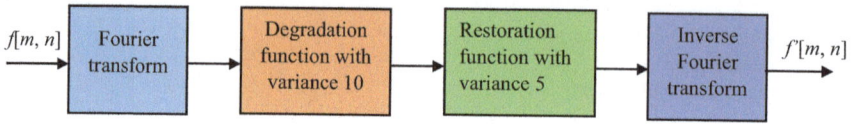

Fig. 5.75 Block diagram depicting problem statement

Experiment 5.35: Effect of Improper Selection of Parameter in the Inverse Filtering

This experiment shows the impact of choosing the wrong parameter in the restoration filter. The input image is corrupted by Gaussian blur. In the case of Gaussian blur, the variance determines its severity. The input image is degraded by a Gaussian blur of variance 10. An attempt is made to restore the image by choosing an inverse filter. While performing the restoration, the variance of the Gaussian blur is assumed to be 5 instead of 10. The block diagram that depicts this study is shown in Fig. 5.75. The Python code to perform this task is given in Fig. 5.76, and the corresponding output is shown in Fig. 5.77.

Inferences

- From Fig. 5.77, it is possible to observe that the restored image is different from the input image.
- It is not possible to restore the original image if the parameter of the inverse filter is chosen wrongly when compared to the parameters of the degradation filter.

Experiment 5.36: Inverse Filtering for Out-of-Focus Blur

In this experiment, the spectrum of the input image is multiplied with out-of-focus blur. Then, inverse filter is applied to obtain the restored image. The block diagram that depicts the problem statement is shown in Fig. 5.78. The Python code that performs this task is shown in Fig. 5.70, and the corresponding output is shown in Fig. 5.80.

Inference

- From Fig. 5.80, it is possible to observe that the inverse filter is not effective in restoring the image that is degraded by out-of-focus blur.

Experiment 5.37: Investing the Inverse Filter in the Presence of Degradation and Noise

In this experiment, the image is blurred by Gaussian blur. It is then affected by additive Gaussian noise. Inverse filter is applied to the blurred and noisy version of the image. The block diagram that depicts the problem statement is shown in Fig. 5.81.

The Python code that implements the above-mentioned task is shown in Fig. 5.82, and the corresponding output is shown in Fig. 5.83.

Inference

- From Fig. 5.83, it is possible to observe that inverse filter is not effective in restoring the image that is both degraded and affected by additive noise.

```
#Case study 1: Inverse filtering
import numpy as np
import matplotlib.pyplot as plt
import cv2
img=cv2.imread('cameraman.tif',0)#Step 1: Reading th input image
IMG=np.fft.fft2(img);#Step 2: Obtaining the spectrum of input image
IMG=np.fft.fftshift(IMG)
#Step 3:PSF of Gaussian blur with variance 10
M,D0,D1=255,10,5
x=np.linspace(-M/2,M/2,M+1)
y=np.linspace(-M/2,M/2,M+1)
X,Y=np.meshgrid(x,y)
D=np.sqrt(X**2+Y**2)
H=np.exp(-D**2/(2*D0**2))
#Step 4: PSF used for restoration with variance 5
H1=np.exp(-D**2/(2*D1**2))
G=np.multiply(IMG,H);#Step 4: Obtaining the degraded image
F_hat = G / H1;#Step 5: Applying Inverse Filter
a = np.nan_to_num(F_hat)
f_hat = np.fft.ifft2( np.fft.ifftshift(a) )
#Step 5: Displaying the results
plt.figure(figsize=(8,6)),plt.subplot(1,4,1),plt.imshow(img,cmap='gray'),
plt.title('Input image'),plt.axis('off'),plt.subplot(1,4,2),plt.imshow(H,cmap='gray'),
plt.title('PSF for degradation'),plt.axis('off'),plt.subplot(1,4,3),
plt.imshow(H1,cmap='gray'),plt.title('PSF for restoration')
plt.axis('off'),plt.subplot(1,4,4),plt.imshow(np.abs(f_hat),cmap='gray'),
plt.title('Restored image'),plt.axis('off')
plt.tight_layout()
```

Fig. 5.76 Python code for inverse filter

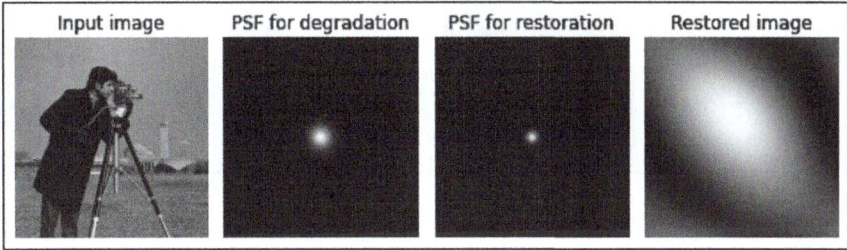

Fig. 5.77 Result of Python code shown in Fig. 5.76

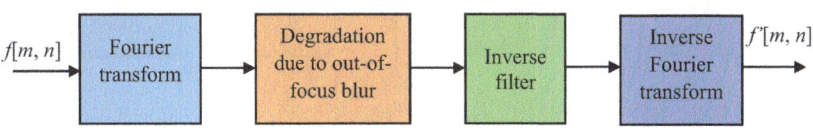

Fig. 5.78 Block diagram depicting the application of inverse filter to out-of-focus blur

```
#Inverse filter for out-of-focus blur
import numpy as np
import matplotlib.pyplot as plt
import cv2
img=cv2.imread('Clock.tiff',0);#Step1: Read the noise free image
IMG=np.fft.fft2(img);#Step 2: FT of the input image
IMG=np.fft.fftshift(IMG)
#Step 3: Define the out-of-focus blur
H=np.zeros([256,256])
m,n=H.shape
R=10
for i in range(m):
    for j in range(n):
        D=((i-128)**2 + (j-128)**2)**0.5
        if(D<=R):
            H[i,j]=1/(np.pi*R**2)
G=np.multiply(IMG,H);# Step 4: Multiply the spectrum of image with out-of-focus blur
blurred_img=np.fft.ifft2(np.fft.ifftshift(G))
F_hat=G/H;# #Step 5: Define the Inverse filter
F_hat=np.nan_to_num(F_hat)
res_img=np.fft.ifft2(np.fft.ifftshift(F_hat))
plt.figure(figsize=(8,6)),plt.subplot(1,4,1),plt.imshow(img,cmap='gray'),
plt.title('Input image'),plt.xticks([]),plt.yticks([]),plt.subplot(1,4,2),plt.imshow(H,cmap='gray'),
plt.title('Blurring function'),plt.axis('off'),plt.subplot(1,4,3),
plt.imshow(np.abs(blurred_img),cmap='gray'),plt.title('Blurred image'),plt.xticks([]),
plt.yticks([]),plt.subplot(1,4,4),plt.imshow(np.abs(res_img),cmap='gray'),
plt.title('Restored image'),plt.xticks([]),plt.yticks([])
plt.tight_layout()
```

Fig. 5.79 Python code to apply inverse filtering for out-of-focus blur

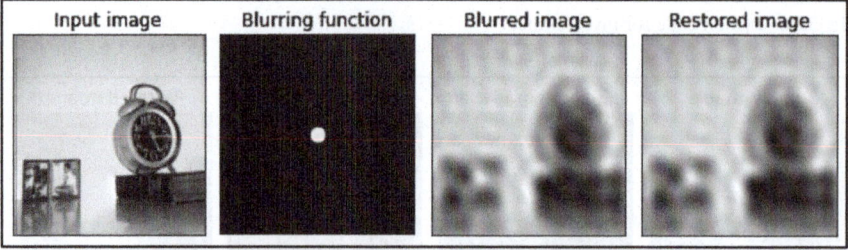

Fig. 5.80 Result of Python code shown in Fig. 5.79

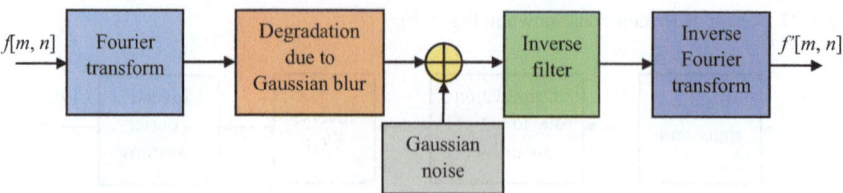

Fig. 5.81 Block diagram representing inverse filter in the presence of noise

```
#Inverse filter in the presence of noise
import numpy as np
import matplotlib.pyplot as plt
import cv2
img=cv2.imread('cameraman.tif',0);#Step1: Read the noise free image
IMG=np.fft.fft2(img);#Step 2: Fourier transform of the input image
IMG=np.fft.fftshift(IMG)
M,D0,mean,var=255,10,0,0.01;
x=np.linspace(-M/2,M/2,M+1)
y=np.linspace(-M/2,M/2,M+1)
X,Y=np.meshgrid(x,y)
D=np.sqrt(X**2+Y**2)
H=np.exp(-D**2/(2*D0**2));#Step 3: Define the Gaussian blur
G=np.multiply(IMG,H)#Step 4: Multiply the spectrum of image with Gaussian blur
blurred_img=np.fft.ifft2(np.fft.ifftshift(G))
sigma = var**0.5
gauss_noise = 100*np.random.normal(mean,sigma,(256,256))
G_noisy=np.add(np.real(blurred_img),gauss_noise);#Step 5: Adding noise to the image
F_hat=G_noisy/H; #Step 6: Define the Inverse filter
F_hat=np.nan_to_num(F_hat)
res_img=np.fft.ifft2(np.fft.ifftshift(F_hat))
plt.figure(figsize=(8,6)),plt.subplot(1,4,1),plt.imshow(img,cmap='gray'),
plt.title('Input image'),plt.xticks([]),plt.yticks([]),plt.subplot(1,4,2),plt.imshow(H,cmap='gray'),
plt.title('Blurring function'),plt.axis('off'),plt.subplot(1,4,3),
plt.imshow((G_noisy),cmap='gray'),plt.title('Blurred noisy image')
plt.xticks([]),plt.yticks([]),plt.subplot(1,4,4),plt.imshow(np.abs(res_img),cmap='gray'),
plt.title('Restored image'),plt.xticks([]),plt.yticks([])
plt.tight_layout()
```

Fig. 5.82   Python code that performs the inverse filtering of the degraded noisy image

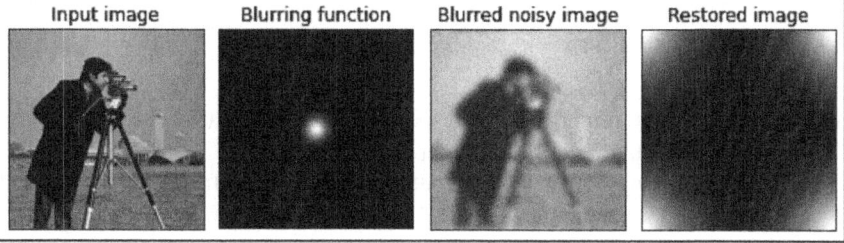

Fig. 5.83   Result of Python code shown in Fig. 5.82

5.12.2   Pseudo-Inverse Filter

Two practical approaches to overcome the drawback of inverse filter are (1) use a low-pass filter to eliminate the very low values often experienced in the high frequencies and (2) constraint division approach. These two approaches are termed as pseudo-inverse filtering. Pseudo-inverse filter is a stabilized version of the inverse filter. To mitigate the effect of zeros in the degradation function, the expression for the restoration filter is given by

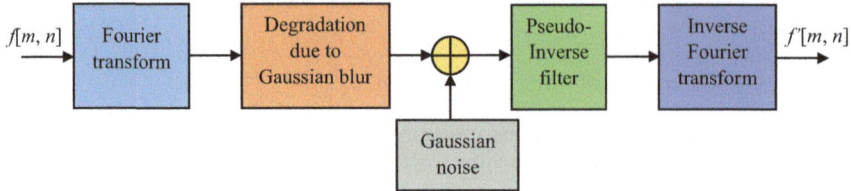

Fig. 5.84 Block diagram representing inverse filter in the presence of noise

$$W[k,l] = \begin{cases} \dfrac{1}{H[k,l]}, & |H[k,l]| \geq \varepsilon, \\ 0, & |H[k,l]| < \varepsilon. \end{cases} \qquad (5.34)$$

Experiment 5.38: Investing the Pseudo-Inverse Filter in the Presence of Degradation and Noise

In this experiment, the image is blurred by Gaussian blur. It is then affected by additive Gaussian noise. Pseudo inverse filter is applied to the blurred and noisy version of the image. The block diagram that depicts the problem statement is shown in Fig. 5.84.

The Python code that implements the above-mentioned task is shown in Fig. 5.85, and the corresponding output is shown in Fig. 5.86.

Inference

- From Fig. 5.86, it is possible to observe that pseudo-inverse filter effectively restores the image that is both degraded and affected by additive noise.

5.12.3 Wiener Filter

Wiener filter is an optimum filter with respect to minimum mean square error sense. The framework of image restoration is depicted in Fig. 5.87.

In Fig. 5.87, $f[m, n]$ represents the input image that is free from degradation and noise, $h[m, n]$ represents the mathematical model of the degradation, $\eta[m, n]$ represents the additive noise, $g[m, n]$ represents the observed image, $w[m, n]$ represents the restoration filter, and $f'[m, n]$ represents the restored image.

From Fig. 5.87, if $h[m, n]$ is assumed to be linear and space invariant, then the expression for the observed image is given by

$$g[m,n] = f[m,n] * h[m,n] + \eta[m,n] \qquad (5.35)$$

The expression for the restored image in terms of observed image and the restoration filter is given by

$$f'[m,n] = g[m,n] * w[m,n] \qquad (5.36)$$

```
#Inverse filter in the presence of noise
import numpy as np
import matplotlib.pyplot as plt
import cv2
img=cv2.imread('Clock.tiff',0); #Step1: Read the noise free image
IMG=np.fft.fft2(img); #Step 2: Fourier transform of the input image
IMG=np.fft.fftshift(IMG)
#Step 3: Define the Gaussian blur
M,D0,mean,var=255,10,0,0.1
x=np.linspace(-M/2,M/2,M+1)
y=np.linspace(-M/2,M/2,M+1)
X,Y=np.meshgrid(x,y)
D=np.sqrt(X**2+Y**2)
H=np.exp(-D**2/(2*D0**2))
W=np.zeros([256,256])
G=np.multiply(IMG,H); #Step 4: Multiply the spectrum of image with Gaussian blur
blurred_img=np.fft.ifft2(np.fft.ifftshift(G))
sigma = var**0.5
gauss_noise=np.random.normal(mean,sigma,(256,256))
G_noisy=np.add((blurred_img),gauss_noise); #Step 5: Adding noise to the image
#Step 6: Define the pseudo Inverse filter
for i in range(H.shape[0]):
    for j in range(H.shape[1]):
        if H[i,j]<=0.01:
            W[i,j]=0
        else:
            W[i,j]=1/H[i,j]
G_Noisy=np.fft.fft2(G_noisy)
G_Noisy=np.fft.fftshift(G_Noisy)
F_hat=np.multiply(G_Noisy,W)
F_hat=np.nan_to_num(F_hat)
res_img=np.fft.ifft2(np.fft.ifftshift(F_hat))
plt.figure(figsize=(8,6)),plt.subplot(1,4,1),plt.imshow(img,cmap='gray'),
plt.title('Input image'),plt.xticks([]),plt.yticks([]),plt.subplot(1,4,2),plt.imshow(H,cmap='gray'),
plt.title('Blurring function'),plt.axis('off'),plt.subplot(1,4,3),
plt.imshow(np.real(G_noisy),cmap='gray'),plt.title('Blurred noisy image')
plt.xticks([]),plt.yticks([]),plt.subplot(1,4,4),plt.imshow(np.abs(res_img),cmap='gray'),
plt.title('Pseudo Inverse output'),plt.xticks([]),plt.yticks([])
plt.tight_layout()
```

Fig. 5.85 Python code that performs the pseudo—inverse filtering of the degraded noisy image

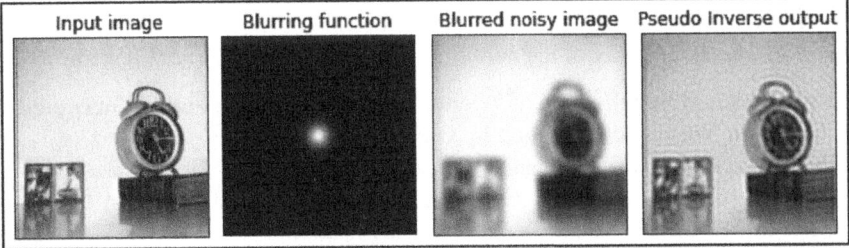

Fig. 5.86 Result of Python code shown in Fig. 5.85

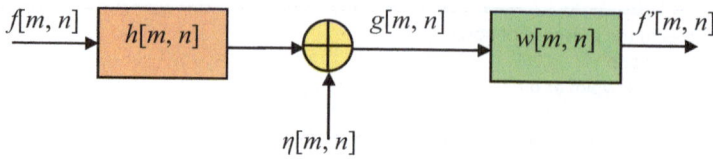

Fig. 5.87 Framework of image restoration

Upon taking Fourier transform of Eq. (5.35), we get

$$G[k,l] = F[k,l] \times H[k,l] + N[k,l] \tag{5.37}$$

Equation (5.37) is obtained using the fact that convolution in spatial domain is equivalent to multiplication in the frequency domain.

The expression for the Wiener filter can be written as

$$W[k,l] = \frac{H^*[k,l]}{H[k,l]H^*[k,l] + \dfrac{S_N[k,l]}{S_f[k,l]}} \tag{5.38}$$

where $H[k,l]$ represents the Fourier transform of the blurring filter, $S_N[k, l]$ denotes the power spectral density of noisy components, and $S_f[k,l]$ indicates the power spectral density of the original input image.

Let $K = \dfrac{S_N[k,l]}{S_f[k,l]}$, then Eq. (5.38) can be written as

$$W[k,l] = \frac{H^*[k,l]}{H[k,l]H^*[k,l] + K} \tag{5.39}$$

If $K = 0$, the above equation can be written as

$$W[k,l] = \frac{1}{H[k,l]} \tag{5.40}$$

From Eq. (5.40), it is possible to state that Wiener filter behaves like inverse filter in the absence of noise.

Drawback of Wiener Filter
To construct Wiener filter, the power spectral density of the undegraded image and the power spectral density of the noise must be known, which is not often known.

Experiment 5.39: Application of Wiener Filter to an Image that is Corrupted by Gaussian Noise and Degraded by Out-of-Focus Blur
In this experiment, the following steps are carried out:

Step 1: The input image that is free from noise and degradation is read.

Step 2: Out-of-focus blur with radius $R = 7$ is generated.

Step 3: The Fourier transform of the noise-free image and out-of-focus blur function are taken.

Step 4: In order to create a blurred image, the results of Step 3 are multiplied, and the inverse Fourier transform is computed.

Step 5: In order to create a noisy image, the result of Step 4 is corrupted by additive white Gaussian noise with zero mean and variance = 10.

Step 6: The Fourier transform of noisy image is taken.

Step 7: Wiener filter is obtained with $K = 0.03$, where "K" represents noise-to-signal ratio.

Step 8: The results of Steps 6 and 7 are multiplied, and the inverse Fourier transform is used to obtain the restored image.

The Python code that performs the above-mentioned task is shown in Fig. 5.88, and the corresponding output is shown in Fig. 5.89.

```
#Wiener filter for out-of-focus blur
import numpy as np
import matplotlib.pyplot as plt
import cv2
img=cv2.imread('cameraman.tif',0);#Step 1: Read the input image
#Step2: Adding Gaussian noise to the image
row,col= img.shape
mean, var, R = 0, 10, 7
IMG= np.fft.fftshift(np.fft.fft2(img));#Ste p 3: Taking the FT of the input image
#Step 4: Creating out-of-focus blur kernel
blur=np.zeros([row,col])
for i in range(row):
    for j in range(col):
            D=((i-np.floor(row/2))**2 + (j-np.floor(col/2))**2)**0.5
            if (D<=R):
                blur[i, j] = 1 / (np.pi * (R ** 2))
BLUR=np.fft.fftshift(np.fft.fft2(blur));#Ste p 5: Taking the FT of the blur kernel
BLURRED_IMG=np.multiply(IMG,BLUR);#Step 6: Creating blurred image in Frequency domain
K=0.02
filter1=np.conj(BLUR)/(BLUR**2 + K);#Step7: Wiener filter step
sigma = var**0.5
gauss = np.random.normal(mean,sigma,(row,col))
gauss = gauss.reshape(row,col)
#Step 8:Obtaining the blurred image in the spatial domain
blurred_img=np.fft.ifft2(BLURRED_IMG)
blurred_img = np.abs(np.fft.ifftshift(blurred_img))
noisy_img=blurred_img+gauss
Noisy_img=np.fft.fftshift(np.fft.fft2(noisy_img));#Step 5: Taking the FT of the blur kernel
out_fre = np.nan_to_num((Noisy_img*filter1))
out = np.fft.ifft2(out_fre)
out = np.fft.ifftshift(out)
#Step 9: Plotting the results
plt.figure(figsize=(8,6)),plt.subplot(1,4,1),plt.imshow(img,cmap='gray'), plt.axis('off'),
plt.title('Noise free image'), plt.subplot(1,4,2),plt.imshow(blurred_img,cmap='gray'),
plt.title('Blurred image'), plt.axis('off'),plt.subplot(1,4,3),plt.imshow(noisy_img,cmap='gray'),
plt.title('Blur+Noise'),plt.axis('off'),plt.subplot(1,4,4),plt.imshow(np.abs(out),cmap='gray'),
plt.title('Restored image'),plt.axis('off'),plt.tight_layout()
```

Fig. 5.88 Wiener filter for an image that is degraded by out-of-focus blur and corrupted by Gaussian noise

Fig. 5.89 Result of Python code shown in Fig. 5.88

Inferences

- From Fig. 5.88, it is possible to observe that the image is blurred using the PSF of out-of-focus blur with radius $R = 7$.
- It is to be noted that increasing the radius will increase the extent of the blur. For this example, it is chosen as 7.
- The image is corrupted by Gaussian noise with variance of 10. The value of "K" chosen for restoration is 0.02.
- From Fig. 5.89, it is possible to observe that in restored image, the impact of blur is considerably reduced.

Experiment 5.40: Vary the Radius of the PSF of Out-of-Focus Blur and Observe Its Effect

In the previous experiment, the radius of PSF of out-of-focus blur is kept as 7. Now it is increased to 30 and its impact is analysed. The Python code that performs this task is shown in Fig. 5.90, and the corresponding output is shown in Fig. 5.91.

Inference

- Increasing the radius of the PSF of out-of-focus blur results in an increased extent of blur. The Wiener filter tries to restore the image, so the value of "K" has to be selected properly.

Experiment 5.41: Wiener Filter for Gaussian Blur

In this experiment, instead of out-of-focus blur, Gaussian blur is introduced and the performance of Wiener filter in the presence of Gaussian blur is analysed. The Python code that performs Wiener filtering of an image that is degraded by Gaussian blur and corrupted by Gaussian noise is shown in Fig. 5.92, and the corresponding output is shown in Fig. 5.93.

Inference

- From Fig. 5.93, it is possible to observe that the impact of blurring being reduced by the application of Wiener filter.

Experiment 5.42: Performance of Wiener Filter for Different Values of "K"

In this experiment, the performance of Wiener filter for different values of "K", namely $K = 0.0001, 0.00001, 0.000001,$ and 0.0000001, is analysed. The Python code that performs this task is shown in Fig. 5.94, and the corresponding output is shown in Fig. 5.95.

```
# #Wiener filter for out-of-focus blur
import numpy as np
import matplotlib.pyplot as plt
import cv2
img=cv2.imread('cameraman.tif',0);#Step 1: Read the input image
#Step2: Adding Gaussian noise to the image
row,col= img.shape
mean, var, R = 0, 2, 30
IMG= np.fft.fftshift(np.fft.fft2(img));#Ste p 3: Taking the FT of the input image
#Step 4: Creating out-of-focus blur kernel
blur=np.zeros([row,col])
for i in range(row):
    for j in range(col):
            D=((i-np.floor(row/2))**2 + (j-np.floor(col/2))**2)**0.5
            if (D<=R):
                blur[i, j] = 1 / (np.pi * (R ** 2))
BLUR=np.fft.fftshift(np.fft.fft2(blur));#Step 5: Taking the FT of the blur kernel
BLURRED_IMG=np.multiply(IMG,BLUR);#Step 6: Creating blurred image in Frequency
domain
K=0.0009
filter1=np.conj(BLUR)/(BLUR**2 + K);#Step7: Wiener filter step
sigma = var**0.5
gauss = np.random.normal(mean,sigma,(row,col))
gauss = gauss.reshape(row,col)
#Step 8:Obtaining the blurred image in the spatial domain
blurred_img=np.fft.ifft2(BLURRED_IMG)
blurred_img = np.abs(np.fft.ifftshift(blurred_img))
noisy_img=blurred_img+gauss
Noisy_img=np.fft.fftshift(np.fft.fft2(noisy_img));#Step 5: Taking the FT of the blur kernel
out_fre = np.nan_to_num((Noisy_img*filter1))
out = np.fft.ifft2(out_fre)
out = np.fft.ifftshift(out)
#Step 9: Plotting the results
plt.figure(figsize=(8,6)),plt.subplot(1,4,1),plt.imshow(img,cmap='gray'),
plt.title('Noise free image'),plt.axis('off'),plt.subplot(1,4,2),
plt.imshow(blurred_img,cmap='gray'),plt.title('Blurred image'), plt.axis('off')
plt.subplot(1,4,3),plt.imshow(noisy_img,cmap='gray'),plt.title('Blur+Noise')
plt.axis('off'),plt.subplot(1,4,4),plt.imshow(np.abs(out),cmap='gray'),
plt.title('Restored image'),plt.axis('off')
plt.tight_layout()
```

Fig. 5.90 Wiener filter for out-of-focus blur with blur radius $R = 30$

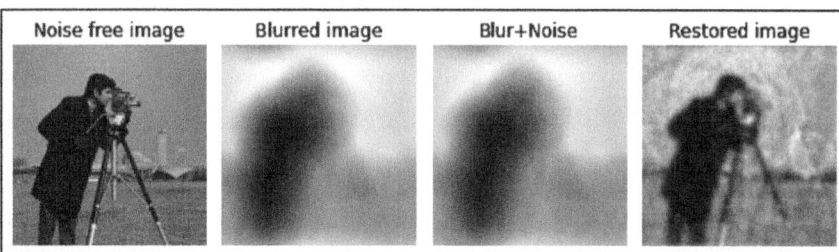

Fig. 5.91 Result of Python code shown in Fig. 5.90

```
#Wiener filter for Gaussian blur
import numpy as np
import matplotlib.pyplot as plt
import cv2
img=cv2.imread('cameraman.tif',0);#Step 1: Read the input image
row,col= img.shape
mean, var, M, D0 =0,100,255,10
sigma = var**0.5
gauss = np.random.normal(mean,sigma,(row,col))
gauss = gauss.reshape(row,col)
img1=img+gauss;#Step2: Adding Gaussian noise to the image
#Step 3: Taking the FT of the input image
IMG= np.fft.fftshift(np.fft.fft2(img1))
#Step 4: Creating Gaussian blur kernel
x=np.linspace(-M/2,M/2,M+1)
y=np.linspace(-M/2,M/2,M+1)
X,Y=np.meshgrid(x,y)
D=np.sqrt(X**2+Y**2)
blur=np.exp(-D**2/(2*D0**2))
#Step 5: Taking the FT of the blur kernel
BLUR=np.fft.fftshift(np.fft.fft2(blur))
BLURRED_IMG=np.multiply(IMG,BLUR);#Step 6: Creating blurred image in Frequency domain
K=0.01
filter1=np.conj(BLUR)/(BLUR**2 + K);#Step7: Wiener filter step
sigma = var**0.5
gauss = np.random.normal(mean,sigma,(row,col))
gauss = gauss.reshape(row,col)
#Step 8: Obtaining the blurred image in the spatial domain
blurred_img=np.fft.ifft2(BLURRED_IMG)
blurred_img = np.abs(np.fft.ifftshift(blurred_img))
noisy_img=blurred_img+gauss
Noisy_img=np.fft.fftshift(np.fft.fft2(noisy_img));#Step 5: Taking the FT of the blur kernel
out_fre = np.nan_to_num((Noisy_img*filter1))
out = np.fft.ifft2(out_fre)
out = np.fft.ifftshift(out)
#Step 9: Plotting the results
plt.figure(figsize=(8,6)),plt.subplot(1,4,1),plt.imshow(img,cmap='gray'), plt.axis('off'),
plt.title('Noise free image'), plt.subplot(1,4,2),plt.imshow(blurred_img,cmap='gray'),
plt.title('Blurred image'),plt.axis('off'),plt.subplot(1,4,3),plt.imshow(noisy_img,cmap='gray'),
plt.title('Blur+Noise'),plt.axis('off'),plt.subplot(1,4,4),plt.imshow(np.abs(out),cmap='gray'),
plt.title('Restored image'),plt.axis('off'),plt.tight_layout()
```

Fig. 5.92 Wiener filter for Gaussian blur

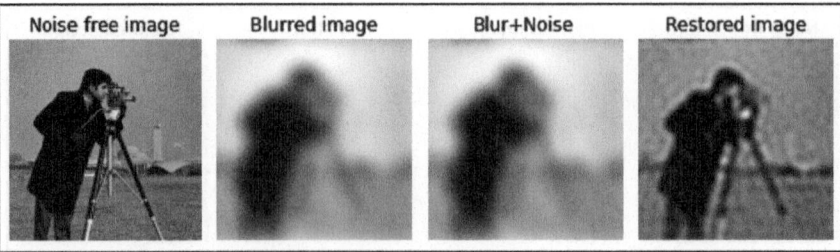

Fig. 5.93 Result of Python code shown in Fig. 5.92

```
#Wiener filter for Gaussian blur
import numpy as np
import matplotlib.pyplot as plt
import cv2
#Step 1: Read the input image
img=cv2.imread('cameraman.tif',0)
#Step2: Adding Gaussian noise to the image
row,col= img.shape
mean, var, M, D0 = 0, 100, 255, 50
sigma = var**0.5
gauss = np.random.normal(mean,sigma,(row,col))
gauss = gauss.reshape(row,col)
img1=img+gauss
#Step 3: Taking the FT of the input image
IMG= np.fft.fftshift(np.fft.fft2(img1))
#Step 4: Creating Gaussian blur kernel
x=np.linspace(-M/2,M/2,M+1)
y=np.linspace(-M/2,M/2,M+1)
X,Y=np.meshgrid(x,y)
D=np.sqrt(X**2+Y**2)
blur=np.exp(-D**2/(2*D0**2))
#Step 5: Taking the FT of the blur kernel
BLUR=np.fft.fftshift(np.fft.fft2(blur))
#Step 6: Creating blurred image in Frequency domain
BLURRED_IMG=np.multiply(IMG,BLUR)
#Step7: Wiener filter step
K=[0.0001,0.00001,0.000001,0.0000001]
fig = plt.figure(figsize=(8,6))
for i in range(len(K)):
    filter1=np.conj(BLUR)/(BLUR**2 + K[i])
    out_fre = np.nan_to_num(BLURRED_IMG* filter1)
    out = np.fft.ifftshift(out_fre)
    out = np.abs(np.fft.ifft2(out))
    plt.subplot(1, 4,i+1),plt.imshow(out,cmap='gray'), plt.title(f'K = {K[i]}'),plt.axis('off')
plt.tight_layout()
```

Fig. 5.94 Python code of Wiener filter for different values of "*K*"

Fig. 5.95 Result of Python code shown in Fig. 5.94

Inference

- From Fig. 5.95, it is possible to observe that the performance of the Wiener filter is better for lower values of "K". As the value of "K" is less, the quality of the restored image is good.

5.12.4   Total Variation Filter

Total variation filter was developed by Rudin, Osher, and Fatemi in the year 1992. Total variation denoising algorithm is an effective filtering method for recovering piece-wise constant signals. Total variation filter is often used for image denoising and image restoration.

Total Variation

The total variation (TV) of a signal measures how much the signal changes between signal values. For the total variation of the 1D signal ($x[n]$) with a length of N is written as

$$TV(x) = \sum_{n=2}^{N} \left| x[n] - x[n-1] \right| \tag{5.41}$$

The total variation of "x" can also be written as using l_1 norm, which is given by

$$TV(x) = Dx_1 \tag{5.42}$$

where the matrix D is written as

$$D = \begin{bmatrix} -1 & 1 & 0 & \cdots & 0 \\ 0 & -1 & 1 & \cdots & 0 \\ \vdots & \vdots & \ddots & \vdots & \vdots \\ 0 & 0 & \cdots & 1 & 0 \\ 0 & 0 & \cdots & -1 & 1 \end{bmatrix} \tag{5.43}$$

with a size of (N—1) × N.

Total Variation Denoising

Let us assume the signal "x" is corrupted by additive white Gaussian noise (η). The corrupted signal is denoted as "y". The mathematical expression of the corrupted image is given by

$$y = x + \eta, \quad y, x, \eta \in \mathbb{R}^N \tag{5.44}$$

The objective of the total variation denoising algorithm is to estimate "x" from "y" by minimizing the objective function, which is given as follows:

$$J(x) = y - x_2^2 + \lambda Dx_1 \tag{5.45}$$

where λ is the regularization parameter, which controls the smoothness of the output signal. If the noise content is large, then λ value will be chosen as large.

Total Variation Denoising Algorithm

The main objective function of the total variation denoising algorithm is given by

$$J(x) = y - x_2^2 + \lambda Dx_1$$

where D is the $M \times N$ matrix, and the optimal value of the objective function is defined as

$$J^*(x) = \min_x y - x_2^2 + \lambda Dx_1 \tag{5.46}$$

The objective function in Eq. (5.46) is a minimization function and is complicated because differentiation of l_1 norm is not possible. Hence, the dual formulation method can minimize the objective function $J(x)$.

Let us consider the absolute value of a signal "x" is a scalar for deriving the dual formulation, which is written as

$$|x| = \max_{|z| \le 1} zx \tag{5.47}$$

Equation (5.47) is a circuitous form and its advantage is that the non-differentiability of the function is converted to the feasible set. Hence, Eq. (5.47) can be written as

$$x_1 = \max_{|z| \le 1} z^T x \tag{5.48}$$

where the condition $|z| \le 1$ is considered as element wise. Similarly,

$$Dx_1 = \max_{|z| \le 1} z^T Dx \tag{5.49}$$

Substituting Eq. (5.49) in the Eq. (5.45), we get

$$J(x) = y - x_2^2 + \lambda \max_{|z| \le 1} z^T Dx \tag{5.50}$$

The above equation can be rewritten as

$$J(x) = \max_{|z| \le 1} y - x_2^2 + \lambda z^T Dx \tag{5.51}$$

The optimal value of the objective function can be written as

$$J^*(x) = \min_x \max_{|z| \le 1} y - x_2^2 + \lambda z^T Dx \tag{5.52}$$

To obtain the minimizing vector "x", it has to be obtained both "x" and auxiliary vector "z". The function of the vector (x, z) in Eq. (5.52) is defined as

$$F(x,z) = y - x_2^2 + \lambda z^T Dx \tag{5.53}$$

Substituting Eq. (5.53) in Eq. (5.52), we get

$$J^*(x) = \min_x \max_{|z| \le 1} F(x,z) \tag{5.54}$$

The function $(F(x, z))$ is convex in "x" and concave in "z", the optimal value $J^*(x)$ is a saddle point of $F(x, z)$. Using min-max property, Eq. (5.54) can be rewritten as

$$J^*(x) = \max_{|z| \le 1} \min_x F(x,z) \tag{5.55}$$

Now, substituting Eq. (5.53) in Eq. (5.55), we get

$$J^*(x) = \max_{|z| \le 1} \min_x y - x_2^2 + \lambda z^T Dx \tag{5.56}$$

Equation (5.56) denotes the dual formulation of the total variation denoising problem. To obtain the optimal value $J^*(x)$, taking the partial derivative of Eq. (5.56) with respect to "x" and equating the result to zero, we get

$$\frac{\partial J(x)}{\partial x} = -2(y - x) + \lambda D^T z = 0$$

Simplifying the above equation, we get

$$(y - x) = \frac{\lambda D^T z}{2} \tag{5.57}$$

and

$$x = y - \frac{\lambda D^T z}{2} \tag{5.58}$$

Substituting Eqs. (5.57) and (5.58) in Eq. (5.56), we get

$$J^*(x) = \max_{|z| \le 1} \frac{\lambda D^T z}{2}^2 + \lambda z^T D\left(y - \frac{\lambda D^T z}{2}\right)$$

Simplifying the above equation, we get

$$J^*(x) = \max_{|z| \le 1} -\frac{\lambda^2}{4} z^T DD^T z + \lambda z^T Dy \tag{5.59}$$

Equation (5.59) is a maximization problem and it is converted into a minimization problem, the above equation can be rewritten as

$$z^* = \underset{|z| \le 1}{\arg\min}\, z^T DD^T z - \frac{4}{\lambda} z^T Dy \tag{5.60}$$

To obtain the optimum value of z^*, differentiating the above equation with respect to "z" and equating the result it to zero, we get

$$\frac{\partial z^*}{\partial z} = 2DD^T z - \frac{4}{\lambda} Dy = 0 \tag{5.61}$$

and

$$DD^T z = \frac{2}{\lambda} Dy \tag{5.62}$$

Solving Eq. (5.62) requires a potentially large system of linear equations and, furthermore, does not yield a solution "z" satisfying the constraint $|z| \le 1$. Therefore, to find "z", this problem has to be treated as a constraint minimization problem and it can be achieved by using majorization–minimization approach. Hence, let us consider the function in Eq. (5.60) as

$$A(z) = z^T DD^T z - \frac{4}{\lambda} z^T Dy \tag{5.63}$$

And setting "$z^{(i)}$" as point of coincidence, a separable majorizer of $A(z)$ by adding the non-negative function, $(z - z^{(i)})^T(\alpha I - DD^T)(z - z^{(i)})$ to $A(z)$, we get

$$A(z) + \left(z - z^{(i)}\right)^T \left(\alpha I - DD^T\right)\left(z - z^{(i)}\right) \tag{5.64}$$

where α is greater than or equal to the maximum eigenvalue of DD^T. Using the majorization–minimization method, the update equation for "z" is given by

$$z^{(i+1)} = \underset{|z| \le 1}{\arg\min}\, A(z) + \left(z - z^{(i)}\right)^T \left(\alpha I - DD^T\right)\left(z - z^{(i)}\right) \tag{5.65}$$

Simplifying the above equation, we get

$$z^{(i+1)} = \underset{|z| \le 1}{\arg\min}\, zz^T - 2\left(\frac{1}{\alpha} D\left(\frac{2}{\lambda} y - D^T z^{(i)}\right) + z^{(i)}\right)^T z \tag{5.66}$$

To find the optimum value of "z" with the constraint of $|z| \le 1$, first let us consider the scalar form of above equation, we get

$$J_1(z) = \underset{|z| \le 1}{\arg\min}\, z^2 - 2bz \tag{5.67}$$

Now, differentiating the above equation with respect to "z" and equating it to zero, we get

$$\frac{\partial J_1(z)}{\partial z} = 2z - 2b = 0;$$

$$z = b \tag{5.68}$$

Therefore, the minimum of the function, $z^2 - 2bz$, is at $z = b$. If $|b| \leq 1$, then the solution is $z = b$, and this solution also can be seen as $z = \text{sign}(b)$. Therefore, the final solution of this function is in the form of a "Clip function", and it is defined as

$$\text{Clip}(b,T) = \begin{cases} b, & \text{for } |b| \leq T \\ T\text{sign}(b), & \text{for } |b| > T \end{cases} \tag{5.69}$$

Based on Eq. (5.69), the "z" update equation can be written as

$$z^{(i+1)} = \text{Clip}\left(z^{(i)} + \frac{1}{\alpha} D\left(\frac{2}{\lambda} y - D^T z^{(i)} \right), 1 \right) \tag{5.70}$$

where "i" is the iteration index and once the $z^{(i)}$ is converged then the signal $x = y - \lambda \frac{D^T z}{2}$. The optimization problem is convex and the iteration will converge from any initialization. This algorithm is also called as "*iterative clipping algorithm*".

Chambolle's Projection Algorithm

The Chambolle's project algorithm can be used for minimizing the total variation of a grayscale image. This algorithm is working based on a dual formulation method. The algorithm of Chambolle's projection method for grayscale image denoising is given in Fig. 5.96. From this figure, it is possible to observe that y is the noisy input image and z is the denoised image.

Algorithm: Chambolle's Projection approach for TV denoising of a grayscale image
Input: A noisy image $y[i,j]$ with a size of $N \times N$, a trade-off parameter $\lambda > 0$, a time step parameter($\delta_t > 0$) and an algorithm tolerance ($\tau > 0$).
$p = 0$
while $\max\limits_{1 \leq i,j \leq N} \{|p^{n+1}[i,j] - p^n[i,j]|\} > \tau$ **do**

    for all pixel $[i,j]$ in the image **do**

    $p(i,j) \leftarrow \frac{p[i,j] + \delta_t D(div\, p - \lambda \eta)[i,j]}{1 + \delta_t |D(div\, p - \lambda \eta)[i,j]|}$

    end *for*

end **while**
Return $z = \eta - \frac{1}{\lambda} div\, p$.
Output: The denoised image $z[i,j]$ as a $N \times N$ matrix.

Fig. 5.96 Chambolle's projection algorithm for TV denoising

```
#Total Variation denoising
import matplotlib.pyplot as plt
from skimage.restoration import denoise_tv_chambolle
from skimage import data, img_as_float
from skimage.util import random_noise
import cv2
Ori_img = cv2.imread('cameraman.tif',0)
sigma,weight = 0.05,[0.1,0.3,0.5,0.8]
noisy = random_noise(Ori_img, var=sigma**2)
fig=plt.figure(figsize=(8,6)),plt.subplot(2,3,1),plt.imshow(Ori_img,cmap='gray')
plt.title('Original Image'),plt.axis('off'),plt.subplot(2,3,2),plt.imshow(noisy,cmap='gray')
plt.title('Noisy Image'),plt.axis('off'),
for i in range(len(weight)):
    Denoise=denoise_tv_chambolle(noisy, weight=weight[i], channel_axis=-1)
    plt.subplot(2,3,3+i),plt.imshow(Denoise,cmap='gray')
    plt.title('Denoised with Weight.{}'.format(weight[i])),plt.axis('off')
plt.tight_layout()
```

Fig. 5.97 Python code of Chambolle TV denoising algorithm

Experiment 5.43: Implementation of Total Variation Denoising Algorithm

This experiment deals with the implementation of total variation denoising algorithm to remove additive white Gaussian noise in an input image. The Cameraman image is read and it is corrupted by additive white Gaussian noise. The corrupted image is passed through total variation denoising algorithm to get denoised image. The Python code to perform the above-mentioned task is given in Fig. 5.97, and its corresponding output is shown in Fig. 5.98.

Inferences

The following inferences can be drawn from this experiment:

- Figure 5.97 shows that the "denoise_tv_chambolle" Python command is imported from "skimage" library. Additive white Gaussian noise is added into the original input image by "random_noise" command. The weight factor (λ) is varied from 0.1 to 0.8.
- From Fig. 5.98, it is possible to infer that the weight factor (λ) increases the burring effect in the denoised image. Therefore, the selection of the weight factor is important in the total variation denoising algorithm.

Exercises

1. Write a Python code to prove that the median filter is a non-linear filter.
2. Write a Python code to prove that the mean filter is a linear filter.
3. Verify that the maximum filter is a non-linear filter.
4. Prove that the minimum operator is a non-linear operator.

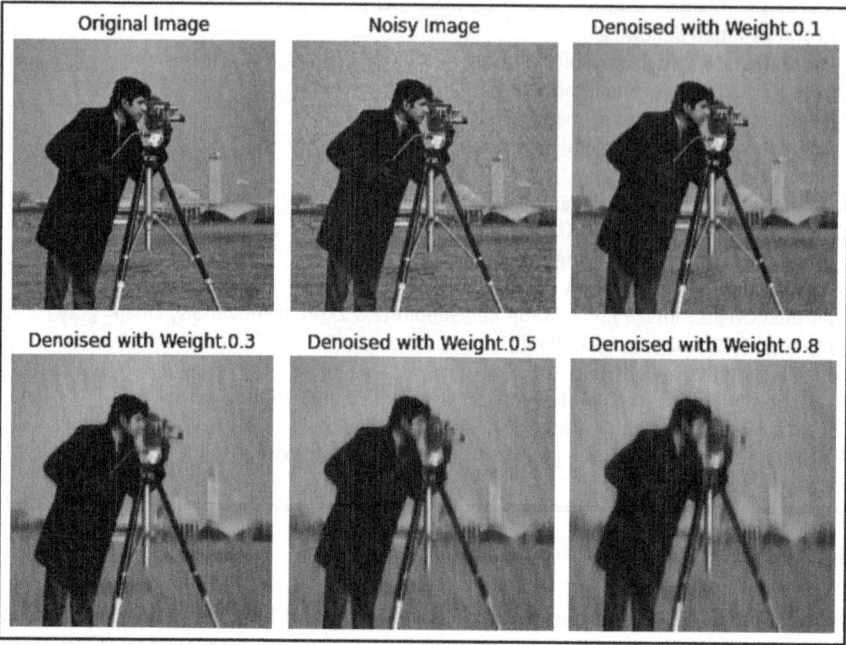

Fig. 5.98 Result of Chambolle's TV denoising algorithm

5. Read the input image and degrade the input image using motion blur. The angle of the blur is kept as 0°, and the distance is varied as 10, 25, 50, and 100 units. Plot the degraded image and comment on the obtained image.
6. In this experiment, fix the distance as of motion blur PSF as 50 units and vary the angle 0°, 45°, 90°, and 135°. Apply this PSF to the input image and comment on the observed output.

Objective Questions

1. Assertion: Maximum filter is a non-linear filter

Reason: Maximum filter violates superposition principle

(A) Assertion and reason are true
(B) Assertion is true, reason is false
(C) Assertion is false, reason may be true
(D) Assertion and reason are false

2. Random occurrence of gray levels "0" and "255" in an 8-bit image is termed as

(A) Periodic noise
(B) Salt and pepper noise
(C) Speckle noise
(D) Gaussian noise

3. An example of a linear filter is

   (A) Minimum filter
   (B) Maximum filter
   (C) Median filter
   (D) Mean filter

4. The filter that is effective in minimizing the impact of salt and pepper noise in digital image is

   (A) Minimum filter
   (B) Maximum filter
   (C) Median filter
   (D) Mean filter

5. Identify the filter that is linear

   (A) Minimum filter
   (B) Maximum filter
   (C) Median filer
   (D) Mean filter

6. Assertion: Median filtering can be implemented efficiently using convolution
Reason: Median filter is a non-linear filter that cannot be implemented via convolution

   (A) Assertion and reason are true
   (B) Assertion is true, reason is false
   (C) Assertion is false, reason may be true
   (D) Assertion and reason are false

7. Statement 1: Mean filter is a non-linear filter
Statement 2: Median filter is a linear filter

   (A) Statements 1 and 2 are true
   (B) Statement 1 is true, Statement 2 is false
   (C) Statement 1 is false, Statement 2 is true
   (D) Statements 1 and 2 are false

8. Median filter is

   (A) Linear filter
   (B) Order statistic filter
   (C) Sharpening filter
   (D) Frequency domain filter

9. The following Python code generates

```
import numpy as np
import matplotlib.pyplot as plt
img=np.zeros([256,256])
R=50
rows=1
columns=2
for i in range(0,256):
    for j in range(0,256):
        D=((i-128)**2 + (j-128)**2)**0.5
        if(D<=R):
            img[i,j]=1/(np.pi*R**2)
```

(A) Out-of-focus blur
(B) Motion blur
(C) Atmospheric turbulence blur
(D) Gaussian blur

10. Wiener filter is an optimal filter with respect to minimum

(A) Absolute error
(B) Mean square error
(C) Mean absolute error
(D) Root mean square error

11. The process of moving a filter mask over the image and computing the sum of product at each location is termed as

(A) Splicing
(B) Convolution
(C) Spectral estimation
(D) Transform

12. Wavelet decomposition decomposes the image into

(A) Space–space representation
(B) Space–frequency representation
(C) Scale–space representation
(D) Space–orientation representation

13. The expression for peak signal-to-noise ratio (PSNR) for 8-bit image representation is

(A) $10\log_{10}\left(\dfrac{255^2}{MSE}\right)$

(B) $10\log_{10}\left(\dfrac{127^2}{MSE}\right)$

(C) $10\log_{10}\left(\dfrac{63^2}{MSE}\right)$

(D) $10\log_{10}\left(\dfrac{31^2}{MSE}\right)$

14. An example of multiplicative noise is

    (A) Gaussian noise
    (B) Salt and pepper noise
    (C) Speckle noise
    (D) Periodic noise

15. The point spread function $h[m,n] = \begin{cases} \dfrac{1}{\pi R^2}, & if \ \sqrt{m^2 + n^2} \le R, \\ 0, & otherwise. \end{cases}$ represents

    (A) No blur
    (B) Out-of-focus blur
    (C) Atmospheric turbulence blur
    (D) Motion blur

Answers to Objective Questions

Q. No.	1	2	3	4	5	6	7	8	9	10
Key	A	B	D	C	D	C	D	B	A	B
Q. No.	11	12	13	14	15					
Key	B	C	A	C	B					

Answers to PreLab Questions

1. Examples of non-linear filters include median filter, Bilateral filter, non-local mean filter, and morphological filter. The non-linear filters effectively suppress non-Gaussian noise, such as spike noise, while preserving the edge information.

2. A filter is considered as a non-linear filter if it does not obey superposition principle. Superposition principle involves (1) homogeneity property and (2) additivity property. The median filter violates the additivity property; hence it is non-linear.

3. Bilateral filter considers both spatial and depth statistics. It can smooth the image as well as it can preserve the edge information in the image. The smoothing effect allows it to minimize the impact of Gaussian noise and salt and pepper noise.

4. Advantages of bilateral filter:

    (a) Bilateral filter performance depends on the choice of domain and range parameters. Improper choice of domain parameter leads to over-smoothing, and inappropriate choice of range parameter leads to insufficient noise reduction.
    (b) Bilateral filter is computationally intensive due to the calculation of spatial and range domains.

5. First, the detection of periodic noise is done using Fourier transform. After knowing the frequency of occurrence of the noise, a notch filter can be used to minimize the impact of periodic noise.

6. Gaussian smoothing is a good option if the image is corrupted with white Gaussian noise. Median filter is an effective tool if the image is corrupted with salt and pepper noise.

7. The degradation function is linear if it obeys superposition principle. According to superposition principle, the operation is linear if it obeys both homogeneity and additive property. The degradation function is shift invariant if the following criteria is satisfied:

If $H[f(x, y)] = g(x, y)$, then $H[f(x - a, y - b)] = g(x - a, y - b)$.

8. The image degradation process is depicted in figure. In figure, if the degradation function $h[m, n]$ is assumed to be linear and shift-invariant, then the expression   for   the   observed   image   is   given   by

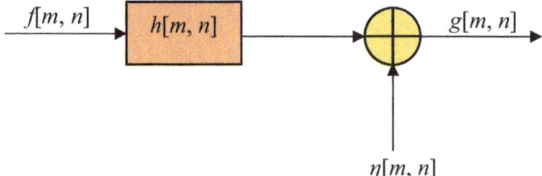

$$\eta[m, n]$$

It is to be known that convolution holds good if the degradation is assumed to be linear and shift invariant.

9. Some of the ways to estimate the degradation function are (1) through mathematical modelling, (2) through observation, and (3) through experimentation.

10. Wiener filter is an optimal filter with respect to minimum mean square error. Wiener filter attempts to minimize the mean square error between the observed signal and the desired signal.

Bibliography

1. Bahadir K. Gunturk, Xin Li, "Image Restoration: Fundamentals and Advances", CRC Press, 2012.
2. Rafael C. Gonzalez and Richard E. Woods, "Digital Image Processing", Pearson Education, 2018.
3. John C. Russ, "The Image Processing Handbook", CRC Press, 2015.
4. Alan C. Bovik, "The Essential Guide to Image Processing", Academic Press, 2009.
5. John W. Woods, "Multidimensional Signal, Image, and Video Processing and Coding", Academic Press, 2011.
6. L. Rudin, S. Osher, and E. Fatemi, "Nonlinear total variation based noise removal algorithms", Physica D, Vol. 60, pp.259-268, 1992.

Chapter 6
Morphological Image Processing

Learning Objectives

After reading this chapter, the reader is expected to

- Understand the operators in morphological image processing.
- Know the impact of dilation and erosion operations.
- Understand the significance of opening and closing operations.
- Use the morphological operations for image processing applications, such as denoising, detection, and so on.
- Perform basic morphological operations on grayscale image.

Roadmap of the Chapter

The roadmap of this chapter is given in the form of a flow diagram, shown in Fig. 6.1.

PreLab Questions

1. What do you mean by morphological image processing?
2. What is a structuring element? Briefly explain the significance of it.
3. List out the basic morphological operations.
4. Compare opening and closing morphological operations.
5. How did you extract the boundary of the object using erosion and dilation operations?
6. What is idempotent operation? Whether opening and closing operations are idempotent?
7. What is a hit-or-miss transform? Mention the significance of it.
8. What do you mean by Top-Hat Transform (THT)? Give some applications of it.
9. How did you perform the thinning operation by using erosion or hit-or-miss transform? List out the significance of it.

Supplementary InformationThe online version contains supplementary material available at https://doi.org/10.1007/978-981-96-6382-8_6.

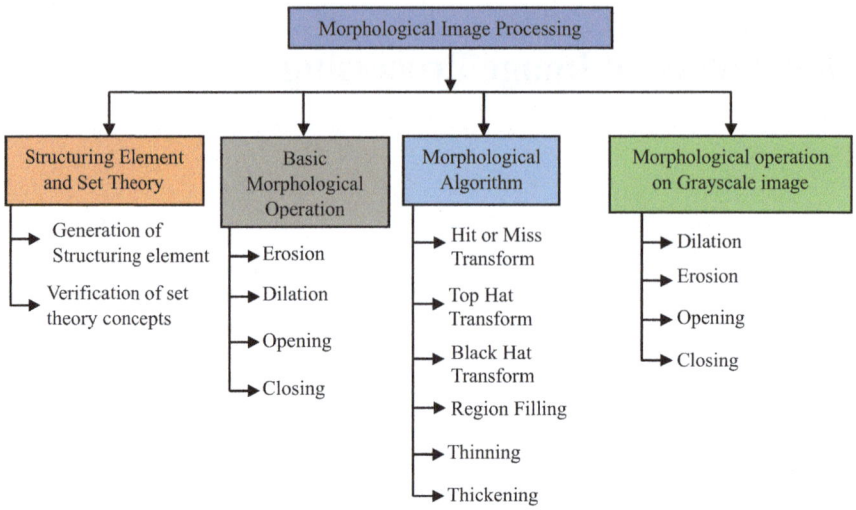

Fig. 6.1 Roadmap of this chapter

10. What do you mean by thickening? How did you perform it using basic morphological operations?
11. Can morphological operations be performed on the grayscale image? If yes, briefly explain how it could be possible.
12. What is morphological smoothing in a grayscale image?
13. What is a morphological gradient? How it could be implemented?
14. What is the difference between internal gradients, external gradients, and thick gradients?
15. Define: Directional gradient in morphological operation.

6.1   Introduction

Morphological image processing is a set of non-linear operations that are related to the shape or morphology features in an image. Morphological approaches probe an image with a small shape or template known as a structuring element. The structuring element is positioned at all possible locations in the image, and it is compared with the corresponding neighbourhood of pixels. A morphological operation on a binary image generates a new binary image in which the pixel has a non-zero value only if the test is successful at that location in the input image. Some form of morphological operation on image with a structuring element is shown in Fig. 6.2. From this figure, it is possible to observe that all the pixels in the structuring element fit on the image; it will create a new binary image as an output, and a few pixels in the structuring element fit with the image pixels, which will create a new binary image.

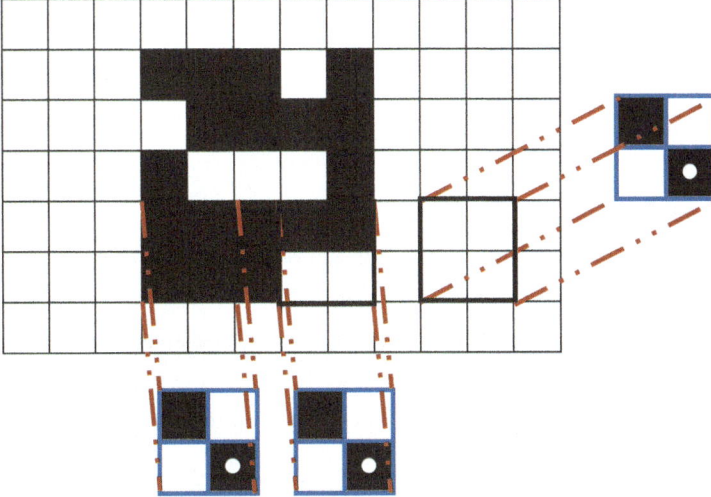

Fig. 6.2 Morphological operation using structuring element

If the pixels in the structuring element do not fit with the pixels in the input image, it will not create a new image (i.e. there is no impact of the morphological operation on the image). Therefore, a morphological operation on a binary image creates a new binary image in which the pixel has a non-zero value only if the operation is successful at that location in the input image.

6.2 Structuring Element

The structuring element is a small binary image that takes the value as either 0s or 1s. The matrix dimension specifies the size of the structuring element. The pattern of 1s and 0s represents the shape of the structuring element. The origin of the structuring element is usually one of its pixels, although generally, the origin can be outside the structuring element. In general, the centre of the element in the structuring element acts as an origin for the odd dimensions of the structuring elements. The structuring elements play an important role in morphological image processing, which is the same role as convolution kernels in linear image filtering. When a structuring element is placed on a binary image, each of its pixels is associated with the corresponding pixel of the neighbourhood under the structuring element. The structuring element is said to fit the image if the value 1 of the structuring element exactly fits into the value of 1 in the image. Similarly, a structuring element is said to hit or intersect an image if, at least for one of its pixels set to 1, the corresponding image pixel is also 1. Zero-valued pixels of the structuring element are ignored, where the corresponding image value is irrelevant.

Experiment 6.1: Generate and Display the Different Samples of Structuring Elements

This experiment discusses the generation and display of the different structuring element using Python. The Python code that generates and displays the structuring element is given in Fig. 6.3, and its corresponding output is displayed in Fig. 6.4.

Inferences

From Figs. 6.3 and 6.4, the following inferences can be made:

- h1, h2, ..., h9 stores the nine different structuring elements with the size of 3×3.
- Figure 6.2 displays the nine different structuring elements with the size of 3×3.

   Task: Generate and display the different structuring elements with the size of 5×5, 7×7, 9×9, and 11×11.

Experiment 6.2: Use the Built-in Python Command to Generate Different Structuring Elements

This experiment helps us to generate different structuring elements by using built-in Python commands. The Python code is to generate different structuring elements given in Fig. 6.5, and its corresponding output is displayed in Fig. 6.6.

```
# This program displays different kernels
import cv2
import numpy as np
import matplotlib.pyplot as plt
h1=np.array([[0., 1., 0.],[1., 1., 1.],[0., 1., 0.]],'uint8');# Structuring Element
h2=np.array([[1., 0., 0.],[0., 1., 0.],[0., 0., 1.]],'uint8');# Structuring Element
h3=np.array([[0., 0., 1.],[0., 1., 0.],[1., 0., 0.]],'uint8');# Structuring Element
h4=np.array([[0., 0., 0.],[1., 1., 1.],[0., 0., 0.]],'uint8');# Structuring Element
h5=np.array([[0., 0., 0.],[0., 1., 1.],[0., 1., 1.]],'uint8');# Structuring Element
h6=np.array([[1., 1., 0.],[1., 1., 0.],[0., 0., 0.]],'uint8');# Structuring Element
h7=np.array([[0., 0., 0.],[1., 1., 0.],[1., 1., 0.]],'uint8');# Structuring Element
h8=np.array([[1., 0., 1.],[0., 1., 0.],[1., 0., 1.]],'uint8');# Structuring Element
h9=np.array([[0., 1., 0.],[0., 1., 0.],[0., 1., 0.]],'uint8');# Structuring Element
plt.subplot(3,3,1),plt.imshow(h1,cmap='gray'),plt.title('Struct. Element 1')
plt.xticks([]),plt.yticks([]),plt.subplot(3,3,2),plt.imshow(h2,cmap='gray'),
plt.title('Struct. Element 2'),plt.xticks([]),plt.yticks([]),plt.subplot(3,3,3),
plt.imshow(h3,cmap='gray'),plt.title('Struct. Element 3'),plt.xticks([]),plt.yticks([])
plt.subplot(3,3,4),plt.imshow(h4,cmap='gray'),plt.title('Struct. Element 4')
plt.xticks([]),plt.yticks([]),plt.subplot(3,3,5),plt.imshow(h5,cmap='gray'),
plt.title('Struct. Element 5'),plt.xticks([]),plt.yticks([]),plt.subplot(3,3,6),
plt.imshow(h6,cmap='gray'),plt.title('Struct. Element 6'),plt.xticks([]),plt.yticks([])
plt.subplot(3,3,7),plt.imshow(h7,cmap='gray'),plt.title('Struct. Element 7')
plt.xticks([]),plt.yticks([]),plt.subplot(3,3,8),plt.imshow(h8,cmap='gray'),
plt.title('Struct. Element 8'),plt.xticks([]),plt.yticks([]),plt.subplot(3,3,9),
plt.imshow(h9,cmap='gray'),plt.title('Struct. Element 9'),plt.xticks([]),plt.yticks([])
plt.tight_layout()
```

Fig. 6.3 Python code for Experiment 6.1

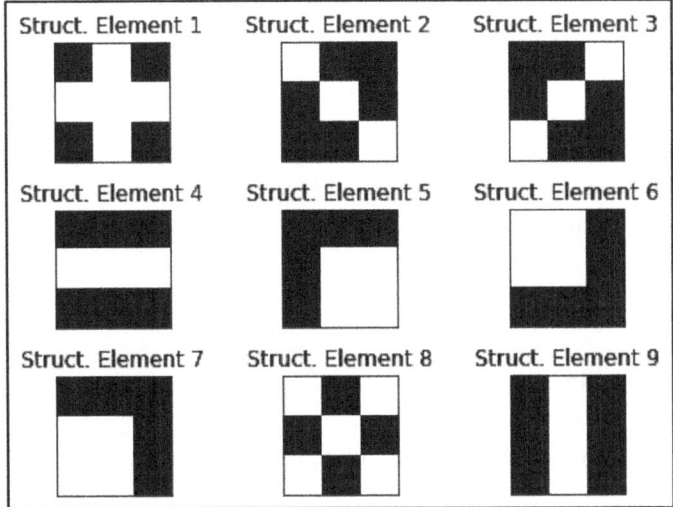

Fig. 6.4 Display of structuring elements

```
#This program is to generate Kernels using built-in command
import cv2
import matplotlib.pyplot as plt
h1=cv2.getStructuringElement(cv2.MORPH_RECT,(111,111))
h2=cv2.getStructuringElement(cv2.MORPH_ELLIPSE,(111,111))
h3=cv2.getStructuringElement(cv2.MORPH_CROSS,(111,111))
plt.subplot(1,3,1),plt.imshow(h1,cmap='binary'),plt.title('Rectangle Kernel')
plt.xticks([]),plt.yticks([]),plt.subplot(1,3,2),plt.imshow(h2,cmap='gray'),
plt.title('Ellipse Kernel'),plt.xticks([]),plt.yticks([]),plt.subplot(1,3,3),
plt.imshow(h3,cmap='gray'),plt.title('Cross Shaped Kernel')
plt.xticks([]),plt.yticks([])
plt.tight_layout()
```

Fig. 6.5 Python code for Experiment 6.2

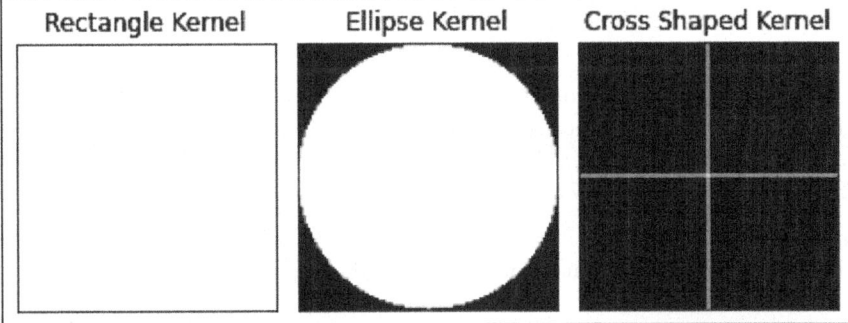

Fig. 6.6 Display of structuring elements

Inferences

The following inferences can be observed from this experiment:

- From Fig. 6.5, it is possible to observe that "cv2.getStructuringElement" command is used to obtain the square, circle, and cross kernels.
- Generated kernels are displayed in Fig. 6.6; from this result, it is possible to infer that the dimensions of the kernels are in square form.

Task: Modify the Python code given in Fig. 6.5 and generate the rectangle and elliptic kernels.

6.3   Set Theory

Set theory is important for the binary image morphological operation. The morphological operation performs the binary image processing using set theory concepts. The major set theory concepts are "OR", "AND", "NOT", and "XOR", which are defined as follows:

The "OR" operation resembles the "union" operation in the set; therefore, let A and B be two sets, then the OR operation of A and B is given by

$$OR(A,B) = A \cup B = \text{bitwise\_}OR(A,B) \tag{6.1}$$

The "AND" operation performs the "intersection" of the two sets, namely, A and B, which is written as

$$AND(A,B) = A \cap B = \text{bitwise\_}AND(A,B) \tag{6.2}$$

The "NOT" operation performs the "compliment" of a set A, which is mathematically defined as

$$NOT(A) = \bar{A} = \text{bitwise\_}NOT(A) \tag{6.3}$$

The "XOR" operation can be defined as

$$XOR(A,B) = A\bar{B} \cup \bar{A}B = \text{bitwise\_}XOR(A,B) \tag{6.4}$$

Experiment 6.3: Verification of Set Theory Concepts

The different set theory concepts such as OR, AND, NOT, and XOR operations are performed with two different binary images and its Python code and simulation result are shown in Figs. 6.7 and 6.8, respectively.

Inferences

The following inferences can be observed from this experiment:

```
# This program performs the set theory concept
import cv2
import matplotlib.pyplot as plt
I1= cv2.imread('Imag11.jpg');
I2= cv2.imread('Imag22.jpg');
OrI=cv2.bitwise_or(I1,I2)
AndI=cv2.bitwise_and(I1,I2)
NotI=cv2.bitwise_not(I1)
XorI=cv2.bitwise_xor(I1,I2)
plt.figure(figsize=(8,6)),plt.subplot(2,3,1),plt.imshow(I1),plt.title('Image 1'),
plt.xticks([]),plt.yticks([]),plt.subplot(2,3,2),plt.imshow(I2),plt.title('Image 2'),
plt.xticks([]),plt.yticks([]),plt.subplot(2,3,3),plt.imshow(OrI),plt.title('Union (OR) '),
plt.xticks([]),plt.yticks([]),plt.subplot(2,3,4),plt.imshow(AndI),plt.title('Intersection (AND)'),
plt.xticks([]),plt.yticks([]),plt.subplot(2,3,5),plt.imshow(NotI),
plt.title('Complement (NOT) of Image 1'),plt.xticks([]),plt.yticks([]),plt.subplot(2,3,6),
plt.imshow(XorI),plt.title('XOR Operation'),plt.xticks([]),plt.yticks([])
plt.tight_layout()
```

Fig. 6.7 Python code for set theory

Fig. 6.8 Simulation result of Python code given in Fig. 6.7

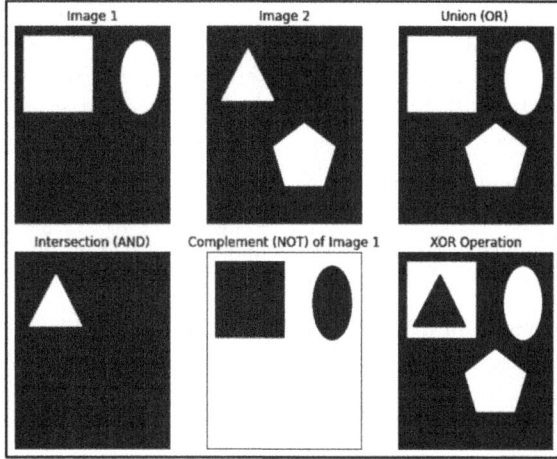

- From Fig. 6.7, it is possible to infer that "cv2" library is used for this experiment, and "bitwise_or", "bitwise_and", "bitwise_not", and "bitwise_xor" commands are used to compute the "OR", "AND", "NOT", and "XOR" operations, respectively.
- Figure 6.8 shows the simulation output of the Python code given in Fig. 6.7. In the output of union or OR operation, the "triangle"in the Image-2 is overlapped with the "square"in the Image-1. Similarly, in the output of the AND operation, the common area between Image-1 and Image-2 is retained (i.e. triangle shape).

- The complement of Image-1 shows the NOT operation, and the XOR operation output displays the common area between Image-1 and Image-2 as zero (black) and the output is one (white).

6.4 Morphological Operations

This section discusses the basic morphological operations such as (1) erosion, (2) dilation, (3) opening, and (4) closing.

6.4.1 Erosion

The erosion operation is the basic operation of morphological image processing, which decreases the number of pixels "1" in the input binary image. The erosion operation is defined as

$$X \ominus B = \left\{ x : B_x \subseteq X \right\} \tag{6.5}$$

where X denotes the input image, B represents the structuring element, and "x" is the pixels of the selected window of "X". The size of the selected window will be the size of the structuring element "B". The symbol "$\ominus$" denotes the erosion operation.

Depth of Operation
The depth of the morphological operation is defined as the number of iterations of a particular morphological operation. That is, the same operation can be performed again and again of the output.

Experiment 6.3: Write a Python Code to Perform "Erosion" Operation
This experiment discusses the erosion operation on binary image and its significance. The Python code to perform the erosion operation is shown in Fig. 6.9. The simulation result of the Python code given in Fig. 6.9 is displayed in Fig. 6.10. From Fig. 6.9, it is possible to infer that cv2 library is imported and "cv2.erode" Python command is used here to compute the erosion operation on "Image11.jpg". "iterations = 10" denotes the same operation repeats 10 times with the previous result. The structuring element is stored in the variable "h".

From Fig. 6.10, it is possible to observe that the size of the white area of the erosion output is lesser than the white area of the input image, which is confirmed by the difference output between the input image and the erosion output.

Inferences
The following inference can be made from this experiment:

```
# This program performs the erosion operation
import cv2
import numpy as np
import matplotlib.pyplot as plt
I1= cv2.imread('Imag11.jpg');
h=np.zeros((3,3),np.uint8)
for i in range(h.shape[0]):
    h[i,i]=1;
    h[i,h.shape[0]-(i+1)]=1
Er=cv2.erode(I1,h,iterations = 10)
plt.subplot(1,4,1),plt.imshow(I1),plt.title('Input Image'),plt.xticks([]),plt.yticks([])
plt.subplot(1,4,2),plt.imshow(h,cmap='gray'),plt.title('Kernel'),plt.xticks([]),plt.yticks([])
plt.subplot(1,4,3),plt.imshow(Er),plt.title('Erosion Output'),plt.xticks([]),plt.yticks([])
plt.subplot(1,4,4),plt.imshow(I1-Er),plt.title('Difference'),plt.xticks([]),plt.yticks([])
plt.tight_layout()
```

Fig. 6.9 Erosion Python code

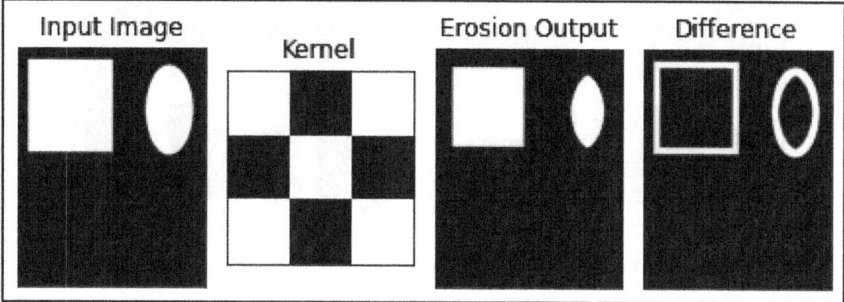

Fig. 6.10 Simulation result

- The erosion operation reduces the white pixel in the input image.
- The erosion operation on binary image is to erode away the boundaries of regions of foreground pixels.

Experiment 6.4: Remove the Salt Noise Using "Erosion"
This experiment deals with the removal of salt noise present in the input image. The Python code that provides the removal of salt noise from the input image is shown in Fig. 6.11, and its corresponding output is displayed in Fig. 6.12.

Inference
- From Fig. 6.12, it is possible to observe that the erosion operation removes the salt noise. Hence, erosion operation can be preferred to remove salt noise in image.

```
# This program performs salt noise removal using erosion
import cv2
import numpy as np
import matplotlib.pyplot as plt
I1= cv2.imread('salt_noise.jpg');
h=np.array([[0., 1., 0.],[1., 1., 1.],[0., 1., 0.]],'uint8');# Structuring Element
Op=cv2.erode(I1,h)
plt.subplot(1,3,1),plt.imshow(I1),plt.title('Input Noisy Image'),plt.xticks([]),
plt.yticks([]),plt.subplot(1,3,2),plt.imshow(h,cmap='gray'),plt.title('Kernel')
plt.xticks([]),plt.yticks([]),plt.subplot(1,3,3),plt.imshow(Op,cmap='binary'),
plt.title('Denoised Image'),plt.xticks([]),plt.yticks([])
plt.tight_layout()
```

Fig. 6.11 Python code to remove salt noise

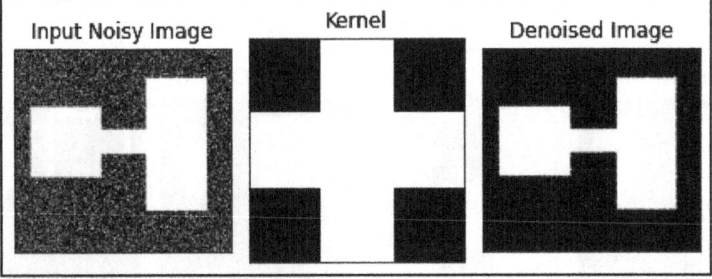

Fig. 6.12 Output of the Python code given in Fig. 6.11

6.4.2 Dilation

Dilation is another basic morphological operation, which performs the opposite operation of erosion. It increases the white pixels of the foreground object. The dilation operation is mathematically defined as

$$X \oplus B = \left\{ x : \hat{B}_x \cap X \neq \emptyset \right\} \tag{6.6}$$

where the symbol "$\oplus$" denotes the dilation operation and $\hat{B}_x$ is the reflection of structuring element "B", and it is mathematically written as

$$\hat{B} = \left\{ x : x = -b, \ for\, b \in B \right\} \tag{6.7}$$

```
# This program performs the dilation operation
import cv2
import numpy as np
import matplotlib.pyplot as plt
I1= cv2.imread('Imag11.jpg');
h=np.zeros((3,3),np.uint8)
for i in range(h.shape[0]):
    h[i,i]=1;
    h[i,h.shape[0]-(i+1)]=1
DI=cv2.dilate(I1,h,iterations = 5)
plt.subplot(1,4,1),plt.imshow(I1),plt.title('Input Image'),plt.xticks([]),plt.yticks([])
plt.subplot(1,4,2),plt.imshow(h,cmap='gray'),plt.title('Kernel')
plt.xticks([]),plt.yticks([]),plt.subplot(1,4,3),plt.imshow(DI),plt.title('Dilation Output')
plt.xticks([]),plt.yticks([]),plt.subplot(1,4,4),plt.imshow(DI-I1),plt.title('Difference')
plt.xticks([]),plt.yticks([])
plt.tight_layout()
```

Fig. 6.13 Python code for "dilation" operation

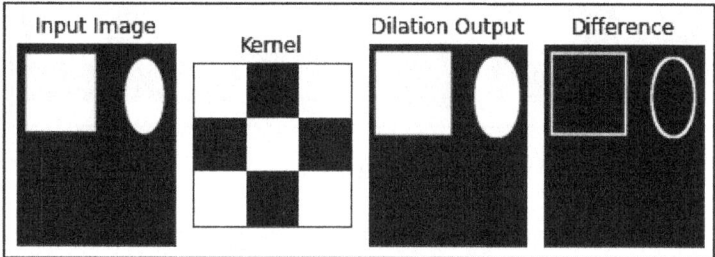

Fig. 6.14 Simulation result of "dilation" operation

Experiment 6.5: Dilation Operation

This experiment performs the dilation operation on binary image "I1" with the structuring element "h". The Python code to perform the dilation operation is given in Fig. 6.13, and its simulation result is shown in Fig. 6.14. Figure 6.13 shows that the "cv2" library is imported and "cv2.dilate" built-in Python command is used to compute the dilation output.

From Fig. 6.14, it is possible to observe that the area of white pixels in the foreground is increased by the dilation operation, which is confirmed by the difference between the dilated and input images.

Inferences

The following inferences can be drawn from this experiment:

- The dilation operation increases the white pixels of the foreground.
- The dilation operation reduces the background pixels.

```
# This program performs pepper noise removal using dilation
import cv2
import numpy as np
import matplotlib.pyplot as plt
I1= cv2.imread('pepper_noise.jpg');
h=np.array([[0., 1., 0.],[1., 1., 1.],[0., 1., 0.]],'uint8');# Structuring Element
Op=cv2.dilate(I1,h)
plt.subplot(1,3,1),plt.imshow(I1),plt.title('Input Noisy Image'),plt.xticks([]),
plt.yticks([]),plt.subplot(1,3,2),plt.imshow(h,cmap='gray'),plt.title('Kernel')
plt.xticks([]),plt.yticks([]),plt.subplot(1,3,3),plt.imshow(Op,cmap='binary'),
plt.title('Denoised Image'),plt.xticks([]),plt.yticks([])
plt.tight_layout()
```

Fig. 6.15 Python code to remove pepper noise

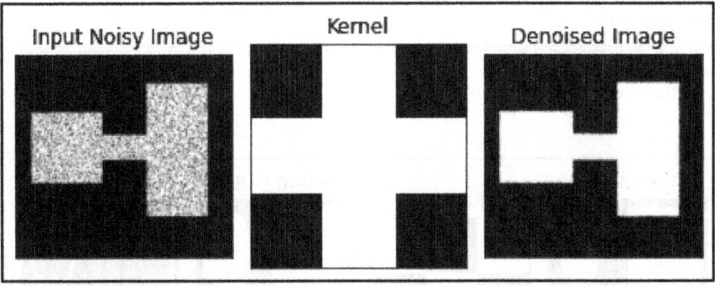

Fig. 6.16 Output of the Python code given in Fig. 6.15

- The dilation operation can be used to remove the black dots present in the foreground.

Experiment 6.6: Removal of Pepper Noise Using "Dilation"
This experiment deals with the removal of pepper noise present in the input image. The Python code that provides the removal of pepper noise from the input image is shown in Fig. 6.15, and its corresponding output is displayed in Fig. 6.16.

Inference
- From Fig. 6.16, it is possible to observe that the dilation operation removes the pepper noise. Hence, dilation operation can be preferred to remove pepper noise.

Experiment 6.7: Prove that Erosion and Dilation Operations Are Dual to Each Other
This experiment explains that the erosion and dilation operations are dual to each other using Python. "Dilation is the dual of erosion", which means that dilating foreground pixels is equivalent to eroding the background pixels. Similarly, "Erosion is the dual of Dilation", which means that eroding the foreground pixels is equivalent to dilating the background pixels.

The dilation and erosion operations are duals of each other with respect to set complementation and reflection, which is given by

$$\left(X\Theta B\right)^{c} = X^{c} \oplus \hat{B} \tag{6.8}$$

or

$$\left(X \oplus B\right)^{c} = X^{c}\Theta\hat{B} \tag{6.9}$$

Equations (6.8) and (6.9) show that erosion and dilation are dual. However, erosion is not the inverse of dilation and vice versa.

The Python code to verify the above statement is shown in Fig. 6.17, and its simulation result is shown in Fig. 6.18.

```python
# This Python code proofs dual of dilation and erosion
import cv2
import numpy as np
import matplotlib.pyplot as plt
I1= cv2.imread('Imag11.jpg');
h=np.zeros((3,3),np.uint8)
for i in range(h.shape[0]):
    h[i,i]=1;
    h[i,h.shape[0]-(i+1)]=1
Er=cv2.erode(I1,h,iterations = 1)# Erosion
Y1=cv2.bitwise_not(Er);# Complement of Erosion output
I1c=cv2.bitwise_not(I1);# Complement of input
h1=cv2.flip(h,-1);#reflection
DI=cv2.dilate(I1c,h1,iterations = 1)# Dilation
plt.subplot(1,4,1),plt.imshow(I1),plt.title('Input Image'),plt.xticks([]),plt.yticks([])
plt.subplot(1,4,2),plt.imshow(h,cmap='gray'),plt.title('Kernel'),plt.xticks([]),plt.yticks([])
plt.subplot(1,4,3),plt.imshow(Y1),plt.title('Erosion Output'),plt.xticks([]),plt.yticks([])
plt.subplot(1,4,4),plt.imshow(DI),plt.title('Dilation output'),plt.xticks([]),plt.yticks([])
plt.tight_layout()
```

Fig. 6.17 Python code for duality of erosion and dilation

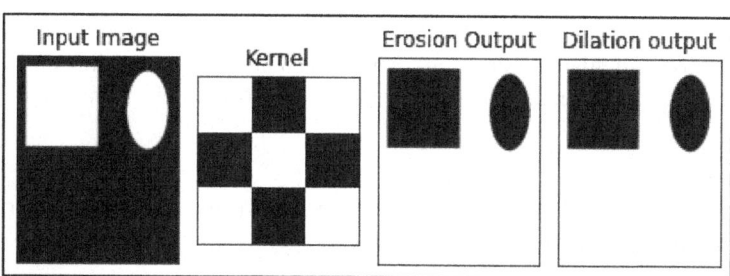

Fig. 6.18 Duality of erosion and dilation

Inferences

The following inferences can be made from this experiment:

- From Fig. 6.17, it is possible to observe that "Er" is the erosion output and "Y1" denotes the complement of erosion output, which resembles the LHS of Eq. (6.8).
- The variable "I1c" is the complement of the input image, "h1" represents the reflection of the structuring element, and "Dl" is the output of dilation, which resembles the RHS of Eq. (6.8).
- From Fig. 6.18, it is possible to infer that the results of erosion and dilation operations are the same (i.e. it confirms the duality of the erosion and dilation operations).

Task: Verify the duality of erosion and dilation equation is given by $(X \oplus B)^c = X^c \ominus \hat{B}$.

6.4.3 Boundary Extraction Using Erosion and Dilation

The boundary of the objects can be obtained by erosion and dilation operations. The erosion operation used to extract the boundary of the object is given by

$$\text{Boundary}(X) = X - (X \ominus B) \qquad (6.10)$$

where X is the input image, B is the structuring element, and Boundary (X) denotes the boundary of the input image (X). The result will be all the foreground pixels that are surrounded by the background. This will be called as "interior boundary" of the object.

The dilation operation can be used to obtain the boundary of the object, which is mathematically written as

$$\text{Boundary}(X) = (X \oplus B) - X \qquad (6.11)$$

The resultant boundary is all the background pixels, which are bordered by the foreground pixels. This will be called as "exterior boundary" of the object.

Experiment 6.8: Boundary Extraction Using "Erosion" and "Dilation"

This experiment deals with the extraction of boundary from the given input image using erosion and dilation operations. The Python code to extract the boundary of the object using erosion and dilation is given in Fig. 6.19, and its simulation result is shown in Fig. 6.20.

Inference

- From Fig. 6.20, it is possible to observe that the erosion and dilation operations extract the boundary of the objects in the image.

Task: Prove that erosion is not the inverse of dilation and vice versa.

```
# This program does the Boundary extraction using erosion and dilation
import cv2
import matplotlib.pyplot as plt
I1= cv2.imread('Imag2.jpg');
h=cv2.getStructuringElement(cv2.MORPH_CROSS,(11,11))# Structuring Element
Er=cv2.erode(I1,h);
Dl=cv2.dilate(I1,h);
plt.figure(figsize=(8,6)),plt.subplot(1,4,1),plt.imshow(I1),plt.title('Input Image'),plt.xticks([]),
plt.yticks([]),plt.subplot(1,4,2),plt.imshow(h,cmap='gray'),plt.title('Kernel'),plt.xticks([]),plt.yticks([])
plt.subplot(1,4,3),plt.imshow(I1-Er,cmap='binary'),plt.title('Boundary-Erosion')
plt.xticks([]),plt.yticks([]),plt.subplot(1,4,4),plt.imshow((Dl-I1),cmap='binary'),
plt.title('Bounadry-Dilation'),plt.xticks([]),plt.yticks([])
plt.tight_layout()
```

Fig. 6.19 Python code for boundary extraction

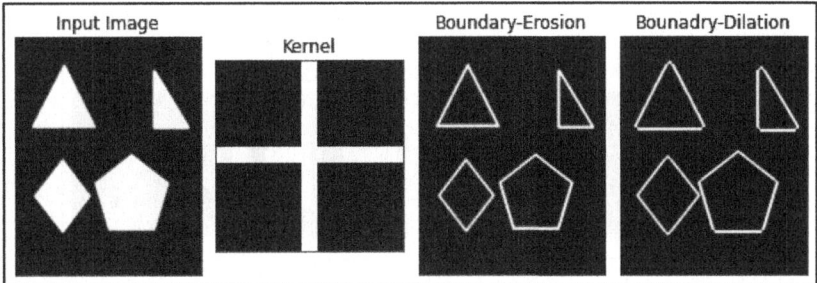

Fig. 6.20 Boundary extraction result

6.4.4   Opening

Opening is another important morphological operation and it can be performed by erosion followed by dilation operation with the same structuring element. The mathematical expression for the opening operation is defined as

$$X \circ B = (X \ominus B) \oplus B \qquad (6.12)$$

The symbol "∘" represents the opening operation. The erosion operation hits all the places where the structuring element fits inside the image and the resultant image, but it only marks these positions at the origin of the structuring element. The erosion followed by dilation operation fills back the full structuring element at places where the structuring element fits inside the object. Therefore, an opening operation is the union of all translated copies of the structuring element that can fit inside the object.

```
# This program performs opening using erosion and dilation
import cv2
import matplotlib.pyplot as plt
I1= cv2.imread('Openclose.jpg');
h=cv2.getStructuringElement(cv2.MORPH_RECT,(55,55));# Structuring Element
E=cv2.erode(I1,h);# Erosion
Op=cv2.dilate(E,h);# Dilation
plt.subplot(1,4,1),plt.imshow(I1),plt.title('Input Image'),plt.xticks([]),plt.yticks([])
plt.subplot(1,4,2),plt.imshow(h,cmap='binary'),plt.title('Kernel'),plt.xticks([]),plt.yticks([])
plt.subplot(1,4,3),plt.imshow(Op),plt.title('Opening Output'),plt.xticks([]),plt.yticks([])
plt.subplot(1,4,4),plt.imshow((I1-Op),cmap='gray'),plt.title('Difference')
plt.xticks([]),plt.yticks([])
plt.tight_layout()
```

Fig. 6.21 Python code for "opening" operation

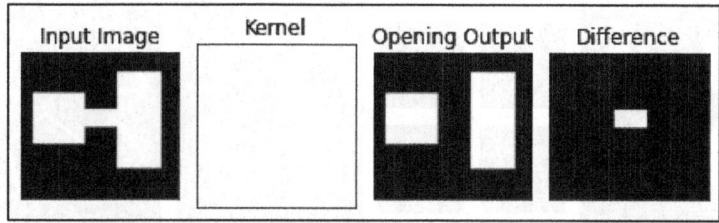

Fig. 6.22 Simulation result

Experiment 6.9: Perform the "Opening" Operation Using Erosion Followed by Dilation

This experiment discusses the opening operation on binary images using Python illustration. The Python code that computes the opening operation on a binary image is depicted in Fig. 6.21, and its simulation result is shown in Fig. 6.22.

Inferences

The following inferences can be made from this experiment:

- From Fig. 6.21, it is possible to observe that erosion operation is done and dilation operation is performed on the resultant image of the erosion.
- From Fig. 6.22, it is possible to confirm that the opening operation can be used to open the joint between two objects that exist in the image.

Experiment 6.10: Perform Opening Operation by Built-in Python Command

In this experiment, the built-in Python command is used to perform the opening operation. Here, the "cv2" library is built with the command "cv2.morphologyEx(I1, cv2.MORPH_OPEN, h, iterations=1)" used to obtain the opening output. The Python code to perform the opening operation is shown in Fig. 6.23, and its simulation result is displayed in Fig. 6.24.

```
# This program performs opening using built-in command
import cv2
import matplotlib.pyplot as plt
I1= cv2.imread('Openclose.jpg');
h=cv2.getStructuringElement(cv2.MORPH_RECT,(55,55));# Structuring Element
Op=cv2.morphologyEx(I1, cv2.MORPH_OPEN,h, iterations=1)
plt.subplot(1,4,1),plt.imshow(I1),plt.title('Input Image')
plt.xticks([]),plt.yticks([]),plt.subplot(1,4,2),plt.imshow(h,cmap='binary'),
plt.title('Kernel'),plt.xticks([]),plt.yticks([]),plt.subplot(1,4,3),
plt.imshow(Op),plt.title('Opening Output'),plt.xticks([]),plt.yticks([])
plt.subplot(1,4,4),plt.imshow((I1-Op),cmap='gray'),plt.title('Difference')
plt.xticks([]),plt.yticks([])
plt.tight_layout()
```

Fig. 6.23 Python code for "opening" operation

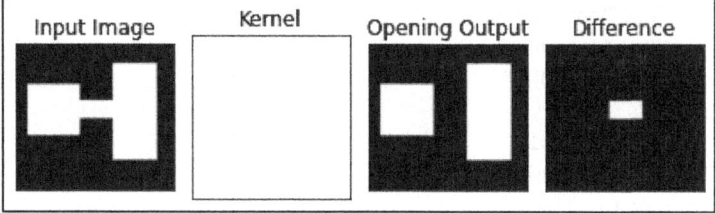

Fig. 6.24 Simulation result

Inferences

The following inferences can be drawn from this experiment:

- From Fig. 6.23, it is evident that the built-in Python command of the "cv2" library "cv2.morphologyEx" is utilized to compute the opening operation.
- Figure 6.24 shows that the output of the opening operation is on par with the output displayed in Fig. 6.22.

6.4.5   Closing

Closing is another important operation of morphological image processing. The closing operation (•) is dilation followed by erosion, and it is mathematically written as

$$X \bullet B = \left(X \oplus B \right) \ominus B \tag{6.13}$$

From Eq. (6.13), it is possible to observe that the dilation operation is performed first and then the erosion operation is done with the same structuring element. The closing is opposite operation of opening. The closing operation fills all places where the structuring element will not fit in the image background.

Experiment 6.11: Perform the "Closing" Operation Using Dilation Followed by Erosion

This experiment discusses how to perform closing operations using dilation and erosion operations. The Python code to perform a closing operation using dilation followed by erosion is shown in Fig. 6.25, and its corresponding output is depicted in Fig. 6.26.

```
# This program performs the closing using dilation and erosion
import cv2
import numpy as np
import matplotlib.pyplot as plt
I1= cv2.imread('toolsbw.bmp');
h=np.zeros((11,11),np.uint8)
for i in range(h.shape[0]):
    h[i,i]=1;
    h[i,h.shape[0]-(i+1)]=1
E=cv2.dilate(I1,h);# Erosion
Op=cv2.erode(E,h);# Dilation
plt.subplot(1,3,1),plt.imshow(I1,cmap='gray'),plt.title('Input Image'),plt.xticks([]),
plt.yticks([]),plt.subplot(1,3,2),plt.imshow(h,cmap='gray'),plt.title('Kernel'),
plt.xticks([]),plt.yticks([]),plt.subplot(1,3,3),plt.imshow(Op,cmap='gray'),
plt.title('Closing Output'),plt.xticks([]),plt.yticks([])
plt.tight_layout()
```

Fig. 6.25 Python code for "closing" operation

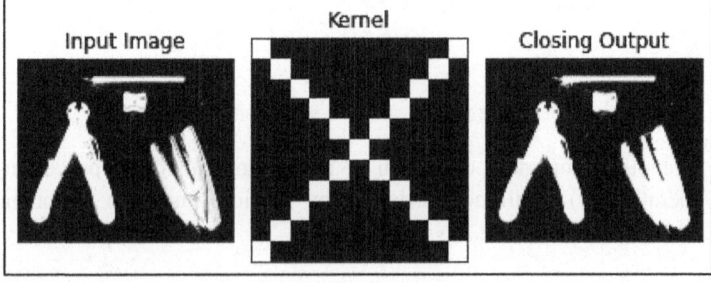

Fig. 6.26 Simulation result

Inferences

The following inferences can be made from this experiment:

- From Fig. 6.25, it is possible to observe that the dilation operation is done first, and the erosion operation is performed next on the resultant image of the dilation.
- From Fig. 6.26, it is possible to confirm that the closing operation can be used to fill the small gaps inside the object.

Experiment 6.12: Perform Closing Operation by Built-in Python Command

In this experiment, the built-in Python command is used to perform the closing operation. Here, the "cv2" library built-in command "cv2.morphologyEx(I1, cv2.MORPH_CLOSE, h, iterations = 1)" is used to obtain the closing result. The Python code to perform the closing operation is shown in Fig. 6.27, and its simulation result is displayed in Fig. 6.28.

```
# This program performs closing operation using built-in command
import cv2
import numpy as np
import matplotlib.pyplot as plt
I1= cv2.imread('toolsbw.bmp');
h=np.zeros((11,11),np.uint8)
for i in range(h.shape[0]):
    h[i,i]=1;
    h[i,h.shape[0]-(i+1)]=1
Op=cv2.morphologyEx(I1, cv2.MORPH_CLOSE,h, iterations=1)
plt.subplot(1,3,1),plt.imshow(I1,cmap='gray'),plt.title('Input Image')
plt.xticks([]),plt.yticks([]),plt.subplot(1,3,2),plt.imshow(h,cmap='gray'),
plt.title('Kernel'),plt.xticks([]),plt.yticks([]),plt.subplot(1,3,3),
plt.imshow(Op,cmap='gray'),plt.title('Closing Output'),plt.xticks([]),plt.yticks([])
plt.tight_layout()
```

Fig. 6.27 Python code for "closing" operation

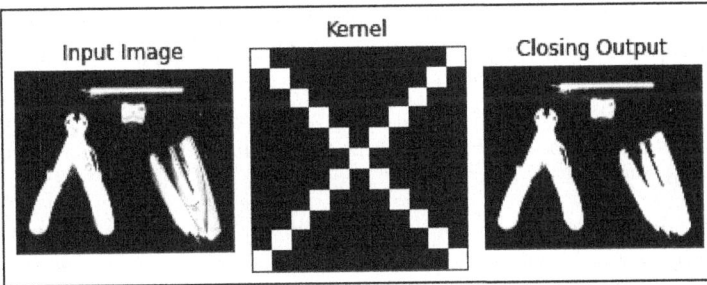

Fig. 6.28 Simulation result

Inferences

The following observations can be drawn from this experiment:

- From Fig. 6.27, it is possible to see that the "cv2" library built-in Python command "cv2.morphologyEx" is used here to compute the closing operation.
- From Fig. 6.28, it is possible to observe that the black line and small portions are filled with white in colour by the closing operation. Therefore, the closing operation can be used to fill the small black dots or gaps with white.

6.4.6   Duality of Opening and Closing Operations

The opening and closing operations are dual to each other. The duality condition of the opening and closing operations is defined as

$$(X \circ B)^c = X^c \bullet \hat{B} \tag{6.14}$$

and

$$(X \bullet B)^c = X^c \circ \hat{B} \tag{6.15}$$

The above Eqs. (6.14) and (6.15) indicate that the opening operation can be performed by the closing operation and vice versa.

Experiment 6.13: Verify the Duality of Opening and Closing Operations

This experiment verifies the duality of opening and closing operations using Python. The Python code for the verification of the duality of opening and closing operations is given in Fig. 6.29, and its simulation result is displayed in Fig. 6.30.

Inferences

The following inferences can be made from this experiment:

- From Fig. 6.29, it is possible to observe that "Op1" is the opening output and "Y1" denotes the complement of opening output, which resembles the LHS of Eq. (6.14).
- The variable "I1c" is the complement of the input image, "h1" represents the reflection of the structuring element, and "Cl" is the output of closing, which resembles the RHS of Eq. (6.14).
- From Fig. 6.30, it is possible to infer that the results of opening and closing operations are the same, which confirms the duality of the opening and closing operations.

Task: Verify that the duality of opening and closing equation is given by $(X \bullet B)^c = X^c \circ \hat{B}$.

```
# This python code proofs the dual of opening and closing
import cv2
import numpy as np
import matplotlib.pyplot as plt
I1= cv2.imread('toolsbw.bmp');
h=np.zeros((3,3),np.uint8)
for i in range(h.shape[0]):
    h[i,i]=1;
    h[i,h.shape[0]-(i+1)]=1
Op1=cv2.morphologyEx(I1, cv2.MORPH_OPEN,h, iterations=1)# Opening
Y1=cv2.bitwise_not(Op1);# Complement of Opening output
I1c=cv2.bitwise_not(I1);# Complement of input
h1=cv2.flip(h,-1);#reflection
Cl=cv2.morphologyEx(I1c, cv2.MORPH_CLOSE,h1, iterations=1)# Closing
plt.subplot(1,4,1),plt.imshow(I1),plt.title('Input Image'),plt.xticks([]),plt.yticks([])
plt.subplot(1,4,2),plt.imshow(h,cmap='gray'),plt.title('Kernel'),plt.xticks([]),plt.yticks([])
plt.subplot(1,4,3),plt.imshow(Y1),plt.title('Opening Output'),plt.xticks([]),plt.yticks([])
plt.subplot(1,4,4),plt.imshow(Cl),plt.title('Closing Output'),plt.xticks([]),plt.yticks([])
plt.tight_layout()
```

Fig. 6.29 Python code for duality of opening and closing operations

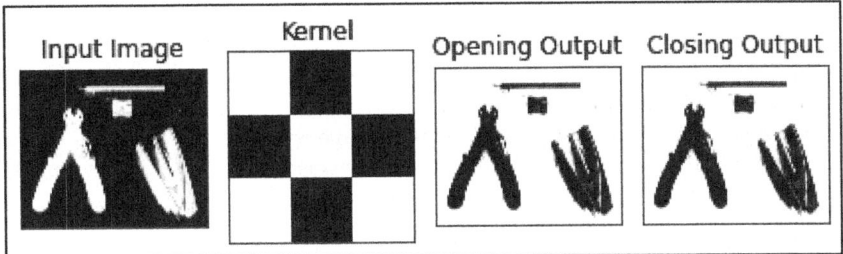

Fig. 6.30 Simulation result

6.4.7 Idempotence of Opening and Closing Operations

As per the *Cambridge Dictionary*, the meaning of the word "idempotent" is that "An idempotent element of a set does not change in value when multiplied or operated by itself". The idempotence of opening and closing operations is written as

$$\left(\left(\left(\left(X \circ B\right) \circ B\right) \circ B\right) \cdots \circ B\right) = X \circ B \tag{6.16}$$

and

$$\left(\left(\left(\left(X \bullet B\right) \bullet B\right) \bullet B\right) \cdots \bullet B\right) = X \bullet B \tag{6.17}$$

The above Eqs. (6.16) and (6.17) indicate that nothing changes after applying more than one opening or closing operation.

Experiment 6.14: Verify the Idempotence of Opening Operation

This experiment verifies the idempotence of opening operation by using Python. The Python code that verifies the above-mentioned task is given in Fig. 6.31, and its simulation result is depicted in Fig. 6.32.

Inferences

The following inferences can be made from this experiment:

- From Fig. 6.31, it is possible to observe that opening operations are repeated by four times with the same structuring element.
- Figure 6.32 displays that the first, second, third, and fourth-time opening results are the same. This indicates that the opening operation is idempotent.

Task: Verify the closing operation is an idempotent.

```
# This program performs idempotence of opening
import cv2
import numpy as np
import matplotlib.pyplot as plt
I1= cv2.imread('Openclose.jpg');
h=np.zeros((51,51),np.uint8)
for i in range(h.shape[0]):
    h[i,i]=1;
    h[i,h.shape[0]-(i+1)]=1
Op=cv2.morphologyEx(I1, cv2.MORPH_OPEN,h, iterations=1)
Op1=cv2.morphologyEx(Op, cv2.MORPH_OPEN,h, iterations=1)
Op2=cv2.morphologyEx(Op1, cv2.MORPH_OPEN,h, iterations=1)
Op3=cv2.morphologyEx(Op2, cv2.MORPH_OPEN,h, iterations=1)
plt.subplot(2,3,1),plt.imshow(I1,cmap='gray'),plt.title('Input Image')
plt.xticks([]),plt.yticks([]),plt.subplot(2,3,2),plt.imshow(h,cmap='gray'),
plt.title('Kernel'),plt.xticks([]),plt.yticks([]),plt.subplot(2,3,3),
plt.imshow(Op,cmap='gray'),plt.title('1st time Opening')
plt.xticks([]),plt.yticks([]),plt.subplot(2,3,4),plt.imshow(Op1,cmap='gray'),
plt.title('2nd time Opening'),plt.xticks([]),plt.yticks([])
plt.subplot(2,3,5),plt.imshow(Op2,cmap='gray'),plt.title('3rd time Opening')
plt.xticks([]),plt.yticks([]),plt.subplot(2,3,6),plt.imshow(Op,cmap='gray'),
plt.title('4th time Opening'),plt.xticks([]),plt.yticks([])
plt.tight_layout()
```

Fig. 6.31 Python code for verification idempotent of opening

Fig. 6.32 Simulation result

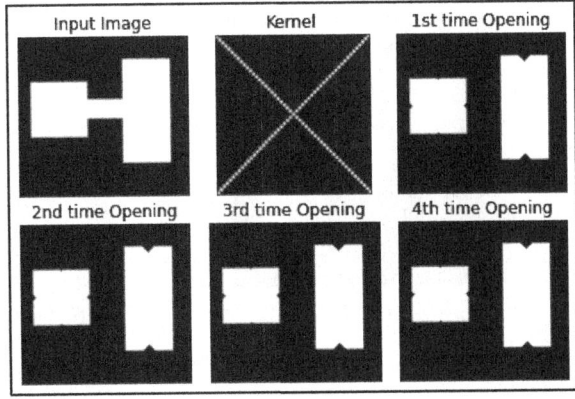

6.5 Hit-or-Miss Transform

The hit-or-miss transform is a morphological algorithm that can be used to look for particular patterns of foreground and background pixels in an image, and also it can be used for template matching. Here, two structuring elements are used to obtain the template matching in the input image. The structuring element "B" acts as a template and "$W - B$" is the background of the template "B". In other words, "B" is the foreground of the template. The size of the "W" will always be greater than the size of the "B". This transform is basically an intersection of the erosion of the input image with the structuring element "B" and the erosion of the complement of the input image with the structuring element "$W - B$".

The mathematical equation of the hit-or-miss transform is given by

$$X \circledast B = (X \ominus B) \cap (X^c \ominus (W - B)) \tag{6.18}$$

where the symbol "$\circledast$" denotes the hit-or-miss transform.

Experiment 6.15: Write a Python Code to Perform the Hit-or-Miss Transform
This experiment deals with the computation of hit-or-miss transform using Python. Let us consider the binary image and structuring element is shown in Fig. 6.33.

The hit-or-miss transform can be used to obtain patterns (kernel) whether it exists in the input image or not, and it also gives the number of patterns present in the image by counting the white pixels in the hit-or-miss transform output. The Python code to perform the hit-or-miss transform is shown in Fig. 6.34. From this figure, it is possible to observe that "cv2.morphologyEx(a,cv2.MORPH_ HITMISS,B1,B2,iterations=1)" command provides the final output. "B1" is the structuring element and "B2" is the complement of "B1". If we say B1 is the foreground, then B2 will be the background, and it is complemented by "B1". After executing the Python code given in Fig. 6.34, the obtained simulation result is shown in Fig. 6.35. From this figure, it is possible to know that there are only three

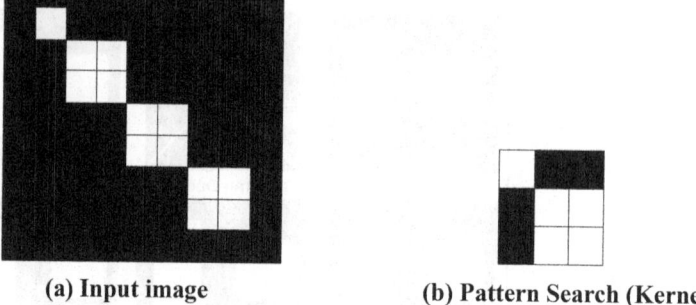

(a) Input image   **(b) Pattern Search (Kernel)**

Fig. 6.33 Input and pattern images: (**a**) input image, (**b**) pattern search (kernel)

```
# This program performs hit-or-miss transform
import cv2
import numpy as np
import matplotlib.pyplot as plt
a = np.zeros((9,9),'uint8')
a[1, 1] = 1; a[2:4, 2:4] = 1; a[4:6, 4:6] = 1;a[6:8, 6:8] = 1;
B1 = np.array([[1, 0, 0], [0, 1, 1], [0, 1, 1]]);
B2=1-B1;
y1=cv2.morphologyEx(a,cv2.MORPH_HITMISS,B1,B2,iterations=1)
plt.subplot(1,2,1),plt.imshow(a,cmap='gray'),plt.title('Input Image')
plt.xticks([]),plt.yticks([]),plt.subplot(1,2,2),plt.imshow(y1,cmap='gray'),
plt.title('Hit-or-Miss output'),plt.xticks([]),plt.yticks([])
plt.tight_layout()
```

Fig. 6.34 Python code for hit-or-miss transform

white pixels, which means that there are three similar patterns ("B1") exist in the given input image.

Inferences

The following inferences can be observed from this experiment:

- From Fig. 6.35, it is possible to observe that hit-or-miss transform can be used for template matching.
- For example, in a printed circuit board (PCB), any electronic components are missed, which are to be identified by using this transform.

Experiment 6.16: Implement Eq. (6.18) Using "Erosion" Operations

This experiment implements the hit-or-miss transform using erosion operations. The Python code to perform this task is shown in Fig. 6.36, and its simulation result is given in Fig. 6.37.

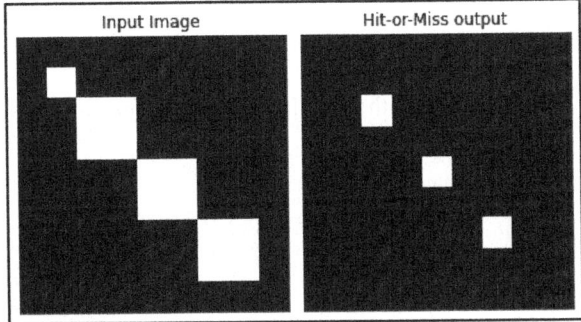

Fig. 6.35 Simulation result

```
# This program computes hit or miss transform using erosion
import cv2
import numpy as np
import matplotlib.pyplot as plt
a = np.zeros((9,9),'uint8')
a[1, 1] = 1; a[2:4, 2:4] = 1; a[4:6, 4:6] = 1;a[6:8, 6:8] = 1;
B1 = np.array([[1, 0, 0], [0, 1, 1], [0, 1, 1]],'uint8');
B2, a1=1-B1,1-a;
y1=cv2.erode(a,B1);
y2=cv2.erode(a1,B2);
y=cv2.bitwise_and(y1,y2)
plt.subplot(1,2,1),plt.imshow(a,cmap='gray'),plt.title('Input Image')
plt.xticks([]),plt.yticks([]),plt.subplot(1,2,2),plt.imshow(y,cmap='gray'),
plt.title('Hit-or-Miss output'),plt.xticks([]),plt.yticks([])
plt.tight_layout()
```

Fig. 6.36 Python code to perform hit-or-miss transform using erosion

Fig. 6.37 Simulation result

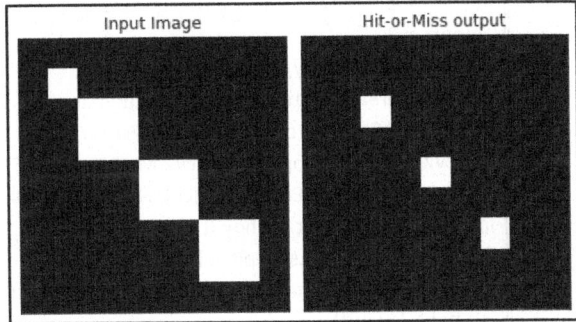

Inferences
- From Fig. 6.36, it is possible to confirm that erosion operations are used to compute the hit-or-miss transform.
- From Fig. 6.37, it shows that the simulation result is on par with the simulation result shown in Fig. 6.35.

6.6 Top-Hat Transform

The top-hat transform is morphological operation in digital image processing, which is used to extract the small elements and details in the given input images. Top-hat transform is defined by some kernel as the difference between the input image and its opening result. The top-hat transform is mathematically represented as

$$\text{Top\_hat}(X) = X - (X \circ B) \tag{6.19}$$

where "X" is the input image, "B" denotes the structuring element or kernel, and "$\circ$" represents the opening operation.

Experiment 6.17: Top-Hat Transform
The Python code to compute the top-hat transform is given in Fig. 6.38, and its simulation result is shown in Fig. 6.39.

Inferences
- From Fig. 6.39, it is possible to observe that output of top-hat transform contains minute details of the image. That is, very small details are enhanced and taken out using the top-hat operation.
- Hence, it is useful in observing the minute details of the inputs when are present as light pixels on a dark background.

```
# This program performs Top Hat Transform
import cv2
import matplotlib.pyplot as plt
I1 = cv2.imread("testing2.png") # Input image
I1 = cv2.cvtColor(I1, cv2.COLOR_BGR2GRAY) #RGB to Gray
B = cv2.getStructuringElement(cv2.MORPH_ELLIPSE,(5,5)) # Kernel
Y = cv2.morphologyEx(I1,cv2.MORPH_TOPHAT,B) # Top hat transform
plt.subplot(1,2,1),plt.imshow(I1,cmap='gray'),plt.title('Input Image')
plt.xticks([]),plt.yticks([]),plt.subplot(1,2,2),plt.imshow(Y,cmap='gray'),
plt.title('Top Hat Transform'),plt.xticks([]),plt.yticks([])
plt.tight_layout()
```

Fig. 6.38 Python code to perform top-hat transform

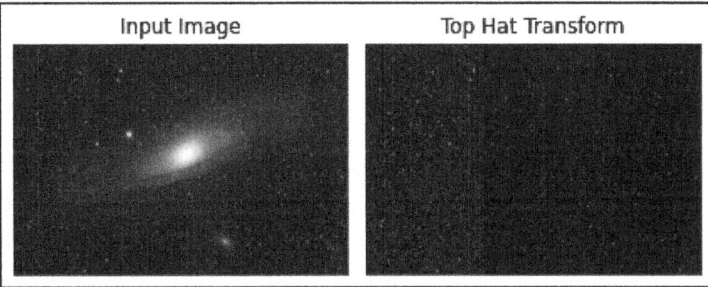

Fig. 6.39 Top-hat transformed output

```
# This program performs Black Hat Transform
import cv2
import matplotlib.pyplot as plt
I1 = cv2.imread("testing1.jpg") # Input image
I1 = cv2.cvtColor(I1, cv2.COLOR_BGR2GRAY) #RGB to Gray
B = cv2.getStructuringElement(cv2.MORPH_ELLIPSE,(5,5)) # Kernel
Y = cv2.morphologyEx(I1,cv2.MORPH_BLACKHAT,B) # Top hat transform
plt.subplot(1,2,1),plt.imshow(I1,cmap='gray'),plt.title('Input Image')
plt.xticks([]),plt.yticks([]),plt.subplot(1,2,2),plt.imshow(Y,cmap='gray'),
plt.title('Black Hat Transform'),plt.xticks([]),plt.yticks([])
plt.tight_layout()
```

Fig. 6.40 Python code to perform black-hat transform

6.7 Black-Hat Transform

The black-hat transform is a morphological operation in digital image processing used to extract the small elements and details in the given input images. Black-hat transform is defined as the difference between the closing result and the input image by some kernel. It enhances dark objects of interest in a bright background. The black-hat transform is mathematically represented as

$$\text{Black hat}(X) = (X \bullet B) - X \tag{6.20}$$

where "X" is the input image, "B" denotes the structuring element or kernel, and "$\bullet$" represents the closing operation.

Experiment 6.18: Black-Hat Transform
The Python code to compute the black-hat transform is given in Fig. 6.40, and its simulation result is shown in Fig. 6.41.

Fig. 6.41 Black-hat transformed output

Inferences
- From Fig. 6.41, it is possible to observe that the output of the black-hat transform contains minute details of the image. That is, very small details are enhanced and taken out using the black-hat operation.
- Also, it is evident that the black-hat transform highlights all the objects that are dark on white background.

6.8   Region Filling

Region filling is an important operation in image processing and computer graphics. It is the process of colouring in a region of interest in an image. Region filling operations can be classified into polygon-based and pixel-based methods. The polygon-based method is also called as "ordered edge list", "scan conversion", or "rasterization" method and is applicable whenever the contour or boundary of the region of interest is given as a polygon. In the pixel-based technique, a region or boundary of the object is described in terms of bounding pixels that outline it or as the totality of pixels that comprise it. In both methods, the boundary region of the object must be computed for the region filling. The morphological operation can be used for the region-filling process. The region-filling process using the dilation operation is mathematically written as

$$Y_k = \left(Y_{k-1} \oplus B\right) \cap A^c \, for \, k = 1, 2, 3, \ldots \tag{6.21}$$

where Y_0 is the initial image with all the elements are zero except the seed point. The seed point must be set "1" within the region of interest. "B" is the structuring element and A^c is the complement of the input image, which is to be region filled. The region filling algorithm begins with a seed point inside the boundary and the objective is to fill the entire region with 1s by iteratively. From Eq. (6.21), it is possible to observe that the region-filling process contains dilation, complementation, and intersection operations. There are two ways to terminate the algorithm: the first one

```
# This program performs Region Filling
import cv2
import numpy as np
import matplotlib.pyplot as plt
X=np.zeros([9,9]);
X[1,4]=1;X[2,(3,5)]=1;X[3,(2,6)]=1;X[4,(1,7)]=1;X[5,(2,6)]=1;X[6,(3,5)]=1;X[7,4]=1;
X1c=1-X;
X1=np.zeros([X.shape[0],X.shape[1]]);
seed=(1,1);# Seed point must be within the boundary
X1[seed[0],seed[1]]=1;
B=np.array([[0, 1, 0],[1, 1, 1],[0, 1, 0]],'uint8');
for i in range(X.shape[0]):
    for j in range(X.shape[1]):
        Y1=cv2.dilate(X1,B,iterations = 1)# Dilation
        X1=cv2.bitwise_and(Y1, X1c) # Intersection
out=cv2.bitwise_or(X, 1-X1)# Union operation
plt.subplot(1,2,1),plt.imshow(X,cmap='gray'),plt.title('Input Image'),
plt.xticks([]),plt.yticks([]),plt.subplot(1,2,2),plt.imshow(out,cmap='gray'),
plt.title('Filled Image'),plt.xticks([]),plt.yticks([])
plt.tight_layout()
```

Fig. 6.42 Python code to perform region filling

Fig. 6.43 Region filling output

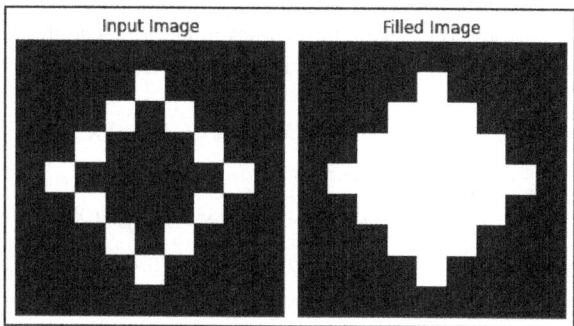

is to fix the number of iterations, and the second one is based on completion of region filling process.

Experiment 6.19: Write a Python Code to Perform Region Filling Eq. (6.21)
This experiment discusses the region-filling process using morphological operations. The Python code to perform the region-filling process is given in Fig. 6.42, and its simulation result is shown in Fig. 6.43. In this experiment, we have considered the boundary of the diamond object as the input image and a cross-structuring element with the size of 3×3 as the kernel.

Inference

- From Fig. 6.43, the bounding pixels of the region of interest are given as input to the region-filling algorithm and output is obtained as a filled region of the object.

Tasks

1. Execute the Python code given in Fig. 6.42 with the incomplete bounding pixels (i.e. X[4,(1,8)]=1, boundary of the object is not closed). Comments on the observed result.
2. Execute the Python code given in Fig. 6.42 and select the seed point outside bounding pixels (seed=(1,1)). Comments on the observed result.

6.9 Thinning

Thinning is a morphological operation, which reduces the foreground of the object. This reduction may be accomplished by obtaining the skeleton of the region. Skeletonization is the process of extracting the skeletons of an object in an image. In this operation, it removes foreground pixels iteratively layer by layer until the thickness of the skeleton is one pixel width. Also, it preserves the topology of the actual shape while removing away most of the foreground pixels. There are many methods currently available to implement the thinning operation such as (1) Zhang Suen fast parallel thinning algorithm, (2) non-max suppression in Canny edge detector, (3) Guo and Hall's two sub-iteration parallel thinning method, and (4) iterative methods using morphological operations.

Thinning operation is similar to operation of erosion or opening and also it can be performed by using hit-or-miss transform. The thinning operation can be implemented by using erosion and opening operations given by

$$S_i(X) = (X_{i-1} \ominus B) - ((X_{i-1} \ominus B) \circ B) \tag{6.22}$$

$$X \otimes B = \bigcup_{i=0}^{N} S_i(X) \tag{6.23}$$

where X_0 is the input binary image, B is the structuring element, $X_i = X_{i-1} \ominus B$, $\otimes$ denotes the thinning operation. S_i is the subset result of erosion and opening operation. Here, "i" indicates the iteration number of erosion. N is the last iterative step before Xi erodes to the empty set is a stopping criterion.

Thinning operation can be implemented by using hit-or-miss transform, which is mathematically written as

$$X \otimes B = X - (X \circledast B) \tag{6.24}$$

where ⊛ represents the hit-or-miss transform output of the input binary image X, and B is set of structuring elements denoted as $B = \{B_1, B_2, ..., B_N\}$. In general, B_i is the rotated version of the B_{i-1}. Here, sequence of structuring elements is used to produce symmetric results, and this operation is mostly applied in an iterative manner until no further changes occur.

Experiment 6.20: Implement a Thinning Operation Using Erosion and Opening Operations

This experiment discusses the implementation of thinning operation using iterative erosion and opening operations. The Python code to perform this task is given in Fig. 6.44 and its simulation result is displayed in Fig. 6.45.

Inferences

The following inferences can be drawn from this experiment:

- From Fig. 6.44, erosion and opening operations are used repeatedly and the stopping condition is the count of non-zero pixels in erosion output is equal to zero.
- From Fig. 6.45, it is possible to infer that the thinning output image shows that the width of the line segment is almost 1.

```
# This program performs Thinning
import cv2
import numpy as np
import matplotlib.pyplot as plt
I = cv2.imread('Skeletonization.bmp') # Input image
I = cv2.cvtColor(I, cv2.COLOR_BGR2GRAY) #RGB to Gray
I=cv2.bitwise_not(I)
I1 = I.copy()
B = cv2.getStructuringElement(cv2.MORPH_ELLIPSE,(3,3))
# Create an empty output image to hold values
thin_out = np.zeros(I.shape,dtype='uint8')
# Loop until erosion leads to an empty set
while (cv2.countNonZero(I1)!=0):
    E = cv2.erode(I1,B); # Erosion
    Op = cv2.morphologyEx(E,cv2.MORPH_OPEN,B) # # Opening on eroded image
    S = E - Op; # Subtract Erode and Opening out
    thin_out = cv2.bitwise_or(S,thin_out); # Union of all previous sets
    I1 = E.copy();  # Set the eroded image for next iteration
plt.subplot(1,2,1),plt.imshow(I,cmap='gray'),plt.title('Input Image')
plt.xticks([]),plt.yticks([]),plt.subplot(1,2,2),plt.imshow(thin_out,cmap='gray'),
plt.title('Thinning output'),plt.xticks([]),plt.yticks([])
plt.tight_layout()
```

Fig. 6.44 Python code to perform "thinning"

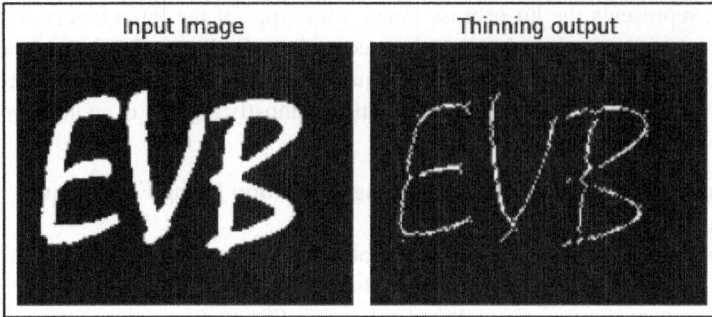

Fig. 6.45 Thinning output

```
# This program performs Thickenning
import cv2
import matplotlib.pyplot as plt
I = cv2.imread("Skeleton.jpg") # Input image
B = cv2.getStructuringElement(cv2.MORPH_ELLIPSE,(3,3))
thick_out = cv2.dilate(I,B,iterations = 3); # Dilation
plt.subplot(1,2,1),plt.imshow(I,cmap='gray'),plt.title('Input Image')
plt.xticks([]),plt.yticks([]),plt.subplot(1,2,2),plt.imshow(thick_out,cmap='gray'),
plt.title('Thickenning output'),plt.xticks([]),plt.yticks([])
plt.tight_layout()
```

Fig. 6.46 Python code to perform "thickening"

6.10   Thickening

Thickening is the duality of the thinning operation and it is used to thicken the width of the skeleton or thinned image. The mathematical expression for the thickening operation "$\odot$" is given by

$$A \odot B = \bigcup_{i=0}^{N} \left(A_i \oplus B \right) \tag{6.25}$$

where "$\oplus$" denotes dilation operation, "$\odot$" represents thickening operation, and N is the number of iterations for the dilation operation. A is the skeleton input image, which is to be thickened.

Experiment 6.21: Write a Python Code to Perform Thickening Operation
This experiment deals with the performing thickening operation on skeleton image using Python. The Python code to perform this task is given in Fig. 6.46, and its simulation result is shown in Fig. 6.47.

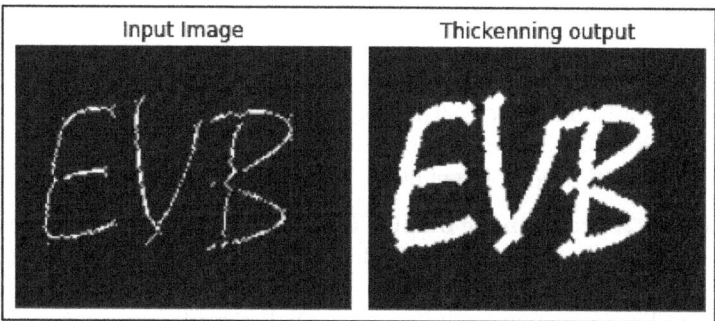

Fig. 6.47 Thickening output

Inferences

The following inference can be made from this experiment:

- From Fig. 6.46, it is possible to observe that dilation operation of skeleton image (I) is done repeatedly with the structuring element (B). That is, the number of iterations is chosen as 3. The number of iterations increases the width of the thickness of the output.
- From Fig. 6.47, it is possible to confirm that the output image is thickened whereas the input image is skeleton.

6.11 Morphological Operation on Grayscale Image

The morphological operations such as dilation, erosion, opening, and closing can be applied on grayscale images. The binary morphological operations can be extended to grayscale images using minimum and maximum operations. This section discusses how to apply morphological operations on grayscale images.

6.11.1 Dilation

The grayscale dilation operation on grayscale image involves assigning to each pixel in an image by the maximum value of the neighbourhood pixels corresponding to the structuring element. The dilation operation on grayscale image is mathematically written as

$$(X \oplus B)(m,n) = \max \left\{ \begin{array}{l} X(m-s,\, n-y) + B(x,y) | (m-s), \\ (n-y) \in W_X;\ (x,y) \in W_B \end{array} \right\} \qquad (6.26)$$

where X is the input grayscale image, B is the structuring element, and W_X and W_B are the size of neighbourhood and size of the structuring element, respectively.

The dilation output depends on the values of the structuring element. If all the values of the structuring element are positive, then the dilation output will be brighter. The size of the structuring element plays a major role in reducing or eliminating the dark details present in the input image.

Experiment 6.22: Perform the Dilation Operation on Grayscale Image
This experiment deals with the effect of dilation operation on grayscale image. The Python code to perform the dilation operation on the grayscale image is shown in Fig. 6.48, and its simulation result is displayed in Fig. 6.49.

```
# Grayscale dilation
import cv2
import matplotlib.pyplot as plt
I = cv2.imread("Fence2.jpg") # Input image
I = cv2.cvtColor(I, cv2.COLOR_BGR2GRAY) #RGB to Gray
I1=255-I
B=cv2.getStructuringElement(cv2.MORPH_CROSS,(55,55))
y=cv2.dilate(I, B, iterations = 1);
y1=cv2.dilate(I1, B, iterations = 1);
plt.subplot(1,4,1),plt.imshow(I,cmap='gray'),plt.title('Input Image-1'),plt.xticks([]),plt.yticks([])
plt.subplot(1,4,2),plt.imshow(y,cmap='gray'),plt.title('Dilation Output-1'),plt.xticks([]),
plt.yticks([]),plt.subplot(1,4,3),plt.imshow(I1,cmap='gray'),plt.title('Input Image-2')
plt.xticks([]),plt.yticks([]),plt.subplot(1,4,4),plt.imshow(y1,cmap='gray'),
plt.title('Dilation Output-2'),plt.xticks([]),plt.yticks([])
plt.tight_layout()
```

Fig. 6.48 Python code to perform "dilation"

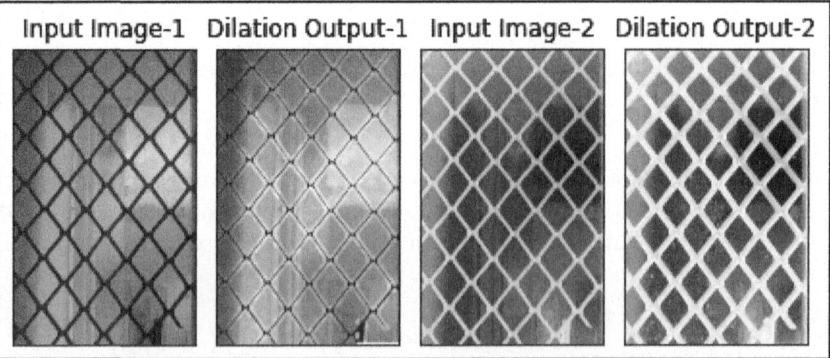

Fig. 6.49 Dilation output

Inference
- From Fig. 6.49, it is possible to infer that dilation operation reduces the width of the dark pixels and increases the width of the bright pixels.

Task: Change the value of iterations to 2 in the Python code shown in Fig. 6.48. Comment on the observed result.

6.11.2   Erosion

The grayscale erosion operation on a grayscale image can be performed by assigning each pixel in an image by the minimum value obtained over the neighbourhood of the structuring element. The grayscale erosion operation on grayscale image is mathematically written as

$$(X \ominus B)(m, n) = \min \left\{ \begin{matrix} X(m-s, n-y) + B(x, y) \mid \\ (m-s), (n-y) \in W_X ; (x, y) \in W_B \end{matrix} \right\} \qquad (6.27)$$

where X is the input greyscale image, B is the structuring element, and W_X and W_B are the size of the neighbourhood and the size of the structuring element, respectively.

The grayscale erosion can be performed by the maximum operation as well. However, the above equation can be modified as

$$(X \ominus B)(m, n) = \max \left\{ \begin{matrix} X(m-s, n-y) - B(x, y) \mid \\ (m-s), (n-y) \in W_X ; (x, y) \in W_B \end{matrix} \right\} \qquad (6.28)$$

The erosion output depends on the values of the structuring element. If all the values of the structuring element are positive then the erosion output is darker. The size of the structuring element plays a major role in reducing or eliminating the brighter details present in the input image.

Experiment 6.23: Perform the Erosion Operation on Grayscale Image
This experiment deals with the effect of erosion operation on grayscale image. The Python code to perform the erosion operation on the grayscale image is shown in Fig. 6.50, and its simulation result is displayed in Fig. 6.51.

Inference
- From Fig. 6.51, it is possible to infer that erosion operation reduces the width of the bright pixels and increases the width of the dark pixels.

Task: Change the value of iterations to 2 in the Python code shown in Fig. 6.50. Comment on the observed result.

```
# Grayscale erosion
import cv2
import matplotlib.pyplot as plt
I = cv2.imread("Fence2.jpg") # Input image
I = cv2.cvtColor(I, cv2.COLOR_BGR2GRAY) #RGB to Gray
I1=255-I
B=cv2.getStructuringElement(cv2.MORPH_CROSS,(55,55))
y=cv2.erode(I, B, iterations = 2);
y1=cv2.erode(I1, B, iterations = 2);
plt.subplot(1,4,1),plt.imshow(I,cmap='gray'),plt.title('Input Image-1'),plt.xticks([]),
plt.yticks([]),plt.subplot(1,4,2),plt.imshow(y,cmap='gray'),plt.title('Erosion Output-1')
plt.xticks([]),plt.yticks([]),plt.subplot(1,4,3),plt.imshow(I1,cmap='gray'),plt.title('Input Image-2')
plt.xticks([]),plt.yticks([]),plt.subplot(1,4,4),plt.imshow(y1,cmap='gray'),
plt.title('Erosion Output-1'),plt.xticks([]),plt.yticks([])
plt.tight_layout()
```

Fig. 6.50 Python code to perform "erosion"

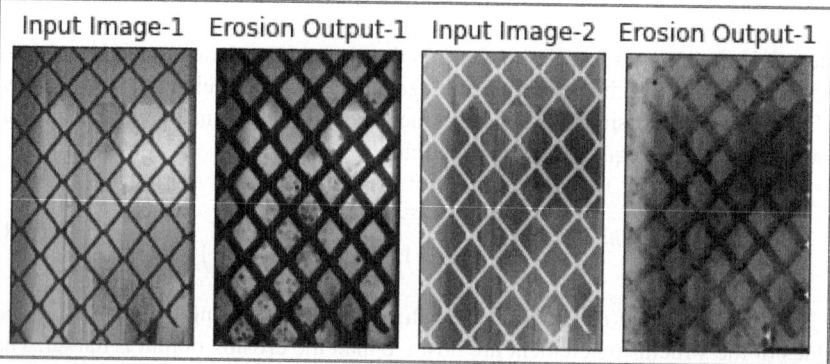

Fig. 6.51 Erosion output

6.11.3 Opening

The grayscale opening operation of an image can be performed by the grayscale erosion operation followed by grayscale dilation operation. The opening output value is the maximum of the minimum value of the image in the surrounding neighbourhood pixels defined by the structuring element.

The opening operation can be mathematically written as

$$(X\ominus B)(m,n) = \min\left\{ \begin{matrix} X(m-s,n-y)+B(x,y)| \\ (m-s),(n-y)\in W_X;\ (x,y)\in W_B \end{matrix} \right\} \qquad (6.29)$$

$$(X\circ B)(m,n) = \max\left\{ \begin{matrix} (X\ominus B)\left[(m-s,n-y)\right]+B(x,y)| \\ (m-s),(n-y)\in W_X;\ (x,y)\in W_B \end{matrix} \right\} \qquad (6.30)$$

From the above equations it is possible to infer that erosion operation is done first, followed by dilation operation.

Experiment 6.24: Implementation of Grayscale Opening Operation

The aim of this experiment is to implement the grayscale opening operation using Python. The Python code to perform the opening operation on the grayscale image is given in Fig. 6.52, and its corresponding simulation output is depicted in Fig. 6.53.

Inferences

The following inferences can be drawn from this experiment:

- From Fig. 6.52, it is possible to infer that "cv2.morphologyEx(I, cv2.MORPH_OPEN,B, iterations=1)" command is used to obtain the opening output, which is imported from the "cv2" library. The structuring element is chosen as a circle with a diameter of 155.
- The output of the Python code given in Fig. 6.52 is depicted in Fig. 6.53. From this figure, it is possible to observe that the morphological operation has opened up the background of the image.

Task: Replace the structuring element with a rectangle and cross instead of the ellipse in the Python code given in Fig. 6.52. Comment on the observed output.

```
# Grayscale Opening
import cv2
import matplotlib.pyplot as plt
I = cv2.imread("tools.jpg") # Input image
I = cv2.cvtColor(I, cv2.COLOR_BGR2GRAY) #RGB to Gray
B=cv2.getStructuringElement(cv2.MORPH_ELLIPSE,(155,155))
y=cv2.morphologyEx(I, cv2.MORPH_OPEN,B, iterations=1)
plt.subplot(1,2,1),plt.imshow(I,cmap='gray'),plt.title('Input Image'),plt.xticks([]),plt.yticks([])
plt.subplot(1,2,2),plt.imshow(y,cmap='gray'),plt.title('Opening Output'),plt.xticks([]),plt.yticks([])
plt.tight_layout()
```

Fig. 6.52 Python code to perform "opening" operation

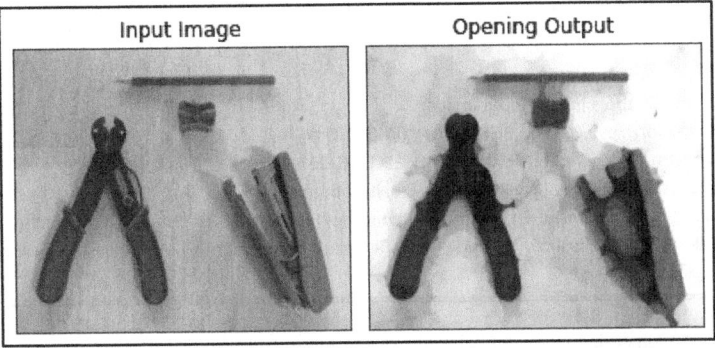

Fig. 6.53 Opening output

6.11.4 Closing

The grayscale closing operation of an image can be performed by the grayscale dilation operation followed by grayscale erosion operation. The closing output value is the minimum of the maximum value of the image in the surrounding neighbourhood pixels defined by the structuring element.

The closing operation can be mathematically written as

$$(X \oplus B)(m, n) = \max \left\{ \begin{matrix} X(m-s, n-y) + B(x, y) | \\ (m-s), (n-y) \in W_X; \ (x,y) \in W_B \end{matrix} \right\} \tag{6.31}$$

$$(X \bullet B)(m, n) = \min \left\{ \begin{matrix} (X \oplus B)[(m-s, n-y)] + B(x, y) | \\ (m-s), (n-y) \in W_X; \ (x,y) \in W_B \end{matrix} \right\} \tag{6.32}$$

From the above equations, it is possible to infer that dilation operation is done first, followed by erosion operation.

Experiment 6.25: Implementation of Grayscale "Closing" Operation
The aim of this experiment is to implement the grayscale closing operation using Python. The Python code to perform the closing operation on the grayscale image is given in Fig. 6.54, and its corresponding simulation output is depicted in Fig. 6.55.

Inferences
The following inferences can be drawn from this experiment:

- From Fig. 6.54, it is possible to infer that the "cv2.morphologyEx(I, cv2. MORPH_CLOSE,B, iterations=1)" command is used to obtain the closing output, which is imported from the "cv2" library. The structuring element is chosen as a circle with a diameter of 155.
- The output of the Python code given in Fig. 6.54 is depicted in Fig. 6.55. From this figure, it is possible to observe that the foreground object approaches to merge with a background of the image.

```
# Grayscale closing
import cv2
import matplotlib.pyplot as plt
I = cv2.imread("tools.jpg") # Input image
I = cv2.cvtColor(I, cv2.COLOR_BGR2GRAY) #RGB to Gray
B=cv2.getStructuringElement(cv2.MORPH_ELLIPSE,(155,155))
y=cv2.morphologyEx(I, cv2.MORPH_CLOSE,B, iterations=1)
plt.subplot(1,2,1),plt.imshow(I,cmap='gray'),plt.title('Input Image'),plt.xticks([]),plt.yticks([])
plt.subplot(1,2,2),plt.imshow(y,cmap='gray'),plt.title('Closing Output'),plt.xticks([]),plt.yticks([])
plt.tight_layout()
```

Fig. 6.54 Python code to perform "closing" operation

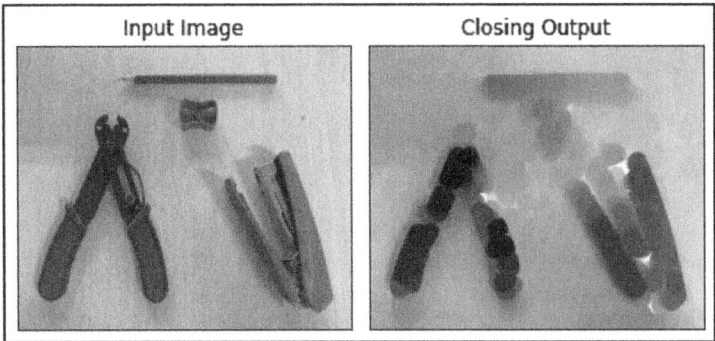

Fig. 6.55 Closing operation output

Task: Replace the structuring element by rectangle and cross instead of ellipse in the Python code given in Fig. 6.54. Comment on the observed output.

6.11.5 Morphological Smoothing

The opening operation followed by closing operation results in morphological smoothing. This operation removes both bright and dark particles in the image. The mathematical expression of morphological smoothing is given by

$$\text{Morphological Smoothing} = \left((X \circ B) \bullet B \right) \tag{6.33}$$

where X is the input image and B represents a structuring element.

The average of erosion and dilation of an image equivalent to morphological smoothing, which is also called "dynamic smoothing". The mathematical expression for the dynamic smoothing is given by

$$\text{Dynamic Smoothing} = \frac{1}{2}\left\{ (X \oplus B) + (X \ominus B) \right\} \tag{6.34}$$

The texture smoothing can be obtained from the average of the opening and closing operations, which is mathematically written as

$$\text{Texture Smoothing} = \frac{1}{2}\left\{ (X \circ B) + (X \bullet B) \right\} \tag{6.35}$$

Experiment 6.26: Morphological Smoothing Operation
This experiment discusses the smoothing operation on grayscale images using morphological operations. The Python code to perform the above-mentioned task is given in Fig. 6.56, and its corresponding output is shown in Fig. 6.57.

```
# Gray scale Smoothing
import cv2
import numpy as np
import matplotlib.pyplot as plt
I = cv2.imread("cropped.jpg",0) # Input image
B=cv2.getStructuringElement(cv2.MORPH_RECT,(3,3))
# Opening followed by closing
y11=cv2.morphologyEx(I, cv2.MORPH_OPEN,B, iterations=1)
y1=cv2.morphologyEx(y11, cv2.MORPH_CLOSE,B, iterations=1)
# Averaging erosion and dilation
y21=cv2.dilate(I, B, iterations = 1);
y22=cv2.erode(I, B, iterations = 1);
y2=np.add(y21,y22)/2
# Averaging Opening and Closing (texture smoothing)
y31=cv2.morphologyEx(I, cv2.MORPH_OPEN,B, iterations=1)
y32=cv2.morphologyEx(I, cv2.MORPH_CLOSE,B, iterations=1)
y3=np.add(y31,y32)/2
plt.figure(figsize=(10,8)),plt.subplot(1,4,1),plt.imshow(I,cmap='gray'),plt.title('Input Image')
plt.xticks([]),plt.yticks([]),plt.subplot(1,4,2),plt.imshow(y1,cmap='gray'),
plt.title('Opening followed by Closing'),plt.xticks([]),plt.yticks([])
plt.subplot(1,4,3),plt.imshow(y2,cmap='gray'),plt.title('Avg. of Dilation & Erosion')
plt.xticks([]),plt.yticks([]),plt.subplot(1,4,4),plt.imshow(y3,cmap='gray'),
plt.title('Avg. of Opening & Closing'),plt.xticks([]),plt.yticks([])
plt.tight_layout()
```

Fig. 6.56 Python code to perform smoothing operation

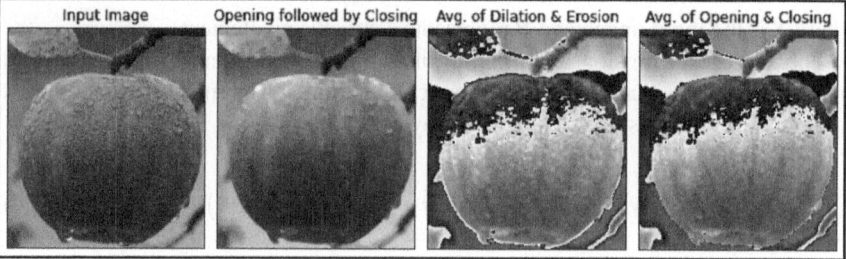

Fig. 6.57 Various smoothing result

Inferences

The following inferences can be drawn from this experiment:

- From Fig. 6.56, it is possible to infer that a grayscale image is read, and a 3×3 square kernel is used as a structuring element for the opening operation followed by the closing operation. The output image is displayed in Fig. 6.57 (second column). From this figure, it is evident that this procedure blurs edge details, and it looks like a smoothened version of the original input image.

- From Fig. 6.56, it is possible to observe that dilation and erosion of the input image are computed, and the average of these two results is displayed in Fig. 6.57 (third column). This figure shows that the inside of the region of interest gets smoothened, whereas the border line of the region of interest is highlighted in white and black lines.
- The Python code for the texture smoothing operation is given in Fig. 6.56 in that opening and closing operations of the input image are performed after the average of those results is displayed in Fig. 6.57. This figure shows a very thin edge line of the region of interest.

Task: Read a grayscale image and add salt and pepper noise to it. Repeat the procedure followed in the Python code given in Fig. 6.56. Comment on the observed results.

6.11.6   Morphological Edge Detection

The basic morphological operations can be used to distinguish the smooth "ramp" edges from ripple "texture" edges. There are three variations of Lee edge detectors: (1) dynamic Lee edge detector, (2) texture Lee edge detector, and (3) ramp Lee edge detector.

Dynamic Lee Edge Detector

It is an edge detector that gives the output similar to the result of the linear Laplacian filter. The mathematical expression for this detector is given by

$$\text{Dynamic Lee}(X) = \min\left(\rho_B^+, \rho_B^-\right) \tag{6.36}$$

where $\rho_B^+ = X \oplus B - X$ and $\rho_B^- = X - (X \ominus B)$. Dynamic Lee edge detector uses the dilation and erosion operations to compute its result.

Texture Lee Edge Detector

The texture Lee edge detector is used to detect the texture edges in an image, which is mathematically defined as

$$\text{Texture Lee }(X) = \min\left\{(X \circ B), (X \bullet B)\right\} \tag{6.37}$$

The above equation shows that the texture Lee edge detector computes the texture edge using opening and closing operations.

Ramp Lee Edge Detector

The ramp Lee edge detector uses the dilation, erosion, opening, and closing operations to compute its edge components, and it is defined as

$$\text{Ramp Lee} \left(X \right) = \min \left(\left\{ \left(X \oplus B \right) - \left(X \circ B \right) \right\}, \left\{ \left(X \bullet B \right) - \left(X \ominus B \right) \right\} \right) \quad (6.38)$$

Experiment 6.27: Implementation of Morphological Edge Detection
This experiment deals with the implementation of morphological edge detection using Python. The Python code to perform the computation of morphological edge detection is given in Fig. 6.58, and its corresponding simulation output is shown in Fig. 6.59.

Inferences
The following inferences can be inferred from this experiment:

- From Fig. 6.58, it is possible to confirm that Eqs. (6.36)–(6.38) are implemented to get morphological edge detection of a grayscale image.
- Figure 6.59 shows the input and three different Lee edge detectors output. This figure clearly distinguishes the difference of those three edge detectors: that is, dynamic Lee edge detector output contains the edge and texture details; texture

```
# Grayscale Edge detection
import cv2
import numpy as np
import matplotlib.pyplot as plt
I = cv2.imread("cropped.jpg",0) # Input image
B=cv2.getStructuringElement(cv2.MORPH_RECT,(3,3))
# Dynamic Lee edge detector
y11=cv2.dilate(I, B, iterations = 1);
y12=cv2.erode(I, B, iterations = 1);
y1=np.minimum((y11-I),(I-y12))
# Texture Lee Edge detector
y21=cv2.morphologyEx(I, cv2.MORPH_CLOSE,B, iterations=1)
y22=cv2.morphologyEx(y11, cv2.MORPH_OPEN,B, iterations=1)
y2=np.minimum((y21-I),(y22-I))
# Ramp Lee edge detector
y3=np.minimum((y11-y21),(y22-y12))
plt.figure(figsize=(10,8)),plt.subplot(1,4,1),plt.imshow(I,cmap='gray'),plt.title('Input Image')
plt.xticks([]),plt.yticks([]),plt.subplot(1,4,2),plt.imshow(y1,cmap='gray'),
plt.title('Dynamic Lee'),plt.xticks([]),plt.yticks([]),plt.subplot(1,4,3),
plt.imshow(y2,cmap='gray'),plt.title('Texture Lee'),plt.xticks([]),plt.yticks([])
plt.subplot(1,4,4),plt.imshow(y3,cmap='gray'),plt.title('Ramp Lee'),plt.xticks([]),plt.yticks([])
plt.tight_layout()
```

Fig. 6.58 Python code to perform different Lee edge detectors

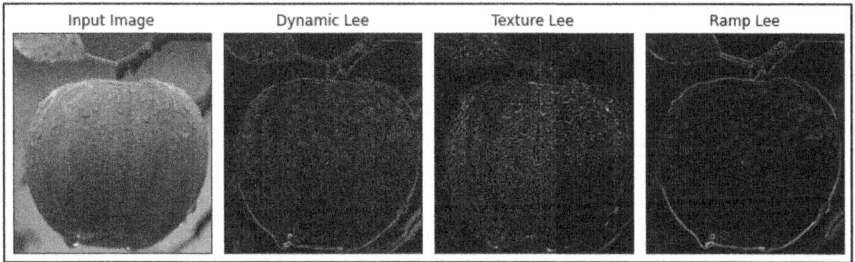

Fig. 6.59 Various edge detection outputs

Lee edge detector output has texture details only, whereas Ramp Lee edge detector contains the line edges and Lee texture edges.

Task: Change the input image in the Python code given in Fig. 6.58 by "squares. tif" and comment on the observed result.

6.11.7   Second-Order Derivative of Morphological Operation

This section discusses the morphological second-order derivatives. It can be achieved by subtracting the smoothed image from its original image. For the variety of smooth operations in the morphological processing, there are three types of second-order derivative morphological operations.

Dynamic Edge Gradient (DYG)

The mathematical expression of dynamic edge gradient (DYG) is defined as

$$DYG(X) = X - DYT(X) \tag{6.39}$$

where $DYT(X)$ denotes the dynamic smoothing of image X. This function will isolate all the edges in the input image.

Texture Edge Gradient (TEG)

The texture edge gradient will isolate only non-ramp edges instead of all edges. The mathematical expression for the texture edge gradient is given by

$$TEG(X) = X - TET(X) \tag{6.40}$$

where $TET(X)$ denotes the texture smoothing of image X.

Ramp Edge Gradient (RAG)

The ramp edge gradient of the image is computed from the difference between the dynamic edge gradient and texture edge gradient, which will retain only the ramp edges and exclude the texture edges and noise. The ramp edge gradient is mathematically written as

$$RAG(X) = DYG(X) - TEG(X) \tag{6.41}$$

where DYG(X) and TEG(X) represent the dynamic edge gradient and texture edge gradient of the image X.

Experiment 6.28: Implementation of Second-Order Derivatives Edge Detector

This experiment deals with the second-order derivative of a morphological edge detector using Python. The Python code to perform this task is given in Fig. 6.60, and its simulation result is depicted in Fig. 6.61.

Inferences

From this experiment, the following inferences can be drawn:

```python
# Second order derivative Edge detector
import cv2
import numpy as np
import matplotlib.pyplot as plt
I = cv2.imread("squares.tif",0) # Input image
B=cv2.getStructuringElement(cv2.MORPH_RECT,(3,3))
# Averaging erosion and dilation (Dynamic Smoothing)
y21=cv2.dilate(I, B, iterations = 1);
y22=cv2.erode(I, B, iterations = 1);
DYT=np.add(y21,y22)/2
DYG = I - DYT; # Dynamic Gradient
# Averaging Opening and Closing (texture smoothing)
y31=cv2.morphologyEx(I, cv2.MORPH_OPEN,B, iterations=1)
y32=cv2.morphologyEx(I, cv2.MORPH_CLOSE,B, iterations=1)
TET=np.add(y31,y32)/2
TEG = I - TET;# Texture Gradient
plt.figure(figsize=(10,8)),plt.subplot(1,4,1),plt.imshow(I,cmap='gray'),plt.title('Input Image')
plt.xticks([]),plt.yticks([]),plt.subplot(1,4,2),plt.imshow(DYG,cmap='gray'),
plt.title('Dynamic Gradient'),plt.xticks([]),plt.yticks([]),plt.subplot(1,4,3),
plt.imshow(TEG,cmap='gray'),plt.title('Texture Gradient'),plt.xticks([]),plt.yticks([])
plt.subplot(1,4,4),plt.imshow((DYG-TEG),cmap='gray'),plt.title('Ramp Gradient')
plt.xticks([]),plt.yticks([])
plt.tight_layout()
```

Fig. 6.60 Python code to perform second-order derivative edge detectors

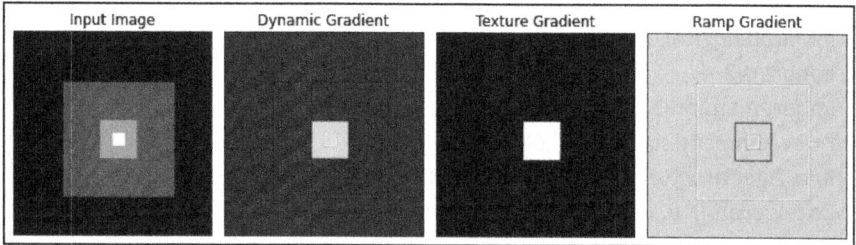

Fig. 6.61 Various second-order derivative edge detector outputs

- Figure 6.60 shows the implementation of Eqs. (6.39)–(6.41) in the Python platform.
- Figure 6.61 depicts the output of the second-order derivative edge detection. The ramp gradient output contains only the ramp edges, and noisy and texture edges are discarded.

6.11.8 Morphological Gradient

The high grayscale differences in the image defines the boundary or edge of the region of interest or object. The edges can be enhanced by gradient operation. The edge enhancement using morphological operation is called as morphological gradient. The basic morphological gradient computation can be achieved by taking the difference between dilation and erosion outputs. This method highlights the sharp gray level transitions in an image. The output depends on the selection of the structuring element. The basic difference between the gradients obtained using Sobel, Prewitt, and morphological gradients is that results tend to depend less on edge directionality due to symmetrical structuring elements.

The basic morphology gradient is also called as "Beucher gradient" and it is defined as the arithmetic difference between the dilation and erosion outputs by the same structuring element. The mathematical expression for the morphological gradient (ρ) is given by

$$\rho_B(X) = (X \oplus B) - (X \ominus B) \tag{6.42}$$

where B denotes the structuring element and X represents the input image.

Experiment 6.29: Basic Morphological Gradient Computation
The aim of this experiment is to obtain the morphological gradient using Python. The Python code to compute the morphological gradient is given in Fig. 6.62, and its corresponding simulation result is shown in Fig. 6.63.

Inferences
The following inferences can be observed from this experiment:

```
# Morphological Gradient
import cv2
import matplotlib.pyplot as plt
I = cv2.imread("squares.tif",0) # Input image
B=cv2.getStructuringElement(cv2.MORPH_RECT,(3,3))
D=cv2.dilate(I, B, iterations = 1); # Dilation operation
E=cv2.erode(I, B, iterations = 1); # Erosion operation
G=D-E;# Difference
plt.figure(figsize=(10,8)),plt.subplot(1,4,1),plt.imshow(I,cmap='gray'),
plt.title('Input Image'),plt.xticks([]),plt.yticks([]),plt.subplot(1,4,2),
plt.imshow(D,cmap='gray'),plt.title('Dilation'),plt.xticks([]),plt.yticks([])
plt.subplot(1,4,3),plt.imshow(E,cmap='gray'),plt.title('Erosion')
plt.xticks([]),plt.yticks([]),plt.subplot(1,4,4),plt.imshow(G,cmap='gray'),
plt.title('Morph_Gradient'),plt.xticks([]),plt.yticks([])
plt.tight_layout()
```

Fig. 6.62 Python code to perform morphological gradient

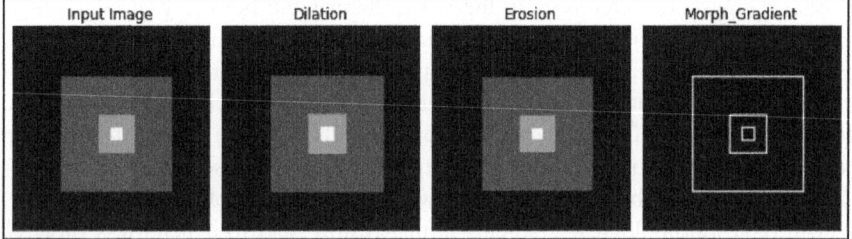

Fig. 6.63 Result of morphological gradient

- Figure 6.62 shows that dilation and erosion operations performed on the input image and the difference of those results gives the image gradient output.
- Figure 6.63 shows that the morphological gradient gives the maximum variation of the grayscale intensities within the neighbourhood defined by the structuring element rather than a local slope.

Experiment 6.30: Morphological Gradient Variants
This experiment discusses the texture gradients and smooth edge gradients using morphological gradients. The morphological gradient for the texture or noisy components in an image is given by

$$\text{Texture Gradient}\,(\text{TEG})\,(X) = (X \bullet B) - (X \circ B) \qquad (6.43)$$

The morphological gradient for the smooth edges in an image is defined as

$$\text{Ramp edge}(X) = \rho_B(X) - \text{TEG}(X)$$

$$= \left\{ (X \oplus B) - (X \ominus B) \right\} - \left\{ (X \bullet B) - (X \circ B) \right\} \tag{6.44}$$

The Python code to implement Eqs. (6.43) and (6.44) is given in Fig. 6.64, and its corresponding output is shown in Fig. 6.65.

```
# Morphological Gradient (Texture and Ramp edge)
import cv2
import matplotlib.pyplot as plt
I = cv2.imread("cropped.jpg",0) # Input image
B=cv2.getStructuringElement(cv2.MORPH_RECT,(3,3))
D=cv2.dilate(I, B, iterations = 1);
E=cv2.erode(I, B, iterations = 1);
G=D-E; # Morphological gradients
O=cv2.morphologyEx(I, cv2.MORPH_OPEN,B, iterations=1)
C=cv2.morphologyEx(I, cv2.MORPH_CLOSE,B, iterations=1)
TEG=C-O;# Texture gradients
RAG=(D-E)-TEG;# Ramp or smooth edge gradients
plt.figure(figsize=(10,8)),plt.subplot(1,3,1),plt.imshow(I,cmap='gray'),
plt.title('Input Image'),plt.xticks([]),plt.yticks([]),plt.subplot(1,3,2),
plt.imshow(TEG,cmap='gray'),plt.title('Texture Gradient'),plt.xticks([]),plt.yticks([])
plt.subplot(1,3,3),plt.imshow(RAG,cmap='gray'),plt.title('Ramp edge Gradient')
plt.xticks([]),plt.yticks([])
plt.tight_layout()
```

Fig. 6.64 Python code to perform texture and ramp edge gradient

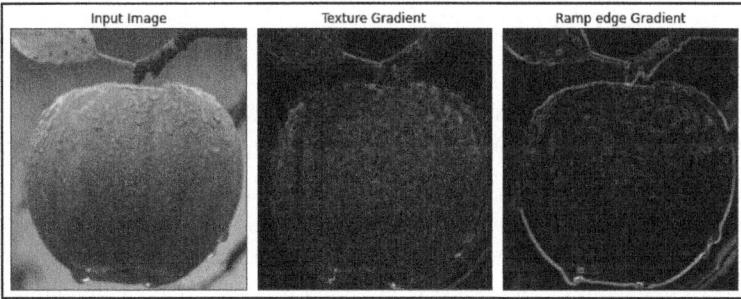

Fig. 6.65 Simulation result of texture and ramp edge gradients

Inferences

The following inferences can be drawn from this experiment:

- From Fig. 6.64, it is possible to observe that dilation, erosion, opening, and closing operations are used to obtain the texture and ramp edge gradients.
- Figure 6.65 shows that the texture edge gradient retains texture edges only, and the ramp edge gradient preserves strong, smooth edge regions only.

6.11.9   Boundary Extraction

This section discusses the boundary extraction of region of interest using basic morphological operations. Here, dilation and erosion operations are used to extract the boundary of the object or region of interest.

Internal Boundary Extraction

The internal boundary of the object is obtained by erosion operation and it is also called as internal gradient or half gradient by erosion. The mathematical expression for the internal gradient of the object is obtained as

$$\text{Internal Gradient}\left(\rho_B^-\right)(X) = X - \{X \ominus B\} \tag{6.45}$$

where B is the structuring element and X is the input image. The internal gradient is obtained by taking difference between input image and its eroded version. The internal gradient enhances the internal boundary of the object brighter than its background and the external boundaries of the object darker than the object.

External Boundary Extraction

The external boundary of the object can be obtained by using dilation operation, and it is termed as external gradient or half gradient by dilation. It can be obtained by taking the difference between the dilated version of the input image and the original input image. The mathematical expression for the external gradient of the object is written as

$$\text{External Gradient}\left(\rho_B^+\right)(X) = \{X \oplus B\} - X \tag{6.46}$$

The external gradient enhances the internal boundary of the objects darker than their background and external boundary of the objects brighter than their background.

Experiment 6.31: Boundary Extraction of an Object

The aim of this experiment is to obtain the internal and external boundary of the object using erosion and dilation operations. The Python code to extract the internal and external boundaries of an object is given in Fig. 6.66, and its simulation result is depicted in Fig. 6.67.

Inferences

From this experiment, the following inferences can be observed:

```
# Boundary extraction
import cv2
import matplotlib.pyplot as plt
I = cv2.imread("squares.tif",0) # Input image
B=cv2.getStructuringElement(cv2.MORPH_RECT,(3,3))
D=cv2.dilate(I, B, iterations = 1);
E=cv2.erode(I, B, iterations = 1);
IG=I-E; # Internal gradients
EG=D-I; # External gradients
plt.figure(figsize=(10,8)),plt.subplot(1,3,1),plt.imshow(I,cmap='gray'),
plt.title('Input Image'),plt.xticks([]),plt.yticks([]),plt.subplot(1,3,2),
plt.imshow(IG,cmap='gray'),plt.title('Internal Gradient'),plt.xticks([]),plt.yticks([])
plt.subplot(1,3,3),plt.imshow(EG,cmap='gray'),plt.title('External Gradient')
plt.xticks([]),plt.yticks([])
plt.tight_layout()
```

Fig. 6.66   Python code to perform boundary extraction

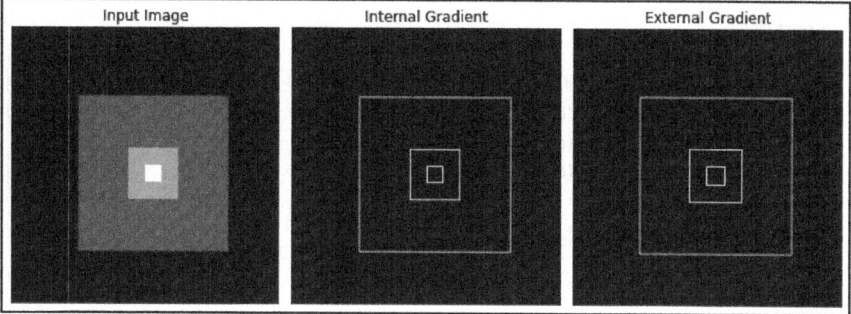

Fig. 6.67   Simulation result of boundary extraction

- From Fig. 6.66, it is possible to infer that dilation and erosion of the input image are obtained, as well as the difference between input and dilated/eroded version of input.
- Figure 6.67 depicts that the size of the internal gradient square is a little smaller than the size of the external gradient square output.

6.11.10   Thick Gradients

The morphological gradient is termed as thick gradient when the size of the structuring element is greater than 1. Thick gradient of an image is computed by dilation and erosion operations, which is expressed as

$$\text{Thick Gradient}\left(X_{nB}\right) = \left\{X \oplus nB\right\} - \left\{X \ominus nB\right\} \tag{6.47}$$

where "n" denotes the size of the structuring element. Thick gradient gives the maximum variation of the function in a neighbourhood of size "n". If the transitions between objects are smooth, then thick gradients are preferred.

Experiment 6.32: Computation of Thick Gradients
This experiment deals with the computation of thick gradients using Python. The Python code to perform the computation of thick gradients of an object is given in Fig. 6.68, and its corresponding simulation output is shown in Fig. 6.69.

Inferences
The following inferences can be observed from this experiment:

- Figure 6.68 shows that the size of the structuring element is chosen as 3×3, 5×5, and 7×7 with a rectangle kernel. Dilation and erosion operations are performed. Thickness gradient is obtained by taking difference between dilation and erosion results.
- From Fig. 6.69, it is possible to observe that the thicknesses of the gradient increase while increasing the size of the structuring element.

```
# Thick Gradients
import cv2
import matplotlib.pyplot as plt
I = cv2.imread("squares.tif",0) # Input image
B1=cv2.getStructuringElement(cv2.MORPH_RECT,(3,3))
B2=cv2.getStructuringElement(cv2.MORPH_RECT,(5,5))
B3=cv2.getStructuringElement(cv2.MORPH_RECT,(7,7))
D1=cv2.dilate(I, B1, iterations = 1);
E1=cv2.erode(I, B1, iterations = 1);
TG1=D1-E1; # Thick gradients
D2=cv2.dilate(I, B2, iterations = 1);
E2=cv2.erode(I, B2, iterations = 1);
TG2=D2-E2; # Thick gradients
D3=cv2.dilate(I, B3, iterations = 1);
E3=cv2.erode(I, B3, iterations = 1);
TG3=D3-E3; # Thick gradients
plt.figure(figsize=(10,8)),plt.subplot(1,4,1),plt.imshow(I,cmap='gray'),plt.title('Input Image'),
plt.xticks([]),plt.yticks([]),plt.subplot(1,4,2),plt.imshow(TG1,cmap='gray'),
plt.title('Thick Gradient (3 x 3)'),plt.xticks([]),plt.yticks([]),plt.subplot(1,4,3),
plt.imshow(TG2,cmap='gray'),plt.title('Thick Gradient (5 x 5)'),plt.xticks([]),plt.yticks([])
plt.subplot(1,4,4),plt.imshow(TG3,cmap='gray'),plt.title('Thick Gradient (7 x 7)'),
plt.xticks([]),plt.yticks([])
plt.tight_layout()
```

Fig. 6.68 Python code to perform boundary extraction

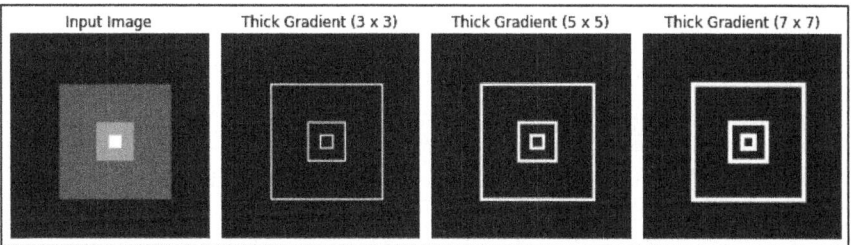

Fig. 6.69 Simulation result of boundary extraction

6.11.11 Directional Gradients

The directional gradient is defined by replacing the isotropic structuring element with a line segment (L) (horizontal, vertical, and diagonal) in a specific direction (α). The mathematical expression for the directional gradient is written as

$$\text{Directional Gradient}\left(\rho_{L\alpha}\right)(X) = \{X \oplus L\alpha\} - \{X \ominus L\alpha\} \qquad (6.48)$$

where "$L\alpha$" is the directional line segment structuring element.

Experiment 6.33: Directional Gradient Extraction
This experiment discusses the computation of directional gradient using Python. The different directional oriented line segments are used as structuring elements. The Python code to perform the task of directional gradient computation is given in Fig. 6.70, and its simulation result is shown in Fig. 6.71.

Inferences
The following inferences can be observed from this experiment:

- From Fig. 6.70, it is possible to observe that different directional structuring elements such as horizontal, vertical, and diagonal are generated, then these structuring elements are used for the dilation and erosion operations to compute directional gradients of the given input image.
- Figure 6.71 shows the directional gradients output of the given input image.

6.11.12 Top-Hat Transformation

The top hat is a morphological operation; it enhances image details such as thin, sharp, and positive variations in an image. The morphological top hat can be defined as the arithmetic difference between the original image and its opening or the closing and the original image. Therefore, it is classified into white top hat and black top hat.

```
# Directional Gradients
import cv2
import numpy as np
import matplotlib.pyplot as plt
I = cv2.imread("Resolution_Chart.tiff",0) # Input image
B1=np.array([[0, 0, 0],[1, 1, 1],[0, 0, 0]],'uint8');
B2=np.array([[0, 1, 0],[0, 1, 0],[0, 1, 0]],'uint8');
B3=np.array([[1, 0, 0],[0, 1, 0],[0, 0, 1]],'uint8');
B4=np.array([[0, 0, 1],[0, 1, 0],[1, 0, 0]],'uint8');
D1=cv2.dilate(I, B1, iterations = 1);
E1=cv2.erode(I, B1, iterations = 1);
DG1=D1-E1; # Horizontal gradients
D2=cv2.dilate(I, B2, iterations = 1);
E2=cv2.erode(I, B2, iterations = 1);
DG2=D2-E2; # Vertical gradients
D3=cv2.dilate(I, B3, iterations = 1);
E3=cv2.erode(I, B3, iterations = 1);
DG3=D3-E3; # Diagonal-1 gradients
D4=cv2.dilate(I, B4, iterations = 1);
E4=cv2.erode(I, B4, iterations = 1);
DG4=D4-E4; # Diagonal-2 gradients
plt.figure(figsize=(12,6)),plt.subplot(2,5,6),plt.imshow(I,cmap='gray'),plt.title('Input Image'),
plt.xticks([]),plt.yticks([]),plt.subplot(2,5,2),plt.imshow(B1,cmap='gray'),
plt.title('Horizontal (SE)'),plt.xticks([]),plt.yticks([]),plt.subplot(2,5,3),
plt.imshow(B2,cmap='gray'),plt.title('Vertical (SE)'),plt.xticks([]),plt.yticks([])
plt.subplot(2,5,4),plt.imshow(B3,cmap='gray'),plt.title('Diagonal-1 (SE)'),
plt.xticks([]),plt.yticks([]),plt.subplot(2,5,5),plt.imshow(B4,cmap='gray'),
plt.title('Diagonal-2 (SE)'),plt.xticks([]),plt.yticks([]),plt.subplot(2,5,7),
plt.imshow(DG1,cmap='gray'),plt.title('DG (Horizontal)'),plt.xticks([]),plt.yticks([]),
plt.subplot(2,5,8),plt.imshow(DG2,cmap='gray'),plt.title('DG (Vertical)'),
plt.xticks([]),plt.yticks([]),plt.subplot(2,5,9),plt.imshow(DG3,cmap='gray'),
plt.title('DG (Diagonal-1)'),plt.xticks([]),plt.yticks([]),plt.subplot(2,5,10),
plt.imshow(DG4,cmap='gray'),plt.title('DG (Diagonal-2)'),plt.xticks([]),plt.yticks([])
plt.tight_layout()
```

Fig. 6.70 Python code to perform directional gradients

The white top hat (WTH) is also termed as the top hat by opening, which can be mathematically expressed as

$$\mathrm{WTH}(X) = X - (X \circ B) \tag{6.49}$$

The white top-hat transform is used to extract the peaks in the image.

The black top hat (BTH) can be defined as the arithmetic difference between the closing and the original image, which is mathematically written as

$$\mathrm{BTH}(X) = (X \bullet B) - X \tag{6.50}$$

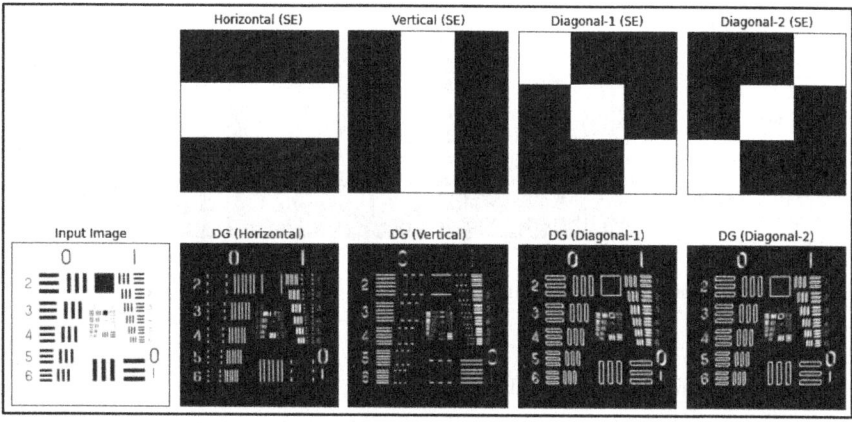

Fig. 6.71 Simulation result of directional gradient extraction

```
# Top Hat Transform
import cv2
import matplotlib.pyplot as plt
I = cv2.imread("Resolution_Chart.tiff",0) # Input image
B=cv2.getStructuringElement(cv2.MORPH_RECT,(5,5))
O=cv2.morphologyEx(I, cv2.MORPH_OPEN,B, iterations=1)
C=cv2.morphologyEx(I, cv2.MORPH_CLOSE,B, iterations=1)
WTH=I-O;# White Top Hat transform
BTH=C-I;# Black Top Hat Transform
diff=BTH-WTH
plt.figure(figsize=(10,8)),plt.subplot(1,4,1),plt.imshow(I,cmap='gray'),
plt.title('Input Image'),plt.xticks([]),plt.yticks([]),plt.subplot(1,4,2),
plt.imshow(WTH,cmap='gray'),plt.title('White Top Hat'),plt.xticks([]),plt.yticks([])
plt.subplot(1,4,3),plt.imshow(BTH,cmap='gray'),plt.title('Black Top Hat')
plt.xticks([]),plt.yticks([]),plt.subplot(1,4,4),plt.imshow(diff,cmap='gray'),
plt.title('Difference'),plt.xticks([]),plt.yticks([])
plt.tight_layout()
```

Fig. 6.72 Python code to perform top-hat transformation

The black top-hat transform is used to extract the troughs in the images.

Experiment 6.34: Implementation of Top-Hat Transform
The aim of this experiment is to perform the top-hat transform using Python. This experiment studies the difference between white top-hat and black top-hat transforms. The Python code to perform the computation of top-hat transform on a grayscale image is given in Fig. 6.72, and its corresponding output is depicted in Fig. 6.73.

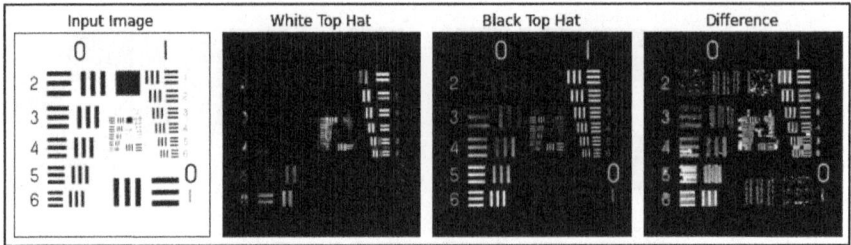

Fig. 6.73 Simulation result of top-hat transform

Inferences

The following inferences can be drawn from this experiment:

- From Fig. 6.72, it is possible to observe that white top-hat and black top-hat transforms are implemented.
- Figure 6.73 displays the results of white top hat, black top hat and the difference between both.

Exercises

1. Read any binary image and apply the dilation operation using two different structuring elements: (1) square, and (2) circle. Choose the size of structuring element as per your choice. Comment on the observed results.
2. Read any binary image and apply the erosion operation using two different structuring elements: (1) square, and (2) ellipse. Choose the size of structuring element as per your choice. Comment on the observed results.
3. Apply opening operation on any binary image with two different structuring elements: (1) ellipse, and (2) cross with the size of 5 × 5. Comment on the observed results.
4. Read a binary image given below and use hit-or-miss transform to extract only a square shape from it. Use suitable structuring element and erosion to perform

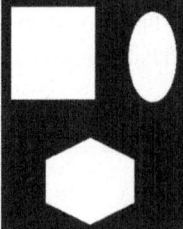

   the same.
5. Read "cameraman.tif" grayscale image and add a pepper noise only in it. Use a suitable structuring element to dilate this image. Comment on the observed result.
6. Read "cameraman.tif" grayscale image and add only a salt noise in it. Use a suitable structuring element to erode this image. Comment on the observed result.
7. Perform the edge detection "cameraman.tif" grayscale image using dilation in conjunction with suitable other morphological operation. Describe how you perform edge detection using dilation.

8. Perform the edge detection "Clock.tiff" grayscale image using erosion in conjunction with suitable other morphological operation. Describe how you perform edge detection using erosion.

Objective Questions

1. What will be the output after executing the following Python code?

```
import cv2
import numpy as np
I1= np.array([[0.,1.,0.],[1.,1.,1.],[0.,1.,0.]],'uint8');
I2= np.array([[1.,0.,1.],[0.,0.,0.],[1.,0.,1.]],'uint8');
out=cv2.bitwise_or(I1,I2)
print(out)
```

(A)
```
[[1 1 1]
 [1 1 1]
 [1 1 1]]
```

(B)
```
[[1 0 1]
 [0 0 0]
 [1 0 1]]
```

(C)
```
[[0 1 0]
 [1 1 1]
 [0 1 0]]
```

(D)
```
[[0 0 0]
 [0 0 0]
 [0 0 0]]
```

2. What will the output be after executing the following Python code?

```
import cv2
import numpy as np
I1= np.array([[0.,1.,0.],[1.,1.,1.],[0.,1.,0.]],'uint8');
I2= np.array([[1.,0.,1.],[0.,0.,0.],[1.,0.,1.]],'uint8');
out=cv2.bitwise_and(I1,I2)
print(out)
```

(A)
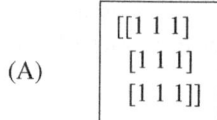

```
[[1 1 1]
 [1 1 1]
 [1 1 1]]
```

(B)
```
[[1 0 1]
 [0 0 0]
 [1 0 1]]
```

(C)
```
[[0 1 0]
 [1 1 1]
 [0 1 0]]
```

(D)
```
[[0 0 0]
 [0 0 0]
 [0 0 0]]
```

3. After executing the following Python code, the output will be

```
import cv2
import numpy as np
I1= np.array([[0.,1.,0.],[1.,1.,1.],[0.,1.,0.]],'uint8');
I2= np.array([[1.,0.,1.],[0.,0.,0.],[1.,0.,1.]],'uint8');
out=cv2.bitwisexor(I1,I2)
print(out)
```

(A)
```
[[1 1 1]
 [1 1 1]
 [1 1 1]]
```

(B)
```
[[1 0 1]
 [0 0 0]
 [1 0 1]]
```

(C)
```
[[0 1 0]
 [1 1 1]
 [0 1 0]]
```

(D)
```
[[0 0 0]
 [0 0 0]
 [0 0 0]]
```

4. What will the output be after executing the Python code below?

```
import cv2
import numpy as np
l1= np.array([[0.,1.,0.],[1.,1.,1.],[0.,1.,0.]],'uint8');
l2=np.pad(l1,[1,1]);
h= np.array([[1.,0.,1.],[0.,0.,0.],[1.,0.,1.]],'uint8');
out=cv2.dilate(l2,h)
print(out)
```

(A)
```
[[0 1 0 1 0]
 [1 1 1 1 1]
 [0 1 0 1 0]
 [1 1 1 1 1]
 [0 1 0 1 0]]
```

(B)
```
[[0 1 0 1 0]
 [1 1 1 1 1]
 [0 1 1 1 0]
 [1 1 1 1 1]
 [0 1 0 1 0]]
```

(C)
```
[[0 1 1 1 0]
 [1 1 1 1 1]
 [1 1 1 1 1]
 [1 1 1 1 1]
 [0 1 1 1 0]]
```

(D)
```
[[1 1 1 1 1]
 [1 1 1 1 1]
 [1 1 1 1 1]
 [1 1 1 1 1]
 [1 1 1 1 1]]
```

5. What will the output be after executing the Python code below?

```
import cv2
import numpy as np
l1= np.array([[0.,1.,0.],[1.,1.,1.],[0.,1.,0.]],'uint8');
l2=np.pad(l1,[1,1]);
h= np.array([[1.,0.,1.],[0.,0.,0.],[1.,0.,1.]],'uint8');
out=cv2.dilate(l2,h)
print(out)
```

(A)
[[0 1 0 1 0]
[1 1 1 1 1]
[0 1 0 1 0]
[1 1 1 1 1]
[0 1 0 1 0]]

(B)
[[0 0 0 0 0]
[0 0 0 0 0]
[0 0 0 0 0]
[0 0 0 0 0]
[0 0 0 0 0]]

(C)
[[0 1 1 1 0]
[1 1 1 1 1]
[1 1 1 1 1]
[1 1 1 1 1]
[0 1 1 1 0]]

(D)
[[1 1 1 1 1]
[1 1 1 1 1]
[1 1 1 1 1]
[1 1 1 1 1]
[1 1 1 1 1]]

6. Morphological opening operation can be defined as

   (A) Dilation followed by erosion operation
   (B) Erosion followed by dilation operation
   (C) Dilation followed by dilation operation
   (D) Erosion followed by erosion operation

7. Morphological closing operation can be defined as

   (A) Dilation followed by erosion operation
   (B) Erosion followed by dilation operation
   (C) Dilation followed by dilation operation
   (D) Erosion followed by erosion operation

8. Morphological gradient can be mathematically defined as

   (A) $(X \oplus B) - (X \ominus B)$
   (B) $(X \ominus B) - (X \oplus B)$
   (C) $(X \oplus B) + (X \ominus B)$
   (D) $(X \oplus B) \, XOR \, (X \ominus B)$

9. Mathematical expression for texture gradients is given by

  (A) $(X \circ B) - (X \bullet B)$
  (B) $(X \bullet B) - (X \circ B)$
  (C) $(X \bullet B) + (X \circ B)$
  (D) $(X \bullet B) \, XOR \, (X \circ B)$

10. The expression for the thick gradient is

  (A) $\{X \oplus nB\} + \{X \ominus nB\}$
  (B) $\{X \ominus nB\} - \{X \oplus nB\}$
  (C) $\{X \oplus nB\} - \{X \ominus nB\}$
  (D) $(X \bullet B) - (X \circ B)$

11. The black top-hat transform can be defined as

  (A) $X - (X \circ B)$
  (B) $X + (X \circ B)$
  (C) $(X \bullet B) - X$
  (D) $(X \bullet B) + X$

12. Statement 1: Dilation operation is commutative
    Statement 2: Erosion operation is commutative

  (A) Statements 1 and 2 are true
  (B) Statement 1 is true, Statement 2 is false
  (C) Statement 1 is false, Statement 2 is true
  (D) Statements 1 and 2 are false

Answers to Objective Questions

Q. No.	1	2	3	4	5	6	7	8	9	10
Key	A	D	A	A	B	B	A	A	B	C
Q. No.	11	12								
Key	C	B								

Answers to PreLab Questions

1. Morphological image processing is a collection of non-linear operations related to the shape or morphology of features in an image. Initially, the morphological operations performed on binary images are extended further into gray-scale image.

2. The structuring element is a small binary matrix; it takes the values of 1s and 0s. The matrix dimensions define the size of the structuring element. The pattern of 1s and 0s specifies the shape of the structuring element. The origin of the structuring element will be any one of the elements in the binary matrix.

3. The basic morphological operations are (1) dilation and (2) erosion. Dilation is a process in which the binary image is expanded from its shape. The expansion of the output image is decided by the size of the structuring element. Erosion is the counter process of dilation; it shrinks the input image (i.e. the number of ones in the output binary image is always lesser than a number of ones in the input binary image). These two operations are used for the other morphological operations such as opening, closing, boundary extraction, and so on.

S. No.	Closing	Opening
1.	Dilation followed by erosion operation	Erosion followed by dilation operation
2.	It fills the small holes and gaps in a single pixel object	It smooths the inside of the object contour, breaks narrow strips, and eliminates thin portions in the image
3.	It protects coarse structures, closes small gaps, and rounds off concave corners	It is used to remove noise in the image

4. The dilation and erosion operations can be used to extract the boundary of the object. The following equations can be used for the boundary extraction:

$$\text{Boundary}(X) = (X \oplus B) - X$$

$$\text{Boundary}(X) = X - (X \ominus B)$$

The dilated output is subtracted by the original input image, providing the boundary output. Similarly, the original input image is subtracted by the eroded output, resulting in boundary output.

5. The operation applies more than once, and it does not affect or change the output. That operation is an idempotent operation. The opening and closing operations are idempotent operations, which do not change the output applied more than once.

6. The hit-or-miss transform (HMT) is a morphological algorithm that can be used to look for particular patterns of foreground and background pixels in an image. The HMT is used for the template matching applications. For example, any missing parts in the PCB can be identified by the HMT using proper structuring element.

7. Top-hat transform is defined as the difference between input image and its opening output or the difference between closing output and the input image. The first one is called the white top-hat transform, and the second one is the black top-hat transform. This can be used to enhance the very thin details in an input image.

8. Thinning operation is a morphological operation, which reduces the foreground pixels of the object. It is similar to erosion or opening operation and it can be performed by using erosion and opening operations given by

$$S_i(X) = (X_{i-1} \ominus B) - ((X_{i-1} \ominus B) \circ B)$$

$$X \otimes B = \bigcup_i^{\substack{i=0 \\ N}} S_i(X)$$

where X_0 is the input binary image, B is the structuring element, $X_i = X_{i-1} \ominus B$, and "$\otimes$" denotes the thinning operation. S_i is the subset result of erosion and opening operation. Here, "i" indicates the iteration number of erosion. N is the last iterative step before X_i erodes to the empty set and is a stopping criterion.

Thinning operation can be implemented by using hit-or-miss transform, which is mathematically written as

$$X \otimes B = X - (X \circledast B)$$

where "$\circledast$" represents the hit-or-miss transform output of the input binary image X, and B is set of structuring elements denoted as $B = \{B_1, B_2, \ldots, B_N\}$. In general, B_i is the rotated version of the B_{i-1}. Here, sequence of structuring elements is used to produce symmetric results, and this operation is mostly applied in an iterative manner until no further changes occur.

9. Thickening is the duality of the thinning operation, which can be used to thicken the width of the thinned image. The mathematical expression for the thickening operation "$\odot$" is given by

$$A \odot B = \bigcup_{i=0}^{N} (A_i \oplus B)$$

where "$\oplus$" denotes dilation operation, "$\odot$" represents thickening operation, and N is the number of iterations for the dilation operation. A is the skeleton input image, which is to be thickened.

10. Yes. The morphological operations such as dilation, erosion, opening, closing, and so on can be applied on the grayscale image. The minimum and maximum non-linear operations can be used to perform the grayscale morphological operations.

11. The morphological smoothing on grayscale image is performed by opening operation followed by closing operation. The morphological smoothing can be obtained by taking average of erosion and dilation output, which is called as dynamic smoothing. The arithmetic average of opening and closing operations will give texture smoothing result.

12. The edge enhancement using morphological operation is termed as morphological gradient. The morphological gradient can be implemented by taking difference between dilation and erosion outputs with the same structuring element. The basic morphology gradient is called as Beucher gradient.

S. No.	Internal gradients	External gradients	Thick gradients
1.	It extracts internal boundary of the object or region of interest	It extracts the external boundary of the object or region of interest	It thickens the boundary of the object by increasing the size of the structuring element
2.	Input image is subtracted by erosion output $(X - \{X\Theta B\})$, which is called as half gradient by erosion	Dilated output is subtracted by the input image $(\{X \oplus B\} - X)$, which is called as half gradient by dilation	It is computed by dilation and erosion operations (i.e. difference between the dilation and erosion outputs) $= \{X \oplus nB\} - \{X\Theta nB\}$, where "$n$" denotes the size of the structuring element

13. The directional gradient is a kind of boundary extraction method that uses the line segment with a specific direction as a structuring element instead of an isotropic structuring element. The mathematical expression for the directional gradient is given by

$$\text{Directional Gradient}\left(\rho_{La}\right)\left(X\right) = \{X \oplus La\} - \{X\Theta La\}$$

where "La" is the directional line segment structuring element.

Bibliography

1. Kenneth R Castleman, Digital Image Processing, Pearson Education India; 1st edition, 2007.
2. Michael A. Wirth, Grayscale Morphological Analysis, Computing and Information Science, University of Guelph, 2004.
3. S. Jayaraman, S. Esakkirajan, and T. Veerakumar, Digital Image Processing, 2nd Edition, Tata McGraw Hill, New Delhi, 2021.
4. Rafael C. Gonzalez, Richard E. Woods, Digital Image Processing, 4th Edition, Pearson Education Limited, 2018.
5. Pierre Soille, "Morphological Image Analysis: Principles and Applications", Springer, 2002.
6. Edward Dougherty and Robert Lotufo, "Hands-on Morphological Image Processing", SPIE Press, 2003

Chapter 7
Image Segmentation

Learning Objectives

After completing this chapter, the reader should be able to

- Perform image segmentation based on discontinuity.
- Perform and analyze different region-based image segmentation.
- Perform and analyze different clustering-based image segmentation.
- Perform and analyze graph-based image segmentation.

Roadmap of the Chapter

The concepts discussed in this chapter are illustrated in the form of a roadmap, which is given in Fig. 7.1.

Prelab Questions

1. What is the objective of image segmentation?
2. Mention different techniques used to perform image segmentation.
3. Why is a Laplacian operator considered an isotropic operator?
4. Compare Canny edge detector with Laplacian-of-Gaussian (LoG) edge detector.
5. What is the objective of performing (1) Non-maxima suppression and (2) Hysteresis threshold operation in Canny edge detector?
6. What is the fundamental principle behind the active contour method of image segmentation?
7. Why is the active contour model also termed the "Snake" algorithm?
8. Mention the pros and cons of the active contour method of image segmentation.
9. Mention valid differences between the k-means clustering algorithm and the mean shift algorithm.

Supplementary Information The online version contains supplementary material available at https://doi.org/10.1007/978-981-96-6382-8_7.

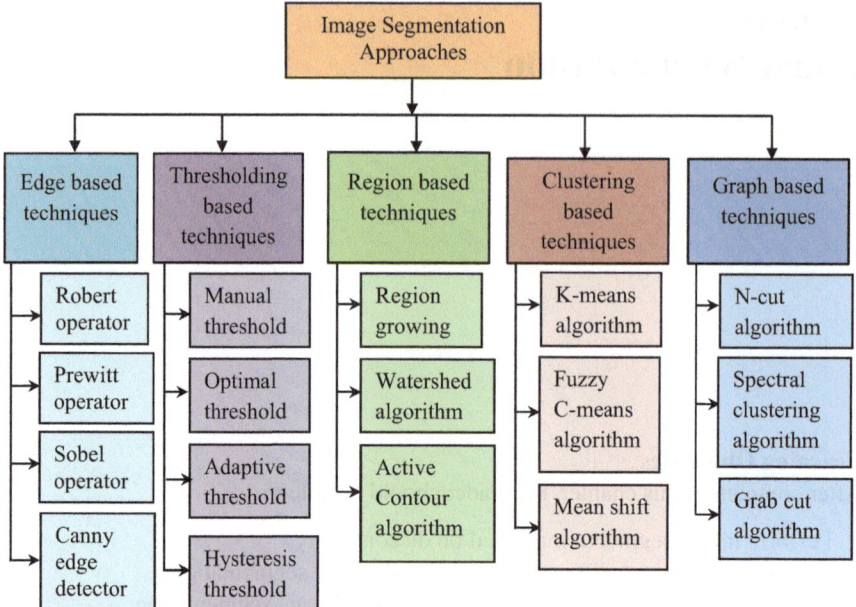

Fig. 7.1 Roadmap of the chapter

10. What is clustering? Mention a valid difference between the k-means clustering algorithm and the Fuzzy C-means clustering algorithm.

7.1   Introduction

Image segmentation partitions the image into its constituent regions. One view of image segmentation is to divide an image into multiple non-overlapping regions. The other view considers it the process of grouping pixels together that have similar attributes. Segmentation algorithms can be grouped into two categories: (1) Segmentation based on discontinuity and (2) Segmentation based on similarity. Segmentation based on discontinuity detects local discontinuity in intensity. Segmentation based on similarity partitions an image into regions that are similar according to a set of predefined criteria. The overall view of different types of image segmentation methods is given in Fig. 7.2.

Image segmentation is an essential building block for most image processing and computer vision tasks. Image segmentation is widely used in medical imaging, face recognition, pedestrian detection, etc.

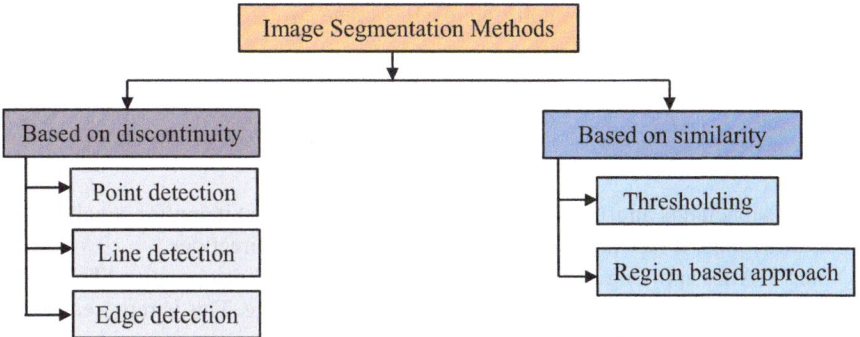

Fig. 7.2 Different methods of image segmentation

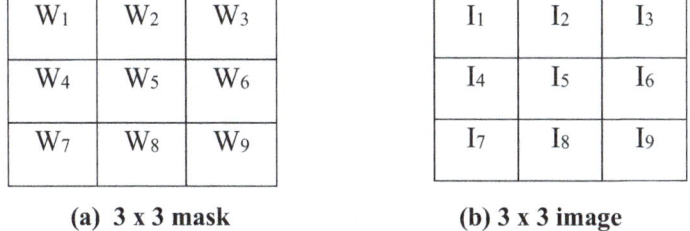

(a) **3 x 3 mask**   (b) **3 x 3 image**

Fig. 7.3 Mask and the corresponding portion of the image. (a) 3×3 mask. (b) 3×3 image

7.2   Edge-Based Image Segmentation

Edges correspond to drastic changes in the gray level of the image. First-order and second-order differential operators are used to detect the discontinuities in the gray level of the image. This section discusses different edge detection algorithms.

7.2.1   Isolated Point Detection

The fundamental idea employed in isolated point detection is that second-order derivatives respond stronger at isolated points and thin lines than first-order derivatives. Hence, the Laplacian mask, which is based on a second-order derivative, is used to detect the isolated points. The steps involved in isolated point detection are

Step 1: Apply Laplacian mask over the input image to detect the isolated points. This is shown in Fig. 7.3.

By applying the 3×3 mask over the image one gets

$$\nabla^2 f\left(x,y\right) = \sum\nolimits_{i=1}^{9} w_i I_i \tag{7.1}$$

The expression for 3×3 Laplacian mask is given by

$$w(x,y) = \begin{bmatrix} -1 & -1 & -1 \\ -1 & 8 & -1 \\ -1 & -1 & -1 \end{bmatrix} \tag{7.2}$$

The Laplacian is an isotropic operator, which implies that it applies equally well in all directions. It has no bias towards a particular set of directions.

Step 2: After applying Laplacian mask, use the thresholding operation (T denotes Threshold value) to identify the isolated points in the image. This is represented as

$$g(x,y) = \begin{cases} 1, & \left| \nabla^2 f(x,y) \right| > T \\ 0, & \text{otherwise} \end{cases} \tag{7.3}$$

Experiment 7.1: Isolated Point Detection

This experiment discusses the implementation of isolated point detection using Laplacian mask. The Python code that performs the above-mentioned task is given in Fig. 7.4, and its corresponding output is shown in Fig. 7.5.

Inferences

The following inferences can be drawn from this experiment:

- From Fig. 7.4, it is possible to infer that the "cv2.Laplacian"command is used here to compute the isolated points in the input image. The "cv2.threshold" command is used for retaining the higher value in the final result and removing the lesser values in the isolated point output.
- From Fig. 7.5, it is possible to observe that some of the isolated points are removed after the thresholding process.

```
#Isolated point detection
import matplotlib.pyplot as plt
import cv2 as cv2
img=cv2.imread('cameraman.tif',0)
Edge_out = cv2.Laplacian(img, -1, ksize=3, scale=1,delta=0,borderType=cv2.BORDER_DEFAULT)
thresh,out = cv2.threshold(Edge_out,225,255,cv2.THRESH_BINARY)
fig = plt.figure(figsize=(9,3))
plt.subplot(1,3,1),plt.imshow(img,cmap='gray'), plt.title('Input Image'),plt.axis('off')
plt.subplot(1,3,2),plt.imshow(Edge_out,cmap='gray'),plt.title('Without Thresholding')
plt.axis('off'),plt.subplot(1,3,3),plt.imshow(out,cmap='gray'),plt.axis('off')
plt.title(r'With Thresholding = {}'.format(thresh))
plt.tight_layout()
```

Fig. 7.4 Python code for isolated point detection

Fig. 7.5 Result of Python code given in Fig. 7.4

7.2.2   Line Detection

There are three different types of line edges such as (1) Step edge, (2) Ramp edge, and (3) Roof edge. Step edge refers to a sudden change in gray level value. Ramp edge refers to a gradual change in the gray level value. For the roof edge profile, the intensity value should first increase, and then proportionately, it should decrease. The image that exhibits step edge can be generated by the black and white image in which 50% of the image exhibits a low gray level value (0), and the remaining 50% should exhibit a high gray level value (255). The image that exhibits a ramp edge is obtained by performing a smoothing operation on the image that exhibits a step edge profile. Smoothing operation converts sudden change in gray level value to gradual change in the gray level value.

Experiment 7.2: Types of Edges in Digital Image
This experiment aims to generate the three types of line edge images and display their edge profile. The Python code that generates the edge images and their edge profile is shown in Figs. 7.6 and 7.7, respectively.

Inferences
The following inferences can be drawn from this experiment:

- Image-1 exhibits step edge profile. Sudden change results in a step-edge profile. Upon observing image-1, it is possible to infer that Image-1 has a gray level value of "1", which immediately takes a value of '0'. This results in discontinuity in the image.
- Image-2 exhibits a ramp edge profile. Image-2 is obtained from Image-1 by passing Image-1 through a low pass filter. The size of the low pass filter mask used in this experiment is 19×19. The sudden change is converted into a gradual change upon performing low-pass filtering.
- Image-3 exhibits the roof edge profile. At the centre, the gray level value is high and is gradually decreasing at both ends from the centre, which results in a roof edge.

```
#Types of edges
import numpy as np
import matplotlib.pyplot as plt
import cv2
#Step1: Generation of image which exhibits step edge
img1=np.zeros([256,256])
img1[0:256,0:128]=255
#Step 2: Generation of image that exhibit ramp edge
kernel = np.ones((19,19), np.float32)/361
img2=cv2.filter2D(img1,-1,kernel)
img3=np.zeros([256,256])
#Step 3: Generation of image that exhibit roof edge
img3[:,100:120]=np.array(np.arange(0,240,12))
img3[:,120:140]=np.array(np.arange(240,0,-12))
#Step 4: Plotting the image and their edge profiles
plt.subplot(2,3,1),plt.imshow(img1,cmap='gray'),plt.title('Image-1')
plt.xticks([]),plt.yticks([]),plt.subplot(2,3,2),plt.imshow(img2,cmap='gray'),
plt.title('Image-2'),plt.xticks([]),plt.yticks([]),plt.subplot(2,3,3),
plt.imshow(img3,cmap='gray'),plt.title('Image-3'),plt.xticks([]),plt.yticks([])
plt.subplot(2,3,4),plt.plot(img1[128,:]),plt.title('Step edge'),plt.xticks([]),
plt.yticks([]),plt.subplot(2,3,5),plt.plot(img2[128,:]),plt.title('Ramp edge')
plt.xticks([]),plt.yticks([]),plt.subplot(2,3,6),plt.plot(img3[128,:]),
plt.title('Roof edge'),plt.xticks([]),plt.yticks([])
plt.tight_layout()
```

Fig. 7.6 Python code which generates images that exhibit different edge profiles

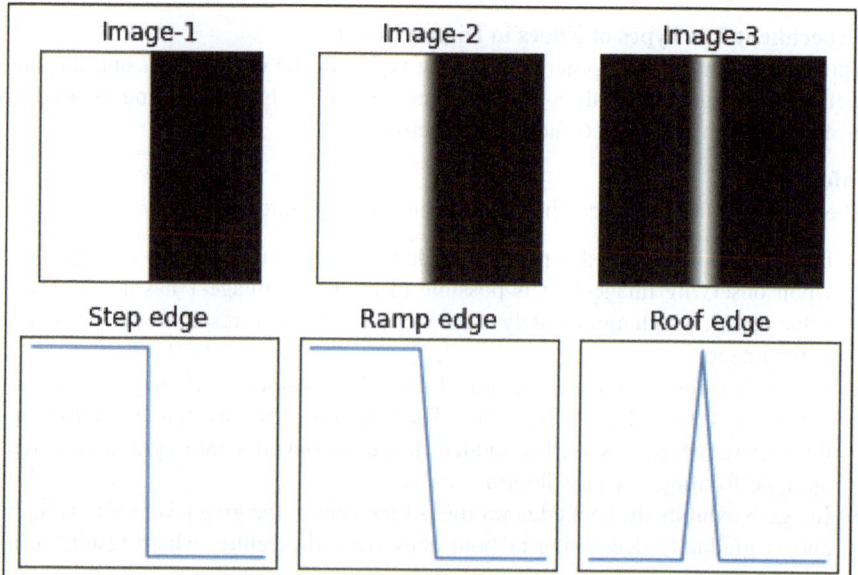

Fig. 7.7 Images and their edge profiles

Experiment 7.3: Generate an Image Which Exhibits Spike Edge

This experiment deals with the generation of spike image using Python. The Python code which generates an image that exhibits a spike-like edge profile is shown in Fig. 7.8, and the corresponding output is shown in Fig. 7.9.

Experiment 7.4: Various Lines Detection in Image

In this experiment, the test image generated has horizontal, vertical, and diagonal lines. The generated image is passed through a horizontal line detection mask, vertical line detection mask, and diagonal line detection mask to obtain the output images. The mask used to detect the horizontal, vertical, and diagonal lines is given in Table 7.1. The Python code that performs this task is shown in Fig. 7.10, and the corresponding output is shown in Fig. 7.11.

```
#Image exhibiting spike edge profile
import numpy as np
import matplotlib.pyplot as plt
#Step1: Generation of image which exhibit step change
img=np.zeros([256,256])
img[:,128]=255
#Step 2: Plotting the image and the edge profile
plt.subplot(2,1,1),plt.imshow(img,cmap='gray'),plt.title('Spike edge like Image')
plt.axis('off'),plt.subplot(2,1,2),plt.plot(img[128,:]),plt.title('Edge profile'),
plt.xticks([]),plt.yticks([])
plt.tight_layout()
```

Fig. 7.8 Python code to generate image with spike edge profile

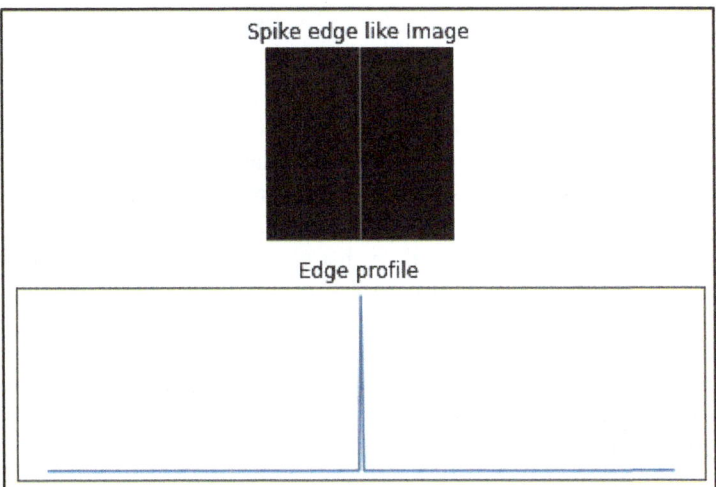

Fig. 7.9 Result of Python code shown in Fig. 7.8

Table 7.1 Mask to detect different types of lines

S. No.	Nature of the mask	Mask
1	Horizontal line detection	$\begin{bmatrix} -1 & -1 & -1 \\ 2 & 2 & 2 \\ -1 & -1 & -1 \end{bmatrix}$
2	Vertical line detection	$\begin{bmatrix} -1 & 2 & -1 \\ -1 & 2 & -1 \\ -1 & 2 & -1 \end{bmatrix}$
3	Diagonal line detection	$\begin{bmatrix} -1 & -1 & 2 \\ -1 & 2 & -1 \\ 2 & -1 & -1 \end{bmatrix}$
4	Diagonal line detection	$\begin{bmatrix} 2 & -1 & -1 \\ -1 & 2 & -1 \\ -1 & -1 & 2 \end{bmatrix}$

Inferences

The following inferences can be observed from this experiment:

- The input image has horizontal, vertical, and diagonal lines.
- The horizontal line detector highlights only the horizontal line. The vertical line detector highlights the vertical line.
- The diagonal edge detector detects or highlights the diagonal line in the input image.
- The point detector highlights all the points in the input image.

7.2.3 Edge Detection

Edges are significant local changes in the intensity of the image. Edge detection is a method of segmenting images into regions of discontinuity. Edge detection can be performed using either first-order or second-order derivative operators. The classification of edge detection algorithm based on first-order or second-order derivatives is shown in Fig. 7.12.

Gradients are mathematical functions that measure the intensity changes of an image. First-order and second-order derivative filters are used to compute image gradients. The gradient-based edge detection procedure is shown in Fig. 7.13. From this figure, it is possible to observe that the computation of gradient along x and y directions is the first step, and then the magnitude and phase angle are computed from the gradient of the input image.

The gradient magnitude is expressed as

$$M = \sqrt{G_x^2 + G_y^2} \tag{7.4}$$

```
#Various Lines detection
import numpy as np
import matplotlib.pyplot as plt
import cv2
#Step 1: Generation of test image
img=np.zeros([256,256])
img[128,:]=255 #Horizontal line
img[:,128]=255 #Vertical line
#Diagonal lines
for i in range(0,256):
   for j in range(0,256):
      if (i==j)|(i==256-j):
         img[i,j]=255
#Step 2: Defining the line detection mask
h1=np.array([[-1,-1,-1],[2,2,2],[-1,-1,-1]]) #Horizontal
h2=np.array([[-1,2,-1],[-1,2,-1],[-1,2,-1]]) #Vertical
h3=np.array([[-1,-1,2],[-1,2,-1],[2,-1,-1]]) #Diagonal
h4=np.array([[2,-1,-1],[-1,2,-1],[-1,-1,2]]) #Diagonal
h5=np.array([[0,-1,0],[-1,4,-1],[0,-1,0]]) #Point
#Step 3: Filtered image
img1=cv2.filter2D(img,-1,h1)
img2=cv2.filter2D(img,-1,h2)
img3=cv2.filter2D(img,-1,h3)
img4=cv2.filter2D(img,-1,h4)
img5=cv2.filter2D(img,-1,h5)
#Step 4: Plotting the result
fig=plt.figure(figsize=(8,6))
plt.subplot(2,3,1),plt.imshow(img,cmap='gray'),plt.title('Input image'),plt.axis('off')
plt.subplot(2,3,2),plt.imshow(img1,cmap='gray', vmin=150,vmax=255),plt.axis('off')
plt.title('Horizontal line detection'),plt.subplot(2,3,3),
plt.imshow(img2,cmap='gray',vmin=150,vmax=255),plt.title('Vertical line detection')
plt.axis('off'),plt.subplot(2,3,4),plt.imshow(img3,cmap='gray',vmin=160,vmax=255)
plt.title('Diagonal line detection'),plt.axis('off'),plt.subplot(2,3,5),
plt.imshow(img4,cmap='gray',vmin=200,vmax=255),plt.title('Diagonal line detection')
plt.axis('off'),plt.subplot(2,3,6),plt.imshow(img5,cmap='gray',vmin=0,vmax=255),
plt.title('All lines detection'),plt.axis('off')
plt.tight_layout()
```

Fig. 7.10 Python code to illustrate horizontal, vertical, and diagonal line detection

The gradient direction is expressed as

$$\varphi = \tan^{-1}\left(\frac{G_y}{G_x}\right) \tag{7.5}$$

The gradient magnitude represents the strength of the edge. The gradient angle describes the direction of the edge.

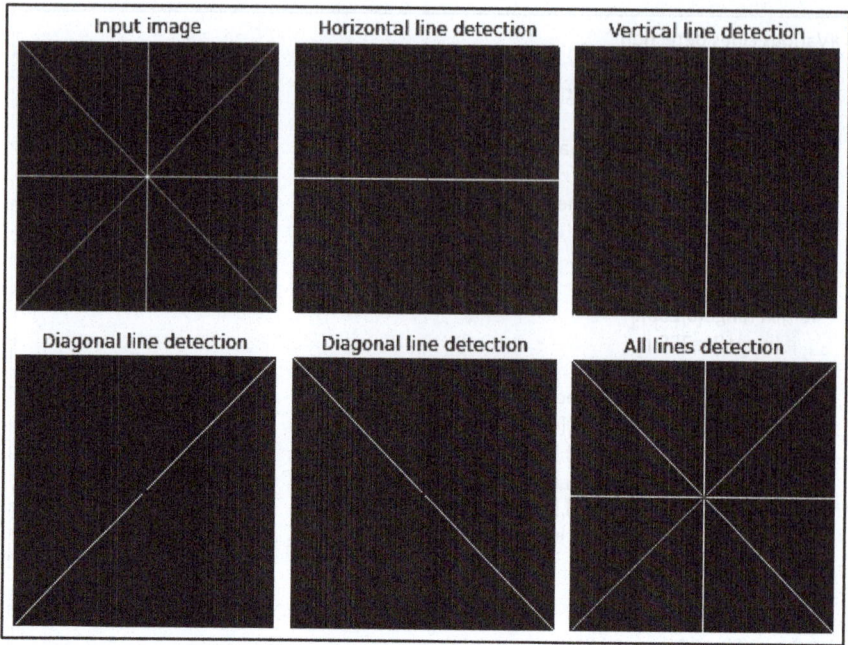

Fig. 7.11 Output of the Python code shown in Fig. 7.10

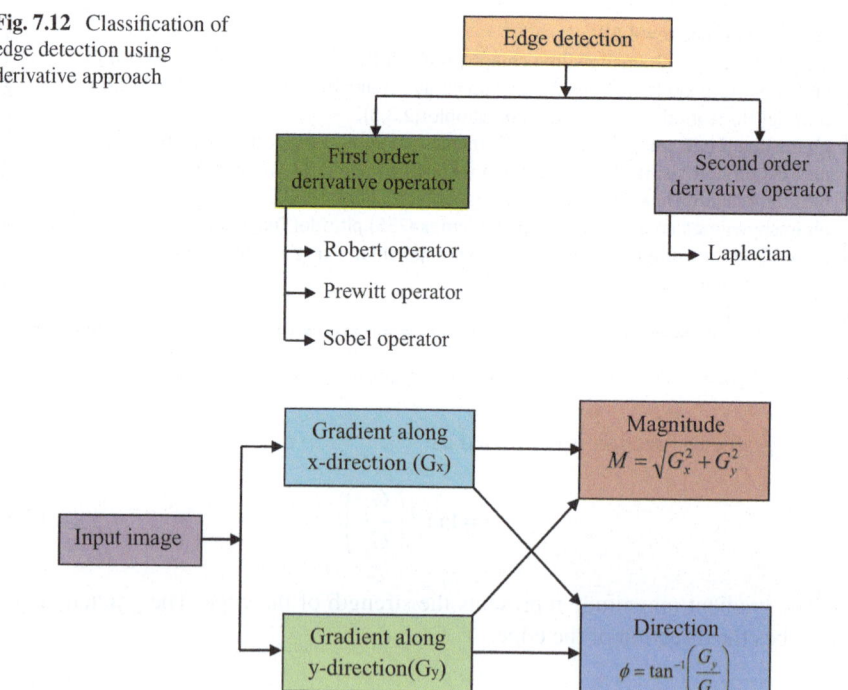

Fig. 7.12 Classification of edge detection using derivative approach

Fig. 7.13 Edge detection using gradient approach

Experiment 7.5: Robert Edge Detection

The aim of this experiment is to implement Robert edge detection approach in a Python environment. The Python code that performs edge detection using the Robert operator is given in Fig. 7.14, and the corresponding output is shown in Fig. 7.15. The steps followed in Robert edge detection are as follows:

Step 1: Generation of test image. The test image is black-and-white, which has a sharp transition from black to white. This implies that the test image exhibits edges along the x and y-directions.

Step 2: Computing the gradient of the input image along x and y directions using Robert operator.

Step 3: Computing the Magnitude of the edge.

Step 4: Computing the Direction of the edge.

Step 5: Displaying the results.

Inferences

- The gradient along *the* x-direction detects the change in intensity of the image along *the* x-direction.

```
# Robert Edge Detection
import numpy as np
import matplotlib.pyplot as plt
import cv2
#Step 1: Generation of test image
img=np.zeros([256,256])
img[78:178,78:178]=255
rows,cols=img.shape
M = cv2.getRotationMatrix2D((cols/2,rows/2),-45,1)
img_input = cv2.warpAffine(img,M,(cols,rows))
#Step2: Defining the Robert mask
gx=np.array([[1,0],[0,-1]])
gy=np.array([[0,1],[-1,0]])
#Step 3: Determining the gradient along x and y direction
Gx=cv2.filter2D(img_input,-1,gx)
Gy=cv2.filter2D(img_input,-1,gy)
#Step 4: Determining the magnitude and direction
magnitude=np.sqrt(np.square(Gx)+np.square(Gy))
direction=np.arctan2(Gy,Gx)/(180*np.pi)
#Step 5: Displaying the results
plt.figure(figsize=(8,6)),plt.subplot(2,3,1),plt.imshow(img_input,cmap='gray')
plt.title('Input image'),plt.xticks([]),plt.yticks([]),plt.subplot(2,3,2),
plt.imshow(Gx,cmap='gray'),plt.title('Gradient along x-direction'),plt.xticks([]),
plt.yticks([]),plt.subplot(2,3,3),plt.imshow(Gy,cmap='gray'),plt.xticks([]),
plt.yticks([]),plt.title('Gradient along y-direction'),plt.xticks([]),plt.yticks([])
plt.subplot(2,3,5),plt.imshow(magnitude,cmap='gray'),plt.title('Magnitude of the edge')
plt.xticks([]),plt.yticks([]),plt.subplot(2,3,6),plt.imshow(direction,cmap='gray')
plt.title('Direction of the edge'),plt.xticks([]),plt.yticks([])
plt.tight_layout()
```

Fig. 7.14 Python code to detect edge using Robert operator

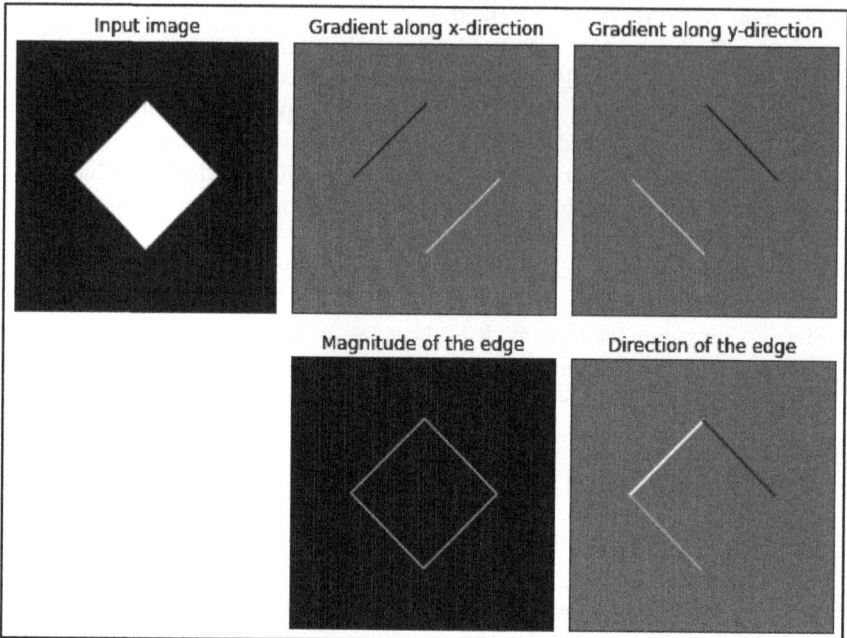

Fig. 7.15 Result of edge detection using Robert operator

- The gradient along *the* y-direction detects the change in intensity of the image along *the* y-direction.
- The magnitude of the edge represents the strength of the edge, whereas the angle represents the direction of the edge.

Experiment 7.6: Prewitt Edge Detection
This experiment discusses the implementation of Prewitt operator-based edge detection. The Python code to detect edges using the Prewitt operator is shown in Fig. 7.16, and the corresponding output is shown in Fig. 7.17.

Inferences

- The Prewitt operator is capable of detecting edges along "*x*" and "*y*" directions.
- The magnitude of the edge displays the strength of the edge.
- The angle of the edge indicates the direction of the edge.

Experiment 7.7: Sobel Edge Detection
This experiment deals with the implementation of the Sobel edge detector using Python. The Python code to detect the gradient along *x* and *y*-directions, the corresponding magnitude and angle is shown in Fig. 7.18, and the corresponding output is shown in Fig. 7.19.

```
# Prewitt Edge Detection
import numpy as np
import matplotlib.pyplot as plt
import cv2
#Step 1: Generation of test image
img_input=cv2.imread('test1.jpg',0)
#Step2: Defining the Prewitt mask
gx=np.array([[-1,0,1],[-1,0,1],[-1,0,1]])
gy=np.array([[-1,-1,-1],[0,0,0],[1,1,1]])
#Step 3: Determining the gradient along x and y direction
Gx=cv2.filter2D(img_input,-1,gx)
Gy=cv2.filter2D(img_input,-1,gy)
#Step 4: Determining the magnitude and direction
magnitude=np.sqrt(np.square(Gx)+np.square(Gy))
direction=np.arctan2(Gy,Gx)/(180*np.pi)
#Step 5: Displaying the results
plt.figure(figsize=(8,4)),plt.subplot(2,3,1),plt.imshow(img_input,cmap='gray')
plt.title('Input image'),plt.xticks([]),plt.yticks([]),plt.subplot(2,3,2),
plt.imshow(Gx,cmap='gray'),plt.title('Gradient along x-direction'),plt.xticks([]),
plt.yticks([]),plt.subplot(2,3,3),plt.imshow(Gy,cmap='gray'),plt.xticks([]),
plt.yticks([]),plt.title('Gradient along y-direction'),plt.xticks([]),plt.yticks([])
plt.subplot(2,3,5),plt.imshow(magnitude,cmap='gray'),plt.title('Magnitude of the edge')
plt.xticks([]),plt.yticks([]),plt.subplot(2,3,6),plt.imshow(direction,cmap='gray')
plt.title('Direction of the edge'),plt.xticks([]),plt.yticks([])
plt.tight_layout()
```

Fig. 7.16 Python code to obtain Prewitt edge detection

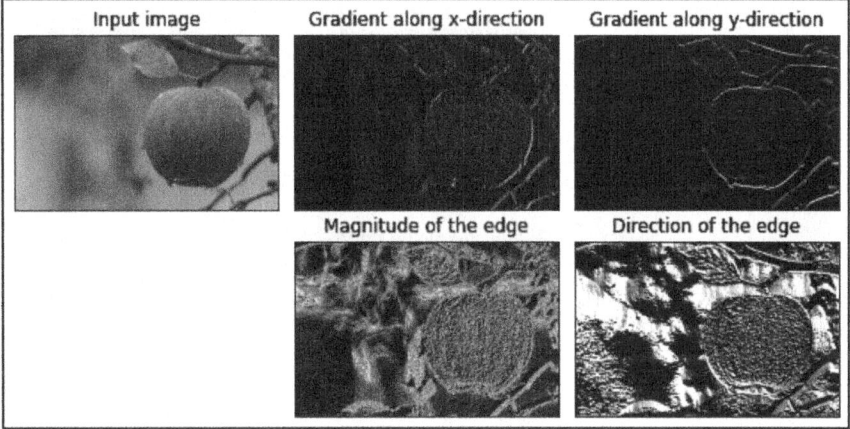

Fig. 7.17 Result of Prewitt edge detection

```
# Sobel Edge Detection
import numpy as np
import matplotlib.pyplot as plt
import cv2
#Step 1: Generation of test image
img_input=cv2.imread('W.png',0)
#Step2: Defining the Sobel mask
gx=np.array([[-1,-2,-1],[0,0,0],[1,2,1]])
gy=np.array([[-1,0,1],[-2,0,2],[-1,0,1]])
#Step 3: Determining the gradient along x and y direction
Gx=cv2.filter2D(img_input,-1,gx)
Gy=cv2.filter2D(img_input,-1,gy)
#Step 4: Determining the magnitude and direction
magnitude=np.sqrt(np.square(Gx)+np.square(Gy))
direction=np.arctan2(Gy,Gx)/(180*np.pi)
#Step 5: Displaying the results
plt.figure(figsize=(8,4)),plt.subplot(2,3,1),plt.imshow(img_input,cmap='gray')
plt.title('Input image'),plt.xticks([]),plt.yticks([]),plt.subplot(2,3,2),
plt.imshow(Gx,cmap='gray'),plt.title('Gradient along x-direction'),plt.xticks([]),
plt.yticks([]),plt.subplot(2,3,3),plt.imshow(Gy,cmap='gray'),plt.xticks([]),
plt.yticks([]),plt.title('Gradient along y-direction'),plt.xticks([]),plt.yticks([])
plt.subplot(2,3,5),plt.imshow(magnitude,cmap='gray'),plt.title('Magnitude of the edge')
plt.xticks([]),plt.yticks([]),plt.subplot(2,3,6),plt.imshow(direction,cmap='gray')
plt.title('Direction of the edge'),plt.xticks([]),plt.yticks([])
plt.tight_layout()
```

Fig. 7.18 Python code to determine the edge using Sobel operator

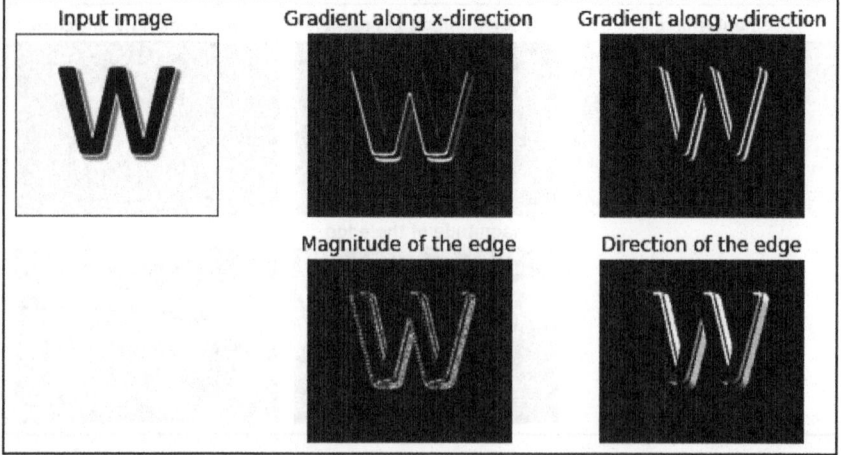

Fig. 7.19 Result of Sobel edge detection

Inferences

- In this experiment, the Sobel mask is used to compute the gradient along the horizontal and vertical directions.
- The magnitude and the angle of Sobel edge detector are also computed.
- From this experiment, it is possible to conclude that Sobel operator effectively captures the intensity change along the horizontal and vertical direction.

Canny Edge Detection

John F. Canny proposed the Canny edge detection algorithm in the year 1986. Canny edge detection is one of the most widely used algorithms to detect edges in a grayscale image. It is a multi-stage edge detection algorithm. The steps involved in Canny edge detection are summarized below:

1. Perform Gaussian smoothing of the input image.
2. Compute gradient along horizontal and vertical directions using the Sobel operator.
3. Perform non-maximum suppression. In non-maximum suppression, the image is scanned along the image gradient direction. If the pixels are not part of the local maxima, they are set to zero. Non-maximum suppression is done to thin out the edges.
4. Hysteresis thresholding is used to classify the edge. Two thresholds are employed in hysteresis thresholding, namely, upper and lower thresholds. Higher threshold is used to identify the strong pixels. Lower threshold is used to identify non-relevant pixels. Pixels having intensity between the upper and lower thresholds are flagged as weak.

Experiment 7.8: Canny Edge Detection
The aim of this experiment is to compute the Canny edge detection using Python. The Python code, which performs the step-by-step edge detection using the Canny edge detection algorithm, is given in Fig. 7.20, and the corresponding output is shown in Fig. 7.21.

Inferences
From Fig. 7.21, the following inferences can be drawn:

- Gaussian smoothing results in smoothing of edge information.
- Sobel operator is used to detect the intensity variation along horizontal and vertical direction.
- Non-maximum suppression is used to remove weak edges in the input image.
- The final result is obtained by performing hysteresis thresholding to the result of non-maximum suppression.

```python
#Canny edge detection
import cv2
import numpy as np
import matplotlib.pyplot as plt
img=cv2.imread('cameraman.tif',0)
# Step 1: Gaussian Smoothing
blurred_img = cv2.GaussianBlur(img, (5, 5), 1.1)
# Step 2: Gradient Calculation
sobel_x = cv2.Sobel(blurred_img, cv2.CV_64F, 1, 0, ksize=5)
sobel_y = cv2.Sobel(blurred_img, cv2.CV_64F, 0, 1, ksize=5)
gradient_magnitude = np.sqrt(sobel_x**2 + sobel_y**2)
gradient_direction = np.arctan2(sobel_y, sobel_x)
# Step 3: Non-Maximum Suppression
suppressed_edges = np.zeros_like(gradient_magnitude)
for i in range(1, gradient_magnitude.shape[0] - 1):
   for j in range(1, gradient_magnitude.shape[1] - 1):
     angle = gradient_direction[i, j]
     if (0 <= angle < 22.5) or (157.5 <= angle <= 180):
       neighbors = [gradient_magnitude[i, j - 1], gradient_magnitude[i, j + 1]]
     elif (22.5 <= angle < 67.5):
         neighbors = [gradient_magnitude[i - 1, j - 1], gradient_magnitude[i + 1, j + 1]]
     elif (67.5 <= angle < 112.5):
       neighbors = [gradient_magnitude[i - 1, j], gradient_magnitude[i + 1, j]]
     else:
       neighbors = [gradient_magnitude[i + 1, j - 1], gradient_magnitude[i - 1, j + 1]]
       if gradient_magnitude[i, j] >= max(neighbors):
         suppressed_edges[i, j] = gradient_magnitude[i, j]
# Step 4: Hysteresis Thresholding
low_threshold, high_threshold = 120, 190 # Adjust as needed
strong_edges = suppressed_edges > high_threshold
weak_edges = (suppressed_edges >= low_threshold) & (suppressed_edges <= high_threshold)
final_edges = np.zeros_like(suppressed_edges)
final_edges[strong_edges] = 255
for i in range(1, final_edges.shape[0] - 1):
   for j in range(1, final_edges.shape[1] - 1):
       if weak_edges[i, j]:
         if np.any(strong_edges[i - 1:i + 2, j - 1:j + 2]):
           final_edges[i, j] = 255
#Step 5: Displaying the results
plt.figure(figsize=(8,6)),plt.subplot(2,3,1),plt.imshow(img,cmap='gray'),plt.title('Input image')
plt.xticks([]),plt.yticks([]),plt.subplot(2,3,2),plt.imshow(blurred_img,cmap='gray')
plt.title('Gaussian smoothed image'),plt.xticks([]),plt.yticks([]),plt.subplot(2,3,3),
plt.imshow(gradient_magnitude,cmap='gray'),plt.title('Magnitude of the edge'),plt.xticks([]),
plt.yticks([]),plt.subplot(2,3,5),plt.imshow(suppressed_edges,cmap='gray'),
plt.title('Edge suppression'),plt.xticks([]),plt.yticks([]),plt.subplot(2,3,6),
plt.imshow(final_edges,cmap='gray'),plt.title('Final result'),plt.xticks([]),plt.yticks([])
plt.tight_layout()
```

Fig. 7.20 Python code to perform step-by-step Canny edge detection algorithm

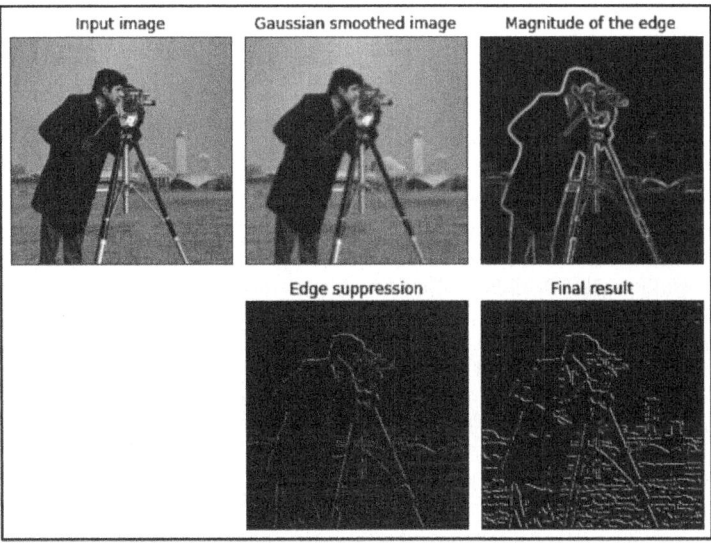

Fig. 7.21 Step-by-step results of Canny edge detection algorithm

$$
\begin{bmatrix} +5 & +5 & +5 \\ -3 & 0 & -3 \\ -3 & -3 & -3 \end{bmatrix}
\quad
\begin{bmatrix} +5 & +5 & -3 \\ +5 & 0 & -3 \\ -3 & -3 & -3 \end{bmatrix}
\quad
\begin{bmatrix} +5 & -3 & -3 \\ +5 & 0 & -3 \\ +5 & -3 & -3 \end{bmatrix}
\quad
\begin{bmatrix} -3 & -3 & -3 \\ +5 & 0 & -3 \\ +5 & +5 & -3 \end{bmatrix}
$$

    (a) North   **(b) North-East**   **(c) East**   **(d) South-East**

$$
\begin{bmatrix} -3 & -3 & -3 \\ -3 & 0 & -3 \\ +5 & +5 & +5 \end{bmatrix}
\quad
\begin{bmatrix} -3 & -3 & -3 \\ -3 & 0 & +5 \\ -3 & +5 & +5 \end{bmatrix}
\quad
\begin{bmatrix} -3 & -3 & +5 \\ -3 & 0 & +5 \\ -3 & -3 & +5 \end{bmatrix}
\quad
\begin{bmatrix} -3 & +5 & +5 \\ -3 & 0 & +5 \\ -3 & -3 & -3 \end{bmatrix}
$$

    (e) South   **(f) South-West**   **(g) West**   **(h) North-West**

Fig. 7.22 Kirsch Compass kernel in eight directions. (**a**) North. (**b**) North-East. (**c**) East. (**d**) South-East. (**e**) South. (**f**) South-West. (**g**) West. (**h**) North-West

Kirsch Compass Edge Detector

Kirsch edge detector is named after computer scientist Russell A. Kirsch. Kirsch edge detection is used to find the maximum edge strength in its eight predetermined compass directions. Kirsch edge detector uses eight 3×3 directional convolutional kernels. The eight directions are North, North-East, East, South-East, South, South-West, West and North-West. The 3×3 Kirsch kernel in eight directions is given in Fig. 7.22. In Kirsch edge detector, the weights are assigned to all pixel positions except the centre pixel.

```
#Kirsch compass operator
import numpy as np
import cv2
import matplotlib.pyplot as plt
#Step 1: Reading the input image
img=cv2.imread('cameraman.tif',0)
#Step 2: Defining the Kirsch compass kernel
kirsch_masks=[np.array([[5,5,5],[-3,0,-3],[-3,-3,-3]]),#North
    np.array([[5,5,-3],[5,0,-3],[-3,-3,-3]]),#North-East
    np.array([[5,-3,-3],[5,0,-3],[5,-3,-3]]),#East
    np.array([[-3,-3,-3],[5,0,-3],[5,5,-3]]),#South-East
    np.array([[-3,-3,-3],[-3,0,-3],[5,5,5]]),#South
    np.array([[-3,-3,-3],[-3,0,5],[-3,5,5]]),#South-West
    np.array([[-3,-3,5],[-3,0,5],[-3,-3,5]]),#West
    np.array([[-3,5,5],[-3,0,5],[-3,-3,-3]])]#North-West
#Step 3: Applying the mask
filtered_img=[cv2.filter2D(img,-1,mask) for mask in kirsch_masks]
#Step 4: Displaying the results
titles=['North','North-East','East','South-East','South','South-West','West','North-West']
plt.figure(figsize=(10,10))
for i in range(8):
    plt.subplot(3,3,i+2),plt.imshow(filtered_img[i],cmap='gray')
    plt.title(titles[i]),plt.axis('off')
plt.subplot(3,3,1),plt.imshow(img,cmap='gray'),plt.title('Input image'),plt.axis('off')
plt.tight_layout()
```

Fig. 7.23 Python code to detect the edge using Kirsch compass operator

Experiment 7.9: Kirsch Compass Edge Detector

The objective of this experiment is to find the edges in the input image in 8 possible directions using the Kirsch compass operator. The Python code that performs the task is shown in Fig. 7.23, and the corresponding output is shown in Fig. 7.24.

Inference

- From Fig. 7.24, it is possible to observe that Kirsch compass operator detects edges in eight directions.

Robinson Edge Detection

Robinson compass mask is a direction mask that is used for edge detection. It has eight orientations namely East, West, North, South, North-East, North-West, South-West, and South-East. Robinson masks are symmetrical about their directional axis. Robinson mask has only three coefficients, namely, 0, 1, and 2. The Robinson mask is given in Fig. 7.25.

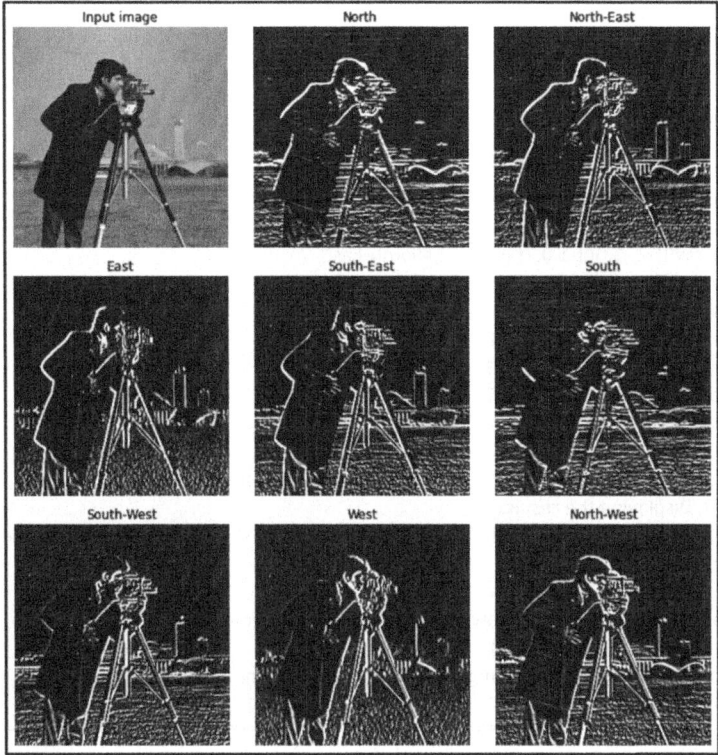

Fig. 7.24 Result of Python code shown in Fig. 7.23

$$\begin{bmatrix} -1 & 0 & 1 \\ -2 & 0 & 2 \\ -1 & 0 & 1 \end{bmatrix} \quad \begin{bmatrix} -1 & 0 & 1 \\ -2 & 0 & 2 \\ -1 & 0 & 1 \end{bmatrix} \quad \begin{bmatrix} 1 & 2 & 1 \\ 0 & 0 & 0 \\ -1 & -2 & -1 \end{bmatrix} \quad \begin{bmatrix} 2 & 1 & 0 \\ 1 & 0 & -1 \\ -1 & -1 & -2 \end{bmatrix}$$

(a) East   **(b) North-East**   **(c) North**   **(d) North-West**

$$\begin{bmatrix} 1 & 0 & -1 \\ 2 & 0 & -2 \\ 1 & 0 & -1 \end{bmatrix} \quad \begin{bmatrix} 0 & -1 & -2 \\ 1 & 0 & -1 \\ -2 & 1 & 0 \end{bmatrix} \quad \begin{bmatrix} -1 & -2 & -1 \\ 0 & 0 & 0 \\ 1 & 2 & 1 \end{bmatrix} \quad \begin{bmatrix} -2 & -1 & 0 \\ -1 & 0 & 1 \\ 0 & 1 & 2 \end{bmatrix}$$

(e) West   **(f) South-West**   **(g) South**   **(h) South-East**

Fig. 7.25 Robinson compass mask. (**a**) East. (**b**) North-East. (**c**) North. (**d**) North-West. (**e**) West. (**f**) South-West. (**g**) South. (**h**) South-East

Experiment 7.10: Robinson Edge Detection
The Python code that obtains the edge detection using the Robinson edge detector is shown in Fig. 7.26, and the corresponding output is shown in Fig. 7.27.

```
#Robinson edge detection
import numpy as np
import cv2
import matplotlib.pyplot as plt
#Step 1: Reading the input image
img=cv2.imread('cameraman.tif',0)
#Step 2: Defining the Kirsch compass kernel
robinson_masks=[np.array([[-1,0,1],[-2,0,2],[-1,0,1]]),#East
    np.array([[-2,-1,0],[-1,0,1],[0,1,2]]),#South-East
    np.array([[-1,-2,-1],[0,0,0],[1,2,1]]),#South
    np.array([[0,-1,-2],[1,0,-1],[2,1,0]]),#South-West
    np.array([[1,0,-1],[2,0,-2],[1,0,-1]]),#West
    np.array([[2,1,0],[1,0,-1],[0,-1,-2]]),#North-West
    np.array([[1,2,1],[0,0,0],[-1,-2,-1]]),#North
    np.array([[0,-1,2],[-1,0,1],[-2,-1,0]])]#South-West
#Step 3: Applying the mask
filtered_img=[cv2.filter2D(img,-1,mask) for mask in robinson_masks]
#Step 4: Displaying the results
titles=['East','South-East','South','South-West','West','North-West','North','South-West']
plt.figure(figsize=(10,10))
for i in range(8):
    plt.subplot(3,3,i+2),plt.imshow(filtered_img[i],cmap='gray')
    plt.title(titles[i]),plt.axis('off')
plt.subplot(3,3,1),plt.imshow(img,cmap='gray'),plt.title('Input image'),plt.axis('off')
plt.tight_layout()
```

Fig. 7.26 Python code which performs edge detection using Robinson kernel

Inference

- Robinson compass mask has the ability to detect the edge in 8 possible directions.

Marr–Hildreth Edge Detection

In Maar–Hildreth method of edge detection, the input image is first smoothened by a Gaussian filter. Then, the Laplacian operator is used to obtain the second-order derivative. When the second-order derivative crosses zero, then that particular location corresponds to the edge location. Marr–Hildreth operator is also termed as Laplacian of Gaussian (LoG) filter. The expression for two-dimensional Gaussian function which is applied to the input image to smoothen the image is expressed as

$$f(x,y) = e^{-\left(\frac{x^2+y^2}{2\sigma^2}\right)} \tag{7.6}$$

Taking partial derivative of the above Gaussian function with respect to "x"

$$\frac{\partial f(x,y)}{\partial x} = e^{-\left(\frac{x^2+y^2}{2\sigma^2}\right)} \times \left(-\frac{2x}{2\sigma^2}\right) \tag{7.7}$$

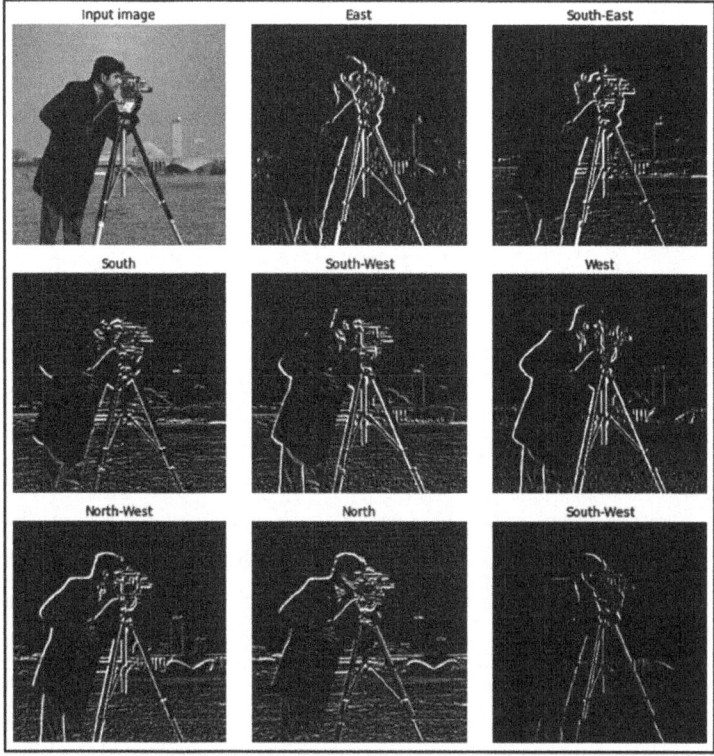

Fig. 7.27 Result of Robinson edge detection

Simplifying the above expression, we get

$$\frac{\partial f(x,y)}{\partial x} = \left(-\frac{x}{\sigma^2}\right) e^{-\left(\frac{x^2+y^2}{2\sigma^2}\right)} \qquad (7.8)$$

Taking partial derivative of the above expression with respect to "x", we get

$$\frac{\partial^2 f(x,y)}{\partial x^2} = \frac{e^{-\left(\frac{x^2+y^2}{2\sigma^2}\right)}}{\sigma^2} \left(\frac{x^2}{\sigma^2} - 1\right) \qquad (7.9)$$

Similarly, taking second-order partial derivative of the Gaussian function with respect to the variable "y", we get

$$\frac{\partial^2 f(x,y)}{\partial y^2} = \frac{e^{-\left(\frac{x^2+y^2}{2\sigma^2}\right)}}{\sigma^2} \left(\frac{y^2}{\sigma^2} - 1\right) \qquad (7.10)$$

The expression for the Laplacian is given by

$$\nabla^2 f(x,y) = \frac{\partial^2 f(x,y)}{\partial x^2} + \frac{\partial^2 f(x,y)}{\partial y^2} \qquad (7.11)$$

Adding Eqs. (7.9) and (7.10), we get

$$\nabla^2 f(x,y) = \frac{e^{-\left(\frac{x^2+y^2}{2\sigma^2}\right)}}{\sigma^2}\left(\frac{x^2}{\sigma^2}-1\right) + \frac{e^{-\left(\frac{x^2+y^2}{2\sigma^2}\right)}}{\sigma^2}\left(\frac{y^2}{\sigma^2}-1\right) \qquad (7.12)$$

The above equation can be simplified as

$$\nabla^2 f(x,y) = e^{-\left(\frac{x^2+y^2}{2\sigma^2}\right)}\left(\frac{x^2+y^2-2\sigma^2}{\sigma^4}\right) \qquad (7.13)$$

In Marr–Hildreth edge detection, the input image is first convolved with a Gaussian filter to perform a smoothing operation; then the Laplacian operator is applied to the smoothened image. This is expressed as

$$\nabla^2\left(f(x,y) * g(x,y)\right) \qquad (7.14)$$

In the above expression, $f(x,y)$ represents the input image, $g(x,y)$ represents the Gaussian kernel. Since convolution is associative, the above expression can be written as

$$f(x,y) * \nabla^2\left(g(x,y)\right) \qquad (7.15)$$

In the above expression, $\nabla^2(g(x,y))$ represents the Laplacian of Gaussian function which is termed as LoG operator.

Experiment 7.11: Laplacian of Gaussian (LoG) filtering or Marr–Hildreth edge detection

The objective of this experiment is to obtain the edge of the input image using Laplacian of Gaussian. The steps followed in Laplacian of Gaussian (LoG) filtering are as follows:

1. The input image is passed through Gaussian low-pass filter to smoothen the image.
2. The second-order derivative of the smoothened image is obtained by applying Laplacian filter.

The Python code that accomplishes the above-mentioned task is shown in Fig. 7.28, and the corresponding output is shown in Fig. 7.29.

```
#Laplacian of Gaussian
import matplotlib.pyplot as plt
import cv2
#Step 1: Reading the input image
img=cv2.imread('squares.tif',0)
#Step2: Performing Gaussian smoothing
img1 = cv2.GaussianBlur(img, (3, 3), 0)
#Step 3: Taking Laplacian of the result
filtered_image = cv2.Laplacian(img1, cv2.CV_16S, ksize=3)
#Step 4: Displaying the result
plt.subplot(1,2,1),plt.imshow(img,cmap='gray'),plt.title('Input image')
plt.xticks([]),plt.yticks([]),plt.subplot(1,2,2),plt.imshow(filtered_image,cmap='gray')
plt.title('LoG filtered image'),plt.xticks([]),plt.yticks([])
plt.tight_layout()
```

Fig. 7.28 Python code to perform LoG filtering of input image

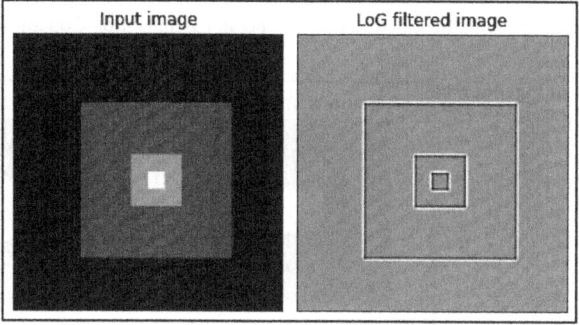

Fig. 7.29 Result of LoG filtering of input image

Inference

- The input image shows variation in intensity level from black to white. The LoG filter extracts the edges of the input image.

Experiment 7.12: Laplacian Operator: An Isotropic Operator

The objective of this experiment is to prove that Laplacian operator is an isotropic operator. An operator is an isotropic operator which applies equally well in all directions in an image. The operator has no bias towards particular directions. The Python code which is used to prove that Laplacian is an isotropic operator is shown in Fig. 7.30, and the corresponding output is shown in Fig. 7.31.

Inferences

- The Laplacian operator is applied to input image and shows the edge information of the input image. The input image is rotated by 45°.

```
#Laplacian is an isotropic operator
import numpy as np
import matplotlib.pyplot as plt
import cv2
#Generation of test image
img=np.zeros([256,256])
img[98:158,98:158]=255
rows,cols=img.shape
M = cv2.getRotationMatrix2D((cols/2,rows/2),-45,1)
img_45 = cv2.warpAffine(img,M,(cols,rows))
Laplacian_img= cv2.Laplacian(img, cv2.CV_64F)
Laplacian_img_45= cv2.Laplacian(img_45, cv2.CV_64F)
plt.subplot(2,2,1),plt.imshow(img,cmap='gray'),plt.title('Input image'),plt.xticks([]),plt.yticks([]),
plt.subplot(2,2,2),plt.imshow(img_45,cmap='gray'),plt.title('Rotated image'),plt.xticks([]),
plt.yticks([]), plt.subplot(2,2,3),plt.imshow(Laplacian_img,cmap='gray',vmin=-255,vmax=255)
plt.title('Laplacian of input image'),plt.xticks([]),plt.yticks([])
plt.subplot(2,2,4),plt.imshow(Laplacian_img_45,cmap='gray',vmin=-255,vmax=255)
plt.title('Laplacian of rotated image'),plt.xticks([]),plt.yticks([])
plt.tight_layout()
```

Fig. 7.30 Python code to illustrate that Laplacian operator is an isotropic operator

Fig. 7.31 Result of Python code shown in Fig. 7.30

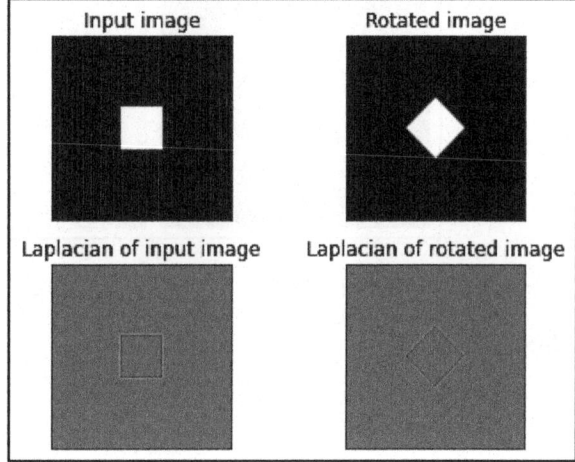

- The edges of the rotated image are obtained using the Laplacian operator.
- The results indicate that the Laplacian operator is not biased towards a particular direction. Hence, it is an isotropic operator.

7.3   Image Segmentation Through Thresholding

The goal of image thresholding is to divide the pixels of an image into several subsets by selecting some intensity values. Thresholding segments a grayscale image into a binary image. In thresholding operation, each pixel of the image is compared with the threshold value. If the pixel value is greater than the threshold, the output pixel value is high, otherwise the pixel value is low. Choosing the threshold is a challenging problem. Different types of thresholding discussed in this section include (1) Manual thresholding, (2) Global thresholding, (3) Thresholding using OTSU method, (4) Adaptive thresholding, and (5) Hysteresis thresholding.

7.3.1 Manual Thresholding

In this approach, the histogram of the input image is plotted first. If the image exhibits bimodal histogram, then suitable threshold operation can be performed to obtain the binary image.

Experiment 7.13: Manual Thresholding Without Built-in Function
In this experiment, the input image is a "cameraman" image. Upon taking the histogram of the input image, it is possible to observe that the image exhibits a bimodal histogram. The threshold value closer to "100" can be chosen to segment the image or to convert the grayscale image into a binary image. A threshold value of "95" is chosen to convert the input grayscale image to a binary image. The Python code that performs this task is shown in Fig. 7.32, and the corresponding output is shown in Fig. 7.33.

```
#Segmentation using thresholding operation
import cv2
import matplotlib.pyplot as plt
#Step 1: Reading the input image
img=cv2.imread('cameraman.tif',0)
#Step 2: Fixing the threshold value
threshold_value=95
#Step 3: Obtaining the binary image
img_thresh=img>threshold_value
#Step 4: Displaying the results
fig=plt.figure(figsize=(8,8))
plt.subplot(2,2,1),plt.imshow(img,cmap='gray')
plt.title('Gray scale image'),plt.axis('off')
plt.subplot(2,2,2),plt.imshow(img_thresh,cmap='gray')
plt.title('Thresholded image'),plt.xticks([]),plt.yticks([])
plt.subplot(2,2,3),plt.hist(img.ravel(),bins = 256, range = [0,256])
plt.title('Histogram of input image')
plt.subplot(2,2,4),plt.hist(img_thresh.ravel(),bins = 100, range = [0,1])
plt.title('Histogram of thresholded image'),plt.xticks([0,1])
plt.tight_layout()
```

Fig. 7.32 Python code to perform manual thresholding operation

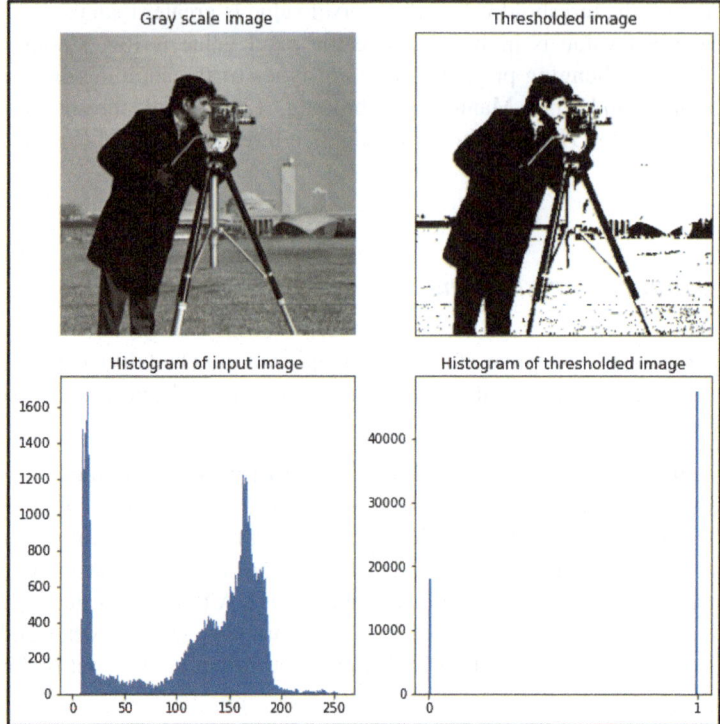

Fig. 7.33   Result of manual thresholding operation

Inferences

The following inferences can be drawn from Fig. 7.33.

- The input "Cameraman" image is an eight-bit grayscale image.
- The histogram of the input image exhibits a bimodal histogram.
- Upon manually choosing the threshold value to "95", it is possible to observe that the resultant image is a binary image.
- The histogram of binary image has only two gray levels which are either "0" or "1".

Experiment 7.14: Manual Thresholding Using Built-in Function From Computer Vision Library

The built-in function "*cv2.threshold*" can be used to perform manual thresholding operations. Different options available in "*cv2.threshold*" are summarized in Table 7.2. In the Table 7.2, $f(m, n)$ represents the input image and $g(m, n)$ represents the output image.

In this experiment, the input "cameraman" image is read and three forms of thresholding, namely, binary thresholding, truncated thresholding, and thresholding to zero operations are performed using the built-in functions given in Table 7.2. The

Table 7.2 Different types of thresholding an image

S. No.	Built-in function	Expression	Meaning
1	cv2.THRESH_BINARY	$g(m,n) = \begin{cases} \text{max\_value}, f(m,n) > th \\ 0, \quad \text{otherwise} \end{cases}$	If the pixel value is greater than the threshold value, it will be set as 255 else "0"
2	cv2.THRESH_BINARY_INV	$g(m,n) = \begin{cases} 0, \quad f(m,n) > th \\ \text{max\_value}, \quad \text{otherwise} \end{cases}$	Inverted case of cv2.THRESH_BINARY
3	cv.THRESH_TRUNC	$g(m,n) = \begin{cases} \text{threshold}, f(m,n) > th \\ f(m,n), \text{otherwise} \end{cases}$	If the pixel value is greater than the threshold, it is truncated to threshold value
4	cv.THRESH_TOZERO	$g(m,n) = \begin{cases} f(m,n), f(m,n) > th \\ 0, \text{otherwise} \end{cases}$	Input image pixel values are set to zero if it is less than the threshold value
5	cv.THRESH_TOZERO_INV	$g(m,n) = \begin{cases} 0, f(m,n) > th \\ f(m,n), \text{otherwise} \end{cases}$	Inverted case of cv.THRESH_TOZERO

Python code that performs this task is shown in Fig. 7.34, and the corresponding output is shown in Fig. 7.35.

Inferences

The following inferences can be drawn from this experiment:

- The input image is an eight-bit grayscale image. The threshold value chosen is 95.
- The binary thresholding and the truncated thresholding yield a binary image.
- The "thresholding to zero value" result is a grayscale image.

```
#Segmentation using different thresholding operation
import cv2
import matplotlib.pyplot as plt
#Step 1: Reading the input image
img=cv2.imread('cameraman.tif',0)
#Step 2: Fixing the threshold value
threshold_value=95
#Step 3: Performing different forms of thresholding
ret, thresh1 = cv2.threshold(img, threshold_value, 255, cv2.THRESH_BINARY)
ret, thresh2 = cv2.threshold(img, threshold_value, 255, cv2.THRESH_TRUNC)
ret, thresh3 = cv2.threshold(img, threshold_value, 255, cv2.THRESH_TOZERO)
#Step 4: Displaying the results
fig=plt.figure(figsize=(8,4)),plt.subplot(1,4,1),plt.imshow(img,cmap='gray')
plt.title('Input image'),plt.axis('off'),plt.subplot(1,4,2),plt.imshow(thresh1,cmap='gray')
plt.title('Binary thresholding'),plt.xticks([]),plt.yticks([]),plt.subplot(1,4,3),
plt.imshow(thresh2,cmap='gray'),plt.title('Truncated thresholding'),plt.xticks([]),
plt.yticks([]),plt.subplot(1,4,4),plt.imshow(thresh3,cmap='gray')
plt.title('Thresholding to zero'),plt.xticks([]),plt.yticks([])
plt.tight_layout()
```

Fig. 7.34 Python code to perform different types of thresholding operation

Fig. 7.35 Result of Python code shown in Fig. 7.34

7.3.2   *Otsu Thresholding*

The main idea behind Otsu's algorithm is to minimize within-class variance or maximize the between-class variance to determine the optimal threshold value. Otsu method assumes a bimodal distribution of gray level values.

The expression for within class variance at specific threshold value "T" is given by

$$\sigma_w^2 = c_1\sigma_1^2 + (1 - c_1)\sigma_2^2 \qquad (7.16)$$

In the above expression, σ_1^2 and σ_2^2 are the variance of the first and second class, respectively, and c_1 is the cumulative sum at threshold "T". Thus, σ_w^2 is the weighted sum of variances of both classes.

The expression for between-class variance at specific value of threshold "T" is given by

$$\sigma_b^2 = c_1(1 - c_1)(\mu_1 - \mu_2)^2 \qquad (7.17)$$

In the above expression, σ_b^2 represents between class variance, and μ_1 and μ_2 are the mean of classes 1 and 2, respectively.

Assuming that the range of grayscale of image is $i = 0, 1, 2, \ldots, L - 1$, and the pixels number with grayscale "k" is n_k, the total number of pixels in the image is given by

$$N = \sum_{k=0}^{L-1} n_k \qquad (7.18)$$

The probability of occurrence of the gray level "k" is given by

$$p_k = \frac{n_k}{N} \qquad (7.19)$$

The gray level threshold "T" can be used to divide the gray level of the image into two parts: $C_1 = (0, 1, 2, \ldots, T)$, $C_2 = (T + 1, T + 2, \ldots, L - 1)$, then the probability and the mean of the class C_1 and C_2 are given by

$$P_r(C_1) = \sum_{i=0}^{T} p_i = C_1 \qquad (7.20)$$

$$P_r(C_2) = \sum_{i=T+1}^{L-1} p_i = 1 - C_1 \qquad (7.21)$$

$$\mu_1 = \sum_{i=0}^{T} \frac{ip_i}{C_1} \qquad (7.22)$$

$$\mu_2 = \sum_{i=T+1}^{L-1} \frac{ip_i}{1 - C_1} \qquad (7.23)$$

The expression for the variance of the classes C_1 and C_2 are expressed as

$$\sigma_1^2 = \sum_{i=1}^{T} \frac{(i-\mu_1)^2 p_i}{C_1} \tag{7.24}$$

$$\sigma_2^2 = \sum_{i=T+1}^{L-1} \frac{(i-\mu_1)^2 p_i}{1-C_1} \tag{7.25}$$

The expression for within-class variance at specific threshold value "T" is given by

$$\sigma_w^2 = c_1 \sigma_1^2 + (1-c_1) \sigma_2^2 \tag{7.26}$$

The expression for between-class variance at specific value of threshold "T" is given by

$$\sigma_b^2 = c_1 (1-c_1)(\mu_1 - \mu_2)^2 \tag{7.27}$$

The objective of Otsu algorithm is to minimize the within-class variance or maximize the between-class variance. The optimum threshold is the value k^* that maximizes $\sigma_b^2(k^*)$, where

$$\sigma_b^2(k^*) = \max_{0 \le k \le L-1} \sigma_b^2(k) \tag{7.28}$$

Thus, the segmented image based on the threshold value is given by

$$g(m,n) = \begin{cases} 1, if & f(m,n) \ge k^* \\ 0, if & f(m,n) < k^* \end{cases} \tag{7.29}$$

The separability measure is expressed as

$$\eta(k^*) = \frac{\sigma_b^2(k^*)}{\sigma^2(G)} \tag{7.30}$$

In the above expression, $\sigma^2(G)$ represents the global variance. $\eta(k^*)$ takes value between 0 and 1.

In summary, Otsu's method looks at every possible value for the threshold between the background and foreground, calculates the variance within each of the two clusters, and selects the value for which the weighted sum of these variances is the least.

Experiment 7.15: Image Segmentation Using Otsu Method
This experiment deals with the concept of Otsu method for the image segmentation. The Python code, which performs image segmentation using the Otsu algorithm, is given in Fig. 7.36, and the corresponding output is shown in Fig. 7.37.

```
# Image segmentation using Otsu method
import cv2
import matplotlib.pyplot as plt
img=cv2.imread('cameraman.tif',0)
ret2,th2 = cv2.threshold(img,0,255,cv2.THRESH_OTSU)
plt.subplot(1,2,1),plt.imshow(img,cmap='gray')
plt.title('Input image'),plt.axis('off')
plt.subplot(1,2,2),plt.imshow(th2,cmap='gray')
plt.title('Otsu Threshold = ${}$ output'.format(ret2)),
plt.xticks([]),plt.yticks([])
plt.tight_layout()
```

Fig. 7.36 Image segmentation using Otsu's thresholding

Fig. 7.37 Result of Otsu's thresholding

Inferences

The following inferences can be made from this experiment:

- The input image is an 8-bit Cameraman image.
- Upon performing thresholding based on Otsu's algorithm, the grayscale image is converted to a binary image. The threshold value using Otsu's algorithm is 88.

7.3.3   Hysteresis Threshold

In hysteresis thresholding is defined by two thresholds, namely, (1) Lower threshold and (2) Higher threshold. Pixels above the higher threshold are classified as objects, and those below the lower threshold are considered background. Pixels between the lower and higher thresholds are classified as objects only if they are adjacent to other object pixels.

```
# Image segmentation using hysteresis thresholding
import matplotlib.pyplot as plt
from skimage import filters
import cv2
#Step 1: Reading the input image
img=cv2.imread('coin_single1.jpg',0)
#Step 2: Edge detection using Sobel opertor
edges = filters.sobel(img)
#Step 3: Defining the lower and higher threshold
low, high = 0.02, 0.18
lowt = (edges > low).astype(int)
hight = (edges > high).astype(int)
#Step 4: Perform hysteresis threshold
img_out= filters.apply_hysteresis_threshold(edges, low, high)
plt.subplot(1,2,1),plt.imshow(img,cmap='gray')
plt.title('Input image'),plt.axis('off')
plt.subplot(1,2,2),plt.imshow(img_out,cmap='gray')
plt.title('Output image'),plt.axis('off')
plt.tight_layout()
```

Fig. 7.38 Python code to perform hysteresis thresholding operation

Fig. 7.39 Result of hysteresis thresholding of the image

Experiment 7.16: Image Segmentation Using Hysteresis Thresholding
This experiment deals with image segmentation using hysteresis thresholding. The Python code that performs hysteresis thresholding using the built-in function available in the "*scikit*" library is shown in Fig. 7.38, and the corresponding output is shown in Fig. 7.39.

Inferences
The following inferences can be observed from this experiment:

•   The input image is a "single coin" image. For this image, the lower threshold is fixed as 0.02, and the higher threshold value is fixed as 0.18.

- Upon performing hysteresis thresholding based on the above threshold values, it is possible to observe that the foreground is separated from the background.

7.3.4   Adaptive Threshold

Global threshold uses fixed threshold value for all the pixels in the image. Global threshold will not work properly if an image has different lighting conditions in different areas. In adaptive threshold, the input image is divided into regions or local neighbourhood. The threshold value is computed for each pixel based on the range of intensity values in its local neighbourhood. Thus, in adaptive thresholding, the threshold values are dynamically calculated for smaller regions of the image. Adaptive thresholding can be broadly classified as (1) Adaptive mean thresholding and (2) Adaptive Gaussian thresholding. In adaptive mean thresholding, the threshold value is computed by taking the mean of the pixel values in the window. In adaptive Gaussian thresholding, the threshold value is computed by taking the weighted sum of pixel values in the neighbourhood area where the weights are assigned using the Gaussian window technique.

Experiment 7.17: Adaptive Thresholding of the Image
The objective of this experiment is to perform adaptive thresholding of the input image. Two approaches to adaptive thresholding discussed in this experiment are adaptive mean thresholding and adaptive Gaussian thresholding. The built-in function "adaptiveThreshold" available in computer vision library is used to perform the adaptive thresholding. The Python code that performs the above-mentioned task is given in Fig. 7.40, and the corresponding output is shown in Fig. 7.41.

```
# Image segmentation using adaptive thresholding
import matplotlib.pyplot as plt
import cv2
img=cv2.imread('coin_single1.jpg',0); #Reading the input image
#Adaptive Mean threshold
img_out1= cv2.adaptiveThreshold(img,255,cv2.ADAPTIVE_THRESH_MEAN_C,\
 cv2.THRESH_BINARY,21,10)
#Adaptive Gaussian threshold
img_out2 = cv2.adaptiveThreshold(img,255,cv2.ADAPTIVE_THRESH_GAUSSIAN_C,\
 cv2.THRESH_BINARY,21,10)
#Displaying the result
plt.subplot(1,3,1),plt.imshow(img,cmap='gray'),plt.title('Input image'),plt.xticks([]),
plt.yticks([]),plt.subplot(1,3,2),plt.imshow(img_out1,cmap='gray'),plt.title('AMT output'),
plt.xticks([]),plt.yticks([]),plt.subplot(1,3,3),plt.imshow(img_out2,cmap='gray')
plt.title('AGT output'),plt.xticks([]),plt.yticks([])
plt.tight_layout()
```

Fig. 7.40 Python code to perform adaptive thresholding

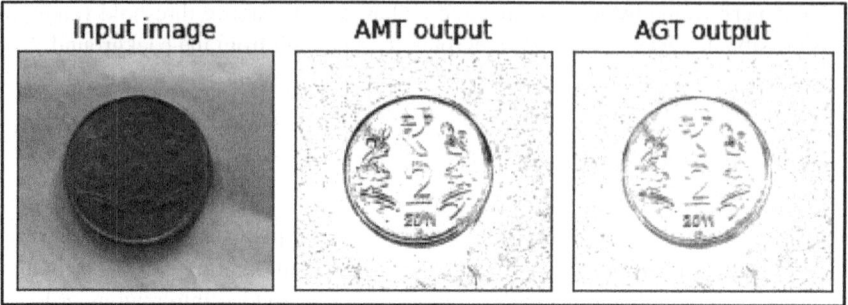

Fig. 7.41 Result of adaptive threshold

Inferences

From this experiment, the following inferences can be made:

- The input image is a "coin image". Two types of adaptive thresholding are performed on the input image.
- The adaptive threshold algorithms used in this example are adaptive mean threshold and adaptive Gaussian threshold.
- The block size chosen is 9, and the constant value used to subtract from the mean or weighted mean is chosen as 3.

7.4 Region-Based Image Segmentation

Region-based approach attempts to split the image into connected disjoint regions such that their union results in the whole image. The partition of the image into regions is based on some logical predicate that is true for each region but false for any union of them.

7.4.1 Region-Growing Algorithm

The region-growing algorithm starts with one or group of pixels which are termed as seed pixels. The seed pixels are compared with neighbouring pixels. If a neighbouring pixel meets certain criteria, it is added to the group, else it is not added. This process is continued until no more neighbouring pixels can be added to the group.

Experiment 7.18: Region-Growing Method for Image Segmentation

Aim of this experiment is to implement a region-growing approach for the image segmentation in Python environment. For this, "cameraman" image is considered as a grayscale input image. The seed point location be fixed as (150, 90). The Python code, which performs image segmentation using the region-growing approach, is shown in Fig. 7.42, and the corresponding output is shown in Fig. 7.43.

```
# Image segmentation using region-growing approach
import matplotlib.pyplot as plt
import cv2
import numpy as np
img = cv2.imread('cameraman.tif', 0);# Read the input image
seed_point = (150, 90);# Set the seed point
# Defining 4-connectivity
neighbors = [(0, 1), (1, 0), (-1, 0), (0, -1)]
region_threshold = 95
region_size = 1
region_mean = float(img[seed_point])
growth_points = [seed_point];# Initialize the list of growth points
# Mark array to indicate whether a pixel has been segmented
segmented_img = np.zeros_like(img)
#Region growing algorithm
while len(growth_points) > 0:
    new_points = []
    for point in growth_points:
        for neighbor in neighbors:
            # Calculate the position of neighboring pixel
            x_new = point[0] + neighbor[0]
            y_new = point[1] + neighbor[1]
            # Check if the neighboring pixel is outside the image boundaries
            if x_new < 0 or y_new < 0 or x_new >= img.shape[0] or y_new >= img.shape[1]:
                continue
            # Check if the neighboring pixel has already been segmented
            if segmented_img[x_new, y_new]:
                continue
            pixel_value = img[x_new, y_new]
            if abs(pixel_value - region_mean) < region_threshold:
                segmented_img[x_new, y_new] = True
                region_size += 1
                region_mean = (region_mean * (region_size - 1) + pixel_value) / region_size
                new_points.append((x_new, y_new))
    growth_points = new_points
#Displaying the result
plt.subplot(1,2,1),plt.imshow(img,cmap='gray'),plt.title('Input image'),plt.axis('off')
plt.subplot(1,2,2),plt.imshow(segmented_img,cmap='gray')
plt.title('Segmented image'),plt.xticks([]),plt.yticks([])
plt.tight_layout()
```

Fig. 7.42 Python code to perform image segmentation using region-growing approach

Inferences

The following inferences can be drawn from this experiment:

- The input image is an eight-bit 256×256 grayscale image.
- The input image is segmented using region-growing approach to obtain the segmented image.
- The segmented image is a binary image that takes a gray level of either "0" or "1".

Fig. 7.43 Result of Python code shown in Fig. 7.42

- The seed point chosen for this test image is (150,90) and the "region_threshold" value chosen is 95. Both these factors influence the performance of the algorithm.

Task: Repeat the above experiment by choosing the region threshold as 110 and comment on the observed result.

7.4.2 Watershed-Based Image Segmentation

Watershed segmentation is a region-based image segmentation technique. Watershed algorithm considers image as a topographic map. It considers the brightness of a pixel as its height. The dark pixels represent the valleys. Water placed on any pixel enclosed by a common watershed line flows downhill to a common local intensity minimum. Pixels draining to a common minimum form a catchment basin, which represents a segment. The watershed transform computes catchment basins and watershed lines (ridgelines), where catchment basins correspond to image regions and ridgelines relate to region boundaries.

Experiment 7.19: Watershed Algorithm-based Image Segmentation
This experiment discusses the implementation of the watershed algorithm in a Python environment. For this, the input test image is read and is then segmented using watershed algorithm. The built-in function is available in "*scikit-learn*" library. The built-in functions used in the Python code are given in Table 7.3. The Python code that performs the segmentation task is shown in Fig. 7.44, and the corresponding output is shown in Fig. 7.45.

Inferences
From this experiment, following inferences can be observed:

- The test image contains different coins. First, the edge information is obtained using "Laplacian operator".

Table 7.3 Built-in function used in watershed-based segmentation

S. No.	Built-in function	Library	Purpose
1	Laplace	Skimage.Filters	To extract the edge information from the input image
2	Watershed	Skimage.Segmentation	To perform segmentation of the image using watershed algorithm

```
#Watershed algorithm based image segmentation
import cv2
import matplotlib.pyplot as plt
import numpy as np
from skimage.filters import laplace
from skimage import segmentation
img=cv2.imread('coins.jpg',0);#Step 1: Read the input image
elevation_map=laplace(img);#Step 2: Extract the edge information
markers=np.zeros_like(img);#Step3: Define the markers
markers[img<100]=1
markers[img>125]=2
#Step 4: Perform watershed based segmentation
segmented_img=segmentation.watershed(elevation_map,markers)
#Step 5: Displaying the results
plt.subplot(1,3,1),plt.imshow(img,cmap='gray')
plt.title('Input image'),plt.xticks([]),plt.yticks([])
plt.subplot(1,3,2),plt.imshow(elevation_map,cmap='gray')
plt.title('Edge map'),plt.xticks([]),plt.yticks([])
plt.subplot(1,3,3),plt.imshow(segmented_img,cmap='gray')
plt.title('Segmented image'),plt.xticks([]),plt.yticks([])
plt.tight_layout()
```

Fig. 7.44 Python code to perform segmentation using watershed algorithm

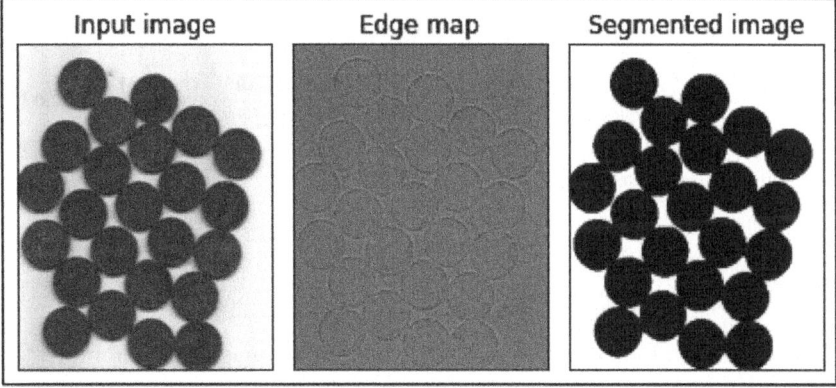

Fig. 7.45 Result of Python code shown in Fig. 7.44

- The markers for watershed algorithm are defined. After defining the markers, the input image is segmented using a watershed algorithm.
- The result implies that the foreground and background are separated and the segmentation task is carried out successfully.

7.5   Clustering-Based Segmentation

Clustering algorithms divide data into clusters of pixels with similar values. Two clustering algorithms discussed in this section include (1) K-means clustering algorithm and (2) Fuzzy C-means clustering algorithm.

7.5.1   K-Means Clustering Algorithm

In the "k-means" clustering algorithm, pixel values are plotted as data points, and "k" random points are selected as the centre of a cluster. Each pixel is assigned to a cluster based on the nearest centroid. Centroids are then relocated to the mean of each cluster, and the process is repeated, with centroids being relocated with each iteration until clusters have stabilized. The objective function of k-means algorithm is given by

$$J = \sum_{i=1}^{n} \sum_{k=1}^{K} w_{ik} \left\| x^i - \mu_k \right\|^2 \tag{7.31}$$

In the above expression, the first summation is with respect to a number of data points, and the second summation is with respect to a number of clusters; μ_k represents the cluster centre. From the expression (7.31), it is possible to interpret that the data point x_i is assigned to the closest cluster by computing the sum of squared distance from the cluster's centroid.

In Eq. (7.31)

$$w_{ik} = \begin{cases} 1, & \text{data point belong to the cluster } k \\ 0, & \text{otherwise} \end{cases} \tag{7.32}$$

The above expression can also be written as

$$w_{ik} = \begin{cases} 1, & \text{if } k = \text{argmin}_j \left\| x^i - \mu_j \right\|^2 \\ 0, & \text{otherwise} \end{cases} \tag{7.33}$$

Experiment 7.20: k-means Clustering Algorithm for Image Segmentation
This experiment aims to implement k-means clustering algorithm for image segmentation in Python environment. For this, a grayscale image is read, the image has four coins. This input image is passed through k-means clustering algorithm. The

value of "k" is varied as 2, 3, 4, 5, and 6. The number of iterations is fixed as 10. The Python code, which performs the task of image segmentation through the k-means algorithm for different values of "k", is shown in Fig. 7.46, and the corresponding output is shown in Fig. 7.47.

Inferences

The following inferences can be observed from this experiment:

- The input image to k-means clustering algorithm is grayscale.
- The input image has four coins of denomination 1, 5, and 10.
- The input image is passed through a k-means clustering algorithm for $k = 2, 3, 4,$ 5, and 6.
- When the value of $k = 2$, the denomination of the coin is not visible in the segmented image. With the increase in the value of "k", the denomination of the coin appears in the output image.

```
# k means clustering algorithm
import cv2
import numpy as np
import matplotlib.pyplot as plt
# Reading the input image
image=cv2.imread('coin_testimg3.jpg',0)
fig=plt.figure(figsize=(8,6)),plt.subplot(2,3,1),plt.imshow(image,cmap='gray')
plt.title('Input image'),plt.xticks([]),plt.yticks([])
# Reshape the image to a 2D array of pixels
pixels = image.reshape((-1, 3))
# Convert the data type to float32
pixels = np.float32(pixels)
# Define the criteria (stopping criteria for the k-means algorithm)
criteria = (cv2.TERM_CRITERIA_EPS + cv2.TERM_CRITERIA_MAX_ITER, 50, 0.82)
k = [2,3,4,5,6]
for i in range(len(k)):
    # Perform K-Means clustering
    _, labels, centers = cv2.kmeans(pixels, k[i], None, criteria, 10,
cv2.KMEANS_RANDOM_CENTERS)
    # Convert back to 8-bit values
    centers = np.uint8(centers)
    # Map the pixel values to their respective centers
    segmented_image = centers[labels.flatten()]
    segmented_image = segmented_image.reshape(image.shape)
    plt.subplot(2,3,i+2),plt.imshow(segmented_image,cmap='binary')
    plt.title('Segmented with k = {}'.format(k[i]))
    plt.xticks([]),plt.yticks([])
plt.tight_layout()
```

Fig. 7.46 Python code to perform segmentation using k-means clustering algorithm

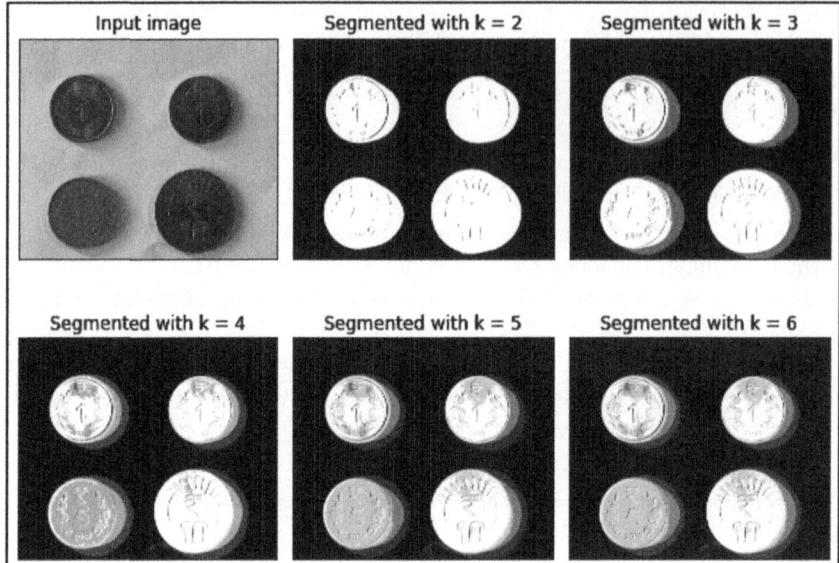

Fig. 7.47   Segmented image using k-means clustering algorithm

7.5.2   Fuzzy C-Means Clustering Algorithm

In k-means clustering algorithm, the data points exclusively belong to one cluster, whereas in fuzzy c-means clustering algorithm, the data points can belong to more than one cluster with a likelihood. Fuzzy c-means clustering involves two processes (1) Calculation of cluster centres (2) Assignment of data points to the cluster centres using a form of Euclidean distance. The above two steps are repeated until the cluster centres stabilize. The algorithm is similar to k-means clustering but it incorporates fuzzy set concepts of partial membership by allowing data points to belong to more than one cluster. The objective function of fuzzy C-means algorithm is given by

$$J = \sum_{i=1}^{n} \sum_{j=1}^{K} \mu_{ij} \parallel x^{i} - c_{j} \parallel^{2} \tag{7.34}$$

In the above expression, μ_{ij} represents the fuzzy membership of the pixel or the data point to the cluster centre. The objective function can reach the global minimum when pixels near the centroid of corresponding clusters are assigned higher membership values, while lower membership values are assigned to pixels far from the centroid.

Experiment 7.21: Image Segmentation Using Fuzzy C Means Clustering Algorithm

This experiment uses fuzzy C-means clustering approach to implement image segmentation. The Python code, which performs the fuzzy C-means clustering algorithm on the input test image "rice.tif," a 256 × 256 grayscale image, is shown in Fig. 7.48, and the corresponding output is shown in Fig. 7.49.

```python
#Fuzzy C-means clustering
import numpy as np
import matplotlib.pyplot as plt
import cv2
import skfuzzy as fuzz
img=cv2.imread('rice.tif',0);#Reading the input image
pixels = img.reshape(-1, 1);# Reshape the image into a 1D array
n_clusters = 2
# Apply fuzzy C-means clustering
cntr, u, u0, d, jm, p, fpc = fuzz.cluster.cmeans(
    pixels.T, n_clusters, 2, error=0.001, maxiter=1000, init=None)
# Get the cluster membership for each pixel
cluster_membership = np.argmax(u, axis=0)
# Reshape the clustered data back to the original image shape
segmented_image = cluster_membership.reshape(img.shape)
plt.subplot(1,2,1),plt.imshow(img,cmap='gray')
plt.title('Input image'),plt.xticks([]),plt.yticks([])
plt.subplot(1,2,2),plt.imshow(segmented_image,cmap='gray')
plt.title('Segmented image'),plt.xticks([]),plt.yticks([])
plt.tight_layout()
```

Fig. 7.48 Python code to perform fuzzy C-means clustering

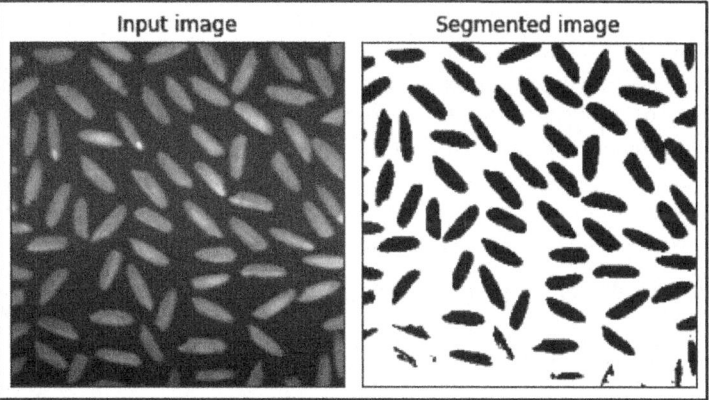

Fig. 7.49 Result of fuzzy C-means clustering

Inferences

The following inferences can be observed from this experiment:

- The input image is a 256 × 256 grayscale "rice" image. The number of clusters chosen is 2.
- The *"Scikit-Fuzzy"* library is used to implement the Fuzzy C-means clustering algorithm.
- The built-in function *"fuzz.cluster.cmeans"* is used to implement the fuzzy C-means clustering algorithm. The input to the function is the data points, number of clusters, array exponentiation applied to the membership function, error which is for the stopping criterion, maximum number of iterations.
- If the initial condition is "None", then the algorithm is randomly initialized.
- From the input and the segmented image, it is possible to observe that the input image is properly segmented using fuzzy C-means clustering algorithm.

7.5.3 Mean Shift Algorithm-Based Image Segmentation

The mean shift algorithm belongs to density-based clustering. Here, density refers to probability density function. Given a set of data points from an unknown probability distribution, density estimation refers to the problem of estimating density function of the given data. Density estimation can be broadly classified into parametric and non-parametric. Parametric density estimation is a model-based approach. The advantage of the parametric method is that the estimates of the values can be made using a small amount of data. In non-parametric method, no assumption is made about the distribution of the data. The density is estimated based only on the available data. The mean shift (MS) algorithm is a non-parametric iterative method introduced by Fukunaga and Hostetler for locating modes of a probability density function via a kernel density estimate from a given dataset. The algorithm was generalized by Cheng to illustrate that mean shift algorithm is a mode-seeking process on a surface constructed with a shadow kernel. The mean shift algorithm iteratively shifts each data point to a weighted average of neighbouring points to find stationary points of the estimated probability density function. The mean shift algorithm can be used as a clustering tool, where each mode represents a cluster. In contrast to the k-mean clustering approach, the mean shift algorithm does not require prior knowledge of the number of clusters, and there is no assumption of the shape of the clusters. The mean shift algorithm can be applied to image segmentation, object tracking, edge detection, and information fusion applications. The steps involved in mean shift algorithm are summarised below:

1. Given a distribution of "N" data in feature space, set $m_i = f_i$ as the initial mean for each data "I".
2. Repeat the following for each mean m_i:

   (a) Place window of size W around m_i.
   (b) Compute centroid (m) within the window. Set $m_i = m$.
   (c) Stop if the shift in m_i is less than a threshold.

3. Label all pixels that have same mode as belonging to the same cluster.

The fundamental parameter in mean shift algorithm is the bandwidth, which determines the number of clusters. Bandwidth refers to the size of the window across which the mean is calculated. Some of the common approaches to select the bandwidth are (1) Scott's rule, (2) Silverman's rule, and (3) Expert's knowledge. The Scott's rule selects a bandwidth that is proportional to the standard deviation of the data. The Silverman's rule selects a bandwidth that is proportional to the median interquartile range of the data. Expert knowledge rule, the bandwidth selection is done manually with rich domain-specific information. The Python "*sklearn*" module offers "*estimate_bandwidth*" function based on nearest neighbour analysis.

Experiment 7.22: Implementation of Mean Shift Algorithm
This experiment explores the implementation of mean shift algorithm for image segmentation in the Python environment. Initially, the input test image is read; it is then passed through mean shift algorithm to obtain the segmented image. The Python code that performs this task is shown in Fig. 7.50, and the corresponding output is shown in Fig. 7.51.

Inferences
The following inferences can be observed from this experiment:

* The "*estimate_bandwidth*" function from "*sklearn.cluster*" is used to find a suitable bandwidth based on a subset of the data. A small bandwidth results in many small clusters, while a larger bandwidth may merge distinct clusters.

```
# Mean Shift algorithm for image segmentation
import cv2
import numpy as np
import matplotlib.pyplot as plt
from sklearn.cluster import MeanShift, estimate_bandwidth
img=cv2.imread('coin_testimg3.jpg');#Read the input image
imgShape = img.shape
flat_image = img.reshape((-1,3));# flatten the image
flat_image = np.float32(flat_image)
#Mean shift algorithm
bandwidth = estimate_bandwidth(flat_image, quantile=.5, n_samples=10)
ms = MeanShift(bandwidth = bandwidth,  bin_seeding=True)
ms.fit(flat_image)
labels=ms.labels_
segments = np.unique(labels)
seg_img = np.reshape(labels, imgShape[:2])
#Displaying the result
plt.subplot(1,2,1),plt.imshow(img,cmap='gray'),plt.xticks([]),plt.yticks([])
plt.title('Input Image'),plt.subplot(1,2,2),plt.imshow(seg_img,cmap='gray'),plt.xticks([]),
plt.yticks([]),plt.title('Segmented Image with Segments (N) = ${}$'.format(segments.shape[0]))
plt.tight_layout()
```

Fig. 7.50 Python code to perform mean shift algorithm

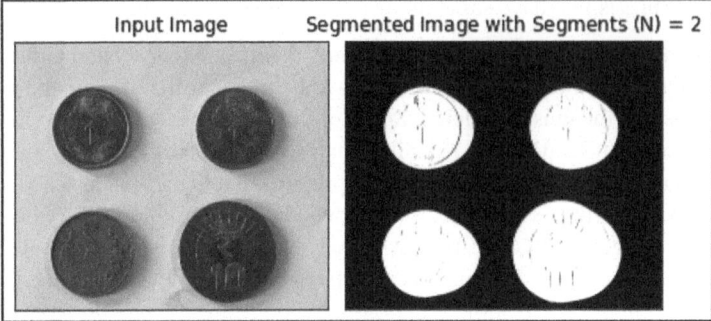

Fig. 7.51 Result of mean shift algorithm-based segmentation

- Bin-seeding is a faster way to compute mean shift. If it is set to true, initial seed points are laced in a grid, reducing the number of iterations needed to converge.
- The input image has four coins of different sizes. It is applied to mean shift algorithm. The mean shift algorithm divides the image into two segments, one corresponding to the foreground (coin) and the other corresponding to the background.

7.5.4 SLIC Algorithm-Based Image Segmentation

SLIC stands for Simple Linear Iterative Clustering. The goal is to cluster image pixels into segments (clusters) based on their colour similarity and proximity in the image plane. This algorithm is inspired by the k-means algorithm, as in the k-means, SLIC takes as input a desired number of segments K. For an image with N pixels, the approximate size of each segment is therefore N/K pixels. There would be a segment centre "C" for roughly equally sized segments at every grid interval $S = \sqrt{\dfrac{N}{k}}$.

The segment centre "C_k" is represented as a 5D vector $[R_k, G_k, B_k, x_k, y_k]$ for $k = 1$, $2, \ldots, K$.

In the SLIC algorithm, as a first step, "K" segment centres are regularly sampled on the image plane and moved to the locations corresponding to the lowest gradient position in a 3×3 neighbourhood. Afterwards, each image pixel is assigned to one of the segments based on the distance, i.e. the distance from a pixel "i" to all the segment centres is computed, and the pixel is assigned to the segment whose centre has the lowest distance to "i". The algorithm assumes that pixels that are associated with a segment lie within a $2S \times 2S$ area around the centre of this segment on the xy plane. After all the pixels are associated with the nearest cluster centre, a new centre is computed as the average $[R, G, B, x, y]$ vector of all the pixels belonging to the cluster. This process of associating pixels with the nearest cluster centre and recomputing the centre is iteratively repeated until convergence.

```
#SLIC Image segmentation
import cv2
import matplotlib.pyplot as plt
from skimage import segmentation
img=cv2.imread('coin_testimg3.jpg')
labels = segmentation.slic(img,n_segments=10,compactness=15.0,enforce_connectivity=True)
seg_img = segmentation.mark_boundaries(img, labels,(1,0,1),(1,0,1),mode='thick')
plt.subplot(1,2,1),plt.imshow(img,cmap='gray'),plt.xticks([]),plt.yticks([])
plt.title('Input Image'),plt.subplot(1,2,2),plt.imshow(seg_img,cmap='gray'),plt.xticks([]),
plt.yticks([]),plt.title('Segmented Image')
plt.tight_layout()
```

Fig. 7.52 Python code to perform image segmentation using SLIC algorithm

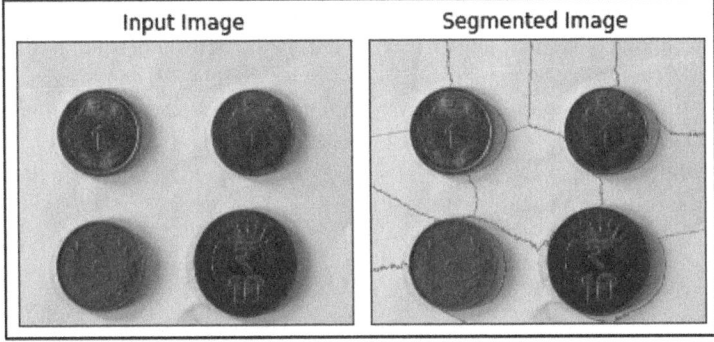

Fig. 7.53 Result of Python code shown in Fig. 7.52

Experiment 7.23: SLIC Algorithm for Image Segmentation

The aim of this experiment is to perform image segmentation using the SLIC algorithm in the Python environment. The "*sci-kit*" library has built-in function "*slic*" to implement SLIC algorithm. The Python code, which performs image segmentation using the "SLIC" algorithm, is given in Fig. 7.52, and the corresponding output is shown in Fig. 7.53.

Inferences

The following inferences can be drawn from this experiment:

- SLIC algorithm generates superpixels by clustering pixels based on their colour similarity and proximity in the image plane.
- The compactness parameter controls the shape of the superpixels.
- A higher value makes superpixels more regularly shaped, a lower value makes superpixels adhere to boundaries better, making them irregularly shaped.
- The compactness parameter is fixed as 15.
- From the result, it is possible to observe the result of "over segmentation".

7.6   Active Contour-Based Image Segmentation

The active contour model is one of the most successful methods of region-of-interest segmentation. It is also referred as snake model. Kass et al. defined the active contour model as an elastic curve that moves through the spatial domain of an image under the influence of internal and external forces. The internal force is computed from the geometrical properties of the contours, and the external force is computed from the image data so that the snake will conform to the object boundary. The internal force is responsible for shrinking and smoothing the snake, and the external force is responsible for pulling the snake to the contour points. The active contour model is based on energy minimization technique. Active contour models can be broadly categorized into (1) Edge-based active contour model and (2) Region based active contour model. Edge-based model uses image gradient to force the active contours to move towards the desired object boundary. Region-based active contour model uses image statistical information to attract the active contours to the object boundaries. Region-based models are more robust when weak edges exist and less sensitive to initialization, but more computationally expensive than edge-based models.

The traditional snake is a curve $v(s) = [x(s), y(s)]$ defined to minimize the energy given by the following equation

$$E = \int_0^1 \left[E_{int}\left(v\left(s\right)\right) + E_{ext}\left(v\left(s\right)\right) \right] ds \tag{7.35}$$

where

$$E_{int}\left(v\left(s\right)\right) = \frac{1}{2}\alpha \left| v'\left(s\right) \right| + \beta \left| v''\left(s\right) \right| \tag{7.36}$$

In the above Eq. (7.36), α and β are weights that control the tension and rigidity of the snake, respectively, and are applied to the first and second derivative of $v(s)$. The external energy is obtained from the image. The expression for the external energy is given by

$$E_{ext}\left(x,y\right) = -\left| \nabla(G_\sigma\left(x,y\right) * I(x,y)) \right|^2 \tag{7.37}$$

In the above expression (7.37), $G_\sigma(x, y)$ represents the Gaussian function, which is used to smoothen the image and ∇ is the gradient operator.

A snake that minimizes the external and internal energy should satisfy the following Euler equation:

$$\alpha v''\left(s\right) - \beta v'''\left(s\right) - \nabla E_{ext} = 0 \tag{7.38}$$

The above equation can be viewed as a force equilibrium, where the internal force is responsible for shrinking and smoothing the snake, and the external force is for pulling the snake to the contour points. The major challenge is to decide the initial contour. For getting better results of segmentation, the initial contour has to be designed near the desired contour.

Experiment 7.24: Active Contour-based Image Segmentation

In this experiment, the input "coin" image is read. It is then passed through Gaussian filter to smoothen the input image. Then an initial contour is defined for the active contour model to perform the image segmentation. The built-in function used in the program are listed in Table 7.4.

The Python code that performs the segmentation of the image using the active contour method is shown in Fig. 7.53, and the corresponding output is shown in Fig. 7.54.

Table 7.4 List of built-in functions used in active contour method of image segmentation

S. No.	Built-in function	Library	Purpose
1	Gaussian	skimage.filters	To perform Gaussian smoothing of the input image. The extent of smoothing is controlled by the standard deviation (σ)
2	active_contour	skimage.segmentation	To perform image segmentation using active contour method.
3	Imread	Computer vision (cv2)	To read the input image
4	Imshow	Matplotlib	To display the image

```
# Active Contour model for image segmentation
import cv2
import numpy as np
import matplotlib.pyplot as plt
import skimage.segmentation as seg
from skimage.filters import gaussian
img=cv2.imread('coin_single1.jpg');#Read the input image
img1 = gaussian(img, sigma=2, preserve_range=False);#Perform Gaussian smoothing
#Define the initial contour
def circle_points(resolution, center, radius):
    radians = np.linspace(0, 2*np.pi, resolution)
    c = center[1] + radius*np.cos(radians)#polar co-ordinates
    r = center[0] + radius*np.sin(radians)
    return (np.array([c, r]).T)
points = circle_points(200, [480, 540], 470)[:-1]
snake = seg.active_contour(img1, points);#Applying the active contour
#Displaying the results
fig,(ax1,ax2,ax3) = plt.subplots(nrows=1, ncols=3)
ax1.imshow(img, cmap='gray'),ax1.set_title('Input Image'),ax1.axis('off')
ax2.imshow(img1,cmap='gray'),ax2.set_title('Smoothened Image'),ax2.axis('off')
ax3.imshow(img,cmap='gray'),ax3.set_title('Active Contour output')
ax3.plot(points[:, 0], points[:, 1], '--r', lw=3)
ax3.plot(snake[:, 0], snake[:, 1], '-b', lw=3),ax3.axis('off')
plt.tight_layout()
```

Fig. 7.54 Python code to perform image segmentation using active contour model

Fig. 7.55   Result of image segmentation

Inferences

The following inferences can be drawn from Fig. 7.55:

- The input image is a "coin" image. The red colour circle represents the initial contour specified by the user.
- The blue colour contour represents the result of active contour model.
- The red colour contour is attracted towards the coin boundary by active contour model. The final result is shown in blue colour.

Experiment 7.25: Verification of Gaussian Smoothing in the Active Contour Model

This experiment tries to verify the importance of the Gaussian smoothing operation in the active contour model. For this, the input image is directly passed to the active contour model without Gaussian smoothening process. The Python code that passes the input image to the active contour model is shown in Fig. 7.56, and the corresponding result is shown in Fig. 7.57.

Inferences

The following inferences can be observed from this experiment:

- From Fig. 7.56, it is possible to observe that the code that performs Gaussian smoothing of the input image is removed.
- In Fig. 7.57, the red colour represents the initial contour, and the blue represents the image segmentation result.
- From Fig. 7.57, it is possible to observe that the contour needs to be pulled towards the image boundary effectively.
- Gaussian smoothing is an essential component in active contour-based image segmentation to obtain effective segmentation results.

Experiment 7.26: Verification of the Impact of Poor Initial Boundary Selection

The objective of the task is to analyze the impact of poor selection of initial boundary on the performance of active contour model performance. For this purpose, the initial contour is defined within the coin image. The Python code that performs this task is shown in Fig. 7.58, and the corresponding output is shown in Fig. 7.59.

```
# Active Contour model without Gaussian filtering for image segmentation
import cv2
import numpy as np
import matplotlib.pyplot as plt
import skimage.segmentation as seg
img=cv2.imread('coin_single1.jpg');#Read the input image
#Define the initial contour
def circle_points(resolution, center, radius):
    radians = np.linspace(0, 2*np.pi, resolution)
    c = center[1] + radius*np.cos(radians)#polar co-ordinates
    r = center[0] + radius*np.sin(radians)
    return (np.array([c, r]).T)
points = circle_points(200, [480, 540], 470)[:-1]
snake = seg.active_contour(img, points);#Applying the active contour
#Displaying the results
fig,(ax1,ax2) = plt.subplots(nrows=1, ncols=2)
ax1.imshow(img, cmap='gray'),ax1.set_title('Input Image'),ax1.axis('off')
ax2.imshow(img,cmap='gray'),ax2.set_title('Active Contour output')
ax2.plot(points[:, 0], points[:, 1], '--r', lw=3)
ax2.plot(snake[:, 0], snake[:, 1], '-b', lw=3),ax2.axis('off')
plt.tight_layout()
```

Fig. 7.56 Python code to perform image segmentation using active contour model

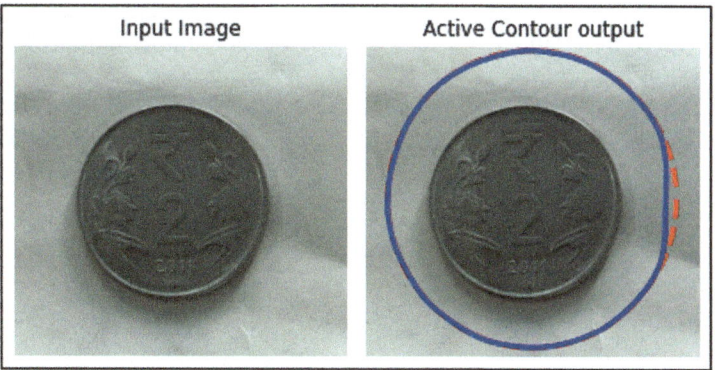

Fig. 7.57 Result of Python code shown in Fig. 7.56

Inferences

From Figs. 7.58 and 7.59, the following inferences can be drawn:

- From Fig. 7.58, it is possible to observe that the initial boundary radius is reduced. The radius is now 230.
- Since the initial contour is within the image, the active contour model is not able to segment the image properly.

```
# Importance of initial contour selection
import cv2
import numpy as np
import matplotlib.pyplot as plt
import skimage.segmentation as seg
from skimage.filters import gaussian
img=cv2.imread('coin_single1.jpg');#Read the input image
img1 = gaussian(img, sigma=2, preserve_range=False);#Perform Gaussian smoothing
#Define the initial contour
def circle_points(resolution, center, radius):
    radians = np.linspace(0, 2*np.pi, resolution)
    c = center[1] + radius*np.cos(radians)#polar co-ordinates
    r = center[0] + radius*np.sin(radians)
    return (np.array([c, r]).T)
points = circle_points(200, [480, 540], 230)[:-1]
snake = seg.active_contour(img1, points);#Applying the active contour
#Displaying the results
fig,(ax1,ax2) = plt.subplots(nrows=1, ncols=2)
ax1.imshow(img, cmap='gray'),ax1.set_title('Input Image'),ax1.axis('off')
ax2.imshow(img,cmap='gray'),ax2.set_title('Active Contour output')
ax2.plot(points[:, 0], points[:, 1], '--r', lw=3)
ax2.plot(snake[:, 0], snake[:, 1], '-b', lw=3),ax2.axis('off')
plt.tight_layout()
```

Fig. 7.58 Python code with poor selection of initial contour

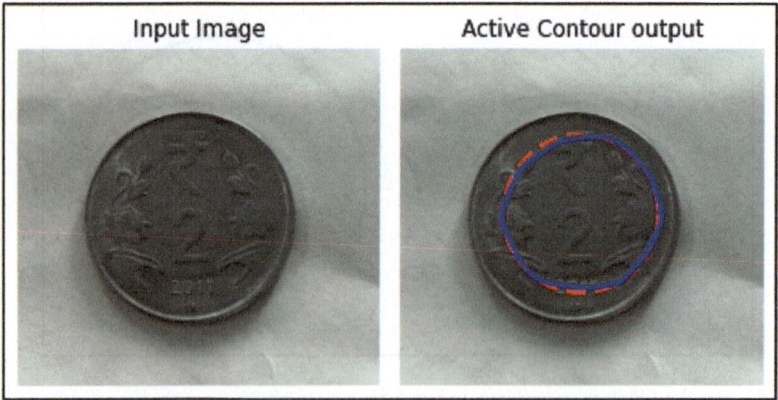

Fig. 7.59 Result of Python code shown in Fig. 7.58

- The final contour after applying active contour model program is shown in red colour. From this, it is possible to infer that the coin image is not segmented properly.
- From this experiment, it is possible to infer that proper initial contour is necessary to obtain an effective segmentation result.
- The "ballooning effect" of the initial contour is not happening for effective segmentation of the coin image.

7.7   Chan–Vese Method for Image Segmentation

The Chan–Vese model is a piecewise constant approximation of global region information based on the Mumford–Shah model. The Chan–Vese model assumes that each region is homogenous with respect to grayscale intensities within a region, and it uses the mean of grayscale intensities within a region as a region descriptor to generate a force that pulls the shape model towards the region of interest. Chan–Vese model is based on the edge function to stop the evolution curve at the desired edge. The Chan–Vese model partitions an input image into foreground (Ω_1) and background (Ω_2) of low intra-region variance and separated by a smooth closed contour. The mathematical model of the Chan–Vese algorithm is given by

$$E = \mu |C| + \lambda_1 \int_{\Omega_1} \left(u_0(X) - c_1 \right)^2 dx + \lambda_2 \int_{\Omega_2} \left(u_0(X) - c_2 \right)^2 dx \qquad (7.39)$$

In the above equation, c_1 and c_2 represent the average intensity levels inside Ω_1 and Ω_2 respectively. In the equation, μ, λ_1 and λ_2 are user-defined parameters. u_0 represents the input image and "C" represents the boundary between the two regions. The optimal segmentation corresponds to the global minimum of the expression given in Eq. (7.39).

Experiment 7.27: Chan–Vese Method for Image Segmentation
This experiment focuses on the segmentation of "coin" image using the Chan–Vese algorithm. The Python code that performs the task of segmentation is shown in Fig. 7.60, and the corresponding output is shown in Fig. 7.61. Chan–Vese segmentation algorithm is an iterative segmentation algorithm. In this experiment, the number of iterations is fixed as 200. Typical values of λ_1 and λ_2 are 1. The value of "μ" is between 0 and 1. Higher values of "μ" are preferable while dealing with ill-defined contours. The "init-level_set" defines the starting level set used by the algorithm. The custom level sets available in the built-in function are "checkerboard", "disk" and "small disk". The "checkerboard" initial level set has fast convergence, but it

```
import cv2
import matplotlib.pyplot as plt
from skimage.segmentation import chan_vese
#Read the input image
img=cv2.imread('coin_testimg10.jpg',0)
#Apply Chan-Vese algorithm
cv = chan_vese(img, mu=0.09, lambda1=1, lambda2=1, tol=1e-3, max_num_iter=100,
            dt=0.2, init_level_set="checkerboard", extended_output=True)
#Displaying the result
plt.subplot(1,2,1),plt.imshow(img,cmap='gray'),plt.title('Input image')
plt.xticks([]),plt.yticks([]),plt.subplot(1,2,2),plt.imshow(cv[1],cmap='gray'),
plt.title('Output image'),plt.xticks([]),plt.yticks([])
plt.tight_layout()
```

Fig. 7.60 Python code to perform segmentation using Chan–Vese algorithm

Fig. 7.61 Result of Python
code shown in Fig. 7.60

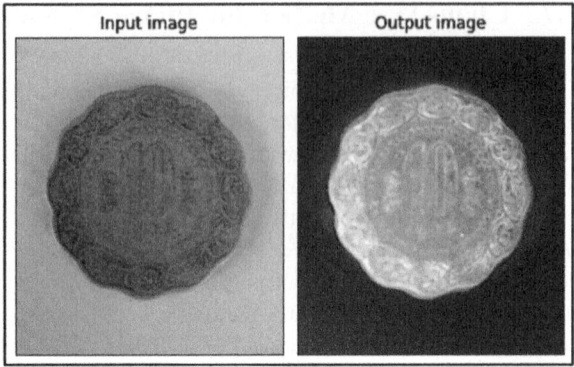

may fail to detect implicit edges. The "disk" initial level set is somewhat slower, but
it is more likely to detect implicit edges. The multiplication factor (dt) serves to
accelerate the algorithm. Higher values of "dt" may speed up the algorithm at the
expense of convergence. The term "tol" represents the level set variation tolerance
between iterations. If the "extended_output" is set as true, then the return value will
be a tuple containing three return values. If it is set to false, only the "segmented
array" will be returned.

Inferences
The following inferences can be made from this experiment:

- The input image is an image that contains coin in a white background. The object
  in the image is the coin.
- After applying Chan–Vese algorithm, it is possible to observe that the algorithm
  separates the foreground and the background. The foreground is the object, and
  the background, in this case, is a black.

7.8   Morphological Geodesic Active Contour

Morphological snakes are a family of image segmentation algorithms whose behav-
iours are similar to active contours, such as geodesic active contours or active contours without edges. Morphological snakes employ operators such as dilation and
erosion, whereas traditional active contour employ partial differential equations
over image arrays. A geometric curve is represented implicitly as a level set and is
evolved based on geometric computations. The level-set refers to a set of point variables for which their function is equal to some constant value. In the geometric
model, the curve is represented with a zero level set $\psi(x, y, t)$. The geometric curve
evolves in time "t" on an image with a speed function which is given by

$$\frac{\partial \psi}{\partial t} = c(k + V_0)|\nabla \psi| \tag{7.40}$$

In the above expression, "k" represents the curvature of the curve which makes it smoother, the parameter V_0 controls the shrinking or expansion of the curve, $\nabla\psi$ is the gradient of the level-set "ψ". The term $c(k + V_0)$ determines the speed of the curve's evolution along its normal direction. The expression for the factor "c" in Eq. (7.40) is given by

$$c = \frac{1}{1 + \left|\nabla\left(G_\sigma * I\right)\right|}$$

(7.41)

In the above expression, $\nabla(G_\sigma * I)$ is the gradient of the Gaussian blurred image. An additional term is included in Eq. (7.40) to pull back the curve in case it overpasses a weak object boundary. After including the addition term Eq. (7.40) is given by

$$\frac{\partial\psi}{\partial t} = c\left(k + V_0\right)\left|\nabla\psi\right| + \nabla c\nabla\psi$$

(7.42)

Morphological geodesic active contour algorithm has four parameters, namely, (1) Preprocessed image, (2) Balloon force, (3) Smoothing parameter, and (4) Number of iterations. The inverse Gaussian gradient operator is used to preprocess the image. The balloon force is used to inflate or deflate the initial contour towards the edges of the image. Smoothing parameter is used to convert the jagged lines into a curve. The algorithm iteratively alters the initial contour to move towards the actual contour of the image.

The advantage of geodesic active contour model is its ability to change a curve's topology in accordance with the shape of the object during the curve evolution process. Geodesic active contour model is useful in applications like object tracking and motion detection.

Experiment 7.28: Morphological Geodesic Active Contour

This experiment explores image segmentation using a morphological geodesic active contour approach. The Python code that performs the ballooning effect in active contour using the geodesic active contour method is given in Fig. 7.62, and the corresponding result is shown in Fig. 7.63.

Inferences

The following inferences can be made from this experiment:

- The input image is a coin image. This input image is Gaussian smoothened first and then applied to get a gradient image using inverse Gaussian gradient method.
- The initial contour is shown in red colour. The initial contour is less than the size of the coin which is to be segmented.
- Here, ballooning effect is required to move the initial contour to wrap the coin.
- The final contour after applying morphological geodesic active contour method is shown in blue colour.
- From the result, it is possible to observe that the initial contour is expanded (ballooning effect) to wrap up the coin.
- The number of iterations required to obtain the above-mentioned result is 400.

```
# morphological_geodesic_active_contour algorithm
import cv2
import numpy as np
import matplotlib.pyplot as plt
from skimage.filters import gaussian
from skimage.segmentation import morphological_geodesic_active_contour,
inverse_gaussian_gradient
img=cv2.imread('coin_single1.jpg',0);#Read the input image
img1 = gaussian(img, sigma=3, preserve_range=False);#Smoothing of the input image
gimg = inverse_gaussian_gradient(img1);#Perform Inverse Gaussian gradient
init_ls = np.zeros(img.shape, dtype=np.int8);#Define the initial contour
m,n=init_ls.shape
r=40
for i in range(0,m):
    for j in range(0,n):
        if(i-m/2)**2+(j-n/2)**2<r**2:
            init_ls[i,j]=1
#Perform Morphological geodesic active contour
ls = morphological_geodesic_active_contour(gimg, 400, init_ls,smoothing=3, balloon=1.2,
                    threshold=0.9)
#Displaying the result
fig,(ax1,ax2,ax3,ax4) = plt.subplots(figsize=(12, 5),nrows=1, ncols=4)
ax1.imshow(img, cmap='gray'),ax1.set_title('Input Image'),ax1.set_xticks([]),ax1.set_yticks([])
ax2.imshow(img1,cmap='gray'),ax2.set_title('Gaussian Smoothened Image'),ax2.set_xticks([]),
ax2.set_yticks([]),ax3.imshow(gimg,cmap='gray'),ax3.set_title('Inverse Gaussian Gradient')
ax3.set_xticks([]),ax3.set_yticks([]),ax4.imshow(img, cmap='gray'),
ax4.set_title('Geodesic Active Contour Output'),ax4.contour(init_ls,colors='r'),
ax4.contour(ls, colors='b'),ax4.set_xticks([]),ax4.set_yticks([])
plt.tight_layout()
```

Fig. 7.62 Python code to perform morphological geodesic active contour

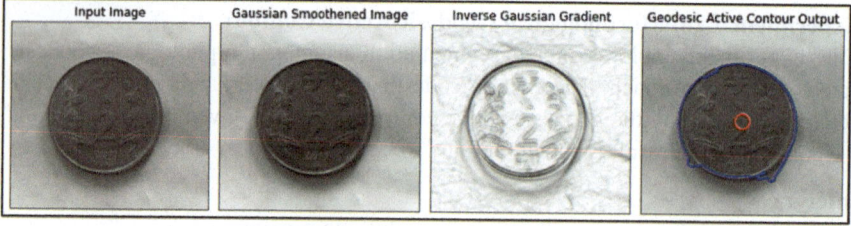

Fig. 7.63 Result of morphological geodesic active contour method

Experiment 7.29: Impact of Number of Iterations and Threshold in Morphological Geodesic Active Contour Method

This experiment discusses the impact of number of iterations and threshold in morphological geodesic active contour method. For this, the number of iterations is reduced from 400 to 200. After changing the number of iterations is 200 in the Python code given in Fig. 7.62, and the simulation result is displayed in Fig. 7.64. Similarly, changing the threshold value from 0.9 to 0.5 and keeping the number of

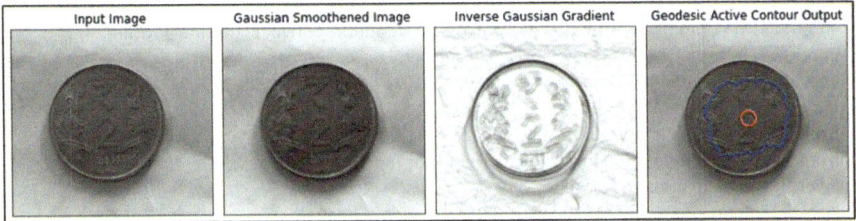

Fig. 7.64 Impact of number of iterations in morphological geodesic active contour method

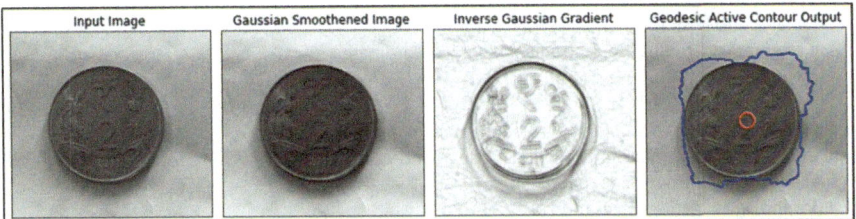

Fig. 7.65 Impact of the threshold value in morphological geodesic active contour method

iterations is 400 in the Python code given in Fig. 7.62, and the simulation result is shown in Fig. 7.65.

Inferences

The following observations can be drawn from this experiment:

- From Fig. 7.64, it is possible to infer that the impact of reducing the number of iterations to half. Upon reducing the number of iterations to half, the ballooning effect of the algorithm is minimum. The algorithm is not able to expand the contour to the exact boundaries of the coin image.
- From Fig. 7.65, it is possible to infer that upon reducing the threshold value from 0.9 to 0.5, the active contour cannot effectively capture the boundary of the coin.

Experiment 7.30: Comparison of Active Contour Versus Morphological Geodesic Active Contour

The objective of this experiment is to compare active contour algorithm with morphological geodesic active contour algorithm. The same test image is applied to both algorithm. The test image contains a coin. The objective is to trace the boundary of the coin using active contour and morphological active contour algorithm. The Python code that performs this task is shown in Fig. 7.66, and the corresponding output is shown in Fig. 7.67.

Inferences

From Fig. 7.66, the following inferences can be drawn:

- For the active contour method of image segmentation, the input image is preprocessed using a Gaussian smoothing filter.

```
# Comparison of Active Contour Vs morphological_geodesic_active_contour algorithm
import cv2
import numpy as np
import matplotlib.pyplot as plt
from skimage.filters import gaussian
from skimage.segmentation import active_contour,morphological_geodesic_active_contour,
inverse_gaussian_gradient
img=cv2.imread('coin_testimg10.jpg',0);#Read the input image
img1 = gaussian(img, sigma=2, preserve_range=False);#Smoothing of the input image
m,n=img.shape
# I) Active contour method
def circle_points(resolution, center, radius):#Define the initial contour
    radians = np.linspace(0, 2*np.pi, resolution)
    c = center[1] + radius*np.cos(radians)#polar co-ordinates
    r = center[0] + radius*np.sin(radians)
    return (np.array([c, r]).T)
points = circle_points(250, [m/2, n/2], 800)[:-1]
#Perform active contour method of image segmentation
snake =active_contour(img1, points,alpha=0.01)
#Morphological geodesic contour
gimg = inverse_gaussian_gradient(img1);#Perform Inverse Gaussian gradient
init_ls = np.zeros(img.shape, dtype=np.int8);#Define the initial contour
m,n=init_ls.shape
r=800
for i in range(0,m):
    for j in range(0,n):
        if(i-m/2)**2+(j-n/2)**2<r**2:
            init_ls[i,j]=1
#II) Perform Morphological geodesic active contour
ls = morphological_geodesic_active_contour(gimg, 190, init_ls,smoothing=3, balloon=-2,
                        threshold=0.9)
#Displaying the result
fig, ax = plt.subplots(figsize=(6, 4),nrows=1, ncols=2),ax[0].imshow(img, cmap='gray'),
ax[0].set_title('Active Contour'),ax[0].set_xticks([]),ax[0].set_yticks([])
ax[0].plot(points[:, 0], points[:, 1], '--b', lw=3),ax[0].plot(snake[:, 0], snake[:, 1], '-r', lw=3)
ax[1].imshow(img, cmap='gray'),ax[1].set_title('Geodesic Active Contour'),ax[1].set_xticks([]),
ax[1].set_yticks([]),ax[1].contour(init_ls,colors='b'),ax[1].contour(ls, colors='r')
plt.tight_layout()
```

Fig. 7.66 Comparison of active contour with morphological geodesic active contour

- The built-in function "*active_contour*" available in "scikit" image library is used to perform the segmentation. The value of "α" in active contour method is chosen as 0.01.
- For morphological geodesic active contour, the input image is preprocessed using the "inverse Gaussian Gradient" function, which is used to obtain the edge of the input image. The initial contour is defined as a circle.
- The number of iterations is fixed as 190, the ballooning factor is chosen as "−2". The negative sign implies that the initial boundary has to be shrunk. The smoothing factor is fixed as 3.

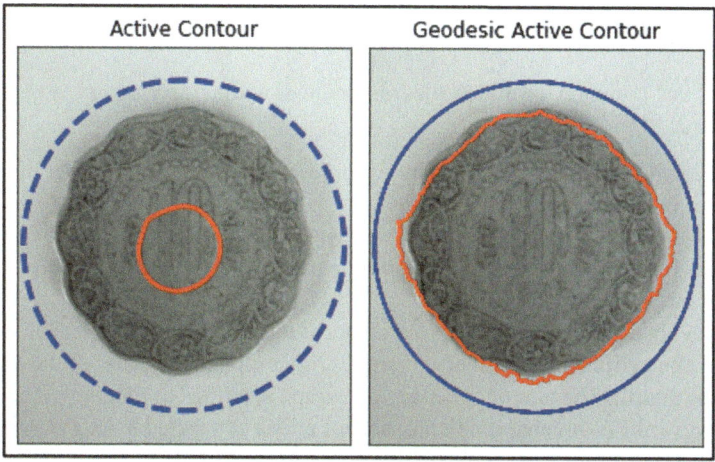

Fig. 7.67 Result of comparison of active contour with morphological geodesic active contour

From Fig. 7.67, the following inferences can be drawn:

- The test image is the same for both the active contour and morphological geodesic active contour. The test image is a 10-paise coin image.
- The blue dotted curve in the active contour represents the initial boundary, and the red represents the final boundary obtained after applying the active contour algorithm.
- The blue circle in the morphological geodesic active contour result represents the initial boundary, and the red circle indicates the final boundary after the algorithm is applied.
- By observing the results of active contour with morphological geodesic active contour, it is possible to infer that the morphological geodesic active contour algorithm encircles the coin better than the active contour algorithm. Thus, morphological geodesic active contour algorithm performs better than the active contour algorithm.

7.9   Graph-Based Image Segmentation

A graph is a structure used to describe a set of objects and the pairwise relations between those objects. A graph consists of nodes and edges. The nodes are referred to as vertices, and the edges are the lines or arcs connecting any two graph nodes.

7.9.1   *Graph Representation*

A graph is represented as $G = (V, E)$, where "V" represents the set of "N" nodes, $|V| = N$. "E" denotes the set of edges connecting the nodes.

7.9.2 Terminologies in Graph Theory

Some of the common terminologies associated with graph theory are summarized below:

Vertex: Geometrically, small solid circles represent vertices. The number of distinct vertices is represented as $|V|$.

Edge: Edge either joins one vertex to another or joins a vertex to itself. Curves or straight-line segments represent geometrical edges. The number of distinct edges in a graph is represented by $|E|$.

Adjacency: In a graph, two vertices are adjacent if they are the endpoints of an edge.

Order of the graph: The number of vertices of a graph is the order of the graph.

Size of the graph: The number of edges of a graph is termed as the size of the graph.

Directed graph: A directed graph has a set of nodes connected by edges, with each node having a direction associated with it. An example of a directed graph is illustrated in Fig. 7.68a.

In Fig. 7.68a, "P" and "Q" represent two nodes. The graph can be traversed from node "P" to node "Q" and not vice-versa.

Cycles: In a directed graph, a cycle is a path that starts and ends at the same vertex.

Degree of a vertex (valency): The degree of a vertex is the number of edges incident to the vertex. It is denoted as $\deg(v)$.

For the graph shown in Fig. 7.68b:

- $\deg(P) = 3$, since the node "P" has three edges. Hence, $\deg(P)$ is equal to three.
- $\deg(R) = 2$, because node "R" has two edges.
- $\deg(Q) = 2$, because two edges are meeting at the node "Q",
- $\deg(S) = 1$, since only one edge meets the node "S".

Undirected graph: In an undirected graph, the edges are bidirectional with no direction associated with them. An example of undirected graph is illustrated in Fig. 7.68c. From this figure, it is possible to observe that the nodes "P" and "Q" are connected by an edge without arrow. This implies that the graph can be traversed from node "P" to node "Q" and vice-versa.

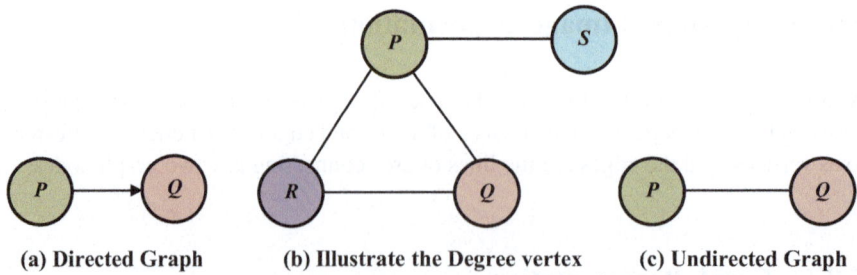

(a) Directed Graph   (b) Illustrate the Degree vertex   (c) Undirected Graph

Fig. 7.68 Sample graphs. (**a**) Directed graph. (**b**) Illustrate the degree vertex. (**c**) Undirected graph

Unweighted graph: In unweighted graphs, the edges do not have weights associated with them. An example of an unweighted graph is shown in Fig. 7.69a.

From Fig. 7.69a, it is possible to observe that there is a connection between the nodes "*P*", "*Q*", and "*R*", but the strength of the connection is not mentioned; hence it is an example of an unweighted graph.

Weighted graph: In a weighted graph, a weight is associated with each edge. The weight may represent attributes like distance, cost, time, etc., based on the type of problem chosen. Figure 7.69b represents a weighted graph in which the connection weight between the nodes "*P*" and "*Q*" is 1, whereas the connection weight between the noises "*Q*" and "*R*" is 2 and the connection weight between the nodes "*P*" and "*R*" is 3.

Bipartite graph: A bipartite graph is a graph where the vertices can be divided into two disjoint sets such that all edges connect a vertex in one set to a vertex in another set. An example of bipartite graph is shown in Fig. 7.70.

Figure 7.70 represents bipartite graph because the vertex of the graph can be decomposed into two sets "*X*" and "*Y*". Set $X = \{P, R\}$ and set $Y = \{Q, S\}$. The vertices of set *X* join only with vertices of set *Y* and vice-versa. The vertices within the same set do not join. Hence, the graph is a bipartite graph.

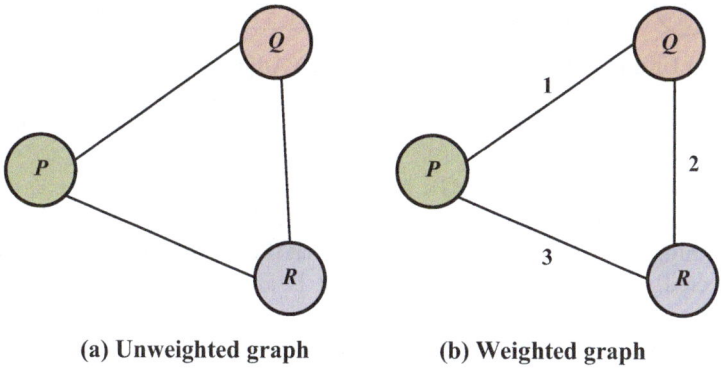

(a) Unweighted graph   (b) Weighted graph

Fig. 7.69 Unweighted and weighted graphs. (a) Unweighted graph. (b) Weighted graph

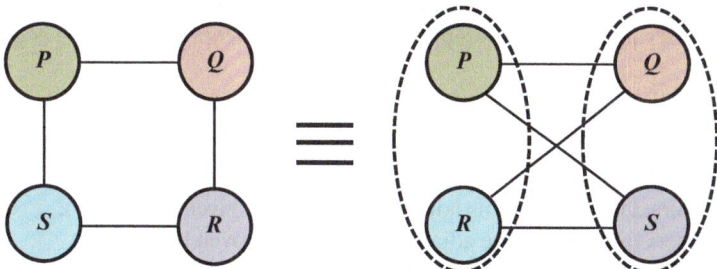

Fig. 7.70 Bipartite graph

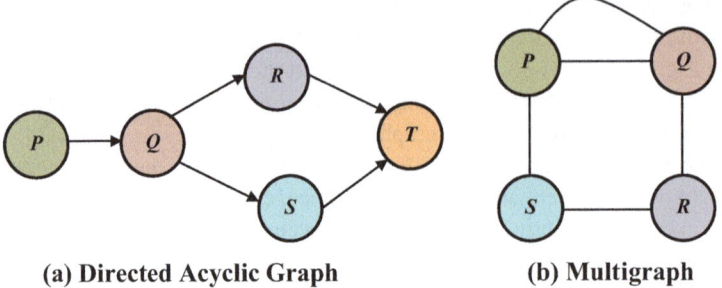

(a) Directed Acyclic Graph   **(b) Multigraph**

Fig. 7.71 Directed acyclic and multigraph. (**a**) Directed acyclic graph. (**b**) Multigraph

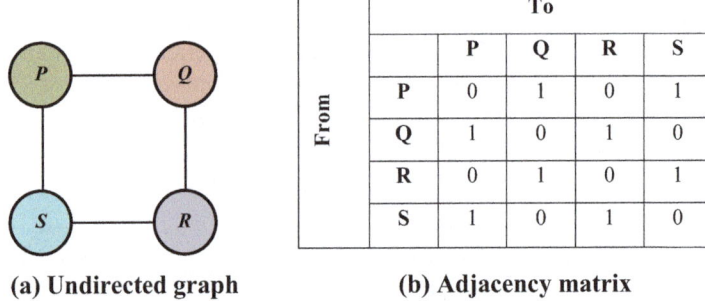

		To			
		P	**Q**	**R**	**S**
From	**P**	0	1	0	1
	Q	1	0	1	0
	R	0	1	0	1
	S	1	0	1	0

(a) Undirected graph   **(b) Adjacency matrix**

Fig. 7.72 Undirected graph and its adjacency matrix. (**a**) Undirected graph. (**b**) Adjacency matrix

Directed acyclic graph (DAG): A directed graph with no cycles is a directed acyclic graph. Figure 7.71a shows an example of a directed acyclic graph.

From Fig. 7.71a, it is possible to observe that the graph is a directed graph, but the directed graph has no cycle. Hence, it is an example of a directed acyclic graph.

Multigraph: A graph with more than one edge between the same two vertices is called multigraph. An example of a multigraph is shown in Fig. 7.71b. It is multigraph because the vertices "*P*" and "*Q*" are connected by more than one edge.

Adjacency matrix: Let "*G*" be a graph with "*n*" vertices. The adjacency matrix of "*G*" is a $n \times n$ matrix. The adjacency matrix describes the connections between any two nodes in "*V*" which is represented as w_{ij}. The expression for w_{ij} is given by

$$
w_{ij} = \begin{cases} 1, & if \left\{ v_i, v_j \right\} \text{ is an edge of } G, \\ 0, & \text{otherwise,} \end{cases} \tag{7.43}
$$

The undirected graph and its adjacency matrix are given in Fig. 7.72. Few observations about the adjacency matrix are given below:

- The diagonal entries of the adjacent matrix are zero; which implies that the graph has no self-loops.

- For an undirected graph, the adjacency matrix is a symmetric matrix.
- The number of nodes (vertex) in the graph determines the size of the adjacency matrix. For a graph with "n" nodes, the size of the adjacency matrix is $n \times n$.

7.9.3   Laplacian Matrix

The Laplacian matrix of $G(V, E)$ is defined as

$$L = D - A \tag{7.44}$$

In the above equation, "D" represents the diagonal matrix (Degree matrix) of node degree and "A" represents the adjacency matrix. The matrix "D" is defined as

$$D_{i,j} = \begin{cases} \text{degree}(v_i), & \text{if } i = j, \\ 0, & \text{otherwise.} \end{cases} \tag{7.45}$$

Let us consider an undirected graph shown in Fig. 7.72a, the Laplacian matrix is computed as follows:

Step 1: Computation of degree matrix "D".

The degree matrix is a diagonal matrix with the entries of the diagonal equal to the number of edges connected to the node. The degree matrix for the undirected graph is shown in Fig. 7.72a, using Eq. (7.45) is given by

$$D = \begin{bmatrix} 2 & 0 & 0 & 0 \\ 0 & 2 & 0 & 0 \\ 0 & 0 & 2 & 0 \\ 0 & 0 & 0 & 2 \end{bmatrix} \tag{7.46}$$

All the four nodes in Fig. 7.72a have two edges; hence all the diagonal entries in "D" are two.

Step 2: Computation of the adjacency matrix (A).

The adjacency matrix describes the connections between any two nodes. The adjacency matrix for the graph depicted in Fig. 7.72a is given by

$$A = \begin{bmatrix} 0 & 1 & 1 & 0 \\ 1 & 0 & 0 & 1 \\ 1 & 0 & 0 & 1 \\ 0 & 1 & 1 & 0 \end{bmatrix} \tag{7.47}$$

Step 3: Computation of Laplacian matrix (L).

Using the definition of Laplacian matrix, $L = D - A$, the Laplacian matrix is given by

$$L = \begin{bmatrix} 2 & 0 & 0 & 0 \\ 0 & 2 & 0 & 0 \\ 0 & 0 & 2 & 0 \\ 0 & 0 & 0 & 2 \end{bmatrix} - \begin{bmatrix} 0 & 1 & 1 & 0 \\ 1 & 0 & 0 & 1 \\ 1 & 0 & 0 & 1 \\ 0 & 1 & 1 & 0 \end{bmatrix} \qquad (7.48)$$

Simplifying the above expression, we get

$$L = \begin{bmatrix} 2 & -1 & -1 & 0 \\ -1 & 2 & 0 & -1 \\ -1 & 0 & 2 & -1 \\ 0 & -1 & -1 & 2 \end{bmatrix} \qquad (7.49)$$

Properties of Laplacian Matrix
The following are the properties of Laplacian matrix.

- The Laplacian matrix is a real symmetric matrix.
- Since the Laplacian matrix is real and symmetric, its eigenvalues are real, and its eigenvectors are orthogonal.
- The row sum of Laplacian matrix is zero.
- The column sum of the Laplacian matrix is zero.
- Laplacian matrix is a positive semi-definite matrix.
- The number of zero eigenvalues of Laplacian matrix is equal to the number of connected components in the graph.

7.9.4   Graph Partitioning

The central idea in graph partitioning is that the vertices are partitioned into disjoint sets. The graph is partitioned such that the edges within the group have high weights, and the edges between groups have small weights. In graph-theoretic language, it is termed as "cut". In graph theory, a cut is a partition of nodes that divides the graph into two disjoint subsets. It is expressed as

$$\text{cut}(A,B) = \sum_{u \in A, v \in B} w(u,v) \qquad (7.50)$$

The Graph "G" is divided into two disjoint sets "A" and "B" such that $A \cup B = V$ and $A \cap B = \varphi$. The degree of dissimilarity between these two sets can be computed as the total weight of the edges that have been removed. The optimal bipartitioning of a graph minimizes the *cut* value. The *cut* algorithm can be classified as (1) minimum cut (Min-Cut), (2) maximum cut, and (3) normalized cut. Min-Cut of a weighted graph is defined as the minimum sum of weights of edges that, when removed from the graph, divides the graph into two groups. Given an undirected graph $G = (V, E)$, if the objective is to partition "V" into two subsets, V_1 and V_2, such that the number of edges between V_1 and V_2 is maximum, is termed as max-cut. The normalized cut is represented as

$$N_{cut}(A,B) = \frac{cut(A,B)}{asso(A,V)} + \frac{cut(A,B)}{asso(B,V)} \tag{7.51}$$

In the above expression, $cut(A, B)$ is the sum of all the edge weights associated with the cut and $asso(A, V)$ is the sum of all the edge weights associated with the cut and all the points in the graph. $asso(B, V)$ is the total connection from nodes in "B" to all the nodes in the graph.

Steps in normalized cut algorithm for image segmentation are summarized below:

Step 1: Generate a graph $G = (V, E)$ for the given image. Here "V" represents the vertex, and "E" denotes the edge. Calculate the weights on each edge.

Step 2: Solve $(D - W)x = \lambda Dx$ for eigenvectors with the smallest eigenvalues. Here, "W" is the affine matrix of the graph, and "D" is a diagonal matrix in which each element along the diagonal represents the degree of correspondent vertex.

Step 3: Use the eigenvector with the second smallest eigenvalue to bipartition the graph.

Step 4: Decide if the current partition should be subdivided, and recursively repartition the segmented parts if necessary.

Experiment 7.31: Construction of Region Adjacency Graph (RAG)

This experiment discusses the construction of a region adjacency graph using Python. The Python code to obtain the Region Adjacency Graph of the input image is given in Fig. 7.73 and the corresponding output is shown in Fig. 7.74. The built-in function "*graph.rag_mean_color*" available in "*sci-kit*" library is used to obtain the RAG. The objective is to construct the region adjacency graph using mean colours. Each node in the RAG represents a set of pixels with image with the same label in "labels". The weight between two adjacent regions represents how similar or dissimilar two regions are depending on "mode" parameter.

Inferences

The input image is a coin image. This image is passed through "SLIC" algorithm to obtain the segmented image. Region adjacency matrix is built on the over segmented image obtained using SLIC algorithm.

Experiment 7.32: Perform Normalized Cut Algorithm in a Region Adjacency Graph (RAG)

Aim of this experiment is to perform normaliZed cut algorithm in a region adjacency graph using Python. The Python code, which performs image segmentation using the normalized cut algorithm, is given in Fig. 7.75, and the corresponding output is shown in Fig. 7.76.

```
## Region Adjacency Graph
import cv2
import matplotlib.pyplot as plt
from skimage import segmentation
from skimage import graph
#Reading the input image
img=cv2.imread('coin_single1.jpg')
#Image segmentation using SLIC algorithm
labels = segmentation.slic(img, compactness=30, n_segments=400)
seg_img = segmentation.mark_boundaries(img, labels, (0, 0, 0))
plt.subplot(1,3,2),plt.imshow(seg_img),plt.title('Segmented image'),
plt.xticks([]),plt.yticks([])
# Obtain the Region Adjacency Graph (RAG)
rag = graph.rag_mean_color(img, labels)
fig, ax = plt.subplots(nrows=1, ncols=3, sharex=True, sharey=True, figsize=(8,4))
ax[0].imshow(img, cmap='gray'),ax[0].set_title('Input Image'),ax[0].set_xticks([]),
ax[0].set_yticks([]),ax[1].imshow(seg_img, cmap='gray'),
ax[1].set_title('Segmented Image'),ax[1].set_xticks([]),ax[1].set_yticks([])
lc = graph.show_rag(labels, rag, img, ax=ax[2])
# specify the fraction of the plot area that will be used to draw the colorbar
fig.colorbar(lc, fraction=0.03, ax=ax[2])
ax[2].set_title('RAG drawn with Input image'),ax[2].set_xticks([]),ax[2].set_yticks([])
plt.tight_layout()
```

Fig. 7.73   Python code to obtain the region adjacency graph

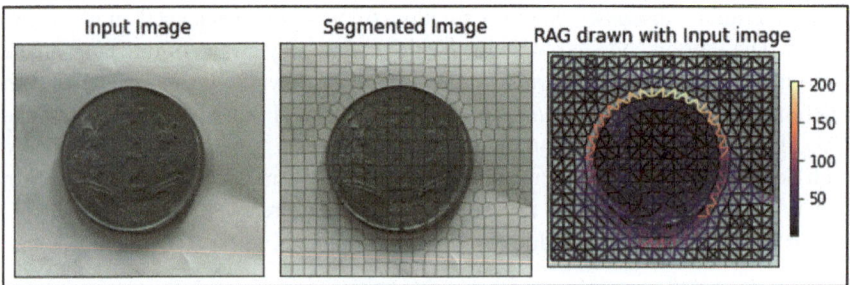

Fig. 7.74   Result of Python code shown in Fig. 7.73

Inferences

- In the Python code, the built-in function "slic" available in scikit library is used to obtain the labels.
- The algorithm constructs region adjacency graph and recursively performs a normalized cut on it.
- Normalized cut is a top-down approach that starts with the graph and breaks it down into smaller parts.

```
# Normalised cut algorithm for image segmentation
import cv2
import matplotlib.pyplot as plt
from skimage import graph
from skimage import segmentation,color
img=cv2.imread('coin_testimg3.jpg')
labels1 = segmentation.slic(img, compactness=35, n_segments=20, start_label=1)
g = graph.rag_mean_color(img, labels1, mode='similarity')
labels2 = graph.cut_normalized(labels1, g)
seg_img = color.label2rgb(labels2, img, kind='avg', bg_label=0)
plt.subplot(1,2,1),plt.imshow(img,cmap='gray')
plt.title('Input image'),plt.xticks([]),plt.yticks([])
plt.subplot(1,2,2),plt.imshow(seg_img,cmap='gray')
plt.title('Segmented image'),plt.xticks([]),plt.yticks([])
plt.tight_layout()
```

Fig. 7.75 Python code to perform normalized cut algorithm for image segmentation

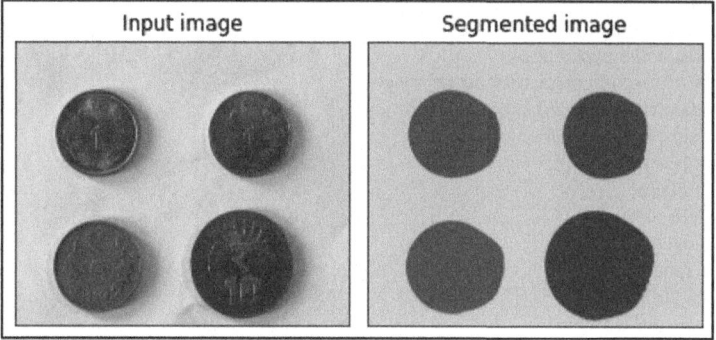

Fig. 7.76 Result of Python code given in Fig. 7.75

- SLIC algorithm gives over segmentation upon which the region adjacency graph is built.
- Normalized cut is performed on the region adjacency graph to obtain the segmented image.

7.9.5   Spectral Clustering

The word spectrum refers to the eigenvalue of the Laplacian matrix. As the name "spectral clustering"implies, spectral clustering algorithm performs clustering as per spectrum (eigenvalues). Laplacian matrix is a positive semidefinite matrix. Spectral clustering is an unsupervised machine learning algorithm that is used to identify clusters within a dataset. It uses eigenvectors of the Laplacian matrix to perform dimensionality reduction before applying k-means algorithm.

The steps followed in spectral clustering are summarized below:

Step 1: Compute the Laplacian matrix (L).

Step 2: Perform Eigen decomposition of Laplacian matrix. Calculate the first "k" eigenvectors corresponding to the "k" smallest eigenvalues of "L".

Step 3: Consider the matrix formed by the first "k" eigenvectors.

Step 4: Cluster the graph nodes using k-means clustering.

Experiment 7.33: Image Segmentation Using Spectral Clustering

This experiment discusses the implementation of spectral clustering algorithm for image segmentation. The Python code that performs spectral clustering of the input image using the built-in function "*spectral_clustering*" available in the "*scikit.cluster*" library is given in Fig. 7.77, and the corresponding output is shown in Fig. 7.78.

```
# Spectral Clustering based image segmentation
import numpy as np
import matplotlib.pyplot as plt
from sklearn.feature_extraction import image
from sklearn.cluster import spectral_clustering
#Step1: Generation of test image
img=np.zeros([100,100])
m,n=img.shape
r1,r2=12,30
for i in range(0,m):
    for j in range(0,n):
        if (i-20)**2+(j-20)**2<r1**2:
            img[i,j]=1
        if (i-50)**2 + (j-50)**2<r2**2:
            img[i,j]=1
        elif(i-20)**2+(j-80)**2<r1**2:
            img[i,j]=1
mask = img.astype(bool);#Step 2: Define the mask
img1 = img + 0.1 * np.random.randn(*img.shape);#Step 3: Adding noise to the input image
graph = image.img_to_graph(img1, mask=mask);#Step 4: Obtaining the graph
graph.data = np.exp(-graph.data / graph.data.std())
#Step 5: Perform the spectral clustering
labels = spectral_clustering(graph, n_clusters=1, eigen_solver="arpack")
label_im = np.full(mask.shape, -1.0)
label_im[mask] = labels
fig, ax = plt.subplots(nrows=1, ncols=3, figsize=(10, 5)),ax[0].matshow(img),
ax[0].set_title('Original image'),ax[0].set_xticks([]),ax[0].set_yticks([]),ax[1].matshow(img1),
ax[1].set_title('Noisy Image'),ax[1].set_xticks([]),ax[1].set_yticks([]),ax[2].matshow(label_im),
ax[2].set_title('Segmented Image'),ax[2].set_xticks([]),ax[2].set_yticks([])
plt.show()
```

Fig. 7.77 Python code to perform spectral clustering of input image

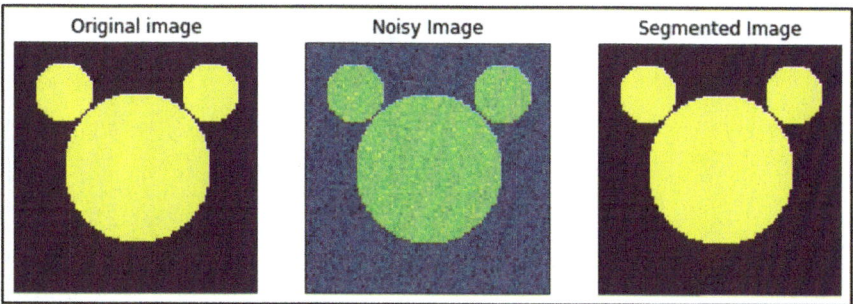

Fig. 7.78   Result of Python code shown in Fig. 7.77

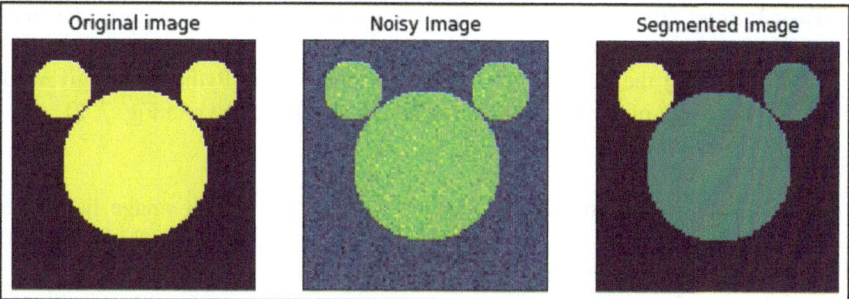

Fig. 7.79   Result of spectral clustering algorithm with the number of clusters as two

Inferences

- The input test image is generated and then corrupted by random noise with normal distribution.
- The noisy image is fed to the spectral clustering algorithm by choosing the number of clusters as "1".
- ARPACK is a Fortran package that provides routines for quickly finding a few eigenvalues/eigenvectors of large sparse matrices.
- Since the number of clusters is chosen as one, the colour of all the circles in the output image is "yellow".

Task 1: Repeat the experiment by changing the number of clusters to two. Display the result and comment on the observed result.

Upon changing the number of clusters to two in the Python code given in Fig. 7.77, the result of the spectral clustering algorithm is shown in Fig. 7.79.

Inferences

- Upon changing the number of clusters as two, the output image has two colours "yellow" and "green" which implies that the given image is partitioned into two clusters.

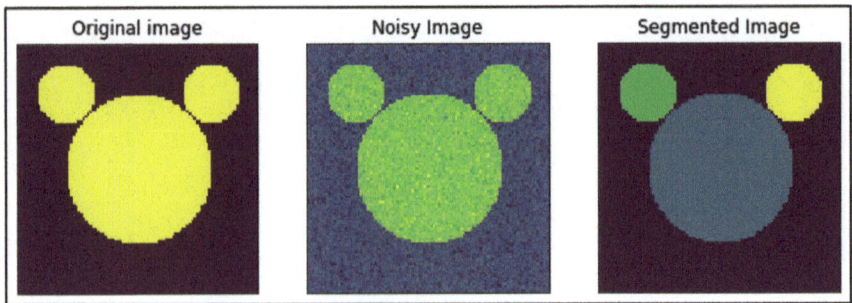

Fig. 7.80 Result of spectral clustering algorithm with the number of clusters as three

Task 2: Repeat the experiment by change the number of clusters as three. Display the result and comment on the observed result.

Upon changing the number of clusters as three in the Python code given in Fig. 7.77, the result of the spectral clustering algorithm is shown in Fig. 7.80.

Inference

- Upon changing the number of clusters to three, the output image has three colours for the three circles, namely "yellow", "green", and "blue", which implies that the given image is partitioned into three clusters.

7.10   GrabCut Algorithm for Image Segmentation

GrabCut algorithm is used to segment the input image into foreground and background. It is a semi-automatic image segmentation method that user intervention is required to perform the segmentation task. The user input is a rectangle on an image. The rectangle should include the subjects of the image. The area lying outside the rectangle is defined as the background. The algorithm defines the area in the rectangle as a colour distribution model using the Gaussian Mixture Model (GMM), where each pixel will be labelled as foreground or background. GrabCut segmentation technique uses graph cuts to perform segmentation. GrabCut makes use of both edge and region information. To perform the segmentation, a graph is built where nodes or vertex in the graph represent pixels in the image. Two special nodes are created which are termed as Source and Sink nodes. The Source node represents the foreground of the image, and the Sink node represents the background. Now, segmentation task is to separate the Source and Sink node. The energy function is incorporated into the graph as weights between pixel nodes and weights between pixel and Source or Sink nodes. Weights between pixel nodes are determined by edge information in the image. A strong indication of the edge between two pixels results in a minimal weight between two-pixel nodes. The region information determines the weights between pixel nodes and the Source and Sink nodes. These weights are calculated by determining the probability of pixel node being part of the background

```
import numpy as np
import matplotlib.pyplot as plt
import cv2
#Reading the input image
img=cv2.imread('cameraman.tif')
#Defining the parameters of GrabCut algorithm
mask = np.zeros(img.shape[:2],np.uint8)
bgdModel = np.zeros((1,65),np.float64)
fgdModel = np.zeros((1,65),np.float64)
rect = (25,25,159,250) #Retangular area which encloses the area of FG
#Grab cut algorithm
new_mask, fg, bg =
cv2.grabCut(img,mask,rect,bgdModel,fgdModel,10,cv2.GC_INIT_WITH_RECT)
mask2 = np.where((new_mask==2)|(new_mask==0),0,1).astype('uint8')
#Segmented image
seg_img = img*mask2[:,:,np.newaxis]
#Displaying the result
plt.subplot(1,2,1),plt.imshow(img,cmap='gray')
plt.title('Input image'),plt.xticks([]),plt.yticks([])
plt.subplot(1,2,2),plt.imshow(seg_img,cmap='gray')
plt.title('Segmented image'),plt.xticks([]),plt.yticks([])
plt.tight_layout()
```

Fig. 7.81 Python code to perform image segmentation using GrabCut algorithm

or foreground region. A Min-cut algorithm is used to segment the graph. Once the Source and Sink nodes are separated, all pixels connected to the Source node become part of the foreground, and the rest become part of the background.

Experiment 7.34: Image Segmentation Using GrabCut Algorithm

This experiment deals with the image segmentation using GrabCut algorithm. The built-in function "*grabCut*" available in "CV2" library is used to segment the image into foreground and background. The Python code, which performs this task, is given in Fig. 7.81 and the corresponding output is shown in Fig. 7.82.

Inferences

- The GrabCut algorithm is fed with "cameraman" image. The algorithm segments the input image into foreground and background.
- The rectangular area defined by the user is used to identify the foreground.
- Proper initialization of the rectangular region is necessary to separate the object in the input image.
- In this experiment, the rectangular area is defined so that the cameraman is considered the foreground and the rest of the image is considered the background.

Exercise

1. Read an input image and perform the following thresholding operation (1) Global thresholding (2) OTSU method of thresholding (3) Adaptive mean thresholding and (4) Adaptive Gaussian mean thresholding. Display each result and comment on the observed result.

Fig. 7.82 Result of GrabCut algorithm

2. Read an input image and add a random noise in it. Apply the different types of thresholding operation on the noisy image. Comment on the observed results.
3. Generate a test image of size 400×400 with alternate white and black pixels each of size "50" unit. Then add white Gaussian noise that follows normal distribution to the generated test image. Apply Robert and Prewitt operators on the input and noisy images and comment on their edge detection performance.
4. Read a "rice.jpg" image and segment the input image using k-means and Fuzzy C-means algorithm. Comment on the observed result.
5. Read a "coin_testimg3.jpg" image and apply Mean shift clustering algorithm and K-means clustering algorithm to get segmentation output. Comment on the observed results.

Objective Questions

1. Canny edge detector removes spurious edges by

    (A) Hysteresis thresholding
    (B) Low pass filtering
    (C) Non-maxima suppression
    (D) Finding zero crossings

2. The image segmentation technique that considers image as topological surface is

    (A) OTSU thresholding-based segmentation
    (B) Watershed algorithm-based segmentation
    (C) Region split and merge type segmentation
    (D) Clustering based segmentation

3. Identify the statement that is false with respect to mean shift algorithm

    (A) Mean shift algorithm is a "mode seeking" algorithm
    (B) Mean shift algorithm is a non-parametric kernel density estimation algorithm
    (C) In mean shift algorithm, it is necessary to define the number of clusters in advance
    (D) Mean shift algorithm does not require the assumption of equal-sized clusters

4. An 8-bit grayscale image is fed to global thresholding operation, then the output image is

   (A) 8-bit grayscale image
   (B) 16-bit grayscale image
   (C) 4-bit grayscale image
   (D) Binary image.

5. Identify the statement that is false with respect to Laplacian matrix

   (A) Laplacian matrix is a symmetric matrix
   (B) Laplacian matrix is a positive semi-definite matrix
   (C) The eigenvalues of Laplacian matrix can be either positive or negative
   (D) The number of zero eigenvalues of Laplacian is equal to the number of connected components in the graph

6. Statement 1: K-means assumes that the clusters are spherical and of equal size
   Statement 2: Mean shift algorithm can handle clusters of arbitrary shape

   (A) Statements 1 and 2 are true
   (B) Statement 1 is true, Statement 2 is false
   (C) Statement 1 is false, Statement 2 is true
   (D) Statements 1 and 2 are false

7. For proper segmentation, the value of $R_i \cap R_j$ for all i, j such that $i \neq j$ is

   (A) Entire region "R"
   (B) R_i
   (C) R_j
   (D) Null set

8. The value of "x" such that the mask $M = \begin{bmatrix} 0 & -1 & 0 \\ -1 & x & -1 \\ 0 & -1 & 0 \end{bmatrix}$ act as Laplacian operator is

   (A) 0
   (B) -1
   (C) 4
   (D) -4

9. The thresholding employed in Canny edge detection algorithm is

   (A) OTSU threshold
   (B) Hysteresis threshold
   (C) Optimal threshold
   (D) Adaptive threshold

10. The thresholding algorithm, which is based on minimizing the with-in class variance, is

   (A) OTSU threshold
   (B) Hysteresis threshold
   (C) Optimal threshold
   (D) Adaptive threshold

11. The test image generated by the following Python code exhibits

```
img=np.zeros([256,256])
img[0:256,0:128]=255
```

(A) Step edge
(B) Ramp edge
(C) Roof edge
(D) Spike edge

12. In the following Python code if the variable "img" contains 8-bit grayscale image, then the variable "img1" will contain

```
Img1=img>128
```

(A) Eight-bit grayscale image
(B) Six-bit grayscale image
(C) Four-bit grayscale image
(D) Binary image

13. In the following Python code, if one plots the histogram of the image returned by cv2.threshold(in this case it is the variable "th2") then the histogram will have

```
img=cv2.imread('cameraman.tif',0)
ret2,th2 = cv2.threshold(img,0,255,cv2.THRESH_OTSU)
```

(A) 256 peaks in the gray level 0–255
(B) 8 peaks in the gray level 0–255
(C) Two peaks in the gray level 0–255
(D) 10 peaks in the gray level 0–255

14. The mask given in the following Python code represents

```
gx=np.array([[-1,-2,-1],[0,0,0],[1,2,1]])
gy=np.array([[-1,0,1],[-2,0,2],[-1,0,1]])
```

(A) Robert mask
(B) Prewitt mask
(C) Sobel mask
(D) Robinson mask

15. The following Python code performs

```
img=cv2.imread('testimage.tif',0)
img1 = cv2.GaussianBlur(img, (3, 3), 0)
filtered_image = cv2.Laplacian(img1, cv2.CV_16S, ksize=3)
```

(A) Laplacian of Gaussian function
(B) Difference of Gaussian function
(C) Canny edge detection
(D) Robinson edge detection

Answers to Objective Questions

Q. No.	01	02	03	04	05	06	07	08	09	10	11	12	13	14	15
Key	C	B	C	D	C	A	D	C	B	A	A	D	C	C	A

Answers to PreLab Questions

1. The objective of image segmentation is to partition an image into sub-regions based on a desired feature.
2. Image segmentation algorithms can be broadly classified into two types (1) based on discontinuity and (2) based on similarity. The different techniques used in segmentation methods are given below in a table.

S. No.	Segmentation methods	Techniques
1	Edge-based segmentation	(1) Robert operator (2) Prewitt operator (3) Sobel operator (4) Laplacian operator (5) Canny edge detector (6) Laplacian of Gaussian
2	Thresholding-based segmentation	(1) Global thresholding (2) Otsu method (3) Adaptive thresholding (4) Hysteresis thresholding
3	Region-based segmentation	(1) Region growing (2) Region splitting (3) Split and merge technique (4) Watershed algorithm
4	Clustering-based segmentation	(1) K-means clustering (2) Mean shift algorithm
5	Active contour-based segmentation	(1) Snake algorithm (2) Gradient vector flow (3) Geodesic active contour
6	Graph-based algorithm for image segmentation	(1) Spectral clustering (2) Normalized cut (3) Minimum cut
7	Artificial intelligence-based segmentation	(1) Neural network (2) Fuzzy logic (3) Evolutionary computation

3. An isotropic operator is an operator that has no bias to any particular direction in an image. Laplacian is a second-order derivative filter that is used to find edges in an image. Laplacian operator is isotropic because the response of the operator is independent of the direction of discontinuities in the image.

S. No.	Canny edge detector	Laplacian-of-Gaussian edge detector
1	Canny edge detector is anisotropic	LoG edge detector is isotropic
2	Canny is a first derivative operator	LoG is a second derivative operator

4. (a) Non-maxima suppression: Non-maximum suppression is used to thin out the edges. The image is scanned along the image gradient direction, and if pixels are not part of the local maxima they are set to zero. (b) Hysteresis thresholding: Hysteresis Thresholding is achieved by setting the lower and upper threshold values. Any edges with an intensity gradient above the upper threshold are sure to be edges, and those below the lower threshold are sure to be non-edges, so they are discarded. Those who lie between these two thresholds are classified as edges or non-edges based on their connectivity. If they are connected to "sure-edge" pixels, they are considered to be part of edges.

5. Active contour is based on deforming an initial contour towards the boundary of the object to be detected. The deformation is obtained by trying to minimize a functional design such that minimum is obtained at the boundary of the object. The energy functional is basically composed of two components: one controls the smoothness of the curve, and another attracts the curve towards the boundary.

6. The basic idea in active contour is to initialize a position for the contour, then define image forces acting on the contour, making it change its position and adapt to the image features. Active contour is an energy-minimization method of image segmentation. The minimization of the energy leads to dynamic behaviour in the segmentation, and because of the way the contours slither while minimizing energy, the active contour method is also termed as a "snake" algorithm.

7. The advantages of active contour over conventional image segmentation are.

   (a) After proper initialization, the active contour or snake converges iteratively to an energy minimum state.

   (b) Energy minimization from a coarse to fine in scale space can enlarge the capture region around the features of interest and decrease the computational complexity.

The drawbacks of active contour method are

   (a) Careful initialization of the contour is necessary to get the desired result. Generally, the initial contour must be close enough to the true contour. Snakes cannot automatically split or merge based on changes in the topology of the image.

   (b) The active contour model cannot handle topological changes, making it difficult to extract multiple objects in an image.

   (c) Active contour algorithm is sensitive to noise. The noise can attract the active contour, deviating it from the actual contour.

S. No.	Mean shift algorithm	K-mean clustering algorithm
1	It automatically determines the number of clusters based on the data	The number of clusters to be specified in advance
2	Mean shift algorithm does not make any assumptions about the shape or size of the clusters, as it relies on the density information of the data	K-means assumes that the clusters are spherical and of equal size

S. No.	Mean shift algorithm	K-mean clustering algorithm
3	Mean shift algorithm is a density-based clustering algorithm that seeks to find dense regions in the data	K-means is a centroid-based clustering algorithm that aims to partition the data into k distinct clusters
4	Mean shift algorithm has a higher time complexity due to its iterative nature	K-means is a faster algorithm compared to mean shift, especially for large datasets. This is because k-means has a linear time complexity

8. Clustering is the partitioning of the data into subsets (clusters) such that data in each cluster share some common trait. The k-means clustering algorithm assigns each data point to one cluster exclusively. Fuzzy C-means clustering algorithm assigns data points to multiple clusters with varying degrees.

Bibliography

1. Tao Lei, Asoke K. Nandi, "Image segmentation: Principles, techniques, and applications", John Wiley and Sons Ltd, 2022.
2. Rafael C. Gonzalez and Richard E. Woods, "Digital Image Processing", Pearson Education, 2018.
3. Richard Szeliski, "Computer Vison: Algorithms and Applications", Springer, 2011.
4. Kenneth R. Castleman, "Digital Image Processing", Pearson Education, 2007.
5. Alan C. Bovik, "Handbook of Image and Video Processing", Academic Press, 2000.

Chapter 8
Feature Extraction

Learning Objectives

After reading this chapter, the reader can be able to

- Understand the different types of features
- Extract the image features
- Know the importance of the image features
- Distinguish the different types of image features
- Appreciate the significance of feature extraction in image processing applications

Roadmap of this Chapter

This chapter discusses the different feature extraction procedures given as a roadmap, as shown in Fig. 8.1.

PreLab Questions

1. What are image features?
2. List out the different types of image features.
3. What is the significance of colour features?
4. What is texture feature? Mention the significance of texture feature.
5. List out the steps involved in the computation of HOG features.
6. Mention a few important GLCM features.
7. What is SIFT? Is it invariant to scale, orientation, and transformation?
8. List out the advantages of local or general features.
9. Distinguish between handcrafted features and deep features.
10. What is an autoencoder?
11. What are the major components of auto encoder?
12. Distinguish between feature extraction and feature selection.

Supplementary Information The online version contains supplementary material available at
https://doi.org/10.1007/978-981-96-6382-8_8.

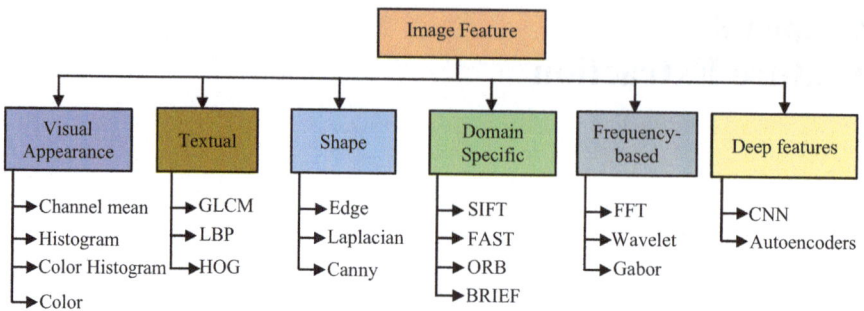

Fig. 8.1 Roadmap of the chapter

8.1   Introduction

Features of an image depict a set of measurements describing the "physical" objects in an image. Features in the image are the prominent properties that represent an image's visual information. The image features are employed for several image processing and analysis tasks. Image features are used in different image analysis/processing tasks, including segmentation, object detection and tracking, object recognition, classification, etc.

The complete features can be categorized into the following categories: visual appearance features, textual features, shape features, domain-specific features, frequency domain features, and deep features.

8.1.1   Visual Appearance Features

Generally, the most important property of any visual appearance feature is its uniqueness, distinguishing the objects in any image in the feature space. Many image processing/analysis tasks include using single or combinations of multiple visual appearance features. A few of such features are described as follows:

8.1.2   Channel Mean Pixel Values

Channel mean pixel values are one of the simple features used by users in image processing industrial applications: thumbnail creation, image compression, and resizing. The channel mean pixel value computes the mean intensity of each colour channel (red, green, and blue) in an image.

The channel mean value of the image is computed as

$$\text{Channel\_Mean}\left(X[:,:,i]\right) = \frac{\text{Sum of all Pixels in image } X[:,:,i]}{\text{Total number of Pixels in image } X[:,:,i]} \tag{8.1}$$

The mean value of the image is calculated using

$$\text{Mean}\left(X\right) = \frac{\text{Sum of all Pixels in image } X}{\text{Total number of Pixels in image } X}$$
$$= \frac{1}{3}\sum_{i=0}^{3}\text{Channel\_Mean}\left(X[:,:,i]\right) \tag{8.2}$$

The colour image can be converted into grayscale image using "rgb2gray" conversion. This method uses the equation is given by

$$\text{Gray}\left(X\right) = 0.299 \times R + 0.587 \times G + 0.114 \times B \tag{8.3}$$

where R, G, and B represent the R, G, and B channels of colour image (X). The mean value of the grayscale image (GX) is computed as

$$\text{Mean}\left(GX\right) = \frac{\text{Sum of all Pixels in image } GX}{\text{Total number of Pixels in image } GX} \tag{8.4}$$

where "GX" denotes the grayscale image, which is converted from colour image using Eq. (8.3).

Experiment 8.1: Channel Mean Pixel Computation
This experiment discusses the computation of channel mean pixel values using Python. In this experiment, the mean value of each channel is computed, and the weighted mean value of the colour image gives the grayscale image using the "rgb2gray" Python command. It also computes the difference between the channel mean and the weighted mean of the pixel values. The Python code to compute the channel and weighted mean pixel values is given in Fig. 8.2, and its simulation result is shown in Fig. 8.3.

Inferences
The following inferences can be made from this experiment:

- From Fig. 8.2, it is possible to infer that the colour image is read, and then the colour image is converted into grayscale by using the mean of all three channels. Also, the colour image is converted into grayscale using "rgb2gray" conversion method.
- From Fig. 8.3a, it is possible to observe that the mean value of the colour image and grayscale image converted by using the average or mean approach are the

```
import matplotlib.pyplot as plt
from skimage import io
from skimage.color import rgb2gray
import numpy as np
I=io.imread("greenredapples.jpg")
plt.figure(figsize=(12, 6))
for c in range(3):
    plt.subplot(2, 3, c+1)
    I_channel = I[..., c]
    mu=np.round(I_channel.mean(),5)
    plt.imshow(I_channel, cmap='gray')
    plt.title(f'Channel {c}, mean {mu}'), plt.axis("off")
I_mean = I.mean(axis=-1)
I_WM = 255*rgb2gray(I)
I_diff = I_mean - I_WM
plt.subplot(2,3,4),plt.imshow(I_mean, cmap='gray')
plt.title('Channel mean image'),plt.axis(False)
plt.subplot(2,3,5),plt.imshow(I_WM, cmap='gray')
plt.title('Weighted mean image'),plt.axis(False)
plt.subplot(2,3,6),plt.imshow(I_diff, cmap='gray'),plt.axis(False)
plt.title('Image mean - weighted mean')
print(f'The mean of img is: {np.round(I.mean(),5)}')
print(f'The mean of img_mean is: {np.round(I_mean.mean(),5)}')
print(f'The mean of img_weighted_mean is: {np.round(I_WM.mean(),5)}')
```

Fig. 8.2 Channel mean pixel values

same. However, the mean value of the grayscale image converted using "rgb2gray" approach is different from the mean value of the original colour image.
- From Fig. 8.3b, it is possible to observe that Channels 0, 1, and 2 give different information on the input image, and this information is image-dependent. Look wise the channel mean and weighted mean images are the same, but there is a difference between them.

8.1.3   Histogram Feature

The histogram of an image is a graphical representation of the frequency of pixels in an image as a function of their intensity. Histograms are made up of bins, each bin representing a certain intensity value or range of values. This histogram result can be used as a feature for image processing applications.

The mean of img is: 106.92093
The mean of img_mean is: 106.92093
The mean of img_weighted_mean is: 116.65623

(a) Mean values

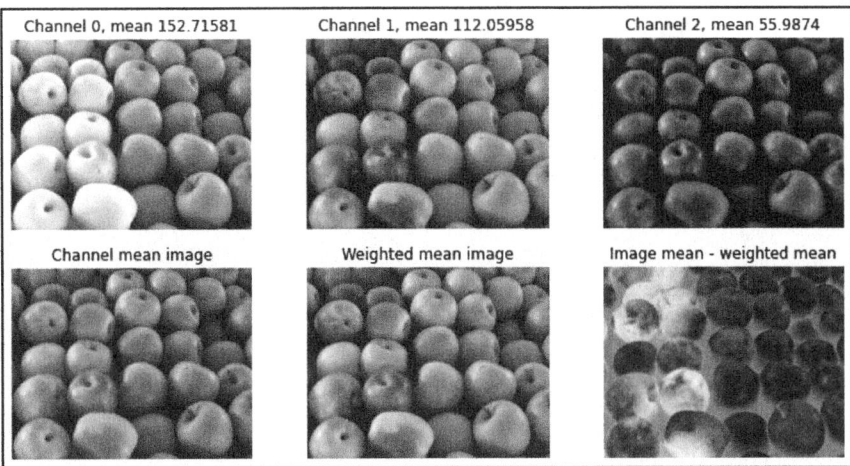

(b) Results of Channels and their mean and weighted mean images

Fig. 8.3 Simulation result of channel mean pixel. (**a**) Mean values. (**b**) Results of channels and their mean and weighted mean images

```
import matplotlib.pyplot as plt
from skimage import io
from skimage.color import rgb2gray
I=io.imread("greenredapples.jpg")
Gray_I = 255*rgb2gray(I)
flatten_I = Gray_I.flatten()
fig, (ax1, ax2) = plt.subplots(1, 2, figsize=(8, 4))
ax1.imshow(Gray_I, cmap='gray'),ax1.set_title('Original Image')
ax1.axis('off'),ax2.hist(flatten_I, bins=256)
ax2.set_xlabel('Pixel Intensity'),ax2.set_ylabel('No.of Occurrence')
ax2.set_title('Histogram')
plt.tight_layout()
```

Fig. 8.4 Histogram feature extraction

Experiment 8.2: Extraction of Histogram Features

This experiment deals with extracting histogram features from the grayscale image. The Python code to compute the histogram feature from the input image is given in Fig. 8.4, and its simulation result is shown in Fig. 8.5.

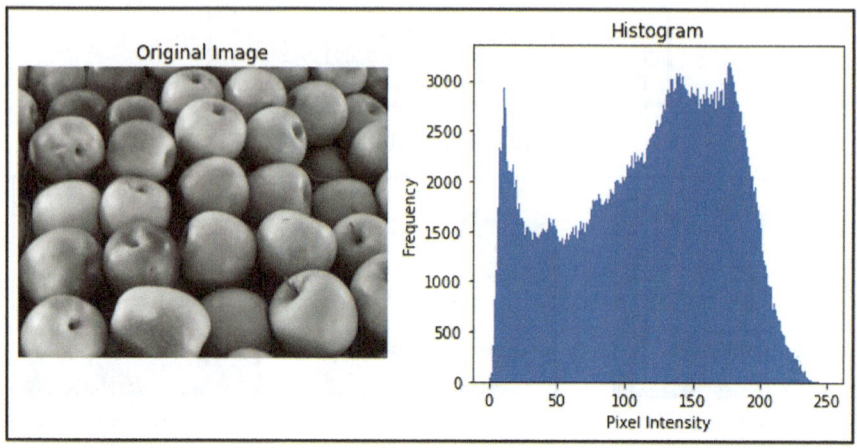

Fig. 8.5 Original image and histogram plot

Inferences

- From Fig. 8.4, it is possible to observe that the colour image is first converted into a grayscale image.
- The "flatten" command is used here to convert a 2D image into a 1D array. "hist" is used to plot the histogram of the flattened image.
- In the "hist' command, the "bins" value decides the pixel intensity range. Here, 256 indicates that the pixel intensity varies from 0 to 255. For example, bins = 100 gives 100 pixels intensity values between 0 and 255.
- From Fig. 8.5, it is possible to infer that the "x-axis" denotes "pixel intensity" and the "y-axis" represents number of occurrences of the gray level of the image.

Task: Vary the value of "bins" in the Python code given in Fig. 8.4 to 50, 100, and 150. Comment on the observed results.

8.1.4   Colour Histogram

A colour histogram is a representation of the distribution of colours in an image. It provides a compact representation of colour distribution. One of the major advantages of the colour histogram is that it is invariant to translation and rotation about the viewing axis of the image.

A colour histogram can be a three-dimensional plot of pixel values for RGB images. In a colour histogram plot, each channel of the RGB image is quantized into multiple bins. The quantization divides the RGB space into an appropriate number of ranges. The colour histogram of an image can be plotted as a function defined over the colour space to approximate the pixel counts.

```
import matplotlib.pyplot as plt
from skimage import io
I=io.imread("greenredapples.jpg")
flatten_IR = I[:,:,0].flatten()
flatten_IG = I[:,:,1].flatten()
flatten_IB = I[:,:,2].flatten()
fig, (ax1, ax2) = plt.subplots(1, 2, figsize=(8, 4))
ax1.imshow(I, cmap='gray'),ax1.set_title('Original Image')
ax1.axis('off'),ax2.hist(flatten_IR, bins=256,color = 'red')
ax2.hist(flatten_IG, bins=256,color = 'green')
ax2.hist(flatten_IB, bins=256,color = 'blue')
ax2.set_xlabel('Pixel Intensity'),ax2.set_ylabel('No.of Occurrence')
ax2.set_title('Histogram')
plt.tight_layout()
```

Fig. 8.6 Colour histogram feature extraction

Fig. 8.7 Original image and its colour histogram

Experiment 8.3: Colour Histogram of an Image

This experiment discusses the computation of histogram features of colour images. The Python code to compute histogram features of colour image is given in Fig. 8.6, and its corresponding output is depicted in Fig. 8.7.

Inferences

The following inferences can be drawn from this experiment:

- From Fig. 8.6, the colour image is read and split separately between the R, G, and B channels. Each channel image was flattened to compute the histogram. All three channels' histogram is plotted in the same plot.
- From Fig. 8.7, it is possible to observe that the input image is a colour image, and its histogram plot contains three colour information.

8.1.5   Colour Features

Colour information gives more detail on an object in the image than the grayscale. For example, a green apple and a red apple are in a basket. The grayscale image shows only the apples in the basket, whereas the colour image shows the type of apple, like green or red. Therefore, colour information is the most widely used feature for image processing because it strongly correlates with the underlying image objects or scenes. Colour is more robust with respect to scaling, orientation, perspective, and occlusion of images.

Experiment 8.4: Importance of Colour Feature
This experiment shows the importance of colour features. Read the green and red apples in a basket image and convert it into a grayscale image. Now display both the grayscale image and colour image. The Python code to perform this task is given in Fig. 8.8, and its simulation result is shown in Fig. 8.9.

Inference

- From Fig. 8.9, it is possible to observe that the grayscale image shows only the apple; it misses whether it is a red or green apple, whereas the colour image clearly distinguishes the type of apple.

```
import cv2
import matplotlib.pyplot as plt
#Step 1: Reading the colour image in BGR format
img_bgr=cv2.imread('greenredapples.jpg')
grayImage = cv2.cvtColor(img_bgr, cv2.COLOR_BGR2GRAY)
#Step 2: Converting BGR to RGB format
img_rgb = cv2.cvtColor(img_bgr, cv2.COLOR_BGR2RGB)
plt.figure(),plt.subplot(1,2,1),plt.imshow(grayImage,cmap='gray'),
plt.title('Gray scale image'),plt.xticks([]),plt.yticks([]),
plt.subplot(1,2,2),plt.imshow(img_rgb),
plt.title('Colour image'),plt.xticks([]),plt.yticks([])
plt.tight_layout()
```

Fig. 8.8 Colour feature importance

Fig. 8.9 Importance of the colour feature

Task: Read the image containing amla and lemon and convert it into a grayscale image. Compare the result with the colour image. Comment on the observed result.

Colour Moments

Colour moments are measures that can be used to differentiate images based on their colour features. These colour moments provide a measurement for colour similarity between images. These colour moments can be used for image retrieval applications. The colour moments are mean, standard deviation, and skewness. A colour pixel can be defined by 3 or more values. Let us consider the RGB colour image, which contains three colour channels. For each colour channel, three colour moments, therefore a total of nine colour moments for the colour image.

Moment 1 (Mean)
The pth channel colour moment mean is computed as

$$CM_p = \frac{1}{MN} \sum_{i=0}^{M-1} \sum_{j=0}^{N-1} X_p(i,j) \tag{8.5}$$

where CM_p represents the average value of the pth channel. MN denotes the size of the image, X_p represents the pth channel of colour image X.

Moment 2 (Standard Deviation (Std))
The pth channel colour moment (standard deviation (std)) is calculated as

$$C\sigma_p = \sqrt{\frac{1}{MN} \sum_{i=0}^{M-1} \sum_{j=0}^{N-1} \left(X_p(i,j) - CM_p\right)^2} \tag{8.6}$$

```
# Python code for colour moments
import cv2
import numpy as np
from scipy.stats import skew
#Read the colour image in BGR format
img_bgr=cv2.imread('greenredapples.jpg');
CM=np.zeros([3,3]);
for i in range(img_bgr.shape[2]):
    X=img_bgr[:,:,i];
    CM[i,0]=np.mean(X.flatten()); # mean color moment
    CM[i,1]=np.std(X.flatten());# standard deviation color moment
    CM[i,2]=skew(X.flatten());# skewness color moment
print('Colour Moments: ',CM)
```

Fig. 8.10   Computation colour moments

```
Colour Moments: [[ 55.99007926  45.51546841   0.41827645]
 [112.06051952  60.98028999  -0.24303716]
 [152.71783315  70.03237591  -0.45355645]]
```

Fig. 8.11   Colour moments of "greenredapples.jpg"

where $C\sigma_p$ represents the standard deviation of the pth channel. MN denotes the size of the image, X_p represents the pth channel of colour image X.

Moment 3 (Skewness)

The pth channel colour moment (skewness) is computed as

$$CS_p = \sqrt[3]{\frac{1}{MN}\sum_{i=0}^{M-1}\sum_{j=0}^{N-1}\left(X_p\left(i,j\right)-CM_p\right)^3} \tag{8.7}$$

where CS_p represents the standard deviation of the pth channel. MN denotes the size of the image, X_p represents the pth channel of colour image X.

Experiment 8.5: Computation of Colour Moments

This experiment discusses the computation of NINE colour moments of the RGB colour image. The Python code to perform this task is shown in Fig. 8.10, and its corresponding result is displayed in Fig. 8.11.

Inferences

- From Fig. 8.10, it is possible to observe that "scipy statistics" library is imported to compute the "skewness".
- Figure 8.11 displays the colour moments of "greenredapples.jpg" there are three channels, and for each channel, three moments are calculated. Thus, the total number of moments is 9.

Colour Coherence Vector (CCV)

The colour coherence vector is an image descriptor that extracts colour-related features from the image, and it can be used as a low-dimensional representation of that image. Coherent vector classifies each pixel in an image as either coherent or incoherent. A coherent pixel is a pixel that is a part of the big connected component. An incoherent pixel is a pixel that is a part of a small connected component. Thus, the output of a coherent colour vector is the number of coherent pixels and the number of incoherent pixels in an image.

The steps to be followed to compute the colour-coherent vector feature are as follows:

Step 1: Blur the input image.
Step 2: Quantize the blurred image to reduce the colour space in "n" distinct colours.
Step 3: Classify each pixel either as coherent or incoherent.

Step 3a: Find the connected component for each quantized colour pixel.
Step 3b: Determine the threshold called "τ"; it is commonly 1% of the image size.
Step 3c: Any connected component with a number of pixels more than or equal to "τ" is considered a coherent pixel; otherwise, it is considered an incoherent pixel.

Step 4: For each quantized colour, compute two values (C and N), where C denotes the number of coherent pixels, and N represents the number of incoherent pixels.

Illustration of CCV Computation
Let us consider a blurred image as

0	1	2	3	4
5	6	7	8	9
10	11	12	7	14
15	2	17	8	19
1	21	22	23	24

Now, quantize the blurred image with the pixel values $\{0{:}8 - 0, 9{:}15 - 1, 16{:}24 - 2\}$. Applying this quantization to the blurred image, we get the quantized image as

0	0	0	0	0
0	0	0	0	1
1	1	1	0	1
1	0	2	0	2
0	2	2	2	2

The connected component of each colour using eight adjacency connectivity, we get

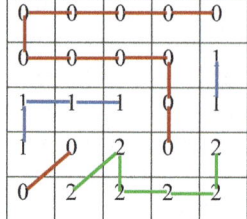

Assume the threshold $\tau = 4$, and for colour "0", there are two connected components (see red line), in that one connected component has more than 4 components, which is more than $\tau = 4$. Therefore, all the pixels that correspond to these connected components are considered coherent pixels. The other connected component has two components, which is less than $\tau = 4$. Therefore, the two pixels in an image corresponding to these two components are classified as incoherent pixels for colour "0". Similarly, for the colour "1", there are two connected components; one has four components, and another has two components. The first one satisfies the coherent component, and the other does not satisfy the condition of the coherent component; hence, its corresponding pixels are incoherent pixels. There is one connected component for the colour "2"; the number of components is 6, which satisfies the coherent pixel condition. Hence, the pixels corresponding to these components are considered coherent pixels.

The final colour-coherent feature vector is given by

Colour	0	1	2
Coherent (C)	11	4	6
Incoherent (N)	2	2	0

The number of coherent and incoherent pixels is 21 and 4, respectively. The total number of pixels in the considered image is 25, and the total number of coherent and incoherent pixels is also 25. Hence, no pixel is missed in this computation.

Experiment 8.6: Computation of Colour Coherence Vector
This experiment deals with the computation of the colour coherence vector feature of an image, which is illustrated in this section. The Python code to perform this task is given in Fig. 8.12, and its corresponding output is shown in Fig. 8.13.

Inferences

- After executing the Python code given in Fig. 8.12, the output obtained is exactly the same as the theoretical computation. The size of the input image is 5×5, whereas the size of the CCV is 2×3, which is observed in Fig. 8.13. Hence, CCV will act as a feature vector for the given input image.

```
# Python code for CCV computation
import cv2
import numpy as np
th=4;
Q_I = np.array([[0,0,0,0,0],[0,0,0,0,1],[1,1,1,0,1],[1,0,2,0,2],[0,2,2,2,2]]);
# Initialise the coherence vectors
c_v = [0] * (Q_I.max() + 1);# Coherent Vector
ic_v = [0] * (Q_I.max() + 1);# Incoherent Vector
color=np.arange(0,Q_I.max()+1)
for value in range(Q_I.max()+1):
    mask = Q_I == value
    connected_components =
cv2.connectedComponentsWithStats(mask.astype(np.uint8), 4, cv2.CV_32S)
    num_labels = connected_components[0]
    stats = connected_components[2]
    for label in range(1, num_labels):
        count = stats[label, cv2.CC_STAT_AREA]
        if count >= th:
            c_v[value] += count
        else:
            ic_v[value] += count
print("Color:        ",color)
print("Coherent Vector:", c_v)
print("Incoherent Vector:", ic_v)
```

Fig. 8.12 Computation of coherent and incoherent vector

Fig. 8.13 Simulation
result

```
Color:        [0 1 2]
Coherent Vector: [11, 4, 6]
Incoherent Vector: [2, 2, 0]
```

Experiment 8.7: CCV Computation of Grayscale Image

This experiment uses Python to discuss the colour coherence vector computation of the grayscale image. The Python code to perform the above-mentioned task is given in Fig. 8.14, and its simulation result is shown in Fig. 8.15.

Inferences

- From Fig. 8.14, it is possible to infer that the input image is a grayscale image, $Q = 16$ and the threshold value is chosen as 8.
- Figure 8.15 displays the input and quantized image with coherent and incoherent vector values.

```
# CCV computation of grayscale image
import cv2
import numpy as np
import matplotlib.pyplot as plt
def grayscale_ccv(I, Q, th):
    Q_I = (I // Q) * Q
    # Initialise the coherence vectors
    c_v = [0] * (Q_I.max() + 1);# Coherent Vector
    ic_v = [0] * (Q_I.max() + 1);# Incoherent Vector
    for value in range(Q_I.max()+1):
        mask = Q_I == value
        connected_components = cv2.connectedComponentsWithStats(mask.astype(np.uint8),
                                    4, cv2.CV_32S)
        num_labels = connected_components[0]
        stats = connected_components[2]
        for label in range(1, num_labels):
            count = stats[label, cv2.CC_STAT_AREA]
            if count >= th:
                c_v[value] += count
            else:
                ic_v[value] += count
    return Q_I, c_v, ic_v
I = cv2.imread('Clock.tiff', 0);# Load the grayscale image
Q,th=16,8;
Q_I,c_v, ic_v = grayscale_ccv(I, Q, th)
plt.subplot(1,2,1),plt.imshow(I,cmap='gray'),plt.title('Input Image'),plt.axis('off')
plt.subplot(1,2,2),plt.imshow(Q_I,cmap='gray'),
plt.title('Quantized with Q = {}'.format(Q)),plt.axis('off')
print("Coherent Vector:", c_v)
print("Incoherent Vector:", ic_v)
```

Fig. 8.14 Computation of coherent and incoherent vector. (**a**) Input and quantized image. (**b**) Coherent and incoherent vectors

Task: Vary the Q and threshold values in the Python code given in Fig. 8.14 and comment on the observed result.

Zernike Moment

The Zernike moment is a geometric-based moment, and it is a 2D orthogonal polynomial function on a unit circle. The orthogonal moments of Zernike moment are scaling and rotation invariant. The Zernike moment contains several orthogonal sets of complex-valued polynomials, which is defined as

$$V_{nm}(x,y) = R_{nm}(x,y)\exp\left(jm \times \tan^{-1}\left(\frac{y}{x}\right)\right) \qquad (8.8)$$

(a) Input and Quantised image

Coherent Vector: [0, 0, 0, 0, 0, 0, 0, 0, 0, 0, 0, 0, 0, 0, 0, 0, 0, 0, 0, 0, 0, 0, 0, 0, 0, 0, 0, 0, 0, 0, 0, 0, 0, 0, 0, 0, 0, 0, 3811, 0, 0, 0, 0, 0, 0, 0, 0, 0, 0, 0, 0, 0, 0, 0, 0, 0, 0, 0, 0, 0, 0, 0, 0, 0, 0, 0, 0, 0, 0, 0, 0, 0, 0, 0, 3257, 0, 0, 0, 0, 0, 0, 0, 0, 0, 0, 0, 0, 0, 0, 0, 0, 0, 0, 0, 0, 0, 0, 0, 0, 0, 0, 0, 0, 0, 0, 0, 0, 0, 0, 4222, 0, 0, 0, 0, 0, 0, 0, 0, 0, 0, 0, 0, 0, 0, 0, 0, 0, 0, 0, 0, 0, 0, 0, 0, 0, 0, 0, 0, 0, 0, 0, 0, 0, 0, 3931, 0, 0, 0, 0, 0, 0, 0, 0, 0, 0, 0, 0, 0, 0, 0, 0, 0, 0, 0, 0, 0, 0, 0, 0, 0, 0, 0, 0, 0, 0, 0, 0, 0, 0, 4786, 0, 0, 0, 0, 0, 0, 0, 0, 0, 0, 0, 0, 0, 0, 0, 0, 0, 0, 0, 0, 0, 0, 0, 0, 0, 0, 0, 0, 0, 0, 0, 16978, 0, 0, 0, 0, 0, 0, 0, 0, 0, 0, 0, 0, 0, 0, 0, 0, 0, 0, 0, 0, 0, 0, 0, 0, 0, 0, 0, 0, 0, 0, 0, 0, 0, 0, 25379]
Incoherent Vector: [0, 0, 0, 0, 0, 0, 0, 0, 0, 0, 0, 0, 0, 0, 0, 0, 0, 0, 0, 0, 0, 0, 0, 0, 0, 0, 0, 0, 0, 0, 0, 0, 0, 0, 0, 0, 0, 95, 0, 0, 0, 0, 0, 0, 0, 0, 0, 0, 0, 0, 0, 0, 0, 0, 0, 0, 0, 0, 0, 0, 0, 0, 0, 0, 0, 0, 0, 0, 0, 0, 0, 0, 0, 0, 498, 0, 0, 0, 0, 0, 0, 0, 0, 0, 0, 0, 0, 0, 0, 0, 0, 0, 0, 0, 0, 0, 0, 0, 0, 0, 0, 0, 0, 0, 0, 0, 0, 715, 0, 0, 0, 0, 0, 0, 0, 0, 0, 0, 0, 0, 0, 0, 0, 0, 0, 0, 0, 0, 0, 0, 0, 0, 0, 0, 0, 0, 0, 0, 0, 0, 0, 703, 0, 0, 0, 0, 0, 0, 0, 0, 0, 0, 0, 0, 0, 0, 0, 0, 0, 0, 0, 0, 0, 0, 0, 0, 0, 0, 0, 0, 0, 0, 535, 0, 0, 0, 0, 0, 0, 0, 0, 0, 0, 0, 0, 0, 0, 0, 0, 0, 0, 0, 0, 0, 0, 0, 0, 0, 0, 0, 0, 0, 486, 0, 0, 0, 0, 0, 0, 0, 0, 0, 0, 0, 0, 0, 0, 0, 0, 0, 0, 0, 0, 0, 0, 0, 0, 0, 0, 0, 0, 0, 0, 0, 0, 0, 140]

(b) Coherent and Incoherent Vectors

Fig. 8.15 Simulation result

where $x^2 + y^2 \leq 1$, $n \geq 0$, $|m| \leq n$. $R_{nm}(x, y)$ denotes the radial polynomial function, which is defined as

$$R_{nm}(x,y) = \sum_{k=0}^{(n-|m|)/2} S_{n,|m|,k}\left(x^2 + y^2\right)^{\left(\frac{n-2k}{2}\right)} \tag{8.9}$$

where

$$S_{n,|m|,k} = (-1)^k \frac{(n-k)!}{k\left(\frac{n+|m|}{2} - k\right)!\left(\frac{n-|m|}{2} - k\right)!} \tag{8.10}$$

```
# Zernike moment
import mahotas
import cv2
import matplotlib.pyplot as plt
img = cv2.imread('Clock.tiff',0);# Load the gray scale image
radius = 5
moment = mahotas.features.zernike_moments(img, radius)
plt.imshow(img,cmap='gray'),plt.title('Input Image'),plt.axis('off')
print(r'Zernike Moment with Radius = {}:'.format (radius),
```

Fig. 8.16 Computation of Zernike moment

Zernike Moment with Radius = 5:
[0.31830989 0.00913481 0.00487709
0.00659642 0.02002878 0.0434792
0.00807039 0.01769842 0.01458258
0.03473163 0.06787538 0.04867104
0.00738682 0.04070637 0.02361825
0.02569884 0.0464545 0.08585966
0.06779415 0.09901887 0.0045254
0.07726935 0.03867746 0.01377074

Fig. 8.17 Simulation result

The Zernike moment of the input image $f(x, y)$ for the value of n and m is computed as

$$ZM_{nm} = \frac{n+1}{\pi}\sum_{x}\sum_{y}f(x,y)V_{nm}^{*}(x,y) \tag{8.11}$$

The positive Zernike moment is computed for the positive value of "m" because $V_{nm}(x,y) = V_{nm}^{*}(x,y)$. The centre of the unit circle is located at the origin of the coordinate; hence, the Zernike moment is independent of scaling and rotation operations.

Experiment 8.8: Computation of Zernike Moment

This experiment discusses the computation of Zernike moment for the grayscale image using Python. The Python code to compute the Zernike moment is given in Fig. 8.16, and its simulation result is shown in Fig. 8.17.

Inferences

- From Fig. 8.16, it is possible to observe that "mahotas" library is imported to obtain the Zernike feature or moment of the input image. The radial parameter is chosen as 5.
- Figure 8.17 indicates that the 25 numbers of Zernike moments are extracted from the given input image.

Legendre Moment

Legendre moment is an orthogonal moment and it can be used to represent an image with minimum amount of information redundancy. The 2D Legendre moment can be computed using the recursive formula of 1D Legendre polynomials. The Legendre moment for a 2D digital image with a size of $N \times N$ can be computed as

$$L_{pq} = \frac{(2p+1)(2q+1)}{(N-1)^2} \sum_{i=1}^{N} \sum_{j=1}^{N} P_p(x_i) P_q(y_j) f(x_i, y_j) \qquad (8.12)$$

where $x_i = \dfrac{2i-N-1}{N-1}, y_i = \dfrac{2j-N-1}{N-1}$.

The recursive relation for the Legendre polynomial is given by

$$P_{p+1}(x) = \frac{2p+1}{p+1} x P_p(x) - \frac{p}{p+1} P_{p-1}(x), p \geq 1 \qquad (8.13)$$

With $P_0(x) = 1, P_1(x) = x$.

Experiment 8.9: Computation of Legendre Moment

This experiment discusses the computation of Legendre moment for the grayscale image using Python. The Python code to compute the Legendre moment is given in Fig. 8.18, and its simulation result is shown in Fig. 8.19.

Inferences

- From Fig. 8.18, it is possible to observe that the 1D Legendre polynomial function is defined as a function and which is utilized to compute the 2D Legendre moment of the 2D grayscale image.
- Figure 8.19 indicates that the 18 Legendre moments are extracted from the given input image.

8.2   Texture Feature

Texture is an essential property of virtually all visual object surfaces, such as papers, clouds, wood, and fabrics. An image can be considered a mosaic of different texture regions, and the texture associated with each can represent the region. The texture of an image provides insights into how colours or intensities are spatially arranged within the image or a specific region of it. Texture plays an important role in human vision and image classification. Pictures of flowers, walls, water, or patterns on a fabric or single objects are distinguished according to their texture. The texture observation depends on certain conditions such as light, angle, distance, or other environmental effects. Texture is the tactile or visual characteristic of a surface. Texture analysis aims to find a unique way of representing the underlying

```
import numpy as np
from math import factorial, pow
import cv2
import matplotlib.pyplot as plt
img = cv2.imread('Clock.tiff',0)
img = np.float32(img)
def LegendrePoly(d,v):
  P=[]
  for k in range(0,d+1):
    if (d-k)%2==0:
      a=pow(-1,(d-k)//2)*(1/pow(2,d))*factorial(d+k)/(factorial((d-k)//2)*
            factorial((d+k)//2)*factorial(k))
      p = a * pow(v, k)
      P.append(p)
    else:
      a=0
  P=sum(P)
  return P
L_moment=[]
M,N=np.shape(img)
d=M*N
m,n=5,5
for s in range(0,m+1):
  for t in range(0,n+1):
    norm = ((2 * s + 1) * (2 * t + 1)) /d
    L=0
    for i in range(0,M):
      for j in range(0,N):
        xi = (2 * i - M - 1) / (M - 1)
        yi = (2 * j - N - 1) / (N - 1)
        T= img[i][j]*LegendrePoly(s,xi)*LegendrePoly(t,yi)
        L=L+T
    L=norm*L
    L_moment.append(L)
plt.imshow(img,cmap='gray'),plt.title('Input Image'),plt.axis('off')
print('Legendre Moments',L_moment)
```

Fig. 8.18 Computation of legendre moment

characteristics of textures and represent them in some simpler but unique form so that they can be used for robust, accurate classification and segmentation of objects.

Textures are classified into two types: (1) touch and (2) visual. Touch textures relate to the touchable feel of a surface and range from the softest to the roughest. Visual textures relate to human image observation.

Legendre Moments [185.9802703857422, -27.139500337488176, -1.1907000127000276, -46.82117148006857, -22.925856264107864, -13.770619366619409, -2.1537561154828584, 25.643070603260878, -38.765662615706994, 23.378280306726076, 17.981972149732457, 6.259999912704703, 27.662217343433323, -0.6171429563900772, 29.723039619555035, -1.8250622205327083, 19.377910989476383, 3.3500939896440136]

Fig. 8.19 Simulation result

Fig. 8.20 Relation between reference and neighbourhood pixels

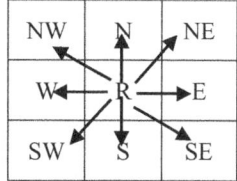

Some of the well-known texture features are (1) co-occurrence matrices, (2) local binary patterns, (3) Gabor features, (4) Tamura feature, (5) simultaneous autoregressive (SAR) models, (6) orientation texture features, (7) wavelet transform features, etc.

8.2.1 GLCM

GLCM stands for Gray Level Co-occurrence Matrix; it is also called the Gray Tone Spatial Dependency Matrix. The GLCM is a tabulation of how often different combinations of pixel occur in an image. GLCM texture depends on the relationship between two pixels at a time. The two pixels are named the "reference pixel (R)" and the "neighbourhood pixel". The relation between reference and neighbouring pixels with the window size is 3×3, as shown in Fig. 8.20. From Fig. 8.20, it is possible to infer that the relation between the reference and its neighbourhood pixels is in the form of horizontal (West (W) or East (E)), vertical (North (N) or south (S)), diagonal (North-East (NE), North-West (NW), South-East (SE), and South-West (SW)). Therefore, there are eight directions; among the eight directions, only four are used for the GLCM computation. W is the opposite of E, and N is the opposite of S, and so on.

Therefore, spatial invariant relations will be chosen by counting in four directions (N, NE, E, SE). Based on these four directions, four GLCM tables or matrices can be obtained for an image. The computation of four GLCM matrices for an image (X) is illustrated as follows:

Each cell in the GLCM matrix gives the count of the combinations in the given image. The combination of reference and neighbouring pixels is given by

Neighbour Reference	0	1	2	3
0	(0, 0)	(0, 1)	(0, 2)	(0, 3)
1	(1, 0)	(1, 1)	(1, 2)	(1, 3)
2	(2, 0)	(2, 1)	(2, 2)	(2, 3)
3	(3, 0)	(3, 1)	(3, 2)	(3, 3)

The four directions GLCM matrix for the given image (X) is shown in Fig. 8.21. Figure 8.22a indicates the count of horizontal combinations between reference and neighbourhood pixels. The first element, "1", indicates the one number of (0, 0) combinations present in the image (X) shown in Fig. 8.21. Similarly, the last element, "1", shows the one number of (3, 3) combinations in the image (X) shown in Fig. 8.21.

Figure 8.22b indicates the vertical combinations of the reference and neighbouring pixels. The first element of this matrix, "1", denotes the one number of $\begin{bmatrix} 0 \\ 0 \end{bmatrix}$ combinations that exist in the image (X) shown in Fig. 8.21. The highest value in this matrix, 4, indicates that four numbers of $\begin{bmatrix} 1 \\ 1 \end{bmatrix}$ combinations are present in the image (X) shown in Fig. 8.21.

Fig. 8.21 Image (X)

0	0	1	1	2
2	0	1	2	2
3	3	1	1	2
2	2	1	1	1

1	2	0	0
0	4	3	0
1	1	2	0
0	1	0	1

1	0	1	1
0	4	1	0
0	2	2	1
0	0	2	0

0	1	0	0
0	2	3	0
1	1	1	1
1	1	0	0

1	2	0	0
0	3	2	0
0	0	1	1
0	1	1	0

(a) Horizontal (East)   (b) Vertical (North)   (c) Diagonal (NE)   (d) Diagonal (SE)

Fig. 8.22 GLCM matrix of image shown in Fig. 8.21. (**a**) Horizontal (East). (**b**) Vertical (North). (**c**) Diagonal (NE). (**d**) Diagonal (SE)

Figure 8.22c gives the GLCM values of diagonal (NE) combinations in the input image (*X*). The highest value in this matrix, "3", denotes the three numbers of $\begin{bmatrix} 0 & 2 \\ 1 & 0 \end{bmatrix}$ combinations in the image (*X*) shown in Fig. 8.21.

Figure 8.22d gives the GLCM values of diagonal (SE) combinations in the input image (*X*) shown in Fig. 8.21. The highest value in this matrix, "3", denotes the three numbers of $\begin{bmatrix} 1 & 0 \\ 0 & 1 \end{bmatrix}$ combinations that occur in the image (*X*) shown in Fig. 8.21.

Experiment 8.10: Computation of GLCM Matrix

This experiment discusses the generation of a GLCM matrix for the input image (X) shown in Fig. 8.21 using Python. The Python code is to compute the GLCM matrix for the input image (*X*) shown in Fig. 8.21, which is given in Fig. 8.23, and its simulation result is depicted in Fig. 8.24.

Inferences

*   From Fig. 8.23, it is possible to observe that the "graycomatrix" imported from the "scikit" library to compute the GLCM matrix from the given image. "dis-

```
# Computation of GLCM matrix
import numpy as np
from skimage.feature import graycomatrix
X=np.array([[0.,0.,1.,1.,2.],[2.,0.,1.,2.,2.],[3.,3.,1.,1.,2.],[2.,2.,1.,1.,1]],'uint8')
# Generate GLCM
distances = [1] # Offset
angles = [0]  # [0, 90, -45,45],[E, N, NE, SE]
glcm = graycomatrix(X, distances=distances, angles=angles,levels=4)
print('Input (X) = \n', X)
out=np.zeros([glcm.shape[0],glcm.shape[1]])
for i in range(glcm.shape[0]):
    for j in range(glcm.shape[1]):
        out[i][j]=glcm[i][j][0][0]
print('GLCM of X with Angle ({}\u00b0) = \n'.format(angles[0]),out)
```

Fig. 8.23 Python code for Computation of GLCM matrix

GLCM of X with Angle (0°) =
[[1. 2. 0. 0.]
[0. 4. 3. 0.]
[1. 1. 2. 0.]
[0. 1. 0. 1.]]

GLCM of X with Angle (-45°) =
[[0. 1. 0. 0.]
[0. 2. 3. 0.]
[1. 1. 1. 1.]
[1. 1. 0. 0.]]

Input (X) =
[[0 0 1 1 2]
[2 0 1 2 2]
[3 3 1 1 2]
[2 2 1 1 1]]

GLCM of X with Angle (90°) =
[[1. 0. 1. 1.]
[0. 4. 1. 0.]
[0. 2. 2. 1.]
[0. 0. 2. 0.]]

GLCM of X with Angle (45°) =
[[1. 2. 0. 0.]
[0. 3. 2. 0.]
[0. 0. 1. 1.]
[0. 1. 1. 0.]]

Fig. 8.24 Four directions GLCM matrices

Table 8.1 Some important GLCM features

S. No.	Name of the feature	Mathematical expression	Significance
1.	Contrast	$\displaystyle\sum_{i,j=0}^{N-1} G_{i,j}(i-j)^2$	• It measures the local variations in the image • A higher value indicates a large difference between neighbouring pixels
2.	Dissimilarity	$\displaystyle\sum_{i,j=0}^{N-1} G_{i,j}\lvert i-j\rvert$	• It measures the average difference in the neighbouring pixels • A higher value indicates greater heterogeneity in texture
3.	Homogeneity	$\displaystyle\sum_{i,j=0}^{N-1} \frac{G_{i,j}}{1+(i-j)^2}$	• It reflects the closeness of the distribution of elements in the GLCM to the GLCM diagonal • A higher value reflects that elements are concentrated along the diagonal and that texture is uniform
4.	Angular second moment (ASM) or energy (E)	$\text{ASM} = \displaystyle\sum_{i,j=0}^{N-1} G_{i,j}^2$ $E = \sqrt{\text{ASM}}$	• It denotes the orderliness or homogeneity of the image • A higher value indicates that the texture is more uniform
5.	Correlation	$\displaystyle\sum_{i,j=0}^{N-1} \frac{G_{i,j}\left(i-\mu_i\right)\left(j-\mu_j\right)}{\sqrt{\sigma_i^2 \sigma_j^2}}$ where $\mu_i = \displaystyle\sum_{i,j=0}^{N-1} iG_{i,j}$ $\mu_j = \displaystyle\sum_{i,j=0}^{N-1} jG_{i,j}$ $\sigma_i^2 = \displaystyle\sum_{i,j=0}^{N-1} G_{i,j}\left(i-\mu_i\right)^2$ $\sigma_j^2 = \displaystyle\sum_{i,j=0}^{N-1} G_{i,j}\left(j-\mu_j\right)^2$	• It measures the linear dependency of pixels on those of neighbouring pixels • The higher value indicates a more predictable texture

tances" parameter decides whether the neighbouring pixel is either a direct neighbour or next neighbour and so on.

- "distances = 1" denotes the direct neighbours to the reference pixel. If "distances = 2" means second neighbours from the reference pixel.
- "Angle" indicates the direction of the combination, and "0" represents the horizontal or East direction. "90" denotes vertical or North direction. "45" and "−45" represent diagonals in the (SE) and (NE) directions, respectively.
- From Fig. 8.24, it is possible to observe that the results are on par with the theoretical results.

GLCM Features

The GLCM features are tabulated in Table 8.1. Some important GLCM features are tabulated in Table 8.1.

```
# Computation of GLCM matrix
import numpy as np
from skimage.feature import graycomatrix, graycoprops
X=np.array([[0.,0.,1.,1.,2.],[2.,0.,1.,2.,2.],[3.,3.,1.,1.,2.],[2.,2.,1.,1.,1]],'uint8')
# Generate GLCM
distances = [1] # Offset
angles = [0]  # Vertical Direction
glcm = graycomatrix(X, distances=distances, angles=angles,levels=4)
print('Input (X) = \n', X)
out=np.zeros([glcm.shape[0],glcm.shape[1]])
for i in range(glcm.shape[0]):
  for j in range(glcm.shape[1]):
    out[i][j]=glcm[i][j][0][0]
print('GLCM of X with Angle ({}\u00b0) = \n'.format(angles[0]),out)
# Calculate Features from GLCM
contrast = graycoprops(glcm, 'contrast')
dissimilarity = graycoprops(glcm, 'dissimilarity')
homogeneity = graycoprops(glcm, 'homogeneity')
energy = graycoprops(glcm, 'energy')
correlation = graycoprops(glcm, 'correlation')
print('           GLCM Features')
print('------------------------------------------------------------ ')
print('Contrast   | Dissimilarity | Homogeneity | Energy   | Correlation ')
print('-----------------------------------------------------------')
print(' %-9s | %-13s | %-11s | %-8s |%-11s' % (np.round(contrast[0],4),
       np.round(dissimilarity[0],4),np.round(homogeneity[0],4),
       np.round(energy[0],4),np.round(correlation[0],4)))
```

Fig. 8.25 Computation of GLCM features

Experiment 8.11: GLCM Feature Extraction

This experiment discusses the GLCM feature extraction from the GLCM matrix. The Python code to perform this task is given in Fig. 8.25, and its simulation result is shown in Fig. 8.26.

Inferences

- Figure 8.25 shows that GLCM features are extracted from the Python command "*graycoprops*", which is available in the "scikit" library.
- Figure 8.26 shows that five GLCM features are extracted, and the values of the features are different for different orientations of the GLCM matrix.

Experiment 8.12: GLCM Features of Grayscale Image

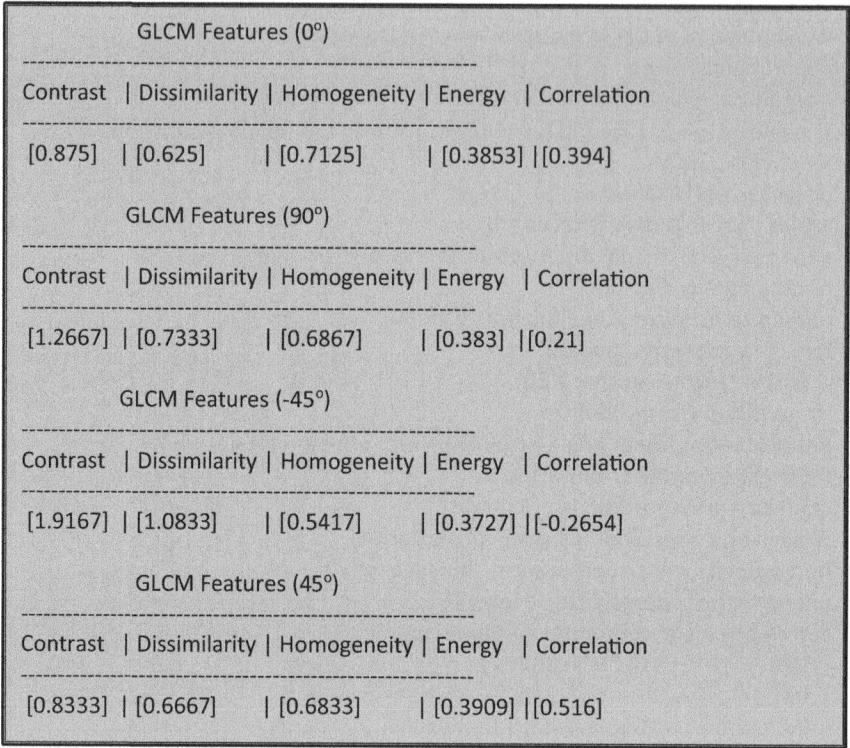

Fig. 8.26 Four directions GLCM features

This experiment discusses the computation of GLCM features of grayscale image using Python. The Python code to perform this task is shown in Fig. 8.27, and its simulation result is displayed in Fig. 8.28.

Inferences

The following inferences can be observed from this experiment:

- From Fig. 8.27, it is possible to observe that "distances = 1" indicates the combination of pixels between reference and direct next pixel as the neighbourhood pixel. The orientation (angles) varied from "0°", "90°", "45°", "−45°".
- Figure 8.28 shows the GLCM features of the Cameraman image; a total of 25 features are extracted from the GLCM matrices of the Cameraman image. These features can be fed into different image-processing applications, such as face recognition, object recognition, image classification, etc.
- Figure 8.29 displays the GLCM matrix of the Cameraman image for four different orientations. The few white colours represent the non-zero GLCM matrix of the Cameraman's image.

Task: Change the value of "distances" to 2, 3, 4, and 5 and comment on the observed GLCM features.

```
# Computation of GLCM matrix for a grayscale image using 'scikit'
import numpy as np
from skimage.io import imread
from skimage.feature import graycomatrix, graycoprops
import matplotlib.pyplot as plt
X=imread('cameraman.tif',0);
# Generate GLCM
distances = [1] # Offset
ang = [0,90,45,-45]  # Directions
plt.imshow(X,cmap='gray'),plt.title('Input Image'),
plt.xticks([]),plt.yticks([])
plt.figure(figsize=(8,8))
print('           GLCM Features')
print('-------------------------------------------------------------------------------- ')
print('Orientation | Contrast   | Dissimilarity | Homogeneity | Energy   | Correlation ')
print('--------------------------------------------------------------------------------')
for k in range(len(ang)):
    glcm = graycomatrix(X, distances=distances, angles = [ang[k]],levels=256)
    out=np.zeros([glcm.shape[0],glcm.shape[1]])
    for i in range(glcm.shape[0]):
        for j in range(glcm.shape[1]):
            out[i][j]=glcm[i][j][0][0]
    plt.subplot(2,2,k+1),plt.imshow(out,cmap='gray')
    plt.title('GLCM of X with Angle ({}\u00b0)'.format(ang[k]))
    plt.xticks([]),plt.yticks([])
# Calculate Features from GLCM
    contrast = graycoprops(glcm, 'contrast')
    dissimilarity = graycoprops(glcm, 'dissimilarity')
    homogeneity = graycoprops(glcm, 'homogeneity')
    energy = graycoprops(glcm, 'energy')
    correlation = graycoprops(glcm, 'correlation')
    print('%-11s | %-9s | %-13s | %-11s | %-8s |%-11s' % (ang[k],np.round(contrast[0],4),
        np.round(dissimilarity[0],4),np.round(homogeneity[0],4),
        np.round(energy[0],4),np.round(correlation[0],4)))
plt.tight_layout()
```

Fig. 8.27 Computation GLCM features

GLCM Features					
Orientation	Contrast	Dissimilarity	Homogeneity	Energy	Correlation
0	[518.6036]	[9.1659]	[0.3131]	[0.0383]	[0.9335]
90	[317.5313]	[8.0933]	[0.2987]	[0.037]	[0.9592]
45	[713.2679]	[11.5019]	[0.2669]	[0.0343]	[0.9087]
-45	[645.7185]	[11.2735]	[0.2668]	[0.0343]	[0.9173]

Fig. 8.28 Four directions GLCM Features of Cameraman image

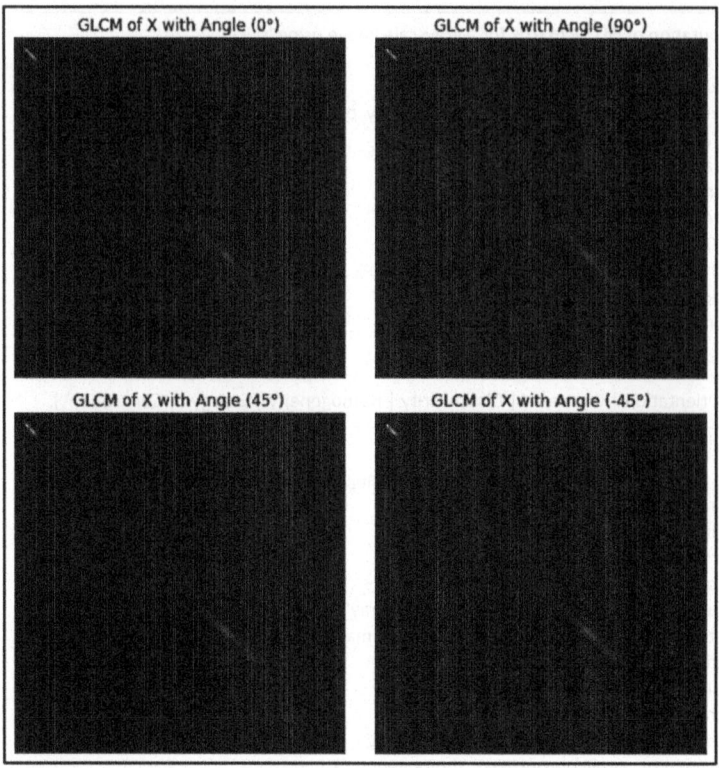

Fig. 8.29 GLCM matrix for Cameraman image

8.2.2   *Local Binary Pattern (LBP)*

LBP is a texture-based feature, which is based on the signs of differences between neighbourhood pixels and centre pixel. The calculation of the LBP of a particular pixel is illustrated in Fig. 8.30. From this figure, it is possible to observe that the centre pixel is compared with the 8 neighbourhoods of it. If the centre pixel value is greater than or equal to neighbourhood pixel, then the output is assigned as 1; otherwise, the output is assigned to 0. For each 3×3 neighbourhood pixel, the output is an eight-bit binary code. This binary code can be considered as a binary pattern. This binary code is multiplied by the respective weight, which is shown in Fig. 8.30. Finally, it sums up all the values in the window after the respective weight is multiplied. The resultant value is the LBP value for the centre pixel. Any odd value can be chosen for the size of the neighbourhood window to avoid the centre pixel issue for the computation. The histogram will be constructed to determine the frequency values of binary patterns. Each pattern represents the possibility of a binary pattern found in the image. The number of histogram bins depends on the number of involved pixels in the LBP calculation. If LBP uses 8 pixels, the number of

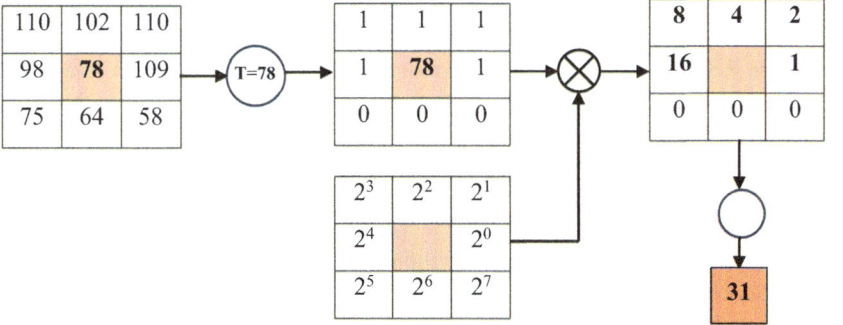

Fig. 8.30 LBP calculation

histogram bins will be 2^8 or equal to 256. Instead of centre pixel as a threshold, any other value may be chosen as a threshold.

The basic version of the LBP operator uses the centre pixel value as a threshold to the 3×3 neighbour pixels. The threshold operation will create a binary pattern representing texture characteristics. The mathematical computation of LBP for 3×3 neighbourhood pixels can be written as

$$\text{LBP}(i,j) = \sum_{n=0}^{7} 2^n f\{X_n - X(i,j)\}$$ (8.14)

where LBP(i, j) is a LBP value at the centre pixel of the image X(i, j). X_n is the neighbourhood pixels. "n" denotes the index of neighbourhood pixels. The function $f\{x\}$ can be mathematically written as

$$f(x) = \begin{cases} 0, & \text{if } x < 0 \\ 1, & \text{if } x \geq 0 \end{cases}$$ (8.15)

For example (see Fig. 8.30), the centre pixel, 78, will be selected as a threshold value. The neighbourhood pixels are assigned 0 if their values are less than the threshold. The neighbourhood pixels are assigned to 1 if their values are greater than or equal to the threshold. The LBP value is computed by applying scalar multiplication between the binary and weight matrices. Finally, the sum of all multiplication results is used to represent the LBP value.

Experiment 8.13: Computation of Local Binary Pattern Texture Feature
This experiment deals with the computation of the LBP texture feature using Python. The Python code to compute the LBP value of the given image is shown in Fig. 8.31a, and its simulation result is depicted in Fig. 8.31b.

Inferences
The following inferences can be drawn from this experiment:

- From Fig. 8.31a, it is possible to observe that the LBP python command "local_binary_pattern", is imported from the "scikit" library. P is the number of points in a neighbourhood is chosen as 8 and the distance between the centre pixel and neighbourhood pixels (R-Radius) is fixed as 1.

- Figure 8.31b shows that the LBP value of the centre pixel (78) in image X is computed as 31, which reflects the theoretical calculation obtained in the example given in Fig. 8.31b.
- The zero padding is used for the LBP computation of border pixels in an image.

Tasks

1. Change the value of P as 4 in the Python code given in Fig. 8.31a and comment on the observed result.
2. Change the value of R as 2 in the Python code given in Fig. 8.31a and comment on the observed result.

Experiment 8.14: LBP Computation of Grayscale Image

This experiment discusses computing the LBP feature of grayscale image using Python. Read the grayscale image, choose the number of points in the neighbourhoods as [2, 4, 8], and fix the radius of the neighbourhood as [1, 2, 4]. The Python code to compute the above-mentioned task is given in Fig. 8.32, and its simulation result is shown in Fig. 8.33.

Inferences

The following inferences can be made from this experiment:

- Figure 8.32 shows that the number of points in the neighbourhood (P) varies from [2, 4, 8]. The distance between the centre pixel and its neighbourhoods (i.e. Radius) (R) is varied from [1, 2, 4].
- From Fig. 8.33, it is possible to observe that the LBP of the grayscale image changes for changing the value of P and R. Therefore, different LBP features can be computed for the same image, which will be useful for extracting more LBP features from the input image for further image processing applications.

```
import numpy as np
from skimage.feature import local_binary_pattern
X=np.array([[110.,102.,110.],[98.,78.,109.],[75.,64.,58.]],'uint8')
P, R = 8, 1
out=local_binary_pattern(X, P, R, method='default')
print('Input matrix, X =\n',X)
print('LBP values of X =\n',out)
```

```
Input matrix, X =
[[110 102 110]
 [ 98  78 109]
 [ 75  64 58]]
LBP values of X =
[[  0. 145.   0.]
 [  6.  31.   4.]
 [  6.  30.  28.]]
```

(a) Python code   **(b) LBP features**

Fig. 8.31 Computation of GLCM features. **(a)** Python code. **(b)** LBP features

```
from skimage.io import imread
from skimage.feature import local_binary_pattern
import matplotlib.pyplot as plt
X = imread('Clock.tiff',0)
P = [2, 4, 8]
R = [1, 2, 4]
plt.figure(figsize=(12,5)),plt.subplot(2,5,1),plt.imshow(X,cmap='gray');
plt.title('Input Image')
plt.xticks([]),plt.yticks([])
out=[]
k=2
for i in range(len(P)):
    for j in range(len(R)):
        out=local_binary_pattern(X, P[i], R[j], method='default')
        plt.subplot(2,5,k),plt.imshow(out,cmap='gray')
        plt.title('P = {}, R = {}'.format(P[i],R[j]))
        plt.xticks([]),plt.yticks([])
        k=k+1;
```

Fig. 8.32 Python code for computation of LBP features

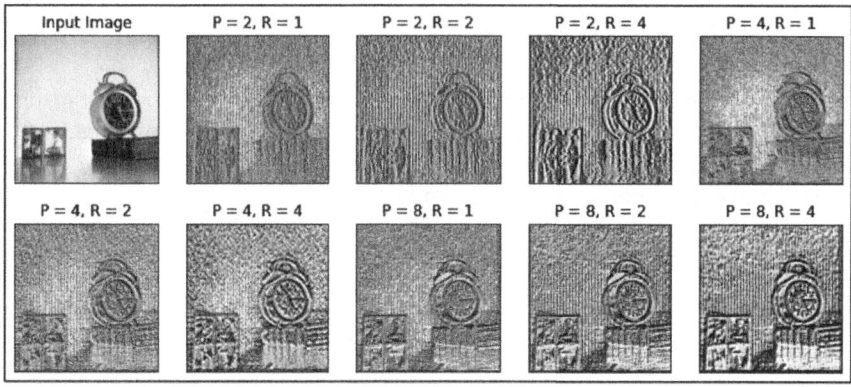

Fig. 8.33 LBP features of "Clock" image

8.2.3 Histogram Oriented Gradients (HOG)

HOG is another texture feature descriptor. It focuses on the structure or shape of the object in an image. It is similar to the Canny edge detector, Scale Invariant Feature Transform (SIFT) feature. The HOG feature contains the magnitude and angle or orientation of the gradient, hence this feature is better than the other feature descriptors like Canny edge detector, SIFT, etc.

The HOG serves as a feature descriptor, extracting gradient details from an image by computing histograms of oriented gradients within localized regions. Widely applied in computer vision tasks like object, face, and pedestrian detection, text classification, and optical character recognition (OCR). HOG offers a valuable alternative to Convolutional Neural Networks (CNNs) in certain scenarios. Specifically, when dealing with limited datasets or constrained computational resources, opting for HOG may prove advantageous. Its simplicity and effectiveness in feature extraction make it seamlessly compatible with traditional machine learning techniques such as Support Vector Machines (SVM). Additionally, HOG shines in cases where images exhibit low resolution or significant pixelation. In these instances, gradients often furnish more reliable features than raw pixel values, making HOG a preferred choice for robust feature extraction.

Approach: The steps involved in the computation of the HOG feature in the image are as follows:

Step 1: Read the image and resize it to 64 × 128 the image into 8 × 8 or 16 × 16 image patches to extract the features.

Step 2: Calculate the gradient in the "x" and "y" directions.

The gradient of the input image in "x" and "y" directions is obtained for each and every pixel in an image with the window size of 3 × 3, and it is calculated using the Eqs. (8.16) and (8.17):

$$G_x(m,n) = I(m,n+1) - I(m,n-1) \qquad (8.16)$$

$$G_y(m,n) = I(m-1,n) - I(m+1,n) \qquad (8.17)$$

where $G_x(m, n)$ and $G_y(m, n)$ denote the gradient in the "x" and "y" directions of the pixel located at (m, n).

Step 3: Compute the magnitude and orientation or angle of each gradient pixel.

The magnitude (H) and orientation or angle (θ) of each pixel are calculated from the gradient of the image, which is computed in Step 2. The computation of the magnitude and angle of each pixel is given by

$$\text{Magnitude}\left(H(m,n)\right) = \sqrt{G_x^2(m,n) + G_y^2(m,n)} \qquad (8.18)$$

$$\text{Orientation or angle}\left(\theta(m,n)\right) = \left| tan^{-1}\left(\frac{G_y(m,n)}{G_x(m,n)}\right) \right| \qquad (8.19)$$

Step 4: Calculate the histogram of gradient.

After obtaining the gradient of each pixel in an image, the magnitude gradient matrix and angle gradient matrix are divided into either 8 × 8 blocks or 16 × 16 blocks. For example, an 8 × 8 block contains a 9 element, and the 9-point histogram can be computed from it. The 9-point histogram develops a histogram with 9 bins, and each bin has an information of angle range of 20°. Therefore, the number of bins in a histogram can be calculated by using the Eq. (8.20):

$$\text{Number of bins} = 9\left(\text{ranging from } 0° to\ 180°\right) \qquad (8.20)$$

$$\text{Step size}\left(\Delta\theta\right) = \frac{180°}{\text{Number of bins}} = \frac{180°}{9} = 20°$$

The above equation indicates that for the 9-point histogram, the number of bins is '9' with a distance of an angle of 20°.

The boundary of the jth bin is computed as $[\Delta\theta \times j, \Delta\theta \times (j + 1)]$. Similarly, the centre value of the jth bin is computed by

$$C_j = \Delta\theta \times \left(j + \frac{1}{2} \right)$$

(8.21)

For each cell in a block, the value of jth and $(j + 1)^{th}$ bin is calculated by

$$j = \frac{\theta}{\Delta\theta} - \frac{1}{2}$$

(8.22)

$$V_j = H \times \left[\frac{\theta}{\Delta\theta} - \frac{1}{2} \right]$$

(8.23)

$$V_{j+1} = H \times \left[\frac{\theta - C_j}{\Delta\theta} \right]$$

(8.24)

The values of V_j and V_{j+1} are appended in the array at the index of jth and $(j + 1)^{th}$ bin in the histogram.

Once the histogram of each block is computed, then 4 blocks from 9-point histogram matrix are clubbed together to form a new block (2×2). This clubbing can be done overlappingly with a stride of 8 pixels. The total number of features in a vector (4×9) 36, which is arranged in the form of

$$f_{b_i} = [b_1, b_2, \cdots, b_{36}]$$

(8.25)

Step 5: Normalize the gradients in 16×16 cell.

The value of f_b for each block is normalized by the L_2 norm which is mathematically written as

$$f_{b_i} = \frac{f_{b_i}}{\sqrt{\| f_{b_i} \|_2^2 + \varepsilon^2}}$$

(8.26)

where ε is a small value to avoid zero division error during the normalization process.

The normalizing constant "k" is obtained as

$$k = \sqrt{b_1^2 + b_2^2 + \ldots + b_{36}^2}$$

(8.27)

The normalized f_{b_i} is used to reduce the effect of changes in the contrast between images of the same object, and it is calculated as

$$f_{b_i} = \left[\frac{b_1}{k}, \frac{b_2}{k}, \cdots, \frac{b_{36}}{k} \right]$$

(8.28)

```
from skimage.io import imread
from skimage.transform import resize
from skimage.feature import hog
import matplotlib.pyplot as plt
img = imread('Clock.tiff',0)
plt.figure(figsize=(8,6)),
plt.subplot(1,3,1),plt.imshow(img,cmap='gray')
plt.title('Input Image: size {}'.format(img.shape)),plt.xticks([]),plt.yticks([])
resized_img = resize(img, (64, 128))
plt.subplot(1,3,2),plt.imshow(resized_img,cmap='gray')
plt.title('Resized Image: size {}'.format(resized_img.shape)),plt.xticks([]),plt.yticks([])
fd, hog_image = hog(resized_img, orientations=9, pixels_per_cell=(8, 8),
                cells_per_block=(2, 2), visualize=True, channel_axis=None)
plt.subplot(1,3,3),plt.imshow(hog_image,cmap='gray')
plt.title('HOG Descriptor: size {}'.format(hog_image.shape)),plt.xticks([]),plt.yticks([])
print('Length of HOG Feature : ', len(fd));
plt.tight_layout()
```

Fig. 8.34 Computation HOG features

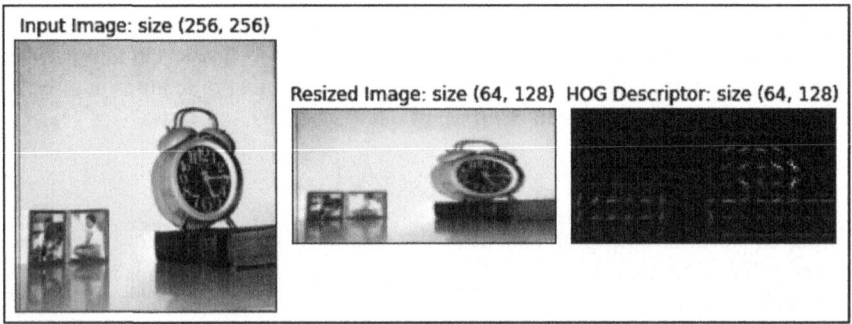

Fig. 8.35 HOG features of "Clock" image

Step 6: Computation of HOG features for the entire image.

The HOG feature of the entire image is computed by combining all the values in each block. For a 36-point feature vector, horizontally, there are 7 blocks, and vertically, there are 15 blocks. Hence, the total length of the HOG feature will be $(7 \times 15 \times 36)$ 3780 feature points.

Experiment 8.15: Computation of HOG Feature for a Grayscale Image Using "scikit" Library

This experiment discusses the extraction of the HOG feature from the given grayscale image using Python. The Python code to compute the HOG feature from a grayscale image is given in Fig. 8.34. From this figure, it is possible to observe that the input image size is resized to 64×128 in the first step. Python command 'hog' is used to compute the HOG feature, which is imported from the "scikit" library. After executing the Python code given in Fig. 8.34, the simulation result is shown in Fig. 8.35.

Inferences

- From Fig. 8.35, it is possible to infer that the size of the input image to the HOG feature extraction is 64 × 128.
- The length of the HOG feature is 3780 for orientation 9, and the image patch size is 8 × 8.

Task: Execute the Python code given in Fig. 8.34 with the value of orientation of 16 and comment on the observed HOG image and length of the HOG feature vector.

```
import cv2
import numpy as np
import matplotlib.pyplot as plt
img = cv2.imread('Clock.tiff',0);# Load the grayscale image
# Specify the parameters of HOG descriptor
win_size = img.shape
cell_size,block_size = (8, 8),(16, 16)
block_stride,num_bins = (8, 8), 9
hog = cv2.HOGDescriptor(win_size, block_size, block_stride, cell_size, num_bins)
# Compute the HOG Descriptor for the grayscale image
hog_descriptor = hog.compute(img)
hog_descriptor_reshaped = hog_descriptor.reshape(31,31,2,2,num_bins).transpose((1, 0, 2, 3, 4))
ave_grad = np.zeros((32, 32, num_bins))# initiaize the average gradients
hist_counter = np.zeros((32, 32, 1))# Initialize the Histogram counter
# Add up all the histograms for each cell and count the number of histograms per cell
for i in range(2):
    for j in range(2):
        ave_grad[i:31 + i, j:31 + j] += hog_descriptor_reshaped[:, :, i, j, :]
        hist_counter[i:31 + i,j:31 + j] += 1
ave_grad /= hist_counter;# Calculate the average gradient for each cell
len_vecs = ave_grad.shape[0] * ave_grad.shape[1] * ave_grad.shape[2]
deg = np.linspace(0, np.pi, num_bins, endpoint=False);# no.of bins from 0 to 180 degree
U = np.zeros((len_vecs))
V = np.zeros((len_vecs))
X = np.zeros((len_vecs))
Y = np.zeros((len_vecs))
counter = 0
for i in range(ave_grad.shape[0]):
    for j in range(ave_grad.shape[1]):
        for k in range(ave_grad.shape[2]):
            U[counter] = ave_grad[i, j, k] * np.cos(deg[k])
            V[counter] = ave_grad[i, j, k] * np.sin(deg[k])
            X[counter] = (cell_size[0] / 2) + (cell_size[0] * i)
            Y[counter] = (cell_size[1] / 2) + (cell_size[1] * j)
            counter = counter + 1
fig, (ax1, ax2) = plt.subplots(1, 2, figsize=(8, 6))
ax1.set(title='Grayscale Image'),ax1.imshow(img, cmap='gray'),ax1.axis('off')
# Plot the feature vector (HOG Descriptor)
ax2.set(title='HOG Descriptor count = {}'.format(len(hog_descriptor)))
ax2.quiver(Y, X, U, V, color='red', headwidth=0, headlength=0, scale_units='inches', scale=3)
ax2.invert_yaxis(),ax2.set_aspect(aspect=1),ax2.set_facecolor('black'),plt.xticks([]),plt.yticks([])
```

Fig. 8.36 Computation HOG features using CV2 library

Fig. 8.37 HOG features of "Clock" image

Experiment 8.16: HOG Feature Extraction from Grayscale Image Using "OpenCV"
This experiment computes the HOG feature of grayscale image using the OpenCV library. The Python code for this computation is given in Fig. 8.36, and its corresponding simulation result is shown in Fig. 8.37.

Inferences
The following inferences can be drawn from this experiment:

- From Fig. 8.36, it is possible to observe that the Python command "cv2. HOGDescriptor" is used for extracting the HOG parameters and "hog.compute" is used here to compute the HOG feature of the input image. Also, it is possible to infer that there is no need to resize the input image into (64 × 128 or 128 × 64). The entire image is given as input to the "hog.compute" Python command. All these commands are imported from the "cv2" library.
- From Fig. 8.37, it is possible to see that the HOG features are displayed in the direction of the feature vector. The length of the HOG feature vector is 34,596.

   Task: Execute the Python code given in Fig. 8.36 with the value of num_bins 4 and 16. Comment on the observed HOG descriptor and count of the HOG feature vectors.

8.3   Shape Feature

Shapes of an object of interest act as a feature. For the shape feature extractions, a good segmentation algorithm has to be used to detect the boundary of the region of interest or object. The shape feature can be split into (1) boundary-based features and (2) region-based features. Boundary-based features can be further classified into rectilinear, polygonal approximation, finite element models, and Fourier-based shape descriptors.

8.3.1 Edges

Edge detection plays a crucial role in various image processing tasks, such as identifying and analyzing image edges or boundaries. It is widely used in applications like object and motion detection, image segmentation, medical imaging, and optical character recognition (OCR). By utilizing edge features, it becomes possible to detect variations in pixel intensity and sharp transitions between different regions within an image. This technique is especially effective for performing simple image processing operations like edge detection or boundary extraction. It is particularly beneficial in scenarios where the image data is straightforward and the edges are clearly defined.

8.3.2 Gradient Edge

An image gradient is defined as a directional change in image pixels. At each pixel of the input grayscale image, a gradient obtains the change in pixel value in a given direction. Computing the magnitude and orientation of the image can detect the region of the image, which is called an edge. Image gradients can be computed by using kernels or filters. The different kernels for the gradient edge detectors are given in Table 8.2.

Experiment 8.17: Computation of Gradient Edge Feature from an Image
This experiment discusses the computation of the gradient edge features from a grayscale image using Python. In this experiment, the edge features of Roberts, Sobel, Scharr, and Prewitt are computed. The Python code to compute the gradient edge features from the grayscale image is given in Fig. 8.38, and its simulation result is shown in Fig. 8.39.

Table 8.2 Different kernels for gradient edge detector

S. No.	Name of the edge detector	Kernel or filter mask
1.	Roberts	$G_x = \begin{bmatrix} +1 & 0 \\ 0 & -1 \end{bmatrix}, G_y = \begin{bmatrix} 0 & +1 \\ -1 & 0 \end{bmatrix}$
2.	Sobel	$G_x = \begin{bmatrix} -1 & 0 & +1 \\ -2 & 0 & +2 \\ -1 & 0 & +1 \end{bmatrix}, G_y = \begin{bmatrix} -1 & -2 & -1 \\ 0 & 0 & 0 \\ +1 & +2 & +1 \end{bmatrix}$
3.	Scharr	$G_x = \begin{bmatrix} +3 & 0 & -3 \\ +10 & 0 & -10 \\ +3 & 0 & -3 \end{bmatrix}, G_y = \begin{bmatrix} +3 & +10 & +3 \\ 0 & 0 & 0 \\ -3 & -10 & -3 \end{bmatrix}$
4.	Prewitt	$G_x = \begin{bmatrix} +1 & 0 & -1 \\ +1 & 0 & -1 \\ +1 & 0 & -1 \end{bmatrix}, G_y = \begin{bmatrix} -1 & -1 & -1 \\ 0 & 0 & 0 \\ +1 & +1 & +1 \end{bmatrix}$

```
# Gradient edge features
from skimage import io
from skimage.filters import roberts,sobel,scharr,prewitt
import matplotlib.pyplot as plt
I = io.imread("Clock.tiff",as_gray=True)
E_roberts = roberts(I)
E_sobel=sobel(I)
E_scharr=scharr(I)
E_prewitt = prewitt(I)
fig,axes = plt.subplots(nrows=1,ncols=5,sharex=True,sharey=True,figsize=(8,4))
ax = axes.ravel()
ax[0].imshow(I,cmap="gray"),ax[0].set_title("Original_image")
ax[1].imshow(E_roberts,cmap="gray"),ax[1].set_title('Roberts')
ax[2].imshow(E_sobel,cmap="gray"),ax[2].set_title("Sobel")
ax[3].imshow(E_scharr,cmap="gray"),ax[3].set_title("Scharr")
ax[4].imshow(E_prewitt,cmap="gray"),ax[4].set_title("Prewitt")
for a in ax:
    a.axis('off')
plt.tight_layout()
```

Fig. 8.38 Computation of gradient edge features using "scikit" library

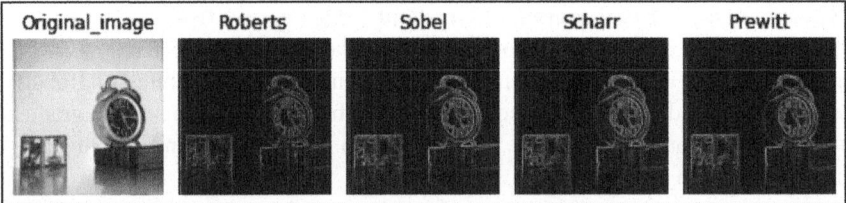

Fig. 8.39 Gradient edge features of "Clock" image

Inferences

- The gradient edge features like Roberts, Sobel, Scharr, and Prewitt are extracted from the "Clock" image using the "scikit" library. The gradient edge or edge map of the "Clock" image is shown in Fig. 8.39.

8.3.3   *Kirsch Gradient Operator*

The Kirsch gradient operator is a non-linear edge detector that detects the maximum edge strength in a few predetermined directions. This operator takes a single kernel and rotates in 45° increments through all 8 directions such as {North (N), South (S), East (E), West (W), North-West (NW), South-West (SW), North-East (NE) and South-East (SE)}. The edge magnitude is calculated as the maximum magnitude across all 8 directions. Each pixel of images uses these 8 kernels to obtain convolution.

Let us consider a 3×3 image, and its centre pixel is denoted as A^*, which is given by

$$\begin{bmatrix} A_3 & A_2 & A_1 \\ A_4 & A^* & A_0 \\ A_5 & A_6 & A_7 \end{bmatrix} \tag{8.29}$$

The gradient magnitude of the centre pixel is computed as

$$M(i,j) = \max\left(1, \max_{k=0}^{7}\left\{\left|5S_k - 3T_k\right|\right\}\right) \tag{8.30}$$

where $S_k = A_k + A_{k+1} + A_{k+2}$ and $T_k = A_{k+3} + A_{k+4} + \cdots + A_{k+7}$. In the computation of S and T modulo-8 operation has to be performed.

Experiment 8.18: Computation of Kirsch Gradient Operator
This experiment discusses the computation of the Kirsch gradient operator of an image using Python. The Python code to compute the gradient of an image using Kirsch operator is given in Fig. 8.40, and its simulation result is shown in Fig. 8.41.

Inferences

- Figure 8.41 shows that the boundary of the objects in a given image is obtained by the Kirsch gradient operator.

```
# Kirsch Operator
import cv2
import numpy as np
import matplotlib.pyplot as plt
I = cv2.imread("testimage2.JPG")
I_G = cv2.cvtColor(I, cv2.COLOR_BGR2GRAY)
I= cv2.cvtColor(I, cv2.COLOR_BGR2RGB)
plt.figure(figsize=(6,6)),plt.subplot(121),plt.imshow(I),
plt.title("Original image"),plt.axis('off')
M,N = I_G.shape
K_Out = np.zeros([M, N], dtype=int)
K_Out[0, :] = I_G[0, :]
K_Out[:, 0] = I_G[:, 0]
K_Out[M-1, :] = I_G[M-1, :]
K_Out[:, N-1] = I_G[:, N-1]
for i in np.arange(1, M-1):
  for j in np.arange(1, N-1):
    Bloc = I_G[i-1:i+2, j-1:j+2]
    n = 8
    BlocFl = np.zeros(n, dtype=int)
    BlocFl[:3] = Bloc[0,:]
    BlocFl[3] = Bloc[1, -1]
    BlocFl[4:7] = Bloc[-1,:][::-1]
    BlocFl[7] = Bloc[1,0]
    mx = 1
    for k in np.arange(n):
      S = BlocFl[k%n]+BlocFl[(k+1)%n]+BlocFl[(k+2)%n]
      T = (BlocFl[(k+3)%n]+BlocFl[(k+4)%n]+BlocFl[(k+5)%n]+
           BlocFl[(k+6)%n]+BlocFl[(k+7)%n]);# Modulo-8 operation
      diff = abs((5*S)-(3*T))
      if diff > mx:
        mx = diff
    K_Out[i, j] = mx
I[K_Out > 150]=[255,0,0]
plt.subplot(122),plt.imshow(I,cmap="gray"),plt.title("Kirsch Gradient Detection"),plt.axis('off')
plt.show()
```

Fig. 8.40 Computation of Kirsch gradient operator

8.3.4   Harris Corner Detector

The Harris corner detector was developed by Chris Harris and Mike Stephens in 1988. This Harris corner detector finds the difference between the centre pixel and its neighbouring pixels in all directions. The mathematical expression of the Harris corner detector is given by

$$E(x,y) = \sum_{m,n} w(m,n)\big[I(m+x,n+y)-I(m,n)\big]^2 \qquad (8.31)$$

Fig. 8.41 Kirsch gradient operator

where "I" denotes the input image, "w" is the window function, which is either a rectangular or Gaussian window and "E" is the corner points. Using Taylor series expansion for 2D function, the term $I(m + x, n + y)$ in the above equation can be written as

$$I(m+x,n+y) = I(m,n) + xI_m(m,n) + yI_n(m,n)$$
$$+ \frac{1}{2!} \left\{ \begin{array}{l} x^2 I_{mm}(m,n) \\ + xyI_{mn}(m,n) + y^2 I_{nn}(m,n) \end{array} \right\}$$
$$+ \frac{1}{3!} \left\{ \begin{array}{l} x^3 I_{mmm}(m,n) + x^2 yI_{mmn}(m,n) \\ + xy^2 I_{mnn}(m,n) + y^3 I_{nnn}(m,n) \end{array} \right\} + \cdots \qquad (8.32)$$

Using the first-order approximation, the above Eq. (8.32) can be written as

$$I(m+x,n+y) \approx I(m,n) + xI_m(m,n) + yI_n(m,n) \qquad (8.33)$$

Now substituting Eq. (8.33) in (8.31), we get

$$E(x,y) = \sum_{m,n} w(m,n) \left[I(m,n) + xI_m(m,n) + yI_n(m,n) - I(m,n) \right]^2 \qquad (8.34)$$

The above equation can be further simplified as

$$E(x,y) = \sum_{m,n} w(m,n) \left[xI_m(m,n) + yI_n(m,n) \right]^2 \qquad (8.35)$$

The above equation can be rewritten as

$$E(x,y) = \sum_{m,n} w(m,n) \left[x^2 I_m^2(m,n) + y^2 I_n^2(m,n) + 2xyI_m(m,n)I_n(m,n) \right] \qquad (8.36)$$

The above equation can be written in the matrix form, we get

$$E(x,y) = \sum_{m,n} w(m,n) \begin{bmatrix} x & y \end{bmatrix} \begin{bmatrix} I_m^2 & I_m I_n \\ I_m I_n & I_n^2 \end{bmatrix} \begin{bmatrix} x \\ y \end{bmatrix} \tag{8.37}$$

The above equation can be rewritten as

$$E(x,y) = \begin{bmatrix} x & y \end{bmatrix} \sum_{m,n} w(m,n) \begin{bmatrix} I_m^2 & I_m I_n \\ I_m I_n & I_n^2 \end{bmatrix} \begin{bmatrix} x \\ y \end{bmatrix} \tag{8.38}$$

For small shifts [x, y], using a bilinear approximation,

$$E(x,y) \cong \begin{bmatrix} x & y \end{bmatrix} M \begin{bmatrix} x \\ y \end{bmatrix} \tag{8.39}$$

where M is a 2 × 2 matrix computed from image derivatives, which represented as

$$M = \sum_{m,n} w(m,n) \begin{bmatrix} I_m^2 & I_m I_n \\ I_m I_n & I_n^2 \end{bmatrix} \tag{8.40}$$

Note that the change of intensity measure E is closely related to the local auto-correlation function, with M denotes shape at the origin. Let λ_1 and λ_2 be the eigen-values of M. λ_1 and λ_2 will be proportional to the principal curvatures of the local autocorrelation function and form a rotationally invariant description of M. The following three cases are to be considered:

1. If both curvatures are small, the local correlation function is flat, and then the windowed image portion is of approximately constant intensity values. Here, arbitrary shifts of the image patch cause little change in the intensity measure E.
2. If one curvature is high and the other one is low, the local autocorrelation is ridge-shaped and then only shifts along the edge; it indicates an edge.
3. If both curvatures are high, the local autocorrelation function sharply peaks and then shifts in any direction will, increase measure E. This highlights a corner.

The above discussions are illustrated in Fig. 8.42.

Experiment 8.19: Computation of Harris Corner Detector
This experiment discusses the computation of the Harris corner in an image using Python. The Python code to compute the Harris corner detector from the grayscale image is given in Fig. 8.43, and its simulation result is shown in Fig. 8.44.

Inferences

• From Fig. 8.43 it is possible to observe that the "cv2.cornerHarris" is used to obtain the corners of the object.

• Block size and aperture size of Sobel and Harris free parameters are chosen as 5, 5, and 0.01, respectively. The boundary or corner points of the objects are shown in Fig. 8.44.

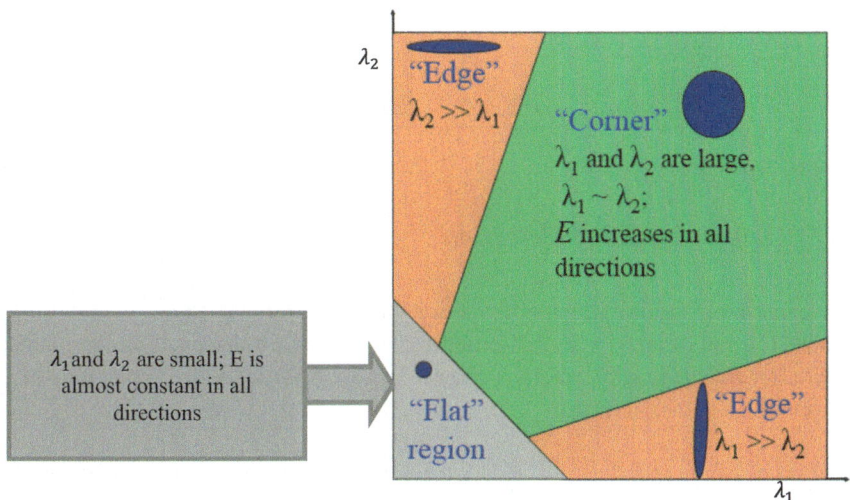

Fig. 8.42 Classification of Edge points using eigenvalues

```
# Harris Corner detector
import cv2
import matplotlib.pyplot as plt
I = cv2.imread("testimage2.JPG")
I_G = cv2.cvtColor(I, cv2.COLOR_BGR2GRAY)
I= cv2.cvtColor(I, cv2.COLOR_BGR2RGB)
plt.figure(figsize=(6,6))
plt.subplot(121),plt.imshow((I)),plt.title("Original image")
plt.xticks([]),plt.yticks([])
B=5;# Neighbourhood size
K=5;# Aperture parameter for Sobel
H_free=0.01;# Harris free parameter
O_I = cv2.cornerHarris(I_G, B, K, H_free)
D_I = cv2.dilate(O_I, None)
I[D_I > 0.001 * D_I.max()]=[255,0,0]
plt.subplot(122),plt.imshow(I,cmap="gray")
plt.title("Harris corner detector"),plt.xticks([]),plt.yticks([])
plt.show()
```

Fig. 8.43 Computation of Harris corner using CV2

Fig. 8.44 Harris corners

8.3.5 Laplacian Edge Detection

This experiment deals with the extraction of the Laplacian edge feature using Python. The Laplacian is a second-order derivative filter. It detects the edge points if there is a change in adjacent pixel values. The 3×3 kernel of the Laplacian filter is given by

$$\begin{bmatrix} 0 & -1 & 0 \\ -1 & 4 & -1 \\ 0 & -1 & 0 \end{bmatrix}$$

The Laplacian filter kernels usually contain negative values in a cross pattern centred within the array. The corners are either zero or positive values. The centre value can be either positive or negative based on the neighbouring values, and the sum of the kernel will always be zero.

Experiment 8.20: Laplacian Edge Detector
This experiment discusses Laplacian edge detection using Python. The Python code to compute the Laplacian edge map of an image is given in Fig. 8.45, and its simulation result is shown in Fig. 8.46.

Inferences

- From Fig. 8.45, it is possible to infer that the "cv2" library is used to compute the Laplacian edge map. The "cv2.Laplacian" python command is used here.
- The original and Laplacian edge map is shown in Fig. 8.46.

Task: Change the values of "ddepth" and "ksize" in the Python code given in Fig. 8.45 and comment on the observed result.

```
# Laplacian Edge detector
import cv2
import matplotlib.pyplot as plt
I = cv2.imread("Clock.tiff",0)
O_I = cv2.Laplacian(I,ddepth = 3,ksize = 3)
plt.figure(figsize=(6,6))
plt.subplot(121),plt.imshow(I,cmap="gray"),plt.title("Original image")
plt.axis('off'),plt.subplot(122),plt.imshow(O_I,cmap="gray")
plt.title("Laplacian Edge detector"),plt.axis('off')
plt.show()
```

Fig. 8.45 Computation of Laplacian edge features using cv2 library

Fig. 8.46 Laplacian edge features of "Clock" image

8.3.6 Canny Edge Detector

This experiment deals with the Canny edge detection using Python. The Python code to extract the Canny edge features is given in Fig. 8.47, and its corresponding output is shown in Fig. 8.48.

Inferences
The following inferences can be drawn from this experiment:

• Figure 8.47 shows that the 'Sobel' operator is used to compute the gradients along the "x" and "y" directions.
• The magnitude and orientation or direction are computed for the Canny edge detection.
• A different orientation threshold is used for the final gradient orientation computation.
• Finally, the edge map is computed by thresholding magnitude and gradient orientation.
• From Fig. 8.48, it is possible to observe that the thickened edge map is computed for the Clock image.

```
import cv2
import numpy as np
import matplotlib.pyplot as plt
I = cv2.imread('Clock.tiff', 0)
Blur = cv2.GaussianBlur(I, (5, 5), 0)
G_x = cv2.Sobel(Blur, cv2.CV_64F, 1, 0, ksize=3)
G_y = cv2.Sobel(Blur, cv2.CV_64F, 0, 1, ksize=3)
M = np.sqrt(G_x**2 + G_y**2)
D = np.arctan2(G_y, G_x) * (180 / np.pi);# direction
G_D = np.zeros_like(D); # Gradient direction
G_D[((D >= 0) & (D < 22.5)) | ((D >= 157.5) & (D < 180))] = 0
G_D[(D >= 22.5) & (D < 67.5)] = 45
G_D[(D >= 67.5) & (D < 112.5)] = 90
G_D[(D >= 112.5) & (D < 157.5)] = 135
Lth = 0; # Lower threshold (Direction)
Hth = 100;# Higher threshold
E = np.zeros_like(I);# Edges
E[(M >= Hth) & (G_D == Lth)] = 255
plt.figure(figsize=(6,6))
plt.subplot(121),plt.imshow(I,cmap="gray"),plt.title("Original image")
plt.axis('off'),plt.subplot(122),plt.imshow(E,cmap="gray")
plt.title("Canny Edge Detection"),plt.axis('off')
plt.show()
```

Fig. 8.47 Computation of Canny edge features using the cv2 library

Fig. 8.48 Laplacian edge features of "Clock" image

8.4 Domain-Specific Features

Domain-specific feature extraction process involves creating features that are specific to a particular domain or application. In image processing, domain-specific features may include edge detection, colour histograms, and texture.

8.4.1 Scale-Invariant Feature Transform (SIFT)

SIFT extracts features that are based on detecting key points and extracting local feature descriptors. SIFT features are invariant to scale, orientation, and affine transformations and are widely used in computer vision tasks such as object recognition, image stitching, and 3D reconstruction.

The steps followed to compute SIFT are as follows:

Step 1: Scale-space extrema detection.

The scale space of an image is a function $I(m, n, \sigma)$, which is produced by using Gaussian filtering at different scales of the input image. The scale space is separated into octaves, and the number of octaves and scale depends on the size of the original image. The size of the octave's image is half the size of the previous image.

The blurred octave images are used to find another set of images called the "Difference of Gaussian" (DoG). These DoG images are very useful for finding interesting key points in the image. The Difference of Gaussian blurring image is obtained from two different "σ" blurred images (σ and $k\sigma$). This process is done for different octaves of the image in the Gaussian pyramid.

The interesting key points are computed based on the pixel, which is compared with its 8 neighbouring pixels, 9 pixels in the next scale, and 9 pixels in the previous scales. Here, 26 checks are made to decide whether a particular pixel is a key point. If the pixel is a local extrema, then it is a potential key point.

Step 2: Key point localization.

In the previous step, lots of key points are identified in an image. Some key points lie along an edge, or they do not have enough contrast. In these two cases, these key points are not useful as features. The low contrast points are removed based on the Taylor series expansion of scale space to get a more accurate location of extrema if the pixel value at this extrema is less than a threshold value. The Hessian (2×2) matrix is used to remove the key points that lie on the edges.

Step 3: Orientation assignment.

A neighbourhood is considered around the key point location, depending on the scale, gradient magnitude, and direction. An orientation histogram with 36 bins covering $360°$ is created. The highest peak in the histogram is taken, and any peak above 80% is also considered to calculate the orientation. It creates key points with the same location and scale but in different directions.

Step 4: Key point descriptor.

In the computation of the key point descriptor, a 16×16 window around the key point is considered. Furthermore, it is split into 16 subblocks with the size of 4×4. For each subblock, 8 bin histogram orientation is computed. Therefore, a total of 128 bin values ($4 \times 4 \times 8$) are represented as a feature vector to form a key point descriptor. Lastly, to compute the rotation and illumination invariant key points, the key point's rotation is subtracted from each orientation. The normalized key points greater than 0.2 give the illumination invariant key points.

Step 5: Key point matching.

```
# SIFT Feature extraction
import cv2
from matplotlib import pyplot as plt
I = cv2.imread('Clock.tiff',0)
sift = cv2.SIFT_create();# SIFT
key, des = sift.detectAndCompute(I, None);#keypoints and descriptors
I_key = cv2.drawKeypoints(I, key, 0, (255, 0, 0),
                        flags=cv2.DRAW_MATCHES_FLAGS_DRAW_RICH_KEYPOINTS)
I_k_rgb = cv2.cvtColor(I_key, cv2.COLOR_BGR2RGB)
plt.figure(figsize=(8,6))
plt.subplot(121),plt.imshow(I,cmap="gray"),plt.title("Original image")
plt.axis('off'),plt.subplot(122),plt.imshow(I_key)
plt.title("SIFT Key points color"),plt.axis('off')
```

Fig. 8.49 Computation of SIFT features using cv2 library

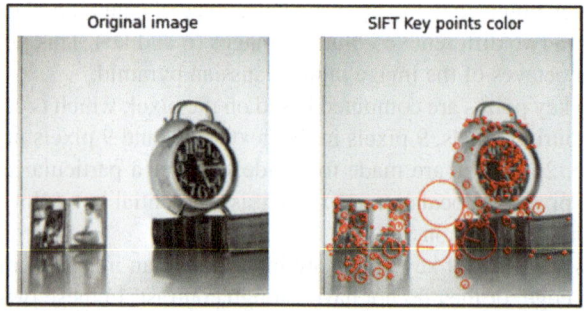

Fig. 8.50 SIFT features of "Clock" image

The key points between two images are matched by identifying their nearest neighbours. For this, the ratio of the closest distance to the second closest distance is considered; if the ratio is greater than 0.8, they are rejected. It eliminates 90% of false matches between the two images.

Experiment 8.21: Computation of SIFT Feature

This experiment discusses the extraction of SIFT features in an image using Python. The Python code to extract the SIFT feature is given in Fig. 8.49, and its corresponding result is displayed in Fig. 8.50.

Inferences

The following inferences can be observed from this experiment:

- From Fig. 8.49, it is possible to infer that "sift.detectAndCompute" is used to compute the SIFT features, and "cv2.drawKeypoints" is used to draw key points on the image.
- Figure 8.50 shows the original and SIFT key points, the radius of the circle decides the rich feature of the input image.

8.4.2 FAST (Features from Accelerated Segment Test)

FAST stands for Features from Accelerated Segment Test. It is a corner detection approach introduced by Edward Rosten and Tom Drummond in 2006. The FAST corner detector is computationally efficient; hence, it is very suitable for real-time video processing applications.

The steps involved in the FAST feature extraction algorithm are as follows:

Step 1: Select a pixel (I_p) in the image to be identified as a corner pixel and choose the appropriate threshold value (t).

Step 2: Select 16 neighbouring pixels of pixel (I_p) as per the diagram shown in Fig. 8.51.

Step 3: Compare the 16 neighbouring pixels with the pixel (I_p) and threshold (t) using the Eq. (8.41) and identify the numbers of dark, brighter, and similar pixels among 16.

$$S_p = \begin{cases} \text{darker,} & I_p \leq I_p - t \\ \text{similar,} & I_p - t < I_p < I_p + t \\ \text{brighter,} & I_p \geq I_p + t \end{cases} \qquad (8.41)$$

Step 4: Speed up the process of the algorithm. Initially, four pixels located at the positions (1, 5, 9, and 13) are compared with pixel (I_p). If at least three pixels out of four are not below $I_p - t$ or above $I_p + t$, then the pixel (I_p) cannot be considered as a corner pixel. Hence, reject the pixel (I_p) as a possible interest point.

Step 5: If at least three pixels out of four are below $I_p - t$ or above $I_p + t$, then check all remaining 12 neighbouring pixels by using Eq. (8.41).

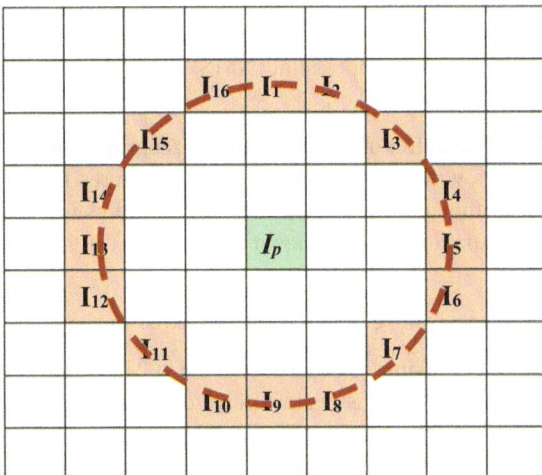

Fig. 8.51 Corner point detection in FAST

```
#FAST feature key points
import cv2
from matplotlib import pyplot as plt
I = cv2.imread('Clock.tiff',0)
fast = cv2.FastFeatureDetector_create();# Initiate FAST object
kp = fast.detect(I,None);# find the key points
I1 = cv2.drawKeypoints(I, kp, None, color=(0,255,0))
fast.setNonmaxSuppression(0);# Disable nonmaxSuppression
kp1 = fast.detect(I, None)
I2 = cv2.drawKeypoints(I, kp1, None, color=(0,255,0))
plt.figure(figsize=(12,6))
plt.subplot(131),plt.imshow(I,cmap="gray"),plt.title("Original image")
plt.axis('off'),plt.subplot(132),plt.imshow(I1),plt.title(f"FAST Key points with NMS ({len(kp)})"),
plt.axis('off'),plt.subplot(133),plt.imshow(I2),
plt.title(f"FAST Key points without NMS ({len(kp1)})"),plt.axis('off')
plt.show()
```

Fig. 8.52 Computation of FAST features using cv2 library

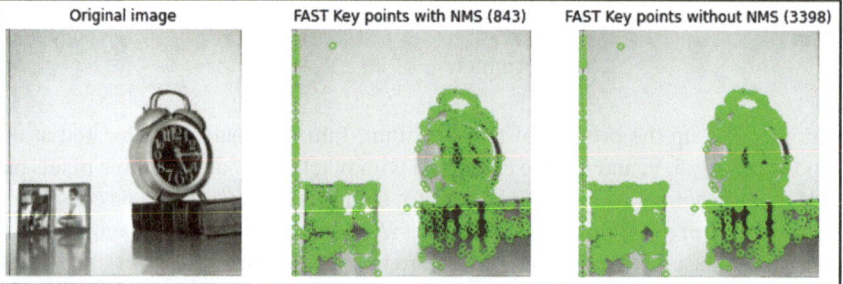

Fig. 8.53 FAST features of "Clock" image

Step 6: Repeat the process for the entire image pixels.

Step 7: Use the nonmaximal suppression (NMS) method to avoid repeatability in the interest point selection.

Experiment 8.22: Extraction of FAST Features from an Image

This experiment deals with the extraction of FAST features from the given image using Python. The Python code to extract the FAST features in an image is given in Fig. 8.52, and its simulation result is shown in Fig. 8.53.

Inferences

The following inferences can be drawn from this experiment:

- From Fig. 8.52, it is possible to observe that the "CV2" library is used to import the Python command "cv2.FastFeatureDetector_create" to compute the FAST features and also observe that the "fast.setNonmaxSuppression" command is used to disable the feature points having the non-maximum value.

- Figure 8.53 displays the input and FAST key points with and without NMS results. From this figure, it is possible to conclude that the number of key points in NMS is lesser than the actual key points in an image.

8.4.3   BRIEF (Binary Robust Independent Elementary Features)

Binary strings (bitstrings) act as a feature vector, and they take the values of 1 and 0 in them. The key points of the image are described as a feature vector, which has a length of 128, 256, and 512 bitstrings. The steps involved in the computation of BRIEF are as follows:

Step 1: Read the input image.
Step 2: Smoothen the input image using Gaussian filtering to reduce the noise sensitivity and increase the stability and repeatability of the descriptors.
Step 3: The smoothened image is split into image patches (P). The binary value of the image patch is computed using a binary test (τ), which is defined as

$$\tau\left(P:x,y\right)=\begin{cases}1, & if\ P\left(x\right)<P\left(y\right)\\0, & if\ P\left(x\right)\geq P\left(y\right)\end{cases} \tag{8.42}$$

where $P(x)$ is the pixel value at location x. The set of location pairs is uniquely defined for the set of binary tests ($n(x,y)$). "n" is the size or length of binary feature vectors and the value will be chosen as 128, 256, and 512.
Step 4: The final BRIEF feature vector or descriptor is computed using

$$f_{n_d}\left(P\right)=\sum_{1\leq i\leq n_d}2^{i-1}\tau\left(P:X_i,Y_i\right) \tag{8.43}$$

where X_i and Y_i denote the location vectors.

Experiment 8.23: Computation of BRIEF Descriptor
This experiment deals with computing the BRIEF descriptor from an image using Python. The Python code to compute the BRIEF feature vector is given in Fig. 8.54, and its simulation result is depicted in Fig. 8.55.

Inferences
The following inferences can be drawn from this experiment:

- Figure 8.54 shows that the "CV2" library is imported, and "*cv2.xfeatures2d. StarDetector_create()*" Python command is used to initialize key points. "*cv2. xfeatures2d.BriefDescriptorExtractor_create()*" Python command is used to initialize the BRIEF descriptor. The BRIEF descriptor does not provide any method

```
# BRIEF Feature
import cv2
from matplotlib import pyplot as plt
I = cv2.imread('Clock.tiff',0)
star = cv2.xfeatures2d.StarDetector_create();# Initialize FAST detector
brief = cv2.xfeatures2d.BriefDescriptorExtractor_create();# Initialize BRIEF extractor
kp = star.detect(I,None);# find the keypoints with STAR
kp, des = brief.compute(I, kp);# compute the descriptors with BRIEF
I2 = cv2.drawKeypoints(I, kp, None, color=(255,0,0),
                    flags=cv2.DRAW_MATCHES_FLAGS_DRAW_RICH_KEYPOINTS)
plt.figure(figsize=(12,6)),plt.subplot(131),
plt.imshow(I,cmap="gray"),plt.title("Original image"),plt.axis('off'),
plt.subplot(132),plt.imshow(I2),plt.title(f"BRIEF Key points ({len(kp)})"),
plt.axis('off'),plt.subplot(133),plt.imshow(des),
plt.title(f"Descriptor ({des.shape})"),plt.axis('off')
plt.show()
```

Fig. 8.54 Computation of BRIEF features using cv2 library

Fig. 8.55 BRIEF features of "Clock" image

to find the features. Therefore, the STAR method is used here to initialize the feature vector.

- Figure 8.55 displays the input image and its BRIEF key points. Also shows the BRIEF descriptor with the size of (35 × 32).

8.4.4   Oriented FAST and Rotated BRIEF (ORB)

The ORB feature descriptor uses the idea of FAST key point detector and BRIEF descriptor. It is a very fast binary descriptor that is rotation-invariant and noise resistant.

Experiment 8.24: Computation ORB Descriptor

This experiment deals with computing the ORB descriptor from an image using Python. The Python code to compute the ORB feature vector is given in Fig. 8.56, and its simulation result is depicted in Fig. 8.57.

Inferences

The following inferences can be drawn from this experiment:

- Figure 8.56 shows that "CV2" library is imported and "*cv2.ORB_create()*" Python command is used to initialize the process. "*orb.detectAndCompute*" Python command is used to compute the ORB key points and descriptor.
- Figure 8.57 displays the input image, ORB key points, and descriptors. The radius of the circle denotes the magnitude of the feature points.

```
# ORB Feature extraction
import cv2
from matplotlib import pyplot as plt
I = cv2.imread('Clock.tiff',0)
orb = cv2.ORB_create(34)
kp, des = orb.detectAndCompute(I, None)
# Draw rich key points on input image
I1 = cv2.drawKeypoints(I,
kp,I,color=(255,0,0),flags=cv2.DRAW_MATCHES_FLAGS_DRAW_RICH_KEYPOINTS)
plt.figure(figsize=(12,6)),plt.subplot(131),
plt.imshow(I,cmap="gray"),plt.title("Original image"),plt.axis('off'),
plt.subplot(132),plt.imshow(I1),plt.title(f"ORB Key points ({len(kp)})"),
plt.axis('off'),plt.subplot(133),plt.imshow(des),
plt.title(f"Descriptor ({des.shape})"),plt.axis('off')
plt.show()
```

Fig. 8.56 Computation of ORB features using cv2 library

Fig. 8.57 ORB features of "Clock' image

8.5   Frequency-Based Features

Frequency-based features, such as Fourier descriptors, are a type of feature extraction method that captures the frequency content of an image. These features are often used in computer vision applications such as object recognition, texture analysis, data compression, and image retrieval. Frequency-based features are used in places with limited data and a requirement of rotational and spatial invariance.

8.5.1   Fourier Transform-Based Features

Fourier transform is a mathematical tool that converts the time domain signal into the frequency domain and vice versa. It uses the Fourier basis function for the conversion. The output of the Fourier transform contains the magnitude and phase information of the input image. It decomposes the input signal into multiple sines, cosines, and a constant signal. The output gives information about the signal at a particular frequency. Therefore, it is capable of converting the highly correlated signal into an uncorrelated spectrum. This uncorrelated spectrum can be used as a feature to represent an input signal.

Experiment 8.25: Fourier Transform-Based Feature Extraction
This experiment extracts the Fourier transform features from an image using Python. The Python code to extract the Fourier transform features is given in Fig. 8.58, and its simulation result is shown in Fig. 8.59.

Inferences
The following inferences can be drawn from this experiment:

- From Fig. 8.58, it is possible to observe that the "*cv2.dft*" Python command is used to find the Fourier features.
- *fftshift( )* command rearranges all frequency components into ascending order from negative to positive with the zero-frequency term in the centre. *fftshift( )* always puts the Nyquist term at the 0-index.
- For the reduction of the Fourier features, the mask within the certain radius is assigned to be one, and outside the radius is assumed to be zero, and it is multiplied with the fftshift output.
- Based on the radius of the mask, the reconstructed output will vary; if the radius of the mask is small, it blurs the image due to the loss of the high-frequency components, which is shown in Fig. 8.59.

```
import numpy as np
import cv2
from matplotlib import pyplot as plt
I = cv2.imread('Clock.tiff', 0)
DFT = cv2.dft(np.float32(I), flags=cv2.DFT_COMPLEX_OUTPUT)
shift = np.fft.fftshift(DFT)
rad=10
row, col = I.shape
center_row, center_col = row // 2, col // 2
mask = np.zeros((row, col, 2), np.uint8)
mask[center_row - rad:center_row + rad, center_col - rad:center_col + rad] = 1
fft_shift = shift * mask
fft_ifft_shift = np.fft.ifftshift(fft_shift)
I_Rec = cv2.idft(fft_ifft_shift)
M_IRec = cv2.magnitude(I_Rec[:,:,0], I_Rec[:,:,1])
P_IRec = cv2.phase(I_Rec[:,:,0], I_Rec[:,:,1])
plt.figure(figsize=(10,10))
plt.subplot(131), plt.imshow(I, cmap='gray')
plt.title('Input Image'), plt.xticks([]), plt.yticks([])
plt.subplot(132),plt.imshow(M_IRec, cmap='gray')
plt.title('Magnitude Output'), plt.xticks([]), plt.yticks([])
plt.subplot(133), plt.imshow(P_IRec, cmap='gray')
plt.title('Phase Output'), plt.xticks([]), plt.yticks([])
plt.show()
```

Fig. 8.58   Computation of FFT features using cv2 library

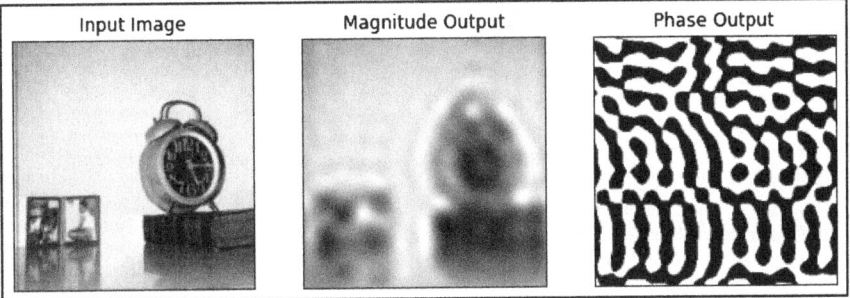

Fig. 8.59   FFT features of "clock" image

8.5.2   Wavelet Feature

Wavelet is a mathematical function that decomposes a signal into different frequency components and then studies each component with a resolution matched to
its multiresolution scale. Wavelet transform decomposes an image into four

different frequency components like "*LL*", "*LH*", "*HL*", and "*HH*" in the first level of decomposition, and then the "*LL*' subband only further decomposed into four subbands in the second level of decomposition and so on. In each level of decomposition, the size of each subband is half of the original size of the input (i.e. (M, N) is the size of the input image, then the size of the output subband will be $(M/2, N/2)$ where M and N should be an integer also the $(M/2, N/2)$ also will be an integer). The frequency components or coefficients of each subband act as wavelet features of the input image.

Experiment 8.26: Wavelet Feature Extraction

This experiment discusses the extraction of wavelet features from an input image using Python. The Python code to obtain the wavelet features from an image is given in Fig. 8.60, and its simulation result is shown in Fig. 8.61.

Inferences

The following inferences can be made from this experiment:

- From Fig. 8.60, it is possible to infer that the "pywt" library is imported to find the wavelet feature. "*pywt.dwt2()*" command is used here to obtain the wavelet coefficients.
- In this experiment, the first level of decomposition is done.
- "*pywt.threshold()*" command is used to retain the significant wavelet features, and insignificant wavelet features are made as zero.
- Figure 8.61 shows the original wavelet subbands and their corresponding thresholded (50) wavelet coefficients. The thresholded wavelet coefficients are less when compared to the original wavelet coefficients shown in the first row of Fig. 8.61.

```
import numpy as np
import matplotlib.pyplot as plt
import pywt
import cv2
I = cv2.imread('Clock.tiff', 0)
O_I=np.array(I)
coeffs = pywt.dwt2(O_I,"bior1.3")
th = 50
coeffs_th=[pywt.threshold(c,th,mode="soft") for c in coeffs]
#C_I = pywt.idwt2(coeffs_th,"bior1.3")
plt.figure(figsize=(8,5)),plt.subplot(241),plt.imshow(coeffs[0],cmap="gray")
plt.title("LL"),plt.axis("off"),plt.subplot(242),plt.imshow(coeffs[1][0],cmap="gray")
plt.title("LH"),plt.axis("off"),plt.subplot(243),plt.imshow(coeffs[1][1],cmap="gray")
plt.title("HL"),plt.axis("off"),plt.subplot(244),plt.imshow(coeffs[1][2],cmap="gray")
plt.title("HH"),plt.axis("off"),plt.subplot(245),plt.imshow(coeffs_th[0],cmap="gray")
plt.title(f"LL (Threshold = {th})"),plt.axis("off"),plt.subplot(246),
plt.imshow(coeffs_th[1][0],cmap="gray"),plt.title(f"LH (Threshold = {th})"),plt.axis("off"),
plt.subplot(247), plt.imshow(coeffs_th[1][1],cmap="gray"),plt.title(f"HL (Threshold = {th})"),
plt.axis("off"),plt.subplot(248),plt.imshow(coeffs_th[1][2].astype(np.uint8),cmap="gray")
plt.title(f"HH (Threshold = {th})"),plt.axis("off")
plt.tight_layout()
```

Fig. 8.60 Computation of biorthogonal wavelet features using pywt library

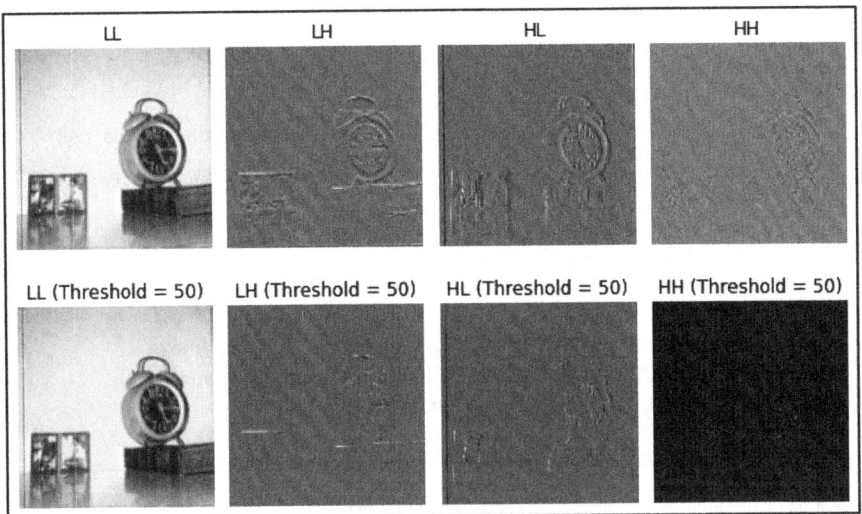

Fig. 8.61 Biorthogonal wavelet features of "Clock" image

8.5.3 Gabor Feature

The Gabor feature extraction process starts with the 2D Gabor filter being applied to the input image. The Gabor filter is a combination of the "Gaussian filter" and a "sinusoidal term". The process of the Gabor filter is guided by Gabor's uncertainty principle, which states that the product of frequency and time resolution must be greater than a constant. This principle helps in the selection of orientation and frequencies in a better way. The Gabor filter is mathematically defined as

$$G\left(x, y; \lambda, \theta, \psi, \sigma, \gamma\right) = e^{\left(-\frac{x'^2 + \gamma^2 y'^2}{2\sigma^2}\right)} e^{\left(j\left(2\pi\frac{x'}{\lambda} + \psi\right)\right)} \tag{8.44}$$

where $x' = x\cos\theta + y\sin\theta$, $y' = -x\sin\theta + y\cos\theta$. λ represents the wavelength of the sinusoidal factor, θ denotes the orientation, ψ represents phase offset, σ denotes the standard deviation of the Gaussian function, γ represents the aspect ratio of the spatial coordinates, and (x, y) is the spatial coordinates of the Gabor filter.

Experiment 8.27: Gabor Feature Extraction
This experiment deals with the Gabor feature extraction using Python. The Python code to compute the Gabor feature extraction is given in Fig. 8.62, and its corresponding output is shown in Fig. 8.63.

Inferences
The following inferences can be observed from this experiment:

- Figure 8.62 shows the Python code for the Gabor feature extraction, "*gabor_filter*" is written as a function in that the "*cv2.filter2D*" function is used to compute the filter output.

```
import cv2
import matplotlib.pyplot as plt
def gabor_filter(I, theta, sigma, lamda, gamma, psi):
    kernel = cv2.getGaborKernel((sigma, sigma), sigma, theta, lamda, gamma, psi)
    gabor_out = cv2.filter2D(I, cv2.CV_8UC3, kernel)
    return gabor_out
I = cv2.imread('Clock.tiff', 0)
theta,sigma,lamda,gamma, psi = 0, 5, 5, 1.5, 0.5
out = gabor_filter(I, theta, sigma, lamda, gamma, psi)
plt.figure(figsize=(10, 5))
plt.subplot(1, 2, 1), plt.imshow(I, cmap='gray'), plt.title('Original Image')
plt.xticks([]),plt.yticks([]),plt.subplot(1, 2, 2),plt.imshow(out, cmap='gray'),
plt.title('Gabor Features'),plt.xticks([]), plt.yticks([])
plt.show()
```

Fig. 8.62 Computation of Gabor features using cv2 library

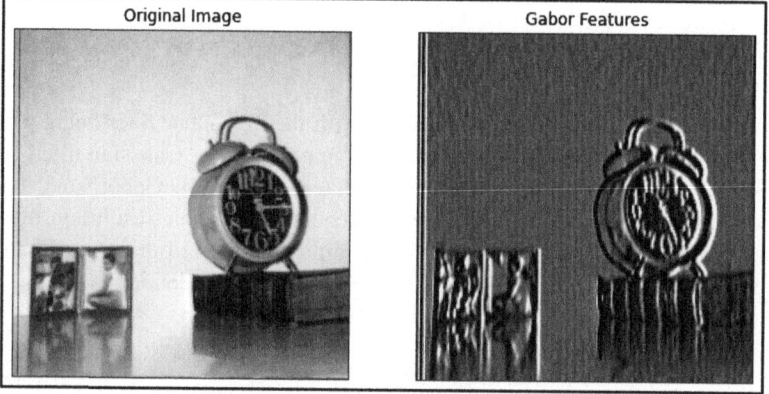

Fig. 8.63 Gabor features of "Clock" image

- Gabor features of the Clock image are shown in Fig. 8.63. Varying the Gabor filter parameters yields different Gabor features. This is the advantage of the Gabor filter.

8.6   Deep Features

Deep features are also called deep learning features or learned features, which are abstract and complex representations derived from the raw data during the neural network training process. The deep features are learned from the input data without explicit programming, allowing the deep learning model to uncover intricate patterns that might be difficult for humans to detect or compute. The deep learning model consists of a neural network with multiple layers, which are used to model the high-level abstractions in data. This model can be supervised or unsupervised learning for computer vision applications.

8.6.1   Convolutional Neural Networks (CNN)

CNNs are generally the preferred choice for feature extraction from images because CNNs are specifically designed for processing colour images and perform more complex tasks such as image classification, object detection, or segmentation, where they can extract complex and descriptive features with any variations such as lighting conditions, scale, and other factors in the image. It is useful in situations where high accuracy is preferred after processing the images, thus making it the most efficient way.

Experiment 8.28: CNN Feature Extraction of MNIST Dataset
This experiment discusses the computation of CNN features from the MNIST dataset using Python. The Python code to extract the CNN features is given in Fig. 8.64, and its corresponding output is shown in Fig. 8.65.

Inferences
The following inferences can be made from this experiment:

- From Fig. 8.64, it is possible to observe that the "*tensorflow*" library is used for the CNN feature computation. "*keras.Sequential*" command is used for CNN modelling, in that the "*Dense*" command receives the number of layers and size of the input as an input, and the "sigmoid" function acts as an activation function.
- The CNN features corresponding to the input test images are plotted, as shown in Fig. 8.65.

8.6.2   Autoencoders

Autoencoders can be used for feature extraction in scenarios where the CNN architecture is too computationally expensive or where the amount of labelled data is limited. In this application, the autoencoder is trained on a dataset of images and used to extract features that can be used in downstream machine-learning models. Autoencoders are generally used for unsupervised learning tasks such as anomaly detection, dimensionality reduction, image denoising, compression, and generation of new data points, the goal of which is to learn a compact representation of the input data. They are particularly useful when the input data is high-dimensional and noisy, as they can help to remove noise and extract relevant features. If the task requires supervised learning, such as image classification or object detection, CNNs are the better choice. In some cases, autoencoders and CNNs can be used together

```
from tensorflow import keras
#import tensorflow as tf
import matplotlib.pyplot as plt
import numpy as np
(x_train,y_train),(x_test,y_test)=keras.datasets.mnist.load_data()
plt.figure(figsize=(20,8)),plt.subplot(241),plt.imshow(x_test[2],cmap='gray'),
plt.title('Test Image-1'),plt.xticks([]), plt.yticks([]),
plt.subplot(242),plt.imshow(x_test[25],cmap='gray'),plt.title('Test Image-2')
plt.xticks([]), plt.yticks([]),plt.subplot(243),plt.imshow(x_test[100],cmap='gray'),
plt.title('Test Image-3'),plt.xticks([]), plt.yticks([]),plt.subplot(244),
plt.imshow(x_test[5000],cmap='gray'),plt.title('Test Image-4'),
plt.xticks([]),plt.yticks([])
x_train=x_train/255
x_test=x_test/255
x_train_flatten = x_train.reshape(len(x_train),28*28)
x_train_flatten.shape
x_test_flattened = x_test.reshape(len(x_test),28*28)
x_test_flattened.shape
model=keras.Sequential([keras.layers.Dense(10,input_shape=(784,),activation='sigmoid')])
model.compile(optimizer='adam',loss='sparse_categorical_crossentropy',metrics=['accuracy'])
model.fit(x_train_flatten,y_train,epochs=5)
model.evaluate(x_test_flattened,y_test)
y_predicted=model.predict(x_test_flattened)
x=np.arange(0,y_predicted.shape[1])
plt.subplot(245),plt.stem(x,y_predicted[2,:]),plt.xticks(x),plt.xlabel('Feature No.'),
plt.ylabel('Feature value'), plt.title('Test Image-1 CNN features')
plt.subplot(246),plt.stem(x,y_predicted[25,:]),plt.xticks(x),plt.xlabel('Feature No.'),
plt.ylabel('Feature value'),plt.title('Test Image-2 CNN features')
plt.subplot(247),plt.stem(x,y_predicted[100,:]),plt.xticks(x),plt.xlabel('Feature No.'),
plt.ylabel('Feature value'),plt.title('Test Image-3 CNN features')
plt.subplot(248),plt.stem(x,y_predicted[5000,:]),plt.xticks(x),plt.xlabel('Feature No.'),
plt.ylabel('Feature value'), plt.title('Test Image-4 CNN features')
plt.show()
```

Fig. 8.64 Computation of CNN features using "TensorFlow" library

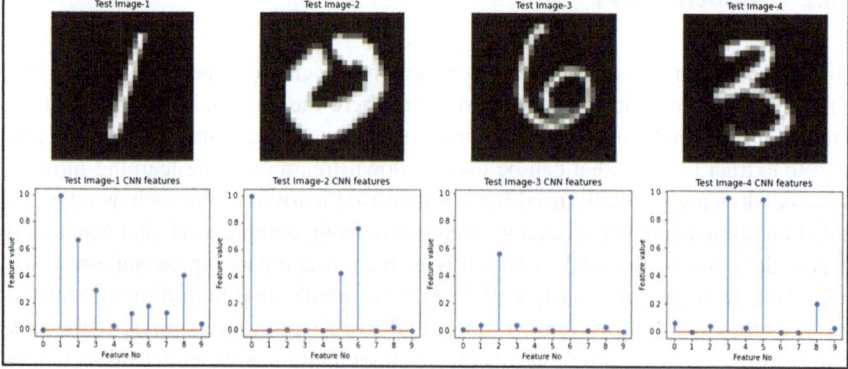

Fig. 8.65 CNN features of sample MNIST data

for feature extraction. For example, in transfer learning, an autoencoder can be used to extract features from an image dataset, which can then be fine-tuned using a smaller labelled dataset using a CNN. The features learned by the autoencoder can act as a starting point for CNN to improve its performance.

ResNet18

ResNet18 is a residual network family with a 72-layer architecture with 18 deep layers. The aim of this architecture is to enable large amounts of convolutional layers to function efficiently. The addition of multiple deep layers to a network creates degradation in the output. This is known as the problem of vanishing gradient where neural networks, while getting trained through the backpropagation mechanism, rely on gradient descent, descending the loss function to find the minimizing weights. The primary idea of ResNet is the use of jumping connections, which are mostly referred to as shortcut connections or identity connections. These shortcut connections remove the vanishing gradient issue by again using the activations of the previous layer. ResNet18 uses batch normalization and ReLU activation functions in the process.

Experiment 8.29: Encoder Feature (ResNet18) Extraction

This experiment discusses the ResNet18 feature extraction using Python. The Python code computes the ResNet18 features given in Fig. 8.66, and its corresponding output is shown in Fig. 8.67.

Inferences

The following inferences can be drawn from this experiment:

- From Fig. 8.66, it is possible to observe that the input image is resized into 224×224, and pretrained 'resnet18' is used for the feature extraction.
- The extracted features with different layers are displayed in Fig. 8.67. The sizes of the feature vectors are reduced.

Exercises

1. Read the RGB colour image and convert it into *YCbCr* format using Python. Also, compute the colour moments for each channel.
2. Write a Python code to compute the remaining GLCM features (other than the five features discussed in this chapter) of a grayscale image.
3. Write a Python code to compute the local binary pattern (LBP) features with the number of points in a neighbourhood as 24 (i.e. a 5×5 window).
4. Execute the Python code given in Fig. 8.34 with the size of the image patch or pixels_per_cell (16, 16) and comment on the observed HOG image and length of the HOG feature vector.
5. Obtain the Laplacian edge features of the "Clock" image with the size of the Laplacian kernel as 5×5.
6. Write a Python code to extract the second-level decomposed wavelet features of the "Cameraman" image. Comment on the observed result.
7. Extract the Gabor feature of the "Clock" image with a standard deviation of 20, orientation of $45°$, and spatial aspect ratio of 2.5. Comment on the observed result.

```
import torch
import torch.nn as nn
from torchvision import models, transforms
import matplotlib.pyplot as plt
from PIL import Image
import numpy as np
transform = transforms.Compose([transforms.Resize((224, 224)),transforms.ToTensor(),
   transforms.Normalize(mean=0., std=1.)])
I = Image.open(str('tools.jpg'))
I1=I;
model = models.resnet18(pretrained=True)
#print('Model',model)
model_weights, conv_layers = [], []
model_children = list(model.children())
counter = 0
for i in range(len(model_children)):
   if type(model_children[i]) == nn.Conv2d:
      counter+=1
      model_weights.append(model_children[i].weight)
      conv_layers.append(model_children[i])
   elif type(model_children[i]) == nn.Sequential:
      for j in range(len(model_children[i])):
         for child in model_children[i][j].children():
            if type(child) == nn.Conv2d:
               counter+=1
               model_weights.append(child.weight)
               conv_layers.append(child)
print(f"Total convolution layers: {counter}")
device = torch.device('cuda' if torch.cuda.is_available() else 'cpu')
model = model.to(device)
I = transform(I)
print(f"I shape before: {I.shape}")
I = I.unsqueeze(0)
print(f"I shape after: {I.shape}")
I = I.to(device)
outputs, names = [], []
for layer in conv_layers[0:]:
   I = layer(I)
   outputs.append(I)
   names.append(str(layer))
print(len(outputs))
```

Fig. 8.66 Computation of autoencoder features using torch library

```
#print feature_maps
for feature_map in outputs:
    print(feature_map.shape)
processed = []
for feature_map in outputs:
    feature_map = feature_map.squeeze(0)
    gray_scale = torch.sum(feature_map,0)
    gray_scale = gray_scale / feature_map.shape[0]
    processed.append(gray_scale.data.cpu().numpy())
# for fm in processed:
#     print(fm.shape)
fig = plt.figure(figsize=(2*len(processed), len(processed)))
a = fig.add_subplot(int(np.ceil(len(processed)/6)), 6, 1)
imgplot = plt.imshow(l1),a.axis("off")
a.set_title('Input image', fontsize=30)
for i in range(len(processed)):
    a = fig.add_subplot(int(np.ceil(len(processed)/6)), 6, i+2)
    imgplot = plt.imshow(processed[i])
    a.axis("off"),a.set_title(names[i].split('(')[0]+''+(f"{processed[i].shape}"), fontsize=30)
plt.savefig(str('feature_maps.jpg'), bbox_inches='tight')
```

Fig. 8.66   (continued)

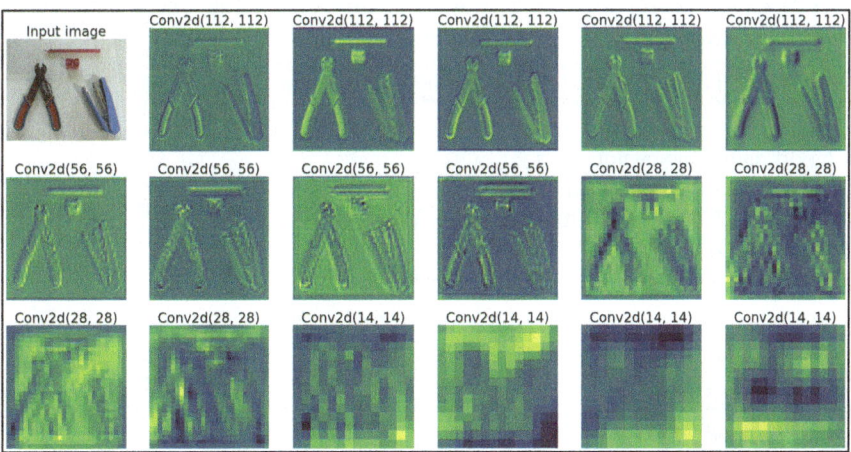

Fig. 8.67   Autoencoder features for tools image

8. Write a Python code to extract the deep encoder features of ResNet50 and comment on the observed result.
9. Write a Python code to extract the deep encoder features of LSTM (Long Short Term Memory) and comment on the observed result.
10. Write a Python code to extract the deep encoder features of GRU (Gated Recurrent Unit) and comment on the observed result.

Objective Questions

1. Which one is the visual appearance feature in the image?

    (A) GLCM
    (B) SIFT
    (C) CNN
    (D) Histogram

2. The example of a shape feature is _____.

    (A) Colour
    (B) LBP
    (C) Wavelet
    (D) Canny

3. The histogram of an image is defined as

    (A) Graphical representation of the frequency of pixels in an image as a function of their intensity.
    (B) Edge map of the image
    (C) Conversion of the spatial information of the image into frequency information.
    (D) Graphical representation of the intensity of an image as a function of frequency.

4. What will be the output after executing the following Python code?

```
import cv2
import matplotlib.pyplot as plt
I1=cv2.imread('greenredapples.jpg')
I2 = cv2.cvtColor(I1, cv2.COLOR_BGR2GRAY)
plt.imshow(I2),plt.axis('off')
```

    (A)

    (B)

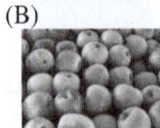

(C)

(D)

5. The input image patch is given by $\begin{bmatrix} 128 & 90 & 101 \\ 88 & [100] & 87 \\ 101 & 99 & 100 \end{bmatrix}$. What will be the LBP of the centre pixel "100'.

    (A) 170

    (B) 100

    (C) 99.33

    (D) 255

6. The Python command for the HOG feature computation using the "scikit" library is

    (A) hog.descriptor

    (B) HoG.descriptor

    (C) hog

    (D) hog.compute

7. The following filter can be used for emphasize the edges in the image.

    (A) Laplacian

    (B) Canny

    (C) Roberts

    (D) Sobel

8. An example of a domain-specific feature is

    (A) Histogram

    (B) LBP

    (C) SIFT

    (D) DFT

9. Which filter is used to compute the Gabor feature?

    (A) Laplacian

    (B) Highpass

    (C) Hessian

    (D) Gaussian

10. ResNet18 contains _____ layer architecture in that _____ deep convolutional layers.

    (A) 64, 18
    (B) 72, 50
    (C) 72, 18
    (D) 18, 72

11. Statement 1: Autoencoders are a supervised learning technique

    Statement 2: Autoencoder's output is exactly same as the input.

    (A) Statements 1 and 2 are true
    (B) Statement 1 is true, Statement 2 is false
    (C) Statement 1 is false, Statement 2 is true
    (D) Statements 1 and 2 are false

12. The concept of zero crossing is employed by

    (A) Robert operator
    (B) Prewitt operator
    (C) Laplacian operator
    (D) Sobel operator

Answers to Objective Questions

Q. No.	1	2	3	4	5	6	7	8	9	10	11	12
Key	D	D	A	A	A	C	A	C	D	C	D	C

Answers to PreLab Questions

1. Image features are parts or patterns of an object in an image that help to identify it. They contain edges and interest points of an object in an image, which provides rich information about the object in an image.
2. The image features are broadly classified into (1) General and (2) Domain-specific features. The general features include colour, texture, and shape features. Domain-specific features are further classified into (1) fingerprint, (2) human face, and (3) conceptual features.
3. Colour is an important feature that helps humans recognize images easily. It is also one of the most widely used low-level visual features, and it is invariant to image size and orientation.
4. Texture is a low-level visual feature that can distinguish the regions of interest in an image. It refers to an object's instinctive surface properties and contains information about the structural arrangement of surfaces and their relationship with the surroundings. For example, texture features can identify whether an object is soft or rough.

5. HOG means a histogram of gradient features or descriptors, and it can be obtained at a specified location. The following steps are involved in HOG computation:

   (a) Compute image gradient magnitudes and orientations or directions over the whole image. Using thresholding, make small gradient magnitudes as zero.
   (b) Centre the cell grid on an image location.
   (c) For each cell, form an orientation histogram by quantizing the gradient directions; add the thresholded gradient magnitudes for each such orientation bin.
   (d) Stack the histograms into a 1D array of length [number of orientation bins × number of cells].
   (e) Normalize the 1D array values, which will be HOG features.

6. The important GLCM features are (1) Contrast, (2) Dissimilarity, (3) Homogeneity, (4) Angular second moment, and (5) Correlation.

7. SIFT stands for scale invariant feature transform features based on detecting key points and extracting local feature descriptors. SIFT features are invariant to scale, orientation, and affine transformations. Therefore, it can be preferred for computer vision applications like object recognition, image stitching, and 3D reconstruction.

8. The advantages of local features are as follows:

   (a) Locality: The features are local and robust to occlusion and clutter.
   (b) Distinctiveness: It can easily differentiate an extensive database of objects.
   (c) Quantity: A single image has hundreds or thousands of features.
   (d) Efficiency: It is used in real-time environment.
   (e) Generality: It can exploit different features in different situations.

9. Handcrafted features refer to manually designed, domain-specific features that are extracted from images for a specific task which include techniques like scale-invariant feature transform (SIFT), histogram of oriented gradients (HOG), speeded-up robust features (SURF), local binary pattern (LBP), etc. Deep features are learned features that are automatically obtained from deep learning algorithms.

10. An autoencoder is a type of neural network designed to learn data representations, typically for unsupervised learning tasks. The autoencoders can capture meaningful patterns in data by compressing the data into a lower-dimensional space and then reconstructing it.

11. The major components of the autoencoder are (1) Encoder, (2) Decoder, and (3) Latent space representation. The encoder compresses data into a lower-dimensional space. The latent space, or the bottleneck layer, is the layer where data is compressed and from where the decoder generates the reconstruction. The decoder reconstructs the compressed data back to the original input space.

12. Feature extraction transforms arbitrary data into a numerical feature. Feature selection is a dimensionality reduction technique. Dimensionality reduction is the process of reducing the number of features in a dataset while retaining the salient features. The feature selection is necessary to reduce the computational complexity, and avoid overfitting problems.

Bibliography

1. Richard Duda, Peter hart and David Stork, "Pattern Classification", Wiley,2007.
2. Christopher M. Bishop, "Pattern Recognition and Machine Learning", Springer, 2006.
3. Sergios Theoridis, Konstantinos Koutroumbas, "Pattern Recognition", Academic Press, 2008.
4. Edward Rosten and Tom Drummond, "Machine learning for high-speed corner detection" in 9th European Conference on Computer Vision, vol. 1, 2006, pp. 430–443.
5. Edward Rosten, Reid Porter, and Tom Drummond, "Faster and better: a machine learning approach to corner detection" in IEEE Trans. Pattern Analysis and Machine Intelligence, 2010, vol 32, pp. 105-119.
6. Michael Calonder, Vincent Lepetit, Christoph Strecha, and Pascal Fua, "BRIEF: Binary Robust Independent Elementary Features", 11th European Conference on Computer Vision (ECCV), Heraklion, Crete. LNCS Springer, September 2010.
7. Deng, L. (2012). The MNIST database of handwritten digit images for machine learning research. IEEE Signal Processing Magazine, 29(6), 141–142.
8. Robert. M. Haralick, K. Shanmugam and I. Dinstein, "Textural Features for Image Classification," in IEEE Transactions on Systems, Man, and Cybernetics, vol. SMC-3, no. 6, pp. 610-621, Nov. 1973.

Chapter 9
Image Compression

Learning Objectives

After reading this chapter, the reader can able to

- Understand terminologies and meanings related to image compression.
- Understand the different types of image compression.
- Perform the lossless compression of the digital images.
- Perform the lossy compression of the digital images.
- Understand the dictionary-based image compression scheme.
- Implement transform-based image compression scheme.

Roadmap of the Chapter

The roadmap of the chapter is given in the form of a flowchart below (Fig. 9.1):

PreLab Questions

1. What is the objective of image compression?
2. What are the types of image compression schemes?
3. Name a few lossless compression schemes.
4. List out the lossy compression algorithm.
5. What do you mean by spatial redundancy?
6. What do you mean by spectral redundancy?
7. What is psychovisual redundancy, and how can it be minimized?
8. What is coding redundancy? And how it could be removed?
9. What is the significance of entropy?
10. How do you evaluate the performance of lossless compression algorithm?
11. What performance metrics are used to evaluate the lossy compression schemes?

Supplementary Information The online version contains supplementary material available at https://doi.org/10.1007/978-981-96-6382-8_9.

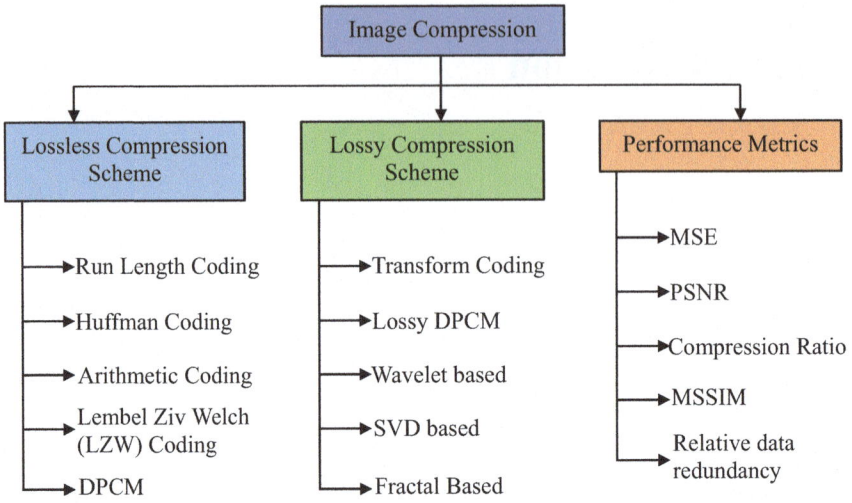

Fig. 9.1 Road map of the chapter

12. Which transform technique is used in the well-known JPEG image compression standard?
13. What is fractal image compression?

9.1   Introduction

Image compression is an algorithm that represents image data with fewer bits without degrading the image quality or information. Image compression can be achieved by reducing the redundancy present in an image. The redundancy of the image is classified into four types (1) Spatial redundancy, (2) Spectral redundancy, (3) Coding redundancy, and (4) Psychovisual redundancy.

9.2   Spatial Redundancy or Interpixel Redundancy

Spatial redundancy exploits the similarity or correlation across different pixels of an image. It is also known as interpixel redundancy. This allows a pixel value to be estimated from its neighbouring pixel. If the neighbouring pixel values are the same, then it contains high spatial redundancy, which will be reduced by any transform technique or run length coding.

An image block is shown in Fig. 9.2, which highlights the high and low spatial redundant information. From this figure, it is possible to observe that the encircled

Fig. 9.2 Image block

15	15	15	100	90	85
15	(15)	15	102	89	80
15	15	15	100	85	79
0	50	100	100	90	85
150	200	0	102	89	80
0	15	50	100	85	79

pixel value, and its closest neighbours take a similar value, which has high spatial redundancy, whereas the pixel marked as square and its neighbouring pixels are different. It shows that the pixel has less spatial redundancy with its neighbourhoods. Generally, a smooth region in an image contains high spatial redundancy, and the edge portion has very less spatial redundancy.

9.3 Spectral Redundancy

Spectral redundancy exists in the colour images. In general, the colour image is a combination of three primary colours like red, green, and blue. Each colour component can represent the information of the image content. The correlation between the colour bands is called spectral redundancy. The spectral redundancy can be minimized by using the sub-sampling process and converting the RGB to YUV, RGB to YCbCr, and RGB to HSI.

Experiment 9.1: Write a Python Code to Prove That the Colour Image Has Redundant Information, and Conversion of RGB to YUV Removes the Redundant Information

This experiment deals with the conversion of RGB to YUV using Python. The Python code to perform this task is shown in Fig. 9.3, and its simulation result is shown in Fig. 9.4. From Fig. 9.3, it is possible to observe that the built-in command "cv2.cvtColor(C_img, cv2.COLOR_RGB2YUV)" is used.

Inferences

From Fig. 9.4, the following inferences can be made

- The information contained in red, green, and blue components are similar to each other. From these figures, we can get information on the input image. Therefore, red, green, and blue information are redundant.
- The second row of Fig. 9.4 is the output of the Y, U, and V components, giving different information about the input image. The Y component gives the luminance component of the input image (i.e. it carries more information about the input image). Whereas U and V are the chrominance components, they carry colour information, and these two are non-redundant.
- Therefore from this experiment, the redundant information in RGB image can be removed by using RGB to YUV conversion.

```
import cv2
import matplotlib.pyplot as plt
C_img = cv2.imread('Seg1.jpeg')
YUV = cv2.cvtColor(C_img,  cv2.COLOR_RGB2YUV)
plt.figure(),plt.subplot(2,3,1),
plt.imshow(C_img[:,:,0],cmap='gray'),plt.title('Red'),plt.axis('off')
plt.subplot(2,3,2),plt.imshow(C_img[:,:,1],cmap='gray'),plt.title('Green'),plt.axis('off')
plt.subplot(2,3,3),plt.imshow(C_img[:,:,2],cmap='gray'),plt.title('Blue'),plt.axis('off')
plt.subplot(2,3,4),plt.imshow(YUV[:,:,0],cmap='gray'),plt.title('Y'),plt.axis('off')
plt.subplot(2,3,5),plt.imshow(YUV[:,:,1],cmap='gray'),plt.title('U'),plt.axis('off')
plt.subplot(2,3,6),plt.imshow(YUV[:,:,2],cmap='gray'),plt.title('V'),plt.axis('off')
```

Fig. 9.3 Python code for RGB to YUV conversion

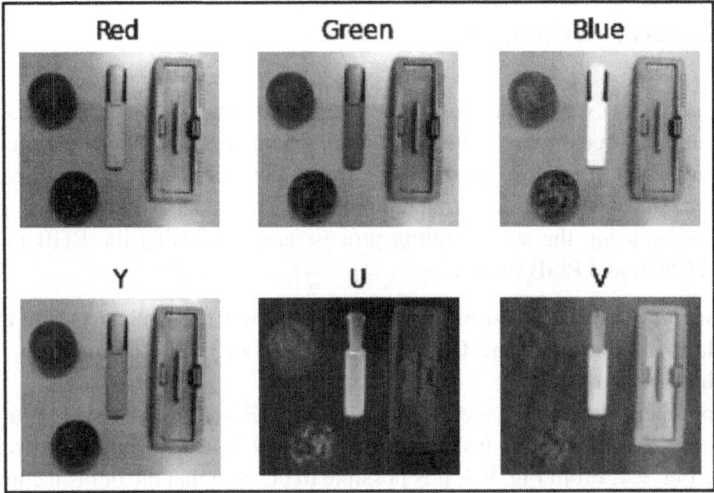

Fig. 9.4 Result of Python code given in Fig. 9.3

Tasks

1. Perform the RGB to L*a*b* conversion and verify the representation of information in both colour spaces. [Hint: Use cv.COLOR_RGB2Lab].
2. Perform the RGB to L*a*b* conversion and verify the representation of information in both colour spaces. [Hint: Use cv2.COLOR_RGB2HSV].
3. Perform the RGB to Lab conversion and verify the representation of information in both colour spaces. [Hint: Use cv2.COLOR_RGB2YCrCb].
4. Write Python code to get the RGB colour image back in YCrCb format. [Hint: Use cv2.COLOR_YCrCb2RGB].

9.4   Coding Redundancy

In general, data can be in the form of symbols, which will be the pixel value of the image data. Those symbols are encoded by the codes, and the length of the codes plays a major role in the image compression. The smaller length code is used to encode the more frequently occurring symbols, and the larger length of the code is used for the symbols that rarely occur. This will achieve the image compression. For example, the probability of the symbols is denoted by

$$P(X_k) = \frac{m_k}{M}, \quad \text{for } k = 0,1,2,\ldots,L-1 \tag{9.1}$$

where X_k is the symbol, m_k denotes the number of occurrences, and M is the length of the data. Total number of unique symbols is L. The length of the code for each symbol is denoted as $l(X_k)$. The average number of bits needed to represent the whole data is measured by

$$L_{avg} = \sum_{k=0}^{L-1} l(X_k) P(X_k) \tag{9.2}$$

Use the variable length code like Huffman coding to represent each symbol. The average length of the code will be less than the actual length of the code. Therefore, the Huffman coding can be used to reduce the coding redundancy by the lesser number of bits allotted to the more probability symbol and a larger number of bits allotted to the less probability symbol. For example, the word to be encoded is "SUCCESS". The probability of each symbol is given by $\{C = 2/7, E = 1/7, S = 3/7, U = 1/7\}$. Based on the higher probability, the following binary code is assigned for each symbol $\{S = $ "1", $C = $ "00", $E = $ "010", $U = $ "011"$\}$. The encoded bitstream of word "SUCCESS" based on the above binary code, we get $\{$"1011000001011"$\}$. The total number of bits in the encoded bitstream is 13. Assume that the symbol uses 8-bit ASCII code, and to transmit the word "SUCCESS", it takes (7×8) 56 bits, whereas by using the binary code assigned for each symbol based on its probability; it takes only 13 bits. Now, the compression ratio will be $(56/13 = 4.3077)$, achieved by the coding redundancy in the input data. Using proper coding techniques like Shannon Fano, Huffman, and Runlength Coding will reduce the coding redundancy.

9.5   Psychovisual Redundancy

Psychovisual redundancy exists due to the inability of human perception to slight variations in the original data. The human visual system is more responsive to slow variations and gradual changes of illumination than perceiving finer details and rapid variations of intensities. For example, the human eye is more sensitive to

Fig. 9.5 Psychovisual
redundancy. (**a**) Original
image. (**b**) Compressed
image

(a) Original image   **(b) Compressed image**

differences between dark intensities than bright ones and differences between different shades of green than red or blue. These considerations of varying sensitivity of the human eye to colours and their intensities contribute to psychovisual redundancies. For human visual perception, certain information has less relative importance. For example, the grayscale image is quantized by a lesser number of bits, the human eye may not notice the difference, that loss of information is called "Psychovisual Redundancy". This redundancy can be observed in Fig. 9.5. From this figure, the first image is the original 8-bit grayscale image, and the second one is the vector (LBG) quantized image. For the human eye is very difficult to notice the error between these two images.

9.6   Performance Metrics

There are many performance metrics that are currently available to verify the performance of the image compression algorithms. In this section, a few performance metrics like compression ratio, compression factor, mean square error, peak signal-to-noise ratio, and mean structural similarity index measure are discussed. These metrics are widely used to analyze the performance of the compression algorithm.

9.6.1   Compression Ratio

Compression ratio (CR) is a measure that is used to quantify the amount of data or input compressed. It is the ratio between the size of the original image and the size of the compressed (encoded) image. The mathematical expression for the compression ratio is given by

$$\text{Compression Ratio}(\text{CR}) = \frac{\text{Size of the original image}}{\text{Size of the Compressed image}} \tag{9.3}$$

9.6.2 *Relative Data Redundancy (R)*

The relative data redundancy is a quantifiable measure of compression that gives a range of values from 0 to 1. The relative data redundancy is calculated as

$$\text{Relative data redundancy}\,(R) = \left(1 - \frac{1}{\text{CR}}\right) \tag{9.4}$$

9.6.3 *PSNR*

The performance of the decompressed image can be quantified by using Peak Signal to Noise Ratio (PSNR) in dB. The mathematical expression for the PSNR in dB is given by

$$\text{PSNR in dB} = 20\log_{10}\left(\frac{\max(X)}{\sqrt{\text{MSE}}}\right) \tag{9.5}$$

where "X" represents the input original image and max(X) denotes the maximum pixel value of the original image. MSE indicates the mean square error between the original image (X) and the reconstructed or decompressed image (Y). The MSE can be obtained by using

$$\text{MSE} = \frac{1}{MN}\sum_{m=0}^{M-1}\sum_{n=0}^{N-1}\left(X(m,n) - Y(m,n)\right)^2 \tag{9.6}$$

where "M" and "N" denote the number of rows and columns of the image, respectively.

9.6.4 *MSSIM*

The structural similarity index measure is a perception-based model. In this measure, image degradation is considered as the change of perception in structural information. It measures the similarity between two images. It compares the similarity between the local regions of the two images. The mathematical expression used to compute SSIM is given by

$$\text{SSIM}_i(X,Y) = \frac{\left(2\mu_X\mu_Y + C_1\right)\left(2\sigma_X\sigma_Y + C_2\right)}{\left(\mu_X^2 + \mu_Y^2 C_1\right)\left(\sigma_X^2 + \sigma_{Y+}^2 C_2\right)} \tag{9.7}$$

where μ_X and μ_Y are local means of the image X and Y, respectively. σ_X and σ_Y are the local standard deviations of the images X and Y, respectively. C_1 and C_2 are the constants. "i" represents the ith local region or block of the image. From Eq. (9.7), it is possible to observe that the input images are subdivided into multiple blocks, SSIM is measured for each block, and the overall SSIM of the image is calculated by the average of the SSIMs. It is called as Mean SSIM and computed as

$$\text{MSSIM}(X,Y) = \frac{1}{K} \sum_{i=1}^{K} \text{SSIM}_i(X,Y) \tag{9.8}$$

where "K" is the number of blocks or local regions.

9.7   Lossless Compression Scheme

The lossless compression scheme is used to compress the input data and get back the original data from the compressed data. In this scheme, there is no loss between the input and reconstructed data. Hence, it is called a "Lossless compression scheme". Some of the lossless schemes are Run Length Encoding, Huffman Coding, Arithmetic Coding, Lembel Ziv coding, Differential Pulse Code Modulation without quantizer, etc.

9.7.1   Entropy

Entropy is a measure, which gives the average number of bits needed to code the symbol in the source. The entropy can be measured by using

$$H = -\sum_{i=1}^{N} p_i \log_2(p_i) \, \text{bits}/\text{symbol} \tag{9.9}$$

where p_i denotes the probability of the ith symbol and N denotes the number of unique symbols in the source data. The sum of the probability of the symbols in the source must be equal to one.

Experiment 9.2: Obtain the Entropy of the Cameraman Image
This experiment discusses the computation of entropy measure of the grayscale image. The Python code to perform this task is shown in Fig. 9.6a, and its simulation result is depicted in Fig. 9.6b.

Inferences

- From Fig. 9.6, it is possible to observe that the input image is a "cameraman" image and it is a grayscale image. It takes a value between 0 and 255.
- The entropy of the cameraman image is 7.0097 bits/symbol. It shows that the 7.0097 bits are needed to represent each pixel or symbol.

```
import cv2
import numpy as np
#Step 1: Reading the image
I1=cv2.imread('cameraman.tif',0)
(m,n)=I1.shape
#Step 2: Obtaining the histograms
hist1 = cv2.calcHist ([I1], [0], None, [256], [0, 256]);
P=hist1/(m*n);
H=[0]
for i in range(len(P)):
  if P[i]>0:
    H1=(-P[i])*np.log2(P[i])
    H=H+H1
print('Entropy =',H,'bits/symbol')
```

Entropy = [7.00971628] bits/symbol

| (a) Python code | (b) Entropy output |

Fig. 9.6 Entropy measure of cameraman image. (**a**) Python code. (**b**) Entropy output

```
import cv2
import numpy as np
I1=np.zeros([8,8],'uint8')
I1[2:6,2:6]=255
I1[(1,6),1:7]=128
(m,n)=I1.shape
hist1 = cv2.calcHist ([I1], [0], None, [256], [0, 256]);
P=hist1/(m*n);# Probability of each pixel
H=[0]
for i in range(len(P)):
  if P[i]>0:
    H1=(-P[i])*np.log2(P[i])
    H=H+H1
print('Input image:', I1)
print('Entropy =',H,'bits/symbol')
```

Input image: [[0   0   0   0   0   0   0   0]
 [0 128 128 128 128 128 128   0]
 [0   0 255 255 255 255   0   0]
 [0   0 255 255 255 255   0   0]
 [0   0 255 255 255 255   0   0]
 [0   0 255 255 255 255   0   0]
 [0 128 128 128 128 128 128   0]
 [0   0   0   0   0   0   0   0]]
Entropy = [1.41973677] bits/symbol

| (a) Python code | (b) Entropy output |

Fig. 9.7 Entropy measure of the three gray level images. (**a**) Python code. (**b**) Entropy output

Experiment 9.3: Generate an Image of Size 8 × 8 with the Pixel Values 0, 128, and 255. Obtain the Entropy of the Image and Comment on the Observed Result

This experiment deals with the generation of 8 × 8 image with three gray levels 0, 128, and 255. Also, it computes the entropy of the input image. The Python code to perform this task is given in Fig. 9.7a, and its entropy result is depicted in Fig. 9.7b.

Inference

From Fig. 9.7b, it is possible to observe that there are three gray levels (0, 128, 255) in an image, and the image size is 8 by 8. The entropy is 1.4197 bits/pixel, and it is

```
import numpy as np
l1=np.zeros([8,8],'uint8')
l1[2:6,2:6]=255
l1[(1,6),1:7]=128
_, occur = np.unique(l1, return_counts=True)
# Frequency of occurrence
occur = occur.astype(np.foat64)
occur /= l1.size; # probability
 # Calculate the entropy of the image using the
normalised counts
H = -np.sum(occur * np.log2(occur))
print('Input image:', l1)
print('Entropy =',H,'bits/symbol')
```

```
Input image: [[ 0  0  0  0  0  0  0  0]
 [ 0 128 128 128 128 128 128  0]
 [ 0  0 255 255 255 255  0  0]
 [ 0  0 255 255 255 255  0  0]
 [ 0  0 255 255 255 255  0  0]
 [ 0  0 255 255 255 255  0  0]
 [ 0 128 128 128 128 128 128  0]
 [ 0  0  0  0  0  0  0  0]]
Entropy = 1.4197367178034825
```

| (a) Python code | (b) Entropy output |

Fig. 9.8 Entropy measure of the three gray level images. (**a**) Python code. (**b**) Entropy output

evident that the number of gray levels or symbols is less in an image, more redundant occur. If the entropy is less, then lesser number of bits is required to represent a pixel or symbol.

Experiment 9.4: Computation Entropy of an Image (Method-2)

This experiment deals with the generation of image 8×8 with three gray levels 0, 128, and 255. Also, the entropy of the input image is computed using only "numpy" library. The Python code to perform this task is given in Fig. 9.8a, and its entropy result is shown in Fig. 9.8b.

Inferences

- From Fig. 9.8b, it is possible to observe that there are three gray levels (0, 128, 255) in an image, and the image size is 8 by 8.
- The entropy is 1.4197 bits/pixel, and it is evident that the number of gray levels or symbols is less in an image, there is more redundancy in the image.
- Entropy is a measure of information content in the input image.

Task: Generate 8×8 binary image, calculate its entropy value, and comment on the observed result.

9.7.2 Run Length Encoding

The run length encoding is a lossless compression scheme, which takes the string of characters as an input and counts the number of characters that are repeated in the string. The output of the RLE is count and character. This coding can be used for data compression. For example, let us consider the input string to the RLE as "AAAAAACCCCCCC" and the output of RLE will be "6A7C". That is, the format of the encoded string is (Run, Repeated Character).

```
I1="AMMAAPPA"
enc_out,count,prev, bits = [], 0, None, 16;
for c in I1:
    if prev==None:
        prev = c
        count+=1
    else:
        if prev!=c:
            enc_out.append((count, prev))
            prev=c
            count=1
        else:
            if count<(2**bits)-1:
                count+=1
            else:
                enc_out.append((count, prev))
                prev=c
                count=1
enc_out.append((count, prev))
print('Input string:',I1)
print('Encoded output:',enc_out)
```

Input string: AMMAAPPA
Encoded output: [(1, 'A'), (2, 'M'), (2, 'A'), (2, 'P'), (1, 'A')]

(a) Python Code   (b) Result

Fig. 9.9 Python code and its result of RLE. (**a**) Python code. (**b**) Result

Experiment 9.5: Write a Python Code to Obtain the Encoded String of Input String Using Run Length Encoding

This experiment discusses the encoding of the input string using run-length coding. The Python code to perform this task is shown in Fig. 9.9a, and its simulation result of the encoded output is shown in Fig. 9.9b.

Inferences

From this experiment, the following inferences can be drawn:

- The input data is string, and the output of the RLE is also string.
- From the output, the first character denotes the run length of the character and the second character is the character of the string.
- The input data contains more repetition of the same character, which implies more redundancy in the input data, hence good compression can be achieved.

Tasks

1. Execute the Python code given in Fig. 9.9a with the input string "AAAAAAAAAAAAABBBBBBBBBBBB" and comment on the observed output.
2. Execute the Python code given in Fig. 9.9a with the input string "ABABABABABABABABABABABABA" and comment on the observed output.

Experiment 9.6: Write a Python Code to Decode the RLE Output

This experiment helps us to get back the input string from the compressed RLE output. The Python code to perform this task is shown in Fig. 9.10a, and its simulation result is depicted in Fig. 9.10b.

```
# RLE decoding for grayscale image
enc_out=[(12, 'A'), (12, 'B')]
De_out=""
for rl in enc_out:
    r,p = rl[0], rl[1]
    for i in range(r):
        De_out=De_out + p
print('Encoded Input:',enc_out)
print('Decoded Output:',De_out)
```

Encoded Input: [(12, 'A'), (12, 'B')]

Decoded Output:
AAAAAAAAAAAABBBBBBBBBBBB

| (a) Python Code | (b) Result |

Fig. 9.10 Python code and its result of Run Length Decoding. (**a**) Python code. (**b**) Result

Inferences

- The outcome of this experiment shows that the length of the output string is larger than the length of the encoded input string.

Experiment 9.7: Encode the Grayscale Image Using Run Length Encoding
This experiment discusses the image encoding using run length encoder. For this, an image is generated with the size of 8 × 8, with the three gray levels {0, 128, 255}. This image is encoded by using run length encoder. The Python code to perform the above-mentioned task is shown in Fig. 9.11, and its simulation result is displayed in Fig. 9.12.

Inferences
From this experiment, the following inferences can be made:

- The size of the input image is 8 × 8 and the gray levels are 0, 128, and 255. That is three unique symbols in this image.
- From the Python code, "bits" indicates the length of the window.
- The encoded output shows the run and its symbol or character. If all the run values are added it results in 64, which is the total symbol or pixels in the given image.

Experiment 9.8: Decode the Grayscale Image from the RLE Output
This experiment explains the decoding of the run length encoder using Python. The encoded output and size of the input are fed as an input to the decoder. The output will be grayscale image with the same size of the input image. The Python code used to decode RLE is given in Fig. 9.13, and its simulation result is shown in Fig. 9.14.

Inference

- From Fig. 9.14, it is possible to confirm that the result of RLE Decoder exactly matches the input shown in Fig. 9.12.
- Therefore, the run length encoding scheme is a lossless compression scheme.

```
# Gray scale image RLE
import numpy as np
l1=np.zeros([8,8])
l1[2:6,2:6]=255
l1[(1,6),1:7]=128
fl1 = l1.flatten()
enc_out,count,prev, bits = [], 0, None, 8;
for c in fl1:
    if prev==None:
        prev = c
        count+=1
    else:
        if prev!=c:
            enc_out.append((count, prev))
            prev=c
            count=1
        else:
            if count<(2**bits)-1:
                count+=1
            else:
                enc_out.append((count, prev))
                prev=c
                count=1
enc_out.append((count, prev))
print('Input Image:',l1)
print('Encoded output:',enc_out)
```

Fig. 9.11 Python code for grayscale image RLE

```
Input Image: [[ 0.  0.  0.  0.  0.  0.  0.  0.]
 [ 0. 128. 128. 128. 128. 128. 128.  0.]
 [ 0.  0. 255. 255. 255. 255.  0.  0.]
 [ 0.  0. 255. 255. 255. 255.  0.  0.]
 [ 0.  0. 255. 255. 255. 255.  0.  0.]
 [ 0.  0. 255. 255. 255. 255.  0.  0.]
 [ 0. 128. 128. 128. 128. 128. 128.  0.]
 [ 0.  0.  0.  0.  0.  0.  0.  0.]]
Encoded output: [(9, 0.0), (6, 128.0), (3, 0.0), (4, 255.0), (4, 0.0), (4, 255.0),
(4, 0.0), (4, 255.0), (4, 0.0), (4, 255.0), (3, 0.0), (6, 128.0), (9, 0.0)]
```

Fig. 9.12 RLE output for grayscale image

Experiment 9.9: Encode and Decode the Cameraman Image Using RLE

This experiment deals with encoding and decoding the cameraman image using run length encoder. The Python code to perform this task is given in Fig. 9.15, and its corresponding output is shown in Fig. 9.16.

Fig. 9.13 Python code for decode the grayscale image from RLE output

```
# RLE decoding for grayscale image
import numpy as np
enc_out=[(9, 0.0), (6, 128.0), (3, 0.0), (4, 255.0), (4, 0.0), (4,
255.0), (4, 0.0), (4, 255.0), (4, 0.0), (4, 255.0), (3, 0.0), (6,
128.0), (9, 0.0)]
De_out=[]
shape=[8,8]
for rl in enc_out:
    r,p = rl[0], rl[1]
    De_out.extend([p]*r)
dimg = np.array(De_out).reshape(shape)
print('Encoded Input:',enc_out)
print('Decoded Output:',dimg)
```

Encoded Input: [(9, 0.0), (6, 128.0), (3, 0.0), (4, 255.0), (4, 0.0), (4, 255.0), (4, 0.0), (4, 255.0), (4, 0.0), (4, 255.0), (3, 0.0), (6, 128.0), (9, 0.0)]
Decoded Output: [[0.   0.   0.   0.   0.   0.   0.   0.]
 [0. 128. 128. 128. 128. 128. 128.   0.]
 [0.   0. 255. 255. 255. 255.   0.   0.]
 [0.   0. 255. 255. 255. 255.   0.   0.]
 [0.   0. 255. 255. 255. 255.   0.   0.]
 [0.   0. 255. 255. 255. 255.   0.   0.]
 [0. 128. 128. 128. 128. 128. 128.   0.]
 [0.   0.   0.   0.   0.   0.   0.   0.]]

Fig. 9.14 Decoded result of RLE

Inference

- From Fig. 9.16, it is possible to observe that the input and decoded images are the same, which indicates that the RLE is a lossless coding algorithm.

9.7.3   Huffman Coding

Huffman coding is a variable-length coding method developed by David Albert Huffman in 1952. The Huffman codes are optimal codes that assign one symbol to one code word. This coding is based on the probability of occurrence of the alphabets used in the data or input string. In this coding, the shorter code words or symbols are used to assign the symbols that occurred more frequently in the data or input. The Huffman coding result will achieve an average length of the codeword that is as close as possible to the source entropy. The probability of the given data is estimated apriori, then the table of Huffman codes can be fixed, and it has to be

```
# Encode and decode the cameraman image using RLE
import numpy as np
import matplotlib.pyplot as plt
import cv2
I1=cv2.imread('cameraman.tif',0);
fl1 = I1.flatten()
enc_out,count,prev, bits = [], 0, None, 16;
for c in fl1:
  if prev==None:
    prev = c
    count+=1
  else:
    if prev!=c:
      enc_out.append((count, prev))
      prev=c
      count=1
    else:
      if count<(2**bits)-1:
        count+=1
      else:
        enc_out.append((count, prev))
        prev=c
        count=1
enc_out.append((count, prev))
De_out=[]
shape=I1.shape
for rl in enc_out:
  r,p = rl[0], rl[1]
  De_out.extend([p]*r)
dimg = np.array(De_out).reshape(shape)
plt.figure(),plt.subplot(1,2,1),plt.imshow(I1,cmap='gray'),plt.title('Input Image'),plt.axis('off')
plt.subplot(1,2,2),plt.imshow(dimg,cmap='gray'),plt.title('Decoded Image'),plt.axis('off')
```

Fig. 9.15 Python code to perform RLE of grayscale image

Fig. 9.16 Input and decoded output using RLE

shared with both the encoder and decoder. Huffman coding follows the prefix code. Prefix code is a code word that does not occur as the prefix of another code word. Therefore, it is uniquely decodable.

Illustration of Huffman Code

Let us consider a word "COLLEGE" and encode this word using Huffman coding. From the given word, it is possible to observe that the alphabets "C", "E", "G", "L", and "O" are used. The probability of each alphabet is obtained as

$$P(X) = \frac{\text{Number of Alphabet } X}{\text{Length of input string}} \tag{9.10}$$

For the character "C", $P(C)$ is calculated as

$$P(C) = \frac{1}{7}$$

Similarly, for other characters, as follows: $P(E) = \frac{2}{7}, P(G) = \frac{1}{7}, P(L) = \frac{2}{7}, P(O) = \frac{1}{7}$. Arrange these probabilities in descending order, and the result is shown in Table 9.1 in the first column. Take the least two probabilities from the bottom and add them together, then perform the descending order, which is depicted in the second column of Table 9.1. Repeat this process till the end of the two probabilities.

Experiment 9.10: Write a Python Code to Compute the Binary Huffman Code for the Word "COLLEGE"

This experiment discusses the implementation of binary Huffman coding using Python. The Python code for the binary Huffman coding is shown in Fig. 9.17. From this figure, it is possible to observe that the formation of the binary tree concept is used to implement the binary Huffman code tree. After executing the Python code given in Fig. 9.17, the simulation result is shown in Fig. 9.18. Here, the alphabet used in the given input word "COLLEGE" and its corresponding binary code is displayed, which is in agreement with the example discussed in the previous section.

Table **9.1** Computation of Huffman coding

Probability	Stage-I	Stage-II	Stage-II
$P(L) = 2/7$ (00)	2/7 (00)	3/7 (1)	4/7 (0)
$P(E) = 2/7$ (01)	2/7 (01)	2/7 (00)	3/7 (1)
$P(C) = 1/7$ (11)	2/7 (10)	2/7 (01)	
$P(O) = 1/7$ (100)	1/7 (11)		
$P(G) = 1/7$ (101)			

```
input_data = 'COLLEGE'
# Node tree creation
class NodeTree(object):
  def __init__(self, L = None, R = None):
    self.L, self.R = L, R
  def children(self):
    return (self.L, self.R)
# Huffman coding
def Huffman_tree(node, L=True, String=''):
  if type(node) is str:
    return {node: String}
  (l, r) = node.children()
  D = dict()
  D.update(Huffman_tree(l, True, String + '1'))
  D.update(Huffman_tree(r, False, String + '0'))
  return D
# Calculation of no.of occurrences
occur = {}
for c in input_data:
  if c in occur:
    occur[c] += 1
  else:
    occur[c] = 1
occur = sorted(occur.items(), key=lambda x: x[1], reverse=True)
nodes = occur
while len(nodes) > 1:
  (key1, c1) = nodes[-1]
  (key2, c2) = nodes[-2]
  nodes = nodes[:-2]
  node = NodeTree(key1, key2)
  nodes.append((node, c1 + c2))
  nodes = sorted(nodes, key=lambda x: x[1], reverse=True)
huffman_Code = Huffman_tree(nodes[0][0])
print(' Alphabet | Huffman code ')
print('---------------------')
for (char, frequency) in occur:
  print(' %-8r |%8s' % (char, huffman_Code[char]))
```

Fig. 9.17 Python code and its result of Binary Huffman coding

Inference

- From Fig. 9.18, it is possible to observe that the simulation result is in agreement with theoretical result.

Fig. 9.18 Simulation
result

Alphabet	Huffman code
'L'	00
'E'	01
'C'	11
'O'	100
'G'	101

Experiment 9.11: Huffman Coding for Grayscale Image

This experiment discusses image encoding using binary Huffman code. For this, an 8 × 8 test image with the three gray levels {0, 128, 255} is generated. This image is encoded by using binary Huffman coder. The Python code to perform the above-mentioned task is shown in Fig. 9.19, and its simulation result is displayed in Fig. 9.20. For the Python implementation of the Huffman encoding algorithm, "Python Counter" is imported from the "Collections" library. Python Counter is a container that holds the count of each of the elements present in the container. The counter is a sub-class available inside the dictionary class.

Inferences

From this experiment, the following inferences can be made:

- The size of the input image is 8 × 8 and the gray levels are 0, 128, and 255. That is, three unique symbols in this image.
- From the output shown in Fig. 9.20, it is possible to infer that the lesser number of bits is assigned for the higher probability of the symbol. That is the code "0" is assigned to the symbol "0", which has higher probability than the other symbols "255" and "128". This illustrates the fact that Huffman code is a variable length code.
- From the Huffman code, it is possible to infer that no code word is a prefix of the next code word. Hence, Huffman code is a "prefix code".

Experiment 9.12: Encode the Eight-Bit Grayscale Image Using Huffman Coding

This experiment discusses the computation of Huffman coding for the given eight-bit grayscale (Cameraman image) image. The Python code to perform this task is shown in Fig. 9.21, and its simulation result is depicted in Fig. 9.22.

Inferences

- From Fig. 9.22b, it is possible to observe that pixels having higher probability take the smaller length of the binary code, whereas pixels having lesser probability take longer lengths of binary code.

Task: Write a Python code to decode the original message from the encoded bitstream.

```
# Huffman Encode for image patch
import numpy as np
from collections import Counter
l1=np.zeros([8,8],'uint8');#input patch
l1[2:6,2:6]=255;
l1[(1,6),1:7]=128
print('Input :', l1)
fimg = l1.flatten().tolist()
pxs = len(fimg)
tbl = Counter(fimg)
occur = {k:v/pxs for k,v in tbl.items()}
occur =(sorted(occur.items(), key=lambda x: x[1], reverse=True))
nodes = occur
# Node tree creation
class NodeTree(object):
   def __init__(self, L = None, R = None):
      self.L, self.R = L, R
   def children(self):
      return (self.L, self.R)
# Huffman coding
def Huffman_tree(node, L=True, String=''):
   if type(node) is int:
      return {node: String}
   (l, r) = node.children()
   D = dict()
   D.update(Huffman_tree(l, True, String + '1'))
   D.update(Huffman_tree(r, False, String + '0'))
   return D
while len(nodes) > 1:
   (key1, c1) = nodes[-1]
   (key2, c2) = nodes[-2]
   nodes = nodes[:-2]
   node = NodeTree(key1, key2)
   nodes.append((node, c1 + c2))
   nodes = sorted(nodes, key=lambda x: x[1], reverse=True)
huffman_Code = Huffman_tree(nodes[0][0])
print('Huffman Encoder Output:')
print(' Pixel | Probability | Huffman code ')
print('-------------------------------------')
i=0;
for (c, frequency) in occur:
   print(' %-8r | %-11s | %-12s' % (c, occur[i][1], huffman_Code[c]))
   i=i+1;
```

Fig. 9.19 Python code for grayscale image Huffman coding

Fig. 9.20 Huffman coding
output for grayscale image

```
Input : [[ 0  0  0  0  0  0  0  0]
 [ 0 128 128 128 128 128 128  0]
 [ 0  0 255 255 255 255  0  0]
 [ 0  0 255 255 255 255  0  0]
 [ 0  0 255 255 255 255  0  0]
 [ 0  0 255 255 255 255  0  0]
 [ 0 128 128 128 128 128 128  0]
 [ 0  0  0  0  0  0  0  0]]
Huffman Encoder Output:
Pixel | Probability | Huffman code
------------------------------------
0        | 0.5625      | 0
255      | 0.25        | 10
128      | 0.1875      | 11
```

9.7.4   Arithmetic Coding

Arithmetic coding is a lossless compression scheme to compress the data based on the probability of occurrence of each unique symbol in the data.

Arithmetic Encoding

The following steps are involved in the arithmetic encoding algorithm:

Step 1: Calculate the frequency of occurrence of each unique symbol in the data. Then, the frequency of occurrence is used to compute the probability of occurrence for each unique symbol.

Step 2: Initially, the entire range will [0, 1). Calculate the cumulative sum using the probability of occurrence calculated in Step 1 and assign each unique symbol to an interval of probabilities.

Step 3: For each symbol in the data, narrow down the entire interval based on the upper bound and lower bound of the interval of probabilities of that symbol. The new lower and upper bound of the symbol (X) can be obtained as

$$\text{low}_{\text{new}}(X) = \text{low} + \text{interval} \times \left(\text{low}_{\text{range}}(X)\right) \tag{9.11}$$

$$\text{high}_{\text{new}}(X) = \text{low} + \text{interval} \times \left(\text{high}_{\text{range}}(X)\right) \tag{9.12}$$

where $\text{low}_{\text{range}}$ refers to the symbol(X) low range and $\text{high}_{\text{range}}$ indicates the symbol (X) high range. Interval can be obtained from the difference between high range and low range of the symbol (X). Then, calculate the new cumulative sum and assign each unique symbol to range in the new interval.

```
import cv2
import matplotlib.pyplot as plt
from collections import Counter
I1=cv2.imread('cameraman.tif',0);
plt.imshow(I1,cmap='gray'),plt.title('Input Image'),plt.axis('off')
fimg = I1.flatten().tolist()
pxs = len(fimg)
tbl = Counter(fimg)
occur = {k:v/pxs for k,v in tbl.items()}
occur =(sorted(occur.items(), key=lambda x: x[1], reverse=True))
nodes = occur
# Node tree creation
class NodeTree(object):
    def __init__(self, L = None, R = None):
        self.L, self.R = L, R
    def children(self):
        return (self.L, self.R)
# Huffman coding
def Huffman_tree(node, L=True, String=''):
    if type(node) is int:
        return {node: String}
    (l, r) = node.children()
    D = dict()
    D.update(Huffman_tree(l, True, String + '1'))
    D.update(Huffman_tree(r, False, String + '0'))
    return D
while len(nodes) > 1:
    (key1, c1) = nodes[-1]
    (key2, c2) = nodes[-2]
    nodes = nodes[:-2]
    node = NodeTree(key1, key2)
    nodes.append((node, c1 + c2))
    nodes = sorted(nodes, key=lambda x: x[1], reverse=True)
huffman_Code = Huffman_tree(nodes[0][0])
print('Huffman Encoder Output:')
print(' Pixel | Probability | Huffman code ')
print('-------------------------------------')
i=0;
for (c, frequency) in occur:
    print(' %-8r | %-20s | %-12s' % (c, occur[i][1], huffman_Code[c]))
    i=i+1;
```

Fig. 9.21 Python code for grayscale image Huffman coding

Huffman Encoder Output:
Pixel | Probability | Huffman code
----
14 | 0.0257110595703125 | 10101
13 | 0.0233306884765625 | 11011
9 | 0.0225372314453125 | 11110
12 | 0.022216796875 | 11111
....
246 | 6.103515625e-05 | 01110111111011
252 | 4.57763671875e-05 | 000100100001100
245 | 3.0517578125e-05 | 0001001000011010
253 | 1.52587890625e-05 | 0001001000011011

(a) Input image   (b) Sample Huffman code output

Fig. 9.22 Huffman coding output for grayscale image. (**a**) Input image. (**b**) Sample Huffman code output

Step 4: Compute the tag value to be encoded, which is the average of the upper bound of the last symbol and lower bound of the last symbol. This can be written as

$$\text{tag} = \frac{\text{Upper bound of last symbol} + \text{Lower bound of last symbol}}{2} \qquad (9.13)$$

The source of the encoder is given by $S = \{w, 0.5, i, 0.25, n, 0.25\}$. Obtain the tag value of the word to be encoded as "*win*".

Encoding in arithmetic coding algorithm starts by representing the cumulative probabilities of all symbols on a line that ranges from 0 to 1.

Now, to encode the word "win", the first letter to be encoded is "*w*". The new low range of the symbol "*w*" can be obtained as

$$\text{low}_{\text{new}}(w) = \text{low} + \text{interval} \times \left(\text{low}_{\text{range}}(w)\right) \qquad (9.14)$$

Substituting the corresponding value (i.e. low(w) = 0, interval = 0.5–0 = 0.5, $\text{low}_{\text{range}}(w) = 0$) in the Eq. (9.14), we get

$$\text{low}_{\text{new}}(w) = 0 + 0.5 \times (0) = 0$$

Similarly for the new high range of symbol "*w*" can be obtained as

$$\text{high}_{\text{new}}(w) = \text{low} + \text{interval} \times \left(\text{high}_{\text{range}}(w)\right) \qquad (9.15)$$

Now, substituting the value of (i.e. low(w) = 0, interval = 0.5–0 = 0.5, $\text{high}_{\text{range}}(w) = 1$) in the Eq. (9.15), we get

$$\text{high}_{new}\left(w\right)=0+0.5\times\left(0.5\right)=0.25$$

similarly the new low range and new high range of symbols "i" and "n" is given by

$$\text{low}_{new}\left(i\right)=0+0.5\times\left(0.5\right)=0.25$$

$$\text{high}_{new}\left(i\right)=0+0.5\times\left(0.75\right)=0.375$$

$$\text{low}_{new}\left(n\right)=0+0.5\times\left(0.75\right)=0.375$$

$$\text{high}_{new}\left(n\right)=0+0.5\times\left(1\right)=0.5$$

After encoding the first letter ("w") from the word "win", the low_{new} and high_{new} are 0 and 0.5, respectively. The updated cumulative sum is shown in Fig. 9.23 (second one).

Now the second letter of the word "win" is "i" and the new low range and new high range of each symbol of the word "win" is updated as follows:

The interval for the letter "i" is (interval = 0.375–0.25 = 0.125), low range is 0.25.

$$\text{low}_{new}\left(w\right)=0.25+0.125\times\left(0\right)=0.25$$

$$\text{high}_{new}\left(w\right)=0.25+0.125\times\left(0.5\right)=0.3125$$

$$\text{low}_{new}\left(i\right)=0.25+0.125\times\left(0.5\right)=0.3125$$

$$\text{high}_{new}\left(i\right)=0.25+0.125\times\left(0.75\right)=0.34375$$

$$\text{low}_{new}\left(n\right)=0.25+0.125\times\left(0.75\right)=0.34375$$

$$\text{high}_{new}\left(n\right)=0.25+0.125\times\left(1\right)=0.375$$

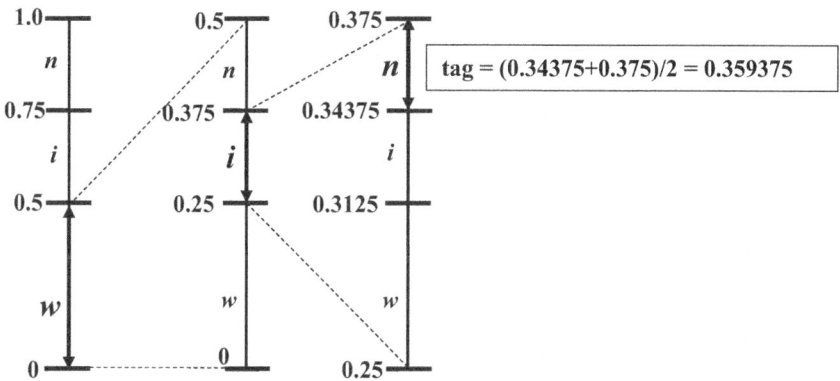

Fig. 9.23 Encoding of the word "win"

The updated cumulative sum after encoding the letter "i" is shown in Fig. 9.23 (see the third vertical).

The last letter of the word "win" is "n". Hence, the tag value is calculated based on the updated low range and high range of "n". Which is given by

$$\text{tag} = \frac{0.34375 + 0.375}{2} = 0.359375$$

Experiment 9.13: Encode the Word "Win" by Using Arithmetic Coding and the Source Encoder Is Given by {w = 0.5, i = 0.25, n = 0.25}
The Python code used to obtain the tag value of the word "win" is given in Fig. 9.24. After executing the Python code given in Fig. 9.24, the output tag value is "0.359375", which is on par with the theoretical result.

Arithmetic Decoding

An arithmetic coder contains an encoding and decoding algorithm; the encoder will generate the tag value as an output based on a given input word. The decoder will get back the original word from the tag value, symbol, probability, and length of the word. The steps of the arithmetic decoding algorithm are as follows:

Step 1: Get the tag value, dictionary of the symbol and its probability, and the length of the word.

Step 2: Initialize the lower bound and upper bound as 0 and 1, respectively. Mention the cumulative sum based on the given symbol and its probability.

Step 3: Find the symbol corresponding to the tag value between the cumulative sums.

Step 4: Update the new lower range and upper range of the decoded symbol (X) using the following equations:

$$\text{low}_{\text{new}}(X) = \text{low} + \text{interval} \times \left(\text{low}_{\text{range}}(X)\right) \tag{9.16}$$

$$\text{high}_{\text{new}}(X) = \text{low} + \text{interval} \times \left(\text{high}_{\text{range}}(X)\right) \tag{9.17}$$

Step 5: Repeat Step 3 to Step 4 up to the length of the word.

The tag value is given as 0.359375 and the probability of each symbol {$w = 0.5$, $i = 0.25$, $n = 0.25$} and length of the word is 3.

First, initialize the lower bound and upper bound as 0 and 1, respectively, and mention the cumulative sum of each symbol.

Now, fit the tag value on the cumulative sum diagram. The tag value corresponding to the symbol is the first decoded symbol. In this case, the tag value is 0.359375 and it fits on the symbol "w", which is indicated in Fig. 9.25 (first diagram).

Based on the low and high range of the symbol "w", the new cumulative sum diagram is updated as follows:

```
def get_cumulative_sum(low, up, prob_ls):
    cum_sum = [round(low,8)]
    interval = round((up - low),8)
    sym_low = round(low,8)
    for prob in prob_ls:
        sym_up = sym_low + (interval * prob)
        cum_sum.append(round(sym_up,8))
        sym_low = round(sym_up,8)
    return cum_sum
#print('Cumulative sum for interval [0, 1): ', cum_sum)
def sym_new_interval(cum_sum, unique_symbol):
    interval_dict = {}
    i = 0
    j = 0
    while i < len(cum_sum) - 1:
        key = unique_symbol[j]
        low = cum_sum[i]
        up = cum_sum[i + 1]
        interval_dict[key] = [low, up]
        i += 1
        j += 1
    return interval_dict
def get_tag(prob, unique_symbol, Inp_data):
    prob_ls = []
    for key, value in prob.items():
        prob_ls.append(value)
    cum_sum = get_cumulative_sum(0.0, 1.0, prob_ls)
    #print('Cumulative sum for interval [0, 1): ', cum_sum)
    interval_dict = sym_new_interval(cum_sum, unique_symbol)
    tag = 0.0
    for c in Inp_data:
        sym_interval = interval_dict.get(c)
        sym_low = sym_interval[0]
        sym_up = sym_interval[1]
        tag = round(((sym_low + sym_up) / 2.0),6)
        cum_sum = get_cumulative_sum(sym_low, sym_up, prob_ls)
        interval_dict = sym_new_interval(cum_sum, unique_symbol)
    return tag
prob={'w': 0.5, 'i': 0.25, 'n': 0.25}
unique_symbol=['w','i','n']
Inp_data='win'
tag = get_tag(prob, unique_symbol, Inp_data);
print('The tag value for ', '"',Inp_data,'"',' is ', tag)
```

Fig. 9.24 Python code for encoding the word "win" using arithmetic coding

Fig. 9.25 Decoding the
word "*win*"

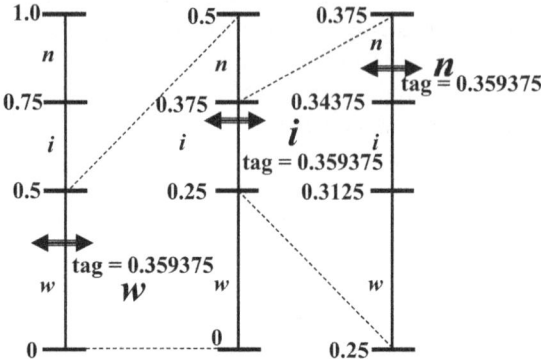

The interval is (0.5–0 = 0.5), substituting this value in the below equations, we get

$$\text{low}_{new}(X) = \text{low} + \text{interval} \times \left(\text{low}_{range}(X)\right)$$

$$\text{high}_{new}(X) = \text{low} + \text{interval} \times \left(\text{high}_{range}(X)\right)$$

$$\text{low}_{new}(w) = 0 + 0.5 \times (0) = 0$$

$$\text{high}_{new}(w) = 0 + 0.5 \times (0.5) = 0.25$$

$$\text{low}_{new}(i) = 0 + 0.5 \times (0.5) = 0.25$$

$$\text{high}_{new}(i) = 0 + 0.5 \times (0.75) = 0.375$$

$$\text{low}_{new}(n) = 0 + 0.5 \times (0.75) = 0.375$$

$$\text{high}_{new}(n) = 0 + 0.5 \times (1) = 0.5$$

The updated cumulative sum diagram is shown in Fig. 9.25 (refer second one).
Now fit the tag value 0.359375 on the updated cumulative sum diagram, and the obtained symbol is "*i*", which is the second decoded symbol. This is illustrated in Fig. 9.25 (second diagram).

The new interval is (0.375–0.25 = 0.125), low is 0.25, and update the new lower range and higher range of each symbol, we get

$$\text{low}_{new}(X) = \text{low} + \text{interval} \times \left(\text{low}_{range}(X)\right)$$

$$\text{high}_{new}(X) = \text{low} + \text{interval} \times \left(\text{high}_{range}(X)\right)$$

$$\text{low}_{new}(w) = 0.25 + 0.125 \times (0) = 0.25$$

$$\text{high}_{new}(w) = 0.25 + 0.125 \times (0.5) = 0.3125$$

$$\text{low}_{new}(i) = 0.25 + 0.125 \times (0.5) = 0.3125$$

$$\text{high}_{\text{new}}(i) = 0.25 + 0.125 \times (0.75) = 0.34375$$

$$\text{low}_{\text{new}}(n) = 0.25 + 0.125 \times (0.75) = 0.34375$$

$$\text{high}_{\text{new}}(n) = 0.25 + 0.125 \times (1) = 0.375$$

The updated cumulative diagram is shown in Fig. 9.25 (third diagram). Now, fit the tag value on the third cumulative diagram, the symbol corresponding to the tag value is "n". hence the third decoded symbol is "n". This is illustrated in Fig. 9.25 (third diagram). Length of the encoded word is 3, therefore stop the decoding process. Finally, the decoded word is "win".

Experiment 9.14: Decode the Word "Win" from the Tag Value and Its Source Encoder Details

This experiment uses Python to decode the word "win" from the tag and the source encoder details. The Python code used to perform this task is given in Fig. 9.26. After executing the Python code given in Fig. 9.26, the decoded output is "win", which is on par with the encoded word.

Experiment 9.15: Arithmetic Coding Implementation

Encode the message "INDIA" using an arithmetic encoding scheme.

This experiment deals with the implementation of arithmetic encoding using Python. The Python code for the arithmetic encoder is given in Fig. 9.27, and its corresponding simulation result is shown in Fig. 9.28.

Inference

- The word to be encoded is "INDIA" and has a length of 5 characters or symbols. The encoded tag value for the word "INDIA" is 0.21385, which can be observed in Fig. 9.28.

Experiment 9.16: Write a Python Code to Decode the Data from the Probability of Each Symbol, Length of the Data and Tag Value Given

This experiment discusses the decoding of the original content from the encoded tag value, probability of each symbol, and data length using Python. The Python code for the arithmetic decoding algorithm is given in Fig. 9.29, and its simulation result is shown in Fig. 9.30.

Inferences

- From Fig. 9.30, it is possible to observe that after executing the Python code given in Fig. 9.29, the simulation output is "INDIA", which was the input to the Python code of the arithmetic encoding algorithm given in Fig. 9.27.
- The decoding algorithm decodes the output as same as the input. Hence, arithmetic coding is a lossless coding scheme.

Task: Make the tag value zero for LSD to MSD in the Python code given in Fig. 9.29 and comment on the observed result.

```
## ARithmetic Decoding
prob={'w': 0.5, 'i': 0.25, 'n': 0.25};
data_len,tag,prob_ls,unique_symbol=3,0.359375,[],[]
print('Probability of each symbol: ',prob)
print('length of the word: ', data_len)
print('Encoded tag value: ',tag)
def get_cum_sum(low, up, prob_ls):
    cum_sum = [round(low,4)]
    interval = round((up - low),4)
    sym_low = round(low,4)
    for prob in prob_ls:
        sym_up = sym_low + (interval * prob)
        cum_sum.append(round(sym_up,4))
        sym_low = round(sym_up,4)
    return cum_sum
def sym_new_interval(cum_sum, unique_symbol):
    interval_dict = {}
    i,j = 0,0
    while i < len(cum_sum) - 1:
        key = unique_symbol[j]
        low = cum_sum[i]
        up = cum_sum[i + 1]
        interval_dict[key] = [low, up]
        i += 1
        j += 1
    return interval_dict
for key, value in prob.items():
    prob_ls.append(value)
    unique_symbol.append(key)
    cum_sum = get_cum_sum(0.0, 1.0, prob_ls)
    interval_dict = sym_new_interval(cum_sum, unique_symbol)
    i,data_char_ls,c_low,c_up = 0,[],0.0,1.0
    while i < data_len:
        for key, value in interval_dict.items():
            low,up = value[0],value[1]
            if (tag > low) and (tag < up):
                c_low = low
                c_up = up
                data_char_ls.append(key)
                break
        cum_sum = get_cum_sum(c_low, c_up, prob_ls)
        interval_dict = sym_new_interval(cum_sum, unique_symbol)
        i += 1
    decode=''
    for e in data_char_ls:
        decode += e;
print('Decoded word: ',decode)
```

Fig. 9.26 Python code for decode the word "win" using arithmetic coding

```
# Arithmetic Encoder
Inp_data = 'INDIA';# input('Enter the message:');
data_len = len(Inp_data)
print('The word to be encoded: ', Inp_data)
print('The length of the word: ', data_len)
#Identify the unique symbol in the input data
unique_symbol = []
for c in Inp_data:
    unique = True
    for e in unique_symbol:
        if e == c:
            unique = False
            break
    if unique:
        unique_symbol.append(c)
print('Unique symbol in the input: ', unique_symbol)
# Calculate the frequency of occurrence of each symbol
freq = {}
for c in unique_symbol:
    symbol_freq = 0
    for e in Inp_data:
        if c == e:
            symbol_freq += 1
    freq[c] = symbol_freq
print('Frequency of each unique symbol: ', freq)
#Obtain the probability of each symbol
prob = {}
for key, value in freq.items():
    prob[key] = round((value/data_len),4);
    # probability of occurrence of a unique symbol = frequency/data length
#print('Occurring probability of each unique symbol: ', prob)
prob_ls = []
def get_cumulative_sum(low, up, prob_ls):
    cum_sum = [round(low,4)]
    interval = round((up - low),4)
    sym_low = round(low,4)
    for prob in prob_ls:
        sym_up = sym_low + (interval * prob)
        cum_sum.append(round(sym_up,4))
        sym_low = round(sym_up,4)
    return cum_sum
#print('Cumulative sum for interval [0, 1): ', cum_sum)
```

Fig. 9.27 Python code for arithmetic encoder

```
def sym_new_interval(cum_sum, unique_symbol):
  interval_dict = {}
  i = 0
  j = 0
  while i < len(cum_sum) - 1:
    key = unique_symbol[j]
    low = cum_sum[i]
    up = cum_sum[i + 1]
    interval_dict[key] = [low, up]
    i += 1
    j += 1
  return interval_dict
def get_tag(prob, unique_symbol, Inp_data):
  prob_ls = []
  for key, value in prob.items():
    prob_ls.append(value)
  cum_sum = get_cumulative_sum(0.0, 1.0, prob_ls)
  #print('Cumulative sum for interval [0, 1): ', cum_sum)
  interval_dict = sym_new_interval(cum_sum, unique_symbol)
  tag = 0.0
  for c in Inp_data:
    sym_interval = interval_dict.get(c)
    sym_low = sym_interval[0]
    sym_up = sym_interval[1]
    tag = round(((sym_low + sym_up) / 2.0),6)
    cum_sum = get_cumulative_sum(sym_low, sym_up, prob_ls)
    interval_dict = sym_new_interval(cum_sum, unique_symbol)
  return tag
tag = get_tag(prob, unique_symbol, Inp_data);
print('The tag value for ', "",Inp_data,"",' is ', tag)
print('Probability of the symbol:',prob)
```

Fig. 9.27 (continued)

The word to be encoded: INDIA

The length of the word: 5

Unique symbol in the input: ['I', 'N', 'D', 'A']

Frequency of each unique symbol: {'I': 2, 'N': 1, 'D': 1, 'A': 1}

The tag value for " INDIA " is 0.21385

Probability of the symbol: {'I': 0.4, 'N': 0.2, 'D': 0.2, 'A': 0.2}

Fig. 9.28 Simulation result

```
## Arithmetic Decoding
prob={'I': 0.4, 'N': 0.2, 'D': 0.2, 'A': 0.2};
data_len,tag,prob_ls,unique_symbol=5,0.21385,[],[]
print('Probability of each symbol: ',prob)
print('length of the word: ', data_len)
print('Encoded tag value: ',tag)
def get_cum_sum(low, up, prob_ls):
    cum_sum = [round(low,4)]
    interval = round((up - low),4)
    sym_low = round(low,4)
    for prob in prob_ls:
        sym_up = sym_low + (interval * prob)
        cum_sum.append(round(sym_up,4))
        sym_low = round(sym_up,4)
    return cum_sum
def sym_new_interval(cum_sum, unique_symbol):
    interval_dict = {}
    i,j = 0,0
    while i < len(cum_sum) - 1:
        key = unique_symbol[j]
        low = cum_sum[i]
        up = cum_sum[i + 1]
        interval_dict[key] = [low, up]
        i += 1
        j += 1
    return interval_dict
for key, value in prob.items():
    prob_ls.append(value)
    unique_symbol.append(key)
    cum_sum = get_cum_sum(0.0, 1.0, prob_ls)
    interval_dict = sym_new_interval(cum_sum, unique_symbol)
    i,data_char_ls,c_low,c_up = 0,[],0.0,1.0
    while i < data_len:
        for key, value in interval_dict.items():
            low,up = value[0],value[1]
            if (tag > low) and (tag < up):
                c_low = low
                c_up = up
                data_char_ls.append(key)
                break
        cum_sum = get_cum_sum(c_low, c_up, prob_ls)
        interval_dict = sym_new_interval(cum_sum, unique_symbol)
        i += 1
    decode=''
    for e in data_char_ls:
        decode += e;
print('Decoded word: ',decode)
```

Fig. 9.29 Python code for arithmetic decoder

Probability of each symbol: {'I': 0.4, 'N': 0.2, 'D': 0.2, 'A': 0.2}

length of the word: 5

Encoded tag value: 0.21385

Decoded word: INDIA

Fig. 9.30 Simulation result

9.7.5   LZW Coding

LZW coding is a lossless data compression scheme, which was developed by Abraham Lempel, Jakob Ziv, and Terry Welch. Therefore, it is named as LZW. It is a dictionary-based lossless compression algorithm that scans an input pattern that occurs more than once. The repeated patterns are then saved in a dictionary, and references are placed within the compressed file wherever repetitive input occurs. LZW algorithm is used in the GIF image format and is part of the widely used Unix file compression utility compress.

The LZW algorithm consists of encoding and decoding processes. In the encoding process, the input data string is converted into an integer code; whereas decoding process gets back the input data string from the encoded integer codes. Both encoding and decoding algorithms have a default table that serves as the initial dictionary. While executing the algorithm, this initial dictionary is updated with the new integers and its corresponding string pattern.

Experiment 9.17: Encode the Word "AMMAAPPA" Using LZW Algorithm
This experiment explains the encoding and decoding of word "AMMAAPPA" using LZW algorithm. The unique characters in the word in the given word is {"A", "M", "P"}. The initial dictionary by default will be {A—0, M—1, P—2}.

String	Integer code
A	0
M	1
P	2

Encoding Process

The first character to be encoded is "A" and its corresponding integer code is "0". Thus, the encoder output is "0".

Encoded input	A	Encoder output	0

The next character in the given word is "M", which is available in the dictionary and its corresponding integer code is "1". Therefore, the encoder output for this character is "1".

| Encoded input | AM | Encoder output | 0,1 |

Now, combining the characters "A" and "M", we get "AM", which is not available in the dictionary; hence, "AM" is the new entry for the dictionary, and its corresponding integer code is assigned as "3'.

String	Integer code
A	0
M	1
P	2
AM	3

The next character to be encoded is "M", which is available in the dictionary. Therefore, include the next character in the given word (M). Now, let us check whether "MM" exists in the dictionary or not. "MM" does not exist in the dictionary, so the output integer code for the character "M" is "1". The updated encoder output is given by

| Encoded input | AMM | Encoder output | 0,1,1 |

From the above integer code, it is possible to observe that only "M" is encoded, not "MM".

Now update the dictionary with the new entry of "MM" and assign the integer code as "4".

String	Integer code
A	0
M	1
P	2
AM	3
MM	4

Until now, AMM is encoded and the next character to be encoded is "A", available in the dictionary and its corresponding integer code is "0". Now, combining the current character with the previously encoded character "M", we get "MA", which is the new entry for the dictionary. The integer code assigned to "MA" is 5. Now consider the next character and combine; we get "AA", which is unavailable in the existing dictionary. Hence, only the character "A" has to be encoded, and its corresponding integer code is "0". The updated encoder output is given by

| Encoded input | AMMA | Encoder output | 0,1,1,0 |

Now update the dictionary with the new entry of "AA" and assign the integer code as "6".

String	Integer code
A	0
M	1
P	2
AM	3
MM	4
MA	5
AA	6

From the above dictionary table, it is possible to understand that two new entries are present in the dictionary.

The encoded characters from the given word are "AMMA". The next character to be encoded is "A", in the dictionary. Now consider the next character in the given word "P" and combine it with "A"; we get "AP", and it is not available in the dictionary. Thus, only "A" has to be encoded, and the output integer code is "0". Include "AP" in the dictionary list and assign the integer code to "7".

String	Integer code
A	0
M	1
P	2
AM	3
MM	4
MA	5
AA	6
AP	7

The updated encoder output is

Encoded input	AMMAA	Encoder output	0,1,1,0,0

Repeat this process till the end of the character in the given word. The final dictionary and encoder output is given below:

String	Integer code
A	0
M	1
P	2
AM	3
MM	4
MA	5
AA	6
AP	7
PP	8
PA	9

Encoded input	AMMAAPPA	Encoder output	0,1,1,0,0,2,2,0

The Python code for the LZW encoding process of the word "AMMAAPPA" is given in Fig. 9.31, and its simulation result is shown in Fig. 9.32.

Inferences

The following inferences can be made from this experiment:

- From Fig. 9.31, it is possible to observe that "np.fromiter" command is used from the numpy library. It is used to create a new 1D array from an iterable object.
- Also, it is possible to see that "tuple" is used to store multiple items in a single variable.
- From Fig. 9.32, it is evident that the input to the LZW is a string, and the output from the LZW is an integer code.

Task: Modify the Unique_symbols in the Python code given in Fig. 9.31 and consider input as "catcatcatcatcatcatcat". Comment on the observed result.

```
# LZW Encoding
import numpy as np
Unique_symbols= ['A','M','P']
txt='AMMAAPPA'
input_txt=np.fromiter(txt, (np.str_,1))
dict = {tuple([ value ]):idx for  idx,value in enumerate(Unique_symbols)}
En_out = []
entry = tuple([input_txt[0]])
I = 1
while I < len(input_txt):
    entry_dict = entry + tuple([ input_txt[I] ])
    if entry_dict in dict:
        entry = entry_dict
    else:
        # add new entry to dictionary
        En_out.append( dict[entry] )
        dict[ entry_dict ] = max(dict.values()) + 1
        entry = tuple([ input_txt[I] ])
    I = I+1
En_out.append(dict[entry])
print('Text to be Encoded: ', txt)
print('--- Dictionary----')
print(' String    | Integer code ')
print('----------------------')
for key, value in dict.items():
    print(' %-10r | % -5r' % (key, value))
print('Encoder Output: ',np.array(En_out))
```

Fig. 9.31 Python code for LZW encoder

Fig. 9.32 Simulation
result

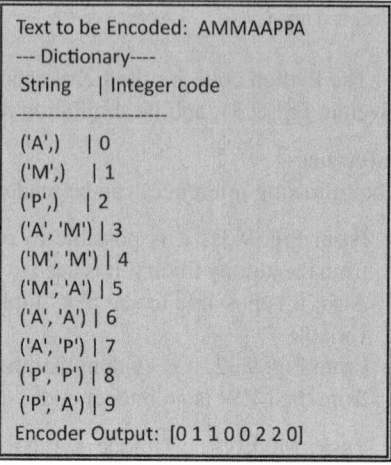

Text to be Encoded: AMMAAPPA
--- Dictionary----
String | Integer code

('A',) | 0
('M',) | 1
('P',) | 2
('A', 'M') | 3
('M', 'M') | 4
('M', 'A') | 5
('A', 'A') | 6
('A', 'P') | 7
('P', 'P') | 8
('P', 'A') | 9
Encoder Output: [0 1 1 0 0 2 2 0]

Experiment 9.18: Decode the LZW Encoded Output [0, 1, 1, 0, 0, 2, 2, 0] with the Initial Dictionary {a→0, m→1, p→2}

This experiment deals with the decoding process of LZW encoded output integer [0, 1, 1, 0, 0, 2, 2, 0] and initial dictionary $\{a{\to}0, m{\to}1, p{\to}2\}$ using Python.

LZW Decoding Process

The decoding process starts with the initial dictionary in the form of reversible, which is given by

Integer code	String
0	A
1	M
2	P

From the encoder integer code, the first code is "0", and its corresponding string in the dictionary is "A". Hence, the decoded output for the first integer code is "A".

Integer code	0	Decoder output	A

The next integer code in the given encoder output is "1", which is available in the dictionary and its corresponding string is "M". Therefore, the decoder output for this integer code is "M".

Integer code	0,1	Decoder output	AM

The dictionary list must be updated based on the decoder output string. Therefore, combining the strings "A" and "M", we get "AM" which is to be included in the dictionary and the corresponding integer code is assigned as "3", which is given below

Integer code	String
0	A
1	M
2	P
3	AM

The next integer code in the given encoder output is "1", which is available in the dictionary and its corresponding string is "M". Therefore, the decoder output for this integer code is "M".

Integer code	0,1,1	Decoder output	AMM

The dictionary list must be updated based on the decoder output string. Therefore, combining the previously decoded string with the current decoded string output, "M" and "M", respectively, we get "MM" which is to be included in the dictionary, and the corresponding integer code is assigned as "4", which is given below

Integer code	String
0	A
1	M
2	P
3	AM
4	MM

The next integer code in the given encoder output is "0", which is available in the dictionary and its corresponding string is "A". Therefore, the decoder output for this integer code is "A".

Integer code	0,1,1,0	Decoder output	AMMA

Based on the decoder output string, the dictionary list has to be updated. Therefore, combining the previously decoded string with current decoded string output, "M" and "A", respectively, we get "MA" which is to be included in the dictionary, and the corresponding integer code is assigned as "5", which is given below.

Integer code	String
0	A
1	M
2	P
3	AM
4	MM
5	MA

The next integer code in the given encoder output is "0", which is available in the dictionary and its corresponding string is "A". Therefore, the decoder output for this integer code is "A".

Integer code	0,1,1,0,0	Decoder output	AMMAA

The dictionary list must be updated based on the decoder output string. Therefore, combining the previously decoded string with current decoded string output, "A" and "A" respectively, we get "AA" which is to be included in the dictionary, and the corresponding integer code is assigned as "6", which is given below.

Integer code	String
0	A
1	M
2	P
3	AM
4	MM
5	MA
6	AA

The next integer code in the given encoder output is "2", which is available in the dictionary, and its corresponding string is "P". Therefore, the decoder output for this integer code is "P".

Integer code	0,1,1,0,0,2	Decoder output	AMMAAP

Based on the decoder output string, the dictionary list has to be updated. Therefore, combining the previously decoded string with current decoded string output, "A" and "P", respectively, we get "AP" which is to be included in the dictionary, and the corresponding integer code is assigned as "7", which is given below.

Integer code	String
0	A
1	M
2	P
3	AM
4	MM
5	MA
6	AA
7	AP

The next integer code in the given encoder output is "2", which is available in the dictionary and its corresponding string is "P". Therefore, the decoder output for this integer code is "P".

| Integer code | 0,1,1,0,0,2,2 | Decoder output | AMMAAPP |

Based on the decoder output string, the dictionary list has to be updated. Therefore, combining the previously decoded string with current decoded string output, "P" and "P", respectively, we get "PP" which is to be included in the dictionary, and the corresponding integer code is assigned as "8", which is given below

Integer code	String
0	A
1	M
2	P
3	AM
4	MM
5	MA
6	AA
7	AP
8	PP

The next integer code in the given encoder output is "0", which is available in the dictionary and its corresponding string is "P". Therefore, the decoder output for this integer code is "P".

| Integer code | 0,1,1,0,0,2,2,0 | Decoder output | AMMAAPPA |

Based on the decoder output string, the dictionary list has to be updated. Therefore, combining the previously decoded string with current decoded string output, "P" and "A", respectively, we get "PA" which is to be included in the dictionary, and the corresponding integer code is assigned as "9", which is given below

Integer code	String
0	A
1	M
2	P
3	AM
4	MM
5	MA
6	AA
7	AP
8	PP
9	PA

There is no further integer code in the encoder output. Therefore, stop the decoding process, and the final result of the decoder is "AMMAAPPA", which is exactly the same as the input. Hence, LZW coding is a lossless coding scheme.

From the encoding and decoding process of LZW, the dictionary has to be updated to avoid transmitting the dictionary to the receiver. Only the integer code, along with the initial dictionary, has to be sent to the receiver. Encoder output, that is integer code is the compressed file of the input data. Therefore, the compression ratio is calculated as

$$\text{Compression Ratio}(\text{CR}) = \frac{\text{Uncompressed original data}}{\text{Compressed file}}$$

The Python code to perform the LZW decoding process is given in Fig. 9.33, and its corresponding output is displayed in Fig. 9.34.

Inferences

The following inferences can be made from this experiment:

- The input to the decoder is an integer code (i.e. the code is assigned to string in the dictionary).

```python
#LZW Decoding
import numpy as np
Unique_symbols= ['A','M','P']
y=np.array([0, 1, 1, 0, 0, 2, 2, 0]);
dict = {idx: [ value ] for idx,value in enumerate(Unique_symbols)}
Dec_out = dict[ y[0] ].copy()#First symbol
entry = dict[ y[0] ].copy()
l = 1
while l < len(y):
    if y[l] in dict:
    # append first character of output and add to dictionary
        entry.append( dict[ y[l] ][0] )
    else:
        entry.append( entry[0] )
    dict[max(dict.keys())+1] = entry.copy()
    Dec_out += dict[ y[l] ].copy()
    entry = dict[ y[l] ].copy()
    l += 1
print('Input to Decoder: ', y)
print('--- Dictionary----')
print(' Integer code | String ')
print('-----------------------')
for key, value in dict.items():
    print(' %-12s | % -10r' % (key, value))
print('Decoder Output: ',np.array(Dec_out))
```

Fig. 9.33 Python code for LZW decoder

Fig. 9.34 Simulation result

```
Input to Decoder: [0 1 1 0 0 2 2 0]
--- Dictionary----
Integer code | String
-----------------------
0       | ['A']
1       | ['M']
2       | ['P']
3       | ['A', 'M']
4       | ['M', 'M']
5       | ['M', 'A']
6       | ['A', 'A']
7       | ['A', 'P']
8       | ['P', 'P']
9       | ['P', 'A']
Decoder Output: ['A' 'M' 'M' 'A' 'A' 'P' 'P' 'A']
```

- The decoder output is the string, and the decoder process also updates the dictionary.
- From this, the dictionary must be updated in both encoder and decoder processes.

9.7.6 DPCM-Based Compression

Differential Pulse Code Modulation (DPCM) is a predictive technique that removes the inter-pixel redundancy of a given input. It predicts the next value based on the values of the previous neighbouring input data elements. It computes the residual value between the actual and predicted value, which is given by

$$\text{Residue} = \text{actual value} - \text{predicted value} \qquad (9.18)$$

The residue data is losslessly compressed by using RLE, Huffman coding, etc. This DPCM decorrelates the data and causes the residual to have lower entropy so that a minimum number of bits are spent to transmit or store the compressed file. This DPCM technique is used in the JPEG lossless compression standard.

Prediction Approach

Let us consider a 1D signal, which is given by $X = \{x_1, x_2, x_3, \ldots, x_N\}$. The predicted value of x_k is obtained as

$$p_k = \alpha x_{k-1} \qquad (9.19)$$

where α is the predictive parameter, which decides the prediction of the current value of the input based on the previous value of the input. In general, the predictive parameter α can be chosen as 1.0 or 0.99. p_k denotes the predicted value.

The residue value (e_k) is calculated by

$$e_k = x_k - p_k \qquad (9.20)$$

where y_k is obtained from Eq. (9.19) with the initial x_0 assumed as 0. The residue is passed through entropy encoder. For the decoding, the original input from the encoder output, entropy decoder is used, and the decoded residue is added with predicted value, which is given by

$$z_k = e_k + p_k \qquad (9.21)$$

The predicted value of the decoder DPCM is calculated as

$$p_k = \alpha z_{k-1} \qquad (9.22)$$

The block diagram of the DPCM is shown in Fig. 9.35.

Experiment 9.19: Implementation of DPCM for 1D Data

This experiment discusses the implementation of DPCM for 1D data using Python. The Python code for this experiment is given in Fig. 9.36a, and its simulation result is depicted in Fig. 9.36b. Here, run length coding is used for the entropy encoder and entropy decoder.

Inference

- From Fig. 9.36b, it is possible to observe that the input and reconstructed data are the same, indicating that DPCM is a lossless compression algorithm.

  Task: Change the value of "alpha" in the Python code given in Fig. 9.36a. Observe the change in compressed data and comment on it.

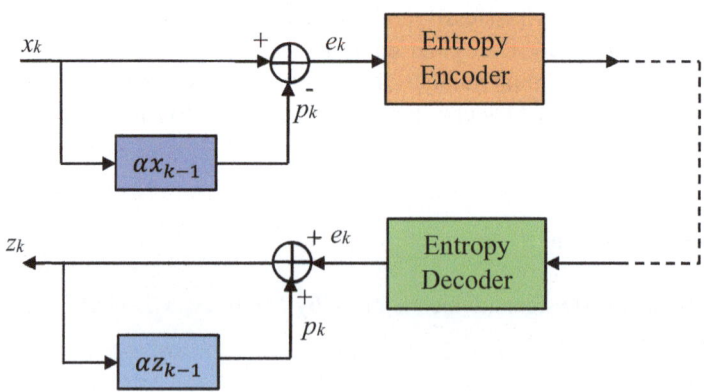

Fig. 9.35 Flow diagram of DPCM

```
# DPCM 1D Array
import numpy as np
x=np.array([100,100,100,100,101,101,101,101,101,101])
alpha=1# it may be 0.99, 0.98 or 1
pe=np.zeros(len(x))
e=np.zeros(len(x))
pe[0]=0
e[0]=x[0]-pe[0];
for i in range(1,len(x)):
    pe[i]=alpha*x[i-1]
    e[i]=x[i]-pe[i]
fl1 = e# RLE Encoding
enc_out,count,prev, bits = [], 0, None, 16;
for c in fl1:
    if prev==None:
        prev = c
        count+=1
    else:
        if prev!=c:
            enc_out.append((count, prev))
            prev=c
            count=1
        else:
            if count<(2**bits)-1:
                count+=1
            else:
                enc_out.append((count, prev))
                prev=c
                count=1
enc_out.append((count, prev))
# RLE decoding
De_out=[]
for rl in enc_out:
    r,p = rl[0], rl[1]
    De_out.extend([p]*r)
z=np.zeros(len(x))
pd=np.zeros(len(x))
z[0]=e[0]+0
for j in range(1,len(De_out)):
    pd[j]=alpha*z[j-1]
    z[j]=e[j]+pd[j]
print('Input Data :',x)
print('Compressed Data',enc_out)
print('Reconstructed Data:',z)
```

```
Input Data : [100 100 100 100
101 101 101 101 101 101]
Compressed Data [(1, 100.0),
(3, 0.0), (1, 1.0), (5, 0.0)]
Reconstructed Data: [100. 100.
100. 100. 101. 101. 101. 101.
101. 101.]
```

(a) **Python code**   (b) **Result**

Fig. 9.36 DPCM with RLE. (a) Python code. (b) Result

Experiment 9.20: Implementation of 2D Data DPCM
This experiment deals with the implementation of 2D DPCM using Python. Let us consider an input is 2D data (X) and the predictor value (P) is calculated as

$$P(i,j) = aX(i,j-1) + bX(i-1,j-1) + cX(i-1,j) \qquad (9.23)$$

where a, b, c are the predictor constants or parameters. For better performance, the values of (a, b, c) can be chosen as $(1, 0, 0)$, $(0, 0, 1)$, $(0.5, 0, 0.5)$, $(1, -1, 1)$, and $(0.75, -0.5, 0.75)$.

Inferences
From this experiment, the following inferences can be made:

- From Fig. 9.37, it is possible to observe that input data is in 2D format. The predictor constant or parameters are chosen as $a = 1$, $b = 0$ and $c = 0$.
- Figure 9.38 shows that both the input and reconstructed output are the same, which indicates that DPCM can be used for the lossless compression.

Task: Vary the predictor parameters value and comment on the observed reconstructed output and compressed file output.

Experiment 9.21: DPCM for Grayscale Image
This experiment discusses the DPCM lossless compression of grayscale image. The input to the DPCM is considered as a "Clock" grayscale image. The predictor parameters of DPCM are chosen as "$a = 0.75$, $b = -0.5$ and $c = 0.75$". The Python code for this task is given in Fig. 9.39, and its corresponding simulation result is depicted in Fig. 9.40.

Inference

- From Fig. 9.40, it is possible to confirm that both input and reconstructed images are the same, which indicates that DPCM can be used as a lossless compression scheme.

9.7.7   Bitplane Coding

The image with more than two intensity levels can be coded using bit-plane coding. An image with N bits intensity value contains N numbers of binary images. Therefore, using gray value to binary converter converts the gray intensity value to its equivalent binary "N" bits. Each binary image is called as a bitplane. Now, flatten each binary image and compress it using run length encoding or any lossless compression scheme. The flow diagram of bitplane coding is shown in Fig. 9.41.

Fig. 9.37 DPCM for 2D data

```
# 2D DPCM
import numpy as np
import matplotlib.pyplot as plt
I1=np.zeros([8,8],'uint8');#input patch
I1[2:6,2:6]=255;
I1[(1,6),1:7]=128;
print('Input data:', I1)
I2=np.pad(I1,[1,1],mode='constant')
(m,n)=I2.shape
Pe=np.zeros([m,n]);
e=np.zeros([m,n]);
a,b,c=0.75,-0.5,0.75
for i in range(0,m):
    for j in range(0,n):
        Pe[i,j]=a*I2[i,j-1]+b*I2[i-1,j-1]+c*I2[i-1,j];
        e[i,j]=I2[i,j]-Pe[i,j];
fl1 = e.flatten()# RLE Encoding
enc_out,count,prev, bits = [], 0, None, 16;
for ch in fl1:
    if prev==None:
        prev = ch
        count+=1
    else:
        if prev!=ch:
            enc_out.append((count, prev))
            prev=ch
            count=1
        else:
            if count<(2**bits)-1:
                count+=1
            else:
                enc_out.append((count, prev))
                prev=ch
                count=1
enc_out.append((count, prev))
print('Compressed file:',enc_out)
# RLE decoding
De_out=[]
for rl in enc_out:
    r,p = rl[0], rl[1]
    De_out.extend([p]*r)
dimg = np.array(De_out).reshape(m,n)
Z1=np.zeros([m,n],'uint8');
Pd=np.zeros([m,n]);
for i in range(0,m):
    for j in range(0,n):
        Pd[i,j]=a*Z1[i,j-1] + b*Z1[i-1,j-1] + c*Z1[i-1,j];
        Z1[i,j]=dimg[i,j]+Pd[i,j];
Recons=Z1[1:m-1,1:n-1]
print('Reconstructed output:',Recons)
```

```
Input data: [[ 0   0   0   0   0   0   0   0]
 [ 0 128 128 128 128 128 128  0]
 [ 0   0 255 255 255 255  0   0]
 [ 0   0 255 255 255 255  0   0]
 [ 0   0 255 255 255 255  0   0]
 [ 0   0 255 255 255 255  0   0]
 [ 0 128 128 128 128 128 128  0]
 [ 0   0   0   0   0   0   0   0]]
Compressed file: [(22, 0.0), (1, 128.0), (5, 32.0), (1, -96.0), (3, 0.0), (1, -96.0), (1, 223.0), (3,
31.75), (1, -223.25), (1, 64.0), (4, 0.0), (1, 63.75), (3, 0.0), (1, -63.75), (5, 0.0), (1, 63.75), (3, 0.0),
(1, -63.75), (5, 0.0), (1, 63.75), (3, 0.0), (1, -63.75), (4, 0.0), (1, 128.0), (1, -159.25), (3, -31.75),
(1, 159.5), (1, -96.0), (3, 0.0), (1, -96.0), (5, -32.0), (1, 64.0), (11, 0.0)]
Reconstructed output: [[ 0   0   0   0   0   0   0   0]
 [ 0 128 128 128 128 128 128  0]
 [ 0   0 255 255 255 255  0   0]
 [ 0   0 255 255 255 255  0   0]
 [ 0   0 255 255 255 255  0   0]
 [ 0   0 255 255 255 255  0   0]
 [ 0 128 128 128 128 128 128  0]
 [ 0   0   0   0   0   0   0   0]]
```

Fig. 9.38 Simulation result

Experiment 9.22: Compress the Grayscale Image Using Bitplane Coding

This experiment discusses the compression of grayscale image using bitplane coding. The Python code to perform this task is given in Fig. 9.42, and its simulation result is shown in Fig. 9.43.

Inferences

The following inferences can be made from Fig. 9.42:

- Run length encoder (RLE) and run length decoder (RLD) are defined in the form of functions.
- The eight bitplanes of the given grayscale image are extracted, and the extracted bitplane is fed as an input to the RLE. Here, the maximum number of bits are used for the "run" is fixed as (bits = 16). This decides the maximum of run value will be within 2^{16}.
- The run length encoder output is the input to the run length decoder (RLD) in addition to the size of the input image (m, n).
- The RLD decodes the original bitplane from the run and the symbol of the RLE output.
- Finally, all the bit planes are summed up to get a final reconstructed image.

```
# 2D DPCM
import numpy as np
import cv2
import matplotlib.pyplot as plt
I1=cv2.imread('Clock.tiff',0);
I2=np.pad(I1,[1,1],mode='constant')
(m,n)=I2.shape
Pe=np.zeros([m,n]);
e=np.zeros([m,n]);
a,b,c=0.75,-0.5,0.75
for i in range(0,m):
    for j in range(0,n):
        Pe[i,j]=a*I2[i,j-1]+b*I2[i-1,j-1]+c*I2[i-1,j];
        e[i,j]=I2[i,j]-Pe[i,j];
fl1 = e.flatten()# RLE Encoding
enc_out,count,prev, bits = [], 0, None, 16;
for ch in fl1:
    if prev==None:
        prev = ch
        count+=1
    else:
        if prev!=ch:
            enc_out.append((count, prev))
            prev=ch
            count=1
        else:
            if count<(2**bits)-1:
                count+=1
            else:
                enc_out.append((count, prev))
                prev=ch
                count=1
enc_out.append((count, prev))
#print('Compressed file:',enc_out)
# RLE decoding
De_out=[]
for rl in enc_out:
    r,p = rl[0], rl[1]
    De_out.extend([p]*r)
dimg = np.array(De_out).reshape(m,n)
Z1=np.zeros([m,n],'uint8');
Pd=np.zeros([m,n]);
for i in range(0,m):
    for j in range(0,n):
        Pd[i,j]=a*Z1[i,j-1] + b*Z1[i-1,j-1] + c*Z1[i-1,j];
        Z1[i,j]=dimg[i,j]+Pd[i,j];
Recons=Z1[1:m-1,1:n-1]
plt.subplot(1,2,1),plt.imshow(I1,cmap='gray'),plt.title('Input image'),plt.axis('off')
plt.subplot(1,2,2),plt.imshow(Recons,cmap='gray'),plt.title('Reconstructed image'),plt.axis('off')
```

Fig. 9.39   DPCM for grayscale image

Input image
Reconstructed image

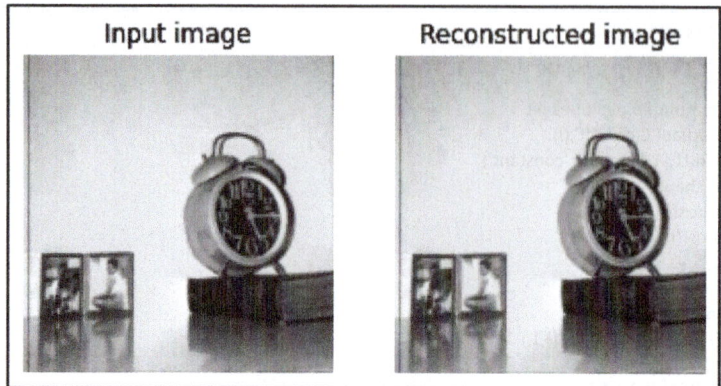

Fig. 9.40 Simulation result

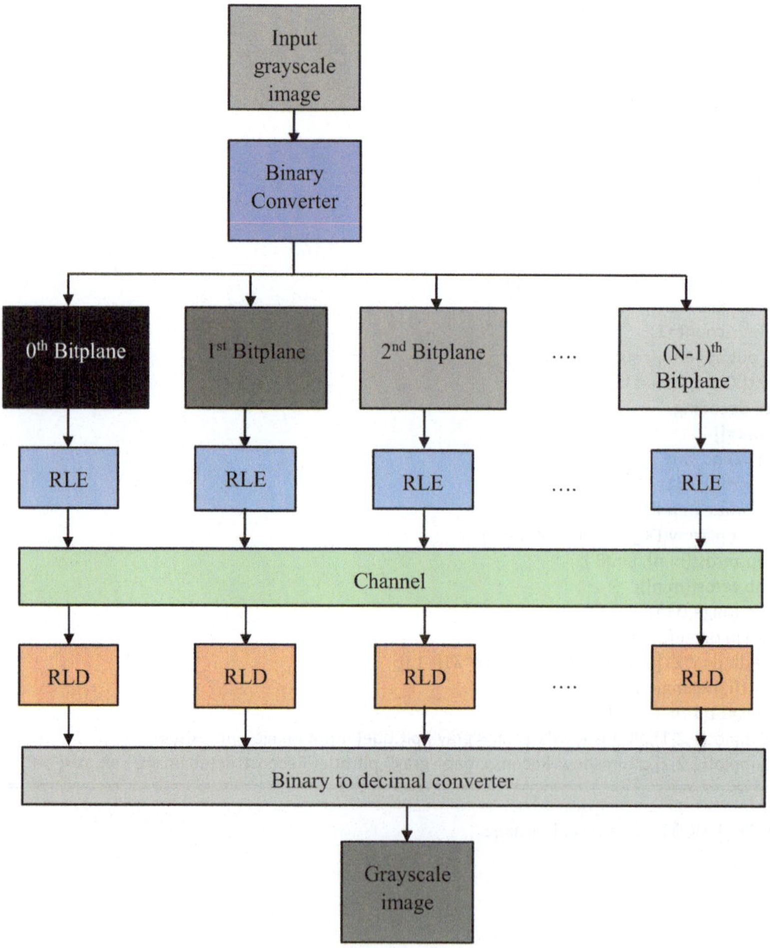
Input grayscale image
Binary Converter
0th Bitplane
1st Bitplane
2nd Bitplane
....
(N-1)th Bitplane
RLE
RLE
RLE
....
RLE
Channel
RLD
RLD
RLD
....
RLD
Binary to decimal converter
Grayscale image

Fig. 9.41 Flow diagram of bitplane coding

- Also, the compression ratio for this image is computed as "4.3477". For the computation of compression ratio, the size of the RLE output is measured for all the bitplanes and the maximum number of bits needed to represent the "run" is 16, and the bitplanes symbol is 0 or 1. Hence, the number of compressed bits is calculated by {length(RLE output)*(16 + 1)}.

From Fig. 9.43, it is possible to observe that there is no difference between the input and reconstructed images.

The uses of lossless compression scheme are shown in Table 9.2.

```
# Bitplane coding compression scheme
import cv2
import numpy as np
import matplotlib.pyplot as plt
#Step 1: Reading the input image
img=cv2.imread('Clock.tiff',0)
m,n=img.shape
out, compress, decompress = [],[],[]
Res=np.zeros([m,n],'uint8')
def RLE(x,bits):   # Run length Encoding
  fl1 = x.flatten()# RLE Encoding
  enc_out,count,prev = [], 0, None;
  for ch in fl1:
    if prev==None:
      prev = ch
      count+=1
    else:
      if prev!=ch:
        enc_out.append((count, prev))
        prev=ch
        count=1
      else:
        if count<(2**bits)-1:
          count+=1
        else:
          enc_out.append((count, prev))
          prev=ch
          count=1
  enc_out.append((count, prev))
  return enc_out
def RLD(enc_out,m,n): # Run length decoding
  De_out=[]
  for rl in enc_out:
    r,p = rl[0], rl[1]
    De_out.extend([p]*r)
  dimg = np.array(De_out).reshape(m,n)
  return dimg
```

Fig. 9.42 Bitplane coding Python program

```
Compressed_bits=0;
bits=16;# maximum run length size
for k in range(8):
    # create an image for each k bit plane
    plane = np.full((img.shape[0], img.shape[1]), 2 ** k, np.uint8)
    res1 = cv2.bitwise_and(plane, img);# bitwise and operation
    x = res1/(2**k);# make only 0s and 1s
    out.append(x)
    y=RLE(out[k],bits);
    Compressed_bits=Compressed_bits+(len(y)*(bits+1))
    compress.append(y)
    z=RLD(compress[k],m,n)
    decompress.append(z)
for t in range(8):
    Res=Res+decompress[t]*(2**t)
plt.subplot(1,2,1),plt.imshow(img,cmap='gray'),plt.title('Input image'),plt.axis('off')
plt.subplot(1,2,2),plt.imshow(Res,cmap='gray'),plt.title('Reconstructed'),plt.axis('off')
print('Compression Ratio CR: ', Compressed_bits/(m*n*8))
```

Fig. 9.42 (continued)

Fig. 9.43 Simulation result

Table 9.2 Usage of lossless compression schemes

Standards and image file formats	Compression algorithm
Joint Binary Image Experts Group (JBIG) and JBIG2	Arithmetic Coding
Grayscale and colour JBIG	Bitplane + Arithmetic coding
Lossless (JPEG) Joint Photograph Expert Group	DPCM
Fax: – Group 3 – Extended 2D Group 3 – Group 4	RLE and Huffman coding
BMP (Microsoft)	RLE
GIF (CompuServe)	LZW
TIFF	Choice of Group 3, Group 4, LZW, or RLE
PNG	Variants of LZ77
MIFF (X Window)	RLE or DPCM
PIX (SGI IRIS)	RLE
BW (SGI IRIS)	RLE
Compress (Unix)	LZW
gzip (Unix)	A variant of LZ77

9.8 Lossy Compression Scheme

In the lossy compression scheme, the exact information in the input data cannot be recovered from the compressed file or data. There are some insignificant details in the input data, which will be removed by the compression algorithm to achieve a high compression ratio. In lossy compression, the reconstructed image has some loss, which is completely imperceptible to a human viewer. For this reason, lossy compression algorithms on images can often get a factor of 2 better compression than lossless compression schemes with an imperceptible loss in quality.

9.9 Transform Coding

Transform coding is a lossy compression technique; it converts the spatial domain image into the frequency domain using transformation techniques. The suitable image transform can be chosen to decorrelate the interpixel redundancy within in the image. The transformed coefficients are coded to achieve high compression. For the decorrelation of the image, orthogonal transforms are preferred so that recon-struction of the original image from the compressed file can be possible. Also, the orthogonal transform has the property of energy preservation while converting from spatial domain to frequency domain. The transform operation itself does not pro-vide any compression; it will decorrelate the original data and compact a large frac-tion of the signal energy into a relatively small set of transform coefficients. Due to the energy compaction of the transformed coefficients, many of the coefficients hold less information which has to be removed by using a quantization process. Then, lossless coding techniques like Huffman, run length, and arithmetic coding can be used as an entropy encoder to get a compressed file. The block diagram of transform coding encoder is shown in Fig. 9.44. From this figure, it is possible to observe that transform coding scheme contains three major blocks in encoder, such as (1) Forward transform, (2) Quantization, and (3) Entropy coding. The reverse processes followed to reconstruct the image from the compressed file, which is depicted in Fig. 9.45. The major blocks in decoder are (1) Entropy decoding, (2) Inverse quantization, and (3) Inverse transform.

Experiment 9.23: Use Fourier Transform to Compress the Image
This experiment discusses the transform coding using Fourier transform. The input image is decorrelated using the 2D Fourier transform and to achieve compression a few of the Fourier coefficients are made as zero instead of quantization. The non-zero coefficients are passed through entropy encoder to get compressed file. The block diagram for the above-mentioned task is shown in Fig. 9.46. The Python code to perform this task is shown in Fig. 9.47, and its simulation result is depicted in Fig. 9.48. The entropy encoder is a lossless scheme. Thus, it is not included in the Python code, and only a few Fourier coefficients are made as zero.

Inferences
The following inferences can be made from this experiment:

- From Fig. 9.47, it is possible to observe that the input image is passed through FFT to obtain its spectrum. Few of the coefficients are made as zero with the dif-ferent radii.

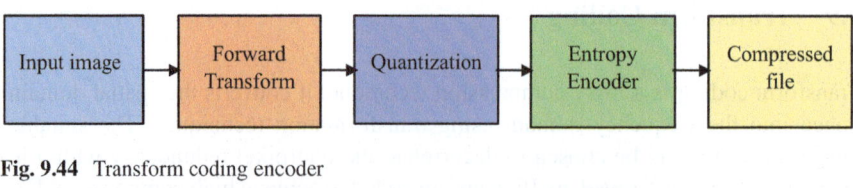

Fig. 9.44 Transform coding encoder

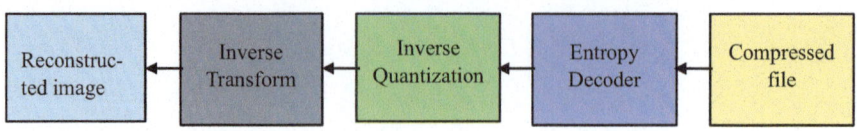

Fig. 9.45 Transform coding decoder

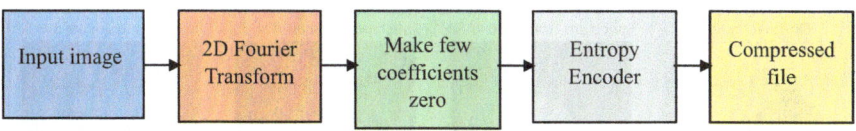

Fig. 9.46 Block diagram for Fourier transform-based transform coding

```
# Fourier transform based Transform Coding
import cv2
import numpy as np
from matplotlib import pyplot as plt
#Read in the image
I1 = cv2.imread('cameraman.tif', 0)
#Apply the fourier transform
FFT_I1 = np.fft.fft2(I1)# 2d DFT
FFT_I1_shifted = np.fft.fftshift(FFT_I1)
FFT_I1_shifted1=FFT_I1_shifted
Mag_F = np.log(np.abs(FFT_I1_shifted) + 1)
out, compress, decompress = [],[],[]
#Plot the images for comparison
plt.figure(figsize=(12,6))
plt.subplot(2,4,1), plt.imshow(I1, cmap='gray'),plt.title('Original Image'), plt.xticks([]), plt.yticks([])
plt.subplot(2,4,5), plt.imshow(Mag_F, cmap='gray'),plt.title('Magnitude Spectrum'), plt.xticks([]),
plt.yticks([])
r,c = I1.shape
radius=[50,25,5]  #Radius of the circle
for k in range(len(radius)):
  for i in range(0,r):
    for j in range(0,c):
      if (i-128)**2 + (j-128)**2 > radius[k]**2:
        FFT_I1_shifted[i,j]=0
  Mag_F1 = np.log(np.abs(FFT_I1_shifted) + 1)
  plt.subplot(2,4,k+2), plt.imshow(Mag_F1, cmap='gray'),
  plt.title(r'Spectrum truncated = {}'.format(radius[k])), plt.xticks([]), plt.yticks([])
  IFFT_I1 = np.fft.ifftshift(FFT_I1_shifted)
  Rec_I1 = np.fft.ifft2(IFFT_I1)
  Rec_I1 = np.abs(Rec_I1)
  plt.subplot(2,4,k+6),plt.imshow(Rec_I1 , cmap='gray'),
  plt.title(r'Reconstructed Image = {}'.format(radius[k])), plt.xticks([]), plt.yticks([])
```

Fig. 9.47 Fourier-based transform coding

- Figure 9.48 shows that the radius of the non-zero Fourier coefficients decides the visual quality of the reconstructed image.

Experiment 9.24: Discrete Cosine Transform (DCT)-Based Transform Coding
This experiment discusses the transform coding using DCT. The input image is decorrelated using the 2D DCT, and to achieve compression, few significant non-zero coefficients are retained by using the thresholding technique. The non-zero coefficients are only used for the reconstruction of the original image in the

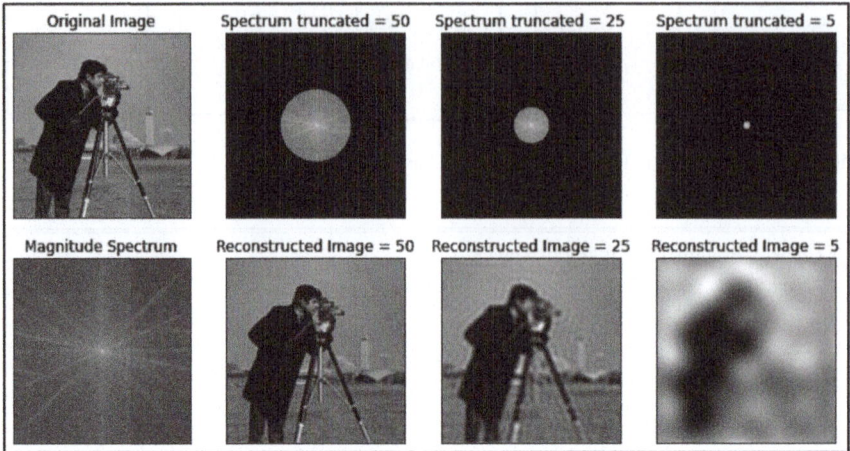

Fig. 9.48 Simulation result

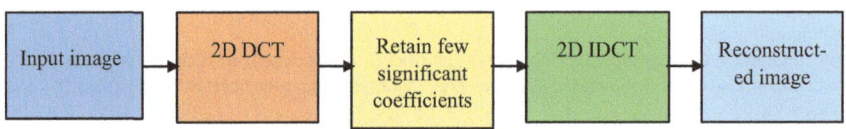

Fig. 9.49 Block diagram for DCT-based transform coding

decoding process. The block diagram for the above-mentioned task is shown in Fig. 9.49. The Python code to perform this task is shown in Fig. 9.50, and its simulation result is depicted in Fig. 9.51.

Inferences

The following inferences can be made from this experiment:

- From Fig. 9.50, it is possible to observe that the input image is split into 8 × 8 subblocks, and each subblock is passed through DCT to obtain its coefficients. By using the thresholding approach, non-zero coefficients are selected for the inverse DCT computation.
- The retained coefficients in percentage and their corresponding reconstructed image are depicted in Fig. 9.51. From this figure, it is possible to observe that more numbers of retained coefficients give better visual quality, and its compression ratio is less.

```
# DCT based transform coding
import numpy as np
import matplotlib.pyplot as plt
from scipy.fftpack import dct,idct
from numpy import r_
import cv2
img=cv2.imread('Clock.tiff',0);#Step 1: Read image
imsize = img.shape
IM = np.zeros(imsize)
block_size = 8
for i in r_[:imsize[0]:block_size]:#Step 2: DCT for 8 x 8 subblock
    for j in r_[:imsize[1]:block_size]:
        IM[i:(i+block_size),j:(j+block_size)] =
dct(dct(img[i:(i+block_size),j:(j+block_size)].T,norm='ortho').T,norm='ortho')
thresh = [0.001,0.25,0.5]# Step 3: Thesholding or Removal of insignificant thresholds
plt.figure(figsize=(10,6)),plt.subplot(2,4,1),plt.imshow(img,cmap='gray'),
plt.title('Input Image'),plt.axis('off'), plt.subplot(2,4,5), plt.imshow(IM,
cmap='gray',vmin=0,vmax=np.max(IM)*0.01),
plt.title('Original Spectrum'),plt.xticks([]), plt.yticks([])
for k in range(len(thresh)):
    I_thresh = IM * (np.abs(IM) > thresh[k]*np.max(np.abs(IM)))
    rimg=np.zeros(imsize)
    for i in r_[:imsize[0]:block_size]: #Step 4: Reconstruction of the image from subblock
        for j in r_[:imsize[1]:block_size]:
            rimg[i:(i+block_size),j:(j+block_size)]
=idct(idct(I_thresh[i:(i+block_size),j:(j+block_size)].T,norm='ortho').T,norm='ortho')
    frac_nonzero = np.sum(I_thresh != 0.0)/img.size;#Compression ratio
    dct_coeff=round((100*frac_nonzero),2);# % of retianed non zero coefficients
    MSE = np.sum((img-rimg)**2)/img.size;# MSE computation
    PSNR = 10*np.log10(np.max(img)**2/MSE);#Compute Peak Signal to Noise Ratio (PSNR)
#Step 4: Displaying the result
    plt.subplot(2,4,k+2),plt.imshow(I_thresh,cmap='gray',vmin=0,vmax=np.max(IM)*0.01)
    plt.title(r'DCT coef. Retained {} %'.format(round((100*frac_nonzero),2))),plt.axis('off')
    plt.subplot(2,4,k+6),plt.imshow(rimg,cmap='gray')
    plt.title('PSNR={}dB; CR={}'.format(round(PSNR,2),round((1/frac_nonzero),2))),plt.axis('off')
plt.tight_layout()
```

Fig. 9.50 DCT-based transform coding

- Therefore, from this experiment, it is possible to conclude that the number of coefficients considered for the reconstruction plays a major role in the quality as well as compression ratio. If the number of retained coefficients in percentage decreases, the compression ratio increases and the PSNR decreases.

Task: Vary the threshold and the block size is 16 in the Python code given in Fig. 9.50. Comment on the observed result.

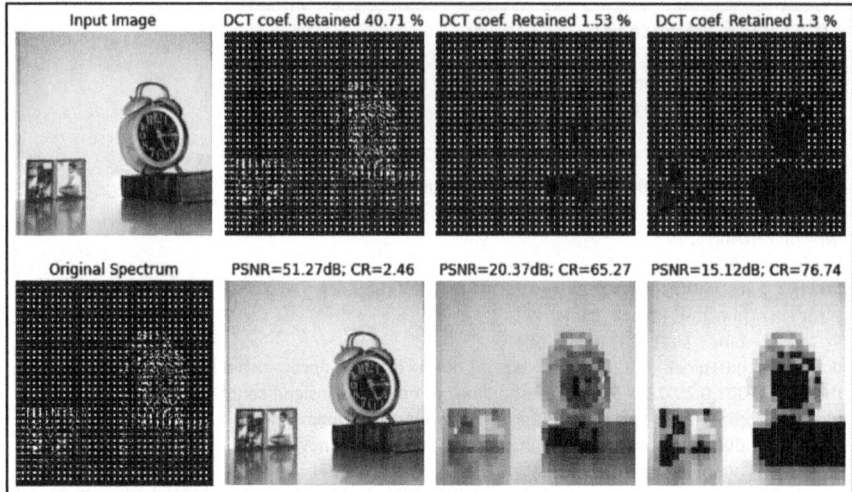

Fig. 9.51 Simulation result

9.10 Lossy DPCM

Generally, image is a 2D matrix, which consists of pixels, the neighbouring pixels may be highly correlated. A high correlation implies that a pixel is predictable based on its neighbourhood pixels. Therefore, one can transmit or store the pixel differences rather than actual pixels. This difference value takes a lesser value than the actual pixel value. Therefore, it helps to achieve compression. The encoder transmits only the difference value instead of the actual pixel value, so a smaller number of bits are allocated for transmission or storage. This concept is called as predictive coding. The block diagram of lossy predictive coding is shown in Fig. 9.52.

From Fig. 9.52, the input signal is $x[n]$ and $\hat{x}[n]$ is the predicted value, the difference is called as error signal, which is computed as

$$e[n] = x[n] - \hat{x}[n] \tag{9.24}$$

The error signal $e[n]$ is passed through the quantizer, the quantized error signal is the encoder output, which is sent through channel to the decoder section.

The predicted or estimated value of $x[n]$ is computed by

$$\hat{x}[n] = f\{x[n-1], x[n-2], \cdots, x[n-N]\} \tag{9.25}$$

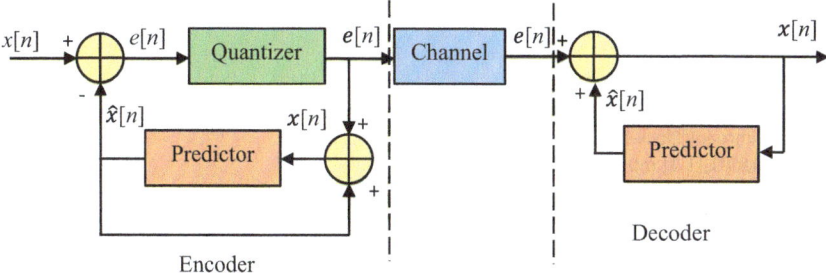

Fig. 9.52 Block diagram of lossy DPCM

where $f\{.\}$ represents the function of prediction and N denotes the order of the prediction function or N number of previous input values used for the predicted value computation.

The reconstructed value is calculated from the predicted value and the quantized error value, which can be expressed as

$$\tilde{x}[n] = \hat{x}[n] + \hat{e}[n] \tag{9.26}$$

Therefore, the estimated or predicted value of current $x[n]$ can be computed from the reconstructed signal also, which is written as

$$\hat{x}[n] = f\{\tilde{x}[n-1], \tilde{x}[n-2], \cdots, \tilde{x}[n-N]\} \tag{9.27}$$

Similarly, in the decoder section, the reconstructed signal is obtained as

$$\tilde{x}[n] = \hat{x}[n] + \hat{e}[n] \tag{9.28}$$

Experiment 9.25: Lossy DPCM Coding
This experiment discusses the compression of grayscale image using 2D lossy DPCM approach. Here, the predicted value is computed from the function of three past input pixels and uniform quantization is used to quantize the error value from the encoder of lossy DPCM. The Python code to perform this task is shown in Fig. 9.53, and its corresponding simulation result is depicted in Fig. 9.54.

Inferences
The following inferences can be made from this experiment:

- From Fig. 9.53, it is possible to observe that the predicted value of current pixel is computed by previous three pixels and by the constant ($a = 1$, $b = -1$, $c = 1$). The number of bits for the uniform quantization varies [1, 2, 4, 6, 8].

```
# 2D lossy DPCM
import numpy as np
import cv2
import matplotlib.pyplot as plt
I1=cv2.imread('Clock.tiff',0);
I2=np.pad(I1,[1,1],mode='constant')
plt.figure(figsize=(10,6)),plt.subplot(2,3,1),plt.imshow(I1,cmap='gray'),
plt.title('Input image'),plt.axis('off')
(m,n)=I2.shape
bits=[1,2,4,6,8];
for k in range(len(bits)):
  Pe=np.zeros([m,n]);
  e=np.zeros([m,n]);
  qe=np.zeros([m,n]);
  Re=np.zeros([m,n],'uint8');
  a,b,c=1,-1,1
  q=255/(2**bits[k]);
  for i in range(0,m):
      for j in range(0,n):
        Pe[i,j]=a*Re[i,j-1]+b*Re[i-1,j-1]+c*Re[i-1,j];
        e[i,j]=I2[i,j]-Pe[i,j];
        qe[i,j]= np.round((np.floor(e[i,j]/ q) * q + (q / 2)),0)
        Re[i,j]=Pe[i,j]+qe[i,j]
  Z1=np.zeros([m,n],'uint8');
  Pd=np.zeros([m,n]);
  for i in range(0,m):
    for j in range(0,n):
      Pd[i,j]=a*Z1[i,j-1] + b*Z1[i-1,j-1] + c*Z1[i-1,j];
      Z1[i,j]=qe[i,j]+Pd[i,j];
  Recons=Z1[1:m-1,1:n-1]
  MSE = np.sum((I1-Recons)**2)/I2.size;# MSE computation
  PSNR = 10*np.log10(np.max(I1)**2/(MSE));#Compute Peak Signal to Noise Ratio (PSNR)
  plt.subplot(2,3,k+2),plt.imshow(Recons,cmap='gray'),
  plt.title(r'RI: B = {}, PSNR = {} dB'.format(bits[k],round(PSNR,2))),plt.axis('off')
plt.tight_layout()
```

Fig. 9.53 Lossy DPCM-based image compression

- From Fig. 9.54, it is evident that the quality of the reconstructed image is improved when the number of bits increases in the uniform quantization. The value of bits per pixel is 8; the PSNR value is infinity, which confirms that both the input and the reconstructed image are exactly the same.
- By looking at the reconstructed image with number of bits is 6 similar to the input image. Therefore, removing the redundant information in an image will not affect the visual quality of the image. This helps to achieve the compression.

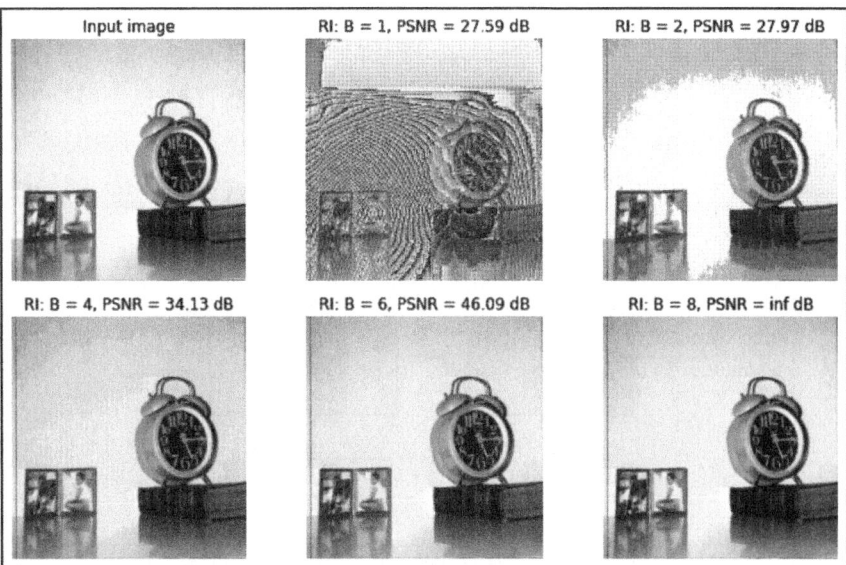

Fig. 9.54 Simulation result of lossy DPCM

9.11   Vector Quantization

Quantization is a key element for data or image compression, and it is a lossy compression method. Generally, it can be seen as many-to-one mapping. That is set of values is represented by a finite set of symbols. Quantization techniques are useful to minimize the psychovisual redundancy in the image. For example, if the data values are between 0 and 0.5, it can be represented by the symbol of "0". From this symbol, the original value cannot be reconstructed, the result will be an approximate value. Hence, this method is a lossy compression approach. The quantization can be classified into scalar and vector quantization. In the scalar quantization, each input data sample is quantized individually, whereas in the vector quantization, the set of input data samples is grouped together to form a cluster and a unique symbol encodes this cluster. From this unique symbol, set of data samples can be decoded.

The vector quantization is a block-based spatial domain approach, and it is used for the image coding. In the vector quantization, the input image is split into L-dimensional input vectors. In the vector quantization, code book plays a major role for the compression. The code book contains code vectors. The number of code vectors in the code book represents the size of the code book. The function of the encoder is to search for the code vector that best matches the input vector according to some distortion measure. The index of this code vector is then transmitted to the

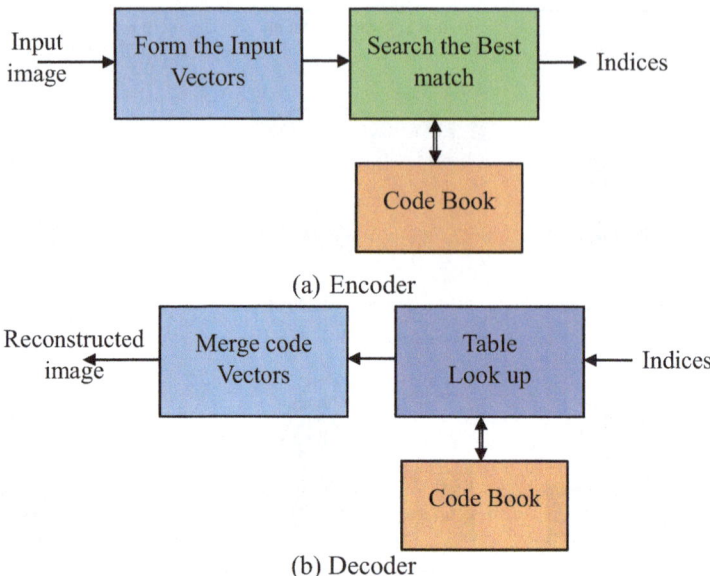

Fig. 9.55 Vector quantization process. (a) Encoder. (b) Decoder

receiver. The received index is used to look up the code vector from the code book. The identified code vector is the replacement of input vector. The block diagram of the vector quantization encoder and the decoder is shown in Fig. 9.55. Code book design and searching strategies are the important process for the vector quantization approach. The commonly used code book generation method is Linde Buzo Gray (LBG) algorithm, which computes a code book with a locally minimum average distortion for a given training set and given code book size. Entropy-constrained vector quantization (ECVQ) extends the LBG algorithm for code book creation under an entropy constraint.

Experiment 9.26: Image Compression Using LBG Vector Quantization
This experiment discusses image compression using LBG vector quantization. LBG stands for Linde-Buzo-Gray algorithm. LBG algorithm is used to create the code book based on the number of code vectors and the length of the code vectors. Assume the dimension of the input vector is 8 and size of the code book is 8. The Python code to perform this task is shown in Fig. 9.56, and its corresponding output is depicted in Fig. 9.57.

```
import numpy as np
import matplotlib.pyplot as plt
import cv2
img = cv2.imread('cameraman.tif',0)
m,n=img.shape
l1=img.flatten()
vec=8
N=len(l1)/vec;
IM=np.zeros([int(N),vec]);
Rec1=np.zeros([int(N),vec]);
for i in range(int(N)): # Input vector formation
   IM[i,:] = l1[i*vec:(i+1)*vec]

epsilon,max_iter = 0.01,100
no_of_clusters = 8
# LBG algorithm
codebook = np.mean(IM, axis=0)[np.newaxis, :] # Step 1: Initialization
while codebook.shape[0] < no_of_clusters:# Step 2: Splitting
    codebook = np.vstack([codebook * (1 + epsilon), codebook * (1 - epsilon)])
    iter_count = 0
    prev_codebook = np.zeros_like(codebook)
    while np.linalg.norm(codebook - prev_codebook) > 1e-6 and iter_count < max_iter:
      iter_count += 1
      # Step 3: Classification
      distances = np.linalg.norm(IM[:, np.newaxis] - codebook, axis=2)
      labels = np.argmin(distances, axis=1)
      # Step 4: Centroid Update
      prev_codebook = np.copy(codebook)
      for i in range(codebook.shape[0]):
         codebook[i] = np.round(np.mean(IM[labels == i], axis=0),0)
# Step 5: Convergence Check is implicitly done at the start of the while loop
#Encoding
indices = np.argmin(np.linalg.norm(IM[:, np.newaxis] - codebook, axis=2), axis=1)
# Decoding
for i in range(len(indices)):
   Rec1[i,:]=codebook[indices[i]]
dimg = Rec1.reshape(m,n)
MSE = np.sum((img-dimg)**2)/img.size;# MSE computation
PSNR = 10*np.log10(np.max(img)**2/MSE);#Compute Peak Signal to Noise Ratio (PSNR)
CR = (img.size * 8) / (len(indices)*np.log2(no_of_clusters) )
fig=plt.figure(figsize=(8,6)),plt.subplot(1,2,1),plt.imshow(img,cmap='gray'),plt.title('Input image'),
plt.xticks([]), plt.yticks([]),plt.subplot(1,2,2),plt.imshow(dimg,cmap='gray'),
plt.title(r'Recons.image PSNR = {}, CR = {}'.format(np.round(PSNR,2), np.round(CR,2)))
plt.xticks([]), plt.yticks([]),plt.tight_layout()
```

Fig. 9.56 Vector quantization-based image compression

Fig. 9.57 Simulation result

Inferences

- From Fig. 9.57, it is possible to infer that the PSNR is 21.76 dB and compression ratio is 21.33.
- The high compression ratio is achieved due to the limited size of the code book, which is only 8 in this illustration. However, the visual quality of the reconstructed image is poor.

Experiment 9.27: Vary the Size of the Code Book in the LBG-Based Vector Quantization and Comment on the Observed Result

This experiment discusses the impact of the size of the code book in the vector quantization-based image compression approach. For this, the sizes of the code book are varied as 4, 8, 16, 64, 128, and 256. The size of each input vector is chosen as 4. The visual quality and the quantitative measures like PSNR and CR are computed. The Python code to perform this task is shown in Fig. 9.58, and its simulation result is displayed in Fig. 9.59.

Inferences

- From Fig. 9.59, it is clearly observed that while increasing the size of the code book, the quality of the reconstructed image increases, at the same time, the compression ratio decreases.
- Therefore, the lossy compression gives trade-off between the quality of the reconstructed image and compression ratio, based on our requirement the parameters of the vector quantization have to be chosen.

```python
import numpy as np
import matplotlib.pyplot as plt
import cv2
img = cv2.imread('Clock.tiff',0)
m,n=img.shape
l1=img.flatten()
vec=4
N=len(l1)/vec;
IM=np.zeros([int(N),vec]);
Rec1=np.zeros([int(N),vec]);
plt.figure(figsize=(12,6)), plt.subplot(2,4,1),plt.imshow(img,cmap='gray'),plt.title('Input image'),
plt.xticks([]), plt.yticks([])
for i in range(int(N)): # Input vector formation
  IM[i,:] = l1[i*vec:(i+1)*vec]
epsilon,max_iter = 0.01,100
no_of_clusters = [4, 8, 16, 32, 64, 128, 256];
for k in range(len(no_of_clusters )):
  # LBG algorithm
  codebook = np.mean(IM, axis=0)[np.newaxis, :] # Step 1: Initialization
  while codebook.shape[0] < no_of_clusters[k]:# Step 2: Splitting
      codebook = np.vstack([codebook * (1 + epsilon), codebook * (1 - epsilon)])
      iter_count = 0
      prev_codebook = np.zeros_like(codebook)
      while np.linalg.norm(codebook - prev_codebook) > 1e-6 and iter_count < max_iter:
        iter_count += 1
        # Step 3: Classification
        distances = np.linalg.norm(IM[:, np.newaxis] - codebook, axis=2)
        labels = np.argmin(distances, axis=1)
        # Step 4: Centroid Update
        prev_codebook = np.copy(codebook)
        for i in range(codebook.shape[0]):
            codebook[i] = np.round(np.mean(IM[labels == i], axis=0),0)
            # Step 5: Convergence Check is implicitly done at the start of the while loop
            #Encoding
  indices = np.argmin(np.linalg.norm(IM[:, np.newaxis] - codebook, axis=2), axis=1)
  # Decoding
  for i in range(len(indices)):
    Rec1[i,:]=codebook[indices[i]]
  dimg = Rec1.reshape(m,n)
  MSE = np.sum((img-dimg)**2)/img.size;# MSE computation
  PSNR = 10*np.log10(np.max(img)**2/MSE);#Compute Peak Signal to Noise Ratio (PSNR)
  CR = (img.size * 8) / (len(indices)*np.log2(no_of_clusters[k]) )
  plt.subplot(2,4,k+2),plt.imshow(dimg,cmap='gray'),
  plt.title(r'N = {}, PSNR = {}, CR = {}'.format(no_of_clusters[k],np.round(PSNR,2), np.round(CR,2)))
  plt.xticks([]), plt.yticks([])
plt.tight_layout()
```

Fig. 9.58 Vector quantization-based image compression

Fig. 9.59 Simulation result

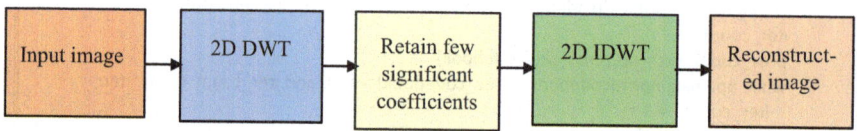

Fig. 9.60 Block diagram for wavelet-based compression

9.12   Wavelet-Based Compression

The wavelet compression approach is used to compress the image and retain the image quality better by removing the high-frequency components. Wavelet transform has the ability to perform multi-resolution analysis of the image. Wavelet family contains rich set of wavelet filters, which can provide better image compression than other transform-based coding like DCT. The drawback of JPEG standard is the blocking artefact due to block processing of DCT. The wavelet transform can remove blocking artefact; therefore, it is used in JPEG2000 image compression standard.

Experiment 9.28: Wavelet Transform-Based Image Compression
This experiment discusses wavelet transform-based compression. The input image is decomposed into wavelet subbands using 2D wavelet transform. These wavelet subbands hold a variety of coefficients, such as approximation, vertical, horizontal, and diagonal details. To achieve the compression in this algorithm, few insignificant wavelet coefficients are made as zero by using thresholding technique. The significant coefficients are used to reconstruct the original image. The block diagram for the above-mentioned task is shown in Fig. 9.60. The Python code to perform this task is shown in Fig. 9.61, and its simulation result is depicted in Fig. 9.62.

```
# Wavelet based Compression
import numpy as np
import matplotlib.pyplot as plt
import cv2
import pywt
I1 = cv2.imread('Clock.tiff',0);
#B = np.mean(A, -1);
n = 3
w = 'db2'
wav_coeff = pywt.wavedec2(I1,wavelet=w,level=n)
Coeff, Coeff_slices = pywt.coeffs_to_array(wav_coeff)
plt.figure(figsize=(12,6)),
plt.subplot(2,4,1),plt.imshow(I1,cmap='gray'),plt.title('Input Image'),plt.axis('off'),
plt.subplot(2,4,5), plt.imshow(Coeff, cmap='gray',vmin=0,vmax=np.max(Coeff)*0.01),
plt.title('Subbands'),plt.xticks([]), plt.yticks([])
Csort = np.sort(np.abs(Coeff.reshape(-1)))
thresh = [0.001,0.1,0.25]
for k in range(len(thresh)):
    I_thresh = Coeff * (np.abs(Coeff) > thresh[k]*np.max(np.abs(Coeff)))
    frac_nonzero = np.sum(I_thresh != 0.0)/I1.size;#Compression ratio
    Coeff_filt = pywt.array_to_coeffs(I_thresh,Coeff_slices,output_format='wavedec2')
    Rec = pywt.waverec2(Coeff_filt,wavelet=w)
    wav_coeff=round((100*frac_nonzero),2);# % of retained non zero coefficients
    MSE = np.sum((I1-Rec)**2)/I1.size;# MSE computation
    PSNR = 10*np.log10(np.max(I1)**2/MSE);#Compute Peak Signal to Noise Ratio (PSNR)
#Step 4: Displaying the result
    plt.subplot(2,4,k+2),plt.imshow(I_thresh,cmap='gray',vmin=0,vmax=np.max(I_thresh)*0.01)
    plt.title(r'Wavelet coef.Retained {}%'.format(round((100*frac_nonzero),2))),
    plt.xticks([]), plt.yticks([]),plt.subplot(2,4,k+6),plt.imshow(Rec,cmap='gray')
    plt.title('PSNR={}dB; CR={}'.format(round(PSNR,2),round((1/frac_nonzero),2))),plt.axis('off')
plt.tight_layout()
```

Fig. 9.61 Wavelet-based compression

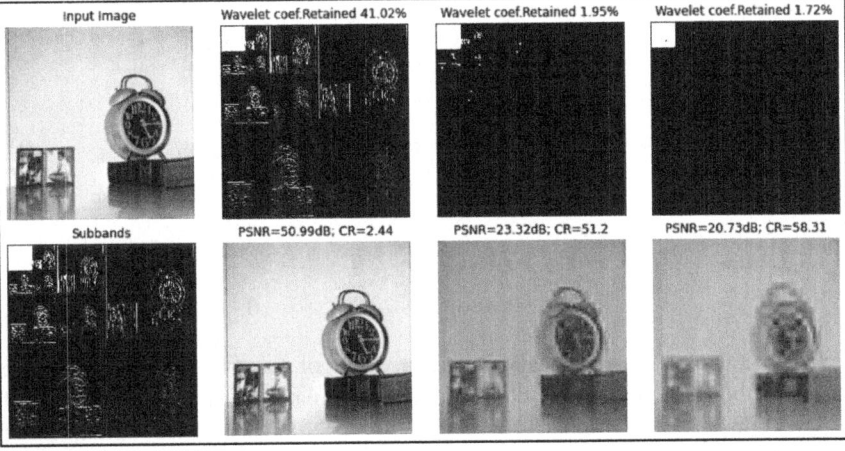

Fig. 9.62 Simulation result

Inferences

The following inferences can be made from this experiment:

- From Fig. 9.61, it is possible to observe that the input image is decomposed by wavelet transform with "db2" wavelet, and the level of decomposition is 3. By using thresholding approach, non-zero coefficients are selected for the inverse discrete wavelet transform computation.
- The retained coefficients in percentage and their corresponding reconstructed image are depicted in Fig. 9.62. From this figure, it is possible to observe that a greater number of retained coefficients gives better visual quality and its compression ratio is less.
- From this experiment, it is possible to conclude that number of coefficients considered for the reconstruction plays a major role in the quality as well as compression ratio. If the number of retained coefficients in percentage decreases, the compression ratio increases, and the PSNR value decreases.

9.13   SVD Based Compression

The singular value decomposition (SVD) is a transform, which decomposes the input matrix "A" with the size ($m \times n$) into three matrices such as U, S, and V. The relationship between the input matrix and decomposed matrices is given by

$$A = USV^{\mathrm{T}} \tag{9.29}$$

where U and V are the orthonormal matrices with the size of ($m \times m$) and ($n \times n$), respectively. S represents the diagonal singular value matrix with the size of ($m \times n$). The SVD representation of matrix A is shown in Fig. 9.63.

The singular values matrix in the form of

$$S = \begin{bmatrix}
\sigma_1 & 0 & \cdots & 0 & 0 & \cdots & 0 \\
0 & \sigma_2 & \cdots & 0 & 0 & \cdots & 0 \\
\vdots & \vdots & \ddots & \vdots & \vdots & \cdots & \vdots \\
0 & 0 & \cdots & \sigma_r & 0 & \cdots & 0 \\
0 & 0 & \cdots & 0 & \sigma_{r+1} & \cdots & 0 \\
\vdots & \vdots & \cdots & \vdots & \vdots & \ddots & \vdots \\
0 & 0 & \cdots & 0 & 0 & \cdots & \sigma_n \\
0 & 0 & \cdots & 0 & 0 & \cdots & 0
\end{bmatrix}$$

For $i = 1, 2, 3, \ldots, n$, σ_i are called singular values of a matrix A. For example, the rank of the matrix A is "r", then the singular values in the form of $\{\sigma_1 \geq \sigma_2 \geq \sigma_3 \cdots \geq \sigma_r > 0$ and $\sigma_{r+1} = \sigma_{r+2} = \cdots = \sigma_n = 0\}$. That is the "$r$" numbers of singular values are non-zero for "n" singular values.

Experiment 9.29: SVD-Based Image Compression

This experiment deals with the singular value decomposition (SVD) based image compression. The input image is decomposed into *U*, *S*, and *V* using SVD. *U* and *V* are the orthonormal matrices, and *S* is the singular value diagonal matrix. Only a few singular values are utilized for the reconstruction process to get compression. For that, few singular values are retained as its, and the remaining singular values are made as zero. The block diagram for the above-mentioned task is shown in Fig. 9.64. The Python code used to perform this task is shown in Fig. 9.65, and its simulation result is depicted in Fig. 9.66.

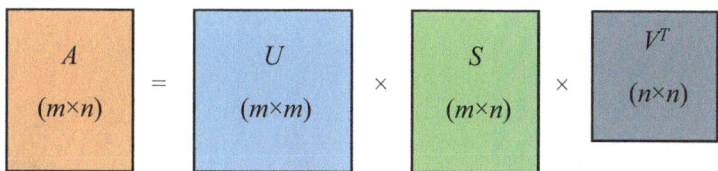

Fig. 9.63 Factorization of SVD

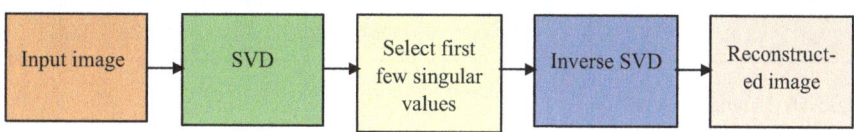

Fig. 9.64 Block diagram for SVD-based compression

```
# SVD based image compression
import cv2
import numpy as np
import matplotlib.pyplot as plt
I1 = cv2.imread('Clock.tiff',0);
plt.figure(figsize=(10,8)),
plt.subplot(2,3,1),plt.imshow(I1,cmap='gray'),plt.title('Input Image'),plt.axis('off')
U, S, V = np.linalg.svd(I1, full_matrices=False)# Singular Value Decomposition
# Reconstruction of Original Image with number of singular values
no_sing=[5, 10, 15, 20, S.shape[0]]
for i in range(len(no_sing)):
    Rec_I = U[:, :no_sing[i]] @ np.diag(S[:no_sing[i]]) @ V[:no_sing[i], :]
    MSE = np.sum((I1-Rec_I)**2)/I1.size;# MSE computation
    PSNR = 10*np.log10(np.max(I1**2)/MSE);#Compute Peak Signal to Noise Ratio (PSNR)
    plt.subplot(2, 3, i+2),plt.imshow(Rec_I, cmap='gray'),plt.axis('off')
    plt.title('PSNR={}dB; S Retained ={}'.format(round(PSNR,2),no_sing[i])),plt.axis('off')
plt.tight_layout()
```

Fig. 9.65 Python code for SVD-based compression

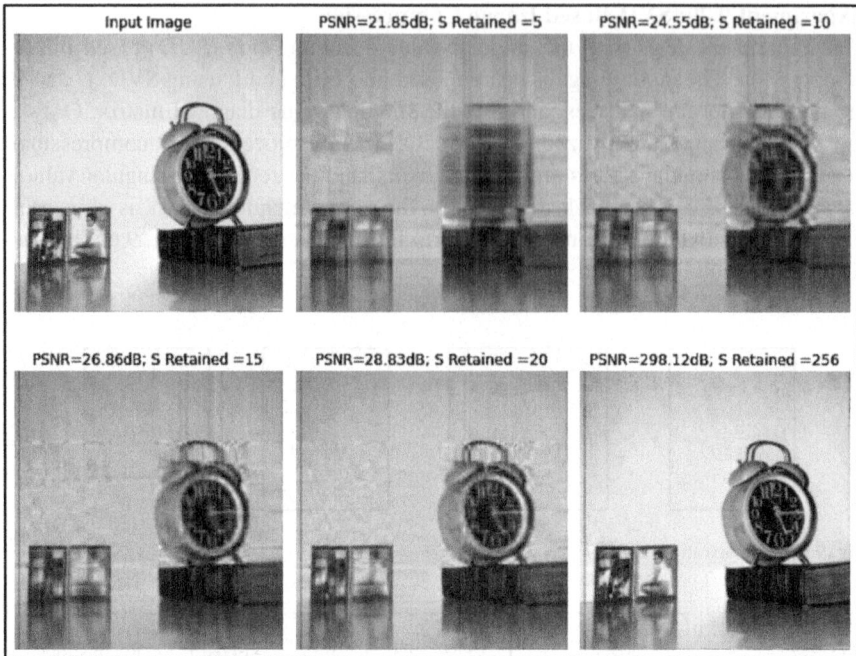

Fig. 9.66 Simulation result

Inferences

The following inferences can be made from this experiment:

- From Fig. 9.65, it is possible to observe that the input image is decomposed by SVD using "np.linalg.svd" numpy library. The result contains three matrices U and V are orthonormal matrices and S is a singular value vector. Only few singular values are used to reconstruct the original image they are [5, 10, 15, 20, and full].
- Figure 9.66 shows the reconstructed image with the different singular values used. From this, it is possible to observe that the reconstructed image quality increases with more singular values included for the reconstruction.

9.14   Fractal Image Compression

The word "fractal" originates from Latin word "fract" or "fractus" meaning "broken" or "uneven" and it was coined by Benoit B. Mandelbrot. Some properties of fractal set (F) are as follows:

1. The fractal set (F) has some self-similarity.
2. Fractal set is detailed on every scale.

3. Fractal dimension does not need to be an integer.
4. Most of the time fractal has some simple mathematical or algorithmic description.

Fractal is a self-repeating geometrical figure. Examples of fractal include Sierpinski triangle, Koch curve, Spiral, Barnsley's fern, fractal tree, pentagon pattern, etc. All these fractals can be generated by iterated function system (IFS). An iterated function system is a finite set of contraction mappings on a complete metric space (X, d), which is mathematically written as

$$\{\omega_i : X \rightarrow X \,|\, i = 1,2,\dots,N\} \tag{9.30}$$

Each contraction mapping ω_i has a corresponding contractivity factor c_i. An alternative notation for the same IFS is given by

$$\{X;,\omega_1;,\omega_2;,\dots;,\omega_N\}. \tag{9.31}$$

The fractal image generation can be achieved by using affine transformations, which are mathematically written as

$$w_i \begin{bmatrix} m \\ n \end{bmatrix} = \begin{bmatrix} a_i & b_i \\ c_i & d_i \end{bmatrix} \begin{bmatrix} m \\ n \end{bmatrix} + \begin{bmatrix} e_i \\ f_i \end{bmatrix} \tag{9.32}$$

where (m, n) denotes the location of the pixel, a_i, b_i, c_i, d_i, e_i and f_i are the parameters that translate, skew, stretch, rotate, and scale an input image pixel.

Experiment 9.30: Generation of Sierpinski Triangle Using IFS
This experiment discusses the generation of the Sierpinski triangle using IFS in a Python environment. The affine transformation matrix for the Sierpinski triangle generation is given by

$$1 = \begin{bmatrix} 0.5 & 0 \\ 0 & 0.5 \end{bmatrix} \begin{bmatrix} m \\ n \end{bmatrix} + \begin{bmatrix} 0 \\ 0 \end{bmatrix}$$

$$2 = \begin{bmatrix} 0.5 & 0 \\ 0 & 0.5 \end{bmatrix} \begin{bmatrix} m \\ n \end{bmatrix} + \begin{bmatrix} 0.5 \\ 0 \end{bmatrix}$$

$$3 = \begin{bmatrix} 0.5 & 0 \\ 0 & 0.5 \end{bmatrix} \begin{bmatrix} m \\ n \end{bmatrix} + \begin{bmatrix} 0.25 \\ 0.8660 \end{bmatrix}$$

The Python code to generate Sierpinski triangle is given in Fig. 9.67 and its simulation result is shown in Fig. 9.68.

Inference

- From Fig. 9.68, it is possible to see that the output is the Sierpinski triangle and it is a fractal pattern.

```
# Python code for Sierpinski traingle generation
import matplotlib.pyplot as plt
from random import randint
x, y = [],[]; # initializing the list
x.append(0) ; # setting first element to 0
y.append(0)
current = 0
for i in range(1, 50000):
    z = randint(1, 3); # generates a random
          # the x and y coordinates of the equations are appended in the lists respectively.
    if z == 1:
        x.append(0.5*(x[current]))
        y.append(0.5*(y[current]))
    if z == 2:
        x.append(0.5*(x[current]) + 0.5)
        y.append(0.5*(y[current]))
    if z == 3:
        x.append(0.5*(x[current]) + 0.25)
        y.append(0.5*(y[current]) + 0.8660)
    current = current + 1
plt.scatter(x, y, s = 0.005, edgecolor ='blue'),plt.xticks([]),
plt.yticks([]),plt.title('Sierpinski traingle')
plt.show()
```

Fig. 9.67 Python code for Sierpinski triangle generation

Fig. 9.68 Simulation result

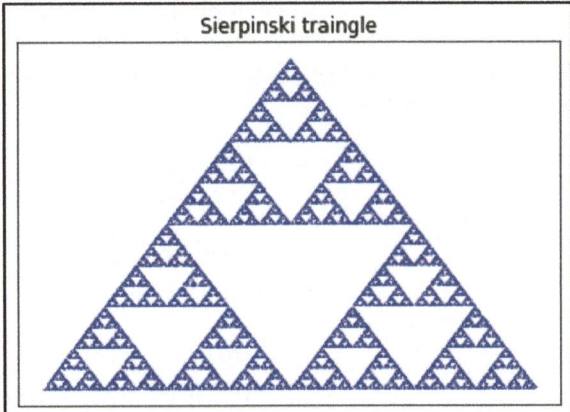

Experiment 9.31: Generation of Fractal Tree Using IFS

This experiment discusses the generation of fractal tree using IFS in Python environment. The affine transformation matrices for the fractal tree generation are given by

$$1 = \begin{bmatrix} 0.195 & -0.488 \\ 0.344 & 0.443 \end{bmatrix} \begin{bmatrix} m \\ n \end{bmatrix} + \begin{bmatrix} 0.722 \\ 0.536 \end{bmatrix} \tag{9.33}$$

```
# Python code for Fractal tree generation
import matplotlib.pyplot as plt
from random import randint
x, y = [],[]; # initializing the list
# setting first element to 0
x.append(0)
y.append(0)
current = 0
for i in range(1, 50000):
    z = randint(1, 4); # generates a random
    if z == 1:
        x.append(0.195*(x[current]) - 0.488*(y[current]) + 0.722)
        y.append(0.344*(x[current]) + 0.443*(y[current]) + 0.536)
    if z==2:
        x.append(0.462*(x[current]) + 0.414*(y[current]) + 0.538)
        y.append(-0.252*(x[current]) + 0.361*(y[current]) + 1.167)
    if z==3:
        x.append(-0.058*(x[current]) - 0.070*(y[current]) + 1.125)
        y.append(0.453*(x[current]) - 0.111*(y[current]) + 0.185)
    if z== 4:
        x.append(-0.045*(x[current]) + 0.091*(y[current]) + 0.863)
        y.append(-0.469*(x[current]) - 0.022*(y[current]) + 0.871)
    current = current + 1
plt.scatter(x, y, s = 0.1, edgecolor ='green'),
plt.title('Fractal Tree'),plt.xticks([]),plt.yticks([])
plt.show()
```

Fig. 9.69 Python code for fractal tree generation

$$2 = \begin{bmatrix} 0.462 & 0.414 \\ -0.252 & 0.361 \end{bmatrix} \begin{bmatrix} m \\ n \end{bmatrix} + \begin{bmatrix} 0.538 \\ 1.167 \end{bmatrix} \tag{9.34}$$

$$3 = \begin{bmatrix} -0.058 & -0.070 \\ 0.453 & -0.111 \end{bmatrix} \begin{bmatrix} m \\ n \end{bmatrix} + \begin{bmatrix} 1.125 \\ 0.185 \end{bmatrix} \tag{9.35}$$

$$4 = \begin{bmatrix} -0.045 & 0.091 \\ -0.469 & -0.022 \end{bmatrix} \begin{bmatrix} m \\ n \end{bmatrix} + \begin{bmatrix} 0.863 \\ 0.871 \end{bmatrix} \tag{9.36}$$

Implementing the Eqs. (9.33–9.36) in the Python can generate "Fractal tree". The Python code to generate a fractal tree is given in Fig. 9.69, and its simulation result is shown in Fig. 9.70.

Inference

- From Fig. 9.70, it is possible to see that the output is the fractal tree and it is a fractal pattern.

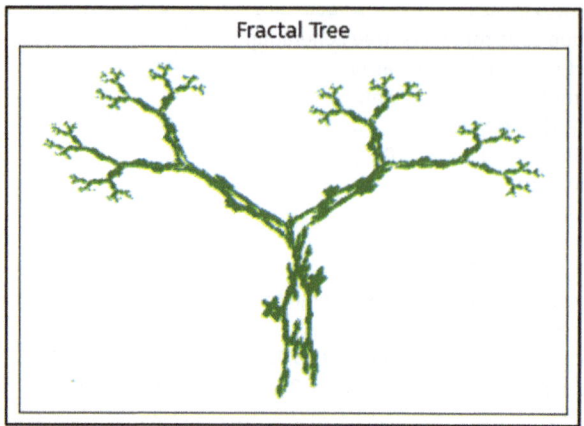

Fractal Tree

Fig. 9.70 Simulation result

9.14.1   *Fractal Image Compression Algorithm*

Fractal image compression is a lossy image compression approach. It was developed by Hutchinson, Barnsley, and Demko. This approach searches the self-similarities among the diverse image blocks and only stores the parameters of the contractual transformation in place of the image pixels. The fractal image compression can be achieved by using affine transformations, which are mathematically written as

$$
w_i \begin{bmatrix} m \\ n \end{bmatrix} = \begin{bmatrix} a_i & b_i \\ c_i & d_i \end{bmatrix} \begin{bmatrix} m \\ n \end{bmatrix} + \begin{bmatrix} e_i \\ f_i \end{bmatrix} \tag{9.37}
$$

where (m, n) denotes the location of the pixel, a_i, b_i, c_i, d_i, e_i, and f_i are the parameters, which translate, skew, stretch, rotate, and scale an input image pixel. Let us consider an image shown in Fig. 9.71a. From this figure, we can make a copy of images, which is depicted in Fig. 9.71b. Comparing these two images, the source image is shown in Fig. 9.71a, and multiple copies of the image are shown in Fig. 9.71b. Now, if we want to store or represent an image shown in Fig. 9.71b, only the original input image, along with the affine transform constants, is enough. That is the advantage of fractal image compression.

The fractal image compression algorithm starts with the partioning of the image into "M" non-overlapping range blocks "R_i". Another partition of the image is made this time into "N" non overlapping domain blocks "D_j". Each domain block has the size of twice the size of the range blocks. The domain and range block of an image is illustrated in Fig. 9.72. With these two image partitions, the fractal block coding algorithm searches each range block "R_i" for the best match amongst the domain blocks "D_j". In order to compare a domain block with a range block, the size of both

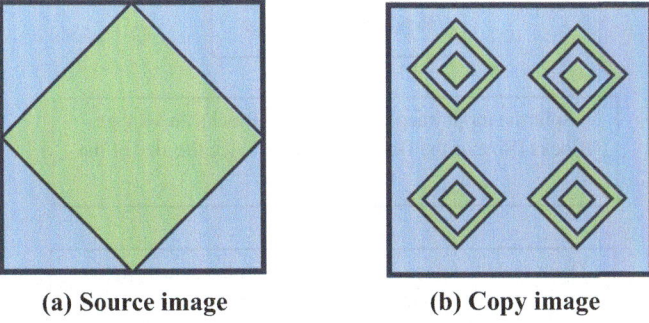

(a) Source image   **(b) Copy image**

Fig. 9.71 Example of fractal concept. (**a**) Source image. (**b**) Copy image

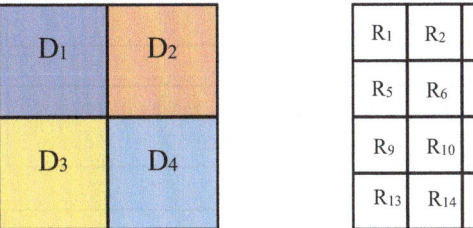

Fig. 9.72 Example of domain and range blocks

blocks should be the same. For this, it may use the average the pixels in the domain block and reduce its size to the size of the range block. Some transformation methods, such as flipping, rotation, change contrast, and brightness operation, can be performed to find the best match between the domain and range blocks. Flipping is a reflection of the scaled-down domain block, and the rotations contain rotating the domain block with 0°, 90°, 180°, or 270°. For these transformations, there are eight variants of each domain block to compare with each range block. That is the domain block may flip or not flip with the four rotation transformations, total eight transformations variants.

Using the root mean square error between the range block and flipping and rotation of the down-scaled domain block with a contrast scaling constant and brightness controlling constant. The function of the domain block is obtained as

$$\omega_i\left(D_{j(i)}\right) = \alpha \times \text{rotate}\left(\text{flip}\left(\hat{D}_{j(i)}\right)\right) + \beta \tag{9.38}$$

That minimizes using the following equation

$$e_{\text{rms}}\left(I,G\right) = \sqrt{\sum_{m=1}^{P}\sum_{n=1}^{Q}\left|I\left(m,n\right) - G\left(m,n\right)\right|^2} \tag{9.39}$$

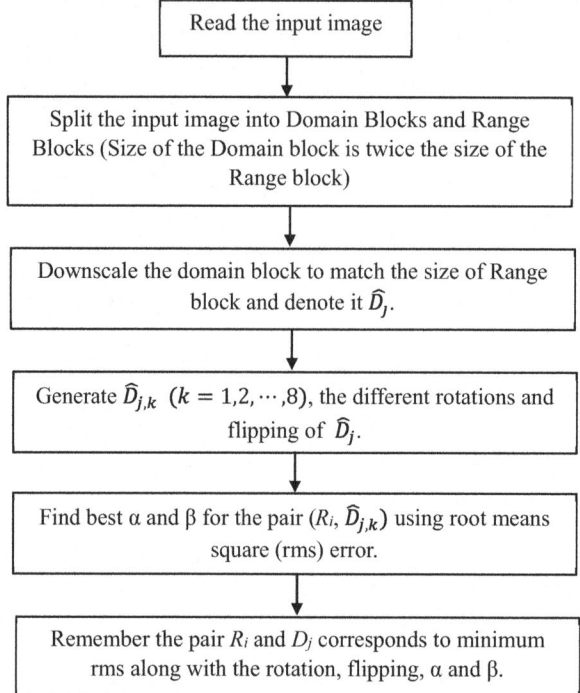

Fig. 9.73 Flow diagram of fractal block coding

where $I = R_i$ and $G = \omega_i(D_{j(i)})$. The flow diagram of the fractal block coding algorithm is shown in Fig. 9.73 and the Python code to perform the image compression using fractal block coding is shown in Fig. 9.74.

Inference

From Fig. 9.75, it is possible to observe that the iteration increases the root mean square error (RMSE) measure decreases and also the output image quality increases.

Exercises

1. Write a Python code to read a colour image. Convert it into YUV space and to get back the original RGB. Comment on the observed result.
2. Generate an 8 × 8 image with gray level values 0, 50, 128, 200, and 255. Obtain the entropy of the image and comment on the observed result.
3. Encode the text "AAAABBBBCCCCXXXX" using run length encoding. Assume that this text is transmitted by using ASCII (7bit) binary code. Obtain the compression ratio of RLE.

```
# Fractal image compression
import matplotlib.pyplot as plt
from scipy import ndimage
import numpy as np
import math
import cv2
def get_greyscale_image(img):
    return np.mean(img[:,:,:2], 2)
# Transformations
def reduce(img, factor):# Downscale
    result = np.zeros((img.shape[0] // factor, img.shape[1] // factor))
    for i in range(result.shape[0]):
        for j in range(result.shape[1]):
            result[i,j] = np.mean(img[i*factor:(i+1)*factor,j*factor:(j+1)*factor])
    return result

def rotate(img, angle):# Rotation
    return ndimage.rotate(img, angle, reshape=False)

def flip(img, direction): # Flipping
    return img[::direction,:]

def apply_transformation(img, direction, angle, contrast=1.0, brightness=0.0):
    return contrast*rotate(flip(img, direction), angle) + brightness

#Contrast and brightness
def find_contrast_and_brightness1(D, S):
    contrast = 0.75;# Fix the contrast and only fit the brightness
    brightness = (np.sum(D - contrast*S)) / D.size
    return contrast, brightness

def find_contrast_and_brightness2(D, S):
    # Fit the contrast and the brightness
    A = np.concatenate((np.ones((S.size, 1)), np.reshape(S, (S.size, 1))), axis=1)
    b = np.reshape(D, (D.size,))
    x, _, _, _ = np.linalg.lstsq(A, b)
    return x[1], x[0]
# Compression for greyscale images
def generate_all_transformed_blocks(img, source_size, destination_size, step):
    factor = source_size // destination_size
    transformed_blocks = []
    for k in range((img.shape[0] - source_size) // step + 1):
        for l in range((img.shape[1] - source_size) // step + 1):
            # Extract the input block and reduce it to the shape of an output block
            S = reduce(img[k*step:k*step+source_size,l*step:l*step+source_size], factor)
            for direction, angle in candidates: # Generate all possible transformed blocks
                transformed_blocks.append((k, l, direction, angle, apply_transformation(S, direction, angle)))
    return transformed_blocks
```

Fig. 9.74 Python code for fractal block coding algorithm

```
def compress(img, inp_size, out_size, step):
  transformations = []
  transformed_blocks = generate_all_transformed_blocks(img, inp_size, out_size, step)
  i_count = img.shape[0] // out_size
  j_count = img.shape[1] // out_size
  for i in range(i_count):
    transformations.append([])
    for j in range(j_count):
      transformations[i].append(None)
      min_d = float('inf')
      # Extract the output block
      D = img[i*out_size:(i+1)*out_size,j*out_size:(j+1)*out_size]
      # Test all possible transformations and take the best one
      for k, l, direction, angle, S in transformed_blocks:
        contrast, brightness = find_contrast_and_brightness2(D, S)
        S = contrast*S + brightness
        d = np.sum(np.square(D - S))
        if d < min_d:
          min_d = d
          transformations[i][j] = (k, l, direction, angle, contrast, brightness)
  return transformations
def decompress(transformations, inp_size, out_size, step, nb_iter=8):
  factor = inp_size // out_size
  h = len(transformations) * out_size
  w = len(transformations[0]) * out_size
  iterations = [np.random.randint(0, 256, (h, w))]
  cur_img = np.zeros((h, w))
  for i_iter in range(nb_iter):
    print(i_iter)
    for i in range(len(transformations)):
      for j in range(len(transformations[i])):
        k, l, flip, angle, contrast, brightness = transformations[i][j];# Apply transform
        S = reduce(iterations[-1][k*step:k*step+inp_size,l*step:l*step+inp_size], factor)
        D = apply_transformation(S, flip, angle, contrast, brightness)
        cur_img[i*out_size:(i+1)*out_size,j*out_size:(j+1)*out_size] = D
    iterations.append(cur_img)
    cur_img = np.zeros((h, w))
  return iterations
def plot_iterations(iterations, target=None):
  plt.figure(figsize=(10,8))
  r = math.ceil(np.sqrt(len(iterations)))
  c = r
  for i, img in enumerate(iterations):
    plt.subplot(r, c, i+1), plt.imshow(img, cmap='gray', vmin=0, vmax=255, interpolation='none')
    plt.xticks([]),plt.yticks([])
    if target is None:
      plt.title(str(i))
    else:
      plt.title('Iter ' + str(i) + '; (RMSE:' + '{0:.2f}'.format(np.sqrt(np.mean(np.square(target - img)))) + ')')
  plt.tight_layout()
```

Fig. 9.74 (continued)

```
# Parameters
directions = [1, -1]
angles = [0, 90, 180, 270]
candidates = [[direction, angle] for direction in directions for angle in angles]

img = cv2.imread('Clock.tiff',0)
img = reduce(img, 4)
plt.figure(),plt.imshow(img, cmap='gray', interpolation='none'),plt.xticks([]),plt.yticks([])
plt.title('Input Image')
transformations = compress(img, 8, 4, 8)
iterations = decompress(transformations, 8, 4, 8)
plot_iterations(iterations, img),
plt.show()
```

Fig. 9.74 (continued)

4. Generate a grayscale image is given by

$$\begin{bmatrix} 0 & 0 & 0 & 0 & 10 & 10 & 10 & 10 \\ 10 & 10 & 10 & 10 & 10 & 10 & 10 & 10 \\ 20 & 20 & 20 & 20 & 20 & 20 & 20 & 20 \\ 25 & 25 & 25 & 25 & 25 & 25 & 25 & 25 \\ 25 & 25 & 25 & 25 & 25 & 25 & 25 & 25 \\ 20 & 20 & 20 & 20 & 20 & 20 & 20 & 20 \\ 20 & 20 & 20 & 20 & 20 & 20 & 20 & 20 \\ 10 & 10 & 10 & 10 & 0 & 0 & 0 & 0 \end{bmatrix}$$

and encode this image using run length encoder with the raster scan method (row-wise). Repeat the encoding process with column-wise. Obtain the compression ratio and comment on it.

5. Generate a grayscale image is given by

$$\begin{bmatrix} 0 & 0 & 0 & 0 & 10 & 10 & 10 & 10 \\ 10 & 10 & 10 & 10 & 10 & 10 & 10 & 10 \\ 20 & 20 & 20 & 20 & 20 & 20 & 20 & 20 \\ 25 & 25 & 25 & 25 & 25 & 25 & 25 & 25 \\ 25 & 25 & 25 & 25 & 25 & 25 & 25 & 25 \\ 20 & 20 & 20 & 20 & 20 & 20 & 20 & 20 \\ 20 & 20 & 20 & 20 & 20 & 20 & 20 & 20 \\ 10 & 10 & 10 & 10 & 0 & 0 & 0 & 0 \end{bmatrix}$$

and encode this image using Huffman coding. Compute the compression ratio and comment on the result.

6. Obtain the tag value for the word "GOOD" using arithmetic coding and modify the tag value ±0.5, decode the word. Also, compute the maximum deviation that can be allowed in the tag value to get back the original message as it is.

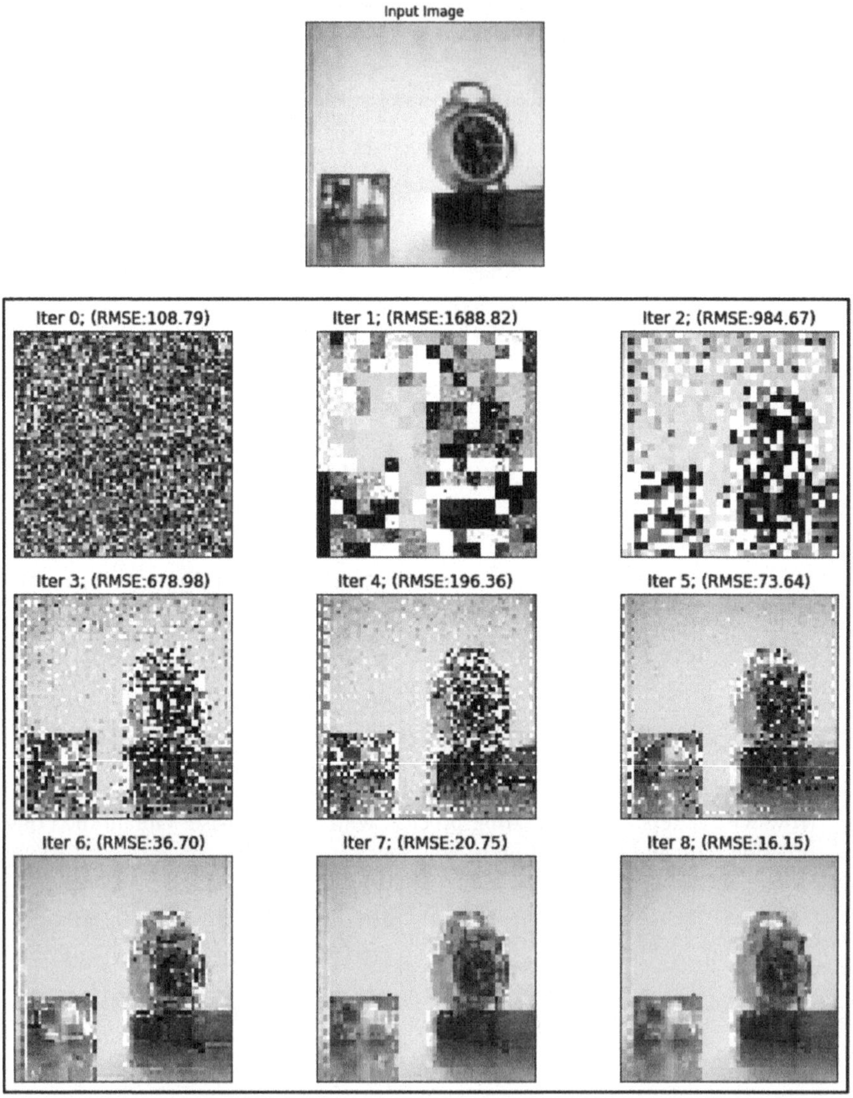

Input Image

Iter 0; (RMSE:108.79)	Iter 1; (RMSE:1688.82)	Iter 2; (RMSE:984.67)
Iter 3; (RMSE:678.98)	Iter 4; (RMSE:196.36)	Iter 5; (RMSE:73.64)
Iter 6; (RMSE:36.70)	Iter 7; (RMSE:20.75)	Iter 8; (RMSE:16.15)

Fig. 9.75 Simulation result

7. The initial dictionary is given by

String	Integer code
C	0
E	1
S	2
U	3

The LZW encoder output is [2 3 0 0 1 2 2], decode the original string. Also, display the updated dictionary.

8. Write a Python code to compress the grayscale image is given by

$$\begin{bmatrix} 0 & 0 & 0 & 0 & 10 & 10 & 10 & 10 \\ 10 & 10 & 10 & 10 & 10 & 10 & 10 & 10 \\ 20 & 20 & 20 & 20 & 20 & 20 & 20 & 20 \\ 25 & 25 & 25 & 25 & 25 & 25 & 25 & 25 \\ 25 & 25 & 25 & 25 & 25 & 25 & 25 & 25 \\ 20 & 20 & 20 & 20 & 20 & 20 & 20 & 20 \\ 20 & 20 & 20 & 20 & 20 & 20 & 20 & 20 \\ 10 & 10 & 10 & 10 & 0 & 0 & 0 & 0 \end{bmatrix}$$ using lossless DPCM approach with the

predictor parameters are chosen to be $\{a = 1, b = -1, c = 1\}$. Compute the compression ratio and comment on it.

9. Read a grayscale image and compress it using bitplane coding with RLE. Obtain the compression ratio and comment on the obtained result.

10. Read a grayscale image and compress it using transform coding. Choices of the transform are (1) Fourier transform and (2) Discrete Cosine Transform. Retain only 25% of maximum energy content coefficients of both the transforms for the reconstruction. Obtain the PSNR values and comment on the reconstructed images.

11. Change the values of predictor constants $\{a, b, c\}$ in the lossy DPCM coding and observe the impact of the reconstructed image. Comment on the observed result.

12. Vary the size of the input vector like (4, 8, 16) in the LBG-based vector quantization and fix the size of the code book is 128. Comment on the observed result.

13. Read a grayscale image, compress it using wavelet-based compression with the "coiflet1" wavelet filter, and level of decomposition is 3. Reconstruct the image with the 25% of the higher energy wavelet filter coefficients. Compute the PNSR and comment on the observed result.

14. The Iterated Function System (IFS) code for Barnsley's fern pattern is given below. Write a Python code to create Barnsley's fern pattern and comment on the observed result.

Ω	a	B	c	d	E	f	
1	0	0	0	0.16	0	0	Stem
2	0.85	0.04	−0.04	0.85	0	1.6	Small leaflet
3	0.2	−0.26	0.23	0.22	0	1.6	Large leaflet—left
4	−0.15	0.28	0.26	0.24	0	0.44	Large leaflet—right

15. The Iterated Function System (IFS) code for Pentagon pattern is given below. Write a Python code to create Pentagon pattern and comment on the observed result.

ω	a	b	c	D	e	f
1	0.382	0	0	0.382	0.3072	0.6190
2	0.382	0	0	0.382	0.6033	0.4044
3	0.382	0	0	0.382	0.0139	0.4044
4	0.382	0	0	0.382	0.1253	0.0595
5	0.382	0	0	0.382	0.4920	0.0595

Objective Questions

1. What will be the output, after executing the following Python code?

```
import numpy as np
I=np.eye(4);
print(I.size)
```

(A) (4, 4)

(B) 16

(C) $\begin{bmatrix} 1 & 0 & 0 & 0 \\ 0 & 1 & 0 & 0 \\ 0 & 0 & 1 & 0 \\ 0 & 0 & 0 & 1 \end{bmatrix}$

(D) $\begin{bmatrix} 1 & 1 & 1 & 1 \\ 1 & 1 & 1 & 1 \\ 1 & 1 & 1 & 1 \\ 1 & 1 & 1 & 1 \end{bmatrix}$

2. What would be the output after executing the following Python code?

```
import numpy as np
I1=np.eye(4)
_, occur = np.unique(I1, return_counts=True)
print(occur)
```

(A) [12, 4]
(B) [4, 12]
(C) [16]
(D) [0]

3. After executing the Python code given below, what will be the output?

```
import numpy as np
I=np.eye(2);
I1 = I.flatten()
print(I1)
```

(A) [1. 1. 0. 0.]
(B) [1. 1. 1. 1.]
(C) [1. 0. 0. 1.]
(D) $\begin{bmatrix} 1 & 0 \\ 0 & 1 \end{bmatrix}$

4. After executing the python code given below, what will be output?

```
import numpy as np
I=np.eye(2);
I1 = I.flatten()
I2 = np.array(I1).reshape(I.shape)
print(I2)
```

(A) [[1. 0.]
     [0. 1.]]
(B) [1. 0. 1. 0.]
(C) (2, 2)
(D) $\begin{bmatrix} 1 & 0 \\ 0 & 1 \end{bmatrix}$

5. What would be the output, after executing the following Python code?

```
import numpy as np
from collections import Counter
I1=np.eye(2);
I2 = I1.flatten().tolist()
pxs = len(I2)
tbl = Counter(I2)
occur = {k:v/pxs for k,v in tbl.items()}
print(occur)
```

(A) {1.0: 4.0, 0.0: 0.0}
(B) {1.0: 0.0, 0.0: 1.0}
(C) {1.0: 2.0, 0.0: 2.0}
(D) {1.0: 0.5, 0.0: 0.5}

6. What would be the output, after executing the following Python code?

```
a=0.123456
b=round(a,4)
print(b)
```

(A) 0.1235
(B) 0.1234
(C) 0.1000
(D) 0.0

7. What would be the output after executing the following Python code?

```
import numpy as np
X='IND'
Y=np.fromiter(X, (np.str_,1))
print(Y)
```

(A) ["I" "N" "D"]
(B) ['IND']
(C) ["I" "N" "D"]
(D) ["IND"]

8. What would be the output, after executing the following Python code?

```
import numpy as np
import cv2
X=np.array([[128., 255.], [0., 64.]],'uint8')
Y = np.full((X.shape[0], X.shape[1]), 2 ** 0, np.uint8)
Z = cv2.bitwise_and(Y, X);
print(Z)
```

(A) $\begin{array}{cc} [[1 & 0] \\ [0 & 1]] \end{array}$

(B) $\begin{array}{cc} [[1 & 1] \\ [0 & 1]] \end{array}$

(C) $\begin{array}{cc} [[0 & 1] \\ [0 & 0]] \end{array}$

(D) $\begin{array}{cc} [[128 & 255] \\ [0 & 64]] \end{array}$

9. The arithmetic lossless coding is used in the following image standard.

(A) JPEG
(B) JBIG
(C) Group 3 Fax
(D) JPEG2000

10. The variants of LZ77 used in the following file format.

    (A) BMP
    (B) MIFF
    (C) PNG
    (D) PIX

11. Statement 1: Huffman code is a prefix code
    Statement 2: Huffman code is a fixed-length code

    (A) Statements 1 and 2 are correct
    (B) Statement 1 is correct, statement 2 is wrong.
    (C) Statement 2 is correct, statement 1 is wrong
    (D) Statements 1 and 2 are wrong

12. Match the techniques which is used to minimize the redundancy

Techniques	**Redundancy**
1. Transform	P. Psychovisual redundancy
2. Quantization	Q. Coding redundancy
3. Encoding	R. Spatial redundancy

    (A) 1-P, 2-Q, 3-R
    (B) 1-R, 2-P, 3-Q
    (C) 1-R, 2-Q, 3-P
    (D) 1-Q, 2-P, 3-R

13. **Statement 1**: Transform used for image compression should have high energy compaction.
    Statement 2: Transform used for image compression should have low energy compaction.

    (A) Statements 1 and 2 are false
    (B) Statement 1 is true, statement 2 is false
    (C) Statement 1 is false, statement 2 is true
    (D) Statements 1 and 2 are true

14. The transform employed in JPEG and JPEG 2000 standards are, respectively

    (A) Fourier, Wavelet
    (B) Discrete Cosine Transform, Wavelet
    (C) Fourier, Discrete Cosine Transform
    (D) Discrete Cosine Transform, Fourier

15. Assertion: Quantization results in loss of information
    Reason: Quantization is many-to-one mapping

    (A) Assertion and reason are true
    (B) Assertion is true, reason is false
    (C) Assertion is false, reason may be true
    (D) Assertion and reason are false

Answers to Objective Questions

Q. No.	01	02	03	04	05	06	07	08	09	10
Key	B	A	C	A	D	A	C	C	B	C
Q. No.	11	12	13	14	15					
Key	B	B	B	B	A					

Answers to PreLab Questions

1. The objective of the image compression is to reduce irrelevant and redundant information in an image data to store and transmit it effectively. Image compression algorithm minimize the number of bits to represent the image data.
2. The image compression scheme is classified into lossless and lossy compression scheme. In the lossless compression scheme, the original image can be reconstructed from its compressed file without any loss of information, whereas the lossy compression scheme cannot reconstruct the original image from its compressed file without the loss of information. In this scheme there will be deviation between the original and reconstructed image. However, these deviations may not be noticed by the human eye.
3. Examples of lossless coding are Run length coding, Huffman coding, arithmetic coding, dictionary-based coding, DPCM without quantizer, etc.
4. The examples of lossy image compression algorithms are transform coding, lossy DPCM, wavelet based compression, scalar quantization, vector quantization, SVD based image compression, fractal based image compression, etc.
5. The spatial redundancy exploits the similarity across the different pixels of an image. It is also called as interpixel redundancy. The spatial redundancy can be removed by the image transform.
6. The spectral redundancy exploits the correlation between the different colour planes like (R, G, B) or colour bands. Colour conversion approaches like, RGB to YUV, RGB to YCbCr, RGB to HSI, RGB to HSV, etc., minimizes the spectral redundancy in the color image.
7. Certain information in an image or data has less relative importance than other information in a normal human visual system. This information is said to be psychovisual redundant. The less relative information in the image will not affect the human perception of the image. Thus, the less relative information can be eliminated by using vector quantization scheme.
8. Coding redundancy normally is present in any natural binary encoding of the gray levels in an image. It can be eliminated by coding the gray level as having a higher probability with the shortest code word and the gray level as having the least probability with a lengthier code word.

9. Entropy is a measure, which gives the average number of bits needed to code the symbol in the source. The entropy can be measured by using

$$H = -\sum_{i=1}^{N} p_i \log_2 (p_i) \, \text{bits} / \text{symbol}$$

It gives a fundamental limit on the amount of data compression that can be achieved for the input image data.

10. The lossless compression algorithm's reconstructed image always has good quality. Hence, the performance of the lossless compression algorithm is measured by the compression ratio and compression factor.

11. The lossy image compression algorithm always compromises the quality of the image to achieve high compression. Therefore, PSNR, MSE, MSSIM, compression ratio, and compression factor can be used to evaluate the performance of the lossy compression algorithms.

12. The JPEG standard is widely used for image compression; DCT is used as a transform in this standard and the input image is split by 8×8 or 16×16 sub-blocks, and DCT, quantization, zig-zag scan and entropy coding in the encoder block process each subblock. The reverse process like entropy decoder, inverse quantization and IDCT is used in the decoder block to decompress the original image from the compressed file.

13. Fractal image compression is a lossy compression scheme based on fractals. Fractals are complex objects which has property of self-similarity. That is, a small section of fractal object is similar to whole object, hence fractal is the repetition of the same structural form. Fractal image compression can be achieved based on affine contractive transforms, which utilize the existence of self-symmetry in the image.

Bibliography

1. Rafael C. Gonzalez, Richard E. Woods, Steven L. Eddins, "Digital Image Processing Using MATLAB", Prentice Hall, 2006.
2. K. R. Rao, and P. C. Yip (Eds.), "The Transform and Data Compression Handbook" First Edition, CRC Press, 2001.
3. David Salomon, "Data compression- The Complete Reference", 4th Edition, Springer, 2007.
4. Khalid Sayood, "Introduction to Data Compression", Morgan Kaufmann Publishers, 2012.
5. S. Jayaraman, S. Esakkirajan, T. Veerakumar, "Digital Image Processing", 2nd Edition, Tata McGraw Hill, New Delhi, 2021.
6. Steve J. Leon; "Linear Algebra with Applications", Macmillan Publishing Company, New York, 1996.
7. Michael F. Barnsley, "Fractals Everywhere", 2nd edition, Academic press, 1993.
8. Yuval Fisher, "Fractal Image Compression, Theory and applications", Springer-Verlag, 1995.

Chapter 10
Colour Image Processing

Learning Objectives

After reading this chapter, the reader is expected to

- Understand the types and significance of colour models.
- Perform denoising of colour image.
- Perform enhancement of colour image.
- Implement Pseudo-colouring algorithm for grayscale image.
- Perform segmentation of colour image using k-means clustering algorithm.
- Perform compression of colour image using principal component analysis.

Roadmap of the Chapter

Different topics discussed in this chapter are given in the form of a road map, which is depicted in Fig. 10.1.

From Fig. 10.1, it is possible to infer that topics covered in this chapter include discussion about different colour models, enhancement of colour image using histogram equalization and contrast limited adaptive histogram equalization, pseudo colouring of grayscale image, segmentation of colour image using k-means clustering algorithm, and compression of colour image using principal component analysis.

PreLab Questions

1. Why *is the RGB* colour model considered an additive colour model? Mention a device in which *RGB* colour model is used.
2. Why *is CMYK* considered a subtractive colour model? Mention one practical application of *CMYK* colour model.
3. Mention the sensor in human eye which is responsible for colour vision.
4. Mention four valid differences between *RGB* colour model and *CMYK* colour model.

Supplementary Information The online version contains supplementary material available at https://doi.org/10.1007/978-981-96-6382-8_10.

S Esakkirajan et al., *Digital Image Processing*,
https://doi.org/10.1007/978-981-96-6382-8_10

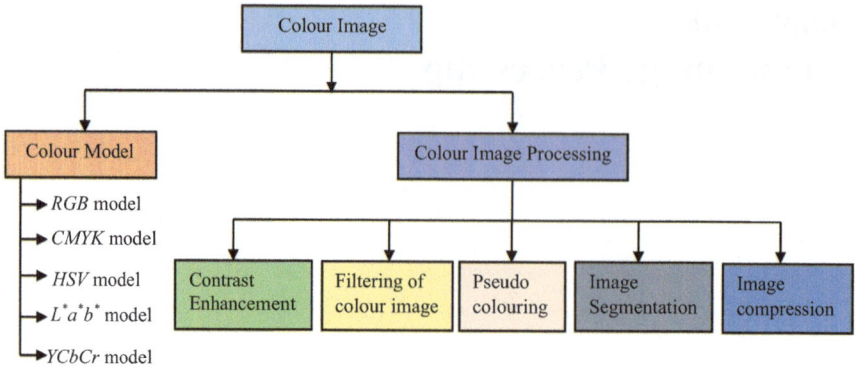

Fig. 10.1   Road map of colour image processing chapter

5. What do "*H*", "*S*", and "*V*" in the *HSV* colour model indicate?
6. What is the impact of changing the sign of the "*a**" plane in *L*a*b** colour space (that is, plane "*a**" is changed to "*−a**")?
7. What is the impact of changing the sign of the "*b**" plane in *L*a*b** colour space (that is, plane "*b**" is changed to "*−b**")?
8. Mention the steps involved in the computation of principal components of a signal or feature.
9. While using PCA to compress the image, how many principal components are needed to compress the image efficiently?
10. Mention two advantages and drawbacks of k-means clustering algorithm.

10.1   Colour

We are living in a world of colour images in the form of print, displays, photographs, the Internet, and movies. Colour is a subjective sensation one can observe when the visible region of electromagnetic radiation reaches the eyes. The perception of colour is important in applications like digital imaging, computer vision, entertainment, consumer electronics, etc. Humans can perceive thousands of colours but only about two dozen shades of gray. The sensors in the human eye, namely, rods and cones, operate in different ways and at various light levels. The rods are utilized for monochromatic vision at low light levels which is termed as "scotopic vision". The cones are the primary source of colour vision in bright light which is termed as "photopic vision". Three types of cones, namely, short (S), medium (M), and long (L), are sensitive to blue, green and green light, respectively.

10.2   Colour Models

A colour model is a multidimensional representation of the colour spectrum. A colour model uses three primary colours to produce a wide array of colours. Colour space is the range of colours a colour model can produce. Colour spaces are used to define a standardized method of representing colours in digital images. Different colour spaces are useful for different purposes.

10.2.1   RGB Colour Model

The RGB colour cube is given in Fig. 10.2. From this figure, it is possible to observe that each colour is represented as a single point. If each colour is represented using 8 bits, then 24 bits will be required to represent an RGB image. Mixing an equal proportion of red, green and blue components will result in a white colour. RGB colour model is a device-dependent colour model. Every device can have its own set of primaries, which may look red, green and blue, but it could be slightly different from primaries used elsewhere.

From the colour cube shown in Fig. 10.2, it is possible to interpret the following:

$$Green + Red = Yellow \qquad\qquad (10.1)$$

$$Green + Blue = Cyan \qquad\qquad (10.2)$$

$$Red + Blue = Magenta \qquad\qquad (10.3)$$

$$Red + Green + Blue = White \qquad\qquad (10.4)$$

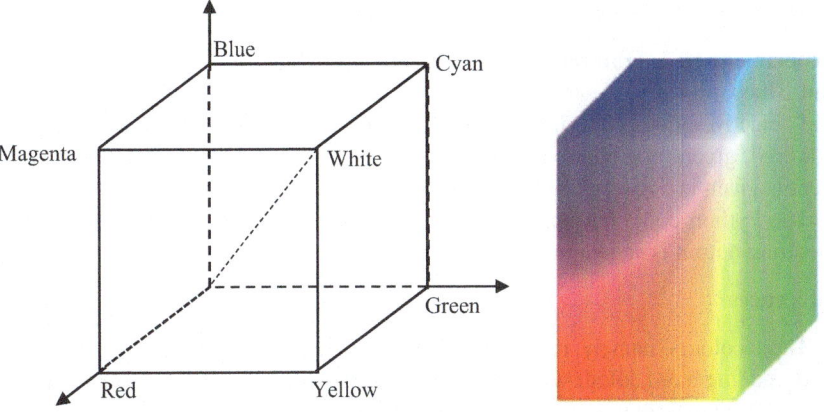

Fig. 10.2 RGB colour cube

Fig. 10.3 Block diagram
of the problem statement

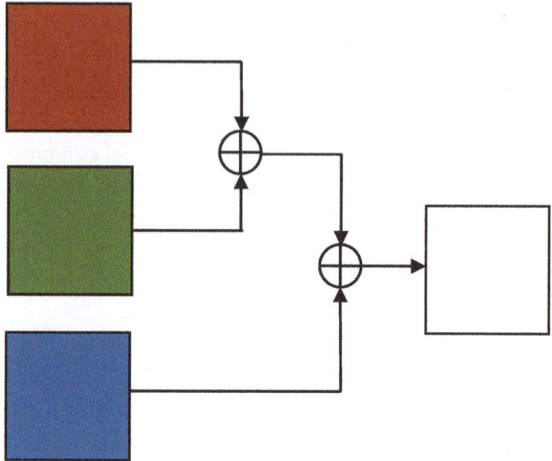

Experiment 10.1: Generation of Red, Green, and Blue Components of Colour and Adding Them Together

The objective of this experiment is to generate 256×256 red, blue, and green colours separately. After the generation of these three colours, they are added together to obtain the white colour. The Python code, which generates the red, green, and blue colours separately and then added together to obtain the white colour, is shown in Fig. 10.3.

The Python code that performs the task illustrated in the block diagram is given in Fig. 10.4, and the corresponding output is shown in Fig. 10.5.

Inferences

From Fig. 10.5, the following inferences can be drawn:

- Three colour images were generated, namely, red, green, and blue colours of size 256×256.
- The three colours are added to obtain the white colour.

Experiment 10.2: Obtaining Yellow, Cyan, and Magenta from Red, Green, and Blue Colour

The objective of this experiment is to obtain the yellow, cyan, and magenta colours from red, green, and blue colour. The block diagram depicting the problem statement is given in Fig. 10.6.

The Python code that performs this task is shown in Fig. 10.7, and the corresponding output is shown in Fig. 10.8.

Inferences

- Three colours, namely, red, green, and blue colours are generated.
- By adding a red colour with a green colour, the yellow colour is generated.
- Cyan colour is obtained by adding green and blue colour.
- Magenta colour is obtained by adding red and blue colour.

```
import numpy as np
import matplotlib.pyplot as plt
import cv2
#Step 1: Define the dimensions of the image
height, width, channel = 64, 64, 3
# Step2: Generation Red, Green, Blue colour components
red1, green1, blue1 = 255, 0, 0
red2, green2, blue2 = 0, 255, 0
red3, green3, blue3 = 0, 0, 255
# Step3 Generate RGB images
im_red = np.full((height, width, channel), [red1, green1, blue1], dtype=('uint8'))
im_green = np.full((height, width, channel), [red2, green2, blue2], dtype=('uint8'))
im_blue = np.full((height, width, channel), [red3, green3, blue3], dtype=('uint8'))
#Step 4: Generation of white image
im_white1=cv2.add(im_red,im_green)
im_white=cv2.add(im_white1,im_blue)
# Step 5: Displaying the result
plt.figure(figsize=(8,4)),plt.subplot(1,4,1),plt.imshow(im_red),plt.title('Red colour'),plt.xticks([]),
plt.yticks([]),plt.subplot(1,4,2),plt.imshow(im_green),plt.title('Green colour'),plt.xticks([]),
plt.yticks([]),plt.subplot(1,4,3),plt.imshow(im_blue),plt.title('Blue colour'),plt.xticks([]),
plt.yticks([]),plt.subplot(1,4,4),plt.imshow(im_white),plt.title('Red+Green+Blue'),plt.xticks([]),
plt.yticks([]),plt.tight_layout()
```

Fig. 10.4 Python code to generate white image from red, green, and blue components

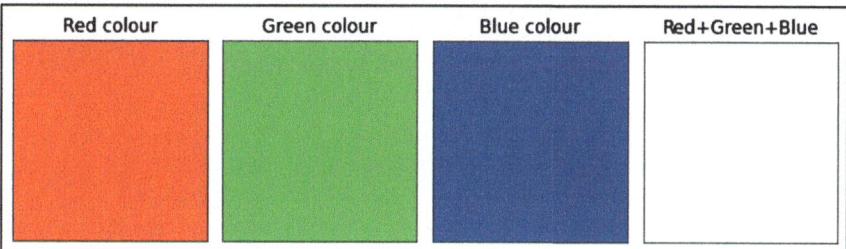

Fig. 10.5 Addition of red, green, and blue colour to obtain white colour

- The conclusion is that mixing two primary colours in equal proportions produces a secondary colour.

Experiment 10.3: Read a Colour Image and Display the Red, Green, and Blue Plane of the Image

The Python code which performs the task of displaying the red, green, and blue planes is shown in Fig. 10.9, and the corresponding output is shown in Fig. 10.10.

Inferences

The following inferences can be made from this experiment:

- The cv2 library reads and displays the RGB image in BGR format.
- The input image is an RGB image, and the output is the red, green, and blue plane of the input RGB image.

Fig. 10.6 Obtaining
yellow, cyan, and magenta
from red, green, and blue
colour

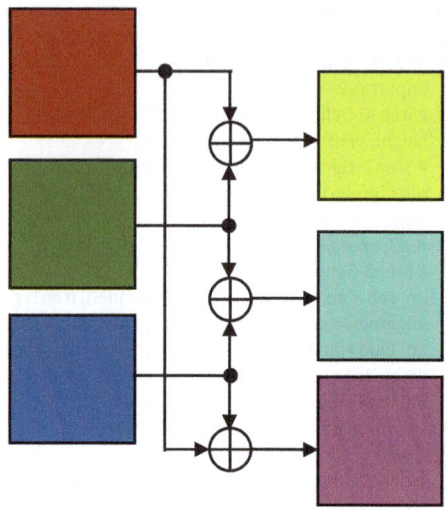

```
#Python code to obtain yellow, cyan and magenta from red, green and blue colours
import numpy as np
import matplotlib.pyplot as plt
import cv2
#Step 1: Define the dimensions of the image
height, width, channel = 256, 256, 3
# Step2: Generation Red, Green, Blue colour components
red1, green1, blue1 = 255, 0, 0
red2, green2, blue2 = 0, 255, 0
red3, green3, blue3 = 0, 0, 255
# Step3 Generate RGB images
im_red = np.full((height, width, channel), [red1, green1, blue1], dtype=('uint8'))
im_green = np.full((height, width, channel), [red2, green2, blue2], dtype=('uint8'))
im_blue = np.full((height, width, channel), [red3, green3, blue3], dtype=('uint8'))
#Step 4: Generation of white image
im_yellow=cv2.add(im_red,im_green)
im_cyan=cv2.add(im_blue,im_green)
im_magenta=cv2.add(im_red,im_blue)
# Step 5: Displaying the result
plt.subplot(2,3,1),plt.imshow(im_red),plt.title('Red colour'),plt.xticks([]),plt.yticks([])
plt.subplot(2,3,2),plt.imshow(im_green),plt.title('Green colour'),plt.xticks([]),plt.yticks([])
plt.subplot(2,3,3),plt.imshow(im_blue),plt.title('Blue colour'),plt.xticks([]),plt.yticks([])
plt.subplot(2,3,4),plt.imshow(im_yellow),plt.title('Red+Green'),plt.xticks([]),plt.yticks([])
plt.subplot(2,3,5),plt.imshow(im_cyan),plt.title('Green+Blue'),plt.xticks([]),plt.yticks([])
plt.subplot(2,3,6),plt.imshow(im_magenta),plt.title('Red+Blue'),plt.xticks([]),plt.yticks([])
plt.tight_layout()
```

Fig. 10.7 Python code to obtain yellow, cyan, and magenta from red, green, and blue colours

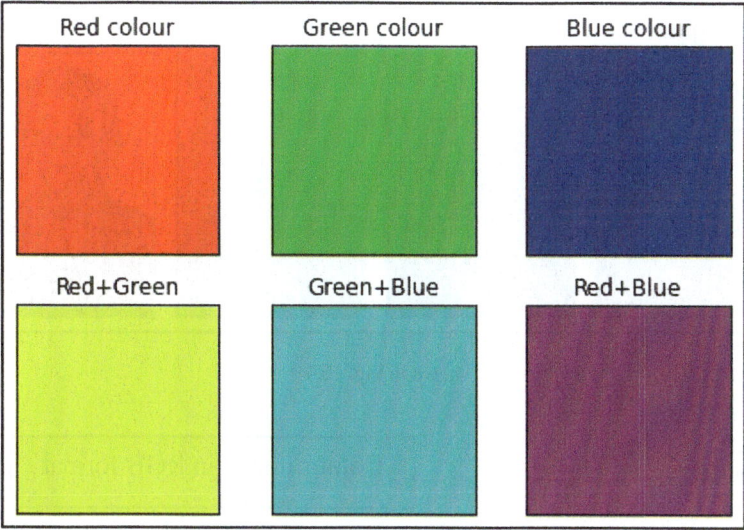

Fig. 10.8 Result of Python code shown in Fig. 10.7

```
#Extracting the three bitplanes of the colour image
import cv2
import matplotlib.pyplot as plt
import numpy as np
im=cv2.imread('esakkirajan.jpg');#Reading the input RGB image
row,col,plane=im.shape
#Extracting the three planes of the digital image
blue_plane = np.zeros((row,col,plane),np.uint8)
blue_plane[:,:,0] = im[:,:,0]
green_plane = np.zeros((row,col,plane),np.uint8)
green_plane[:,:,1] = im[:,:,1]
red_plane = np.zeros((row,col,plane),np.uint8)
red_plane[:,:,2] = im[:,:,2]
plt.figure(figsize=(6,4)),plt.subplot(1,4,1),plt.imshow(cv2.cvtColor(im, cv2.COLOR_BGR2RGB)),
plt.xticks([]),plt.yticks([]),plt.title('Original'),plt.subplot(1,4,2),
plt.imshow(cv2.cvtColor(blue_plane, cv2.COLOR_BGR2RGB)),plt.title('Blue Plane')
,plt.xticks([]),plt.yticks([]),plt.subplot(1,4,3),
plt.imshow(cv2.cvtColor(green_plane, cv2.COLOR_BGR2RGB)),plt.xticks([]),plt.yticks([]),
plt.title('Green Plane'),plt.subplot(1,4,4),
plt.imshow(cv2.cvtColor(red_plane, cv2.COLOR_BGR2RGB)),plt.xticks([]),plt.yticks([]),
plt.title('Red Plane'),plt.tight_layout()
```

Fig. 10.9 Python code to display the three planes of the colour image

Fig. 10.10 Result of the Python code shown in Fig. 10.9

Fig. 10.11 Processing of colour image

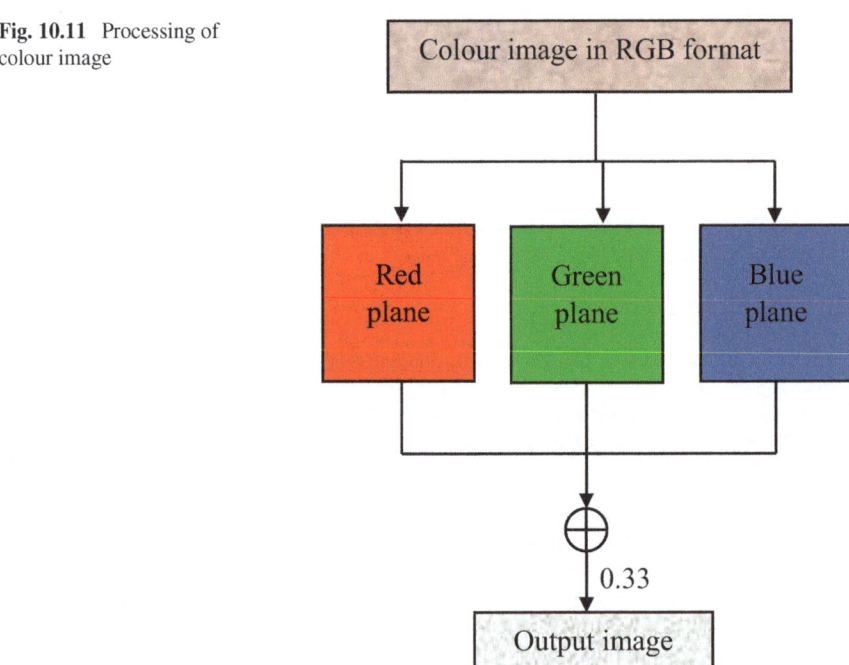

Experiment 10.4: Read a Colour Image in RGB Format. Separate the Red, Green, and Blue Planes. Then Add the Three Planes and Divide It by a Factor of 3 to Obtain a New Image. Comment on the Nature of the New Image
The problem statement is depicted in the form of block diagram in Fig. 10.11.

The Python code that performs the task shown in Fig. 10.11 is given in Fig. 10.12, and the corresponding output is shown in Fig. 10.13.

Inference

• From Fig. 10.13, it is possible to observe that the input image is a colour image, and the output image is a grayscale version of the input colour image.

```
import cv2
import matplotlib.pyplot as plt
import numpy as np
#Step 1: Reading the colour image in BGR format
img_bgr=cv2.imread('colourimg1.jpg')
img_rgb = cv2.cvtColor(img_bgr, cv2.COLOR_BGR2RGB)
row,col=img_bgr.shape[0:2]
img=np.zeros([row,col])
for i in range (row):
   for j in range (col):
      img[i,j]=np.sum(img_bgr[i,j,:])*0.33
plt.subplot(1,2,1),plt.imshow(img_rgb),plt.title('Input image'),plt.xticks([]),
plt.yticks([]),plt.subplot(1,2,2),plt.imshow(img,cmap='gray'),
plt.title('Output image'),plt.xticks([]),plt.yticks([])
plt.tight_layout()
```

Fig. 10.12 Python code to process the colour image

Fig. 10.13 Result of Python code shown in Fig. 10.12

10.2.2   CMY Colour Model

CMY stands for Cyan, Magenta, and Yellow. It is a subtractive colour model. CMY colour model is widely preferred in printing. The relationship between CMY and RGB colour model is given by

$$C = 1 - R \tag{10.5}$$

$$M = 1 - G \tag{10.6}$$

$$Y = 1 - B \tag{10.7}$$

A black colour is introduced along with C, M, and Y to obtain CMYK model where "K" represents the black colour. The CMYK colours are also known as "four colour printing". Similarly, the relationship between RGB and CMY models is given by

$$\begin{bmatrix} R \\ G \\ B \end{bmatrix} = \begin{bmatrix} 1 \\ 1 \\ 1 \end{bmatrix} - \begin{bmatrix} C \\ M \\ Y \end{bmatrix} \tag{10.8}$$

Experiment 10.5: Relationship Between RGB and CMY Models
The objective of this experiment is to illustrate the relationship between RGB and CMY models. The Python code that establishes the relationship between the RGB and CMY models is given in Fig. 10.14, and the corresponding output is shown in Fig. 10.15.

```
#Relationship between RGB and CMY colour model
import numpy as np
import matplotlib.pyplot as plt
#Step 1: Define the dimensions of the image
height, width, channel = 256, 256, 3
# Step2: Generation Red, Green, Blue colour components
red1, green1, blue1 = 255, 0, 0
red2, green2, blue2 = 0, 255, 0
red3, green3, blue3 = 0, 0, 255
# Step3 Generate RGB images
im_red = np.full((height, width, channel), [red1, green1, blue1], dtype=('uint8'))
im_green = np.full((height, width, channel), [red2, green2, blue2], dtype=('uint8'))
im_blue = np.full((height, width, channel), [red3, green3, blue3], dtype=('uint8'))
#Step 4: Generation of white image
im_cyan=1-im_red/255
im_magenta=1-im_green/255
im_yellow=1-im_blue/255
# Step 5: Displaying the result
plt.figure(figsize=(8,6)),plt.subplot(2,3,1),plt.imshow(im_red),plt.title('Red colour'),
plt.xticks([]),plt.yticks([]),plt.subplot(2,3,2),plt.imshow(im_green),plt.title('Green colour'),
plt.xticks([]),plt.yticks([]),plt.subplot(2,3,3),plt.imshow(im_blue),plt.title('Blue colour'),
plt.xticks([]),plt.yticks([]),plt.subplot(2,3,4),plt.imshow(im_cyan),plt.title('Cyan = 1 - Red'),
plt.xticks([]),plt.yticks([]),plt.subplot(2,3,5),plt.imshow(im_magenta),
plt.title('Magenta = 1 - Green'),plt.xticks([]),plt.yticks([]),plt.subplot(2,3,6),
plt.imshow(im_yellow),plt.title('Yellow = 1 - Blue'),plt.xticks([]),plt.yticks([])
plt.tight_layout()
```

Fig. 10.14 Python code to illustrate the relationship between RGB and CMY colour model

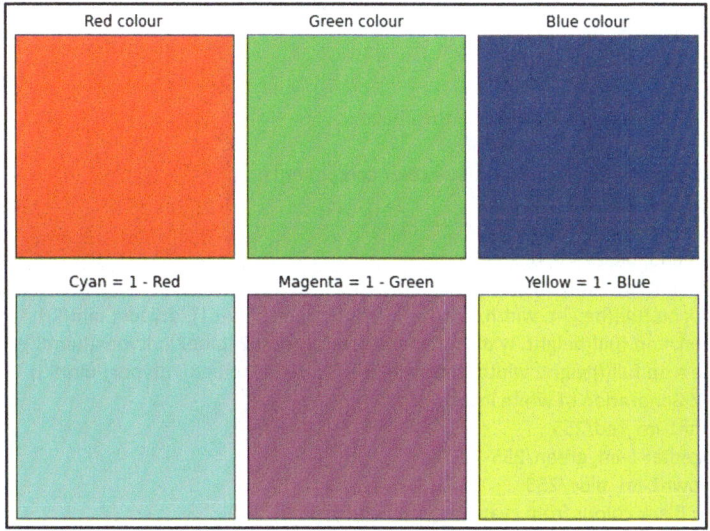

Fig. 10.15   Relationship between RGB and CMY colour model

Inferences
The following inferences can be drawn from Fig. 10.15

- Cyan colour is obtained from red colour using the relation $C = 1 - R$.
- Magenta is obtained from green colour using the relation $M = 1 - G$.
- Yellow colour is obtained from blue colour using the relation $Y = 1 - B$.

Experiment 10.6: Obtaining Black Colour from Cyan, Magenta, and Yellow.
This experiment aims to illustrate that adding equal amounts of cyan, magenta, and yellow components results in black colour. The Python code which performs the task of adding an equal proportion of cyan, magenta, and yellow colour is given in Fig. 10.16, and the corresponding output is shown in Fig. 10.17.

Inference

- From Fig. 10.17, it is possible to observe that adding equal proportions of cyan, magenta, and yellow colours results in black colour.

10.2.3   HSV Colour Model

The HSV colour model is based on polar coordinates. In the HSV colour model, "H" stands for "Hue", "S" stands for "Saturation" and "V" stands for "Value". Hue is a quantity that distinguishes one colour from another colour. The intensity of a distinctive hue or degree of colour sensation is defined by Saturation. The "value" determines whether the colour is light or dark.

```
import numpy as np
import matplotlib.pyplot as plt
import cv2
#Step 1: Define the dimensions of the image
height, width, channel = 256, 256, 3
# Step2: Generation Red,Green,Blue color components
red1, green1, blue1 = 255, 0, 0
red2, green2, blue2 = 0, 255, 0
red3, green3, blue3 = 0, 0, 255
# Step3 Generate RGB images
im_red = np.full((height, width, channel), [red1, green1, blue1], dtype=('uint8'))
im_green = np.full((height, width, channel), [red2, green2, blue2], dtype=('uint8'))
im_blue = np.full((height, width, channel), [red3, green3, blue3], dtype=('uint8'))
#Step 4: Generation of white image
im_cyan=1-im_red/255
im_magenta=1-im_green/255
im_yellow=1-im_blue/255
#Step 5: Black colour from cyan, magenta and yellow
im_black1=cv2.add(im_cyan,im_magenta)
im_black=cv2.add(im_black1,im_yellow)
im_blcak=im_black/255
#Step 6: Displaying the results
plt.figure(figsize=(8,6)),plt.subplot(1,4,1),plt.imshow(im_cyan),plt.title('Cyan colour'),
plt.xticks([]),plt.yticks([]),plt.subplot(1,4,2),plt.imshow(im_magenta)
plt.title('Magenta colour'),plt.xticks([]),plt.yticks([]),plt.subplot(1,4,3),
plt.imshow(im_yellow),plt.title('Yellow colour'),plt.xticks([]),plt.yticks([])
plt.subplot(1,4,4),plt.imshow(im_black.astype('uint8')),plt.title('Cyan+Magenta+Yellow')
plt.xticks([]),plt.yticks([])
plt.tight_layout()
```

Fig. 10.16 Python code to obtain black colour from cyan, magenta, and yellow colours

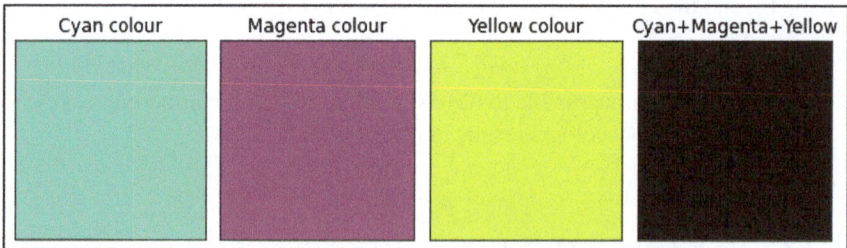

Fig. 10.17 Black colour by adding cyan, magenta, and yellow colour

In HSV colour model, the red colour is represented at 0°, yellow at 60°, green colour at 120°, cyan at 180°, blue at 240°, and magenta at 300°. From Fig. 10.18, it is possible to observe that complementary colours like yellow and cyan are on opposite sides of the hexagon.

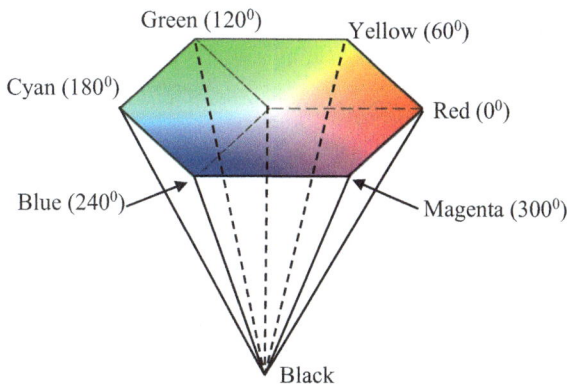

Fig. 10.18 HSV colour model

Experiment 10.7: RGB to HSV Conversion

In this example, an RGB test image is generated first. The test image is a 256×256 image which is divided into four quadrants. The first quadrant is red in colour; the second, third, and fourth quadrants are green, blue, and cyan, respectively. This test image is then converted to the HSV model, and then the Hue, Saturation, and Value are displayed as separate images. The Python code that performs this task is shown in Fig. 10.19, and the corresponding output is shown in Fig. 10.20.

Inferences

- The input test image (RGB image) is a 256×256 image with red, green, blue, and cyan colour.
- The hue plane image corresponding to the RGB image displays dark colour (black) for red and white for blue.
- "Saturation" refers to the purity of the colour. The colours with the highest saturation are represented as white, and the colours with the lowest saturation are represented as black.
- The "value" represents brightness. Brightest areas of the value plane correspond to the brightest colours in the original image.

Experiment 10.8: Impact of Adding 120° to the Hue Component of the Input Test Image

In this experiment, a test image is generated. The test image has red, green, and blue colour components. Each size 100×100 gets concatenated horizontally. The test image is converted to HSV format. After conversion, 120° is added to only Hue component. After this, the new Hue, Saturation, and Value components will be merged. Then it is converted back to RGB format. The block diagram which depicts this problem statement is shown in Fig. 10.21.

The Python code that performs the task shown in Fig. 10.21 is given in Fig. 10.22, and the corresponding output is shown in Fig. 10.23.

```
import numpy as np
import matplotlib.pyplot as plt
import cv2
#Step 1: Generation of test image
height, width, channel = 128, 128, 3
# Step2: Generation Red, Green, Blue colour components
red1, green1, blue1 = 255, 0, 0
red2, green2, blue2 = 0, 255, 0
red3, green3, blue3 = 0, 0, 255
im_red = np.full((height, width, channel), [red1, green1, blue1], dtype=('uint8'))
im_green = np.full((height, width, channel), [red2, green2, blue2], dtype=('uint8'))
im_blue = np.full((height, width, channel), [red3, green3, blue3], dtype=('uint8'))
im_cyan=cv2.add(im_blue,im_green)
im_white=cv2.add(im_cyan,im_red)
img_color=np.zeros([256,256,3],dtype='uint8')
img_color[0:128,0:128]=im_red
img_color[128:256,0:128]=im_blue
img_color[0:128,128:256]=im_green
img_color[128:256,128:256]=im_cyan
#Step 2: Conversion of test image to HSV format
img_hsv = cv2.cvtColor(img_color, cv2.COLOR_RGB2HSV)
#Step 3: Displaying the results
plt.figure(figsize=(8,4)),plt.subplot(1,4,1),plt.imshow(img_color),plt.title('RGB image')
plt.xticks([]),plt.yticks([]),plt.subplot(1,4,2),plt.imshow(img_hsv[:,:,0],cmap='gray')
plt.title('Hue component'),plt.xticks([]),plt.yticks([]),plt.subplot(1,4,3),
plt.imshow(img_hsv[:,:,1],cmap='gray'),plt.title('Saturation component'),
plt.xticks([]),plt.yticks([]),plt.subplot(1,4,4),plt.imshow(img_hsv[:,:,2],cmap='gray')
plt.title('Value component'),plt.xticks([]),plt.yticks([])
plt.tight_layout()
```

Fig. 10.19 Python code to convert RGB to HSV image

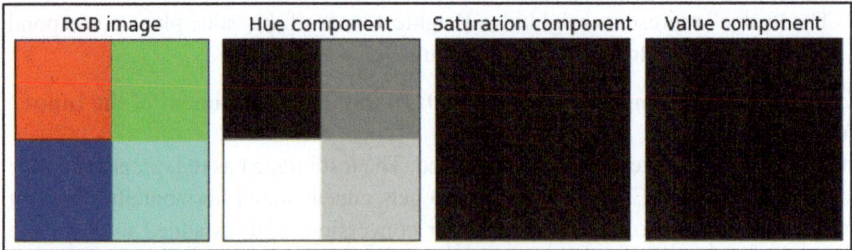

Fig. 10.20 Hue, saturation, and value component of an RGB image

Inferences
From Fig. 10.23, it is possible to observe the following facts when 120° is added to the Hue component of the image:

- The red colour in the input image turns out to be blue colour in the output image.
- The green colour in the input image appears as red colour in the output image.
- The blue colour in the input image appears as green colour in the output image.

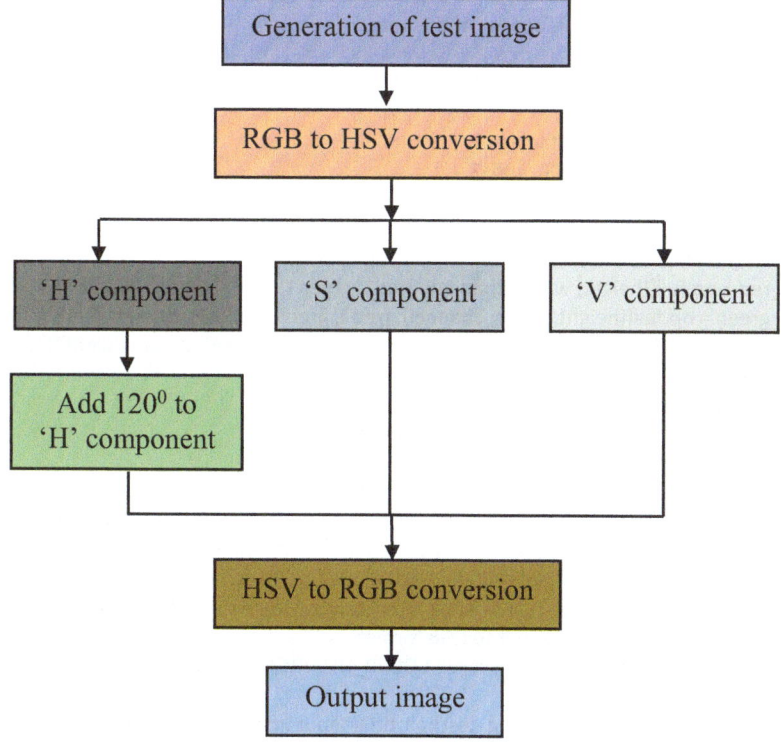

Fig. 10.21 Block diagram representing the problem statement

Task: Change the value 90° instead of 120° in the Python code given in Fig. 10.22. Comment on the observed result.

Colour Segmentation in HSV Space

The HSV colour space can be used to filter a particular colour. In order to filter a colour, it is necessary to set boundaries for which colour needs to be detected. The objective is to detect specific regions in specific colours. To identify a region of a specific colour, the first step is to fix the threshold and create a mask to separate the different colours. HSV colour space is much more useful for this purpose as the colours in HSV space are much more localized and thus can be easily separated.

Experiment 10.9: Segmentation of Red Colour in the Input Image

In this experiment, a test image is chosen in such a way that the test image contains four lemons (yellow in colour) and one tomato (red in colour). The threshold value is chosen so that the region corresponding to the tomato has to be separated from the rest of the image. The Python code that performs this task is shown in Fig. 10.24, and the corresponding output is shown in Fig. 10.25.

```
# Add 120o to the Hue component of the image
import cv2
import matplotlib.pyplot as plt
import numpy as np
#Step 1: Generation of test image
height, width, channel = 100, 100, 3
red1, green1, blue1 = 255, 0, 0
red2, green2, blue2 = 0, 255, 0
red3, green3, blue3 = 0, 0, 255
im_red = np.full((height, width, channel), [red1, green1, blue1], dtype=('uint8'))
im_green = np.full((height, width, channel), [red2, green2, blue2], dtype=('uint8'))
im_blue = np.full((height, width, channel), [red3, green3, blue3], dtype=('uint8'))
img_test=cv2.hconcat((im_red,im_green,im_blue))
#Step 2: Convert the image to HSV format
img_hsv = cv2.cvtColor(img_test, cv2.COLOR_RGB2HSV)
#Step 3: Extract the HSV components
img_h=img_hsv[:,:,0]
img_s=img_hsv[:,:,1]
img_v=img_hsv[:,:,2]
img_h=np.add(img_h,120);#Step 4: Add 120 degree to 'H' component
img_nhsv=cv2.merge([img_h,img_s,img_v]);#Step 5: Merge the HSV components
#Step 6: Convert the HSV format to RGB format
img_nrgb = cv2.cvtColor(img_nhsv, cv2.COLOR_HSV2RGB)
#Step 7: Displaying the result
plt.subplot(2,1,1),plt.imshow(img_test),plt.title('Input image'),plt.xticks([]),
plt.yticks([]),plt.subplot(2,1,2),plt.imshow(img_nrgb),plt.title('Output image'),
plt.xticks([]),plt.yticks([])
plt.tight_layout()
```

Fig. 10.22 Python code to add $120°$ to the Hue component of the image

Fig. 10.23 Result of
Python code shown in
Fig. 10.22

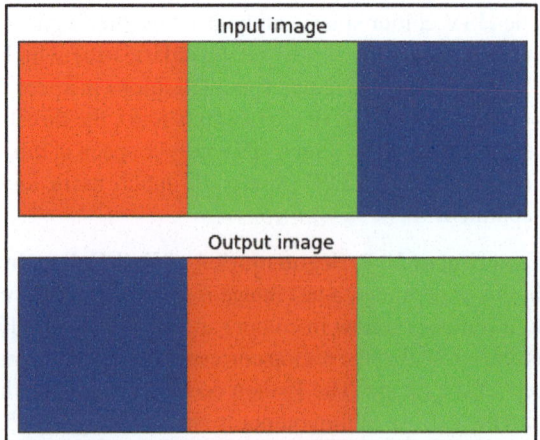

```
#Segmentation of red colour region
import cv2
import matplotlib.pyplot as plt
import numpy as np
#Step 1: Reading the colour image in BGR format
img_bgr=cv2.imread('colour_testimage3.jpg')
#Step 2: Converting BGR to RGB format
img_rgb = cv2.cvtColor(img_bgr, cv2.COLOR_BGR2RGB)
#Step 3: Converting to HSV format
img_hsv = cv2.cvtColor(img_bgr, cv2.COLOR_BGR2HSV)
# Step 4:  Defining the boundary values to highlight red colour
lower = np.array([0, 100, 100])
upper = np.array([20, 255, 255])
#Step 5: Creating the mask
mask1 = cv2.inRange(img_hsv, lower, upper)
#Step 6: Applying the mask to the image
img_out = cv2.bitwise_and(img_bgr, img_bgr, mask=mask1)
#Step 7: Displaying the results
plt.subplot(1,2,1),plt.imshow(img_rgb),plt.title('Input image'),plt.xticks([]),plt.yticks([])
plt.subplot(1,2,2),plt.imshow(cv2.cvtColor(img_out, cv2.COLOR_BGR2RGB)),
plt.title('Output image'),plt.xticks([]),plt.yticks([])
plt.tight_layout()
```

Fig. 10.24 Python code to segment red colour region in the test image

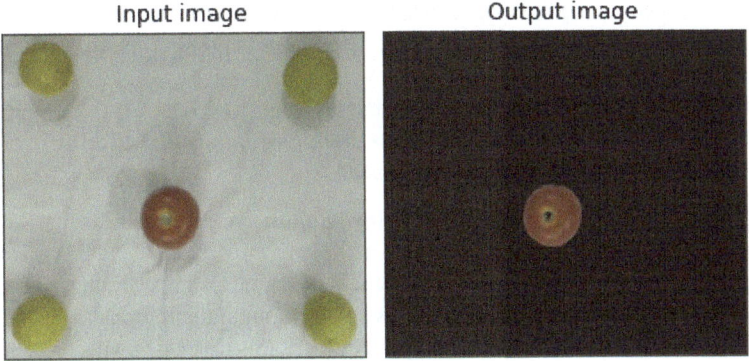

Fig. 10.25 Segmentation of red colour region in the test image

Inferences

The following inferences can be made from Fig. 10.25:

- The input image has four lemons (yellow) and one tomato (red) at the centre.
- By properly fixing the threshold, a mask is generated. The generated mask is applied to the image in HSV format to segment the red colour, which is the region corresponding to the tomato.

```
#Segmentation of Yellow colour region
import cv2
import matplotlib.pyplot as plt
import numpy as np
#Step 1: Reading the colour image in BGR format
img_bgr=cv2.imread('colour_testimage3.jpg')
#Step 2: Converting BGR to RGB format
img_rgb = cv2.cvtColor(img_bgr, cv2.COLOR_BGR2RGB)
#Step 3: Converting to HSV format
img_hsv = cv2.cvtColor(img_bgr, cv2.COLOR_BGR2HSV)
# Step 4:  Defining the boundary values to highlight red colour
lower = np.array([20, 100, 30])
upper = np.array([50, 255, 255])
#Step 5: Creating the mask
mask1 = cv2.inRange(img_hsv, lower, upper)
#Step 6: Applying the mask to the image
img_out = cv2.bitwise_and(img_bgr, img_bgr, mask=mask1)
#Step 7: Displaying the results
plt.subplot(1,2,1),plt.imshow(img_rgb),plt.title('Input image'),plt.xticks([]),plt.yticks([])
plt.subplot(1,2,2),plt.imshow(cv2.cvtColor(img_out, cv2.COLOR_BGR2RGB)),
plt.title('Output image'),plt.xticks([]),plt.yticks([])
plt.tight_layout()
```

Fig. 10.26 Python code to segment the yellow colour in the test image

- From the result (output image), it is possible to observe that the region corresponding to tomato (red colour) is isolated (segmented) from the rest of the regions in the image.
- This example can be considered as image filtering (filtering of specific colour in the image). It can also be interpreted as the segmentation of a specific region in the image based on the colour of the image.

Experiment 10.10: Segmentation of Yellow Colour Region in the Input Test Image

The test image considered in this experiment is the same as the test image chosen in the previous experiment. Here the objective is to segment the region corresponding to yellow (lemon). The Python code which performs this task is shown in Fig. 10.26, and the corresponding output is shown in Fig. 10.27.

Inferences

The following inferences can be made from this experiment:

- The objective is to segment the yellow colour in the input test image.
- The threshold is fixed so that the yellow region alone is segmented in the output image.
- From the output image, it is possible to observe that the yellow colour in the input image is segmented from the rest of the regions in the test image.

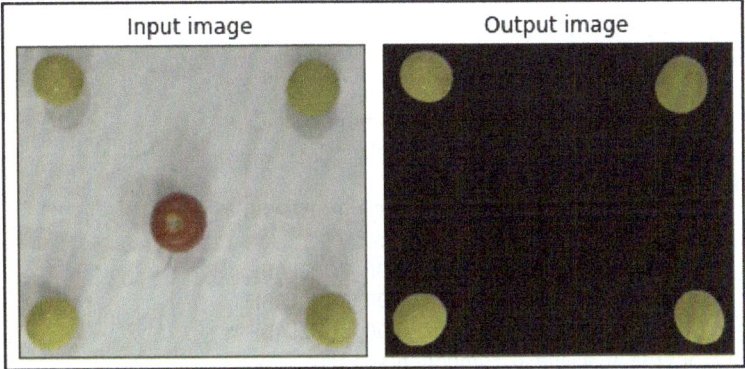

Fig. 10.27 Segmentation of yellow colour in the test image

10.2.4 L*a*b* *Colour Space*

The letters L^*, a^*, and b^* represent each of the three values the CIELAB colour space uses to measure objective colour and calculate colour differences. In $L^*a^*b^*$ colour space, "L^*" represents the lightness from black to white on a scale of 0–100, whereas "a^*" and "b^*" represent the chromaticity. "a^*" value represents the colour from red to green. The negative axis is green, and the positive is red. "b^*" value goes from yellow to blue. Blue lies on the negative side, and yellow is on the positive side. $L^*a^*b^*$ colour space is device independent.

Experiment 10.11: Conversion of RGB to L*a*b* Colour Space
This experiment discusses the conversion of RGB colour image into $L^*a^*b^*$ colour space. Set the "L^*", "a^*", and "b^*" components to zero. After zeroing the components, convert the image back to RGB space and display the result. The Python code that performs the desired task mentioned in the problem statement is shown in Fig. 10.28, and the corresponding output is shown in Fig. 10.29.

Inferences
The following inferences can be drawn from this experiment:

- The input image is an RGB image. The white patches in the input image appear black when setting the "L^*" component to zero.
- Component "a^*" represents greenness to redness with values of -128 to $+127$. With the zeroing of the "a^*" channel, the image appears to be green.
- Component "b^*" blueness to yellowness with values from -128 to $+127$. The image appears to be blue with zeroing of "b^*" channel.

Experiment 10.12: Changing the Sign of "b*" in L*a*b* Colour Space
In this experiment, read the test image containing four lemons on a white background. Convert the image into $L^*a^*b^*$ space. In the $L^*a^*b^*$ space, change the sign of the "b^*" space, then convert the image back to RGB image. Comment on the observed image.

```
#RGB to L*a*b* colour space manipulation
import cv2
import matplotlib.pyplot as plt
#Step 1: Reading the colour image in BGR format
img_bgr=cv2.imread('colour_testimg4.jpg')
#Step 2: Convert the BGR to RGB format
img_rgb = cv2.cvtColor(img_bgr, cv2.COLOR_BGR2RGB)
#Step 3: Convert the RGB to Lab colour space
img_lab1=cv2.cvtColor(img_bgr,cv2.COLOR_BGR2LAB)
img_lab2=cv2.cvtColor(img_bgr,cv2.COLOR_BGR2LAB)
img_lab3=cv2.cvtColor(img_bgr,cv2.COLOR_BGR2LAB)
#Step 4: Set the 'L' 'a' and 'b' components to zero
img_lab1[:,:,0]=0
img_lab2[:,:,1]=0
img_lab3[:,:,2]=0
#Step 5: Convert the image back to RGB space
img_rgb1=cv2.cvtColor(img_lab1,cv2.COLOR_LAB2RGB)
img_rgb2=cv2.cvtColor(img_lab2,cv2.COLOR_LAB2RGB)
img_rgb3=cv2.cvtColor(img_lab3,cv2.COLOR_LAB2RGB)
#Step 6: Display the results
plt.subplot(2,2,1),plt.imshow(img_rgb),plt.title('Original RGB image')
plt.xticks([]),plt.yticks([]),plt.subplot(2,2,2),plt.imshow(img_rgb1)
plt.title('"L*" component set to zero'),plt.xticks([]),plt.yticks([])
plt.subplot(2,2,3),plt.imshow(img_rgb2),plt.xticks([]),plt.yticks([])
plt.title('"a*" component set to zero'),plt.xticks([]),plt.yticks([])
plt.subplot(2,2,4),plt.imshow(img_rgb3),plt.title('"b*" component set to zero')
plt.xticks([]),plt.yticks([])
plt.tight_layout()
```

Fig. 10.28 Python code to convert RGB to $L*a*b*$ space

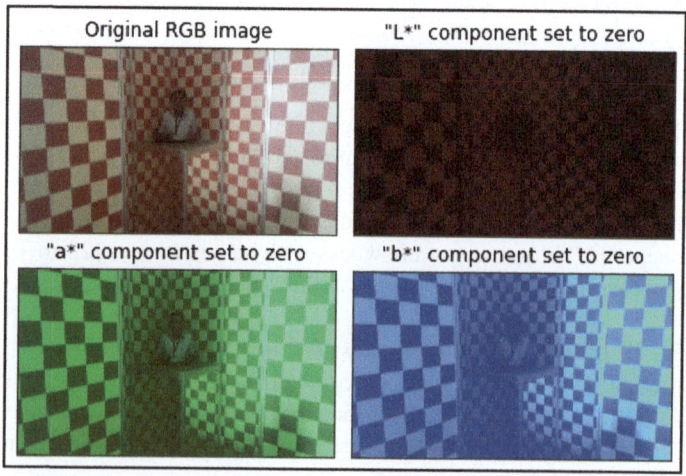

Fig. 10.29 Result of Python code shown in Fig. 10.28

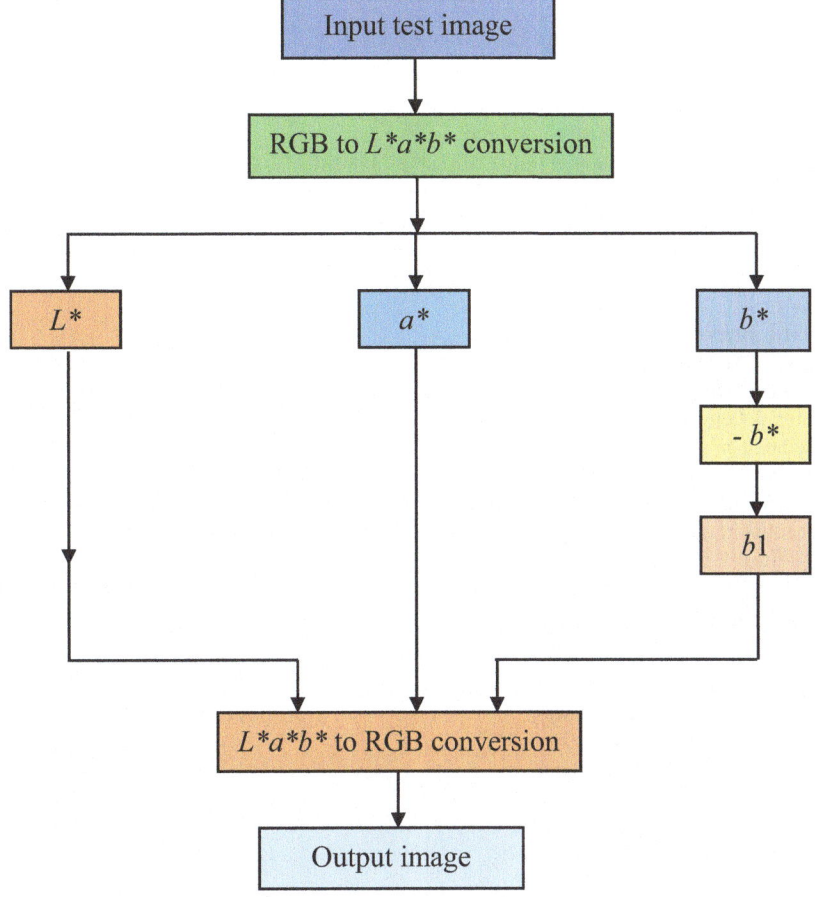

Fig. 10.30 Block diagram of problem statement

The problem statement is represented in the form of a block diagram, which is shown in Fig. 10.30. From Fig. 10.30, it is possible to observe that the following steps are involved in the solution to the problem statement.

Step 1: Reading the input RGB image.
Step 2: Converting the RGB image to $L*a*b*$ colour space.
Step 3: Reversing the sign of colour plane "$b*$".
Step 4: Merging the modified $L*a*b*$ space.
Step 5: Converting the modified $L*a*b*$ space to RGB to obtain the output image.

The Python code that performs the task shown in the block diagram is given in Fig. 10.31, and the corresponding output is shown in Fig. 10.32.

Inferences
The following inferences can be drawn from Fig. 10.32:

```
import cv2
import matplotlib.pyplot as plt
#Step 1: Reading the colour image in BGR format
img_bgr=cv2.imread('testimage_lemon.jpg')
#Step 2: Converting BGR to RGB format
img_rgb = cv2.cvtColor(img_bgr, cv2.COLOR_BGR2RGB)
#Step 3: Processing in LAB colour space
lab = cv2.cvtColor(img_bgr, cv2.COLOR_BGR2LAB)
l, a, b = cv2.split(lab)
#Step 4: Changing the sign of 'b' plane
b1=-b
b1=b1.astype('uint8')
#Step 5: Merging of Lab plane
modified_lab = cv2.merge([l, a, b1])
#Step 6: Conversion from Lab to RGB space
modified_img = cv2.cvtColor(modified_lab, cv2.COLOR_LAB2RGB)
#Step 7: Displaying the result
plt.subplot(1,2,1),plt.imshow(img_rgb),plt.title('Input image'),plt.xticks([]),plt.yticks([])
plt.subplot(1,2,2),plt.imshow(modified_img),plt.title('Output image')
plt.xticks([]),plt.yticks([]),plt.tight_layout()
```

Fig. 10.31 Python code to change the sign of "$b*$" plane in $L*a*b*$ colour space

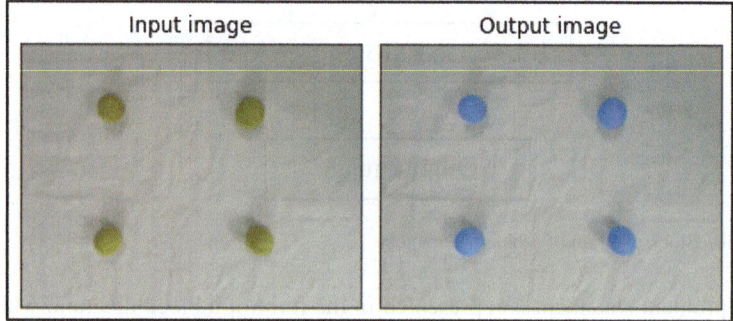

Fig. 10.32 Result of Python code shown in Fig. 10.31

- The input test image has four lemons, which appear a yellow colour.
- The yellow colour is modified into blue after changing the sign of the "$b*$" plane in $L*a*b*$ space.

Experiment 10.13: Impact of Changing the Sign of Colour Plane "$a*$" in $L*a*b*$ Colour Space

The objective of this experiment is to illustrate the impact of changing the sign of the colour plane "$a*$" in $L*a*b*$ colour space. To do this, the input test image, which consists of four tomatoes, is read first. The image is converted to $L*a*b*$ colour space. Then the sign of the colour plane "$a*$" is reversed. After that, the modified $L*a*b*$ colour plane is merged which is then converted back to RGB colour plane. The block diagram of the problem statement is shown in Fig. 10.33.

The Python code that performs the task mentioned in the block diagram is given in Fig. 10.34, and the corresponding output is shown in Fig. 10.35.

Inferences

From this experiment, the following inferences can be made:

- The input test image has four tomatoes on a white background. The tomatoes are 'red' in colour.
- Upon changing the sign of "$a*$" plane in $L*a*b*$ colour space, the "red" colour changes to "green" colour. In the output image, it is possible to observe that there is a transition of red colour to green colour.

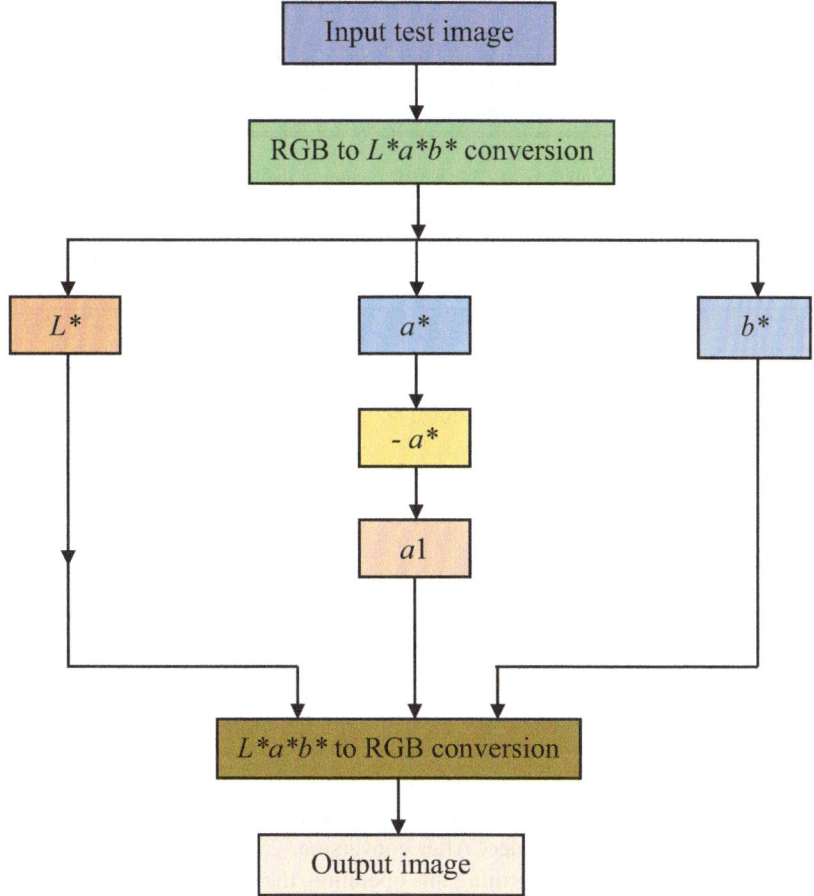

Fig. 10.33 Block diagram of analyzing the impact of changing the sign of plane "$a*$" in $L*a*b*$ space

```
import cv2
import matplotlib.pyplot as plt
#Step 1: Reading the colour image in BGR format
img_bgr=cv2.imread('testimage_tomato.jpg')
#Step 2: Converting BGR to RGB format
img_rgb = cv2.cvtColor(img_bgr, cv2.COLOR_BGR2RGB)
#Step 3: Processing in LAB colour space
lab = cv2.cvtColor(img_bgr, cv2.COLOR_BGR2LAB)
l, a, b = cv2.split(lab)
#Step 4: Changing the sign of 'b' plane
a1=-a
a1=a1.astype('uint8')
#Step 5: Merging of Lab plane
modified_lab = cv2.merge([l, a1, b])
#Step 6: Conversion from Lab to RGB space
modified_img = cv2.cvtColor(modified_lab, cv2.COLOR_LAB2RGB)
#Step 7: Displaying the result
plt.subplot(1,2,1),plt.imshow(img_rgb),plt.title('Input image'),plt.xticks([]),plt.yticks([])
plt.subplot(1,2,2),plt.imshow(modified_img),plt.title('Output image')
plt.xticks([]),plt.yticks([]),plt.tight_layout()
```

Fig. 10.34 Python code to analyze the impact of changing the sign of plane "$a*$" in $L*a*b*$ colour space

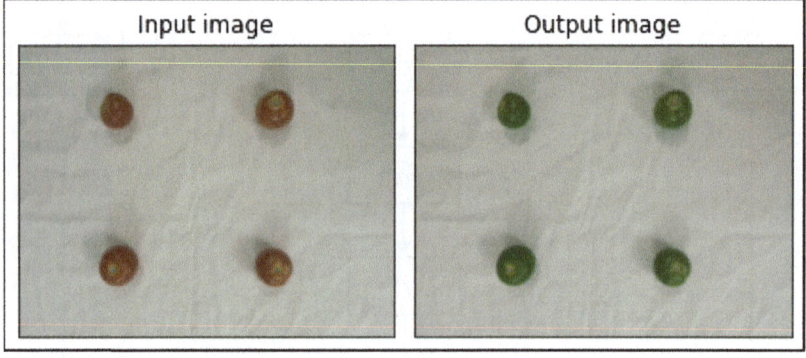

Fig. 10.35 Result of Python code shown in Fig. 10.34

Experiment 10.14: Impact of Inversion of Colour Plane "$L*$" in $L*a*b*$ Colour Space

The objective of this experiment is to observe the impact of inverse of the plane "$L*$" in $L*a*b*$ colour space. To do this, the input test image is read, and it is then converted to $L*a*b*$ colour space. After conversion, 255 is subtracted from each value of plane "$L*$". After performing this operation, the modified "$L*$", along with the original "$a*$" and "$b*$" planes, are merged. Finally, a colour space conversion from $L*a*b*$ to RGB is performed to obtain the output image. The block diagram which depicts the problem statement is shown in Fig. 10.36.

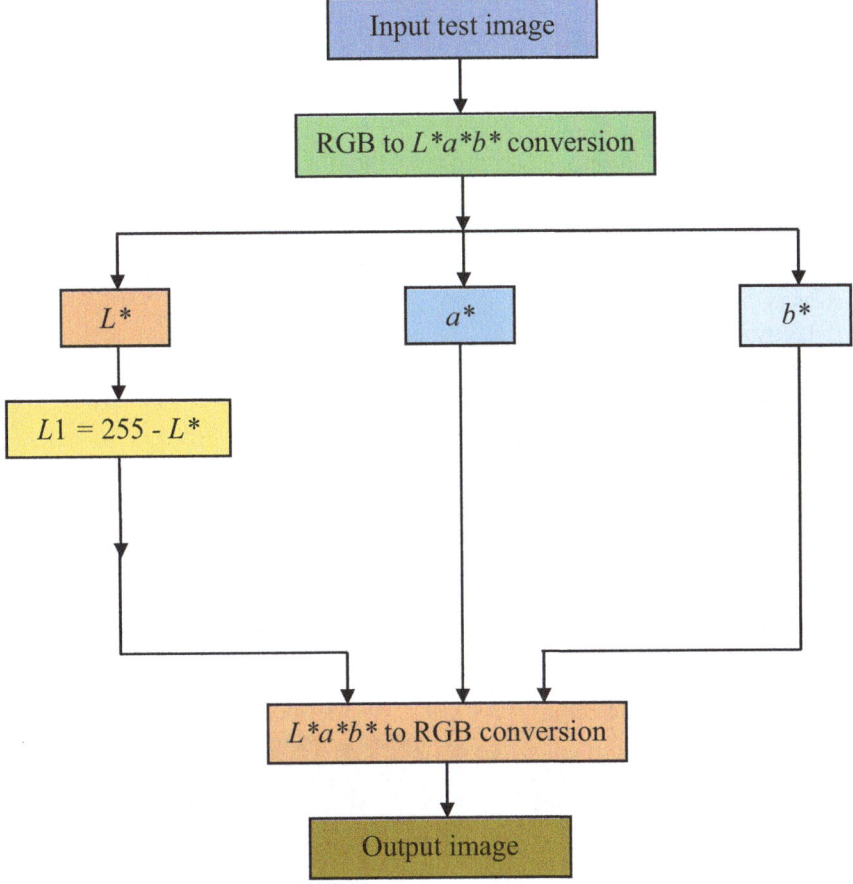

Fig. 10.36 Block diagram depicting the problem statement

The Python code which performs the task shown in the block diagram is given in Fig. 10.37, and the corresponding output is shown in Fig. 10.38.

Inferences

The following inferences can be drawn from this experiment:

- The input test image displays a plate with bread, sandwiches, and snacks.
- The white colour in the input image appears as black in the output image. Gray level inversion occurs if a value of 255 is subtracted from each value in "$L*$" plane.

10.2.5 YCbCr Colour Space

In YCbCr colour space, "Y" represents the luminance channel, whereas "Cb" and "Cr" represent the chrominance channels. The human eye is less sensitive to changes in chrominance. The luminance channel (Y) carries most information from the point

```
import cv2
import matplotlib.pyplot as plt
#Step 1: Reading the colour image in BGR format
img_bgr=cv2.imread('testimage2.jpg')
#Step 2: Converting BGR to RGB format
img_rgb = cv2.cvtColor(img_bgr, cv2.COLOR_BGR2RGB)
#Step 3: Processing in LAB colour space
lab = cv2.cvtColor(img_bgr, cv2.COLOR_BGR2LAB)
l, a, b = cv2.split(lab)
#Step 4: Inversion of 'L' plane
l1=255-l
l1=l1.astype('uint8')
#Step 5: Merging of Lab plane
modified_lab = cv2.merge([l1, a, b])
#Step 6: Conversion from Lab to RGB space
modified_img = cv2.cvtColor(modified_lab, cv2.COLOR_LAB2RGB)
#Step 7: Displaying the result
plt.subplot(1,2,1),plt.imshow(img_rgb),plt.title('Input image'),plt.xticks([]),plt.yticks([])
plt.subplot(1,2,2),plt.imshow(modified_img),plt.title('Output image')
plt.xticks([]),plt.yticks([]),plt.tight_layout()
```

Fig. 10.37 Python code to analyze the impact of inversion of "*L**" plane in *L*a*b** colour space

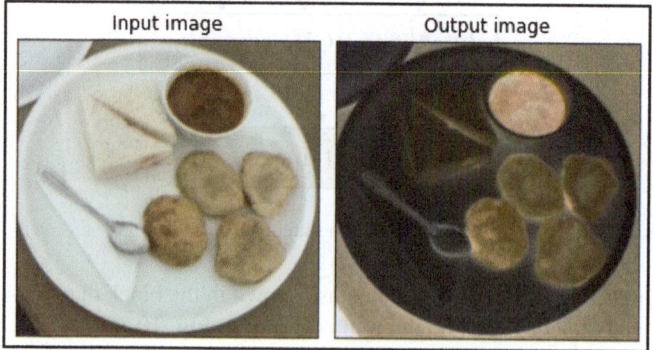

Fig. 10.38 Result of Python code shown in Fig. 10.37

of view of human perception. YCbCr colour space is extensively used in the development of JPEG standard. The relationship between "RGB" and "YCbCr" colour space is given by

$$Y = 16 + \frac{65.738R}{256} + \frac{129.057G}{256} + \frac{25.064B}{256} \tag{10.9}$$

$$Cb = 128 - \frac{37.945R}{256} - \frac{74.494G}{256} + \frac{112.439B}{256} \tag{10.10}$$

$$Cr = 128 + \frac{112.439R}{256} - \frac{94.1544G}{256} - \frac{18.285B}{256} \qquad (10.11)$$

Experiment 10.15: Conversion of YCbCr Colour Space

The objective of this experiment is to convert a colour image in YCbCr format and then display the "Y", "Cr", and "Cb" components of the colour image. The Python code, which reads the colour image and converts it into YCbCr format and then displays the luminance and the chrominance component of the image, is given in Fig. 10.39, and the corresponding output is shown in Fig. 10.40.

Inferences

The following inferences can be made from Fig. 10.40:

- The input image is a "Butterfly image". The black colour butterfly has red and white spots on its wings.

```
import cv2
import matplotlib.pyplot as plt
#Step 1: Reading the colour image in BGR format
img_bgr=cv2.imread('colourimg1.jpg')
#Step 2: Converting BGR to RGB format
img_rgb = cv2.cvtColor(img_bgr, cv2.COLOR_BGR2RGB)
#Step 3: Converting the image to YCbCr format
img_ycbcr=cv2.cvtColor(img_bgr, cv2.COLOR_BGR2YCR_CB)
#Step 4: Displaying the results
fig = plt.figure(figsize=(8,4)),plt.subplot(1,4,1),plt.imshow(img_rgb),plt.title('RGB image'),
plt.xticks([]),plt.yticks([]),plt.subplot(1,4,2),plt.imshow(img_ycbcr[:,:,0]),
plt.title('Luminance (Y) component'),plt.xticks([]),plt.yticks([]),plt.subplot(1,4,3),
plt.imshow(img_ycbcr[:,:,1]),plt.title('Cr component'),plt.xticks([]),plt.yticks([]),
plt.subplot(1,4,4),plt.imshow(img_ycbcr[:,:,2]),plt.title('Cb component'),plt.xticks([]),
plt.yticks([]),plt.tight_layout()
```

Fig. 10.39 Python code to display the luminance and chrominance components of the image

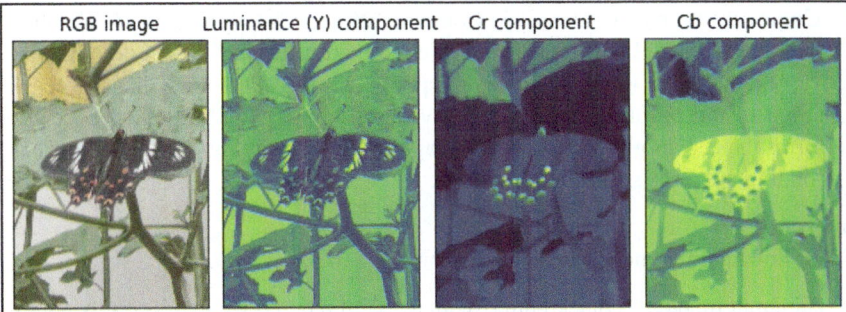

Fig. 10.40 Luminance and chrominance component of the input image

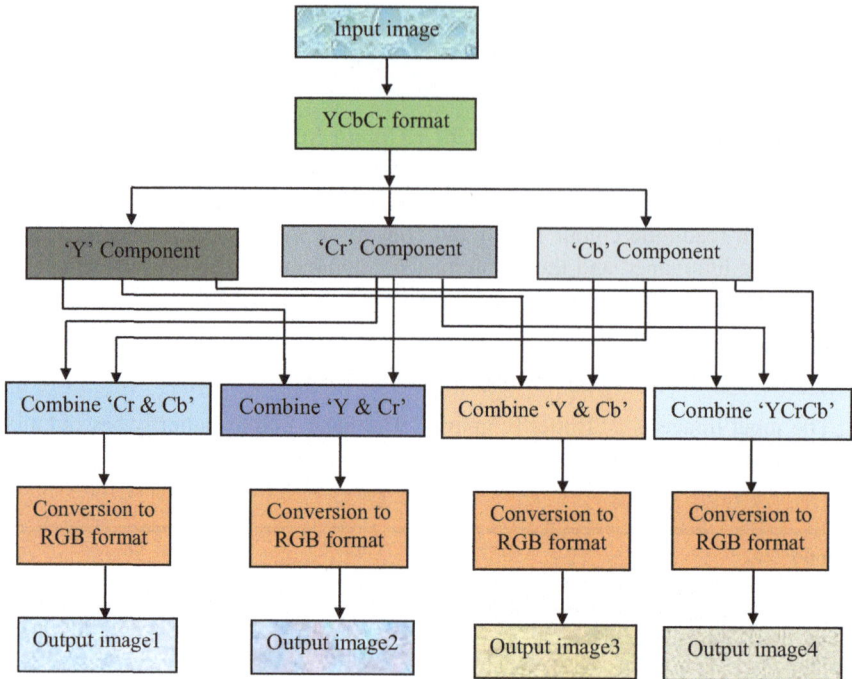

Fig. 10.41   Block diagram representation of the problem statement

- The luminance component resembles the input image. It carries much of the information of the input image.
- The "Cr" component displays bright spots wherever the input image has a red component.
- The "Cb" component represents another chroma information of the input image.

Experiment 10.16: Impact of Luminance and Chrominance Components

The objective of this experiment is to understand the impact of luminance and chrominance components. The input image is read first. It is then converted into YCbCr format. Now four different combinations are done: (1) Combine "Cb and Cr" alone, (2) Combine "Y and Cr" alone, (3) Combine "Y and Cb" alone, and (4) Combine "Y, Cb and Cr" to obtain four different combinations. After these combinations, convert the image to RGB format and display the result. The block diagram representation of the problem statement is given in Fig. 10.41. The Python code that performs the task as given in the block diagram is shown in Fig. 10.42, and the corresponding output is shown in Fig. 10.43.

Inference

The following inferences can be made from Fig. 10.43:

- The input image is a black butterfly image with red and white dots on its wings.
- "OI" represents the output image. The output image obtained using only chrominance components "Cb and Cr", no longer resembles the input image. This

```
import cv2
import matplotlib.pyplot as plt
import numpy as np
#Step 1: Reading the colour image in BGR format
img_bgr=cv2.imread('colourimg1.jpg')
#Step 2: Converting BGR to RGB format
img_rgb = cv2.cvtColor(img_bgr, cv2.COLOR_BGR2RGB)
#Step 3: Converting the image to YCbCr format
img_ycbcr=cv2.cvtColor(img_bgr, cv2.COLOR_BGR2YCR_CB)
img_y=img_ycbcr[:,:,0]
img_cb=img_ycbcr[:,:,1]
img_cr=img_ycbcr[:,:,2]
zeros = np.zeros_like(img_cb)
img_only_crcb=cv2.merge((zeros,img_cb,img_cr))
img_only_ycr=cv2.merge((img_y,zeros,img_cr))
img_only_ycb=cv2.merge((img_y,img_cb,zeros))
img_all=cv2.merge((img_y,img_cb,img_cr))
img_out1= cv2.cvtColor(img_only_crcb, cv2.COLOR_YCR_CB2RGB)
img_out2= cv2.cvtColor(img_only_ycr, cv2.COLOR_YCR_CB2RGB)
img_out3= cv2.cvtColor(img_only_ycb, cv2.COLOR_YCR_CB2RGB)
img_out4= cv2.cvtColor(img_all, cv2.COLOR_YCR_CB2RGB)
plt.figure(figsize=(10,8)),plt.subplot(1,5,1),plt.imshow(img_rgb),plt.title('Input image')
plt.xticks([]),plt.yticks([]),plt.subplot(1,5,2),plt.imshow(img_out1),plt.title('OI:Combine Cr and Cb')
plt.xticks([]),plt.yticks([]),plt.subplot(1,5,3),plt.imshow(img_out2),plt.title('OI:Combine Y and Cr')
plt.xticks([]),plt.yticks([]),plt.subplot(1,5,4),plt.imshow(img_out3),plt.title('OI:Combine Y and Cb')
plt.xticks([]),plt.yticks([]),plt.subplot(1,5,5),plt.imshow(img_out4),plt.title('OI:Combine Y Cr and Cb')
plt.xticks([]),plt.yticks([]),plt.tight_layout()
```

Fig. 10.42 Python code to analyze the impact of luminance and chrominance components

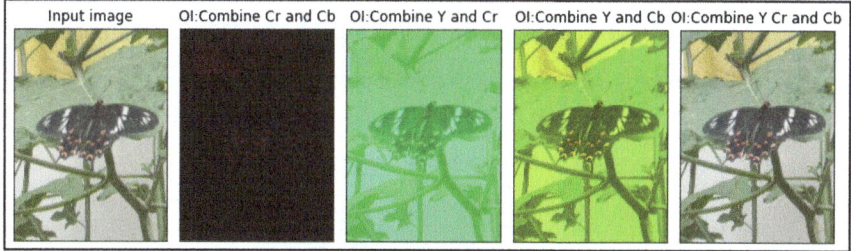

Fig. 10.43 Result of Python code shown in Fig. 10.42

illustrates the fact that the human eye is more sensitive to luminance than chrominance information.

- The output image obtained using "Y and Cr" resembles the input image with cyan background.
- The output image obtained using "Y and Cr" resembles the input image with yellow background.
- The output image obtained using "Y, Cr, and Cb" exactly resembles the input image.

10.3   Histogram of Colour Image

Histogram is a plot of gray level against the frequency of occurrence of the gray level. The colour image has three planes, namely, red, green, and blue. The histogram of the colour image computes the histogram of the red plane, green plane, and blue plane separately.

Experiment 10.17: Histogram of a Colour Image

In this experiment, a colour image is first read using the library "cv2", and then the histogram of the colour image is computed by individually obtaining the histogram of the red, green, and blue planes. The Python code that performs this task is shown in Fig. 10.44, and the corresponding output is shown in Fig. 10.45.

```
#Histogram of colour image
import cv2
from matplotlib import pyplot as plt
#Step 1: Reading the colour image
img = cv2.imread('testcolourimg1.jpg')
#Step 2: Computing the histogram of the image
color = ('b','g','r')
plt.figure(figsize=(5,4)),plt.subplot(2,1,1),plt.imshow(img),plt.xticks([]),
plt.yticks([]),plt.title('Input Image')
for i,col in enumerate(color):
    histr = cv2.calcHist([img],[i],None,[256],[0,256])
    plt.subplot(2,1,2),plt.plot(histr,color = col),plt.xlim([0,256]),plt.xlabel('Gray level')
    plt.ylabel('Freq. of occur.'),plt.title('Histogram')
plt.tight_layout()
```

Fig. 10.44   Python code to compute the histogram of the colour image

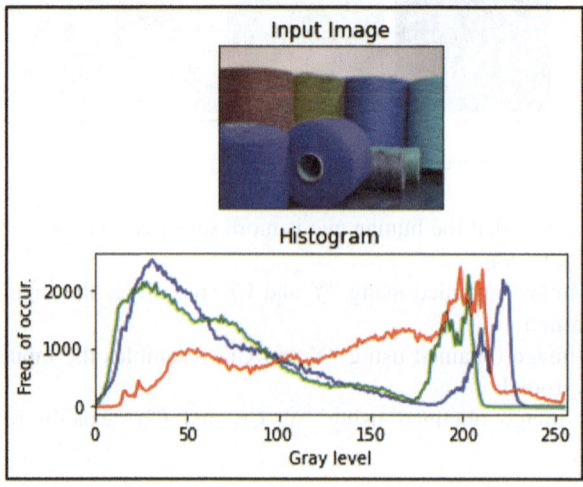

Fig. 10.45   Histogram of the colour image

Inference

- The colour image has three planes, namely, red, green, and blue; the histograms of the three planes are computed and displayed together to obtain the histogram of the colour image.

Experiment 10.18: Histogram of Red Image

Read a colour image that is completely red. Extract the red, green, and blue plane of the input image. Plot the histogram of the three planes and comment on the observed output. The Python code that performs the above-mentioned task is shown in Fig. 10.46, and the corresponding output is shown in Fig. 10.47.

Inferences

- From Fig. 10.47, it is possible to observe that the gray level 0 appears for blue and green planes, whereas the gray level 255 occurs for the red plane, which implies that the input test image is a pure red image.

Experiment 10.19: Histogram of White Image

In this experiment, instead of reading a pure red image, read a pure white image, extract the three-colour plane of the white image, and the histogram of three colour planes are plotted. The Python code and its corresponding result are shown in Figs. 10.48 and 10.49, respectively.

From Fig. 10.49, it is possible to observe that all three colours, blue, green, and red, appear equally in a white image. This is because the gray level 255 is the

```
import matplotlib.pyplot as plt
import numpy as np
#Reading the input RGB image
im=np.zeros([128,128,3],'uint8')
im[:,:,0]=255*np.ones([128,128])
im[:,:,1]=np.zeros([128,128])
im[:,:,2]=np.zeros([128,128])
#Extracting the three color planes
red_plane = im[:,:,0]
green_plane = im[:,:,1]
blue_plane = im[:,:,2]
plt.figure(figsize=(10,8)),plt.subplot(2,2,1),plt.imshow(im),plt.title('Red image'),
plt.xticks([]),plt.yticks([])
#Plotting the histogram of three color planes
plt.subplot(2,2,2),plt.hist(red_plane.ravel(),bins=256,range=[0,255],color='red')
plt.title('Histogram of red plane'),plt.xlabel('gray level'),plt.ylabel('Freq. Occur')
plt.subplot(2,2,3),plt.hist(green_plane.ravel(),bins=256,range=[0,255],color='green')
plt.title('Histogram of green plane'),plt.xlabel('gray level'),plt.ylabel('Freq. Occur')
plt.subplot(2,2,4),plt.hist(blue_plane.ravel(),bins=256,range=[0,255],color='blue')
plt.title('Histogram of blue plane'),plt.xlabel('gray level'),plt.ylabel('Freq. Occur')
plt.tight_layout()
```

Fig. 10.46 Python code to obtain the histogram of red, green, and blue planes

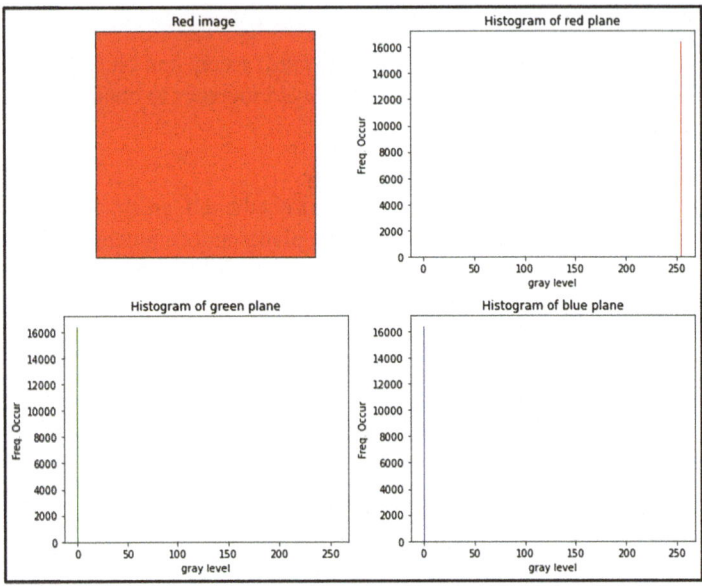

Fig. 10.47 Simulation result

```
import matplotlib.pyplot as plt
import numpy as np
#Reading the input RGB image
im=np.zeros([128,128,3],'uint8')
im[:,:,0]=255*np.ones([128,128])
im[:,:,1]=255*np.ones([128,128])
im[:,:,2]=255*np.ones([128,128])
#Extracting the three color planes
red_plane = im[:,:,0]
green_plane = im[:,:,1]
blue_plane = im[:,:,2]
plt.figure(figsize=(10,8))
plt.subplot(2,2,1),plt.imshow(im),plt.title('White image'),plt.xticks([]),plt.yticks([])
#Plotting the histogram of three colour planes
plt.subplot(2,2,2),plt.hist(red_plane.ravel(),bins=256,range=[0,255],color='red')
plt.title('Histogram of red plane'),plt.xlabel('gray level'),plt.ylabel('Freq. Occur')
plt.subplot(2,2,3),plt.hist(green_plane.ravel(),bins=256,range=[0,255],color='green')
plt.title('Histogram of green plane'),plt.xlabel('gray level'),plt.ylabel('Freq. Occur')
plt.subplot(2,2,4),plt.hist(blue_plane.ravel(),bins=256,range=[0,255],color='blue')
plt.title('Histogram of blue plane'),plt.xlabel('gray level'),plt.ylabel('Freq. Occur')
plt.tight_layout()
```

Fig. 10.48 Histogram of three colour planes for pure white image

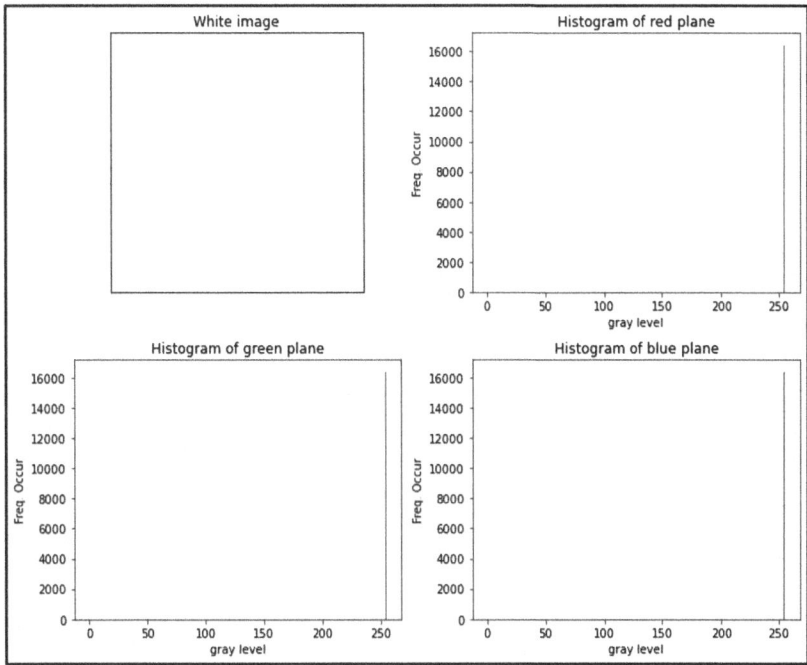

Fig. 10.49 Simulation result

maximum for all the three red, green, and blue planes, which is observed in Fig. 10.49. This implies that white colour has an equal proportion of red, green, and blue colours.

10.4   Histogram Equalization of Colour Image

Histogram equalization employs a monotonic, non-linear mapping that re-assigns the intensity values of pixels in the input image such that the output image contains a uniform distribution of intensities. Histogram equalization is employed to improve the contrast in the image. This section discusses histogram equalization of the colour image in two different approaches. In the first approach, the histogram equalization is applied to red, green, and blue channels separately in an RGB image. In the second approach, the RGB image is converted to *HSV* colour space, where the histogram equalization is performed in the "*V*" plane, and the image is again converted back to RGB space.

Experiment 10.20: Histogram Equalization in RGB Planes
In this method, the input colour image is read and histogram equalization is performed by applying histogram equalization to blue, green, and red channels

separately. The Python code, which performs the histogram equalization of the given colour image by applying the histogram equalization function individually to blue, green, and red channels, is given in Fig. 10.50, and the corresponding output is shown in Fig. 10.51.

Inferences

- From Fig. 10.50, it is possible to observe that four steps are followed to equalize the histogram of the colour image. The steps are
- Step 1: Reading the input colour image.
- Step 2: Apply histogram equalization to blue, green, and red channels separately. The built-in function "equalizeHist" available in the "CV" library performs the task.
- Step 3: The concatenation of the histogram equalized channels using the built-in function "stack" available in "numpy" library is used to combine the channels together.
- Step 4: deals with displaying the input image and histogram equalised image.
- From Fig. 10.51, it is possible to infer that the boy's hand and ear are clearly visible in the histogram-equalized image.

Experiment 10.21: Histogram Equalization by Converting BGR to HSV Plane
Histogram equalization of the colour image by converting the BGR image to HSV image and then performing histogram equalization in the HSV plane. After performing histogram equalization, the image is converted back to RGB. The Python code, which performs histogram equalization by converting BGR to HSV and performing equalization in HSV format, is given in Fig. 10.52, and the corresponding output is shown in Fig. 10.53.

```
import cv2
from matplotlib import pyplot as plt
import numpy as np
#Step 1: Reading the colour image
img = cv2.imread('testimage_colour.jpg')
#Step 2: Apply histogram equalisation to the three channels
colorimage_b = cv2.equalizeHist(img[:,:,0])
colorimage_g = cv2.equalizeHist(img[:,:,1])
colorimage_r = cv2.equalizeHist(img[:,:,2])
#Step 3: Combine the histogram equalised channels
colorimage_enh = np.stack((colorimage_b,colorimage_g,colorimage_r), axis=2)
#Step 4: Displaying the results
plt.subplot(1,2,1),plt.imshow(img),plt.title('Input image'),plt.xticks([]),
plt.yticks([]),plt.subplot(1,2,2),plt.imshow(colorimage_enh),
plt.title('Histogram equalized image'),plt.xticks([]),plt.yticks([])
plt.tight_layout()
```

Fig. 10.50 Python code to perform histogram equalization of colour image

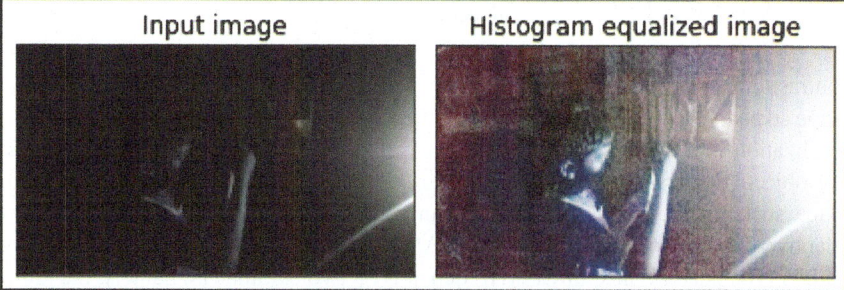

Fig. 10.51   Result of histogram equalization of the colour image

```
import cv2
from matplotlib import pyplot as plt
#Step 1: Reading the colour image
img = cv2.imread('testimage_colour.jpg')
#Step 2: Convertig BGR to HSV format
img_hsv = cv2.cvtColor(img, cv2.COLOR_BGR2HSV)
#Step 3: Performing histogram equalisation in HSV
img_hsv[:, :, 2] = cv2.equalizeHist(img_hsv[:, :, 2])
#Step 4: Converting the image back to RGB format
img_eql= cv2.cvtColor(img_hsv, cv2.COLOR_HSV2RGB)
#Step 5: Displaying the results
plt.subplot(1,2,1),plt.imshow(img),plt.title('Input image'),plt.xticks([]),plt.yticks([]),
plt.subplot(1,2,2),plt.imshow(img_eql),plt.title('Histogram equalized image'),
plt.xticks([]),plt.yticks([]),plt.tight_layout()
```

Fig. 10.52   Python code to perform histogram equalization in HSV format

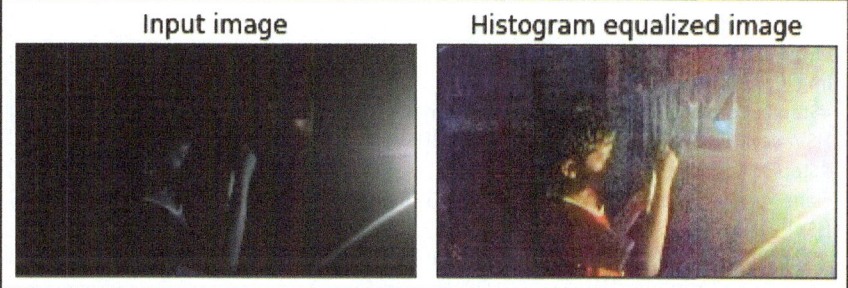

Fig. 10.53   Result of Python code shown in Fig. 10.52

Inference

• From Fig. 10.53, it is possible to observe that the histogram equalized image has better visual quality than the input image.

10.5   CLAHE to Colour Image

Contrast enhancement techniques are devised to enhance the visual quality of the image so as to provide better details for different image processing tasks. Histogram equalization is a widely adopted technique to enhance the contrast of the images. The objective of histogram equalization is to distribute the intensity values in an image such that lower contrast areas can gain higher contrast. Contrast Limited Adaptive Histogram Equalization (CLAHE) is a local histogram equalization method. The performance of CLAHE depends on two parameters, namely, the number of tiles and clip limit. Proper choice of these two parameters ensures better visual quality after the application of CLAHE. This section deals with the application of CLAHE algorithm to the colour image, in which the input colour image is converted to HSV format, and CLAHE is applied to the "V" plane. After enhancing the contrast of "V" plane, the image is again converted back to RGB plane for visualization.

Experiment 10.22: Colour Image Enhancement Using CLAHE
In this experiment, the input colour image is read, and it is then converted to HSV colour space. After conversion, the contrast-limited adaptive histogram equalization (CLAHE) is applied to "V" channel. Then, the image is converted back to RGB for display. The Python code which performs the above-mentioned task is given in Fig. 10.54, and the corresponding output is shown in Fig. 10.55.

Inferences

- From Fig. 10.55, the visual quality of the processed image using CLAHE algorithm is better than the input image.
- The "Laptop" on the table is blurred in the input image, but it is clearly visible in the processed image.

```
import cv2
from matplotlib import pyplot as plt
#Step 1: Reading the colour image
img = cv2.imread('testimg3.jpg')
#Step 2: Converting the image to HSV format
HSV = cv2.cvtColor(img, cv2.COLOR_BGR2HSV)
#Step 3: Applying CLAHE to 'V' plane
clahe = cv2.createCLAHE(clipLimit=10,tileGridSize=(4,4))
HSV[:,:,2] = clahe.apply(HSV[:,:,2])
#Step 4: Converting the image back to RGB
im_out = cv2.cvtColor(HSV, cv2.COLOR_HSV2RGB)
#Step 5: Displaying the results
plt.subplot(1,2,1),plt.imshow(img),plt.title('Input image'),plt.xticks([]),plt.yticks([]),
plt.subplot(1,2,2),plt.imshow(im_out),plt.title('CLAHE output image'),
plt.xticks([]),plt.yticks([]),plt.tight_layout()
```

Fig. 10.54   Python code to apply CLAHE algorithm to colour image

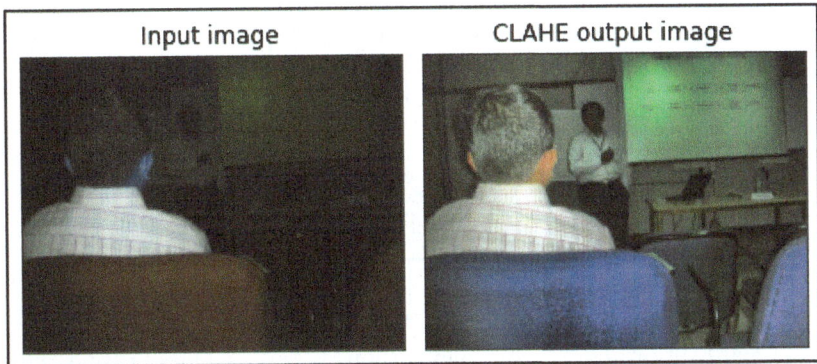

Fig. 10.55 Result of applying CLAHE algorithm to the colour image

10.6 Quantization of Colour Image

Quantization is mapping a large set of values to a smaller set of values. Quantization is a non-linear and irreversible process. Quantization can be broadly classified into (1) Scalar quantization and (2) Vector quantization. Scalar quantization deals with the approximation of scalar values, whereas vector quantization deals with the approximation of a group of values.

Experiment 10.23: Quantization of Colour Image
In this experiment, an RGB image is read, and it is then divided into red, green, and blue planes. Scalar quantization is applied to individual red, green, and blue planes. The quantized colour planes are merged to obtain the quantized colour image. The block diagram which depicts the problem statement is shown in Fig. 10.56. The Python code which performs the scalar quantization of the colour image is shown in Fig. 10.57, and the corresponding output is shown in Fig. 10.60.

Inferences
The following inferences can be made from Fig. 10.58:

- The input image is quantized by varying the bit rate as 1, 2, 4, 6, and 8.
- When the bit rate is 1, the quality of the reconstructed image is poor.
- With the increase in bit rate, the reconstructed or quantized image quality increases. When the bit rate is 8, the quantized image resembles the input image.
- To get the better quality image, the bit rate has to be higher; with an increase in bit rate, the storage complexity increases. There should be a compromise between the storage space and the quality of the image.

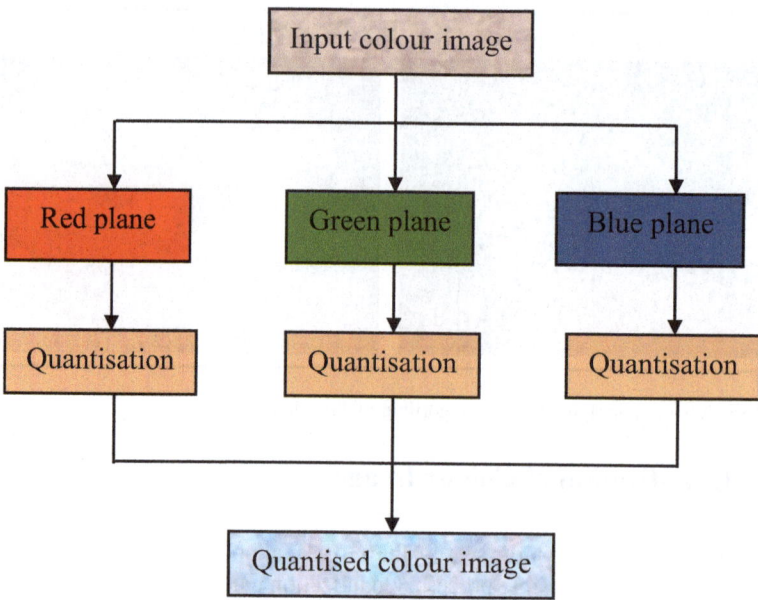

Fig. 10.56 Block diagram depicting problem statement

```
# Quantisation of colour image
import cv2
import matplotlib.pyplot as plt
import numpy as np
#Step 1: Reading the colour image in BGR format
img_bgr=cv2.imread('colourtestimg2.jpg')
#Step 2: Converting BGR to RGB format
img_rgb = cv2.cvtColor(img_bgr, cv2.COLOR_BGR2RGB)
plt.figure(figsize=(8,4)),plt.subplot(2,3,1),plt.imshow(img_rgb),plt.title('Input image'),
plt.xticks([]),plt.yticks([])
#Step 3: Separating the colour image into R, G and B planes
img1=img_rgb[:,:,0]
img2=img_rgb[:,:,1]
img3=img_rgb[:,:,2]
#Step 4: Function to perform quantisation
def imquant(img,b):
    dr = np.max(img) - np.min(img) #Dynamic range
    l = 2 ** b   #Reconstruction level
    q = dr / l     #Quantization step size
    q_im = np.floor(img/q)*q + (q/2)
    return(q_im.astype(np.uint8))
#Step 5: Applying quantisation to R, G, B plane
b=[1,2,4,6,8]  #Number of bits used to represent pixel
for i in range(len(b)):
    imgq1=imquant(img1,b[i])
    imgq2=imquant(img2,b[i])
    imgq3=imquant(img3,b[i])
    #Step 6: Combining the quantised colour planes
    img_rec=cv2.merge([imgq1,imgq2,imgq3])
    plt.subplot(2,3,i+2),plt.imshow(img_rec),plt.title('Quantized image with b={}'.format(b[i]))
    plt.xticks([]),plt.yticks([])
plt.tight_layout()
```

Fig. 10.57 Python code to perform quantization of colour image

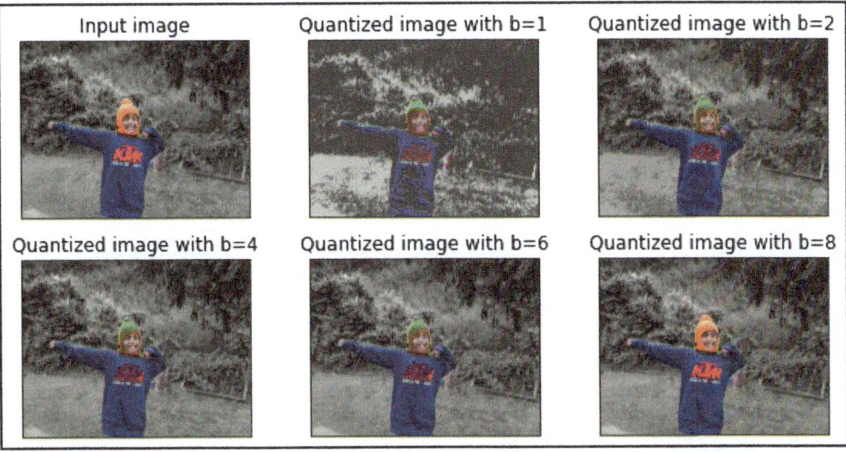

Fig. 10.58 Input and quantized image with different bit rate

10.7   Colour Image Filtering: Median Filter

Digital images are corrupted by noise during acquisition, storage, processing, and transmission. Different types of noises in digital images include additive white Gaussian noise, speckle noise, which is multiplicative in nature, impulse noise, and periodic noise. This section discusses the minimization of impact of impulse noise in colour image. Impulse noise appears as isolated bright or dark pixels in the image. It is due to random bit errors during transmission. Median filter is effective in minimizing the impact of salt and pepper noise. The principle of median filter is to replace the gray level of each pixel by the median of the gray levels in a neighbourhood of the pixels.

Experiment 10.24: Median Filtering of Colour Image

This experiment discusses the median filtering of colour image. Read a colour image, and add salt and pepper noise to the colour image. Pass the noisy image through a median filter whose kernel size is varied as 3, 7, 9, and 11. The Python code, which performs the task of adding salt and pepper noise to the colour image and filtering it using a median filter of different kernel sizes, is shown in Fig. 10.59, and the corresponding outputs are shown in Fig. 10.60.

Inferences

- From Fig. 10.60, it is possible to observe that the impact of salt and pepper noise is minimized by increasing the size of the kernel of median filter.
- The 11×11 kernel minimizes the impact of salt and pepper noise than 3×3 kernel.

```
import cv2
from matplotlib import pyplot as plt
import random
import numpy as np
#Step 1: Reading the colour image
img = cv2.imread('testimage_cake.jpg')
#Step 2: Adding salt and pepper noise
prob=0.4
noisy_img = np.zeros(img.shape,np.uint8)
thres = 1 - prob
for i in range(img.shape[0]):
    for j in range(img.shape[1]):
        rdn = random.random()
        if rdn < prob:
          noisy_img[i][j] = 0
        elif rdn > thres:
          noisy_img[i][j] = 255
        else:
          noisy_img[i][j] = img[i][j]
plt.figure(figsize=(8,6)),plt.subplot(2,3,1),plt.imshow(img),plt.title('Input image')
plt.xticks([]),plt.yticks([]),plt.subplot(2,3,2),plt.imshow(noisy_img),
plt.xticks([]),plt.yticks([]),plt.title('Noisy image')
#Step 3: Applying median filter
kernel_size=[3,7,9,11]
for i in range(len(kernel_size)):
   medfilt_img=cv2.medianBlur(noisy_img,kernel_size[i])
   plt.subplot(2,3,i+3),plt.imshow(medfilt_img),plt.xticks([]),plt.yticks([])
   plt.title('MF with kernel size ={}'.format(kernel_size[i]))
plt.tight_layout()
```

Fig. 10.59 Python code to denoise salt and pepper noise in colour image

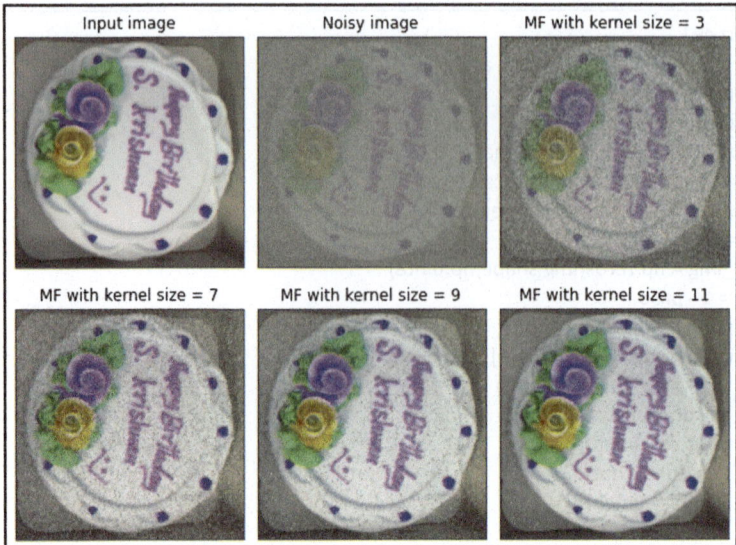

Fig. 10.60   Impact of median filter to minimize salt and pepper noise in colour image

10.8   Pseudo Colour

In general, human eye cannot distinguish more than 50 gray levels in an image. Subtle details can easily be lost when looking at grayscale images. To enhance the variations in gray level and make them more intuitive, grayscale images are pseudo-coloured, where each grayscale is mapped to a colour level through Look Up Table (LUT).

Experiment 10.25: Conversion of Binary Image to Two Colours
This experiment discusses the input grayscale image is converted into two colours output image. The two colours C_1 and C_2 chosen for the intensity levels in the grayscale image are illustrated in Fig. 10.61.

In Fig. 10.61, the x-axis represents the gray level of the input image, the y-axis represents the colour. If the gray level of the input image is from 0 to L_1, the output colour is C_1. If the input gray level is beyond L_1, the output colour is C_2.

To verify this concept, the checkerboard pattern is generated, and it is the input binary image. The checkerboard pattern takes only two gray levels, which are either 0 or 255. If the gray level is greater than zero, the output colour is red; otherwise, the output colour is green. The Python code that performs this operation is given in Fig. 10.62, and the corresponding output is shown in Fig. 10.63.

Inferences
From Fig. 10.63, the following inference can be drawn:

- The input image is a 256 × 256 checkerboard pattern, which is a binary image.
- The input image takes only two gray levels which are either 0 or 255.

Fig. 10.61 Pseudo
colouring using intensity
slicing

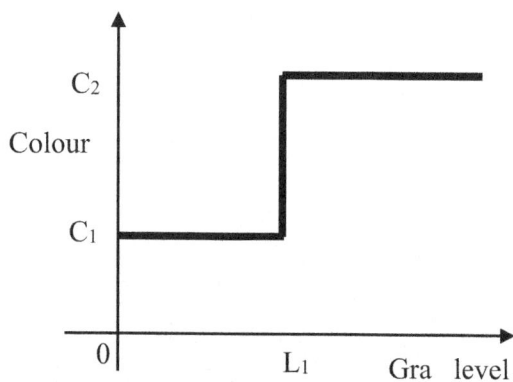

```
import matplotlib.pyplot as plt
import numpy as np
#Step 1: Generate 256 x 256 checkerboard pattern
x, y = np.meshgrid(np.arange(256), np.arange(256))
img_chess = np.zeros((256, 256), dtype=np.uint8)
img_chess[(x // 32 + y // 32) % 2 == 0] = 1
m,n=img_chess.shape
#Step 2: Create a red, green and blue pattern
height, width, channel = 256, 256, 3
red1, green1, blue1 = 255, 0, 0
red2, green2, blue2 = 0, 255, 0
red3, green3, blue3 = 0, 0, 255
im_red = np.full((height, width, channel), [red1, green1, blue1], dtype=('uint8'))
im_green = np.full((height, width, channel), [red2, green2, blue2], dtype=('uint8'))
im_blue = np.full((height, width, channel), [red3, green3, blue3], dtype=('uint8'))
#Step 3: Generate colour image template
img_color=np.zeros([256,256,3],dtype='uint8')
# Step 4: Obtaining the colour image based on intensity of input image
for i in range (m):
    for j in range(n):
        if img_chess[i,j]>0:
            img_color[i,j]=im_red[i,j]
        else:
            img_color[i,j]=im_green[i,j]
#Step 5: Displaying the results
plt.subplot(1,2,1),plt.imshow(img_chess,cmap='gray'),plt.title('Binary image')
plt.xticks([]),plt.yticks([]),plt.subplot(1,2,2),plt.imshow(img_color)
plt.title('Pseudo colour image'),plt.xticks([]),plt.yticks([])
plt.tight_layout()
```

Fig. 10.62 Python code to perform pseudo colouring based on intensity slicing

- The output image turns red if the input gray level is greater than 0. The output
  image is green if the input gray level is 0.
- The output image is a pseudo colour version of the input binary image.

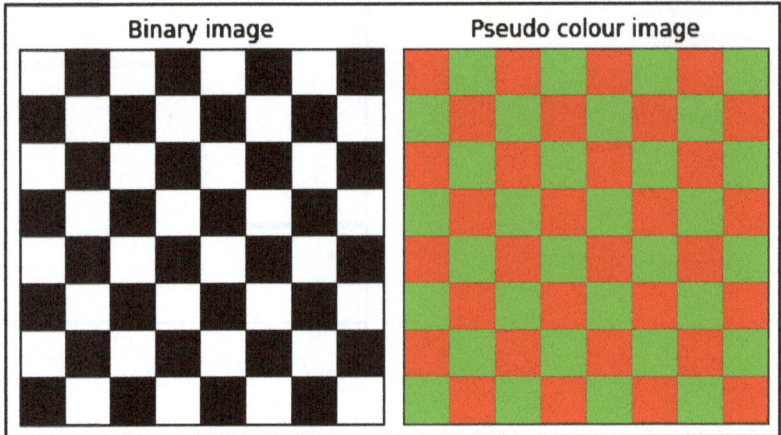

Fig. 10.63 Pseudo colouring of grayscale image

Task: Modify the code shown in Fig. 10.62, such that if the input gray level is greater than 0, the output is green colour. On the other hand, if the input gray level is zero, the output should be a blue colour.

Experiment 10.26: Pseudo Colouring of Grayscale Image
In this experiment, a gradient test image is generated. The gray level varies from black to white. Three gray levels exist in the input image which are −1, 0, and 1. If the gray level is −1, then it will be replaced by red colour; if the gray level is 0, it will be replaced by green colour, and if the gray level is 1 then that gray level is replaced by blue colour. The Python code that performs this operation is shown in Fig. 10.64, and the corresponding output is shown in Fig. 10.65.

Inferences
The following inferences can be made from this experiment:

- The input image has three gray levels, which appear as black, gray, and white.
- Corresponding to the grayscale image, a colour image is generated.
- For the black colour, the red colour is generated, for grayscale, green colour is generated, and for the white colour, blue colour is generated to obtain the pseudo colour image.

Experiment 10.27: Pseudo Colour of the Input Grayscale Image Using Different Colormaps
Matplotlib has number of built-in colour maps which can be used to obtain the pseudo colour. OpenCV defines 12 colour maps that can be applied to a grayscale image. The built-in function applyColorMap() can be used to produce pseudo coloured image. In this experiment, a grayscale image is read, and then an attempt is made to obtain a different colourmap representations of the grayscale image. The Python code that performs this task is shown in Fig. 10.66, and the corresponding output is shown in Fig. 10.67.

```
#Pseudo colouring of grayscale image
import numpy as np
import matplotlib.pyplot as plt
#Step 1: Generation of test image
img=np.zeros([3,3])
for i in range(0,3):
    for j in range(0,3):
        img[i,j]=j-1
m,n=img.shape
#Colour patern
height, width, channel = 3, 3, 3
red1, green1, blue1 = 255, 0, 0
red2, green2, blue2 = 0, 255, 0
red3, green3, blue3 = 0, 0, 255
im_red = np.full((height, width, channel), [red1, green1, blue1], dtype=('uint8'))
im_green = np.full((height, width, channel), [red2, green2, blue2], dtype=('uint8'))
im_blue = np.full((height, width, channel), [red3, green3, blue3], dtype=('uint8'))
#Step 3: Generate colour image template
img_color=np.zeros([3,3,3],dtype='uint8')
for i in range (m):
    for j in range(n):
        if img[i,j]<0:
            img_color[i,j]=im_red[i,j]
        elif img[i,j]==0:
            img_color[i,j]=im_green[i,j]
        else:
            img_color[i,j]=im_blue[i,j]
#Step 5: Displaying the results
plt.subplot(1,2,1),plt.imshow(img,cmap='gray'),plt.title('Grayscale image')
plt.xticks([]),plt.yticks([]),plt.subplot(1,2,2),plt.imshow(img_color)
plt.title('Pseudo colour image'),plt.xticks([]),plt.yticks([])
plt.tight_layout()
```

Fig. 10.64 Python code to perform pseudo colouring of grayscale image

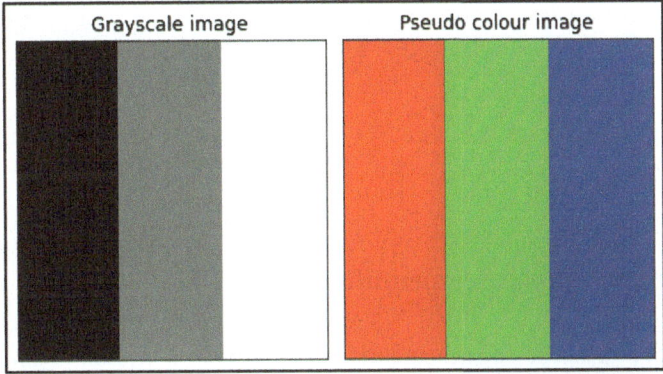

Fig. 10.65 Result of Python code shown in Fig. 10.64

```
#Pseudo colouring
import matplotlib.pyplot as plt
import cv2
#Step 1: Reading the image
img_gray=cv2.imread('Clock.tiff',0)
#Step 2: Defining different colormap
colormap1 = cv2.COLORMAP_HOT
colormap2=cv2.COLORMAP_HSV
colormap3=cv2.COLORMAP_JET
#Step 3: Different pseduo color representation
img_color1 = cv2.applyColorMap(img_gray, colormap1)
img_color2 = cv2.applyColorMap(img_gray, colormap2)
img_color3 = cv2.applyColorMap(img_gray, colormap3)
#Step 4: Displaying the result
plt.figure(figsize=(8,6)),plt.subplot(1,4,1),plt.imshow(img_gray,cmap='gray'),
plt.title('Grayscale image'),plt.xticks([]),plt.yticks([]),plt.subplot(1,4,2),
plt.imshow(img_color1),plt.title('Colormap = HOT'),plt.xticks([]),plt.yticks([])
plt.subplot(1,4,3),plt.imshow(img_color2),plt.title('Colormap = HSV')
plt.xticks([]),plt.yticks([]),plt.subplot(1,4,4),plt.imshow(img_color3)
plt.title('Colormap = JET'),plt.xticks([]),plt.yticks([])
plt.tight_layout()
```

Fig. 10.66   Python code to obtain pseudo colour representation of grayscale image

Fig. 10.67   Psuedo colouring of grayscale image

Inference

- Different colour maps give different colour representations of the input grayscale image.

10.9   Colour Image Segmentation

The objective of image segmentation is to partition an image into homogeneous regions such that they are semantically meaningful with respect to characteristics like colour, intensity, texture, etc. Different techniques for image segmentation include thresholding, edge-based segmentation, region-based approach, and cluster-based approach. Threshold segmentation is suitable for images where the target and background occupy different gray level ranges. This section discusses image segmentation using k-means clustering algorithm. Clustering is an unsupervised learning method. The purpose of clustering is to divide the data points into several categories.

10.9.1   k-Means Clustering Algorithm

The steps in k-means clustering algorithm are summarized below:

Step 1: Initialize number of cluster "k" and centre.
Step 2: For each pixel of an image, calculate the Euclidean distance "d" between the center and each pixel of an image using the formula

$$d = p(x,y) - c_k \tag{10.12}$$

In the above expression, $p(x, y)$ represents the pixels, c_k represents the cluster centre.
Step 3: Assign all the pixels to the nearest centre based on distance "d".
Step 4: After all pixels have been assigned, recalculate the new position of the centre using the relation

$$c_k = \frac{1}{k} \sum_{y \in c_k} \sum_{x \in c_k} p(x,y) \tag{10.13}$$

Step 5: Repeat the process until it satisfies the tolerance or error value.
Step 6: Reshape the cluster pixels into image.

Experiment 10.28: k-Means Clustering Algorithm for Colour Image Segmentation
In this experiment, the retinal image is read, and then it is passed through the k-means clustering algorithm. The k-means clustering algorithm is an iterative algorithm. The termination of the algorithm can be fixed either as the number of iterations or if the specified accuracy is reached. In this experiment, the number of iterations is specified as 100 and the accuracy is specified as 0.85. The number of clusters "k" varies as 2, 3, 4, and 5. The Python code that performs the task of image segmentation using k-means clustering is shown in Fig. 10.68, and the outputs are displayed in Fig. 10.69. The built-in functions used in the program are listed in Table 10.1.

Inference
The following inferences can be observed from Fig. 10.69:

- The input image contains four objects with multiple colours.
- The output of k-means clustering with k = 1, the complete image becomes only one colour.

```
import cv2
import matplotlib.pyplot as plt
import numpy as np
#Step 1: Reading the colour image in BGR format
img_bgr=cv2.imread('tools.jpg')
#Step 2: Converting BGR to RGB format
img_rgb = cv2.cvtColor(img_bgr, cv2.COLOR_BGR2RGB)
plt.figure(figsize=(8,4)),plt.subplot(2,3,1),plt.imshow(img_rgb),
plt.title('Input image'),plt.xticks([]),plt.yticks([])
pixel_vals = img_rgb.reshape((-1,3))
pixel_vals = np.float32(pixel_vals)
criteria = (cv2.TERM_CRITERIA_EPS + cv2.TERM_CRITERIA_MAX_ITER, 100, 0.85)
k = [1,2,4,6,8]              `
for i in range(len(k)):
    retval, labels, centers = cv2.kmeans(pixel_vals, k[i], None, criteria, 10,
cv2.KMEANS_RANDOM_CENTERS)
    centers = np.uint8(centers)
    segmented_data = centers[labels.flatten()]
    segmented_image = segmented_data.reshape((img_rgb.shape))
    plt.subplot(2,3,i+2),plt.imshow(segmented_image)
    plt.title('Segmented with k = {}'.format(k[i])),plt.xticks([]),plt.yticks([])
plt.tight_layout()
```

Fig. 10.68 Python code to perform image segmentation using k-means clustering algorithm

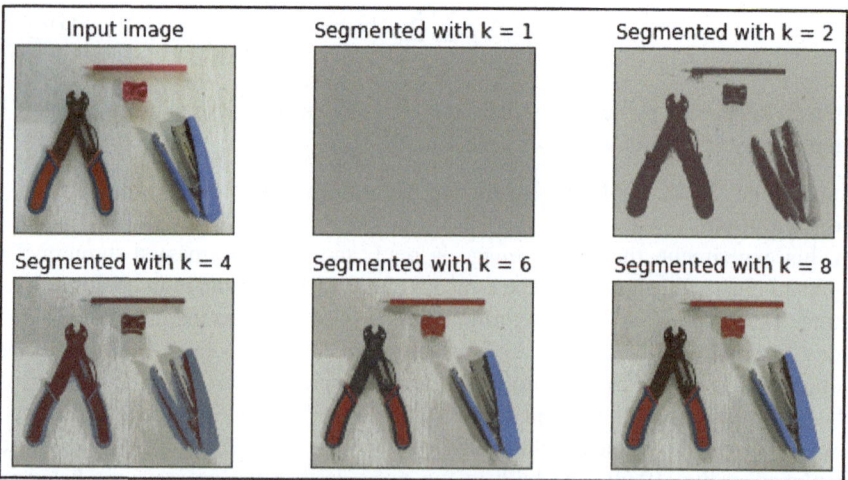

Fig. 10.69 Input and result of k-means clustering algorithm

Table 10.1 The built-in function used in image segmentation program

S. no.	Built-in function	Library	Purpose
1	K-means	CV2	To perform k-means clustering on the input data
2	float32	Numpy	To convert the data type to float
3	uint8	Numpy	To convert the data type of unsigned integer "8" bits
4	Reshape	Numpy	Change the shape of an array

- When the k = 2, the input image is segmented into two categories (i.e. foreground objects and the background blank).
- When k = 4, the output image contains four colours, it starts distinguishing the individual objects.
- When k = 6 and 8, all the colours present in the object are retained by the k means clustering algorithm.

Task: Repeat the above experiment by modifying the following parameters. The number of iterations to be fixed as 100, and the accuracy as 0.95. The number of cluster "k" to be fixed as "8".

10.10   Colour Image Compression Using PCA

PCA stands for principal component analysis. PCA is widely used in dimensionality reduction. PCA represents the data in a new coordinate system in which basis vectors follow modes of greatest variance in the data. The steps followed in image compression using PCA are represented in the form of a block diagram, which is given in Fig. 10.70.

The steps followed in PCA-based colour image compression which is depicted in Fig. 10.70 is summarized below:

Step 1: First the three components of the RGB image are extracted.
Step 2: For reach channel, first "n" principal components are retained.
Step 3: The forward transform projects the image matrix along the principal components.
Step 4: The inverse transform is used to reconstruct the image using only "n" principal components.

Experiment 10.29: PCA-Based Colour Image Compression

The objective of this experiment is to compress the input colour image using PCA. First, the colour image in BGR format is converted to RGB format. Then PCA is applied to red, green, and blue components to compress the image. After that image is reconstructed using modified red, green, and blue components. The Python code that performs this task is given in Fig. 10.71, and the corresponding output is shown in Fig. 10.72.

The built-in functions used in the program and its purpose are summarized in Table 10.2.

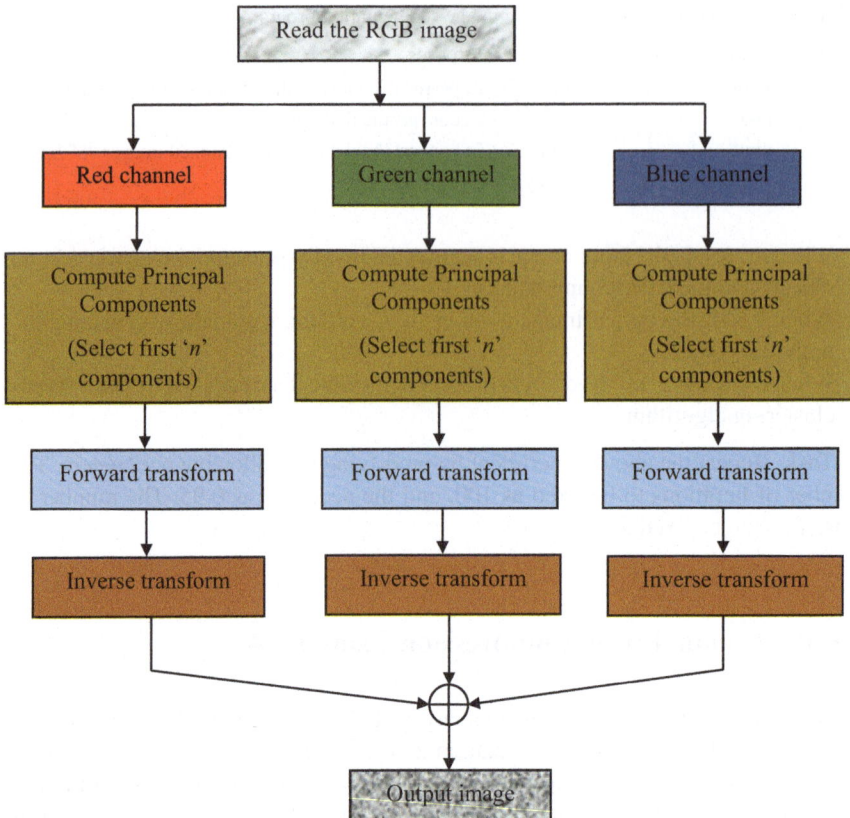

Fig. 10.70   Block diagram of PCA-based colour image compression

Inferences

From Fig. 10.72, the following inferences can be drawn

- The term "RI" represents the reconstructed image.
- When the number of principal components is 10, the reconstructed image is a distorted version of the input image.
- With increase in the number of principal components, the reconstructed image resembles the input image.

Exercise

1. Read a colour image and convert the colour image to a grayscale image. From the grayscale image obtain the binary image. Display the input colour image, converted grayscale, and binary image.
2. Generate a test image that is a white circle on a black background. The size of the image is 256×256, and the radius of the circle is 40 units. Now, create a pseudo-coloured image such that the circle should be red and the background blue.

```
import cv2
import matplotlib.pyplot as plt
from sklearn.decomposition import PCA
import numpy as np
#Step 1: Reading the colour image in BGR format
img_bgr=cv2.imread('Rose.jpg')
#Step 2: Converting BGR to RGB format
img_rgb = cv2.cvtColor(img_bgr, cv2.COLOR_BGR2RGB)
plt.figure(figsize=(10,8)),plt.subplot(2,3,1),plt.imshow(img_rgb),plt.title('Input image')
plt.xticks([]),plt.yticks([])
r,g,b=cv2.split(img_rgb)
r,g,b=r/255,g/255,b/255
pca_components=[10,50,100,200,300]
for i in range(len(pca_components)):
    pca_r=PCA(pca_components[i])
    reduced_r=pca_r.fit_transform(r)
    pca_g=PCA(pca_components[i])
    reduced_g=pca_g.fit_transform(g)
    pca_b=PCA(pca_components[i])
    reduced_b=pca_b.fit_transform(b)
    recons_r=pca_r.inverse_transform(reduced_r)
    recons_g=pca_g.inverse_transform(reduced_g)
    recons_b=pca_b.inverse_transform(reduced_b)
    img_recons=cv2.merge((recons_r,recons_g,recons_b))
    plt.subplot(2,3,i+2),plt.imshow((img_recons * 255).astype(np.uint8))
    plt.title('RI:# of PCA components = {}'.format(pca_components[i]))
    plt.xticks([]),plt.yticks([])
plt.tight_layout()
```

Fig. 10.71 Python code to perform image compression using PCA

3. Generate a 256×256 RGB test image in which the first, second, third, and fourth quadrants are red, green, blue, and cyan colours. Now convert this test RGB image to HSV format. After conversion, set the "H" component, "S" component, and "V" components to zero. Then convert the HSV image back to the RGB image and comment on the observed result.

4. Segmentation of green colour region in the test image. The test image has two apples (red colour), two oranges (yellow colour), and a cucumber (green colour). Segment the green colour in the test image by converting the image into HSV space and applying a suitable threshold to separate the green colour.

5. Observe the impact of adding 90° to the Hue component of the test image. The test image has red, green, and blue colours. Each size 100×100 gets concatenated horizontally. The test image is converted to HSV format. After conversion, 90° is added to only Hue component. After this, the new Hue, Saturation, and Value components will be merged. Then it is converted back to RGB format. Display the input (test image) and output image and comment on the observed result.

Fig. 10.72 Original and reconstructed images using different principal components

Table 10.2 Built-in function used in Python code shown in Fig. 10.71

S. no.	Built-in function	Library	Purpose
1	PCA	Sklearn	To perform principal component analysis. PCA is built under sklearn.decomposition
2	Split	CV2	To split the RGB planes of the colour image
3	Transform	Sklearn	Project the image into the basis of the calculated principal components

6. Observe the impact of adding 90° to the Hue component of the test image. The test image has red, green, and blue colours. Each size 100 × 100 gets concatenated horizontally. The test image is converted to HSV format. After conversion, 60° is added to only Hue component. After this, the new Hue, Saturation, and Value components are merged. Then it is converted back to RGB format. Display the input (test image) and output image and comment on the observed result.

7. Read the colour image, convert it into $L*a*b*$ format. Separate the "$L*$", "$a*$", "$b*$" components. Force the value of "$L*$" component to zero without altering the values of "$a*$" and "$b*$" components. Then convert the image back to RGB plane to obtain the output image. Comment on the observed result.

8. Apply pseudo colouring to the eight-bit grayscale image given below:

$$\begin{bmatrix} 252 & 185 & 101 & 35 \\ 212 & 132 & 112 & 114 \\ 54 & 60 & 142 & 151 \\ 32 & 52 & 134 & 201 \end{bmatrix}$$

A colour map of four colours, namely, red, green, blue, and white, is used in the order of darkest to lightest intensities. Assume that the grayscale intensity values are linearly mapped to the new colours.

Objective Questions

1. If the following Python code is executed, which plane will be extracted in the variable "im1"?

```
import cv2
im=cv2.imread('testimg.jpg')
im1=im[:,:,2]
```

(A) Red plane
(B) Green plane
(C) Blue plane
(D) Either Red or Green plane

2. Which colour plane is set to zero if the following Python code is executed?

```
import cv2
img=cv2.imread('testimg.jpg')
img[:,:,0]=0
```

(A) Red plane
(B) Blue plane
(C) Green plane
(D) None of the plane is set to zero

3. Which colour plane is set to zero, if the following Python code is executed?

```
import cv2
img=cv2.imread('testimg.jpg')
img1 = cv2.cvtColor(img_bgr, cv2.COLOR_BGR2RGB)
img1[:,:,0]=0
```

(A) Red plane
(B) Blue plane
(C) Green plane
(D) None of the plane is set to zero

4. What will the colour of the image (test_image) be if the following Python code is executed?

```
import numpy as np
height, width, channel = 256, 256, 3
test_image = np.full((height, width, channel), [0,0,255], dtype=('uint8'))
```

(A) Red
(B) Green
(C) Blue
(D) Purple

5. What will the colour of the image (test_image) be if the following Python code is executed?

```
import numpy as np
height, width, channel = 256, 256, 3
test_image = np.full((height, width, channel), [0,255,255], dtype=('uint8'))
```

(A) Red
(B) Green
(C) Blue
(D) Cyan

6. What will the colour of the image (test_image) be if the following Python code is executed?

```
import numpy as np
height, width, channel = 256, 256, 3
test_image = np.full((height, width, channel), [255,255,255], dtype=('uint8'))
```

(A) White
(B) Red
(C) Green
(D) Blue

7. What will the image's nature be in the variable "img" if the following python code is executed?

```
import cv2
import matplotlib.pyplot as plt
import numpy as np
#Step 1: Reading the colour image in BGR format
img_bgr=cv2.imread('testimg.jpg')
img_rgb = cv2.cvtColor(img_bgr, cv2.COLOR_BGR2RGB)
row,col=img_bgr.shape[0:2]
img=np.zeros([row,col])
for i in range (row):
    for j in range (col):
        img[i,j]=sum(img_bgr[i,j])*0.33
```

(A) Contrast enhanced RGB image
(B) Red channel filtered RGB image
(C) Grayscale image
(D) Blue channel filtered RGB image

8. What will be colour of the resultant image if equal proportions of red, green, and blue colours are added?

(A) Yellow
(B) Cyan
(C) Magenta
(D) White

9. Consider a display device with the maximum intensities for the red, green, and blue channels of 100, 200, and 200, respectively. The intensity of white colour of this device is

(A) 100
(B) 200
(C) 400
(D) 500

10. An example of a subtractive colour model is

(A) RGB colour model
(B) CMY colour model
(C) HSV colour model
(D) YC_bC_r colour model

11. The colour model which is used in computer monitor is

(A) RGB colour model
(B) CMY colour model
(C) HSV colour model
(D) YC_bC_r colour model

12. Match the following
    Colour model   Appropriate
    (i) RGB   (P) Human visual system
    (ii) CMYK   (Q)Computer display
    (iii) HSV   (R) Printer

    (A) (i)-(P),(ii)-Q, (iii)-(R)
    (B) (i)-(Q),(ii)-(R), (iii)-(P)
    (C) (i)-(R), (ii)-Q, (iii)-(P)
    (D) (i)-(R), (ii)-(P), (iii)-(Q)

13. By adding 30° to the Hue component of the HSV colour model, the red colour
    changes to

    (A) Blue colour
    (B) Green colour
    (C) Cyan colour
    (D) Magenta colour

14. Statement 1: Rods are responsible for chromatic vision.
    Statement 2: Cones are responsible for chromatic vision

    (A) Statements 1 and 2 are false
    (B) Statement 1 is true, Statement 2 is false
    (C) Statement 1 is false, Statement 2 is true
    (D) Statements 1 and 2 are true

15. In HSV colour space, the primary colours are separated by

    (A) 45°
    (B) 60°
    (C) 90°
    (D) 120°

Answers to Objective Questions

Q. No.	01	02	03	04	05	06	07	08	09	10
Key	A	B	A	C	D	A	C	D	D	B
Q. No.	11	12	13	14	15					
Key	A	B	B	C	D					

Answers to PreLab Questions

1. In the RGB colour model, colour is produced by adding varying amounts of red, green, and blue light together. Hence, the RGB colour model is considered as an additive colour model. RGB colour model is employed in computer monitor.

2. In the CMYK colour model, the pigments used to form the image absorb or subtract some of the colours from white light; the remaining colours reach the eye to produce the image, and the CMYK colour model is considered as a subtractive colour model. CMYK colour model is employed in printers.

3. In the human eye, there are two types of sensors, namely, rods and cones. Cones are responsible for colour vision, which is termed as photopic vision.

4. The valid differences between RGB colour model and CMYK colour model are tabulated below:

S. no.	RGB colour model	CMYK colour model
1	Additive colour model	Subtractive colour model
2	The model uses light to display colours	This model uses ink to display colours
3	RGB colour model is employed in computer displays	CMYK colour model is employed in printers
4	Colours result from transmitted light	Colours result from reflected light
5	Red + Green + Blue = White	Cyan + Magenta + Yellow = Black

5. In HSV colour model, "H" represents "Hue", "S" stands for "Saturation" and "V" stands for "Value". Hue is a degree on the colour wheel from $0°$ to $360°$. Saturation is a percentage value. Zero percentage represents shades of gray and 100% represents a full colour. Value represents the lightness in percentage. 0% value indicates black and 100% indicates white.

6. Upon changing the colour plane "a*" as "−a*", the red colour is converted to a green colour and vice versa.

7. Upon changing the colour plane "b*" as "−b*", the blue colour is converted to yellow colour and vice versa.

8. The following steps are involved in computing the principal components: Step 1: Computing the covariance matrix, Step 2: Computing the eigenvalues and eigenvectors of the covariance matrix. The eigenvector of the covariance matrix is the principal component.

9. The number of principal components required depends on the nature of the input image. Different images can be compressed with different artefact levels using the same principal components. The number of principal components depends on the total variance in the image that is taken into account in the principal components.

10. Advantages of k-means algorithm are

(a) Simplicity: The algorithm starts with a set of randomly chosen initial centres; one repeatedly assigns each input point to its nearest centre and then recomputes the centres given the point assignment

(b) Scalability: Scaling k-means to massive data is simple because of its iterative nature

Drawbacks of k-means clustering algorithm are

(a) Choice of number of clusters: Choosing an optimal number of clusters (k) is challenging in k-means clustering.

(b) K-means clustering works well with numerical data, however it cannot handle categorical data. Categorical data does not have natural notion of distance or similarity.

Bibliography

1. Stephen J. Sangwine, Robin E.N. Horne, "The Colour Image Processing Handbook", Springer, 2012.
2. Rastislav Luckac and Kostantinos N. Plataniotis, "Color Image Processing: Methods and Applications", CRC Press, 2006.
3. Kostantinos N. Plataniotis, Anastasios N. Venetsanopoulos, "Color Image Processing and Applications", Springer, 2000.
4. Rangaraj M. Rangayyan, "Color Image Processing with Biomedical Applications", SPIE Press, 2011.
5. Alan C. Bovik, "Handbook of Image and Video Processing", Academic Press, 2000.

Chapter 11
Image Analysis Using Machine Learning and Deep Learning

Learning Objectives

After learning this chapter, the reader is expected to

- Know different types of learning, such as supervised, unsupervised, and reinforcement learning.
- Understand the principles and applications of machine learning algorithms like linear regression, logistic regression, support vector machine, decision tree, k-nearest neighbour classifier, and Naïve Bayes classifier.
- Understand the functionalities of different layers of convolutional and recurrent neural networks.
- Comparison of different machine learning and deep learning techniques using performance measures.

Roadmap of the Chapter

The concepts discussed in this chapter are illustrated as a roadmap, which is given in Fig. 11.1.

PreLab Questions

1. What is a feedforward neural network?
2. What is activation function? How is it helpful in neural networks?
3. What is loss function? What is the role in creating a neural network model?
4. What is backpropagation?
5. What is VGG16?
6. During training a model one realizes that data is insufficient. Mention three data augmentation techniques to overcome the shortage of data. Assume the data to be an image.

Supplementary Information The online version contains supplementary material available at https://doi.org/10.1007/978-981-96-6382-8_11.

S Esakkirajan et al., *Digital Image Processing*, https://doi.org/10.1007/978-981-96-6382-8_11

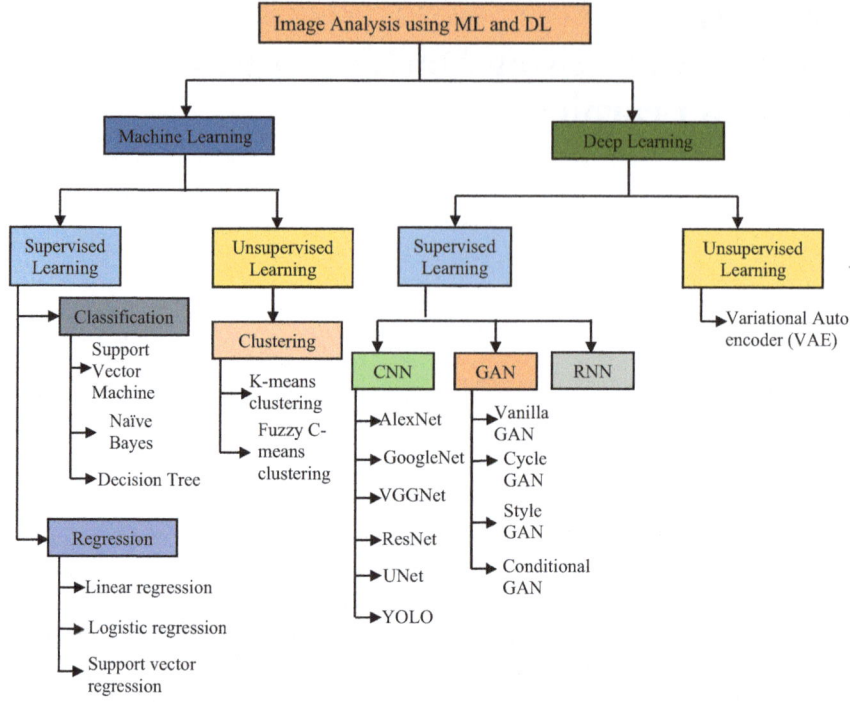

Fig. 11.1 Roadmap of the chapter

7. What is the bias-variance trade-off?
8. What is "dropout" with respect to neural network? Mention the advantage of using the "dropout" phenomenon in neural networks.
9. Mention the three prominent layers in the Convolutional Neural Network (CNN). Also mention the application of each layer.
10. What is the vanishing gradient problem in deep neural networks? What are the main causes of the vanishing gradient problem? Also, mention the impact of the vanishing gradient problem.
11. Explain the phenomenon of "batch normalization" in deep neural networks. Mention the advantages of employing batch normalization.
12. State the relationship between autoencoders and principal component analysis (PCA).
13. Explain the term "transfer learning" employed in the deep learning approach.
14. Mention the essential blocks of an autoencoder.
15. What are the types of auto encoders? Mention two applications of the autoencoder.

11.1   Introduction

Artificial intelligence (AI) is the study of computers or machines that attempt to model and apply the intelligence of the human mind. AI can perform the task on its own or combine it with other technologies like sensors, robotics, etc. AI can improve their problem-solving skills by encompassing machine learning and deep learning. The AI can be categorized into weak AI and strong AI. The weak AI is trained and focused to perform specific tasks. Hence, it is also known as artificial narrow intelligence or narrow AI. Some examples of the narrow AI used in real-time applications are Apple's Siri, Amazon's Alexa, IBM Watsonx, Gemini, ChatGPT, and self-driving vehicles. Strong AI is made up of artificial general intelligence and artificial super intelligence. It is a theoretical form of AI where a machine can behave as intelligent as human. This AI would be self-aware with a consciousness that would have the ability to solve problems, learn, and plan for the future.

11.2   Classical Programming

In classical programming, input and the predefined rules or algorithm are given to the computer or machine, and the computer or machine produces output based on the input and algorithm. The flow diagram of classical programming is shown in Fig. 11.2a. From this figure, it is possible to infer that the computer or machine receives the input data and the predefined rule algorithm and produces the output. Hence, in classical programming, the computer or machine is used for only computation; it does not learn from the input data, which will give the output based on the predefined rule.

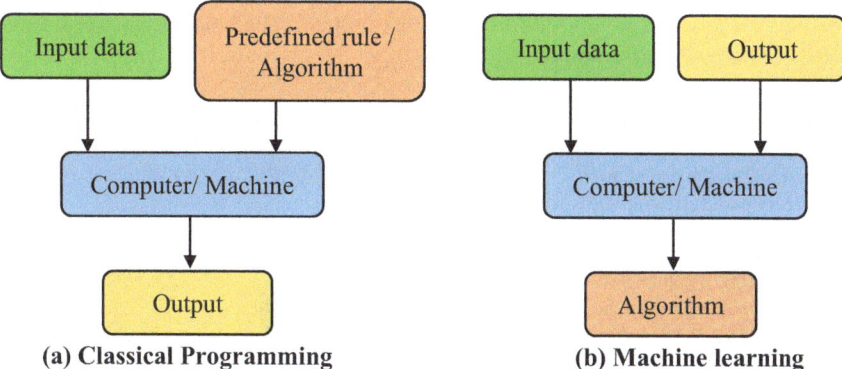

(a) Classical Programming   **(b) Machine learning**

Fig. 11.2 Flow diagram of classical programming and machine learning. (**a**) Classical programming. (**b**) Machine learning

Experiment 11.1: Classical Programming

This experiment performs the classical programming concept with input data and a predefined rule. Let us consider a basic image processing operation like image negative, and the predefined rule to compute image negative is "$255 - x$", where "x" is the input image. The Python code used to perform the classical programming concept is given in Fig. 11.3a, and its corresponding result is shown in Fig. 11.3b.

Inferences

The following inferences can be drawn from this experiment: (1) From Fig. 11.3a, it is possible to observe that the output equation (i.e. $255 - I1$) is a predefined rule, which is implemented, and the machine is used here to compute the output. (2) Figure 11.3b shows the input and output images.

11.3 Machine Learning

In machine learning, the machine learns from the input data and the output, generating the algorithm. The flow diagram of the machine learning is shown in Fig. 11.2b. From this figure, it is possible to observe that the input data and output are fed to the computer or machine. The machine trains itself with the input to produce the output as an algorithm or mathematical model. The types of machine learning are classified into (1) supervised learning, (2) unsupervised learning, (3) semi-supervised learning, and (4) reinforcement learning.

11.3.1 Supervised Learning

Supervised learning is one of the categories of the machine learning, which uses the labelled datasets to train algorithms to predict outputs. The labelled dataset means that it contains the information of both the input details as well as output labels or

```
import cv2
import matplotlib.pyplot as plt
I = cv2.imread('testcolourimg1.jpg')
I1 = cv2.cvtColor(I, cv2.COLOR_BGR2RGB)
O = 255 - I1
plt.subplot(1,2,1),plt.imshow(I1),
plt.title('Input Image'),plt.axis('off')
plt.subplot(1,2,2),plt.imshow(O),
plt.title('Image Negative'),plt.axis('off')
plt.tight_layout()
```

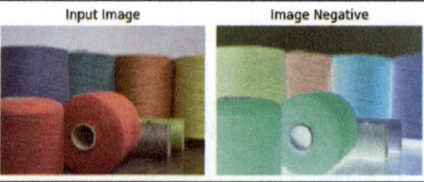

| **(a) Classical Programming** | **(b) Simulation result** |

Fig. 11.3 Classical programming. (**a**) Classical programming. (**b**) Simulation result

details. The machine uses these information in the training process to generate the mathematical model or algorithm. Some popular examples of supervised machine learning methods are: linear regression, random forest, and support vector machine (SVM).

Experiment 11.2: Supervised Machine Learning
This experiment tries to explain the concept of a supervised machine-learning approach using Python. This experiment discusses the linear regression machine learning approach, a type of supervised learning used to obtain the mathematical model from the inputs and responses. 1D input and output vectors are chosen to understand machine learning concepts. A detailed explanation of linear regression will be discussed in the next section. The Python code used to perform the machine learning process is given in Fig. 11.4, and its simulation result is shown in Fig. 11.5.

Inferences
The following inferences can be drawn from this experiment:

- Figure 11.4 shows that input and output vectors are given as an input and the linear regression model gives the output as coefficients [b_0, b_1]. The predicted output is computed using the linear equation which is mentioned as {y_pred = b_0 + b_1*x}.

```
# Machine learning approach Linear regression
import numpy as np
import matplotlib.pyplot as plt
x = np.array([0, 1, 2, 3, 4, 5, 6, 7, 8, 9]);# Independent value
y = np.array([10, 15, 30, 45, 60, 85, 75, 95, 110, 125]);# Dependent value
n = np.size(x);#number of observations/points
m_x = np.mean(x);# mean of x vector
m_y = np.mean(y);# mean of y vector
SS_xy = np.sum(y*x) - n*m_y*m_x; # Cross deviation
SS_xx = np.sum(x*x) - n*m_x*m_x;# deviation
b_1 = SS_xy / SS_xx; # regression coefficients
b_0 = m_y - b_1*m_x; # regression coefficients
b=[b_0,b_1]
plt.scatter(x, y, color = "m", marker = "o", s = 100)
y_pred = b_0 + b_1*x;# predicted response vector
plt.scatter(x, y_pred, color = "g", marker = "d", s = 100)
plt.legend(['Actual output','Predicted output'])
plt.xlabel('Input Value (Independent)'),plt.ylabel('Output/Predicted Value')
plt.title('Modeling Coefficients : {}'.format(b))
plt.tight_layout()
```

Fig. 11.4 Python code for supervised machine learning modelling

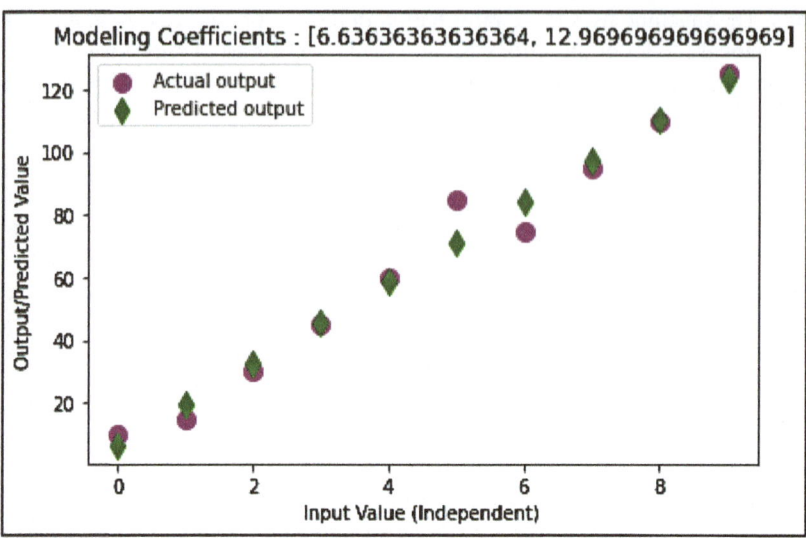

Fig. 11.5 Simulation result of supervised machine learning model

- Figure 11.5 shows the actual output and the predicted output value by using a linear regression model. The model coefficients also displayed in Fig. 11.5. From this figure, it is possible to observe that the machine learning approach generates the predicted output value. Here, the machine learns the output response based on the input and output vectors. If the machine produces the mathematical model based on the input data with the output label or output data, then that learning is called as supervised learning.

11.3.2   Unsupervised Machine Learning

The unsupervised machine learning algorithm is another machine learning algorithm that works for the unlabelled data. The unlabelled data means the input dataset does not contain the output labels or details. The unlabelled dataset is used for the training process in the machine learning process. Only input data without an output label is given as input to the machine learning algorithm to obtain the output.

Experiment 11.3: Unsupervised Machine Learning Algorithm
This experiment discusses the implementation of an unsupervised machine-learning approach using Python. For this implementation, the k-means clustering algorithm is used to cluster the input data without an output label. The Python code used to perform the unsupervised machine learning algorithm for clustering the input data in the data classification problem is given in Fig. 11.6, and its simulation result is shown in Fig. 11.7. IRIS data is used in this experiment, where the IRIS dataset contains the

```
# Unsupervised Learning-Kmeans clustering
from sklearn import datasets
import matplotlib.pyplot as plt
from sklearn.cluster import KMeans
iris_data = datasets.load_iris();# Loading IRIS dataset
print('Features name :',iris_data.feature_names); # # Features
# Dataset Slicing
x_axis = iris_data.data[:, 2]  # Petal Length
y_axis = iris_data.data[:, 3]  # Petal Width
plt.figure(figsize=(8,4)),plt.subplot(1,2,1)
plt.scatter(x_axis, y_axis,color = "r", marker = "o")
plt.title('Input Data'),plt.xlabel('Petal Length Feature'),plt.ylabel('Petal Width Feature')
model = KMeans(n_clusters=3, n_init=10);#Unsupervised Learning
model.fit(iris_data.data[:,(2,3)]);# Fitting Model
# Prediction on the entire data
Predicted_output = model.predict(iris_data.data[:,(2,3)])
plt.subplot(1,2,2),plt.scatter(x_axis, y_axis, c=Predicted_output)
plt.title('Clustered Data using Unsupervised Learning')
plt.xlabel('Petal Length Feature'),plt.ylabel('Petal Width Feature')
plt.tight_layout()
```

Fig. 11.6 Python code for unsupervised machine learning modelling

three different types of irises such as Setosa, Versicolor, and Virginica; the features are sepal length and sepal width, petal length and petal width. Out of four features, only two are considered "petal length" and "petal width" for easy display in 2D plots.

Inferences

The following inferences can be observed from this experiment:

- From Fig. 11.6, it is possible to infer that input to the *"KMeans"* model is only the input data vector, there is no output label in it. The number of clusters is chosen as 3 because the IRIS dataset contains three different types of irises.
- The simulation output of the Python code given in Fig. 11.6 is shown in Fig. 11.7. From this figure, it is possible to observe that the input data plotted before the machine learning algorithm all are in one colour (i.e. red). These input data are fed into the unsupervised machine learning model; the output contains three different colours, which shows the three clusters are formed by the K-means clustering algorithm based on the given input vector.

11.3.3 Semi-supervised Machine Learning

Semi-supervised machine learning is another type of machine learning algorithm in which the input data is partially labelled and partially unlabelled. These kinds of datasets are trained by using a semi-supervised machine learning approach.

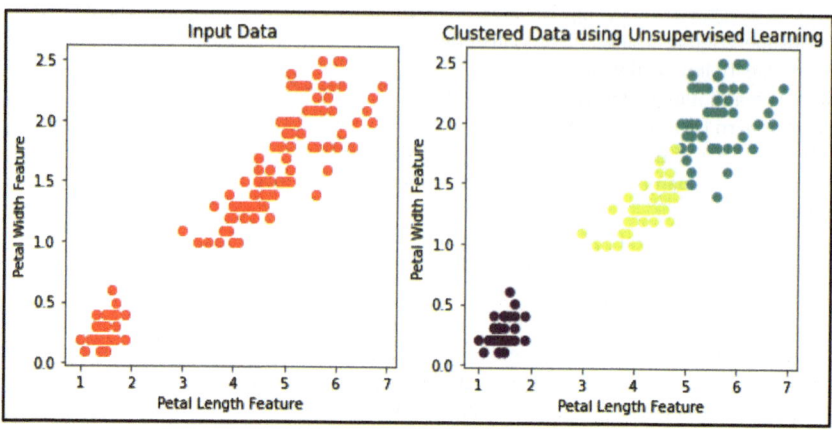

Fig. 11.7 Simulation result of unsupervised machine learning model

Experiment 11.4: Semi-supervised Machine Learning Algorithm

This experiment discusses the implementation of semi-supervised machine learning approach using Python. For this implementation, eXtreme Gradient Boosting (XGBoost) algorithm is used for the input data classification. The XGBoost is a machine learning algorithm under ensemble learning. It builds a predictive model by combining the predictions of multiple individual models iteratively. The Python code to perform the semi-supervised machine learning method for the data classification problem is given in Fig. 11.8, and its simulation result is shown in Fig. 11.9. IRIS data is used in this experiment, where the IRIS dataset contains the three different types of irises such as Setosa, Versicolor, and Virginica; the features are sepal length and width, petal length and width. IRIS dataset is a fully labelled one. However, the input data is split into labelled and unlabelled data to verify semi-supervised learning. The labelled data is trained by XGBoost algorithm as it is, whereas the unlabelled data is labelled by using the prediction value of XGBoost algorithm is greater than 0.9, then included these data into the labelled dataset and removed it from the unlabelled dataset, continue this process till the unlabelled dataset length is zero by using self-learning approach.

Inferences

The following inferences can be observed from this experiment:

- From Fig. 11.8, it is possible to observe that the input data is split into training (80%) and testing (20%) sets. The training set is further split into labelled (40%) and unlabelled (40%) datasets. Further, this dataset is converted from a "*numpy*" array to a "pandas" format.
- Also, it is possible to infer that input to the "*XGBoost*" model is used here to train the labelled data first, then, based on the predicted probability, the unlabelled data is labelled and appended with labelled dataset. After that, the final labelled dataset is trained using the XGBoost modelling algorithm.

```
# Semi-supervised Learning
from sklearn import datasets
from sklearn.model_selection import train_test_split
import pandas as pd
import numpy as np
from xgboost import XGBClassifier
import matplotlib.pyplot as plt
iris_data = datasets.load_iris();## Loading IRIS dataset
D_train, D_test, O_label_train_true, O_label_test_true =
train_test_split(iris_data.data[:,(2,3)],
                        iris_data.target,test_size=0.2, random_state=10)
D_label,O_label = D_train[:60],O_label_train_true[:60]
D_unlabelled = D_train[60:]
#sklearn.datasets Converting to pandas
D_label = pd.DataFrame(D_label)
O_label = pd.Series(O_label)
D_unlabelled = pd.DataFrame(D_unlabelled)
while True: # Self Learning Algorithm
    model = XGBClassifier(objective='multi:softmax',num_class=3,random_state=10)
    model.fit(D_label, O_label);# Train the model with labelled data
    D_unlabelled.reset_index(drop=True, inplace=True);# Get probability of unlabelled data
    if D_unlabelled.empty: # Check if D_unlabelled is empty before prediction
        break
    Predicted_output = model.predict_proba(D_unlabelled);
    index = [ index for index,x in enumerate(np.max(Predicted_output,axis=1)) if x > 0.90]
    if len(index)==0:
        break
    temp = D_unlabelled.iloc[index]
    D_unlabelled.drop(index,inplace=True)
    pred = pd.Series(model.predict(temp))
    D_label = pd.concat([D_label, temp], ignore_index=True)
    O_label = pd.concat([O_label, pred], ignore_index=True)
model = XGBClassifier(objective='multi:softmax',num_class=3,random_state=10)
model.fit(D_label, O_label);# Train the model
# Make predictions on the test set
y_pred = model.predict(D_test)
plt.figure(figsize=(8,4)),plt.subplot(1,2,1)
plt.scatter(D_test[:,0], D_test[:,1],color = "r", marker = "o")
plt.title('Input Test Data'),plt.xlabel('Petal Length Feature'),plt.ylabel('Petal Width Feature')
plt.subplot(1,2,2),plt.scatter(D_test[:,0], D_test[:,1], c=y_pred)
plt.title('Classification:Semisupervised Learning')
plt.xlabel('Petal Length Feature'),plt.ylabel('Petal Width Feature')
plt.tight_layout()
```

Fig. 11.8 Python code for unsupervised machine learning modelling

- Figure 11.9 shows the testing classification (20%) data. From this figure, it is possible to observe that the input data plotted before the machine learning process all are in one colour (i.e. red). These input data are classified into three categories using the semi-supervised XGBoost algorithm.

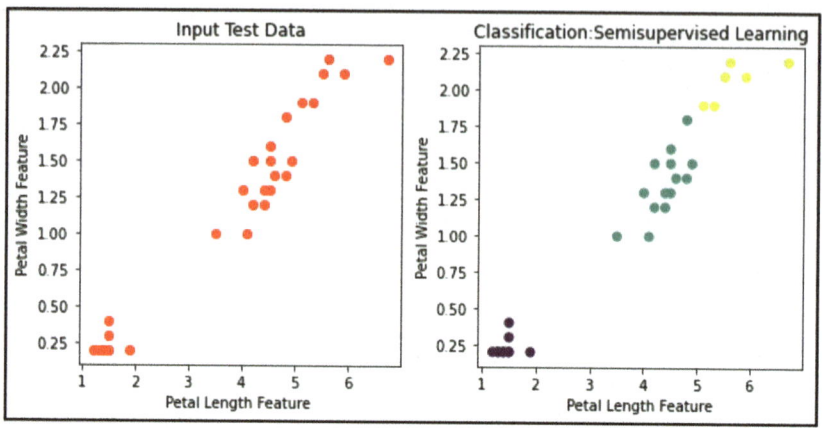

Fig. 11.9 Simulation result of semi-supervised machine learning model

11.3.4   Reinforcement Learning

Reinforcement learning is a feedback-based machine learning technique. The agent learns to behave in an environment by performing the actions and looking at the outcomes of actions. For each good action, the agent gets positive feedback or reward, and for each bad action, the agent gets negative feedback or penalty. In reinforcement learning, the agent learns automatically using feedback without labelled data. Since the unlabelled data, the agent is bound to learn only by experience. Reinforcement learning solves a specific type of problem where decision-making is sequential, and the goal is long-term, such as automatic car driving, robotics, and game playing like a chess game, mazes, etc. In this learning, the agent interacts with and explores the environment by itself. The primary goal of an agent in reinforcement learning is to improve performance by getting the maximum positive rewards. The agent learns with the process of hit and trial, and based on the experience, it learns to perform the task in a better way. The reinforcement learning procedure is shown in Fig. 11.10.

Agent is an entity that can perceive or explore the environment and act upon it. Environment is a situation in which an agent is present or surrounded by. It may be assumed that stochastic or random environment. Action is the move taken by an agent within the environment. State is a situation returned by the environment after each action taken by the agent. Reward is feedback returned to the agent from the environment to evaluate the action of the agent. Policy is a strategy the agent applies for the following action based on the current state. Value is expected long-term return with the discount factor and opposite to the short-term reward. Q-value is similar to the Value, but it takes one additional parameter as a current action.

The implementation of reinforcement learning in machine learning is value-based, policy-based, and model-based. In the value-based approach, the final task is to find the optimal value function, which is the maximum value at a state under any

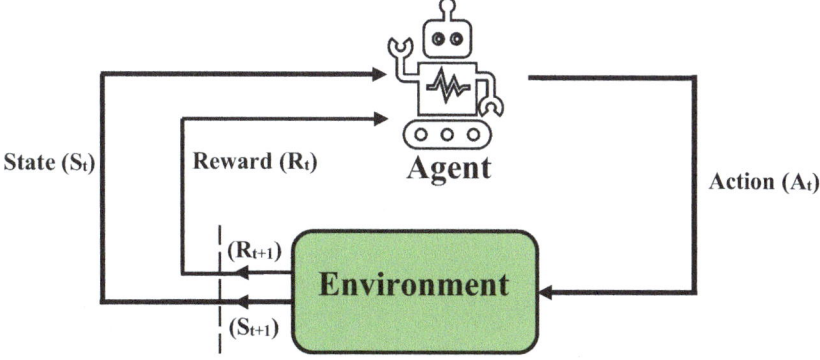

Fig. 11.10 Reinforcement machine learning

policy. Hence, the agent expects the long-term return at any state(s) under the policy. In the policy-based approach, the final task is to obtain the optimal policy for the maximum future rewards without using the value function. In this method, the agent tries to apply such a policy that the action performed in each step helps to maximize the future reward. There are two types of policy-based approaches; the first one is deterministic, in which the policy produces the same action in any state. The second one is stochastic; here, the probability determines the produced action. In the model-based approach, a virtual model is created for the environment, and the agent explores that environment to learn it. Therefore, this approach has no particular solution or algorithm since the model representation is different for each environment.

11.4 Machine Learning Algorithms

Machine learning algorithms can detect patterns and learn from them. This section discusses the different machine learning algorithms like Linear regression, Logistic regression, Decision tree, Support Vector Machine (SVM), Naïve Bayes, k-nearest neighbour (KNN), K-means, Random forest, Dimensionality reduction and AdaBoosting algorithm, etc.

11.4.1 Linear Regression

Linear regression is a machine learning technique and statistical approach used for predictive analysis. Linear regression gives a linear relationship between an output/dependent variable and one or more independent variables. Hence, it is called linear regression. The linear regression model provides a sloped straight line representing

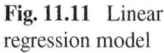

Fig. 11.11 Linear regression model

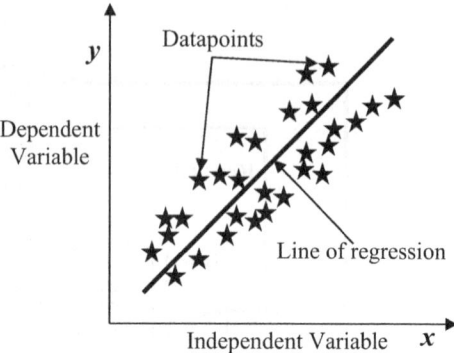

the relationship between the dependent and independent variables, which is shown in Fig. 11.11. The mathematical representation of linear regression is given by

$$y = \alpha_0 + \alpha_1 x + \varepsilon \tag{11.1}$$

where y represents the dependent variable or output or target, x is an independent variable or predictor variable, α_0 is a weight or coefficient that gives an additional degree of freedom, α_1 is a linear regression coefficient, and ε is a random error. The values of x and y act as training datasets.

The linear regression is classified into simple linear regression and multiple linear regression. In a simple linear regression, a single independent variable is used to predict the value of a numerical target variable. In multiple linear regression, more than one independent variable is used to predict the value of a numerical target. The linear line, which shows the relationship between the dependent and independent variables, is called a regression line. The slope of the regression line is positive, then it is called a positive linear relationship, whereas the slope of the regression line is negative, which is called a negative linear relationship.

The linear regression algorithm aims to find the best-fitted line of regression for the given data points. The different values of the weights or coefficients (α_0 and α_1) give a different line of regression. Hence, linear regression is used to calculate the best values for α_0 and α_1 so that it can give the best-fit line of regression for the dataset. The cost function is used to find the best values for α_0 and α_1. The cost function optimizes the linear regression coefficients or weights. Therefore, the cost function can be used to find the accuracy of the mapping function, which maps the input variable to the output variable. This mapping function is called the Hypothesis function. The cost function for the linear regression approach is the mean squared error (MSE), which is the average squared error between the predicted output and actual output. The mathematical expression for the MSE cost function is given by

$$\text{MSE} = \frac{1}{N} \sum_{i=1}^{N} \left(y_i - \left(\alpha_0 + \alpha_1 x_i \right) \right)^2 \tag{11.2}$$

where y_i is the actual value, $\alpha_0 + \alpha_1 x_i$ is the predicted value, and N denotes the number of observations.

The distance between the actual value and the predicted value is called *residual*. If the observed points or data points are far from the line of regression, then the residual will be high, and the cost function will be high. If the data points are close to the line of regression, then the residual will be small, and the cost function will also be less. Therefore, the line of regression has to be as close to the observed points, and then the line of regression will be the best-fit line of regression.

The line of regression depends on the values of coefficients or weights. The values of the weights are computed by applying a gradient descent approach to the cost function (MSE). The regression model uses gradient descent to update the weights of the line of regression by reducing the cost function. It may be done by randomly selecting the weights' values and then updating them to reach the minimum cost function iteratively.

Experiment 11.5: Simple Linear Regression
This experiment deals with the Python implementation of simple linear regression. The simple linear regression contains a single independent and dependent variable. The Python code to implement the simple linear regression algorithm for the "*salary data*" is given in Fig. 11.12. After executing the Python code given in Fig. 11.12, the simulation result is shown in Fig. 11.13.

```
# Simple Linear regression
import numpy as np
import matplotlib.pyplot as plt
import pandas as pd
from sklearn.model_selection import train_test_split
from sklearn.linear_model import LinearRegression
data_set= pd.read_csv('House_Rent_Dataset.csv')
id_x1= data_set.iloc[0:1500, 3].values;# Independent Variable
id_x=np.reshape(id_x1,[-1,1])
d_y= data_set.iloc[0:1500,2].values; # Dependent Variable
# Splitting the dataset into training and test set.
id_x_train, id_x_test, d_y_train, d_y_test= train_test_split(id_x, d_y,
                        test_size= 0.2, random_state=0)
#Fitting the Simple Linear Regression model to the training dataset
simple_regression= LinearRegression()
simple_regression.fit(id_x_train, d_y_train)
#Prediction of Test and Training set result
y_pred= simple_regression.predict(id_x_test)
x_pred= simple_regression.predict(id_x_train)
plt.scatter(id_x_train, d_y_train, color="black", marker='*',s=100)
plt.plot(id_x_train, x_pred, color="magenta")
plt.title("Rent vs Area (Training Dataset)") ,plt.xlabel("Area in Square feet")
plt.ylabel("Rent (In Rupees)")
plt.show()
```

Fig. 11.12 Python code for simple linear regression model

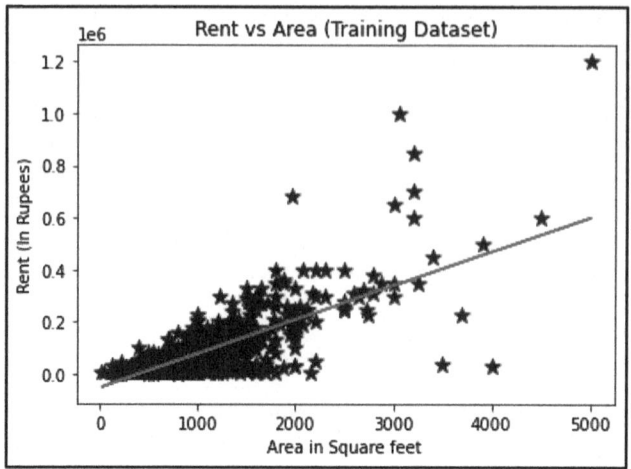

Fig. 11.13 Simulation output of simple linear regression model

Inferences

The following inferences can be drawn from Fig. 11.12:

- The dataset is in the form of a ".*csv*" file; hence, the "read_csv" command is used from the "*panda*" library to read a CSV file. In the machine learning algorithm, the dataset must be split into training and testing data. Here, the trained data should not be used for the testing process, and testing data should not be used in the training process. For this, the dataset is split into training and testing data by using the command "*train_test_split*" from the "*sklearn*" library.
- The linear regression algorithm is available in the "*sklearn*" library in the name of "*LinearRegression*", which is imported. The "simple_regression.fit" command is used to obtain the best-fit line of regression from the training dataset.
- The command "simple_regression.predict" is used to find the predicted value for the test data. For plotting the line of regression, the training data is fed into the linear regression model, and the predicted output is utilized.
- The "plt.scatter" command is used here to display the data points in the plot.
- The "plt.plot" command is used to plot the line of regression.
- From Fig. 11.13, it is possible to observe that the input data points are represented by "★", and the fitted line of regression is in the form of linear. The slope of the line of regression is positive; hence, the independent and dependent variables have a positive linear relationship.

Task: Apply the dataset, which has the nature of a negative linear relationship between independent and dependent variables, and obtain the line of regression.

Experiment 11.6: Multiple Linear Regression

This experiment discusses multiple linear regression using Python. Multiple linear regression is one of the important regression algorithms that model the linear relationship between a single dependent variable and more than one independent variable. In multiple linear regression, the target variable (y) is a linear combination of multiple predictor variables $\{x_1, x_2, \cdots, x_n\}$. It is an extension of simple linear regression, which is written as

$$y = \alpha_0 + \alpha_1 x_1 + \alpha_2 x_2 + \cdots + \alpha_n x_n \qquad (11.3)$$

where $\{\alpha_0, \alpha_1, \cdots, \alpha_n\}$ weights or coefficients of the multiple linear regression model. In this experiment, the input data is considered "50_Startups.csv", which contains the 50 startup companies' details {R&D Spend, Administration, Marketing Spend, State and Profit}. The first four details are considered independent variables, and the "Profit" is assumed to be a dependent or target variable. This experiment aims to create a model that can predict which company has the maximum profit and the most affecting factor for the profit of a company. The input dataset contains more than one independent variable. Hence, the linear regression model used for this experiment is a multiple linear regression model. The Python code to implement the multiple linear regression (MLR) model for the input dataset is given in Fig. 11.14. After executing the Python code given in Fig. 11.14, the simulation result is shown in Fig. 11.15. The initial input dataset contains the categorical features or details ("California", "Florida", "New York"), which is shown in Fig. 11.15a. The machine learning algorithm can handle the data in form of numbers. Therefore, the name of the "states" in the dataset is replaced by the number (0, 1, 2),

```
# Multiple Linear Regression approach
import numpy as np
import pandas as pd
from sklearn.preprocessing import LabelEncoder, OneHotEncoder
from sklearn.compose import ColumnTransformer
from sklearn.model_selection import train_test_split
from sklearn.linear_model import LinearRegression
data_set= pd.read_csv('50_Startups.csv')
Id_x= data_set.iloc[:, :-1].values;# Independent variables
D_y= data_set.iloc[:, 4].values; # Dependent variable
print('Independent Variables (Actual):',Id_x)
labelencoder_Idx= LabelEncoder()
Id_x[:, 3]= labelencoder_Idx.fit_transform(Id_x[:,3])
print('Independent Variables :',Id_x)
ct = ColumnTransformer([('encoder', OneHotEncoder(), [3])], remainder='passthrough')
Id_x = np.array(ct.fit_transform(Id_x))
print('Independent Variables (final):',Id_x)
Id_x = Id_x[:, 1:]
# Splitting the dataset into training and test set.
x_train, x_test, y_train, y_test= train_test_split(Id_x, D_y, test_size= 0.2, random_state=0)
MLR= LinearRegression()
MLR.fit(x_train, y_train);#Fitting the MLR model to the training set:
y_pred= MLR.predict(x_test); #Predicting the Test set result;
print('Train Score: ', MLR.score(x_train, y_train)),print('Test Score: ', MLR.score(x_test, y_test))
print('Y_Predict:',y_pred), print('Y_Actual : ', y_test)
```

Fig. 11.14 Python code for multiple linear regression

Independent Variables (Actual):
[[165349.2 136897.8 471784.1 'New York']
[162597.7 151377.59 443898.53 'California']
[153441.51 101145.55 407934.54 'Florida']
[144372.41 118671.85 383199.62 'New York']
[142107.34 91391.77 366168.42 'Florida']
[131876.9 99814.71 362861.36 'New York']
[134615.46 147198.87 127716.82 'California']
[130298.13 145530.06 323876.68 'Florida']
[120542.52 148718.95 311613.29 'New York']
...

(a) Actual Input Dataset

Independent Variables:
[[165349.2 136897.8 471784.1 2]
[162597.7 151377.59 443898.53 0]
[153441.51 101145.55 407934.54 1]
[144372.41 118671.85 383199.62 2]
[142107.34 91391.77 366168.42 1]
[131876.9 99814.71 362861.36 2]
[134615.46 147198.87 127716.82 0]
[130298.13 145530.06 323876.68 1]
[120542.52 148718.95 311613.29 2]
...

(b) After relacing by numbers

Independent Variables (final):
[[0.0 0.0 1.0 165349.2 136897.8 471784.1]
[1.0 0.0 0.0 162597.7 151377.59 443898.53]
[0.0 1.0 0.0 153441.51 101145.55 407934.54]
[0.0 0.0 1.0 144372.41 118671.85 383199.62]
[0.0 1.0 0.0 142107.34 91391.77 366168.42]
[0.0 0.0 1.0 131876.9 99814.71 362861.36]
[1.0 0.0 0.0 134615.46 147198.87 127716.82]
[0.0 1.0 0.0 130298.13 145530.06 323876.68]
[0.0 0.0 1.0 120542.52 148718.95 311613.29]
...

(c) One-hot encoder output

Train Score: 0.9501847627493607
Test Score: 0.9347068473282858
Y_Predict: [103015.20159796 132582.27760816
132447.73845175 71976.09851259
178537.48221054 116161.24230163
67851.69209676 98791.73374688
113969.43533012 167921.0656955]
Y_Actual : [103282.38 144259.4 146121.95
77798.83 191050.39 105008.31 81229.06
97483.56 110352.25 166187.94]

(d) Prediction Score

Fig. 11.15 Simulation output. (**a**) Actual input dataset. (**b**) After replacing by numbers. (**c**) One-hot encoder output. (**d**) Prediction score

respectively. This can be done by using "Label Encoding" technique that is used to convert categorical columns into numerical values so that machine learning models can fit the dataset. The dataset after the process of label encoding is depicted in Fig. 11.15b. The "*ColumnTransformer*" is handy for the case of datasets that contain heterogeneous data types. One hot encoding is the standard technique used to convert categorical variables into numerical variables. Here, each category is represented as a binary vector; that is, only one element is "1", and all other elements are "0". In this experiment, one hot encoding converts categorical variables into a binary matrix, where each category is represented by a separate binary feature, where the corresponding category is marked as "1", and all other categories are marked with "0". For example, if the categorical variable is "California", then the numerical variable will be (1, 0, 0). The output after the one-hot encoding of the input dataset is depicted in Fig. 11.15c.

After converting the categorical dataset into the numerical dataset, the dataset is split into training and testing data using the "train_test_split" command, and the training data is fed into linear regression modelling. The prediction score for the testing and training data, the predicted output for the test data and the actual output of the test data are shown in Fig. 11.15d.

Inferences

- This experiment deals with the input data having more than one independent variable and heterogeneous data types (Numerical and Categorical variables).
- A one-hot encoding approach converts the categorical variable into numerical value.
- The same simple linear regression model is used for multiple linear regression.
- The error between the predicted and actual value is less, which concludes that this model can be used to predict the profit of startups.

11.4.2   Polynomial Regression

Polynomial regression is a regression algorithm that models the relationship between the dependent and independent variables as being nth-degree polynomial. The mathematical expression for the polynomial regression is given by

$$y = \alpha_0 + \alpha_1 x + \alpha_2 x^2 + \alpha_3 x^3 + \cdots + \alpha_n x^n \tag{11.4}$$

From the Eq. (11.4), it is possible to infer that the independent variable is only one (i.e. x). The polynomial regression is a special case of multiple linear regression. It is a linear model with some modifications to increase the accuracy of the regression model. It makes use of a linear regression model to fit the complicated and non-linear functions and datasets. Therefore, in polynomial regression, the original input features or data are converted into polynomial features or data of the required degree and then modelled using a linear model. Thus, polynomial regression can be used for the data in a non-linear fashion.

Experiment 11.7: Polynomial Regression

This experiment deals with the polynomial regression-based machine learning technique using Python. In this experiment, the input data is considered "Position_Salaries. csv", which contains the information on "Position", "Levels" and "Salary". However, only two parameters ("Levels" and "Salaries") are considered for the polynomial regression modelling. The Python code used to perform the polynomial regression modelling is given in Fig. 11.16, and its simulation result is shown in Fig. 11.17.

Inferences

The following inferences can be drawn from this experiment:

- From Fig. 11.16, it is possible to observe that the "PolynomialFeatures" command is used to preprocess the data, and the preprocessed data is utilized for the linear regression to get a polynomial regression modelling.
- From Fig. 11.17, it is possible to observe that the polynomial fitted line is exactly fitted with input data when the degree of a polynomial function is chosen as 5 and 6. Therefore, the degree of the polynomial function plays a major role in proper prediction.

```
# Polynomial Regression
import matplotlib.pyplot as plt
import pandas as pd
from sklearn.preprocessing import PolynomialFeatures
from sklearn.linear_model import LinearRegression
data_set= pd.read_csv('Position_Salaries.csv')
Id_x=data_set.iloc[:, 1:2].values; # Independent Variable
D_y=data_set.iloc[:, 2].values;# Dependent Variable
plt.figure(figsize=(12,10))
for i in range(6):
    poly= PolynomialFeatures(degree= i+1)
    x_poly= poly.fit_transform(Id_x)
    Poly_Reg =LinearRegression()
    Poly_Reg.fit(x_poly, D_y)
    plt.subplot(2,3,(i+1)),plt.scatter(Id_x,D_y,color="black",marker='*', s=100)
    plt.plot(Id_x, Poly_Reg.predict(poly.fit_transform(Id_x)), color="blue")
    plt.title("Polynomial Regression with degree = {}".format(i+1))
    plt.xlabel("Position Levels"),plt.ylabel("Salary")
    plt.tight_layout()
```

Fig. 11.16   Python code for polynomial regression

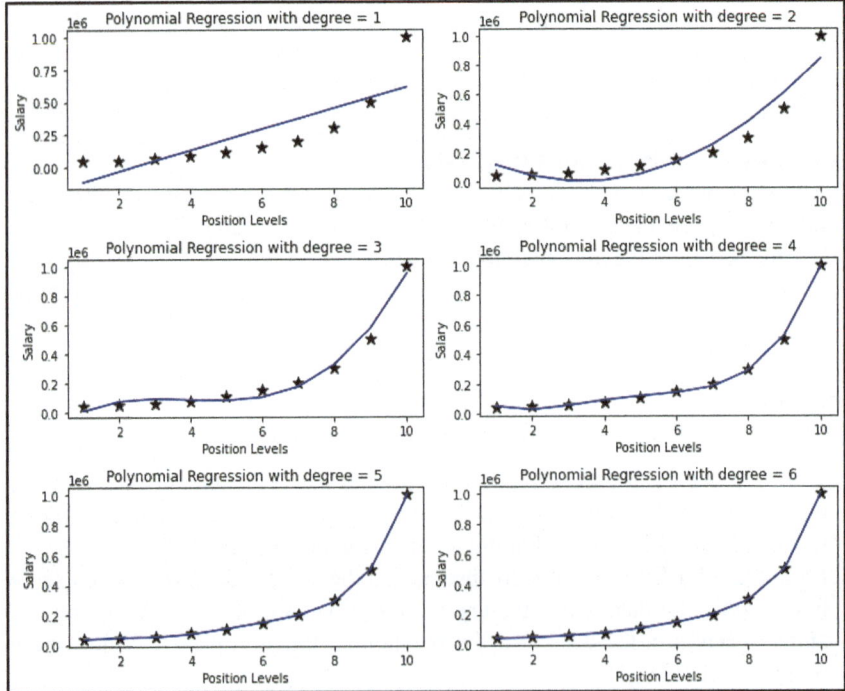

Fig. 11.17   Simulation result of polynomial regression

11.4.3 Logistic Regression

Logistic regression is a supervised machine learning algorithm that uses logistic functions to predict the probability of a binary outcome. The logistic regression model delivers a binary output like yes or no, 1 or 0, true or false. The logistic regression analyses the relationship between one or more independent variables and classifies data into discrete classes. Therefore, it is mostly used in predictive modelling, where the model estimates the mathematical probability of whether an instance belongs to a specific category or not. The logistic function uses the "S" shaped fitted line to predict two maximum values, either 0 or 1. The curve from the logistic function indicates the likelihood of something such as whether the cells are cancerous or not, ripped fruits or not, etc.

Logistic regression uses the sigmoid mathematical function to map the predicted values to probabilities. It maps any real value into another value between 0 and 1. The values of the logistic regression must be between 0 and 1, which cannot cross the limit. Hence, it forms a curve like the "S" form. The S-form curve is called the Sigmoid or logistic function, as shown in Fig. 11.18. From this figure, it is possible to observe that the threshold value is fixed as 0.5. If the function $f(x)$ is greater than 0.5, then the output will be one or else the output will be zero.

The logistic regression equation can be derived from the linear regression equation. The straight-line linear equation is given by

$$y = \alpha_0 + \alpha_1 x_1 + \alpha_2 x_2 + \cdots + \alpha_n x_n \tag{11.5}$$

The output of the logistic regression takes a value between 0 and 1, hence the above equation can be written as

$$f(y) = \begin{cases} \dfrac{y}{1-y}; & y \neq 1 \\ \infty, & y = 1 \end{cases} \tag{11.6}$$

The logarithmic function is used to convert the range of values of logistic regression from 0 to 1 into $-\infty$ to $+\infty$. The following equation can be used:

$$\log(f(y)) = \alpha_0 + \alpha_1 x_1 + \alpha_2 x_2 + \cdots + \alpha_n x_n \tag{11.7}$$

Fig. 11.18 Sigmoid or logistic function

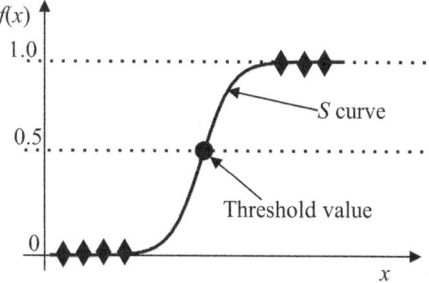

The Eq. (11.7) is the final logistic regression modelling equation.

The logistic regression modelling is classified into three types: (1) Binomial logistic regression, (2) Multinomial logistic regression, and (3) Ordinal logistic regression. The binomial logistic regression contains only two types of dependent or output variables (i.e. true or false, 1 or 0, pass or fail, etc.). In the multinomial logistic regression, the output dependent variables will be more than two, which are unordered types (i.e. types of categories of domestic animals like cats, dogs, cows, etc). For the ordinal logistic regression, the output dependent variables are more than two similar to the multinomial logistic regression. But these dependent variables are ordered one (i.e. low, medium, or high).

Experiment 11.8: Binomial Logistic Regression
This experiment tries to explain the implementation of binomial logistic regression using Python. The "Machine" dataset is used for this experiment, which contains the details of whether the machine is a failure or not is output or dependent variable, and the independent variables are football—the number of people or objects passing by the machine, tempMode-temperature mode or setting of the machine, AQ-air quality index near the machine, USS-Ultrasonic sensor data (proximity measurements), CS-electrical current usage of the machine, VOC-Volatile organic compounds level, RP-RPM (revolutions per minute), IP-input pressure to the machine, temperature-Operating temperature of the machine. Out of nine dependent variables, only two independent variables were chosen for this experiment to visualize the dataset better. The Python code used to perform the binomial logistic regression is given in Fig. 11.19 and its simulation result is shown in Fig. 11.20.

Inferences
The following inferences can be made from this experiment:

- From Fig. 11.19, it is possible to observe that the "StandardScaler()" command is imported from the "sklearn" library. This command preprocesses the input dataset, standardising the input features by removing the mean and scaling to unit variance. The standard score of a sample x is calculated as $= \dfrac{x - \mu}{\sigma}$, where μ and σ are mean and standard deviation, respectively.
- "LogisticRegression" is a Python command that models logistic regression, and it is imported from the "sklearn" library.
- The confusion matrix is a performance metric for classification problems. The confusion matrix is shown in Fig. 11.20a. The diagonal ($-45°$) value represents the correct prediction, and the diagonal ($+45°$) value gives the wrong prediction result.
- The visualization of the training dataset is shown in Fig. 11.20b, which indicates the two input independent variables in *the x* and *y* axes. The output of the failure and not failure is marked as "1" and "0". Here, "1" denotes the machine is a failure, and '0' represents the machine is not a failure.

```
# Binomial logistic regression
import numpy as np
import matplotlib.pyplot as plt
import pandas as pd
from sklearn.model_selection import train_test_split
from sklearn.linear_model import LogisticRegression
from sklearn.preprocessing import StandardScaler
from sklearn import metrics
from matplotlib.colors import ListedColormap
data_set= pd.read_csv('Machine_data.csv')
id_x= data_set.iloc[:, [2,3]].values;# Independent Variable
d_y= data_set.iloc[:, 9].values; # Dependent Variable
x_train, x_test, y_train, y_test= train_test_split(id_x, d_y, test_size= 0.25, random_state=0)
st_x= StandardScaler()
x_train= st_x.fit_transform(x_train)
x_test= st_x.transform(x_test)
classifier= LogisticRegression(random_state=0)
classifier.fit(x_train, y_train)
y_pred= classifier.predict(x_test)
cm = metrics.confusion_matrix(y_test, y_pred)
cm_display = metrics.ConfusionMatrixDisplay(confusion_matrix = cm, display_labels = [0, 1])
cm_display.plot(),plt.show()
x_set, y_set = x_train, y_train
x1, x2 = np.meshgrid(np.arange(start = x_set[:, 0].min() - 1, stop = x_set[:, 0].max() + 1, step
=0.01),
np.arange(start = x_set[:, 1].min() - 1, stop = x_set[:, 1].max() + 1, step = 0.01))
plt.contourf(x1, x2, classifier.predict(np.array([x1.ravel(), x2.ravel()]).T).reshape(x1.shape),
alpha = 0.75,
cmap = ListedColormap(('magenta','green' )))
plt.xlim(x1.min(), x1.max()),plt.ylim(x2.min(), x2.max())
for i, j in enumerate(np.unique(y_set)):
    plt.scatter(x_set[y_set == j, 0], x_set[y_set == j, 1],
        c = ListedColormap(('black', 'red'))(i), label = j)
plt.title('Logistic Regression (Training set)'),plt.xlabel('Air Quality Index')
plt.ylabel('Proximity Measurement'),plt.legend(),plt.show()
```

Fig. 11.19 Python code for binomial logistic regression

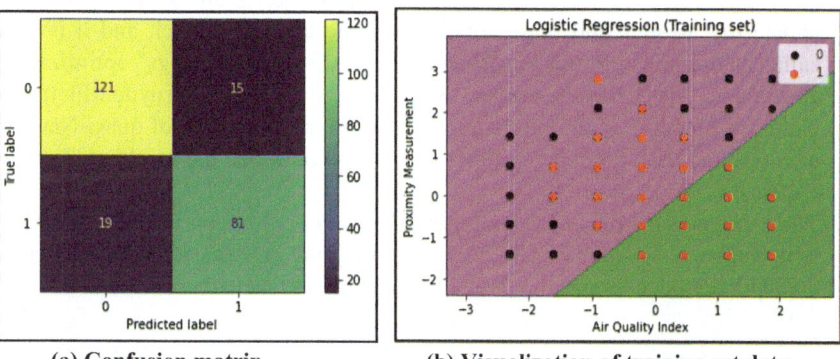

(a) Confusion matrix   (b) Visualization of training set data

Fig. 11.20 Simulation result. (**a**) Confusion matrix. (**b**) Visualization of training set data

```
# Multinomial Logistic Regression
from sklearn import datasets
from sklearn.linear_model import LogisticRegression
from sklearn.model_selection import train_test_split
from sklearn import metrics
import matplotlib.pyplot as plt
data_set = datasets.load_iris();# Loading IRIS dataset
X=data_set.data;
y=data_set.target;
x_train, x_test, y_train, y_test= train_test_split(X, y, test_size= 0.25, random_state=0)
# Define the multinomial logistic regression model
MLR = LogisticRegression(multi_class='multinomial', solver='lbfgs',max_iter=1000)
MLR.fit(x_train, y_train)
y_pred= MLR.predict(x_test)
cm = metrics.confusion_matrix(y_test, y_pred)
cm_display = metrics.ConfusionMatrixDisplay(confusion_matrix = cm, display_labels = [0, 1, 2])
cm_display.plot(),plt.title('Confusion Matrix'),plt.xlabel('Predicted Output')
plt.ylabel('True Output'),plt.show()
```

Fig. 11.21 Python code for multinomial logistic regression

Experiment 11.9: Multinomial Logistic Regression

This experiment deals with multinomial logistic regression for data classification using Python. The "IRIS" dataset is used as an input to this model. The three output variables: "setosa", "versicolor", and "virginica", are represented as output variables 0, 1, and 2, respectively. The four input variables are "sepal length (cm)", "sepal width (cm)", "petal length (cm)", "petal width (cm)". There are three output variables; hence, multinomial logistic regression can be used for data classification. The Python code used to perform the multinomial logistic regression modelling is given in Fig. 11.21, and its confusion matrix is shown in Fig. 11.22.

Inferences

The following inferences can be drawn from this experiment:

- From Fig. 11.21, it is possible to observe that "LogisticRegression" command is imported from the "sklearn" library. The multi_class is chosen as "multinomial" and solver is selected as "lbfgs". The solver is an algorithm used to update the weights and biases of the machine learning model, and it is also called an optimizer. In this experiment, the solver uses the "lbfgs" optimization algorithm. The LBFGS means that "Limited memory Broyden-Fletcher-Goldfarb-Shanno" is an optimization algorithm in the family of quasi-Newton methods and uses limited computer memory to optimize the machine learning parameters.

- The confusion matrix of the multinomial logistic regression modelling for the IRIS dataset is shown in Fig. 11.22. From this figure, it is possible to observe that the input dataset contains the three types of flowers labelled as 0, 1, and 2.

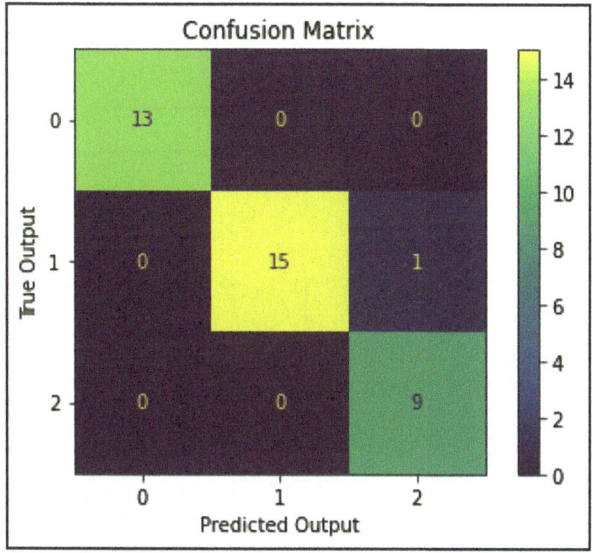

Fig. 11.22 Confusion matrix

11.4.4   Decision Tree

A decision tree is a supervised machine-learning approach that can be used for both classification and regression problems. However, it is widely preferred for solving classification problems. This approach is a tree-structured classifier, containing internal nodes, branches, and leaf nodes. The internal nodes represent the features or input of a dataset. Branches denote the decision rules and the leaf node gives the final outcome of the classifier. There are two nodes in the decision tree approach. They are called the decision node and leaf node. The decision node is used to make any decision with multiple branches, whereas leaf nodes are the output of those decisions and do not contain any further branches. The structure of the decision tree looks like tree, which starts from the root node and it expands on further branches and constructs a tree-like structure; hence it is called as a decision tree. The structure of the decision tree is shown in Fig. 11.23. From this figure, it is possible to observe that the decision tree contains decision nodes, branches, and leaf nodes.

The decision tree contains the following terminologies. They are

1. Root Node: The starting of the decision node of the decision tree is called as Root Node. It represents the entire dataset, which is further divided into two or more homogeneous sets.
2. Leaf Node: This is the end of the decision tree and it cannot be further divided.
3. Splitting: Splitting is the process of dividing the decision node or root node into sub-nodes according to the decision rule.
4. Branch/Sub tree: A tree formed by splitting the tree.

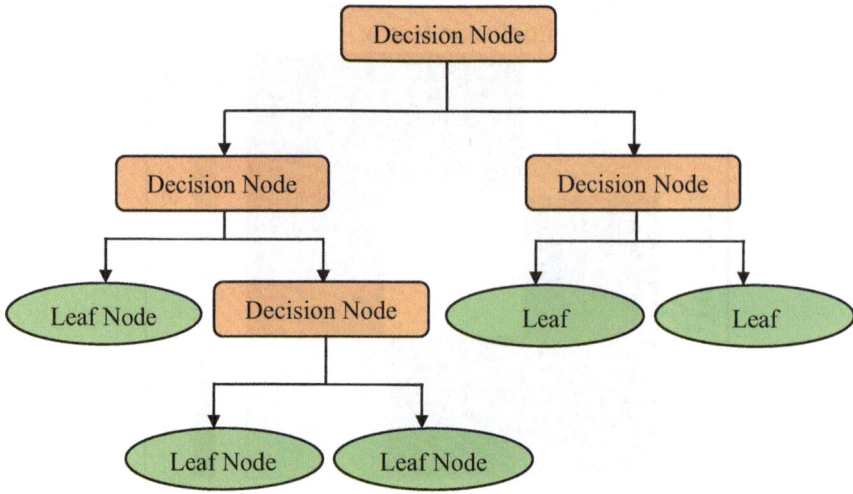

Fig. 11.23 General structure of decision tree

5. Pruning: It is the process of removing unwanted branches from the tree.
6. Parent/Child node: The root node of the tree is called the parent node, and other nodes are called the child nodes.

Decision tree algorithm is used for predicting the class of the given input data-set. The algorithm starts with the root node of the tree, and the algorithm compares the values of the root attribute with the real dataset attribute. Based on the comparison results, the branch jumps to the next node. For the next node, the decision tree algorithm again compares the attribute value with the other sub-nodes, and it repeats this further. Therefore, the decision tree algorithm is a continuous process; it continues until it reaches the leaf node of the tree.

Decision Tree Algorithm
The steps involved in the decision tree algorithm are as follows:

Step 1: Start the tree with the root node (R), which contains the complete dataset.
Step 2: Obtain the best attribute in the dataset using Attribute Selection Measure (ASM).
Step 3: Split the Set (R) into subsets that contain possible values for the best attributes.
Step 4: Generate the decision tree node, which contains the best attribute.
Step 5: Repeatedly make new decision trees using the subsets of the dataset created in Step 3. Repeat this process until a stage is reached where it cannot further classify the nodes and call the final node a leaf node.

Attribute Selection Measure (ASM) is an important factor in the Decision tree algorithm. Information gain and Gini Index are the two popular measures for ASM.

Information Gain

The information gain is the measurement of entropy changes after the dataset segmentation based on an attribute, which calculates information a feature provides for the classes. The information gain is calculated by

$$\text{Information gain} = \text{Entropy}\left(\text{Parent}\right) - \left[W_{\text{avg}} * \text{Entropy}\left(\text{Children}\right)\right] \quad (11.8)$$

where "Entropy" is a metric to measure the impurity in a given attribute. It specifies randomness in the dataset. In a decision tree, the goal is to decrease the entropy of the dataset by creating more pure subsets of data. Since entropy is a measure of impurity, decreasing the entropy increases the purity of the data. W_{avg} is the average weight of each child (class or feature) in the dataset.

The entropy can be computed as

$$\text{Entropy}\left(E\right) = -\sum_{i=1}^{N} p_i \log_2 \left(p_i\right) \quad (11.9)$$

where "p_i" is the probability of randomly selected class 'i'.

Experiment 11.10: Decision Tree-Based Classification

This experiment discusses the data classification using a decision tree algorithm. To explain the concept of the decision tree algorithm, "IRIS dataset" is considered, and the Python code for the decision tree algorithm is shown in Fig. 11.24, and its simulation result is displayed in Fig. 11.25.

Inferences

The following inferences can be drawn from Experiment 11.10:

- Figure 11.24 shows that the "tree.DecisionTreeClassifier" command from "sklearn" library is used to classify the IRIS dataset.
- "tree.plot_tree" command is used here to display the "entropy", "samples" and "values", which is depicted in Fig. 11.25a.
- The confusion matrix of the testing IRIS data is shown in Fig. 11.25b. From this figure, it is possible to observe that the number of classes in the IRIS dataset is three, and its predicted results are also displayed.

11.4.5 Support Vector Machine

Support vector machine (SVM) is a more powerful machine learning algorithm for linear or non-linear classification, regression, and outlier detection. It can be used for text classification, image classification, spam detection, handwriting identification, gene expression analysis, face detection, and anomaly detection. SVM algorithms are used to find the maximum separating hyperplane between the different classes present in the target feature set. Therefore, the SVM algorithm aims to create the best line or decision boundary to separate n-dimensional space into classes

```
# Decision tree algorithm for classification
from sklearn.datasets import load_iris
from sklearn import tree
from matplotlib import pyplot as plt
from sklearn.model_selection import train_test_split
from sklearn import metrics
iris = load_iris()
X = iris.data
y = iris.target
x_train, x_test, y_train, y_test= train_test_split(X, y, test_size= 0.25, random_state=0)
#build decision tree
clf = tree.DecisionTreeClassifier(criterion='entropy', max_depth=4,min_samples_leaf=4)
#fit the tree to iris dataset
clf.fit(x_train, y_train)
#plot decision tree
fig, ax = plt.subplots(figsize=(6, 6)) #figsize value changes the size of plot
tree.plot_tree(clf,ax=ax,feature_names=['sepal length','sepal width','petal length','petal width'])
plt.show()
y_pred= clf.predict(x_test)
cm = metrics.confusion_matrix(y_test, y_pred)
plt.figure()
cm_display = metrics.ConfusionMatrixDisplay(confusion_matrix = cm, display_labels = ['Setosa',
'Versicolor', 'Virginica'])
cm_display.plot(),plt.title('Confusion Matrix'),plt.xlabel('Predicted Output')
plt.ylabel('True Output'),plt.show()
```

Fig. 11.24 Python code for Decision tree algorithm

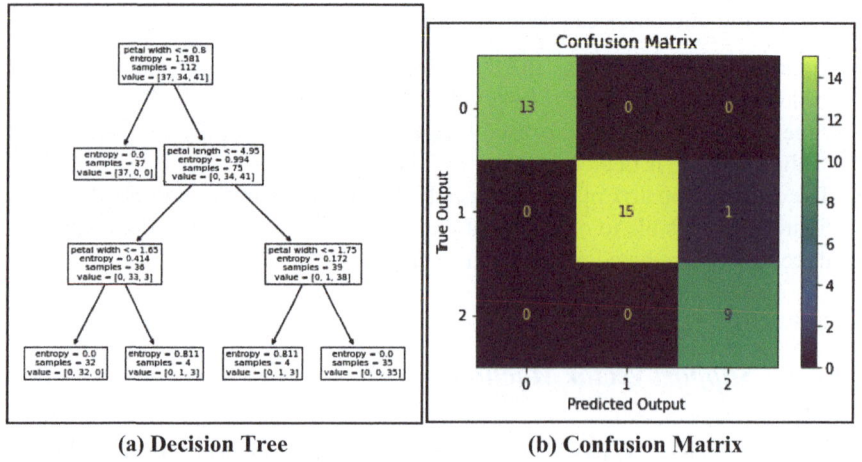

(a) **Decision Tree**   (b) **Confusion Matrix**

Fig. 11.25 Decision tree result of IRIS dataset. (**a**) Decision tree. (**b**) Confusion matrix.

so that the new data point can be correctly classified during testing. The best boundary line or decision boundary is called a *hyperplane*.

The support vector machine selects the extreme points/vectors for the hyperplane creation. These extreme points or vectors are called "*support vectors*"; hence, the

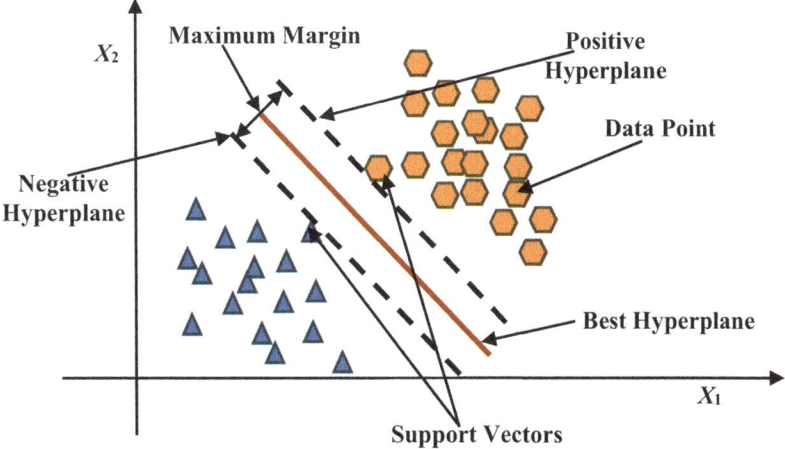

Fig. 11.26 Illustration of linear support vector machine

algorithm is named "*Support Vector Machine*". The hyperplane of the SVM is illustrated in Fig. 11.26.

Figure 11.26 shows the different terms in the SVM algorithm, like data point, positive hyperplane, negative hyperplane, maximum margin, support vectors, and best hyperplane. The orange and blue data points are feature 1 (X_1) and feature 2 (X_2) of the input dataset. The distance between the support vectors and the hyperplane is called as *the margin*. The goal of SVM is to maximize this margin. The hyperplane with the maximum margin is called the *optimal or best hyperplane*.

SVM can be classified into (1) Linear SVM and (2) Non-linear SVM. The linear SVM uses a single straight line to classify the input dataset into two classes, which is called a linearly separable dataset. The non-linear SVM is used to classify the non-linearly separable dataset. Here, this dataset cannot be classified by using a straight line. The non-linear curve can be used to separate the dataset. The non-linear SVM classifier is illustrated in Fig. 11.27a. From Fig. 11.27a, it is possible to observe that a straight line cannot separate the data points as it is in their present form. Hence, these data points are mapped from 2D to 3D by using the equation given by

$$z = X_1^2 + X_2^2 \qquad (11.10)$$

By adding the z dimension, the data can be plotted as shown in Fig. 11.27b. From this figure, it is evident that the data points are segregated by using linear single straight line. Finally, the 3D space is converted into a 2D space, as shown in Fig. 11.27c.

Experiment 11.11: Implementation of Linear SVM Classifier
This experiment discusses the implementation of a linear SVM classifier using Python. In this experiment, the IRIS dataset is considered in that "Petal Width" and

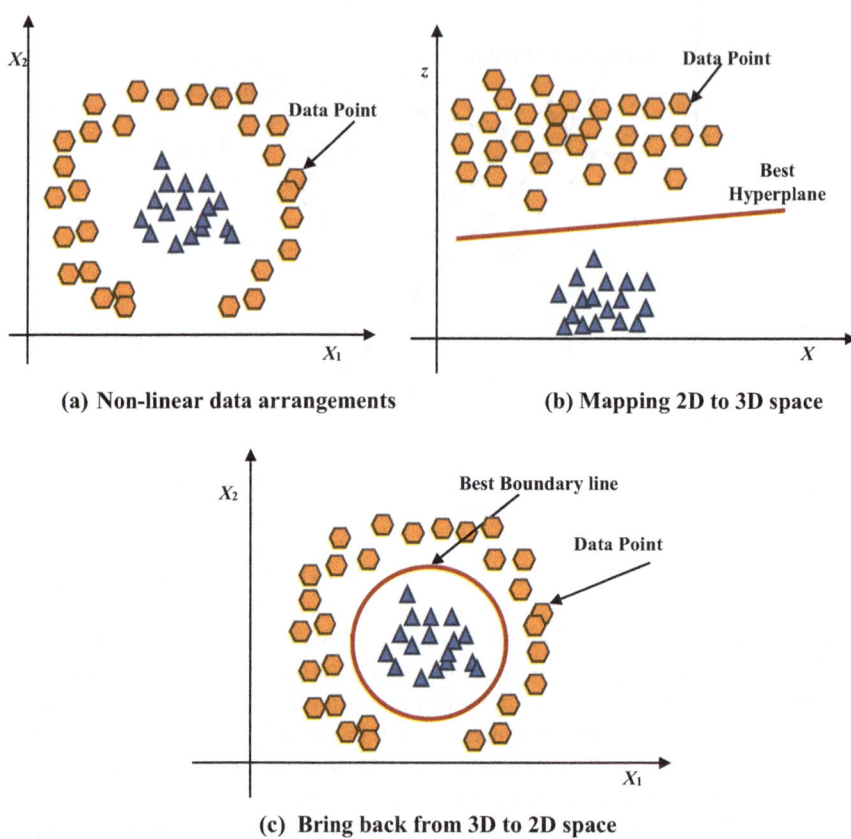

(a) Non-linear data arrangements

(b) Mapping 2D to 3D space

(c) Bring back from 3D to 2D space

Fig. 11.27 Non-linear SVM illustration. (**a**) Non-linear data arrangements. (**b**) Mapping 2D to 3D space. (**c**) Bring back from 3D to 2D space

"Petal Length" features are chosen for the training and testing of the linear SVM. The Python code to perform the linear SVM classification is given in Fig. 11.28, and its simulation result is shown in Fig. 11.29.

Inferences
The following inferences can be made from this experiment:

- From Fig. 11.28, it is possible to observe that "The IRIS dataset" is used for this experiment and that "Petal Width" and "Petal Length" features are considered for the linear SVM classifier implementation.
- Mesh grid plot is used to visualize the linear SVM model with the training data.
- A confusion matrix measure is used to verify the performance of the linear SVM.
- Figures 11.29a, b visualize the linear SVM model for training and testing data, which splits the input features into three classes by using two hyperplanes.
- Fig. 11.29c displays the confusion matrix of the testing IRIS dataset.

```
# Linear SVM Classifier
import numpy as np
import matplotlib.pyplot as plt
from sklearn import datasets
from sklearn.svm import SVC
from sklearn.model_selection import train_test_split
from sklearn import metrics
iris = datasets.load_iris()
X = iris.data[:, 2:4]  # Input features only last two features for visualization
y = iris.target;# Output Label
x_train, x_test, y_train, y_test= train_test_split(X, y, test_size= 0.2, random_state=0)
SVM_linear = SVC(kernel='linear');#Train SVM with linear kernel
SVM_linear.fit(x_train, y_train)
# Create a mesh to plot decision boundaries
h = 0.01  # step size in the mesh
x_min, x_max = x_train[:, 0].min() - 1, x_train[:, 0].max() + 1
y_min, y_max = x_train[:, 1].min() - 1, x_train[:, 1].max() + 1
xx, yy = np.meshgrid(np.arange(x_min, x_max, h),np.arange(y_min, y_max, h))
# Plot decision boundary of Linear SVM
Z_linear = SVM_linear.predict(np.c_[xx.ravel(), yy.ravel()])
Z_linear = Z_linear.reshape(xx.shape)
y_pred= SVM_linear.predict(x_test)
cm = metrics.confusion_matrix(y_test, y_pred)
plt.figure(),plt.contourf(xx, yy, Z_linear, cmap='winter', alpha=0.8)
plt.scatter(x_train[:, 0], x_train[:, 1], c=y_train, cmap='plasma')
plt.title('Linear SVM_Training'),plt.xlabel('Petal Length')
plt.ylabel('Petal Width'),plt.xlim(xx.min(), xx.max()),plt.ylim(yy.min(), yy.max()),plt.show()
plt.figure(),plt.contourf(xx, yy, Z_linear, cmap='winter', alpha=0.8)
plt.scatter(x_test[:, 0], x_test[:, 1], c=y_pred, cmap='Spectral')
plt.title('Linear SVM_Testing'),plt.xlabel('Petal Length'),plt.ylabel('Petal Width'),
plt.xlim(xx.min(), xx.max()),plt.ylim(yy.min(), yy.max()),plt.show()
plt.figure()
cm_display = metrics.ConfusionMatrixDisplay(confusion_matrix = cm, display_labels = ['Setosa',
'Versicolor', 'Virginica'])
cm_display.plot(),plt.title('Confusion Matrix'),plt.xlabel('Predicted Output')
plt.ylabel('True Output'),plt.show()
```

Fig. 11.28 Python code for linear SVM classifier

Experiment 11.12: Implementation of Non-linear SVM Classifier

This experiment discusses the implementation of non-linear SVM classifier using Python. The "IRIS dataset" is used for the non-linear SVM classifier; in particular, "Petal Width" and "Petal Length" features are considered. Also, the radial basis function "RBF" kernel is utilized to generate the SVM classifier model. The radial basis function is a non-linear function. Hence, the SVM classifier is called a non-linear SVM classifier. The Python code for the non-linear SVM classifier is given in Fig. 11.30, and its corresponding simulation result is displayed in Fig. 11.31.

Inferences

The following inferences can be drawn from this experiment:

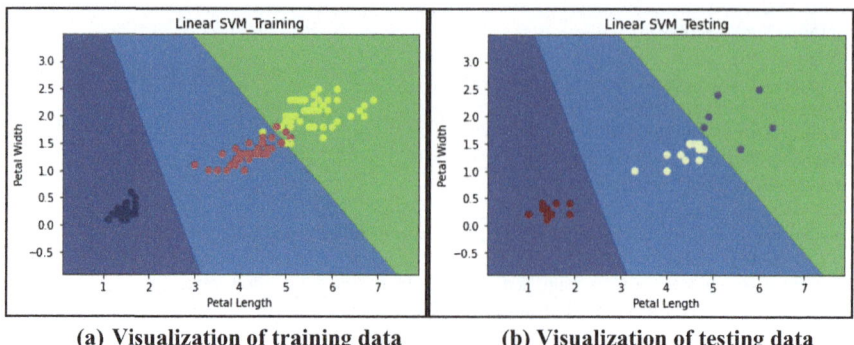

(a) Visualization of training data   **(b) Visualization of testing data**

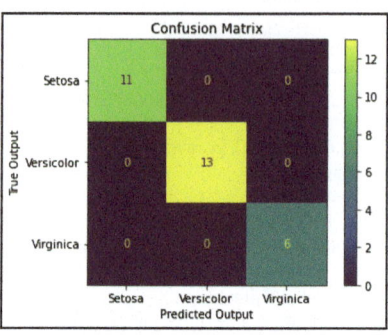

(c) Confusion Matrix

Fig. 11.29 Linear SVM result of IRIS dataset. (**a**) Visualization of training data. (**b**) Visualization of testing data. (**c**) Confusion matrix

- From Fig. 11.30, it is possible to infer that "rbf" non-linear kernel is used for the SVM classifier modelling, and "gamma" value is chosen as 10. "Meshgrid function is used to display the decision boundary of the SVM classifier.
- Figure 11.31a shows the decision boundary of the SVM classifier for the training IRIS dataset.
- Figure 11.31b displays the predicted output of the testing IRIS dataset, which are lies within the boundary of each class.
- Figure 11.31c confirms the predicted result is exactly matched with true result by using the confusion matrix.

11.4.6   Naïve Bayes Algorithm

Naïve Bayes is a supervised machine learning algorithm and it works based on the Bayes theorem. Naïve Bayes algorithm can be used for solving classification tasks like text classification, spam filtration, sentimental analysis, and classifying articles. This algorithm comprises two words: "Naïve" and "Bayes". This algorithm simply

```
# Non-linear SVM Classifier using RBF kernel
import numpy as np
import matplotlib.pyplot as plt
from sklearn import datasets
from sklearn.svm import SVC
from sklearn.model_selection import train_test_split
from sklearn import metrics
iris = datasets.load_iris()
X = iris.data[:, 2:4]  # Input features only last two features for visualization
y = iris.target;# Output Label
x_train, x_test, y_train, y_test= train_test_split(X, y, test_size= 0.2, random_state=0)
SVM_nonlinear = SVC(kernel='rbf', gamma=10);#Train SVM with RBF kernel
SVM_nonlinear.fit(x_train, y_train)
# Create a mesh to plot decision boundaries
h = 0.01  # step size in the mesh
x_min, x_max = x_train[:, 0].min() - 1, x_train[:, 0].max() + 1
y_min, y_max = x_train[:, 1].min() - 1, x_train[:, 1].max() + 1
xx, yy = np.meshgrid(np.arange(x_min, x_max, h),np.arange(y_min, y_max, h))
# Plot decision boundary of non-linear SVM
Z_nonlinear = SVM_nonlinear.predict(np.c_[xx.ravel(), yy.ravel()])
Z_nonlinear = Z_nonlinear.reshape(xx.shape)
y_pred= SVM_nonlinear.predict(x_test)
cm = metrics.confusion_matrix(y_test, y_pred)
plt.figure(),plt.contourf(xx, yy, Z_nonlinear, cmap='winter', alpha=0.8)
plt.scatter(x_train[:, 0], x_train[:, 1], c=y_train, cmap='plasma')
plt.title('Nonlinear SVM using RBF_Training'),plt.xlabel('Petal Length'),plt.ylabel('Petal Width'),
plt.xlim(xx.min(), xx.max()),plt.ylim(yy.min(), yy.max()),plt.show()
plt.figure(),plt.contourf(xx, yy, Z_nonlinear, cmap='winter', alpha=0.8)
plt.scatter(x_test[:, 0], x_test[:, 1], c=y_pred, cmap='Spectral')
plt.title('Nonlinear SVM using RBF_Testing'),plt.xlabel('Petal Length'),plt.ylabel('Petal Width'),
plt.xlim(xx.min(), xx.max()),plt.ylim(yy.min(), yy.max()),plt.show()
plt.figure()
cm_display = metrics.ConfusionMatrixDisplay(confusion_matrix = cm, display_labels = ['Setosa',
'Versicolor', 'Virginica'])
cm_display.plot(),plt.title('Confusion Matrix'),plt.xlabel('Predicted Output')
plt.ylabel('True Output'),plt.show()
```

Fig. 11.30 Python code for non-linear SVM classifier

assumes the occurrence of a particular feature is independent of the occurrence of other features, and it uses the principle of Bayes theorem for the prediction; hence, it is called a Naïve Bayes algorithm.

Bayes Theorem

Bayes theorem is used to determine the probability of a hypothesis with prior knowledge, and it depends on the conditional probability. The Bayes theorem states that the given class variable (y) and dependent feature vector (X), which contains the features $\{x_1, x_2, x_3, \ldots, x_n\}$:

$$P(X) = \frac{P(y)P(y)}{P(x_1, x_2, \cdots, x_n)} \tag{11.11}$$

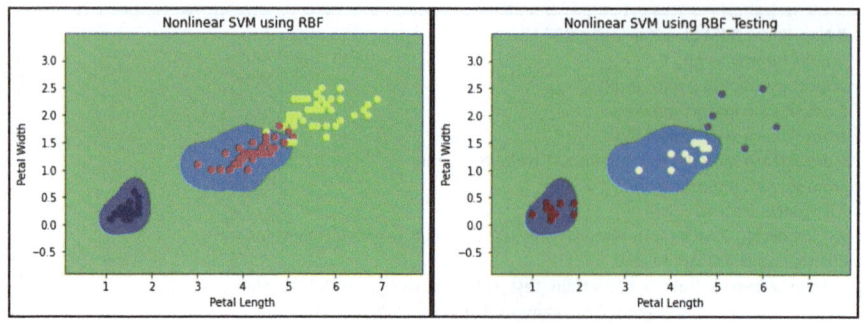

(a) Visualization of training data   (b) Visualization of testing data

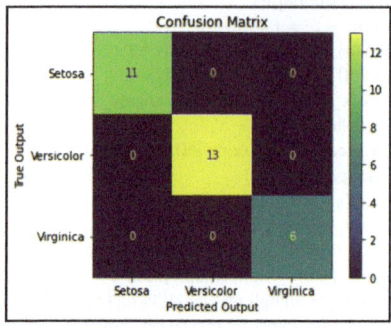

(c) Confusion Matrix

Fig. 11.31 Non-linear SVM result of IRIS dataset. (a) Visualization of training data. (b) Visualization of testing data. (c) Confusion matrix

Using the naïve conditional independence assumption that

$$P(y,x_1,x_2,\cdots,x_n) = P(y) \text{ for all } i \qquad (11.12)$$

The above equation can be simplified as

$$P(x_1,x_2,\cdots,x_n) = \frac{P(y)\prod_{i=1}^{n}P(y)}{P(x_1,x_2,\cdots,x_n)} \qquad (11.13)$$

Since $P(x_1, x_2, \cdots, x_n)$ is constant given the input vector, the classification rule can be written as

$$P(x_1,x_2,\cdots,x_n) \propto P(y)\prod_{i=1}^{n}P(y) \qquad (11.14)$$

The final predicted class output can be obtained by using

$$\hat{y} = \arg P(y)\prod_{i=1}^{n}P(y) \qquad (11.15)$$

Here, maximum A posteriori (MAP) estimation is used to estimate $P(y)$. $P(y)$ denotes the relative frequency of class "y" in the training set. The different Naïve Bayes classifiers differ mainly by the assumptions of making the distribution of $P(y)$. The different assumptions of distributions of $P(y)$ are Gaussian Naïve Bayes, Multinomial Naïve Bayes, Complement Naïve Bayes, Bernoulli Naïve Bayes, Categorical Naïve Bayes and Out-of-core Naïve Bayes, etc.

Experiment 11.13: Implementation of Naïve Bayes Classifier
This experiment discusses the implementation of Naïve Bayes classifier using Python. The "IRIS dataset" is used for the Naïve Bayes classifier, in particular, "Petal Width" and "Petal Length" features are considered. Gaussian function is used as maximum A posteriori (MAP) to estimate the $P(y)$. The Python code for the Gaussian Naïve Bayes classifier is given in Fig. 11.32, and its corresponding simulation result is shown in Fig. 11.33.

```
# Naive Bayes Classifier
import numpy as np
import matplotlib.pyplot as plt
from sklearn import datasets
from sklearn.model_selection import train_test_split
from sklearn.naive_bayes import GaussianNB
from sklearn import metrics
iris = datasets.load_iris()
X = iris.data[:, 2:4]  # Input features only last two features for visualization
y = iris.target;# Output Label
X_train, X_test, y_train, y_test= train_test_split(X, y, test_size= 0.2, random_state=0)
Gauss_NaiveBayes = GaussianNB()
Gauss_NaiveBayes.fit(X_train, y_train)
# Create a mesh to plot decision boundaries
h = 0.01  # step size in the mesh
x_min, x_max = X_train[:, 0].min() - 1, X_train[:, 0].max() + 1
y_min, y_max = X_train[:, 1].min() - 1, X_train[:, 1].max() + 1
xx, yy = np.meshgrid(np.arange(x_min, x_max, h),np.arange(y_min, y_max, h))
# Plot decision boundary of Gaussian Naive Bayes
Z_nonlinear = Gauss_NaiveBayes.predict(np.c_[xx.ravel(), yy.ravel()])
Z_nonlinear = Z_nonlinear.reshape(xx.shape)
y_pred= Gauss_NaiveBayes.predict(X_test)
cm = metrics.confusion_matrix(y_test, y_pred)
plt.figure(figsize=(10,6)),plt.subplot(1,2,1),plt.contourf(xx, yy, Z_nonlinear, cmap='winter', alpha=0.8)
plt.scatter(X_train[:, 0], X_train[:, 1], c=y_train, cmap='plasma')
plt.title('Gaussian Naive Bayes-Training'),plt.xlabel('Petal Length'),plt.ylabel('Petal Width'),
plt.xlim(xx.min(), xx.max()),plt.ylim(yy.min(), yy.max()),plt.subplot(1,2,2)
plt.contourf(xx, yy, Z_nonlinear, cmap='winter', alpha=0.8)
plt.scatter(X_test[:, 0], X_test[:, 1], c=y_pred, cmap='Spectral'),
plt.title('Gaussian Naive Bayes-Testing'),plt.xlabel('Petal Length'),plt.ylabel('Petal Width'),
plt.xlim(xx.min(), xx.max()),plt.ylim(yy.min(), yy.max()),plt.tight_layout()
plt.figure()
cm_display = metrics.ConfusionMatrixDisplay(confusion_matrix = cm, display_labels = ['Setosa',
'Versicolor', 'Virginica'])
cm_display.plot(),plt.title('Confusion Matrix'),plt.xlabel('Predicted Output')
plt.ylabel('True Output'),plt.show()
```

Fig. 11.32 Python code for Gaussian Naïve Bayes classifier

Inferences

The following inferences can be drawn from this experiment:

- From Fig. 11.32, it is possible to infer that "GaussianNB()" function is imported from "sklearn.naive_bayes" library and which is used to build a classifier model using the IRIS dataset. Meshgrid function is used to display the decision boundary of the classifier.
- Figure 11.33a shows the decision boundary of the Gaussian Naïve Bayes classifier for the training and testing IRIS dataset.

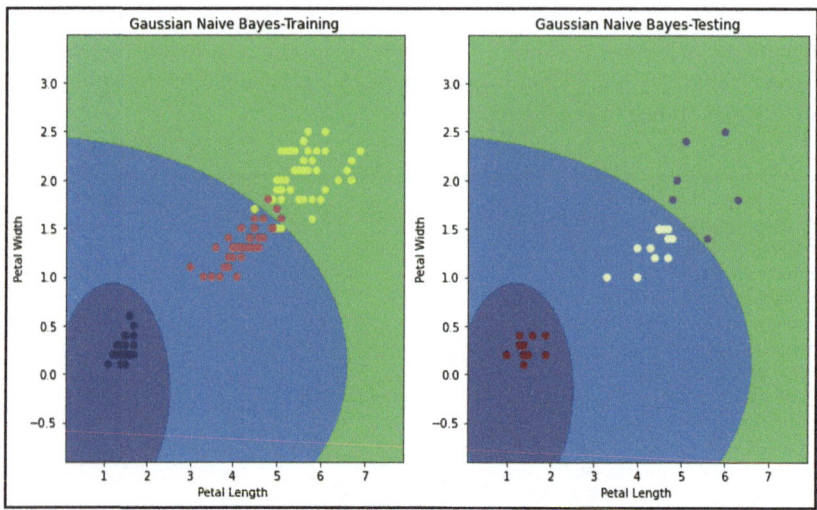

(a) Visualization of training and testing data

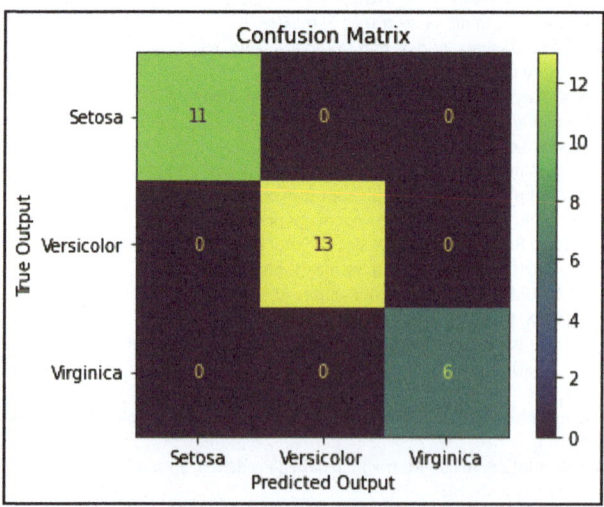

(c) Confusion Matrix

Fig. 11.33 Result of Gaussian Naïve Bayes for IRIS dataset. (**a**) Visualization of training and testing data. (**b**) Confusion matrix

- Figure 11.33b confirms the predicted result is exactly matched with true result by using the confusion matrix.

11.4.7 K-Nearest Neighbour (KNN)

K-nearest neighbour algorithm is a machine learning algorithm that works both the supervised and unsupervised leanings. The KNN algorithm assumes the similarity between the new data and the available training data and puts the new data into the category that is most similar to the available training categories. Initially, the KNN algorithm stores all the training data and classifies the new data based on the similarity between the new data and training data. KNN is a non-parametric approach; it does not make any assumption on underlying data, and it is also known as lazy learner algorithm because it does not learn from the training data. This algorithm works directly on the input dataset. In the training phase of the KNN algorithm stores the dataset and when it gets new data, then it classifies that data into a particular category based on the similarity between the new data and the training data. The illustration of KNN algorithm is shown in Fig. 11.34. From Fig. 11.34a, it is

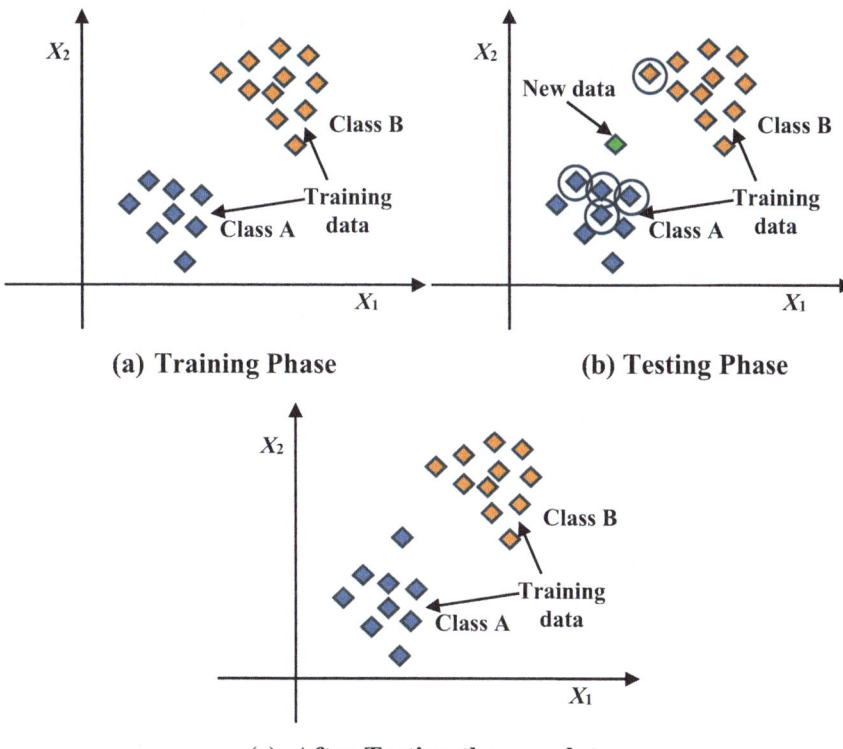

Fig. 11.34 Illustration of KNN algorithm. (**a**) Training phase. (**b**) Testing phase. (**c**) After testing the new data

possible to observe that in the training phase input data or training data are stored. For the new data, which is to be classified into a particular category or class, the similarity between the new data and the available training data is computed, which is shown in Fig. 11.34b and based on the similarity value. For this, K numbers of neighbours are chosen and distance between the new data and K neighbours is calculated. The maximum number of neighbours (the circled training data are closest neighbours) from particular class is close to the new data then the new data is assigned to the particular class, which is shown in Fig. 11.34c. The K numbers of neighbours are utilized to classify the new data into a particular class, hence this algorithm is named as "K Nearest Neighbour" (KNN) algorithm.

KNN Algorithm

The steps of KNN algorithm are as follows:

Step 1: Select the number K of the neighbours to calculate the similarity between the new data and K-neighbours.
Step 2: Calculate the Euclidean distance or some other distance measure between the new data and K neighbours.
Step 3: Take the K-nearest neighbours as the calculated distance measure.
Step 4: Count the number of data points in each class or category among these K neighbours.
Step 5: Assign the new data to that class or category for which the number of the neighbour is maximum.
Step 6: Repeat Steps (2)–(5) for the new data.

Different distance metrics can be used for the KNN classifier modelling. They are (1) Euclidean distance, (2) Minkowski distance, (3) Manhattan distance, (4) Cosine distance, (5) Jaccard distance, (6) Hamming distance, etc. The expression for the different distance metrics is given in Table 11.1.

Table 11.1 Distance metrics for KNN classifier

S. no.	Name of the distance metric	Mathematical expression	Significance
1.	Euclidean	$d(x,y) = \sqrt{\sum_{i=1}^{n}(x_i - y_i)^2}$	It is a measure of the true straight-line distance between two points in Euclidean space
2.	Minkowski	$d(x,y) = \left(\sum_{i=1}^{n}|x_i - y_i|^p\right)^{1/p}$	It is a metric intended for real-valued vector spaces
3.	Manhattan	$d(x,y) = \sum_{i=1}^{n}|x_i - y_i|$	This distance is preferred over Euclidean distance for the high-dimensionality dataset
4.	Cosine	$\cos(x,y) = \dfrac{\vec{x}.\vec{y}}{\|\vec{x}\| \, \|\vec{y}\|}$	It is measured by the cosine of the angle between two vectors and determines whether two vectors are pointing in the same direction
5.	Jaccard	$d(x,y) = 1 - J(x,y) = 1 - \dfrac{|x \cap y|}{|x \cup y|}$	The Jaccard approach looks at the two datasets and finds the incident where both values are equal to 1

Experiment 11.14: Implementation of KNN Classifier

This experiment discusses the implementation of KNN classifier using Python. The "IRIS dataset" is used for the KNN classifier, in particular, "Petal Width" and "Petal Length" features are considered. The Python code for the KNN classifier is given in Fig. 11.35, and its corresponding simulation result is shown in Fig. 11.36.

Inferences

The following inferences can be drawn from this experiment:

- From Fig. 11.35, it is possible to infer that "KNeighborsClassifier" function is imported from "sklearn.neighbors" library and which is used to build a classifier model using the IRIS dataset. Meshgrid function is used to display the decision boundary of the classifier.

```
# KNN Classifier
import numpy as np
import matplotlib.pyplot as plt
from sklearn import datasets
from sklearn.model_selection import train_test_split
from sklearn.neighbors import KNeighborsClassifier
from sklearn import metrics
iris = datasets.load_iris()
X = iris.data[:, 2:4]  # Input features only last two features for visualization
y = iris.target;# Output Label
X_train, X_test, y_train, y_test= train_test_split(X, y, test_size= 0.2, random_state=0)
KNN= KNeighborsClassifier(n_neighbors=5, metric='euclidean', p=2 )
KNN.fit(X_train, y_train)
# Create a mesh to plot decision boundaries
h = 0.01  # step size in the mesh
x_min, x_max = X_train[:, 0].min() - 1, X_train[:, 0].max() + 1
y_min, y_max = X_train[:, 1].min() - 1, X_train[:, 1].max() + 1
xx, yy = np.meshgrid(np.arange(x_min, x_max, h),np.arange(y_min, y_max, h) )
# Plot decision boundary of Gaussian Naive Bayes
Z_nonlinear = KNN.predict(np.c_[xx.ravel(), yy.ravel()])
Z_nonlinear = Z_nonlinear.reshape(xx.shape)
y_pred= KNN.predict(X_test)
cm = metrics.confusion_matrix(y_test, y_pred)
plt.figure(figsize=(10,6)),plt.subplot(1,2,1),plt.contourf(xx, yy, Z_nonlinear, cmap='winter', alpha=0.8)
plt.scatter(X_train[:, 0], X_train[:, 1], c=y_train, cmap='plasma'),plt.title('KNN Classifier-Training'),
plt.xlabel('Petal Length'),plt.ylabel('Petal Width'),plt.xlim(xx.min(), xx.max()),
plt.ylim(yy.min(), yy.max()),plt.subplot(1,2,2),
plt.contourf(xx, yy, Z_nonlinear, cmap='winter', alpha=0.8)
plt.scatter(X_test[:, 0], X_test[:, 1], c=y_pred, cmap='Spectral'),plt.title('KNN Classifier-Testing'),
plt.xlabel('Petal Length'),plt.ylabel('Petal Width'),plt.xlim(xx.min(), xx.max())
plt.ylim(yy.min(), yy.max()),plt.tight_layout(),plt.figure()
cm_display = metrics.ConfusionMatrixDisplay(confusion_matrix = cm, display_labels = ['Setosa',
'Versicolor', 'Virginica'])
cm_display.plot(),plt.title('Confusion Matrix'),plt.xlabel('Predicted Output')
plt.ylabel('True Output'),plt.show()
```

Fig. 11.35 Python code for KNN classifier

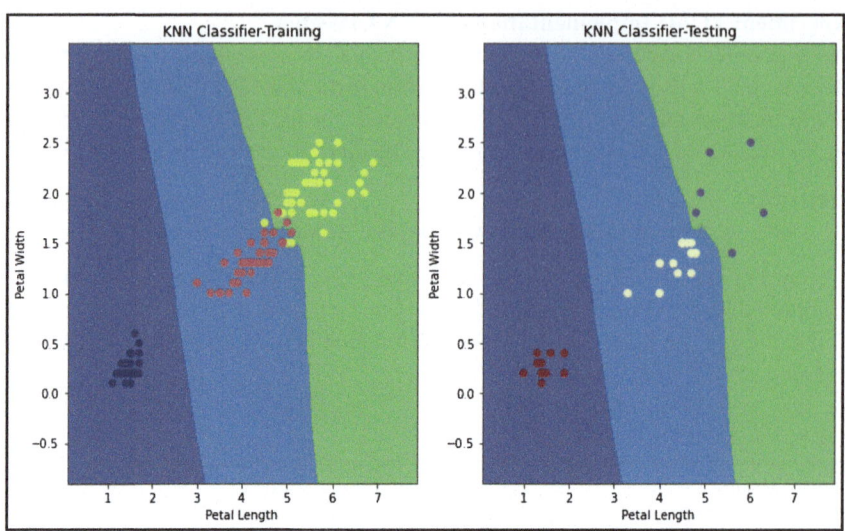

(a) Visualization of training and testing data

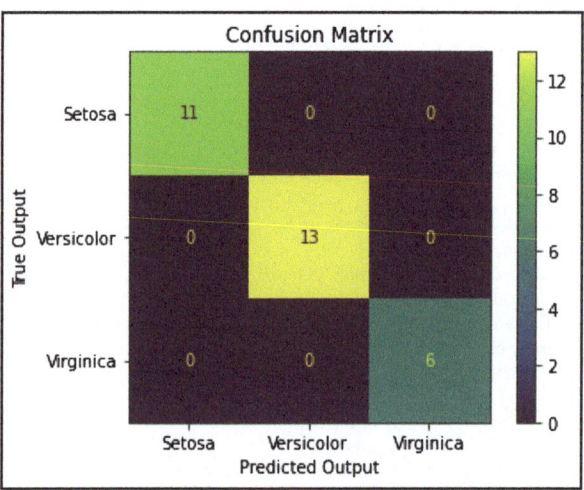

(b) Confusion Matrix

Fig. 11.36 Result of KNN classifier for IRIS dataset. (**a**) Visualization of training and testing data. (**b**) Confusion matrix

- Figure 11.36a shows the decision boundary of the KNN classifier for the training and testing IRIS dataset. Here, "Euclidean" metric is used as a distance metric.
- Figure 11.36b confirms the predicted result is exactly matched with true result by using the confusion matrix.

11.4.8   K-Means Algorithm

The K-means clustering algorithm is an unsupervised machine-learning technique used for data classification and segmentation. The unlabelled dataset is grouped into different clusters based on the value of "K". Here, K denotes the number of pre-defined clusters that need to be created in the process of clustering the dataset. It is an iterative approach that separates the unlabelled dataset into K different clusters so that each dataset belongs to only one group with similar properties. Each cluster is associated with its own centre, which is called as "centroid". The K-means cluster algorithm is to minimize the distance between the datapoint and their corresponding cluster centroid.

K-Means Clustering Algorithm
The step-by-step approach of the K-means clustering algorithm is given below:

Step 1: Choose the number of clusters (i.e. K).

Step 2: Select the random K points in the given training dataset, which are the initial centroid of the cluster.

Step 3: Assign each data point to its closest centroid, which forms the predefined K clusters.

Step 4: Calculate the variance and update the position of the new centroid for each cluster.

Step 5: Repeat Step 3 until each data point is assigned to the new nearest centroid of each cluster.

Step 6: If any reassignment occurs, then go to Step 4. Else, stop the assigning process, and the obtained centroids are the final centroid for each cluster.

Illustration of the K-Means Clustering Algorithm
This section discusses the illustration of K-means clustering algorithm. The initial dataset is called as "training dataset", which is shown in Fig. 11.37. Then, the number of clusters is chosen as 3, and the 3 numbers of cluster centroid are fixed randomly in the given dataset, which is displayed in Fig. 11.37b. Figure 11.37c shows the random centroid's movement in each cluster to the actual cluster centre. Figure 11.37d displays the final centroid of each cluster. The final clustering output is shown in Fig. 11.37e. The Elbow method can be used to find the optimum number of clusters in the given dataset. This approach uses the "Within Cluster Sum of Squares" concept to obtain the optimum "K" value. Distance measures like Euclidean, Manhattan, Minkowski, etc., can be used to find the gap between the data points and the cluster centroid.

Experiment 11.15: Implementation of K-means Clustering Algorithm
This experiment discusses the implementation of K-means clustering algorithm using Python. The "IRIS dataset" is used here, and in particular, "Petal Width" and "Petal Length" features are considered. The Python code for the K-means clustering is given in Fig. 11.38, and its corresponding simulation result is shown in Fig. 11.39.

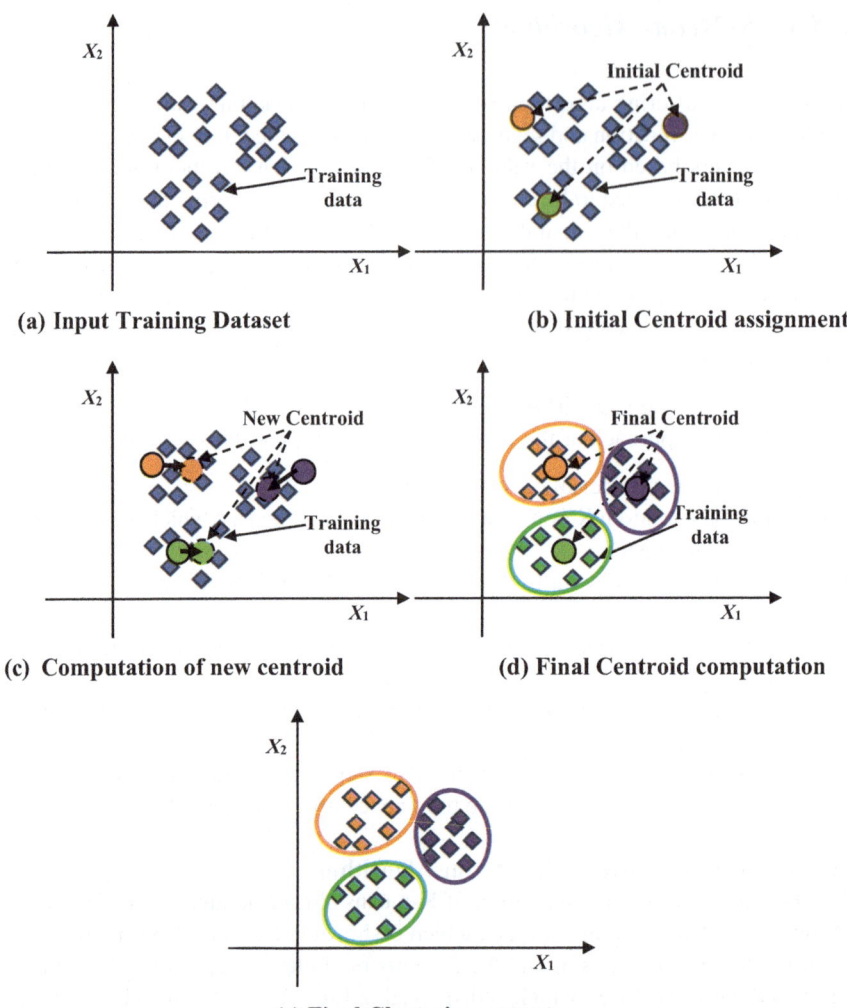

Fig. 11.37 Illustration of K-means clustering algorithm. (**a**) Input training dataset. (**b**) Initial centroid assignment. (**c**) Computation of new centroid. (**d**) Final centroid computation. (**e**) Final clustering output

Inferences

The following inferences can be drawn from this experiment:

- From Fig. 11.38, it is possible to infer that "KMeans" function is imported from "sklearn.cluster" library and which is used to build a clustering model for the IRIS dataset. "scatter" function is used to display the IRIS feature vectors.

```
# K-means clustering algorithm
import matplotlib.pyplot as plt
from sklearn import datasets
from sklearn.cluster import KMeans
iris = datasets.load_iris()
X = iris.data[:, 2:4]  # Input features only last two features for visualization
y = iris.target;# Output Label
KmC= KMeans(n_clusters=3, init='k-means++', random_state= 0 )
y_pred=KmC.fit_predict(X)
plt.scatter(X[y_pred == 0, 0], X[y_pred == 0, 1], s = 100, c = 'blue', label = 'Setosa')
plt.scatter(X[y_pred == 1, 0], X[y_pred == 1, 1], s = 100, c = 'green', label = 'Versicolor')
plt.scatter(X[y_pred == 2, 0], X[y_pred == 2, 1], s = 100, c = 'red', label = 'Virginica')
plt.scatter(KmC.cluster_centers_[:, 0], KmC.cluster_centers_[:, 1], s = 300, c = ['black'], label =
'Centroid'),plt.title('Kmeans Clustering Output'),plt.xlabel('Petal Length'),plt.ylabel('Petal Width')
plt.legend(),plt.show()
```

Fig. 11.38   Python code for K-means clustering

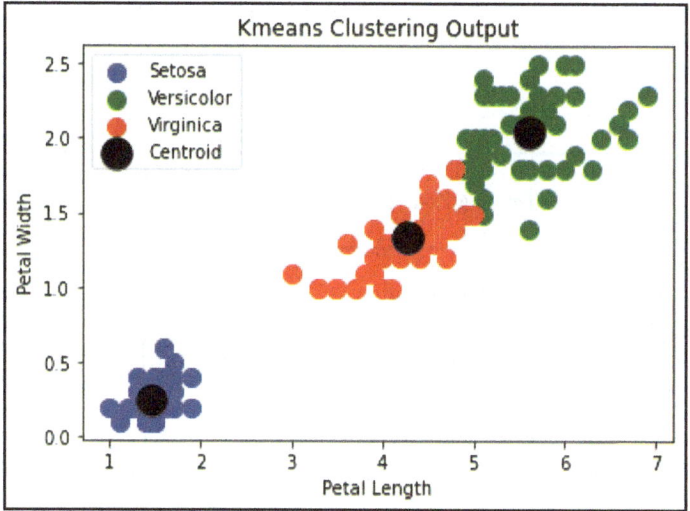

Fig. 11.39   Result of K-means clustering for IRIS dataset

- The number of clusters (K), "n_clusters" is chosen as 3. "K-means++" is a centroid initialization method, which is used to improve the K-means algorithm by intelligently selecting initial cluster centroids.
- Figure 11.39 displays the final output of the K-means clustering for the IRIS dataset. From this figure, it is possible to infer that the number of clusters is chosen as 3, and the output of the K-means clustering algorithm divides the input dataset into three sets of clusters.

11.4.9   *Random Forest Algorithm*

Random forest is a supervised machine learning algorithm that can be used for classification and regression. The basic concept of the random forest algorithm is based on ensemble learning. It is a process of combining multiple classifiers to solve a complex problem and to improve the performance of the model. The name of random forest suggests that it is a classifier that contains a number of decision trees on various subsets of the given dataset and takes the average to improve the predictive accuracy of that dataset. That is, the decision tree algorithm contains a single tree, whereas the random forest takes the prediction from each decision tree and is based on the majority votes of predictions, which gives a final output. Therefore, the higher number of trees in the forest leads to higher accuracy and prevents the problem of overfitting. The block diagram of the random forest algorithm is shown in Fig. 11.40.

From Fig. 11.40, it is possible to observe that the input dataset is divided into M number of training sets, and each training set is applied to the decision tree algorithm. The output of each decision tree is used for the majority voting to identify the class. The majority class will be the final output of the random forest algorithm.

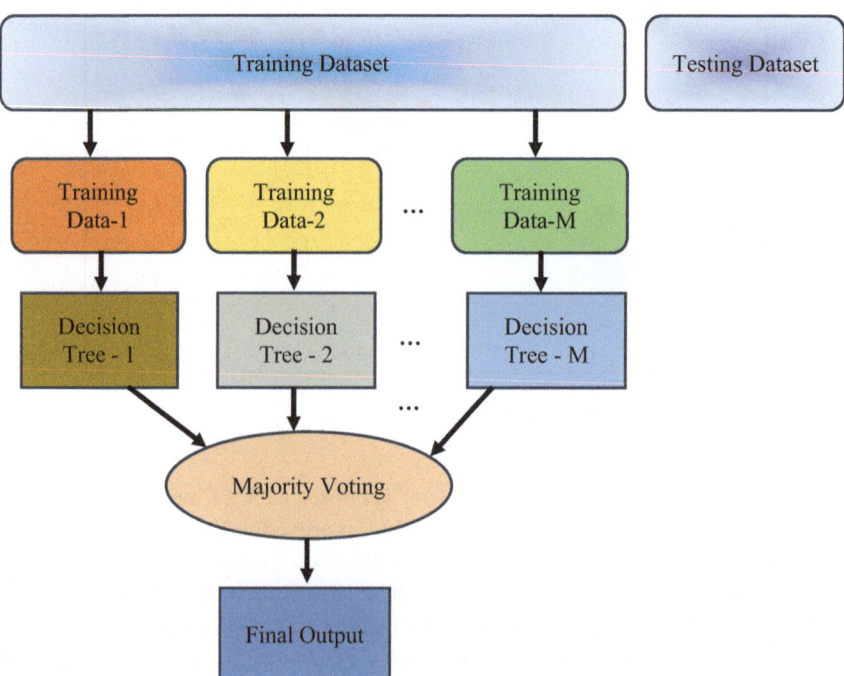

Fig. 11.40 Flowchart of the random forest algorithm

Advantages

1. The random forest algorithm can be used to solve both classification and regression problems.
2. It is considered as very accurate and robust model because it uses large number of decision tree to make predictions.
3. It takes the average of all the decision tree predictions and nullifies the biases. Hence, it does not affect the overfitting problem.
4. It can handle the missing values. There are two ways to handle the missing values they are (a) to use median values to replace continuous variables and (b) to compute the proximity-weighted average of missing values.
5. Random forest algorithm can be used for feature selection.

Disadvantages

1. Random forest takes more computational complexity. That is, it is very slow in making predictions because a large number of decision trees are used to make predictions. All the trees in the forest have to make a prediction for the same input and then perform majority voting on it. Hence, it is a time-consuming process.
2. The model is difficult to interpret as compared to a decision tree. The predictions can easily be made as compared to decision tree.

Experiment 11.16: Random Forest Algorithm for Classification
This experiment discusses image classification using a random forest algorithm. For the image classification, the input dataset is considered IRIS data. The Python code to implement the above-mentioned task is given in Fig. 11.41, and its corresponding output is shown in Fig. 11.42.

Inferences
The following inferences can be observed from this experiment:

- From Fig. 11.41, it is evident that the "*RandomForestClassifier*" command is used here to build a model. "*n_estimators* = 10" denotes the number of decision trees used for this model building is 10, and the "*entropy*" is considered for the information gain in the decision tree algorithm.
- The confusion matrix of the random forest algorithm is shown in Fig. 11.42, which indicates that the input dataset contains three different classes of input.

Experiment 11.17: Random Forest Algorithm for Regression
Random forest regression in machine learning is an ensemble method; it uses multiple decision trees and a technique called Bootstrap and Aggregation, commonly called "bagging". There are various types of ensemble learning approaches: (1) Bagging or Bootstrap Aggregating, (2) Boosting, and (3) Stacking. Bagging method involves training multiple models on random subsets of the training data. The individual model's predictions are combined by averaging to get a final prediction. Boosting method involves training a sequence of models, where each subsequent

```
# Random forest algorithm for classification
from sklearn.datasets import load_iris
from sklearn.ensemble import RandomForestClassifier
from matplotlib import pyplot as plt
from sklearn.model_selection import train_test_split
from sklearn import metrics
iris = load_iris()
X = iris.data
y = iris.target
x_train, x_test, y_train, y_test= train_test_split(X, y, test_size= 0.25, random_state=0)
#Random forest
clf= RandomForestClassifier(n_estimators= 10, criterion="entropy")
clf.fit(x_train, y_train)
y_pred= clf.predict(x_test)
cm = metrics.confusion_matrix(y_test, y_pred)
plt.figure()
cm_display = metrics.ConfusionMatrixDisplay(confusion_matrix = cm, display_labels = ['Setosa',
'Versicolor', 'Virginica'])
cm_display.plot(),plt.title('Confusion Matrix'),plt.xlabel('Predicted Output')
plt.ylabel('True Output'),plt.show()
```

Fig. 11.41 Python code for random forest classifier

Fig. 11.42 Confusion
matrix for random forest
algorithm of IRIS dataset

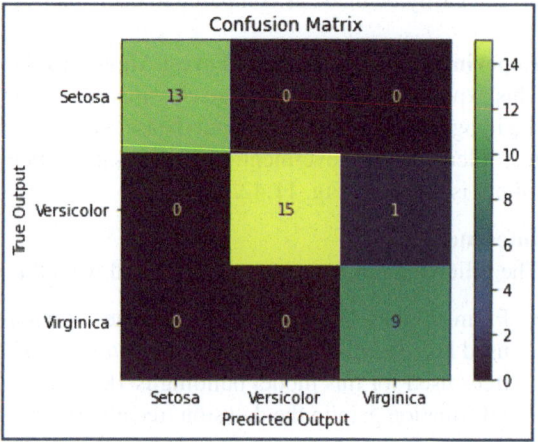

model works on the errors made by the previous model. The final prediction is combined predictions using a weighted voting mechanism. Stacking involves using the predictions from one set of models as input features for another model. The second level model makes the final prediction.

This experiment deals with the random forest regression-based machine learning technique using Python. In this experiment, the input data is considered as "Position_ Salaries.csv", which contains the information on Position, Levels, and Salary. However, only two parameters (Levels and Salaries) are considered for the random forest regression modelling. The Python code used to perform the random forest

```
# Random Forest Regression
import matplotlib.pyplot as plt
import pandas as pd
from sklearn.ensemble import RandomForestRegressor
data_set= pd.read_csv('Position_Salaries.csv')
Id_x=data_set.iloc[:, 1:2].values; # Independent Variable
D_y=data_set.iloc[:, 2].values;# Dependent Variable
RF_regressor = RandomForestRegressor(n_estimators=10, random_state=0, oob_score=True)
RF_regressor.fit(Id_x, D_y)
plt.plot(Id_x, D_y, marker='o', color="red")
plt.plot(Id_x, RF_regressor.predict((Id_x)), marker='d', color="blue")
plt.legend(['Original','Predicted']),plt.title("Random Forest Regression")
plt.xlabel("Position Levels"),plt.ylabel("Salary")
plt.tight_layout()
```

Fig. 11.43 Python code for random forest regression

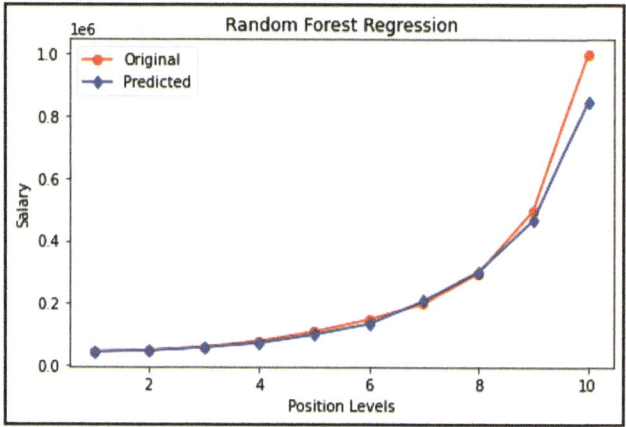

Fig. 11.44 Simulation result

regression modelling is given in Fig. 11.43, and its simulation result is shown in Fig. 11.44.

Inferences

The following inferences can be drawn from this experiment:

- From Fig. 11.43, it is possible to observe that "*RandomForestRegressor*" command is used to model the random forest regressor. "*n_estimators* = 10" denotes the number of decision trees used for this model building is 10 and the "*oob_score*" is the out of bag score or OOB score, which estimates the model's generalization performance. The OOB score is mainly used in bagging algorithms to validate the bagging algorithm.
- From Fig. 11.44, it is possible to observe that the random forest regressor predicted output is in line with the actual input data.

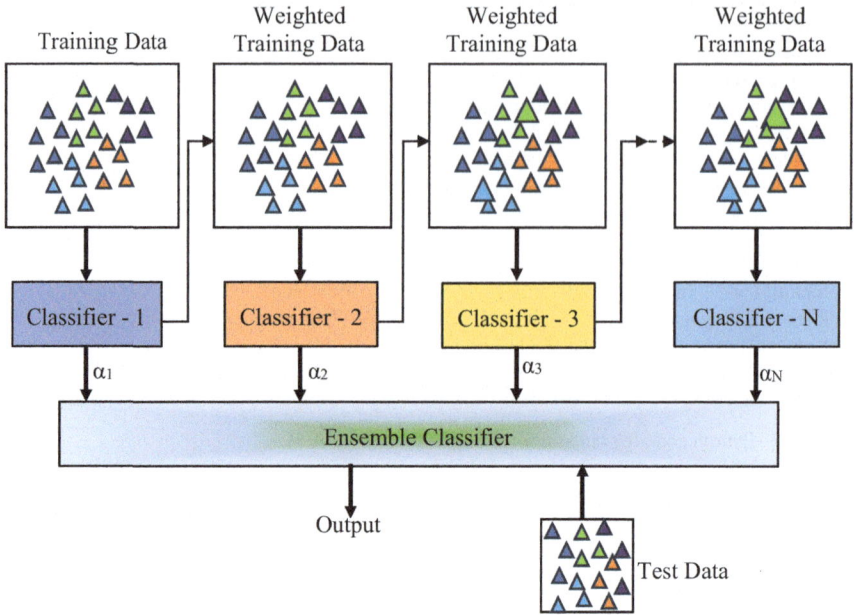

Fig. 11.45 Illustration of AdaBoost multi-class classifier

11.4.10   AdaBoost Algorithm

AdaBoost stands for Adaptive Boosting, which is a machine-learning algorithm that works for classification and regression tasks. It uses the ensemble learning process to iteratively train the weak classifier on the training dataset, with each successive classifier giving more weight to the data points that are misclassified. The final output of the AdaBoost model is decided by combining all the weak classifiers that have been used for training with the weightage given to the models according to their performance metrics, such as accuracies. The model that has the highest accuracy is assigned the highest weightage, and the lowest weightage is given to the model that has the lowest accuracy. The illustration of the AdaBoost classifier is shown in Fig. 11.45. From Fig. 11.45, it is possible to observe that the size of the initial training data is the same, which is the input to the "Classifier-1". From the output of Classifier-1, the misclassified training data are weighted and given as input to "Classifier-2". The size of the misclassified weighted data is bigger than the correctly classified input data. The misclassified weighted training data of Classifier-2 is further weighted before giving as input to the next classifier (i.e. Classifier-3). From Fig. 11.45, it is possible to see that the size of the misclassified weighted training data of Classifier-2 is larger than the previously correctly classified data. In the final stage of the Classifier-N, only one input training data is larger than the other training data because in the previous classifier output, there is only one input data is misclassified, and that training data alone weighted further, which can be seen in Fig. 11.45.

The AdaBoost algorithm combines many weak machine learning classifier models to create a powerful classification model. The step-by-step approach of the AdaBoost classifier is given below:

Step 1: Initialize the weights.

Let us consider the input and output pairs of the training dataset containing "n" data points, which are given by $D = \left\{ \left(X_i, y_i \right) \right\}_{i=1}^{n}$ and these data points are uniformly weighted by $\omega_i = \dfrac{1}{n}$.

Step 2: Train the weak classifiers.
Assume that there are "N" weak classifiers $\{C_k\}$ and all these weak classifiers are trained with the uniformly weighted training dataset.
Step 3: After the training process of Step 2, compute the error rate (ε_k) of each weak classifier by using

$$\varepsilon_k = \sum_{C_k(X_i) \neq y_i} \frac{\omega_i}{\sum_{X_i} \omega_i}, \ 1 \leq i \leq n \tag{11.16}$$

Step 4: From the error rate obtained from Step (3), the weight of the weak classifier for the ensemble output (α_k) is calculated as:

$$\alpha_k = \log \left(\frac{1 - \varepsilon_k}{\varepsilon_k} \right) \tag{11.17}$$

Step 5: Finally, the distribution of the weights ω_i corresponding to each X_i, which will be used as training data for the next weak classifier, is proportionally adjusted to the probability that a sample is correctly estimated and inversely proportional to the error rate of the weak classifier (ε_k).
Step 6: The final output of the AdaBoost classifier is defined as

$$\hat{y}(X) = \sum_{k=1}^{N} \left[\alpha_k \left(C_k (X) = l \right) \right] \tag{11.18}$$

Experiment 11.18: AdaBoost Classifier Algorithm for IRIS Data Classification

This experiment discusses image classification using the AdaBoost algorithm. For the image classification, the input dataset is considered as IRIS data. The Python code to implement the above-mentioned task is given in Fig. 11.46, and its corresponding output is shown in Fig. 11.47.

Inferences
The following inferences can be observed from this experiment:

- Figure 11.46 shows that the "*AdaBoostClassifier*" command is used here to build a model.
- The confusion matrix of the random forest algorithm is shown in Fig. 11.47, which indicates that the input dataset contains three different classes of input.

```
# AdaBoostClassifier
import matplotlib.pyplot as plt
from sklearn import datasets
from sklearn.model_selection import train_test_split
from sklearn.ensemble import AdaBoostClassifier
from sklearn import metrics
iris = datasets.load_iris()
X = iris.data
y = iris.target;# Output Label
X_train, X_test, y_train, y_test= train_test_split(X, y, test_size= 0.2, random_state=0)
ADB=AdaBoostClassifier()
ADB.fit(X_train, y_train)
y_pred= ADB.predict(X_test)
cm = metrics.confusion_matrix(y_test, y_pred)
plt.figure()
cm_display = metrics.ConfusionMatrixDisplay(confusion_matrix = cm, display_labels = ['Setosa',
'Versicolor', 'Virginica'])
cm_display.plot(),plt.title('Confusion Matrix'),plt.xlabel('Predicted Output')
plt.ylabel('True Output'),plt.show()
```

Fig. 11.46 Python code for AdaBoost classifier

Fig. 11.47 Confusion
matrix for AdaBoost of
IRIS dataset

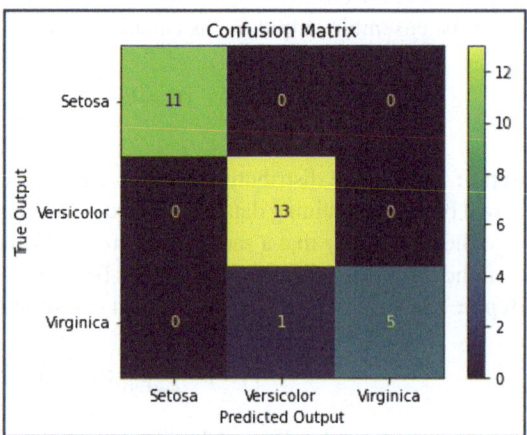

11.5   Dimensionality Reduction

Dimensionality reduction is a method used to reduce the number of features in a dataset. The reduced number of features is enough to represent the information about the actual dataset. It can also be defined as "the process of converting the higher dimensional dataset into lesser dimensions dataset ensuring that it provides similar information". In machine learning, higher dimensional data refers to data with a large number of features. Therefore, the curse of dimensionality is a common issue in machine learning, where the performance of the model weakens as the number of features increases. Also, the complexity of the model increases with the number of features increases. It may also lead to overfitting, where the model fits the training data too closely and does not generalize well to new data.

The dimensionality reduction methods are widely used in machine learning for obtaining a better-fit predictive model while solving classification and regression problems. Dimensionality reduction techniques are majorly classified into feature selection and dimensionality reduction. There are several ways to select features: missing value ratio, low variance filter, high correlation filter, random forest, backward feature extraction, and forward feature selection. Dimensionality reduction can be done through components or factors-based and projection-based reduction. The components or factors-based reduction methods are factor analysis, principal component analysis (PCA), and independent component analysis (ICA). Some of the projection-based reduction methods are ISOMAP (Isometric Mapping), t-SNE (t-distributed Stochastic Neighbour Embedding), and UMAP (Uniform Manifold Approximation and Projection).

11.5.1 Feature Selection

The process of selecting the subset of the relevant features and leaving out the irrelevant features from the dataset is called as feature selection. The selection of relevant features in a dataset plays a major role in building a high-accuracy model. The process of selecting the optimal features from the input dataset is known as feature selection. Three possible methods can be used for the feature selection: (1) Filters method, (2) Wrappers method, and (3) Embedded method. In the filters method, the irrelevant features in the dataset are filtered out, and only the relevant features are retained in the dataset. The most commonly used filter methods are correlation, chi-square test, ANOVA (Analysis of Variance), information gain, etc. In the wrappers method, some features are given as input to the machine learning algorithm and evaluate the performance. If the performance improves, then those features are added; otherwise, they are removed from the list. This method is more accurate than the filtering method, but it is complex. Some examples of wrapper methods are forward selection, backward selection, and bi-directional elimination. Embedded approaches use the feature in the different training iterations and evaluate the importance of each feature. The used feature has some importance; that feature is added to the feature selection list or else not included in the feature selection list. Examples of the embedded methods are LASSO, Elastic Net, Ridge Regression, etc.

11.5.2 Feature Extraction

Feature extraction is an algorithm that transforms the higher-dimensional space input data into lower-dimensional space. In other words, the feature extraction algorithm involves creating new features by combining or transforming the original features of the input data. The final aim of the feature extraction algorithm is to create a set of features that captures the essence of the original data in a lower dimensional space. Some of the widely used feature extraction methods are principal component analysis (PCA), linear discriminant analysis (LDA), Kernel PCA, Quadratic Discriminant Analysis, autoencoder, and t-distributed stochastic neighbour embedding (t-SNE), etc.

11.5.3 Principle Component Analysis (PCA)

Principal component analysis is an unsupervised machine learning algorithm that is used for dimensionality reduction. It is a statistical process that converts the correlated features of the data into a set of linearly uncorrelated features by using orthogonal transformation. The outputs of the orthogonal transformed features are called as "Principal Components". PCA is one of the most commonly used tools for exploratory data analysis and predictive modelling. PCA tries to find the lower dimensional surface to project the high dimensional data. It works by considering the variance of each attribute because the high attribute shows the good split between the classes, and it reduces the dimensionality. Also, it retains the important attributes and drops out the least important attributes. The flow chart of the PCA algorithm is shown in Fig. 11.48.

Experiment 11.19: Dimensionality Reduction Using PCA
This experiment discusses the implementation of principal component analysis for the IRIS dataset using Python. The IRIS dataset contains four features such as sepal length, sepal width, petal length, and petal width. The Python code for the

Fig. 11.48 Flow chart of the PCA algorithm

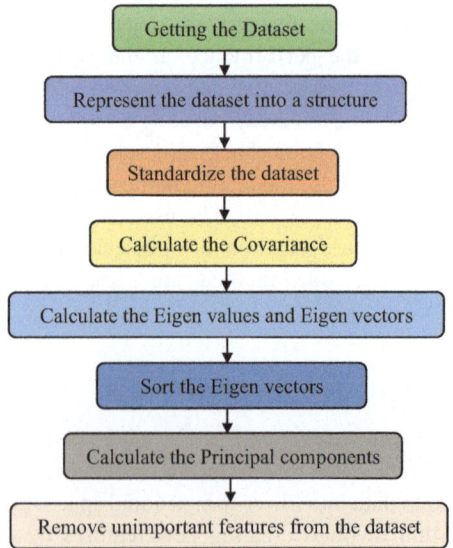

```
# Dimensionality Reduction using PCA
from sklearn import datasets
import pandas as pd
from sklearn.preprocessing import StandardScaler
from sklearn.decomposition import PCA
import seaborn as sns # to plot the heat maps
import matplotlib.pyplot as plt
iris = datasets.load_iris();#Load the Dataset
#Convert the dataset into a pandas data frame
df = pd.DataFrame(iris['data'], columns = iris['feature_names'])
print('Input Features:'),print(df.head())#display the head of the dataset
scalar = StandardScaler() #Standardize the features
scaled_data = pd.DataFrame(scalar.fit_transform(df)) #scaling the data
print('Scaled Features:'),print(scaled_data)
#Check the Correlation between input features (before PCA)
plt.figure(figsize=[8,3]),plt.subplot(1,2,1),sns.heatmap(scaled_data.corr())
plt.title('Correlated features before PCA ')
pca = PCA(n_components = 4);#Applying PCA
pca.fit(scaled_data);# PCA Model
```

Fig. 11.49 Python code for PCA

dimensionality using PCA is given in Fig. 11.49, and its simulation result is displayed in Fig. 11.50.

Inferences

The following inferences can be made from this experiment:

- From Fig. 11.49, it is possible to infer that "*sklearn*" library is used in this experiment, and "*StandardScaler*" and "PCA" Python commands are imported to standardize the dataset and obtain the principal components of the dataset, respectively. The dimensionality reduction can be done by changing the value of "*n_components*" in the Python command given by "*PCA(n_components = 4)*".
- Figure 11.50 shows the input features in the different stages of the dimensionality reduction process using PCA. Figure 11.50a displays the input features, which contain four features. Figure 11.50b, c shows the features value of scaled and PCA. Figure 11.50d confirms the correlation between the PCA features is zero compared to the correlation between the scaled features. These highly correlated features can be used for further image processing applications like image classification, object detection, etc.

```
Input Features:
      0     1     2     3
0    5.1   3.5   1.4   0.2
1    4.9   3.0   1.4   0.2
2    4.7   3.2   1.3   0.2
3    4.6   3.1   1.5   0.2
4    5.0   3.6   1.4   0.2
..   ...   ...   ...   ...
145  6.7   3.0   5.2   2.3
146  6.3   2.5   5.0   1.9
147  6.5   3.0   5.2   2.0
148  6.2   3.4   5.4   2.3
149  5.9   3.0   5.1   1.8
```

(a) Input Features

```
Scaled Features:
      0          1          2          3
0   -0.900681   1.019004  -1.340227  -1.315444
1   -1.143017  -0.131979  -1.340227  -1.315444
2   -1.385353   0.328414  -1.397064  -1.315444
3   -1.506521   0.098217  -1.283389  -1.315444
4   -1.021849   1.249201  -1.340227  -1.315444
..     ...        ...        ...        ...
145  1.038005  -0.131979   0.819596   1.448832
146  0.553333  -1.282963   0.705921   0.922303
147  0.795669  -0.131979   0.819596   1.053935
148  0.432165   0.788808   0.933271   1.448832
149  0.068662  -0.131979   0.762758   0.790671
```

(b) Scaled features

```
PCA Features:
      PC1        PC2        PC3        PC4
0   -2.264703   0.480027  -0.127706  -0.024168
1   -2.080961  -0.674134  -0.234609  -0.103007
2   -2.364229  -0.341908   0.044201  -0.028377
3   -2.299384  -0.597395   0.091290   0.065956
4   -2.389842   0.646835   0.015738   0.035923
..     ...        ...        ...
145  1.870503   0.386966   0.256274  -0.389257
146  1.564580  -0.896687  -0.026371  -0.220192
147  1.521170   0.269069   0.180178  -0.119171
148  1.372788   1.011254   0.933395  -0.026129
149  0.960656  -0.024332   0.528249   0.163078
```

(c) PCA Features

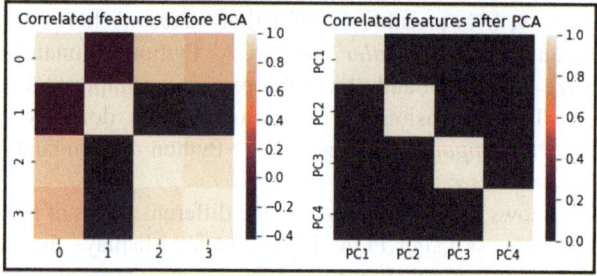

(d) Correlation between features before and after PCA

Fig. 11.50 Simulation result of PCA for IRIS dataset. (**a**) Input features. (**b**) Scaled features. (**c**) PCA features. (**d**) Correlation between features before and after PCA

11.5.4   Linear Discriminative Analysis (LDA)

The LDA is similar to a PCA, but it has the capability of finding the component axes that maximize the variance of the input features. Also, it maximizes the separation gap between multiple classes. LDA is a transformation technique that uses the output labels; therefore, it is generally a supervised learning approach.

Experiment 11.20: Dimensionality Reduction Using LDA
This experiment discusses the implementation of linear discriminative analysis for the IRIS dataset using Python. The IRIS dataset contains four features: sepal length, sepal width, petal length, and petal width. The Python code for the dimensionality using LDA is given in Fig. 11.51, and its simulation result is displayed in Fig. 11.52.

Inferences
The following inferences can be made from this experiment:

- From Fig. 11.51, it is possible to infer that "*sklearn*" library is used in this experiment, and "*StandardScaler*" and "LDA" Python commands are imported to standardize the dataset and obtain the LDA components of the dataset, respectively.

```
# Dimensionality Reduction using LDA
from sklearn import datasets
import pandas as pd
from sklearn.preprocessing import StandardScaler
from sklearn.discriminant_analysis import LinearDiscriminantAnalysis as LDA
import seaborn as sns # to plot the heat maps
import matplotlib.pyplot as plt
iris = datasets.load_iris();#Load the Dataset
y = iris.target
#Convert the dataset into a pandas data frame
df = pd.DataFrame(iris['data'], columns = iris['feature_names'])
print('Input Features:'),print(df)#display the head of the dataset
scalar = StandardScaler() #Standardize the features
scaled_data = pd.DataFrame(scalar.fit_transform(df)) #scaling the data
print('Scaled Features:'),print(scaled_data)
#Check the Correlation between input features (before LDA)
plt.figure(figsize=[8,3]),plt.subplot(1,2,1),sns.heatmap(scaled_data.corr())
plt.title('Correlated features before LDA')
lda = LDA(n_components = 2);#Applying LDA
data_lda = lda.fit_transform(scaled_data,y)
data_lda = pd.DataFrame(data_lda,columns=['LDA1','LDA2'])
print('LDA Features:'),print(data_lda)
#Check Correlation between features after LDA
plt.subplot(1,2,2),sns.heatmap(data_lda.corr())
plt.title('Correlated features after LDA')
```

Fig. 11.51 Python code for LDA

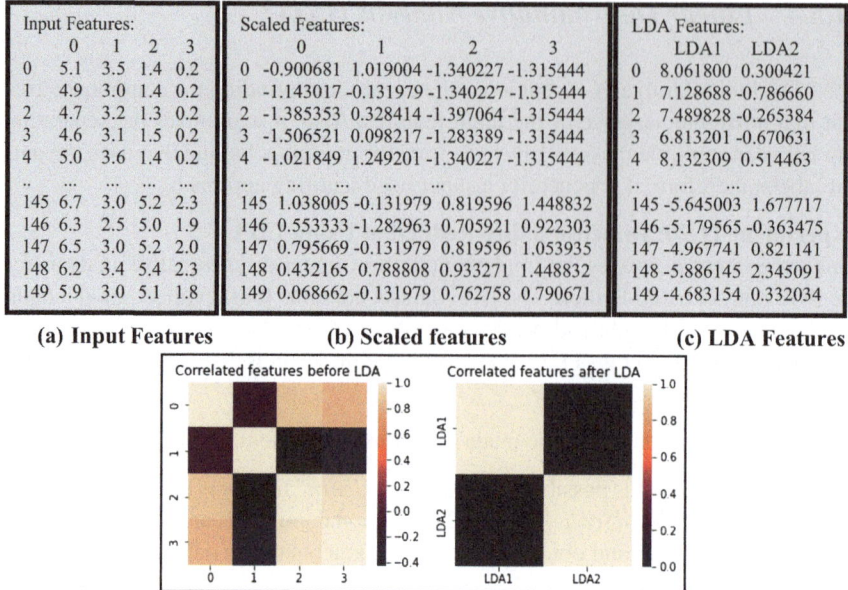

Input Features:				Scaled Features:				LDA Features:	
0	1	2	3	0	1	2	3	LDA1	LDA2
0 5.1	3.5	1.4	0.2	0 -0.900681	1.019004	-1.340227	-1.315444	0 8.061800	0.300421
1 4.9	3.0	1.4	0.2	1 -1.143017	-0.131979	-1.340227	-1.315444	1 7.128688	-0.786660
2 4.7	3.2	1.3	0.2	2 -1.385353	0.328414	-1.397064	-1.315444	2 7.489828	-0.265384
3 4.6	3.1	1.5	0.2	3 -1.506521	0.098217	-1.283389	-1.315444	3 6.813201	-0.670631
4 5.0	3.6	1.4	0.2	4 -1.021849	1.249201	-1.340227	-1.315444	4 8.132309	0.514463
.. ...	...	...	...	.. ...	...	...	...	.. ...	...
145 6.7	3.0	5.2	2.3	145 1.038005	-0.131979	0.819596	1.448832	145 -5.645003	1.677717
146 6.3	2.5	5.0	1.9	146 0.553333	-1.282963	0.705921	0.922303	146 -5.179565	-0.363475
147 6.5	3.0	5.2	2.0	147 0.795669	-0.131979	0.819596	1.053935	147 -4.967741	0.821141
148 6.2	3.4	5.4	2.3	148 0.432165	0.788808	0.933271	1.448832	148 -5.886145	2.345091
149 5.9	3.0	5.1	1.8	149 0.068662	-0.131979	0.762758	0.790671	149 -4.683154	0.332034

(a) **Input Features**   (b) **Scaled features**   (c) **LDA Features**

(d) **Correlation between features before and after LDA**

Fig. 11.52 Simulation result of LDA for IRIS dataset. (**a**) Input features. (**b**) Scaled features. (**c**) LDA features. (**d**) Correlation between features before and after LDA

- The dimensionality reduction can be done by changing the value of "*n_components*" in the Python command given by "*LDA(n_components = 2)*". However, the value of "*n_components*" must be less than the number of classes in the dataset. The IRIS dataset contains three classes, hence the number of LDA components is chosen as 2.
- Figure 11.52 shows the input features in the different stages of the dimensionality reduction process using LDA. Figure 11.52a displays the input features, which contain four features.
- Figure 11.52b, c shows the features value of scaled and LDA. Figure 11.52d confirms the correlation between the LDA features is zero compared to the correlation between the scaled features.
- These highly correlated features can be used for further image processing applications like image classification, object detection, etc.

11.5.5   Kernel PCA

The Kernel PCA (KPCA) is an extension algorithm of traditional PCA. It is used to reduce the dimensionality of the non-linear dataset with the help of kernels, which implicitly map inputs into high-dimensional feature spaces. Kernels are functions that compute the dot product between image data points in a high-dimensional feature space without requiring the coordinates of the data in that space. The steps followed in the computation of Kernel PCA as follows:

Step 1: Select a kernel function: Choose the appropriate kernel function based on the properties of the dataset.

Step 2: Compute the kernel matrix: Using the selected kernel function, compute the pairwise similarity between data points in the dataset. The resultant matrix will be a symmetric positive semi-definite matrix.

Step 3: Select the eigenvalues and eigenvectors: The greatest eigenvalues and top "k" eigenvectors are the primary components of the given input dataset and are the reduced dimensional representation of the given dataset.

Experiment 11.21: Dimensionality Reduction Using Kernel PCA
This experiment discusses the implementation of Kernel PCA for the IRIS dataset using Python. The IRIS dataset contains four features: sepal length, sepal width, petal length, and petal width. The Python code for the dimensionality reduction using Kernel PCA is given in Fig. 11.53, and its simulation result is displayed in Fig. 11.54.

Inferences
The following inferences can be made from this experiment:

- From Fig. 11.53, it is possible to infer that "*sklearn*" library is used in this experiment, and "*StandardScaler*" and "*KernelPCA*" Python commands are imported to standardize the dataset and obtain the KPCA components of the dataset, respectively. The dimensionality reduction can be done by changing the value of "*n_components*" in the Python command given by "*KernelPCA(n_components = 2, kernel = 'rbf')*".

- Figure 11.54 shows the input features in the different stages of the dimensionality reduction process using KPCA. Figure 11.54a displays the input features, which contain four features. Figure 11.54b, c shows the feature value of scaled and KPCA. Figure 11.54d confirms the correlation between the KPCA features is zero compared to the correlation between the scaled features. These highly correlated features can be used for further image processing applications like image classification, object detection, etc.

11.6 Deep Learning Algorithm

Deep learning is a subset of machine learning, and it is based on artificial neural network architecture. An artificial neural network (ANN) uses layers of interconnected nodes called neurons that work together to process and learn from the input data. ANN consists of an input layer, a hidden layer, and an output layer, whereas a deep neural network consists of an input layer, multiple hidden layers, and an output layer. Each neuron receives input from the previous layer neurons or the input

```
# Dimensionality Reduction using Kernel PCA
from sklearn import datasets
import pandas as pd
from sklearn.preprocessing import StandardScaler
from sklearn.decomposition import KernelPCA
import seaborn as sns # to plot the heat maps
import matplotlib.pyplot as plt
iris = datasets.load_iris();#Load the Dataset
y = iris.target
#Convert the dataset into a pandas data frame
df = pd.DataFrame(iris['data'], columns = iris['feature_names'])
print('Input Features:'),print(df)#display the head of the dataset
scalar = StandardScaler() #Standardize the features
scaled_data = pd.DataFrame(scalar.fit_transform(df)) #scaling the data
print('Scaled Features:'),print(scaled_data)
#Check the Correlation between input features (before KPCA)
plt.figure(figsize=[8,3]),plt.subplot(1,2,1),sns.heatmap(scaled_data.corr())
plt.title('Correlated features before Kernel PCA')
kpca = KernelPCA(n_components = 2,kernel = 'rbf');#Applying Kernel PCA
data_kpca = kpca.fit_transform(scaled_data,y)
data_kpca = pd.DataFrame(data_kpca,columns=['KPCA1','KPCA2'])
print('Kernel PCA Features:'),print(data_kpca)
#Check Correlation between features after KPCA
plt.subplot(1,2,2),sns.heatmap(data_kpca.corr())
plt.title('Correlated features after Kernel PCA')
```

Fig. 11.53 Python code for Kernel PCA

layer. The output of one neuron becomes the input to other neurons in the next layer of the network, and this process continues until the final layer produces the network output. The neural network layers transform the input data through a series of non-linear transformations, permitting the network to learn complex representations of the input data. The base of the deep learning network is the artificial neural networks. The architecture of the artificial neural network is shown in Fig. 11.55. From this figure, it is possible to observe that the neural network architecture consists of the input, hidden, and output layers. The input layer is the first layer of the neural network architecture; it receives input from external sources and transfers it to the hidden layer. The hidden layer is the second layer of the ANN; it gets information from the input or previous layer, computes the weighted total, and transfers the result to the next layer. The weights of each input from the preceding layer are more or less optimized by giving each input a distinct weight. These weights are then adjusted during the training process to enhance the performance of the model. Each circle in Fig. 11.55 shows the artificial neuron, which is also called a unit. The complete ANN comprises the artificial neurons, which are arranged in a series of layers.

Input Features:					Scaled Features:					Kernel PCA Features:	
	0	1	2	3		0	1	2	3	KPCA1	KPCA2
0	5.1	3.5	1.4	0.2	0	-0.900681	1.019004	-1.340227	-1.315444	0 0.802038	-0.093750
1	4.9	3.0	1.4	0.2	1	-1.143017	-0.131979	-1.340227	-1.315444	1 0.665623	0.109343
2	4.7	3.2	1.3	0.2	2	-1.385353	0.328414	-1.397064	-1.315444	2 0.758616	0.012529
3	4.6	3.1	1.5	0.2	3	-1.506521	0.098217	-1.283389	-1.315444	3 0.706189	0.056918
4	5.0	3.6	1.4	0.2	4	-1.021849	1.249201	-1.340227	-1.315444	4 0.793607	-0.126192
..	...	...	...	...	..	...	...	...	...	..	...
145	6.7	3.0	5.2	2.3	145	1.038005	-0.131979	0.819596	1.448832	145 -0.474052 -	
146	6.3	2.5	5.0	1.9	146	0.553333	-1.282963	0.705921	0.922303	0.464977	
147	6.5	3.0	5.2	2.0	147	0.795669	-0.131979	0.819596	1.053935	146 -0.439752	0.154730
148	6.2	3.4	5.4	2.3	148	0.432165	0.788808	0.933271	1.448832	147 -0.536161 -	
149	5.9	3.0	5.1	1.8	149	0.068662	-0.131979	0.762758	0.790671	0.322908	

(a) **Input Features**   (b) **Scaled features**   (c) **Kernel PCA Features**

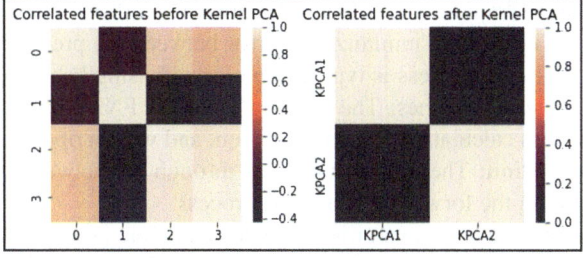

(d) **Correlation between features before and after Kernel PCA**

Fig. 11.54 Simulation result of Kernel PCA for IRIS dataset. (**a**) Input features. (**b**) Scaled features. (**c**) Kernel PCA features. (**d**) Correlation between features before and after Kernel PCA

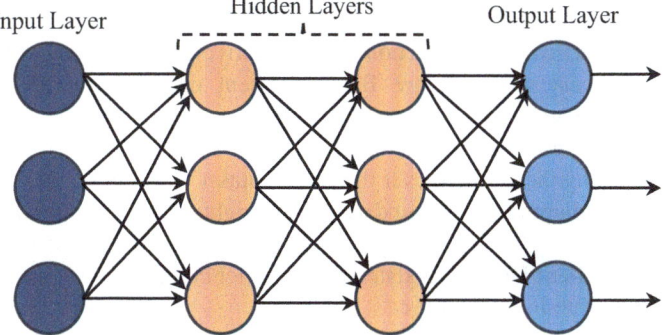

Fig. 11.55 Architecture of artificial neural network

Deep learning models are capable of learning features from the data automatically, and those learned features are well suited for image processing applications such as image recognition, speech recognition, object detection, etc. The most widely used architectures in deep learning models are feedforward neural networks (FNNs), convolutional neural networks (CNNs), and recurrent neural networks (RNNs).

11.6.1   Feedforward Neural Networks

The feedforward neural network is the core of many other neural networks, such as convolution neural networks, RNN, etc. The process of getting an input to produce some output to make some kind of prediction is known as "feed forward". The feedforward neural network has no feedback loops or connections in the network architecture. It has an input layer, hidden layers, and an output layer. The important terminologies of Neural Network are as follows:

Activation Functions: Activation functions are used to introduce the non-linearity into the network, enabling it to learn and model complex data patterns. The commonly used activation functions are sigmoid, tanh, ReLU, and Leaky ReLU.

Training Process: Training a feedforward neural network involves adjusting the weights of the neurons to minimize the error between the predicted output and the true output. This process is typically performed using backpropagation and gradient descent approaches. The training phase of FNN consists of forward propagation, loss calculation, backpropagation, and weight optimization.

Forward Propagation: The input data passes through the network, and output is calculated during the forward propagation process.

Loss Calculation: The loss or error is calculated using the loss function like mean square error (MSE) for regression problems and Cross entropy for classification problems during the Loss calculation process.

Backpropagation Process: In backpropagation process, the loss is propagated back through the network to update the weights of the neural network.

Optimization of the weights of the neural network is done by the gradient descent approach based on the loss function. The gradient descent approach is an optimization algorithm used to minimize the error function in an iterative manner to update the weights in the direction of the negative gradient. The variants of the gradient descent approach are Batch gradient descent, stochastic gradient descent, mini-batch gradient descent, etc.

Batch Gradient Descent: The batch gradient descent approach updates the weights after computing the gradient over the entire dataset.

Stochastic Gradient Descent updates the weights for each training sample individually.

Min-batch Gradient Descent updates weights after computing the gradient over a small batch of training samples.

After the training process, the evaluation of the feedforward neural network is based on metrics like accuracy, precision, recall, F1 score, and confusion matrix.

Implementation of Feedforward Neural Network

This experiment discusses the Python implementation of a feedforward neural network for image classification tasks. For this implementation, TensorFlow and Keras are used to build, train, and evaluate a neural network model to classify handwritten digits from the MNIST dataset.

TensorFlow: TensorFlow is an open-source machine learning library developed by Google. TensorFlow is used to build and train deep learning models as it

Fig. 11.56 TensorFlow
diagram

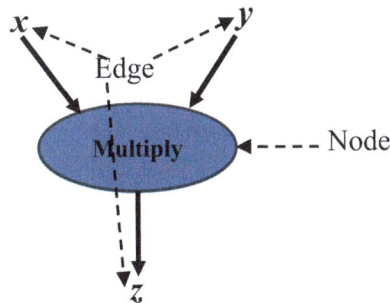

simplifies the creation of computational graphs and efficient execution on various hardware platforms. TensorFlow is basically a software library for numerical computation using data flow graphs, which contain nodes and edges. The nodes in the graph denote the mathematical operations, whereas edges in the graph represent the multidimensional data arrays, which are called as "tensors" communicated between them. Let us consider a TensorFlow diagram, which is shown in Fig. 11.56. In this figure "multiply" is a node, which denotes multiplication operation and x and y are input edges or tensors and z is the result edge or tensor. This flexible architecture permits us to deploy computation to one or more CPUs or GPUs in PC, server, or mobile device with a single application programming interface (API).

The important terminologies in TensorFlow are as follows:

1. **Computational Graph:** It is a series of TensorFlow operations arranged into a graph of nodes. Running the computational graph is to evaluate the nodes, it should be run the computational graph within a session. The computational graph is created using "*node = tensorflow.constant*(10, dtype=tf.int32)" Python command.

2. **Session:** It summarizes the control and state of the TensorFlow runtime. To run the computational graph, "*session*" must be created by using "ss = tensorflow. Session()" and after the execution of the computational graph, the session must be closed by using "ss.close()".

3. **Variables:** TensorFlow has variable nodes, which are used to hold variable data. These variables are used to hold and update the parameters of a training model. Variables are in memory buffers containing tensors. It must be explicitly initialized and saved to disk during and after training. The difference between a constant and a variable is that a constant value is stored in the graph, and its value is replicated wherever the graph is loaded, whereas a variable is stored separately and may live on a parameter server. The variable can be created using "*tensorflow.Variable*()" command.

4. **Placeholder:** A graph can be parameterized to accept external inputs, called as "placeholders". A placeholder is a promise to provide a value later. While evaluating the graph involving placeholder nodes, a feed_dict parameter is passed to the session's run method to specify tensors that provide concrete values to the placeholders. The "*tensorflow.placeholder*()" command creates a placeholder.

Keras: It is a high-level and user-friendly API for building and training neural networks. It is an open-source library built in Python that runs on top of TensorFlow. It is developed to enable fast experimentation and iteration, and it lowers the barrier to entry with deep learning.

Sequential Model: A sequential model is a linear stack of layers used for building a simple feedforward neural network architecture. A sequential model represents a straightforward way to create a neural network where each layer is stacked sequentially, and the data flows sequentially through each layer. Because of the sequential way of data flow, it is more suitable for designing a feedforward neural network. In feedforward neural networks, the data or information passes through the layers in a fixed order, from the input layer through hidden layers to the output layer. The following Python commands can be used to build a feedforward NN, they are:

Sequential(): This function initializes an empty sequential model, which is imported from TensorFlow and Keras.

Flatten(): This function denotes the flatten layer, which converts the 2D image into a 1D array.

Dense(): This function denotes Dense layer, which specifies the number of units or neurons in the first layer based on the input and activation function. Mostly the first layer activation function will be "ReLU". Suppose the Dense layer is used for the output layer with a number of output neurons. The "softmax" activation function is commonly preferred for multiclass classification tasks.

Experiment 11.22: Feedforward NN Using Sequential Model

This experiment deals with the implementation of feedforward neural network using a sequential model for MNIST data classification. It demonstrates the process of network building, training, and testing the MNIST data classification using TensorFlow and Keras. In the first step, the MNIST dataset is loaded and normalized by scaling the pixel values within the range of 0 and 1. The model architecture is represented using the sequential model, consisting of flatten and dense layers. The Python code to build a feedforward NN using the Sequential model is given in Fig. 11.57, and its simulation result is shown in Fig. 11.58.

Inferences

The following inferences can be drawn from Fig. 11.57:

- *"TensorFlow"* and *"Keras"* libraries are imported. Also, in the sequential model, layers like Input, Flatten, and Dense are imported for creating the feedforward NN.
- The *"Adam"* optimizer and *"SparseCategoricalCrossentropy"* loss functions are imported to train the model for the weights update.
- MNIST dataset is loaded for the training and evaluation of the feedforward NN model.
- The *"Sequential"* command is used to create an empty feedforward NN model. The Flatten layer is used to flatten the input image, two hidden layers are created using a Dense layer with a number of neurons 512 and 128, and the "ReLU" activation function is used in both hidden layers formation. The output layer is

```
# Feedforward Neural network using Sequential model
import tensorflow as tf
from tensorflow.keras.models import Sequential
from tensorflow.keras.layers import Input, Dense, Flatten
from tensorflow.keras.optimizers import Adam
from tensorflow.keras.losses import SparseCategoricalCrossentropy
from tensorflow.keras.metrics import SparseCategoricalAccuracy
mnist = tf.keras.datasets.mnist;# Load MNIST dataset
(x_train, y_train), (x_test, y_test) = mnist.load_data()
x_train, x_test = x_train / 255.0, x_test / 255.0; # Normalise the dataset
# Define Sequential model
FNN = Sequential([
    Input(shape=(28, 28)),  # Define input shape as the first layer
    Flatten(),  # Flatten the input
    Dense(units=512, activation='relu'), # Hidden layer 1
    Dense(units=128, activation='relu'), # Hidden layer 2
    Dense(units=10, activation='softmax') # Output layer
])
FNN.compile(optimizer=Adam(),loss=SparseCategoricalCrossentropy(),
        metrics=[SparseCategoricalAccuracy()]);# Compile the model
FNN.fit(x_train, y_train, epochs=10);# Training phase
test_loss, test_acc = FNN.evaluate(x_test, y_test); # Testing or evaluating phase
print(f'\nTest accuracy: {test_acc}'),print(f'\nTest Loss: {test_loss}')
print('Model Summary:'),FNN.summary()
```

Fig. 11.57 Creation of Feedforward neural network using sequential model

created using the Dense with a number of output neurons 10 because the number of digits in the MNIST dataset is 10 digits (0–9) handwritten characters and the "Sigmoid" activation function is used.

- Compilation of the build model is done by "compile" Python command with the "*Adam*" optimizer, "*SparseCategoricalCrossentropy*" loss function, and "*SparseCategoricalAccuracy*" performance metric function.
- The "*fit*" and "*evaluate*" commands are used to train and test the model, respectively.

The following inferences can be made from Fig. 11.58:

- The model is a sequential model, which contains a Flatten layer and three Dense layers, in which two are hidden layers and the final one is an output layer.
- The test accuracy is obtained as 98%, and the test loss is 8%.
- From the summary of the model, it is possible to observe that the size of the output of each layer and the number of parameters in each layer were also obtained.

Test accuracy: 0.9814000129699707
Test Loss: 0.08104995638132095
Model Summary:
Model: "sequential"

Layer (type)	Output Shape	Param #
flatten (Flatten)	(None, 784)	0
dense (Dense)	(None, 512)	401,920
dense_1 (Dense)	(None, 128)	65,664
dense_2 (Dense)	(None, 10)	1,290

Total params: 1,406,624 (5.37 MB)
Trainable params: 468,874 (1.79 MB)
Non-trainable params: 0 (0.00 B)
Optimizer params: 937,750 (3.58 MB)

Fig. 11.58 Simulation result

Experiment 11.23: Feedforward NN Using Functional Model
This experiment deals with the implementation of feedforward neural network using functional model for MNIST data classification. It demonstrates the process of network building, training, and testing the MNIST data classification using TensorFlow and Keras. In the first step, the MNIST dataset is loaded and normalized by scaling the pixel values within the range of 0 and 1. The model architecture is represented using the functional model, which consists of flatten, and dense layers. The Python code to build a feedforward NN using a functional model is given in Fig. 11.59, and its simulation result is shown in Fig. 11.60.

Inferences
The following inferences can be drawn from Fig. 11.59:

- *"TensorFlow"* and *"Keras"* libraries are imported. Also, layers like input, flatten, and dense are imported to create the feedforward NN.
- MNIST dataset is loaded and normalized for training and evaluating the feedforward NN model.
- "to_categorical" command is imported and used to create a matrix with binary values and columns equal to the number of categories in the data. For example, in the MNIST dataset, the output labels vary from 0 to 9. This command converts a single output label into a 1 by 10 array, which contains 1 corresponding to the actual output label and other elements are zero.

```
import tensorflow as tf
from tensorflow.keras.layers import Input, Dense, Flatten
from tensorflow.keras.models import Model
from tensorflow.keras.utils import to_categorical
mnist = tf.keras.datasets.mnist;# Load MNIST dataset
(x_train, y_train), (x_test, y_test) = mnist.load_data()
x_train, x_test = x_train / 255.0, x_test / 255.0; # Normalise the dataset
y_train = to_categorical(y_train, num_classes=10)
y_test = to_categorical(y_test, num_classes=10)
# Define input layer
input_layer = Input(shape=(28, 28))
flatten_layer=Flatten()(input_layer)
# Create hidden layer 1
hidden_layer = Dense(units=128, activation='relu')(flatten_layer)
# Create hidden layer 2
hidden_layer1 = Dense(units=64, activation='relu')(hidden_layer)
# Create output layer
output_layer = Dense(units=10, activation='softmax')(hidden_layer1)
# Define the model
FNN = Model(inputs=input_layer, outputs=output_layer)
# Compile the model and specify loss, optimizer, etc.
FNN.compile(optimizer='adam', loss='categorical_crossentropy', metrics=['accuracy'])
FNN.fit(x_train, y_train, epochs=10);# Training phase
test_loss, test_acc = FNN.evaluate(x_test, y_test); # Testing or evaluating phase
print(f'\nTest accuracy: {test_acc}'),print(f'\nTest Loss: {test_loss}')
print('Model Summary:')
FNN.summary()
```

Fig. 11.59 Creation of feedforward neural network using functional model

- Initially, input, flatten, hidden, and output layers are created using "Input", "Flatten", "Dense", and "Dense" commands. Then finally, "Model" command is used to build a feedforward NN model.
- Two hidden layers are created with the size of neurons 128 and 64, respectively.
- An output layer is created with a size of neurons 10 for 10 class classification tasks.
- Compilation of the build model is done by the "compile" Python command with the "*Adam*" optimizer, "*SparseCategoricalCrossentropy*" loss function, and "*SparseCategoricalAccuracy*" performance metric function.
- The "*fit*" and "*evaluate*" commands are used to train and test the model, respectively.

The following inferences can be made from Fig. 11.60:

- The functional model contains a flatten layer and three dense layers, in which two are hidden layers and the final one is an output layer.
- The test accuracy is obtained as 97.6%, and the test loss is 9%.

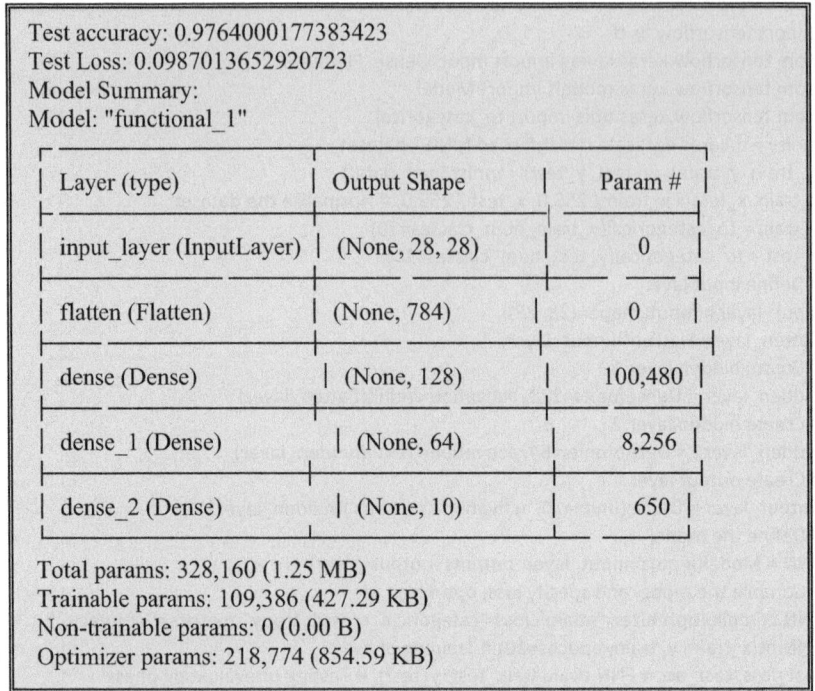

Test accuracy: 0.9764000177383423
Test Loss: 0.09870013652920723
Model Summary:
Model: "functional_1"

Layer (type)	Output Shape	Param #
input_layer (InputLayer)	(None, 28, 28)	0
flatten (Flatten)	(None, 784)	0
dense (Dense)	(None, 128)	100,480
dense_1 (Dense)	(None, 64)	8,256
dense_2 (Dense)	(None, 10)	650

Total params: 328,160 (1.25 MB)
Trainable params: 109,386 (427.29 KB)
Non-trainable params: 0 (0.00 B)
Optimizer params: 218,774 (854.59 KB)

Fig. 11.60 Simulation result

- From the summary of the model, it is possible to observe that the size of the output of each layer and the number of parameters in each layer was also obtained.

11.6.2   Convolutional Neural Network

A convolutional neural network (CNN) is a type of deep learning model that's particularly well-suited for analyzing images and videos. CNNs have gained popularity because they can automatically identify features in visual data, which makes them ideal for tasks like recognizing objects in pictures, classifying images, or even detecting faces. Unlike traditional machine learning techniques that require a lot of manual feature extraction, CNNs learn directly from the data. The convolutional neural network consists of six different layers such as (1) Input layer, (2) Convoluation layer (Convolution + ReLU), (3) Pooling layer, (4) Fully connected layer, (5) Softmax/logistic layer, and (6) Output layer.

The convolutional layers at the heart of a CNN use small filters to scan images and pick up basic patterns like edges, textures, and simple shapes. As the network processes the data, these basic features combine to form more complex structures in the deeper layers, helping the model understand what objects or features are present in the image.

Another important part of CNNs is the pooling layers, which helps to reduce the size of the data by down-sampling, making the model faster and more efficient. This also helps to prevent overfitting by keeping the most important information and discarding the noise.

Overall, CNNs have revolutionized how computers interpret visual information, powering everything from self-driving cars to medical image analysis. By learning directly from the raw data, they are able to outperform traditional methods in many real-world applications.

Experiment 11.24: Design of CNN Model for CIFAR10 Data Classification
This experiment discusses the development of the CNN model for CIFAR10 data classification. The CIFAR-10 dataset consists of 60,000 (32 × 32 × 3 (colours)) images in 10 different classes like "airplane", "automobile", "bird", "cat", "deer", "dog", "frog", "horse", "ship", and "truck". Each class contains 6000 images and, in total, 50,000 images for training and 10,000 images for testing. The dataset is split into five training batches and one test batch, each with 10,000 images. The test batch contains exactly 1000 randomly selected images from each class. The training batches contain the remaining images in random order. This dataset was created by Alex Krizhevsky, Vinod Nair, and Geoffrey Hinton. The CNN model architecture is shown in Fig. 11.61. This experiment explores the creation of the above-mentioned CNN architecture using Python. The CNN architecture contains a few convolution layers with ReLU activation followed by a max pooling layer and then a dropout layer. This same structure may be followed by different dimensions of the convolution kernels, which are used to extract more features from the input data, and the flatten layer is used to convert the multidimensional features into a 1D array then followed by a dense layer, which is a fully connected layer with the ReLU activation

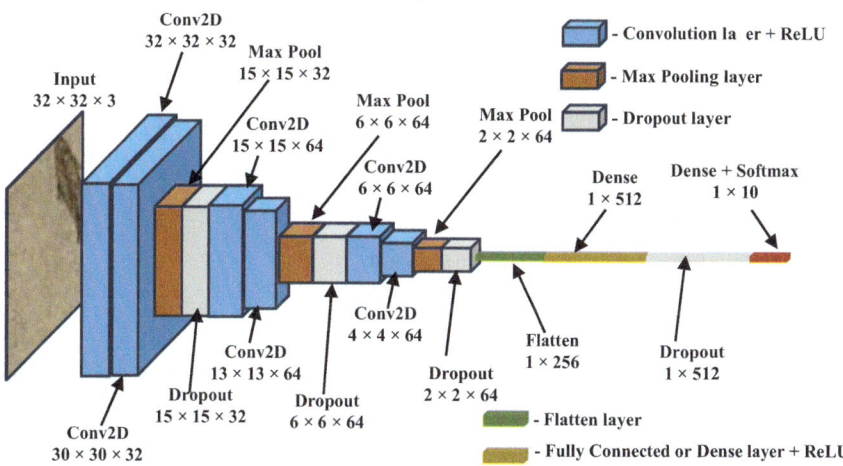

Fig. 11.61 Architecture of CNN model for CIFAR10 data classification

function. Finally, the dense layer with softmax activation function is the output layer for the classification tasks.

The Python code for the CNN model for CIFAR10 data classification is shown in Fig. 11.62. The simulation result of this classification task is shown in Fig. 11.63.

```python
# CNN model creation for classification
import numpy as np
import matplotlib.pyplot as plt
from keras.models import Sequential
from keras.utils import to_categorical
from keras.layers import Dense, Conv2D, MaxPooling2D, Dropout, Flatten
from keras.datasets import cifar10
(train_images, train_labels), (test_images, test_labels) = cifar10.load_data()
# Find the unique numbers from the train labels
classes = np.unique(train_labels)
nClasses = len(classes)
plt.figure(figsize=[8,6]),plt.subplot(121);# Display the first image in testing data
plt.imshow(train_images[10,:,:], cmap='gray')
plt.title("{}th Ground Truth (Train)".format(train_labels[10])),plt.axis('off')
plt.subplot(122),plt.imshow(test_images[10,:,:], cmap='gray')
plt.title("{}th Ground Truth (Test)".format(test_labels[15])),plt.axis('off')
nRows,nCols,nDims = train_images.shape[1:]
train_data = train_images.reshape(train_images.shape[0], nRows, nCols, nDims)
test_data = test_images.reshape(test_images.shape[0], nRows, nCols, nDims)
input_shape = (nRows, nCols, nDims)
train_data = train_data.astype('float32')
test_data = test_data.astype('float32')
train_data /= 255
test_data /= 255
train_labels_one_hot = to_categorical(train_labels)
test_labels_one_hot = to_categorical(test_labels)
def CNN_Model():
    CNN = Sequential()
    # The first two layers with 32 filters of window size 3x3
    CNN.add(Conv2D(32, (3, 3), padding='same', activation='relu', input_shape=input_shape))
    CNN.add(Conv2D(32, (3, 3), activation='relu'))
    CNN.add(MaxPooling2D(pool_size=(2, 2)))
    CNN.add(Dropout(0.25))
   # The second two layers with 64 filters of window size 3x3
    CNN.add(Conv2D(64, (3, 3), padding='same', activation='relu'))
    CNN.add(Conv2D(64, (3, 3), activation='relu'))
    CNN.add(MaxPooling2D(pool_size=(2, 2)))
    CNN.add(Dropout(0.25))
  # The third two layers with 64 filters of window size 3x3
    CNN.add(Conv2D(64, (3, 3), padding='same', activation='relu'))
    CNN.add(Conv2D(64, (3, 3), activation='relu'))
    CNN.add(MaxPooling2D(pool_size=(2, 2)))
    CNN.add(Dropout(0.25))
  # Flatten, Fully connected and output layer
    CNN.add(Flatten())
    CNN.add(Dense(512, activation='relu'))
    CNN.add(Dropout(0.5))
    CNN.add(Dense(nClasses, activation='softmax'))
    return CNN
```

Fig. 11.62 Python code for CNN modelling

```
CNN = CNN_Model()
batch_size, epochs = 256, 50
CNN.compile(optimizer='rmsprop', loss='categorical_crossentropy', metrics=['accuracy'])
history = CNN.fit(train_data, train_labels_one_hot, batch_size=batch_size, epochs=epochs,
verbose=1, validation_data=(test_data, test_labels_one_hot))
test_loss, test_acc=CNN.evaluate(test_data, test_labels_one_hot)
print('Test accuracy: {test_acc}'),print('Test Loss: {test_loss}')
print('Model Summary:'),CNN.summary()
```

Fig. 11.62 (continued)

Inferences

The following inferences can be drawn from this experiment:

- From Fig. 11.62, it is possible to infer that the "Sequential" model is imported from the "Keras.models" library, different layers of the CNN model like Dense, Conv2D, MaxPooling2D, Dropout, and Flatten from the "Keras.layers" library. CIFAR10 dataset is imported for training and testing.
- The "to_categorical" is a numpy array (or) a vector that has integers that represent different categories, can be converted into a numpy array (or) a matrix that has binary values and has columns equal to the number of categories in the data.
- The CNN model is created using the imported different layers from "Keras.layers".
- Initial Conv2D contains 32 convolution filters size of 3×3 and with "ReLU" activation function, and the second convolution layer also contains 32 convolution filters with the size of 3×3, and the activation function used is "ReLU". The next layer is the max pooling layer with a reduction size of 2×2, and the final one is the Dropout layer, which randomly sets 25% of the neuron units to zero during training, effectively dropping them out of the network for that iteration.
- In the final stage, the flatten layer is used to convert the 2D array to a 1D array, passed through a fully connected layer with the "ReLU" activation function and finally, another fully connected layer with the "softmax" activation function, giving the final classification output.
- The "CNN.compile" command is used to configure the created model with suitable parameters like, "loss function", "optimizer" and "metrics".
- The "CNN.fit" command is used to train the model, and the "CNN.evaluate" command is used to test the model and obtain performance metrics of the created model.
- From Fig. 11.63, it is possible to observe that the summary of the created model is displayed, and test accuracy and test loss are also seen from it.

Task: Vary the values of batch_size and epochs in the Python code given in Fig. 11.62 and comment on the test accuracy and test loss results.

Test accuracy: 0.7777000069618225
Test Loss: 0.6984601616859436
Model Summary:
Model: "sequential"

Layer (type)	Output Shape	Param #
conv2d (Conv2D)	(None, 32, 32, 32)	896
conv2d_1 (Conv2D)	(None, 30, 30, 32)	9,248
max_pooling2d (MaxPooling2D)	(None, 15, 15, 32)	0
dropout (Dropout)	(None, 15, 15, 32)	0
conv2d_2 (Conv2D)	(None, 15, 15, 64)	18,496
conv2d_3 (Conv2D)	(None, 13, 13, 64)	36,928
max_pooling2d_1 (MaxPooling2D)	(None, 6, 6, 64)	0
dropout_1 (Dropout)	(None, 6, 6, 64)	0
conv2d_4 (Conv2D)	(None, 6, 6, 64)	36,928
conv2d_5 (Conv2D)	(None, 4, 4, 64)	36,928
max_pooling2d_2 (MaxPooling2D)	(None, 2, 2, 64)	0
dropout_2 (Dropout)	(None, 2, 2, 64)	0
flatten (Flatten)	(None, 256)	0
dense (Dense)	(None, 512)	131,584
dropout_3 (Dropout)	(None, 512)	0
dense_1 (Dense)	(None, 10)	5,130

Total params: 552,278 (2.11 MB)
Trainable params: 276,138 (1.05 MB)
Non-trainable params: 0 (0.00 B)
Optimizer params: 276,140 (1.05 MB)

Fig. 11.63 Simulation result of CNN model

11.6.3   AlexNet

AlexNet was first proposed by Alex Krizhevsky, Ilya Sutskever, and Geoffrey Hinton in the 2012 "ImageNet Large Scale Visual Recognition Challenge" (ILSVRC-2012). It is a fundamental, simple, and effective CNN architecture containing convolution layers, pooling layers, rectified linear unit (ReLU) layers, and fully connected layers. Specifically, AlexNet is composed of five convolutional

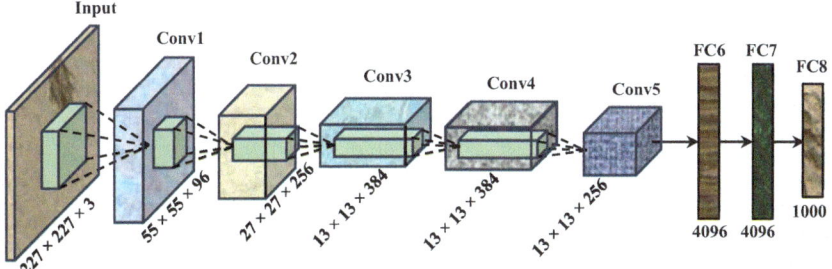

Fig. 11.64 AlexNet architecture

layers: the first layer, the second layer, the third layer, and the fourth layer, followed by the pooling layer, and the fifth layer, followed by three fully connected layers, which is shown in Fig. 11.64. For the AlexNet architecture, the convolutional kernels are extracted during the back-propagation optimization procedure by optimizing the whole cost function with the stochastic gradient descent (SGD) algorithm. Generally, the convolutional layers act upon the input feature maps with the sliding convolutional kernels to generate the convolved feature maps, and the pooling layers operate on the convolved feature maps to aggregate the information within the given neighbourhood window with a max pooling operation or average pooling operation. The reason why AlexNet is successful can be attributed to some practical strategies, such as the ReLU non-linearity layer and the dropout regularization technique. The ReLU is a half-wave rectifier function, which can significantly accelerate the training phase and prevent overfitting. The dropout technique can be regarded as a kind of regularization by stochastically setting a number of the input neurons or hidden neurons to be zero to reduce the co-adaptations of the neurons, which is usually utilized in the fully connected layers in the AlexNet architecture. The important features of AlexNet are as follows: (1) The input image size could be $227 \times 227 \times 3$; if the input image is other than this size, it could be resized by using some padding approach. (2) The Batch size is fixed as 128. (3) Stochastic Gradient Descent optimization algorithm is used as a learning algorithm.

Experiment 11.25: Implementation of AlexNet Model for Image Classification
This experiment discusses the implementation and training of the AlexNet architecture using "PyTorch" for image classification tasks. It outlines the model architecture, data preprocessing, and training methodology. The Python code for image classification using AlexNet is given in Fig. 11.65, and its simulation result is shown in Fig. 11.66. The AlexNet model consists of five convolution layers, three max pooling layers, and three fully connected layers. ReLU activation function is applied after each layer to introduce non-linearity. Data preprocessing is used to ensure compatibility with AlexNet and improve model generation, which includes resizing, normalization, and data augmentation. The dataset is loaded using PyTorch's "ImageFolder" class, and data is batched using "DataLoader" with a batch size of 32. The training process involves (1) Initialization-Number of output classes and weights. (2) Loss function-Cross Entropy Loss is used to compute classification

```
# AlexNet
import torch
import torch.nn as nn
import torch.optim as optim
import torch.nn.functional as F
from torch.utils.data import DataLoader
from torchvision import transforms, datasets
import matplotlib.pyplot as plt
# Define the AlexNet Model in PyTorch
class AlexNet(nn.Module):
    def __init__(self, num_classes=20):
        super(AlexNet, self).__init__()
        self.conv1 = nn.Conv2d(3, 64, kernel_size=3, stride=1, padding=1)
        self.pool = nn.MaxPool2d(kernel_size=2, stride=2)
        self.conv2 = nn.Conv2d(64, 192, kernel_size=3, stride=1, padding=1)
        self.conv3 = nn.Conv2d(192, 384, kernel_size=3, stride=1, padding=1)
        self.conv4 = nn.Conv2d(384, 384, kernel_size=3, stride=1, padding=1)
        self.conv5 = nn.Conv2d(384, 256, kernel_size=3, stride=1, padding=1)
        # Placeholder size for the fully connected layer
        self.fc1 = nn.Linear(256 * 28 * 28, 4096)
        self.fc2 = nn.Linear(4096, 4096)
        self.fc3 = nn.Linear(4096, num_classes)
    def forward(self, x):
        x = F.relu(self.conv1(x))
        x = self.pool(x)
        x = F.relu(self.conv2(x))
        x = self.pool(x)
        x = F.relu(self.conv3(x))
        x = F.relu(self.conv4(x))
        x = F.relu(self.conv5(x))
        x = self.pool(x)
        # Flatten the tensor for fully connected layers
        x = x.view(x.size(0), -1)  # Flatten dynamically based on input size
        x = F.relu(self.fc1(x))
        x = F.relu(self.fc2(x))
        x = self.fc3(x)
        return x
# Data augmentation and normalization for training
train_transforms = transforms.Compose([transforms.Resize((224, 224)),
    transforms.ToTensor(),transforms.Normalize(mean=[0.485, 0.456, 0.406],
                          std=[0.229, 0.224, 0.225]),])
val_test_transforms = transforms.Compose([
    transforms.Resize((224, 224)),transforms.ToTensor(),
    transforms.Normalize(mean=[0.485, 0.456, 0.406], std=[0.229, 0.224, 0.225]),])
train_dir = 'D:\\Veeraa 2021\\PSG\\DIP using Python\\data_h\\train'
val_dir = 'D:\\Veeraa 2021\\PSG\\DIP using Python\\data_h\\valid'
test_dir = 'D:\\Veeraa 2021\\PSG\\DIP using Python\\data_h\\test'
train_data = datasets.ImageFolder(root=train_dir, transform=train_transforms)
val_data = datasets.ImageFolder(root=val_dir, transform=val_test_transforms)
test_data = datasets.ImageFolder(root=test_dir, transform=val_test_transforms)
```

Fig. 11.65 Python code for AlexNet

```
train_loader = DataLoader(train_data, batch_size=32, shuffle=True)
val_loader = DataLoader(val_data, batch_size=32, shuffle=False)
test_loader = DataLoader(test_data, batch_size=32, shuffle=False)
model = AlexNet(num_classes=20);# Initialize model, criterion, and optimizer
device = torch.device('cuda' if torch.cuda.is_available() else 'cpu')
model.to(device)  # Move model to GPU if available
print(device)
criterion = nn.CrossEntropyLoss()
optimizer = optim.RMSprop(model.parameters(), lr=0.001)
# Train the model
epochs,train_acc_history,test_acc_history = 5,[],[]
for epoch in range(epochs):
  model.train()
  correct_train = 0
  total_train = 0
  for inputs, labels in train_loader:
    inputs, labels = inputs.to(device), labels.to(device)  # Move data to GPU
    optimizer.zero_grad()
    outputs = model(inputs)
    loss = criterion(outputs, labels)
    loss.backward()
    optimizer.step()
    _, predicted = torch.max(outputs, 1)
    total_train += labels.size(0)
    correct_train += (predicted == labels).sum().item()
  train_accuracy = 100 * correct_train / total_train
  train_acc_history.append(train_accuracy)
  model.eval();# Evaluate on validation set
  correct_val,total_val = 0, 0
  with torch.no_grad():
    for inputs, labels in val_loader:
      inputs, labels = inputs.to(device), labels.to(device)  # Move data to GPU
      outputs = model(inputs)
      _, predicted = torch.max(outputs, 1)
      total_val += labels.size(0)
      correct_val += (predicted == labels).sum().item()
  test_accuracy = 100 * correct_val / total_val
  test_acc_history.append(test_accuracy)
  print(f"Epoch {epoch+1}/{epochs} - Train Accuracy: {train_accuracy:.2f}% - Test Accuracy:
{test_accuracy:.2f}%")
plt.figure(figsize=(10, 5));# Plot accuracy vs epoch
plt.plot(range(epochs), train_acc_history, label="Train Accuracy")
plt.plot(range(epochs), test_acc_history, label="Test Accuracy"),plt.xlabel('Epochs'),
plt.ylabel('Accuracy (%)'),plt.title('Training and Test Accuracy vs Epoch')
plt.legend(),plt.show()
```

Fig. 11.65 (continued)

error. (3) Optimizer-RMSProp is chosen with a learning rate of 0.001 for weight updates. (4) Training Loop-For each epoch: Inputs are applied through the model to compute predictions, Gradients are calculated using backpropagation, optimizer updates model weights, and training and validation accuracies are obtained.

Inferences

The following inferences can be drawn from this experiment:

- From Fig. 11.65, it is possible to infer that "torch.nn" is imported from the "PyTorch" library, different layers of CNN model like Conv2d, MaxPooling2d, and Linear from "torch.nn" library. "Headgear" dataset is used for the training, validation and testing of the model. The Headgear dataset contains 20 classes of head gear-hats, caps, helmets, etc., 3620 train images, 100 test and 100 validation images. All images are $224 \times 224 \times 3$ in jpg format.
- Initial Conv2D contains 64 convolution filters with a size of 3×3 and with a "ReLU" activation function followed by a Max pooling layer with a pool size of 2×2 and a stride of 2×2.
- The second convolution layer contains 192 convolution filters with the size of 3×3, and the activation function used is "ReLU", followed by the Max pooling layer with a pool size of 2×2 and a stride of 2×2.
- The third and fourth convolution layers contain 384 convolution filters with the size of 3×3, and the activation function used is "ReLU".
- The fifth convolution layer contains 256 convolution filters with the size of 3×3, and the activation function used is "ReLU", followed by a Maxpooling layer with a pool size of 2×2 and a stride of 2×2.
- The next three layers are fully connected; the first two have a ReLU activation function with the size of 1×4096, and the last one has a softmax activation function with 1×20. Here "20" denotes the number of classes in the input dataset.
- The AlexNet compiled with the "rmsprop" optimizer, "categorical_crossentropy" loss function and "accuracy" performance metric.
- The AlexNet is trained with a batch size of 32 and the number of epochs is fixed as 5.
- The overall summary of the AlexNet is shown in Fig. 11.66. The test accuracy obtained by this model is 31.00%.

```
Epoch 1/5 - Train Accuracy: 11.69% - Test Accuracy: 9.00%
Epoch 2/5 - Train Accuracy: 21.05% - Test Accuracy: 23.00%
Epoch 3/5 - Train Accuracy: 29.78% - Test Accuracy: 30.00%
Epoch 4/5 - Train Accuracy: 37.54% - Test Accuracy: 22.00%
Epoch 5/5 - Train Accuracy: 43.09% - Test Accuracy: 31.00%
AlexNet(
  (conv1): Conv2d(3, 64, kernel_size=(3, 3), stride=(1, 1), padding=(1, 1))
  (pool): MaxPool2d(kernel_size=2, stride=2, padding=0, dilation=1, ceil_mode=False)
  (conv2): Conv2d(64, 192, kernel_size=(3, 3), stride=(1, 1), padding=(1, 1))
  (conv3): Conv2d(192, 384, kernel_size=(3, 3), stride=(1, 1), padding=(1, 1))
  (conv4): Conv2d(384, 384, kernel_size=(3, 3), stride=(1, 1), padding=(1, 1))
  (conv5): Conv2d(384, 256, kernel_size=(3, 3), stride=(1, 1), padding=(1, 1))
  (fc1): Linear(in_features=200704, out_features=4096, bias=True)
  (fc2): Linear(in_features=4096, out_features=4096, bias=True)
  (fc3): Linear(in_features=4096, out_features=20, bias=True)
)
```

Fig. 11.66 Simulation result

Task: Vary the values of batch_size and epochs in the Python code given in Fig. 11.65 and comment on the test accuracy and loss outputs.

11.6.4 GoogleNet

GoogleNet, also called Inception-v1, is a convolutional neural network architecture created by Google specifically for image classification tasks. It was unveiled in 2014 and achieved notable success by winning the ImageNet Large Scale Visual Recognition Challenge (ILSVRC) 2014, attaining a top-5 error rate of 6.67%, which marked a substantial improvement over the prior year's winner. The overall architecture of GoogleNet is shown in Fig. 11.67. The GoogleNet architecture is composed of 22 layers, which include convolutional layers, pooling layers, Inception modules, fully connected layers, and softmax layers. It takes a 224 × 224 × 3 RGB image as input and produces a probability distribution across 1000 classes as output. The main contribution of GoogleNet was the development of the Inception module, which allows for the efficient use of network depth and width, leading to improved accuracy with fewer parameters and reduced computational cost. Inception module of GoogleNet is displayed in Fig. 11.68.

Summary of the GoogleNet architecture is as follows:

Input Layer: The input network receives a 224 × 224 × 3 RGB image.

Convolutional Layer: The first layer applies convolution with 64 filters of size 7 × 7 and a stride of 2, focusing on local feature extraction from the input image.

Max Pooling Layer: The output from the initial convolutional layer is processed through a max pooling layer with a 3 × 3 filter size and a stride of 2, reducing the spatial dimensions and providing translation invariance.

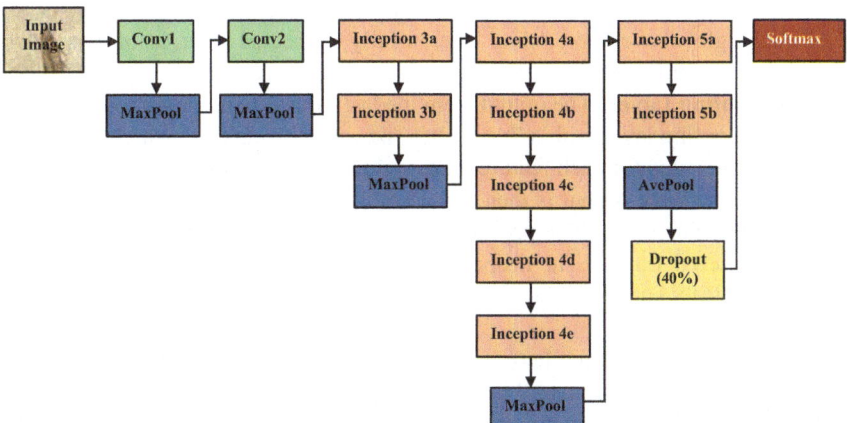

Fig. 11.67 GoogleNet architecture

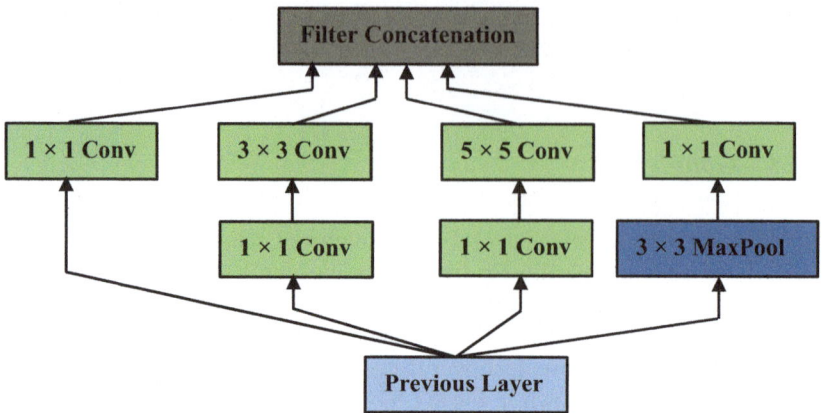

Fig. 11.68 Inception size-reduction module

Local Response Normalization Layer: This layer normalizes the responses of neighbouring neurons to help prevent overfitting.

Convolutional Layer: The output is then passed through another convolutional layer that utilizes 64 filters of size 1 × 1, effectively reducing dimensionality.

Convolutional Layer: The next step involves another convolutional layer with 192 filters of size 3 × 3.

Max Pooling Layer: Following this, the output undergoes another max pooling operation with a 3 × 3 filter size and a stride of 2.

Inception Modules: The result is then processed through a series of nine inception modules, where multiple branches of convolutional and pooling layers with varying filter sizes are concatenated before moving to the subsequent layer. This setup leverages the network's depth and width efficiently.

Auxiliary Classifiers: Three intermediate layers incorporate auxiliary classifiers to facilitate the learning of discriminative features and reduce overfitting. Each consists of a global average pooling layer, a fully connected layer, a softmax layer, and a cross-entropy loss layer.

Average Pooling Layer: The output from the last Inception module proceeds to an average pooling layer with a 7 × 7 filter size and a stride of 1, which calculates the average value for each feature map, yielding a single scalar per map.

Dropout Layer: The output is then passed through a dropout layer that randomly omits some neurons to help prevent overfitting.

Fully Connected Layer: The dropout layer's output is flattened and transmitted through a fully connected layer with 1000 neurons, corresponding to each class in the dataset.

Softmax Layer: The output here goes into a softmax layer, which calculates the probability distribution over the 1000 classes.

Output Layer: The final layer produces the predicted class label based on the highest probability from the softmax outcomes.

In total, GoogleNet comprises 22 parameterized layers, which include convolutional and fully connected layers. Considering the non-parameterized layers, such as max pooling, the architecture consists of a total of 27 layers.

Experiment 11.26: Implementation of GoogleNet or Inception-v1 Model for Image Classification

This experiment discusses the implementation and training of the GoogleNet architecture using PyTorch for image classification tasks. It outlines the model architecture, data preprocessing, and training methodology. The Python code for image classification using GoogleNet is given in Fig. 11.69, and its simulation result is shown in Fig. 11.70.

Inferences

The following inferences can be drawn from this experiment:

- From Fig. 11.69, it is possible to infer that "torch.nn" is imported from the "PyTorch" library, different layers of CNN model like Conv2d, MaxPooling2d, and Linear from "torch.nn" library. "Headgear" dataset is used to train, validate, and test the model. The Headgear dataset contains 20 classes of head gear-hats, caps, helmets, etc., 3620 train images,100 test and 100 validation images. All images are $224 \times 224 \times 3$ in jpg format.
- The GoogleNet is implemented with submodules like Conv_Block, Inception_ Block, and Auxillary.
- The GoogleNet is compiled with the "Adam" optimizer, "cross entropy" loss function, and "accuracy" performance metric.
- The AlexNet is trained with the number of epochs fixed as 3.
- The training and validation accuracy and loss are shown in Fig. 11.70. The best validation accuracy is obtained as 48%.

11.6.5   VGG-16

VGG16 means "Visual Geometry Group" with 16 layers network. The Visual Geometry Group from the University of Oxford developed this deep neural network. VGG16 has the distinctive features of architectural simplicity. The network consists of several convolutional layers, followed by max-pooling layers, and ends with three fully connected layers. VGG16 primarily uses 3×3 filters for its convolutional layers, which is a key design choice. By using smaller filters, the model can learn finer details in the image while still capturing complex patterns as the network deepens. A notable benefit of this approach is that stacking multiple small 3×3 filters results in a receptive field equivalent to larger filters (e.g. 5×5 or 7×7), but with fewer parameters. For example, three consecutive 3×3 convolutional layers have the same receptive field as a single 7×7 layer but require fewer parameters and computational resources. The architecture of VGG16 is shown in Fig. 11.71.

```
# GoogleNet
import time
import copy
import torch
import torch.nn as nn
import torch.optim as optim
from torch.utils.data import DataLoader
from torchvision import transforms, datasets
# Define the GoogleNet Model in PyTorch
class GoogleNet(nn.Module):
    def __init__(self, in_channels=3, use_auxiliary=True, num_classes=20):
        super(GoogleNet, self).__init__()
        self.conv1 = Conv_Block(in_channels, 64, kernel_size=7, stride=2, padding=3)
        self.conv2 = Conv_Block(64, 192, kernel_size=3, stride=1, padding=1)
        self.maxpool = nn.MaxPool2d(kernel_size=3, stride=2, padding=1)
        self.avgpool = nn.AvgPool2d(kernel_size=7, stride=1)
        self.dropout = nn.Dropout(0.4)
        self.linear = nn.Linear(1024, num_classes)
        self.use_auxiliary = use_auxiliary
        if use_auxiliary:
            self.auxiliary4a = Auxiliary(512, num_classes)
            self.auxiliary4d = Auxiliary(528, num_classes)
        self.inception3a = Inception_Block(192, 64, 96, 128, 16, 32, 32)
        self.inception3b = Inception_Block(256, 128, 128, 192, 32, 96, 64)
        self.inception4a = Inception_Block(480, 192, 96, 208, 16, 48, 64)
        self.inception4b = Inception_Block(512, 160, 112, 224, 24, 64, 64)
        self.inception4c = Inception_Block(512, 128, 128, 256, 24, 64, 64)
        self.inception4d = Inception_Block(512, 112, 144, 288, 32, 64, 64)
        self.inception4e = Inception_Block(528, 256, 160, 320, 32, 128, 128)
        self.inception5a = Inception_Block(832, 256, 160, 320, 32, 128, 128)
        self.inception5b = Inception_Block(832, 384, 192, 384, 48, 128, 128)
    def forward(self, x):
        y = None
        z = None
        x = self.conv1(x)
        x = self.maxpool(x)
        x = self.conv2(x)
        x = self.maxpool(x)
        x = self.inception3a(x)
        x = self.inception3b(x)
        x = self.maxpool(x)
        x = self.inception4a(x)
        if self.training and self.use_auxiliary:
            y = self.auxiliary4a(x)
        x = self.inception4b(x)
        x = self.inception4c(x)
        x = self.inception4d(x)
```

Fig. 11.69 Python code for GoogleNet

```
      if self.training and self.use_auxiliary:
        z = self.auxiliary4d(x)
      x = self.inception4e(x)
      x = self.maxpool(x)
      x = self.inception5a(x)
      x = self.inception5b(x)
      x = self.avgpool(x)
      x = x.reshape(x.shape[0], -1)
      x = self.dropout(x)
      x = self.linear(x)
      return x, y, z
class Conv_Block(nn.Module):
  def __init__(self, in_channels, out_channels, kernel_size, **kwargs):
    super(Conv_Block, self).__init__()
    self.conv = nn.Conv2d(in_channels, out_channels, kernel_size, **kwargs)
    self.bn = nn.BatchNorm2d(out_channels)
    self.relu = nn.ReLU()
  def forward(self, x):
    return self.relu(self.bn(self.conv(x)))
class Inception_Block(nn.Module):
  def __init__(self, im_channels, num_1x1, num_3x3_red, num_3x3, num_5x5_red, num_5x5,
num_pool_proj):
    super(Inception_Block, self).__init__()
    self.one_by_one = Conv_Block(im_channels, num_1x1, kernel_size=1)
    self.tree_by_three_red = Conv_Block(im_channels, num_3x3_red, kernel_size=1)
    self.tree_by_three = Conv_Block(num_3x3_red, num_3x3, kernel_size=3, padding=1)
    self.five_by_five_red = Conv_Block(im_channels, num_5x5_red, kernel_size=1)
    self.five_by_five = Conv_Block(num_5x5_red, num_5x5, kernel_size=5, padding=2)
    self.maxpool = nn.MaxPool2d(kernel_size=3, stride=1, padding=1)
    self.pool_proj = Conv_Block(im_channels, num_pool_proj, kernel_size=1)
  def forward(self, x):
    x1 = self.one_by_one(x)
    x2 = self.tree_by_three_red(x)
    x2 = self.tree_by_three(x2)
    x3 = self.five_by_five_red(x)
    x3 = self.five_by_five(x3)
    x4 = self.maxpool(x)
    x4 = self.pool_proj(x4)
    x = torch.cat([x1, x2, x3, x4], 1)
    return x
```

Fig. 11.69 (continued)

```
class Auxiliary(nn.Module):
  def __init__(self, in_channels, num_classes):
    super(Auxiliary, self).__init__()
    self.avgpool = nn.AvgPool2d(kernel_size=5, stride=3)
    self.conv1x1 = Conv_Block(in_channels, 128, kernel_size=1)
    self.fc1 = nn.Linear(2048, 1024)
    self.fc2 = nn.Linear(1024, num_classes)
    self.dropout = nn.Dropout(0.7)
    self.relu = nn.ReLU()
  def forward(self, x):
    x = self.avgpool(x)
    x = self.conv1x1(x)
    x = x.reshape(x.shape[0], -1)
    x = self.relu(self.fc1(x))
    x = self.dropout(x)
    x = self.fc2(x)
    return x
# Data augmentation and normalization for training
train_transforms = transforms.Compose([transforms.Resize((224, 224)),transforms.ToTensor(),
transforms.Normalize(mean=[0.485, 0.456, 0.406], std=[0.229, 0.224, 0.225]),])
val_test_transforms = transforms.Compose([transforms.Resize((224,
224)),transforms.ToTensor(),
  transforms.Normalize(mean=[0.485, 0.456, 0.406], std=[0.229, 0.224, 0.225]),])
train_dir = 'D:\\Veeraa 2021\\PSG\\DIP using Python\\data_h\\train'
val_dir = 'D:\\Veeraa 2021\\PSG\\DIP using Python\\data_h\\valid'
test_dir = 'D:\\Veeraa 2021\\PSG\\DIP using Python\\data_h\\test'
train_data = datasets.ImageFolder(root=train_dir, transform=train_transforms)
val_data = datasets.ImageFolder(root=val_dir, transform=val_test_transforms)
test_data = datasets.ImageFolder(root=test_dir, transform=val_test_transforms)
train_loader = DataLoader(train_data, batch_size=32, shuffle=True)
val_loader = DataLoader(val_data, batch_size=32, shuffle=False)
test_loader = DataLoader(test_data, batch_size=32, shuffle=False)
model = GoogleNet();# Initialize model, criterion, and optimizer
device = torch.device('cuda' if torch.cuda.is_available() else 'cpu')
model.to(device)  # Move model to GPU if available
print(device)
epochs = 3
criterion = nn.CrossEntropyLoss()
optimizer = optim.Adam(model.parameters(), lr=0.0001, weight_decay=1e-4)
lr_scheduler = optim.lr_scheduler.ReduceLROnPlateau(optimizer, patience=5, verbose=True)
# Train the model
def train_model(model, dataloaders, criterion, optimizer, num_epochs=50, use_auxiliary=True):
  since = time.time()
  val_acc_history = []
  best_model_wts = copy.deepcopy(model.state_dict())
  best_acc = 0.0
  for epoch in range(num_epochs):
    print('Epoch {}/{}'.format(epoch, num_epochs - 1))
    print('-' * 10)
```

Fig. 11.69   (continued)

```
for phase in ['train', 'val']: # Each epoch has a training and validation phase
    if phase == 'train':
        model.train()  # Set model to training mode
    else:
        model.eval()   # Set model to evaluate mode
    running_loss = 0.0
    running_corrects = 0
    for inputs, labels in dataloaders[phase]: # Iterate over data
        inputs = inputs.to(device)
        labels = labels.to(device)
        optimizer.zero_grad() # Zero the parameter gradients
        with torch.set_grad_enabled(phase == 'train'): # Forward. Track history if only in train
            if phase == 'train': # Backward + optimize only if in training phase
                if use_auxiliary:
                    outputs, aux1, aux2 = model(inputs)
                    loss = criterion(outputs, labels) + 0.3 * criterion(aux1, labels) + 0.3 * criterion(aux2,
labels)
                else:
                    outputs, _, _ = model(inputs)
                    loss = criterion(outputs, labels)
                _, preds = torch.max(outputs, 1)
                loss.backward()
                optimizer.step()
            if phase == 'val':
                outputs, _, _ = model(inputs)
                loss = criterion(outputs, labels)
                _, preds = torch.max(outputs, 1)
        running_loss += loss.item() * inputs.size(0)
        running_corrects += torch.sum(preds == labels.data)
    epoch_loss = running_loss / len(dataloaders[phase].dataset)
    if phase == 'val': # Adjust learning rate based on val loss
        lr_scheduler.step(epoch_loss)
    epoch_acc = running_corrects.double() / len(dataloaders[phase].dataset)
    print('{} Loss: {:.4f} Acc: {:.4f}'.format(phase, epoch_loss, epoch_acc))
    if phase == 'val' and epoch_acc > best_acc:
        best_acc = epoch_acc
        best_model_wts = copy.deepcopy(model.state_dict())
    if phase == 'val':
        val_acc_history.append(epoch_acc)
    print()
time_elapsed = time.time() - since
print('Training complete in {:.0f}m {:.0f}s'.format(time_elapsed // 60, time_elapsed % 60))
print('Best val Acc: {:4f}'.format(best_acc))
model.load_state_dict(best_model_wts); # load best model weights
return model, val_acc_history
model, _ = train_model(model, {"train": train_loader, "val": val_loader}, criterion, optimizer, epochs)
```

Fig. 11.69 (continued)

The architecture of VGG16 is divided into blocks of convolutional layers, followed by max-pooling layers. The first few blocks of the network contain fewer filters (e.g. 64 filters in the first block, 128 in the second block), while deeper layers have progressively more filters, reflecting the increasing complexity of the features being learned. Max-pooling layers, typically with a 2×2 window and a stride of 2,

Fig. 11.70 Simulation result of GoogleNet for Headgear dataset

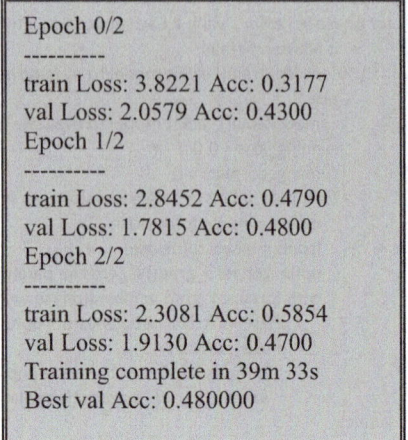

Epoch 0/2
----
train Loss: 3.8221 Acc: 0.3177
val Loss: 2.0579 Acc: 0.4300
Epoch 1/2
----
train Loss: 2.8452 Acc: 0.4790
val Loss: 1.7815 Acc: 0.4800
Epoch 2/2
----
train Loss: 2.3081 Acc: 0.5854
val Loss: 1.9130 Acc: 0.4700
Training complete in 39m 33s
Best val Acc: 0.480000

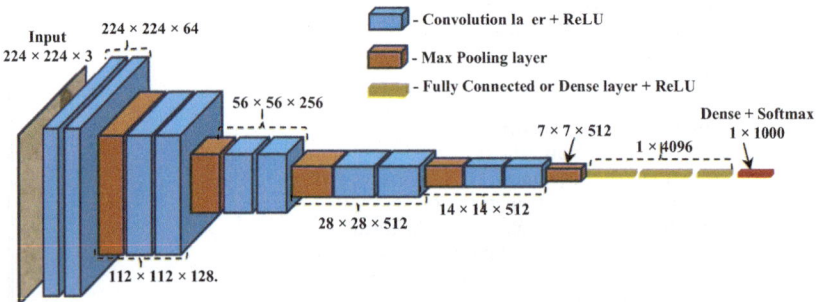

Fig. 11.71 VGG16 architecture

reduce the spatial dimensions of the feature maps and help with the computational efficiency of the model. These pooling layers also contribute to making the network more invariant to small translations and distortions in the input images.

The last part of the VGG16 architecture consists of three fully connected layers, with the final layer serving as the output layer. The fully connected layers are dense layers that connect every neuron from the previous layer to each neuron in the current layer. In the case of image classification tasks, the final fully connected layer uses a softmax activation function to output a probability distribution across different classes.

Experiment 11.27: Implementation of VGG16 Using Keras
This experiment discusses the implementation of VGG16 deep neural network model using "Keras" in the Python environment. The implementation of the VGG16 model is given in the form of flow diagram and it is shown in Fig. 11.72. The Python code for VGG16 model is given in Fig. 11.73, and its simulation result is shown in Fig. 11.74.

Fig. 11.72 Flow diagram
of VGG16 model creation

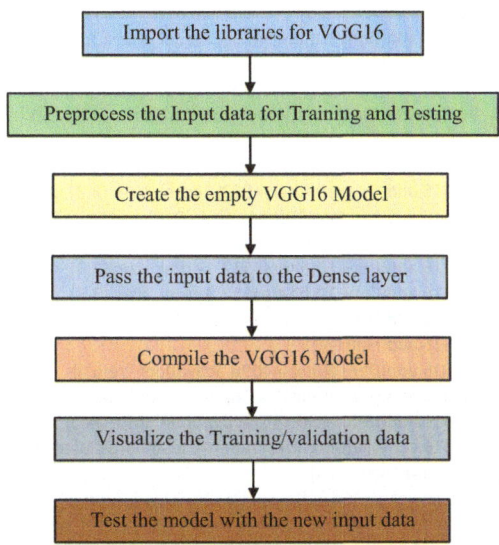

```
# VGG16 Model
import keras
from keras.models import Sequential
from keras.layers import Dense, Conv2D, MaxPool2D , Flatten
from keras.preprocessing import image
from keras.models import load_model
from tensorflow.keras.preprocessing.image import ImageDataGenerator
import numpy as np
from keras.optimizers import Adam
from keras.callbacks import ModelCheckpoint, EarlyStopping
import matplotlib.pyplot as plt
train_data_dir=r"D:\Veeraa 2021\PSG\DIP using Python\Dataset_for_testing2"
trdata = ImageDataGenerator()
traindata = trdata.flow_from_directory(directory="Dataset_for_testing2",target_size=(256,256))
tsdata = ImageDataGenerator()
testdata = tsdata.flow_from_directory(directory="Dataset_for_testing2", target_size=(256,256))
VGG16 = Sequential()
VGG16.add(Conv2D(input_shape=(256,256,3),filters=64,kernel_size=(3,3),padding="same",
activation="relu"))
VGG16.add(Conv2D(filters=64,kernel_size=(3,3),padding="same", activation="relu"))
VGG16.add(MaxPool2D(pool_size=(2,2),strides=(2,2)))
VGG16.add(Conv2D(filters=128, kernel_size=(3,3), padding="same", activation="relu"))
VGG16.add(Conv2D(filters=128, kernel_size=(3,3), padding="same", activation="relu"))
VGG16.add(MaxPool2D(pool_size=(2,2),strides=(2,2)))
```

Fig. 11.73 Python code for VGG16 modelling

```
VGG16.add(Conv2D(filters=256, kernel_size=(3,3), padding="same", activation="relu"))
VGG16.add(Conv2D(filters=256, kernel_size=(3,3), padding="same", activation="relu"))
VGG16.add(Conv2D(filters=256, kernel_size=(3,3), padding="same", activation="relu"))
VGG16.add(MaxPool2D(pool_size=(2,2),strides=(2,2)))
VGG16.add(Conv2D(filters=512, kernel_size=(3,3), padding="same", activation="relu"))
VGG16.add(Conv2D(filters=512, kernel_size=(3,3), padding="same", activation="relu"))
VGG16.add(Conv2D(filters=512, kernel_size=(3,3), padding="same", activation="relu"))
VGG16.add(MaxPool2D(pool_size=(2,2),strides=(2,2)))
VGG16.add(Conv2D(filters=512, kernel_size=(3,3), padding="same", activation="relu"))
VGG16.add(Conv2D(filters=512, kernel_size=(3,3), padding="same", activation="relu"))
VGG16.add(Conv2D(filters=512, kernel_size=(3,3), padding="same", activation="relu"))
VGG16.add(MaxPool2D(pool_size=(2,2),strides=(2,2)))
VGG16.add(Flatten())
VGG16.add(Dense(units=4096,activation="relu"))
VGG16.add(Dense(units=4096,activation="relu"))
VGG16.add(Dense(units=9, activation="softmax"))
VGG16.compile(optimizer=Adam(), loss=keras.losses.categorical_crossentropy,
metrics=['accuracy'])
checkpoint = ModelCheckpoint("VGG16_1.keras", monitor='val_accuracy', verbose=1,
save_best_only=True, save_weights_only=False, mode='auto', save_freq='epoch')
early = EarlyStopping(monitor='val_accuracy', min_delta=0, patience=20, verbose=1, mode='max')
hist = VGG16.fit(traindata, epochs=10, steps_per_epoch=10, validation_data=testdata,
validation_steps=10, callbacks=[checkpoint,early])
plt.plot(hist.history["accuracy"]),plt.plot(hist.history['val_accuracy']),plt.plot(hist.history['loss']),
plt.plot(hist.history['val_loss']),plt.title("model
accuracy"),plt.ylabel("Accuracy"),plt.xlabel("Epoch")
plt.legend(["Accuracy","Validation Accuracy","loss","Validation Loss"]),plt.show()
img = image.load_img("TUNGRO_0002.jpg",target_size=(256,256))
img = np.asarray(img)
plt.imshow(img),plt.title('Input Test Image')
img = np.expand_dims(img, axis=0)
saved_model = load_model("VGG16_1.keras")
output = VGG16.predict(img)
output1=output[0];
out=np.argmax(output1)
out_label=['Bacterial_Blight','Blast','Brownspot','Healthy','Hispa','Leaf_scald','Leaf_smut','Narro w
_Brown','Tungro']
print('Output Class',out_label[out])
```

Fig. 11.73 (continued)

Inferences

The following inferences can be drawn from Fig. 11.73:

- The "Sequential" model is imported from the "Keras" library.
- The following layers like "Dense", "Conv2D", "MaxPool2D", and Flatten are imported from the "Keras.layers" library.
- The "ImageDataGenerator" is imported to preprocess the image data or dataset.
- By using ".add" Python command, various layers like convolution, dense, max pooling and flatten can be added into the sequential model to form the VGG16 network.

Model: "sequential"

Layer (type)	Output Shape	Param #
conv2d (Conv2D)	(None, 256, 256, 64)	1,792
conv2d_1 (Conv2D)	(None, 256, 256, 64)	36,928
max_pooling2d (MaxPooling2D)	(None, 128, 128, 64)	0
conv2d_2 (Conv2D)	(None, 128, 128, 128)	73,856
conv2d_3 (Conv2D)	(None, 128, 128, 128)	147,584
max_pooling2d_1 (MaxPooling2D)	(None, 64, 64, 128)	0
conv2d_4 (Conv2D)	(None, 64, 64, 256)	295,168
conv2d_5 (Conv2D)	(None, 64, 64, 256)	590,080
conv2d_6 (Conv2D)	(None, 64, 64, 256)	590,080
max_pooling2d_2 (MaxPooling2D)	(None, 32, 32, 256)	0
conv2d_7 (Conv2D)	(None, 32, 32, 512)	1,180,160
conv2d_8 (Conv2D)	(None, 32, 32, 512)	2,359,808
conv2d_9 (Conv2D)	(None, 32, 32, 512)	2,359,808
max_pooling2d_3 (MaxPooling2D)	(None, 16, 16, 512)	0
conv2d_10 (Conv2D)	(None, 16, 16, 512)	2,359,808
conv2d_11 (Conv2D)	(None, 16, 16, 512)	2,359,808
conv2d_12 (Conv2D)	(None, 16, 16, 512)	2,359,808
max_pooling2d_4 (MaxPooling2D)	(None, 8, 8, 512)	0
flatten (Flatten)	(None, 32768)	0
dense (Dense)	(None, 4096)	134,221,824
dense_1 (Dense)	(None, 4096)	16,781,312
dense_2 (Dense)	(None, 9)	36,873

Total params: 497,264,093 (1.85 GB)
Trainable params: 165,754,697 (632.30 MB)
Non-trainable params: 0 (0.00 B)
Optimizer params: 331,509,396 (1.23 GB)

Fig. 11.74   Simulation result of VGG16 model

Fig. 11.75 Residual
learning block

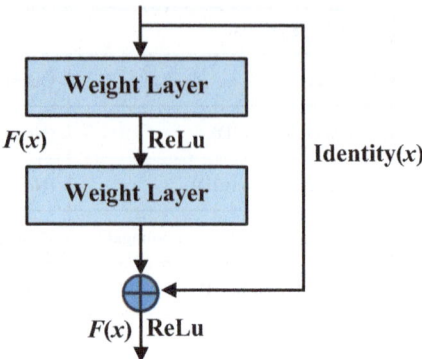

- "Adams" optimizer, "categorical_crossentropy" loss, and "accuracy" performance metric are used to compile the VGG16 model.
- The "EarlyStopping" command is utilized to stop the training process when a monitored metric has stopped improving.
- Also, "ModelCheckpoint" callback is used in conjunction with training using model.fit() to save a model or weights at some interval, so the model or weights can be loaded later to continue the training from the state saved.

The following observations can be made from Fig. 11.74:

- The VGG16 model is a sequential model.
- There are a total 16 number of layers with trainable parameters in the network, which includes both the 13 convolutional layers and the 3 fully connected/dense layers. The weights of 16 layers can be adjusted during the training process.

11.6.6   ResNet-50

ResNet-50 is a deep convolutional neural network architecture that belongs to the Residual Networks (ResNet) family, introduced by Microsoft Research in 2015. The "50" in ResNet-50 refers to the number of layers, including convolutional layers and residual blocks. ResNet-50 sets itself apart from other deep networks by using residual connections, or skip connections, which helps to address the problem of vanishing gradients that can occur in very deep networks. In a typical neural network, as the network depth increases, gradients can become too small to update weights during training effectively. ResNet overcomes this by adding shortcut connections that allow the input of a layer to bypass one or more intermediate layers and be added directly to the output. This "residual learning" allows the model to focus on learning only the difference (residuals) between the input and output, making it easier to train very deep models. The "residual learning block" is shown in Fig. 11.75. The overall architecture of ResNet50 is displayed in Fig. 11.76.

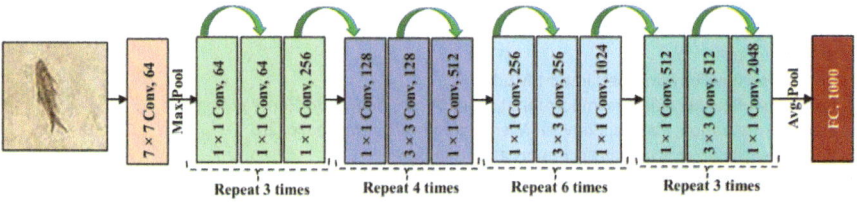

Fig. 11.76 ResNet50 architecture

ResNet-50 comprises 50 layers, including 49 convolutional layers organized into residual blocks, each typically containing two or three convolutional layers. These residual blocks are the foundation of ResNet's architecture and help to ensure that information can flow more easily through the network. The model also uses batch normalization and ReLU activations to improve training stability and performance. ResNet-50 is highly effective for image classification tasks, as evidenced by its strong performance on benchmarks like ImageNet. Its innovative design has made it a cornerstone in deep learning, and it is widely used for transfer learning in various computer vision applications. By enabling the training of very deep networks, ResNet-50 has significantly advanced the capabilities of neural networks, making it a go-to model for many research and industry projects.

Experiment 11.28: Implementation of ResNet50 Model for Image Classification

This experiment discusses the implementation and training of the ResNet50 architecture using Keras for image classification tasks. The "Hand sign" dataset in ".h5" format is used as an input to the ResNet50. "h5py" package is used to load the data. Then, ".h5" format data is converted into the data in numpy array. Each image is a three-channel image with 64 × 64 dimensions. There are 1080 images in the train data and 120 in test data. The Python code for image classification using ResNet50 is given in Fig. 11.77, and its simulation result is shown in Fig. 11.78.

Inferences

The following inferences can be drawn from this experiment:

- From Fig. 11.77, it is possible to infer that "h5py" python package is imported, which provides both a high and low-level interface to the HDF5 library from Python. The low-level interface is intended to be a complete wrapping of the HDF5 API, while the high-level component supports access to HDF5 files, datasets, and groups using established Python and NumPy concepts.
- Different layers of CNN model like Input, Add, Dense, Activation, ZeroPadding2D, BatchNormalization, Flatten, Conv2D, AveragePooling2D, and MaxPooling2D are imported from Keras library.
- The "glorot_uniform" is an initializer, it is also called as Yoshua Bengio and Xavier Glorot initializer, which is imported from the Keras initializer library. This initializer is used to initialize the weights in a network to maintain the objective of activation variances in forward propagation and back-prop.

```python
import h5py
import numpy as np
from tensorflow.keras.models import Model
from tensorflow.keras.layers import Input, Add, Dense, Activation, ZeroPadding2D,
BatchNormalization, Flatten, Conv2D, AveragePooling2D, MaxPooling2D
from tensorflow.keras.initializers import glorot_uniform
import matplotlib.pyplot as plt
import tensorflow.keras.backend as K
K.set_image_data_format('channels_last')
def load_dataset():
    train_dataset = h5py.File("D:\\Veeraa 2021\\PSG\\DIP using Python\\train_signs.h5", "r")
    train_set_x_orig = np.array(train_dataset["train_set_x"][:]) # train set features
    train_set_y_orig = np.array(train_dataset["train_set_y"][:]) # train set labels
    test_dataset = h5py.File("D:\\Veeraa 2021\\PSG\\DIP using Python\\test_signs.h5", "r")
    test_set_x_orig = np.array(test_dataset["test_set_x"][:]) # test set features
    test_set_y_orig = np.array(test_dataset["test_set_y"][:]) # test set labels
    classes = np.array(test_dataset["list_classes"][:]); # list of classes
    train_set_y_orig = train_set_y_orig.reshape((1, train_set_y_orig.shape[0])); # reshape
    test_set_y_orig = test_set_y_orig.reshape((1, test_set_y_orig.shape[0]))
    return train_set_x_orig, train_set_y_orig, test_set_x_orig, test_set_y_orig, classes

def convert_to_one_hot(Y, C):
    Y = np.eye(C)[Y.reshape(-1)].T
    return Y

def plotImages(images_arr, labels):
 fig, axes = plt.subplots(1,10, figsize=(20,20))
 axes = axes.flatten()
 for ax, img in zip(axes, images_arr):
   ax.imshow(img)
   ax.axis('off')
 plt.tight_layout()
 plt.show()
 print(labels[0][0:10])
train_set_x_orig, Y_train_orig, test_set_x_orig, Y_test_orig, classes = load_dataset()
# normalize image vectors
X_train = train_set_x_orig/255
X_test  = test_set_x_orig/255
# Convert training and test labels to one hot matrices
Y_train = convert_to_one_hot(Y_train_orig, classes.shape[0]).T
Y_test = convert_to_one_hot(Y_test_orig, classes.shape[0]).T
print ("number of training examples = " + str(X_train.shape[0]))
print ("number of test examples = " + str(X_test.shape[0]))
# Note channels are last dimensions for images
print ("X_train shape: " + str(X_train.shape))
print ("Y_train shape: " + str(Y_train.shape))
print ("X_test shape: " + str(X_test.shape))
print ("Y_test shape: " + str(Y_test.shape))
plotImages(X_train, Y_train_orig)
```

Fig. 11.77 Python code for ResNet50

```
def identity_block(X, f, filters, stage, block):
  # defining base name for block
  conv_base_name = 'res' + str(stage) + block + '_'
  bn_base_name = 'bn' + str(stage) + block + '_'
  f1, f2, f3 = filters
  bn_axis = 3
  X_skip_connection = X
  # First component/layer of main path
  X = Conv2D(filters= f1, kernel_size = (1,1), strides = (1,1), padding='valid',
name=conv_base_name+'first_component', kernel_initializer = glorot_uniform(seed=0))(X)
  X = BatchNormalization(axis=bn_axis, name=bn_base_name+'first_component')(X)
  X = Activation('relu')(X)
  # Second component/layer of main path
  X = Conv2D(filters= f2, kernel_size = (f,f), strides = (1,1), padding='same',
name=conv_base_name+'second_component', kernel_initializer = glorot_uniform(seed=0))(X)
  X = BatchNormalization(axis=bn_axis, name=bn_base_name+'second_component')(X)
  X = Activation('relu')(X)
  # Third component/layer of main path
  X = Conv2D(filters= f3, kernel_size = (1,1), strides = (1,1), padding='valid',
name=conv_base_name+'third_component', kernel_initializer = glorot_uniform(seed=0))(X)
  X = BatchNormalization(axis=bn_axis, name=bn_base_name+'third_component')(X)
  X = Add()([X, X_skip_connection])
  X = Activation('relu')(X)
  return X
def convolutional_block(X, f, filters, stage, block, s = 2):
   conv_base_name = 'res' + str(stage) + block + '_'
   bn_base_name = 'bn' + str(stage) + block + '_'
   f1, f2, f3 = filters
   bn_axis = 3
   X_skip_connection = X
   # First component of main path
   X = Conv2D(f1, (1, 1), strides = (s,s), padding = 'valid', name = conv_base_name +
'first_component', kernel_initializer = glorot_uniform(seed=0))(X)
   X = BatchNormalization(axis = bn_axis, name = bn_base_name + 'first_component')(X)
   X = Activation('relu')(X)
   # Second component of main path
   X = Conv2D(f2,  kernel_size = (f, f), strides = (1,1), padding = 'same', name = conv_base_name +
'second_component', kernel_initializer = glorot_uniform(seed=0))(X)
   X = BatchNormalization(axis = bn_axis, name = bn_base_name + 'second_component')(X)
   X = Activation('relu')(X)
   X = Conv2D(f3, kernel_size = (1, 1), strides = (1,1), padding = 'valid', name = conv_base_name +
'third_component', kernel_initializer = glorot_uniform(seed=0))(X)
   X = BatchNormalization(axis = bn_axis, name = bn_base_name + 'third_component')(X)
   X_skip_connection = Conv2D(f3, (1, 1), strides = (s,s), padding = 'valid', name = conv_base_name +
'merge', kernel_initializer = glorot_uniform(seed=0))(X_skip_connection)
   X_skip_connection = BatchNormalization(axis = 3, name = bn_base_name +
'merge')(X_skip_connection)
   X = Add()([X, X_skip_connection])
   X = Activation('relu')(X)
   return X
```

Fig. 11.77 (continued)

```
def ResNet50(input_shape = (64, 64, 3), classes = 6):
  X_input = Input(input_shape);# plug in input_shape to define the input tensor
  X = ZeroPadding2D((3, 3))(X_input);# Zero-Padding : pads the input with a pad of (3,3)
  # Stage 1
  X = Conv2D(64, (7, 7), strides = (2, 2), name = 'conv_1', kernel_initializer =
glorot_uniform(seed=0))(X)
  X = BatchNormalization(axis = 3, name = 'bn_1')(X)
  X = Activation('relu')(X)
  X = MaxPooling2D((3, 3), strides=(2, 2))(X)
  # Stage 2
  X = convolutional_block(X, f = 3, filters = [64, 64, 256], stage = 2, block='a', s = 1)
  X = identity_block(X, 3, [64, 64, 256], stage=2, block='b')
  X = identity_block(X, 3, [64, 64, 256], stage=2, block='c')
  # Stage 3
  X = convolutional_block(X, f=3, filters=[128, 128, 512], stage=3, block='a', s=2)
  X = identity_block(X, 3, [128, 128, 512], stage=3, block='b')
  X = identity_block(X, 3, [128, 128, 512], stage=3, block='c')
  X = identity_block(X, 3, [128, 128, 512], stage=3, block='d')
  # Stage 4
  X = convolutional_block(X, f=3, filters=[256, 256, 1024], stage=4, block='a', s=2)
  X = identity_block(X, 3, [256, 256, 1024], stage=4, block='b')
  X = identity_block(X, 3, [256, 256, 1024], stage=4, block='c')
  X = identity_block(X, 3, [256, 256, 1024], stage=4, block='d')
  X = identity_block(X, 3, [256, 256, 1024], stage=4, block='e')
  X = identity_block(X, 3, [256, 256, 1024], stage=4, block='f')
  # Stage 5
  X = convolutional_block(X, f=3, filters=[512, 512, 2048], stage=5, block='a', s=2)
  X = identity_block(X, 3, [512, 512, 2048], stage=5, block='b')
  X = identity_block(X, 3, [512, 512, 2048], stage=5, block='c')
  # Average Pooling
  X = AveragePooling2D((2, 2), name='avg_pool')(X)
  # output layer
  X = Flatten()(X)
  X = Dense(classes, activation='softmax', name='fc' + str(classes), kernel_initializer =
glorot_uniform(seed=0))(X)
  # Create model
  model = Model(inputs = X_input, outputs = X, name='ResNet50')
  return model
model = ResNet50(input_shape = (64, 64, 3), classes = 6)
model.compile(optimizer='adam', loss='categorical_crossentropy', metrics=['accuracy'])
model.fit(X_train, Y_train, epochs = 20, batch_size = 32)
predictions = model.evaluate(X_test, Y_test)
print("Loss = " + str(predictions[0]))
print("Test Accuracy = " + str(predictions[1]))
```

Fig. 11.77 (continued)

- The "backend" library is imported from Keras, the backend refers to the computational engine executing operations and computations in deep learning models. The backend configuration determines which computational engine runs numeric expressions in Keras, providing flexibility and compatibility with different frameworks.

```
number of training examples = 1080
number of test examples = 120
X_train shape: (1080, 64, 64, 3)
Y_train shape: (1080, 6)
X_test shape: (120, 64, 64, 3)
Y_test shape: (120, 6)
```

(a) Details about the dataset

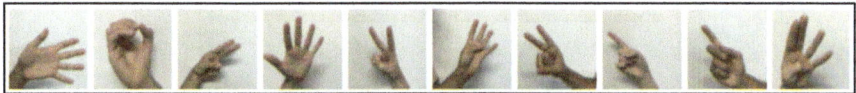

(b) Sample images

```
Loss = 0.3500302731990814
Test Accuracy = 0.925000011920929
```

(c) Test Accuracy

Fig. 11.78 Simulation result of ResNet50 for SIGNS dataset. (**a**) Details about the dataset. (**b**) Sample images. (**c**) Test accuracy

- ResNet architecture consists of "identity block" and "convolutional block", which are defined as functions and these functions are called while designing ResNet50 network.
- The ResNet50 model is compiled with the "Adam" optimizer, "categorical cross entropy" loss function, and the performance metric function used as "accuracy".
- The model is trained with the input dataset, 20 epochs, and 32 batch size.
- The detail about the input dataset is shown in Fig. 11.78a, and sample images are displayed in Fig. 11.78b.
- Figure 11.78c shows the loss and test accuracy of the ResNet50 for the "SIGNS" dataset.

11.6.7   UNET

UNet is a convolutional neural network architecture developed for image segmentation. It consists of the contracting path (encoder) and an expansive path (decoder). The contracting path contains encoder layers that extract high-level features in the input image and reduce the spatial dimension of the input image. This encoder layer consists of repeated blocks of convolutional layers followed by max pooling layers. The max pooling layer effectively reduces the spatial dimension of the input image. The expansive path contains the decoder, which is responsible for upsampling or upscaling the low-resolution feature maps to bring back the original size of the input image. The decoder layer has repeated blocks of transposed convolutions followed by concatenation with corresponding feature maps from the contracting path. The UNet has a bottleneck layer, which exists between the encoder and decoder paths. This bottleneck layer captures the most critical features while maintaining the

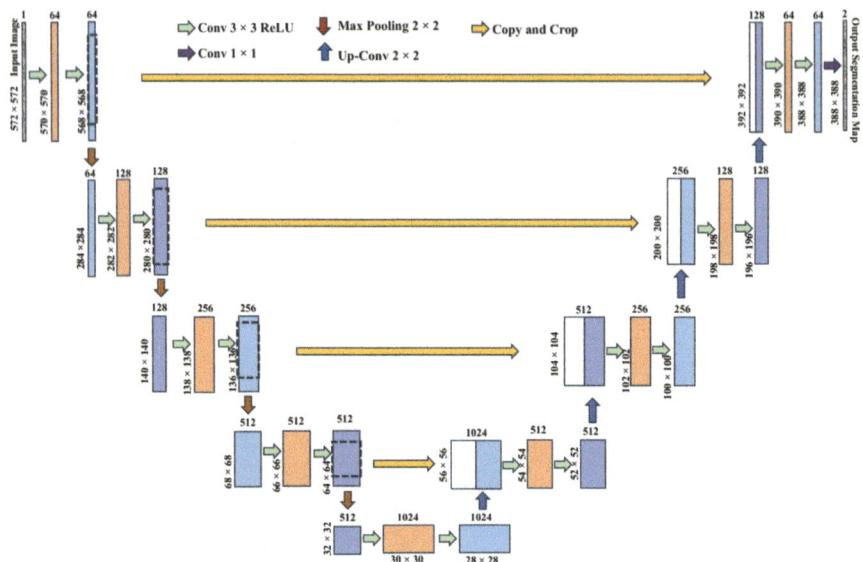

Fig. 11.79 UNET architecture

spatial information of the input image. The architecture of UNET is shown in Fig. 11.79.

Experiment 11.29: Implementation of UNET

This experiment discusses image segmentation using UNET architecture. For this, "Forest Segmentation Dataset" is chosen to verify the performance of the UNET. The "Forest Segmentation Dataset" contains 5108 satellite images with its ground truth mask images. The semantic segmentation of this dataset is done by using UNET. The Python code to perform the semantic segmentation of Forest Segmentation dataset is given in Fig. 11.80, and its simulation result is shown in Fig. 11.81.

Inferences

The following inferences can be made from this experiment:

- From Fig. 11.80, it is possible to infer that "Keras" library is used to build the UNET model, and "Forest Segmentation dataset" is imported to train and test the UNET architecture.
- The UNET model is built using convolution, encoder, and decoder blocks.
- Intersection of Union (IoU) measure is used to validate the performance of the UNET model.
- The output or predicted mask is the output of the UNET model trained with 20 epochs, and the accuracy obtained is 83%, as shown in Fig. 11.81a. When increasing the number of epochs in training, the accuracy may increase, and the predicted mask may be similar to the actual mask.

```
# Semantic Image Segmentation using UNET
import numpy as np
import pandas as pd
import matplotlib.pyplot as plt
import os
import tensorflow as tf
from tensorflow.keras.preprocessing.image import ImageDataGenerator
#from tensorflow.python.keras.callbacks import ModelCheckpoint, EarlyStopping
from tensorflow.keras.layers import Conv2D, BatchNormalization, Activation, MaxPool2D,
Conv2DTranspose, Concatenate, Input
from tensorflow.keras.models import Model
from skimage.morphology import label
import tensorflow.keras.backend as K
base_directory = 'D:/Veeraa 2021/PSG/DIP using Python/UNET/Forest Segmented/Forest
Segmented'
images_folder = os.path.join(base_directory, 'images')
masks_folder = os.path.join(base_directory, 'masks')
data = pd.read_csv(os.path.join(base_directory, 'meta_data.csv'))
data.head()
img_dim = 256
image_datagen = ImageDataGenerator(rescale=1./255,validation_split=0.15)
mask_datagen = ImageDataGenerator(rescale=1./255,validation_split=0.15)

train_image_generator = image_datagen.flow_from_directory(
    'D:/Veeraa 2021/PSG/DIP using Python/UNET/Forest Segmented/Forest Segmented',
    target_size=(img_dim, img_dim),class_mode = None,classes = ['images'],
    batch_size = 32,seed=42,subset='training')
train_mask_generator = mask_datagen.flow_from_directory(
    'D:/Veeraa 2021/PSG/DIP using Python/UNET/Forest Segmented/Forest Segmented',
    target_size=(img_dim, img_dim),class_mode = None,classes = ['masks'],
    color_mode = 'grayscale',batch_size = 32,seed=42,subset='training')

val_image_generator = image_datagen.flow_from_directory(
    'D:/Veeraa 2021/PSG/DIP using Python/UNET/Forest Segmented/Forest Segmented',
    target_size=(img_dim, img_dim),class_mode = None,classes = ['images'],
    batch_size = 32,seed=42,subset='validation')

val_mask_generator = mask_datagen.flow_from_directory(
    'D:/Veeraa 2021/PSG/DIP using Python/UNET/Forest Segmented/Forest Segmented',
    target_size=(img_dim, img_dim),class_mode = None,classes = ['masks'],
    color_mode = 'grayscale',batch_size = 32,seed=42,subset='validation')

def custom_generator(image_generator, mask_generator):
    while True:
        images = image_generator.__next__() # Use __next__() here
        masks = mask_generator.__next__()   # Use __next__() here
        yield images, masks
train_generator = custom_generator(train_image_generator, train_mask_generator)
val_generator = custom_generator(val_image_generator, val_mask_generator)
```

Fig. 11.80 Python code for UNET

- From Fig. 11.81b, it is possible to observe that the training image dataset contains both the input image and its corresponding ground truth (i.e. segmentation mask). This UNET model works like a supervised learning algorithm.
- From Fig. 11.81c, it is possible to infer that the UNET model tries to predict the segmentation mask image from the test image.

```
training_samples_size = train_image_generator.samples
val_samples_size = val_image_generator.samples
n = 0
fig, axs = plt.subplots(5, 2, figsize=(6,12))
for i,m in train_generator:
  img,mask = i,m
  if n < 5:
    axs[n,0].imshow(img[0]),axs[n,0].set_title('Input Image'),axs[n,0].set_xticks([]),
    axs[n,0].set_yticks([]),axs[n,1].imshow(mask[0],cmap='gray'),axs[n,1].set_title('Mask Image'),
    axs[n,1].set_xticks([]),axs[n,1].set_yticks([])
    fig.tight_layout()
    n+=1
  else:
    break

def conv_block(input, num_filters):
  x = Conv2D(num_filters, 3, padding="same")(input)
  x = BatchNormalization()(x)
  x = Activation("relu")(x)
  x = Conv2D(num_filters, 3, padding="same")(x)
  x = BatchNormalization()(x)
  x = Activation("relu")(x)
  return x

def encoder_block(input, num_filters):
  x = conv_block(input, num_filters)
  p = MaxPool2D((2, 2))(x)
  return x, p

def decoder_block(input, skip_features, num_filters):
  x = Conv2DTranspose(num_filters, (2, 2), strides=2, padding="same")(input)
  x = Concatenate()([x, skip_features])
  x = conv_block(x, num_filters)
  return x

def build_unet(input_shape):
  inputs = Input(input_shape)
  s1, p1 = encoder_block(inputs, 32)
  s2, p2 = encoder_block(p1, 64)
  s3, p3 = encoder_block(p2, 128)
  s4, p4 = encoder_block(p3, 256)
  b1 = conv_block(p4, 512)
  d1 = decoder_block(b1, s4, 256)
  d2 = decoder_block(d1, s3, 128)
  d3 = decoder_block(d2, s2, 64)
  d4 = decoder_block(d3, s1, 32)
  outputs = Conv2D(1, 1, padding="same", activation="sigmoid")(d4)
  model = Model(inputs, outputs, name="U-Net")
  return model
```

Fig. 11.80   (continued)

```
def iou_coef(y_true, y_pred, smooth=1):
    intersection = K.sum(K.abs(y_true * y_pred), axis=[1,2,3])
    union = K.sum(y_true,[1,2,3])+K.sum(y_pred,[1,2,3])-intersection
    iou = K.mean((intersection + smooth) / (union + smooth), axis=0)
    return iou

def iou_coef_loss(y_true, y_pred):
    return -iou_coef(y_true, y_pred)

def iou_metric(y_true_in, y_pred_in, print_table=False):
    labels = label(y_true_in > 0.5)
    y_pred = label(y_pred_in > 0.5)
    true_objects = len(np.unique(labels))
    pred_objects = len(np.unique(y_pred))
    intersection = np.histogram2d(labels.flatten(), y_pred.flatten(), bins=(true_objects,
pred_objects))[0]
# Compute areas (needed for finding the union between all objects)
    area_true = np.histogram(labels, bins = true_objects)[0]
    area_pred = np.histogram(y_pred, bins = pred_objects)[0]
    area_true = np.expand_dims(area_true, -1)
    area_pred = np.expand_dims(area_pred, 0)
    union = area_true + area_pred - intersection;# Compute union
    intersection = intersection[1:,1:]
    union = union[1:,1:]
    union[union == 0] = 1e-9
    iou = intersection / union; # Compute the intersection over union
# Precision helper function
    def precision_at(threshold, iou):
        matches = iou > threshold
        true_positives = np.sum(matches, axis=1) == 1   # Correct objects
        false_positives = np.sum(matches, axis=0) == 0  # Missed objects
        false_negatives = np.sum(matches, axis=1) == 0  # Extra objects
        tp, fp, fn = np.sum(true_positives), np.sum(false_positives), np.sum(false_negatives)
        return tp, fp, fn
    prec = []
    if print_table:
        print("Thresh\tTP\tFP\tFN\tPrec.")
    for t in np.arange(0.5, 1.0, 0.05):
        tp, fp, fn = precision_at(t, iou)
        if (tp + fp + fn) > 0:
            p = tp / (tp + fp + fn)
        else:
            p = 0
        if print_table:
            print("{:1.3f}\t{}\t{}\t{}\t{:1.3f}".format(t, tp, fp, fn, p))
        prec.append(p)
        if print_table:
        print("AP\t-\t-\t-\t{:1.3f}".format(np.mean(prec)))
    return np.mean(prec)
```

Fig. 11.80 (continued)

```
def iou_metric_batch(y_true_in, y_pred_in):
    batch_size = y_true_in.shape[0]
    metric = []
    for batch in range(batch_size):
        value = iou_metric(y_true_in[batch], y_pred_in[batch])
        metric.append(value)
    return np.array(np.mean(metric), dtype=np.float32)

def my_iou_metric(label, pred):
    metric_value = tf.compat.v1.py_func(iou_metric_batch, [label, pred], tf.float32)
    return metric_value
input_shape = (img_dim, img_dim, 3)
model = build_unet(input_shape)
model.compile(optimizer='rmsprop',loss='binary_crossentropy',metrics=['accuracy', iou_coef])
model.summary()
model.fit(train_generator,steps_per_epoch=training_samples_size//32,
          validation_data=val_generator,validation_steps=val_samples_size//32,epochs=20)
random_val_samples = val_generator.__next__()
val_image_samples = random_val_samples[0]
val_mask_samples = random_val_samples[1]
predicted_masks = model.predict(val_image_samples)
predicted_masks[predicted_masks >= 0.5] = 1
predicted_masks[predicted_masks < 0.5] = 0
f, axarr = plt.subplots(5,3,figsize=(6, 12))
for i in range(0,5):
    axarr[i,0].imshow(val_image_samples[i],cmap='gray'),axarr[i,0].title.set_text('Original Image')
    axarr[i,0].set_xticks([]),axarr[i,0].set_yticks([]),
    axarr[i,1].imshow(val_mask_samples[i],cmap='gray'),axarr[i,1].title.set_text('Actual Mask')
    axarr[i,1].set_xticks([]),axarr[i,1].set_yticks([])
    axarr[i,2].imshow(predicted_masks[i],cmap='gray'),axarr[i,2].title.set_text('Predicted Mask')
    axarr[i,2].set_xticks([]),axarr[i,2].set_yticks([])
    plt.tight_layout()
```

Fig. 11.80 (continued)

```
Epoch 1/20
135/135 ─ 1370s 10s/step - accuracy: 0.7180 - iou_coef: 0.4654 - loss: 0.5620 - val_accuracy: 0.3742 -
val_iou_coef: 0.0050 - val_loss: 4.5304
Epoch 10/20
135/135 ─ 1341s 10s/step - accuracy: 0.8142 - iou_coef: 0.5739 - loss: 0.3995 - val_accuracy: 0.7660 -
val_iou_coef: 0.4971 - val_loss: 0.5482
Epoch 20/20
135/135 ─ 1408s 10s/step - accuracy: 0.8338 - iou_coef: 0.6000 - loss: 0.3589 - val_accuracy: 0.8276 -
val_iou_coef: 0.5804 - val_loss: 0.3919
```

(a) Performance measures of different epoch for Image segmentation using UNET

Fig. 11.81 Simulation result of UNET for forest segmentation dataset. (**a**) Performance measures of different epochs for image segmentation using UNET. (**b**) Sample training images. (**c**) Sample test images and UNET results

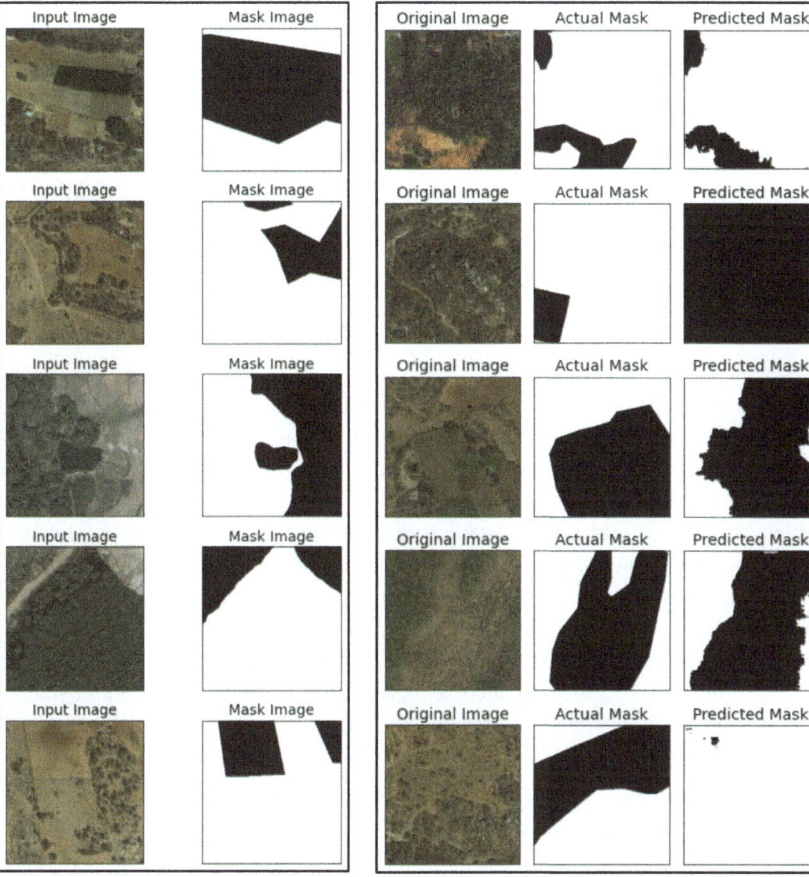

(b) Sample Training images   **(c) Sample Test images and UNET results**

Fig. 11.81 (continued)

11.6.8 YOLO

You Only Look Once, or YOLO, is a type of convolutional neural network (CNN) similar to GoogleNet. It is designed to detect objects in images using a single-step process. YOLO takes an image as input and processes it through a deep convolutional neural network to find and categorize objects all at once. The YOLO architecture has 24 convolutional layers, 4 max-pooling layers, and 2 fully connected layers, which are shown in Fig. 11.82. First, the input image is resized to 448 × 448 pixels. Then, a 1 × 1 convolution is applied to reduce the number of channels in the image, followed by a 3 × 3 convolution to create a three-dimensional output. Most layers use the ReLU activation function, but the final layer uses a linear activation function. Methods like batch normalization and dropout are included to prevent overfitting.

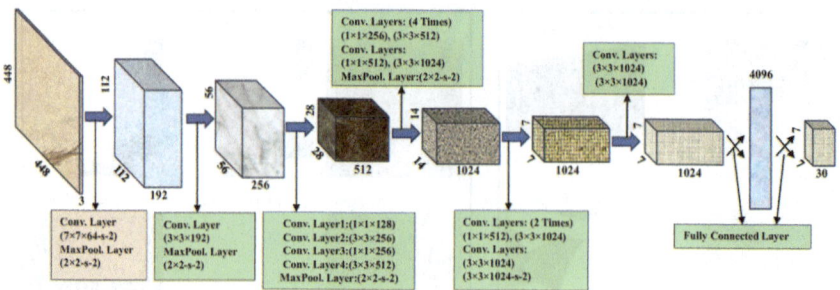

Fig. 11.82 YOLO architecture

The YOLO algorithm uses several techniques, such as residual blocks, bounding box regression, intersection over union (IoU), and non-maximum suppression, to detect objects. YOLO divides the input image into a grid of S × S sections. If an object's centre falls within a grid section, that section is responsible for detecting the object. Each grid section can predict multiple bounding boxes and associated confidence scores, indicating how likely it is that an object is present. During training, only one bounding box predictor is assigned to each object. The IoU metric helps the model to determine how well the predicted boxes match the actual objects. YOLO selects the predictor that has the highest IoU with the ground truth for each object, enabling it to improve its accuracy over time for different sizes and shapes of objects. This approach helps to enhance the overall effectiveness of object detection in images.

Experiment 11.30: Object Detection Using YOLOv3 Model
YOLO has been developed in several versions, such as YOLOv1, YOLOv2, YOLOv3, YOLOv4, YOLOv5, YOLOv6, and YOLOv7. Each version has been built on top of the previous version with enhanced features such as improved accuracy, faster processing, and better handling of small objects. This experiment uses YOLOv3 model to detect the objects in the input image. The Python code for the object detection using YOLOv3 is given in Fig. 11.83, and its simulation result is shown in Fig. 11.84.

Inferences
The following inferences can be drawn from this experiment:

- From Fig. 11.83, it is possible to observe that the following Conv2D, Input, BatchNormalization, LeakyReLU, ZeroPadding2D, UpSampling2D, add, and concatenate layers were imported from "Keras" library. It confirms that all those layers are involved in creating the YOLOv3 model.
- This Python code consists of Convolution Block, Bounding Box, and WeightReader functions.
- Figure 11.84 shows the object detection of different test images and their accuracy for the classes.

```
# YOLOv3 Model
import struct
import numpy as np
from numpy import expand_dims
from tensorflow.keras.layers import Conv2D, Input, BatchNormalization, LeakyReLU,
ZeroPadding2D, UpSampling2D, add, concatenate
from keras.models import Model
from keras.preprocessing.image import load_img
from keras.preprocessing.image import img_to_array
import matplotlib.pyplot as plt
from matplotlib.patches import Rectangle
def conv_block(inp, convs, skip=True):
  x = inp
  count = 0
  for conv in convs:
    if count == (len(convs) - 2) and skip:
      skip_connection = x
    count += 1
    if conv['stride'] > 1: x = ZeroPadding2D(((1,0),(1,0)))(x)
# peculiar padding as darknet prefer left and top
    x = Conv2D(conv['filter'],
          conv['kernel'],
          strides=conv['stride'],
          padding='valid' if conv['stride'] > 1 else 'same',
# peculiar padding as darknet prefer left and top
          name='conv_' + str(conv['layer_idx']),
          use_bias=False if conv['bnorm'] else True)(x)
    if conv['bnorm']: x = BatchNormalization(epsilon=0.001, name='bnorm_' +
str(conv['layer_idx']))(x)
    if conv['leaky']: x = LeakyReLU(alpha=0.1, name='leaky_' + str(conv['layer_idx']))(x)
```

Fig. 11.83 Python code for object detection using YOLOv3 model

```
def make_yolov3_model():
    input_image = Input(shape=(None, None, 3))
    # Layer  0 => 4
    x = conv_block(input_image, [{'filter': 32, 'kernel': 3, 'stride': 1, 'bnorm': True, 'leaky': True, 'layer_idx':
0},
                         {'filter': 64, 'kernel': 3, 'stride': 2, 'bnorm': True, 'leaky': True, 'layer_idx': 1},
                         {'filter': 32, 'kernel': 1, 'stride': 1, 'bnorm': True, 'leaky': True, 'layer_idx': 2},
                         {'filter': 64, 'kernel': 3, 'stride': 1, 'bnorm': True, 'leaky': True, 'layer_idx': 3}]))
    # Layer  5 => 8
    x = conv_block(x, [{'filter': 128, 'kernel': 3, 'stride': 2, 'bnorm': True, 'leaky': True, 'layer_idx': 5},
                   {'filter':  64, 'kernel': 1, 'stride': 1, 'bnorm': True, 'leaky': True, 'layer_idx': 6},
                   {'filter': 128, 'kernel': 3, 'stride': 1, 'bnorm': True, 'leaky': True, 'layer_idx': 7}])
    # Layer  9 => 11
    x = conv_block(x, [{'filter':  64, 'kernel': 1, 'stride': 1, 'bnorm': True, 'leaky': True, 'layer_idx': 9},
                   {'filter': 128, 'kernel': 3, 'stride': 1, 'bnorm': True, 'leaky': True, 'layer_idx': 10}])
    # Layer 12 => 15
    x = conv_block(x, [{'filter': 256, 'kernel': 3, 'stride': 2, 'bnorm': True, 'leaky': True, 'layer_idx': 12},
                   {'filter': 128, 'kernel': 1, 'stride': 1, 'bnorm': True, 'leaky': True, 'layer_idx': 13},
                   {'filter': 256, 'kernel': 3, 'stride': 1, 'bnorm': True, 'leaky': True, 'layer_idx': 14}])
    # Layer 16 => 36
    for i in range(7):
        x = conv_block(x, [{'filter': 128, 'kernel': 1, 'stride': 1, 'bnorm': True, 'leaky': True, 'layer_idx':
16+i*3},{'filter': 256, 'kernel': 3, 'stride': 1, 'bnorm': True, 'leaky': True, 'layer_idx': 17+i*3}])
    skip_36 = x
    # Layer 37 => 40
    x = conv_block(x, [{'filter': 512, 'kernel': 3, 'stride': 2, 'bnorm': True, 'leaky': True, 'layer_idx': 37},
                   {'filter': 256, 'kernel': 1, 'stride': 1, 'bnorm': True, 'leaky': True, 'layer_idx': 38},
                   {'filter': 512, 'kernel': 3, 'stride': 1, 'bnorm': True, 'leaky': True, 'layer_idx': 39}])
    # Layer 41 => 61
    for i in range(7):
        x = conv_block(x, [{'filter': 256, 'kernel': 1, 'stride': 1, 'bnorm': True, 'leaky': True, 'layer_idx':
41+i*3},{'filter': 512, 'kernel': 3, 'stride': 1, 'bnorm': True, 'leaky': True, 'layer_idx': 42+i*3}])
    skip_61 = x
    # Layer 62 => 65
    x = conv_block(x, [{'filter': 1024, 'kernel': 3, 'stride': 2, 'bnorm': True, 'leaky': True, 'layer_idx': 62},
                   {'filter':  512, 'kernel': 1, 'stride': 1, 'bnorm': True, 'leaky': True, 'layer_idx': 63},
                   {'filter': 1024, 'kernel': 3, 'stride': 1, 'bnorm': True, 'leaky': True, 'layer_idx': 64
    # Layer 66 => 74
    for i in range(3):
        x = conv_block(x, [{'filter': 512, 'kernel': 1, 'stride': 1, 'bnorm': True, 'leaky': True, 'layer_idx':
66+i*3},{'filter': 1024, 'kernel': 3, 'stride': 1, 'bnorm': True, 'leaky': True, 'layer_idx': 67+i*3}], skip=True)
    # Layer 75 => 79
    x = conv_block(x, [{'filter':  512, 'kernel': 1, 'stride': 1, 'bnorm': True, 'leaky': True, 'layer_idx': 75},
                   {'filter': 1024, 'kernel': 3, 'stride': 1, 'bnorm': True, 'leaky': True, 'layer_idx': 76},
                   {'filter':  512, 'kernel': 1, 'stride': 1, 'bnorm': True, 'leaky': True, 'layer_idx': 77},
                   {'filter': 1024, 'kernel': 3, 'stride': 1, 'bnorm': True, 'leaky': True, 'layer_idx': 78},
                   {'filter':  512, 'kernel': 1, 'stride': 1, 'bnorm': True, 'leaky': True, 'layer_idx': 79}], skip=False)
```

Fig. 11.83 (continued)

```
    # Layer 80 => 82
    yolo_82 = conv_block(x, [{'filter': 1024, 'kernel': 3, 'stride': 1, 'bnorm': True, 'leaky': True, 'layer_idx':
80},
                    {'filter':  255, 'kernel': 1, 'stride': 1, 'bnorm': False, 'leaky': False, 'layer_idx': 81}],
skip=False)
    # Layer 83 => 86
    x = conv_block(x, [{'filter': 256, 'kernel': 1, 'stride': 1, 'bnorm': True, 'leaky': True, 'layer_idx': 84}],
skip=False)
    x = UpSampling2D(2)(x)
    x = concatenate([x, skip_61], axis=-1)
    # Layer 87 => 91
    x = conv_block(x, [{'filter': 256, 'kernel': 1, 'stride': 1, 'bnorm': True, 'leaky': True, 'layer_idx':
87},{'filter': 512, 'kernel': 3, 'stride': 1, 'bnorm': True, 'leaky': True, 'layer_idx': 88},{'filter': 256, 'kernel':
1, 'stride': 1, 'bnorm': True, 'leaky': True, 'layer_idx': 89},{'filter': 512, 'kernel': 3, 'stride': 1, 'bnorm':
True, 'leaky': True, 'layer_idx': 90},{'filter': 256, 'kernel': 1, 'stride': 1, 'bnorm': True, 'leaky': True,
'layer_idx': 91}], skip=False)
    # Layer 92 => 94
    yolo_94 = conv_block(x, [{'filter': 512, 'kernel': 3, 'stride': 1, 'bnorm': True, 'leaky': True, 'layer_idx':
92},{'filter': 255, 'kernel': 1, 'stride': 1, 'bnorm': False, 'leaky': False, 'layer_idx': 93}], skip=False)
    # Layer 95 => 98
    x = conv_block(x, [{'filter': 128, 'kernel': 1, 'stride': 1, 'bnorm': True, 'leaky': True,  'layer_idx': 96}],
skip=False)
    x = UpSampling2D(size=(2, 2))(x)
    # x = UpSampling2D(2)(x)
    x = concatenate([x, skip_36],axis=-1)
    # Layer 99 => 106
    yolo_106 = conv_block(x, [{'filter': 128, 'kernel': 1, 'stride': 1, 'bnorm': True, 'leaky': True, 'layer_idx':
99},{'filter': 256, 'kernel': 3, 'stride': 1, 'bnorm': True, 'leaky': True, 'layer_idx': 100},{'filter': 128,
'kernel': 1, 'stride': 1, 'bnorm': True, 'leaky': True, 'layer_idx': 101},{'filter': 256, 'kernel': 3, 'stride': 1,
'bnorm': True, 'leaky': True, 'layer_idx': 102},{'filter': 128, 'kernel': 1, 'stride': 1, 'bnorm': True, 'leaky':
True, 'layer_idx': 103},{'filter': 256, 'kernel': 3, 'stride': 1, 'bnorm': True, 'leaky': True, 'layer_idx': 104},
{'filter': 255, 'kernel': 1, 'stride': 1, 'bnorm': False, 'leaky': False, 'layer_idx': 105}], skip=False)
    model = Model(input_image, [yolo_82, yolo_94, yolo_106])
    return model

class WeightReader:
    def __init__(self, weight_file):
        with open(weight_file, 'rb') as w_f:
            major,   = struct.unpack('i', w_f.read(4))
            minor,   = struct.unpack('i', w_f.read(4))
            revision, = struct.unpack('i', w_f.read(4))
            if (major*10 + minor) >= 2 and major < 1000 and minor < 1000:
                w_f.read(8)
            else:
                w_f.read(4)
            transpose = (major > 1000) or (minor > 1000)
            binary = w_f.read()
        self.offset = 0
        self.all_weights = np.frombuffer(binary, dtype='float32')
```

Fig. 11.83 (continued)

```
def read_bytes(self, size):
    self.offset = self.offset + size
    return self.all_weights[self.offset-size:self.offset]
def load_weights(self, model):
    for i in range(106):
        try:
            conv_layer = model.get_layer('conv_' + str(i))
            print("loading weights of convolution #" + str(i))
            if i not in [81, 93, 105]:
                norm_layer = model.get_layer('bnorm_' + str(i))
                size = np.prod(norm_layer.get_weights()[0].shape)
                beta  = self.read_bytes(size) # bias
                gamma = self.read_bytes(size) # scale
                mean  = self.read_bytes(size) # mean
                var   = self.read_bytes(size) # variance
                weights = norm_layer.set_weights([gamma, beta, mean, var])
            if len(conv_layer.get_weights()) > 1:
                bias   = self.read_bytes(np.prod(conv_layer.get_weights()[1].shape))
                kernel = self.read_bytes(np.prod(conv_layer.get_weights()[0].shape))
                kernel = kernel.reshape(list(reversed(conv_layer.get_weights()[0].shape)))
                kernel = kernel.transpose([2,3,1,0])
                conv_layer.set_weights([kernel, bias])
            else:
                kernel = self.read_bytes(np.prod(conv_layer.get_weights()[0].shape))
                kernel = kernel.reshape(list(reversed(conv_layer.get_weights()[0].shape)))
                kernel = kernel.transpose([2,3,1,0])
                conv_layer.set_weights([kernel])
        except ValueError:
            print("no convolution #" + str(i))
def reset(self):
    self.offset = 0
class BoundBox:
    def __init__(self, xmin, ymin, xmax, ymax, objness=None, classes=None):
        self.xmin = xmin
        self.ymin = ymin
        self.xmax = xmax
        self.ymax = ymax
        self.objness = objness
        self.classes = classes
        self.label = -1
        self.score = -1
    def get_label(self):
        if self.label == -1:
            self.label = np.argmax(self.classes)
        return self.label
    def get_score(self):
        if self.score == -1:
            self.score = self.classes[self.get_label()]
        return self.score
```

Fig. 11.83 (continued)

```python
def sigmoid(x):
    return 1. / (1. + np.exp(-x))
def decode_netout(netout, anchors, obj_thresh, net_h, net_w):
    grid_h, grid_w = netout.shape[:2]
    nb_box = 3
    netout = netout.reshape((grid_h, grid_w, nb_box, -1))
    nb_class = netout.shape[-1] - 5
    boxes = []
    netout[..., :2]  = sigmoid(netout[..., :2])
    netout[..., 4:]  = sigmoid(netout[..., 4:])
    netout[..., 5:]  = netout[..., 4][..., np.newaxis] * netout[..., 5:]
    netout[..., 5:] *= netout[..., 5:] > obj_thresh
    for i in range(grid_h*grid_w):
        row = i / grid_w
        col = i % grid_w
        for b in range(nb_box):
            # 4th element is objectness score
            objectness = netout[int(row)][int(col)][b][4]
            if(objectness.all() <= obj_thresh): continue
                # first 4 elements are x, y, w, and h
            x, y, w, h = netout[int(row)][int(col)][b][:4]
            x = (col + x) / grid_w # center position, unit: image width
            y = (row + y) / grid_h # center position, unit: image height
            w = anchors[2 * b + 0] * np.exp(w) / net_w # unit: image width
            h = anchors[2 * b + 1] * np.exp(h) / net_h # unit: image height
            # last elements are class probabilities
            classes = netout[int(row)][col][b][5:]
            box = BoundBox(x-w/2, y-h/2, x+w/2, y+h/2, objectness, classes)
            boxes.append(box)
    return boxes
def correct_yolo_boxes(boxes, image_h, image_w, net_h, net_w):
        new_w, new_h = net_w, net_h
        for i in range(len(boxes)):
                x_offset, x_scale = (net_w - new_w)/2./net_w, float(new_w)/net_w
                y_offset, y_scale = (net_h - new_h)/2./net_h, float(new_h)/net_h
                boxes[i].xmin = int((boxes[i].xmin - x_offset) / x_scale * image_w)
                boxes[i].xmax = int((boxes[i].xmax - x_offset) / x_scale * image_w)
                boxes[i].ymin = int((boxes[i].ymin - y_offset) / y_scale * image_h)
                boxes[i].ymax = int((boxes[i].ymax - y_offset) / y_scale * image_h)
def interval_overlap(interval_a, interval_b):
        x1, x2 = interval_a
        x3, x4 = interval_b
        if x3 < x1:
                if x4 < x1:
                        return 0
                else:
                        return min(x2,x4) - x1
        else:
                if x2 < x3:
                        return 0
                else:
                        return min(x2,x4) - x3
```

Fig. 11.83 (continued)

```
def bbox_iou(box1, box2):
        intersect_w = interval_overlap([box1.xmin, box1.xmax], [box2.xmin, box2.xmax])
        intersect_h = interval_overlap([box1.ymin, box1.ymax], [box2.ymin, box2.ymax])
        intersect = intersect_w * intersect_h
        w1, h1 = box1.xmax-box1.xmin, box1.ymax-box1.ymin
        w2, h2 = box2.xmax-box2.xmin, box2.ymax-box2.ymin
        union = w1*h1 + w2*h2 - intersect
        return float(intersect) / union
def do_nms(boxes, nms_thresh):
        if len(boxes) > 0:
                nb_class = len(boxes[0].classes)
        else:
                return
        for c in range(nb_class):
                sorted_indices = np.argsort([-box.classes[c] for box in boxes])
                for i in range(len(sorted_indices)):
                        index_i = sorted_indices[i]
                        if boxes[index_i].classes[c] == 0: continue
                        for j in range(i+1, len(sorted_indices)):
                                index_j = sorted_indices[j]
                                if bbox_iou(boxes[index_i], boxes[index_j]) >= nms_thresh:
                                        boxes[index_j].classes[c] = 0
def get_boxes(boxes, labels, thresh):
        v_boxes, v_labels, v_scores = list(), list(), list()
        # enumerate all boxes
        for box in boxes:
                for i in range(len(labels)):
                        if box.classes[i] > thresh:
                                v_boxes.append(box)
                                v_labels.append(labels[i])
                                v_scores.append(box.classes[i]*100)
        return v_boxes, v_labels, v_scores
def draw_boxes(filename, v_boxes, v_labels, v_scores):
    plt.figure(figsize=(20,10))
    data = plt.imread(filename)
    plt.imshow(data)# plot the image
    ax = plt.gca()
    for i in range(len(v_boxes)):
        box = v_boxes[i]
        y1, x1, y2, x2 = box.ymin, box.xmin, box.ymax, box.xmax
        width, height = x2 - x1, y2 - y1
        rect = Rectangle((x1, y1), width, height, fill=False, color='red',lw=3)
        ax.add_patch(rect)
        label = "%s (%.3f)" % (v_labels[i], v_scores[i])
        plt.text(x1-20, y1-20, label, color='blue',fontsize=18)
        plt.axis('off')
    plt.show()
```

Fig. 11.83 (continued)

```
def load_image(filename, shape):
    img = load_img(filename)
    width, height = img.size
    img = load_img(filename, target_size=shape)
    img = img_to_array(img);# convert to numpy array
    img = img.astype('float32');# scale pixel values to [0, 1]
    img /= 255.0
    img = expand_dims(img, 0)
    return img, width, height
model = make_yolov3_model()
weight_reader = WeightReader("D:\Veeraa 2021\PSG\DIP using Python\YOLO\yolov3.weights")
weight_reader.load_weights(model)
input_w, input_h = 416, 416
input_filename = "D:\Veeraa 2021\PSG\DIP using Python\YOLO\office.jpg"
l1, image_w, image_h = load_image(input_filename, (input_w, input_h))
out = model.predict(l1);# make prediction
print([a.shape for a in out])
anchors = [[116,90, 156,198, 373,326], [30,61, 62,45, 59,119], [10,13, 16,30, 33,23]]
class_threshold = 0.7
boxes = list()
for i in range(len(out)):
        boxes += decode_netout(out[i][0], anchors[i], class_threshold, input_h, input_w)
correct_yolo_boxes(boxes, image_h, image_w, input_h, input_w)
do_nms(boxes, 0.4)
labels = []
with open("D:\Veeraa 2021\PSG\DIP using Python\YOLO\coco.names", "r") as f:
    labels = [line.strip() for line in f.readlines()]
v_boxes, v_labels, v_scores = get_boxes(boxes, labels, class_threshold)
for i in range(len(v_boxes)):
        print(v_labels[i], v_scores[i])
draw_boxes(input_filename, v_boxes, v_labels, v_scores)
```

Fig. 11.83 (continued)

(a) "office" image

Fig. 11.84 Object detection result of YOLOv3 model. (**a**) "Office" image. (**b**) "Dog" image. (**c**) "Dining_table" image. (**d**) "Soccer" image

truck 94.48875784873962
bicycle 98.66693615913391
dog 99.73618984222412

(b) "dog" image

bottle 99.31203722953796
wine glass 98.65633845329285
wine glass 85.87427735328674
vase 99.93102550506592

(c) "dining_table" image

person 99.99862909317017
person 99.89579916000366
person 99.97996687889099
person 99.92873668670654
person 89.49975371360779
sports ball 99.93001818656921

(d) "soccer" image

Fig. 11.84   (continued)

11.6.9 Recurrent Neural Network (RNN)

A recurrent neural network (RNN) is a type of artificial neural network designed for processing and analyzing sequential data, where the order of inputs matters. Unlike traditional feedforward neural networks, RNNs have connections that loop back on themselves, enabling them to maintain an internal state or memory of past inputs. This ability to "remember" previous information allows RNNs to model temporal dependencies in sequential data, making them particularly effective for tasks such as time series forecasting, natural language processing, speech recognition, and video analysis. In an RNN, the output of each time step is not only influenced by the current input but also by the hidden state, which encodes information from prior time steps.

A recurrent neural network (RNN) is composed of multiple fixed activation function units, each corresponding to a specific time step in the sequence. The architecture of RNN is shown in Fig. 11.85. From this figure, it is possible to observe that the architecture contains an input layer (X), a hidden layer (h) with a loop, an output layer (Y), and weights (U, V, and W). At each time step, these units maintain an internal state known as the hidden state (h), which stores the knowledge that the network has accumulated from previous time steps. The hidden state essentially represents the "memory" of the network, encoding past information that influences the current output (Y). As the network processes the sequence, the hidden state is updated at every time step, reflecting changes in the network's understanding of the input data over time. The input layer (X) receives and processes the external input before passing it onto the next layer. In the middle layer, the hidden layers (h) contain multiple units, each equipped with its own activation function, weights, and biases. These hidden layers work together to transform the input data into a form that allows the network to make predictions or generate outputs based on the temporal patterns in the sequence. As information flows through the RNN, each hidden layer updates its activation based on both the current input and the previous hidden state, allowing the network to capture dependencies and relationships over time. This unique structure enables RNNs to handle sequential data, making them effective for speech recognition, language modelling, and time series forecasting tasks.

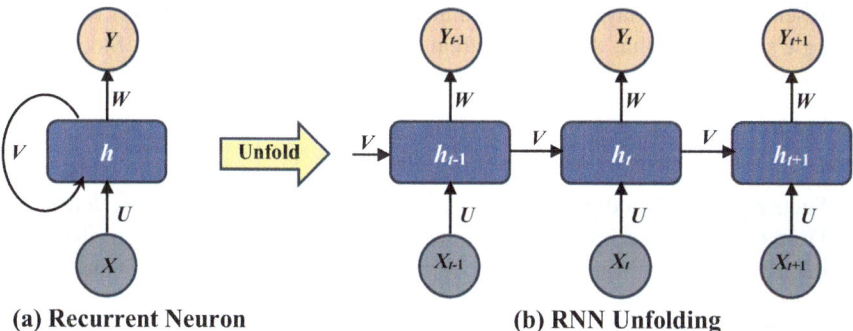

(a) Recurrent Neuron   (b) RNN Unfolding

Fig. 11.85 Architecture of recurrent neural network. (**a**) Recurrent neuron. (**b**) RNN unfolding

Steps of the RNN Network:

- **Step 1:** For each time step t, the current input X_t is provided to the network.
- **Step 2:** The hidden state h_t is computed by combining the input at the current time step and the previous hidden state h_{t-1}, using an activation function (like tanh or ReLU).
- **Step 3:** The current hidden state h_t becomes the previous hidden state h_{t-1} for the next time step.
- **Step 4:** After processing all time steps, the final hidden state h_t is calculated using the output activation function to calculate the output Y_t.
- **Step 5:** The output Y_t is compared to the actual target output Y_{true}, and the error is computed. The error is then propagated back through the network to adjust the weights, using gradient descent or another optimization method.

However, standard RNNs face challenges when it comes to learning long-term dependencies due to the problem of vanishing gradients. As the network learns through backpropagation, gradients can become extremely small, making it difficult for the model to update weights in earlier layers when dealing with long sequences. This limitation can cause the network to forget crucial information from earlier in the sequence. To overcome this, variations of RNNs like Long Short-Term Memory (LSTM) networks and Gated Recurrent Units (GRU) were introduced. These models use special gating mechanisms to control the flow of information and allow the network to retain important information over longer sequences, mitigating the vanishing gradient problem.

RNNs, including LSTMs and GRUs, have been foundational in the development of models for tasks involving sequential data. They have been widely used for applications such as machine translation, speech synthesis, sentiment analysis, and even in generating text. While newer architectures like Transformers have surpassed RNNs in some areas, particularly in natural language processing, RNNs remain a crucial part of the deep learning toolbox for certain sequence modelling tasks.

Experiment 11.31: Simple Recurrent Neural Network for Regression Task
This experiment discusses the prediction of Google Stock Price using RNN. Google Stock Price Dataset consists of two CSV (Comma Separated Values) files containing historical stock price data for training and evaluation. Each row in the dataset represents a trading day, and the columns provide various information related to Google's stock for that day. The Python code to predict the Google Stock Price using RNN is shown in Fig. 11.86, and its simulation result is shown in Fig. 11.87.

Inferences
The following inferences can be drawn from Fig. 11.86:

- Sequential CNN model is imported from the Keras and SimpleRNN, Dense and Drop out layers are imported from the Keras layers. Preprocessing of the input dataset is done by MinMaxScaler, which is imported from sklearn library.

```
## RNN
import numpy as np
import pandas as pd
import matplotlib.pyplot as plt
from sklearn.preprocessing import MinMaxScaler
from keras.models import Sequential
from keras.layers import Dense, SimpleRNN, Dropout
train_DS = pd.read_csv('Google_Stock_Price_Train.csv')
train = train_DS.loc[:, ['Open']].values
scaler = MinMaxScaler(feature_range = (0, 1))
train_scaled = scaler.fit_transform(train)
X_train, y_train = [], []
timesteps = 75
for i in range(timesteps, 1250):
    X_train.append(train_scaled[i - timesteps:i, 0])
    y_train.append(train_scaled[i, 0])
X_train, y_train = np.array(X_train), np.array(y_train)
X_train = np.reshape(X_train, (X_train.shape[0], X_train.shape[1], 1))
RNN = Sequential();#Initialize of RNN
RNN.add(SimpleRNN(units = 75, activation='relu', return_sequences=True, input_shape=
(X_train.shape[1],1)))
RNN.add(Dropout(0.2));# First RNN Layer
RNN.add(SimpleRNN(units = 75, activation='relu', return_sequences=True))
RNN.add(Dropout(0.2));# Second RNN Layer
RNN.add(SimpleRNN(units = 75, activation='relu', return_sequences=True))
RNN.add(Dropout(0.2));# Third RNN Layer
RNN.add(SimpleRNN(units = 75))
RNN.add(Dropout(0.2))
RNN.add(Dense(units = 1));# Output Layer
RNN.compile(optimizer='adam', loss= 'mean_squared_error');#Compile
RNN.fit(X_train, y_train, epochs=100, batch_size=32);# Training
print('RNN Model:', RNN.summary())
test_DS = pd.read_csv('Google_Stock_Price_Test.csv')
True_stock_price = test_DS.loc[:, ['Open']].values
total_DS = pd.concat((train_DS['Open'], test_DS['Open']), axis=0)
inputs = total_DS[len(total_DS)-len(test_DS) - timesteps:].values.reshape(-1,1)
inputs = scaler.transform(inputs) # min-max scaler
X_test = []
for i in range(timesteps, 95):
    X_test.append(inputs[i-timesteps:i,0])
X_test = np.array(X_test)
X_test = np.reshape(X_test, (X_test.shape[0], X_test.shape[1], 1))
predicted_stock_price = RNN.predict(X_test)
predicted_stock_price = scaler.inverse_transform(predicted_stock_price)
plt.plot(True_stock_price, color='green', label='True Google Stock Price')
plt.plot(predicted_stock_price, color='black', label='Predicted Google Stock Price')
plt.title('Google Stock Price Prediction'),plt.xlabel('Time')
plt.ylabel('Google Stock Price'),plt.legend(),plt.show()
```

Fig. 11.86 Python code for RNN model

Model: "sequential"

Layer (type)	Output Shape	Param #
simple_rnn (SimpleRNN)	(None, 75, 75)	5,775
dropout (Dropout)	(None, 75, 75)	0
simple_rnn_1 (SimpleRNN)	(None, 75, 75)	11,325
dropout_1 (Dropout)	(None, 75, 75)	0
simple_rnn_2 (SimpleRNN)	(None, 75, 75)	11,325
dropout_2 (Dropout)	(None, 75, 75)	0
simple_rnn_3 (SimpleRNN)	(None, 75)	11,325
dropout_3 (Dropout)	(None, 75)	0
dense (Dense)	(None, 1)	76

Total params: 119,480 (466.72 KB)
Trainable params: 39,826 (155.57 KB)
Non-trainable params: 0 (0.00 B)
Optimizer params: 79,654 (311.15 KB)

(a) Summary of RNN model

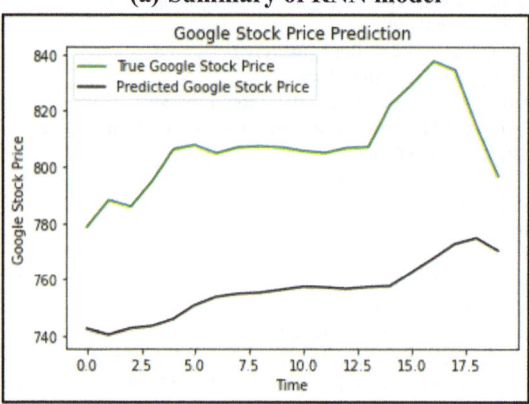

(b) True and predicted result of RNN model

Fig. 11.87 Simulation result of RNN model. (**a**) Summary of RNN model. (**b**) True and predicted result of RNN model

- Using the SimpleRNN, Drop out and Dense layers, the RNN model is created. Here, the ReLU activation function and the Adam optimizer is used to compile the RNN model with the mean square error loss function.

  The following inferences can be observed from Fig. 11.87:

- The RNN consists of Four SimpleRNN layers with ReLu activation function and the last layer is the Dense layer, which acts as an output layer.
- The true and predicted google stock price is plotted.

11.6.10 Generative Adversarial Networks (GANs)

Generative Adversarial Networks (GANs) are a revolutionary concept in deep learning, introduced by Ian Goodfellow and his collaborators in 2014. The primary aim of generative modelling is to autonomously learn patterns from input data, allowing the model to generate new examples that closely resemble the original dataset. GANs are designed to generate new data samples that resemble a given dataset by utilizing two neural networks, a generator and a discriminator, which compete with each other in a dynamic, game-like framework. Adversarial training enables these models to engage in a competitive process, where the generator gradually improves its ability to produce realistic samples, ultimately achieving a level where it can successfully deceive the discriminator about half the time. This competition fosters the creation of highly realistic synthetic data, which has wide-ranging applications in areas such as image synthesis, video generation, and data augmentation. The block diagram of GAN is shown in Fig. 11.88.

Generative Adversarial Networks (GANs) consist of two key components:

Generator: Focuses on learning a generative model that captures how data is created, using a probabilistic framework to simulate the data generation process.

Discriminator: Refers to the competitive dynamic where the generated samples are evaluated against real images from the dataset. A discriminator is employed to differentiate between authentic and generated images, fostering the adversarial setup.

Generator in a GAN The generator is a crucial component of a Generative Adversarial Network (GAN), responsible for creating new, realistic data samples. It takes random noise as input and transforms it into complex data representations, such as images or text, typically using a deep neural network. The generator is a kind of neural network tasked with creating synthetic data from a random noise vector, typically drawn from a Gaussian or uniform distribution. Its goal is to generate samples that are indistinguishable from real data. The generator transforms the low-dimensional noise input into high-dimensional data by passing it through layers of upsampling or deconvolution (in the case of image data). Over time, as the generator improves, it becomes increasingly adept at producing realistic outputs.

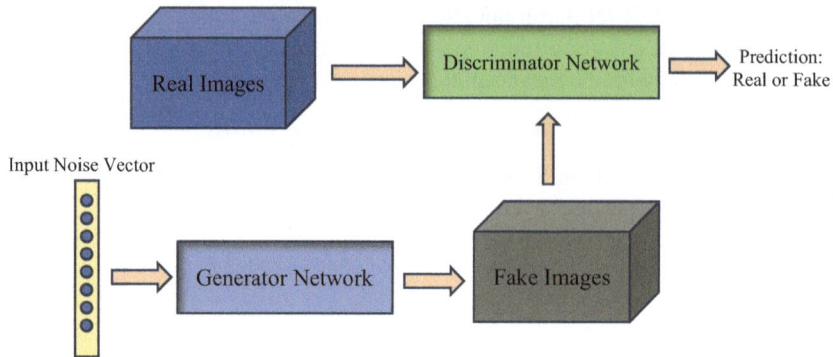

Fig. 11.88 Block diagram for GAN model

Through training, the generator learns the underlying distribution of the training data by adjusting its parameters. This is achieved using backpropagation, where the generator fine-tunes its layers to produce outputs that closely resemble real data. The success of the generator lies in its ability to create high-quality, diverse samples that effectively deceive the discriminator.

Generator Loss The generator's objective in a GAN is to produce synthetic samples that are realistic enough to fool the discriminator. This is achieved by minimizing its loss function (JG), which encourages the discriminator to classify the generated samples as real. The loss function is defined as:

$$JG = -\frac{1}{m}\sum\nolimits_{i=1}^{m} \log D\big(G(Z_i)\big) \tag{11.19}$$

where "JG" measures how effectively the generator fools the discriminator. The "$\log D(G(Z_i))$" represents the log probability of the discriminator classifying the generated samples as real.
The generator aims to minimize this loss by maximizing the discriminator's likelihood of misclassifying the generated data as real $\log D(G(Z_i))$ by approaching highly realistic synthetic samples.

Discriminator in GAN In Generative Adversarial Networks (GANs), the discriminator is an artificial neural network designed to classify inputs as real (from the training dataset) or fake (generated by the generator). It acts as a binary classifier, evaluating input samples and assigning a probability score indicating their authenticity. It evaluates the authenticity of the data by learning to recognize patterns and features characteristic of real samples. The discriminator's architecture often involves convolutional layers for feature extraction and fully connected layers for binary classification. As training progresses, the discriminator learns to become more accurate in identifying fake data.

During training, the discriminator learns to differentiate genuine data from the dataset and artificial samples created by the generator. Over time, it refines its parameters to improve accuracy and proficiency. For image data, its architecture often incorporates convolutional layers or other domain-specific structures. The goal of adversarial training is to maximize the discriminator's ability to correctly identify real samples as authentic and generated samples as fake. Through the iterative interaction between the generator and discriminator, the GAN evolves to produce highly realistic synthetic data.

Discriminator Loss   The discriminator's objective is to minimize the negative log-likelihood of accurately classifying both real and generated samples. This is achieved using the following loss function:

$$JD = -\frac{1}{m}\sum\nolimits_{i=1}^{m} \log D\left(X_i\right) - \frac{1}{m}\sum\nolimits_{i=1}^{m}\left(1 - \log D\left(G\left(Z_i\right)\right)\right) \qquad (11.20)$$

where "JD" measures the discriminator's ability to distinguish between real and generated samples. The "$\log D(X_i)$" represents the log probability of the discriminator correctly classifying real samples. The "$\log D(G(Z_i))$" is the log probability of the discriminator correctly identifying generated samples as fake. The discriminator minimizes this loss to accurately classify real and artificial samples, improving its performance in the adversarial process.

Minimax Loss   The overall adversarial training objective in GANs is based on a minimax optimization problem, expressed as:

$$\min_{G}\max_{D} E_{X\sim pdata(X)}\left[\log D\left(X\right)\right] + E_{Z\sim pz(Z)}\left[\log\left(1 - D\left(G\left(Z\right)\right)\right)\right] \qquad (11.21)$$

where "G" is the generator network, "D" is the discriminator network, "X" is the real data samples drawn from the true data distribution "$pdata(X)$". "Z" is the random noise sampled from a prior distribution $pz(Z)$. "$D(X)$" is the probability that the discriminator correctly identifies real data as authentic. $D(G(Z))$ is the probability that the discriminator classifies generated data as authentic. The generator aims to minimize this objective, while the discriminator seeks to maximize it, leading to a dynamic balance that drives both networks to improve iteratively. The objective is to reach a Nash equilibrium where the generator produces samples so indistinguishable from real data that the discriminator classifies both real and fake data with equal probability (0.5).

However, training GANs is not without challenges. One major issue is mode collapse, where the generator learns to produce a limited variety of outputs, ignoring the full data distribution. Another difficulty is training instability, which can arise when the discriminator becomes too strong, causing the generator to stagnate. Furthermore, GANs are sensitive to hyperparameters such as learning rates, batch sizes, and architectural design, requiring meticulous tuning for effective training.

The applications of GANs are vast and transformative. In the domain of image synthesis, GANs can create realistic images of objects, scenes, or people. They are used for style transfer, where one image's artistic style is applied to another. GANs enable super-resolution, enhancing low-resolution images to high resolutions for improved quality. In data augmentation, GANs generate synthetic training samples to improve model performance in cases of limited data. Additionally, GANs find applications in video synthesis, creating animations or sequences, and anomaly detection, identifying unusual patterns by comparing generated data with observed inputs. Overall, GANs have become a cornerstone of generative modelling, pushing the boundaries of artificial intelligence in creating realistic and high-quality synthetic data. They continue to evolve, addressing their inherent challenges and opening up new possibilities for innovation across industries.

Implementation of GAN   The following steps have to be followed for the implementation of GAN:

> **Step 1:** Initialization: A Generator (G) creates synthetic data, and a Discriminator (D) evaluates whether data is real or fake.
> **Step 2:** Generation: "G" takes a random noise vector as input and transforms it into a data sample (e.g. an image).
> **Step 3:** Discrimination: "D" analyzes both real data (from the training set) and generated data, outputting a probability of authenticity.
> **Step 4:** Adversarial Training: "G" improves by trying to "fool" D into classifying fake data as real. "D" refines its ability to distinguish real data from fake.
> **Step 5:** Progression: As training continues, "G" generates increasingly realistic data, making it harder for "D" to differentiate real from fake. When "G" consistently produces data indistinguishable from real samples, it is considered well-trained.

Experiment 11.32: Implementation of DCGAN for Image Generation

This experiment discusses the implementation of DCGAN using Python environment. The DCGAN is a kind of Generative Adversarial Network, which is used to generate 2D image using deep learning mechanism. For the implementation, MNIST dataset is used to train the DCGAN model, and input noisy data is given as an input to the trained model, which generates the MNIST data. The Python code for the GAN is given in Fig. 11.89, and its simulation result is shown in Fig. 11.90.

Inferences

The following inferences can be drawn from this experiment:

- From Fig. 11.89, it is possible to observe that MNIST data is loaded and two main functions such as "Generator" and "Discriminator" are implemented using the deep learning concepts. The "make_generator_model()" function is used as a generator model, which generates the 2D image when noisy data is given as an input in it.
- The "make_discriminator_model()" function is used as a discriminator model, which discriminates the output generated by the generator model.

```
#DCGAN
import tensorflow as tf
import matplotlib.pyplot as plt
import os
import PIL
from tensorflow.keras import layers
import time
from IPython import display
(train_images, train_labels), (_, _) = tf.keras.datasets.mnist.load_data()
train_images = train_images.reshape(train_images.shape[0], 28, 28, 1).astype('float32')
train_images = (train_images - 127.5) / 127.5  # Normalize the images to [-1, 1]
BUFFER_SIZE, BATCH_SIZE = 10000,128
train_dataset =
tf.data.Dataset.from_tensor_slices(train_images).shuffle(BUFFER_SIZE).batch(BATCH_SIZE)
def make_generator_model():
  Generator = tf.keras.Sequential()
  Generator.add(layers.Dense(7*7*256, use_bias=False, input_shape=(100,)))
  Generator.add(layers.BatchNormalization())
  Generator.add(layers.LeakyReLU())
  Generator.add(layers.Reshape((7, 7, 256)))
  assert Generator.output_shape == (None, 7, 7, 256)  # Note: None is the batch size
  Generator.add(layers.Conv2DTranspose(128, (5, 5), strides=(1, 1), padding='same',
use_bias=False))
  assert Generator.output_shape == (None, 7, 7, 128)
  Generator.add(layers.BatchNormalization())
  Generator.add(layers.LeakyReLU())
  Generator.add(layers.Conv2DTranspose(64, (5, 5), strides=(2, 2), padding='same',
use_bias=False))
  assert Generator.output_shape == (None, 14, 14, 64)
  Generator.add(layers.BatchNormalization())
  Generator.add(layers.LeakyReLU())
  Generator.add(layers.Conv2DTranspose(1, (5, 5), strides=(2, 2), padding='same',
use_bias=False, activation='tanh'))
  assert Generator.output_shape == (None, 28, 28, 1)
  return Generator
Generator = make_generator_model()
noise = tf.random.normal([1, 100])
generated_image = Generator(noise, training=False)
plt.imshow(generated_image[0, :, :, 0], cmap='gray'),
plt.title('Noisy Image'),plt.xticks([]),plt.yticks([])
```

Fig. 11.89   Python code for DCGAN model

```
def make_discriminator_model():
  Discriminator = tf.keras.Sequential()
  Discriminator.add(layers.Conv2D(64, (5, 5), strides=(2, 2), padding='same',input_shape=[28,
28, 1]))
  Discriminator.add(layers.LeakyReLU())
  Discriminator.add(layers.Dropout(0.3))
  Discriminator.add(layers.Conv2D(128, (5, 5), strides=(2, 2), padding='same'))
  Discriminator.add(layers.LeakyReLU())
  Discriminator.add(layers.Dropout(0.3))
  Discriminator.add(layers.Flatten())
  Discriminator.add(layers.Dense(1))
  return Discriminator
Discriminator = make_discriminator_model()
decision = Discriminator(generated_image)
print (decision)
cross_entropy = tf.keras.losses.BinaryCrossentropy(from_logits=True)
def Discriminator_loss(real_output, fake_output):
  real_loss = cross_entropy(tf.ones_like(real_output), real_output)
  fake_loss = cross_entropy(tf.zeros_like(fake_output), fake_output)
  total_loss = real_loss + fake_loss
  return total_loss
def Generator_loss(fake_output):
  return cross_entropy(tf.ones_like(fake_output), fake_output)
Generator_optimizer = tf.keras.optimizers.Adam(1e-4)
Discriminator_optimizer = tf.keras.optimizers.Adam(1e-4)
checkpoint_dir = './training_checkpoints'
checkpoint_prefix = os.path.join(checkpoint_dir, "ckpt")
checkpoint = tf.train.Checkpoint(generator_optimizer=Generator_optimizer,
                 discriminator_optimizer=Discriminator_optimizer,
                 generator=Generator,discriminator=Discriminator)
EPOCHS, noise_dim, num_examples_to_generate  = 50, 100, 9
seed = tf.random.normal([num_examples_to_generate, noise_dim])
@tf.function
def train_step(images):
  noise = tf.random.normal([BATCH_SIZE, noise_dim])
  with tf.GradientTape() as gen_tape, tf.GradientTape() as disc_tape:
    generated_images = Generator(noise, training=True)
    real_output = Discriminator(images, training=True)
    fake_output = Discriminator(generated_images, training=True)
    gen_loss = Generator_loss(fake_output)
    disc_loss = Discriminator_loss(real_output, fake_output)
  gradients_of_generator = gen_tape.gradient(gen_loss, Generator.trainable_variables)
  gradients_of_discriminator = disc_tape.gradient(disc_loss, Discriminator.trainable_variables)
  Generator_optimizer.apply_gradients(zip(gradients_of_generator,
Generator.trainable_variables))
  Discriminator_optimizer.apply_gradients(zip(gradients_of_discriminator,
Discriminator.trainable_variables))
```

Fig. 11.89 (continued)

```
def train(dataset, epochs):
  for epoch in range(epochs):
    start = time.time()
    for image_batch in dataset:
      train_step(image_batch)
    display.clear_output(wait=True)
    generate_and_save_images(Generator,epoch + 1,seed)
    if (epoch + 1) % 15 == 0:
      checkpoint.save(file_prefix = checkpoint_prefix)
    print ('Time for epoch {} is {} sec'.format(epoch + 1, time.time()-start))
  display.clear_output(wait=True)
  generate_and_save_images(Generator,epochs,seed)

def generate_and_save_images(model, epoch, test_input):
  predictions = model(test_input, training=False)
  fig = plt.figure(figsize=(4, 4))
  for i in range(predictions.shape[0]):
    plt.subplot(3, 3, i+1)
    plt.imshow(predictions[i, :, :, 0] * 127.5 + 127.5, cmap='gray')
    plt.axis('off')
train(train_dataset, EPOCHS)
checkpoint.restore(tf.train.latest_checkpoint(checkpoint_dir))

def display_image(epoch_no):
    return PIL.Image.open('image_at_epoch_{:04d}.png'.format(epoch_no))
display_image(EPOCHS)
```

Fig. 11.89 (continued)

- The "Discriminator_loss" function is used to identify whether the image generated by the generator is true or fake image with the help of "BinaryCrossentropy" loss measure.
- During train process "train_step(images)", the input to the generator is "noisy" and discriminator gets two inputs like real input image and image generated by generator, and its corresponding outputs are "real output" and "fake output".
- The generator loss is obtained by the fake output of the discriminator and discriminator loss is obtained by real output of the discriminator.
- Figure 11.90 shows the input noisy image and 9 images generated by the DCGAN at 50th Epoch.

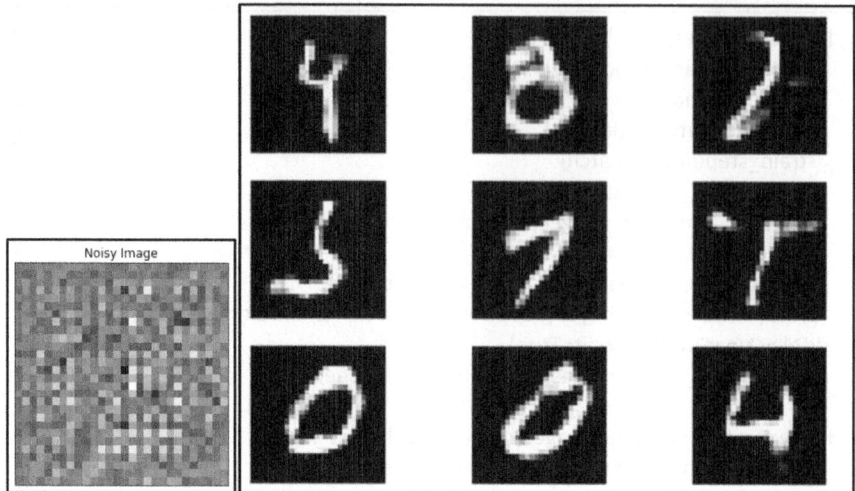

(a) Input to the Generator   (b) Output image from GAN at 50 epoch

Fig. 11.90 Simulation result. (a) Input to the generator. (b) Output image from GAN at 50 epoch

11.6.11   CycleGAN

CycleGAN (Cycle-Consistent Generative Adversarial Network) is a type of GAN architecture designed for unsupervised image-to-image translation. It enables the conversion of images from one domain to another (e.g. Horses to Zebras, Summer to Winter landscapes) without requiring paired examples for training. This is particularly useful in situations where paired data is unavailable or impractical to collect.

CycleGAN is designed to transfer the characteristics of one set of images to another or map the distribution of images from one domain to another. It frames the task as an image reconstruction problem. First, an input image (X) is processed through a generator "G" to create a translated version. Then, this translated image is passed through another generator "F" to reconstruct the original image. The mean squared error (MSE) loss is calculated between the original image and its reconstruction to evaluate the quality of the process. A key feature of CycleGAN is its ability to perform image translation with unpaired datasets, where no direct correspondence exists between the input and output images.

There are two key features of Cycle GAN as compared to Vanilla GAN. Those are as follows. Unlike traditional GANs, which require paired images (e.g. a horse image and its zebra equivalent), CycleGAN learns the mapping between two image domains (e.g. horses and zebras) using unpaired datasets. The core innovation of CycleGAN lies in its cycle consistency loss. It ensures that when an image from domain "A" is translated to domain "B" and then back to domain "A", the resulting image should closely resemble the original. This constraint stabilizes the training

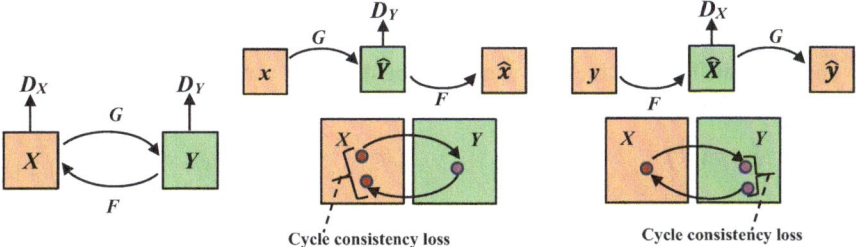

Fig. 11.91 Training procedure for CycleGAN

process and preserves essential details. CycleGAN is a powerful framework for unsupervised image-to-image translation, leveraging adversarial training and cycle consistency to achieve remarkable results in unpaired datasets. Its flexibility and versatility make it a popular choice for tasks spanning art, medical imaging, and data augmentation. The training procedure of CycleGAN is illustrated in Fig. 11.91.

CycleGAN consists of two main components: a generator and a discriminator. The generator's role is to produce samples that mimic the desired distribution, while the discriminator's job is to distinguish whether a given sample is from the actual distribution (real) or generated by the generator (fake). The basic difference between the CycleGAN apart from Vanilla GAN architectures is its use of two mapping functions (*GG* and *FF*), which serve as generators, along with their corresponding discriminators (DBD_B and DAD_A). These mapping functions are defined as:

$$G : X \to Y \quad \text{and} \quad F : Y \to X, G : X \to Y \tag{11.22}$$

Here, X represents the input image distribution, and Y denotes the target output distribution. The discriminators corresponding to these mappings are designed to evaluate the authenticity of samples in their respective domains.

Cycle GAN Architecture

The CycleGAN architecture consists of two generators and two discriminators. The first generator (GG) transforms images from domain A to domain B and the second generator (FF) transforms images from domain B to domain A. Similarly, the first discriminator (DBD_B) distinguishes real images from domain B and fake images generated by GG(G(A)G(A)). The second discriminator (DAD_A) distinguishes real images from domain A and fake images generated by FF(F(B)F(B)).

The CycleGAN framework combines several loss functions to achieve its objectives: They are (1) adversarial loss, (2) cycle consistency loss, and (3) total loss.

1. Adversarial Loss: Each generator aims to produce images that can fool the corresponding discriminator, while each discriminator learns to distinguish between real and fake images. The adversarial loss function is given by

$$L_{\text{GAN}} \left(G, DB, A, B \right) = E_{b \sim pdata(b)} \left[\log DB(b) \right] + E_{a \sim pdata(a)} \left[1 - \log DB(G(a)) \right] \tag{11.23}$$

Similarly, FF and DAD_A have their adversarial loss.

2. Cycle Consistency Loss: Ensures that the translation process preserves the original content. This is achieved by minimizing the discrepancy between the original image and the image reconstructed after a round-trip translation.

$$L_{\text{cyc}}(G, F) = E_{a \sim pdata(a)} \Big[F\big(G(a)\big) - a_1 \Big] + E_{b \sim pdata(b)} \Big[G\big(F(b)\big) - b_1 \Big] \qquad (11.24)$$

3. Total Loss: The total objective combines adversarial loss and cycle consistency loss, which is mathematically written as

$$L\big(G, F, DA, DB\big) = L_{\text{GAN}}\big(G, DB, A, B\big) + L_{\text{GAN}}\big(G, DA, B, A\big) + \lambda L_{\text{cyc}}\big(G, F\big) \ (11.25)$$

where λ is a weight factor that balances the two losses.

Training Process of CycleGAN

The training process of the cycle GAN is as follows:

Step 1: Initialization: Two generators, G and F, and two discriminators, DAD_A and DBD_B, are initialized. Random noise or real images are used as inputs to the generators.

Step 2: Adversarial training: Generators G and F are trained to produce images that can deceive discriminators DBD_B and DAD_A, respectively. Discriminators are trained to improve their ability to classify real and fake images.

Step 3: Cycle consistency: For each input image, the round-trip consistency is enforced by minimizing the cycle consistency loss.

Step 4: Iterative updates: The generator and discriminator networks are updated alternately in a competitive process until convergence.

Advantages of Cycle GAN

- No Need for Paired Data: CycleGAN is highly effective in scenarios where collecting paired datasets is infeasible.
- Cycle Consistency: Ensures that the transformation preserves the semantic content of the original image.
- Versatility: Can be applied across various domains, including medical imaging, art, and data augmentation.

11.6.12   StyleGAN

StyleGAN (Style Generative Adversarial Network) is an advanced variant of GANs that focuses on generating high-quality images with controllable visual features. It was introduced by NVIDIA in 2018 and has since become a popular tool for generating realistic images, such as human faces, artworks, and more. The key feature of StyleGAN is its ability to generate images by separating different levels of control, allowing for greater flexibility in controlling fine-grained visual aspects, such as facial features, background, and overall style.

The StyleGAN algorithm follows four major steps:

Step 1: Separation of Latent Space: StyleGAN introduces a new approach to manipulating the latent space, where instead of directly mapping a random noise vector to the output, the model operates in a hierarchical manner by controlling different aspects of image generation at multiple layers.

Step 2: Style Modulation: In StyleGAN, the input latent vector "z" is first mapped to an intermediate latent space "w", which is then used to modulate the feature maps in the generator at different scales. This modulation, known as "style", allows the model to control different levels of image attributes.

Step 3: Progressive Growing: StyleGAN uses a technique called progressive growing, where the network starts by generating low-resolution images and gradually increases the resolution during training. This process helps improve the quality of generated images by allowing the model to learn coarse features first before refining them at higher resolutions.

Step 4: Adaptive Instance Normalization (AdaIN): To apply style at each layer, StyleGAN uses AdaIN, a method that normalizes feature maps at each layer of the generator by scaling and shifting them using parameters derived from the latent vector "w". This allows the model to control the style of the generated image at different levels of detail, leading to more refined control over the final output.

StyleGAN consists of two main components: the Generator and the Discriminator. However, the generator in StyleGAN operates differently compared to the other versions of the GANs due to the style-based approach. The architecture of StyleGAN is shown in Fig. 11.92.

Generator: The generator takes in a latent vector "z" and processes it through a mapping network, which outputs an intermediate latent vector "w". This vector is then used to modulate the feature maps in the generator. The generator's architecture progressively adds layers to produce higher-resolution images. Key features include:

- Mapping Network: Transforms the random noise vector z into an intermediate latent space w.
- Style Modulation: The intermediate latent vector w is used to modulate the features at each layer, allowing for control over the generated image's style.
- Progressive Upsampling: The image is generated in a series of stages, starting from low resolution and gradually increasing in size, with each stage progressively refining the image.

Discriminator: The discriminator evaluates the authenticity of the images produced by the generator. It distinguishes between real images (from the training set) and fake images (generated by the generator). The discriminator is typically a convolutional neural network (CNN) that outputs a probability indicating whether an image is real or fake.

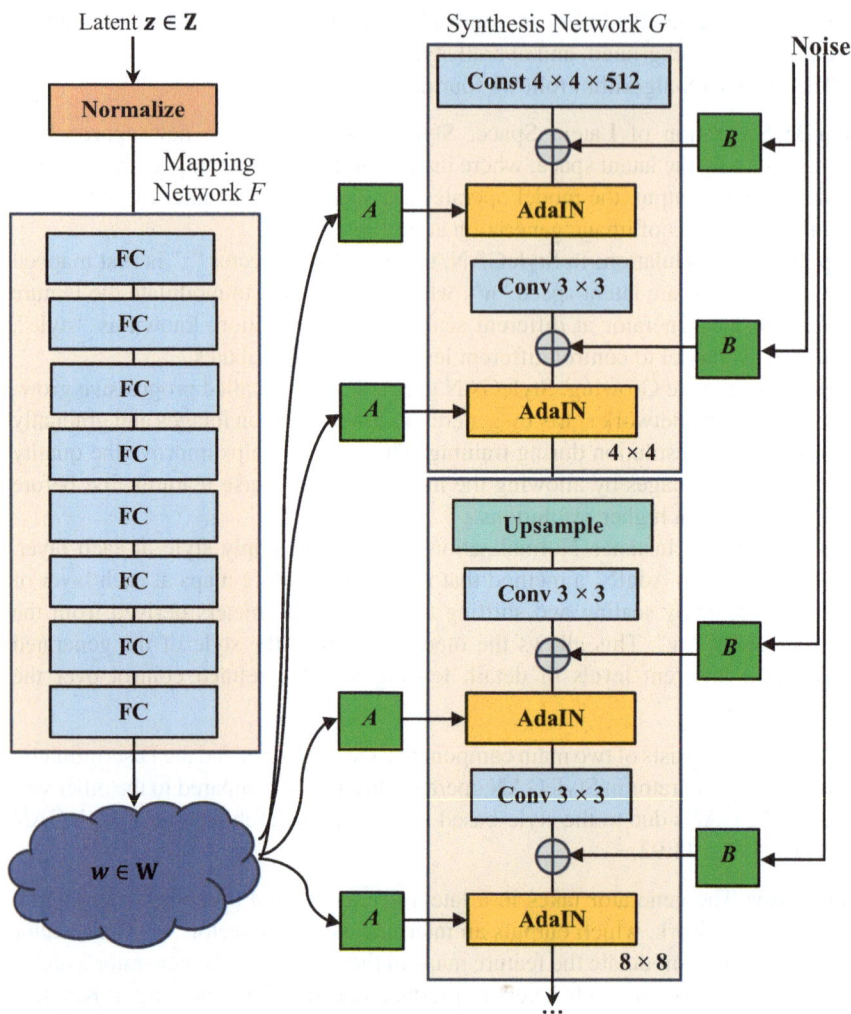

Fig. 11.92 Architecture of StyleGAN

Loss Functions in StyleGAN: StyleGAN uses a combination of loss functions to train the generator and discriminator effectively:

Adversarial Loss: The core loss for training GANs, encouraging the generator to produce images that can fool the discriminator, and the discriminator to correctly distinguish real from fake images.

$$L_{\text{GAN}} = E_{x \sim pdata(x)}\Big[\log D(x)\Big] + E_{z \sim pz(z)}\Big[1 - D\big(G(z)\big)\Big] \qquad (11.26)$$

Perceptual Path Length Regularization: To stabilize training and improve the quality of generated images, StyleGAN incorporates a perceptual path length regularization, which helps the generator produce smooth transitions in the latent space, preventing issues like mode collapse.

Style Loss: StyleGAN introduces an additional loss function that ensures the generated image maintains the intended style at different layers of the generator. This loss encourages the generator to modulate features in a way that matches the desired style.

Advantages of StyleGAN

- Control Over Image Features: The style-based approach allows users to have fine-grained control over various aspects of the generated image, such as pose, color, and texture, making it more versatile compared to traditional GANs.
- High-Quality Images: StyleGAN is capable of generating highly detailed and photorealistic images, especially with its progressive growth and style modulation techniques.
- Flexibility in Application: StyleGAN is widely applicable in diverse fields, from entertainment (creating synthetic faces for movies) to medicine (generating medical images for training purposes).

11.6.13 Conditional GAN

A Conditional Generative Adversarial Network (CGAN) is an advanced variation of the standard Generative Adversarial Network (GAN), where the generation of output is conditioned on specific input data. A GAN can be adapted into a conditional model by introducing additional information (denoted as y) to both the generator and discriminator. This extra information could be anything from class labels to data from other sources, which is provided alongside the usual input to guide the generation process.

Generator Architecture: In a CGAN, the generator receives two inputs: the prior input noise (z) and the conditioning information (y). These are combined into a joint hidden representation, from which the generator produces synthetic data. The adversarial training framework allows flexibility in how this hidden representation is constructed.

Discriminator Architecture: Similarly, the discriminator receives both real data (x) and the conditioning information (y) as inputs. Its task is to distinguish between real data and synthetic data generated by the generator, based on the given condition (y).

Loss Function: The objective function for the conditional GAN is framed as a two-player minimax game:

$$\min_G \max_D V(D,G) = E_{x \sim pdata(x)}\Big[\log D(x|y)\Big] + E_{z \sim pz(z)}\Big[\log\big(1 - D\big(G(z|y)\big)\big)\Big] \quad (11.27)$$

Here, E represents the expected operator, which denotes the expected value of a random variable. $E_{X \sim pdata(X)}$ denotes the expected value with respect to the real data distribution $pdata(x)$, while $E_{Z \sim pz(Z)}$ denotes the expected value with respect to the prior noise distribution $pz(Z)$.

The goal is to balance the generator and discriminator's abilities. The first term $logD(x|y)$ encourages the discriminator to correctly classify real data. The second term $log(1 - D(G(z|y)))$ encourages the generator to create data that the discriminator will classify as real. This balance helps the generator improve its ability to produce realistic data, while the discriminator becomes more adept at distinguishing between real and generated data based on the given conditions.

11.6.14   Variational Autoencoder (VAE)

The Variational Autoencoders (VAEs) are generative models used in machine learning to generate new data in the form of variations of the input data trained in the model. Autoencoder is a neural architecture that consists of two parts: encoder and decoder. The decoder follows the encoder, and in the middle, there is the so-called hidden layer that has various names and can sometimes be referred to as the bottleneck layer, latent space, hidden layer, encoding layer, or code layer. Like autoencoders (AE), the VAEs are deep learning models that consist of an encoder and a decoder. The encoder learns to isolate the important latent variables from the training dataset, and a decoder uses those latent variables to reconstruct the original input data. The VAE architecture was originally developed by Diederik O. Kingma and Max Welling in 2013. Most autoencoder architectures encode a discrete dataset with a fixed representation of latent variables, whereas VAE architecture encodes a continuous dataset with the probabilistic representation of that latent space. The advantage of VAE over AE is that VAE not only reconstructs the exact original input but also uses variational inference to generate new data output that resembles the original input data. VAEs are probabilistic models. VAEs encode latent variables of training data not as a fixed discrete value z but as a continuous range of possibilities expressed as a probability distribution $p(z)$. The VAEs encode two latent vectors: a vector of means (μ) and standard deviations (σ). These two vectors represent the range of possibilities for each latent variable and the expected variance within each range of possibilities. Using the methodologies, reconstruction loss, Kullback-Leibler (KL) divergence, evidence lower bound, and reparameterization trick, VAEs can synthesize new data samples that are unique and original unto themselves and resemble the original training data.

Reconstruction Loss: VAEs use reconstruction loss, also called reconstruction error, as a primary loss function in training. Reconstruction loss measures the difference between the original input data and the reconstructed output by the decoder. The cross-entropy loss or mean squared error (MSE) can be used as the reconstruction loss function in the training of VAE. In general, the autoencoder model creates a bottleneck that allows only a subset of the original input data to pass through to the decoder. The training process starts with a randomized initialization of model parameters; the encoder has not yet learned which parts of the data to weigh more heavily. As a result, it will initially output a suboptimal latent representation, and the decoder will output a somewhat inaccurate or incomplete reconstruction of the original input. By minimizing reconstruction loss through gradient descent over the parameters of the encode and decoder blocks, the weights of the autoencoder model will be adjusted to yield a more useful encoding of latent space. The reconstruction loss alone is sufficient to optimize the encoders. However, a variational autoencoder aims to reconstruct the original input and generate new samples that resemble the original input. An additional optimization algorithm like Kullback-Leibler (KL) divergence can be utilized for this.

Kullback-Leibler (KL) Divergence: The KL divergence is a metric used to compare two probability distributions. Minimizing the KL divergence between the learned distribution of latent variables and a simple Gaussian distribution whose values range from 0 to 1 forces the learned encoding of latent variables to follow a normal distribution. This distribution helps smooth the interpolation of any point in latent space, thereby generating new images. The issue with using KL divergence for variational inference is that the denominator of the equation is intractable, meaning it would take a theoretically infinite amount of time to compute directly. VAEs approximate the minimization of KL divergence by maximizing the evidence lower bound (ELBO).

Evidence Lower Bound (ELBO): Evidence Lower Bound (ELBO) refers to the probability of observable input data, which is responsible for the reconstruction. Those observable variables in the input data are the "evidence" for the latent variables discovered by the autoencoder. The "lower bound" refers to the worst-case estimate for the log-likelihood of a given distribution. The actual log-likelihood may be higher than the ELBO. A specific output of the autoencoder is conditioned by both the KL divergence loss term and the reconstruction loss term, which fits the "evidence" of the training data. Hence, training a model for variational inference can be referred to as maximizing the ELBO. The variation autoencoder aims to generate new output data in random variations of the training dataset. VAE uses a function that selects a random value for the latent variable, which the decoder can then use to generate an approximate reconstruction of the input data. However, an inherent randomness property cannot be optimized because there is no best random or vector of random values. Therefore, using any gradient descent approach, such a random vector cannot be optimized through backpropagation. To overcome this issue, VAE uses the reparameterization trick.

Reparameterization Trick: The reparameterization trick introduces a new parameter (ε), a random value selected from the normal distribution between 0 and 1. This new parameter modifies the latent variable (z) as $=\mu_x + \varepsilon\sigma_x$. Because the random value ε is not derived from and has no relation to the autoencoder model's parameters, it can be ignored during backpropagation. This model is updated through some form of gradient descent, a gradient-based optimization algorithm also developed by Kingma to maximize the ELBO.

Experiment 11.33: Implementation of Variational Autoencoder (VAE)
This experiment discusses the implementation of a variational autoencoder (VAE) using a Python environment. The VAE is an autoencoder, but it can generate new images. The "fashion MNIST" dataset is used to train the VAE model for implementation. This is a dataset of 60,000 28 × 28 grayscale images of 10 fashion categories and a test set of 10,000 images. The 10 fashion categories are {"T-shirt/top", "Trouser", "Pullover", "Dress", "Coat", "Sandal", "Shirt", "Sneaker", "Bag", "Ankle boot"}. The VAE model is initially trained with the fashion MNIST dataset, and based on the latent variable, the decoder can generate a new output. The Python code for the VAE is given in Fig. 11.93, and its simulation results are shown in Figs. 11.94 and 11.95.

Inferences
The following inferences can be drawn from this experiment:
   From Fig. 11.93, it is possible to infer that

- The Fashion MNIST dataset is imported to train and test the VAE model.
- The encoder of the VAE is modelled with an input image, mean, variance and sampling value.
- The decoder of the VAE model predicts the output or generates the output based on the latent vector.
- "Adam" optimizer is used to train the model.

   From Figs. 11.94 and 11.95, the following inferences can be made:

- Figure 11.94 shows the various layers of the encoder and decoder of VAE in the form of a summary.
- The encoder block of VAE consists of input layer, two convolutional layers, a flatten layer, and three dense layers. Finally, it contains a sampling layer.
- The decoder block of VAE consists of an input layer that receives input as a latent dimension, one dense layer, a reshape layer, and three convolutional transpose layers. The final output of the decoder layer is getting from the last convolutional transpose layer.
- Figure 11.95 shows the image generated by the VAE for the specific latent points varied from (−1 to 1). The number of epochs is chosen as 10.
- The number of latent points is fixed as 25. Hence, the resultant image contains 25 generated images, as evident in Fig. 11.95.

Exercises

1. Write a Python code to perform gray level slicing operation on 2D image using classical programming.
2. Read the "Penguin dataset". Apply a multinomial logistic regression algorithm to classify the data and obtain the accuracy of it.

```
# Variational Autoencoder (VAE)
import numpy as np
import tensorflow as tf
import keras
from keras import layers
import matplotlib.pyplot as plt
(x_train, _), (x_test, _) = keras.datasets.fashion_mnist.load_data()
fashion_mnist = np.concatenate([x_train, x_test], axis=0)
fashion_mnist = np.expand_dims(fashion_mnist, -1).astype("float32") / 255

class Sampling(layers.Layer):
  def call(self, inputs):
    mean, log_var = inputs
    batch = tf.shape(mean)[0]
    dim = tf.shape(mean)[1]
    epsilon = tf.random.normal(shape=(batch, dim))
    return mean + tf.exp(0.5 * log_var) * epsilon
latent_dim = 2
# Encoder Block
encoder_inputs = keras.Input(shape=(28, 28, 1))
x = layers.Conv2D(64, 3, activation="relu", strides=2, padding="same")(encoder_inputs)
x = layers.Conv2D(128, 3, activation="relu", strides=2, padding="same")(x)
x = layers.Flatten()(x)
x = layers.Dense(16, activation="relu")(x)
mean = layers.Dense(latent_dim, name="mean")(x)
log_var = layers.Dense(latent_dim, name="log_var")(x)
z = Sampling()([mean, log_var])
encoder = keras.Model(encoder_inputs, [mean, log_var, z], name="encoder")
encoder.summary()
#Decoder Block
latent_inputs = keras.Input(shape=(latent_dim,))
x = layers.Dense(7 * 7 * 64, activation="relu")(latent_inputs)
x = layers.Reshape((7, 7, 64))(x)
x = layers.Conv2DTranspose(128, 3, activation="relu", strides=2, padding="same")(x)
x = layers.Conv2DTranspose(64, 3, activation="relu", strides=2, padding="same")(x)
decoder_outputs = layers.Conv2DTranspose(1, 3, activation="sigmoid", padding="same")(x)
decoder = keras.Model(latent_inputs, decoder_outputs, name="decoder")
decoder.summary()
class VAE(keras.Model):
        def __init__(self, encoder, decoder, **kwargs):
                super().__init__(**kwargs)
                self.encoder = encoder
                self.decoder = decoder
                self.total_loss_tracker = keras.metrics.Mean(name="total_loss")
                self.reconstruction_loss_tracker =
keras.metrics.Mean(name="reconstruction_loss")
                self.kl_loss_tracker = keras.metrics.Mean(name="kl_loss")
```

Fig. 11.93 Python code for VAE model

```
        @property
        def metrics(self):
        return[self.total_loss_tracker,self.reconstruction_loss_tracker,self.kl_loss_tracker]

        def train_step(self, data):
                with tf.GradientTape() as tape:
                        mean,log_var, z = self.encoder(data)
                        reconstruction = self.decoder(z)
                        reconstruction_loss = tf.reduce_mean(
                                tf.reduce_sum(keras.losses.binary_crossentropy(data,
reconstruction),axis=(1, 2)))
                        kl_loss = -0.5 * (1 + log_var - tf.square(mean) - tf.exp(log_var))
                        kl_loss = tf.reduce_mean(tf.reduce_sum(kl_loss, axis=1))
                        total_loss = reconstruction_loss + kl_loss
                grads = tape.gradient(total_loss, self.trainable_weights)
                self.optimizer.apply_gradients(zip(grads, self.trainable_weights))
                self.total_loss_tracker.update_state(total_loss)
                self.reconstruction_loss_tracker.update_state(reconstruction_loss)
                self.kl_loss_tracker.update_state(kl_loss)
                return {"loss": self.total_loss_tracker.result(),
                        "reconstruction_loss": self.reconstruction_loss_tracker.result(),
                        "kl_loss": self.kl_loss_tracker.result()}
vae = VAE(encoder, decoder)
vae.compile(optimizer=keras.optimizers.Adam())
vae.fit(fashion_mnist, epochs=10, batch_size=128)
def plot_latent_space(vae, n=5, figsize=5):
        img_size, scale = 28,1
        figure = np.zeros((img_size * n, img_size * n))
        grid_x = np.linspace(-scale, scale, n)
        grid_y = np.linspace(-scale, scale, n)[::-1]
        for i, yi in enumerate(grid_y):
                for j, xi in enumerate(grid_x):
                        sample = np.array([[xi, yi]])
                        x_decoded = vae.decoder.predict(sample, verbose=0)
                        images = x_decoded[0].reshape(img_size, img_size)
                        figure[i * img_size : (i + 1) * img_size,
                                j * img_size : (j + 1) * img_size] = images
        plt.figure(figsize=(figsize, figsize))
        start_range = img_size // 2
        end_range = n * img_size + start_range
        pixel_range = np.arange(start_range, end_range, img_size)
        sample_range_x = np.round(grid_x, 1)
        sample_range_y = np.round(grid_y, 1)
        plt.xticks(pixel_range, sample_range_x)
        plt.yticks(pixel_range, sample_range_y)
        plt.xlabel("z[0]"),plt.ylabel("z[1]")
        plt.imshow(figure, cmap="gray"),plt.axis('off'),plt.show()
plot_latent_space(vae)
```

Fig. 11.93 (continued)

3. Read the "Hawks dataset". Use the Decision tree classifier approach to classify the dataset and display the confusion matrix.
4. Use support vector machine learning algorithm to classify the "Mushrooms dataset". Plot the confusion matrix of the result and obtain the accuracy of the classifier.

Model: "encoder"

Layer (type)	Output Shape	Param #	Connected to
input_layer (InputLayer)	(None, 28, 28, 1)	0	-
conv2d (Conv2D)	(None, 14, 14, 64)	640	input_layer_33[0···
conv2d_1 (Conv2D)	(None, 7, 7, 128)	73,856	conv2d_33[0][0]
flatten (Flatten)	(None, 6272)	0	conv2d_34[0][0]
dense (Dense)	(None, 16)	100,368	flatten_16[0][0]
mean (Dense)	(None, 2)	34	dense_32[0][0]
log_var (Dense)	(None, 2)	34	dense_32[0][0]
sampling (Sampling)	(None, 2)	0	mean[0][0], log_var[0][0]

Total params: 174,932 (683.33 KB)
Trainable params: 174,932 (683.33 KB)
Non-trainable params: 0 (0.00 B)
Model: "decoder"

Layer (type)	Output Shape	Param #
input_layer_1 (InputLayer)	(None, 2)	0
dense_1 (Dense)	(None, 3136)	9,408
reshape (Reshape)	(None, 7, 7, 64)	0
conv2d_transpose (Conv2DTranspose)	(None, 14, 14, 128)	73,856
conv2d_transpose_1 (Conv2DTranspose)	(None, 28, 28, 64)	73,792
conv2d_transpose_2 (Conv2DTranspose)	(None, 28, 28, 1)	577

Total params: 157,633 (615.75 KB)
Trainable params: 157,633 (615.75 KB)
Non-trainable params: 0 (0.00 B)

Fig. 11.94 Summary of encoder and decoder of VAE

5. Use "Cars dataset" to evaluate the performance of the Naïve Bayes classifier algorithm. Also visualize the training and test data of the "Cars dataset".
6. Download the "glass.csv" file from the Internet source and apply this data to the KNN classifier algorithm with the Jaccard distance metric. Plot the confusion matrix of the KNN classifier and comment on the observed result.
7. Cluster the following eight points (with (x, y) represent locations) into three clusters: I1(2, 10), I2(2, 5), I3(8, 4), I4(5, 8), I5(7, 5), I6(6, 4), I7(1, 2), I8(4, 9). Initial cluster centres are: I1(2, 10), I4(5, 8) and I7(1, 2). The distance measure between two points $a = (x_1, y_1)$ and $b = (x_2, y_2)$ is defined as $D(a,b) = |x_2 - x_1| + |y_2 - y_1|$. Use K-means clustering algorithm to find the three cluster centres after the third iteration.

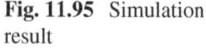

Fig. 11.95 Simulation result

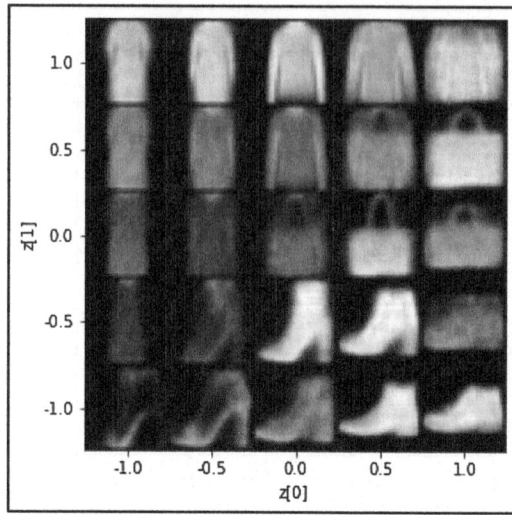

8. Download the "glass.csv" file from Internet source and apply this data into random forest algorithm to classify the dataset. Plot the confusion matrix and comment on the observed result.

9. Use PCA dimensionality reduction approach to reduce the features of "Cars dataset". Comment on the observed result.

10. Apply the dimensionality reduction algorithms like LDA and Kernel PCA to the "glass.csv" dataset. Comment on which algorithm gives better performance in the dimensionality reduction point of view and why.

11. Construct a CNN model consisting of five convolution layers. Each convolution layer would be followed by ReLU activation function and a max-pooling layer. After this one dense layer followed by output layer containing ten neurons. The input layer must be compatible with the images with the size of $227 \times 227 \times 3$ in the dataset. What is the total number of computations involved in this CNN model? Also mention the total number of parameters in the CNN model.

12. Build a CNN model to classify the MNIST dataset. The CNN can be constructed using Keras Sequential API, which allows for building of sequential models layer-by-layer. The architecture should typically include convolutional layers, pooling layers, and fully connected layers. Consider accuracy as a performance measure to evaluate the model.

13. Given a sequence of character from a dataset, train a model to predict the next character in the sequence using Recurrent Neural Network.

14. Segment the optic cup from optic disc in retinal image dataset using UNET architecture. The retinal images can be downloaded from publicly available dataset.

15. Implement GAN to generate realistic images from CIFAR-10 dataset. Choose the dimensionality of the noise vector as 100, learning rate of the optimizer as

0.0001, Adam optimizer coefficients beta1 = 0.45 and beta2 = 0.998, and the number of eopchs as 20.

Objective Questions

1. Which of the following statements is FALSE with respect to regression?

   (A) It relates inputs to outputs
   (B) It is used for prediction
   (C) It may be used for interpretation
   (D) It discovers causal relationships

2. The term "overfitting" in supervised learning refers to

   (A) Model is too simple to capture patterns
   (B) Model learns the training data too well but does not generalize
   (C) Model is not learning from the data
   (D) Model performs well on both training and testing data

3. Increasing the regularization of a model will typically

   (A) Decrease the bias and variance
   (B) Increase its bias and decrease its variance
   (C) Decrease its bias and increase its variance
   (D) Increase its bias and varianceaa

4. Irreducible error in machine learning is caused by

   (A) Noise in the data
   (B) Bias in the model
   (C) Variance in the model
   (D) Overfitting of the model

5. An input image of dimension $256 \times 256 \times 3$ is applied to convolutional layer which has fifty 3×3 kernels. The dimension of the resulting tensor with stride = 1 and no zero padding is

   (A) $256 \times 256 \times 50$
   (B) $254 \times 254 \times 50$
   (C) $128 \times 128 \times 3$
   (D) $256 \times 256 \times 3$

6. What are support vectors in an SVM without slack?

   (A) The most important features in the dataset.
   (B) The data points that do not fall into a specific classification.
   (C) All points within the dataset are considered support vectors.
   (D) The data points on the margin of the SVM.

7. Identify the statement that is correct with respect to the activation function of a neural network

   (A) Activation function always outputs values between 0 and 1.
   (B) Activation functions are applied only to the output units.
   (C) Activation functions are essential for learning non-linear decision boundaries.
   (D) Activation functions are needed to speed up the gradient computation during backpropagation.

8. Which of the following would be the most appropriate loss function to use when training a neural network on a multi-class classification problem?

   (A) Mean Absolute Error
   (B) Mean Squared Error
   (C) Cross Entropy
   (D) Hinge loss

9. Which of the following methods would not help when a model suffers from high variance?

   (A) Reduce training data
   (B) Decrease model size
   (C) Increase the amount of regularization
   (D) Perform feature extraction

10. The purpose of sigmoid function in classification algorithm is

    (A) It converts continuous input into categorical data
    (B) It standardizes the input to have zero mean and variance one
    (C) It optimizes the weights to reduce loss
    (D) It transforms the output to a probability

11. Which of the following is NOT a valid way to reduce the over fitting problem?

    (A) Increase the amount of training data.
    (B) Improve the optimization algorithm being used for error minimization.
    (C) Decrease the model complexity.
    (D) Reduce the noise in the training data

12. What is the main drawback of using Gradient Descent in regression models?

    (A) It is computationally intensive for large datasets.
    (B) It cannot be used with non-linear relationships.
    (C) It may get struck in local minima.
    (D) It is highly sensitive to data scaling.

13. For the matrix $\begin{bmatrix} 1 & 1 & 2 & 4 \\ 4 & 6 & 6 & 8 \\ 3 & 2 & 1 & 0 \\ 1 & 2 & 3 & 4 \end{bmatrix}$, the output after applying 2×2 Max pooling filter with a stride of two is

(A) $\begin{bmatrix} 6 & 8 \\ 3 & 4 \end{bmatrix}$

(B) $\begin{bmatrix} 6 & 2 \\ 4 & 3 \end{bmatrix}$

(C) $\begin{bmatrix} 1 & 2 \\ 3 & 4 \end{bmatrix}$

(D) $\begin{bmatrix} 1 & 3 \\ 2 & 4 \end{bmatrix}$

14. Which type of neural network is used in the competitive learning paradigm?

(A) Self-Organizing map
(B) Radial Basis Function network
(C) Multi-layer Perceptron
(D) Recurrent Neural Network

15. Which activation function is used to reduce the vanishing gradient problem in deep learning?

(A) Tanh
(B) Softmax
(C) Sigmoid
(D) ReLU

16. The purpose of validation set in machine learning is

(A) To train the model
(B) To fine-tune hyperparameters
(C) To test the model's generalization
(D) To provide additional training data

17. What is the primary purpose of a decision tree's leaf nodes?

(A) To split the data
(B) To represent features
(C) To store feature values
(D) To make predictions

18. Which machine learning algorithm is sensitive to the scale of features and requires feature scaling?

    (A) Decision Trees
    (B) K-means clustering
    (C) Naïve Baye's algorithm
    (D) Support Vector Machines

19. The purpose of bias term in a linear regression model is

    (A) To handle outliers
    (B) To avoid over fitting
    (C) To model the noise in the data
    (D) To shift the regression line up or down

20. Which evaluation metric is commonly used for accessing the performance of a classification model when dealing with imbalanced datasets?

    (A) Accuracy
    (B) F1-score
    (C) Mean Absolute error
    (D) Mean square error

21. Which of the following guidelines is applicable to initialization of the weight vector in a fully connected neural network?

    (A) Weight vector should not be set it to zero as it will cause over fitting
    (B) Weight vector should not be set to zero because gradient descent will explore a very small space
    (C) Weight vector should set it to zero otherwise it causes a bias
    (D) Weight vector should set it to zero in order to preserve symmetry across all neurons

22. Averaging the output of multiple decision trees helps to

    (A) Increase bias
    (B) Decrease bias
    (C) Increase variance
    (D) Decrease variance

23. Statement 1: An autoencoder is a neural network designed to learn feature representations in an unsupervised manner.
    Statement 2: An autoencoder is a neural network designed to learn feature representations in a supervised manner.

    (A) Statements 1 and 2 are true
    (B) Statement 1 is true, Statement 2 is false
    (C) Statement 1 is false, Statement 2 is true
    (D) Statements 1 and 2 are false

24. Which of the following statement is true about activation function in a neural network?

    (A) Activation function speed up the gradient calculation in back propagation
    (B) Action functions are applied only to the output units
    (C) Activation functions help to learn nonlinear decision boundaries
    (D) Activation function always output values as either 0 or 1

25. Which of the following condition would serve as a sensible stopping condition while building a decision tree?

    (A) Stop if the validation error decreases as the tree grows
    (B) Do not split the treenode that an equal number of sample points from each class
    (C) Do not split treenode if the split would cause a large reduction in the weighted average entropy
    (D) Do not split a tree node whose depth exceeds a specified threshold

26. Statement 1: Pruning in decision tree improves training accuracy
    Statement 2: Pruning in decision tree improves validation accuracy.

    (A) Statements 1 and 2 are true
    (B) Statement 1 is true, Statement 2 is false
    (C) Statement 1 is false, Statement 2 is true
    (D) Statements 1 and 2 are false

27. Consider the sigmoid function represented as $f(x) = \dfrac{1}{1+e^{-x}}$. The expression for the derivative of this function is given by

    (A) $f(x) = f(x)(1 + f(x))$
    (B) $f(x) = f(x)(1 - f(x))$
    (C) $f(x) = f(x) \ln (1 - f(x))$
    (D) $f(x) = f(x)/(1 - f(x))$

28. In linear regression, L_2 regularization is equivalent to imposing a

    (A) Logistic prior
    (B) Laplace prior
    (C) Gaussian class-conditional
    (D) Gaussian prior

29. The kernel trick

    (A) Can be applied to any learning algorithm
    (B) Can improve the speed of high-degree polynomial regression
    (C) Is necessary if one wants to add polynomial feature to a learning algorithm
    (D) Can improve the speed of learning algorithms when the number of samples is very large

30. Which of the following regression methods always have just one unique optimum, regardless of the data?

    (A) Least Square Regression
    (B) Lasso Regression
    (C) Ridge Regression
    (D) Logistic Regression

31. An input image of dimension $256 \times 256 \times 3$ is applied to convolutional layer which has fifty 3×3 kernels. How many parameters does this convolution layers have?

    (A) 1200
    (B) 1400
    (C) 1600
    (D) 1800

32. The built-in function in tensor flow to train the model with given inputs is

    (A) model.predict
    (B) model.fit
    (C) model.compile
    (D) model.evaluate

33. The built-in function in tensor flow which can be used to access the model's performance in terms of loss and accuracy is

    (A) model.predict
    (B) model.fit
    (C) model.compile
    (D) model.evaluate

34. The built-in function in tensor flow is used for making predictions on new or unseen data

    (A) model.predict
    (B) model.fit
    (C) model.compile
    (D) model.evaluate

35. Which evaluation metric is commonly used for classification tasks when class imbalance is present?

    (A) Accuracy
    (B) F1-Score
    (C) Mean Square Error
    (D) R-Squared

36. A machine learning method that reuses a trained model designed for a particular task to accomplish a different et related task is

(A) Hybrid learning
(B) Ensemble learning
(C) Transfer learning
(D) Cooperative learning

Answers to Objective Questions

Q. No.	01	02	03	04	05	06	07	08	09	10
Key	D	B	B	A	B	D	C	C	A	D
Q. No.	11	12	13	14	15	16	17	18	19	20
Key	B	D	A	A	D	B	D	D	D	B
Q. No.	21	22	23	24	25	26	27	28	29	30
Key	B	D	B	C	D	C	B	D	D	C
Q. No.	31	32	33	34	35	36				
Key	B	B	D	A	B	C				

Answers to PreLab Questions

1. A feedforward neural network is a type of neural network where data or information flows in one direction from the input layer to the output layers. It does not contain any cycles or loops within it.
2. The activation function is a mathematical equation that computes the output of each node of the neural network. Mostly the activation function maps the linear data into non-linear manner, because of its non-linear nature property, which enables the neural network to learn complex patterns. Some of the common activation functions are ReLU, Sigmoid and Tanh.
3. The loss function quantifies the measure of neural network predictions with the actual target values. This loss function can be used while training the neural network model. This quantifiable result fine tunes the optimization process to obtain the optimum weights of the neural networks. Some of the examples of loss functions are mean squared error, Cross entropy loss, etc.
4. Backpropagation is an algorithm used to train Feedforward Neural Networks. It consists of calculating the gradient of the loss function with respect to each weight by the chain rule and updating the weights to minimize the loss using an optimization algorithm like Gradient Descent or Adam optimizer.
5. VGG16 is a convolutional neural network model that's used for image recognition. It's unique in that it has only 16 layers that have weights, as opposed to relying on a large number of hyper-parameters. It's considered one of the best vision model architectures.

6. Data augmentation can be achieved through (1) Flipping the image (2) Cropping the image (3) Rotating the image (4) More images can be generated by adding noise to the image.

7. The bias is the difference between the prediction of the model and the correct value. The variability of model prediction for a given data points is the spread of the data termed as the variance of the model. If the algorithm is too simple, then it may be on high bias and low variance condition. If algorithms fit too complex then it may be on high variance and low bias. Bias-variance trade off in machine learning is crucial as it directly impacts a model's predictive performance. The goal of bias-variance trade-off is the delicate equilibrium between under fitting and over fitting. The goal is to find the optimal level of complexity that allows a model to generalize effectively to an unseen data.

8. Dropout refers to dropping out of some nodes either in the input or hidden layer in a neural network so that all the forward and backwards connections with a dropped node are temporarily removed. Dropout is used to reduce the overfitting problem. By randomly dropping a few units, it forces the layers to take more or less responsibility for the input by taking a probabilistic approach. This ensures that the model is getting generalized hence reducing the problem of overfitting.

9. The three main layers of CNN are (1) Convolution layer (2) Polling layer and (3) Fully connected layer. The convolution layer performs feature extraction, the polling layer performs dimensionality reduction and extracts the dominant features, whereas the fully connected layer is responsible for mapping extracted features into a final output such as classification.

10. The vanishing gradient problem occurs when the gradients used to update the network's weight become very small or vanish as they are backpropagated through the network. The problem of vanishing gradient is due to the nature of certain activation functions and the chain rule of calculus. Vanishing gradient problem can lead to (1) slow convergence (2) Network getting stuck to local minima (3) Poor learning performance.

11. In deep neural network, training is complicated due to the fact that the distribution of each layer's inputs changes during training, as the parameters of the previous layers change. This phenomenon is termed as internal covariate shift. Batch normalization is a technique to normalize activations in intermediate layers of deep neural networks. Batch normalization avoids activation explosion by repeatedly correcting all activations to be zero-mean and of unit standard deviation. The advantages of performing batch normalization are (1) Networks train faster (2) Batch normalization allows one to use high learning rates which increases the speed at which networks train.

12. PCA is a linear transformation to the subspace whereas autoencoder is a non-linear transformation to the hidden units. If the autoencoder's activation functions are linear, then its function will be very similar to that of PCA.

13. Transfer learning is a machine learning method that reuses a trained model designed for a particular task to accomplish a different yet related task.

14. An autoencoder essentially contains an (1) Encoder layer (2) Bottleneck layer and (3) Decoder layer. The encoder layer compress the input data into a compressed representation. The bottle neck layer is used to represent the compressed input. The decoder layer reconstructs the encoded information (image) back to the original dimension.

15. Different types of autoencoders include (1) Vanilla autoencoder which is the basic autoencoder that efficiently encodes and decodes data (2) Sparse autoencoder which can learn more compact and efficient data representations (3) Variational autoencoder which can generate new data points that resemble in some form of the training data (4) Denoising autoencoder which has improved robustness to noise and irrelevant information. Autoencoders can be used for (1) Dimensionality reduction (2) Feature extraction (3) Image denoising (4) Image Compression (5) Anomaly detection.

Bibliography

1. P. A. Flach, "Machine Learning. The Art and Science of Algorithms That Make Sense of Data", Cambridge University Press, 2012.
2. S. Marsland, "Machine Learning: An Algorithmic Perspective" 2nd ed. Chapman and Hall/ CRC Press, 2014.
3. T. M. Mitchell, "Machine Learning", McGraw-Hill, 1997.
4. S. Russell and P. Norvig, "Artificial Intelligence: A Modern Approach", 4th ed. Prentice-Hall, 2021.
5. Ian Goodfellow, Yoshua Bengio and Aaron Courville, "Deep Learning", An MIT Press book, 2016.
6. Charu C. Aggarwal, "Neural Networks and Deep Learning: A Textbook", Springer, 2019.

Index

© The Editor(s) (if applicable) and The Author(s), under exclusive license to
Springer Nature Singapore Pte Ltd. 2025
S Esakkirajan et al., *Digital Image Processing*,
https://doi.org/10.1007/978-981-96-6382-8

The manufacturer's authorised representative in the EU is Springer
Nature Customer Service Centre GmbH, Europaplatz 3, 69115 Heidelberg,
Germany. If you have any concerns regarding our products, please
contact ProductSafety@springernature.com

Printed and bound by CPI Group (UK) Ltd, Croydon, CR0 4YY
23/04/2026
02095594-0014